(continued on inside back cover)

THE WAITE GROUP'S

WINDOWS API BIBLE

The Definitive Programmer's Reference

James L. Conger

WAITE GROUP PRESS
Corte Madera, California

Development Editor ▼ *Mitchell Waite*
Content Editor ▼ *Mark Peterson*
Reviewer ▼ *Paul J. Perry*
Copy Editor ▼ *Kathy Carlyle*
Production Manager ▼ *Julianne Ososke*
Illustrations ▼ *Pat Rogondino*
Design and Production ▼ *Barbara Gelfand Design*
Editorial Director ▼ *Scott Calamar*

Printed in the United States of America
  94 95 • 10 9 8 7 6 5 4

Library of Congress Cataloging in Publication Data

Conger, Jim.
    The Waite Group's Windows API bible : the definitive programmer's reference / by James L. Conger.
        p.   cm.
    Includes index.
    ISBN 1-878739-15-8 : $39.95
    1. Windows (Computer programs)   2. Application software.
I. Title.   II. Title: Windows API bible.
QA76.76.W56C67   1992
005.4'3--dc20   91-48075
                                                                              CIP

To Claire

Acknowledgments

I wish I could say that I knew every aspect of Windows programming before I began to write this book. I was surprised to find out how much of Windows I had never used, and in many cases, never noticed. Spelunking the remote corners of Windows was an enjoyable experience, but I needed a lot of help.

I am particularly indebted to Mark Peterson, who edited the book and provided many insights and useful examples. I also received help from Don Stegall, who kindly contributed a keyboard hook example and helped on several weird problems I encountered. When I became desperate, I turned to Dennis Cook, Len Gray, Rudyard Merrian, and many other contributors to the MSOPSYS forum on CompuServe.

Although this book was processed almost exclusively through electronic media, it was amazing how much work was needed to get the book in its final form. Scott Calamar supervised the entire operation, with a lot of help from Julianne Ososke, Pat Rogondino, Kathy Carlyle, and K.D. Sullivan. Finally, I would like to thank Mitchell Waite for proposing the book, guiding its design and content, and for being the constant champion of the project.

Introduction

The purpose of this book is to save Windows programers time. Most of us who have been programming with Windows for a few years have become accustomed to having our desks cluttered with various books. Mine seems to always have four or five Windows Software Development Kit manuals, a well thumbed copy of Charles Petzold's excellent book *Programming Windows*, several printouts of example programs, and perhaps a few other books buried under the pile.

The *Windows Bible* is an attempt to assemble most of the information you need in one place. Following the organization of the other Waite Group bibles, the *Windows Bible* is organized by subject. Each chapter covers a separate topic. The chapter introductions cover basic concepts. The details are covered in the function and message descriptions.

A key element to making the book useful is the use of short example programs. They are particularly important with Windows, where functions are seldom used alone. Most functions require the support of a series of related functions and messages to do their task. The example programs show a function or message in context, with supporting functions in place, and with variables properly declared.

The example programs in this book are different from examples used in Windows tutorials. Tutorials generally use longer example programs, with many functions and messages demonstrated at one time. The examples in the *Windows Bible* are as short as possible. Their only purpose is to demonstrate one function or message or at most a few related functions or messages. They *do* show the proper use of the function or message, without a lot of other distractions.

In some cases, the emphasis on keeping the examples short and clear caused me to write what borders on writing simplistic code. For example, the preferred way to find out the correct text line spacing is to use the GetTextMetrics() function. It determines character heights on the screen. This assures that the spacing will be correct, regardless of the video resolution used. In the *Windows API Bible* examples, fixed line spacing is used for demonstration output in chapters that do not focus on display of text. This avoids the distraction of having GetTextMetrics() show up in every example. The correct usage of GetTextMetrics() is explained in the chapter on text output.

The structure of the book groups related subjects. Chapter 1 is an introduction for those new to Windows. Chapters 2 to 5 deal with the creation of windows, and the related menu and scrolling functions. Chapters 6 to 9 cover the various aspects of Windows messages. Chapters 10 to 12 deal with output to the screen and printers. The remaining chapters cover separate topics which are only loosely related.

One disadvantage to the organization by related subjects is that it is not possible to introduce the reader to each subject in succession. For example, several of the message hook functions in Chapter 8, *Message Processing Functions,* require the use of dynamic link libraries. DLLs are not covered until Chapter 28, *Dynamic Link Libraries*. Cross references are included in these cases.

While writing the book I was surprised to find a number of functions that I had not run into in four years of Windows programming. Some of these more obscure functions turned out to be remarkably useful. The experienced reader may find the discussions of message hooks, communications and sound support, atoms, and dynamic data exchange (DDE), and the multiple document interface (MDI) worth reviewing.

Good luck with your Windows projects!

Jim Conger

Windows 3.1 Note

The *Waite Group's Windows API Bible* was originally written using Microsoft Windows 3.0. Towards the end of the project Microsoft released their first beta test version of Windows 3.1. We knew immediately that Windows 3.1 was much more than a minor maintenance release, and included many new features. Unfortunately, the physical limits of how many pages can be bound into one book made it impossible to put all of the Windows 3.1 additions into the *Windows API Bible*. We therefore made the decision to put the elements of Windows common to both Windows 3.0 and 3.1 into the *Windows API Bible*, and start work on a second volume to cover the unique features of Windows 3.1. Microsoft made additional enhancements during the Windows 3.1 development period, culminating with the addition of the multimedia extensions. These will be covered in the second volume, along with OLE (object linking and embedding) and True Type fonts. This first volume discusses DDE (dynamic data exchange) using the message-based protocols, but not using the version 3.1 DDEML library.

The *Windows API Bible* continues to document the "core" of Windows. Feedback from readers has been very positive, and we are proceeding with the companion book tentativelly entitled *Windows Bible: The New Testament*. This second volume will document all of the new features in Windows 3.1 with the same combination of text and example programs used in the *Windows API Bible*. We hope that these books will continue to serve their intended purpose: Saving Windows programmers time.

Table of Contents

Table of Contents

This chapter introduces Windows programming and develops the GENERIC.C program. GENERIC.C will serve as the basis for all of the examples in this book.

Windows Programming Overview

If you have been programming in DOS or in a minicomputer environment, your first look at a Windows program may be a little disconcerting. Windows programs *are* different. The differences boil down to a few basic principles.

1. Instead of telling the computer what to do one step at a time, Windows programs are structured to wait there until the program receives a message from Windows. Messages are statements like "The user just clicked a button with the mouse pointer—do something!"

2. The Windows environment has built-in support for all the basic hardware such as the video display, memory, mouse, keyboard, and printers. Microsoft takes care of worrying about all of the latest hardware—freeing you to create applications. Programmers spend their time learning and using the 600 Windows functions, rather than writing their own code to support multiple printers, video cards, etc.

3. Windows moves programs and data around in memory to make room for other program pieces and data. This movement allows many programs to coexist in a fairly limited amount of memory, but it also means that the programmer cannot assume that anything will stay put for long. Windows gives you all of the tools you need to deal with moveable memory, but it takes a little getting used to.

Despite these differences, Windows is not a difficult environment in which to work. When you have gotten over the initial hurdle of writing a few simple programs, the tremendous built-in power of Windows will spoil you. It will be difficult for you to ever go back to more primitive environments.

If you are new to programming with the Windows environment, my main advice is to dive in and try it. You will find that most Windows programs are remarkably similar, so that when you have one running, the second one is a matter of modification. One of the main goals of this book is to provide working examples for all of the Windows functions, saving you the time it takes by figuring out how every one of them is used. For efficiency, a simple "GENERIC" program, which is described in the next section, is used as the basis for most of the programming examples.

Structure of a Windows Program

Most Windows programs have two C functions in common, WinMain() and WndProc(). Only WinMain() is required, although WndProc() shows up in almost every Windows program. WndProc() can be named anything you want, but most programmers name it WndProc(). WinMain() must be named "WinMain," just like the main() function in a conventional C program. Any large program will have many other functions doing tasks for WndProc(), but these two functions will be there to begin.

WinMain( ) - Calls several functions that tell the Windows environment about the properties of the program's main window. This includes what color to paint the window, the name of the icon to show when the program is initialized, where to find the program's menu, etc. WinMain() also contains some standard code to process Windows messages to and from the program you are writing. WinMain() is also the entry and exit point of the program, again like main() in a conventional C program.

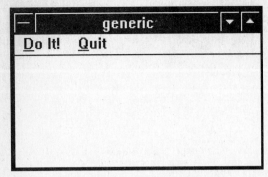

Figure 1-1. The GENERIC Program's Window.

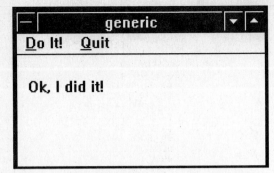

Figure 1-2. GENERIC After Clicking the "Do It!" Menu Item.

WndProc() - This is where you write the program logic. This function is usually called the "message processing function" as Windows messages are interpreted and acted upon within this function.

Let's take a look at a simple example. We will create a program that looks like Figure 1-1. The program creates a window with the title "generic" and with two menu items, "Do It!" and "Quit". When the program is first run, it just sits there.

Moving the mouse pointer to "Do It!" and clicking the left mouse button causes text to appear in the window, as shown in Figure 1-2. Clicking the "Quit" menu item causes the program to stop and the window to disappear. The minimize and maximize buttons in the upper right corner work per standard Windows conventions, as does the system button in the upper left corner.

GENERIC.C Example Windows Program

Listing 1-1 shows all of the C code needed to make GENERIC.C. Although the code looks complex at first glance, it is remarkably short. Remember that this program creates a window that can be moved and sized on the screen, shrunken to an icon, expanded to the size of the screen, and which has a functioning menu.

➪ **Listing 1-1. GENERIC.C**

```
/* generic.c   generic windows application */
#include <windows.h>            /* window's header file - always included */
#include "generic.h"            /* the application's header file */

int PASCAL WinMain (HANDLE hInstance, HANDLE hPrevInstance, LPSTR lpszCmdLine, int nCmdShow)
{                               /* variable types defined in windows.h */

        HWND            hWnd ;          /* a handle to a message */
        MSG             msg ;           /* a message */
        WNDCLASS        wndclass ;      /* the window class */

        ghInstance = hInstance ; /* store instance handle as global var. */

        if (!hPrevInstance)             /* load data into window class struct. */
        {
                wndclass.style                  = CS_HREDRAW | CS_VREDRAW ;
                wndclass.lpfnWndProc            = WndProc ;
                wndclass.cbClsExtra             = 0 ;
                wndclass.cbWndExtra             = 0 ;
                wndclass.hInstance              = hInstance ;
                wndclass.hIcon                  = LoadIcon (hInstance, gszAppName) ;
                wndclass.hCursor                = LoadCursor (NULL, IDC_ARROW) ;
                wndclass.hbrBackground          = GetStockObject (WHITE_BRUSH) ;
                wndclass.lpszMenuName           = gszAppName ;
```

```
        wndclass.lpszClassName          = gszAppName ;
                        /* register the window class */
        if (!RegisterClass (&wndclass))
                return FALSE ;
}
hWnd = CreateWindow (            /* create the program's window here */
        gszAppName,             /* class name */
        gszAppName,             /* window name */
        WS_OVERLAPPEDWINDOW,    /* window style */
        CW_USEDEFAULT,          /* x position on screen */
        CW_USEDEFAULT,          /* y position on screen */
        CW_USEDEFAULT,          /* width of window */
        CW_USEDEFAULT,          /* height of window */
        NULL,                   /* parent window handle (null = none) */
        NULL,                   /* menu handle (null = use class menu) */
        hInstance,              /* instance handle */
        NULL) ;                 /* lpstr (null = not used) */

    ShowWindow (hWnd, nCmdShow) ;           /* make window visible */
    UpdateWindow (hWnd) ;                   /* send first WM_PAINT message */
                    /* the next while() loop is the "message loop" */

    while (GetMessage (&msg, NULL, 0, 0))   /* wait for a message */
    {
        TranslateMessage (&msg) ;           /* does some key conversions */
        DispatchMessage (&msg) ;            /* sends message to WndProc() */
    }
    return msg.wParam ;                     /* returns application's exit code */
}


long FAR PASCAL WndProc (HWND hWnd, unsigned iMessage, WORD wParam, LONG lParam)
{
    HDC     hDC ;                           /* device context handle */

    switch (iMessage)                       /* process windows messages */
    {
        case WM_COMMAND:                    /* process menu items */
            switch (wParam)
            {
            case IDM_DOIT:                  /* User hit the "Do it" menu item */
                hDC = GetDC (hWnd) ;        /* get device context */
                TextOut (hDC, 10, 20, "Ok, I did it!", 13) ;
                ReleaseDC (hWnd, hDC) ;     /* release device context */
                break ;
            case IDM_QUIT:                  /* send end of application message */
                DestroyWindow (hWnd) ;
                break ;
            }
            break ;
        case WM_DESTROY:                    /* stop application */
            PostQuitMessage (0) ;
            break ;
        default:                            /* default windows message processing */
            return DefWindowProc (hWnd, iMessage, wParam, lParam) ;
    }
    return (0L) ;
}
```

The WinMain() function looks more complex than it is. The saving grace is that this function remains almost unchanged from one program to the next. You just copy that part into your next project. I will explain what it does in a moment. Let's deal with the WinProc() function first.

WinProc() processes messages from Windows. The messages are all integers, but for clarity they are given names in the WINDOWS.H header file. The two messages that GENERIC.C has to process are WM_COMMAND (a menu item was pressed), and WM_DESTROY (stop the application and close its window). The menu items are labeled IDM_DOIT and IDM_QUIT. These names are defined in the program's header file GENERIC.H, shown in Listing 1-2.

➪ Listing 1-2. GENERIC.H Header File

```
/* generic.h
#define IDM_DOIT   1                /* menu item id values */
#define IDM_QUIT   2
        /* global variables */
int     ghInstance ;
char    gszAppName [] = "generic" ;
        /* function prototypes */
Long FAR PASCAL WndProc (HWND, unsigned, WORD, LONG) ;
```

When the user clicks the "Do It!" menu item, Windows sends the GENERIC program a WM_COMMAND message. Part of this message is the menu item number, in this case IDM_DOIT which we defined equal to one in GENERIC.H. When the WndProc() function in GENERIC.C gets this message, it executes the code:

```
case IDM_DOIT:*/
        hDC = GetDC (hWnd) ;               /* get device context */
        TextOut (hDC, 10, 20, "Ok, I did it!", 13) ;
        ReleaseDC (hWnd, hDC) ;            /* release device context */
        break ;
```

The program uses the Windows function GetDC() to get some information about the video screen. Using this information (called the device context), the program writes the words "Ok, I did it!" using the Windows function TextOut(). Finally, the memory tied up with the screen information is released by using ReleaseDC(). Those three functions put the words on the screen.

Similarly, if the user clicks the "Quit" menu item, the program executes the DestroyWindow() function. DestroyWindow() deletes the program's window, causing the program to end. This is called "terminating" an application. Windows sends the program the WM_DESTROY message, which is processed to exit the program.

We have covered the operation of the WinProc() function. What about all of the code in the upper WinMain() function of GENERIC.C? Most of this code deals with creating the program's main window. Creating a window is a three step process:

1. First, you have to create a window "class." The class is described by filling in a bunch of data in a structure called *wndclass*. Here is an example of one of those lines.

```
wndclass.hIcon = LoadIcon (hInstance, gszAppName) ;
```

In this case, every window created with this window class will refer to an icon with the same name as the program "generic." The global variable *gszAppName* is defined in the GENERIC.H header file. Once all of the window class data is filled in, you notify Windows that you have created a new class of windows by using the function RegisterClass().

2. Second, you use the CreateWindow() function to create one or more windows based on the window class. CreateWindow() passes more information on to windows, such as the style of the window, the background color, etc.

3. Finally, you display the window by calling the ShowWindow() function. At the bottom of the WinMain() function you will see the rather odd loop:

```
while (GetMessage (&msg, NULL, 0, 0))            /* the message loop */
{
        TranslateMessage (&msg) ;
        DispatchMessage (&msg) ;
}
```

This loop, called the *message loop*, is in every Windows program. Windows passes all of the messages to the program via the functions in this loop. There are a few other functions that can be used in the message loop for special purposes like menu accelerator keys, but usually the loop will look exactly like this one.

If you want to type in the GENERIC.C program, compile it, and run it, you will need a couple of other small files. These files are the resource file that defines the menu, icon, and other resources used by the program; the definition file that gives the compiler some guidance when creating the program; and the make file, to help automate compiling and linking the program.

The resource file GENERIC.RC is simple. It includes an icon file GENERIC.ICO that was created with the SDKPaint application that comes with the Windows Software Development Kit. It also defines the program's menu. Note that the menu items are given ID numbers, which are defined in the header file.

▷ **Listing 1-3. GENERIC.RC Resource File**

```
/* generic.rc
#include <windows.h>
#include "generic.h"

generic          ICON    generic.ico

generic          MENU
BEGIN
    MENUITEM "&Do It!"          IDM_DOIT
    MENUITEM "&Quit",           IDM_QUIT
END
```

The .DEF definition file provides the linker with information on how to assemble the finished program. Chapter 14, *Memory Management*, contains a full discussion of all of the statements that can be put in definition files. Here is a brief description of this example file.

The DESCRIPTION string is added into the file, usually to contain copyright information. EXETYPE of WINDOWS tells the linker that this will be a Windows 3.0 version program. The STUB line names a small file that ends up becoming the beginning of the finished program. The WINSTUB file is the code that prints out a warning message if a user tries to run a Windows program from DOS.

The CODE and DATA statements control how memory will be managed for this program. Listing 1.4. shows the normal settings. HEAPSIZE and STACKSIZE control the amount of memory allocated for the program's local data heap and stack. Finally, the EXPORTS section names all of the functions (besides the mandatory WinMain()) that the program will want Windows to call.

▷ **Listing 1-4. GENERIC.DEF Definition File**

```
NAME            GENERIC
DESCRIPTION     'generic windows program'
EXETYPE         WINDOWS
STUB            'WINSTUB.EXE'
CODE            PRELOAD MOVEABLE
DATA            PRELOAD MOVEABLE MULTIPLE
HEAPSIZE        1024
STACKSIZE       5120
EXPORTS         WndProc
```

NMAKE.EXE is a program that runs other programs, typically compilers and linkers. NMAKE automates compilation of a program based on an NMAKE control file. The convention is to name the NMAKE control file the same as the main C program, but without an extension. For example, the NMAKE file for GENERIC.C is GENERIC, shown in Listing 1.5. The GENERIC listing starts with the ALL statement. This tells NMAKE that we are trying to create GENERIC.EXE and that any file that has been saved more recently than GENERIC.EXE is going to need to be included in the next compilation.

The next two lines define macros. Anytime the CFLAGS word is found preceded by a dollar sign and parentheses, the line of compiler switches "-c -D LINT_ARGS -A -Os -Gsw -W2" is substituted. These are the standard compiler switches for compiling a small Windows C program. Similarly, LFLAGS is replaced by /NOD, a linker control switch. These flags are discussed in Chapter 14 on memory management.

The remaining lines tell NMAKE which files to compare to decide if a file needs to be recompiled. For example, if either GENERIC.C or GENERIC.H has been saved more recently than GENERIC.OBJ, the next line is executed. The resource compiler, RC.EXE is controlled by the next group of commands. The last group controls the linker. Note that RC is run again at the very end of the NMAKE file. The resource compiler adds the compiled resource data (from our resource file above) to the program file and then marks the completed program as a Windows 3.0 version application.

▷ **Listing 1-5. GENERIC—The NMAKE File**

```
ALL: generic.exe

CFLAGS=-c -D LINT_ARGS -AS -Os -Gsw -W2
LFLAGS=/NOD

generic.obj : generic.c generic.h                    ; compile the C file
    $(CC) $(CFLAGS) generic.c

generic.res: generic.rc generic.ico                  ; compile the resource file
    rc -r generic.rc

generic.exe : generic.obj generic.def generic.res        ; link'm together
    link $(LFLAGS) generic, , ,libw slibcew, generic
    rc generic.res
```

The last file you have to create is the program's icon. This is done using the SDKPaint application, choosing the icon file type. Save the icon you create as GENERIC.ICO. Once you have all of these files, you can create the working program by typing the command

```
NMAKE GENERIC
```

from within DOS. If you have not done all of this, I suggest you try it. The GENERIC application serves as the basis for most of the programming examples in the rest of the book. You can run the program by double-clicking the GENERIC.EXE file name from within the file manager, or by using the "Program Run" menu item from the program manager, or by typing WIN GENERIC from the DOS command line.

How Windows Programs Are Compiled and Linked

In a conventional C program, you build the program by first compiling all of the C language files and then linking them to make the final executable file (an .EXE file in DOS). Windows works the same way, but with an added step: the resource compiler. One of the many clever aspects of the Windows environment is the separation of programming code (C code) from programming resources. In Windows, resources refer to things like menus, dialog box outlines, icons, bitmaps, and blocks of text. They are stored in a resource file, separate from the C language files. Resource files are compiled using the resource compiler, RC.EXE.

If you look at the GENERIC.RC file, you will see that only two resources are included in this simple example. The first is the icon. The resource compiler reads the line

```
generic         ICON    generic.ico
```

and pulls in the icon data from the file GENERIC.ICO. The name "generic" on the left is then associated with the data from this file.

Similarly the lines

```
generic         MENU
BEGIN
    MENUITEM "&Do It!"          IDM_DOIT
    MENUITEM "&Quit",           IDM_QUIT
END
```

define a menu with two items ("Do It!" and "Quit"), which are associated with the menu item numbers IDM_DOIT and IDM_QUIT (defined in GENERIC.H). Given this simple definition, Windows knows to space the menu items along the menu line of the window, highlight the items when clicked with the mouse, etc. The only thing left for the programmer to worry about is what action to take when the menu items are activated.

The other added file needed for Windows programs is the definition file. GENERIC.DEF provides basic information about how to build the Windows program. For example, you specify the amount of memory to reserve for the program's stack and free memory area, how memory is to be managed (MOVEABLE...), and the name of the functions that Windows will be passing messages to (EXPORTS...). We will discuss this file in the chapter on memory management functions. For now, just realize that a file like this is needed for every Windows program and that .DEF files tend to all be similar. The full sequence of events in the creation of the GENERIC.EXE program is as follows:

GENERIC.C —> compiled by CL —> GENERIC.OBJ
GENERIC.RC —> compiled by RC —> GENERIC.RES
GENERIC.OBJ + GENERIC.RES + GENERIC.DEF —> linked by LINK and RC —> GENERIC.EXE

The NMAKE file takes care of all of this for us, so that you only have to issue one command (NMAKE GENERIC) to create the complete program.

How Windows Programs Work

If you check the file size of the GENERIC.EXE file, you will find that it is about 8200 bytes. This is remarkably small, considering that you have a resizeable graphics window, icon and menu functions built in, and full mouse support. The secret to this small size is that Windows programs do not contain even a fraction of the program code needed to do all of these operations. The program you create makes uses of a large collection of functions that are part of the Windows environment when Windows is running on your computer. Every Windows program shares these working libraries of functions for control of the screen, printers, keyboard, mouse, menus, bitmaps, and a long list of other functions.

This collection of working functions is maintained in files stored in the SYSTEM directory on your hard disk. The SYSTEM directory was created when you installed Windows. The three primary files are

GDI.EXE   Video display and printer functions.
USER.EXE   Mouse, keyboard, sound, communications port and timer support.
KERNEL.EXE   File and memory management.

Each of these programs in turn calls driver files (like DISPLAY.DRV) for specific functions. Windows only loads the modules it needs into memory and swaps them out of memory when they are no longer needed. Besides saving you, the programmer, from having to create all of this logic every time you write a complete program, Windows also greatly reduces memory consumption. All of the application programs running at once share the same basic support library for the hardware.

As we will see in Chapter 14, *Memory Management*, Windows does even more than this to conserve memory. If you write a large program with a number of C files linked together, Windows will load just the parts it needs to start up. Later, as the user makes use of other functions, Windows will load the other parts as needed. Windows will also move data and programs around in memory to make room for new material. All of this is transparent to the user. The bottom line is: Our little GENERIC.C program may not look like much in its raw C language form, but when it is operating as a running program, it has an army of Windows functions behind it.

Windows Naming Conventions—WINDOWS.H

Windows has a lot of functions. To minimize the chance of passing the wrong kind of data to a function, the developers of Windows developed a consistent naming convention so that the name of the variable indicates the type of data to which it refers. This system of names is often call "Hungarian notation" in honor of its inventor, Charles Simonyi. The basic system of prefixes is shown in Table 1-1.

Prefix	Data Type	⊠
b	BOOL (int, use only TRUE and FALSE values, 1 and 0)	
by	BYTE (unsigned char)	
c:	char	
dw	DWORD (doubles word, an unsigned long integer)	
fn	function	
g	global (the author's use of "g")	
h	handle (explained below)	
i	int (two byte integer)	
l	long	
n	short (int) or near pointer	
p	pointer	
s	string	
sz	string terminated by zero	
w	word (two bytes)	

Table 1-1. Variable name prefix codes used in Hungarian notation

For example, the variable *lpszBigName* is a long pointer to a zero terminated string (l = long, p = pointer, sz = zero terminated string). Also note the use of capital letters in the name to make the word breaks clear without wasting space. Extending this concept, Windows makes extensive use of the C language preprocessor to create and use new data types. In many cases these data types are just another name for an integer or long variable. Using the Windows name, rather than the underlying data type, helps keep your program clear and reduces the chances of making a silly mistake.

All of these typedefs and defines are in a large header file called WINDOWS.H. You can see a reference to this file at the top of GENERIC.C and GENERIC.H. Every program you write under Windows will need this header file at the top, so that the compiler can keep track of all the preprocessor directives. Listing 1-6 provides a few examples from WINDOWS.H.

▷ **Listing 1-6. WINDOWS.H Excerpt**

```
typedef int                 BOOL;
typedef unsigned char       BYTE;
typedef unsigned int        WORD;
typedef unsigned long       DWORD;
typedef char near           *PSTR;
typedef char far            *LPSTR;
...
typedef WORD                HANDLE;
typedef HANDLE              HWND;
typedef HANDLE              HICON;
typedef HANDLE              HDC;
typedef HANDLE              HMENU;
typedef HANDLE              HFONT;
...
typedef struct tagPOINT
  {
    int  x;
    int  y;
  } POINT;
typedef POINT               *PPOINT;
typedef POINT NEAR          *NPPOINT;
typedef POINT FAR           *LPPOINT;
```

```
typedef struct tagRECT
{
        int     left;
        int     top;
        int     right;
        int     bottom;
} RECT ;
typedef RECT                    *PRECT;
typedef RECT NEAR               *NPRECT;
typedef RECT FAR                *LPRECT;
...
#define WM_CREATE               0x0001
#define WM_DESTROY              0x0002
#define WM_MOVE         0x0003
#define WM_SIZE         0x0004
```

The first six lines in Listing 1-6 give shorthand names for common data types. This saves time by allowing you to use the word "BYTE" in place of "unsigned char" any time you declare a variable name. Note that the shorthand names follow the prefix rules. For example PSTR is a pointer to a string, while LPSTR is a long (far) pointer to a string. The next group of typedefs define "HANDLE" and then define a bunch of different handles for icons, menus, etc. If you trace the lineage of typedefs, you will realize that all of these handles are just unsigned ints. Windows uses them to keep track of all sorts of data in memory, including bitmaps, memory blocks, icons, logical brushes, etc. Handles are definitely NOT addresses in memory. Just think of a handle as an ID value for a data item.

The third group in the example shows the creation of a new data types POINT and RECT for points and rectangles. In this case , the typedefs include the creation of structures to hold the x and y coordinates. Three pointer data types are then based on the data types. The handy thing about complex data types like these is that you can refer to all four data points that define a rectangular area with a single variable name. The last group of defines in Listing 1-6 provides names for the numeric values of a series of Windows messages. These names make it a lot easier to read the program. A complete listing of WINDOWS.H is included at the end of this book. As you start programming in Windows, you will probably find yourself referring to this listing frequently.

Improving GENERIC

If you try to resize the GENERIC program's window, you will notice that the "Ok, I did it!" message disappears every time you change the window's size. That is because Windows repaints the center of the window (called the *client area*) every time a part of the window is changed or resized.

To keep some text on the client area, we can retype it every time the window is repainted. How do we know when Windows wants to refresh the screen? Simple, we just look for the WM_PAINT message in our WinProc() function. Listing 1-7 shows the WinProc() function for the modified GENERIC.C program. The changed portions are emphasized.

▷ **Listing 1-7. GENERIC2.C—Changes to Process the WM_PAINT Message**

```
long FAR PASCAL WndProc (HWND hWnd, unsigned iMessage, WORD wParam, LONG lParam)
{
        HDC                     hDC ;           /* device context handle */
        PAINTSTRUCT             ps ;

        switch (iMessage)                       /* process windows messages */
        {
                case WM_PAINT:
                        hDC = BeginPaint(hWnd, &ps) ;
                        TextOut (hDC, 1, 1,
                                "I'm here because of WM_PAINT.", 29) ;
                        EndPaint (hWnd, &ps) ;
                        break ;
                case WM_COMMAND:        /* process menu items */
                        switch (wParam)
                        {
                        case IDM_DOIT:  /* User hit the "Do it" menu item */
```

```
                                        hDC = GetDC (hWnd) ;
                                        TextOut (hDC, 10, 20, "Ok, I did it!", 13) ;
                                        ReleaseDC (hWnd, hDC) ;
                                        break ;
                                case IDM_QUIT:
                                        DestroyWindow (hWnd) ;
                                        break ;
                                }
                                break ;
                        case WM_DESTROY:
                                PostQuitMessage (0) ;
                                break ;
                        default:
                                return DefWindowProc (hWnd, iMessage, wParam, lParam) ;
                }
        return (0L) ;
}
```

Now when you run the GENERIC.EXE program, the window always shows the message "I'm here because of WM_PAINT." This message persists after resizing the window, as it is repainted every time a WM_PAINT message is received. The result looks like Figure 1-3. The old message "Ok, I did it!" still appears if you click the "Do It!" menu item, but continues to disappear if you resize the window.

Besides demonstrating how the WM_PAINT message is used, this example is typical of how Windows programs are developed. You start with a simple outline such as GENERIC.C, then gradually add the functions you need for your specific application. The end results can be as different as a spreadsheet and communications program. They all have their roots in the basic structure of GENERIC.C.

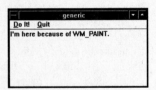

Figure 1-3. The Improved GENERIC.C Processing the WM_PAINT Messages.

Instances and Message Loops

We went over the code in GENERIC.C's WinMain() function pretty fast. Although all of the functions used in WinMain() are discussed in more detail in later chapters, there are a few points worth noting here. You may have noticed that both WinMain() and WndProc() are declared with the PASCAL statement. This saves a few bytes when the compiler pushes the function's parameters on the stack. The trade-off is that the PASCAL convention does not allow functions to have a variable number of parameters. Functions like printf() cannot use the PASCAL calling convention, as you do not know in advance how many parameters will be passed to the function. Windows uses the PASCAL statement wherever possible to make the code as small and fast as possible.

The WndProc() function is also preceded by the FAR statements. This makes the address of the function a FAR pointer. As Windows will use all available memory to hold programs, FAR pointers are needed for functions that Windows calls directly.

The first two parameters passed by Windows to WinMain() when the program starts are *hInstance* and *hPrevInstance*. These are "instance handles." You can run more than one copy of a program at the same time under Windows. Each version of the program is called a "program instance." Windows keeps only one copy of the program's code in memory, but keeps separate data for each instance.

GENERIC.C's WinMain() function stores the instance handle in a global variable *ghInstance*, defined in GENERIC.H. This is done because the instance handle is frequently needed in calling other functions, and it saves a little time if you keep a copy of the handle. If the program is starting for the first time (no other copy is running), the *hPrevInstance* will be NULL (zero). If another copy is running, *hPrevInstance* will be an integer value. GENERIC.C checks this and does not bother trying to register the window class for the program if another instance exists. That is because the first instance of the program will have already registered the class.

WinMain() passes two other parameters. *nCmdLine* is a pointer to a null-terminated character string containing the command line that launched the program. You can set the command line from within the program manager using the "File/Properties" menu item. This is rarely used in Windows. Windows programs tend to use initialization files such as WIN.INI to pass data to the application on startup. Support for initialization files is discussed in Chapter 20, *MS DOS and Disk File Access*.

The *nCmdShow* parameter is an integer. This value is passed to the ShowWindow() function later in WinMain() to control the initial appearance of the window. You do not have to use this value with ShowWindow(). The ShowWindow() function description in Chapter 3 discusses other options, such as starting the window in a minimized (iconic) state.

The WindProc() function also has four parameters. *hWnd* is the handle of the window receiving messages from Windows. Windows maintains a list of all windows in memory, using the handle (an unsigned integer) as an index. We will use this handle to refer to the window in many functions.

iMessage is the message from Windows. This is an unsigned integer, usually referred to by the symbolic name defined in WINDOWS.H, such as WM_PAINT. The "WM" stands for Windows Message. The *wParam* and *lParam* parameters are data that are passed along with each message. *wParam* is a WORD (two bytes), while *lParam* is a LONG value (four bytes). Their meaning will depend on the message being sent. For example, if you change the size of a window, Windows will send a WM_SIZE message. With this message, *lParam* will hold the new height and width of the window after resizing. *lParam* and *wParam* have different meanings with every Windows message.

In the simple GENERIC example, only a few Windows messages are acted on by the WndProc() function. The rest of the messages fall through to the bottom of WndProc() and end up sent to DefWindowProc(). This function does the default actions for all Windows messages. Default actions are things like processing WM_SIZE messages to change the window's size. You can stop the default action from occurring by intercepting the message in the WndProc() function, and then just returning zero from WndProc(), rather than passing the message on to DefWindowProc(). More on this in Chapter 8, *Message Processing Functions*.

Program Listing Conventions In This Book

The GENERIC application described above forms the basis for every example in this book. To save space, repeated portions of the program listings are not shown unless some change must be made. In most cases, the only changes are to the WndProc() function. If the example listing shows only the WndProc() function, you can assume that WinMain() and the support files (GENERIC, GENERIC.H, GENERIC.DEF, GENERIC.RC) are all identical to those listed in this chapter.

You will also note the use of two global variables in many of the examples. *ghInstance* and *gszAppName* are defined in GENERIC.H. They contain the program's instance handle and program name, respectively. The instance handle and application name are used in many different function calls. You can easily write code that avoids the use of these global variables. They are used in the examples to save space and improve clarity.

One final space saving trick is used in simple examples where only the top few lines of WndProc() are used to demonstrate a function. If the rest of WndProc() is identical to the GENERIC.C , the bottom portion is replaced with: *[Other program lines]*.

Creating Windows

Usually the word "window" brings to mind the application program's full client area, frame, menu, and caption bar. It turns out that Windows uses the same low-level logic to control all sorts of similar objects, including windows, buttons, list boxes and scroll bars. All of these are forms of "windows." They are all created using the CreateWindow() function. The main elements of a window are illustrated in Figure 2.1.

CreateWindow() is the most complex function in Windows. It is so complex because this one function can create a wide range of objects. Within each family of objects, such as scroll bars and buttons, there are a range of options. These options give you control over what the object looks like, where the text goes, if lists are sorted, and so on. The different options are given names in the WINDOWS.H file. In many cases, you can use several of the options at once, combining their effects. For example, a list box control, where you want the contents sorted and the parent window notified of any selections, would have the series of Windows styles

```
LBS_NOTIFY | LBS_SORT
```

The C language binary OR operator (|) combines these binary values before they are passed to the CreateWindow() function.

The other important control over a window is the window class upon which it is based. There are two basic choices here: Use an existing window class such as "BUTTON" or the parent window's base class, or create a new class from scratch. We will look at an example using both methods in the next two sections.

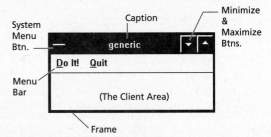

Figure 2-1. Elements of a Window.

Using CreateWindow() Based on an Existing Class

Let's modify the GENERIC.C application to show some window types in the program's client area (the work area below the menu bar). The only changes will be in the WinProc() function. We will put in four calls to CreateWindow(), making button, static text, edit, and scroll bar "windows" when the user clicks the "Do It!" menu item.

▷ **Listing 2-1. Creating Different Windows Using the Same Base Class**

```
long FAR PASCAL WndProc (HWND hWnd, unsigned iMessage, WORD wParam, LONG lParam)
{
        HWND    hButton, hStaticText, hEdit, hScroll ;

        switch (iMessage)                       /* process windows messages */
        {
                case WM_COMMAND:                /* process menu items */
                        switch (wParam)
                        {
                        case IDM_DOIT:          /* User hit the "Do it" menu item */
                                                /* create and show a button */
                                hButton = CreateWindow ("BUTTON", "Button",
                                        WS_CHILD | WS_VISIBLE | BS_PUSHBUTTON,
                                        10, 10, 100, 40, hWnd, CHILD1, ghInstance, NULL) ;
                                ShowWindow (hButton, SW_SHOW) ;
                                                /* create and show static text */
                                hStaticText = CreateWindow ("STATIC", "Static Text",
                                        WS_CHILD | WS_VISIBLE | BS_PUSHBUTTON,
```

```
                              150, 10, 100, 15, hWnd, CHILD2, ghInstance, NULL) ;
            ShowWindow (hStaticText, SW_SHOW) ;
                                /* create and show an edit control */
            hEdit = CreateWindow ("EDIT", "Edit Me",
                    WS_CHILD | WS_VISIBLE | WS_BORDER,
                    150, 40, 100, 25, hWnd, CHILD3, ghInstance, NULL) ;
            ShowWindow (hEdit, SW_SHOW) ;
                                /* create and show a scroll bar */
            hScroll = CreateWindow ("SCROLLBAR", "",
                    WS_CHILD | WS_VISIBLE | SBS_HORZ,
                    10, 100, 200, 20, hWnd, CHILD4, ghInstance, NULL) ;
            ShowWindow (hScroll, SW_SHOW) ;
            break ;
```

[Other program lines]

The rest of the program is the same as GENERIC.C)

The button, scroll bar, static text, and edit controls are all called "child window controls." The word "control" means that they were created with a predefined window class such as BUTTON, rather than registering a new window class. They are child windows because each is related to the parent window and will only be shown if the parent is visible. The WS_CHILD flag used in each call to CreateWindow() creates child windows. CreateWindow() was also passed the parent window's handle *hWnd*. This allows CreateWindow() to make the correct linkup of child and parent.

Notice that the first parameter in each of the calls to CreateWindow() is a word that specifies the type of child window control being created: BUTTON, STATIC, EDIT, and SCROLLBAR. The second parameter is the text string that will show up inside the control. Scroll bars do not have text, so a null string ("") is included. The series of numbers, such as "10, 10, 100, 40", sets the size and location of the child window. The parameter third from the last is the ID value for the window. In this case, the four controls have been numbered in sequence CHILD1, CHILD2, CHILD3, CHILD4. These values are normally defined in the program's header file

```
#define CHILD1          100
#define CHILD2          101
#define CHILD3          102
...
```

Also note that the program's instance handle (saved as the global variable *ghInstance*) is passed to CreateWindow().

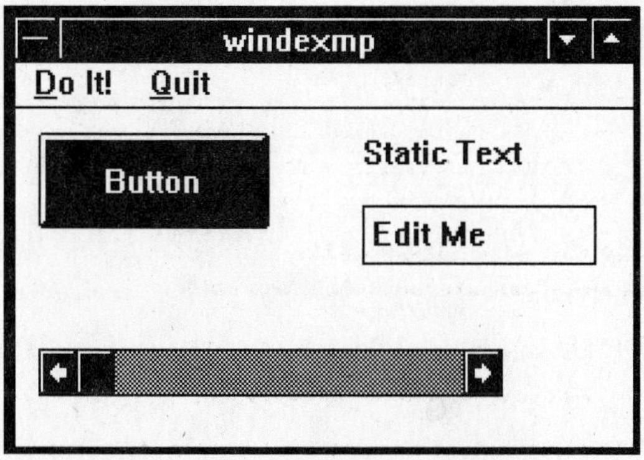

Figure 2-2. Four Types of Child Window Controls.

When you compile and run this program, clicking the "Do It!" button results in a screen like that shown in Figure 2-2. Experienced programmers will note that this example looks like a dialog box (the subject of Chapter 13). However, this is a normal window containing child window controls.

When you resize this window, the child windows in the client area are automatically redrawn. This is a big improvement over our GENERIC.C program in Chapter 1, where we had to explicitly redraw the text every time a WM_PAINT message was received. We have taken advantage of Windows' built in logic for child windows. Windows keeps track of child windows and updates them along with their parent.

If you click the "Edit Me" edit control with the mouse, a beam cursor (caret) appears in the control, and you can type in new letters, backspace to delete, etc. There is a lot of built-in logic in the edit control, which saves the programmer from doing a bunch of mundane code. You can create a serviceable text editor with nothing more than a large edit control. Edit controls are covered in more detail in Chapter 9, *Windows Messages*.

The example in Lisitng 2-1 does not do anything when you click one of the four controls. If you want to use the button control in a real program, you will need to process the messages Windows generates. If you click the button control with the mouse, Windows sends a WM_COMMAND with *wParam* equal to the ID value of the control. A code fragment for this type of processing might look like Listing 2-2.

▷ **Listing 2-2. Example Code for Recognizing Button Controls**

```
long FAR PASCAL WndProc (HWND hWnd, unsigned iMessage, WORD wParam, LONG lParam)
{
        switch (iMessage)                    /* process windows messages */
        {
            case WM_COMMAND:              /* process menu items */
                switch (wParam)
                {
                case CHILD1:     /* control 1 pressed */
                        /* do something here */
                        break ;
                case CHILD2:                /* control 2 pressed */
                        /* etc. */
```

[Other program lines]

This simple interception of WM_COMMAND messages is typically used for buttons. For more complex controls such as the scroll bar and edit controls, a number of messages are possible, depending on what the user does with the control. Scroll bars are the subject of Chapter 5. Edit controls are discussed in Chapter 9 under the EM and EN message section (Edit Message and Edit Notify).

Creating New Window Classes with Separate Message Processing

The previous example used four of the predefined control classes to create child window controls. We can also create child windows that are complete windows, including menus, captions, minimize and maximize boxes, etc. The child window becomes its own "little world" and can display information and process Windows messages independently from its parent window. The best way to deal with more complicated child windows is to give them their own message processing function. This allows you to break up your program logic into a set of similar message processing functions, each modeled after WinProc().

To show how child windows can process their own messages, let's create a program that looks like Figure 2-3. The WINDEXM2 program's main window will be identical to the GENERIC.C program from Chapter 1. In the client area we will put a child window. The child window will be built from a separate window class, and have its own message processing function to deal with screen updates, etc.

Creating this program will require modifications to several parts of the GENERIC.C application. It is best to make a copy of all the GENERIC.* files and then modify each of them.

WINDEXM2.C (Listing 2-3) has an identical WinMain() function to GENERIC.C. In the WinProc() function, WINDEXM2 picks up the WM_CREATE message that Windows sends when a program is started. When this message is received, WINDEXM2 creates a new window class called "SecondClass." This class has several changes compared to the base class we used to create the WINDEXM2 window. The following line sets the message processing function equal to "ChildProc."

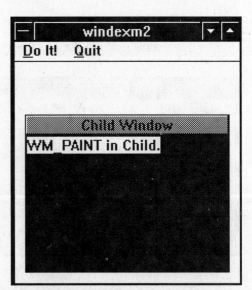

Figure 2-3. WINDEXM2—A Child Window with Separate Message Processing.

```
wndclass.lpfnWndProc = ChildProc ;
```

This function is shown at the bottom of WINDEXM2.C. The class also uses a different cursor shape than the base window class because we specified the predefined IDC_CROSS cursor shape. Similarly, a predefined "brush" used to paint the background color LTGRAY_BRUSH is loaded using the GetStockObject() function. Stock objects are pens and brushes that are always available in Windows. Chapter 11, *Painting the Screens*, explores creating custom pens and brushes. Chapter 6 covers cursors.

```
wndclass.hCursor        = LoadCursor (NULL, IDC_CROSS) ;
wndclass.hbrBackground  = GetStockObject (LTGRAY_BRUSH) ;
```

The changes to the cursor and background brush mean that any time a window is created from the "SecondClass" window class, the mouse will switch to a cross shape in the child window's area and the background will be painted light gray.

➪ Listing 2-3. WINDEXM2.C

```
/* windexm2.c  example of creating a child window with message processing */

#include <windows.h>            /* window's header file - always included */
#include "windexm2.h"           /* the application's header file */


int PASCAL WinMain (HANDLE hInstance, HANDLE hPrevInstance, LPSTR lpszCmdLine,
     int nCmdShow)
{
     /* Exactly the same as WinMain() in generic.c - chapter 1 */
}




long FAR PASCAL WndProc (HWND hWnd, unsigned iMessage, WORD wParam,      LONG lParam)
{
     HDC                hDC ;           /* device context handle */
     static WNDCLASS wndclass ;         /* the window class */
     static HWND        hListBox ;      /* the window handle */

     switch (iMessage)                  /* process windows messages */
     {
          case WM_CREATE: /* build child window when program starts */
               wndclass.style          = CS_HREDRAW | CS_VREDRAW |
                                              CS_PARENTDC ;
               wndclass.lpfnWndProc    = ChildProc ;
               wndclass.cbClsExtra     = 0 ;
               wndclass.cbWndExtra     = 0 ;
               wndclass.hInstance      = ghInstance ;
               wndclass.hIcon          = NULL ;
               wndclass.hCursor        = LoadCursor (NULL, IDC_CROSS) ;
               wndclass.hbrBackground  = GetStockObject (LTGRAY_BRUSH) ;
               wndclass.lpszMenuName   = NULL ;
               wndclass.lpszClassName  = "SecondClass" ;
                         /* register the window class */
               if(RegisterClass (&wndclass))
               {
                    hListBox = CreateWindow ("SecondClass", "Child Window",
                         WS_CHILD | WS_VISIBLE | WS_BORDER | WS_CAPTION,
                         10, 50, 200, 150, hWnd, NULL, ghInstance, NULL) ;
                    ShowWindow (hListBox, SW_SHOW) ;
               }
               break ;
          case WM_COMMAND:                  /* process menu items */
               switch (wParam)
               {
               case IDM_DOIT:            /* User hit the "Do it" menu item */
                    hDC = GetDC (hWnd) ;     /* get device context */
                    TextOut (hDC, 10, 20, "Ok, I did it!", 13) ;
                    ReleaseDC (hWnd, hDC) ;  /* release device context */
                    break ;
               case IDM_QUIT:            /* stop application */
                    DestroyWindow (hWnd) ;
                    break ;
               }
```

```
                               break ;
                   case WM_DESTROY:
                           PostQuitMessage (0) ;
                               break ;
                   default:                          /* default windows message processing */
                           return DefWindowProc (hWnd, iMessage, wParam, lParam) ;
           }
           return (0L) ;
}


/* Here is a separate message processing procedure for the child window */

long FAR PASCAL ChildProc (HWND hWnd, unsigned iMessage, WORD wParam,
       LONG lParam)
{
       HDC                     hDC ;               /* device context handle */
       PAINTSTRUCT             ps ;                /* paint structure */

       switch (iMessage)                           /* process windows messages */
       {
           case WM_PAINT:                          /* just write in the window */
                   hDC = BeginPaint(hWnd, &ps) ;
                   TextOut (hDC, 1, 1, "WM_PAINT in Child.", 18) ;
                   EndPaint (hWnd, &ps) ;
                   break ;
           default:                                /* default windows message processing */
                   return DefWindowProc (hWnd, iMessage, wParam, lParam) ;
       }
       return (0L) ;
}
```

The function ChildProc() at the end of Listing 2-3 looks similar to the WinProc() function from GENERIC.C. Any message processing for our child window will be handled in this function. In this example, all we do is put some text into the window every time a WM_PAINT message is received. We have to make a couple of other changes to files to get all of this to work. One simple thing is to add the function prototype for ChildProc() to our header file so that the compiler can figure out what data types are used. WINEXM2.H is shown in Listing 2-4.

▷ **Listing 2-4. WINEXM2.H Header File**

```
/* windexm2.h    */

#define IDM_DOIT    1                              /* menu item id values */
#define IDM_QUIT    2

/* global variables */
int     ghInstance ;
char    gszAppName []= "windexm2" ;

/* function prototypes */
long FAR PASCAL WndProc (HWND, unsigned, WORD, LONG) ;
long FAR PASCAL ChildProc (HWND, unsigned, WORD, LONG) ;
```

The other change is to put a reference to ChildProc() in our definition file, such as where shown in Listing 2-5. This is needed only when the function will be accessed directly by Windows, processing Windows messages. That's exactly what ChildProc() does, so it is important not to forget to add it to the .DEF file. Details on .DEF files are covered in Chapter 13, *Dialog Boxes*.

▷ **Listing 2-5. WINDEXM2.DEF Definition File**

```
NAME          WINDEXM2
DESCRIPTION   'create windows example'
EXETYPE       WINDOWS
STUB          'WINSTUB.EXE'
CODE          PRELOAD MOVEABLE
DATA          PRELOAD MOVEABLE MULTIPLE
HEAPSIZE      1024
```

```
STACKSIZE    5120
EXPORTS      WndProc
             ChildProc
```

If you compile WINDEXM2.C and try it, you will notice that the child window is updated (painted) automatically whenever the parent window is resized. The child window has a gray client area (from the class definition), and the cursor changes from the normal arrow to a cross shape when it is within the child window's bounds.

Messages Generated by CreateWindow()

In WINDEXM2.C, the WndProc() function processes the WM_CREATE message. It is at this point that WndProc() creates the child window. Where did WM_CREATE come from? It turns out that Windows sends five messages to WndProc() when the program's main window is created by calling CreateWindow() in WinMain(). WINDEXM2.C chooses to act on one of them, WM_CREATE, but just passes the other four on to DefWindowProc(). Windows knows to send the messages to WndProc(), as that was the name of the window message processing function specified in the class definition for the program's main window. We also included WndProc() in the EXPORTS section of the program's .DEF definition file, so that Windows would have the full address.

The sequence of messages that are generated by CreateWindow() is shown in Table 2-1. The actions described for each message are taken care of by the DefWindowProc() function at the bottom of WndProc(). You can get an idea of how important DefWindowProc() is from the complexity of these actions. Fortunately, DefWindowProc() comes with Windows, so we can take advantage of all of these built-in features without any extra coding.

Message	Meaning	⊠
WM_GETMINMAXINFO	Determines the size and position of the window.	
WM_NCCREATE	Window nonclient area about to be created. Memory for the window is allocated internally by Windows. Scroll bars are initialized.	
WM_NCCALCSIZE	Calculation of the window's client area and scroll bar positions.	
WM_CREATE	Notification that a window is about to be created.	
WM_SHOWWINDOW	Display the window.	

Table 2-1. Messages Generated by CreateWindow().

An interesting point to mention here is the order of execution of different parts of the WINDEXM2 program. If you get into the CodeView For Windows debugger and set a few breakpoints, you will find that the five messages are processed by WndProc() right after CreateWindow() is called and before the next line in WinMain() is executed.

This behavior is completely different from a C program running under DOS. Under DOS you can expect one program line to be executed right after the previous one. Windows programs are different. Windows sends messages to WndProc() when Windows feels like it, not necessarily when you might expect it. Function calls within WndProc() may also generate messages that in turn are processed by WndProc(). Message processing functions such as WndProc() are said to be "reentrant," as they may be called many times in a single logical activity. More on this in Chapter 8, *Message Processing Functions*.

Other Uses for Window Controls

In the function description for CreateWindow() that follows, there is a long table of window styles. There are so many window styles available that it is difficult to keep track of them all. Here are a few unusual ones that might come in handy.

The static class is normally used to display text on a window. Using the static class is more convenient than repainting the text every time a WM_PAINT message comes along because the static window class is automatically redrawn. Some of the options for the static class allow items other than text. The SS_BLACKRECT style fills the region with the system color for the edge of windows (usually black). Similarly, SS_GRAYRECT and SS_WHITERECT fill rectangles with the screen (desktop) background and window background colors (defaults are gray and white). You can use a series of these controls to shade areas of your window's client area, again with automatic updating.

If you use an ampersand character (&) in a button class, the letter after the & will be underlined. Windows then uses this letter as an accelerator key. Pressing that letter on the keyboard is equivalent to moving to the button with the mouse. If you need to display & characters in a window style, disable the accelerator functions by using the SS_NOPREFIX style, or use a double && in the text string.

The scroll bar class has a couple of styles that are handy if you want to have the scroll bar along one of the sides of the client area—typical for a word processing application. The SBS_BOTTOMALIGN, SBS_TOPALIGN, SBS_RIGHTALIGN, and SBS_LEFTALIGN styles all fit the scroll bar to the parent window's client area, using the default scroll bar width. More on this in Chapter 5, *Scroll Bars*.

If you want to have an icon on your parent window to pretty things up, there is an SS_ICON style for the static class. This will save you from having to use DrawIcon() on every WM_PAINT cycle. You can also create your own custom buttons, using bitmaps or painting on the button's client area by using the BS_OWNERDRAW button style. You will have to create images for not only the button in its normal state, but also for an inverted image reflecting being pressed and a disabled (no input focus) state. See the owner-drawn menu example in Chapter 4 for an example of processing the messages for owner-drawn items.

Function Descriptions

Table 2-2 summarizes the three window creation functions. The detailed descriptions follow.

Function	Purpose	
CreateWindow()	Creates new windows and child window controls.	
CreateWindowEx()	Creates new windows with an extended style.	
RegisterClass()	Creates new windows classes.	

Table 2-2. Functions for Creating Windows and Controls.

CREATEWINDOW   ■ Win 2.0   ■ Win 3.0   ■ Win 3.1

Purpose	Creates new windows and child window controls.
Syntax	HWND **CreateWindow**(LPSTR *lpClassName*, LPSTR *lpWindowName*, DWORD *dwStyle*, int *X*, int *Y*, int *nWidth*, int *nHeight*, HWND *hWndParent*, HMENU *hMenu*, HANDLE *hInstance*, LPSTR *lpParam*);
Description	CreateWindow() builds a window based on a window class created with RegisterClass() or based on a predefined control class. The location, size, and style of window are passed to CreateWindow() as parameters. ShowWindow() is used after the window is created to display it on the screen.
Uses	The CreateWindow function is used both in the WinMain() function to create the application's main window and also within the program to create child windows and child window controls such as buttons and scroll bars.
Returns	HWND, a handle to the window created. The handle is a unique identifier for the particular window or control created with each call to CreateWindow().
See Also	RegisterClass(), ShowWindow(), DestroyWindow(), CreateWindowEx()
Parameters	
lpClassName	LPSTR: Pointer to a null-terminated string which contains the name of the window class. Classes can either be created using RegisterClass(), or they can be chosen from one of the predefined control classes described in Table 2-3. The class names are case sensitive.

Class	Meaning	⊠
BUTTON	A rectangular push button control.	
COMBOBOX	Combination of a list box, with an edit field on top.	
EDIT	Rectangular region where the user can enter and edit text.	
LISTBOX	A list of character strings. If the list length overflows the length of the box, a vertical scroll control will automatically appear on the right hand side. The listbox can contain graphics items, if the LB_OWNERDRAWFIXED or LBOWNERDRAWVARIABLE styles are used. See Chapter 9, *Windows Messages*.	
MDICLIENT	A Multiple Document Interface window. This style is used for multiple overlapping child windows within the parent window's client area. See Chapter 29, *Multiple Document Interface*.	
SCROLLBAR	A scroll bar control.	
STATIC	Static text. This style is used to place text on the parent window.	

Table 2-3. Predefined Windows Control Classes.

lpWindowName	LPSTR: Points to a null-terminated character string that contains the window's name. For BUTTON styles this string becomes the button's text. For EDIT and STATIC styles the string is shown in the center of the control. For popup windows it is used as the title.
dwStyle	DWORD: Determines the style of window. The styles can be combined by using the C language binary OR operator. For example: WS_CHILD	WS_HSCROLL. Styles can be any of those listed in Table 2-4.
X	int: The horizontal position of the upper left corner of the child window or control. You can use CW_USEDEFAULT to let Windows decide where to put a program's window.
	The *X,Y* location is from the upper left corner of the screen or parent window client area (for child windows), measured in pixels (device units).
Y	int: The vertical position of the upper left corner of the child window or control. You can use CW_USEDEFAULT to let Windows decide where to put a program's window.
nWidth	int: The horizontal size of the window or control. You can use CW_USEDEFAULT to let Windows decide what size to make a program's window.
	The width and height are measured in device units (pixels).
nHeight	int: The horizontal size of the window or control. You can use CW_USEDEFAULT to let Windows decide what size to make a program's window.
hWndParent	HWND: A handle to the window's parent. Specify NULL if there is no parent window. In this case the window will not be destroyed automatically when the main program window is destroyed. Use DestroyWindow() to remove a window from memory.
hMenu	HMENU: A handle to the window's menu. NULL if the class menu is to be used. Use the *dwStyle* parameter to add or eliminate a menu from child windows.
	For controls, *hMenu* is used to set an integer ID value. This value will be passed as the *wParam* parameter of a WM_COMMAND message when the control is activated by a mouse click or keypress.
hInstance	HANDLE: The instance handle for the program module creating the windows.
lpParam	LPSTR: A long pointer to a data structure passed to the window. For example the MDI (Multiple Document Interface) style passes the CLIENTCREATESTRUCT data here. Normally set to NULL, meaning that no data is passed via CreateWindow().
Related Messages	WM_PARENTNOTIFY, WM_NCCREATE, WM_CREATE

Example This example shows the creation of a pushbutton control. The button will have the text "Press Me" in the center. The upper left corner of the button will be at 10,10 relative to the upper left corner of the client area. The button will be 100 pixels wide and 40 high. The parent window's handle is *hWnd*, and has an instance handle of *hInstance*. The button has an ID value of 101. Creating a window does not make it visible; the ShowWindow() does.

```
HWND      hButton ;

hButton = CreateWindow ("BUTTON", "Press Me",
        WS_CHILD | WS_VISIBLE | BS_PUSHBUTTON,
        10, 10, 100, 40, hWnd, 101, hInstance, NULL) ;
ShowWindow (hButton, SW_SHOW) ;
```

Table 2-4 summarizes all of the values that can be used in the *dwstyle* parameter.

Button Styles	Meaning
BS_AUTOCHECKBOX	Small rectangular button with text to the right. The rectangle can either be open or checked. This style toggles automatically between checked and open.
BS_AUTORADIOBUTTON	Small circular button with text to the right. The circle can either be filled or open. This style toggles automatically between checked and open.
BS_AUTO3STATE	Small rectangular button with text to the right. The button can either be filled, grayed, or open. This style toggles automatically between checked, grayed, and open.
BS_CHECKBOX	Small rectangular button with text to the right. The rectangle can either be open or checked.
BS_DEFPUSHBUTTON	Button with text in the center and with a defined (dark) border. This is the button that is pressed when the user presses the (ENTER) key. There can be only one DEFPUSHBUTTON on a window.
BS_GROUPBOX	A box outline with text at the upper left. Used to group other controls.
BS_LEFTTEXT	Causes text to be on the left side of the button. Use this with other button styles.
BS_OWNERDRAW	Designates a button that will be drawn by the program. Windows sends messages to request paint, invert, and disable. Use this style for custom button controls. See the example in Chapter 4 on owner-drawn menu items.
BS_PUSHBUTTON	A rectangular button with text in the center.
BS_RADIOBUTTON	Small circular button with text to the right. The circle can either be filled or open.
BS_3STATE	Small rectangular button with text to the right. The button can either be filled, grayed, or open.

Combo Box Styles	
CBS_AUTOHSCROLL	Combo box control. This is a list box with an edit control at the top to display the current selection. Chapter 9, *Window Messages*, includes a combo box example and message descriptions. With the CBS_AUTOHSCROLL style, the edit area at the top automatically scrolls when typing fills the edit box.
CBS_DISABLENOSCROLL (Win 3.1)	The list box of the combo box control shows a disabled vertical scroll bar when the list box does not contain enough items to fill the list box window. Without this style, the scroll bar disappears when there are not enough items.
CBS_DROPDOWN	Combo box control with a drop down scroll area. This reduces the space taken by the combo box when the list is not needed.

CBS_DROPDOWNLIST	Combo box control with a drop down scroll area. The edit area at top is a static text item which only displays the current selection in the list box.
CBS_HASSTRINGS	The combo box control maintains the list box strings in memory. Fetch them by sending a CB_GETLBTEXT message.
CBS_OEMCONVERT	Combo box edit text is converted to OEM character set and then back to ANSI. Useful for lists of file names.
CBS_OWNERDRAWFIXED	An owner-drawn combo box. The combo box items are of fixed height. See the combo box example in Chapter 9, *Window Messages*, for an example owner-drawn combo box.
CBS_OWNERDRAWVARIABLE	An owner-drawn combo box. The combo box items can be of different heights.
CBS_SIMPLE	The combo box has a list box that is displayed at all times.
CBS_SORT	The combo box items are sorted automatically.

Dialog Box Styles ☒

DS_LOCALEDIT	Forces all memory used by dialog boxes into the application's data segment.
DS_MODALFRAME	Creates a dialog box with a modal frame. Note that this can be combined with the WS_CAPTION and WS_SYSMENU styles.
DS_NOIDLEMSG	No WM_ENTERIDLE messages are sent from the dialog box if created with this style. Normally, WM_ENTERIDLE messages are used to alert the application that the dialog box is displayed, but no user activity has happened yet.
DS_SYSMODAL	System modal dialog box. No other window can gain the input focus until this style dialog box is closed. Used for serious error messages.

Edit Control Styles ☒

ES_AUTOHSCROLL	Edit control with automatic horizontal scrolling if the text will not fit within the edit box.
ES_AUTOVSCROLL	Automatic vertical scrolling for an edit control. Used with ES_MULTILINE. See the example in Chapter 9 of a multiline edit control with a vertical scroll bar.
ES_CENTER	Text is centered within the edit control.
ES_LEFT	Text is left-aligned within the edit control.
ES_LOWERCASE	All characters within the edit control are converted to lowercase as they are entered.
ES_MULTILINE	Allows multiple lines of input within an edit control. This type of control provides basic text processing functions. The discussion of edit control messages that work with this control style is in Chapter 9.
ES_NOHIDESEL	Edit control where the text is left unchanged when the control loses the input focus.
ES_OEMCONVERT	Edit control text is converted to OEM character set and then back to ANSI. Useful for file names.
ES_PASSWORD	Displays typed-in letters as astersik characters "*". The actual typed letters are stored by the edit control. See the EM_SETPASSWORDCHAR message description in Chapter 9.
ES_READONLY (Win 3.1)	The edit text can be viewed, but not changed by the user.
ES_RIGHT	Right-aligned letters within the edit control.
ES_UPPERCASE	All characters within the edit control are converted to uppercase as they are entered.

List Box Styles

LBS_DISABLENOSCROLL (Win 3.1)	The list box control shows a disabled vertical scroll bar when the list box does not contain enough items to fill the list box window. Without this style, the scroll bar disappears when there are not enough items.
LBS_EXTENDEDSEL	List box control where more than one item can be selected by using the mouse and the shift key.
LBS_HASSTRINGS	List box control containing lists of strings. Send the LB_GETTEXT message to retrieve the strings.
LBS_MULTICOLUMN	List box with multiple columns. Can be scrolled horizontally and vertically. Send LB_SETCOLUMNWIDTH to set the column widths.
LBS_MULTIPLESEL	Any number of strings can be selected within the list box. Selection by mouse clicking, deselection by double-clicking.
LBS_NOINTEGRALHEIGHT	A list box of fixed size. The list box height is not scaled to match an even number of items (the default case).
LBS_NOREDRAW	A list box which is not automatically redrawn. Convert the control back to normal by sending the WM_SETREDRAW message.
LBS_NOTIFY	A list box that sends the parent window messages when the user selects one or more items. The list box messages are discussed in Chapter 9.
LBS_OWNERDRAWFIXED	A list box where the program is responsible for drawing all items. Items are of fixed vertical size. There is a similar example using an owner-drawn combo box in Chapter 9, *Windows Messages*.
LBS_OWNERDRAWVARIABLE	A list box where the program is responsible for drawing all items. Items can be of different vertical sizes.
LBS_SORT	A list box where the items are maintained in sort order.
LBS_STANDARD	A list box containing stings, automatically sorted, with messages sent to the parent window when selections are made.
LBS_USETABSTOPS	A list box that recognizes and expands tab characters. By default, tabs are every eight spaces. See the EM_SETTABSTOPS message to change this value.
LBS_WANTKEYBOARDINPUT	The parent window receives WM_VKEYTOITEM and WM_CHARTOITEM messages from the list box when it has the input focus and keys are pressed. Handy for setting key combinations.

Scroll Bar Styles

SBS_BOTTOMALIGN	A scroll bar control, aligned with the bottom edge of the rectangle specified by the *X, Y, nWidth,* and *nHeight* parameters used in calling CreateWindow() for the parent window. The default scroll bar height is used.
SBS_HORZ	A horizontal scroll bar control.
SBS_LEFTALIGN	A scroll bar control, aligned with the left edge of the rectangle specified by the *X, Y, nWidth,* and *nHeight* parameters used in calling CreateWindow() for the parent window. The default scroll bar width is used.
SBS_RIGHTALIGN	A scroll bar control, aligned with the right edge of the rectangle specified by the *X, Y, nWidth,* and *nHeight* parameters used in calling CreateWindow() for the parent window. The default scroll bar width is used.
SBS_SIZEBOX	A scroll bar size box control. This is a small box that allows sizing of a window from one location.

SBS_SIZEBOXBOTTOMRIGHTALIGN	Used with the SBS_SIZEBOX style. A size box control, aligned with the lower right edge of the rectangle specified by the *X, Y, nWidth,* and *nHeight* parameters used in calling CreateWindow() for the parent window. The default size box size is used.
SBS_SIZEBOXTOPLEFTALIGN	Used with the SBS_SIZEBOX style. A size box control, aligned with the top left edge of the rectangle specified by the *X, Y, nWidth,* and *nHeight* parameters used in calling CreateWindow() for the parent window. The default size box size is used.
SBS_TOPALIGN	Used with the SBS_HORZ style. Puts the scroll bar at the top of the parent window's client area.
SBS_VERT	A vertical scroll bar control.

Static Control Styles ⊠

SS_BLACKFRAME	A static control with a black frame outline.
SS_BLACKRECT	A static control with the entire center filled with the color used to draw the window frame. This is black with the default Windows color scheme.
SS_CENTER	A static text control with the text centered.
SS_GRAYFRAME	A static control with the frame color equal to the Windows desktop background. This is gray with the default Windows color scheme.
SS_GRAYRECT	A static control with the entire center filled with the color used to draw the Windows desktop background. This is gray with the default Windows color scheme.
SS_ICON	A static control containing an icon. The text name specifies the name of the icon to use.
SS_LEFT	A static text control with the text left-aligned.
SS_LEFTNOWORDWRAP	A static text control. Text is flush left and truncated to the size of the control.
SS_NOPREFIX	A static control when it is desirable to display ampersands (&) in the text of the control.
SS_RIGHT	A static text control with the text string right-aligned.
SS_SIMPLE	A static text control.
SS_USERITEM	A user-defined static control.
SS_WHITEFRAME	A static text control with a frame matching the Windows background color (default is white).
SS_WHITERECT	A static control with the entire center filled with the color used to draw the parent windows background. This is white with the default Windows color scheme.

Window Styles ⊠

WS_BORDER	Specifies a border on a window .
WS_CAPTION	Specifies a caption (title) on a window. This cannot be used with the WS_DLGFRAME style.
WS_CHILD	Creates a child window. This cannot be used with the WS_POPUP style.
WS_CHILDWINDOW	Same as WS_CHILD.
WS_CLIPCHILDREN	Used when creating the parent window. Specifies that child windows will not extend past the boundary of the parent.
WS_CLIPSIBLINGS	Use with WS_CHILD style. Keeps child windows from overlapping in painting operations.
WS_DISABLED	Creates a window that is initially disabled (cannot receive the input focus).
WS_DLGFRAME	A window with a double border.
WS_GROUP	This style marks a control that the user can reach by using the direction (arrow) keys. Used in dialog boxes.

Window Styles

WS_HSCROLL	A window with a horizontal scroll bar.
WS_ICONIC	A window that is initially iconic. Use with the WS_OVERLAPPED style.
WS_MAXIMIZE	A window that is initially maximized.
WS_MAXIMIZEBOX	A window with a maximize box in the upper right corner.
WS_MINIMIZE	Same as WS_ICONIC.
WS_MINIMIZEBOX	A window with a minimize box in the upper right corner.
WS_OVERLAPPED	A window with a caption and a border.
WS_OVERLAPPEDWINDOW	Combines the WS_OVERLAPPED, WS_CAPTION, WS_SYSMENU, and WS_THICK-FRAME styles. This is a standard parent window.
WS_POPUP	A popup window. Cannot be used with the WS_CHILD style. The window can be displayed outside of the parent's boundaries.
WS_POPUPWINDOW	Combines the WS_POPUP, WS_BORDER, and WS_SYSMENU styles. This is a standard popup window.
WS_SYSMENU	A window with a system menu. This is the square at the upper left corner of the window. Clicking the system menu reveals menu items for "Restore," "Move," etc.
WS_TABSTOP	Used in dialog boxes to specify at which control the tab key stops.
WS_THICKFRAME	A window with a thick frame. The frame is used to size the window.
WS_VISIBLE	A window that is initially visible. Used with overlapped and popup windows.
WS_VSCROLL	A window with a vertical scroll bar.

Table 2-4. Window Styles.

CREATEWINDOWEX   ☐ Win 2.0   ■ Win 3.0   ■ Win 3.1

Purpose   Creates new windows with an extended style.

Syntax   HWND **CreateWindowEx**(DWORD *dwExStyle*,LPSTR *lpClassName*, LPSTR *lpWindowName*, DWORD *dwStyle*, int *X*, int *Y*, int *nWidth*, int *nHeight*, HWND *hWndParent*, HMENU *hMenu*, HANDLE *hInstance*, LPSTR *lpParam*);

Description   The CreateWindowEx() function is used to create child windows with a double border style and/or with WM_PARENTNOTIFY messages disabled. Otherwise, it is identical to CreateWindow(). This is an addition to the 3.0 version of Windows.

Returns   HWND, a handle to the window created.

See Also   RegisterClass(), ShowWindow(), DestroyWindow(), CreateWindow()

Parameters

dwExStyle   DWORD: Specifies the extended style to use in creating the window. The only three styles currently defined are:

Style	Meaning
WS_EX_DLGMODALFRAME	A window with a double border. You can use the WS_CAPTION style in the *dwStyle* parameter to add a title.
WS_EX_NOPARENTNOTIFY	Prevents WM_PARENTNOTIFY messages from being sent to the parent window when a child with this style is created.
WS_EX_TOPMOST (Win 3.1)	Windows created with this style remain above all other non-topmost windows, even when deactivated. The SetWindowPos() function can be used to change this status.

Table 2-5. Extended Window Styles.

lpClassName   LPSTR: Pointer to a null-terminated string which contains the name of the window class. Classes can be created using RegisterClass().

lpWindowName   LPSTR: Points to a null-terminated character string that contains the window's name. For BUTTON styles, this string becomes the button's text. For EDIT and STATIC styles, the string is shown in the center of the control.

dwStyle   DWORD: Determines the style of window. The styles can be combined by using the C language binary OR operator (|). For example: WS_CHILD | WS_HSCROLL. Styles can be any of those listed in Table 2-4 of CreateWindow().

X   int: The horizontal position of the upper left hand corner or the child window or control. You can use CW_USEDEFAULT to let Windows decide where to put a program's window.
                  The *X* and *Y* positions, as well as the *nWdith* and *nHeight* values, are given in device units (pixels).

Y   int: The vertical position of the upper left corner or the child window or control. You can use CW_USEDEFAULT to let Windows decide where to put a program's window.

nWidth   int: The horizontal size of the window or control. You can use CW_USEDEFAULT to let Windows decide what size to make a program's window.

nHeight   int: The horizontal size of the window or control. You can use CW_USEDEFAULT to let Windows decide what size to make a program's window.

hWndParent   HWND: A handle to the window's parent. NULL if there is no parent window.

hMenu   HMENU: A handle to the window's menu. NULL if the class menu is to be used. Use the window styles to add or eliminate a menu line from child windows.

hInstance   HANDLE: The instance handle for the program module creating the windows.

lpParam   LPSTR: A long pointer to a data structure passed to the window. Normally set to NULL, meaning that no data is passed via CreateWindow().

Related Messages WM_PARENTNOTIFY, WM_NCREATE

Example   The following code fragment shows the creation of a window with an extended style as the main program window.

```
WNDCLASS         wndclass ;

wndclass.style            = CS_HREDRAW | CS_VREDRAW | CS_PARENTDC ;
wndclass.lpfnWndProc      = WndProc ;
wndclass.cbClsExtra       = 0 ;
wndclass.cbWndExtra       = 0 ;
wndclass.hInstance        = ghInstance ;
wndclass.hIcon            = NULL ;
wndclass.hCursor          = LoadCursor (NULL, IDC_ARROW) ;
wndclass.hbrBackground    = GetStockObject (WHITE_BRUSH) ;
wndclass.lpszMenuName     = NULL ;
wndclass.lpszClassName    = "SecondClass" ;

            /* register the window class */
if(RegisterClass (&wndclass))
{
        hListBox = CreateWindow Ex(WS_EX_DLGMODALFRAME
                "SecondClass", "Child Window",
                WS_CHILD | WS_VISIBLE | WS_CAPTION,
                10, 50, 200, 150, hWnd, NULL, ghInstance, NULL) ;
        ShowWindow (hListBox, SW_SHOW) ;
}
```

REGISTERCLASS
■ Win 2.0   ■ Win 3.0   ■ Win 3.1

Purpose	Creates new Windows classes.
Syntax	BOOL **RegisterClass**(LPWNDCLASS *lpWndClass*);
Description	RegisterClass() creates a new Windows class that can be used to create any number of new windows and child controls.
Uses	Used in the WinMain() function to create the base class for the parent window. Can be used in the body of the program to create other Windows classes.
Returns	Non-zero (TRUE) if the new class was registered. Zero (FALSE) if the function failed.
See Also	CreateWindow(), CreateWindowEx(), UnregisterClass(), GetClassInfo(), GetClassLong(), GetClassName(), GetClassWord(), SetClassLong(), SetClassWord()
Parameters	
lpWndClass	LPWNDCLASS: A long pointer to a WNDCLASS data structure. This is defined in WINDOWS.H as:

```
typedef struct tagWNDCLASS
{
    WORD        style;
    LONG        (FAR PASCAL *lpfnWndProc)();
    int         cbClsExtra;
    int         cbWndExtra;
    HANDLE      hInstance;
    HICON       hIcon;
    HCURSOR     hCursor;
    HBRUSH      hbrBackground;
    LPSTR       lpszMenuName;
    LPSTR       lpszClassName;
} WNDCLASS;
typedef WNDCLASS         *PWNDCLASS;
typedef WNDCLASS NEAR    *NPWNDCLASS;
typedef WNDCLASS FAR     *LPWNDCLASS;
```

The elements of the WNDCLASS structure are as follows:

style   WORD: The style parameter can be any of those listed in Table 2-6, combined as desired using the C language binary OR operator (|).

Style	Meaning
CS_BYTEALIGNCLIENT	Aligns a window's client area on the byte boundaries horizontally. This makes a small savings in memory consumed by Windows.
CS_BYTEALIGNWINDOW	Aligns a window on the byte boundaries horizontally.
CS_CLASSDC	Gives the window class its own device context. Every window created from this class will share the DC.
CS_DBLCLKS	Mouse double-click messages are sent to the window.
CS_GLOBALCLASS	Makes an application global class. Available to all applications while the program that created the class is running.
CS_HREDRAW	Redraws the window if the horizontal size changes.
CS_NOCLOSE	Stops the close option on the system menu.
CS_OWNDC	Gives each window instance its own device context. Note that each device context requires 800 bytes of memory.
CS_PARENTDC	The window class uses the parent window's device context.
CS_SAVEBITS	Instructs window to save the bitmap of parts of the window that may be obscured by overlapping windows.
CS_VREDRAW	Redraws the window when the vertical size changes.

Table 2-6. RegisterClass() Window Styles

lpfnWndProc   (FAR PASCAL *lpfnWndProc)(): Pointer to the window function. This is usually called "WndProc" for the default window function, or another name for a separate message processing function that you create for a class of windows. These functions should be referenced in the EXPORTS section of the program's .DEF definition file.

cbClsExtra   int: Sets the number of bytes to include at the end of the window class structure. These extra bytes can be used to store information with the class. See the SetClassLong() function description.

cbWndExtra   int: Sets the number of bytes to include after each window instance. This allows data to be stored with each window created. See the SetWindowWord() function description. Set this value to DLGWINDOWEXTRA if you are using the CLASS directive in your resource (.RC) script file to register a dialog box.

hInstance   HANDLE: The instance handle of the module (application program) registering the class.

hIcon   HICON: Handle for the class icon. If set to NULL, the program must draw the icon if the window is minimized. Set to NULL for window classes that are never minimized.

hCursor   HCURSOR: Handle to the class cursor. Usually set to the default arrow cursor, as shown in the following example. May be set to NULL, if the application explicitly sets the cursor shape when processing WM_MOUSEMOVE messages. This is typical of an application that uses one or more custom cursor shapes.

hbrBackground   HBRUSH: Handle to the brush used to paint the background. Besides any of the stock brushes (see GetStockObject()), the brush can also be set to any of the system colors:

COLOR_ACTIVEBORDER
COLOR_ACTIVE CAPTION
COLOR_APPWORKSPACE
COLOR_BACKGROUND
COLOR_BTNFACE
COLOR_BTNSHADOW
COLOR_BTNTEXT
COLOR_CAPTIONTEXT
COLOR_GRAYTEXT
COLOR_HIGHLIGHT
COLOR_HIGHLIGHTEXT
COLOR_INACTIVEBORDER
COLOR_INACTIVECAPTION
COLOR_MENU
COLOR_MENUTEXT
COLOR_SCROLLBAR
COLOR_WINDOW
COLOR_WINDOWFRAME
COLOR_WINDOWTEXT

Add 1 to these values in the class definition. Although unusual, you can set *hbrBackground* to NULL. This requires that the application paint the background when a WM_ERASEBKGND message is received.

lpszMenuName   LPSTR: Points to the class menu name string. If NULL, the class of windows has no default menu.

lpszClassName   LPSTR: Points to the class menu name string. This is the name that will be used in the Create-Window() function's *lpClassName* parameter when creating windows based on the class.

Example

```
WNDCLASS wndclass ;

wndclass.style         = CS_HREDRAW | CS_VREDRAW ;
wndclass.lpfnWndProc   = WndProc ;
wndclass.cbClsExtra    = 0 ;
wndclass.cbWndExtra    = 0 ;
wndclass.hInstance     = hInstance ;
wndclass.hIcon         = LoadIcon (hInstance, gszAppName) ;
wndclass.hCursor       = LoadCursor (NULL, IDC_ARROW) ;
wndclass.hbrBackground = GetStockObject (WHITE_BRUSH) ;
wndclass.lpszMenuName  = "generic" ;
wndclass.lpszClassName = "generic" ;

                /* register the window class */
RegisterClass (&wndclass) ;
```

The Windows programming environment provides a wide range of support functions for manipulating windows and the data that controls the window's appearance and function. Essentially every aspect of a window's behavior can be determined and changed as the program operates. This frees you from having to keep track of where windows are or what they are doing.

Direct Changes to Window Attributes

The simplest support functions act directly on a window's behavior or appearance. For example, GetWindowText() retrieves the window's title, while SetWindowText() changes the title to a new string constant.

You can check the status of a given window with the IsChild(), IsIconic(), IsWindow(), and IsWindowVisible() functions. Of these, the IsIconic() is the most frequently used. It is commonly put into the WinProc() function to change how the client area is painted for windows that do not use a class icon (the icon listed in the RegisterClass() call in WinMain()). You can paint directly on the little bit of window shown when the program's window is iconized with the normal painting and text functions. Use IsIconic() to find out if just the icon is showing or if the full window is visible.

MoveWindow() can move and change the size of a window. This is handy if your program uses several child or popup windows. You can use the SetFocus() function to change which window or control gets the keyboard input. The window receiving keyboard input is said to have the "input focus." GetFocus() will tell you which window has the input focus. The SetActiveWindow() and GetActiveWindow() functions are similar. The active window is the parent window that has the highlighted title bar and currently receives messages from Windows for mouse movements, etc. Active status applies only to parent windows. Focus can apply to a parent or child window.

Changing the Class Data

As we saw in Chapter 2, creating a window is a two-step process. You first need to create a window class using RegisterClass(). Then you create one or more windows based on this class using the CreateWindow() function. As the program operates, you may want to change some of the data in either the class structure or in the parameters passed to the CreateWindow() function. The several functions reading or changing a class data structure work on the different data types in the window class structure, WNDCLASS, as shown in Listing 3-1.

▷ **Listing 3-1. WNDCLASS Definition in WINDOWS.H**

```
typedef struct tagWNDCLASS
  {
    WORD          style;
    LONG          (FAR PASCAL *lpfnWndProc)();
    int           cbClsExtra;
    int           cbWndExtra;
    HANDLE        hInstance;
    HICON         hIcon;
    HCURSOR       hCursor;
    HBRUSH        hbrBackground;
    LPSTR         lpszMenuName;
    LPSTR         lpszClassName;
  } WNDCLASS;
```

GetClassWord() retrieves WORD long values, while GetClassLong() retrieves LONG values. To use these , you will have to mentally convert between the Windows naming conventions defined in WINDOWS.H. For example,

WORD = unsigned int, HANDLE, HICON, HCURSOR, HBRUSH = 2 Bytes

Changing a class value with SetClassWord() or SetClassLong() affects every window that was created from that class. This is handy for globally changing the cursor shape or using a different color brush for every window's background. Changes to an individual window are less drastic. SetWindowWord() and SetWindowLong() affect just one window, not every one in the class. These modified windows are a "subclass." An interesting possibility here is to change the window message function referenced by a window to a new function. This is called "window subclassing." The example shown after the SetWindowLong() function description changes the default processing for a scroll bar to include the handling of arrow keys and page-up/page-down keys. These logic items are added to the normal Windows processing of scroll bar messages, providing a custom version for that one window control.

Data Attached to a Window or Class

Windows has a powerful ability to associate data with a window or window class. A typical use would be in an application with several similar child windows. Each child window can store its own data to work on, while making use of a single message processing function. For small amounts of data, the data can be made a part of the class definition. The *cbClsExtra* element in the WNDCLASS structure sets the amount of extra data stored with the window class. This is common to all windows created from the class. The *cbWndExtra* element in WNDCLASS sets the amount of extra data stored with each window. This is the more common use.

The problem with using extra bytes in the WNDCLASS definition is that the data is not structured. The program must keep track of the meaning and location of each byte. A good way to use this data is to simply store a handle to a memory block with the window (memory allocation is discussed in Chapter 14). The memory block can then contain a large amount of data, defined by a custom data structure. This technique is used in Chapter 29 for the child windows in the MDI (Multiple Document Interface) example.

A more elaborate way to store data with a window is provided with the "property" functions. Properties amount to named data. Each property is given a name and a handle pointing to a memory area allocated to store the data. You attach the property to the window with the SetProp() function. A typical call might be

```
SetProp (hWnd, "Prop1");
```

Any time the window *hWnd* wants to get the handle to the data, it uses GetProp() something like

```
hDataHandle = GetProp (hWnd, "Prop1") ;
```

The data is then extracted from memory after locking the data (see Chapter 14 on memory functions for details). You can also release the property from the window using ReleaseProp(). There is also an EnumProp() function for finding all of the properties associated with a window. With well-designed structures for your data, the property facility will greatly improve the "object oriented" nature of your windows and reduce the need for global data structures.

Notes: Enumeration Functions

The most powerful, but most difficult to use of the windows support functions are the enumeration functions. They are used in a series of situations where you want to get a list of information, but you do not know how many items there will be in the list. For example, asking for a list of child windows attached to a parent: EnumChildWindows(); a list of property data attached to a window's definition: EnumProps(); a list of the program "tasks" running on the system EnumTasks(); or just a list of windows on the screen: EnumWindows(). ("Tasks" are application programs running on the system. This does not include dynamic link libraries (DLL's). "Modules" is the term Windows uses for all running programs, including DLLs.)

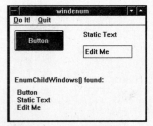

To deal with these problems, the enumeration functions require that you write a short function in your program that the Windows enumeration function will call every time it finds an item that needs to be remembered. You write the enumeration function to make an ever-expanding list of the items, adding one to the list each time the function is called. In general, these items will be of equal length. The following listings are provided to show an example. In this case, a list of all of the

Figure 3-1. Child Windows Enumerated

names of the child windows for a program are enumerated. When the user clicks the "Do It!" menu item, the names are shown on the parent window's client area. The result is shown in Figure 3-1.

Note in the header file that a new data type is created, called ENUMER. This contains a handle pointer to memory and a count of the number of items which are stored in the memory location. Also note the declaration for the enumeration function at the bottom, as shown in Listing 3-2.

▷ **Listing 3-2. WINDENUM.H—Header File for Child Window Enumeration**

```
/* windenum.h    */
/* menu item id values */
#define IDM_DOIT   1
#define IDM_QUIT   2

/* definitions */
#define TITLEWIDE          20

typedef struct
{
        GLOBALHANDLE              hGMem ;
        int                       nCount ;
} ENUMER ;

/* global variables */
int      ghInstance ;
char     gszAppName [] = "WndEnum" ;

/* function prototypes */
long FAR PASCAL WndProc (HWND, unsigned, WORD, LONG) ;
BOOL FAR PASCAL WndEnumFunc (HWND, ENUMER FAR *) ;
```

The enumeration function must be declared in the EXPORTS section of the program's .DEF definition file, as Windows. (See Listing 3-3.)

▷ **Listing 3-3. WINDENUM.DEF**

```
NAME           WINDENUM
DESCRIPTION    'windows enumeration example'
EXETYPE        WINDOWS
STUB           'WINSTUB.EXE'
CODE           PRELOAD MOVEABLE
DATA           PRELOAD MOVEABLE MULTIPLE
HEAPSIZE       1024
STACKSIZE      5120
EXPORTS        WndProc
               WndEnumFunc
```

Note in the C language Listing 3-4 that the enumeration function must be registered with Windows using the MakeProcInstance() function before it is used. Also note in the enumeration function that each new chunk of data is added to the end of the last bit.

▷ **Listing 3-4. WINDENUM.C WndProc() Function**

```
long FAR PASCAL WndProc (HWND hWnd, unsigned iMessage, WORD wParam,        LONG lParam)
{
        static  HWND              hButton ;
        static  HWND              hStaticText ;
        static  HWND              hEdit ;
        static  FARPROC           lpfEnumProc ;
        static  ENUMER            enumer ;
        LPSTR                     lpWindName ;
        HDC                       hDC ;
        int                       i ;

        switch (iMessage)                            /* process windows messages */
        {
                case WM_CREATE:

                        hButton = CreateWindow ("BUTTON", "Button",
```

```
                            WS_CHILD | WS_VISIBLE | BS_PUSHBUTTON,
                            10, 10, 100, 40, hWnd, NULL, ghInstance, NULL) ;
                ShowWindow (hButton, SW_SHOW) ;
                                            /* create and show static text */
                hStaticText = CreateWindow ("STATIC", "Static Text",
                            WS_CHILD | WS_VISIBLE | BS_PUSHBUTTON,
                            150, 10, 100, 15, hWnd, NULL, ghInstance, NULL) ;
                ShowWindow (hStaticText, SW_SHOW) ;
                                            /* create and show an edit control */
                hEdit = CreateWindow ("EDIT", "Edit Me",
                            WS_CHILD | WS_VISIBLE | WS_BORDER,
                            150, 40, 100, 25, hWnd, NULL, ghInstance, NULL) ;
                ShowWindow (hEdit, SW_SHOW) ;

                lpfEnumProc = MakeProcInstance (WndEnumFunc,
                            ghInstance) ;
                break ;
        case WM_COMMAND:                        /* process menu items */
                switch (wParam)
                {
                case IDM_DOIT:          /* User hit the "Do it" menu item */
                        if (enumer.hGMem)       /* if not first time tried */
                                GlobalFree (enumer.hGMem) ; /* free the memory */
                                                /* initialize storage area */
                        enumer.hGMem = GlobalAlloc (GMEM_MOVEABLE | GMEM_ZEROINIT,
                                1L) ;
                        enumer.nCount = 0 ;
                                                /* let Windows run callback func. */
                        EnumChildWindows (hWnd, lpfEnumProc,
                                (DWORD) &enumer) ;
                        hDC = GetDC (hWnd) ;            /* get ready to output */
                        lpWindName = GlobalLock (enumer.hGMem) ;/* lock memory */
                        TextOut (hDC, 10, 100, "EnumChildWindows() found:", 25) ;
                        for (i = 0 ; i < enumer.nCount ; i++)   /* display window */
                        {                               /* titles found */
                        TextOut (hDC, 15, 125 + (15 * i),
                                (LPSTR) (lpWindName + (i * TITLEWIDE)),
                                lstrlen (lpWindName + (i * TITLEWIDE))) ;
                        }
                        GlobalUnlock (enumer.hGMem) ;    /* unlock memory */
                        ReleaseDC (hWnd, hDC) ;
                        break ;
                case IDM_QUIT:
                        DestroyWindow (hWnd) ;
                        break ;
                }
                break ;
        case WM_DESTROY:                    /* stop application */
                GlobalFree (enumer.hGMem) ;              /* release all memory */
                PostQuitMessage (0) ;
                break ;
        default:                    /* default windows message processing */
                return DefWindowProc (hWnd, iMessage, wParam, lParam) ;
        }
        return (0L) ;
}

/* this is the enumeration function, called once for each window */

BOOL FAR PASCAL WndEnumFunc (HWND hWindow, ENUMER FAR *enumer)
{
        LPSTR   lpWindName ;
        char    cBuf [TITLEWIDE + 1] ;

        if (!GlobalReAlloc (enumer->hGMem,
                (DWORD) TITLEWIDE * (enumer->nCount + 1),
                GMEM_MOVEABLE))                 /* make room for 10 more */
                return (0) ;                    /* quit if can't make room */
```

```
      GetWindowText (hWindow, (LPSTR) cBuf, TITLEWIDE) ;        /* get title */
      cBuf [GetWindowTextLength (hWindow)] = '\0' ;             /* add end null */
      lpWindName = GlobalLock (enumer->hGMem) ;                 /* lock the memory area */
                                /* put next name at end */
      lstrcpy (lpWindName + ((enumer->nCount) * TITLEWIDE), (LPSTR) cBuf) ;
      GlobalUnlock (enumer->hGMem) ;           /* unlock the memory area */
      enumer->nCount++ ;                       /* keep track of how many */
      return (1) ;
}
```

All enumeration functions use this basic structure, although the parameters passed to the callback function will be different.

Cautions

It is fairly easy to create an infinite loop of Windows messages. This bombs the program in a hurry. For example, if you decide to create a number of child windows in the WM_CREATE portion of your WinProc() function, you will have trouble. Each time you create a new window, a WM_CREATE message is sent. Use a static BOOL variable to track if this is the first time the WM_CREATE message was issued. Be careful when changing the background color of a window class. The change will not show up immediately if you do not force the window to be repainted using UpdateWindow().

Function Descriptions

Table 3-1 summarizes the Windows support functions. The detailed function descriptions are immediately after the table.

Function	Purpose
AdjustWindowRect	Computes how big the entire window must be to produce a window with a given client area size.
AdjustWindowRectEx	Computes how big the entire window must be to produce a window with a given client area size for a window with an extended style.
AnyPopup	Determines if any popup windows are on the screen.
BeginDeferWindowPos	Begins rapid movement of a window on the screen.
BringWindowToTop	Makes a window visible, if it is underneath other overlapping windows.
ChildWindowFromPoint	Determine which child window occupies a given point on the parent window.
CloseWindow	Minimizes a window.
DeferWindowPos	Causes rapid movement of a window on the screen.
DestroyWindow	Removes a window from the system.
EnableWindow	Enables or disables mouse and keyboard input for the specified window.
EndDeferWindowPos	Completes a rapid movement of a window on the screen. The movement occurs when this function is called.
EnumChildWindows	Calls an enumeration function for all of the child windows of a parent.
EnumProps	Retrieves all of the entries in the property list of a window.
EnumTaskWindows	Lists all of the top-level windows associated with a task.
EnumWindows	Retrieves data on all of the parent windows running on the system.
FindWindow	Retrieves a handle to a window.
FlashWindow	Highlights the window's caption bar.
GetActiveWindow	Finds which parent or popup window is active.
GetClassLong	Retrieves a long value from a class structure.

Table 3.1 continued

Function	Purpose
GetClassName	Retrieves the class name upon which a window is based.
GetClassWord	Retrieves information from a class.
GetClientRect	Retrieves a window's client area size.
GetCurrentTask	Retrieves a handle to the currently executing task.
GetDesktopWindow	Retrieves the handle of the background window that covers the entire screen.
GetFocus	Finds which window has the input focus.
GetLastActivePopup	Finds which popup window was last active.
GetNextWindow	Finds parent and child windows.
GetNumTasks	Finds the number of tasks running in the system.
GetParent	Retrieves a handle to a parent window.
GetProp	Retrieves a property (data) associated with a window.
GetSysModalWindow	Retrieves a handle to a system modal window.
GetTopWindow	Finds the child window on top of any other child windows.
GetVersion	Retrieves the version number of Windows running on the system.
GetWindow	Retrieves a window's handle.
GetWindowLong	Retrieves a long value from a window's data.
GetWindowRect	Retrieve a window's outer dimensions.
GetWindowTask	Retrieves a handle to a task.
GetWindowText	Retrieves a window's title string.
GetWindowTextLength	Finds the number of characters in a window's title string.
GetWindowWord	Retrieves a two byte value from a window's data.
GetWinFlags	Determines what computer CPU and memory model are in operation.
IsChild	Determines if a window is the child of a given parent window.
IsIconic	Checks if a window is minimized.
IsWindow	Checks if a window handle still points to a valid window.
IsWindowEnabled	Checks if a window is enabled for keyboard input.
IsWindowVisible	Checks if a window has been made visible.
IsZoomed	Checks if a window is maximized.
MoveWindow	Moves or resizes a window.
RemoveProp	Removes a property (data) which was associated with a window.
SetActiveWindow	Makes a window visible.
SetClassLong	Changes one of the LONG values in a window class.
SetClassWord	Changes a WORD sized value in a window class.
SetFocus	Gives a window the input focus.
SetParent	Changes the parent window of a child window.
SetProp	Attaches named data to a window.
SetSysModalWindow	Makes a window system-modal.

SetWindowLong	Changes a LONG value associated with a window.
SetWindowPos	Simultaneously changes the size, position, and ordering of windows.
SetWindowText	Changes the title of a window.
SetWindowWord	Changes a WORD value associated with a window's class structure.
ShowOwnedPopups	Shows or hides all popup windows associated with the parent window.
ShowWindow	Displays, hides, or changes the size of a window.
SystemParametersInfo	Determines and/or changes system wide parameters.
UnregisterClass	Frees the memory holding an unneeded class description.
WindowFromPoint	Finds which window (if any) is at a given point on the screen.

Table 3-1. Windows Support Functions Summary.

ADJUSTWINDOWRECT
■ Win 2.0   ■ Win 3.0   ■ Win 3.1

Purpose   Computes how big the entire window must be to produce a window with a given client area size.

Syntax   void **AdjustWindowRect** (LPRECT *lpRect*, LONG *dwStyle*, BOOL *bMenu*);

Description   Changes the contents of the *lpRect* from those of the client rectangle to that of the bounding rectangle. The bounding rectangle encloses the caption, menu bar, and window frame.

Uses   Generally used with CreateWindow() to make a new window of a given size.

Returns   No return value (void).

See Also   AdjustWindowRectEx(), CreateWindow(), MoveWindow().

Parameters

lpRect   LPRECT: A pointer to a RECT rectangle structure.

dwStyle   DWORD: The window style. This includes any of the window style values from the CreateWindow() function (Chapter 2).

bMenu   BOOL: Specifies if the window size calculated should include space for a menu. Set to TRUE to include the menu space, FALSE to omit.

Example   In this example the adjusted rectangle is used in the CreateWindow() function. The final window in this case is converted from the client size of 50, 50, 150, 150 to the total window dimensions 49, 30, 151, 151.

```
long FAR PASCAL WndProc (HWND hWnd, unsigned iMessage, WORD wParam, LONG lParam)
{
        HDC                     hDC ;                   /* device context handle */
        static  WNDCLASS        wndclass ;              /* the window class */
        static  HWND            hListBox ;              /* the window handle */
        RECT                    rWindRect ;

        switch (iMessage)                               /* process windows messages */
        {
                case WM_CREATE:         /* build the child window when program starts */
                        rWindRect.top = 50 ;            /* client area size desired */
                        rWindRect.left = 50 ;
                        rWindRect.bottom = 150 ;
                        rWindRect.right = 150 ;

                        AdjustWindowRect(&rWindRect,    /* rectangle to convert */
                                WS_CHILD | WS_VISIBLE | WS_BORDER | WS_CAPTION,
                                FALSE) ;                /* no menu */

                        wndclass.style          = CS_HREDRAW | CS_VREDRAW | CS_PARENTDC ;
                        wndclass.lpfnWndProc    = ChildProc ;
```

```
                    wndclass.cbClsExtra      = 0 ;
                    wndclass.cbWndExtra      = 0 ;
                    wndclass.hInstance       = ghInstance ;
                    wndclass.hIcon           = NULL ;
                    wndclass.hCursor         = LoadCursor (NULL, IDC_CROSS) ;
                    wndclass.hbrBackground   = GetStockObject (LTGRAY_BRUSH) ;
                    wndclass.lpszMenuName    = NULL ;
                    wndclass.lpszClassName   = "SecondClass" ;
                                             /* register the window class */
                    if(RegisterClass (&wndclass))
                    {
                            hListBox = CreateWindow ("SecondClass", "Child Window",
                                    WS_CHILD | WS_VISIBLE | WS_BORDER | WS_CAPTION,
                                    rWindRect.left, rWindRect.top,
                                    rWindRect.right, rWindRect.bottom,
                                    hWnd, NULL, ghInstance, NULL) ;
                            ShowWindow (hListBox, SW_SHOW) ;
                    }
                    break ;
```

[Other program lines]

ADJUSTWINDOWRECTEX   □ Win 2.0   ■ Win 3.0   ■ Win 3.1

Purpose	Computes how big the entire window must be to produce a window with a given client area size for a window with an extended style.
Syntax	void **AdjustWindowRectEx**(LPRECT *lpRect*, LONG *dwStyle*, BOOL *bMenu*, DWORD *dwExStyle*);
Description	Changes the contents of the *lpRect* from those of the client rectangle to those of the bounding rectangle. The bounding rectangle encloses the caption, menu bar, and window frame.
Uses	Generally used with CreateWindowEx() to make a new window of a given size.
Returns	No returned value (void).
See Also	AdjustWindowRectEx(), CreateWindowEx(), MoveWindow().
Parameters	
lpRect	LPRECT: A pointer to a rectangle structure.
dwStyle	DWORD: The window style. This includes any of the window style values from the CreateWindow() function.
bMenu	BOOL: Specifies if the window size calculated should include space for a menu. Set to TRUE to include menu space, FALSE to omit.
dwExStyle	DWORD: The extended style values used in the CreateWindowEx() function.
Example	Note that the adjusted rectangle is used in the CreateWindowEx() function. The final window in this case is converted from the client size of 50, 50, 100, 100 to the total window dimensions 45, 29, 155, 155.

```
long FAR PASCAL WndProc (HWND hWnd, unsigned iMessage, WORD wParam,  LONG lParam)
{
        HDC                     hDC ;             /* device context handle */
        static WNDCLASS         wndclass ;        /* the window class */
        static HWND             hTextBox ;        /* the window handle */
        RECT                    rWindRect ;

        switch (iMessage)                         /* process windows messages */
        {
                case WM_CREATE: /* build the child window when program starts */
                        rWindRect.top = 50 ;      /* client area size desired */
                        rWindRect.left = 50 ;
                        rWindRect.bottom = 150 ;
                        rWindRect.right = 150 ;

                        AdjustWindowRectEx(&rWindRect,
```

```
                                    WS_CHILD | WS_VISIBLE | WS_BORDER | WS_CAPTION,
                                    FALSE, WS_EX_DLGMODALFRAME) ;

                    wndclass.style          = CS_HREDRAW | CS_VREDRAW | CS_PARENTDC ;
                    wndclass.lpfnWndProc    = ChildProc ;
                    wndclass.cbClsExtra     = 0 ;
                    wndclass.cbWndExtra     = 0 ;
                    wndclass.hInstance      = ghInstance ;
                    wndclass.hIcon          = NULL ;
                    wndclass.hCursor        = LoadCursor (NULL, IDC_CROSS) ;
                    wndclass.hbrBackground  = GetStockObject (LTGRAY_BRUSH) ;
                    wndclass.lpszMenuName   = NULL ;
                    wndclass.lpszClassName  = "SecondClass" ;
                                                /* register the window class */
                    if(RegisterClass (&wndclass))
                    {
                            hTextBox = CreateWindowEx (WS_EX_DLGMODALFRAME,
                                    "SecondClass", "Child Window",
                                    WS_CHILD | WS_VISIBLE | WS_BORDER | WS_CAPTION,
                                    rWindRect.left, rWindRect.top,
                                    rWindRect.right, rWindRect.bottom,
                                    hWnd, NULL, ghInstance, NULL) ;
                            ShowWindow (hTextBox, SW_SHOW) ;
                    }
                    break ;
```

[Other program lines]

ANYPOPUP   ■ Win 2.0   ■ Win 3.0   ■ Win 3.1

Purpose	Determines if any popup windows are on the screen.
Syntax	BOOL **AnyPopup**(void);
Uses	Popup windows can overlap any portion of the parent's window. This function will tell you if any popups exist.
Returns	BOOL, TRUE, or FALSE.
Parameters	None (void).
Example	This fragment shows a WndProc() function checking if there is a popup window before starting to refresh the screen. It may be desirable to close the popup window before painting to eliminate hidden areas.

```
long FAR PASCAL WndProc (HWND hWnd, unsigned iMessage, WORD wParam, LONG lParam)
{
        HDC             hDC ;
        static BOOL     bPopupExist ;

        switch (iMessage)               /* process windows messages */
        {
                case WM_PAINT:
                        if (AnyPopup())
                                bPopupExist = TRUE ;
                        else
                                bPopupExist = FALSE ;
                        break ;
```

[Other program lines]

BEGINDEFERWINDOWPOS   □ Win 2.0   ■ Win 3.0   ■ Win 3.1

Purpose	Begins rapid movement of a window on the screen.
Syntax	HANDLE **BeginDeferWindowPos**(int *nNumWindows*);
Description	This function is the first step in the sequence of functions BeginDeferWindowPos(), DeferWindowPos(), and EndDeferWindowPos(), used to move one or more windows in a single screen refresh cycle.

Uses	Animation of windows by repeatedly moving them, or just fast movement of a single window to a new location.
Returns	A handle to the multiple-window data structure used by DeferWindowPos().
See Also	BeginDeferWindowPos(), DeferWindowPos(), EndDeferWindowPos(), MoveWindow(), SetWindowPos()

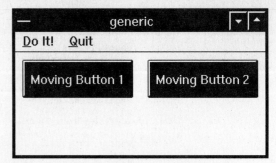

Figure 3-2. BeginDeferWindowPos( ) Example.

Parameters

nNumWindows   int: Sets the number of windows that will be affected by the window movement. This initializes the data structure. Getting the correct value is not critical, as the data structure will be expanded (with some loss of speed) if DeferWindowPos() requires more windows to be updated.

Example   This example, illustration Figure 3-2, creates two button child windows at the bottom of the client area. When the user clicks the "Do It!" menu item, both buttons are relocated to the top of the client area.

```
long FAR PASCAL WndProc (HWND hWnd, unsigned iMessage, WORD wParam, LONG lParam)
{
        HWND                    hTestBox1, hTestBox2 ;
        static  HANDLE          hDeferData ;       /* handle for DeferWindowPos() */

        switch (iMessage)                          /* process windows messages */
        {
                case WM_CREATE: /* create a button when program starts */
                        hTestBox1 = CreateWindow ("BUTTON", "Moving Button 1",
                                WS_CHILD | WS_VISIBLE ,
                                200, 200, 150, 50, hWnd, NULL, ghInstance, NULL) ;
                        ShowWindow (hTestBox1, SW_SHOW) ;
                        hTestBox2 = CreateWindow ("BUTTON", "Moving Button 2",
                                WS_CHILD | WS_VISIBLE ,
                                0, 200, 150, 50, hWnd, NULL, ghInstance, NULL) ;
                        ShowWindow (hTestBox2, SW_SHOW) ;
                        hDeferData = BeginDeferWindowPos (2) ;
                        hDeferData = DeferWindowPos (hDeferData, hTestBox1,
                                hTestBox2, 10, 10, 200, 50, SWP_NOSIZE) ;
                        hDeferData = DeferWindowPos (hDeferData, hTestBox2,
                                NULL, 180, 10, 200, 50, SWP_NOSIZE) ;
                        break ;
                case WM_COMMAND:                   /* process menu items */
                        switch (wParam)
                        {
                        case IDM_DOIT:             /* move the button */
                                EndDeferWindowPos (hDeferData) ;        /* move windows */
                                InvalidateRect (hWnd, NULL, TRUE) ;    /* force paint */
                                break ;
                        case IDM_QUIT:
                                DestroyWindow (hWnd) ;
                                break ;
                        }
                        break ;
                case WM_DESTROY:                   /* stop application */
                        PostQuitMessage (0) ;
                        break ;
                default:                           /* default windows message processing */
                        return DefWindowProc (hWnd, iMessage, wParam, lParam) ;
        }
        return (0L) ;
}
```

BRINGWINDOWTOTOP
■ Win 2.0   ■ Win 3.0   ■ Win 3.1

Purpose	Makes a window visible and activates it (for a popup or top-level window) if the window is underneath other overlapping windows.
Syntax	void **BringWindowToTop**(HWND *hWnd*);
Description	The window chosen is superimposed over any other overlapping windows on the screen. The window is activated if it is a popup or top-level window.
Uses	Most often used with popup windows.
Returns	No return value (void).
See Also	SetFocus(), IsWindowVisible(), SetActiveWindow(), EnableWindow()
Parameters	
hWnd	HWND: Handle of the window to bring to the top.
Example	This example swaps the superposition of the two button controls on the screen when the "Do It!" menu item is clicked.

```
Long FAR PASCAL WndProc (HWND hWnd, unsigned iMessage, WORD wParam, LONG lParam)
{
        static HWND             hTestBox1, hTestBox2 ;   /* the window handles */

        switch (iMessage)                               /* process windows messages */
        {
            case WM_CREATE: /* build the child windows when program starts */
                hTestBox1 = CreateWindow ("BUTTON", "BUTTON 1",
                    WS_CHILD | WS_VISIBLE ,
                    10, 50, 110, 100, hWnd, NULL, ghInstance, NULL) ;
                ShowWindow (hTestBox1, SW_SHOW) ;
                hTestBox2 = CreateWindow ("BUTTON", "BUTTON 2",
                    WS_CHILD | WS_VISIBLE ,
                    30, 70, 130, 130, hWnd, NULL, ghInstance, NULL) ;
                ShowWindow (hTestBox2, SW_SHOW) ;
                break ;
            case WM_COMMAND:                            /* process menu items */
                switch (wParam)
                {
                case IDM_DOIT:          /* User hit the "Do it" menu item */
                    BringWindowToTop (hTestBox2) ;          /* no 1 to top */
                    ShowWindow (hTestBox1, SW_HIDE) ;       /* refresh screen */
                    ShowWindow (hTestBox1, SW_SHOWNORMAL) ;
                    break ;
```
[Other program lines]

CHILDWINDOWFROMPOINT
■ Win 2.0   ■ Win 3.0   ■ Win 3.1

Purpose	Determines which child window occupies a given point on the parent window.
Syntax	HWND **ChildWindowFromPoint**(HWND *hWndParent*, POINT *Point*);
Description	Returns a handle to the child window at a given point.
Uses	Handy if the application uses several child windows, which may be obscuring data on the screen. Typically used with the mouse cursor to determine which child the cursor is over, independent of the mouse buttons being pressed.
Returns	A handle to the child window, NULL if no child window is at the point.
See Also	WindowFromPoint(), ScreenToClient()
Parameters	
hWndParent	HWND: The parent window's handle.
Point	POINT: The client area coordinates to check.
Related Messages	WM_MOUSEMOVE

Cautions   This function will not work properly over pushbutton controls.

Example   This example, as shown in Figure 3-3, displays the name of the window the mouse is pointing to as the cursor is moved over the client area. Two static text windows are placed on the client area. The figure shows the mouse cursor over the lower one. The handle of the child window is retrieved using ChildWindowFromPoint(). The name of the window (the caption string) is determined with GetWindowText().

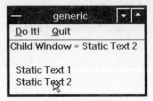

Figure 3-3. ChildWindow-FromPoint( )Example.

```
long FAR PASCAL WndProc (HWND hWnd, unsigned iMessage, WORD wParam, LONG lParam)
{
        HWND            hStatic1, hStatic2, hWndTest ;
        HDC             hDC ;
        POINT           pMouse ;
        char            cBuf [128], cBuf2 [256] ;

        switch (iMessage)                                   /* process windows messages */
        {
        case WM_CREATE:
                hStatic1 = CreateWindow ("STATIC", "Static Text 1",
                        WS_CHILD | WS_VISIBLE | BS_PUSHBUTTON,
                        10, 40, 100, 20, hWnd, 100, ghInstance, NULL) ;
                ShowWindow (hStatic1, SW_SHOW) ;
                hStatic2 = CreateWindow ("STATIC", "Static Text 2",
                        WS_CHILD | WS_VISIBLE | BS_PUSHBUTTON,
                        10, 60, 100, 20, hWnd, 101, ghInstance, NULL) ;
                ShowWindow (hStatic2, SW_SHOW) ;
                break ;
        case WM_MOUSEMOVE:
                pMouse = MAKEPOINT (lParam) ;
                hDC = GetDC (hWnd) ;
                hWndTest = ChildWindowFromPoint (hWnd, pMouse) ;
                if (hWndTest)
                        GetWindowText (hWndTest, cBuf, 127) ;
                else
                        lstrcpy (cBuf, "<none>") ;
                TextOut (hDC, 0, 0, cBuf2, wsprintf (cBuf2,
                        "Child Window = %s", (LPSTR) cBuf)) ;
                ReleaseDC (hWnd, hDC) ;
                break ;
        case WM_COMMAND:/* process menu items */
                switch (wParam)
                {
                case IDM_QUIT:
                        DestroyWindow (hWnd) ;
                        break ;
                }
                break ;
        case WM_DESTROY:/* stop application */
                PostQuitMessage (0) ;
                break ;
        default:                        /* default windows message processing */
                return DefWindowProc (hWnd, iMessage, wParam, lParam) ;
        }
        return (0L) ;
}
```

CLOSEWINDOW   ■ Win 2.0   ■ Win 3.0   ■ Win 3.1

Purpose   Minimizes a window.

Syntax   void **CloseWindow**(HWND *hWnd*);

Description   If the window's class structure contains an icon, the minimized window will display the icon image. Otherwise, the minimized window will be a blank client area, which will receive WM_PAINT messages and can be painted on using normal painting functions.

Uses	Used in applications with several child windows. The closed windows remain on the bottom of the parent's client area. Double-clicking the minimized windows automatically restores them to their previous size.
Returns	No return value (void).
See Also	IsIconic(), IsWindowVisible(), IsZoomed(), OpenIcon()
Parameters	
hWnd	HWND: The window's handle.
Related Messages	WM_SIZE, WM_PAINT
Example	In this example, clicking the "Do It!" menu item causes the button child window to be minimized to the bottom of the parent window's client area. Double-clicking the minimized button restores it.

```
Long FAR PASCAL WndProc (HWND hWnd, unsigned iMessage, WORD wParam, LONG lParam)
{
    static HWND    hButton ;

    switch (iMessage)                            /* process windows messages */
    {
        case WM_CREATE:
                hButton = CreateWindow ("BUTTON", "Button",
                WS_CHILD | WS_VISIBLE | BS_PUSHBUTTON,
                10, 10, 100, 40, hWnd, NULL, ghInstance, NULL) ;
                ShowWindow (hButton, SW_SHOW) ;
                break ;
        case WM_COMMAND:                         /* process menu items */
        switch (wParam)
        {
        case IDM_DOIT:
        CloseWindow (hButton) ;                  /* minimize button */
        break ;
```
[Other program lines]

DEFERWINDOWPOS
□ Win 2.0 ■ Win 3.0 ■ Win 3.1

Purpose	Produces rapid movement of a window on the screen.
Syntax	HANDLE **DeferWindowPos**(HANDLE *hWndPosInfo*, HWND *hWnd*, HWND *hWndInsertAfter*, int *x*, int *y*, int *cx*, int *cy*, WORD *wFlags*);
Description	This is the second function in the series BeginDeferWindowPos(), DeferWindowPos(), EndDeferWindowPos() that allows rapid movement of a window on the screen, all within one screen refresh cycle. DeferWindowPos() sets values in an internal data structure created by BeginDeferWindowPos(). These values are then used by EndDeferWindowPos() to do the actual movement of the window on the screen.
Uses	Animation of windows by repeatedly moving them, or just fast movement of a single window to a new location.
Returns	A handle to the data structure used by DeferWindowPos().
See Also	BeginDeferWindowPos(), EndDeferWindowPos()
Parameters	
hWindPosInfo	HANDLE: The handle to the internal data structure returned by BeginDeferWindowPos().
hWnd	HWND: The window handle of the window to be moved.
hWndInsertAfter	HWND: The window handle of the previous window to be moved. NULL if *hWnd* is the first one.
x	int: The *X*-coordinate of the upper left corner of the window after it has been moved in client coordinates (pixels from the upper left corner of the client area).
y	int: The *Y*-coordinate of the upper left corner of the window after it has been moved in client coordinates.

cx	int: The new width of the window in pixels.
cy	int: The new height of the window in pixels.
wFlags	WORD: One of the values in Table 3-2.

Value	Meaning	
SWP_DRAWFRAME	Draws the frame specified in the window's class description when redrawn.	
SWP_HIDEWINDOW	Hides the window when redrawn.	
SWP_NOACTIVATE	Does not activate the window.	
SWP_NOMOVE	Does not move the window, but the size can be changed with the *cx,cy* parameters.	
SWP_NOREDRAW	Does not redraw the window at the new size/location.	
SWP_NOSIZE	Does not resize the window, but the position can be changed with the *x,y* parameters.	
SWP_NOZORDER	Retains the current ordering in the reposition list. If *hWndInsertAfter* is NULL, *hWnd* is placed at the top of the list. If *hWndInsertAfter* is 1, *hWnd* is placed at the bottom of the list.	
SWP_SHOWWINDOW	Displays the window when redrawn.	

Table 3-2. DeferWindowPos( ) Flags.

Example   See the example under the BeginDeferWindowPos() function description.

DESTROYWINDOW   ■ Win 2.0   ■ Win 3.0   ■ Win 3.1

Purpose	Removes a window from the system.
Syntax	BOOL **DestroyWindow**(HWND *hWnd*);
Description	The window referenced by *hWnd* is deleted. Any child windows of *hWnd* are deleted first, followed by the parent. The window's class is not affected, unless this is the last window on the system using the class.
Uses	Removing popup and child windows from the screen when not needed. Also used to stop an application by destroying the parent window.
Returns	BOOL. TRUE if the window was destroyed, FALSE if the function failed (normally meaning that *hWnd* did not exist).
See Also	UnregisterClass(), CreateWindow()
Parameters	
hWnd	HWND: Handle of the window to be destroyed.
Related Messages	WM_DESTROY, WM_NCDESTROY, WM_OTHERWINDOWDESTROYED
Example	In this example, clicking the "Do It!" menu item causes the popup window to be destroyed and its class to be unregistered.

The ChildProc() function needs to be listed in the EXPORTS section of the program's .DEF file, and a function prototype needs to be added to the header file to use this example code.

```
long FAR PASCAL WndProc (HWND hWnd, unsigned iMessage, WORD wParam, LONG lParam)
{
        static WNDCLASS        wndclass ;       /* the window class */
        static HWND            hPopup ;

        switch (iMessage)                        /* process windows messages */
        {
                case WM_CREATE: /* build the child window when program starts */
```

```
                        wndclass.style          = CS_HREDRAW | CS_VREDRAW | CS_PARENTDC;
                        wndclass.lpfnWndProc    = ChildProc ;
                        wndclass.cbClsExtra     = 0 ;
                        wndclass.cbWndExtra     = 0 ;
                        wndclass.hInstance      = ghInstance ;
                        wndclass.hIcon          = NULL ;
                        wndclass.hCursor        = LoadCursor (NULL, IDC_ARROW) ;
                        wndclass.hbrBackground  = GetStockObject (LTGRAY_BRUSH) ;
                        wndclass.lpszMenuName   = NULL ;
                        wndclass.lpszClassName  = "SecondClass" ;
                                                /* register the window class */
                        if(RegisterClass (&wndclass))
                        {
                                hPopup = CreateWindow ("SecondClass", "Popup Window",
                                        WS_POPUP | WS_VISIBLE | WS_BORDER | WS_CAPTION,
                                        10, 50, 200, 150, hWnd, NULL, ghInstance, NULL) ;
                                ShowWindow (hPopup, SW_SHOW) ;
                        }
                        break ;
                case WM_COMMAND:                /* process menu items */
                        switch (wParam)
                        {
                        case IDM_DOIT:  /* User hit the "Do it" menu item */
                                DestroyWindow (hPopup) ;
                                UnregisterClass ("SecondClass", ghInstance) ;
                                break ;
                        case IDM_QUIT:  /* terminate this application */
                                DestroyWindow (hWnd) ;
                                break ;
                        }
                        break ;
                case WM_DESTROY:
                        PostQuitMessage (0) ;
                        break ;
                default:                        /* default windows message processing */
                        return DefWindowProc (hWnd, iMessage, wParam, lParam) ;
        }
        return (0L ;
}


/* Here is a separate message processing procedure for the child window */

long FAR PASCAL ChildProc (HWND hWnd, unsigned iMessage, WORD wParam,  LONG lParam)
{
        switch (iMessage)               /* process windows messages */
        {
                case WM_DESTROY:
                        break ;
                default:                /* default windows message processing */
                        return DefWindowProc (hWnd, iMessage, wParam, lParam) ;
        }
        return (0L) ;
}
```

ENABLEWINDOW   ■ Win 2.0   ■ Win 3.0   ■ Win 3.1

Purpose	Enables or disables mouse and keyboard input or the specified window.
Syntax	BOOL **EnableWindow**(HWND *hWnd*, BOOL *bEnable*);
Uses	Handy for controlling where a user is allowed to input data. For example, an edit control may be enabled to input a file name only after a subdirectory has been chosen. A window must be enabled before it can be activated. Windows are automatically enabled when created.
Returns	BOOL. TRUE if successful, FALSE if the function failed.

See Also   SetFocus(), GetFocus(), SetActiveWindow()

Parameters

hWnd   HWND: The handle of the window to affect.

bEnable   BOOL : TRUE to enable, FALSE to disable.

Example   This example shows the creation of an edit control. The control is initially disabled and shows gray text inside the edit area. When the user clicks the "Do It!" menu item, the edit control is enabled (can be edited), and displays normal color text inside the edit area.

```
long FAR PASCAL WndProc (HWND hWnd, unsigned iMessage, WORD wParam, LONG lParam)
{
        static HWND    hEdit ;

        switch (iMessage)                          /* process windows messages */
        {
        case WM_CREATE:
                hEdit = CreateWindow ("EDIT", "Edit Me",
                WS_CHILD | WS_VISIBLE | WS_BORDER,
                150, 40, 100, 25, hWnd, NULL, ghInstance, NULL) ;
                ShowWindow (hEdit, SW_SHOW) ;
                EnableWindow (hEdit, FALSE) ;      /* disable input */
        break ;
        case WM_COMMAND:                           /* process menu items */
        switch (wParam)
        {
        case IDM_DOIT:           /* User hit the "Do it" menu item */
                EnableWindow (hEdit, TRUE) ;       /* enable input */
                break ;
```

[Other program lines]

ENDDEFERWINDOWPOS
☐ Win 2.0 ■ Win 3.0 ■ Win 3.1

Purpose   Completes a rapid movement of a window on the screen. The movement occurs when this function is called.

Syntax   void **EndDeferWindowPos**(HANDLE *hWinPosInfo*);

Description   This is the last of the sequence of three functions BeginDeferWindowPos(), DeferWindowPos(), and EndDeferWindowPos(). These functions work together to update the position and size of the one or more windows in a single screen refresh cycle. The actual movement is done when EndDeferWindowPos() is called.

Uses   Animation of windows by repeatedly moving them, or for fast movement of a single window to a new location.

Returns   No returned value (void).

See Also   BeginDeferWindowPos(), DeferWindowPos()

Parameters

hWindPosInfo   HANDLE: Handle to the window position data structure created with BeginDeferWindowPos().

Example   See the example under the BeginDeferWindowPos() function description.

ENUMCHILDWINDOWS
■ Win 2.0 ■ Win 3.0 ■ Win 3.1

Purpose   Calls an enumeration function for all of the child windows of a parent.

Syntax   BOOL **EnumChildWindows**(HWND *hWndParent*, FARPROC *lpEnumFunc*, LONG *lParam*);

Description   Enumerates data from all child windows of the parent. You must supply an enumeration function. The enumeration function is called once for each child window. The child window's handle and the *lParam* value are passed to the enumeration function each time it is called. Typically, the enumeration function collects data for a child window, and stores it in a memory area. *lParam* can be used to pass a handle to the memory area to the enumeration function. Note that although the child window handle will be different each time the enumeration function is called, the *lParam* value remains the same.

Uses   Retrieving handles to all child windows, or other data associated with the child window. You do not need to know how many child windows there are in advance.

Returns   BOOL. TRUE if all child windows have been enumerated, FALSE if not.

See Also   See the description in the *Notes* section at the beginning of this chapter.

Parameters

hWndParent   HANDLE: Handle to the parent window.

lpEnumFunc   FARPROC: Pointer to the enumeration function.

lParam   DWORD: This is the value to be passed to each processing of the enumeration function.

The enumeration (callback) function must have the form

BOOL FAR PASCAL **EnumFunc** (HWND *hWndChild*, DWORD *lParam*)

This function will be called for each child window. You must include the EnumFunc() in the EXPORTS portion of the .DEF file. The EnumFunc() must also be registered with Make-ProcInstance() prior to use. The enumeration function will return TRUE if enumeration continues, FALSE if enumeration stops

The meaning of the parameters on each call is

hWndChild   HWND: The handle of a child window.

lParam   DWORD: This is the *lParam* value passed by EnumChild-Windows(). It can be used to pass any data, including a handle to a memory block that can be used by the enumeration function to store or retrieve data about the child windows.

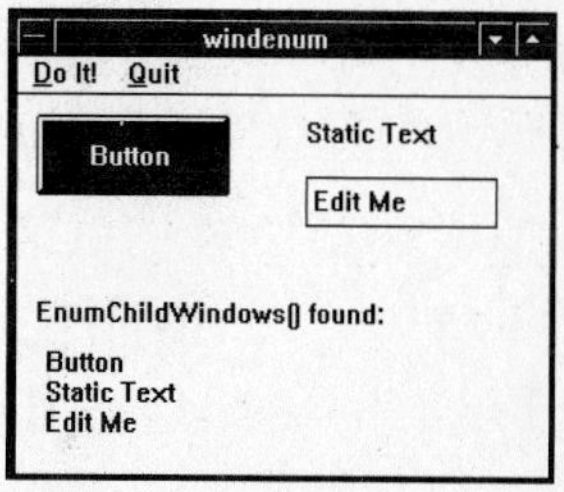

Example   This example creates a window with three children, as shown in Figure 3-4. When the user clicks the "Do It!" menu item, the enumeration function is called to store the names of each of the children. The names are then displayed on the parent window's client area.

Figure 3-4. EnumChild-Windows( ) Example.

Note that the enumeration function keeps expanding the memory area allocated, and adds each new child window name to the end of the memory space.

⇨ **WINDENUM.H Header File**

```
/* windenum.h    */

#define IDM_DOIT   1                                  /* menu item id values */
#define IDM_QUIT   2
       /* definitions */
#define TITLEWIDE       20
typedef struct
{
       GLOBALHANDLE            hGMem ;
       int                     nCount ;
} ENUMER ;
       /* global variables */
int    ghInstance ;
char   gszAppName [] = "WindEnum" ;
       /* function prototypes */
long FAR PASCAL WndProc (HWND, unsigned, WORD, LONG) ;
BOOL FAR PASCAL WndEnumFunc (HWND, ENUMER FAR *) ;
```

⇨ **WindProc( ) Portion of C Program**

```
Long FAR PASCAL WndProc (HWND hWnd, unsigned iMessage, WORD wParam, LONG lParam)
```

```
{
        static  HWND            hButton ;
        static  HWND            hStaticText ;
        static  HWND            hEdit ;
        static  FARPROC         lpfEnumProc ;
        static  ENUMER          enumer ;
        LPSTR                   lpWindName ;
        HDC                     hDC ;
        int                     i ;

        switch (iMessage)                       /* process windows messages */
        {
            case WM_CREATE:
                    hButton = CreateWindow ("BUTTON", "Button",
                            WS_CHILD | WS_VISIBLE | BS_PUSHBUTTON,
                            10, 10, 100, 40, hWnd, NULL, ghInstance, NULL) ;
                    ShowWindow (hButton, SW_SHOW) ;
                                            /* create and show static text */
                    hStaticText = CreateWindow ("STATIC", "Static Text",
                            WS_CHILD | WS_VISIBLE | BS_PUSHBUTTON,
                            150, 10, 100, 15, hWnd, NULL, ghInstance, NULL) ;
                    ShowWindow (hStaticText, SW_SHOW) ;
                                            /* create and show an edit control */
                    hEdit = CreateWindow ("EDIT", "Edit Me",
                            WS_CHILD | WS_VISIBLE | WS_BORDER,
                            150, 40, 100, 25, hWnd, NULL, ghInstance, NULL) ;
                    ShowWindow (hEdit, SW_SHOW) ;

                    lpfEnumProc = MakeProcInstance (WndEnumFunc,
                                                ghInstance) ;
                    break ;
            case WM_COMMAND:                    /* process menu items */
                    switch (wParam)
                    {
                    case IDM_DOIT:              /* User hit the "Do it" menu item */

                            if (enumer.hGMem)       /* if not first time tried */
                                    GlobalFree (enumer.hGMem) ;    /* free the memory */
                                                    /* initialize storage area */
                            enumer.hGMem = GlobalAlloc
                                    (GMEM_MOVEABLE | GMEM_ZEROINIT,        1L) ;
                            enumer.nCount = 0 ;
                                                    /* let Windows run callback func. */
                            EnumChildWindows (hWnd, lpfEnumProc,
                                    (DWORD) &enumer) ;
                            hDC = GetDC (hWnd) ;            /* get ready to output */
                            lpWindName = GlobalLock (enumer.hGMem) ; /* lock memory */
                            TextOut (hDC, 10, 100, "EnumChildWindows() found:", 25) ;
                            for (i = 0 ; i < enumer.nCount ; i++)    /* display window */
                            {                                         /* titles found */
                                    TextOut (hDC, 15, 125 + (15 * i),
                                            (LPSTR) (lpWindName + (i * TITLEWIDE)),
                                            lstrlen (lpWindName + (i * TITLEWIDE))) ;
                            }
                            GlobalUnlock (enumer.hGMem) ;             /* unlock memory */
                            ReleaseDC (hWnd, hDC) ;
                            break ;
                    case IDM_QUIT:
                            DestroyWindow (hWnd) ;
                            break ;
                    }
                    break ;
            case WM_DESTROY:                    /* stop application */
                    GlobalFree (enumer.hGMem) ;        /* release all memory */
                    PostQuitMessage (0) ;
                    break ;
            default:                            /* default windows message processing */
                    return DefWindowProc (hWnd, iMessage, wParam, lParam) ;
        }
        return (0L) ;
}
```

```
BOOL FAR PASCAL WndEnumFunc (HWND hWindow, ENUMER FAR *enumer)
{
        LPSTR   lpWindName ;
        char    cBuf [TITLEWIDE + 1] ;

        if (!GlobalReAlloc (enumer->hGMem,
                    (DWORD) TITLEWIDE * (enumer->nCount + 1),
                    GMEM_MOVEABLE))              /* make room for 10 more */
                return (0) ;                    /* quit if can't make room */

        GetWindowText (hWindow, (LPSTR) cBuf, TITLEWIDE) ;        /* get title */
        cBuf [GetWindowTextLength (hWindow)] = '\0' ;            /* add end null */
        lpWindName = GlobalLock (enumer->hGMem) ;        /* lock the memory area */
                                                         /* put next name at end */
        lstrcpy (lpWindName + ((enumer->nCount) * TITLEWIDE), (LPSTR) cBuf) ;
        GlobalUnlock (enumer->hGMem) ;           /* unlock the memory area */
        enumer->nCount++ ;                       /* keep track of how many */
        return (1) ;
}
```

ENUMPROPS   ■ Win 2.0   ■ Win 3.0   ■ Win 3.1

Purpose	Retrieves all of the entries in the property list of a window.
Syntax	int **EnumProps**(HWND *hWnd*, FARPROC *lpEnumFunc*);
Description	Uses a callback function to repeatedly fetch properties (data) associated by the window with the SetProp() function.

Uses	Allows any amount of data to be associated directly with the window.
Returns	int. −1 on error. Otherwise returns the last value returned by the callback function.
See Also	EnumChildWindows(), SetProp(), GetProp()

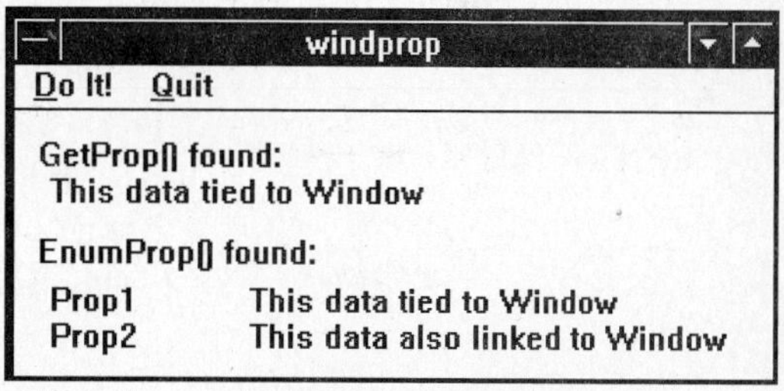

Figure 3-5. Properties Retrieved from a Window.

Parameters

hWnd   HWND: Handle of the window that has a property list to be enumerated.

lpEnumFunc   FARPROC: Pointer to the enumeration function, The enumeration function must be of the form:

int FAR PASCAL **EnumFunc** (HWND *hWnd*, LPSTR *lpString*, HANDLE *hData*);

The enumeration function must be listed in the EXPORTS section of the program's .DEF definition file. The enumeration function is called once for each property associated with the window. The enumeration function should return zero to stop enumeration, or a non-zero value (1) to continue.
    The parameters passed to the enumeration function have the following meanings:

hWnd   HWND: The handle of the window that has a property list to be enumerated.

lpSting   LPSTR: The character string that was used by SetProp() to name the data. This can also be an atom. In this case, the atom is the LOWORD, while the HIWORD is set to zero. Atoms are discussed in Chapter 22, *Atom Functions*.

hDATA   HANDLE: Is a data handle, pointing to the memory where the data is stored.

Example   In this case, two properties are associated with the window. Each of the properties (called "Prop1" and "Prop2") is associated with a handle to memory containing a string. The WinProc() function demonstrates recovering the property data with both the GetProp() and EnumProp() functions. Note that the enumeration function WindPropFunc() must be referenced in the EXPORTS section of the program's .DEF file. When this program executes the "Do It!" menu item, the program window appears as shown in Figure 3-5.

⇨ Header File

```
/* windprop.h   */

#define IDM_DOIT   1                        /* menu item id values */
#define IDM_QUIT   2
        /* definitions */
#define PROPSTRINGWIDE  10
#define MAXPROP         30
        /* global variables */
typedef struct
{
        HANDLE          hPropData ;
        char            cPropName [PROPSTRINGWIDE] ;
} PROPERTY ;

PROPERTY                gPropertyList [MAXPROP] ;
int                     gnPropertyCount ;

int     ghInstance ;
char    gszAppName [] = "windprop" ;
        /* function prototypes */
long FAR PASCAL WndProc (HWND, unsigned, WORD, LONG) ;
BOOL FAR PASCAL WindPropFunc (HWND hWindow, WORD nDummy,
        PSTR pString, HANDLE hData) ;
```

⇨ WindProc( ) Portion of C Program

```
long FAR PASCAL WndProc (HWND hWnd, unsigned iMessage, WORD wParam, LONG lParam)
{
        static  HANDLE  hMemory ;
        static  FARPROC lpfEnumProc ;
        LPSTR           lpName ;
        HDC             hDC ;
        int             i ;
        char            cBuf [128] ;

        switch (iMessage)                               /* process windows messages */
        {
                case WM_CREATE:
                        strcpy (cBuf, "This data tied to Window") ;
                        hMemory = GlobalAlloc (GMEM_MOVEABLE | GMEM_ZEROINIT,
                                (LONG) strlen (cBuf)) ;
                        lpName = GlobalLock (hMemory) ;
                        lstrcpy (lpName, cBuf) ;
                        GlobalUnlock (hMemory) ;
                        SetProp (hWnd, "Prop1", hMemory) ;        /* link data to window */

                        strcpy (cBuf, "This data also linked to Window") ;
                        hMemory = GlobalAlloc (GMEM_MOVEABLE | GMEM_ZEROINIT,
                                (LONG) strlen (cBuf)) ;
                        lpName = GlobalLock (hMemory) ;
                        GlobalUnlock (hMemory) ;
                        lstrcpy (lpName, cBuf) ;
                        SetProp (hWnd, "Prop2", hMemory) ;
                        lpfEnumProc = MakeProcInstance (WindPropFunc, ghInstance) ;
                        break ;
                case WM_COMMAND:                /* process menu items */
                        switch (wParam)
                        {
                        case IDM_DOIT:          /* User hit the "Do it" menu item */
                                hMemory = GetProp (hWnd, "Prop1") ;
                                lpName = GlobalLock (hMemory) ;
                                hDC = GetDC (hWnd) ;            /* get ready to output */
                                TextOut (hDC, 10, 10, "GetProp() found:", 16) ;
                                TextOut (hDC, 15, 25, lpName, lstrlen (lpName)) ;
                                GlobalUnlock (hMemory) ;
                                ReleaseDC (hWnd, hDC) ;
```

```
                                        gnPropertyCount = 0 ;
                                                        /* let Windows run callback func. */
                                        EnumProps (hWnd, lpfEnumProc) ;
                                        hDC = GetDC (hWnd) ;       /* get ready to output */
                                        TextOut (hDC, 10, 50, "EnumProp() found:", 17) ;
                                        for (i = 0 ; i < gnPropertyCount ; i++)
                                        {                               /* display titles found */
                                                TextOut (hDC, 15, 70 + (15 * i),
                                                        (LPSTR) gPropertyList [i].cPropName,
                                                        strlen (gPropertyList [i].cPropName)) ;
                                                lpName = GlobalLock (gPropertyList [i].hPropData) ;
                                                TextOut (hDC, 100, 70 + (15 * i), lpName,
                                                        lstrlen (lpName)) ;
                                                GlobalUnlock (gPropertyList [i].hPropData) ;
                                        }
                                        ReleaseDC (hWnd, hDC) ;
                                        break ;
                                case IDM_QUIT:
                                        DestroyWindow (hWnd) ;
                                        break ;
                                }
                                break ;
                        case WM_DESTROY:          /* stop application */
                                RemoveProp (hWnd, "User Prop") ;
                                PostQuitMessage (0) ;
                                break ;
                        default:                              /* default windows message processing */
                                return DefWindowProc (hWnd, iMessage, wParam, lParam) ;
                }
        return (0L) ;
}


BOOL FAR PASCAL WindPropFunc (HWND hWindow, WORD nDummy, PSTR pString,
        HANDLE hData)
{
        gPropertyList [gnPropertyCount].hPropData = hData ;
        strcpy (gPropertyList [gnPropertyCount].cPropName, pString) ;
        gnPropertyCount++ ;
        return (1) ;
}
```

ENUMTASKWINDOWS   ■ Win 2.0   ■ Win 3.0   ■ Win 3.1

Purpose	Lists all of the top-level windows associated with a task.
Syntax	BOOL **EnumTaskWindows**(HANDLE *hTask*, FARPROC *lpEnumFunc*, LONG *lParam*);
Description	Calls an enumeration function to collect the handle for every top-level window associated with a task. Tasks are running applications in memory. Windows keeps track of all running tasks in the "task handler." Note that dynamic link libraries (DLLs) are not tasks. Each instance of a program is a separate task.
Returns	BOOL. TRUE if all tasks were successfully enumerated, FALSE if not.
See Also	EnumChildWindows(), GetCurrentTask(), GetWindowTask()
Parameters	
hTask	HANDLE: The handle to the task. Use GetCurrentTask() to retrieve the handle of the currently running task, or GetWindowTask() to retrieve the task handle of a specific window.
lpEnumFunc	FARPROC: Pointer to the enumeration function.
lParam	DWORD: The 32-bit value that is to be sent to the callback function each time a task is found. This can be data or a handle to a memory block.

The enumeration function must be in the form:

BOOL FAR PASCAL **EnumFunc** (HWND *hWnd*, DWORD *lParam*);

The function name must be listed in the EXPORTS section of the program's .DEF definition file. The enumeration function must return TRUE to continue enumeration, FALSE to stop enumeration (such as if an error is detected). The meaning of the parameters passed to the enumeration function are as follows:

hWnd   HWND: Handle to the parent window for a task. This value will be different each time the callback function is called.

lParam   DWORD: The data or pointer that is passed on each call to the enumeration function. This is the *lParam* value set when EnumTaskWindows() was called. It will be the same each time the callback function is called.

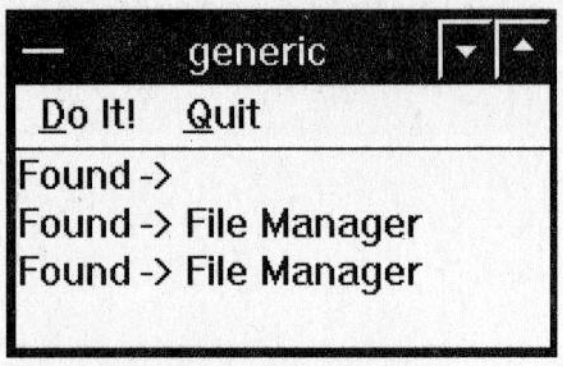

Figure 3-6. EnumTask-Windows( ) Example.

Example   Here the enumeration function is used to determine the top-level windows associated with the Windows File Manager application. There turn out to be three tasks. The first is related to a hidden unnamed window, while the second two are related to a window titled "File Manager." (See Figure 3-6.)

▷ **GENERIC.H Header File**

```
/* generic.h   */

#define IDM_DOIT    1              /* menu item id values */
#define IDM_QUIT    2
            /* definitions */
#define TITLEWIDE          20
typedef struct
{
        GLOBALHANDLE         hGMem ;
        int                  nCount ;
} ENUMER ;
            /* global variables */
int     ghInstance ;
char    gszAppName [] = "generic" ;
            /* function prototypes */
long FAR PASCAL WndProc (HWND, unsigned, WORD, LONG) ;
BOOL FAR PASCAL WindTaskFunc (HWND, ENUMER FAR *) ;


long FAR PASCAL WndProc (HWND hWnd, unsigned iMessage, WORD wParam, LONG lParam)
{
        static  FARPROC          lpfEnumProc ;
        static  ENUMER           enumer ;
        HANDLE                   hTaskWind, hFileMgr ;
        int                      i ;
        HDC                      hDC ;
        LPHANDLE                 lpTaskMem ;
        char                     cBuf [128], cWindName [64] ;

        switch (iMessage)                /* process windows messages */
        {
                case WM_CREATE:          /* tell windows about WindTaskFunc() */
                        lpfEnumProc = MakeProcInstance (WindTaskFunc,
                                                ghInstance) ;
                        break ;
                case WM_COMMAND:                 /* process menu items */
                        switch (wParam)
                        {
                        case IDM_DOIT:           /* User hit the "Do it" menu item */
                                if (enumer.hGMem)        /* if not first time tried */
                                        GlobalFree (enumer.hGMem) ;    /* free the memory */
                                                        /* initialize storage area */
                                enumer.hGMem = GlobalAlloc
```

```
                         (GMEM_MOVEABLE | GMEM_ZEROINIT, 1L) ;
                enumer.nCount = 0 ;
                                /* let Windows run callback func. */
                hFileMgr = FindWindow (NULL, "File Manager") ;
                hTaskWind = GetWindowTask (hFileMgr) ;
                EnumTaskWindows (hTaskWind, lpfEnumProc,
                        (DWORD) (LPSTR) &enumer) ;

                hDC = GetDC (hWnd) ;        /* see which tasks were found */
                lpTaskMem = (LPHANDLE) GlobalLock (enumer.hGMem) ;
                for (i = 0 ; i < enumer.nCount ; i++)
                {
                        hTaskWind = * (lpTaskMem +
                                (i * sizeof (HANDLE))) ;
                        GetWindowText (hTaskWind, cWindName, 63) ;
                        TextOut (hDC, 0, 20*i, cBuf, wsprintf (cBuf,
                                "Found -> %s", (LPSTR) cWindName)) ;
                }
                GlobalUnlock (enumer.hGMem) ;
                ReleaseDC (hWnd, hDC) ;
                break ;
        case IDM_QUIT:
                DestroyWindow (hWnd) ;
                break ;
        }
        break ;
case WM_DESTROY:                         /* stop application */
        GlobalFree (enumer.hGMem) ;      /* release memory */
        FreeProcInstance (lpfEnumProc) ;
        PostQuitMessage (0) ;
        break ;
default:                                 /* default windows message processing */
        return DefWindowProc (hWnd, iMessage, wParam, lParam) ;
}
return (0L) ;
}


/* here is the function to find all of the asks running */
BOOL FAR PASCAL WindTaskFunc (HWND hWind, ENUMER FAR *enumer)

        LPSTR          lpMemory, lpDest ;

        if (!GlobalReAlloc (enumer->hGMem,
                        (DWORD) sizeof (HANDLE) * (enumer->nCount + 1),
                        GMEM_MOVEABLE))           /* make room for 1 more */
                return (0) ;                      /* quit if can't make room */
        lpMemory = GlobalLock (enumer->hGMem) ;   /* lock the memory area */
        lpDest = lpMemory + ((enumer->nCount) * sizeof (HANDLE)) ;
        (HANDLE) *lpDest = hWind ;                /* store handle to task window */
        GlobalUnlock (enumer->hGMem) ;            /* unlock the memory area */
        enumer->nCount++ ;                        /* keep track of how many */
        return (1) ;
}
```

ENUMWINDOWS

■ Win 2.0   ■ Win 3.0   ■ Win 3.1

Purpose	Retrieves data on all of the parent windows running on the system.
Syntax	BOOL **EnumWindows**(FARPROC *lpEnumFunc*, LONG *lParam*);
Description	Calls an enumeration function for every parent window running on the system. The enumeration function can collect whatever data is desired from each window as it is processed.
Uses	Useful for determining what other applications are running.
Returns	TRUE if all parent windows were enumerated, FALSE if not.
See Also	EnumChildWindows(), EnumTaskWindows()

Parameters

lpEnumFunc   FARPROC: The procedure instance address of the enumeration callback function. Use MakeProcInstance() to create this pointer.

lParam   DWORD: The 32-bit value to be passed to the callback function. This can either be data or a pointer.

The enumeration callback function must be in the following format:

BOOL FAR PASCAL **EnumFunc** (HWND *hWnd*, DWORD *lParam*);

The function must be declared in the EXPORTS section of the program's .DEF definition file. The function must return TRUE to continue enumeration, FALSE to stop. The parameters have the following meanings:

hWnd   HWND: The window handle for each window enumerated.

lParam   DWORD: The *lParam* value passed in the call to Enum-Windows(). This value will be the same each time the enumeration function is called.

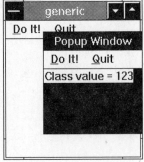

Figure 3-7. EnumWindows() Example.

Example   This example, as shown in Figure 3-7, lists all of the windows active on the screen when the user clicks the "Do It!" menu item.

▷ **WINDENUM.H Header File**

```
/* windenum.h   */

#define IDM_DOIT   1                    /* menu item id values */
#define IDM_QUIT   2

/* definitions */
#define TITLEWIDE        20
typedef struct
{
        GLOBALHANDLE          hGMem ;
        int                   nCount ;
} ENUMER ;

        /* global variables */
int     ghInstance ;
char    gszAppName [] = "windenum" ;
        /* function prototypes */
long FAR PASCAL WndProc (HWND, unsigned, WORD, LONG) ;
BOOL FAR PASCAL WndEnumFunc (HWND, ENUMER FAR *) ;
```

▷ **WINDENUM.C WindProc() Function and Enumeration Function from C Source File**

```
long FAR PASCAL WndProc (HWND hWnd, unsigned iMessage, WORD wParam, LONG lParam)
{
        static  FARPROC       lpfEnumProc ;
        static  ENUMER        enumer ;
        LPSTR                 lpWindName ;
        HDC                   hDC ;
        int                   i ;

        switch (iMessage)              /* process windows messages */
        {
                case WM_CREATE:
                        lpfEnumProc = MakeProcInstance (WndEnumFunc,
                                ghInstance) ;
                        break ;

                case WM_COMMAND:        /* process menu items */
```

```
                        switch (wParam)
                        {
                        case IDM_DOIT:   /* User hit the "Do it" menu item */

                                if (enumer.hGMem)          /* if not first time tried */
                                        GlobalFree (enumer.hGMem) ;    /* free the memory */
                                                          /* initialize storage area */
                                enumer.hGMem = GlobalAlloc (GMEM_MOVEABLE | GMEM_ZEROINIT,
                                        1L) ;
                                enumer.nCount = 0 ;
                                                   /* let Windows run callback func. */
                                EnumWindows (lpfEnumProc, (DWORD) &enumer) ;
                                hDC = GetDC (hWnd) ;          /* get ready to output */
                                lpWindName = GlobalLock (enumer.hGMem) ; /* lock memory */
                                TextOut (hDC, 10, 100, "EnumWindows() found:", 20) ;
                                for (i = 0 ; i < enumer.nCount ; i++)       /* display window */
                                        {                     /* titles found */
                                        TextOut (hDC, 15, 125 + (15 * i),
                                                (LPSTR) (lpWindName + (i * TITLEWIDE)),
                                                lstrlen (lpWindName + (i * TITLEWIDE))) ;
                                        }

                                GlobalUnlock (enumer.hGMem) ;    /* unlock memory */
                                ReleaseDC (hWnd, hDC) ;
                                break ;

                        case IDM_QUIT:
                                DestroyWindow (hWnd) ;
                                break ;
                        }
                        break ;
                case WM_DESTROY:/* stop application */
                        GlobalFree (enumer.hGMem) ;      /* release all memory */
                        PostQuitMessage (0) ;
                        break ;

                default:                /* default windows message processing */
                        return DefWindowProc (hWnd, iMessage, wParam, lParam) ;
        }
    return 0L ;
}

BOOL FAR PASCAL WndEnumFunc (HWND hWindow, ENUMER FAR *enumer)
{
        LPSTR   lpWindName ;
        char    cBuf [TITLEWIDE + 1] ;

        if (!GlobalReAlloc (enumer->hGMem,
                (DWORD) TITLEWIDE * (enumer->nCount + 1),
                GMEM_MOVEABLE))                     /* make room for 10 more */
                return (0) ;                        /* quit if can't make room */

        GetWindowText (hWindow, (LPSTR) cBuf, TITLEWIDE) ;       /* get title */
        cBuf [GetWindowTextLength (hWindow)] = '\0' ;            /* add end null */
        lpWindName = GlobalLock (enumer->hGMem) ;     /* lock the memory area */
                                                     /* put next name at end */
        lstrcpy (lpWindName + ((enumer->nCount) * TITLEWIDE), (LPSTR) cBuf) ;
        GlobalUnlock (enumer->hGMem) ;                /* unlock the memory area */
        enumer->nCount++ ;                           /* keep track of how many */
        return (1) ;
}
```

FINDWINDOW   ■ Win 2.0   ■ Win 3.0   ■ Win 3.1

Purpose	Retrieves a handle to a window.
Syntax	HWND **FindWindow** (LPSTR *lpClassName*, LPSTR *lpWindowName*);
Description	Finds the window's handle given the class name and/or the window's title.

Uses	Useful to find specific applications in memory. For example, an application may need to load the notepad application if it is not already in memory.
Returns	HWND, a handle to a window. Returns NULL if a match was not found.
See Also	ChildWindowFromPoint(), WinExec(), GetClassName(), GetWindowText()
Parameters	
lpClassName	LPSTR: Pointer to a null-terminated string containing the window's class name. If this parameter is NULL, all classes will be searched to find the window name.
lpWindowName	LPSTR: Pointer to a null-terminated string containing the window's title. If this value is NULL, all names will be searched to find the class name.
Example	This example checks to see if the Windows file manager is running.

```
long FAR PASCAL WndProc (HWND hWnd, unsigned iMessage, WORD wParam, LONG lParam)
{
        HDC             hDC ;                           /* device contxt handle */
        HWND            hWindow ;

        switch (iMessage)                       /* process windows messages */
        {
                case WM_COMMAND:                        /* process menu items */
                        switch (wParam)
                        {
                        case IDM_DOIT:                  /* User hit the "Do it" menu item */
                                hWindow = FindWindow (NULL, "File Manager") ;
                                hDC = GetDC (hWnd) ;
                                if (hWindow)
                                        TextOut (hDC, 10, 20,
                                                "I found the file manager!", 25) ;
                                else
                                        TextOut (hDC, 10, 20,
                                                "File manager not found.", 22) ;
                                ReleaseDC (hWnd, hDC) ;
                                break ;
```

[Other program lines]

FLASHWINDOW   ■ Win 2.0   ■ Win 3.0   ■ Win 3.1

Purpose	Highlights the window's caption bar if the window is not minimized, or flashes the window's icon if minimized.
Syntax	BOOL **FlashWindow** (HWND hWnd, BOOL bInvert);
Uses	Informs the user that a window needs attention, even if it does not have the input focus.
Returns	TRUE if the window was active before the call, FALSE if not.
See Also	GetFocus(), SetActiveWindow()
Parameters	
hWnd	HWND: Handle to the window to flash.
bInvert	BOOL: If TRUE, the window is toggled between the active appearance and inactive on each call to FlashWindow(). If FALSE, the window is returned to the same state it started (active or inactive).
Related Messages	WM_SETFOCUS, WM_KILLFOCUS
Example	

```
long FAR PASCAL WndProc (HWND hWnd, unsigned iMessage, WORD wParam, LONG lParam)
{
        switch (iMessage)                       /* process windows messages */
        {
                case WM_COMMAND:                        /* process menu items */
                        switch (wParam)
```

```
        {
        case IDM_DOIT:              /* User hit the "Do it" menu item */
                FlashWindow (hWnd, TRUE) ;
                break ;
```

[Other program lines]

GETACTIVEWINDOW   ■ Win 2.0   ■ Win 3.0   ■ Win 3.1

Purpose	Finds which parent or popup window is active.
Syntax	HWND **GetActiveWindow**(void);
Description	Retrieves a handle to the parent or popup window that is currently active. Active windows have highlighted title bars. Windows are made active by the user selecting the window (the window gets the input focus) or by calling SetFocus().
Uses	In applications with multiple popup windows. Your program can use GetActiveWindow() to find which popup is active.
Returns	A handle to the active window.
See Also	SetActiveWindow(), SetFocus()
Parameters	None (void).
Example	This example changes the title of the currently active window to "I'm Active!" when the user clicks the "Do It!" menu item.

```
long FAR PASCAL WndProc (HWND hWnd, unsigned iMessage, WORD wParam, LONG lParam)
{
        static HWND     hActive ;

        switch (iMessage)                       /* process windows messages */
        {
        case WM_COMMAND:                        /* process menu items */
                switch (wParam)
                {
                case IDM_DOIT:          /* User hit the "Do it" menu item */
                        hActive = GetActiveWindow() ;
                        SetWindowText (hActive, "I'm Active!") ;
                        break ;
```

[Other program lines]

GETCLASSINFO   □ Win 2.0   ■ Win 3.0   ■ Win 3.1

Purpose	Retrieves information about a window class.
Syntax	BOOL **GetClassInfo**(HANDLE *hInstance*, LPSTR *lpClassName*, LPWNDCLASS *lpWindClass*);
Description	Fills in the data in a WNDCLASS structure, based on the instance handle and class name.
Uses	Handy if you are modifying a class with SetClassWord() and SetClassLong() as the program operates. Eliminates the need to keep track of what is in the operating version of the class.
Returns	BOOL. Returns TRUE if a class was found and the data loaded, FALSE if not. The class data is copied into WNDCLASS structure pointed to by the *lpWndClass* parameter. The *lpszClassName*, *lpszMenuName*, and *hInstance* fields are not filled in by this function.

```
typedef struct tagWNDCLASS
  {
        WORD    style;
        LONG    (FAR PASCAL *lpfnWndProc)();
        int     cbClsExtra;
        int     cbWndExtra;
        HANDLE  hInstance;                      /* no */
        HICON   hIcon;
        HCURSOR hCursor;
        HBRUSH  hbrBackground;
```

```
        LPSTR    lpszMenuName;           /* no */
        LPSTR    lpszClassName;          /* no */
} WNDCLASS;

typedef WNDCLASS         *PWNDCLASS;
typedef WNDCLASS NEAR    *NPWNDCLASS;
typedef WNDCLASS FAR     *LPWNDCLASS;
```

See Also   SetClassWord(), SetClassLong(), GetClassLong(), GetClassWord(), RegisterClass(), Unregister-Class()

Parameters

hInstance   HANDLE: The instance of the program that created the window class. Set to NULL if you would like to retrieve information on classes defined by Windows (buttons, list boxes, etc.).

lpClassName   LPSTR: Points to a null-terminated string containing the class name. If the high order word is NULL, the function assumes that the low order word is a value returned by the MAKE-INTRESOURCE macro.

lpWndClass   LPWNDCLASS: Points to the memory area reserved to hold the window class data.

Example   This example determines the handle to the brush used to paint the background for the application's window class.

```
Long FAR PASCAL WndProc (HWND hWnd, unsigned iMessage, WORD wParam, LONG lParam)
{
        static WNDCLASS          WndClass ;
        static HBRUSH            hbrWindBrush ;

        switch (iMessage)                                /* process windows messages */
        {
                case WM_COMMAND:                         /* process menu items */
                        switch (wParam)
                        {
                        case IDM_DOIT:  /* get the class background brush */
                                GetClassInfo (ghInstance, gszAppName, &WndClass) ;
                                hbrWindBrush = WndClass.hbrBackground ;
                                break ;
```

[Other program lines]

GetClassLong   ■ Win 2.0   ■ Win 3.0   ■ Win 3.1

Purpose   Retrieves a long value from the class structure.

Syntax   LONG **GetClassLong**(HWND *hWnd*, int *nIndex*);

Uses   Used to retrieve a pointer to the class message processing function. If the class was created reserving space for extra four-byte data, GetClassLong() can be used to retrieve it.

Returns   The value requested, usually the message processing function address.

See Also   GetClassInfo(), SetClassWord(), SetClassLong(), GetClassWord()

Parameters

hWnd   HWND: A handle to the window using the class.

nIndex   int: Set to one of the values in Table 3-3.

Value	Meaning	⊠
GCL_WNDPROC	Retrieve a far pointer to the window's message processing procedure.	
GCL_MENUNAME	Retrieve a far pointer to a character string containing the menu name.	

Table 3-3. GetClassLong( ) Index Values.

These index values are defined as negative values in WINDOWS.H. Alternatively, if you are retrieving the extra four-byte data from the window class, set *nIndex* equal to the byte number to retrieve (0, 4, 8…).

Example   This example creates a new window class and uses the class to create a popup window. The class definition contains extra space for four bytes (DWORD). These values are set to the integer "123" as the popup is created.

In the popup's own message processing procedure ChildProc(), the class value is recovered and displayed in the popup's client area every time a WM_PAINT message is received. (See Figure 3-8.)

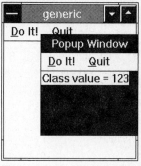

Figure 3-8. GetClassLong( ) Example.

```
long FAR PASCAL WndProc (HWND hWnd, unsigned iMessage, WORD wParam, LONG lParam)
{
        WNDCLASS          wndclass ;                  /* the window class */
        HWND              hPopup ;

        switch (iMessage)                             /* process windows messages */
        {
                case WM_CREATE: /* build the child window when program starts */
                        wndclass.style          = CS_HREDRAW | CS_VREDRAW | CS_PARENTDC;
                        wndclass.lpfnWndProc    = ChildProc ;
                        wndclass.cbClsExtra     = sizeof (DWORD) ;
                        wndclass.cbWndExtra     = 0 ;
                        wndclass.hInstance      = ghInstance ;
                        wndclass.hIcon          = NULL ;
                        wndclass.hCursor        = LoadCursor (NULL, IDC_ARROW) ;
                        wndclass.hbrBackground  = GetStockObject (LTGRAY_BRUSH) ;
                        wndclass.lpszMenuName   = gszAppName ;
                        wndclass.lpszClassName  = "SecondClass" ;
                                        /* register the window class */
                        if(RegisterClass (&wndclass))
                        {
                                hPopup = CreateWindow ("SecondClass", "Popup Window",
                                        WS_POPUP | WS_VISIBLE | WS_BORDER | WS_CAPTION,
                                        10, 50, 150, 150, hWnd, NULL, ghInstance, NULL) ;
                                SetClassLong (hPopup, 0, 123) ;
                                ShowWindow (hPopup, SW_SHOW) ;
                        }
                        break ;
                case WM_COMMAND:        /* process menu items */
                        switch (wParam)
                        {
                        case IDM_QUIT:
                                DestroyWindow (hWnd) ;
                                break ;
                        }
                        break ;
                case WM_DESTROY:        /* stop application */
                        PostQuitMessage (0) ;
                        break ;

                default:                /* default windows message processing */
                        return DefWindowProc (hWnd, iMessage, wParam, lParam) ;
        }
        return (0L) ;
}

/* Here is a separate message processing procedure for the child window */

long FAR PASCAL ChildProc (HWND hWnd, unsigned iMessage, WORD wParam,
```

```
                LONG lParam)
{
        char                    cBuf [128] ;
        int                     n ;
        PAINTSTRUCT             ps ;

        switch (iMessage)               /* process windows messages */
        {
                case WM_PAINT:
                        BeginPaint (hWnd, &ps) ;
                        n = (int) GetClassLong (hWnd, 0) ;
                        TextOut (ps.hdc, 0, 0, cBuf, wsprintf (cBuf,
                                "Class value = %d", n)) ;
                        EndPaint (hWnd, &ps) ;
                        break ;
                case WM_COMMAND:                /* process menu items */
                        switch (wParam)
                        {
                        case IDM_QUIT:
                                DestroyWindow (hWnd) ;
                                break ;
                        }
                        break ;
                default:                /* default windows message processing */
                        return DefWindowProc (hWnd, iMessage, wParam, lParam) ;
        }
        return (OL) ;
}
```

GetClassName   ■ Win 2.0   ■ Win 3.0   ■ Win 3.1

Purpose	Retrieves the class name upon which a window is based .
Syntax	int **GetClassName**(HWND *hWnd*, LPSTR *lpClassName*, int *nMaxCount*);
Description	Copies the class name to a memory area pointed to by *lpClassName*.
Uses	Generally used before GetClassInfo() to load the class name into a string array.
Returns	The number of characters read. Zero if *hWnd* is not a valid window handle.
See Also	GetClassInfo()
Parameters	
hWnd	HWND: Handle to the window which was created based on the class.
lpClassName	LPSTR: Pointer to a memory area to hold the class name.
nMaxCount	int: The maximum number of bytes to retrieve. This allows you to keep the class name from overflowing the *lpClassName* area.
Example	This example displays the class name when the user clicks the "Do It!" menu item.

```
Long FAR PASCAL WndProc (HWND hWnd, unsigned iMessage, WORD wParam, LONG lParam)
{
        char    cBuf[128] ;
        int     nLenStr ;
        HDC     hDC ;

        switch (iMessage)                               /* process windows messages */
        {
                case WM_COMMAND:                        /* process menu items */
                        switch (wParam)
                        {
                        case IDM_DOIT:                  /* User hit the "Do it" menu item */
                                nLenStr = GetClassName (hWnd, cBuf, 127) ;
                                hDC = GetDC(hWnd) ;
                                TextOut (hDC, 10, 10, "The class name is:", 17) ;
                                TextOut (hDC, 10, 25, cBuf, nLenStr) ;
```

```
                              ReleaseDC (hWnd, hDC) ;
                              break ;
```
[Other program lines]

GetClassWord   ■ Win 2.0   ■ Win 3.0   ■ Win 3.1

Purpose	Retrieves information from a class.
Syntax	WORD **GetClassWord**(HWND *hWnd*, int *nIndex*);
Description	Returns two-byte data from a class.
Uses	Generally used to retrieve the class cursor, icon, or background brush. More efficient than GetClassInfo() if you are only retrieving one value.
Returns	The two-byte data value requested.
See Also	GetClassWord(), GetClassLong(), GetClassName(), SetClassLong(), SetClassWord(), GetClassInfo()

Figure 3-9. GetClassWord() Example.

Parameters

hWnd   HWND: The handle of the window that was created based on the class.

nIndex   int: The byte offset for the specific data item. It can be any of the values described in Table 3-4.

Value	Meaning
GCW_CBCLSEXTRA	Retrieve the number of bytes of extra data associated with the class. A second call to GetClassWord() can be used to retrieve a word of data. Use an *nIndex* value of 0, 2, 4… for the first, second, third… words of extra data.
GCW_CBWNDEXTRA	Retrieve the number of bytes of extra data associated with the window. GetWindowWord() can be used to retrieve a word of data. Use an *nIndex* value of 0, 2, 4… for the first, second, third…words of extra data.
GCW_HBRBACKGROUND	Retrieve a handle to the class background brush.
GCW_HCURSOR	Retrieve a handle to the class cursor.
GCW_HICON	Retrieve a handle to the class icon.
GCW_HMODULE	Retrieve a handle to the class module.
GCW_STYLE	Retrieve the window class style.

Table 3-4. GetClassWord() Index Values.

The GCW_ values are defined as negative values in WINDOWS.H. This is how the function differentiates between positive offsets you supply to retrieve extra data stored with the class and a request for a predefined element of class data.

Example   This example retrieves the class icon, as shown in Figure 3-9, in order to display the icon in the window's client area.

```
long FAR PASCAL WndProc (HWND hWnd, unsigned iMessage, WORD wParam, LONG lParam)
{
        HICON           hIcon ;
        HDC             hDC ;

        switch (iMessage)                              /* process windows messages */
        {
                case WM_COMMAND:                       /* process menu items */
                        switch (wParam)
                        {
```

```
                         case IDM_DOIT:  /* Paint the program's icon */
                                  hIcon = GetClassWord (hWnd, GCW_HICON) ;
                                  hDC = GetDC (hWnd) ;
                                  DrawIcon (hDC, 10, 10, hIcon) ;
                                  ReleaseDC (hWnd, hDC) ;
                                  break ;
```

[Other program lines]

GETCLIENTRECT   ■ Win 2.0   ■ Win 3.0   ■ Win 3.1

Purpose	Retrieves a window's client area size.
Syntax	void **GetClientRect**(HWND *hWnd*, LPRECT *lpRect*);
Description	The client area dimensions are copied into the RECT structure pointed to by *lpRect*. As client coordinates are used, the upper left corner is always 0,0. The bottom right corner gives the client area dimensions in device units (pixels).
Uses	Use at the start of WM_PAINT refresh cycles to find out how big an area is visible.
Returns	No returned value (void).
See Also	InvalidateRect(), UpdateWindow(), IsIcon(), BeginPaint(), GetWindowExt(), GetWindowRect()
Parameters	
hWnd	HWND: Handle to the window.
lpRect	LPRECT: Long pointer to a RECT rectangle data structure.
Related Messages	WM_PAINT
Example	This example shows an explicit erasure of the client area rectangle. The client rectangle is passed to InvalidateRect(). The same functionality can be achieved without using GetClientRect(), but having the second parameter in the InvalidateRect() call set to NULL. This causes the entire client area to be updated.

```
long FAR PASCAL WndProc (HWND hWnd, unsigned iMessage, WORD wParam, LONG lParam)
{
        HDC     hDC ;
        RECT    rClient ;
        int     i ;

        switch (iMessage)                         /* process windows messages */
        {
                case WM_COMMAND:                  /* process menu items */
                        switch (wParam)
                        {
                        case IDM_DOIT:            /* User hit the "Do it" menu item */
                                hDC = GetDC (hWnd) ;      /* put text in client area */
                                for (i = 0 ; i < 10 ; i++)
                                {
                                        TextOut (hDC, 10, 10 + (i*15),
                                                "This text will be erased.", 25) ;
                                }
                                ReleaseDC (hWnd, hDC) ;
                                GetClientRect (hWnd, &rClient) ;
                                InvalidateRect (hWnd, &rClient, TRUE) ;
                                UpdateWindow (hWnd) ;    /* force WM_PAINT now */
                                break ;
```

[Other program lines]

GETCURRENTTASK   ■ Win 2.0   ■ Win 3.0   ■ Win 3.1

Purpose	Retrieves a handle to the currently executing task.
Syntax	HANDLE **GetCurrentTask**(void);

Uses	A task is an application program running on the system. Windows keeps track of all running tasks in the "task handler." Each instance of a program is a separate task. This function is used to initialize a callback function made for EnumTaskWindows(). Also used to return the task handle for PostAppMessage().
Returns	HANDLE, a handle to the task executing.
See Also	EnumTaskWindows(), PostAppMessage(), GetWindowTask()
Parameters	None (void).
Example	This example is similar to the example under EnumTaskWindows(). In this case, the handle to the currently executing task is passed to the enumeration function, rather than the task handle for the file manager. The remainder of the program is identical to the example under the EnumTaskWindows() function description.

```
long FAR PASCAL WndProc (HWND hWnd, unsigned iMessage, WORD wParam, LONG lParam)
{
        static  FARPROC         lpfEnumProc ;
        static  ENUMER          enumer ;
        static  HANDLE          hTask, hFoundTask ;
        int                     i ;
        HDC                     hDC ;
        LPHANDLE                lpTaskMem ;

        switch (iMessage)               /* process windows messages */
        {
        case WM_CREATE:                 /* tell windows about WindTaskFunc() */
                lpfEnumProc = MakeProcInstance (WindTaskFunc, ghInstance) ;
                break ;
        case WM_COMMAND:                /* process menu items */
                switch (wParam)
                {
                case IDM_DOIT:  /* User hit the "Do it" menu item */
                        if (enumer.hGMem)       /* if not first time tried */
                                GlobalFree (enumer.hGMem) ;/* free the memory */
                                        /* initialize storage area */
                        enumer.hGMem = GlobalAlloc
                                (GMEM_MOVEABLE | GMEM_ZEROINIT, 1L) ;
                        enumer.nCount = 0 ;
                        hTask = GetCurrentTask () ;
                                        /* let Windows run callback func. */
                        EnumTaskWindows (hTask, lpfEnumProc, (DWORD) &enumer) ;
```
[Other program lines]

GetDesktopWindow   □ Win 2.0   ■ Win 3.0   ■ Win 3.1

Purpose	Retrieves the handle of the background window that covers the entire screen.
Syntax	HWND **GetDesktopWindow**(void);
Uses	Painting on the Windows desktop background. Some specialized utility programs paint on the desktop window to provide utilitarian buttons, such as disk icons and button controls, to launch applications.
Returns	A handle to the desktop background window.
Parameters	None (void).
Comments	The background on which all windows are shown is another window. You can use all painting and text output functions on it, as you would the client area of any other window. This area should be reserved for special purposes such as screen "saving" and printing programs, as painting on the background violates the basic principle of sharing the screen resources between applications.

Example This example prints the string "This text will be on the background." on the upper left corner of the background. It is for demonstration purposes only. Printing text on the background is not a good practice.

```
Long FAR PASCAL WndProc (HWND hWnd, unsigned iMessage, WORD wParam, LONG lParam)
{
        HDC      hDC ;
        HWND     hDesktop ;

        switch (iMessage)                        /* process windows messages */
        {
                case WM_COMMAND:                 /* process menu items */
                        switch (wParam)
                        {
                        case IDM_DOIT:           /* User hit the "Do it" menu item */
                                hDesktop = GetDesktopWindow () ;
                                hDC = GetDC (hDesktop) ;
                                TextOut (hDC, 0, 0,
                                        "This text will be on the background.", 36) ;
                                ReleaseDC (hDesktop, hDC) ;
                                break ;
```

[Other program lines]

GETFOCUS   ■ Win 2.0   ■ Win 3.0   ■ Win 3.1

Purpose	Finds which window has the input focus.
Syntax	HWND **GetFocus**(void);
Description	Retrieves a handle to the window that has the input focus. The window with the input focus will be the next one to receive keyboard input.
Uses	Handy if you have multiple edit controls. Determines which one the user has selected to receive text input.
Returns	HWND, a handle to the window with the input focus.
See Also	SetFocus()
Parameters	None (void).
Related Messages	WM_SETFOCUS, WM_KILLFOCUS

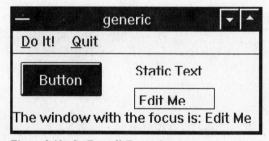

Example This example checks which window has the input focus when the user clicks the "Do It!" menu item. (See Figure 3-10.) Note that this is assured to be either the parent window or one of the children, as

Figure 3-10. GetFocus( ) Example.

clicking the menu will force the focus back to the application. In other circumstances, the focus may be in an outside window when GetFocus() is called. Use SetActiveWindow() to make sure the application is active before calling GetFocus().

```
Long FAR PASCAL WndProc (HWND hWnd, unsigned iMessage, WORD wParam, LONG lParam)
{
        static HWND    hButton ;
        static HWND    hStaticText ;
        static HWND    hEdit ;
        HWND           hFocus ;
        HDC            hDC ;
        static char    cBuf [25] ;

        switch (iMessage)                                  /* process windows messages */
        {
```

```
        case WM_CREATE:

                hButton = CreateWindow ("BUTTON", "Button",
                        WS_CHILD | WS_VISIBLE | BS_PUSHBUTTON,
                        10, 10, 100, 40, hWnd, NULL, ghInstance, NULL) ;
                ShowWindow (hButton, SW_SHOW) ;
                                        /* create and show static text */
                hStaticText = CreateWindow ("STATIC", "Static Text",
                        WS_CHILD | WS_VISIBLE | BS_PUSHBUTTON,
                        150, 10, 100, 15, hWnd, NULL, ghInstance, NULL) ;
                ShowWindow (hStaticText, SW_SHOW) ;
                                        /* create and show an edit control */
                hEdit = CreateWindow ("EDIT", "Edit Me",
                        WS_CHILD | WS_VISIBLE | WS_BORDER,
                        150, 40, 100, 25, hWnd, NULL, ghInstance, NULL) ;
                ShowWindow (hEdit, SW_SHOW) ;
                break ;

        case WM_COMMAND:                   /* process menu items */
                switch (wParam)
                {
                case IDM_DOIT:             /* User hit the "Do it" menu item */
                        hFocus = GetFocus () ;
                        GetWindowText (hFocus, cBuf, 24) ;
                        hDC = GetDC (hWnd) ;
                        TextOut (hDC, 10, 65, "The window with the focus is:", 29) ;
                        TextOut (hDC, 15, 80, cBuf, strlen (cBuf)) ;
                        ReleaseDC (hWnd, hDC) ;
                        break ;
```

[Other program lines]

GETLASTACTIVEPOPUP
□ Win 2.0   ■ Win 3.0   ■ Win 3.1

Purpose	Finds the popup window that was active last.
Syntax	HWND **GetLastActivePopup**(HWND *hwndOwner*);
Uses	In programs with multiple popup windows.
Returns	A handle to the popup window that was active last. Active windows have their title bars or outline borders highlighted. Will return *hwndOwner* if *hwndOwner* does not own any popups or *hwndOwner* was the last active window, or if *hwndOwner* is not a top-level window (if it is owned by another window).
See Also	GetActiveWindow(), SetActiveWindow()

Figure 3-11. GetLast-ActivePopup() Example.

Parameters

hwndOwner   HWND: The handle of the parent window that spawned the popup windows.

Example   This example creates a popup child window. When the user clicks the "Do It!" menu item on the parent window, a handle to the last active popup window is retrieved. This handle is used to change the popup window's caption to "I was Active!". (See Figure 3-11.)

```
long FAR PASCAL WndProc (HWND hWnd, unsigned iMessage, WORD wParam, LONG lParam)
{
        HDC                     hDC ;      /* device context handle */
        static WNDCLASS wndclass ;         /* the window class */
        static HWND             hPopup, hActive ;

        switch (iMessage)                           /* process windows messages */
        {
           case WM_CREATE: /* build the child window when program starts */

                wndclass.style          =
                        CS_HREDRAW | CS_VREDRAW | CS_PARENTDC ;
```

```
                        wndclass.lpfnWndProc      = PopupProc ;
                        wndclass.cbClsExtra       = 0 ;
                        wndclass.cbWndExtra       = 0 ;
                        wndclass.hInstance        = ghInstance ;
                        wndclass.hIcon            = NULL ;
                        wndclass.hCursor          = LoadCursor (NULL, IDC_ARROW) ;
                        wndclass.hbrBackground    = GetStockObject (LTGRAY_BRUSH) ;
                        wndclass.lpszMenuName     = NULL ;
                        wndclass.lpszClassName    = "SecondClass" ;
                                                  /* register the window class */
                        if(RegisterClass (&wndclass))
                        {
                                hPopup = CreateWindow ("SecondClass", "Popup Window",
                                        WS_POPUP | WS_VISIBLE | WS_BORDER | WS_CAPTION,
                                        10, 50, 200, 150, hWnd, NULL, ghInstance, NULL) ;
                                ShowWindow (hPopup, SW_SHOW) ;
                        }
                        break ;
                case WM_COMMAND:                  /* process menu items */
                        switch (wParam)
                        {
                        case IDM_DOIT:            /* User hit the "Do it" menu item */
                                SetFocus (hPopup) ;
                                hActive = GetLastActivePopup (hWnd) ;
                                SetWindowText (hActive, "I was Active!") ;
                                break ;
                        case IDM_QUIT:            /* send end of application message */
                                DestroyWindow (hWnd) ;
                                break ;
                        }
                        break ;

                case WM_DESTROY:          /* stop application */
                        PostQuitMessage (0) ;
                        break ;

                default:                          /* default windows message processing */
                        return DefWindowProc (hWnd, iMessage, wParam, lParam) ;
        }
        return (0L) ;
}

/* Here is a separate message processing procedure for the popup window */

long FAR PASCAL PopupProc (HWND hWnd, unsigned iMessage, WORD wParam,
        LONG lParam)
{
        HDC                     hDC ;             /* device context handle */
        PAINTSTRUCT             ps ;              /* paint structure */
        switch (iMessage)                         /* process windows messages */
        {
                case WM_PAINT:                    /* just write in the window */
                        hDC = BeginPaint(hWnd, &ps) ;
                        TextOut (hDC, 1, 1, "WM_PAINT in Child.", 18) ;
                        EndPaint (hWnd, &ps) ;
                        break ;
                case WM_DESTROY:                  /* stop the application */
                        PostQuitMessage (0) ;
                        break ;
                default:                          /* default windows message processing */
                        return DefWindowProc (hWnd, iMessage, wParam, lParam) ;
        }
        return (0L) ;
}
```

GetNextWindow

■ Win 2.0 ■ Win 3.0 ■ Win 3.1

Purpose	Finds parent and child windows.
Syntax	HWND **GetNextWindow**(HWND *hWnd*, WORD *wFlag*);
Description	Searches the window manager's list for the next or previous window. If *hWnd* points to a top-level window, GetNextWindow() looks for other top-level windows. If *hWnd* points to a child window, GetNextWindow() looks for other child windows.
Uses	To locate child windows in applications with only two or three child windows. EnumWindows() and EnumChildWindows() are more efficient where there are many windows.
Returns	HWND, a handle to the next or previous window in the window manager's list.
See Also	EnumWindows(), EnumChildWindows(), GetWindow()
Parameters	
hWnd	HWND: Handle to a window. If *hWnd* points to a top-level window, GetNextWindow() looks for other top-level windows. If *hWnd* points to a child window, GetNextWindow() looks for other child windows.
wFlag	WORD: Specifies if the handle returned is to be for the next or previous window. It can be either GW_HWNDNEXT or GW_HWNDPREV.

Example

```
Long FAR PASCAL WndProc (HWND hWnd, unsigned iMessage, WORD wParam, LONG lParam)
{
        HDC             hDC ;
        HWND      hNextWindow ;
        char            cBuf[25] ;

        switch (iMessage)                       /* process windows messages */
        {
                case WM_COMMAND:                /* process menu items */
                        switch (wParam)
                        {
                        case IDM_DOIT:          /* User hit the "Do it" menu item */
                                hNextWindow = GetNextWindow (hWnd, GW_HWNDNEXT) ;
                                hDC = GetDC (hWnd) ;
                                TextOut (hDC, 10, 10, "The next window is:", 19) ;
                                itoa (hNextWindow, cBuf, 10) ;
                                TextOut (hDC, 15, 30, cBuf, lstrlen (cBuf)) ;
                                GetWindowText (hNextWindow, cBuf, 24) ;
                                TextOut (hDC, 15, 50, cBuf, lstrlen (cBuf)) ;
                                ReleaseDC (hNextWindow, hDC) ;
                                break ;
```

[Other program lines]

GetNumTasks

■ Win 2.0 ■ Win 3.0 ■ Win 3.1

Purpose	Finds the number of tasks running in the system.
Syntax	int **GetNumTasks**(void);
Description	The number of tasks is the number of unique program instances in operation. If more than one copy of the same program is operating, each will count as a separate task.
Uses	Used in shell applications such as the Program Manager. The shell can determine if it is the only task running by seeing if the returned value from GetNumTasks()is one.
Returns	int, the number of running tasks.
See Also	EnumTaskWindows()
Parameters	None (void).

Example   This example displays the number of tasks running on the system in the example program's client area. The example assumes that the C library STRING.H has been included.

```
Long FAR PASCAL WndProc (HWND hWnd, unsigned iMessage, WORD wParam, LONG lParam)
{
        HDC     hDC ;
        char    cBuf[25] ;
        int     nNumTasks ;

        switch (iMessage)                       /* process windows messages */
        {
                case WM_COMMAND:                /* process menu items */
                        switch (wParam)
                        {
                        case IDM_DOIT:          /* User hit the "Do it" menu item */
                                nNumTasks = GetNumTasks () ;
                                hDC = GetDC (hWnd) ;
                                TextOut (hDC, 10, 10,
                                        "The number of tasks running is:", 31) ;
                                itoa (nNumTasks, cBuf, 10) ;
                                TextOut (hDC, 15, 30, cBuf, strlen (cBuf)) ;
                                ReleaseDC (hWnd, hDC) ;
                                break ;
```

[Other program lines]

GETPARENT   ■ Win 2.0   ■ Win 3.0   ■ Win 3.1

Purpose	Retrieves a handle to a parent window.
Syntax	HWND **GetParent**(HWND *hWnd*);
Description	Windows maintains a table of window handles, and their linkages between parent and children, in memory at all times. Any degree of nesting (children of children of children...) is possible. GetParent() looks for the parent of the window whose handle is *hWnd*.
Uses	Useful if a child or popup window has a separate message processing function. GetParent() allows the child window to retrieve its parent's handle for sending messages to the parent's message function.
Returns	HWND, a handle to the parent window. NULL if *hWnd* does not have a parent.
See Also	ChildWindowFromPoint(), EnumWindows(), GetWindow().
Parameters	
hWnd	HWND: The starting window's handle.
Example	In this example, the parent window creates a popup window. The parent sends the popup window a WM_USER message when the user clicks the "Do It!" menu item. The WM_USER message has the parent's window handle set as *wParam*, so that the popup window can print out the parent's name. GetParent() could just as easily been used within the popup window's message processing function to retrieve the parent window's handle.

```
Long FAR PASCAL WndProc (HWND hWnd, unsigned iMessage, WORD wParam, LONG lParam)
{
        HDC                     hDC ;
        static WNDCLASS         wndclass ;
        static HWND             hPopup, hParent ;

        switch (iMessage)                               /* process windows messages */
        {
                case WM_CREATE: /* build the child window when program starts */
                        wndclass.style          = CS_HREDRAW | CS_VREDRAW | CS_PARENTDC;
                        wndclass.lpfnWndProc    = ChildProc ;
                        wndclass.cbClsExtra     = 0 ;
                        wndclass.cbWndExtra     = 0 ;
                        wndclass.hInstance      = ghInstance ;
```

```
                        wndclass.hIcon          = NULL ;
                        wndclass.hCursor        = LoadCursor (NULL, IDC_ARROW) ;
                        wndclass.hbrBackground  = GetStockObject (LTGRAY_BRUSH) ;
                        wndclass.lpszMenuName   = NULL ;
                        wndclass.lpszClassName  = "SecondClass" ;
                                                /* register the window class */
                        if(RegisterClass (&wndclass))
                        {
                                hPopup = CreateWindow ("SecondClass", "Popup Window",
                                        WS_POPUP | WS_VISIBLE | WS_BORDER | WS_CAPTION,
                                        10, 50, 200, 150, hWnd, NULL, ghInstance, NULL) ;
                                ShowWindow (hPopup, SW_SHOW) ;
                        }
                        break ;
                case WM_COMMAND:                /* process menu items */
                        switch (wParam)
                        {
                        case IDM_DOIT:  /* User hit the "Do it" menu item */
                                hParent = GetParent (hPopup) ;
                                                /* Tell popup window its parentage */
                                SendMessage (hPopup, WM_USER, hParent, OL) ;
                                break ;
                        case IDM_QUIT:
                                DestroyWindow (hWnd) ;
                                break ;
                        }
                        break ;
                case WM_DESTROY:        /* stop application */
                        PostQuitMessage (0) ;
                        break ;
                default:                /* default windows message processing */
                        return DefWindowProc (hWnd, iMessage, wParam, lParam) ;
        }
        return (OL) ;
}

/* Here is a separate message processing procedure for the popup window */

long FAR PASCAL ChildProc (HWND hWnd, unsigned iMessage, WORD wParam, LONG lParam)
{
        HDC             hDC ;
        HWND            hParent ;
        char            cBuf [25] ;

        switch (iMessage)               /* process windows messages */
        {
                case WM_USER:   /* message from parent - wParam is parent handle */
                        hDC = GetDC (hWnd) ;
                        TextOut (hDC, 1, 1, "My Parent window is:", 21) ;
                        GetWindowText ((HWND) wParam, cBuf, 24) ;
                        TextOut (hDC, 1, 15, cBuf, strlen (cBuf)) ;
                        ReleaseDC (hWnd, hDC) ;
                        break ;
                case WM_DESTROY:        /* stop the application */
                        PostQuitMessage (0) ;
                        break ;
                default:                /* default windows message processing */
                        return DefWindowProc (hWnd, iMessage, wParam, lParam) ;
        }
        return (OL) ;
}
```

GetProp   ■ Win 2.0   ■ Win 3.0   ■ Win 3.1

Purpose	Retrieves a property (data) associated with a window.
Syntax	HANDLE **GetProp**(HWND *hWnd*, LPSTR *lpString*);
Description	Retrieves a handle to the memory area associated with the property named by *lpString*.

Uses   The property functions allow data to be associated with a window. This is an excellent way to deal with data that is specific to a certain window, avoiding the need for global data storage.

Returns   HANDLE, a handle to the memory area containing the data. The data must have been previously stored with SetProp().

See Also SetProp(), EnumProp, RemoveProp()

Parameters

hWnd   HWND: Handle to the window which has property data associated with it.

lpString   LPSTR: Pointer to a null-terminated string that contains the name associated with the data. This can also be an atom. In that case the high-order word must be set to zero, while the low-order word should contain the atom value.

Example   This example stores a handle to a global memory block as a window property. The memory block contains the string "This data tied to Window," as shown in Figure 3-12. When the user clicks the "Do It!" menu item, the handle to the memory block is retrieved and the string is displayed in the window's client area. Real uses of property data are most frequent in applications that have a number of similar child windows, such as MDI applications (see Chapter 29). Note that deleting the property does not remove the data pointed to by the memory handle. The memory block is deleted separately from the property when processing the WM_DESTROY message.

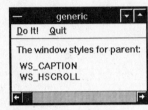

Figure 3-12. GetProp() Example.

```
long FAR PASCAL WndProc (HWND hWnd, unsigned iMessage, WORD wParam, LONG lParam)
{
        HANDLE          hMemory ;
        LPSTR           lpName ;
        HDC             hDC ;
        char            cBuf[] = "This data tied to Window";

        switch (iMessage)               /* process windows messages */
        {
        case WM_CREATE:
                hMemory = GlobalAlloc (GMEM_MOVEABLE | GMEM_ZEROINIT,
                        (LONG) lstrlen (cBuf)) ;
                lpName = GlobalLock (hMemory) ;
                lstrcpy (lpName, cBuf) ;
                GlobalUnlock (hMemory) ;
                SetProp (hWnd, "User Prop", hMemory) ;
                break ;
        case WM_COMMAND:                /* process menu items */
                switch (wParam)
                {
                case IDM_DOIT:  /* User hit the "Do it" menu item */
                        hMemory = GetProp (hWnd, "User Prop") ;
                        lpName = GlobalLock (hMemory) ;
                        hDC = GetDC (hWnd) ;
                        TextOut (hDC, 10, 10, "GetProp() found:", 16) ;
                        TextOut (hDC, 10, 30, lpName, lstrlen (lpName)) ;
                        GlobalUnlock (hMemory) ;
                        ReleaseDC (hWnd, hDC) ;
                        break ;
                case IDM_QUIT:
                        DestroyWindow (hWnd) ;
                        break ;
                }
                break ;
        case WM_DESTROY:                /* stop application */
                hMemory = GetProp (hWnd, "User Prop") ;
                GlobalFree (hMemory) ;
                RemoveProp (hWnd, "User Prop") ;
```

```
                        PostQuitMessage (0) ;
                        break ;
                default:                 /* default windows message processing */
                        return DefWindowProc (hWnd, iMessage, wParam, lParam) ;
        }
        return (0L) ;
}
```

GetSysModalWindow   ■ Win 2.0   ■ Win 3.0   ■ Win 3.1

Purpose	Retrieves a handle to a system modal window.
Syntax	HWND **GetSysModalWindow**(void);
Description	System modal windows take over the input focus from all other windows. GetSysModalWindow() allows you to get a handle to this window and send it messages if desired.
Uses	Passing messages to system modal windows.
Returns	HWND, a handle to the system modal window. NULL if none exists.
See Also	SetSysModalWindow()
Parameters	None (void).
Example	This example shows the creation of a system modal dialog box. A timer is set up in the parent window's message function that checks every ten seconds if a system modal window exists. If so, the timer is shut down and the system modal window is sent a WM_DESTROY message. This saves the user from having to hit the "OK" button to cancel the dialog box. Note that this example will delete any system modal window. A more complete application would discriminate between the window handle(s) of system modal windows created by the application and those belonging to other programs. The GetParent() function is frequently useful in doing these checks.

⇨ **Header File**

```
/* timer.h              */

#define IDM_DOIT  1                      /* menu item id values */
#define IDM_QUIT  2
        /* global variables */
int     ghInstance ;
char    gszAppName [] = "timer" ;
        /* function prototypes */
long FAR PASCAL WndProc (HWND, unsigned, WORD, LONG) ;
BOOL FAR PASCAL DialogProc (HWND hDlg, WORD wMess, WORD wParam, LONG lParam) ;
```

Note that the resource file contains the dialog box definition. The style DS_SYSMODAL has been added to the definition to force the dialog box to be a system modal window.

⇨ **Resource File**

```
/* timer.rc             */

#include <windows.h>
#include "timer.h"
timer        ICON    generic.ico
timer        MENU
BEGIN
   MENUITEM "&Do It!"            IDM_DOIT
   MENUITEM "&Quit",            IDM_QUIT
END
TimerDialog DIALOG 20, 20, 160, 80
CAPTION "SYSTEM MODAL"
STYLE DS_SYSMODAL
{
      CTEXT                 "Timer Example"          -1, 0, 12, 160, 10
      CTEXT                 "This window will go away if you wait.",
                                                     -1, 0, 30, 160, 10
      ICON                  "timer"                  -1, 10, 10, 0, 0
      DEFPUSHBUTTON  "OK"                            IDOK, 50, 50, 30, 14
}
```

⇨ C Listing for WindProc() and Dialog Box Functions

```c
long FAR PASCAL WndProc (HWND hWnd, unsigned iMessage, WORD wParam, LONG lParam)
{
        HWND            hSysModal ;
        static FARPROC  lpfnDlgProc ;

        switch (iMessage)               /* process windows messages */
        {
                case WM_TIMER:          /* kill sys modal window - if any */
                        hSysModal = GetSysModalWindow() ;
                        if (hSysModal)
                                SendMessage (hSysModal, WM_DESTROY, 0, 0L) ;
                        KillTimer (hWnd, 1) ;
                        SetActiveWindow (hWnd) ;
                        break ;
                case WM_COMMAND:        /* process menu items */
                        switch (wParam)
                        {
                        case IDM_DOIT:
                                        /* set timer 1 to every 10 sec. */
                                if (!SetTimer (hWnd, 1, 10000, NULL))
                                {
                                        MessageBox (hWnd, "Too many clocks or timers!",
                                                "Warning",
                                                MB_ICONEXCLAMATION | MB_OK) ;
                                }
                                else            /* Create a system modal dialog box */
                                {
                                        lpfnDlgProc = MakeProcInstance (DialogProc,
                                                ghInstance) ;
                                        DialogBox (ghInstance, "TimerDialog", hWnd,
                                                lpfnDlgProc) ;
                                        FreeProcInstance (lpfnDlgProc) ;
                                }
                                break ;
                        case IDM_QUIT:
                                DestroyWindow (hWnd) ;
                                break ;
                        }
                        break ;
                case WM_DESTROY:        /* stop application */
                        PostQuitMessage (0) ;
                        break ;
                default:                /* default windows message processing */
                        return DefWindowProc (hWnd, iMessage, wParam, lParam) ;
        }
  return 0L ;
}

BOOL FAR PASCAL DialogProc (HWND hDlg, WORD wMess, WORD wParam, LONG lParam)
{
        switch (wMess)
        {
                case WM_INITDIALOG:
                        return TRUE ;
                case WM_COMMAND:                        /* there is only one command - quits */
                case WM_DESTROY:
                        EndDialog (hDlg, 0) ;
                        return TRUE ;
        }
        return FALSE ;
}
```

GetTopWindow   ■ Win 2.0   ■ Win 3.0   ■ Win 3.1

Purpose	Finds the Host child window of a parent.
Syntax	HWND **GetTopWindow**(HWND *hWnd*);

Description   Windows maintains a list of window handles in memory, including the linkage from parent to child. GetTopWindow() can be called repeatedly to find "children of children." This function searches for the first child window in a parent window's internal list of linked child windows.

Returns   HWND, a handle to the top level child window. Returns NULL if the parent does not have child windows.

See Also   ChildWindowFromPoint(), GetWindow()

Parameters

hWnd   HWND: The handle to the parent window.

Example   This example displays the name to the first child window when the "Do It!" menu item is clicked. In this case, there is only one child window: a pushbutton with the window text "Button."

```
long FAR PASCAL WndProc (HWND hWnd, unsigned iMessage, WORD wParam, LONG lParam)
{
        static HWND     hButton ;
        HWND            hTopWindow ;
        HDC             hDC ;
        char            cBuf [25] ;

        switch (iMessage)                /* process windows messages */
        {
        case WM_CREATE:
                hButton = CreateWindow ("BUTTON", "Button",
                        WS_CHILD | WS_VISIBLE | BS_PUSHBUTTON,
                        10, 10, 100, 40, hWnd, NULL, ghInstance, NULL) ;
                ShowWindow (hButton, SW_SHOW) ;
                break ;
        case WM_COMMAND:           /* process menu items */
                switch (wParam)
                {
                case IDM_DOIT:  /* User hit the "Do it" menu item */
                        if (hTopWindow = GetTopWindow (hWnd))
                        {
                                GetWindowText (hTopWindow, cBuf, 24) ;
                                hDC = GetDC (hWnd) ;
                                TextOut (hDC, 10, 60, "The top window is:", 17) ;
                                TextOut (hDC, 15, 75, cBuf, lstrlen (cBuf)) ;
                                ReleaseDC (hWnd, hDC) ;
                        }
                        break ;
```

[Other program lines]

GETVERSION   ■ Win 2.0   ■ Win 3.0   ■ Win 3.1

Purpose   Retrieves the version number of Windows and DOS running on the system.

Syntax   DWORD **GetVersion**(void);

Description   Both the major and minor version numbers (before and after the decimal point) are returned.

Uses   Disabling part of a program if an older version of Windows is in operation.

Returns   DWORD. The high-order word contains the DOS version number. The low-order word contains the Windows version number. In both cases, the high-order byte of the word contains the minor version number, while the low-order byte contains the major version number. For example, Windows version 3.1 running under DOS 5.0 would be coded 0x 00050103 hexadecimal.

See Also   GetWinFlags()

Parameters   None (void).

Note   This function was incorrectly documented in the Windows 2.0 and 3.0 SDK documents and WINDOWS.H file.

Example   This example displays the Window's version number when the user clicks the "Do It!" menu item.

```
long FAR PASCAL WndProc (HWND hWnd, unsigned iMessage, WORD wParam, LONG lParam)
{
        HDC     hDC ;
        char    cBuf[25] ;
        int     nWindVersion, nMajor, nMinor ;

        switch (iMessage)                       /* process windows messages */
        {
                case WM_COMMAND:                /* process menu items */
                        switch (wParam)
                        {
                        case IDM_DOIT:          /* User hit the "Do it" menu item */
                                nWindVersion = (int) GetVersion () ;
                                nMajor = LOBYTE (nWindVersion) ;
                                nMinor = HIBYTE (nWindVersion) ;
                                hDC = GetDC (hWnd) ;
                                TextOut (hDC, 10, 10,
                                        "The current version of Windows:", 31) ;
                                itoa (nMajor, cBuf, 10) ;
                                TextOut (hDC, 15, 30, cBuf, lstrlen (cBuf)) ;
                                TextOut (hDC, 25, 30, ".", 1) ;
                                itoa (nMinor, cBuf, 10) ;
                                TextOut (hDC, 35, 30, cBuf, lstrlen (cBuf)) ;
                                ReleaseDC (hWnd, hDC) ;
                                break ;
```

[Other program lines]

GetWindow   ■ Win 2.0   ■ Win 3.0   ■ Win 3.1

Purpose	Retrieves a window's handle.
Syntax	HWND **GetWindow**(HWND *hWnd*, WORD *wCmd*);
Description	Searches the window manager's list of parent and child windows for the next entry matching the search criteria specified in the *wCmd* parameter.
Uses	An alternative to EnumWindows() and EnumChildWindows(). GetWindow() is simpler to use if there are not very many windows involved in the search.
Returns	HWND, a handle to the window retrieved from the search. NULL if the end of the window manager's list was found, or if the function failed (wrong *wCmd* parameter).
See Also	EnumWindows(), EnumChildWindows(), EnumTasks()
Parameters	
hWnd	HWND: The handle of the window from which to base the search.
wCmd	WORD: The search criteria value. This can be any of the values in Table 3-5.

Value	Meaning	⊠
GW_CHILD	Find the window's first child window.	
GW_HWNDFIRST	Find a child window's first sibling window. If none found, it returns the first top-level window in the window manager's list.	
GW_HWNDLAST	Find a child window's last sibling window. If not found, it returns the last top-level window in the window manager's list.	
GW_HWNDNEXT	Returns the next window in the window manager's list.	
GW_HWNDPREV	Returns the previous window in the window manager's list.	
GW_OWNER	Returns the owner of a window.	

Table 3-5. GetWindow( ) Criteria.

Example   This example creates a child window from the parent window's class when the WM_CREATE message is processed. When the user clicks the "Do It!" menu item, the child window handle is found with GetWindow(), and its caption string determined with GetWindowText(). The child name is displayed in the parent's client area.

```
Long FAR PASCAL WndProc (HWND hWnd, unsigned iMessage, WORD wParam, LONG lParam)
{
        HDC             hDC ;
        HWND            hChild, hGotWind ;
        char            cBuf [25] ;
        static BOOL     bFirstTime = TRUE ;

        switch (iMessage)                       /* process windows messages */
        {
                case WM_CREATE:         /* build the child window when program starts */
                        if (bFirstTime)
                        {
                                bFirstTime = FALSE ;
                                hChild = CreateWindow (gszAppName, "Child Window",
                                        WS_CHILD | WS_VISIBLE | WS_BORDER | WS_CAPTION,
                                        10, 50, 200, 150, hWnd, NULL, ghInstance, NULL) ;
                                ShowWindow (hChild, SW_SHOW) ;
                        }
                        break ;
                case WM_COMMAND:                /* process menu items */
                        switch (wParam)
                        {
                        case IDM_DOIT:          /* User hit the "Do it" menu item */
                                hGotWind = GetWindow (hWnd, GW_CHILD) ;
                                hDC = GetDC (hWnd) ;            /* get device context */
                                TextOut (hDC, 10, 20, "My child is:", 12) ;
                                GetWindowText (hGotWind, cBuf, 24) ;
                                TextOut (hDC, 15, 40, cBuf, strlen (cBuf)) ;
                                ReleaseDC (hWnd, hDC) ;  /* release device context */
                                break ;
```

[Other program lines]

GetWindowLong   ■ Win 2.0   ■ Win 3.0   ■ Win 3.1

Purpose	Retrieves a long value from a window's data.
Syntax	LONG **GetWindowLong**(HWND *hWnd*, int *nIndex*);
Uses	Useful where one or more windows has been subclassed by modifying the basic class structure with SetWindowLong(). Also used to retrieve 32 bit values saved with SetWindowLong().
Returns	The LONG value specified.
See Also	GetWindowWord(), SetWindowLong(), SetWindowWord(), GetClassLong(), GetClassWord()
Parameters	
hWnd	HWND: The window's handle.
nIndex	int: The index to the value to retrieve. This can be any of the values in Table 3-6.

Value	Meaning	⊠
GWL_EXSTYLE	Retrieve the extended window style.	
GWL_STYLE	Retrieve the window style.	
GWL_WNDPROC	Retrieve a long pointer to the window's message processing function.	

Table 3-6. GetWindowLong( ) Index Values.

These GWL_ values are all defined as negative offsets in WINDOWS.H. To retrieve extra four-byte data associated with a window's class structure, use a positive byte offset for *nIndex*. 0 for the first value, 4 for the second, etc.

Related Messages GetWindowWord(), SetWindowLong(), SetWindowWord()

Example This example displays the style parameters of the main window when the user clicks the "Do It!" menu item. (See Figure 3-13.)

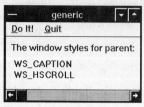

Figure 3-13. GetWindow-Long() Example.

```
Long FAR PASCAL WndProc (HWND hWnd, unsigned iMessage, WORD wParam, LONG lParam)
{
        HDC     hDC ;
        char    cBuf[25] ;
        LONG    lStyle ;

        switch (iMessage)                       /* process windows messages */
        {
                case WM_COMMAND:                /* process menu items */
                        switch (wParam)
                        {
                        case IDM_DOIT:          /* User hit the "Do it" menu item */
                                lStyle = GetWindowLong (hWnd, GWL_STYLE) ;
                                hDC = GetDC (hWnd) ;
                                TextOut (hDC, 10, 10,
                                        "The window styles for parent:", 29) ;
                                if (lStyle & WS_CHILD)
                                        TextOut (hDC, 15, 20, "WS_CHILD", 8) ;
                                if (lStyle & WS_CAPTION)
                                        TextOut (hDC, 15, 30, "WS_CAPTION", 10) ;
                                if (lStyle & WS_HSCROLL)
                                        TextOut (hDC, 15, 40, "WS_HSCROLL", 10) ;
                                /* etc */
                                ReleaseDC (hWnd, hDC) ;
                                break ;
```

[Other program lines]

GETWINDOWRECT ■ Win 2.0 ■ Win 3.0 ■ Win 3.1

Purpose	Retrieves a window's outer dimensions.
Syntax	void **GetWindowRect**(HWND *hWnd*, LPRECT *lpRect*);
Description	Copies the dimensions of the bounding rectangle that exactly encompasses the window into the rectangle structure pointed to by *lpRect*. The dimensions are in screen coordinates (pixels measured from the upper left corner of the screen).
Uses	Window movement and sizing.
Returns	No returned value (void).
See Also	GetClientRect()
Parameters	
hWnd	HWND: A handle to the window.
lpRect	LPRECT: A pointer to a RECT structure that will contain the window's bounding rectangle. The points will be computed in screen coordinates, with 0,0 being the upper left corner of the screen.
Related Messages	WM_SIZE
Example	This example moves a window across the screen diagonally. GetWindowRect() is used to provide the initial window position and size.

```
Long FAR PASCAL WndProc (HWND hWnd, unsigned iMessage, WORD wParam, LONG lParam)
{
        RECT    rWindow ;
        int     i ;

        switch (iMessage)                        /* process windows messages */
        {
                case WM_COMMAND:                 /* process menu items */
                        switch (wParam)
                        {
                        case IDM_DOIT:           /* User hit the "Do it" menu item */
                                GetWindowRect (hWnd, &rWindow) ;
                                for (i = 0 ; i < 10 ; i++)
                                {
                                        MoveWindow (hWnd, rWindow.left + i*10,
                                                rWindow.top + i*10,
                                                rWindow.right + i*10,
                                                rWindow.bottom + i*10, TRUE) ;
                                }
                                break ;
```

[Other program lines]

GetWindowTask

■ Win 2.0   ■ Win 3.0   ■ Win 3.1

Purpose	Retrieves a handle to a task.
Syntax	HANDLE **GetWindowTask**(HWND *hWnd*);
Description	A task is any operating program. Each instance of a program running is a separate task. This function finds the task handle when given the window handle.
Uses	Used to determine the task handle, when given the window handle. This may be done before calling EnumTaskWindows() to provide the *hTask* parameter.
Returns	HANDLE to the task.
See Also	EnumTaskWindows()
Parameters	
hWnd	HWND: The window's handle.

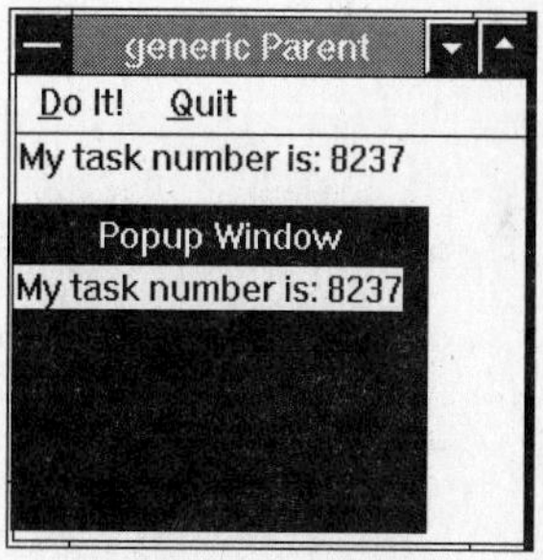

Figure 3-14. GetWindow-Task( ) Example.

Example   This example creates a parent window and a popup window. Both windows display their task handle number. Figure 3-14 provides a graphical example illustrating that all of a top-level window's child windows are part of the same task.

The popup window's message processing function ChildProc() must be listed in the EXPORTS section of the program's .DEF definition file. A function prototype should also be placed in the program's header file.

```
Long FAR PASCAL WndProc (HWND hWnd, unsigned iMessage, WORD wParam, LONG lParam)
{
        PAINTSTRUCT             ps ;
        WNDCLASS                wndclass ;
        HWND                    hPopup ;
        HANDLE                  hTask ;
        char                    cBuf [128] ;

        switch (iMessage)                 /* process windows messages */
        {
                case WM_CREATE: /* build the child window when program starts */
                        wndclass.style
                                = CS_HREDRAW | CS_VREDRAW | CS_PARENTDC ;
                        wndclass.lpfnWndProc    = ChildProc ;
                        wndclass.cbClsExtra     = 0 ;
```

```
                wndclass.cbWndExtra       = 0 ;
                wndclass.hInstance        = ghInstance ;
                wndclass.hIcon            = NULL ;
                wndclass.hCursor          = LoadCursor (NULL, IDC_ARROW) ;
                wndclass.hbrBackground    = GetStockObject (LTGRAY_BRUSH) ;
                wndclass.lpszMenuName     = NULL ;
                wndclass.lpszClassName    = "SecondClass" ;
                                                /* register the window class */
                if(RegisterClass (&wndclass))
                {
                        hPopup = CreateWindow ("SecondClass", "Popup Window",
                                WS_POPUP | WS_VISIBLE | WS_BORDER | WS_CAPTION,
                                110, 50, 200, 150, hWnd, NULL, ghInstance, NULL) ;
                        ShowWindow (hPopup, SW_SHOW) ;
                }
                break ;
        case WM_PAINT:
                BeginPaint (hWnd, &ps) ;
                hTask = GetWindowTask (hWnd) ;
                TestOut (ps.hdc, 0, 0, cBuf, wsprintf (cBuf,
                        "My task number is: %d", hTask)) ;
                EndPaint (hWnd, &ps) ;
                break ;
        case WM_COMMAND:          /* process menu items */
                switch (wParam)
                {
                case IDM_QUIT:
                        DestoryWindow (hWnd) ;
                        break ;
                }
                break ;
        case WM_DESTROY:          /* stop application */
                PostQuitMessage (0) ;
                break ;
        default:                  /* default windows message processing */
                return DefWindowProc (hWnd, iMessage, wParam, lParam) ;
        }
        return (OL) ;
}


/* Here is a separate message processing procedure for the popup window *

long FAR PASCAL ChildProc (HWND hWnd, unsigned iMessage, WORD wParam
        LONG lParam

        PAINTSTRUC           ps
        HANDL                hTask
        cha                  cBuf [128]

        switch (iMessage              /* process windows messages *

                case WM_PAINT
                        BeginPaint (hWnd, &ps)
                        hTask = GetWindowTask (hWnd)
                        TextOut (ps.hdc, 0, 0, cBuf, wsprintf (cBuf
                                "My task number is: %d", hTask))
                        EndPaint (hWnd, &ps)
                        break
                case WM_DESTROY          /* stop the application *
                        PostQuitMessage (0)
                        break
                default                  /* default windows message processing *
                        return DefWindowProc (hWnd, iMessage, wParam, lParam)

        return (OL)
```

GetWindowText
■ Win 2.0　■ Win 3.0　■ Win 3.1

Purpose	Retrieves a window's caption (title string)
Syntax	int **GetWindowText**(HWND *hWnd*, LPSTR *lpString*, int *nMaxCount*);
Uses	For parent, popup, and child windows, the title string shows above the menu bar. For buttons, the title string shows in the center of the button.
Returns	The number of characters copied. Zero if there is no caption.
See Also	SetWindowText(), GetWindowTextLength()
Parameters	
hWnd	HWND: The handle to the window with a title.
lpString	LPSTR: A pointer to the memory area that will contain the title string.
nMaxCount	int: The maximum number of characters to copy. This helps avoid overrunning the end of the character buffer set aside to hold the title string.
Example	This example displays the title of the window in the window's client area.

```
long FAR PASCAL WndProc (HWND hWnd, unsigned iMessage, WORD wParam, LONG lParam)
{
        HDC     hDC ;
        char    cBuf[25] ;

        switch (iMessage)                       /* process windows messages */
        {
            case WM_COMMAND:                    /* process menu items */
                switch (wParam)
                {
                case IDM_DOIT:          /* User hit the "Do it" menu item */
                    GetWindowText (hWnd, cBuf, 24) ;
                    hDC = GetDC (hWnd) ;
                    TextOut (hDC, 10, 10, "The window title for the parent:",
                            32) ;
                    TextOut (hDC, 15, 25, cBuf, GetWindowTextLength (hWnd)) ;
                    ReleaseDC (hWnd, hDC) ;
                    break ;
```

[Other program lines]

GetWindowTextLength
■ Win 2.0　■ Win 3.0　■ Win 3.1

Purpose	Finds the number of characters in a window's title string.
Syntax	int **GetWindowTextLength**(HWND *hWnd*);
Uses	Used prior to GetWindowText() to set up a memory buffer big enough to hold the title string.
Returns	int, the number of characters in the window's title. This can be zero if the window does not have a title.
See Also	GetWindowText(), SetWindowText()
Parameters	
hWnd	HWND: The handle of the window with the title.
Example	See the previous example under the GetWindowText() function description.

GetWindowWord
■ Win 2.0　■ Win 3.0　■ Win 3.1

Purpose	Retrieves a two-byte value from a window's data.
Syntax	WORD **GetWindowWord**(HWND *hWnd*, int *nIndex*);

Uses	Most commonly used to get the window's instance handle (*hInstance*). Can also be used to determine the ID value of a child control, or retrieve 16-bit data stored with the window data by SetWindowWord().
Returns	WORD, the value specified by the *nIndex* parameter.
See Also	GetWindowLong(), SetWindowWord(), SetWindowLong()
Parameters	
hWnd	HWND: The handle to the window.
nIndex	int: Specifies which value to retrieve. This can be any of the values described in Table 3-7.

Value	Meaning	☒
GWW_HINSTANCE	Retrieve the window's instance handle.	
GWW_HWNDPARENT	Retrieve the handle of the parent window.	
GWW_ID	Retrieve a child window's control ID value.	

Table 3-7. GetWindowWord( ) Index Values.

The GWW_ index values are defined as negative numbers in WINDOWS.H. To retrieve extra 16-bit data stored with the window's class definition, use a positive offset for *nIndex*. 0 for the first entry, 2 for the second, etc. The amount of space available is set by the *cbWndExtra* element of the WNDCLASS structure passed to RegisterClass() when the class was registered. 16-bit data is added to the extra data area with SetWindowWord().

Example

```
Long FAR PASCAL WndProc (HWND hWnd, unsigned iMessage, WORD wParam, LONG lParam)
{
        HDC             hDC ;
        char            cBuf[25] ;
        HANDLE          hInstance ;

        switch (iMessage)                               /* process windows messages */
        {
                case WM_COMMAND:                        /* process menu items */
                        switch (wParam)
                        {
                        case IDM_DOIT:          /* User hit the "Do it" menu item */
                                hInstance = GetWindowWord (hWnd, GWW_HINSTANCE) ;
                                hDC = GetDC (hWnd) ;
                                TextOut (hDC, 10, 10,
                                        "The instance handle of the parent:",    35) ;
                                itoa (hInstance, cBuf, 10) ;
                                TextOut (hDC, 15, 25, cBuf, strlen (cBuf)) ;
                                ReleaseDC (hWnd, hDC) ;
                                break ;
```
[Other program lines]

GETWINFLAGS
☐ Win 2.0   ■ Win 3.0   ■ Win 3.1

Purpose	Determines what computer CPU and memory model are in operation.
Syntax	DWORD **GetWinFlags**(void);
Uses	Convenient for determining the approximate performance of the system.
Returns	DWORD value with the parameters encoded as bit values. They may be any of the values described in Table 3-8.

Value	Meaning	☒
WF_80x87	The system has a math coprocessor.	
WF_CPU086	The system has an 8086 CPU.	
WF_CPU186	The system has an 80186 CPU.	
WF_CPU286	The system has an 80286 CPU.	
WF_CPU386	The system has an 80386 CPU.	
WF_CPU486	The system has an 80486 CPU.	
WF_ENHANCED	Windows is running in Enhanced Mode.	
WF_LARGEFRAME	Windows is running with the EMS large-frame memory configuration.	
WF_PMODE	Windows is running in protected mode. This is always set if the mode is WF_ENHANCED or WF_STANDARD.	
WF_SMALLFRAME	Windows is running with the EMS small-frame memory configuration.	
WF_STANDARD	Windows is running in standard mode.	

Table 3-8. GetWinFlags( ) Flags.

You can detect if Windows is running in Real Mode by verifying that neither WF_ENHANCED nor WF_STANDARD has been set.

See Also   GetVersion()

Parameters   None (void).

Example

```
long FAR PASCAL WndProc (HWND hWnd, unsigned iMessage, WORD wParam, LONG lParam)
{
        HDC             hDC ;
        DWORD           dwWinFlags ;

        switch (iMessage)                       /* process windows messages */
        {
        case WM_COMMAND:                        /* process menu items */
                switch (wParam)
                {
                case IDM_DOIT:          /* User hit the "Do it" menu item */
                        dwWinFlags = GetWinFlags () ;
                        hDC = GetDC (hWnd) ;    /* get device context */
                        TextOut (hDC, 10, 20, "GetWinFlags Found:", 18) ;
                        if (dwWinFlags & WF_CPU286)
                                TextOut (hDC, 10, 40, "80286 CPU", 9) ;
                        else if (dwWinFlags & WF_CPU386)
                                TextOut (hDC, 10, 40, "80386 CPU", 9) ;
                        else if (dwWinFlags & WF_CPU486)
                                TextOut (hDC, 10, 40, "80486 CPU", 9) ;

                        if (dwWinFlags & WF_ENHANCED)
                                TextOut (hDC, 10, 60, "Enhanced Mode", 13) ;

                        if (dwWinFlags & WF_80x87)
                                TextOut (hDC, 10, 80, "Math Coprocessor", 16) ;
                        ReleaseDC (hWnd, hDC) ;  /* release device context */
                        break ;
```

[Other program lines]

IsChild

Purpose	Determines if a window is the child of a given parent window.
Syntax	BOOL **IsChild**(HWND *hWndParent*, HWND *hWnd*);
Description	Finds out if *hWnd* is the direct descendant of the *hWndParent* window. Windows maintains the relationship of child windows to their parents in memory at all time. Descendents may also be popup windows.
Uses	Useful in determining the relationship of a series of child windows located with EnumChildWindows()
Returns	BOOL. TRUE if *hWnd* is a child of *hWndParent*, FALSE if not.
See Also	EnumChildWindows(), ChildWindowFromPoint(), WindowFromPoint()
Parameters	
hWndParent	HWND: A handle to the potential parent window.
hWnd	HWND: A handle to the child window to be checked as a descendant of *hWndParent*.
Example	The parentage of the child window is checked and displayed in the parent's client area when the user types the "Do It!" menu item.

```
long FAR PASCAL WndProc (HWND hWnd, unsigned iMessage, WORD wParam, LONG lParam)
{
        HDC             hDC ;
        static HWND     hChild ;
        char            cBuf1 [25], cBuf2 [25] ;
        static BOOL     bFirstTime = TRUE ;
        BOOL            bIsChild ;

        switch (iMessage)              /* process windows messages */
        {
                case WM_CREATE:        /* build the child window when program starts */
                        if (bFirstTime)
                        {
                                bFirstTime = FALSE ;
                                hChild = CreateWindow (gszAppName, "Child Window",
                                        WS_CHILD | WS_VISIBLE | WS_BORDER | WS_CAPTION,
                                        100, 50, 200, 150, hWnd, NULL, ghInstance, NULL) ;
                                ShowWindow (hChild, SW_SHOW) ;
                        }
                        break ;
                case WM_COMMAND:                /* process menu items */
                        switch (wParam)
                        {
                        case IDM_DOIT:          /* User hit the "Do it" menu item */
                                bIsChild = IsChild (hWnd, hChild) ;
                                GetWindowText (hWnd, cBuf1, 24) ;
                                GetWindowText (hChild, cBuf2, 24) ;
                                hDC = GetDC (hWnd) ;
                                TextOut (hDC, 10, 10, cBuf2, strlen (cBuf2)) ;
                                if (bIsChild)
                                        TextOut (hDC, 10, 30, "Is a child of:", 14) ;
                                else
                                        TextOut (hDC, 10, 30, "Is NOT a child of:", 18) ;
                                TextOut (hDC, 15, 50, cBuf1, strlen (cBuf1)) ;
                                ReleaseDC (hWnd, hDC) ;   /* release device context */
                                break ;
```

[Other program lines]

IsIconic

Purpose	Checks to see if a window is minimized
Syntax	BOOL **IsIconic**(HWND *hWnd*);

Description   Normally, windows that are to be minimized have an icon as part of their class definition. When the window is minimized, the icon is displayed. If the class definition has NULL for the class icon, the program is expected to paint in the little bit of client area that is displayed when the window is minimized.

Uses   Handy in processing WM_PAINT messages. If the window is minimized, a separate painting routine can be used.

Returns   BOOL. TRUE if the window is minimized, FALSE if not.

Parameters

hWnd   HWND: The handle to the window which may be minimized.

Related Messages   WM_PAINT, WM_SIZE

Example   In this example, the parent's window class does not have an icon. Instead the program detects if the window is iconized and writes different text if it is during the WM_PAINT cycle.

```
#include <windows.h>            /* window's header file - always included */
#include "generic.h"           /* the application's header file */

int PASCAL WinMain (HANDLE hInstance, HANDLE hPrevInstance, LPSTR lpszCmdLine,
      int nCmdShow)
{

      HWND      hWnd ;                  /* a handle to a message */
      MSG             msg ;            /* a message */
      WNDCLASS        wndclass ;       /* the window class */

      ghInstance = hInstance ;         /* store instance handle as global var. */

      if (!hPrevInstance)              /* load data into window class struct. */
      {
            wndclass.style          = CS_HREDRAW | CS_VREDRAW ;
            wndclass.lpfnWndProc    = WndProc ;
            wndclass.cbClsExtra     = 0 ;
            wndclass.cbWndExtra     = 0 ;
            wndclass.hInstance      = hInstance ;
            wndclass.hIcon          = NULL ;
            wndclass.hCursor        = LoadCursor (NULL, IDC_ARROW) ;
            wndclass.hbrBackground  = GetStockObject (WHITE_BRUSH) ;
            wndclass.lpszMenuName   = gszAppName ;
            wndclass.lpszClassName  = gszAppName ;
                                          /* register the window class */
            if (!RegisterClass (&wndclass))
                    return FALSE ;
      }
      hWnd = CreateWindow (            /* create the program's window here */
            gszAppName,                /* class name */
            gszAppName,                /* window name */
            WS_OVERLAPPEDWINDOW,       /* window style */
            CW_USEDEFAULT,             /* x position on screen */
            CW_USEDEFAULT,             /* y position on screen */
            CW_USEDEFAULT,             /* width of window */
            CW_USEDEFAULT,             /* height of window */
            NULL,                      /* parent window handle (null = none) */
            NULL,                      /* menu handle (null = use class menu) */
            hInstance,                 /* instance handle */
            NULL) ;                    /* lpstr (null = not used) */

      ShowWindow (hWnd, nCmdShow) ;
      UpdateWindow (hWnd) ;            /* send first WM_PAINT message */

      while (GetMessage (&msg, NULL, 0, 0))           /* the message loop */
      {
            TranslateMessage (&msg) ;
            DispatchMessage (&msg) ;
```

```
        }
        return msg.wParam ;
}

long FAR PASCAL WndProc (HWND hWnd, unsigned iMessage, WORD wParam, LONG lParam)
{
        HDC             hDC ;
        PAINTSTRUCT     psPaintStruct ;

        switch (iMessage)                       /* process windows messages */
        {
            case WM_PAINT:
                    hDC = BeginPaint (hWnd, &psPaintStruct) ;
                    if (IsIconic (hWnd))
                            TextOut (hDC, 1, 1, "Icon", 4) ;
                    else
                            TextOut (hDC, 10, 10, "Not iconized now.", 17) ;
                    EndPaint (hWnd, &psPaintStruct) ;
                    break ;
            case WM_COMMAND:                    /* process menu items */
                    switch (wParam)
                    {
                    case IDM_DOIT:              /* User hit the "Do it" menu item */
                            CloseWindow (hWnd) ;      /* minimize window */
                            break ;
                    case IDM_QUIT:              /* send end of application message */
                            DestroyWindow (hWnd) ;
                            break ;
                    }
                    break ;
            case WM_DESTROY:                    /* stop application */
                    PostQuitMessage (0) ;
                    break ;

            default:                    /* default windows message processing */
                    return DefWindowProc (hWnd, iMessage, wParam, lParam) ;
        }
        return (0L) ;
}
```

IsWindow   ■ Win 2.0   ■ Win 3.0   ■ Win 3.1

Purpose	Checks to see if a window handle still points to a valid window.
Syntax	BOOL **IsWindow**(HWND *hWnd*);
Description	Windows keeps a list of all active windows in the system. This function compares the handle to the list of windows to see if the window exists.
Uses	Useful in applications where the user can destroy child windows or popups.
Returns	BOOL. TRUE if *hWnd* refers to a valid window, FALSE if not.
See Also	IsWindowEnabled(), IsWindowVisible(), DestroyWindow()
Parameters	
hWnd	HWND: The window handle to check.
Example	

```
long FAR PASCAL WndProc (HWND hWnd, unsigned iMessage, WORD wParam, LONG lParam)
{
        HDC             hDC ;
        static  HWWD    hchild ;
        char            cBuf [25] ;
        static  BOOL    bfirstTime = TRUE ;
        BOOL            bisWindow ;

        switch (iMessage)       /* process windows messages */
        {
                caseWM_CREATE:  /* build the child window when program starts */
```

```
                if (bFirstTime)
                {
                        bfirstTime = FASLE ;
                        hchild = CreateWindow (gszAppName, "Child Window",
                                WS_CHILD | WS_VISIBLE | WS_BORDER | WS_CAPTION
                                100, 50, 200, 150, hWnd, NULL, ghInstance, NULL);
                        ShowWindow (hChild, SW_SHOW) ;
                }
                break ;
        case WM_COMMAND:                /* process menu items */
                switch (wParam)
                {
                case IDM_DOIT:          /* User hit the "Do it" menu item */
                        hDC = GetDC (hWnd) ;
                        bIsWindow = IsWindow (hChild) ;
                        if (bIsWindow)
                        {
                                GetWindowText (hChild, cBuf, 24) ;
                                TextOut (hDC, 15, 20, cBuf, strlen (cBuf)) ;
                                TextOut (hDC, 10, 40, "was created OK.", 15) ;
                        }
                        ReleaseDC (hWnd, hDC) ;
                        break ;
```

[Other program lines]

IsWindowEnabled   ■ Win 2.0   ■ Win 3.0   ■ Win 3.1

Purpose	Checks to see if a window is enabled for keyboard input.
Syntax	BOOL **IsWindowEnabled**(HWND *hWnd*);
Uses	Most often used with edit controls to see if the control is enabled for keyboard input.
Returns	BOOL. TRUE if the window is enabled, FALSE if not.
See Also	EnableWindow(), IsWindowVisible(), IsWindow()
Parameters	
hWnd	HWND: A handle to a window (or child window control).
Related Messages	WM_ENABLE
Example	Here the edit control is initially disabled. The text in the edit control shows up grayed and cannot be edited. After the user clicks the "Do It!" menu item, the control is enabled and can be edited.

```
long FAR PASCAL WndProc (HWND hWnd, unsigned iMessage, WORD wParam, LONG lParam)
{
        static HWND             hEdit ;
        static BOOL             bFirstTime = TRUE ;

        switch (iMessage)                       /* process windows messages */
        {
                case WM_CREATE:
                        if (bFirstTime)
                        {
                                hEdit = CreateWindow ("EDIT", "This is edit text",
                                        WS_CHILD | WS_VISIBLE,
                                        10, 10, 100, 40, hWnd, NULL, ghInstance, NULL) ;
                                ShowWindow (hEdit, SW_SHOW) ;
                                EnableWindow (hEdit, FALSE) ;   /* starts disabled */
                                bFirstTime = FALSE ;
                        }
                        break ;
                case WM_COMMAND:                /* process menu items */
                        switch (wParam)
                        {
                        case IDM_DOIT:          /* User hit the "Do it" menu item */
                                if (!IsWindowEnabled (hEdit))           /* if disabled */
                                        EnableWindow (hEdit, TRUE) ;    /* enable */
                                break ;
```

[Other program lines]

IsWindowVisible

Purpose	Checks to see if a window has been made visible.
Syntax	BOOL **IsWindowVisible**(HWND *hWnd*);
Description	Windows are made visible by calling ShowWindow(). IsWindowVisible() will return TRUE for any window that has been activated with ShowWindow(), even if the window is completely obscured on the screen by other windows.
Uses	Use if you want to reduce Window's overhead workload by not "showing" the window until it is needed, or if you need to know if the window was hidden with a call to ShowWindow().
Returns	BOOL. TRUE if ShowWindow() has displayed the window, FALSE if not or if the window does not exist.
See Also	ShowWindow()
Parameters	
hWnd	HWND: A handle to the window to check.
Related Messages	WM_CREATE
Example	This example toggles a child window from hidden to visible each time the "Do It!" menu item is clicked.

```
Long FAR PASCAL WndProc (HWND hWnd, unsigned iMessage, WORD wParam, LONG lParam)
{
        HDC                     hDC ;
        static HWND     hChild ;
        char            cBuf [25] ;
        static BOOL     bFirstTime = TRUE ;
        BOOL            bIsVisible ;

        switch (iMessage)               /* process windows messages */
        {
                case WM_CREATE:         /* build the child window when program starts */
                        if (bFirstTime)
                        {
                                bFirstTime = FALSE ;
                                hChild = CreateWindow (gszAppName, "Child Window",
                                        WS_CHILD | WS_VISIBLE | WS_BORDER | WS_CAPTION,
                                        100, 50, 200, 150, hWnd, NULL, ghInstance, NULL) ;
                                ShowWindow (hChild, SW_SHOW) ;
                        }
                        break ;
                case WM_COMMAND:                /* process menu items */
                        switch (wParam)
                        {
                        case IDM_DOIT:          /* User hit the "Do it" menu item */
                                hDC = GetDC (hWnd) ;
                                bIsVisible = IsWindowVisible (hChild) ;
                                if (bIsVisible)
                                {
                                        GetWindowText (hChild, cBuf, 24) ;
                                        TextOut (hDC, 10, 20, cBuf, strlen (cBuf)) ;
                                        TextOut (hDC, 10, 40, "is now visible.", 15) ;
                                        TextOut (hDC, 10, 60, "Now hiding Child...", 19) ;
                                        ShowWindow (hChild, SW_HIDE) ;
                                }
                                else
                                        TextOut (hDC, 10, 20,
                                                "Child window not visible.", 25) ;
                                ReleaseDC (hWnd, hDC) ;  /* release device context */
                                break ;
```

[Other program lines]

IsZoomed

Purpose	Checks to see if a window is maximized.
Syntax	BOOL **IsZoomed**(HWND *hWnd*);
Uses	Many programs do not show the full client region data if their window is not maximized. This function checks to see if the window fills the screen.
Returns	BOOL. TRUE if the window is maximized, FALSE if not.
See Also	IsIconic(), MoveWindow(), CloseWindow(), OpenIcon()
Parameters	
hWnd	HWND: A handle to the window to check.
Related Messages	WM_SIZE
Example	The main window displays a text string indicating if the window is maximized or not when the user clicks the "Do It!" menu item.

```
long FAR PASCAL WndProc (HWND hWnd, unsigned iMessage, WORD wParam, LONG lParam)
{
        HDC     hDC ;

        switch (iMessage)                               /* process windows messages */
        {
                case WM_COMMAND:                        /* process menu items */
                        switch (wParam)
                        {
                        case IDM_DOIT:          /* User hit the "Do it" menu item */

                                hDC = GetDC (hWnd) ;
                                if (IsZoomed (hWnd))
                                        TextOut (hDC, 10, 10,
                                                "Window is now maximized.", 24) ;
                                else
                                        TextOut (hDC, 10, 10,
                                                "Window is NOT maximized.", 24) ;
                                ReleaseDC (hWnd, hDC) ;
                                break ;
```

[Other program lines]

MoveWindow

Purpose	Moves or resizes a window
Syntax	void **MoveWindow**(HWND *hWnd*, int *X*, int *Y*, int *nWidth*, int *nHeight*, BOOL *bRepaint*);
Description	Sends WM_SIZE and/or WM_MOVE messages to the window's message processing function. The *nWidth* and *nHeight* parameters are passed with the WM_SIZE message. The *X,Y* values are passed with the WM_MOVE message. The default message processing logic in DefWindowProc() will handle these messages if the program does not intercept them.
Uses	Moving, resizing, or repainting a window.
Returns	No returned value (void).
See Also	ShowWindow(), GetClientRect(), GetWindowRect(), SetWindowSize()
Parameters	
hWnd	HWND: A handle to the window.
X	int: The new horizontal position of the window's upper left corner. For parent and popup windows, *X* is in screen coordinates. For child windows, *X* is in client coordinates.

Y	int: The new vertical position of the window's upper left corner. For parent and popup windows, *Y* is in screen coordinates. For child windows, *Y* is in client coordinates.
nWidth	int: The new client area width.
nHeight	int: The new client area height.
bRepaint	BOOL: Specifies if the window should be repainted. TRUE if yes, FALSE if not.

Related Messages WM_SIZE, WM_MOVE

Example This program fragment shows a window being moved ten times, each time changing its size. Note how GetWindowRect() is used to determine the window's initial size.

```
Long FAR PASCAL WndProc (HWND hWnd, unsigned iMessage, WORD wParam, LONG lParam)
{
        static RECT    rWindow ;
        static int     i ;

        switch (iMessage)                       /* process windows messages */
        {
                case WM_COMMAND:                /* process menu items */
                        switch (wParam)
                        {
                        case IDM_DOIT:          /* User hit the "Do it" menu item */
                                GetWindowRect (hWnd, &rWindow) ;
                                for (i = 0 ; i < 10 ; i++)
                                {
                                        MoveWindow (hWnd, rWindow.left + i*10,
                                                rWindow.top + i*10,
                                                rWindow.right + i*10,
                                                rWindow.bottom + i*10, TRUE) ;
                                }
                                break ;
```

[Other program lines]

REMOVEPROP   ■ Win 2.0   ■ Win 3.0   ■ Win 3.1

Purpose	Removes a property (data) that was associated with a window.
Syntax	HANDLE **RemoveProp**(HWND *hWnd*, LPSTR *lpString*);
Description	Frees the memory associated with the properties data.
Uses	Use when the property is no longer needed, or when shutting down an application (processing a WM_DESTROY message).
Returns	A handle. The handle points to the property name if the function was successful. Otherwise, the function returns NULL.
See Also	SetProp(), GetProp(), EnumProp()
Parameters	
hWnd	HWND: A handle to the window which has property data.
lpString	LPSTR: A pointer to the string that contains the property name. If atoms are used to name the property, the high-order word will be zero, and the low-order word will be equal to the atom's value.
Example	This example uses a window property value to hold a handle for a global memory block containing a character string. The property is removed when the program terminates. Note that the memory block must be separately freed using GlobalFree().

```
Long FAR PASCAL WndProc (HWND hWnd, unsigned iMessage, WORD wParam, LONG lParam)
{
        static HANDLE       hMemory ;
        LPSTR               lpName ;
        char                cBuf[] = "This data tied to Window";
```

```
        switch (iMessage)                           /* process windows messages */
        {
            case WM_CREATE:
                    hMemory = GlobalAlloc (GMEM_MOVEABLE | GMEM_ZEROINIT,
                        (LONG) strlen (cBuf)) ;
                    lpName = GlobalLock (hMemory) ;
                    lstrcpy (lpName, cBuf) ;
                    GlobalUnlock (hMemory) ;
                    SetProp (hWnd, "User Prop", hMemory) ;
                    break ;
            case WM_COMMAND:                    /* process menu items */
                    switch (wParam)
                    {
                    case IDM_QUIT:
                            DestroyWindow (hWnd) ;
                            break ;
                    }
                    break ;
            case WM_DESTROY:          /* stop application */
                    GlobalFree (hMemory) ;
                    RemoveProp (hWnd, "User Prop") ;
                    PostQuitMessage (0) ;
                    break ;
            default:                    /* default windows message processing */
                    return DefWindowProc (hWnd, iMessage, wParam, lParam) ;
        }
        return (0L) ;
}
```

SETACTIVEWINDOW   ■ Win 2.0   ■ Win 3.0   ■ Win 3.1

Purpose	Makes a window active.
Syntax	HWND **SetActiveWindow**(HWND *hWnd*);
Description	Sets the active window. The active window is the parent window with the input focus. The active window can be iconic.
Uses	Used in applications that coordinate the actions of several independent windows. See Chapter 30 on dynamic data exchange (DDE) for how to exchange data and commands between running applications.
Returns	HWND, a handle to the previously active window.
Comments	This function should not normally be used, as it risks violating one of the basic principles of Windows programing: letting the user determine which window should be active at any time. You may find it useful when a function key or key combination activates a window, as an alternative to mouse control.
See Also	GetActiveWindow(), GetLastActivePopup(), EnableWindow(), BringWindowToTop()
Parameters	
hWnd	HWND: A handle to the window to activate.
Related Messages	WM_ACTIVATE
Example	This code example creates a window that refuses to be covered up. Ten seconds after the "Do It!" menu item is clicked, this program will come back to the top, even if it has been covered by several other windows.

```
long FAR PASCAL WndProc (HWND hWnd, unsigned iMessage, WORD wParam, LONG lParam)
{
        switch (iMessage)                           /* process windows messages */
        {
            case WM_TIMER:
                    KillTimer (hWnd, 1) ;
                    SetActiveWindow (hWnd) ;/* make window reappear */
```

```
                              break ;
           case WM_COMMAND:                    /* process menu items */
                  switch (wParam)
                  {
                  case IDM_DOIT:
                                         /* set timer 1 to every 10 sec. */
                          if (!SetTimer (hWnd, 1, 10000, NULL))
                                MessageBox (hWnd, "Too many clocks or timers!",
                                       "Warning", MB_ICONEXCLAMATION | MB_OK) ;
                          break ;
```

[Other program lines]

SetClassLong   ■ Win 2.0   ■ Win 3.0   ■ Win 3.1

Purpose	Changes one of the LONG values in a window class.
Syntax	LONG **SetClassLong**(HWND *hWnd*, int *nIndex*, LONG *dwNewLong*);
Uses	Allows you to change the window procedure or menu for an existing class. This allows you to make use of an old class, with a new window procedure or menu applied to all subsequent windows created from the class.
	Also allows you to set the values of extra four-byte data that was allocated as part of the class data when the class was registered. Room is made for these values as the *cbClsExtra* element of the WNDCLASS data structure is passed to RegisterClass(). GetClassLong() can be used to retrieve the values set.
Returns	Returns the previous value held by the window class.
See Also	SetClassWord(), GetClassLong(), GetClassWord(), RegisterClass, SetWindowLong()
Parameters	
hWnd	HWND: A handle to a window.
nIndex	int: The index of the value to change. This can be either of the values in Table 3-9.

Value	Meaning	⊠
GCL_MENUNAME	Set a new long pointer to the menu name.	
GCL_WNDPROC	Set a new long pointer to the window function.	

Table 3-9. SetClassLong( ) Flags.

	The GCL_ flags are defined as negative values in WINDOWS.H. To change extra four-byte data in the class definition, use a positive byte offset for *nIndex*. Zero for the first value, 4 for the second, etc.
dwNewLong	LONG: The new four-byte data to insert into the class data.
Notes	Using the GCL_WNDPROC index to set a new window message processing function is called "window subclassing." All windows created from the class after the window function is changed will use the new message processing function.
	Do not change the class settings for predefined child window controls, such as buttons and scroll bars, as these global classes are used by other applications. Instead, change the values for the individual controls using SetWindowLong().
Example	This program modifies the existing window class by changing the window procedure name. All subsequent calls to CreateWindow() create child windows referencing WindProc2(). Note that WindProc2 must be added to the EXPORTS section of the program's .DEF definition file, and a function prototype must be added to the header file.

```
Long FAR PASCAL WndProc (HWND hWnd, unsigned iMessage, WORD wParam, LONG lParam)
{
        HDC                      hDC ;
```

```
        PAINTSTRUCT             PS ;
        HWND                    hChild ;

        switch (iMessage)                               /* process windows messages */
        {
                case WM_PAINT:
                        hDC = BeginPaint (hWnd, &PS) ;
                        TextOut (hDC, 10, 10, "Now in primary WndProc.", 23) ;
                        EndPaint (hWnd, &PS) ;
                        break ;
                case WM_COMMAND:                /* process menu items */
                        switch (wParam)
                        {
                        case IDM_DOIT:          /* create a child window - use sWindProc2() */
                                SetClassLong (hWnd, GCL_WNDPROC, (LONG) WndProc2) ;
                                hChild = CreateWindow (gszAppName, "Child Window",
                                        WS_CHILD | WS_VISIBLE | WS_BORDER | WS_CAPTION,
                                        100, 50, 200, 150, hWnd, NULL, ghInstance, NULL) ;
                                ShowWindow (hChild, SW_SHOW) ;
                                break ;
                        case IDM_QUIT:
                                DestroyWindow (hWnd) ;
                                break ;
                        }
                        break ;
                case WM_DESTROY:                        /* stop application */
                        PostQuitMessage (0) ;
                        break ;
                default:                        /* default windows message processing */
                        return DefWindowProc (hWnd, iMessage, wParam, lParam) ;
        }
        return (0L) ;
}

/* This is the new WindProc() referenced by the SetClassLong() function. */
/* All new children created use this one. */
long FAR PASCAL WndProc2 (HWND hWnd, unsigned iMessage, WORD wParam, LONG lParam)
{
        HDC                     hDC ;
        PAINTSTRUCT     PS ;

        switch (iMessage)                                       /* process windows messages */
        {
                case WM_PAINT:
                        hDC = BeginPaint (hWnd, &PS) ;
                        TextOut (hDC, 10, 10, "Now in SECOND WndProc.", 22) ;
                        EndPaint (hWnd, &PS) ;
                        break ;
                case WM_DESTROY:                        /* stop application */
                        PostQuitMessage (0) ;
                        break ;
                default:                                /* default windows message processing */
                        return DefWindowProc (hWnd, iMessage, wParam, lParam) ;
        }
        return (0L) ;
}
```

SETCLASSWORD
■ Win 2.0 ■ Win 3.0 ■ Win 3.1

Purpose	Changes a WORD sized value in a window class.
Syntax	WORD **SetClassWord**(HWND *hWnd*, int *nIndex*, WORD *wNewWord*);
Description	This function allows you to change the properties of every window created from an existing class. It is often used to change the cursor shape, but can also be used to change any of the extra two-byte wide data stored with the window class structure.
Returns	Returns the previous value.

See Also   SetClassLong(), GetClassWord(), GetClassLong()

Parameters

hWnd   HWND: Handle to the window that was created based on the class.

nIndex   int: The byte offset for the specific data item. It can be any of the values in Table 3-10.

Value	Meaning
GCW_CBCLSEXTRA	Retrieve the number of bytes of extra data associated with the class. A second call to GetClassWord( ) can be used to retrieve a word of data. Use an *nIndex* value of 0, 2, 4... for the first, second, third... words of extra data.
GCW_CBWNDEXTRA	Retrieve the number of bytes of extra data associated with the window. A second call to GetClassWord( ) can be used to retrieve a word of data. Use an *nIndex* value of 0, 2, 4... for the first, second, third... words of extra data.
GCW_HBRBACKGROUND	Retrieve a handle to the class background brush.
GCW_HCURSOR	Retrieve a handle to the class cursor.
GCW_HICON	Retrieve a handle to the class icon.
GCW_HMODULE	Retrieve a handle to the class module.
GCW_STYLE	Retrieve a handle to the window class style.

Table 3-10. SetClassWord( ) Flags.

The GCW_ flags are defined as negative values in WINDOWS.H. To change extra word-sized data associated with the window, use a positive offset for *nIndex*. Zero for the first byte, 2 for the second, etc.

wNewWord   WORD: The new word-sized value to insert into the class structure.

Note   Do not change the class settings for predefined child window controls such as buttons and scroll bars, as these global classes are used by other applications. Instead, change the values for the individual controls using SetWindowWord().

Example   Here the "Do It!" menu item causes the window's class to be altered to a light gray background. This affects all of the child windows created and also affects the parent window's client area on the next refresh (WM_PAINT) cycle.

```
long FAR PASCAL WndProc (HWND hWnd, unsigned iMessage, WORD wParam, LONG lParam)
{
        HWND    hChild ;

        switch (iMessage)                  /* process windows messages */
        {
           case WM_COMMAND:                /* process menu items */
                switch (wParam)
                {
                case IDM_DOIT:             /* User hit the "Do it" menu item */
                     SetClassWord (hWnd, GCW_HBRBACKGROUND,
                            (WORD) GetStockObject (LTGRAY_BRUSH)) ;
                     hChild = CreateWindow (gszAppName, "Child Window",
                            WS_CHILD | WS_VISIBLE | WS_BORDER | WS_CAPTION,
                            100, 50, 200, 150, hWnd, NULL, ghInstance, NULL) ;
                     ShowWindow (hChild, SW_SHOW) ;
                     break ;

                case IDM_QUIT:
                     DestroyWindow (hWnd) ;
                     break ;
                }
                break ;
           case WM_DESTROY:          /* stop application */
```

```
                        PostQuitMessage (0) ;
                        break ;
                default:                /* default windows message processing */
                        return DefWindowProc (hWnd, iMessage, wParam, lParam) ;
        }
        return (0L) ;
}
```

SETFOCUS
■ Win 2.0   ■ Win 3.0   ■ Win 3.1

Purpose	Gives a window the input focus
Syntax	HWND **SetFocus**(HWND *hWnd*);
Description	A window with the input focus gets all of the keyboard input.
Uses	Frequently used where there are multiple child windows. Controls which one has the input focus.
Returns	A handle to the window that previously had the input focus. NULL if *hWnd* is not a valid window handle, or if the window is disabled.
See Also	GetFocus(), EnableWindow()
Parameters	
hWnd	HWND: A handle to the window which is to receive the input focus.
Related Messages	WM_SETFOCUS, WM_GETFOCUS
Example	Here the "Do It!" menu item causes the keyboard input focus to be moved to the edit control. This shows up in the changed appearance of the edit line in the edit box. The text in the edit control goes from gray to black, and an edit cursor appears inside the control. This is the same effect that clicking the edit control with the mouse would have.

```
Long FAR PASCAL WndProc (HWND hWnd, unsigned iMessage, WORD wParam, LONG lParam)
{
        static  HWND            hEdit ;
        static  BOOL            bFirstTime = TRUE ;

        switch (iMessage)                       /* process windows messages */
        {
                case WM_CREATE:                 /* create and show an edit control */
                        if (bFirstTime)
                        {
                                hEdit = CreateWindow ("EDIT", "Edit Me",
                                        WS_CHILD | WS_VISIBLE | WS_BORDER,
                                        150, 40, 100, 25, hWnd, NULL, ghInstance, NULL) ;
                                ShowWindow (hEdit, SW_SHOW) ;
                                bFirstTime = FALSE ;
                        }
                        break ;
                case WM_COMMAND:                /* process menu items */
                        switch (wParam)
                        {
                        case IDM_DOIT:          /* User hit the "Do it" menu item */
                                SetFocus (hEdit) ;
                                break ;
```
[Other program lines]

SETPARENT
■ Win 2.0   ■ Win 3.0   ■ Win 3.1

Purpose	Changes the parent window of a child window.
Syntax	HWND **SetParent**(HWND *hWndChild*, HWND *hWndNewParent*);
Uses	Child windows can be children of child windows, to any desired level of nesting. The advantage is that child windows do not exceed the bounds of their parent's client area and are moved with the parent.

Returns	HWND, a handle to the previous parent window of *hWndChild*.	
See Also	GetParent(), GetNextWindow(), IsWindow()	
Parameters		
hWndChild	HWND: A handle to the child window which is to receive a new parent.	
hWndNewParent	HWND: A handle to the new parent window of *hWndChild*.	

Example   In this example, two child windows are created. Initially, they overlap each other on the screen, as both have the same parent window. When the user clicks the "Do It!" menu item, the second child window becomes the child of the first child window, forcing child2 to be visible only within the client area of child1. Note that these child windows share the message processing function WndProc() of their parent, as they are based on the parent's class. Real child windows would have their own message processing functions. (See Figure 3-15.)

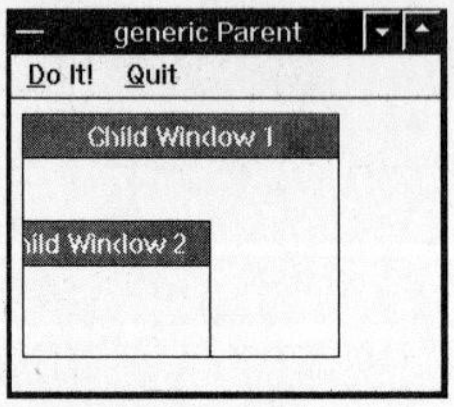

Figure 3-15. Child Windows After Clicking "Do It!".

```
long FAR PASCAL WndProc (HWND hWnd, unsigned iMessage, WORD wParam, LONG lParam)
{
        static HWND     hChild1, hChild2 ;
        static BOOL     bFirstTime = TRUE ;

        switch (iMessage)               /* process windows messages */
        {
                case WM_CREATE:         /* build the child window when program starts */

                        if (bFirstTime)
                        {
                                bFirstTime = FALSE ;
                                hChild1 = CreateWindow (gszAppName, "Child Window 1",
                                        WS_CHILD | WS_VISIBLE | WS_BORDER | WS_CAPTION,
                                        10, 50, 300, 250, hWnd, NULL, ghInstance, NULL) ;
                                ShowWindow (hChild1, SW_SHOW) ;
                                hChild2 = CreateWindow (gszAppName, "Child Window 2",
                                        WS_CHILD | WS_VISIBLE | WS_BORDER | WS_CAPTION,
                                        10, 50, 200, 150, hWnd, NULL, ghInstance, NULL) ;
                                ShowWindow (hChild2, SW_SHOW) ;
                        }
                        break ;
                case WM_COMMAND:                /* process menu items */
                        switch (wParam)
                        {
                        case IDM_DOIT:          /* User hit the "Do it" menu item */
                                SetParent (hChild2, hChild1) ;
                                break ;
```

[Other program lines]

SetProp   ■ Win 2.0   ■ Win 3.0   ■ Win 3.1

Purpose	Attaches named data to a window.
Syntax	BOOL **SetProp**(HWND *hWnd*, LPSTR *lpString*, HANDLE *hData*);
Description	SetProp() allows any data to be associated with the window *hWnd*. The data is given a name, pointed to by *lpString*, to make recall simple. Normally *hData* is a handle to a memory block containing the actual data. *hData* can be a 16-bit value.
Uses	An excellent way to keep track of data that is specific to a given window. Avoids the use of global variables in many cases.
Returns	BOOL. TRUE if the data was added to the window's property list, FALSE if not.
See Also	GetProp(), ReleaseProp(), EnumProp()

Parameters

hWnd   HWND: A handle to the window which is to receive the property data.

lpString   LPSTR: A pointer to a string containing the name to be used for the data. This can also be an atom. In that case the high-order word of *lpString* should be zero, while the low-order word contains the atom's 16-bit value.

hData   HANDLE: A 16-bit value. Normally a handle to a memory block allocated with either LocalAlloc() or GlobalAlloc().

Example   See the example under the GetProp() function description.

SETSYSMODALWINDOW   ■ Win 2.0   ■ Win 3.0   ■ Win 3.1

Purpose   Makes a window system-modal.

Syntax   HWND **SetSysModalWindow**(HWND *hWnd*);

Description   System-modal windows take over the screen, so only they can have the input focus. A typical example is the final message from Windows' program manager, which confirms that the user wants to exit Windows. If a system-modal window creates another system-modal child window, the new window takes over the system. Control returns to the first system-modal window after the second one is destroyed.

Uses   For critical messages and responses to/from the user. This function is seldom called directly, as normally system-modal windows are created as dialog boxes. The window style DS_SYSMODAL automatically creates a system-modal dialog box, eliminating the need to call SetSysModal-Window().

Returns   HWND, a handle to the previous system-modal window (if any).

See Also   GetSysModalWindow()

Parameters

hWnd   HWND: A handle to the window which is to become system-modal.

Example   In this example, the focus can be switched back and forth between the parent and client window until the "Do It!" menu item is clicked. After that, the popup window becomes a system-modal window and will not give up the focus. Hitting a key deletes the window, and stops the program.

```
long FAR PASCAL WndProc (HWND hWnd, unsigned iMessage, WORD wParam, LONG lParam)
{
        HDC                     hDC ;                   /* device context handle */
        static WNDCLASS         wndclass ;              /* the window class */
        static HWND             hPopup, hParent ;

        switch (iMessage)               /* process windows messages */
        {
                case WM_CREATE: /* build the child window when program starts */
                        wndclass.style
                                = CS_HREDRAW | CS_VREDRAW | CS_PARENTDC;
                        wndclass.lpfnWndProc    = ChildProc ;
                        wndclass.cbClsExtra     = 0 ;
                        wndclass.cbWndExtra     = 0 ;
                        wndclass.hInstance      = ghInstance ;
                        wndclass.hIcon          = NULL ;
                        wndclass.hCursor        = LoadCursor (NULL, IDC_ARROW) ;
                        wndclass.hbrBackground  = GetStockObject (LTGRAY_BRUSH) ;
                        wndclass.lpszMenuName   = NULL ;
                        wndclass.lpszClassName  = "SecondClass" ;
                                        /* register the window class */
                        if(RegisterClass (&wndclass))
                        {
                                hPopup = CreateWindow ("SecondClass", "Popup Window",
```

```
                                WS_POPUP | WS_VISIBLE | WS_BORDER | WS_CAPTION,
                                10, 50, 200, 150, hWnd, NULL, ghInstance, NULL) ;
                        ShowWindow (hPopup, SW_SHOW) ;
                }
                break ;
        case WM_COMMAND:        /* process menu items */
                switch (wParam)
                {
                case IDM_DOIT:  /* User hit the "Do it" menu item */
                        SetSysModalWindow (hPopup) ;
                        break ;
                case IDM_QUIT:  /* send end of application message */
                        DestroyWindow (hWnd) ;
                        break ;
                }
                break ;
        case WM_DESTROY:        /* stop application */
                PostQuitMessage (0) ;
                break ;
        default:                /* default windows message processing */
                return DefWindowProc (hWnd, iMessage, wParam, lParam) ;
        }
        return (0L) ;
}

/* Here is a separate message processing procedure for the popup window */
long FAR PASCAL ChildProc (HWND hWnd, unsigned iMessage, WORD wParam,
        LONG lParam)
{
        HDC                     hDC ;
        PAINTSTRUCT             PS ;

        switch (iMessage)               /* process windows messages */
        {
        case WM_PAINT:
                hDC = BeginPaint (hWnd, &PS) ;
                TextOut (hDC, 5, 5, "Hit a key.", 10) ;
                EndPaint (hWnd, &PS) ;
                break ;
        case WM_KEYDOWN:
        case WM_DESTROY:                /* stop the application */
                PostQuitMessage (0) ;
                break ;
        default:                        /* default windows message processing */
                return DefWindowProc (hWnd, iMessage, wParam, lParam) ;
        }
        return (0L) ;
}
```

SETWINDOWLONG   ■ Win 2.0   ■ Win 3.0   ■ Win 3.1

Purpose	Changes a LONG value associated with a window.
Syntax	LONG **SetWindowLong**(HWND *hWnd*, int *nIndex*, LONG *dwNewLong*);
Description	Used to change the style of a window, or to change the window's message processing function. Can also set extra 16-bit data stored with the window if the window's class definition includes space as the *cbWndExtra* element of the WNDCLASS data structure passed to RegisterClass().
Uses	Most often used to do window subclassing. It allows you to add to, or replace the existing window's message processing logic by passing a new window message function to the specific window or control. Also used to associate extra data with the window. It can be used in place of setting window property data, if the amount of data stored with each window is small.
Returns	The previous LONG value.
See Also	SetWindowWord(), GetWindowLong(), GetWindowWord()

Parameters

hWnd   HWND: A handle to the window.

nIndex   int: An integer offset, determining which value is to be changed. This can be any of the values in Table 3-11.

Value	Meaning	☒
GWL_EXSTYLE	Sets a new extended window style. See CreateWindowEx() in Chapter 2, *Creating Windows*, for a list of styles.	
GWL_STYLE	Sets a new window style. See CreateWindow() in Chapter 2 for a list of styles.	
GWL_WNDPROC	Sets a new long pointer to the window procedure.	

Table 3-11. SetWindowLong() Flags.

The GWL_ values are defined as negative values in WINDOWS.H. To access any extra four-byte data defined in the window's class structure, use a positive *nIndex* value. Zero for the first value, four for the second, etc.

dwNewLong   DWORD: The new 32-bit value.

Problems   Take care not to include functions in the new message processing function that cause Windows to call the function again. This sets up an infinite loop and overflows the stack. For example, adding the GetScrollPos() function into NewScrollPos() shown below will fail, as GetScrollPos() ends up forcing another call to the subclassed NewScrollPos() function.

Example   In this example, a scroll bar is placed at the bottom of the window's client area. After clicking the "Do It!" menu item, the scroll bar has the input focus. The scroll bar window is subclassed, providing additional message processing logic from the NewScrollPos() function listed at the bottom. The scroll bar thumb responds to both the left and right arrow keys and the page-up and page-down keys. Note that the NewScrollPos() function must be added to the EXPORTS section of the program's .DEF definition file. A function prototype must also be added to the program's header file.

```
FARPROC         lpfnOldScrollProc ;             /* static to hold old proc pointer */
int             nScrollPos ;                    /* static to hold thumb position */

long FAR PASCAL WndProc (HWND hWnd, unsigned iMessage, WORD wParam, LONG lParam)
{
        static HWND     hScroll ;
        FARPROC         lpfnNewScrollProc ;
        HDC             hDC ;
        RECT            rClient ;

        switch (iMessage)               /* process windows messages */
        {
        case WM_CREATE:

                GetClientRect (hWnd, &rClient) ;
                hScroll = CreateWindow ("SCROLLBAR", "",
                        WS_CHILD | WS_VISIBLE | SBS_BOTTOMALIGN | SBS_HORZ,
                        rClient.left, rClient.top, rClient.right,
                        rClient.bottom, hWnd, NULL, ghInstance, NULL) ;
                ShowWindow (hScroll, SW_SHOW) ;
                SetScrollRange (hScroll, SB_CTL, 0, 9, FALSE) ;
                SetScrollPos (hScroll, SB_CTL, 0, TRUE) ;
                nScrollPos = 0 ;

                        /* subclass the scroll bar to a new procedure */

                lpfnNewScrollProc = MakeProcInstance
                        ((FARPROC) NewScrollProc,  ghInstance) ;
                lpfnOldScrollProc = (FARPROC) GetWindowLong (hScroll,
```

```
                         GWL_WNDPROC) ;
                SetWindowLong (hScroll, GWL_WNDPROC,
                        (LONG) lpfnNewScrollProc) ;
                FreeProcInstance (lpfnNewScrollProc)
                break ;
        case WM_SETFOCUS:
                SetFocus (hScroll) ;
                break ;
        case WM_COMMAND:                  /* process menu items */
                switch (wParam)
                {
                case IDM_DOIT:            /* User hit the "Do it" menu item */
                        hDC = GetDC (hWnd) ;
                        TextOut (hDC, 10, 10,
                                "Try left/right arrow and pg up/dn.",    34) ;
                        ReleaseDC (hWnd, hDC) ;
                        SetFocus (hScroll) ;
                        break ;
                case IDM_QUIT:            /* send end of application message */
                        DestroyWindow (hWnd) ;
                        break ;
                }
                break ;
        case WM_DESTROY:                  /* stop application */
                PostQuitMessage (0) ;
                break ;
        default:                          /* default windows message processing */
                return DefWindowProc (hWnd, iMessage, wParam, lParam) ;
        }
        return (0L) ;
}

long FAR PASCAL NewScrollProc (HWND hWnd, WORD mess, WORD wParam, LONG lParam)
{
        int             nOldScrollPos ;

        nOldScrollPos = nScrollPos ;

        switch (mess)
        {
        case WM_KEYDOWN:
                switch (wParam)
                {
                case VK_RIGHT:                 /* process left and right arrow keys */
                case VK_NEXT:                  /* and page-up, page-down keys */
                        nScrollPos++ ;
                        break ;
                case VK_LEFT:
                case VK_PRIOR:
                        nScrollPos-- ;
                        break ;
                }
                if (nOldScrollPos != nScrollPos)
                        SetScrollPos (hWnd, SB_CTL, nScrollPos, TRUE) ;
        }
        return CallWindowProc (lpfnOldScrollProc, hWnd, mess, wParam, lParam) ;
}
```

SETWINDOWPOS   ■ Win 2.0   ■ Win 3.0   ■ Win 3.1

Purpose	Simultaneously changes the size, position, and ordering of windows.
Syntax	void **SetWindowPos**(HWND *hWnd*, HWND *hWndInsertAfter*, int *X*, int *Y*, int *cx*, int *cy*, WORD *wFlags*);
Description	Windows are ordered in Windows' internal list based on their appearance on the screen. The window on top of all the others is the highest ranked. This function changes that ordering, allowing you to bring a window to the top.

SetWindowPos() does not work if window is maximized.
Use: if (IsMaximized(hWnd)) SendMessage(hWind, WM_SYSCOMMAND, SC_RESTORE, 0L);

Uses   Used with applications that have multiple child and popup windows that can become obscured. Use GetTopWindow() to find the current top window.

Returns   No returned value (void).

See Also   GetTopWindow(), MoveWindow()

Parameters

hWnd   HWND: A handle to the window that will be affected.

hWndInsertAfter   HWND: The handle of the window after which the *hWnd* window is to be inserted. Can be set to NULL, which places *hWnd* at the top-most position. Set to one to place *hWnd* above all top-most windows, even when deactivated.

X   int: The new horizontal position of the *hWnd's* top left corner. For child windows this is in client coordinates. For popup windows, this is in screen coordinates. Can be zero if the SWP_NOMOVE value is used for *wFlags*, meaning no change to the window's position after reordering.

Y   int: The new vertical position of the *hWnd's* top left corner. For child windows, this is in client coordinates. For popup windows, this is in screen coordinates. Can be zero if the SWP_NOMOVE value is used for *wFlags*, meaning no change to the window's position after reordering.

cx   int: The new width of the *hWnd* window. Can be zero if the SWP_NOSIZE value is used for *wFlags*, meaning no change in the window's size after reordering.

cy   int: The new height of the *hWnd* window. Can be zero if the SWP_NOSIZE value is used for *wFlags*, meaning no change in the window's size after reordering.

wFlags   WORD: Can be any combination of the flags shown in Table 3-12, combined using the C language binary OR operator (|).

Value	Meaning
SWP_DRAWFRAME	Draw the window's frame when redrawing. The frame style is defined in the window's class definition. See RegisterClass().
SWP_HIDEWINDOW	Hide the window after reordering.
SWP_NOACTIVATE	Do not make the window active after reordering.
SWP_NOMOVE	Do not change the position of the window after reordering. The *X* and *Y* parameters are ignored if this flag is used.
SWP_NOSIZE	Do not change the size of the window after reordering. The cx and cy parameters are ignored if this flag is used.
SWP_NOREDRAW	Do not redraw the window after reordering.
SWP_NOZORDER	Do not change the window's order in the window list. This makes SetWindowPos() equivalent to MoveWindow().
SWP_SHOWWINDOW	Redraw the window after reordering.

Table 3-12. SetWindowPos() Flags.

Related Messages   WM_SIZE, WM_MOVE, WM_PAINT

Example   Two popup windows are created in the following WndProc() fragment. If the user clicks the "Do It!" menu item, the first child window is positioned above the second. Because of the three SWP_ parameters used in SetWindowPosition(), the size and location of the window is not affected. This is why the four size parameters are set to zero.

```
Long FAR PASCAL WndProc (HWND hWnd, unsigned iMessage, WORD wParam, LONG lParam)
{
```

```
HDC             hDC ;
static HWND     hChild1, hChild2 ;
char            cBuf [25] ;
static BOOL     bFirstTime = TRUE ;
BOOL            bIsVisible ;

switch (iMessage)               /* process windows messages */
{
        case WM_CREATE:         /* build the child window when program starts */
                if (bFirstTime)
                {
                        bFirstTime = FALSE ;
                        hChild1 = CreateWindow (gszAppName, "Child Window 1",
                                WS_POPUP | WS_VISIBLE | WS_BORDER | WS_CAPTION,
                                10, 10, 300, 250, hWnd, NULL, ghInstance, NULL) ;
                        ShowWindow (hChild2, SW_SHOW) ;
                        hChild2 = CreateWindow (gszAppName, "Child Window 2",
                                WS_POPUP | WS_VISIBLE | WS_BORDER | WS_CAPTION,
                                20, 20, 200, 150, hWnd, NULL, ghInstance, NULL) ;
                        ShowWindow (hChild2, SW_SHOW) ;
                }
                break ;
        case WM_COMMAND:                        /* process menu items */
                switch (wParam)
                {
                case IDM_DOIT:                  /* User hit the "Do it" menu item */

                        SetWindowPos (hChild1, hChild2, 0, 0, 0, 0,
                                SWP_NOSIZE | SWP_DRAWFRAME | SWP_NOMOVE) ;
                        break ;
```

[Other program lines]

SETWINDOWTEXT   ■ Win 2.0   ■ Win 3.0   ■ Win 3.1

Purpose	Changes the caption (title) of a window.
Syntax	void **SetWindowText**(HWND *hWnd*, LPSTR *lpString*);
Description	For windows with a title bar, the title shows up in the center of the caption area. For buttons, the title is inside of the button.
Uses	Changes a window's title. Note that the title string is displayed at the bottom of the window icon when the window is minimized. You can use this function to shorten the title when the window is minimized so that the title string fits under the icon, rather than running into other icons' titles.
Returns	No returned value (void).
See Also	GetWindowText()
Parameters	
hWnd	HWND: A handle to the window.
lpString	LPSTR: A pointer to a null-terminated string containing the new title. Windows will truncate the title if it does not fit within the title area of *hWnd*.
Example	This example changes the caption of the main window when the user clicks the "Do It!" menu item.

```
Long FAR PASCAL WndProc (HWND hWnd, unsigned iMessage, WORD wParam, LONG lParam)
{
        switch (iMessage)               /* process windows messages */
        {
                case WM_COMMAND:        /* process menu items */
                        switch (wParam)
                        {
                        case IDM_DOIT:  /* User hit the "Do it" menu item */
                                SetWindowText (hWnd, "I'm the new title!") ;
                                break ;
```

[Other program lines]

SETWINDOWWORD

■ Win 2.0   ■ Win 3.0   ■ Win 3.1

Purpose	Changes a WORD value associated with a window's class structure.
Syntax	WORD **SetWindowWord**(HWND *hWnd*, int *nIndex*, WORD *wNewWord*);
Uses	Normally used to change the control ID of a child window control. Can also be used to set 16-bit data associated with the window. This assumes that room for the data provided by the *cbWndExtra* element of the WNDCLASS data structure was set large enough to hold the data when the class was registered with RegisterClass().
Returns	WORD, the previous value.
See Also	GetWindowWord(), SetWindowLong(), GetWindowLong()
Parameters	
hWnd	HWND: A handle to the window.
nIndex	int: An index to the value to be changed. This can be either of the values in Table 3-13.

Value	Meaning	
GWW_HINSTANCE	Change the instance handle of the module that owns the window.	⊠
GWW_ID	Change the control ID of a child window control.	

Table 3-13. SetWindowWord( ) Flags.

The GWW_ values are defined as negative integers in WINDOWS.H. To change extra WORD sized data defined in the window's class structure, use a positive *nIndex* offset. Zero for the first value, 2 for the second, etc.

wNewWord	WORD: The new 16-bit value.
Example	The button control's ID value is changed to 1000 when the user clicks the "Do It!" menu item.

```
long FAR PASCAL WndProc (HWND hWnd, unsigned iMessage, WORD wParam, LONG lParam)
{
        static HWND         hButton ;
        HDC                 hDC ;
        int                 nID ;
        char                cBuf [25] ;

        switch (iMessage)                /* process windows messages */
        {
        case WM_CREATE:              /* initially created with ID = 99 */
                hButton = CreateWindow ("BUTTON", "Button",
                        WS_CHILD | WS_VISIBLE | BS_PUSHBUTTON,
                        10, 10, 100, 40, hWnd, 99, ghInstance, NULL) ;
                ShowWindow (hButton, SW_SHOW) ;
                break ;
        case WM_COMMAND:             /* process menu items */
                switch (wParam)
                {
                case IDM_DOIT:   /* User hit the "Do it" menu item */
                        hDC = GetDC (hWnd) ;
                        TextOut (hDC, 10, 60, "The button's ID was:", 20) ;
                        nID = GetWindowWord (hButton, GWW_ID) ;
                        itoa (nID, cBuf, 10) ;
                        TextOut (hDC, 10, 80, cBuf, strlen (cBuf)) ;
                        TextOut (hDC, 10, 100, "The new ID is:", 14) ;
                        SetWindowWord (hButton, GWW_ID, 1000) ;
                        nID = GetWindowWord (hButton, GWW_ID) ;
                        itoa (nID, cBuf, 10) ;
                        TextOut (hDC, 10, 120, cBuf, strlen (cBuf)) ;
                        ReleaseDC (hWnd, hDC) ;
                        break ;
```

[Other program lines]

SHOWOWNEDPOPUPS
■ Win 2.0　■ Win 3.0　■ Win 3.1

Purpose	Shows or hides all popup windows associated with the parent window.
Syntax	void **ShowOwnedPopups**(HWND *hWnd*, BOOL *bShow*);
Uses	Allows a "one shot" update of all the popup windows, without needing to individually call ShowWindow() for each one.
Returns	No returned value (void).
See Also	ShowWindow()
Parameters	
hWnd	HWND: A handle to the parent window which may own popups.
bShow	BOOL: TRUE to show all owned popup windows, FALSE to hide all of them.
Related Messages	WM_SHOWWINDOW
Example	Here the two popup windows created vanish and reappear when the user repeatedly clicks the "Do It!" menu item.

```
long FAR PASCAL WndProc (HWND hWnd, unsigned iMessage, WORD wParam, LONG lParam)
{
        static  HWND    hChild1, hChild2 ;
        static  BOOL    bFirstTime = TRUE ;
        static  BOOL    bPopupsShowing = TRUE ;

        switch (iMessage)                   /* process windows messages */
        {
                case WM_CREATE:             /* build the child window when program starts */

                        if (bFirstTime)
                        {
                                bFirstTime = FALSE ;
                                hChild1 = CreateWindow (gszAppName, "Popup Window 1",
                                        WS_POPUP | WS_VISIBLE | WS_BORDER | WS_CAPTION,
                                        10, 10, 300, 250, hWnd, NULL, ghInstance, NULL) ;
                                ShowWindow (hChild2, SW_SHOW) ;
                                hChild2 = CreateWindow (gszAppName, "Popup Window 2",
                                        WS_POPUP | WS_VISIBLE | WS_BORDER | WS_CAPTION,
                                        20, 20, 200, 150, hWnd, NULL, ghInstance, NULL) ;
                                ShowWindow (hChild2, SW_SHOW) ;
                        }
                        break ;
                case WM_COMMAND:                    /* process menu items */
                        switch (wParam)
                        {
                        case IDM_DOIT:              /* User hit the "Do it" menu item */
                                if (bPopupsShowing)
                                {
                                        bPopupsShowing = FALSE ;
                                        ShowOwnedPopups (hWnd, FALSE) ;
                                }
                                else
                                {
                                        bPopupsShowing = TRUE ;
                                        ShowOwnedPopups (hWnd, TRUE) ;
                                }
                                break ;
```

[Other program lines]

SHOWWINDOW
■ Win 2.0　■ Win 3.0　■ Win 3.1

Purpose	Displays, hides, or changes the size of a window.
Syntax	BOOL **ShowWindow**(HWND *hWnd*, int *nCmdShow*);
Description	ShowWindow() is normally called right after a window is created to make it visible.

Uses	Minimizing and maximizing the window, as well as making the window visible. Note that calling ShowWindow() does not guarantee that the window will not be obscured by other windows on the screen. Use SetActiveWindow() or SetWindowPos() to bring windows to the top.
Returns	BOOL. TRUE if the window was visible, FALSE if the window was hidden.
See Also	CreateWindow(), SetActiveWindow(), SetWindowPos()
Parameters	
hWnd	HWN: The handle to the window.
nCmdShow	int: An integer value specifying the action to be taken. It can be any one of the values in Table 3-14 (not a combination).

Value	Meaning	☒
SW_HIDE	Hides the window. The top window on Window's list is activated.	
SW_MINIMIZE	Minimizes the window. The top window on Window's list is activated.	
SW_RESTORE	Activates and displays the window (same as SW_SHOWNORMAL).	
SW_SHOW	Activates and displays the window in its current size and position.	
SW_SHOWMAXIMIZED	Activates and maximizes the window.	
SW_SHOWMINIMIZED	Activates and minimizes the window to an icon.	
SW_SHOWMINNOACTIVE	Displays and minimizes the window. The currently active window remains active.	
SW_SHOWNA	Displays the window, but does not change which window is active.	
SW_SHOWNOACTIVE	Displays the window, but does not change which window is active.	
SW_SHOWNORMAL	Activates and displays the window. If the window was minimized or maximized, the window is returned to its previous size and position.	

Table 3-14. ShowWindow( ) Flags.

Related Messages WM_SHOWWINDOW

Example This example hides a child window when the user clicks the "Do It!" menu item.

```
Long FAR PASCAL WndProc (HWND hWnd, unsigned iMessage, WORD wParam, LONG lParam)
{
        HDC             hDC ;
        static HWND     hChild ;
        char            cBuf [25] ;
        static BOOL     bFirstTime = TRUE ;
        BOOL            bIsVisible ;

        switch (iMessage)               /* process windows messages */
        {
                case WM_CREATE:         /* build the child window when program starts */
                        if (bFirstTime)
                        {
                                bFirstTime = FALSE ;
                                hChild = CreateWindow (gszAppName, "Child Window",
                                        WS_CHILD | WS_VISIBLE | WS_BORDER | WS_CAPTION,
                                        100, 50, 200, 150, hWnd, NULL, ghInstance, NULL) ;
                                ShowWindow (hChild, SW_SHOW) ;
                        }
                        break ;
                case WM_COMMAND:                /* process menu items */
                        switch (wParam)
                        {
                        case IDM_DOIT:          /* User hit the "Do it" menu item */
                                hDC = GetDC (hWnd) ;
                                bIsVisible = IsWindowVisible (hChild) ;
                                if (bIsVisible)
```

```
                    {
                            GetWindowText (hChild, cBuf, 24) ;
                            TextOut (hDC, 10, 20, cBuf, strlen (cBuf)) ;
                            TextOut (hDC, 10, 40, "is now visible.", 15) ;
                            TextOut (hDC, 10, 60, "Now hiding Child...", 19) ;
                            ShowWindow (hChild, SW_HIDE) ;
                    }
                    else
                            TextOut (hDC, 10, 20,
                                    "Child window not visible.", 25) ;
                    ReleaseDC (hWnd, hDC) ;
                    break ;
```

[Other program lines]

SYSTEMPARAMETERSINFO   ☐ Win 2.0   ☐ Win 3.0   ■ Win 3.1

Purpose	Determines and/or change ssystem wide parameters.
Syntax	BOOL **SystemParametersInfo** (WORD *wAction*, WORD *wParam*, LPVOID *lpvParam*, WORD *fWinIni*);
Description	This function allows a wide range of system parameters that control the way applications look and behave to be checked and changed. The changes can optionally be written to the WIN.INI file, making the changes effective in subsequent Windows sessions.
Uses	Used in replacing the Windows Control Panel program.
Returns	BOOL. TRUE if successful, FALSE on error.
See Also	GetSystemMetrics(), WriteProfileString()
Parameters	
wAction	WORD: Any of the following values. The *wParam* and *lpvParam* values are used differently for each value of *wAction*, so their meanings are listed together.

wAction	Meaning ☒
SPI_GETBEEP	Determine if the warning beeper is on or off.
wParam	Set to 0.
lpvParam	A pointer to a BOOL variable that will receive TRUE if the beeper is on, FALSE if the beeper is off.
SPI_GETBORDER	Determine the width of window sizing borders.
wParam	Set to 0.
lpvParam	A pointer to an integer that will receive the border multiplying factor.
SPI_GETGRIDGRANULARITY	Determine the spacing between items placed on the Windows desktop.
wParam	Set to 0.
lpvParam	A pointer to an integer that will receive the current spacing (granularity) factor.
SPI_GETICONTITLELOGFONT	Retrieve the logical font data for icon titles.
wParam	Set to the sizeof() a LOGFONT structure.
lpvParam	A pointer to a LOGFONT structure that will be filled in when the function returns. See the CreateFontIndirect() function description for a description of the LOGFONT data structure.
SPI_GETICONTITLEWRAP	Determine if icon title wrapping is set on or off.
wParam	Set to 0.
lpvParam	A pointer to a BOOL variable that will receive TRUE if title wrapping is on, FALSE if title wrapping is off.

SPI_GETKEYBOARDDELAY	Determine the current keyboard repeat speed.
wParam	Set to 0.
lpvParam	A pointer to an integer that will receive the current keyboard repeat-delay.
SPI_GETKEYBOARDSPEED	Determine the current keyboard auto-repeat speed.
wParam	Set to 0.
lpvParam	A pointer to an integer that will receive the current keyboard auto-repeat speed.
SPI_GETMENUDROPALIGNMENT	Determine if popup menus appear left-aligned or right-aligned relative to the top menu-bar item.
wParam	Set to 0.
lpvParam	A pointer to a BOOL variable that will receive TRUE if popup menus are right-aligned, FALSE if popup menus are left-aligned.
SPI_GETMOUSE	Determine the mouse speed and the X and Y mouse threshold values. Movements smaller than the threshold do not result in mouse activity.
wParam	Set to 0.
lpvParam	A pointer to a three integer array (int value[3]) where: value[0] = X direction mouse threshold; value[1] = Y direction mouse threshold; value[2] = The mouse speed value.
SPI_GETSCREENSAVEACTIVE	Determine if screen saving is on or off.
wParam	Set to 0.
lpvParam	A pointer to a BOOL variable that will receive TRUE if screen saving is on, FALSE if screen saving is off.
SPI_GETSCREENSAVETIMEOUT	Determine the screen save time period.
wParam	Set to 0.
lpvParam	A pointer to an integer that will receive the current screen save delay in seconds.
SPI_ICONHORIZONTALSPACING	Changes the horizontal icon spacing.
wParam	Set to the horizontal icon spacing in pixels.
lpvParam	Set to NULL.
SPI_ICONVERTICALSPACING	Changes the vertical icon spacing.
wParam	Set to the vertical icon spacing in pixels.
lpvParam	Set to NULL.
SPI_LANGDRIVER	Determine the language driver.
wParam	Set to 0.
lpvParam	A pointer to a character buffer that will contain the language driver file name.
SPI_SETBEEP	Turn the system beeper on or off.
wParam	Set to TRUE to turn the beeper on, FALSE to turn the beeper off.
lpvParam	Set to NULL.
SPI_SETBORDER	Change the window sizing border width.
wParam	Set to the new border multiplier factor.
lpvParam	Set to NULL.

Table 3-15. continued

wAction	Meaning
SPI_SETDESKPATTERN	Sets the desktop background pattern by reading the "Pattern=" parameter in the WIN.INI file. Use WriteProfileString() to change the WIN.INI file.
wParam	Set to 0.
lpvParam	Set to NULL.
SPI_SETDESKWALLPAPER	Change the bitmap used for the desktop background.
wParam	Set to 0.
lpvParam	A pointer to a character string that contains the name of the bitmap file.
SPI_SETDOUBLECLKHEIGHT	Change the vertical distance within which a second mouse button click must occur to be registered as a double-click.
wParam	Set to the double-click vertical height in pixels.
lpvParam	Set to NULL.
SPI_SETDOUBLECLICKTIME	Change the maximum number of milliseconds between two mouse button clicks to have the second click register as a double-click.
wParam	Set to double-click time in milliseconds.
lpvParam	Set to NULL.
SPI_SETDOUBLECLKWIDTH	Change the horizontal distance within which a second mouse button click must occur to be registered as a double-click.
wParam	Set to the double-click horizontal height in pixels.
lpvParam	Set to NULL.
SPI_SETGRIDGRANULARITY	Change the size (granularity) of the desktop sizing grid.
wParam	Set to the grid size.
lpvParam	Set to NULL.
SPI_SETICONTITLEWRAP	Turn title wrapping of icon title strings on or off.
wParam	Set to TRUE to turn title wrapping on, FALSE to turn title wrapping off.
lpvParam	Set to NULL.
SPI_SETKEYBOARDDELAY	Change the keyboard delay setting.
wParam	Set to the new delay value.
lpvParam	Set to NULL.
SPI_SETKEYBOARDSPEED	Change the keyboard auto-repeat speed.
wParam	Set to the new auto-repeat speed.
lpvParam	Set to NULL.
SPI_SETMENUDROPALIGNMENT	Change the alignment of popup menus relative to the corresponding item in the top menu bar.
wParam	Set to TRUE for right alignment, FALSE for left alignment.
lpvParam	Set to NULL.
SPI_SETMOUSE	Change the mouse speed and the X and Y mouse threshold values. Movements smaller than the threshold do not result in mouse activity.

wParam	Set to 0.

lpvParam	Set to a pointer to a three integer array (int value[3]) where:
	value[0] = new X direction mouse threshold;
	value[1] = new Y direction mouse threshold;
	value[2] = new mouse speed value.

Table 3-15. SystemParametersInfo( ) wActionValues.

fWinIni   WORD: This value determines if any changes made to system settings are recorded in the WIN.INI file, and if the WM_WININICHANGE message is broadcast to all applications after the change is made. Changing WIN.INI causes the new system settings to be used in subsequent Windows sessions, as WIN.INI is read when Windows starts. Possible settings are shown in Table 3-16.

Value	Meaning
NULL	No change to WIN.INI.
SPIF_UPDATEINIFILE	Writes the new system parameters to the WIN.INI file.
SPIF_SENDWININICHANGE	Writes the new system parameters to the WIN.INI file, and broadcasts the WM_WININICHANGE message to all applications running on the system.

Table 3-16. SystemParametersInfo( ) Flag Settings.

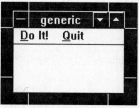

Figure 3-16. SystemParametersInfo( ) Example.

Related Messages WM_WININICHANGE\

Example   This example increases the width of the border of every window running on the system when the user clicks the "Do It!" menu item. The borders are all restored to normal width when the application exits. (See Figure 3-16.)

```
long FAR PASCAL WndProc (HWND hWnd, unsigned iMessage, WORD
wParam, LONG lParam)
{
        static          int       nOldBorderWide ;

        switch (iMessage)                 /* process windows messages */
          {
          case WM_CREATE:          /* save original window border width */
                  SystemParametersInfo (SPI_GETBORDER, 0, &nOldBorderWide,
                          NULL) ;
                  break ;
          case WM_COMMAND:                    /* process menu items */
                  switch (wParam)
                    {                  /* increase border width * 5 */
                          case IDM_DOIT:
                                  SystemParametersInfo (SPI_SETBORDER,
                                          5 * nOldBorderWide, NULL, NULL) ;
                                  break ;
                          case IDM_QUIT:
                                  DestroyWindow (hWnd) ;
                                  break ;
                    }
                  break ;
          case WM_DESTROY:         /* set border width back to normal */
                  SystemParametersInfo (SPI_SETBORDER, nOldBorderWide,
                          NULL, NULL) ;
                  PostQuitMessage (0) ;
                  break ;
```

```
            default:
                    return DefWindowProc (hWnd, iMessage, wParam, lParam) ;
        }
        return (0L) ;
}
```

UNREGISTERCLASS

□ Win 2.0   □ Win 3.0   ■ Win 3.1

Purpose	Frees the memory holding an unneeded class description.
Syntax	BOOL **UnregisterClass**(LPSTR *lpClassName*, HANDLE *hInstance*);
Description	This function completely removes the window class from the system. Make sure all windows based on the class are destroyed before the class is eliminated.
Uses	In applications with several modules. UnregisterClass() can be used to free memory space if the new module does not need certain classes. Classes registered within an application are destroyed automatically when the application terminates.
Returns	BOOL. TRUE if the class was removed, FALSE if the class could not be found, or if a window exists that uses this class.
See Also	RegisterClass()
Parameters	
lpClassName	LPSTR: A pointer to a null-terminated character string containing the class name. Do not attempt to remove predefined window classes, such as buttons and edit controls.
hInstance	HANDLE: The handle to the program instance that created the class.
Example	In this example, clicking the "Do It!" menu item causes the popup window to be destroyed, and its class to be unregistered. Note that the child window's procedure does not issue a PostQuitMessage() function call when it gets a WM_DESTROY message. If it did, removing the popup would close the parent application program as well.

The ChildProc() function needs to be referenced in the EXPORTS section of the program's .DEF definition file, and a function prototype added to the header file.

```
long FAR PASCAL WndProc (HWND hWnd, unsigned iMessage, WORD wParam, LONG lParam)
{
        static WNDCLASS     wndclass ;        /* the window class */
        static HWND         hPopup ;

        switch (iMessage)                     /* process windows messages */
        {
                case WM_CREATE:        /* build the child window when program starts */
                        wndclass.style        = CS_HREDRAW | CS_VREDRAW | CS_PARENTDC;
                        wndclass.lpfnWndProc  = ChildProc ;
                        wndclass.cbClsExtra   = 0 ;
                        wndclass.cbWndExtra   = 0 ;
                        wndclass.hInstance    = ghInstance ;
                        wndclass.hIcon        = NULL ;
                        wndclass.hCursor      = LoadCursor (NULL, IDC_ARROW) ;
                        wndclass.hbrBackground = GetStockObject (LTGRAY_BRUSH) ;
                        wndclass.lpszMenuName = NULL ;
                        wndclass.lpszClassName = "SecondClass" ;
                                              /* register the window class */
                        if(RegisterClass (&wndclass))
                        {
                                hPopup = CreateWindow ("SecondClass", "Popup Window",
                                        WS_POPUP | WS_VISIBLE | WS_BORDER | WS_CAPTION,
                                        10, 50, 200, 150, hWnd, NULL, ghInstance, NULL) ;
                                ShowWindow (hPopup, SW_SHOW) ;
                        }
                        break ;
                case WM_COMMAND:                    /* process menu items */
                        switch (wParam)
```

```
                               {
                               case IDM_DOIT:           /* User hit the "Do it" menu item */
                                       DestroyWindow (hPopup) ;
                                       UnregisterClass ("SecondClass", ghInstance) ;
                                       break ;
                               case IDM_QUIT:
                                       DestroyWindow (hWnd) ;
                                       break ;
                               }
                               break ;
                       case WM_DESTROY:          /* stop application */
                               PostQuitMessage (0) ;
                               break ;
                       default:                  /* default windows message processing */
                               return DefWindowProc (hWnd, iMessage, wParam, lParam) ;
               }
       return (0L) ;
}

/* Here is a separate message processing procedure for the child window */

long FAR PASCAL ChildProc (HWND hWnd, unsigned iMessage, WORD wParam, LONG lParam)
{
       switch (iMessage)               /* process windows messages */
       {
               case WM_DESTROY:
                       break ;
               default:                  /* default windows message processing */
                       return DefWindowProc (hWnd, iMessage, wParam, lParam) ;
       }
       return (0L) ;
}
```

WINDOWFROMPOINT   ■ Win 2.0   ■ Win 3.0   ■ Win

Purpose	Finds which window (if any) is at a given point on the screen.
Syntax	HWND **WindowFromPoint**(POINT *Point*);
Description	Finds a window based on the screen coordinates given in *Point*.
Returns	A handle to the window occupying the given point on the screen. NULL if no window is at that point.
See Also	ChildWindowFromPoint()
Parameters	
Point	POINT: A point structure holding the x and y coordinates of the screen coordinates to check. POINT is defined in WINDOWS.H as

```
typedef struct tagPOINT
{
        int    x;
        int    y;
} POINT;
typedef POINT *PPOINT;
```

Example	This example shows the title of the window located at screen coordinates 100,100 (from the top left corner) when the "Do It!" menu item is clicked.

```
long FAR PASCAL WndProc (HWND hWnd, unsigned iMessage, WORD wParam, LONG lParam)
{
        HDC           hDC ;
        char          cBuf [25] ;
        HWND          FoundWindow ;
        POINT         pScreen ;

        switch (iMessage)                         /* process windows messages */
        {
```

```
        case WM_COMMAND:                    /* process menu items */
              switch (wParam)
              {
              case IDM_DOIT:                /* User hit the "Do it" menu item */

                      pScreen.x = 100 ;
                      pScreen.y = 100 ;
                      hFoundWindow = WindowFromPoint (pScreen) ;
                      hDC = GetDC (hWnd) ;
                      TextOut (hDC, 10, 10,
                              "At 100, 100 is the window:", 26) ;
                      if (hFoundWindow)
                      {
                              GetWindowText (hFoundWindow, cBuf, 24) ;
                              TextOut (hDC, 15, 25, cBuf, strlen (cBuf)) ;
                      }
                      else
                              TextOut (hDC, 15, 25, "None found", 10) ;
                      ReleaseDC (hWnd, hDC) ;
                      break ;
```

[Other program lines]

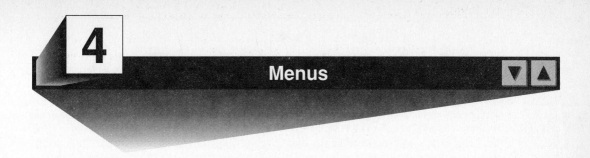

Menus

Menus are used in essentially every Windows program to allow the user to select actions as the program is running. The Windows Software Development Kit (SDK) provides a comprehensive set of tools for building menus and modifying them as the program runs.

Main Menus and Popup Menus

Windows recognizes two basic types of menus: top-level menus and popup menus. The top-level menu (also called the "main" menu of a program is the series of commands that are visible in the window's menu bar at all times, assuming the program has a menu. For simple programs, the menu bar will contain all of the program's menu options. If there is not enough room for all of the menu items on one line, Windows will automatically "break" the line, creating a two-line menu bar. For more complex programs, there is not enough space on the menu bar for all the commands you may need. This is where popup menus (sometimes called submenus, "pull down," or "drop down" menus come in. When clicked, the top menu bar items can spawn popup menu items with many more options from which to choose. Figure 4-1 shows a typical example.

Building Menus in the Resource File

For most programs, defining a menu is simply a matter of writing a few lines in the resource .RC file. Here is an example which produces the menu structure shown in Figure 4-1.

▷ **GENERIC.RC Resource Script File**

Figure 4-1. Top Level Menus and Popup Menus.

```
/* genmenu.rc    1 */
#include <windows.h>
#include "genmenu.h"

genmenu         ICON    generic.ico

genmenu         MENU
BEGIN
        POPUP "&Top Item",
        BEGIN
                MENUITEM "Item &One",     IDM_POP1
                MENUITEM "Item &Two".     IDM_POP2
        END
        MENUITEM "&Quit",                 IDM_QUIT
        MENUITEM "\a&Help",               IDM_HELP
END
```

In this case there are three items on the top level menu bar, "Top Item," "Quit," and "Help." The first item is a headline for a popup menu containing "Item One" and "Item Two." The values behind the menu item ID numbers (IDM_POP1, etc.) are defined in the program's header file as a series of integers. They should be numbered between 0 and 0x7FFF. The numbering sequence is not important.

There are a few extra things to notice about this menu definition. The ampersand (&) characters are used to create keyboard alternatives to clicking menu items with the mouse. The letter following the ampersand is underlined in the menu. Holding down the (ALT) key and the key for the underlined letter causes that menu item to be selected. This amounts to an almost instant keyboard interface. If you need to display the ampersand character, use a double ampersand (&&). If more than one menu item has the same letter preceded by an ampersand, the first one will be underlined and will respond to the (ALT) key combination. A double quote ("") will insert a single quote mark in a string. Within popup menus, you can also use it for a tab character. This will not work on top-level menus. Also note that the "Help" item is preceded by "\a". This moves that item to the right side of the window's menu bar. This is typically used for help information menus.

Menu definitions can also include commands for changing the way a menu item is displayed. "Graying" a menu item causes Windows to display the menu letters with gray text, rather than the usual black. Graying is used to give a visible indication that a menu item is not operating at a given time. Typically grayed items are also disabled, so that no Windows' messages are sent if the user attempts to select the item. Menu items can also be checked, which means that a small checkmark is displayed to the left of the menu item. This is handy when there are options that the user can turn on or off, but not enough options to justify a dialog box with radio buttons to make the selection. You can also control where menus and submenus break, if you use multiline menus.

The control over graying, checking, etc. within the resource .RC file menu definition is achieved by adding the control word to the end of a MENUITEM statement. For example, here is a menu definition with two levels of popup menus, a grayed item, a checked item, and a specification of a break in a popup menu.

▷ **Resource Script File with Menu Items Grayed and Checked**

```
/* genmenu.rc    */
#include <windows.h>
#include "genmenu.h"
genmenu         ICON    generic.ico
genmenu         MENU
BEGIN
        POPUP "&First Menu"
        BEGIN
                MENUITEM "&Top Item",           IDM_TOP1
                MENUITEM "&1st Option",          IDM_OPT1, CHECKED
                MENUITEM "&2nd Option",          IDM_OPT2, GRAYED
                MENUITEM SEPARATOR
                POPUP "&Popup"
                BEGIN
                        MENUITEM "&Left One",    IDM_POP1
                        MENUITEM "&Right One",   IDM_POP2, MENUBREAK
                END
        END
        MENUITEM "&Quit",                       IDM_QUIT
        MENUITEM "\a&Help",                     DM_HELP, HELP
END
```

The full list of menu item options is given in Table 4-1.

Option	Meaning
CHECKED	The item has a checkmark next to it.
GRAYED	The item's text is inactive and appears in gray letters.
HELP	The item has a vertical line to the left. You may also want to put the characters "\a" at the beginning of the menu text to force this item to the menu bar's far right side.
INACTIVE	The item name is displayed, but cannot be selected. No WM_COMMAND messages are sent from this item until it is enabled.
MENUBARBREAK	For menus, places the item on a new line, creating a multiline menu. For popups, places the new item on a new column, creating a multicolumn (rectangular) popup menu. A line is used to separate this item from the previous one.
MENUBREAK	Same as MENUBARBREAK, except for popup menus. For menus, places the item on a new line, creating a multiine menu. For popups, places the new item on a new column, creating a multicolumn (rectangular) popup menu without a dividing line.

Table 4-1. Menu Item Options—Used to the Right of the Menu Item.

Popup menu names (the line that says "POPUP" in the resource file) can also use all of these parameters, but do not have a menu item ID value associated with them. Only the items within the popup menus have ID values for selection. You can also place a line between any two menu items by using MENUITEM SEPARATOR as a menu item. The line cannot be selected, but can help it to clarify long popup menus by breaking the list into logical sections.

Adding a Menu to the Program's Window

Defining a menu in the resource .RC file does not automatically make it visible, or make it a part of the program's window. Normally, you will attach the program's menu to the window's class definition in the WinMain() function. This is done by setting the *lpszMenuName* element of the *wndclass* structure to point to the menu name. RegisterClass() then associates this menu name with any window created from the class.

```
wndclass.style          = CS_HREDRAW | CS_VREDRAW ;
wndclass.lpfnWndProc    = WndProc ;
wndclass.cbClsExtra     = 0 ;
wndclass.cbWndExtra     = 0 ;
wndclass.hInstance      = hInstance ;
wndclass.hIcon          = LoadIcon (hInstance, gszAppName) ;
wndclass.hCursor        = LoadCursor (NULL, IDC_ARROW) ;
wndclass.hbrBackground  = GetStockObject (WHITE_BRUSH) ;
wndclass.lpszMenuName   = "genmenu" ;
wndclass.lpszClassName  = "generic" ;
                        /* register the window class */
if (!RegisterClass (&wndclass))
        return FALSE ;
```

The menu name can be any valid name. The name in the class definition must match the one defined in the resource file for the menu.

Changing Menus

Normally, you will use the resource .RC file to define the menu. If your program allows the user to add new menu options (such as macro names), you may need to modify menu items or build entire new menus after the program starts running. New menus are created with the CreateMenu() function. The new menu is initially empty. Menu items are added to the menu using AppendMenu() and InsertMenu(). As soon as the menu is built, you can attach it to the window using SetMenu(). The memory associated with an old, unneeded menu can be freed using DestroyMenu(). You can also create new popup menus by using CreatePopupMenu(). Items are added to the popup menu using AppendMenu() and InsertMenu(), just like a main menu. When the popup is built, it can be added to the menu using AppendMenu() or InsertMenu(). If your program switches between a few fairly constant menus, you will probably find it simpler to define all of the menus in the resource .RC file. Each menu is given a different name. During the execution of the program, you can switch between menus by calling LoadMenu() to make the menu available and SetMenu() to attach it to the program's window. LoadMenu() only loads one copy of the menu into memory. You can call it multiple times without wasting memory. If you use two or more predefined menus, only one will be attached to the application's main window at any one time. Only the attached menu will end up removed from memory when the application terminates. Use DestroyMenu() to remove any other menus as the program exits, to avoid tying up memory.

Essentially, every aspect of a menu can be changed as the program is running. The most common changes are to change a menu's character string, check and uncheck menu items, gray and disable them, and to delete items. ModifyMenu() allows several of these operations to be carried out in one function call. There are also more specific functions for single operations, such as DeleteMenu() to remove an item, CheckMenuItem() to add and remove checkmarks, and EnableMenuItem() to enable and disable items. If you change the top-level menu, be sure to call DrawMenuBar(). This causes the menu bar to be redrawn. Otherwise, the changes will not become visible until the user attempts to select a menu item. This is not necessary if the changes are made while processing the WM_CREATE message, as that message is processed before the window is drawn for the first time.

Bitmaps as Menu Items

Menu items are normally text strings. In some cases it may be far better to have a visual image for the menu items, rather than using words. Good examples are the "tools" items for paint programs. A picture of a brush is more intuitive than the word "Brush." Figure 4-2 shows a simple example with two menu items, a pen and a pair of scissors.

Figure 4-2. Bitmaps As Menu Items.

You cannot define a bitmap menu item in the resource .RC file. Instead, you add or insert the bitmap item into the menu using AppendMenu() and Insert-Menu(). Typically, the menu bitmaps are created using the SDKPaint program that comes with the software development kit. A 32 by 32 pixel bitmap is good for a small menu item, while 64 by 64 pixels makes a big one. The bitmaps are referenced in the top of the resource file. A typical series of AppendMenu() function calls to load in a menu containing bitmaps is

```
hMenu = CreateMenu () ;
hSubMenu = CreatePopupMenu () ;
hPenBm = LoadBitmap (ghInstance, (LPSTR) "pen") ;
hCutBm = LoadBitmap (ghInstance, (LPSTR) "cut") ;
AppendMenu (hSubMenu, MF_BITMAP, IDM_POP1, (LPSTR)(LONG)hPenBm) ;
AppendMenu (hSubMenu, MF_BITMAP, IDM_POP2, (LPSTR)(LONG)hCutBm) ;
AppendMenu (hMenu, MF_POPUP, hSubMenu, (LPSTR) "&Tools") ;
AppendMenu (hMenu, MF_STRING, IDM_QUIT, (LPSTR) "&Quit") ;
AppendMenu (hMenu, MF_STRING, IDM_HELP, (LPSTR) "&Help") ;
SetMenu (hWnd, hMenu) ;
```

In this case, the bitmaps are loaded into a popup menu. The popup menu is then appended to the main menu with the popup heading of "Tools." Two normal menu items "Quit" and "Help" are then added, before the menu is attached to the program's window with SetMenu(). The resulting menu structure is shown in Figure 4-2. A more complete listing of this program is given in the AppendMenu() function description.

Windows automatically sizes the popup menu to accommodate the largest bitmap loaded. Windows does not put a border around the bitmaps, so you may want to draw the borders when you create the bitmaps in SDKPaint.

The Checkmark Bitmap

A new addition with Windows version 3.0 is the ability to change the bitmap used to show a checkmark next to a checked menu item. This gets a little involved, as the size of the checkmark depends on the video resolution of the screen on which the program is displayed.

GetMenuCheckmarkDimensions() retrieves the size of the menu item checkmarks, while SetMenuItemBitmaps() establishes a new bitmap for a menu item to use for checkmarks. You can go wild and have a different checkmark bitmap for each menu item. Don't confuse these functions with loading bitmaps as the menu items themselves.

Owner-Drawn Menu Items

The most flexible, but most complex, of the menu options is the owner-drawn style. In this case your program paints directly on a popup menu, which is a little window. This allows you to scale graphics images to match the resolution of the screen or the size of the parent window. As an example, consider a program that has two graphics images for the first two popup selections. For simplicity, we will use a blue rectangle and a red ellipse as the choices. The window will appear as shown in Figure 4-3 when the first top-level menu item is selected.

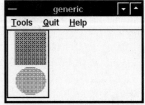

Figure 4-3. Owner-Drawn Menu Items.

Like bitmaps, this type of menu cannot be created from within a resource script file. The menu must be built from within the program. The key to creating owner-drawn menu items is to use the MF_OWNERDRAW flag when AppendMenu() is used to add the items. Listing 4-1 shows the code to create and use the menu shown in Figure 4-3.

▷ **Listing 4-1. WndProc( ) Function Creating Owner-Drawn Menu Items**

```
Long FAR PASCAL WndProc (HWND hWnd, unsigned iMessage, WORD wParam, LONG lParam)
{
        HMENU                           hMenu, hSubMenu ;
        LPMEASUREITEMSTRUCT             MIS ;
        LPDRAWITEMSTRUCT                DIS ;
        static DWORD                    dwRColor, dwEColor ;
        HBRUSH                          hBrush ;
        static   int                    nCheckWide ;

        switch (iMessage)                               /* process windows messages */
        {
              case WM_CREATE:
                    hMenu = CreateMenu () ;
                    hSubMenu = CreatePopupMenu () ;
                    AppendMenu (hSubMenu, MF_OWNERDRAW, IDM_POP1,
                          (LPSTR) (DWORD) RGB (0, 0, 255)) ;
                    AppendMenu (hSubMenu, MF_OWNERDRAW, IDM_POP2,
                          (LPSTR) (DWORD) RGB (255, 0, 0)) ;
                    AppendMenu (hMenu, MF_POPUP, hSubMenu, (LPSTR) "&Tools") ;
                    AppendMenu (hMenu, MF_STRING, IDM_QUIT, (LPSTR) "&Quit") ;
                    AppendMenu (hMenu, MF_STRING, IDM_HELP, (LPSTR) "&Help") ;
                    SetMenu (hWnd, hMenu) ;
                    nCheckWide = LOWORD (GetMenuCheckMarkDimensions ()) ;
                    break ;
              case WM_MEASUREITEM:
                    MIS= (LPMEASUREITEMSTRUCT) lParam ;
                    if (MIS->itemID == IDM_POP1)     /* rectangle item */
                    {
                            MIS->itemWidth = 64;
                            MIS->itemHeight = 64 ;
                            dwRColor = MIS->itemData ;
                    }
                    else if (MIS->itemID == IDM_POP2)/* ellipse */
                    {
                            MIS->itemWidth = 64;
                            MIS->itemHeight = 64 ;
                            dwEColor = MIS->itemData ;
                    }
                    return (OL) ;
              case WM_DRAWITEM:
                    DIS = (LPDRAWITEMSTRUCT) lParam ;
                    if (DIS->itemID == IDM_POP1)      /* rectangle */
                    {
                            if (DIS->itemState == ODS_SELECTED)
                                    hBrush = GetStockObject (BLACK_BRUSH) ;
                            else
                                    hBrush = CreateSolidBrush (dwRColor) ;
                            SelectObject (DIS->hDC, hBrush) ;
                            Rectangle (DIS->hDC, nCheckWide, 0,
                                    64 + nCheckWide, 64) ;
                    }
                    else if (DIS->itemID == IDM_POP2)
                    {
                            if (DIS->itemState == ODS_SELECTED)
                                    hBrush = GetStockObject (BLACK_BRUSH) ;
                            else
                                    hBrush = CreateSolidBrush (dwEColor) ;
                            SelectObject (DIS->hDC, hBrush) ;
                            Ellipse (DIS->hDC, nCheckWide, 65, 64 + nCheckWide,
                                    128) ;
                    }
                    SelectObject (DIS->hDC, GetStockObject (BLACK_BRUSH)) ;
                    DeleteObject (hBrush) ;
                    break ;
              case WM_COMMAND:                          /* process menu items */
                    switch (wParam)
                    {
```

```
                        case IDM_POP1:
                                MessageBox (hWnd, "The rectangle was selected",
                                            "Message", MB_OK) ;
                                break ;
                        case IDM_POP2:
                                MessageBox (hWnd, "The ellipse was selected",
                                            "Message", MB_OK) ;
                                break ;
                        case IDM_QUIT:
                                PostQuitMessage (NULL) ;
                                break ;
                        }
                        break ;
                case WM_DESTROY:            /* stop application */
                        PostQuitMessage (0) ;
                        break ;
                default:                        /* default windows message processing */
                        return DefWindowProc (hWnd, iMessage, wParam, lParam) ;
        }
        return (0L) ;
}
```

The menu is created when the WM_CREATE message is processed. Two of the menu items are set to MF_OWNERDRAW. AppendMenu() has the ability to associate a 32-bit value with the menu item. This ability does not have to be used, but it is a convenient way to pass the color of an owner-drawn menu item. This is done in the example code, using the RGB() macro to specify the desired color value.

Drawing the owner-drawn menu items is a matter of processing two Windows messages. WM_MEASUREITEM is sent when a menu is activated that contains owner-drawn items. This is the same message used for owner-drawn buttons, list boxes, and combo boxes. The *lParam* value passed with the message points to a MEASUREITEMSTRUCT structure. This is defined in WINDOWS.H as

```
/* MEASUREITEMSTRUCT for ownerdraw */

typedef struct tagMEASUREITEMSTRUCT
  {
  WORD CtlType;        /* ODT_MENU, ODT_LISTBOX, ODT_COMBOBOX, ODT_BUTTON */
  WORD CtlID;          /* not used with menu items */
  WORD itemID;         /* the menu item's id number */
  WORD itemWidth;      /* the program fills in these two values to set */
  WORD itemHeight;     /*  the size of the menu item in pixels */
  DWORD  itemData;     /* the 32-bit data from AppendMenu ends up here */
  } MEASUREITEMSTRUCT;
typedef MEASUREITEMSTRUCT NEAR *PMEASUREITEMSTRUCT;
typedef MEASUREITEMSTRUCT FAR  *LPMEASUREITEMSTRUCT;
```

The program must set the *itemWidth* and *itemHeight* values when it processes the WM_MEASUREITEM message, and then it must return to Windows. This is how the program specifies how big the owner-drawn menu item(s) will be. This message is processed once for each owner-drawn menu item in the currently active menu. The actual drawing of the menu items occurs when WM_DRAWITEM messages are sent from WINDOWS. This is a little more complex than you might expect, as the owner-drawn menu item can do graying, checking, changing shape or color on selection, etc. The *lParam* value passed with WM_DRAWITEM is a pointer to a DRAWITEMSTRUCT data structure, defined in WINDOWS.H as

```
/* DRAWITEMSTRUCT for ownerdraw */
typedef struct tagDRAWITEMSTRUCT
  {
  WORD        CtlType;       /* ODT_MENU, ODT_LISTBOX, ODT_COMBOBOX, ODT_BUTTON */
  WORD        CtlID;         /* not used with menu items */
  WORD        itemID;        /* the menu item's id number */
  WORD        itemAction;    /* ODA_DRAWITEM, ODA_SELECT, or ODA_FOCUS */
  WORD        itemState;     /* ODS_SELECTED,ODS_GRAYED,ODS_DISABLED,ODS_CHECKED */
  HWND        hwndItem;      /* the item's handle */              /* or ODS_FOCUS */
  HDC         hDC;           /* the item's device context */
  RECT        rcItem;        /* the bounding rectangle of the item */
  DWORD       itemData;      /* here is where the 32-bit data goes */
```

```
} DRAWITEMSTRUCT;
typedef DRAWITEMSTRUCT NEAR *PDRAWITEMSTRUCT;
typedef DRAWITEMSTRUCT FAR  *LPDRAWITEMSTRUCT;
```

This is a convenient structure, as it contains both the menu window's handle (the menu is a window), bounding rectangle, and device context. The 32-bit value set by AppendMenu() is also available. The program can modify the painting operation depending on the state of the menu (grayed, selected, checked, etc.). In the simple example above, the objects are painted black to show selection. One point of confusion here is that the entire popup menu is a single window. The painting operations for separate items must determine the correct location to paint each item within the menu. In the example, each menu item is 64 pixels high, so spacing is simple. Note that the items are offset to the right by the width of a menu item checkmark, to be consistent with the normal shape of menu items.

Menu Messages

As mentioned above, Windows sends the WM_COMMAND message every time a menu item is selected. This is normally the only message that you will process from a menu. However, you may find use for the WM_INITMENU and WM_INITMENUPOPUP messages. They are sent right before a main menu or popup menu is activated. They provide some advance warning, in case the application needs to change the status of items from enabled to disabled, re-create bitmaps, etc. The WM_MENUCHAR message is sent if the user attempts to use a keyboard shortcut key that does not match any of the menu names preceded by an ampersand character (&). This allows more than one keyboard shortcut to be programmed per menu item, or it can be used to display an error message. The WM_MENUSELECT message is also sent when a menu item is selected. This message is more versatile than the WM_COMMAND message, as it is sent even if the menu item is grayed. Normally, this message is used for warning messages. The messages are documented in Chapter 9, *Window Messages*.

Menu Function Summary

Table 4-2 summarizes the menu support functions. The detailed function descriptions follow immediately after the table.

Function	Purpose
AppendMenu	Adds a new menu item to the end of a menu.
CheckMenuItem	Checks or unchecks a menu item.
CreatePopupMenu	Creates a popup menu
CreateMenu	Create a new, empty menu.
DeleteMenu	Removes an item from a menu.
DestroyMenu	Removes a menu from memory.
DrawMenuBar	Forces a window's menu bar to be repainted.
EnableMenuItem	Changes a menu item to/from enabled and grayed.
GetMenu	Retrieves a handle to a window's menu.
GetMenuCheckMarkDimensions	Retrieves the size and width of the bitmap used to create checkmarks next to menu items.
GetMenuItemCount	Gets the number of menu items in a menu.
GetMenuItemID	Retrieves the ID value associated with a menu item.
GetMenuState	Finds the number of items in a menu, or the status of an item.
GetMenuString	Retrieves the label displayed in a menu item.
GetSubMenu	Retrieves a handle to a popup menu.
GetSystemMenu	Retrieves a handle to the system menu.
HiliteMenuItem	Highlights a top-level menu item.
InsertMenu	Inserts a new menu item into an existing menu.

Table 4-2. continued

Function	Purpose	⊠
LoadMenu	Retrieves a handle to a menu defined in the resource .RC file.	
ModifyMenu	Changes the properties of a menu item.	
RemoveMenu	Removes a menu item from a menu.	
SetMenu	Attaches a menu to a window.	
SetMenuItemBitmaps	Replaces the default menu checkmark bitmap with a custom bitmap.	
TrackPopupMenu	Displays a submenu anywhere on the screen.	

Table 4-2. Menu Function Summary.

APPENDMENU   □ Win 2.0   ■ Win 3.0   ■ Win 3.1

Purpose   Adds a new menu item to the end of a menu.

Syntax   BOOL **AppendMenu**(HMENU *hMenu*, WORD *wFlags*, WORD *wIDNewItem*, LPSTR *lpNewItem*);

Description   Similar to InsertMenu(), except that AppendMenu() only adds menu items to the end of the menu.

Uses   Creating menus from within the body of the program, instead of building them in the resource file. Also useful in modifying existing menus.

Returns   BOOL. TRUE if the new menu item was added successfully, FALSE if not.

See Also   InsertMenu(), CreateMenu(), SetMenu(), DrawMenuBar()

Parameters

hMenu   HMENU: A handle to the menu being changed. Use GetMenu() to retrieve a window's menu handle.

wFlags   WORD: Specifies how the *wIDNewItem* and *lpNewItem* parameters are to be interpreted. These values can be combined using the C language binary OR operator (|)with any of the menu item control flags in Table 4-3.

Value	Meaning	⊠
MF_BITMAP	The menu item will be a bitmap. The low-order word of the *lpNewItem* parameter should contain a handle to the bitmap.	
MF_CHECKED	Places a checkmark next to the menu item.	
MF_DISABLED	Makes it impossible to select the menu item. Does not gray the menu item.	
MF_ENABLED	Makes it possible to select the menu item. This is the default.	
MF_GRAYED	Grays the menu item text and disables the menu item so that it cannot be selected.	
MF_MENUBARBREAK	In popup menus, it separates a new column of items and displays a separator bar between them. In main menus, it starts a new line of menu items.	
MF_MENUBREAK	In popup menu, it separates a new column of items. No separator bar is displayed. In main menus, it breaks the menu into a new line of menu items (two rows of menu items at the window's top).	
MF_OWNERREDRAW	Specifies that the parent window is to paint the menu item each time it is needed. This is not possible for the top menu line, but can be done for drop-down and popup menu items. The parent window will receive WM_MEASUREITEM and WM_DRAWITEM messages to update the drawing area.	
MF_POPUP	Specifies a popup menu. The *wIDNewItem* parameter will be a handle to the popup menu.	
MF_SEPARATOR	Draws a horizontal line in the menu. This line cannot be selected, checked, enabled, or grayed. The *lpNewItem* and *wIDNewItem* parameters are ignored.	

MF_STRING	Specifies that the new item is a character string. *lpNewItem* points to the string.
MF_UNCHECKED	Does not place a checkmark next to the menu item. This is the default.

Table 4-3. AppendMenu( ) Flags.

lpNewItem   LPSTR: Points to the contents of the new menu item. The type of data depends on the *wFlags* setting, as described in Table 4-4.

wFlags	lpNewItem	
MF_STRING	Long pointer to a character string.	
MF_BITMAP	A bitmap handle. The bitmap handle is stored in the low-order word of *lpNewItem*. Use LoadBitmap() to retrieve this value.	
MF_OWNERDRAW	You specify to what the 32-bit value *lpNewItem* points. Windows will send WM_MEASUREITEM and WM_DRAWITEM messages to the window's message processing function when the menu item needs to be redrawn. The value in the *lpNewItem* parameter will end up passed to the window's function as an element of the structures pointed to by the *lParam* value. See the example owner-drawn menu at the beginning of this chapter.	

Table 4-4. AppendMenu( ) Data Types.

Related Messages   WM_MEASUREITEM, WM_DRAWITEM

Example   Here the program does not have a menu specified in the resource .RC file. Instead, the menu is created when the program starts up. Figure 4-4 illustrates the following example.

Figure 4-4. AppendMenu( ) Example.

⇨ **The Program Header File**
```
/* genmenu.h    */
#define IDM_TOP1       1          /* menu item id values */
#define IDM_QUIT       2
#define IDM_POP1       6
#define IDM_POP2       7
#define IDM_HELP       8
        /* global variables */
int     ghInstance ;
char    gszAppName [] = "genmenu" ;
        /* function prototypes */
long FAR PASCAL WndProc (HWND, unsigned, WORD, LONG) ;
```

The Resource .RC File

Note that the two bitmaps which will be used in the menu are named here. Also note that no menu is defined, as it will be created within the program logic.

⇨ **Resource File**
```
/* genmenu.rc    */
#include <windows.h>
#include "genmenu.h"
genmenu        ICON     generic.ico

pen                     BITMAP       pen.bmp
cut                     BITMAP       cut.bmp
```

The WinProc( ) Function

The menu is created when the program starts execution (WM_CREATE message received). The main menu, and the popup menu containing the bitmaps, are created one item at a time. DrawMenuBar() is not required in this case, as the WM_CREATE message is processed before the window and menu bar are painted the first time.

```
long FAR PASCAL WndProc (HWND hWnd, unsigned iMessage, WORD wParam, LONG lParam)
{
        HMENU                   hMenu, hSubMenu ;
        static HBITMAP          hPenBm, hCutBm ;

        switch (iMessage)               /* process windows messages */
        {
                case WM_CREATE:         /* build the program's menu at startup */
                        hMenu = CreateMenu () ;
                        hSubMenu = CreatePopupMenu () ;
                        hPenBm = LoadBitmap (ghInstance, (LPSTR) "pen") ;
                        hCutBm = LoadBitmap (ghInstance, (LPSTR) "cut") ;
                        AppendMenu (hSubMenu, MF_BITMAP, IDM_POP1,
                                (LPSTR)(LONG)hPenBm) ;
                        AppendMenu (hSubMenu, MF_BITMAP, IDM_POP2,
                                (LPSTR)(LONG)hCutBm) ;
                        AppendMenu (hMenu, MF_POPUP, hSubMenu,
                                (LPSTR) "&Tools") ;
                        AppendMenu (hMenu, MF_STRING, IDM_QUIT,
                                (LPSTR) "&Quit") ;
                        AppendMenu (hMenu, MF_STRING, IDM_HELP,
                                (LPSTR) "&Help") ;
                        SetMenu (hWnd, hMenu) ;
                        break ;
                case WM_COMMAND:                /* process menu items */
                        switch (wParam)
                        {
                        case IDM_POP1:          /* Prove that bitmap menu item works! */
                                MessageBox (hWnd, "The pen tool was selected",
                                        "Message", MB_OK) ;
                                break ;
                        case IDM_POP2:
                                MessageBox (hWnd, "The cut tool was selected",
                                        "Message", MB_OK) ;
                                break ;
                        case IDM_QUIT:
                                DestroyWindow (hWnd) ;
                                break ;
                        }
                        break ;
                case WM_DESTROY:                                /* stop application */
                        DeleteObject (hPenBm) ;
                        DeleteObject (hCutBm) ;
                        PostQuitMessage (0) ;
                        break ;
                default:                        /* default windows message processing */
                        return DefWindowProc (hWnd, iMessage, wParam, lParam) ;
        }
        return (0L) ;
}
```

CHECKMENUITEM
■ Win 2.0   ■ Win 3.0   ■ Win 3.1

Purpose	Checks or unchecks a menu item.
Syntax	BOOL **CheckMenuItem**(HMENU *hMenu*, WORD *wIDCheckItem*, WORD *wCheck*);
Description	Works for both main menu items and popup menus.
Uses	Checkmarks generally are used to signify that an option has been turned on or off. For large numbers of options, use a dialog box with radio buttons for selections.
Returns	Returns the previous value of the item, MF_CHECKED or MF_UNCHECKED. Returns −1 on error.
See Also	GetMenuState(), EnableMenuItem(), ModifyMenu()
Parameters	
hMenu	HMENU: A handle to the menu. Use GetMenu() to retrieve a window's menu.

wIDCheckItem	WORD: The menu item number to be checked or unchecked.
wCheck	WORD: Specifies how the command is to be executed. Two of the following four possibilities, see Table 4-5, are always combined with a C language binary OR operator (|) to make the *wCheck* parameter.

Value	Meaning	⊠
MF_BYCOMMAND	The *nIDCheckItem* value is the menu item ID value.	
MF_BYPOSITION	The *nIDCheckItem* value is interpreted relative sequential numbering of existing menu items: 0 is the first item, 1 the second, etc.	
MF_CHECKED	Places a checkmark next to the menu item.	
MF_UNCHECKED	Does not place a checkmark next to the menu item.	

Table 4-5. CheckMenuItem( ) Flags.

Related Messages WM_MENUSELECT

Example Here the menu item IDM_OPT1 toggles between being checked and unchecked each time it is selected. Note that GetMenuState() is used to find the current menu item status (checked or unchecked).

```
Long FAR PASCAL WndProc (HWND hWnd, unsigned iMessage, WORD wParam, LONG lParam)
{
        HMENU           hMenu ;
        BOOL            bChecked ;

        switch (iMessage)                       /* process windows messages */
        {
        case WM_COMMAND:                        /* process menu items */
                switch (wParam)
                {
                case IDM_OPT1:
                        hMenu = GetMenu (hWnd) ;
                        bChecked = GetMenuState (hMenu, IDM_OPT1,
                                MF_BYCOMMAND) ;
                        if (bChecked & MF_CHECKED)
                                CheckMenuItem (hMenu, IDM_OPT1,
                                        MF_BYCOMMAND | MF_UNCHECKED) ;
                        else
                                CheckMenuItem (hMenu, IDM_OPT1,
                                        MF_BYCOMMAND | MF_CHECKED) ;
                        break ;
```

[Other program lines]

CREATEPOPUPMENU
☐ Win 2.0   ■ Win 3.0   ■ Win 3.1

Purpose	Creates an empty popup menu.
Syntax	HMENU **CreatePopupMenu**(void);
Description	Any menu other than the top menu bar is considered to be a popup menu. This function creates an empty popup menu, ready to have items added using AppendMenu() and InsertMenu().
Uses	Creating menus within the body of a program. Can be used with TrackPopupMenu() to create floating popup menus (menus not attached to other menus).
Returns	A handle to the menu created. NULL if a menu cannot be created.
See Also	CreateMenu(), AppendMenu(), InsertMenu()
Parameters	None (void).

Example   Here the program creates its menu on startup. The popup menu is created with two items, a text item "First Popup" and a bitmap "pen." The main menu is then created. The popup menu is added as the second item in the main menu. Finally, the completed menu is attached to the window with SetMenu().

```
Long FAR PASCAL WndProc (HWND hWnd, unsigned iMessage, WORD wParam, LONG lParam)
{
        HMENU           hMenu, hPopup ;
        HBITMAP         hBitmap ;
        switch (iMessage)                       /* process windows messages */
        {
                case WM_CREATE:
                        hPopup = CreatePopupMenu () ;
                        hBitmap = LoadBitmap (ghInstance, "pen") ;
                        AppendMenu (hPopup, MF_STRING, IDM_OPT1, "First Popup") ;
                        AppendMenu (hPopup, MF_BITMAP, IDM_OPT2,
                                (LPSTR) (LONG) hBitmap) ;
                        hMenu = CreateMenu () ;
                        AppendMenu (hMenu, MF_STRING, IDM_TOP1, "First Main") ;
                        AppendMenu (hMenu, MF_POPUP, hPopup, "Popup Item") ;
                        AppendMenu (hMenu, MF_STRING, IDM_QUIT, "Quit") ;
                        SetMenu (hWnd, hMenu) ;
                        break ;
```
[Other program lines]

CREATEMENU   ■ Win 2.0   ■ Win 3.0   ■ Win 3.1

Purpose	Creates a new, empty menu.
Syntax	HMENU **CreateMenu**(void);
Description	This is the first step in creating a menu within the body of an application program. Use AppendMenu() to add items to the menu, and use SetMenu() to attach the menu to a window.
Uses	Typically used to create menus for child windows. An alternative to defining all menus in the program's resource .RC file. Menus created with this function cannot be floating menus. Use CreatePopupMenu() to create floating menus.
Returns	HMENU, a handle to the menu created.
See Also	CreatePopupMenu(), AppendMenu(), SetMenu(), ModifyMenu()
Parameters	None (void).
Example	Here the program does not have a menu specified in the resource .RC file. Instead, the menu is created when the program starts. In this case, there are only two menu items. The IDM_TOP1 and IDM_QUIT values need to be defined in the header file for this example to function.

```
Long FAR PASCAL WndProc (HWND hWnd, unsigned iMessage, WORD wParam, LONG lParam)
{
        HMENU           hMenu ;
        switch (iMessage)                       /* process windows messages */
        {
                case WM_CREATE:
                        hMenu = CreateMenu() ;
                        AppendMenu (hMenu, MF_STRING, IDM_TOP1, "First Menu Item") ;
                        AppendMenu (hMenu, MF_STRING, IDM_QUIT, "Quit") ;
                        SetMenu (hWnd, hMenu) ;
                        break ;
                case WM_COMMAND:                /* process menu items */
                        switch (wParam)
                        {
                        case IDM_TOP1:          /* User hit the "Help" menu item */
                                MessageBox (hWnd, "The first menu item was clicked",
                                        "Message", MB_OK | MB_ICONASTERISK) ;
                                break ;
```
[Other program lines]

DELETEMENU

☐ Win 2.0   ■ Win 3.0   ■ Win 3.1

Purpose	Removes an item from a menu.
Syntax	BOOL **DeleteMenu**(HMENU *hMenu*, WORD *nPosition*, WORD *wFlags*);
Description	This function is poorly named, as it sounds like DestroyMenu(), which removes the entire menu from memory. DeleteMenu() only deletes a single menu item. If the menu item is a popup menu, the popup is destroyed, and its memory freed. Use DrawMenuBar() after this function to repaint the menu bar.
Uses	Small changes to menus as a program runs. This is an alternative to having more than one menu and switching between them.
Returns	BOOL. TRUE if the item was deleted, FALSE otherwise.
See Also	InsertMenu(), AppendMenu(), GetMenu(), DrawMenuBar()
Parameters	
hMenu	HMENU: A handle to the menu. Use GetMenu() to retrieve a window's menu.
nPosition	WORD: The menu item ID value.
wFlags	WORD: Specifies how the *nPosition* parameter is to be interpreted, as shown in Table 4-6.

Value	Meaning	⊠
MF_BYCOMMAND	The *nPosition* value is the menu item ID value.	
MF_BYPOSITION	The *nPosition* value is interpreted relative sequential numbering of existing menu items: 0 is the first item, 1 the second, etc.	

Table 4-6. DeleteMenu( ) Flags.

Example   Note that DrawMenuBar() is used immediately after DeleteMenu() to repaint the menu bar.

```
Long FAR PASCAL WndProc (HWND hWnd, unsigned iMessage, WORD wParam, LONG lParam)
{
        HMENU           hMenu ;

        switch (iMessage)                              /* process windows messages */
        {
                case WM_COMMAND:                       /* process menu items */
                        switch (wParam)
                        {
                        case IDM_TOP1:                 /* Delete a menu item */
                                hMenu = GetMenu (hWnd) ;
                                DeleteMenu (hMenu, IDM_TOP1, MF_BYCOMMAND) ;
                                DrawMenuBar (hWnd) ;
                                break ;
```

[Other program lines]

DESTROYMENU

■ Win 2.0   ■ Win 3.0   ■ Win 3.1

Purpose	Removes a menu from memory.
Syntax	BOOL **DestroyMenu**(HMENU *hMenu*);
Description	Removes menus created in the resource .RC file and those created within the body of a program with the CreateMenu() function.
Uses	Used with applications that have more than one menu. Only the menu attached to the application's window will be deleted when the application terminates. Any other menus will remain in memory. Use DestroyMenu() before the application terminates to free the memory consumed by the unattached menus.
Returns	BOOL. Non-zero if the menu was destroyed, NULL otherwise.

See Also   CreateMenu(), CreatePopupMenu(), GetMenu()

Parameters

hMenu   HMENU: A handle to the menu to remove. Use GetMenu() to find a window's menu.

Example   The resource .RC file contains two menus that are loaded as resources into the program. The "genmenu" menu is attached to the program's window in the WinMain() function. The second menu "genmenu2" is held in reserve until it is time to change menus.

```
/* genmenu.rc    */
#include <windows.h>
#include "genmenu.h"
genmenu        ICON    generic.ico
genmenu        MENU
BEGIN
      POPUP "&First Menu"
      BEGIN
            MENUITEM "&Top Item (Change Menu)",     IDM_TOP1
            MENUITEM "&1st Option",                 IDM_OPT1, GRAYED
            MENUITEM "&2nd Option",                 IDM_OPT2
      END
      MENUITEM "&Quit",                             IDM_QUIT
      MENUITEM "\a&Help",                           IDM_HELP, HELP
END
genmenu2       MENU
BEGIN
      POPUP "&Second Menu"
      BEGIN
            MENUITEM "&Revised Items",     IDM_TOP1
            MENUITEM "&1st Option",        IDM_OPT1
            MENUITEM "&2nd Option",        IDM_OPT2, GRAYED
            MENUITEM "&3rd Option",        IDM_OPT3
      END
      MENUITEM "&Quit",                             IDM_QUIT
      MENUITEM "\a&Help",                           IDM_HELP, HELP
END
```

Part of the WndProc() Function

Note that the old menu is destroyed only if the new menu is successfully added to the window with SetMenu().

```
long FAR PASCAL WndProc (HWND hWnd, unsigned iMessage, WORD wParam, LONG lParam)
{
      HMENU          hMenu1, hMenu2 ;
      BOOL           bStatus ;
      switch (iMessage)                         /* process windows messages */
      {
            case WM_COMMAND:                    /* process menu items */
                  switch (wParam)
                  {
                  case IDM_TOP1:                /* swap menus, destroy old one */
                        hMenu1 = GetMenu (hWnd) ;
                        hMenu2 = LoadMenu (ghInstance, "genmenu2") ;
                        bStatus = SetMenu (hWnd, hMenu2) ;
                        if (bStatus)
                              DestroyMenu (hMenu1) ;
                        else
                              MessageBox (hWnd, "Could not change menus.",

                                    "Warning", MB_OK | MB_ICONINFORMATION) ;
                        break ;
```

[Other program lines]

DrawMenuBar   ■ Win 2.0   ■ Win 3.0   ■ Win 3.1

Purpose   Forces repainting of the window's menu bar.

Syntax   void **DrawMenuBar**(HWND *hWnd*);

Description   The menu bar is not part of the client region of the window and, therefore, is not updated when you use UpdateWindow().

Uses   Use right after any change to the top-level menu.

Returns   No returned value (void).

See Also   DeleteMenu(), GetMenu()

Parameters
hWnd   HWND: A handle to the window which has the menu. Use GetMenu() to retrieve the window's menu handle.

Related Messages   WM_NCPAINT

Example

```
long FAR PASCAL WndProc (HWND hWnd, unsigned iMessage, WORD wParam, LONG lParam)
{
        HMENU           hMenu ;

        switch (iMessage)                               /* process windows messages */
        {
                case WM_COMMAND:                        /* process menu items */
                        switch (wParam)
                        {
                        case IDM_TOP1:                  /* Delete a menu item */

                                hMenu = GetMenu (hWnd) ;
                                DeleteMenu (hMenu, IDM_TOP1, MF_BYCOMMAND) ;

                                DrawMenuBar (hWnd) ;
                                break ;
```
[Other program lines]

ENABLEMENUITEM   ■ Win 2.0   ■ Win 3.0   ■ Win 3.1

Purpose   Changes a menu item to/from enabled and grayed.

Syntax   WORD **EnableMenuItem**(HMENU *hMenu*, WORD *wIDEnableItem*, WORD *wEnable*);

Description   Menu items are normally enabled, meaning that selecting a menu item causes a WM_COMMAND message to be sent to the window's message function. Menu items can be disabled, stopping the messages from being sent. Normally disabled menu items are shown in gray text so that the user can easily see which commands function.

Uses   Some menu actions may not be possible under all situations in a program. For example, it should not be possible to paste data if no data has been cut or copied into the clipboard. In these situations, it is best to disable and gray the menu items that have no function, so that the user intuitively knows that certain actions are not possible.

Returns   WORD holding the previous state of the menu item (MF_GRAYED, etc.). −1 is returned if the menu or menu item does not exist.

See Also   GetMenuState(), ModifyMenu(), GetMenu()

Parameters
hMenu   HMENU: A handle to the menu. Use GetMenu() to retrieve a window's menu.

wIDEnableItem   WORD: The menu item number to change.

wEnable   WORD: The action to take, and how *wIDEnableItem* is to be interpreted. The values shown in Table 4-7 can be combined with the C language binary OR (|) operator.

Value	Meaning
MF_BYCOMMAND	The *nIDEnableItem* value is the menu item ID value.
MF_BYPOSITION	The *nIDEnableItem* value is interpreted relative sequential numbering of the menu items: 0 is the first item, 1 the second, etc.
MF_DISABLED	The menu item is disabled.
MF_ENABLED	The menu item is enabled (and not grayed).
MF_GRAYED	The menu item is grayed.

Table 4-7. EnableMenuItem( ) Flags.

Related Messages WM_COMMAND

Example This example's window has a menu with one drop-down popup menu. The second item on the drop-down menu (IDM_OPT1) alternately disables and enables the third menu item (IDM_OPT2). When disabled, the menu item is also grayed. Here is the resource file. Note that the menu items all start enabled, the default condition.

```
/* genmenu.rc   */
#include <windows.h>
#include "genmenu.h"
genmenu          ICON    generic.ico

genmenu          MENU
BEGIN
        POPUP "&First Menu"
        BEGIN
                MENUITEM "&Top Item",         IDM_TOP1
                MENUITEM "&Disable 2nd",      IDM_OPT1
                MENUITEM SEPARATOR
                MENUITEM "&2nd Option",       IDM_OPT2
        END
   MENUITEM "&Quit",                          IDM_QUIT
END
```

The following code is the first part of the WndProc() function. GetMenuState() is used to find out whether the IDM_OPT2 menu item is currently enabled. If so, EnableMenuItem() is used to disable it. Also, the IDM_OPT1 menu item text is changed with ModifyMenu() to switch between "Enable 2nd" and "Disable 2nd" as appropriate.

```
long FAR PASCAL WndProc (HWND hWnd, unsigned iMessage, WORD wParam,  LONG lParam)
{
        HMENU   hMenu ;
        WORD    wStatus ;

        switch (iMessage)                      /* process windows messages */
        {
                case WM_COMMAND:               /* process menu items */
                        switch (wParam)
                        {
                        case IDM_OPT1:  /* Toggle menu item enable/disable */
                                hMenu = GetMenu (hWnd) ;
                                wStatus = GetMenuState (hMenu, IDM_OPT2,
                                        MF_BYCOMMAND) ;
                                if (wStatus == MF_ENABLED)
                                {
                                        EnableMenuItem (hMenu, IDM_OPT2,
                                                MF_DISABLED | MF_GRAYED |
                                                MF_BYCOMMAND) ;
                                        ModifyMenu (hMenu, IDM_OPT1,
                                                MF_BYCOMMAND | MF_STRING,
                                                IDM_OPT1, "Enable 2nd") ;
                                }
```

```
                              else
                              {
                                  EnableMenuItem (hMenu, IDM_OPT2,
                                          MF_ENABLED | MF_BYCOMMAND) ;
                                  ModifyMenu (hMenu, IDM_OPT1,
                                          MF_BYCOMMAND | MF_STRING,
                                          IDM_OPT1, "Disable 2nd") ;
                              }
                              break ;
```

[Other program lines]

GET MENU   ■ Win 2.0   ■ Win 3.0   ■ Win 3.1

Purpose	Retrieves a handle to a window's menu.
Syntax	HMENU **GetMenu**(HWND *hWnd*);
Uses	Used prior to modifying or destroying the menu. This function will not return a valid handle for child windows with menus.
Returns	HMENU, a handle to the menu. NULL if the window does not have a menu.
See Also	SetMenu(), AppendMenu(), DeleteMenu(), DestroyMenu(), InsertMenu(), ModifyMenu(), RemoveMenu,
Parameters	
hWnd	HWND: A handle to the window that has the menu.
Example	This example deletes the IDM_TOP1 menu item when it is selected.

```
Long FAR PASCAL WndProc (HWND hWnd, unsigned iMessage, WORD wParam, LONG lParam)
{
        HMENU            hMenu ;

        switch (iMessage)                                /* process windows messages */
        {
              case WM_COMMAND:                           /* process menu items */
                    switch (wParam)
                    {
                    case IDM_TOP1:                        /* Delete a menu item */
                          hMenu = GetMenu (hWnd) ;
                          DeleteMenu (hMenu, IDM_TOP1, MF_BYCOMMAND) ;
                          DrawMenuBar (hWnd) ;
                          break ;
```

[Other program lines]

GET MENU CHECK MARK DIMENSIONS   □ Win 2.0   ■ Win 3.0   ■ Win 3.1

Purpose	Retrieves the size and width of the bitmap used to create checkmarks next to menu items.
Syntax	DWORD **GetMenuCheckMarkDimensions**(void);
Description	Windows uses a default checkmark bitmap to check menu items. This can be replaced with custom bitmaps using the SetMenuItemBitmaps() function. GetMenuCheckMarkDimensions() is used to find the size of the bitmap to use for custom checkmarks.
Uses	Custom checkmarks can dress up an application program, with little penalty in memory consumption. As soon as the new bitmap is assigned to the menu item, the CheckMenuItem() function will automatically use this bitmap when checking or unchecking an item.
Returns	DWORD, the HIWORD contains the bitmap height in pixels, the LOWORD contains the bitmap width in pixels.
See Also	SetMenuItemBitmaps(), CheckMenuItem()

Parameters   None (void).

Example   In this example, a bitmap called "pen" is to be used as the checkmark for the IDM_OPT1 menu item. As the program does not know in advance how big the menu checkmarks are going to be (this depends on the video display resolution), the bitmap must be sized to fit the dimensions found when the program starts running. Size the bitmap by copying the bitmap from one device context to another using the StretchBlt() function. The resource .RC file loads the "pen" bitmap.

```
/* genmenu.rc                  */

#include <windows.h>
#include "genmenu.h"
genmenu       ICON          generic.ico
pen           BITMAP        smallpen.bmp
genmenu       MENU
BEGIN
        POPUP "&First Menu"
        BEGIN
                MENUITEM "&Top Item",       IDM_TOP1
                MENUITEM "&Check Me!",       IDM_OPT1
                MENUITEM SEPARATOR
                MENUITEM "&2nd Option",      IDM_OPT2
        END
    MENUITEM "&Quit",                        IDM_QUIT
END
```

The new menu item bitmap is sized and loaded when the WM_CREATE message is received at program startup. In this simple example, the IDM_OPT1 menu item just toggles between being checked with the "pen" bitmap, and being unchecked.

```
long FAR PASCAL WndProc (HWND hWnd, unsigned iMessage, WORD wParam, LONG lParam)
{
        HMENU           hMenu ;
        DWORD           dwCheckSize ;
        HDC             hDC, hSourceDC, hDestDC ;
        static HBITMAP  hPenBitmap ;
        HBITMAP         hMemBitmap ;
        BITMAP          bm ;
        int             nBx, nBy ;
        BOOL            bChecked ;

        switch (iMessage)                       /* process windows messages */
        {
                case WM_CREATE:
                                        /* find out how big the checkmarks are */
                        hMenu = GetMenu (hWnd) ;
                        dwCheckSize = GetMenuCheckMarkDimensions () ;
                        nBx = LOWORD (dwCheckSize) ;
                        nBy = HIWORD (dwCheckSize) ;
                                        /* load a bitmap into a device context */
                        hDC = GetDC (hWnd) ;
                        hSourceDC = CreateCompatibleDC (hDC) ;
                        hPenBitmap = LoadBitmap (ghInstance, "pen") ;
                        SelectObject (hSourceDC, hPenBitmap) ;
                        GetObject (hPenBitmap, sizeof (BITMAP), (LPSTR) &bm) ;
                                        /* create a second DC for scaled bitmap */
                        hDestDC = CreateCompatibleDC (hDC) ;
                        hMemBitmap = CreateCompatibleBitmap (hDestDC, nBx, nBy) ;
                        SelectObject (hDestDC, hMemBitmap) ;
                                        /* fit the bitmap into the menu sized DC */
                        StretchBlt (hDestDC, 0, 0, nBx, nBy, hSourceDC, 0, 0,
                                bm.bmWidth, bm.bmHeight, SRCCOPY) ;
                                        /* attach the sized bitmap to the menu item */
                        SetMenuItemBitmaps (hMenu, IDM_OPT1, MF_BYCOMMAND, NULL,
                                hMemBitmap) ;
                                        /* release unneeded memory consumers */
```

```
                        ReleaseDC (hWnd, hDC) ;
                        DeleteDC (hSourceDC) ;
                        DeleteDC (hDestDC) ;
                        DeleteObject (hPenBitmap) ;
                        break ;
        case WM_COMMAND:                 /* process menu items */
                switch (wParam)
                {
                case IDM_OPT1:           /* Toggle menu item  checked/unchecked */
                        hMenu = GetMenu (hWnd) ;
                        bChecked = GetMenuState (hMenu, IDM_OPT1,
                                MF_BYCOMMAND) ;
                        if (bChecked & MF_CHECKED)
                                CheckMenuItem (hMenu, IDM_OPT1,
                                        MF_BYCOMMAND | MF_UNCHECKED) ;
                        else
                                CheckMenuItem (hMenu, IDM_OPT1,
                                        MF_BYCOMMAND | MF_CHECKED) ;
                        break ;
                case IDM_QUIT:
                        DestroyWindow (hWnd) ;
                        break ;
                }
                break ;
        case WM_DESTROY:/* stop application */
                DeleteObject (hPenBitmap) ;
                PostQuitMessage (0) ;
                break ;
        default:                         /* default windows message processing */
                return DefWindowProc (hWnd, iMessage, wParam, lParam) ;
        }
        return (0L) ;
}
```

GETMENUITEMCOUNT   ■ Win 2.0   ■ Win 3.0   ■ Win 3.1

Purpose	Gets the number of menu items in a menu.
Syntax	WORD **GetMenuItemCount**(HMENU *hMenu*);
Description	GetMenuItemCount() counts the number of menu items. This includes the top-level heading of any popup menus, but does not include the popup items themselves.
Uses	Used to find out how many menu items there are, prior to retrieving data on the menu items such as their ID numbers, strings, etc.
Returns	WORD, the number of menu items. Returns –1 on error.
See Also	GetMenu(), GetMenuItemID(), GetMenuState(), GetMenuString()
Parameters	
hMenu	HMENU: A handle to the menu. Use GetMenu() to find a window's menu handle.

Figure 4-5. GetMenu-
ItemCount() Example.

Example   This example uses several menu functions to determine the number, IDs, status, and menu strings associated with the program's main menu. After execution of the first popup menu selection under "First Menu," the window looks like Figure 4-5.

      Note that the string "First Menu" is a popup menu name, so it does not have a selectable ID value (shown as –1). The "Quit" option is selectable, with an ID value of 2. The popup menu items are not displayed and must be separately examined using GetSubMenu(). Also note that the ampersand characters used to define the (ALT)-key combinations are extracted with GetMenuString().

⇨ The Resource File

```
/* genmenu.rc    */
#include <windows.h>
#include "genmenu.h"
genmenu        ICON    generic.ico
genmenu        MENU
BEGIN
      POPUP "&First Menu"
      BEGIN
              MENUITEM "&Display Items",      IDM_TOP1
              MENUITEM "&1st Option",         IDM_OPT1
              MENUITEM SEPARATOR
              MENUITEM "&2nd Option",         IDM_OPT2
      END
   MENUITEM "&Quit",                          IDM_QUIT
END
```

⇨ The Top of the WndProc( ) Function

```
Long FAR PASCAL WndProc (HWND hWnd, unsigned iMessage, WORD wParam, LONG lParam)
{
        HMENU           hMenu ;
        HDC             hDC ;
        char            cBuf [128], cNumBuf [10] ;
        int             i, nItems, nValue, nChecked, nChars ;

        switch (iMessage)                               /* process windows messages */
        {
                case WM_COMMAND:                        /* process menu items */
                        switch (wParam)
                        {
                        case IDM_TOP1:                  /* Show menu item attributes */
                                hDC = GetDC (hWnd) ;
                                hMenu = GetMenu (hWnd) ;
                                nItems = GetMenuItemCount (hMenu) ;
                                TextOut (hDC, 0, 0, "ID  Checked  String", 19) ;
                                for (i = 0 ; i < nItems ; i++)
                                {
                                        nValue = GetMenuItemID (hMenu, i) ;
                                        nChecked = GetMenuState (hMenu, i,
                                                MF_BYPOSITION | MF_CHECKED) ;
                                        nChars = GetMenuString (hMenu, i, cBuf, 127,
                                                MF_BYPOSITION) ;

                                        itoa (nValue, cNumBuf, 10) ;
                                        TextOut (hDC, 10, 15 + (i * 15), cNumBuf,
                                                strlen (cNumBuf)) ;
                                        if (nChecked == MF_CHECKED)
                                                TextOut (hDC, 30, 15 + (i * 15),
                                                        "Checked", 7) ;
                                        else
                                                TextOut (hDC, 30, 15 + (i * 15),
                                                        "Unchecked", 9) ;
                                        TextOut (hDC, 150, 15 + (i * 15), cBuf, nChars) ;

                                }
                                ReleaseDC (hWnd, hDC) ;
                                break ;
```

[Other program lines]

GETMENUITEMID   ■ Win 2.0   ■ Win 3.0   ■ Win 3.1

Purpose	Retrieves the ID value associated with a menu item.
Syntax	WORD **GetMenuItemID**(HMENU *hMenu*, int *nPos*);
Description	The menu ID values are associated with each item when the menu is defined, either in the resource .RC file or when the menu items are added during program execution with the AppendMenu() and InsertMenu() functions.

Uses	ID values remain constant, even as other menu items are added and deleted. Retrieving the menu item IDs can be useful in programs which allow the user to add and subtract custom menu items such as macro names.

Returns WORD, the ID value for the menu item at position *nPos*. –1 on error.

See Also GetMenuItemCount(), GetMenuState(), GetMenuString().

Parameters
hMenu HMENU: A handle to the menu. Use GetMenu() to retrieve a handle to a window's menu. Use GetSubMenu() to retrieve a handle to a popup menu.

Example See the previous example under the GetMenuItemCount() function description.

GETMENUSTATE   ■ Win 2.0   ■ Win 3.0   ■ Win 3.1

Purpose Finds the number of items in a menu or the status of an item.

Syntax WORD **GetMenuState**(HMENU *hMenu*, WORD *wID*, WORD *wFlags*);

Uses Most often used to determine if a menu item is checked, grayed, or disabled.

Returns WORD. Returns –1 on error. If *wID* identifies a pupup menu, the high-order byte contains the number of items in the popup menu. The low-order byte contains a combination of the flags shown in Table 4-8, logically ORed together.

Value	Meaning	☒
MF_CHECKED	There is a checkmark next to the menu item.	
MF_DISABLED	The menu item is disabled and cannot be selected.	
MF_ENABLED	The menu item is enabled, so it can be selected.	
MF_GRAYED	The menu item text is grayed and disabled so that it cannot be selected.	
MF_MENUBARBREAK	In popup menus, it separates a new column of items and displays a separator bar between them. In normal menus, it starts a new line of menu items.	
MF_MENUBREAK	In popup menus, it separates a new column of items. No separator bar is displayed. In normal menus, it breaks the menu into a new line of menu items (two rows of menu items at the window's top).	
MF_SEPARATOR	A horizontal line in the menu.	
MF_UNCHECKED	No checkmark next to the menu item.	

Table 4-8. GetMenuState() Return Flags.

See Also CheckMenuItem(), GetMenu()

Parameters
hMenu HMENU: A handle to the menu. Use GetMenu() to obtain a window's menu.
wID WORD: The menu item ID value.
wFlags WORD: Specifies how the *wID* is to be interpreted, as shown in Table 4-9.

Value	Meaning	☒
MF_BYCOMMAND	The *wID* value is the menu item ID value.	
MF_BYPOSITION	The *wID* value is interpreted relative sequential numbering of existing menu items: 0 is the first item, 1 the second, etc.	

Table 4-9. GetMenuState() wFlags Settings.

Example   Here the menu item IDM_OPT1 toggles between being checked and unchecked each time it is selected. Note that GetMenuState() is used to find the current menu item status (checked or unchecked).

```
Long FAR PASCAL WndProc (HWND hWnd, unsigned iMessage, WORD wParam, LONG lParam)
{
        HMENU           hMenu ;
        BOOL            bChecked ;

        switch (iMessage)                       /* process windows messages */
        {
                case WM_COMMAND:                /* process menu items */
                        switch (wParam)
                        {
                        case IDM_OPT1:
                                hMenu = GetMenu (hWnd) ;
                                bChecked = GetMenuState (hMenu, IDM_OPT1,
                                        MF_BYCOMMAND) ;
                                if (bChecked & MF_CHECKED)
                                        CheckMenuItem (hMenu, IDM_OPT1,
                                                MF_BYCOMMAND | MF_UNCHECKED) ;
                                else
                                        CheckMenuItem (hMenu, IDM_OPT1,
                                                MF_BYCOMMAND | MF_CHECKED) ;
                                break ;
```

[Other program lines]

GETMENUSTRING   ■ Win 2.0   ■ Win 3.0   ■ Win 3.1

Purpose	Retrieves the label displayed in a menu item.
Syntax	int **GetMenuString**(HMENU *hMenu*, WORD *wIDItem*, LPSTR *lpString*, int *nMaxCount*, WORD *wFlag*);
Description	The menu item's string, including the ampersand (&) character used to specify the accelerator key, is retrieved into a character buffer.
Uses	Handy in programs that allow the user to add and subtract menu items for user-defined functions such as macros.
Returns	int, the number of characters retrieved.
See Also	GetMenu(), GetMenuItemCount(), GetMenuItemID(), GetMenuState(), GetSubMenu()
Parameters	
hMenu	HMENU: A handle to the menu. Use GetMenu() to obtain a window's menu.
wIDItem	WORD: The menu item ID value.
lpString	LPSTRING: A pointer to the character buffer that will hold the menu item string.
nMaxCount	int: The maximum number of characters to write to the buffer. Use this parameter to avoid writing beyond the buffer's end.
wFlags	WORD: Specifies how the *wIDItem* is to be interpreted, as shown in Table 4-10.

Value	Meaning ⊠
MF_BYCOMMAND	The *nIDItem* value is the menu item ID value.
MF_BYPOSITION	The *nIDItem* value is interpreted relative to the sequential numbering of existing menu items: 0 is the first item, 1 the second, etc.

Table 4-10. GetMenuString( ) wFlags Settings.

Example   See the example under the GetMenuItemCount() function description.

GETSUBMENU
■ Win 2.0   ■ Win 3.0   ■ Win 3.1

Purpose   Retrieves a handle to a popup menu.

Syntax   HMENU **GetSubMenu**(HMENU *hMenu*, int *nPos*);

Description   A handle to a popup menu can only be found after the handle to the main menu is located, usually with GetMenu(). When the popup menu handle is obtained, all of the functions that allow reading and changing menu items can be applied to the popup menu.

Uses   In programs that change the elements of popup menus.

Returns   HMENU, a handle to the popup menu. Returns NULL on error, such as *nPos* not referring to a popup menu.

See Also   GetMenu(), GetMenuItemCount(), GetMenuItemID(), GetMenuItemState(), GetMenuItemString(), AppendMenu(), ModifyMenu()

Parameters

hMenu   HMENU: A handle to the parent menu of the popup menu.

nPos   int: The position of the popup menu in the main menu: 0 for the first, 1 for the second, etc. Because popup menus do not have ID values associated with them, it is not possible to retrieve the menu handle based on an ID.

Example   Here the program examines the first popup menu, and shows each of the popup menu items on the screen. Note that the third item in the popup menu is a separator bar. This has an ID of 0. The MF_SEPARATOR status for this item could have been detected using the GetMenuState() function. Figure 4-6 illustrates the example.

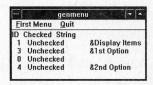

Figure 4-6. GetSubMenu() Example.

The following code represents the resource .RC file that defines the menu structure, including the popup menu.

```
/* genmenu.rc */
#include <windows.h>
#include "genmenu.h"
genmenu        ICON    generic.ico
genmenu        MENU
BEGIN

      POPUP "&First Menu"
      BEGIN
            MENUITEM "&Display Items",      IDM_TOP1
            MENUITEM "&1st Option",         IDM_OPT1
            MENUITEM SEPARATOR
            MENUITEM "&2nd Option",         IDM_OPT2
      END
   MENUITEM "&Quit",                        IDM_QUIT
END
```

The following code represents the top of the WinMain() function. Note that the submenu is retrieved after the main menu is found using GetMenu().

```
long FAR PASCAL WndProc (HWND hWnd, unsigned iMessage, WORD wParam, LONG lParam)
{
      HMENU          hMenu, hSubMenu ;
      HDC            hDC ;
      char           cBuf [128], cNumBuf [10] ;
      int            i, nItems, nValue, nChecked, nChars ;

      switch (iMessage)                            /* process windows messages */
      {
            case WM_COMMAND:                       /* process menu items */
                  switch (wParam)
```

```
                                {
                                case IDM_TOP1:                          /* Show menu item attributes */
                                        hDC = GetDC (hWnd) ;
                                        hMenu = GetMenu (hWnd) ;
                                        hSubMenu = GetSubMenu (hMenu, 0) ;
                                        nItems = GetMenuItemCount (hSubMenu) ;
                                        TextOut (hDC, 0, 0, "ID  Checked  String", 19) ;
                                        for (i = 0 ; i < nItems ; i++)
                                        {
                                                nValue = GetMenuItemID (hSubMenu, i) ;
                                                nChecked = GetMenuState (hSubMenu, i,
                                                        MF_BYPOSITION | MF_CHECKED) ;
                                                nChars = GetMenuString (hSubMenu, i,
                                                        cBuf, 127, MF_BYPOSITION) ;
                                                itoa (nValue, cNumBuf, 10) ;
                                                TextOut (hDC, 10, 15 + (i * 15), cNumBuf,
                                                        strlen (cNumBuf)) ;
                                                if (nChecked == MF_CHECKED)
                                                        TextOut (hDC, 30, 15 + (i * 15),
                                                                "Checked", 7) ;
                                                else
                                                        TextOut (hDC, 30, 15 + (i * 15),
                                                                "Unchecked", 9) ;
                                                TextOut (hDC, 150, 15 + (i * 15),
                                                        cBuf, nChars) ;
                                        }
                                        ReleaseDC (hWnd, hDC) ;
                                        break ;
```

[Other program lines]

GETSYSTEMMENU   ■ Win 2.0   ■ Win 3.0   ■ Win 3.1

Purpose	Retrieves a handle to the system menu.
Syntax	HMENU **GetSystemMenu**(HWND *hWnd*, BOOL *bRevert*);
Description	The system menu is the popup menu that is displayed when you click the button at the top left corner of the program's main window. The system menu generates WM_SYSCOMMAND messages, not WM_COMMAND messages. When a menu item on the system menu is activated, the WM_SYSCOMMAND messages have the *wParam* parameter set as shown in Table 4-11.

System Menu Item	Sends WM_SYSCOMMAND with wParam Set To	⊠
Restore	SC_RESTORE	
Move	SC_MOVE	
Size	SC_SIZE	
Minimize	SC_MINIMUM	
Maximize	SC_MAXIMUM	
Close	SC_CLOSE	
Switch To	SC_TASKLIST	

Table 4-11. WM_SYSCOMMAND Message wParam Values.

You can also modify and add to the system menu using all of the menu modification commands, such as AppendMenu() and InsertMenu(). If you add menu items, their ID values should be below 0xF000 to avoid overlapping the definitions of the default ID values listed above.

Uses	Modifying the system menu is appropriate for small utility programs that may be able to avoid having a menu bar if a few commands are added to the system menu.
Returns	HMENU, a handle to the system menu.

See Also	AppendMenu(), InsertMenu(), ModifyMenu()

Parameters

hWnd   HWND: A handle to the window which contains the system menu.

bRevert   BOOL: If TRUE, the function destroys the current system menu and returns a handle to a new copy of the original system menu. If FALSE (zero), the function returns a handle to the current system menu, retaining any changes.

Related Messages   WM_SYSCOMMAND, WM_INITMENU

Comments   In processing the WM_SYSCOMMAND messages for the default system menu items, it is critical to pass the WM_SYSCOMMAND message on to the default window's message processing function DefWindowProc(). Otherwise the program will stop functioning. The example shows this message pass-through.

Example   Here a single menu item is added to the bottom of the system menu, called "Added Item." When this item is clicked, the WM_SYSCOMMAND message is caught and some text written to the window's client area. Note how the message logic passes any other WM_SYSCOMMAND message straight through to DefWindowProc(), to avoid hanging the program.

```
long FAR PASCAL WndProc (HWND hWnd, unsigned iMessage, WORD wParam, LONG lParam)
{
        HMENU          hSysMenu ;
        HDC            hDC ;

        switch (iMessage)                          /* process windows messages */
        {
                case WM_CREATE:
                        hSysMenu = GetSystemMenu (hWnd, 0) ;
                        AppendMenu (hSysMenu, MF_STRING, IDM_SYSTYPE, "Added Item") ;
                        break ;
                case WM_COMMAND:                    /* process menu items */
                        switch (wParam)
                        {
                        case IDM_QUIT:
                                DestroyWindow (hWnd) ;
                                break ;
                        }
                        break ;
                case WM_DESTROY:                            /* stop application */
                        PostQuitMessage (0) ;
                        break ;
                case WM_SYSCOMMAND:
                        if (wParam == IDM_SYSTYPE)/* added system menu item */
                        {
                                hDC = GetDC (hWnd) ;
                                TextOut (hDC, 10, 10,
                                        "The new system menu item was hit.",    33) ;
                                ReleaseDC (hWnd, hDC) ;
                                return (0) ;
                        }                       /* no break statement here */
                default:                        /* default windows message processing */
                        return DefWindowProc (hWnd, iMessage, wParam, lParam) ;
        }
        return (0L) ;
}
```

HILITEMENUITEM   ■ Win 2.0   ■ Win 3.0   ■ Win 3.1

Purpose	Highlights a top-level menu item.
Syntax	BOOL **HiliteMenuItem**(HWND *hWnd*, HMENU *hMenu*, WORD *wIDHiliteItem*, WORD *wHilite*);
Description	Normally, the mouse and default keyboard accelerator key's automatic actions take care of highlighting top-level menu items. If you need to do this directly, you can use HiliteMenuItem().

Uses	Seldom used. Can be used to provide additional keyboard functionality for menu selections (see example).
Returns	BOOL. TRUE if the item was highlighted, FALSE on error.
See Also	CheckMenuItem(), EnableMenuItem()

Parameters

hWnd	HWND: A handle to the program's window.
hMenu	HMENU: A handle to the program's menu. Use GetMenu() to retrieve this handle.
wIDHiliteItem	WORD: The menu item number to change. Only top-level menu items may be changed.
wHilite	WORD: Flags to set how the *wIDHiliteItem* parameter is interpreted and whether to highlight or unhighlight the menu item. Combine two of the values in Table 4-12 with the C language OR operator (I).

Value	Meaning	⊠
MF_BYCOMMAND	The *nIDHiliteItem* value is the menu item ID value.	
MF_BYPOSITION	The *nIDHiliteItem* value is interpreted relative to the sequential numbering of existing menu items: 0 is the first item, 1 the second, etc.	
MF_HILITE	Highlight the menu item.	
MF_UNHILITE	Remove highlighting from the menu item.	

Table 4-12. HiliteMenuItem( ) Flags.

Example   This example implements a simple keyboard interface for a two-item menu. If the user hits the left or right arrow keys, one of the menu items is highlighted. Hitting the return key selects the highlighted menu item. The only two actions in this case are to display a message box or to exit the program.

▷ **The Resource .RC file**

```
/* genmenu.rc          jim conger 1991 */
#include <windows.h>
#include "genmenu.h"
genmenu         ICON    generic.ico
genmenu         MENU
BEGIN
      MENUITEM "&1st Option",         IDM_TOP1
      MENUITEM "&Quit",               IDM_QUIT
END
```

The following code represents the WndProc() function. Note that the return key action is implemented by sending the same message that would have been received if a mouse click had selected the item (WM_COMMAND). This allows the same logic to perform the functions, regardless if a mouse or keyboard is used.

```
long FAR PASCAL WndProc (HWND hWnd, unsigned iMessage, WORD wParam, LONG lParam)
{
        HMENU           hMenu ;
        static int      nSide = 0 ;

        switch (iMessage)                       /* process windows messages */
        {
                case WM_COMMAND:                /* process menu items */
                        switch (wParam)
                        {
                        case IDM_TOP1:
                                MessageBox (hWnd, "First menu item was hit",
                                        "Message", MB_OK) ;
```

```
                                break ;

                        case IDM_QUIT:
                                DestroyWindow (hWnd) ;
                                break ;
                        }
                        break ;
                case WM_DESTROY:                    /* stop application */
                        PostQuitMessage (0) ;
                        break ;
                case WM_KEYDOWN:
                        switch (wParam)
                        {
                        case VK_LEFT:            /* left arrow key, so hilite "top1" */
                                hMenu = GetMenu(hWnd) ;
                                HiliteMenuItem (hWnd, hMenu, 0,
                                        MF_BYPOSITION | MF_HILITE) ;
                                HiliteMenuItem (hWnd, hMenu, 1,
                                        MF_BYPOSITION | MF_UNHILITE) ;
                                DrawMenuBar (hWnd) ;
                                nSide = 0 ;
                                break ;

                        case VK_RIGHT:           /* right arrow key, so hilite "Quit" */
                                hMenu = GetMenu(hWnd) ;
                                HiliteMenuItem (hWnd, hMenu, 0,
                                        MF_BYPOSITION | MF_UNHILITE) ;
                                HiliteMenuItem (hWnd, hMenu, 1,
                                        MF_BYPOSITION | MF_HILITE) ;
                                DrawMenuBar (hWnd) ;
                                nSide = 1 ;
                                break ;
                        case VK_RETURN:          /* simulate mouse select of menu item */
                                if (nSide)
                                        SendMessage (hWnd, WM_COMMAND, IDM_QUIT, 0L) ;
                                else
                                        SendMessage (hWnd, WM_COMMAND, IDM_TOP1, 0L) ;
                        }
                        break ;
                default:                     /* default windows message processing */
                        return DefWindowProc (hWnd, iMessage, wParam, lParam) ;
        }
        return (0L) ;
}
```

INSERTMENU

□ Win 2.0 ■ Win 3.0 ■ Win 3.1

Purpose	Inserts a new menu item into an existing menu.
Syntax	BOOL **InsertMenu**(HMENU *hMenu*, WORD *nPosition*, WORD *wFlags*, WORD *wIDNewItem*, LPSTR *lpNewItem*);
Description	Adds a new item into any location within a menu. This is more useful than AppendMenu(), which only adds items to the end of the menu.
Uses	Ideal for adding bitmap menu items
Returns	BOOL. TRUE if the item was successfully added, FALSE if not.
See Also	AppendMenu(), ChangeMenu(), CreateMenu(), DrawMenuBar()
Parameters	
hMenu	HMENU: A handle to the menu being changed. Use GetMenu() to retrieve a window's menu handle.
nPosition	WORD: The menu item number in front of which the new item will be inserted. The *wFlags* parameter will either contain the MF_BYPOSITION or MF_BYCOMMAND flag, specifying how the *nPosition* value is to be interpreted.

wFlags	WORD: Specifies how the *nPosition* parameter is to be interpreted in positioning the new menu item. Also sets the status of the new menu item. These values can be combined using the C language binary OR operator (|) with any of the following menu item control flags, as shown in Table 4-13.

Value	Meaning	⊠
MF_BITMAP	The menu item will be a bitmap. The low-order word of the *lpNewItem* parameter should contain a handle to the bitmap.	
MF_BYCOMMAND	The *nPosition* value is interpreted as a menu item ID value. The new item is inserted before the exiting one.	
MF_BYPOSITION	The *nPosition* value is interpreted relative to the sequential numbering of existing menu items: 0 is the first item, 1 the second, etc. The new item is inserted before the exiting one. Use an *nPosition* value of −1 for the end of the menu.	
MF_CHECKED	Places a checkmark next to the menu item.	
MF_DISABLED	Makes it impossible to select the menu item. Does not gray the menu item.	
MF_ENABLED	Makes it possible to select the menu item. This is the default.	
MF_GRAYED	Grays the menu item text and disables the menu item so that it cannot be selected.	
MF_MENUBARBREAK	In popup menus, it separates a new column of items and displays a separator bar between them. In normal menus, it starts a new line of menu items.	
MF_MENUBREAK	In popup menus, it separates a new column of items. No separator bar is displayed. In normal menus, it breaks the menu into a new line of menu items (two rows of menu items at the window's top).	
MF_OWNERREDRAW	Specifies that the parent window is to paint the menu item each time it is needed. This is not possible for the top menu line, but can be done for drop-down and popup menu items. The parent window will receive WM_MEASUREITEM and WM_DRAWITEM messages to update the drawing area.	
MF_POPUP	Specifies a popup menu. The *wIDNewItem* parameter will be a handle to the popup menu.	
MF_SEPARATOR	Draws a horizontal line in the menu. This line cannot be selected, checked, enabled, or grayed. The *lpNewItem* and *wIDNewItem* parameters are ignored.	
MF_STRING	Specifies that the new item is a character string. *lpNewItem* points to the string.	
MF_UNCHECKED	Does not place a checkmark next to the menu item. This is the default.	

Table 4-13. InsertMenu( ) wFlags Values.

wIDNewItem	WORD: Specifies the ID value for the menu item. If *wFlags* is set to MF_POPUP, *wIDNewItem* is the menu handle of the new popup menu.
lpNewItem	LPSTR: Points to the contents of the new menu item. The type of data depends on the *wFlags* setting, as shown in Table 4-14.

wFlags	lpNewItem	⊠
MF_STRING	Long pointer to a character string.	
MF_BITMAP	A bitmap handle. The bitmap handle is stored in the low-order word of *lpNewItem*.	
MF_OWNERDRAW	You specify to what 32-bit value the *lpNewItem* points. Windows will send WM_MEASUREITEM and WM_DRAWITEM messages to the window's message processing function when the menu item needs to be redrawn. See the example owner-drawn menu program in the introduction to this chapter.	

Table 4-14. InsertMenu( ) Data Types.

Related Messages WM_MEASUREITEM, WM_DRAWITEM

Example   This example adds a bitmap to the window's menu, right before the WM_TOP1 menu item. The new menu item has the ID value of ID_PEN.

▷ Header File

```
/* genmenu.h    */

#define IDM_TOP1        1                      /* menu item id values */
#define IDM_QUIT        2
#define IDM_PEN         3
#define IDM_HELP        8
        /* global variables */
int     ghInstance ;
char    gszAppName [] = "genmenu" ;
        /* function prototypes */
long FAR PASCAL WndProc (HWND, unsigned, WORD, LONG) ;
```

▷ Resource File

```
/* genmenu.rc    */
#include <windows.h>
#include "genmenu.h"

genmenu         ICON      generic.ico
menubitmap      BITMAP    pen.bmp

genmenu         MENU
BEGIN
        POPUP "&First Menu"
        BEGIN
                MENUITEM "&Top Item",    IDM_TOP1
        END
        MENUITEM "&Quit",                IDM_QUIT
        MENUITEM "\a&Help",              IDM_HELP, HELP
END
```

▷ Part of the Program File

```
long FAR PASCAL WndProc (HWND hWnd, unsigned iMessage, WORD wParam, LONG lParam)
{
        HMENU           hMenu ;
        HBITMAP         hBitmap ;

        switch (iMessage)                            /* process windows messages */
        {
                case WM_CREATE:
                        hMenu = GetMenu (hWnd) ;
                        hBitmap = LoadBitmap (ghInstance, "menubitmap") ;
                        InsertMenu (hMenu, IDM_TOP1, MF_BITMAP | MF_BYCOMMAND,
                                IDM_PEN, (LPSTR) (LONG) hBitmap) ;
                        break ;
```

[Other program lines]

LOADMENU   ■ Win 2.0   ■ Win 3.0   ■ Win 3.1

Purpose	Retrieves a handle to a menu defined in the resource .RC file.
Syntax	HMENU **LoadMenu**(HANDLE *hInstance*, LPSTR *lpMenuName*);
Uses	Used in the WinMain() function to load the program's main menu. Can be used in the body of a program to load new menus to change menus as the program operates.
Returns	HMENU, a handle to the menu. NULL if no menu was found.
See Also	SetMenu(), DestroyMenu()

Parameters

hInstance   HANDLE: The handle of the program instance.

lpMenuName   LPSTR: A pointer to a string containing the menu name. The menu name is defined in the resource .RC file as the first word in the MENU statement.

Example   See the example under the DestroyMenu() function description.

LoadMenuIndirect   □ Win 2.0   ■ Win 3.0   ■ Win 3.1

Purpose   Loads a new menu, defined in a memory block.

Syntax   HMENU **LoadMenuIndirect** (LPSTR *lpMenuTemplate*);

Description   This function reads a menu definition in a memory block and returns a handle to the menu created. The menu can then be attached to a window with SetMenu(). This function is used internally by Windows, but can be called directly if you take the trouble to create the menu definition template.

Uses   Provides an alternative to the normal menu creation and modification functions.

Returns   HMENU, a handle to the menu created. Returns NULL on error.

See Also   LoadMenu(), ModifyMenu(), AppendMenu(), DrawMenuBar()

Parameters

lpMenuTemplate LPSTR: A pointer to a memory block containing the menu definition. The format of the memory block must start with a MENUITEMTEMPLATEHEADER structure, followed by one or more MENUITEMTEMPLATE structures defining each menu item.

The MENUITEMTEMPLATEHEADER structure is defined in WINDOWS.H as follows:

```
typedef struct
  {
    WORD versionNumber;        /* set to 0 */
    WORD offset;               /* byte offset to first menuitem */
  } MENUITEMTEMPLATEHEADER;
```

The *versionNumber* is a placeholder for future updates to Windows. For now, set this value to zero. The *offset* is the number of bytes from the end of the header to the first MENUITEMTEMPLATE data. This is normally zero, assuming that the menu item data follows immediately in memory. Each menu item is defined in a MENUITEMTEMPLATE data structure. This is a bit difficult to work with for two reasons. One is that the *mtID* field is part of the structure for all template types except MF_POPUP. In that case it is omitted. The other problem is that the *mtString* is variable length. The end of the string is detected by the ending zero byte.

```
typedef struct
  {
    WORD  mtOption;            /* MF_CHECKED, MF_END, etc. */
    WORD  mtID;               /* item ID - not for MF_POPUP */
    char  mtString[1];        /* start of menu item string */
  } MENUITEMTEMPLATE;
```

The *mtOption* element can be a combination of the flags in Table 4-15, combined with the C language binary OR operator (|).

Value	Meaning	⊠
MF_CHECKED	Places a checkmark next to the menu item.	
MF_END	Specifies the end of a popup menu or static menu.	
MF_GRAYED	Grays the menu item text and disables the menu item so that it cannot be selected.	
MF_HELP	The menu item has a vertical bar to the left.	

MF_MENUBARBREAK	In popup menus, it separates a new column of items and displays a separator bar between them. In normal menus, it starts a new line of menu items.
MF_MENUBREAK	In popup menus, it separates a new column of items. No separator bar is displayed. In normal menus, it breaks the menu into a new line of menu items (two rows of menu items at the window's top).
MF_OWNERREDRAW	Specifies that the parent window is to paint the menu item each time it is needed. This is not possible for the top menu line, but can be done for drop-down and popup menu items. The parent window will receive WM_MEASUREITEM and WM_DRAWITEM messages to update the drawing area.
MF_POPUP	Specifies a popup menu. The *mtID* element of the MENUITEMTEMPLATE structure does not exist for this type.

Table 4-15. MENUITEMTEMPLATE mtOption Flags.

Example   This example creates a new menu, as shown in Figure 4-7, when the WM_CREATE message is processed. The menu is defined in a global memory block. The AppendMemory() function at the bottom of the listing is used to simplify dealing with the variable-length fields used to define menus. It adds consecutive chunks of data to the end of a memory block.

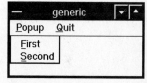

Figure 4-7. LoadMenu-Indirect() Example.

➪ Header File
```
/* generic.h  */

#define IDM_FIRST            1
#define IDM_SECOND           2
#define IDM_QUIT             3

#define MAXMENULONG          20
        /* global variables */
int     ghInstance ;
char    gszAppName [] = "generic" ;
        /* function prototypes */
long FAR PASCAL WndProc (HWND, unsigned, WORD, LONG) ;
void AppendMemory (LPSTR lpDest, LPSTR lpSource, int nBytes, BOOL bReset) ;
```

➪ WndProc() and AppendMemory() C Functions
```
long FAR PASCAL WndProc (HWND hWnd, unsigned iMessage, WORD wParam,        LONG lParam)
{
        HANDLE          hMem ;
        LPSTR           lpMem ;
        WORD            wValue ;
        HMENU           hMenu ;

        switch (iMessage)               /* process windows messages */
        {
                case WM_CREATE:
                        hMem = GlobalAlloc (GMEM_FIXED | GMEM_ZEROINIT,
                                sizeof (MENUITEMTEMPLATEHEADER) +
                                6 * (sizeof (MENUITEMTEMPLATE) + MAXMENULONG)) ;
                        lpMem = GlobalLock (hMem) ;

                        wValue = 0 ;
                        AppendMemory (lpMem, (LPSTR) &wValue, sizeof (WORD), TRUE) ;
                        wValue = 0 ;
                        AppendMemory (lpMem, (LPSTR) &wValue, sizeof (WORD), FALSE) ;

                        wValue = MF_POPUP ;
                        AppendMemory (lpMem, (LPSTR) &wValue, sizeof (WORD), FALSE)
```

```
                        AppendMemory (lpMem, "&Popup", 7, FALSE) ;

                        wValue = 0 ;
                        AppendMemory (lpMem, (LPSTR) &wValue, sizeof (WORD), FALSE) ;
                        wValue = IDM_FIRST ;
                        AppendMemory (lpMem, (LPSTR) &wValue, sizeof (WORD), FALSE) ;
                        AppendMemory (lpMem, "&First", 7, FALSE) ;

                        wValue = MF_END ;
                        AppendMemory (lpMem, (LPSTR) &wValue, sizeof (WORD), FALSE) ;
                        wValue = IDM_SECOND ;
                        AppendMemory (lpMem, (LPSTR) &wValue, sizeof (WORD), FALSE) ;
                        AppendMemory (lpMem, "&Second", 8, FALSE) ;

                        wValue = MF_END ;
                        AppendMemory (lpMem, (LPSTR) &wValue, sizeof (WORD), FALSE) ;
                        wValue = IDM_QUIT ;
                        AppendMemory (lpMem, (LPSTR) &wValue, sizeof (WORD), FALSE) ;
                        AppendMemory (lpMem, "&Quit", 6, FALSE) ;

                        hMenu = LoadMenuIndirect (lpMem) ;
                        SetMenu (hWnd, hMenu) ;
                        GlobalFree (hMem) ;
                        break ;
                case WM_COMMAND:           /* process menu items */
                        switch (wParam)
                        {
                        case IDM_FIRST:            /* User hit the first menu item */
                                MessageBox (hWnd, "First Menu Item Works!",
                                        "Message", MB_OK) ;
                                break ;
                        case IDM_SECOND:/* User hit the second menu item */
                                MessageBox (hWnd, "Second Menu Item Works!",
                                        "Message", MB_OK) ;
                                break ;
                        case IDM_QUIT:             /* User hit the Quit menu item */
                                DestroyWindow (hWnd) ;
                                break ;
                        }
                        break ;
                case WM_DESTROY:/* stop application */
                        PostQuitMessage (0) ;
                        break ;
                default:                   /* default windows message processing */
                        return DefWindowProc (hWnd, iMessage, wParam, lParam) ;
        }
        return (0L) ;
}

void AppendMemory (LPSTR lpDest, LPSTR lpSource, int nBytes, BOOL bReset)
{
        int             i ;
        LPSTR           lps, lpd ;
        static  int     nLastEnd ;

        lps = lpSource ;
        lpd = lpDest ;
        if (bReset)
                nLastEnd = 0 ;
        else
        {
                for (i = 0 ; i < nLastEnd ; i++)
                        lpd++ ;
        }

        for (i = 0 ; i < nBytes ; i++)
        {
                nLastEnd++ ;
                *lpd++ = *lps++ ;
        }
}
```

MODIFYMENU   □ Win 2.0   ■ Win 3.0   ■ Win 3.1

Purpose	Changes the properties of a menu item.
Syntax	BOOL **ModifyMenu**(HMENU *hMenu*, WORD *nPosition*, WORD *wFlags*, WORD *wIDNewItem*, LPSTR *lpNewItem*);
Description	This is a powerful function for changing several attributes of a menu item at the same time. The status (grayed, checked, etc.), the menu item's string or bitmap, and its ID value can all be changed in one function call.
Uses	Modifying a menu while the program operates.
Returns	BOOL. TRUE if the changes were made, FALSE on error.
See Also	CheckMenuItem(), GetMenu(), DrawMenuBar()
Parameters	
hMenu	HMENU: The handle to the menu. Use GetMenu() to retrieve a window's menu handle.
nPosition	WORD: The menu item to change. If the *wFlags* parameter contains MF_BYCOMMAND, *nPosition* refers to the menu item ID number. If *wFlags* contains MF_BYPOSITION, *nPosition* refers to the absolute number of the menu item, 0 for the first, 1 for the second, etc.
wFlags	WORD: The attributes of the menu item after the changes. This parameter is made up from the list, in Table 4-16, using the C language binary OR (|) operator to combine effects.

Value	Meaning
MF_BITMAP	The menu item will be a bitmap. The low-order word of the *lpNewItem* parameter should contain a handle to the bitmap.
MF_BYCOMMAND	The *nPosition* value is interpreted as a menu item ID value. This is the default.
MF_BYPOSITION	The *nPosition* value is interpreted relative to the sequential numbering of existing menu items: 0 is the first item, 1 the second, etc. The new item is inserted before the exiting one. Use an *nPosition* value of −1 for the end of the menu.
MF_CHECKED	Places a checkmark next to the menu item.
MF_DISABLED	Makes it impossible to select the menu item. Does not gray the menu item.
MF_ENABLED	Makes it possible to select the menu item. This is the default.
MF_GRAYED	Grays the menu item text and disables the menu item so that it cannot be selected.
MF_MENUBARBREAK	In popup menus, it separates a new column of items and displays a separator bar between them. In normal menus, it starts a new line of menu items.
MF_MENUBREAK	In popup menus, it separates a new column of items. No separator bar is displayed. In normal menus, it breaks the menu into a new line of menu items (two rows of menu items at the window's top).
MF_OWNERREDRAW	Specifies that the parent window is to paint the menu item each time it is needed. This is not possible for the top menu line, but can be done for drop-down and popup menu items. The parent window will receive WM_MEASUREITEM and WM_DRAWITEM messages to update the drawing area.
MF_POPUP	Specifies a popup menu. The *wIDNewItem* parameter will be a handle to the popup menu.
MF_SEPARATOR	Draws a horizontal line in the menu. This line cannot be selected, checked, enabled, or grayed. The *lpNewItem* and *wIDNewItem* parameters are ignored.
MF_STRING	Specifies that the new item is a character string. *lpNewItem* points to the string.
MF_UNCHECKED	Does not place a checkmark next to the menu item. This is the default.

Table 4-16. ModifyMenu( ) Flags.

wFlags	lpNewItem	⊠
MF_STRING	Long pointer to a character string.	
MF_BITMAP	A bitmap handle. The bitmap handle is stored in the low-order word of *lpNewItem*.	
MF_OWNERDRAW	You specify to which 32-bit value the *lpNewItem* points. Windows will send WM_MEASURE-ITEM and WM_DRAWITEM messages to the window's message processing function when the menu item needs to be redrawn. The value in the *lpNewItem* parameter will end up passed to the window's function as an element of the structure pointed to by the *lParam* value. See the example owner-drawn menu program in the introduction to this chapter.	

Table 4-17. ModifyMenu( ) Data Types.

Related Messages WM_MEASUREITEM, WM_DRAWITEM

Example This example uses ModifyMenu() to simultaneously change the IDM_OPT2 menu item from grayed to normal text and change it's character string to read "Now not Grayed."

```
Long FAR PASCAL WndProc (HWND hWnd, unsigned iMessage, WORD wParam, LONG lParam)
{
        HMENU           hMenu ;

        switch (iMessage)                               /* process windows messages */
        {
                case WM_COMMAND:                        /* process menu items */
                        switch (wParam)
                        {
                        case IDM_TOP1:
                                hMenu = GetMenu (hWnd) ;
                                ModifyMenu (hMenu, IDM_OPT2,
                                        MF_BYCOMMAND | MF_ENABLED | MF_STRING,
                                        IDM_OPT2, (LPSTR) "Now not Grayed") ;

                                break ;
```

[Other program lines]

REMOVEMENU
☐ Win 2.0 ■ Win 3.0 ■ Win 3.1

Purpose	Removes a menu item from a main menu.
Syntax	BOOL **RemoveMenu**(HMENU *hMenu*, WORD *nPosition*, WORD *wFlags*);
Description	The menu item is removed from the main menu. Any popup menus are removed, but are not destroyed. Popups freed in this way can be reused. Be sure that all menus are either attached to the application's main menu, or erased with DestroyMenu() before the application terminates to avoid leaving unattached menus in memory.
Uses	Using RemoveMenu() is considerably simpler in these situations than DeleteMenu(), as RemoveMenu() allows the popup menu to be reattached, rather than rebuilt from scratch. Call GetSubMenu() to obtain the popup menu handle before using RemoveMenu().
Returns	BOOL. TRUE if the menu item was removed, FALSE on error.
See Also	GetSubMenu(), DeleteMenu(), AppendMenu(), InsertMenu()
Parameters	
hMenu	HMENU: A handle to the menu. Use GetMenu() to obtain a handle to a window's menu.

| *nPosition* | WORD: The menu item to be removed. |
| *wFlags* | WORD: Sets how the *nPostion* value is interpreted (Refer to Table 4-18). |

Value	Meaning	⊠
MF_BYCOMMAND	The *nPosition* value is the menu item ID value.	
MF_BYPOSITION	The *nPosition* value is interpreted relative to the sequential numbering of existing menu items: 0 is the first item, 1 the second, etc.	

Table 4-18. RemoveMenu( ) Flags.

Comments   Use DrawMenuBar() after changing the menu items to force Windows to redraw the menu line.

Example   In this example, clicking the IDM_TOP1 menu item causes the first popup menu to be moved from the left of the menu bar to the far right. All of the popup menu items remain intact.

```
long FAR PASCAL WndProc (HWND hWnd, unsigned iMessage, WORD wParam, LONG lParam)
{
        HMENU           hMenu, hPopupMenu ;
        static BOOL     bMovedMenu = FALSE ;

        switch (iMessage)                       /* process windows messages */
        {
        case WM_COMMAND:                        /* process menu items */
                switch (wParam)
                {
                case IDM_TOP1:          /* move first popup menu to menu end */
                        if (!bMovedMenu)
                        {
                                hMenu = GetMenu (hWnd) ;
                                hPopupMenu = GetSubMenu (hMenu, 0) ;
                                RemoveMenu (hMenu, 0, MF_BYPOSITION) ;
                                AppendMenu (hMenu, MF_POPUP, hPopupMenu,
                                        (LPSTR) "New Position") ;
                                DrawMenuBar (hWnd) ;    /* redraw menu bar */
                                bMovedMenu = TRUE ;     /* don't try it twice */
                        }
                        break ;
```
[Other program lines]

SETMENU   ■ Win 2.0   ■ Win 3.0   ■ Win 3.1

Purpose	Attaches a menu to a window.
Syntax	BOOL **SetMenu**(HWND *hWnd*, HMENU *hMenu*);
Description	The menu attached can either be defined in a resource .RC file or created within the program with the CreateMenu() function. Any existing menu is removed.
Uses	Changing to a new menu, or removing a menu from the window.
Returns	BOOL. TRUE if the menu has been changed, FALSE otherwise.
See Also	CreateMenu(), DestroyMenu(), LoadMenu(), DrawMenuBar()
Parameters	
hWnd	HWND: A handle to the window which will change menus.
hMenu	HMENU: A handle to the menu to add. Use LoadMenu() to retrieve the handle to a menu defined in the resource .RC file. Set *hMenu* equal to NULL to remove the menu from a window without replacing it.
Example	See the example under the DestroyMenu() function description.

SETMENUITEMBITMAPS

☐ Win 2.0 ■ Win 3.0 ■ Win 3.1

Purpose	Replaces the default menu checkmark bitmap with a custom bitmap.
Syntax	BOOL **SetMenuItemBitmaps**(HMENU *hMenu*, WORD *nPosition*, WORD *wFlags*, HBITMAP *hBitmapUnchecked*, HBITMAP *hBitmapChecked*);
Description	Windows uses a default checkmark bitmap for checking menu items. This can be replaced with custom bitmaps using the SetMenuItemBitmaps() function. The size of the checkmark bitmaps is dependant on the video resolution of the system the program is running on. GetMenuCheckMarkDimensions() is used to find this size for scaling the bitmap to fit.
Uses	Custom checkmarks can dress up an application program, with little penalty in memory consumption. When the new bitmap is assigned to the menu item, the CheckMenuItem() function automatically will use this bitmap when checking or unchecking an item.
Returns	BOOL. TRUE if the bitmap was set properly, FALSE on error.
See Also	SetMenuItemBitmaps(), CheckMenuItem(), GetMenuCheckMarkDimensions()
Parameters	
hMenu	HMENU: A handle to a menu. Use GetMenu() to retrieve a window's menu.
nPosition	WORD: The menu item number to change.
wFlags	WORD: Specifies whether *nPosition* refers to the menu item ID number or the sequential numbering of menu items. This can be either of the values shown in Table 4-19.

Value	Meaning
MF_BYCOMMAND	The *nPosition* value is the menu item ID value.
MF_BYPOSITION	The *nPosition* value is interpreted relative sequential numbering of existing menu items: 0 is the first item, 1 the second, etc.

Table 4-19. SetMenuItemBitmaps( ) Flags.

hBitmapUnchecked	HBITMAP: A handle to the bitmap to display when the menu item is not checked. This can be NULL, leaving the side of the menu bar blank when unchecked (the normal case).
hBitmapChecked	HBITMAP: A handle to the bitmap to display when the menu item is checked. This can be NULL, leaving the side of the menu bar blank when checked. A NULL value is not recommended.
Example	See the example under the GetMenuCheckMarkDimensions() function description.

TRACKPOPUPMENU

☐ Win 2.0 ■ Win 3.0 ■ Win 3.1

Purpose	Displays a submenu anywhere on the screen.
Syntax	BOOL **TrackPopupMenu**(HMENU *hMenu*, WORD *wFlags*, int *x*, int *y*, int *nReserved*, HWND *hWnd*, LPRECT *lpReserved*);
Description	This is a new option, added with the 3.0 version of Windows. The popup menu is displayed with its upper left corner at *x,y* on the screen. Screen coordinates are used, so the menu can be out of your program's client area. Normal Windows menu item selection and WM_COMMAND messages occur for the popup. The popup disappears after a selection is made, or after another screen area is clicked.
Uses	Convenient if the normal drop-down submenu options obscure an important part of the window's client area.
Returns	BOOL. TRUE if the function displayed the submenu, FALSE on error.
See Also	CreatePopupMenu(), AppendMenu(), GetSubMenu()

Parameters

hMenu   HMENU: A handle to the popup menu to be displayed. Use CreatePopupMenu() to make a new floating popup menu, and add the desired menu items with AppendMenu().

wFlags   WORD: Not used. Always set to NULL.

x   int

y   int: The screen coordinates of the upper left corner. Use ClientToScreen() to convert from a desired location on the window's client area to screen coordinates.

nReserved   int: Not used. Always set to NULL.

hWnd   HWND: A handle to the window that owns the popup menu. This is the window that will receive the WM_COMMAND messages from Windows as the submenu items are selected.

lpReserved   LPRECT: A pointer to a RECT data structure that contains the screen coordinates of a rectangle within which the user can click the mouse button without dismissing the popup menu. If set to NULL, the popup menu is dismissed if the mouse button is clicked anywhere outside of the popup menu boundary. Prior to Windows 3.1, NULL was the only value permitted.

Related Messages WM_COMMAND

Example   This example produces a window as shown in Figure 4-8. If the "Top Item" menu item is clicked, a floating popup appears at the lower left. Clicking the "Item one" menu item in the floating popup causes a simple message box to appear.

The resource .RC file does not include the definition of the floating popup.

Figure 4-8. Floating Popup Menu.

```
/* genmenu.rc              */
#include <windows.h>
#include "genmenu.h"
genmenu        ICON   generic.ico

genmenu        MENU
BEGIN
        MENUITEM "&Top Item",    IDM_TOP1
        MENUITEM "&Quit",        IDM_QUIT
        MENUITEM "\a&Help",      IDM_HELP, HELP
END
```

The floating popup menu is created when the program starts (WM_CREATE message received). It is displayed when the IDM_TOP1 menu item is clicked. Note that TrackPopupMenu() uses screen units for the *X* and *Y* position. The ClientToScreen() function converts the desired coordinates in the window's client rectangle prior to calling TrackPopupMenu().

```
long FAR PASCAL WndProc (HWND hWnd, unsigned iMessage, WORD wParam, LONG lParam)
{
        HMENU                   hMenu ;
        static HMENU            hPopupMenu ;
        POINT                   pFloater ;

        switch (iMessage)                       /* process windows messages */
        {
                case WM_CREATE:
                        hPopupMenu = CreatePopupMenu () ;
                        AppendMenu (hPopupMenu, MF_STRING, IDM_POP1, "Item &one.") ;
                        AppendMenu (hPopupMenu, MF_STRING, IDM_POP2, "Item &two.") ;
                        break ;
                case WM_COMMAND:                /* process menu items */
                        switch (wParam)
                        {
```

```
                 case IDM_TOP1:            /* Top menu item disp. the float. popup */
                         pFloater.x = 0 ;            /* put floating popup on left side */
                         pFloater.y = 100 ;                  /* down 100 units */
                         ClientToScreen (hWnd, &pFloater) ;        /* pt to screen */
                         TrackPopupMenu (hPopupMenu, NULL, pFloater.x,
                                 pFloater.y,      NULL, hWnd, NULL) ;
                         break ;
                 case IDM_POP1:            /* The first item in floating popup hit */
                         MessageBox (hWnd, "This floating menu works!",
                                 "Message", MB_OK) ;
                         break ;

                 case IDM_QUIT:
                         DestroyWindow (hWnd) ;
                         break ;
                 }
                 break ;
```

[Other program lines]

Mechanical equipment designed for people to manipulate settings (stereos, aircraft instruments, etc.) generally make use of buttons, knobs, and slide bars for changing values. These devices are much faster and more intuitive to use than typing at a keyboard. With aircraft instruments, keyboard entry is generally reserved for data that requires great precision, such as navigational settings. Buttons and slide bars (called "scroll bars" in Windows) are excellent ways to get user input. Rotating knobs do not have an exact match on the computer screen (rotating the mouse does not work well), so scroll bars are generally used in places where a machine might use a knob. In general, if your program requires the user to enter data on the keyboard, look for a way to provide a mouse alternative: Scroll bars for numerical values, buttons for choices, and list boxes for selections from a list. This does not mean that keyboard input should be unsupported. Accelerator keys and other keyboard shortcuts find their way into most well-designed Windows programs. The ideal program provides both keyboard and mouse alternatives for every action.

Scroll Bar Concepts

Scroll bar controls are child windows. They are initially created using the CreateWindow() function discussed in Chapter 2, *Creating Windows*. Once created, scroll bars can either be placed on the program's client area, creating windows, or added as part of the window's border, for scrolling the client area. Figure 5-1 illustrates three different scroll bars.

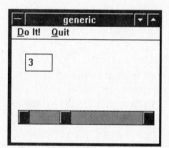 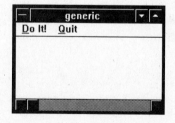 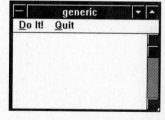

Figure 5-1A (left), B (middle), C (right). Three Examples of Scroll Bar Controls.

Figure 5-1A shows a horizontal scroll bar that is attached to the window's client area. It uses the SBS_HORZ style in CreateWindow(). Moving the scroll bar changes the numeric value in the edit control above it. The control could have been made into a vertical scroll bar by using the SBS_VERT style in CreateWindow(). This would also require changing the dimensions, to make the control thin in the X direction, and tall in the Y direction. Figures 5-1B and C show scroll bars that are attached to the window's border and are not part of the client area. They are generally used as a way of scrolling the client area (moving the contents of the client area horizontally or vertically). If the scroll bar type shown in Figure 5-1A were used to scroll the client area, the scroll bar itself would be moved during scrolling!

The attachment of scroll bars to the window's border is done when the scroll bar control is made visible. ShowScrollBar() is used for scroll bars the same way that ShowWindow() was used for other types of child windows. The difference is that ShowScrollBar() will attach scroll bars to the window's border if the SB_HORZ or SB_VERT style is specified. Windows automatically subtracts the width of the scroll bar from the client area, so that painting on the client area does not run over the scroll bars. The other way to get a scroll bar attached to a window's frame is to create the window with one or two scroll bars specified when CreateWindow() is called. For example, to create a window with a horizontal scroll bar at the bottom (Figure 5-1B), add the WS_HSCROLL window style, as shown in the following code.

```
hWnd = CreateWindow (              /* create the program's window here */

        gszAppName,               /* class name */
        gszAppName,               /* window name */
        WS_OVERLAPPEDWINDOW | WS_HSCROLL,      /* window style */
        CW_USEDEFAULT,            /* x position on screen */
        CW_USEDEFAULT,            /* y position on screen */
        CW_USEDEFAULT,            /* width of window */
        CW_USEDEFAULT,            /* height of window */
        NULL,                     /* parent window handle (null = none) */
        NULL,                     /* menu handle (null = use class menu) */
        hInstance,                /* instance handle */
        NULL) ;                   /* lpstr (null = not used) */
ShowWindow (hWnd, nCmdShow) ;
```

The WS_VSCROLL adds a vertical scroll bar, which can be done with WS_HSCROLL or separately.

Defining the scroll bar as part of the parent window's CreateWindow() call is a handy shortcut, as it saves you from having to create the window's scroll bars as separate child windows. The WndProc() function for the parent window will receive WM_HSCROLL and/or WM_VSCROLL messages if the scroll bar is moved with the mouse. The messages from the scroll bar will be sent using the parent window's handle.

Scroll bars are attached automatically to list boxes when the number of items exceeds the size of the list window. List and combo boxes are discussed in Chapter 9, *Windows Messages*. Edit controls can also have scroll bars attached. Single line edit controls can only take advantage of the horizontal scroll bar, but multiline edit controls can use both vertical and horizontal scroll bars. As edit controls are simply small windows, add the WS_HSCROLL and/or WS_VSCROLL styles when creating the edit control. An example of a multiline edit control with a scroll bar is given in Chapter 9 under *Edit Control Messages*.

Scroll Bar Position and Range

When a scroll bar is first created, the range of values reflected by the two ends of the control are 0 to 100. This is only handy if you happen to be working with a parameter that varies over this range. In most cases, you will want to change the scroll bar range to match the data you are changing. For scrolling text, the range is probably equal to the number of lines of text. The SetScrollRange() function allows the scroll bar range to be reset at any time. The value reflected by the scroll bar thumb (the rectangle in the center of the scroll bar that moves) depends on the scroll bar range. If the range is from one to ten, a value of five will set the thumb in the center. If the range is changed from one to twenty, a value of five will fall only one quarter of the way along the scroll bar. One thing you cannot do is reverse the top and bottom of a scroll bar. This is unfortunate, as the vertical scroll bars are set up with low values at the top and high values at the bottom. This is logical for scrolling text, but is reversed relative to what you would expect for entering a number. You can get around this by subtracting the scroll bar position from the maximum position to get the value the user meant when entering a number.

Scroll Bar Messages

When the user clicks part of a scroll bar, Windows sends either a WM_HSCROLL or WM_VSCROLL message, corresponding to the action on a horizontal or vertical scroll bar, respectively. The *wParam* parameter that gets passed to your WinProc() function with the message will tell where on the scroll bar the mouse was located when the user clicked the mouse button. These *wParam* values have names in WINDOWS.H (like SB_LINEUP for the top or left side arrow). Figure 5-2 shows the *wParam* values for each part of the scroll bar. If you look in WINDOWS.H, you will find two additional scroll bar messages, SB_TOP and SB_BOTTOM. The author has been unable to get a scroll bar to send one of these messages. When the mouse button is released after an action on the scroll bar, Windows sends an SB_ENDSCROLL message. The exception to this is if the user was moving the scroll bar thumb. In this case, releasing the mouse generates the SB_THUMBPOSITION message. The complete description of each of these messages is given in Chapter 9, *Windows Messages*.

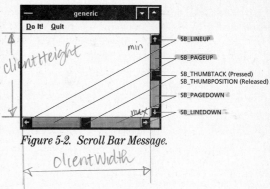

Figure 5-2. Scroll Bar Message.

Scroll Bar Function Summary

The functions relating directly to scroll bars are summarized in Table 5-1. Most of them deal with the simple tasks of setting and retrieving the scroll bar range and thumb position.

Function	Purpose
EnableScrollBar	Enable or disable a scroll bar control (Win 3.1).
GetScrollPos	Retrieve the current position of the scroll bar's thumb.
GetScrollRange	Retrieve the minimum and maximum value range of a scroll bar.
ScrollDC	Scroll a region in a device context and compute the update areas.
ScrollWindow	Scroll a region in a window's client area.
SetScrollPos	Set the position of the scroll bar thumb.
SetScrollRange	Set the minimum and maximum values of a scroll bar.
ShowScrollBar	Display the scroll bar, optionally attaching it to the window's border.

Table 5-1. Scroll Bar Function Summary.

The two functions that are more complex are ScrollWindow() and ScrollDC(). They both scroll an area horizontally and/or vertically. ScrollDC() is more sophisticated, as it computes the areas on the screen that need to be updated after scrolling. Scrolling always uncovers areas on the screen that need to be repainted. Your program logic can determine what action to take depending on the size and location of the areas that need to be updated.

ENABLESCROLLBAR

☐ Win 2.0   ☐ Win 3.0   ■ Win 3.1

Purpose	Enables or disables a scroll bar control.
Syntax	BOOL **EnableScrollBar** (HWND *hWnd*, WORD *wSBFlags*, WORD *wArrowFlags*);
Description	When a scroll bar is disabled, the thumb disappears and the center portion is not shaded. No action or messages occur if the user attempts to use the scroll bar. When activated, the thumb reappears, and the center portion is shaded.
Uses	The scroll bar can be disabled when the control it is attached to loses the input focus. See the example below for an edit control.
Returns	BOOL. TRUE if the function was successful, FALSE on error.
See Also	SetFocus()

Parameters

hWnd HWND: The scroll bar window handle. This can be either a stand-alone scroll bar or a scroll bar attached to another window, depending on the *wSBFlags* value. If the scroll bar is created as part of the window's style (WS_VSCROLL or WS_HSCROLL), the created window's handle is used for *hWnd*.

wSBFlags WORD: The type of scroll bar. This can be any of the types described in Table 5-2.

Value	Meaning
SB_BOTH	Both horizontal and vertical scroll bars attached to a window.
SB_CTL	A scroll bar control. In this case, set *hWnd* equal to the scroll bar handle.
SB_HORZ	A horizontal scroll bar tied to the window. In this case, *hWnd* should be the window's handle.
SB_VERT	A vertical scroll bar tied to the window. In this case, *hWnd* should be the window's handle.

Table 5-2. Scroll Bar Types.

wArrowFlags WORD: Specifies whether the scroll bar is enabled or disabled. It can be any of the following values described in Table 5-3.

Value	Meaning
ESB_ENABLE_BOTH	Enables both arrows of the scroll bar.
ESB_DISABLE_LTUP	Disables the left arrow of a horizontal scroll bar, or the down arrow of a vertical scroll bar.
ESB_DISABLE_RTDN	Disables the right arrow of a horizontal scroll bar, or the up arrow of a vertical scroll bar.
ESB_DISABLE_BOTH	Disables both arrows of a scroll bar.

Table 5-3. Scroll Bar Types.

Example This example creates an edit control with an attached horizontal scroll bar. The scroll bar is only activated when the edit control has the input focus. If the focus shifts to another window, the scroll bar is deactivated. Windows sends a WM_COMMAND message with the edit control's ID value as *wParam* when the scroll bar is activated. The scroll bar notification code is decoded by examining the high-order word of the *lParam* value passed with WM_COMMAND. EN_SETFOCUS is the notification code sent when an edit control gains the input focus. EN_KILLFOCUS is the notification code when the edit control loses the input focus. Figure 5-3 illustrates the use of EnableScrollBar().

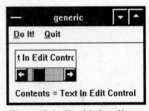

Figure 5-3. EnableScroll-Bar() Example.

```
Long FAR PASCAL WndProc (HWND hWnd, unsigned iMessage, WORD wParam, LONG lParam)
{
        static   HWND    hEdit ;
        HDC              hDC ;
        char             cEditBuf [64], cBuf [128] ;

        switch (iMessage)                  /* process windows messages */
        {
                case WM_CREATE:
                        hEdit = CreateWindow ("EDIT", "",
                                WS_CHILD | WS_BORDER | WS_HSCROLL | ES_AUTOHSCROLL |
                                ES_MULTILINE,
```

```
                              10, 10, 100, 50, hWnd, 101, ghInstance, NULL) ;
                     SetWindowText (hEdit, "Text In Edit Control") ;
                     ShowWindow (hEdit, SW_SHOW) ;
                     break ;
          case WM_COMMAND:          /* process menu items */
                     switch (wParam)
                     {
                     case 101:                   /* edit control notification */
                            switch (HIWORD (lParam))
                            {
                                    case EN_SETFOCUS:
                                            EnableScrollBar (hEdit, SB_HORZ,
                                                    ESB_ENABLE_BOTH) ;
                                            break ;
                                    case EN_KILLFOCUS:
                                            EnableScrollBar (hEdit, SB_HORZ,
                                                    ESB_DISABLE_BOTH) ;
                                            break ;
                            }
                            break ;
                     case IDM_DOIT:              /* retrieve edit text and display */
                            GetWindowText (hEdit, cEditBuf, 63) ;
                            hDC = GetDC (hWnd) ;
                            TextOut (hDC, 10, 70, cBuf, wsprintf (cBuf,
                                    "Contents = %s", (LPSTR) cEditBuf)) ;
                            ReleaseDC (hWnd, hDC) ;
                            break ;
                     case IDM_QUIT:
                            PostQuitMessage (NULL) ;
                            break ;
                     }
                     break ;
          case WM_DESTROY:
                     PostQuitMessage (0) ;
                     break ;
          default:
                     return DefWindowProc (hWnd, iMessage, wParam, lParam) ;
          }
     return (0L) ;
}
```

GetScrollPos   ■ Win 2.0   ■ Win 3.0   ■ Win 3.1

Purpose	Finds the location of the scroll bar thumb.
Syntax	int **GetScrollPos**(HWND *hWnd*, int *nBar*);
Description	Reads the position of the scroll bar thumb. The number returned will depend on the scroll bar range that was set with SetScrollRange().
Returns	int, the scroll bar position.
See Also	SetScrollPos(), SetScrollRange, GetScrollRange()
Parameters	
hWnd	HWND: The scroll bar control handle if *nBar* is SB_CTL, or the window handle if *nBar* is SB_HORZ or SB_VERT.
nBar	int: The type of scroll bar. This can be any of the types listed in Table 5-4.

Value	Meaning	⊠
SB_CTL	A scroll bar control. In this case, set *hWnd* equal to the scroll bar handle.	
SB_HORZ	A horizontal scroll bar tied to the window. In this case, *hWnd* should be the window's handle.	
SB_VERT	A vertical scroll bar tied to the window. In this case, *hWnd* should be the window's handle.	

Table 5-4. Scroll Bar Types.

Related Messages WM_HSCROLL, WM_VSCROLL

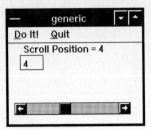

Example

Here the program creates a scroll bar control that sets the numeric value inside the edit control when the scroll bar is moved. When the user clicks the "Do It!" menu item, the current scroll bar position is retrieved by GetScrollPos() and displayed in the client area, as illustrated in Figure 5-4.

*Figure 5-4. GetScrollPos()
Example.*

```
long FAR PASCAL WndProc (HWND hWnd, unsigned iMessage, WORD wParam, LONG lParam)
{
        static          HWND    hEdit, hScroll ;
        static          int     nScrollValue ;
        char                    cBuf [128] ;
        HDC                     hDC ;
        int                     n ;

        switch (iMessage)                       /* process windows messages */
        {
            case WM_CREATE:                     /* create edit control */
                hEdit = CreateWindow ("EDIT", "0",
                        WS_CHILD | WS_VISIBLE | WS_BORDER,
                        20, 20, 40, 25, hWnd, NULL, ghInstance, NULL) ;
                ShowWindow (hEdit, SW_SHOW) ;
                                                /* create scroll bar control */
                hScroll = CreateWindow ("SCROLLBAR", "",
                        WS_CHILD | WS_VISIBLE | SBS_HORZ,
                        10, 100, 200, 20, hWnd, NULL , ghInstance, NULL) ;
                ShowScrollBar (hScroll, SB_CTL, SW_SHOW) ;
                SetScrollRange (hScroll, SB_CTL, 0, 10, FALSE) ;
                nScrollValue = 0 ;
                SetScrollPos (hScroll, SB_CTL, nScrollValue, TRUE) ;
                break ;
            case WM_HSCROLL:
                switch (wParam)
                {
                case SB_THUMBPOSITION:          /* user has moved scroll thumb */
                        nScrollValue = LOWORD (lParam) ;
                        SetScrollPos (hScroll, SB_CTL, nScrollValue, TRUE) ;
                        wsprintf (cBuf, "%d", nScrollValue) ;
                        SetWindowText (hEdit, (LPSTR) cBuf) ;
                        break ;
                case SB_LINEDOWN:               /* user clicked scroll rt arrow */
                        nScrollValue++ ;
                        nScrollValue = nScrollValue > 10 ? 10 : nScrollValue ;
                        SetScrollPos (hScroll, SB_CTL, nScrollValue, TRUE) ;
                        wsprintf (cBuf, "%d", nScrollValue) ;
                        SetWindowText (hEdit, (LPSTR) cBuf) ;
                        break ;
                case SB_LINEUP:                 /* user clicked scroll lf arrow */
                        nScrollValue-- ;
                        nScrollValue = nScrollValue < 0 ? 0 : nScrollValue ;
                        SetScrollPos (hScroll, SB_CTL, nScrollValue, TRUE) ;
                        wsprintf (cBuf, "%d", nScrollValue) ;
                        SetWindowText (hEdit, (LPSTR) cBuf) ;
                        break ;
                }
                break ;
            case WM_COMMAND:                    /* process menu items */
                switch (wParam)
                {
                case IDM_DOIT:                  /* User hit the "Do it" menu item */
```

```
                              n = GetScrollPos (hScroll, SB_CTL) ;
                              hDC = GetDC (hWnd) ;
                              TextOut (hDC, 25, 0, cBuf, wsprintf (cBuf,
                                      "Scroll Position = %d", n)) ;
                              ReleaseDC (hWnd, hDC) ;
                              break ;
                     case IDM_QUIT:
                              DestroyWindow (hWnd) ;
                              break ;
                     }
                     break ;
           case WM_DESTROY:          /* stop application */
                     PostQuitMessage (0) ;
                     break ;
           default:                  /* default windows message processing */
                     return DefWindowProc (hWnd, iMessage, wParam, lParam) ;
     }
     return (0L) ;
}
```

GETSCROLLRANGE   ■ Win 2.0   ■ Win 3.0   ■ Win 3.1

Purpose	Retrieves the minimum and maximum range values for a scroll bar.
Syntax	void **GetScrollRange**(HWND *hWnd*, int *nBar*, LPINT *lpMinPos*, LPINT *lpMaxPos*);
Description	Sets the integer values pointed to by *lpMinPos* and *lpMaxPos* to the scroll bar limits.
Uses	Avoids having to keep track of scroll bar limits in static variables. You can retrieve the scroll bar limits when you use GetScrollPos() to retrieve the scroll bar position.
Returns	No returned value (void).
See Also	GetScrollPos(), SetScrollRange, SetScrollPos()
Parameters	
hWnd	HWND: The scroll bar control handle if *nBar* is SB_CTL, or the window handle if *nBar* is SB_HORZ or SB_VERT.
nBar	int: The type of scroll bar. This can be any of the types listed in Table 5-5.

Value	Meaning	⊠
SB_CTL	A scroll bar control. In this case, set *hWnd* equal to the scroll bar handle.	
SB_HORZ	A horizontal scroll bar tied to the window. In this case, *hWnd* should be the window's handle.	
SB_VERT	A vertical scroll bar tied to the window. In this case, *hWnd* should be the window's handle.	

Table 5-5. Scroll Bar Types.

lpMinPos	LPINT: A pointer to the integer variable that will receive the minimum scroll bar value range.
lpMaxPos	LPINT: A pointer to the integer variable that will receive the maximum scroll bar value range.
Related Messages	WM_HSCROLL, WM_VSCROLL

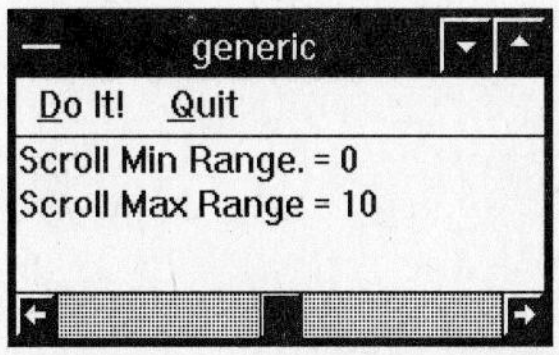

Figure 5-5. GetScrollRange() Example.

Example   This example (illustrated in Figure 5-5) demonstrates a window with an attached horizontal scroll bar. The scroll bar is created with the window during the CreateWindow() call in WinMain(). The scroll bar range and initial position are set when the WndProc() function processes the WM_CREATE message. When the user clicks the "Do It!" menu item, the scroll bar ranges are displayed in the client area.

```
/* generic.c   generic windows application */

#include <windows.h>              /* window's header file - always included */
#include "generic.h"              /* the application's header file */

int PASCAL WinMain (HANDLE hInstance, HANDLE hPrevInstance, LPSTR lpszCmdLine,
        int nCmdShow)
{
        HWND              hWnd ;
        MSG               msg ;
        WNDCLASS          wndclass ;
        ghInstance = hInstance ;      /* store instance handle as global var. */
        if (!hPrevInstance)           /* load data into window class struct. */
        {
                wndclass.style          = CS_HREDRAW | CS_VREDRAW ;
                wndclass.lpfnWndProc    = WndProc ;
                wndclass.cbClsExtra     = 0 ;
                wndclass.cbWndExtra     = 0 ;
                wndclass.hInstance      = hInstance ;
                wndclass.hIcon          = LoadIcon (hInstance, gszAppName) ;
                wndclass.hCursor        = LoadCursor (NULL, IDC_ARROW) ;
                wndclass.hbrBackground  = GetStockObject (WHITE_BRUSH) ;
                wndclass.lpszMenuName   = gszAppName ;
                wndclass.lpszClassName  = gszAppName ;

                                        /* register the window class */
                if (!RegisterClass (&wndclass))
                        return FALSE ;
        }

        hWnd = CreateWindow (           /* create the program's window here */
                gszAppName,             /* class name */
                gszAppName,             /* window name */
                WS_OVERLAPPEDWINDOW | WS_HSCROLL,      /* window style */
                CW_USEDEFAULT,          /* x position on screen */
                CW_USEDEFAULT,          /* y position on screen */
                CW_USEDEFAULT,          /* width of window */
                CW_USEDEFAULT,          /* height of window */
                NULL,                   /* parent window handle (null = none) */
                NULL,                   /* menu handle (null = use class menu) */
                hInstance,              /* instance handle */
                NULL) ;                 /* lpstr (null = not used) */

        ShowWindow (hWnd, nCmdShow) ;
        UpdateWindow (hWnd) ;           /* send first WM_PAINT message */

        while (GetMessage (&msg, NULL, 0, 0))                    /* the message loop */
        {
                TranslateMessage (&msg) ;
                DispatchMessage (&msg) ;
        }
        return msg.wParam ;
}


long FAR PASCAL WndProc (HWND hWnd, unsigned iMessage, WORD wParam,       LONG lParam)
{
        char              cBuf [128] ;
        HDC               hDC ;
        int               nMin, nMax ;

        switch (iMessage)               /* process windows messages */
        {
                case WM_CREATE:
                        SetScrollRange (hWnd, SB_HORZ, 0, 10, FALSE) ;
                        SetScrollPos (hWnd, SB_HORZ, 5, TRUE) ;
                        break ;
```

```
        case WM_COMMAND:           /* process menu items */
               switch (wParam)
               {
               case IDM_DOIT:    /* User hit the "Do it" menu item */
                      GetScrollRange (hWnd, SB_HORZ, &nMin, &nMax) ;
                      hDC = GetDC (hWnd) ;
                      TextOut (hDC, 0, 0, cBuf, wsprintf (cBuf,
                              "Scroll Min Range. = %d", nMin)) ;
                      TextOut (hDC, 0, 20, cBuf, wsprintf (cBuf,
                              "Scroll Max Range = %d", nMax)) ;
                      ReleaseDC (hWnd, hDC) ;
                      break ;
               case IDM_QUIT:
                      DestroyWindow (hWnd) ;
                      break ;
               }
               break ;
        case WM_DESTROY:           /* stop application */
               PostQuitMessage (0) ;
               break ;
        default:                   /* default windows message processing */
               return DefWindowProc (hWnd, iMessage, wParam, lParam) ;
        }
     return (0L) ;
}
```

SCROLLDC   ■ Win 2.0   ■ Win 3.0   ■ Win 3.1

Purpose	Scrolls all or part of a device context vertically and/or horizontally.
Syntax	BOOL **ScrollDC**(HDC *hDC*, int *dx*, int *dy*, LPRECT *lprcScroll*, LPRECT *lprcClip*, HRGN *hrgnUpdate*, LPRECT *lprcUpdate*);
Description	This function is the most powerful method of moving a rectangular region of bits. The movement can be both horizontal and vertical in one function call. A subregion within the scrolling rectangle can be picked out, limiting the area scrolled. The function also computes the size of either an update region or update rectangle, capturing the area that needs to be repainted after scrolling to keep the image intact.
Uses	Scrolling a window's client area, or scrolling all or part of a bitmap in a memory device context.
Returns	BOOL. TRUE if the function executed correctly, FALSE on error.
See Also	ScrollWindow()
Parameters	
hDC	HDC: The device context that contains the image to be scrolled. Use GetDC() to obtain a window's device context.
dx	int: The number of units to scroll horizontally. Positive numbers scroll right, negative numbers scroll left.
dy	int: The number of units to scroll vertically. Positive numbers scroll down, negative numbers scroll up.
lprcScroll	LPRECT: Pointer to the rectangle structure that contains the coordinates of the scrolling rectangle. Use GetClientRect() to obtain a window's client area rectangle.
lprcClip	LPRECT: Pointer to the rectangle structure that contains the coordinates of the clipping rectangle. If the *lprcClip* rectangle is smaller than *lprcScroll*, only the area inside the *lprcClip* rectangle is scrolled.
hrgnUpdate	HRGN: A handle to the update region uncovered by the scrolling process. If scrolling is in both the *X* and *Y* directions simultaneously, the region will not be rectangular. If *hrgnUpdate* and *lprcUpdate* are both NULL, Windows does not compute the update region.

lprcUpdate	LPRECT: A pointer to a rectangle structure that is filled with the dimensions of the smallest rectangle that bounds the update region uncovered by the scrolling process. Set to NULL if you do not want Windows to compute the update rectangle.	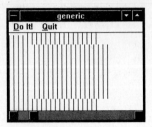

Related Messages WM_HSCROLL, WM_VSCROLL

Example   This example uses ScrollDC to scroll the center part of the window's client region, based on the window's horizontal scroll bar position. The clipping region is set smaller than the client area by 20 units, so that the outermost 20 units are not scrolled. After the user clicks the "Do It!" menu item (drawing the lines) and gives one mouse click of the right scroll bar arrow, the window looks like Figure 5-6.

Figure 5-6. ScrollDC() Example.

```
long FAR PASCAL WndProc (HWND hWnd, unsigned iMessage, WORD wParam, LONG lParam)
{
        static          HWND            hScroll ;
        static          int             nScrollValue, nOldValue ;
        HDC                             hDC ;
        int                             i ;
        RECT                            rWind, rClip, rUpdate ;
        HRGN                            hrgnUpdate ;
        HANDLE                          hPen ;

        switch (iMessage)                       /* process windows messages */
        {
                case WM_CREATE:
                        GetClientRect (hWnd, &rWind) ;
                        hScroll = CreateWindow ("SCROLLBAR", "",
                                WS_CHILD | WS_VISIBLE | SBS_HORZ | SBS_BOTTOMALIGN,
                                rWind.left, rWind.top, rWind.right, rWind.bottom,
                                hWnd, NULL , ghInstance, NULL) ;
                        ShowScrollBar (hWnd, SB_HORZ, TRUE) ;
                        SetScrollRange (hWnd, SB_HORZ, 0, 10, FALSE) ;
                        nScrollValue = nOldValue = 0 ;
                        SetScrollPos (hWnd, SB_HORZ, nScrollValue, TRUE) ;
                        break ;
                case WM_HSCROLL:
                        hrgnUpdate = CreateRectRgn (0, 1, 2, 3) ;
                        hDC = GetDC (hWnd) ;
                        GetClientRect (hWnd, &rWind) ;   /* get client rectangle */
                        rClip.left = rWind.left + 20 ;    /* set clipping region */
                        rClip.right = rWind.right - 20 ; /* inside of client rect */
                        rClip.top = rWind.top + 20 ;
                        rClip.bottom = rWind.bottom - 20 ;
                        switch (wParam)
                        {
                        case SB_THUMBPOSITION:          /* user has moved scroll thumb */
                                nScrollValue = LOWORD (lParam) ;
                                if (nScrollValue != nOldValue)
                                {
                                        SetScrollPos (hWnd, SB_HORZ, nScrollValue, TRUE) ;
                                        ScrollDC (hDC,
                                                20 * (nScrollValue - nOldValue), 0,
                                                (LPRECT) &rWind, (LPRECT) &rClip,
                                                hrgnUpdate,     (LPRECT) &rUpdate) ;
                                        nOldValue = nScrollValue ;
                                }
                                break ;
                        case SB_LINEDOWN:               /* user clicked scroll rt arrow */
                                nScrollValue++ ;
                                nScrollValue = nScrollValue > 10 ? 10 : nScrollValue ;
                                if (nScrollValue != nOldValue)
                                {
```

```
                                    SetScrollPos (hWnd, SB_HORZ, nScrollValue, TRUE) ;
                                    ScrollDC (hDC,
                                            20 * (nScrollValue - nOldValue), 0,
                                            (LPRECT) &rWind, (LPRECT) &rClip,
                                            hrgnUpdate,     (LPRECT) &rUpdate) ;
                                    nOldValue = nScrollValue ;
                            }
                            break ;
                    case SB_LINEUP:                     /* user clicked scroll lf arrow */
                            nScrollValueñ ;
                            nScrollValue = nScrollValue < 0 ? 0 : nScrollValue ;
                            if (nScrollValue != nOldValue)
                            {
                                    SetScrollPos (hWnd, SB_HORZ, nScrollValue, TRUE) ;
                                    ScrollDC (hDC,
                                            20 * (nScrollValue - nOldValue), 0,
                                            (LPRECT) &rWind, (LPRECT) &rClip,
                                            hrgnUpdate,     (LPRECT) &rUpdate) ;
                                    nOldValue = nScrollValue ;
                            }
                            break ;
                    }
                    ReleaseDC (hWnd, hDC) ;
                    DeleteObject (hrgnUpdate) ;
                    break ;
            case WM_COMMAND:                            /* process menu items */
                    switch (wParam)
                    {
                    case IDM_DOIT:                      /* User hit the "Do it" menu item */
                            hDC = GetDC (hWnd) ;
                            hPen = GetStockObject (BLACK_PEN) ;
                            for (i = 0 ; i < 20 ; i++)          /* paint 20 lines */
                            {
                                    MoveTo (hDC, i * 8, 0) ;
                                    LineTo (hDC, i * 8, 400) ;
                            }
                            DeleteObject (hPen) ;
                            ReleaseDC (hWnd, hDC) ;
                            break ;
                    case IDM_QUIT:
                            DestroyWindow (hWnd) ;
                            break ;
                    }
                    break ;
            case WM_DESTROY:            /* stop application */
                    PostQuitMessage (0) ;
                    break ;
            default:                    /* default windows message processing */
                    return DefWindowProc (hWnd, iMessage, wParam, lParam) ;
    }
    return (0L) ;
}
```

SCROLLWINDOW   ■ Win 2.0   ■ Win 3.0   ■ Win 3.1

Purpose	Scrolls a window's client area in the X and Y directions.
Syntax	void **ScrollWindow**(HWND *hWnd*, int *XAmount*, int *YAmount*, LPRECT *lpRect*, LPRECT *lpClipRect*);
Description	This is a simpler scrolling function than ScrollDC(), but it lacks the ability to compute regions or rectangles uncovered by the scrolling process. Instead the uncovered areas are automatically placed into the window's update region for painting on the next WM_PAINT cycle.
Uses	Scrolling small windows where separate logic is applied to compute the uncovered regions.
Returns	No returned value (void).

See Also   ScrollDC()

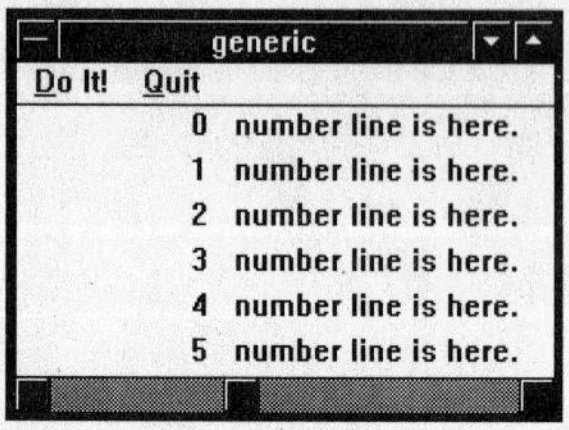

Parameters

hWnd   HWND: The handle of the window that has the client area that will be scrolled.

XAmount   int: The amount to scroll the window in the *X* direction. Device units are used. Positive values scroll right, negative values scroll left.

YAmount   int: The amount to scroll the window in the *Y* direction. Device units are used. Positive values scroll down, negative values scroll up.

Figure 5-7. ScrollWindow() Example.

lpRect   LPRECT: A pointer to a rectangle structure containing the portion of the client area to be scrolled. NULL if the entire client area is to be scrolled. Use GetClientRect() to determine the bounding rectangle of the client area if you will be scrolling a portion of it.

lpClipRect   LPRECT: A pointer to a rectangle structure that contains the clipping rectangle to be scrolled. If the clipping rectangle is within the *lpRect* area, only points within *lpClipRect* will be scrolled. Set equal to NULL if the entire window is to be scrolled.

Related Messages WM_HSCROLL, WM_VSCROLL

Example   This example, illustrated in Figure 5-7, scrolls some text in the client area, based on the position of the horizontal scroll bar at the window's bottom. The text is initially painted when the user clicks the "Do It!" menu item. Because there is no automatic repainting of clipped text on the right side, scrolling the text into the window's side causes the end of the text to be lost.

```
long FAR PASCAL WndProc (HWND hWnd, unsigned iMessage, WORD wParam, LONG lParam)
{
        static          HWND    hScroll ;
        static          int     nScrollValue, nOldValue ;
        char            cBuf [10] ;
        HDC             hDC ;
        int             i ;
        RECT            rWind ;

        switch (iMessage)                       /* process windows messages */
        {
                case WM_CREATE:
                        GetClientRect (hWnd, &rWind) ;
                        hScroll = CreateWindow ("SCROLLBAR", "",
                                WS_CHILD | WS_VISIBLE | SBS_HORZ | SBS_BOTTOMALIGN,
                                rWind.left, rWind.top, rWind.right, rWind.bottom,
                                hWnd, NULL , ghInstance, NULL) ;
                        ShowScrollBar (hWnd, SB_HORZ, TRUE) ;
                        SetScrollRange (hWnd, SB_HORZ, 0, 10, FALSE) ;
                        nScrollValue = nOldValue = 0 ;
                        SetScrollPos (hWnd, SB_HORZ, nScrollValue, TRUE) ;
                        break ;
                case WM_HSCROLL:
                        switch (wParam)
                        {
                        case SB_THUMBPOSITION:   /* user has moved scroll thumb */
                                nScrollValue = LOWORD (lParam) ;
                                if (nScrollValue != nOldValue)
                                {
                                        SetScrollPos (hWnd, SB_HORZ, nScrollValue, TRUE) ;
                                        ScrollWindow (hWnd,
                                                20 * (nScrollValue - nOldValue), 0,
                                                NULL, NULL) ;
                                        nOldValue = nScrollValue ;
```

```
                        }
                        break ;
             case SB_LINEDOWN:       /* user clicked scroll rt arrow */
                        nScrollValue++ ;
                        nScrollValue = nScrollValue > 10 ? 10 : nScrollValue ;
                        if (nScrollValue != nOldValue)
                        {
                                SetScrollPos (hWnd, SB_HORZ, nScrollValue, TRUE) ;
                                ScrollWindow (hWnd,
                                        20 * (nScrollValue - nOldValue), 0,
                                        NULL, NULL) ;
                                nOldValue = nScrollValue ;
                        }
                        break ;
             case SB_LINEUP:         /* user clicked scroll lf arrow */
                        nScrollValueñ ;
                        nScrollValue = nScrollValue < 0 ? 0 : nScrollValue ;
                        if (nScrollValue != nOldValue)
                        {
                                SetScrollPos (hWnd, SB_HORZ, nScrollValue, TRUE) ;
                                ScrollWindow (hWnd,
                                        20 * (nScrollValue - nOldValue), 0,
                                        NULL, NULL) ;
                                nOldValue = nScrollValue ;
                        }
                        break ;
             }
             break ;
       case WM_COMMAND:                 /* process menu items */
             switch (wParam)
             {
             case IDM_DOIT:             /* User hit the "Do it" menu item */
                        hDC = GetDC (hWnd) ;
                        for (i = 0 ; i < 20 ; i++)        /* draw some text */
                        {
                                itoa (i, cBuf, 10) ;
                                TextOut (hDC, 0, i * 20, cBuf, strlen (cBuf)) ;
                                TextOut (hDC, 20, i * 20,
                                        "number line is here.", 20) ;
                        }
                        ReleaseDC (hWnd, hDC) ;
                        break ;
             case IDM_QUIT:
                        DestroyWindow (hWnd) ;
                        break ;
             }
             break ;
       case WM_DESTROY:            /* stop application */
             PostQuitMessage (0) ;
             break ;
       default:                    /* default windows message processing */
             return DefWindowProc (hWnd, iMessage, wParam, lParam) ;
       }
       return (0L) ;
}
```

SETSCROLLPOS   ■ Win 2.0   ■ Win 3.0   ■ Win 3.1

Purpose	Sets the position of the scroll bar thumb.
Syntax	int **SetScrollPos**(HWND *hWnd*, int *nBar*, int *nPos*, BOOL *bRedraw*);
Description	The physical location after the thumb depends on the ranges set for the scroll bar's minimum and maximum values. The thumb's position will be ratioed between these two extremes. Values beyond the limits of the scroll bar range result in the thumb at an end of the scroll bar (no danger of going past limits).

Uses	Generally used when the scroll bar is first created or shown, to make the thumb position match the value represented. It can also be used for building keyboard interface functionality.
Returns	int, the previous position of the scroll bar thumb.
See Also	SetScrollRange(), GetScrollPos(), GetScrollRange()
Parameters	
hWnd	HWND: The scroll bar control handle if *nBar* is SB_CTL, or the window handle if *nBar* is SB_HORZ or SB_VERT.
nBar	int: The type of scroll bar. This can be any of the types listed in Table 5-6.

Value	Meaning	⊠
SB_CTL	A scroll bar control. In this case, set *hWnd* equal to the scroll bar handle.	
SB_HORZ	A horizontal scroll bar tied to the window. In this case, *hWnd* should be the window's handle.	
SB_VERT	A vertical scroll bar tied to the window. In this case, *hWnd* should be the window's handle.	

Table 5-6. Scroll Bar Types.

nPos	int: The new scroll bar thumb position.
bRedraw	BOOL: TRUE if the scroll bar should be redrawn to show the new thumb position, FALSE if not. Use it if you are going to call another scroll bar function, which will then redraw.
Related Messages	WM_HSCROLL, WM_VSCROLL
Example	See the following example under the SetScrollRange() function description.

SETSCROLLRANGE ■ Win 2.0　■ Win 3.0　■ Win 3.1

Purpose	Establishes the upper and lower ranges of a scroll bar.
Syntax	void **SetScrollRange**(HWND *hWnd*, int *nBar*, int *nMinPos*, int *nMaxPos*, BOOL *bRedraw*);
Uses	Used when the scroll bar is created to establish the upper and lower limits of the scroll bar range.
Returns	No returned value (void).
See Also	SetScrollPos(), GetScrollRange(), GetScrollPos()
Parameters	
hWnd	HWND: The scroll bar control handle if *nBar* is SB_CTL, or the window handle if *nBar* is SB_HORZ or SB_VERT.
nBar	int: The type of scroll bar. This can be any of the types listed in Table 5-7.

Value	Meaning	⊠
SB_CTL	A scroll bar control. In this case, set *hWnd* equal to the scroll bar handle.	
SB_HORZ	A horizontal scroll bar tied to the window. In this case, *hWnd* should be the window's handle.	
SB_VERT	A vertical scroll bar tied to the window. In this case, *hWnd* should be the window's handle.	

Table 5-7. Scroll Bar Types.

nMinPos	int: The scroll bar lower limit.
nMaxPos	int: The scroll bar upper limit.
bRedraw	BOOL: TRUE if the scroll bar should be redrawn to show the new thumb position, FALSE if not. Use it if you are going to call another scroll bar function, which will then redraw.

Related Messages WM_HSCROLL, WM_VSCROLL

Example This example creates a scroll bar control and attaches it to the main window. The scroll bar range is set from 0 to 10, and the thumb moved to a value of zero. Note how ShowScrollBar() is used to attach the scroll bar (a child window) to the application's main window.

```
long FAR PASCAL WndProc (HWND hWnd, unsigned iMessage, WORD wParam, LONG lParam)
{
        static          HWND    hScroll ;
        RECT                    rWind ;

        switch (iMessage)                           /* process windows messages */
        {
                case WM_CREATE:
                        GetClientRect (hWnd, &rWind) ;
                        hScroll = CreateWindow ("SCROLLBAR", "",
                                WS_CHILD | WS_VISIBLE | SBS_HORZ | SBS_BOTTOMALIGN,
                                rWind.left, rWind.top, rWind.right, rWind.bottom,
                                hWnd, NULL , ghInstance, NULL) ;
                        ShowScrollBar (hWnd, SB_HORZ, TRUE) ;
                        SetScrollRange (hWnd, SB_HORZ, 0, 10, FALSE) ;
                        nScrollValue = nOldValue = 0 ;
                        SetScrollPos (hWnd, SB_HORZ, nScrollValue, TRUE) ;
                        break ;
```
[Other program lines]

SHOWSCROLLBAR   ■ Win 2.0   ■ Win 3.0   ■ Win 3.1

Purpose	Makes a scroll bar visible and establishes its links to the parent window (if any).
Syntax	void **ShowScrollBar**(HWND *hWnd*, WORD *wBar*, BOOL *bShow*);
Description	Shows or hides a scroll bar. This function should be used rather than ShowWindow() to make scroll bars visible. ShowScrollBar() allows a horizontal or vertical scroll bar to be linked to a window's frame.
Uses	Used during the initial creation of a scroll bar, or later to hide or redisplay the scroll bar. Do **not** call this function while processing a scroll bar message.
Returns	No returned value (void).
See Also	ShowWindow()
Parameters	
hWnd	HWND: The scroll bar control handle if *nBar* is SB_CTL, or the window handle if *nBar* is SB_HORZ or SB_VERT.
nBar	int: The type of scroll bar. This can be any of the types listed in Table 5-8.

Value	Meaning
SB_BOTH	Both horizontal and vertical scroll bars attached to a window.
SB_CTL	A scroll bar control. In this case, set *hWnd* equal to the scroll bar handle.
SB_HORZ	A horizontal scroll bar tied to the window. In this case, *hWnd* should be the window's handle.
SB_VERT	A vertical scroll bar tied to the window. In this case, *hWnd* should be the window's handle.

Table 5-8. Scroll Bar Types.

bShow   BOOL: TRUE if the scroll bar is to be visible, FALSE if it is to be hidden.

Example   See the previous example under the SetScrollRange() function description.

The mouse is used extensively in Windows programs for many purposes. Windows provides excellent built-in support for controlling the mouse. Windows also supports a related concept, the "caret." This is a blinking line (or shape) that can be positioned in the client area to highlight a position. Typically, it is used in word processing applications to show where the next keyboard input will be as text is entered on the screen. Using the caret to fix locations on the screen allows the mouse cursor to be free for menu selections and other uses that take it off the window's client area. Physically, the mouse cursor is a small bitmap that is displayed and erased at different locations on the screen to produce the illusion of movement. This bitmap shape can be changed as the program runs. Many applications can be improved by having the mouse cursor shape change from the usual arrow shape to something more appropriate for the activity. "Pen" shapes for drawing, "hands" for pushing buttons, and even "little men" for playing games are possible. The Windows versions 3.0 and higher support dynamically changing the shape of the cursor as the program runs and basing the cursor shape on bitmap images.

Mouse Message Overview

From the programmer's point of view, the mouse interacts with a program by sending a series of messages. A good way to get a feel for this message flow is to turn on the Windows Spy program that comes with the Software Development Kit (SDK). Set Spy to receive messages from *all* windows. A typical Spy screen is shown in Figure 6-1.

In this example, Spy is tracking messages sent to a program called SNAP3. Here are the first three messages and how to interpret them.

WM_SETCURSOR

Windows uses this message if it needs to change the cursor shape.

WM_NCMOUSEMOVE

The mouse cursor has moved within a nonclient area of the window.

WM_NCHITTEST

This message tests what type of object the cursor is over (for example, border, caption, client area, etc.).

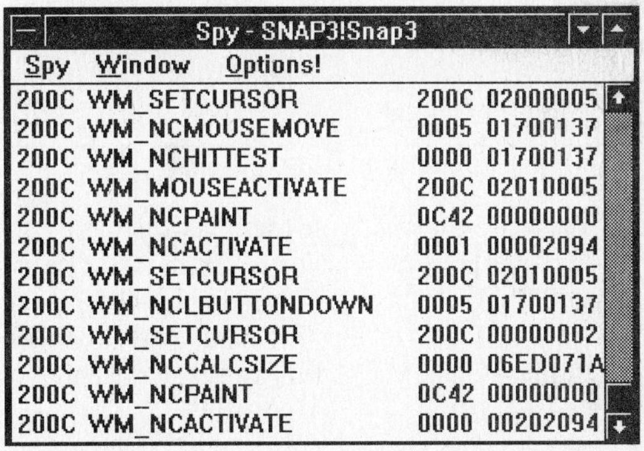

The values shown in hexadecimal on the right side of the Spy window are the *wParam* and *lParam* data that is sent with the message. *wParam* is a WORD, so it

Spy - SNAP3!Snap3		
Spy Window Options!		
200C WM_SETCURSOR	200C	02000005
200C WM_NCMOUSEMOVE	0005	01700137
200C WM_NCHITTEST	0000	01700137
200C WM_MOUSEACTIVATE	200C	02010005
200C WM_NCPAINT	0C42	00000000
200C WM_NCACTIVATE	0001	00002094
200C WM_SETCURSOR	200C	02010005
200C WM_NCLBUTTONDOWN	0005	01700137
200C WM_SETCURSOR	200C	00000002
200C WM_NCCALCSIZE	0000	06ED071A
200C WM_NCPAINT	0C42	00000000
200C WM_NCACTIVATE	0000	00202094

Figure 6-1. Windows Spy Program Viewing Mouse Messages.

only has 16 bits of information, but *lParam* contains 32 bits. These parameters are used to encode the mouse position on the screen, and encode the data about what type of object the mouse cursor is above. We will examine these fields in a moment.

After a little fooling around with Spy, you will realize that Windows sends a lot of messages to your program as you move the mouse or use its buttons. Fortunately, most programs can ignore the majority of these messages and just pass them to the default window's procedure. The messages that you are most likely to use are WM_MOUSEMOVE, WM_LBUTTONDOWN, and its cousins (WM_RBUTTONDOWN, etc.) for detecting the left, right, or center mouse button being pressed or released.

Common Mouse Messages

When you move the mouse, Windows sends a WM_MOUSEMOVE message. The message is not sent every time the mouse cursor moves from one screen pixel to the next. How often the message is sent depends on how fast a computer is running Windows. In general terms, you can expect to get this message about every tenth pixel as the user sweeps the mouse cursor across the screen, more often if the cursor is moved slowly.

When your program receives a WM_MOUSEMOVE message, the *lParam* value contains the cursor's *X,Y* position on the screen. The *Y* position is the high-order 16 bits, while the *X* position is in the low-order 16. Extracting the two WORD-sized values from a LONG parameter is such a common task that the WINDOWS.H file provides the LOWORD and HIWORD macros to automate the task. A typical program fragment for dealing with WM_MOUSEMOVE messages in the WinProc() function is

```
long FAR PASCAL WndProc (HWND hWnd, unsigned iMessage, WORD wParam, LONG lParam)
{
        int     nXpos, nYpos ;

        switch (iMessage)                                      /* process windows messages */
        {
                case WM_MOUSEMOVE:
                        nXpos = LOWORD (lParam) ;
                        nYpos = HIWORD (lParam) ;
                ...
```

Note that the mouse cursor position is given relative to the upper left corner of the window's client area. Windows provides two functions for converting back and forth between screen and client coordinates: ScreenToClient() and ClientToScreen(). These functions are often used as part of the mouse message processing logic. The other basic set of messages have to do with pressing and releasing the mouse button(s). Windows supports one, two, and three button mice, but provides no method to determine which type is in use. In practice, most programmers assume the conservative case and only use the left mouse button. The messages passed to your program from the mouse button active inside the program's client area are summarized in Table 6-1.

Button	Pressed	Released	Pressed a Second Time	☒
Left	WM_LBUTTONDOWN	WM_LBUTTONUP	W_LBUTTONDBLCLK	
Middle	WM_MBUTTONDOWN	WM_MBUTTONUP	WM_MBUTTONDBLCLK	
Bottom	WM_RBUTTONDOWN	WM_RBUTTONUP	WM_RBUTTONDBLCLK	

Table 6-1. Client Area Mouse Button Messages.

You will not normally use them, but there is a parallel set of messages that are sent for mouse button activity outside of the program's client area. These messages have the homolog names such as WM_NCLBUTTONDOWN, etc., where "NC" stands for "Nonclient." Double-clicking the mouse will not automatically generate a double-click message. You must specify that you want these messages in the window's class definition. This involves adding the CS_DBLCLKS value to the class style as shown here.

```
        wndclass.style = CS_HREDRAW | CS_VREDRAW | CS_DBLCLKS ;
```

This would be a typical setting prior to calling RegisterClass(). All of the mouse button messages return the *X* and *Y* coordinates of the cursor in the *lParam* parameter, just like WM_MOUSEMOVE. They also use *wParam* encodes if one of the other mouse buttons, or the shift or control keys, are down when the specified mouse button is pressed. The full descriptions of the messages are given in Chapter 9, *Windows Messages*.

You can find out if the system has a mouse by calling

```
        bMouse = GetSystemMetrics (SM_MOUSEPRESENT) ;
```

The function will return TRUE if there is a mouse, FALSE if not. You can provide an imitation of mouse control by converting from keyboard cursor keypresses to mouse movements. The SetCursorPos() function allows direct control of the cursor location without reference to a mouse. There is no direct way to find out out how many buttons the system mouse has.

Caution: The mouse is a shared resource between all running programs under Windows. Some of the mouse control functions, such as GetCapture() and SetDoubleClickTime(), will affect all of the programs running. Care must be taken to free the mouse, and return the system parameters to their original state, as quickly as possible.

Mouse Functions

The most frequently used mouse function is LoadCursor. It either loads one of the predefined cursor shapes or allows you to load a custom cursor created with the SDKPaint program. Custom cursors have to be referenced in the program's resource .RC file and given a name. For example, to load the cursor file HAND.CUR created with SDKPaint and give the resulting cursor shape the name "hand," add the following line to the resource file

```
hand            CURSOR       hand.cur
```

The cursor shape can be attached to a window's class definition. Windows then switches to that cursor shape any time the mouse cursor is within the window's client area. The function LoadCursor() does the work of pulling the cursor out of the resource data so that it can be attached to the class definition. Use a statement like

```
wndclass.hCursor        = LoadCursor (ghInstance, "hand") ;
```

prior to using RegisterClass() to create the class definition. If you plan to switch between cursor shapes within the bounds of one window, you are better off not assigning a cursor to the window's class. In this case, set the class cursor to NULL, as shown here.

```
wndclass.hCursor        = NULL:
```

Then you can turn on the right cursor shape as the program receives WM_SETCURSOR . A typical code fragment for a program that uses two cursors would be

```
long FAR PASCAL WndProc (HWND hWnd, unsigned iMessage, WORD wParam, LONG lParam)
{
        static          HCURSOR hHandCursor, hArrowCursor ;
        static          BOOL    bUseHand = FALSE ;

        switch (iMessage)                       /* process windows messages */
        {
                case WM_CREATE:
                        hArrowCursor = LoadCursor (NULL, IDC_ARROW) ;
                        hHandCursor = LoadCursor (ghInstance, (LPSTR) "hand") ;
                        break ;
                case WM_SETCURSOR:
                        if (bUseHand)
                                SetCursor (hHandCursor) ;
                        else
                                SetCursor (hArrowCursor) ;
                        break ;
```

[Other program lines]

The ultimate cursor shape control is the CreateCursor() function, added with the 3.0 version of Windows. This function allows you to change the shape of the cursor as the program runs, or as the mouse moves. It can be used to create a cursor that shows the numeric values of the cursor position as the mouse moves. Other creative uses are possible. CreateCursor() defines a cursor with two memory areas that contain bitmaps of the cursor shape. The bitmaps are combined using logical AND and XOR operations to provide black, white, transparent, and inverse screen coloring on every pixel of the cursor.

Caret Functions

The caret is a blinking line or object that marks a temporary location on the screen. It is used in word processing applications to mark where the next typed letter will be displayed. Similar uses appear in music score programs. The caret automatically appears in edit controls (created with CreateWindow()). Carets inside edit controls do not have to be controlled by your program, as the edit control has all of the built-in logic for moving the caret. The caret is a system global resource. This means that there can only be one caret visible on the screen, no matter how many windows or edit controls are visible. If you open a new window and it displays a caret, any other caret on the screen will vanish. This is logical, as otherwise the user would not be able to tell where the next keyboard input would end up. Carets are manipulated as static objects. They do not send messages back to windows. Generally, carets are defined (using CreateCaret()) as vertical lines, although they can be bitmap images. Windows provides support for moving the caret, changing its blinking speed, and hiding it when not needed. If you use a caret in an application, you will need to process the WM_SETFOCUS and WM_KILLFOCUS messages. When the application gains the input focus, create and show the caret using CreateCaret() and ShowCaret(). When it loses the input focus, call DestroyCaret() to eliminate it. There is an example of this logic under the CreateCaret() function description.

Mouse and Cursor Function Summaries

Table 6-2 summarizes the mouse and cursor functions. The complete function descriptions are after the table.

Function	Purpose	⊠
ClientToScreen	Converts a point from client coordinates to screen coordinates.	
ClipCursor	Confines the mouse cursor to an area on the screen.	
CreateCaret	Creates a caret shape.	
CreateCursor	Builds a cursor shape.	
DestroyCaret	Removes a caret from a window.	
DestroyCursor	Deletes a cursor created with CreateCursor().	
GetCapture	Retrieves a handle to the window that has captured the mouse.	
GetCaretBlinkTime	Finds the current rate at which the caret is flashing.	
GetCaretPos	Determines the location of the caret in a window's client area.	
GetClipCursor	Determines the rectangle that the mouse was last confined to by ClipBursor(). (Win 3.1)	
GetCursorPos	Retrieves the X,Y position of the mouse cursor.	
GetDoubleClickTime	Retrieves the double-click time value for the mouse.	
HideCaret	Makes a caret invisible.	
LoadCursor	Loads a new cursor shape.	
ReleaseCapture	Releases capture of the mouse.	
ScreenToClient	Converts from screen coordinates to client window coordinates.	
SetCapture	Captures the mouse so that only the program with the mouse captured receives mouse messages.	
SetCaretBlinkTime	Sets the rate at which the caret shape flashes on the screen.	
SetCaretPos	Sets the position of the caret.	
SetCursor	Establishes which cursor shape to display.	
SetCursorPos	Moves the mouse cursor to a new location.	
SetDoubleClickTime	Changes the mouse button double-click time.	
ShowCaret	Makes the caret visible at its current location.	
ShowCursor	Shows or hides the cursor shape.	
SwapMouseButton	Reverses the right and left mouse buttons.	

Table 6-2. Mouse and Cursor Function Summaries.

CLIENTTOSCREEN   ■ Win 2.0   ■ Win 3.0   ■ Win 3.1

Purpose   Converts a point from client coordinates to screen coordinates.

Syntax   void **ClientToScreen**(HWND *hWnd*, LPPOINT *lpPoint*);

Description	The point structure pointed to by *lpPoint* is updated using screen coordinates. Screen coordinates are pixels measured from the upper left corner of the screen. Client coordinates are pixels measured from the upper left corner of the window's client area.
Uses	Use in programs that use the mouse to capture images off of the screen.
Returns	No returned value (void).
See Also	SetCapture(), ScreenToClient()
Parameters	
hWnd	HWND: The parent window's handle.
lpPoint	LPPOINT: A long pointer to a point structure. Initially, this point contains the client point coordinates.
Related Messages	WM_LBUTTONDOWN, WM_MOUSEMOVE
Example	Here is a useful function which you can use in screen capture programs. The function takes two points in client coordinates (as might be retrieved from the *lParam* data from a WM_LBUTTON-DOWN message) and converts them to window coordinates. The function then draws a rectangle onto the screen, outlining an area between the two points.

```
/* OutlineBlock() writes a rectangle on the screen given the two corner */
/* points.  The R2_NOT style is used, so drawing twice on the same location */
/* erases the outline. */

void OutlineBlock (HWND hWnd, POINT beg, POINT end)
{
        HDC    hDC ;

        hDC = CreateDC ("DISPLAY", NULL, NULL, NULL) ;
        ClientToScreen (hWnd, &beg) ;        /* convert to screen units */
        ClientToScreen (hWnd, &end) ;
        SetROP2 (hDC, R2_NOT) ;               /* use logical NOT brush */
        MoveTo (hDC, beg.x, beg.y) ;          /* draw rectangle */
        LineTo (hDC, end.x, beg.y) ;
        LineTo (hDC, end.x, end.y) ;
        LineTo (hDC, beg.x, end.y) ;
        LineTo (hDC, beg.x, beg.y) ;
        DeleteDC (hDC) ;
}
```

CLIPCURSOR   ■ Win 2.0   ■ Win 3.0   ■ Win 3.1

Purpose	Confines the mouse cursor to an area on the screen.
Syntax	void **ClipCursor**(LPRECT *lpRect*);
Description	After calling this function, the mouse pointer can only be moved within the bounds set by the *lpRect* rectangle.
Uses	Use sparingly, if at all. If the mouse bounds are set in a program, they will continue to be in effect after the program terminates. This basically makes the mouse useless, forcing the user to reboot the computer. A better way for a program to limit mouse's activities is with GetCapture().
Returns	No returned value (void).
See Also	GetCapture(), SetCursor(), GetClipCursor()
Parameters	
lpRect	LPRECT: A long pointer to a rectangle structure. Use SetRect() to quickly fill in the rectangle's dimensions. Set *lpRect* equal to NULL to free the mouse to move anywhere on the screen.
Related Messages	WM_MOUSEMOVE
Example	When the user clicks the "Do It!" menu item, the mouse is confined to a region bounded by a

rectangle with screen coordinates 10,10 and 200,200. The program frees the mouse when the user clicks the "Quit" menu item.

```
long FAR PASCAL WndProc (HWND hWnd, unsigned iMessage, WORD wParam, LONG lParam)
{
        RECT    rMouseCage ;

        switch (iMessage)                       /* process windows messages */
        {
                case WM_COMMAND:                /* process menu items */
                        switch (wParam)
                        {
                        case IDM_DOIT:                  /* User hit the "Do it" menu item */
                                SetRect ((LPRECT) &rMouseCage, 10, 10, 200, 200) ;
                                ClipCursor ((LPRECT) &rMouseCage) ;     /* trap mouse */
                                break ;
                        case IDM_QUIT:
                                ClipCursor (NULL) ;     /* let the mouse loose again */
                                DestroyWindow (hWnd) ;
                                break ;
                        }
                        break ;
                case WM_DESTROY:                        /* stop application */
                        PostQuitMessage (0) ;
                        break ;
                default:                                /* default windows message processing */
                        return DefWindowProc (hWnd, iMessage, wParam, lParam) ;
        }
        return (0L) ;
}
```

CREATECARET   ■ Win 2.0   ■ Win 3.0   ■ Win 3.1

Purpose	Creates a caret shape.
Syntax	void **CreateCaret**(HWND *hWnd*, HBITMAP *hBitmap*, int *nWidth*, int *nHeight*);
Description	Only one caret can exist for any window at a given time. This function creates a caret, removing any existing caret. The caret can either be a bitmap or a vertical line of set size.
Uses	The first step in displaying a caret. This function is followed by SetCaretPos() and ShowCaret().
Returns	No returned value (void).
See Also	DestroyCaret(), SetCaretPos(), ShowCaret(), LoadBitmap()
Parameters	
hWnd	HWND: A handle to the window that owns the caret.
hBitmap	HBITMAP: A handle to the bitmap to use as the caret. The handle is obtained using the LoadBitmap() function. *hBitmap* can be NULL. In this case, a black caret *nWidth* wide by *nHeight* tall is constructed. If *hBitmap* is 1, a gray caret is created.
nWidth	int: The width of the caret in logical units. The size will depend on the mapping mode in effect. Ignored if *hBitmap* is not NULL. Set to NULL to use the default width, equal to the window border width.
nHeight	int: The height of the caret in logical units. The size will depend on the mapping mode in effect. Ignored if *hBitmap* is not NULL. Set to NULL to use the default height, a multiple of the window border width.
Related Message	WM_SETFOCUS, WM_KILLFOCUS
Example	This example shows the creation of two carets. The first is created when the program starts. This is a black cursor, 3 pixels wide by 20 high. When the user clicks the "Do It!" menu item, a bitmap caret is loaded and displayed.

⇨ **The Resource .RC File**

```
/* generic.rc */
#include <windows.h>
#include "generic.h"
generic          ICON            generic.ico
ibeam            BITMAP          ibeam.bmp

generic MENU
BEGIN
    MENUITEM "&Do It!"           IDM_DOIT
    MENUITEM "&Quit",               IDM_QUIT
END
```

The program's WndProc() function uses a static variable *bNewCaret* to keep track of which caret to display. The caret shape is created when the application gains the input focus and is destroyed when the focus is lost. Note how the caret is hidden before painting (WM_PAINT message) and then displayed again. This avoids having the caret bitmap interfere with the painting of the client area.

```
Long FAR PASCAL WndProc (HWND hWnd, unsigned iMessage, WORD wParam, LONG lParam)
{
        static          HBITMAP         hbmCursor ;
        PAINTSTRUCT                     ps ;
        static          BOOL            bNewCaret = FALSE ;

        switch (iMessage)                       /* process windows messages */
        {
                case WM_SETFOCUS:
                        if (bNewCaret)
                        {
                                hbmCursor = LoadBitmap (ghInstance, (LPSTR)"ibeam") ;
                                CreateCaret (hWnd, hbmCursor, NULL, NULL) ;
                        }
                        else
                                CreateCaret (hWnd, NULL, 3, 20) ;
                        SetCaretPos (10, 10) ;
                        ShowCaret (hWnd) ;
                        break ;
                case WM_KILLFOCUS:
                        DestroyCaret () ;
                        break ;
                case WM_PAINT:
                        HideCaret (hWnd) ;
                        BeginPaint (hWnd, &ps) ;
                        TextOut (ps.hdc, 10, 10, "Text output.", 12) ;
                        EndPaint (hWnd, &ps) ;
                        ShowCaret (hWnd) ;
                        break ;
                case WM_COMMAND:                /* process menu items */
                        switch (wParam)
                        {
                        case IDM_DOIT:          /* Change caret shapes */
                                bNewCaret = TRUE ;
                                PostMessage (hWnd, WM_SETFOCUS, 0, OL) ;
                                break ;
                        case IDM_QUIT:          /* send end of application message */
                                DestroyWindow (hWnd) ;
                                break ;
                        }
                        break ;

                case WM_DESTROY:        /* stop application */
                        DeleteObject (hbmCursor) ;
                        PostQuitMessage (0) ;
                        break ;

                default:                /* default windows message processing */
                        return DefWindowProc (hWnd, iMessage, wParam, lParam) ;
```

```
        }
        return (0L) ;
}
```

CREATECURSOR

Purpose   Builds a cursor shape.

Syntax   HCURSOR **CreateCursor**(HANDLE *hInstance*, int *nXhotspot*, int *nYhotspot*, int *nWidth*, int *nHeight*, LPSTR *lpANDbitPlane*, LPSTR *lpXORbitPlane*);

Description   This function allows you to create a mouse cursor shape while the program is running. The cursor shape is controlled by two memory areas that contain masks for the cursor. The bits in these memory blocks are compared to the screen pixels using a logical AND and logical exclusive OR operations. The results are shown in Table 6-3.

AND Bit Mask Value	XOR Bit Mask Value	Result on Screen	⊠
0	0	Black	
0	1	White	
1	0	Transparent	
1	1	Inverted color	

Table 6-3. Cursor Boolean Masks.

Uses   Modifying a cursor shape as the program runs. The cursor can be made to change depending on where it is on the screen, or what action is occurring.

Returns   A handle to the cursor created, NULL on error.

See Also   LoadCursor(), DestroyCursor(), SetCursor()

Parameters

hInstance   HANDLE: The instance handle for the running program.

nXhotspot   int: The horizontal position on the cursor's rectangle that is logically the point with which the cursor points.

nYhotspot   int: The vertical position on the cursor's rectangle that is logically the point with which the cursor points.

nWidth   int: The width of the cursor bitmap in pixels.

nHeight   int: The height of the cursor bitmap in pixels.

lpANDbitPlane   LPSTR: A pointer to the memory area containing the AND mask for the cursor. The Microsoft mouse documentation calls this the "screen mask." See Table 6-3 for the meaning of the AND mask bits.

lpXORbitPlane   LPSTR: A pointer to the memory area containing the XOR mask for the cursor. The Microsoft mouse documentation calls this the "cursor mask." See Table 6-3 for the meaning of the AND mask bits.

Related Messages WM_MOUSEMOVE, WM_SETCURSOR

Example   This example uses CreateCursor() to build a rectangular cursor shape filled with a gray pattern. When the user clicks the "Do It!" menu item, the cursor shape is modified by drawing an *X* on the gray background. The cursor shape is only active in the window's client area. The normal arrow cursor is displayed in the menu, title, and borders of the window, as well as outside of the application's window area. The example takes a shortcut to fill in the background. The cursor data is actually loaded from a bitmap. The bitmap is painted with the stock object "LTGRAY_BRUSH" to come up with the gray pattern. This saves having to figure out how to set each of the memory bits in the areas that CreateCursor() looks to find the cursor shape data. Similarly, the *X* is drawn on the bitmap image and then loaded into the cursor memory area.

```
Long FAR PASCAL WndProc (HWND hWnd, unsigned iMessage, WORD wParam, LONG lParam)
{
        static          HCURSOR hCursor ;
        static          int             nCursX, nCursY, nByteArea ;
        static          HBITMAP hBM ;
        HDC                             hDC ;
        static          HDC             hDCBitmap ;
        static          HANDLE          hmemAND, hmemXOR ;
        LPSTR                           lpAND, lpXOR ;

        switch (iMessage)                       /* process windows messages */
        {
                case WM_CREATE:
                        nCursX = GetSystemMetrics (SM_CXCURSOR) ;        /* get curs size */
                        nCursY = GetSystemMetrics (SM_CYCURSOR) ;
                        hBM = CreateBitmap (nCursX, nCursY, 1, 1, NULL) ;
                        hDC = GetDC (hWnd) ;
                        hDCBitmap = CreateCompatibleDC (hDC) ;    /* get bitmap DC */
                        ReleaseDC (hWnd, hDC) ;
                        nByteArea = (nCursX/8) * nCursY ;
                        SelectObject (hDCBitmap, hBM) ;
                                        /* reserve memory for cursor shape data */
                        hmemAND = GlobalAlloc (GMEM_MOVEABLE, (DWORD) nByteArea) ;
                        hmemXOR = GlobalAlloc (GMEM_MOVEABLE, (DWORD) nByteArea) ;
                                        /* lock the memory areas to work with them */
                        lpAND = GlobalLock (hmemAND) ;
                        lpXOR = GlobalLock (hmemXOR) ;
                                        /* create a gray rectangle cursor */
                        SelectObject (hDCBitmap, GetStockObject (LTGRAY_BRUSH)) ;
                        PatBlt (hDCBitmap, 0, 0, nCursX, nCursY, PATCOPY) ;
                        GetBitmapBits (hBM, (DWORD) nByteArea, lpAND) ;  /* in mem */
                        _fmemset (lpXOR, 0, nByteArea) ; /* XOR mem to all 0's */

                        GlobalUnlock (hmemAND) ;
                        GlobalUnlock (hmemXOR) ;
                        break ;
                case WM_MOUSEMOVE:      /* draw the custom cursor */
                        SetCursor (NULL) ;
                        if (hCursor)
                                DestroyCursor (hCursor) ;/* kill old cursor, if any */
                        lpAND = GlobalLock (hmemAND) ;
                        lpXOR = GlobalLock (hmemXOR) ;
                        hCursor = CreateCursor (ghInstance, 0, 0, nCursX,
                                nCursY, lpAND, lpXOR) ;
                        GlobalUnlock (hmemAND) ;
                        GlobalUnlock (hmemXOR) ;
                        SetCursor (hCursor) ;
                        break ;
                case WM_COMMAND:        /* process menu items */
                        switch (wParam)
                        {
                        case IDM_DOIT:  /* add an X to the cursor bitmap */
                                lpAND = GlobalLock (hmemAND) ;
                                SelectObject (hDCBitmap, GetStockObject (BLACK_PEN)) ;
                                MoveTo (hDCBitmap, 0, 0) ;
                                LineTo (hDCBitmap, nCursX, nCursY) ;
                                MoveTo (hDCBitmap, 0, nCursY) ;
                                LineTo (hDCBitmap, nCursX, 0) ;
                                GetBitmapBits (hBM, (DWORD) nByteArea, lpAND) ;
                                GlobalUnlock (hmemAND) ;
                                break ;
                        case IDM_QUIT:
                                DestroyWindow (hWnd) ;
                                break ;
                        }
```

```
                          break ;
                case WM_DESTROY:           /* stop application */
                          DestroyCursor (hCursor) ;
                          DeleteObject (hBM) ;
                          DeleteDC (hDCBitmap) ;
                          GlobalFree (hmemAND) ;
                          GlobalFree (hmemXOR) ;
                          PostQuitMessage (0) ;
                          break ;
                default:                            /* default windows message processing */
                          return DefWindowProc (hWnd, iMessage, wParam, lParam) ;
        }
        return (0L) ;
}
```

DESTROYCARET   ■ Win 2.0   ■ Win 3.0   ■ Win 3.1

Purpose	Removes a caret from a window.
Syntax	void **DestroyCaret**(void);
Description	Used to destroy cursors created with the CreateCaret() function. Frees any memory associated with the caret, but does not eliminate a bitmap if it was used to create the caret.
Uses	Permanent removal of a caret. Use HideCaret() and ShowCaret() for temporary hiding and displaying of the caret. This function will only work if the current task (running application) owns the caret.
Returns	No returned value (void).
See Also	ShowCaret(), HideCaret(), CreateCaret(), DeleteObject()
Parameters	None (void).
Related Messages	WM_SETFOCUS, WM_KILLFOCUS
Example	See the example under the CreateCaret() function description.

DESTROYCURSOR   □ Win 2.0   ■ Win 3.0   ■ Win 3.1

Purpose	Deletes a cursor created with CreateCursor().
Syntax	BOOL **DestroyCursor**(HCURSOR *hCursor*);
Description	Frees the memory associated with a cursor created with CreateCursor(). Do not use this with cursors loaded from the program's resource .RC file. Also, do not forget to delete the other objects used to create the cursor (see the example under CreateCursor()).
Returns	BOOL. TRUE if the cursor was destroyed, FALSE on error.
See Also	CreateCursor(), DeleteObject()
Parameters	
hCursor	HCURSOR: A handle the cursor created with CreateCursor().
Example	See the example under the CreateCursor() function description.

GETCAPTURE   ■ Win 2.0   ■ Win 3.0   ■ Win 3.1

Purpose	Retrieves a handle to the window that has captured the mouse.
Syntax	HWND **GetCapture**(void);
Description	Once a window captures the mouse, no other application will receive messages from the mouse. GetCapture() allows you to find out which window has captured the mouse.
Uses	Capturing the mouse is normally used in applications that use the mouse to outline or store images off of the screen. GetCapture() can be used to locate the window that has the mouse captive, so that you can send that window a message to release the mouse.

Returns	HWND, the handle of the window that has captured the mouse. NULL if no window has captured the mouse.
See Also	SetCapture(), ReleaseCapture()
Parameters	None (void).
Related Messages	WM_MOUSEMOVE
Example	This example prints the name of the window with the mouse captured on the window's client area every time the window receives a WM_MOUSEMOVE message. When the user clicks the "Do It!" menu item, the program captures the mouse itself. Clicking the left mouse button releases the mouse.

```
long FAR PASCAL WndProc (HWND hWnd, unsigned iMessage, WORD wParam, LONG lParam)
{
        HDC             hDC ;
        HWND            hwndCapture ;
        char            cBuf [25] ;

        switch (iMessage)              /* process windows messages */
        {
                case WM_COMMAND:       /* process menu items */
                        switch (wParam)
                        {
                        case IDM_DOIT:  /* User hit the "Do it" menu item */
                                SetCapture (hWnd) ;
                                break ;
                        case IDM_QUIT:  /* send end of application message */
                                DestroyWindow (hWnd) ;
                                break ;
                        }
                        break ;
                case WM_MOUSEMOVE:
                        hwndCapture = GetCapture () ;
                        hDC = GetDC (hWnd) ;
                        TextOut (hDC, 10, 10,
                                "The window with the mouse captured is:", 38) ;
                        if (!hwndCapture)
                                TextOut (hDC, 10, 40, "<None>", 6) ;
                        else
                        {
                                GetWindowText (hwndCapture, cBuf, 24) ;
                                TextOut (hDC, 10, 40, cBuf, strlen (cBuf) ) ;
                        }
                        ReleaseDC (hWnd, hDC) ;
                        break ;
                case WM_LBUTTONDOWN:
                        ReleaseCapture () ;
                        break ;
                case WM_DESTROY:        /* stop application */
                        PostQuitMessage (0) ;
                        break ;
                default:                        /* default windows message processing */
                        return DefWindowProc (hWnd, iMessage, wParam, lParam) ;
        }
        return (0L) ;
}
```

GETCARETBLINKTIME   ■ Win 2.0   ■ Win 3.0   ■ Win 3.1

Purpose	Finds the current rate at which the caret is flashing.
Syntax	WORD **GetCaretBlinkTime**(void);
Description	Returns the time, in milliseconds, between flashes of the caret. The time is returned even if the caret is not visible.
Returns	WORD, the time in milliseconds between flashes.

See Also	SetCaretBlinkTime(), CreateCaret()
Parameters	None (void).
Example	In this example, the blink rate of the caret is slowed down by 0.1 sec every time the user clicks the "Do It!" menu item. The blink rate is restored to 0.5 sec (500 milliseconds) when the user clicks the "Quit" menu item and exits the program. This example is interesting if two instances of the program are run at the same time. Starting a second copy steals the caret from the first program's client area. Clicking the "Do It!" menu item in either instance of the program slows the blink rate in the window that displays it. The changed blinking rate remains in effect in any application that gains the caret. This visually demonstrates that the caret is a shared resource between applications and instances.

```
Long FAR PASCAL WndProc (HWND hWnd, unsigned iMessage, WORD wParam, LONG lParam)
{
        PAINTSTRUCT             ps ;
        static          BOOL    bNewCaret = FALSE ;
        int                     nTime ;

        switch (iMessage)                       /* process windows messages */
        {
                case WM_SETFOCUS:
                        CreateCaret (hWnd, NULL, 3, 20) ;
                        SetCaretPos (10, 10) ;
                        ShowCaret (hWnd) ;
                        break ;
                case WM_KILLFOCUS:
                        DestroyCaret () ;
                        break ;
                case WM_COMMAND:        /* process menu items */
                        switch (wParam)
                        {
                        case IDM_DOIT:  /* Change caret blink time */
                                nTime = GetCaretBlinkTime () ;
                                nTime += 50 ;
                                SetCaretBlinkTime (nTime) ;
                                break ;
                        case IDM_QUIT:  /* send end of application message */
                                DestroyWindow (hWnd) ;
                                break ;
                        }
                        break ;
                case WM_DESTROY:                /* stop application */
                        SetCaretBlinkTime (500) ;       /* normal blink time*/
                        PostQuitMessage (0) ;
                        break ;
                default:                /* default windows message processing */
                        return DefWindowProc (hWnd, iMessage, wParam, lParam) ;
        }
        return (0L) ;
}
```

GETCARETPOS   ■ Win 2.0   ■ Win 3.0   ■ Win 3.1

Purpose	Determines the location of the caret in a window's client area.
Syntax	void **GetCaretPos**(LPPOINT *lpPoint*);
Description	The current *X* and *Y* positions are loaded into the POINT structure pointed to by *lpPoint*. The program should be sure to use ShowCaret() before using this function. Otherwise, the location returned will be in whatever window currently displays the caret.
Returns	No returned value (void).
See Also	SetCaretPos(), CreateCaret()

Parameters

lpPoint   LPPOINT: A pointer to a point structure that will hold the caret's *X* and *Y* client coordinates. The values are given in logical units.

Example   In this example, the caret is moved 10 units to the right every time the user clicks the "Do It!" menu item. The current caret position is also displayed on the client area.

```
long FAR PASCAL WndProc (HWND hWnd, unsigned iMessage, WORD wParam, LONG lParam)
{
        POINT           ptCaretPos ;
        char            cBuf [10] ;
        HDC             hDC ;

        switch (iMessage)                     /* process windows messages */
        {
                case WM_CREATE:
                        CreateCaret (hWnd, NULL, 3, 20) ;
                        SetCaretPos (10, 10) ;
                        ShowCaret (hWnd) ;
                        break ;
                case WM_COMMAND:           /* process menu items */
                        switch (wParam)
                        {
                        case IDM_DOIT:   /* User hit the "Do it" menu item */
                                GetCaretPos ((LPPOINT) &ptCaretPos) ;
                                SetCaretPos (ptCaretPos.x + 10, ptCaretPos.y) ;
                                itoa (ptCaretPos.x + 10, cBuf, 10) ;
                                hDC = GetDC (hWnd) ;
                                TextOut (hDC, 10, 50, cBuf, strlen (cBuf)) ;
                                TextOut (hDC, 10, 80,
                                        "= current caret X position.", 27) ;
                                ReleaseDC (hWnd, hDC) ;
                                break ;
                        case IDM_QUIT:
                                DestroyWindow (hWnd) ;
                                break ;
                        }
                        break ;
                case WM_DESTROY:/* stop application */
                        PostQuitMessage (0) ;
                        break ;
                default:                        /* default windows message processing */
                        return DefWindowProc (hWnd, iMessage, wParam, lParam) ;
        }
        return (0L) ;
}
```

GetClipCursor   □ Win 2.0   □ Win 3.0   ■ Win 3.1

Purpose   Determines the rectangle that the mouse was last confined to by ClipCursor().

Syntax   void **GetClipCursor** (LPRECT *lpRect*);

Description ClipCursor() is used to limit the mouse cursor to a rectangular area on the screen. GetClipCursor() can be used to determine the current clipping rectangle.

Uses   Seldom used. The cursor is a shared resource between all applications running on the system. Limiting the cursor to an area on the screen violates the Windows design principle of allowing programs to behave independently.

Returns   No returned value (void).

See Also   ClipCursor(), GetWindowRect()

Parameters

lpRect   LPRECT: A pointer to a RECT data structure. GetClipCursor() will fill in the four rectangle coordinate values for the current mouse clipping rectangle. If the mouse is not confined, the screen dimensions are retrieved.

Example   This example, illustrated in Figure 6-2, confines the mouse cursor to the limits of the application's window. The rectangle is recalculated when either a WM_MOVE or WM_SIZE message is received. The coordinates of the clipping rectangle are displayed in the client area. Clicking the "Do It!" menu item temporarily removes the mouse limits.

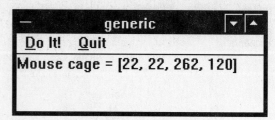

Figure 6-2. GetClipCursor( ) Example.

```
Long FAR PASCAL WndProc (HWND hWnd, unsigned iMessage, WORD wParam, LONG lParam)
{
        RECT                    rCage ;
        PAINTSTRUCT             ps ;
        char                    cBuf [128] ;

        switch (iMessage)                       /* process windows messages */
        {
                case WM_MOVE:
                case WM_SIZE:
                        GetWindowRect (hWnd, &rCage) ;
                        ClipCursor ((LPRECT) &rCage) ;   /* trap mouse in window */
                        InvalidateRect (hWnd, NULL, TRUE) ;      /* force paint */
                        break ;
                case WM_PAINT:
                        BeginPaint (hWnd, &ps) ;
                        GetClipCursor (&rCage) ;
                        TextOut (ps.hdc, 0, 0, cBuf, wsprintf (cBuf,
                                "Mouse cage = [%d, %d, %d, %d]",
                                rCage.left, rCage.top, rCage.right, rCage.bottom)) ;
                        EndPaint (hWnd, &ps) ;
                        break ;
                case WM_COMMAND:                /* process menu items */
                        switch (wParam)
                        {
                        case IDM_DOIT:
                                ClipCursor (NULL) ;     /* free mouse */
                                break ;
                        case IDM_QUIT:
                                DestroyWindow (hWnd) ;
                                break ;
                        }
                        break ;
                case WM_DESTROY:
                        ClipCursor (NULL) ;     /* free mouse */
                        PostQuitMessage (0) ;
                        break ;
                default:
                        return DefWindowProc (hWnd, iMessage, wParam, lParam) ;
        }
        return (0L) ;
}
```

GetCursorPos   ■ Win 2.0   ■ Win 3.0   ■ Win 3.1

Purpose   Retrieves the *X, Y* position of the mouse cursor.

Syntax   void **GetCursorPos**(LPPOINT *lpPoint*);

Description The *X,Y* position of the mouse cursor is loaded into the *lpPoint* structure. Screen coordinates are used. To convert to client coordinates use, ScreenToClient().

Uses	Any time you need to locate the mouse cursor. This is seldom necessary, as moving the mouse generates WM_MOUSEMOVE messages, and clicking the mouse buttons generates WM_LBUTTONDOWN, etc. messages. These messages encode the cursor position in the *lParam* value (Chapter 9, *Windows Messages*, includes all of the message descriptions).

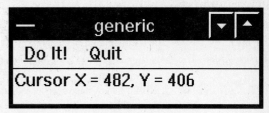

Figure 6-3. GetCursorPos( ) Example.

Returns No returned value (void).

See Also SetCursorPos(), ScreenToClient(), SetCapture(), ReleaseCapture()

Parameters

lpPoint LPPOINT: A pointer to a POINT structure.

Related Messages WM_MOUSEMOVE

Example When the user clicks the "Do It!" menu item, a timer is set. WM_TIMER messages are sent every second, causing the cursor position to be displayed on the screen at these time intervals. (See Figure 6-3.) This updating continues even if the window loses the input focus to another application.

```
long FAR PASCAL WndProc (HWND hWnd, unsigned iMessage, WORD wParam, LONG lParam)
{
        HDC     hDC ;
        POINT   pCursor ;
        char    cBuf [128] ;

        switch (iMessage)                       /* process windows messages */
        {
                case WM_TIMER:
                        GetCursorPos (&pCursor) ;
                        hDC = GetDC (hWnd) ;
                        SetBkMode (hDC, OPAQUE) ;
                        TextOut (hDC, 0, 0, cBuf, wsprintf (cBuf,
                                "Cursor X = %d, Y = %d    ", pCursor.x, pCursor.y)) ;
                        ReleaseDC (hWnd, hDC) ;
                        break ;
                case WM_COMMAND:                /* process menu items */
                        switch (wParam)
                        {
                        case IDM_DOIT:          /* set 1 sec timer */
                                if (!SetTimer (hWnd, 1, 1000, NULL))
                                        MessageBox (hWnd, "Too many clocks or timers!",
                                                "Warning", MB_ICONEXCLAMATION | MB_OK) ;
                                break ;
                        case IDM_QUIT:          /* send end of application message */
                                DestroyWindow (hWnd) ;
                                break ;
                        }
                        break ;
                case WM_DESTROY:                /* stop application */
                        KillTimer (hWnd, 1) ;
                        PostQuitMessage (0) ;
                        break ;
                default:                        /* default windows message processing */
                        return DefWindowProc (hWnd, iMessage, wParam, lParam) ;
        }
        return (0L) ;
}
```

GETDOUBLECLICKTIME
■ Win 2.0   ■ Win 3.0   ■ Win 3.1

Purpose   Retrieves the double-click time value for the mouse.

Syntax   WORD **GetDoubleClickTime**(void);

Description   The double-click time is the number of milliseconds between two mouse clicks. Clicking faster than this value generates a WM_LBUTTONDBLCLK, WM_MBUTTONDBLCLK, or WM_RBUT-TONDBLCLK message for the left, middle, or right mouse buttons, respectively. Note that the WM_LBUTTONDOWN, etc. messages will always be received prior to getting the double-click message.

Uses   Used in advance of SetDoubleClickTime() to find the current double-click time value, prior to changing it.

Returns   WORD, the double-click time in milliseconds.

See Also   SetDoubleClickTime().

Parameters   None (void).

Related Messages   WM_LBUTTONDBLCLK, WM_MBUTTONDBLCLK, WM_RBUTTONDBLCLK

Note   The double-click messages will only be generated if the CS_DBLCLKS style is added to the window's class definition (see the example).

Example   This program detects right button single- and double-clicks and prints messages in the client area for each. The messages are erased by overwriting them with blanks when WM_MOUSEMOVE messages are received. Clicking the "Do It!" menu item increases the double-click time by 100 milliseconds, after displaying the current double-click time. Receiving double-clicks requires that the CS_DBLCLKS style be added to the window's class definition in the WinMain() function

```
wndclass.style = CS_HREDRAW | CS_VREDRAW | CS_DBLCLKS ;
```

Note that the doube-click time is reset to the original timing when the program exits. Other-wise the slower double-click time would continue to affect all of the other programs on the system.

```
Long FAR PASCAL WndProc (HWND hWnd, unsigned iMessage, WORD wParam, LONG lParam)
{
        HDC             hDC ;
        char            cBuf [25] ;
        int             nDoubleTime ;
        static  int     nOldDClick ;

        switch (iMessage)               /* process windows messages */
        {
                case WM_CREATE:
                        nOldDClick = GetDoubleClickTime () ;
                        break ;
                case WM_COMMAND:        /* process menu items */
                        switch (wParam)
                        {
                        case IDM_DOIT:
                                nDoubleTime = GetDoubleClickTime () ;
                                hDC = GetDC (hWnd) ;
                                TextOut (hDC, 10, 10, "The Double Click Time =", 23) ;
                                itoa (nDoubleTime, cBuf, 10) ;
                                TextOut (hDC, 200, 10, cBuf, strlen (cBuf)) ;
                                ReleaseDC (hWnd, hDC) ;
                                SetDoubleClickTime (nDoubleTime + 100) ;
                                break ;
                        case IDM_QUIT:  /* send end of application message */
                                DestroyWindow (hWnd) ;
                                break ;
                        }
                        break ;
```

```
        case WM_MOUSEMOVE:        /* writes over old messages as mouse moves */
              hDC = GetDC (hWnd) ;
              SetBkMode (hDC, OPAQUE) ;
              TextOut (hDC, 10, 30, "                         ", 30) ;
              TextOut (hDC, 10, 50, "                         ", 30) ;
              ReleaseDC (hWnd, hDC) ;
              break ;
        case WM_LBUTTONDOWN:       /* detected the left mouse button down */
              hDC = GetDC (hWnd) ;
              TextOut (hDC, 10, 30, "Got a left button!", 17) ;
              ReleaseDC (hWnd, hDC) ;
              break ;
        case WM_LBUTTONDBLCLK:   /* detected a double click of left button */
              hDC = GetDC (hWnd) ;
              TextOut (hDC, 10, 50, "Got a double click!", 18) ;
              ReleaseDC (hWnd, hDC) ;
              break ;
        case WM_DESTROY:/* stop application */
              SetDoubleClickTime (nOldDClick) ;
              PostQuitMessage (0) ;
              break ;
        default:                  /* default windows message processing */
              return DefWindowProc (hWnd, iMessage, wParam, lParam) ;
      }
      return (0L) ;
}
```

HideCaret   ■ Win 2.0   ■ Win 3.0   ■ Win 3.1

Purpose	Makes a caret invisible.
Syntax	void **HideCaret**(HWND *hWnd*);
Description	The caret must be created with CreateCaret() before it can be visible. As soon as ShowCaret() is called, the caret starts blinking. The caret remains visible until HideCaret() or DestroyCaret() is called. If HideCaret() has been called more than once, an equal number of ShowCaret() calls will be needed before the caret becomes visible.
Uses	It is frequently desirable to hide the caret while the user is doing operations that take the focus of activities away from the client area (menu selections, etc.), or during WM_PAINT processing. As soon as the activity is done, the caret can be made visible again with ShowCaret(). The caret is shared by all applications. If a caret is displayed on one program's window, a caret in another running program's window will disappear automatically.
Returns	No returned value (void).
See Also	ShowCaret(), DestroyCaret(), SetCaretBlinkTime()
Parameters	
hWnd	HWND: A handle for the window that owns the caret. A window can only own one caret at one time. Use CreateCaret() to add a caret shape to a window. Setting *hWnd* to NULL will hide the caret if any window in the current task owns the caret.
Example	See the example under the CreateCaret() function description.

LoadCursor   ■ Win 2.0   ■ Win 3.0   ■ Win 3.1

Purpose	Loads a new cursor shape.
Syntax	HCURSOR **LoadCursor**(HANDLE *hInstance*, LPSTR *lpCursorName*);
Description	This function allows you to load predefined cursors that Window's supplies, or a custom cursor designed with the SDKPaint program. For the latter, the cursor name is included in the resource .RC file. Cursors must be loaded prior to calling SetCursor() to make them visible.

Uses
If the cursor is loaded as part of the window's class definition, the mouse cursor will change to the loaded cursor shape any time the mouse is within the windows client area. If the goal is to have different cursor shapes within the same window's client area at different times, then the window class cursor shape should be set to NULL, and the cursor specified by calling SetCursor() every time a WM_SETCURSOR message is received. See the SetCursor() example code to see this in practice.

Returns
A handle to the new cursor. NULL if new cursor was found.

See Also
SetCursor(), CreateCursor()

Parameters

hInstance
INSTANCE: The instance handle for the executable file that contains the cursor. *hInstance* should be NULL if you are loading one of the predefined cursor shapes listed below.

lpCursorName
LPSTR: A pointer to a string containing the cursor name. For custom cursors, this should be the name used to reference the cursor in the resource .RC file. For predefined cursors, where *hInstance* has been set to NULL, *lpCursorName* should be one of the values described in Table 6-4.

Value	Meaning
IDC_ARROW	The standard arrow shape.
IDC_CROSS	A thin crosshair cursor.
IDC_IBEAM	An I-beam cursor. Used for positioning text.
IDC_ICON	An empty icon.
IDC_SIZE	A square with a smaller square in the lower right corner. Looks like a window being reduced in size.
IDC_SIZENESW	The double-headed arrow Windows uses when adjusting the upper left and lower right sizing borders. Points "NE by SW."
IDC_SIZENS	The double-headed arrow Windows uses when adjusting the top and bottom sizing borders. Points "North/South."
IDC_SIZENWSE	The double-headed arrow Windows uses when adjusting the upper right and lower left sizing borders. Points "NW by SE."
IDC_SIZEWE	The double-headed arrow Windows uses when adjusting the right or left sizing borders. Points "West/East."
IDC_UPARROW	An arrow pointing up.
IDC_WAIT	The hourglass cursor shape.

Table 6-4. Predefined Cursor Names.

Related Messages WM_MOUSEMOVE, WM_SETCURSOR

Example
In this example, a cursor was created using the SDKPaint program. The cursor is named in the resource .RC file as "hand." The program creates a popup window when processing a WM_CREATE message. The popup window has its own window class, which specifies the "hand" icon. When the popup window is visible, the mouse shape will change to the "hand" icon anytime the mouse position is within the popup window's client area.

▷ **Resource File**

```
/* generic.rc          */

#include <windows.h>
#include "generic.h"
popup           ICON            generic.ico
hand            CURSOR          hand.cur
```

```
popup           MENU
BEGIN
   MENUITEM "&Do It!"          IDM_DOIT
   MENUITEM "&Quit",           IDM_QUIT
END
```

➭ WndProc( ) Function

```
long FAR PASCAL WndProc (HWND hWnd, unsigned iMessage, WORD wParam, LONG lParam)
{
        HDC                     hDC ;           /* device context handle */
        static WNDCLASS         wndclass ;      /* the window class */
        static HWND             hPopup, hParent ;

        switch (iMessage)                                       /* process windows messages */
        {
                case WM_CREATE: /* build the child window when program starts */
                        wndclass.style
                                = CS_HREDRAW | CS_VREDRAW | CS_PARENTDC ;
                        wndclass.lpfnWndProc    = WndProc ;
                        wndclass.cbClsExtra     = 0 ;
                        wndclass.cbWndExtra     = 0 ;
                        wndclass.hInstance      = ghInstance ;
                        wndclass.hIcon          = NULL ;
                        wndclass.hCursor        = LoadCursor (ghInstance, "hand") ;
                        wndclass.hbrBackground  = GetStockObject (LTGRAY_BRUSH) ;
                        wndclass.lpszMenuName   = NULL ;
                        wndclass.lpszClassName  = "SecondClass" ;

                        if(RegisterClass (&wndclass))    /* register the window class */
                        {
                                hPopup = CreateWindow ("SecondClass", "Popup Window",
                                        WS_POPUP | WS_VISIBLE | WS_BORDER | WS_CAPTION,
                                        10, 50, 200, 150, hWnd, NULL, ghInstance, NULL) ;
                                ShowWindow (hPopup, SW_SHOW) ;
                        }
                        break ;
```
[Other program lines]

RELEASECAPTURE   ■ Win 2.0   ■ Win 3.0   ■ Win 3.1

Purpose	Releases capture of the mouse.
Syntax	void **ReleaseCapture**(void);
Description	The mouse is captured with the SetCapture() function. When a window captures the mouse, no other window receives mouse messages. ReleaseCapture() returns the mouse to the system, so that all windows can receive messages from the mouse.
Uses	SetCapture() is usually used with programs that outline or copy areas off the screen.
Returns	No returned value (void).
See Also	SetCapture(), GetCapture()
Parameters	None (void).
Related Messages	WM_MOUSEMOVE

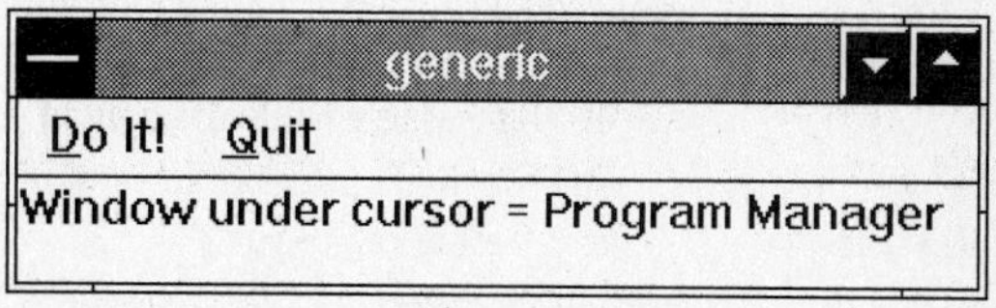

Figure 6-4. ReleaseCapture( ) Example.

Example This example, as illustrated in Figure 6-4, displays the name of the window under the mouse cursor when the left mouse button is clicked. The mouse is captured when the user clicks the "Do It!" menu item. The mouse must be captured for this type of activity to avoid having control pass to the other window. The mouse remains captured until the right mouse button is clicked.

```
long FAR PASCAL WndProc (HWND hWnd, unsigned iMessage, WORD wParam, LONG lParam)
{
        HDC                     hDC ;
```

```
        HWND            hWndUnder ;
        POINT           pMouse ;
        char            cBuf [128], cWinName [64] ;

    switch (iMessage)                       /* process windows messages */
    {
        case WM_COMMAND:                    /* process menu items */
            switch (wParam)
            {
            case IDM_DOIT:                  /* User hit the "Do it" menu item */
                    SetCapture (hWnd) ;             /* capture mouse */
                    break ;
            case IDM_QUIT:
                    DestroyWindow (hWnd) ;
                    break ;
            }
            break ;
        case WM_LBUTTONDOWN:                /* show window under cursor */
            pMouse = MAKEPOINT (lParam) ;
            ClientToScreen (hWnd, &pMouse) ;
            hWndUnder = WindowFromPoint (pMouse) ;
            GetWindowText (hWndUnder, cWinName, 63) ;
            hDC = GetDC (hWnd) ;
            SetBkMode (hDC, OPAQUE) ;
            TextOut (hDC, 0, 0, cBuf, wsprintf (cBuf,
                    "Window under cursor = %s   ", (LPSTR) cWinName)) ;
            ReleaseDC (hWnd, hDC) ;
            break ;
        case WM_RBUTTONDOWN:     /* right mouse button releases */
            ReleaseCapture () ;     /* mouse */
            break ;
        case WM_DESTROY:/* stop application */
            ReleaseCapture () ;
            PostQuitMessage (0) ;
            break ;
        default:        /* default windows message processing */
            return DefWindowProc (hWnd, iMessage, wParam, lParam) ;
    }
  return 0L ;
}
```

SCREENTOCLIENT
■ Win 2.0   ■ Win 3.0   ■ Win 3.1

Purpose	Converts from screen coordinates to client window coordinates.
Syntax	void **ScreenToClient**(HWND *hWnd*, LPPOINT *lpPoint*);
Description	The *X* and *Y* values in the *lpPoint* point structure are changed from screen coordinates (used by the mouse cursor) to client coordinates (used by painting functions).
Uses	Frequently used in conjunction with GetCursorPos() to convert the mouse cursor's location to an *X,Y* location in the window's client area. This is typically done when processing WM_MOUSEMOVE messages while drawing lines or positioning text in the client area.
Returns	No returned value (void).
See Also	GetCursorPos(), ClientToScreen()

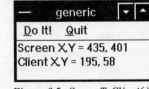

Figure 6-5. ScreenToClient( ) Example.

Parameters

hWnd   HWND: A handle to the window which specifies the client area to use in converting to client coordinates.

lpPoint   LPPOINT: A pointer to a POINT data structure. Initially holds the screen coordinates. After ScreenToClient() is called, the POINT data contains the equivalent client coordinates.

Related Messages WM_MOUSEMOVE, WM_LBUTTONDOWN, WM_NCMOUSEMOVE

Example   This example, as illustrated in Figure 6-5, shows the cursor's location in both screen and client coordinates when the cursor passes over the nonclient area of the window. This includes the borders, caption, and menu bars. The WM_NCMOUSEMOVE message passes the screen coordinates of the cursor location as the *lParam* value. This is converted to a POINT with the MAKEPOINT macro. ScreenToClient() converts the screen coordinates to client coordinates.

```
long FAR PASCAL WndProc (HWND hWnd, unsigned iMessage, WORD wParam, LONG lParam)
{
        HDC             hDC ;
        POINT           pMouse ;
        char            cBuf [128] ;

        switch (iMessage)                       /* process windows messages */
        {
                case WM_COMMAND:                /* process menu items */
                        switch (wParam)
                        {
                        case IDM_QUIT:                  /* send end of application message */
                                DestroyWindow (hWnd) ;
                                break ;
                        }
                        break ;
                case WM_NCMOUSEMOVE:                    /* nonclient mouse movement */
                        pMouse = MAKEPOINT (lParam) ;
                        hDC = GetDC (hWnd) ;
                        SetBkMode (hDC, OPAQUE) ;
                        TextOut (hDC, 0, 0, cBuf, wsprintf (cBuf,
                                "Screen X,Y = %d, %d    ", pMouse.x, pMouse.y)) ;
                        ScreenToClient (hWnd, &pMouse) ;
                        TextOut (hDC, 0, 20, cBuf, wsprintf (cBuf,
                                "Client X,Y = %d, %d    ", pMouse.x, pMouse.y)) ;
                        ReleaseDC (hWnd, hDC) ;
                        break ;
                case WM_DESTROY:                /* stop application */
                        PostQuitMessage (0) ;
                        break ;
                default:                        /* default windows message processing */
                        return DefWindowProc (hWnd, iMessage, wParam, lParam) ;
        }
        return (0L) ;
}
```

SETCAPTURE   ■ Win 2.0   ■ Win 3.0   ■ Win 3.1

Purpose	Captures the mouse so that only the program with the mouse captured receives mouse messages.
Syntax	HWND **SetCapture**(HWND *hWnd*);
Description	Normally, any active program running on the system can receive mouse messages. If a program calls SetCapture(), mouse messages are sent only to it. This makes it impossible to switch focus to another window until ReleaseCapture() is called.
Uses	Programs that grab screen images off of the screen. During the process of outlining an area to be copied, the mouse must be captured to avoid activating a window that the program is trying to copy.
Returns	A handle to the window that previously had the mouse captured. NULL if no window had captured the mouse.
See Also	ReleaseCapture(), GetCapture()
Parameters	
hWnd	HWND: A handle to the window that will capture the mouse.
Related Messages	WM_MOUSEMOVE, WM_SETFOCUS
Example	See the example under the ReleaseCapture() function description.

SetCaretBlinkTime

■ Win 2.0　　■ Win 3.0　　■ Win 3.1

Purpose	Sets the rate at which the caret shape flashes on the screen.
Syntax	void **SetCaretBlinkTime**(WORD *wMSeconds*);
Description	Sets the time, in milliseconds, between caret flashes.
Uses	As the caret is a shared resource between all applications, changing the blink time in one application affects the blink time in all other programs running at that time.
Returns	No returned value (void).
See Also	GetCaretBlinkTime()
Parameters	
wMSeconds	WORD: The time in milliseconds between caret flashes. The default value is 500. This value can be changed from the Control Panel application.
Example	See the example under the GetCaretBlinkTime() function description.

SetCaretPos

■ Win 2.0　　■ Win 3.0　　■ Win 3.1

Purpose	Sets the position of the caret.
Syntax	void **SetCaretPos**(int *X*, int *Y*);
Description	The position is relative to the client region. The position of the cursor is changed even if the caret is hidden.
Uses	This is the basic function for moving a caret shape on the window's client area. A window can own a maximum of one caret at any one time. Use CreateCaret() to load or build a caret.
Returns	No returned value (void).
See Also	CreateCaret(), HideCaret(), ShowCaret(), DPtoLP()
Parameters	
X	int: The horizontal position in logical units in the window's client area.
Y	int: The vertical position in logical units in the window's client area.
	In the default mapping mode, the origin is the upper left corner and the *X,Y* locations are measured in pixels. Use SetMapMode() to change the coordinate system of the client area (see Chapter 10, *Device Contexts*).
Example	When the user clicks the left mouse button, the caret is relocated to that position in the client area of the window. The mouse location has to be converted from screen coordinates to the client location used by SetCaretPos() using the ScreenToClient() function. This example is simplified by using the MM_TEXT mapping mode. In this mode, the logical units equal the client area pixels, measured from the upper left corner of the client area. See Chapter 10, *Device Contexts*, for a discussion of mapping modes and logical coordinates.

```
Long FAR PASCAL WndProc (HWND hWnd, unsigned iMessage, WORD wParam, LONG lParam)
{
        POINT           pCursPoint ;

        switch (iMessage)                       /* process windows messages */
        {
                case WM_CREATE:
                        CreateCaret (hWnd, NULL, 3, 20) ;
                        SetCaretPos (10, 10) ;
                        ShowCaret (hWnd) ;
                        break ;
                case WM_COMMAND:        /* process menu items */
                        switch (wParam)
                        {
                        case IDM_QUIT:  /* send end of application message */
```

```
                                DestroyWindow (hWnd) ;
                                break ;
                        }
                        break ;
                case WM_LBUTTONDOWN:
                        GetCursorPos (&pCursPoint) ;              /* get cursor x,y */
                        ScreenToClient (hWnd, &pCursPoint) ;      /* to client coord */
                        SetCaretPos (pCursPoint.x, pCursPoint.y) ;
                        break ;
                case WM_DESTROY:/* stop application */
                        PostQuitMessage (0) ;
                        break ;

                default:                    /* default windows message processing */
                        return DefWindowProc (hWnd, iMessage, wParam, lParam) ;
        }
        return (0L) ;
}
```

SetCursor   ■ Win 2.0   ■ Win 3.0   ■ Win 3.1

Purpose	Establishes which cursor shape to display.
Syntax	HCURSOR **SetCursor**(HCURSOR *hCursor*);
Description	Cursor shapes must first be loaded with LoadCursor(). SetCursor() is normally used to change the shape of the cursor when processing WM_SETCURSOR or WM_MOUSEMOVE messages. This function is fast if the cursor has already been used once, so it can be called repeatedly to change a cursor shape without noticeably slowing the program.
Uses	Used to change the cursor shape in windows that do not have a cursor loaded as part of the window class definition. If you attempt to use this function within the bounds of a window that has a cursor defined in its class definition, the cursor shape will flicker. This is because Windows is switching back and forth between the class cursor and the cursor loaded with SetCursor() every time a WM_MOUSEMOVE message is sent. Set the class cursor to NULL to avoid this problem.
Returns	A handle to the previous cursor shape.
See Also	LoadCursor()
Parameters	
hCursor	HCURSOR: A handle to the cursor to show. Use LoadCursor() to obtain this handle. You can combine these functions into a single line:

```
SetCursor (LoadCursor (NULL, IDC_WAIT)) ;
```

Related Messages	WM_SETCURSOR, WM_MOUSEMOVE
Example	This example shows a program that switches between two different cursor shapes. The window's class definition in WinMain() does not load a cursor shape (NULL value). Two different cursors are loaded when the program processes a WM_CREATE message. One is the predefined Windows arrow, and the second is a custom cursor called "hand," which is referenced in the resource .RC file. When the user clicks the "Do It!" menu item, the program switches to showing the hand cursor shape.

▷ The Resource File

```
/* generic.rc    */
#include <windows.h>
#include "generic.h"
generic ICON     generic.ico
hand             CURSOR          hand.cur

generic MENU
BEGIN
```

185

```
   MENUITEM "&Do It!"    IDM_DOIT
   MENUITEM "&Quit",     IDM_QUIT
END
```

One line of the WinMain() function is shown here because it is a little unusual. It has no defined cursor shape in the class definition.

▷ **WinMain( ) Function Excerpt**

```
      wndclass.hCursor                    = NULL ;
```

WINCREATE message triggers loading of the cursor shapes. The "word" cursor is loaded from the resource data.

▷ **The WndProc( ) Function**

```
long FAR PASCAL WndProc (HWND hWnd, unsigned iMessage, WORD wParam, LONG lParam)
{
      static          HCURSOR hHandCursor, hArrowCursor ;
      static          BOOL    bUseHand = FALSE ;

      switch (iMessage)                       /* process windows messages */
      {
            case WM_CREATE:
                  hArrowCursor = LoadCursor (NULL, IDC_ARROW) ;
                  hHandCursor = LoadCursor (ghInstance, (LPSTR) "hand") ;
                  break ;
            case WM_SETCURSOR:
                  if (bUseHand)
                        SetCursor (hHandCursor) ;
                  else
                        SetCursor (hArrowCursor) ;
                  break ;
            case WM_COMMAND:                   /* process menu items */
                  switch (wParam)
                  {
                  case IDM_DOIT:               /* User hit the "Do it" menu item */
                        bUseHand = TRUE ;/* switch to a hand shaped cursor */
                        break ;
                  case IDM_QUIT:               /* send end of application message */
                        PostQuitMessage (NULL) ;
                        break ;
                  }
                  break ;
            case WM_DESTROY:                   /* stop application */
                  PostQuitMessage (0) ;
                  break ;
            default:                /* default windows message processing */
                  return DefWindowProc (hWnd, iMessage, wParam, lParam) ;
      }
      return (0L) ;
}
```

SETCURSORPOS   ■ Win 2.0   ■ Win 3.0   ■ Win 3.1

Purpose	Moves the mouse cursor to a new location.
Syntax	void **SetCursorPos**(int X, int Y);
Description	The location is given in screen coordinates. Use ClientToScreen() to convert from client window coordinates to screen coordinates.
Uses	Not often used. SetCursorPos() could be used to provide keyboard support for mouse movements. For example, the arrow keys might move the mouse cursor.
Returns	No returned value (void).
See Also	GetCursorPos(), ClientToScreen()

Parameters

X int: The horizontal location for the mouse cursor, in screen coordinates. Zero is the left side of the screen.

Y int: The vertical location for the mouse cursor, in screen coordinates. Zero is the top of the screen.

Related Messages WM_MOUSEMOVE

Example When the user clicks the "Do It!" menu item, the mouse cursor is moved to the upper left corner of the window's client area. This location is computed by loading 0,0 into a point structure, and then using ClientToScreen() to convert to screen coordinates. SetCursorPos() uses the screen coordinates to relocate the mouse cursor.

```
long FAR PASCAL WndProc (HWND hWnd, unsigned iMessage, WORD wParam, LONG lParam)
{
        POINT           pCursPoint ;

        switch (iMessage)                      /* process windows messages */
        {
                case WM_COMMAND:               /* process menu items */
                        switch (wParam)
                        {
                        case IDM_DOIT:         /* User hit the "Do it" menu item */
                                pCursPoint.x = 0 ;/* specify 0,0 - top left corner */
                                pCursPoint.y = 0 ;
                                ClientToScreen (hWnd, &pCursPoint) ;     /* screen coord. */
                                SetCursorPos (pCursPoint.x, pCursPoint.y) ;
                                break ;
                        case IDM_QUIT:         /* send end of application message */
                                DestroyWindow (hWnd) ;
                                break ;
                        }
                        break ;
                case WM_DESTROY:               /* stop application */
                        PostQuitMessage (0) ;
                        break ;
                default:               /* default windows message processing */
                        return DefWindowProc (hWnd, iMessage, wParam, lParam) ;
        }
        return (0L) ;
}
```

SetDoubleClickTime
■ Win 2.0 ■ Win 3.0 ■ Win 3.1

Purpose Changes the mouse button double-click time.

Syntax void **SetDoubleClickTime**(WORD *wCount*);

Description The double-click time is the number of milliseconds between two mouse clicks. Clicking faster than this value generates a WM_LBUTTONDBLCLK, WM_MBUTTONDBLCLK, or WM_RBUTTONDBLCLK message for the left, middle, or right mouse buttons, respectively. Note that the WM_LBUTTONDOWN, etc. messages will always be received prior to getting the double-click message.

Uses Used to change the current double-click time value. The double-click time is only changed for the duration of the Windows session. To permanently change the double-click time setting in WIN.INI, use the Control Pannel application or WriteProfileString() (see Chapter 20, *MS-DOS and Disk Fill Access*).

Returns No returned value (void).

See Also SetDoubleClickTime().

Parameters

wCount WORD: The new-double click time in milliseconds.

Related Messages WM_LBUTTONDBLCLK, WM_MBUTTONDBLCLK, WM_RBUTTONDBLCLK

Example See the example under the GetDoubleClickTime() function description.

SHOWCARET
■ Win 2.0   ■ Win 3.0   ■ Win 3.1

Purpose Makes the caret visible at its current location.

Syntax void **ShowCaret**(HWND *hWnd*);

Description The caret must be created with CreateCaret() before it can be visible. As soon as ShowCaret() is called, the caret immediately starts blinking. The caret remains visible until HideCaret() or DestroyCaret() is called. If HideCaret() has been called more than once, an equal number of ShowCaret() calls will be needed before the caret becomes visible.

Uses It is frequently desirable to hide the caret while processing WM_PAINT messages, or while the user is doing operations that take the focus of activities away from the client area (menu selections, etc.). When the user returns to the work area, the caret can be made visible again with ShowCaret(). The caret is shared by all applications. If a caret is displayed on one program's window, a caret in another running program's window will disappear.

Returns No returned value (void).

See Also HideCaret(), DestroyCaret(), SetCaretBlinkTime()

Parameters

hWnd HWND: A handle for the window that owns the caret. A window can only own one caret at one time. Use CreateCaret() to add a caret shape to a window.

Example See the example under the CreateCaret() function description.

SHOWCURSOR
■ Win 2.0   ■ Win 3.0   ■ Win 3.1

Purpose Shows or hides the cursor.

Syntax int **ShowCursor**(BOOL *bShow*);

Description If *bShow* is FALSE (zero), ShowCursor() hides the cursor. If *bShow* is TRUE, the cursor is displayed. Multiple calls to ShowCursor() to hide the cursor require an equal number of calls with *bShow* TRUE to restore it.

Uses Used to show the cursor on systems that do not have a mouse.

Returns int, the new display count. Each call with *bShow* TRUE increases the count. Each call with *bShow* FALSE decreases it. The cursor is shown as long as the display count is zero or greater. On systems without a mouse, the display count is initially set to –1.

Parameters

bShow BOOL: TRUE to show the cursor, FALSE to hide it.

Example This example shows a crude emulation of the mouse for a program running on a machine that does not have a mouse. The cursor shape is displayed in the upper left corner of the client area when the program begins. Pressing the arrow keys moves the cursor. Activating the "Do It!" menu item (with (ALT)-D) hides the cursor.

```
long FAR PASCAL WndProc (HWND hWnd, unsigned iMessage, WORD wParam, LONG lParam)
{
        static          POINT   pCursor ;

        switch (iMessage)                       /* process windows messages */
        {
```

```
            case WM_CREATE:
                    pCursor.x = 10 ; /* start with cursor in client area */
                    pCursor.y = 10 ;
                    ClientToScreen (hWnd, &pCursor) ;
                    ShowCursor (TRUE) ;
                    SetCursorPos (pCursor.x, pCursor.y) ;
                    break ;
            case WM_COMMAND:                    /* process menu items */
                    switch (wParam)
                    {
                    case IDM_DOIT:              /* erase the cursor shape */
                            ShowCursor (FALSE) ;
                            break ;
                    case IDM_QUIT:
                            DestroyWindow (hWnd) ;
                            break ;
                    }
                    break ;
            case WM_KEYDOWN:
                    switch (wParam)             /* simple mouse emulation */
                    {
                            case VK_LEFT:       /* left cursor key */
                                    pCursor.x -= 10 ;
                                    break ;
                            case VK_RIGHT:      /* right cursor key */
                                    pCursor.x += 10 ;
                                    break ;
                            case VK_UP:         /* up cursor key */
                                    pCursor.y -= 10 ;
                                    break ;
                            case VK_DOWN:       /* down cursor key */
                                    pCursor.y += 10 ;
                                    break ;
                    }
                    SetCursorPos (pCursor.x, pCursor.y) ;
                    break ;
            case WM_DESTROY:        /* stop application */
                    PostQuitMessage (0) ;
                    break ;
            default:                /* default windows message processing */
                    return DefWindowProc (hWnd, iMessage, wParam, lParam) ;
    }
    return (0L) ;
}
```

SWAPMOUSEBUTTON ■ Win 2.0 ■ Win 3.0 ■ Win 3.1

Purpose	Reverses the right and left mouse buttons.
Syntax	BOOL **SwapMouseButton**(BOOL *bSwap*);
Description	If *bSwap* is TRUE, the right mouse button generates left mouse button messages (WM_LBUTTONDOWN), and the left button generates right mouse button messages (WM_RBUTTONDOWN). If *bSwap* is FALSE, the normal mouse messages are sent.
Uses	Handy for adapting the mouse to left-handed users. Calling this function only changes the mouse button orientation for the duration of the Windows session. Use the Control Pannel application to make a permanent change in the WIN.INI file, or call WriteProfileString() (see Chapter 20, *MS-DOS and File Access*).
Returns	BOOL. TRUE if the mouse buttons are reversed, FALSE if they are normal.
Parameters	
bSwap	BOOL: TRUE if the mouse buttons are to be reversed, FALSE if they are to be normal.
Related Messages	WM_LBUTTONDOWN, WM_RBUTTONDOWN

Example   A message is printed on the client area when a WM_LBUTTONDOWN message is received. The message is erased when a WM_MOUSEMOVE message appears. Clicking the "Do It!" menu item swaps the two mouse buttons, so the right button ends up generating the WM_LBUTTONDOWN messages. Clicking the "Do It!" menu item a second time (using the right mouse button) restores the mouse to normal operation.

```
long FAR PASCAL WndProc (HWND hWnd, unsigned iMessage, WORD wParam, LONG lParam)
{
        HDC                     hDC ;
        static          BOOL    bMouseSwap = FALSE ;

        switch (iMessage)                       /* process windows messages */
        {
                case WM_COMMAND:                /* process menu items */
                        switch (wParam)
                        {
                        case IDM_DOIT:
                                if (bMouseSwap)
                                {
                                        bMouseSwap = FALSE ;
                                        SwapMouseButton (FALSE) ;
                                }
                                else
                                {
                                        bMouseSwap = TRUE ;
                                        SwapMouseButton (TRUE) ;
                                }
                                break ;
                        case IDM_QUIT:          /* send end of application message */
                                DestroyWindow (hWnd) ;
                                break ;
                        }
                        break ;
                case WM_MOUSEMOVE:              /* writes over old messages as mouse moves */
                        hDC = GetDC (hWnd) ;
                        SetBkMode (hDC, OPAQUE) ;
                        TextOut (hDC, 10, 30, "                           ", 30) ;
                        ReleaseDC (hWnd, hDC) ;
                        break ;
                case WM_LBUTTONDOWN:                    /* left mouse button down */
                        hDC = GetDC (hWnd) ;
                        TextOut (hDC, 10, 30, "Got a left button!", 17) ;
                        ReleaseDC (hWnd, hDC) ;
                        break ;
                case WM_DESTROY:                        /* stop application */
                        SwapMouseButton (TRUE) ;
                        PostQuitMessage (0) ;
                        break ;
                default:                /* default windows message processing */
                        return DefWindowProc (hWnd, iMessage, wParam, lParam) ;
        }
        return (0L) ;
}
```

Keyboard Support

All Windows programs use the keyboard to some extent. In general you will find that much of the support for keyboard input is built into predefined tools such as edit controls and menu accelerators. These tools free the programmer from having to deal directly with the keyboard in many cases. Some programs, such as word processors, make heavy use of the keyboard for input. Windows provides extensive support for the keyboard to satisfy these demands.

Virtual Keys

PC keyboards have evolved to include more keys and several "standard" layouts. Realizing that no end to keyboard changes was in sight, the designers of Windows came up with the concept of a "virtual key." The idea is that no matter what make or model of keyboard the user has, the virtual key code for the first function key would always be the same. This frees the programmer from having to consider what type of keyboard is installed.

The definitions of all the virtual key codes are given in the WINDOWS.H header file. Table 7-1 gives all of the codes and their meanings. The vitural code for the character and number keys is the same as their ASCII equivalents (in uppercase) and are not included in the table. Chapter 19, *Character Sets and Strings*, includes a table of the ASCII and ANSI character sets, which both have the same codes for unaccented letters and numbers. Note that the numeric keypad numbers are given different codes from the numbers on the top row of the conventional keyboard. Also note that there is only one virtual key code for the shift keys. Both shift keys generate the same VK_SHIFT.

Be cautious in assuming that a given virtual key will be available on any keyboard. For example, many keyboards only have ten function keys, even though Windows makes provision for 16. Also note that the ASCII value for the "*", "/", "-", and "+" keys generally are sent from the numeric keypad, not VK_MULTIPLY, etc. which are specific to certain OEM keyboards.

Virtual Key Code	Value (hex)	Meaning
VK_ACCEPT	0x1E	Kanji only (Japanese characters)
VK_ADD	0x6B	Plus key
VK_BACK	0x08	Backspace
VK_CANCEL	0x03	Control-break
VK_CAPITAL	0x14	Shift lock
VK_CLEAR	0x0C	Clear key (Numeric keypad 5)
VK_CONTROL	0x11	Control (CTRL) key
VK_CONVERT	0x1C	Kanji only (Japanese characters)
VK_DECIMAL	0x6E	Decimal point
VK_DELETE	0x2E	Delete
VK_DIVIDE	0x6F	Divide (/) key
VK_DOWN	0x28	Down arrow
VK_END	0x23	End

Table 7-1. continued

Virtual Key Code	Value (hex)	Meaning	⊠
VK_ESCAPE	0x1B	Escape (Esc)	
VK_EXECUTE	0x2B	Execute key (if any)	
VK_F1	0x70	Function keys	
VK_F2	0x71		
VK_F3	0x72		
VK_F4	0x73		
VK_F5	0x74		
VK_F6	0x75		
VK_F7	0x76		
VK_F8	0x77		
VK_F9	0x78		
VK_F10	0x79		
VK_F11	0x7A	Enhanced keyboard only	
VK_F12	0x7B	Enhanced keyboard only	
VK_F13	0x7C	Specialized keyboards only	
VK_F14	0x7D	Specialized keyboards only	
VK_F15	0x7E	Specialized keyboards only	
VK_F16	0x7F	Specialized keyboards only	
VK_HIRAGANA	0x18	Kanji only (Japanese characters)	
VK_HOME	0x24	Home	
VK_INSERT	0x2D	Insert	
VK_KANA	0x15	Kanji only (Japanese characters)	
VK_KANJI	0x19	Kanji only (Japanese characters)	
VK_LBUTTON	0x01	Left mouse button	
VK_LEFT	0x25	Left arrow	
VK_MBUTTON	0x04	Middle mouse button	
VK_MENU	0x12	Menu key (if any)	
VK_MODECHANGE	0x1F	Kanji only (Japanese characters)	
VK_MULTIPLY	0x6A	Multiply key	
VK_NEXT	0x22	Next	
VK_NONCONVERT	0x1D	Kanji only (Japanese characters)	
VK_NUMLOCK	0x90	Num Lock	
VK_NUMPAD0	0x60	Numeric keypad keys	
VK_NUMPAD1	0x61		
VK_NUMPAD2	0x62		
VK_NUMPAD3	0x63		
VK_NUMPAD4	0x64		

VK_NUMPAD5	0x65	
VK_NUMPAD6	0x66	
VK_NUMPAD7	0x67	
VK_NUMPAD8	0x68	
VK_NUMPAD9	0x69	
VK_PAUSE	0x13	Pause
VK_PRINT	0x2A	Print Screen (Windows versions below 3.0)
VK_PRIOR	0x21	Page up
VK_RBUTTON	0x02	Right mouse button
VK_RETURN	0x0D	Return
VK_RIGHT	0x27	Right arrow
VK_ROMAJI	0x16	Kanji only (Japanese characters)
VK_SELECT	0x29	Select key (if any)
VK_SEPARATOR	0x6C	Separator key (if any)
VK_SHIFT	0x10	Shift
VK_SNAPSHOT	0x2C	Print Screen (Windows 3.0 and later)
VK_SPACE	0x20	Spacebar
VK_SUBTRACT	0x6D	Subtraction key
VK_TAB	0x09	Tab key
VK_UP	0x26	Up arrow
VK_ZENKAKU	0x17	Kanji only (Japanese characters)

*(The vitural key codes for the letters A to Z and the digits 0 to 9 are their ASCII values)

*Table 7-1. Virtual Key Codes.**

Keyboard Messages

Windows lets your program know about keypresses by sending messages. The most common series of messages is the following:

WM_KEYDOWN   Notification that a key has been depressed.

WM_CHAR   The ASCII code for the letter—if a character (not a function key, cursor arrow, etc.) was pressed.

WM_KEYUP   Notification that a key has been released.

The WM_CHAR message is generated by the TranslateMessage() function in the message loop of the application's WinMain() function. This function is discussed in Chapter 9, *Windows Messages.* Generally you will use the WM_KEYDOWN message to look for function keys, cursor keys, the numeric keypad, and the edit keys such as (PGUP), (PGDN), etc. These are the keys which make the best use of Windows' virtual key code system. WM_CHAR is used to retrieve ASCII keyboard inputs such as letters, numbers, and printable symbols. Using the WM_CHAR message is simpler for letters, as the upper and lowercase letters have different ASCII values. With WM_KEYDOWN, you have to check whether the (SHIFT) key is depressed and check the virtual key code for the letter, which is always the capital letter's ASCII value. If the user depresses the (ALT) key while pressing another key, Windows sends system key messages. The sequence is WM_SYSKEYDOWN, WM_SYSCHAR, and WM_SYSKEYUP. It is unusual to process these messages directly, as they are normally used for keyboard accelerators. Accelerators are explained in the *Keyboard Accelerators* section. Like all Windows messages, the keyboard messages pass information to your program's WinProc() function(s) in the *wParam* and *lParam* parameters. The information you will use most often is in *wParam.* (See Table 7-2.)

Windows Message	Meaning of the *wParam* Parameter	⊠
WM_KEYDOWN	The virtual key code for the key pressed.	
WM_CHAR	The ASCII code for the character represented by the key.	
WM_KEYUP	The virtual key code for the key pressed.	
WM_SYSKEYDOWN	The virtual key code for the key pressed ((ALT) key depressed at the same time).	
WM_SYSCHAR	The ASCII code for the character represented by the key ((ALT) key depressed at the same time).	
WM_SYSKEYUP	The virtual key code for the key pressed ((ALT) key depressed at the same time).	

Table 7-2. wParam Meaning in Keyboard Messages.

There is a lot of other information encoded in the *lParam* parameter, such as the hardware (OEM) code for the key pressed, how many times the key was pressed, etc. This information is fully explained in Chapter 9, *Windows Messages*. For the most part, you will not need this information, and can use the *wParam* data directly in your program. Listing 7-1 shows an example of how these messages are processed. In this case, a single line of text is created on the program's client area. Typing adds to this line, hitting the backspace key removes text from the end. This is an extremely simplified example, but it does provide an outline for how text messages are processed.

▷ **Listing 7-1. Keyboard Input Message Processing***

```
#define BUFSIZE        256

long FAR PASCAL WndProc (HWND hWnd, unsigned iMessage, WORD wParam, LONG lParam)
{
        HDC             hDC ;
        static char     cCharBuf [BUFSIZE] ;
        static int      nCharPos = 0 ;

        switch (iMessage)              /* process windows messages */
        {
        case WM_CREATE:
                cCharBuf [0] = 0 ;         /* start with null string */
                break ;
        case WM_CHAR:              /* add and display char input from keyboard */
                if (wParam >= ' ' & nCharPos < BUFSIZE)
                {
                        cCharBuf [nCharPos++] = wParam ; /* add new letter */
                        cCharBuf [nCharPos] = 0 ;        /* new terminal null */
                }
                InvalidateRect (hWnd, NULL, TRUE) ;/* show updated line */
                UpdateWindow (hWnd) ;
                hDC = GetDC (hWnd) ;
                TextOut (hDC, 0, 0, cCharBuf, strlen (cCharBuf)) ;
                ReleaseDC (hWnd, hDC) ;
                break ;
        case WM_KEYDOWN:
                switch (wParam)           /* rudimentary editing commands */
                {
                        case VK_BACK:                     /* backspace */
                                if (nCharPos > 0)
                                {
                                        nCharPos --;
                                        cCharBuf [nCharPos] = 0 ;
                                }
                                break ;
                        case VK_RIGHT:                    /* right arrow key */
                                /* other edit procedures */
                                break ;
                }
                InvalidateRect (hWnd, NULL, TRUE) ;        /* show updated line */
                UpdateWindow (hWnd) ;
                hDC = GetDC (hWnd) ;
```

```
                TextOut (hDC, 0, 0, cCharBuf, strlen (cCharBuf)) ;
                ReleaseDC (hWnd, hDC) ;
                break ;
        case WM_COMMAND:          /* process menu items */
                switch (wParam)
                {
                case IDM_DOIT:
                        MessageBox (hWnd, "Type something!", "Message", MB_OK) ;
                        break ;
                case IDM_QUIT:   /* send end of application message */
                        DestroyWindow (hWnd) ;
                        break ;
                }
                break ;
        case WM_DESTROY:          /* stop application */
                PostQuitMessage (0) ;
                break ;
        default:                  /* default windows message processing */
                return DefWindowProc (hWnd, iMessage, wParam, lParam) ;
        }
        return (0L) ;
}
```

*Only the WndProc() function is shown. The remainder of the program is identical to the GENERIC application in Chapter 1.

Messages with Non-English Keyboards

English uses a simple alphabet of 26 characters in two cases (upper- and lowercase). Many other languages also have accent characters and other symbols. When you install Windows, you select the assumed language. This loads a file which ends up named OEMANSI.BIN in the Windows directory. You can find out which language file is loaded by calling the GetKBCodePage() function. The OEMANSI.BIN file contains all of the data Windows needs to adjust the keyboard map for the different language's symbols and key layout.

To generate accented characters, users of non-English keyboards use key combinations that tell Windows that the next key combination is to be accented. For example, a French accent circumflex (^) over a character is set by (CTRL)-[and then the letter key. This only works if you have the French OEMANSI.BIN file loaded as part of Windows' install. You can track these extra keystrokes through the WM_DEADCHAR message. For the creation of an accented letter, your WinProc() function would see the following sequence of messages:

WM_KEYDOWN   Pressing the accent key.

WM_DEADCHAR   The character message for the accent.

WM_KEYUP   Releasing the accent key.

WM_KEYDOWN   Pressing the letter key (that will end up accented).

WM_CHAR   The character code for the accented letter.

WM_KEYUP   Releasing the letter key.

Normally you will not need to track all of this, as the accented character has a different character code than the unaccented version. Tables of the character values are given in Chapter 19, *Character Sets and Strings*.

Keyboard Accelerators

Another built-in convenience provided by Windows is a direct way to provide keyboard shortcuts for menu commands and other commands. These are called "accelerators." You do not have to use accelerators in your program. The same effect can be achieved by interpreting keyboard input messages. The main reason to use accelerators is that they are so simple. A few minutes of work will provide a complete set of keyboard alternatives to your mouse driven menu commands. This is in addition to the normal key alternatives for menu items with names that are proceeded by "&" characters. See Chapter 4 on menus if this is not familiar.

An important difference when using keyboard accelerators is that Windows will translate the keystroke message into the equivalent menu command. In other words, pressing an (ALT)-key combination will generate a WM_COMMAND message, not the WM_KEYDOWN sequence that follows a normal keypress. Your application can process the menu item WM_COMMAND message as if the menu item were selected with a mouse click. The user will even see the menu item flash for selection as the accelerator keypress is acted on. The keyboard accelerators are defined in your program's resource .RC file. Listing 7-2 is an example of a complete .RC file, with both a menu and keyboard accelerators defined.

⇨ **Listing 7-2. A Resource File with Keyboard Accelerators**

```
/* generic.rc            */

#include <windows.h>
#include "generic.h"

generic                 ICON   generic.ico

generic                 MENU
BEGIN
        POPUP "&First Menu"
        BEGIN
                MENUITEM "&Display Items (Ctrl-D)",    IDM_TOP1
                MENUITEM "&1st Option (F1)",           IDM_OPT1
                MENUITEM SEPARATOR
                MENUITEM "&2nd Option (F2)",           IDM_OPT2
        END
    MENUITEM "&Quit (End key)",                        IDM_QUIT
END

generic                 ACCELERATORS
BEGIN
        "D",            IDM_TOP1,       VIRTKEY, CONTROL
        VK_F1,          IDM_OPT1,       VIRTKEY
        VK_F2,          IDM_OPT2,       VIRTKEY, NOINVERT
        VK_END,         IDM_QUIT,       VIRTKEY
        VK_F1,          NOTMENU,        VIRTKEY, ALT
END
```

The accelerator table is structured like a menu definition, although there is no equivalent to a popup menu. The table is given a name, in this case "generic." This is the name which your program will use to get the accelerator table ready for use with LoadAccelerators(). You can have more than one table of accelerators in the .RC file, each with a different name. The lines for each keyboard accelerator are between the BEGIN and END lines of the ACCELERATOR definition. The format is

```
tablename       ACCELERATORS
BEGIN
event,          idvalue,        [ASCII or VIRTKEY], [ALT], [CONTROL], [NOINVERT], [SHIFT]
....
END
```

ASCII and VIRTKEY are "event types." The events can be any of the ones listed in Table 7-3.

Event Type	Meaning	
"char" (No Event Type)	A single ASCII character enclosed in double quotes. The character can also be preceded by a "^" to signify a control character.	
ASCII	An integer value for an ASCII character. In this case, specify ASCII after the *idvalue*.	
Virtual key	The uppercase letter or single digit enclosed in double quotes (eg., "A" or "1"). For non-ASCII use the VK_ code for the key. Specify VIRTKEY after the *idvalue*.	

Table 7-3. Keyboard Accelerator Event Types.

The *idvalue* can be any integer. The *idvalues* are normally defined in the program's header file and, in most cases, will be the same as the corresponding menu item ID value. This integer *idvalue* will be the *wParam* parameter when the program receives a WM_COMMAND message from Windows after the user presses the accelerator. The ID values do not have to correspond to menu items. For example, you might have an accelerator key for scrolling the window's client area. The scroll bar control is not part of the menu, so no equivalent menu ID value will exist. Create separate ID values in the header file for these items, and then put the corresponding logic in your WM_COMMAND message processing code to handle the scrolling. The last parameters in the definition of accelerator keys are the options. They can be any of the values shown in Table 7-4. The ALT, CONTROL, and SHIFT options apply only to virtual key (VIRTKEY) accelerators.

Accelerator Option	Meaning	⊠
ALT	The keyboard accelerator is activated only if the (ALT) key is depressed.	
CONTROL	The keyboard accelerator is activated only if the (CTRL) key is depressed. This has the same effect as putting a "^" in front of the accelerator character, but is more readable.	
NOINVERT	The corresponding menu item is not flashed when the accelerator is activated. Normally, the top menu line flashes.	
SHIFT	The keyboard accelerator is activated only if either of the (SHIFT) keys is depressed.	

Table 7-4. Accelerator Options.

The only other changes necessary to include accelerators are two added lines in the WinMain() function. Without accelerators, the window's message loop looks like:

```
while (GetMessage (&msg, NULL, 0, 0))            /* the message loop */
{
        TranslateMessage (&msg) ;
        DispatchMessage (&msg) ;
}
```

This functions simply to pull messages in from the message queue and send them on to the program's message processing function (like WinProc()) to be handled. To have keyboard accelerators interpreted, change the message loop to look like

```
hAccel = LoadAccelerators (hInstance, gszAppName) ;

while (GetMessage (&msg, NULL, 0, 0))                 /* the message loop */
{
        if (!TranslateAccelerator (hWnd, hAccel, &msg))
        {
                TranslateMessage (&msg) ;
                DispatchMessage (&msg) ;
        }
}
```

LoadAccelerators() reads the accelerator table in from the resource data and provides a handle to the table. The TranslateAccelerator() function checks incoming keystrokes for a match in the accelerator table. If a match is found, a WM_COMMAND message is sent directly to the program's message function. The *wParam* parameter passed with WM_COMMAND is set equal to the accelerator ID value. If no match is found, the character messages for the keypress are sent. Notice that the modified message loop with TranslateAccelerator() is set up so that messages that do not match an entry in the accelerator table still get passed to the regular TranslateMessage() and DispatchMessage() functions. If a match is found, TranslateAccelerator() returns a nonzero value, so the normal message functions are bypassed. This stops your program from getting both the accelerator message and the untranslated keyboard messages.

Note: You can create accelerators for the system menu commands (the commands that show up when you click the button in the upper right corner of the program's main window). In this case, the SC_RESTORE, SC_MOVE, SC_SIZE, SC_MINIMUM, SC_MAXIMUM, or SC_CLOSE values will be used for the ID values, and the message processing function will receive a WM_SYSKEYDOWN message instead of WM_KEYDOWN.

Caution: Accelerator keys are easy to program, but not necessarily easy for the user to remember. A good practice is to include the accelerator equivalent to each menu item to the right of the menu name for each menu item that has an accelerator. Including the description in the program's help file is a good idea too! There are a few "standard" keyboard accelerators defined in the CUA Advanced Interface Design Guide. Use the assignments in Table 7-5 if at all possible.

Keys	Meaning	⊠
(ALT)-(←)	Undo previous action.	
(DEL)	Clear selection (not saving the selection to the clipboard).	
(CTRL)-(INS)	Copy (put selection into clipboard).	
(SHIFT)-(INS)	Paste (insert clipboard contents at the current active location).	
(SHIFT)-(DEL)	Cut (put selection into clipboard, and clear it from the screen).	
(F1)	Help. See Chapter 27 for how to construct context-sensitive help files.	
(F3)	File. Activates a file dialog box is most cases.	
(F6)	Next window.	
(SHIFT)-(F6)	Previous window.	

Table 7-5. Recommended Keyboard Accelerators.

Keyboard Function Summary

Table 7-6 summarizes the keyboard functions. The detailed function descriptions follow the table.

Function	Purpose	⊠
EnableHardwareInput	Enable or disable the mouse and keyboard.	
GetAsyncKeyState	Find out if a key has been pressed.	
GetInputState	Determine if there are mouse button, keyboard, or timer events in the message queue.	
GetKBCodePage	Find out which OEM/ANSI keyboard driver table is loaded.	
GetKeyboardState	Find out the status of all of the keys in one function call.	
GetKeyboardType	Retrieve the type of keyboard or the number of function keys.	
GetKeyNameText	Retrieve the name of a key.	
GetKeyState	Determine if a key is currently down, or if a toggle key is active.	
LoadAccelerators	Load the accelerator key combinations from the resource file.	
MapVirtualKey	Convert between virtual key codes, ASCII, and scan codes.	
OemKeyScan	Convert from ASCII, to the keyboard's OEM scan code.	
SetKeyboardState	Set the keyboard status for all 256 virtual keys in one function call.	
TranslateAccelerator	Translate keystrokes into commands using the accelerator table.	
VkKeyScan	Translate an ANSI character to the corresponding virtual key code.	

Table 7-6. Keyboard Function Summary.

Keyboard Function Descriptions

ENABLEHARDWAREINPUT   ■ Win 2.0   ■ Win 3.0   ■ Win 3.1

Purpose	Enables or disables the mouse and keyboard.
Syntax	BOOL **EnableHardwareInput**(BOOL *bEnableInput*);

Description   This function allows you to completely disable all input from the mouse and keyboard. The mouse cursor is frozen on the screen, and the only key combination that has any effect is the (CTRL)-(ALT)-(DEL) combination for a warm boot of the computer.

Uses   Use with great care. EnableHardwareInput() may be useful in time-critical applications such as real-time data acquisition. Be sure to set a system timer (see the example) so that the system will restore itself at intervals. Otherwise, the only way to revive the computer is with a warm or cold boot.

Returns   BOOL. TRUE if the system is enabled, FALSE if disabled.

See Also   EnableWindow()

Parameters
bEnableInput   BOOL: Set to TRUE to enable the system, FALSE to disable it.

Related Messages WM_TIMER

Example   When the user hits the "Do It!" menu item, the mouse and keyboard are disabled for 10 seconds. A timer revives the system when a WM_TIMER message is received.

```
long FAR PASCAL WndProc (HWND hWnd, unsigned iMessage, WORD wParam, LONG lParam)
{
        HDC     hDC ;

        switch (iMessage)               /* process windows messages */
        {
                case WM_TIMER:          /* Restore mouse and keyboard operation */
                        EnableHardwareInput (TRUE) ;
                        KillTimer (hWnd, 1) ;
                        hDC = GetDC (hWnd) ;
                        TextOut (hDC, 10, 10, "Should be enabled now.", 22) ;
                        ReleaseDC (hWnd, hDC) ;
                        break ;
                case WM_COMMAND:                        /* process menu items */
                        switch (wParam)
                        {
                        case IDM_DOIT:
                                if (!SetTimer (hWnd, 1, 10000, NULL))
                                {
                                        MessageBox (hWnd,
                                                "Too many clocks or timers!", "Warning",
                                                MB_ICONEXCLAMATION | MB_OK) ;
                                }
                                else    /* Disable mouse and keyboard for 10 sec */
                                {
                                        EnableHardwareInput (FALSE) ;
                                        hDC = GetDC (hWnd) ;
                                        TextOut (hDC, 10, 10,
                                                "Disabled for 10 sec.", 21) ;
                                        ReleaseDC (hWnd, hDC) ;
                                }
                                break ;
                        case IDM_QUIT:          /* send end of application message */
                                DestroyWindow (hWnd) ;
                                break ;
                        }
                        break ;
                case WM_DESTROY:        /* stop application */
                        PostQuitMessage (0) ;
                        break ;
                default:                        /* default windows message processing */
                        return DefWindowProc (hWnd, iMessage, wParam, lParam) ;
        }
        return (0L) ;
}
```

GetAsyncKeyState
■ Win 2.0 ■ Win 3.0 ■ Win 3.1

Purpose	Finds out if a key is depressed.
Syntax	int **GetAsyncKeyState**(int *vKey*);
Description	This function will determine if a key is currently pressed, or if it has been pressed after the last call to GetAsyncKeyState().
Uses	Particularly useful for applications that use shifted keys or function keys to change an operation. For example, GetAsyncKeyState() can determine if the user hit a function key prior to selecting an item with the mouse.
Returns	int. The high-order byte is 1 if the key is currently down, 0 if not. The low-order byte is 1 if the key was pressed since the last call to GetAsyncKeyState(), 0 if not. Use the LOBYTE and HIBYTE macros to retrieve these values (see the example).
See Also	GetKeyboardState(), GetKeyState()
Parameters	
vKey	int: The virtual key code for the key. See Table 7-1, *Virtual Key Code*s, for a complete list.
Related Messages	WM_KEYDOWN, WM_KEYUP
Example	This example displays the current status of the shift keys when the "Do It!" menu item is clicked.

```
long FAR PASCAL WndProc (HWND hWnd, unsigned iMessage, WORD wParam, LONG lParam)
{
        HDC     hDC ;
        int     nKeyState ;

        switch (iMessage)                          /* process windows messages */
        {
                case WM_COMMAND:                   /* process menu items */
                        switch (wParam)
                        {
                        case IDM_DOIT:
                                InvalidateRect (hWnd, NULL, TRUE) ;
                                UpdateWindow (hWnd) ;   /* clear client area */
                                hDC = GetDC (hWnd) ;
                                nKeyState = GetAsyncKeyState (VK_SHIFT) ;
                                if (HIBYTE (nKeyState))
                                        TextOut (hDC, 10, 10,
                                                "Shift is pressed.", 17) ;
                                else
                                        TextOut (hDC, 10, 10,
                                                "Shift is not now pressed.", 24) ;
                                if (LOBYTE (nKeyState))
                                        TextOut (hDC, 10, 30,
                                                "Shift was pressed.", 18) ;
                                else
                                        TextOut (hDC, 10, 30,
                                                "Shift was not pressed before.", 28) ;
                                ReleaseDC (hWnd, hDC) ;
                                break ;
                        case IDM_QUIT:  /* send end of application message */
                                DestroyWindow (hWnd) ;
                                break ;
                        }
                        break ;
                case WM_DESTROY:/* stop application */
                        PostQuitMessage (0) ;
                        break ;
                default:                    /* default windows message processing */
                        return DefWindowProc (hWnd, iMessage, wParam, lParam) ;
        }
        return (0L) ;
}
```

GetInputState

■ Win 2.0 ■ Win 3.0 ■ Win 3.1

Purpose	Determines if there are mouse button, keyboard, or timer events in the message queue.
Syntax	BOOL **GetInputState**(void);
Description	Windows sends messages to the system message queue when the mouse buttons are clicked or released, when keys are pressed or released, and when a timer is activated. This function checks if there are any pending messages from these events at the time the function is called.
Uses	Handy in lengthy calculations to check whether or not the user has pressed a key or the mouse button. This may indicate that the user wants to abort the procedure. As GetInputState() does not pull the messages off of the input queue, they are still there to be processed by the program's WindProc() function.
Returns	BOOL. TRUE if there are mouse button, keyboard, or timer events on the system message queue, FALSE if not.
See Also	EnableHardwareInput()
Parameters	None (void).
Related Messages	WM_KEYDOWN, WM_KEYUP, WM_TIMER, WM_LBUTTONDOWN
Example	This example sets a one second timer when the user clicks the "Do It!" menu item. Every time a WM_TIMER message is sent, the GetInputState() function checks for mouse button or keyboard input pending in the system message queue. The WM_TIMER events are not detected, as GetInputState() is called after the WM_TIMER event is pulled off of the queue and processed.

```
Long FAR PASCAL WndProc (HWND hWnd, unsigned iMessage, WORD wParam, LONG lParam)
{
        HDC     hDC ;

        switch (iMessage)               /* process windows messages */
        {
        case WM_TIMER:                  /* Restore mouse and keyboard operation */
                InvalidateRect (hWnd, NULL, TRUE) ;
                UpdateWindow (hWnd) ;
                hDC = GetDC (hWnd) ;
                if (GetInputState())
                        TextOut (hDC, 10, 10,
                        "Keyboard or mouse messages ARE in the queue.", 44) ;
                else
                        TextOut (hDC, 10, 10,
                        "NO Keyboard or mouse messages in the queue.", 43) ;
                ReleaseDC (hWnd, hDC) ;
                break ;

        case WM_COMMAND:                      /* process menu items */
                switch (wParam)
                {
                case IDM_DOIT:             /* set timer 1 to every sec. */
                        if (!SetTimer (hWnd, 1, 1000, NULL))
                        {
                                MessageBox (hWnd, "Too many clocks or timers!",
                                        "Warning", MB_ICONEXCLAMATION | MB_OK) ;
                        }
                        break ;
                case IDM_QUIT:             /* send end of application message */
                        DestroyWindow (hWnd) ;
                        break ;
                }
                break ;
        case WM_DESTROY:/* stop application */
                KillTimer (hWnd, 1) ;
                PostQuitMessage (0) ;
                break ;
```

```
        default:                    /* default windows message processing */
                 return DefWindowProc (hWnd, iMessage, wParam, lParam) ;
        }
        return (OL) ;
}
```

GetKBCodePage   ☐ Win 2.0   ■ Win 3.0   ■ Win 3.1

Purpose	Finds out which OEM/ANSI keyboard driver table is loaded.
Syntax	int **GetKBCodePage**(void);
Description	Returns a code for the type of keyboard driver table in use. These drivers are for the characters used in different languages. If the file OEMANSI.BIN is in the windows directory when Windows is started, the translation table is read and used to create the correct set of characters.
Uses	For international programs. Use this function to determine which language is in use. Then switch to the correct resource data to retrieve the correct text for menus, etc.
Returns	int, the code page currently in use by Windows. This can be any of the codes in Table 7-7.

Value	Meaning ⊠
437	Default. USA settings. Implies that the OEMANSI.BIN file is not in the windows directory.
850	International (OEMANSI.BIN was copied from XLAT850.BIN when Windows was installed).
860	Portugal (OEMANSI.BIN was copied from XLAT860.BIN when Windows was installed).
861	Iceland (OEMANSI.BIN was copied from XLAT861.BIN when Windows was installed).
863	French Canadian (OEMANSI.BIN was copied from XLAT863.BIN when Windows was installed).
865	Norway/Denmark (OEMANSI.BIN was copied from XLAT865.BIN when Windows was installed).

Table 7-7. Keyboard Code Page Values.

Parameters	None (void).
Example	This simple example just displays the code page value when the "Do It!" menu item is clicked.

```
Long FAR PASCAL WndProc (HWND hWnd, unsigned iMessage, WORD wParam, LONG lParam)
{
        HDC     hDC ;
        int     KBCode ;
        char    cBuf [25] ;

        switch (iMessage)                              /* process windows messages */
        {
                case WM_COMMAND:                       /* process menu items */
                        switch (wParam)
                        {
                        case IDM_DOIT:
                                KBCode = GetKBCodePage () ;
                                itoa (KBCode, cBuf, 10) ;
                                hDC = GetDC (hWnd) ;
                                TextOut (hDC, 10, 10, cBuf, strlen (cBuf)) ;
                                TextOut (hDC, 10, 40, "= Oem Code Table.", 17) ;
                                ReleaseDC (hWnd, hDC) ;
                                break ;
```
[Other program lines]

GetKeyboardState   ■ Win 2.0   ■ Win 3.0   ■ Win 3.1

Purpose	Finds out the status of all of the keys in one function call.
Syntax	void **GetKeyboardState**(BYTE FAR *lpKeyState);

Description	Copies the status of all 256 virtual keyboard keys to an array of bytes.
Uses	Reading more than one key's status. For example, (SHIFT)-(ALT) key combinations.
Returns	No returned value (void).
See Also	GetInputState(), SetKeyboardState()

Parameters

lpKeyState   BYTE FAR *: An array of 256 bytes. Use the virtual key codes listed at the beginning of the chapter as indices into the array of key states. After the function is called, a given key's byte will have the high bit set to 1 if the key is down, or 0 if the key is up. The low bit is set to 1 if the key has been pressed an odd number of times, otherwise 0. This is only useful for the keys that toggle on and off, such as the (CAPS LOCK) and (SCROLL LOCK) keys.

Related Messages   WM_KEYDOWN

Example   This example checks whether or not the shift key is depressed when any keydown message is received.

```
long FAR PASCAL WndProc (HWND hWnd, unsigned iMessage, WORD wParam, LONG lParam)
{
        HDC             hDC ;
        static char     cKeyBuf [256] ;

        switch (iMessage)                               /* process windows messages */
        {
        case WM_KEYDOWN:
                InvalidateRect (hWnd, NULL, TRUE) ;
                UpdateWindow (hWnd) ;
                hDC = GetDC (hWnd) ;
                GetKeyboardState (cKeyBuf) ;
                if (cKeyBuf [VK_SHIFT] & 0x80)
                        TextOut (hDC, 10, 40, "Shift key pressed.", 18) ;
                else
                        TextOut (hDC, 10, 10, "Shift key NOT pressed.", 22) ;
                ReleaseDC (hWnd, hDC) ;
                break ;
```
[Other program lines]

GETKEYBOARDTYPE   □ Win 2.0   ■ Win 3.0   ■ Win 3.1

Purpose	Retrieves the type of keyboard or the number of function keys.
Syntax	int **GetKeyboardType**(int *nTypeFlag*);
Description	Depending on the value of the *nTypeFlag*, this function will retrieve either a code to the type of keyboard in use, or the number of function keys on the keyboard. The older PC type keyboards had only ten function keys, and they were on the left side of the keyboard. These keyboards also had the arrow and numeric keypads superimposed. This forces a few limits when designing a keyboard interface, which are not a problem with the newer keyboards. Most programmers avoid the issue by not using function keys 11 and 12, and by not creating situations that require simultaneous use of the cursor keys and numeric keypad.
Uses	Determining how many function keys are on the keyboard, and if the direction keys are combined on the numeric keypad.
Returns	int, the keyboard type or number of function keys. If *nTypeFlag* == 0, the returned value is as listed in Table 7-8.

Value	Meaning	
1	IBM PC/XT, or compatible 83 key keyboard.	
2	Olivetti M24 "ICO" 102 key keyboard.	
3	IBM AT 84 key keyboard (early ATs).	
4	IBM Enhanced 101 or 102 key keyboards.	
5	Nokia 1050 and compatible keyboards.	
6	Nokia 9140 and compatible keyboards.	

Table 7-8. Keyboard Type Values.

If *nTypeFlag* = 1, the keyboard subtype is returned. This is not normally used.
If *nTypeFlag* = 2, the number of function keys is returned.

Parameters

nTypeFlag   int: Set to 0, 1, or 2. Controls if the returned value is the keyboard type, subtype, or number of function keys. Normally set to zero to determine if an enhanced keyboard is in use.

Example   This example displays the type of keyboard and the number of function keys when the user clicks the "Do It!" menu item.

```
long FAR PASCAL WndProc (HWND hWnd, unsigned iMessage, WORD wParam, LONG lParam)
{
        HDC     hDC ;
        int     nKeyboard, nFuncKeys ;
        char    cBuf [5] ;

        switch (iMessage)                               /* process windows messages */
        {
                case WM_COMMAND:                        /* process menu items */
                        switch (wParam)
                        {
                        case IDM_DOIT:
                                hDC = GetDC (hWnd) ;
                                nKeyboard = GetKeyboardType (0) ;
                                nFuncKeys = GetKeyboardType (2) ;
                                switch (nKeyboard)
                                {
                                        case 1:
                                                TextOut (hDC, 10, 10,
                                                        "PC keyboard.", 12) ;
                                                break ;
                                        case 3:
                                                TextOut (hDC, 10, 10,
                                                        "Old AT keyboard.", 16) ;
                                                break ;
                                        case 4:
                                                TextOut (hDC, 10, 10,
                                                        "Enhanced keyboard.", 18) ;
                                                break ;
                                        default:
                                                TextOut (hDC, 10, 10,
                                                        "Unusual keyboard.", 17) ;
                                                break ;
                                }
                                itoa (nFuncKeys, cBuf, 10) ;
                                TextOut (hDC, 10, 30, cBuf, strlen (cBuf)) ;
                                TextOut (hDC, 30, 30, "Function keys.", 14) ;
                                break ;
                        case IDM_QUIT:          /* send end of application message */
                                DestroyWindow (hWnd) ;
                                break ;
                        }
                        break ;
```

```
                    case WM_DESTROY:        /* stop application */
                            PostQuitMessage (0) ;
                            break ;
                    default:                /* default windows message processing */
                            return DefWindowProc (hWnd, iMessage, wParam, lParam) ;
            }
        return (OL) ;
}
```

GetKeyNameText   ☐ Win 2.0 ■ Win 3.0 ■ Win 3.1

Purpose	Retrieves the name of a key.
Syntax	int **GetKeyNameText**(LONG *lParam*, LPSTR *lpBuffer*, int *nSize*);
Description	Used in processing of WM_KEYDOWN and WM_KEYUP messages. The *lParam* parameter is passed to GetKeyNameText(). The function then puts the key description into a character buffer pointed to by *lpBuffer*.
Uses	Handy for making error messages. The *lpBuffer* character string is a readable description of the key that was pressed.
Returns	The length of the character string returned.
See Also	GetInputState()
Parameters	
lParam	DWORD: This is the 32-bit parameter passed when a WM_KEYDOWN or WM_KEYUP message is received. See these message descriptions in Chapter 9, *Windows Messages*, for a description of the meaning of each bit.
lpBuffer	LPSTR: Pointer to the buffer to receive the string name.
nSize	WORD: Specifies the maximum length in bytes for the key name, not including the terminating NULL character.
Related Messages	WM_KEYDOWN, WM_KEYUP

Example   This program excerpt shows the key name any time a key is pressed. In most cases (the letter and number keys), this is just the letter itself. The function keys are returned as "F1." The numeric keypad keys are preceded by "Num," as shown in Figure 7-1.

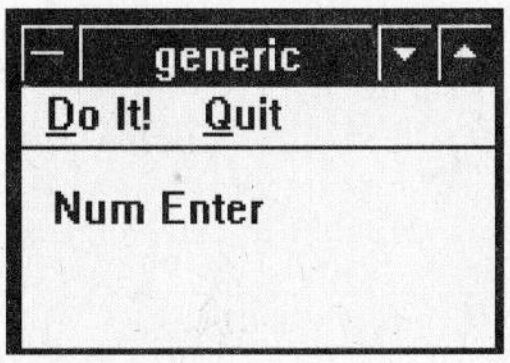

Figure 7-1. GetKeyNameText( ) Example.

```
long FAR PASCAL WndProc (HWND hWnd, unsigned iMessage, WORD wParam, LONG lParam)
{
        HDC     hDC ;
        char    cBuf [15] ;

        switch (iMessage)                               /* process windows messages */
        {
                case WM_KEYDOWN:
                        InvalidateRect (hWnd, NULL, TRUE) ;
                        UpdateWindow (hWnd) ;
                        GetKeyNameText (lParam, cBuf, 14) ;
                        hDC = GetDC (hWnd) ;
                        TextOut (hDC, 10, 10, cBuf, strlen (cBuf)) ;
                        ReleaseDC (hWnd, hDC) ;
                        break ;
```
[Other program lines]

GetKeyState   ■ Win 2.0 ■ Win 3.0 ■ Win 3.1

Purpose	Determines if a key was down when the current message was generated, or if a toggle key was active.
Syntax	int **GetKeyState**(int *nVertKey*);
Description	GetKeyState() allows a key's status to be determined.

Uses   Normally used to check the status of the toggled keys: (CAPS LOCK), (SCROLL LOCK), and (NUM LOCK).

Returns   int. The status of the key is encoded in two bits. The high-order bit is set to 1 if the key was depressed when the current message was sent, otherwise 0. The low-order bit is set to 1 if the key was pressed an odd number of times. This signifies a toggle key being active.

See Also   GetInputState(), GetAsyncKeyState()

Parameters

nVertKey   int: The virtual key code. See Table 7-1 for the complete list.

Related Messages WM_KEYDOWN, WM_KEYUP

Example   This example program fragment shows the name of the key pressed (retrieved by GetKey-NameText()). If the (CAPS LOCK) key is toggled on, the text is printed in capital letters. Otherwise, it is printed in lowercase letters. The C runtime library functions strupr() and strlwr() convert the characters to upper- and lowercase respectively. AnsiLower() and AnsiUpper() could have been used (see Chapter 19, *Character Sets and Strings*).

```
long FAR PASCAL WndProc (HWND hWnd, unsigned iMessage, WORD wParam, LONG lParam)
{
        HDC     hDC ;
        char    cBuf [15] ;

        switch (iMessage)                               /* process windows messages */
        {
        case WM_KEYDOWN:
                InvalidateRect (hWnd, NULL, TRUE) ;        /* clear client area */
                UpdateWindow (hWnd) ;
                GetKeyNameText (lParam, cBuf, 14) ;             /* get key name */
                if (0x0001 & GetKeyState (VK_CAPITAL))    /* caps lock on?*/
                        strupr (cBuf) ;              /* all caps */
                else
                        strlwr (cBuf) ;             /* all lower case */
                hDC = GetDC (hWnd) ;
                TextOut (hDC, 10, 10, cBuf, strlen (cBuf)) ;
                ReleaseDC (hWnd, hDC) ;
                break ;
```

[Other program lines]

LOADACCELERATORS   ■ Win 2.0   ■ Win 3.0   ■ Win 3.1

Purpose   Loads the accelerator key combinations from the resource file.

Syntax   HANDLE **LoadAccelerators**(HANDLE *hInstance*, LPSTR *lpTableName*);

Description   The accelerator key combinations are defined in the resource .RC file. Before they can be used, you must use LoadAccelerators() to retrieve a handle to the accelerator table. This handle is used in the TranslateAccelerator() function to decode incoming keystrokes that may be in the accelerator table. Like menu items, accelerators generate WM_COMMAND messages where the *wParam* value is set to the accelerator ID value. In most cases, this will be the same ID value as a menu item, allowing the accelerator to duplicate exactly a menu command.

Uses   Accelerators are used for keystroke shortcuts to common functions that might otherwise require several mouse actions. Accelerators can be used to generate command messages that do not have menu equivalents. The example program gives one case of this action.

Returns   HANDLE. Returns a handle to the accelerator table if the function was successful, NULL on error. Multiple calls to LoadAccelerators() continue to return the handle to the accelerator table without reloading the data.

See Also   TranslateAccelerator()

Parameters

hInstance   HANDLE: The instance handle for the program containing the accelerator definitions in its resource data.

lpTableName   LPSTR: A pointer to a character string containing the name of the accelerator table. This is the same name given in the ACCELERATORS line of the .RC resource file.

Related Messages WM_COMMAND

Example   This example defines a window with a small menu. The menu items are given keystroke equivalents in the accelerator table. In addition, a command with the ID value code of NOTMENU is defined that can only be driven by the keyboard accelerator _here is no menu equivalent. In all cases, the commands just generate message boxes. As shown in this example the header file contains the define statements for all of the menu and accelerator ID values.

```
/* generic.h */

#define IDM_DOIT        1                       /* menu item id values */
#define IDM_TOP1        2
#define IDM_OPT1        3
#define IDM_OPT2        4
#define IDM_QUIT        5
#define NOTMENU         6                       /* a non-menu id value */
        /* global variables */
int     ghInstance ;
char    gszAppName [] = "generic" ;
        /* function prototypes */
long FAR PASCAL WndProc (HWND, unsigned, WORD, LONG) ;
```

The resource .RC file defines both the menu and the accelerator table. The first accelerator assigns (CTRL)-D to the ID value IDM_TOP1. The second and third definitions define the function keys F1 and F2 to IDM_OPT1 and IDM_OPT2, respectively. IDM_OPT2 is set to not flash the menu item when it is activated (NOINVERT). The END key is equated to the "Quit" menu item ID of IDM_QUIT. Finally, a non-menu command ID of NOTMENU is assigned to the (ALT)-F1 key combination.

```
/* generic.rc */
#include <windows.h>
#include "generic.h"
generic         ICON    generic.ico

generic         MENU
BEGIN
        POPUP "&First Menu"
        BEGIN
                MENUITEM "&Display Items (Ctrl-D)",     IDM_TOP1
                MENUITEM "&1st Option (F1)",    IDM_OPT1
                MENUITEM SEPARATOR
                MENUITEM "&2nd Option (F2)",    IDM_OPT2
        END
        MENUITEM        "&Quit (End key)",      IDM_QUIT
END

generic                 ACCELERATORS
BEGIN
        "D",            IDM_TOP1,       VIRTKEY, CONTROL
        VK_F1,          IDM_OPT1,       VIRTKEY
        VK_F2,          IDM_OPT2,       VIRTKEY, NOINVERT
        VK_END,         IDM_QUIT,       VIRTKEY
        VK_F1,          NOTMENU,        VIRTKEY, ALT
END
```

LoadAccelerators() is used before the program's message loop in WinMain() to retrieve a handle to the accelerator table. The message loop is also modified to include the Translate-

Accelerator() function. Note how the NOTMENU item is treated just like a menu ID in the message processing logic, even though it is only defined in the accelerator table.

```
/* generic.c   accelerator table demonstration */
#include <windows.h>
#include "generic.h"

int PASCAL WinMain (HANDLE hInstance, HANDLE hPrevInstance, LPSTR lpszCmdLine,
        int nCmdShow)
{
        HWND            hWnd ;
        MSG             msg ;
        WNDCLASS        wndclass ;
        HANDLE          hAccel ;

        ghInstance = hInstance ;            /* store instance handle as global var. */
        if (!hPrevInstance)
        {
                wndclass.style          = CS_HREDRAW | CS_VREDRAW ;
                wndclass.lpfnWndProc    = WndProc ;
                wndclass.cbClsExtra     = 0 ;
                wndclass.cbWndExtra     = 0 ;
                wndclass.hInstance      = hInstance ;
                wndclass.hIcon          = LoadIcon (hInstance, gszAppName) ;
                wndclass.hCursor        = LoadCursor (NULL, IDC_ARROW) ;
                wndclass.hbrBackground  = GetStockObject (WHITE_BRUSH) ;
                wndclass.lpszMenuName   = gszAppName ;
                wndclass.lpszClassName  = gszAppName ;
                                        /* register the window class */
                if (!RegisterClass (&wndclass))
                        return FALSE ;
        }
        hWnd = CreateWindow (                   /* create the program's window here */
                gszAppName,                     /* class name */
                gszAppName,                     /* window name */
                WS_OVERLAPPEDWINDOW,            /* window style */
                CW_USEDEFAULT,                  /* x position on screen */
                CW_USEDEFAULT,                  /* y position on screen */
                CW_USEDEFAULT,                  /* width of window */
                CW_USEDEFAULT,                  /* height of window */
                NULL,                           /* parent window handle (null = none) */
                NULL,                           /* menu handle (null = use class menu) */
                hInstance,                      /* instance handle */
                NULL) ;                         /* lpstr (null = not used) */
        ShowWindow (hWnd, nCmdShow) ;
        UpdateWindow (hWnd) ;                   /* send first WM_PAINT message */
        hAccel = LoadAccelerators (hInstance, gszAppName) ;
        while (GetMessage (&msg, NULL, 0, 0))              /* the message loop */
        {
                if (!TranslateAccelerator (hWnd, hAccel, &msg))
                {
                        TranslateMessage (&msg) ;
                        DispatchMessage (&msg) ;
                }
        }
        return msg.wParam ;
}

long FAR PASCAL WndProc (HWND hWnd, unsigned iMessage, WORD wParam, LONG lParam)
{
        switch (iMessage)                       /* process windows messages */
        {
                case WM_COMMAND:                /* process menu items */
                        switch (wParam)
                        {
                        case IDM_TOP1:
                                MessageBox (hWnd,
                                        "The top menu item was activated.",
```

```
                                    "Code IDM_TOP1", MB_OK) ;
                    break ;
            case IDM_OPT1:
                    MessageBox (hWnd,
                            "The second menu item was activated.",
                            "Code IDM_OPT1", MB_OK) ;
                    break ;
            case IDM_OPT2:
                    MessageBox (hWnd,
                            "The third menu item was activated.",
                            "Code IDM_OPT2", MB_OK) ;
                    break ;
            case NOTMENU:
                    MessageBox (hWnd,
                            "This command activated only via an accelerator.",
                            "Code NOTMENU", MB_OK) ;
                    break ;
            case IDM_QUIT:              /* send end of application message */
                    DestroyWindow (hWnd) ;
                    break ;
            }
            break ;
    case WM_DESTROY:            /* stop application */
            PostQuitMessage (0) ;
            break ;
    default:                    /* default windows message processing */
            return DefWindowProc (hWnd, iMessage, wParam, lParam) ;
    }
    return (0L) ;
}
```

MAPVIRTUALKEY   □ Win 2.0   ■ Win 3.0   ■ Win 3.1

Purpose	Converts between virtual key codes, ASCII, and scan codes.
Syntax	WORD **MapVirtualKey**(WORD *wCode*, WORD *wMapType*);
Description	This function performs three separate operations, depending on the value set for *wMapType*. One is the conversion of a virtual key code used in Windows messages to the computer's OEM scan code. (The OEM scan code is the numeric value assigned to each physical key that is returned at a low level through the computer's ROM BIOS functions.) The second mode does the reverse: converts from OEM scan code to the virtual key code used by Windows. The third mode converts virtual key codes to ASCII values.
Uses	The most common use is to convert the virtual key code used in Windows messages to ASCII values that can be printed on the screen. You may find yourself dealing with the OEM scan codes in rare cases, such as destinguishing between the left and right (SHIFT) keys (both generate the same virtual key code).
Returns	WORD, the value returned depends on *wMapType*, explained below.
See Also	OemKeyScan()

Parameters

wCode WORD: The virtual key code to translate if *wMapType* is 0 or 2. This value is normally obtained from the *wParam* parameter received when a WM_KEYDOWN or WM_KEYUP message is interpreted. If *wMapType* is 1, *wCode* is the OEM scan code to translate. See Chapter 9, *Windows Messages*, for a description of how the keyboard data is encoded with the messages.

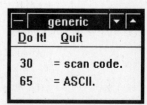

Figure 7-2. MapVirtualKey() Example.

wMapType WORD: Specifies the type of translation to do. The values are shown in Table 7-9.

Value	Meaning	⊠
0	*wCode* is a virtual key code. MapVirtualKey() returns the corresponding OEM scan code for the same key.	
1	*wCode* is an OEM scan code. MapVirtualKey() returns the corresponding virtual key code for the same key.	
2	*wCode* is a virtual key code. MapVirtualKey() returns the corresponding ASCII value.	

Table 7-9. MapVirtualKey( ) Codes.

Related Messages WM_KEYDOWN, WM_KEYUP, WM_CHAR

Example This code fragment shows two uses of the MapVirtualKey() function. The virtual key code is encoded in the *wParam* parameter when the WM_KEYDOWN message is received. MapVirtualKey() is used to convert the virtual key code to the OEM scan code and the ASCII value. The picture below shows the window after the "A" key was pressed.

```
Long FAR PASCAL WndProc (HWND hWnd, unsigned iMessage, WORD wParam, LONG lParam)
{
        HDC             hDC ;
        WORD            wCode ;
        char            cBuf [10] ;

        switch (iMessage)                       /* process windows messages */
        {
                case WM_KEYDOWN:
                        InvalidateRect (hWnd, NULL, TRUE) ;
                        UpdateWindow (hWnd) ;
                        hDC = GetDC (hWnd) ;
                        wCode = MapVirtualKey (wParam, 0) ;
                        itoa (wCode, cBuf, 10) ;
                        TextOut (hDC, 10, 10, cBuf, strlen (cBuf)) ;
                        TextOut (hDC, 50, 10, "= scan code.", 12) ;
                        wCode = MapVirtualKey (wParam, 2) ;
                        itoa (wCode, cBuf, 10) ;
                        TextOut (hDC, 10, 30, cBuf, strlen (cBuf)) ;
                        TextOut (hDC, 50, 30, "= ASCII.", 8) ;
                        ReleaseDC (hWnd, hDC) ;
                        break ;
```

[Other program lines]

OEMKEYSCAN
☐ Win 2.0 ■ Win 3.0 ■ Win 3.1

Purpose Converts from ASCII to the keyboard's OEM scan code.

Syntax DWORD **OemKeyScan**(WORD *wOemChar*);

Description The OEM scan code is part of the *lParam* message accompanying every WM_KEYDOWN and WM_KEYUP message. OemKeyScan() allows you to get the OEM keyboard scan code that matches an ASCII character.

Uses Used in sending other Windows messages that simulate keypresses. This can be an efficient way to pass information between windows that already have message processing logic to handle keyboard input.

Returns DWORD, the OEM scan code in the low-order WORD. The high-order WORD has bit 1 set to 1 if a (SHIFT) key must be pressed to generate the letter, and bit 2 set to 1 if the (CTRL) key must be pressed. If there is no OEM equivalent to *wOemChar*, –1 is returned in both the high-order and low-order WORDS.

See Also VkKeyScan (), MapVirtualKey()

Parameters
wOemChar WORD: The ASCII value to convert.

Related Messages WM_KEYDOWN, WM_KEYUP

Example   In this case, there is a popup window (illustrated in Figure 7-3) which has its own message processing function. When the popup has the input focus, any keypress results in the key's ASCII letter being displayed in the popup's client area. If the user clicks the "Do It!" menu item, the parent window sends the popup a simulated WM_KEYDOWN message, with both *wParam* and *lParam* set to match the letter "A" key. This is a miniature example of how windows can communicate with each other without necessarily adding extra program logic to decode the messages.

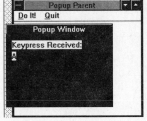

Figure 7-3. OemKeyScan( ) Example.

Because the child window has its own message procedure, the procedure name must be added to the EXPORTS section of the program's .DEF definition file and declared in the header file.

```
Long FAR PASCAL WndProc (HWND hWnd, unsigned iMessage, WORD wParam, LONG lParam)
{
        HDC                     hDC ;                   /* device context handle */
        static WNDCLASS         wndclass ;              /* the window class */
        static HWND             hPopup ;
        WORD                    wVirtKey ;
        DWORD                   dwOemField ;

        switch (iMessage)                               /* process windows messages */
        {
                case WM_CREATE:                         /* build popup window as program starts */
                        wndclass.style
                                = CS_HREDRAW | CS_VREDRAW | CS_PARENTDC ;
                        wndclass.lpfnWndProc    = ChildProc ;
                        wndclass.cbClsExtra     = 0 ;
                        wndclass.cbWndExtra     = 0 ;
                        wndclass.hInstance      = ghInstance ;
                        wndclass.hIcon          = NULL ;
                        wndclass.hCursor        = LoadCursor (NULL, IDC_ARROW) ;
                        wndclass.hbrBackground  = GetStockObject (LTGRAY_BRUSH) ;
                        wndclass.lpszMenuName   = NULL ;
                        wndclass.lpszClassName  = "SecondClass" ;
                                                        /* register the window class */
                        if(RegisterClass (&wndclass))
                        {
                                hPopup = CreateWindow ("SecondClass", "Popup Window",
                                        WS_POPUP | WS_VISIBLE | WS_BORDER | WS_CAPTION,
                                        10, 50, 200, 150, hWnd, NULL, ghInstance, NULL) ;
                                ShowWindow (hPopup, SW_SHOW) ;
                        }
                        break ;
                case WM_COMMAND:        /* process menu items */
                        switch (wParam)
                        {
                        case IDM_DOIT:  /* send popup window a fake keypress */
                                wVirtKey = VkKeyScan ((WORD) 'A') ;
                                dwOemField =
                                        ((OemKeyScan
                                                ((WORD) 'A') & 0x00FF) << 16) | 1 ;
                                SendMessage (hPopup, WM_KEYDOWN, wVirtKey, dwOemField) ;
                                break ;
                        case IDM_QUIT:          /* send end of application message */
                                DestroyWindow (hWnd) ;
                                break ;
                        }
                        break ;
                case WM_DESTROY:        /* stop application */
                        PostQuitMessage (0) ;
                        break ;
                default:                /* default windows message processing */
                        return DefWindowProc (hWnd, iMessage, wParam, lParam) ;
```

```
        }
        return (OL) ;
}


/* Here is a separate message processing procedure for the popup window */
long FAR PASCAL ChildProc (HWND hWnd, unsigned iMessage, WORD wParam,
        LONG lParam)
{
        HDC             hDC ;
        char            cBuf [2] ;

        switch (iMessage)                       /* process windows messages */
        {
                case WM_KEYDOWN:
                        InvalidateRect (hWnd, NULL, TRUE) ;
                        UpdateWindow (hWnd) ;
                        hDC = GetDC (hWnd) ;
                        TextOut (hDC, 10, 10, "Keypress Received:", 18) ;
                        cBuf [0] = (char) MapVirtualKey (wParam, 2) ;
                        TextOut (hDC, 10, 30, cBuf, 1) ;
                        ReleaseDC (hWnd, hDC) ;
                        break ;
                default:                        /* default windows message processing */
                        return DefWindowProc (hWnd, iMessage, wParam, lParam) ;
        }
        return (OL) ;
}
```

SETKEYBOARDSTATE   ■ Win 2.0   ■ Win 3.0   ■ Win 3.1

Purpose	Sets the keyboard status for all 256 virtual keys in one function call.
Syntax	void **SetKeyboardState**(BYTE FAR *lpKeyState*);
Description	The status of all 256 virtual keys is held in an array of bytes pointed to by the *lpKeyState* parameter. In each of these bytes, the high-order bit is set to 1 if the key is down, and the low-order bit is set to 1 if the key has been pressed an odd number of times. The latter is useful for the toggle keys such as (CAPS LOCK) and (NUM LOCK). Generally this function is used after calling GetKeyboardState() to retrieve the current keyboard status. Individual values can be changed in the 256 byte data array, and then sent back to Windows by calling SetKeyboardState().
Uses	Used to change the (SHIFT LOCK), (NUM LOCK), and (SCROLL LOCK) key states. These have the virtual key codes of VK_CAPITAL, VK_NUMLOCK and VK_OEM_SCROLL, respectively. To set one of these toggle keys on, use a value of 0x81 in the 256 byte array. To set a nontoggle (normal) key on, use a value of 0x80. The virtual key code is the index to the item in the array. For example, to set the shift lock item ON in a buffer called cVKBuf[256], use

```
cVKBuf [VK_CAPITAL] = 0x81 ;
```

Returns	No returned value (void).
See Also	GetKeyboardState()
Parameters	
lpKeyState	BYTE FAR *: A pointer to an array of 256 bytes. Generally, initialized to the current keyboard status by calling GetKeyboardState() prior to changing values.
Related Messages	WM_KEYDOWN, WM_KEYUP, WM_CHAR
Example	This WndProc() function toggles the (CAPS LOCK) key on and off when the user clicks the "Do It!" menu item.

```
long FAR PASCAL WndProc (HWND hWnd, unsigned iMessage, WORD wParam, LONG lParam)
{
        HDC             hDC ;
```

```
        char            cKeyBuf [256] ;
        static BOOL     bCapsOn ;

        switch (iMessage)                               /* process windows messages */
        {
                case WM_COMMAND:                        /* process menu items */
                        switch (wParam)
                        {
                        case IDM_DOIT:
                                InvalidateRect (hWnd, NULL, TRUE) ;
                                UpdateWindow (hWnd) ;
                                hDC = GetDC (hWnd) ;
                                GetKeyboardState (cKeyBuf) ;    /* read all VK_ values */
                                if ((cKeyBuf [VK_CAPITAL]) & 0x01)
                                {
                                        cKeyBuf [VK_CAPITAL] = 0 ;      /* shift lock off */
                                        TextOut (hDC, 10, 40,
                                                "Shift key NOT pressed.", 22) ;
                                }
                                else
                                {
                                        cKeyBuf [VK_CAPITAL] = 0x81 ;   /* shift lock on */
                                        TextOut (hDC, 10, 10,
                                                "Shift key pressed.", 18) ;
                                }
                                SetKeyboardState (cKeyBuf) ;    /* set all VK_ values */
                                ReleaseDC (hWnd, hDC) ;
                                break ;
                        case IDM_QUIT:
                                DestroyWindow (hWnd) ;
                                break ;
                        }
                        break ;
                case WM_DESTROY:        /* stop application */
                        PostQuitMessage (0) ;
                        break ;
                default:                        /* default windows message processing */
                        return DefWindowProc (hWnd, iMessage, wParam, lParam) ;
        }
        return (0L) ;
}
```

TRANSLATEACCELERATOR   ■ Win 2.0   ■ Win 3.0   ■ Win 3.1

Purpose	Translates keystrokes into commands using the accelerator table.
Syntax	int **TranslateAccelerator**(HWND *hWnd*, HANDLE *hAccTable*, LPMSG *lpMsg*);
Description	Accelerator key combinations are defined in the ACCELERATOR portion of the resource .RC file. Prior to using the accelerator table, use LoadAccelerators() to retrieve the handle to the table. TranslateAccelerator() is used within the program's message loop to convert from the keystrokes entered to the command specified in the accelerator table.
Uses	Accelerators are used to provide keystroke shortcuts for menu commands. They can also be used to send command messages to the system that do not have keyboard equivalents.

      If TranslateAccelerator() returns a nonzero value, it has successfully translated the keystroke and sent the command to the program's message processing function. The application should not allow the normal TranslateMessage() and DispatchMessage() functions to process the keystrokes again. To avoid this, use the following structure for the program's message loop in WinMain().

```
while (GetMessage (&msg, NULL, 0, 0))                    /* the message loop */
{
        if (!TranslateAccelerator (hWnd, hAccel, &msg))
        {
```

```
                            TranslateMessage (&msg) ;
                            DispatchMessage (&msg) ;
                }
        }
```

When an accelerator is translated, the message is sent directly to the program's message processing function, bypassing the message queue. The accelerator ID value is sent as the *wParam* parameter of either a WM_COMMAND message (normal case) or a WM_SYSCOMMAND message (if the ID value is one of the system menu ID values SC_RESTORE, SC_MOVE, SC_SIZE, SC_MINIMUM, SC_MAXIMUM, SC_CLOSE).

Returns	int, TRUE if a keystroke entry was translated into an accelerator command, FALSE if not.
See Also	LoadAccelerators()
Parameters	
hWnd	HWND: The handle of the window with a message processing function (WinProc()) which is to receive the translated messages.
hAccTable	HANDLE: The handle to the accelerator table retrieved with LoadAccelerators().
lpMsg	LPMSG: A pointer to a message structure. This structure holds the message data received when GetMessage() was called.
Related Messages	WM_COMMAND, WM_SYSCOMMAND
Comments	You can determine if a command message was sent via a menu selection or accelerator by examining the *lParam* parameter when the program receives a WM_COMMAND or WM_SYSCOMMAND message. If the high-order word of *lParam* is one, the message came from an accelerator table translation. Because of the *hWnd* parameter, TranslateAccelerator() sends messages to the message processing function of the main window (the window with the handle *hWnd*), and not to child windows that have separate message processing functions.
Example	See the example under the LoadAccelerators() function description.

VKKEYSCAN
■ Win 2.0   ■ Win 3.0   ■ Win 3.1

Purpose	Translates an ANSI character to the corresponding virtual key code.
Syntax	int **VkKeyScan**(WORD *cChar*);
Description	The returned value contains the VK_ code in the low-order byte and (SHIFT) key information in the high-order byte.
Uses	Sending WM_KEYDOWN and WM_KEYUP messages to other windows. This can be an efficient way to pass information between windows if the receiving window already has keyboard input logic in its message processing (WinProc()) function.
Returns	int. The virtual key code is in the low-order byte returned. The shift state is encoded in the high-order byte as shown in Table 7-10.

Value	Meaning	⊠
0	No shifted keys.	
1	The character is shifted with either of the (SHIFT) keys.	
2	The character is a control character.	
3, 4, 5	A (SHIFT) key combination that is not used for characters.	
6	The (CTRL)-(ALT) key combination.	
7	The (SHIFT)-(CTRL)-(ALT) key combination.	

Table 7-10. VkKeyScan( ) Codes.

See Also   OemKeyScan(), MapVirtualKey()

Parameters
cChar   char: The ANSI char value to be translated into a virtual key code.

Related Messages WM_KEYDOWN, WM_KEYUP

Example   See the example under the OemKeyScan() function description.

8 Message Processing Functions

Message handling is the biggest difference between programming under Windows and programming under a more conventional environment, such as DOS. There is no real equivalent to a message in the DOS world. Message processing is the basic concept behind Windows' ability to run several applications at the same time, and allow the user to easily switch between them. Most programs only use the most basic message functions: a message loop in WinMain() and a series of actions based on received messages in the WndProc() function. Significantly more control over message processing is possible. Messages can be intercepted and modified by hook functions, prior to being passed to the program. Separate programs can also communicate with each other by exchanging messages as they operate.

Message Flow

Figure 8-1 shows a simplified diagram of a message being processed by a Windows program. Windows loads low-level functions for dealing with the keyboard, mouse, and screen when Windows starts. When a hardware event such as a keystroke occurs, Windows sends a message to the active program's message queue. The message queue is just a memory location to hold message data that has not yet been processed by the running program.

The "message" is actually a small data structure defined in the WINDOWS.H header file.

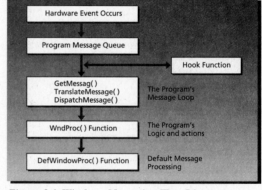

Figure 8-1. Windows Messaging Flow Diagram.

```
/* Message structure */
typedef struct tagMSG
{
        HWND            hwnd;
        WORD            message;
        WORD            wParam;
        LONG            lParam;
        DWORD           time;
        POINT           pt;
} MSG;
typedef MSG                 *PMSG;
typedef MSG NEAR            *NPMSG;
typedef MSG FAR             *LPMSG;
```

The message data contains the window handle (*hwnd*), the coded message type (*message*), the *wParam* and *lParam* data that will be passed to the WndProc() function, the time the message was sent (in milliseconds after Windows started), and a POINT structure containing the *X* and *Y* location of the mouse cursor when the message was sent (*pt*). The cursor location is given in screen coordinates (pixels from the upper left corner of the screen). When most programmers talk about a "message," they usually are referring just to the *message* element in the MSG structure. This is a value, such as WM_PAINT or WM_KEYDOWN defined in WINDOWS.H. Keep in mind that the real message stored in the application's message queue is in the form of the MSG data structure.

Processing Messages

An application program pulls messages off the message queue in the "message loop" at the bottom of the WinMain() function. Message loops typically have the form

```
while (GetMessage (&msg, NULL, 0, 0))        /* pulls messages from message queue */
{
        TranslateMessage (&msg) ;            /* translates keyboard messages to WM_CHAR */
        DispatchMessage (&msg) ;             /* sends the message to WndProc() function */
}
```

The GetMessage() function fetches the message and can give control to other programs if there are no messages to process. GetMessage() is followed by TranslateMessage() and DispatchMessage(). DispatchMessage() sends the message data to the WndProc() function you write to handle the program's logic. DispatchMessage() knows which function should receive the messages because you defined the message function in the window's class definition.

TranslateMessage() is a utility function that takes raw input from the keyboard and generates a new message (WM_CHAR) that is placed on the message queue. The message with WM_CHAR contains the ASCII value for the key pressed, which is easier to deal with than the raw keyboard scan codes and virtual key codes. You can leave TranslateMessage() out if you will not be directly processing keystrokes.

The program's WndProc() function typically deals only with a few of the 250 Windows messages. Depending on the program, messages for menu items, mouse movements, or keyboard input may be important, or ignored. Those that are not processed by the WndProc() logic are passed to the default message handling function, DefWindowProc(), shown at the bottom of Figure 8-1.

Program Control

If you build a long calculation into the body of a Windows program, it will not be possible to switch to another program while the program is calculating. The program is said to "have control" of the Windows environment. This is clearly not how Windows programs should behave. Users expect to be able to switch between applications quickly. Perhaps the single most critical concept to understand about a Windows program is that **Windows programs are not interrupted**. Windows programs must be designed to give up control frequently so that other programs have a chance to operate. (There is one exception to the "no interrupts" statement. When Windows runs a DOS application in 386 mode, the DOS application is handled via interrupts.)

There are only three functions that give up control: GetMessage(), PeekMessage(), and WaitMessage(). Of these, GetMessage() is used most frequently. The difference between these three is in how actively they attempt to keep control of the system. GetMessage() is the most active, and it will keep control until it empties out the application program's message queue. PeekMessage() gives up control as soon as it is called, and it gets control back only if other applications run out of messages to process. WaitMessage() gives up control as soon as it is called and will not recover control until a message within a certain range is found on the program's message queue and all other applications have run out of messages to process. Any program that will remain running under Windows for a length of time must call one of these three functions to allow Windows to pass control between applications.

One way to think about this situation is to imagine the opposite: a Windows program that never gives up control. These are easy to create (too easy). Just put all of the program logic in the WinMain() function, and eliminate the message loop. Once the program is started, no other Windows application will be able to run until the program quits.

Sources of Messages

Figure 8-1 provides a simplified flow diagram for a single message from the mouse or keyboard flowing through the messaging logic. There are a few more possibilities for how a message might originate. Figure 8-2 shows more detail surrounding the program's message loop.

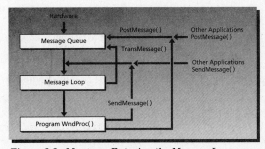

Figure 8-2. Messages Entering the Message Loop.

Messages do not all start from hardware actions. You may find it convenient to send a program messages from within the body of the program. This is frequently done in place of using a *goto:* statement. The messages can be sent either to the program's message queue with PostMessage() or directly to the WndProc() function with SendMessage(). Experienced programmers use PostMessage() and SendMessage() within a program as an alternative to *goto:* statements. Another reason to send a message from within a program is to request repainting of the window's client area. This is such a common request that a shorthand version of SendMessage() is provided just for this purpose. UpdateWindow() sends a WM_PAINT message directly to the program's WndProc() function, bypassing the message queue. Whether or not a message is queued is not normally important to writing a Windows program. Your WndProc() function will deal with both types of messages in the same way.

Other programs can also send messages to running applications. These are often specialized messages, unique to a group of programs. Windows provides RegisterWindowMessage() to generate unique message codes while the programs are running. The codes are sequenced so as to not overlap other message numbers used by unrelated programs. There is a standard protocol for exchanging messages between running programs called "dynamic data exchange" (DDE), which is covered in Chapter 30.

Reentrant Functions

Messages are not like interrupts. Windows will not jump in and halt the execution of a program to go to some more critical task. For example, if a calculation is still running after a menu item is clicked, you do not have to worry about calculation being stopped half way through because a new message is received. Windows will not be able to pass another message to your program until the calculation is done and the execution returns to the message loop for another call to GetMessage(). One situation that *will* start a message from within your function's calculation is if the program uses a Windows function that sends a message, bypassing the message queue. For example, if SendMessage() is called from within the calculation, the message sent will go directly to the WndProc() function and will be acted upon *before* the rest of the calculation has completed.

If WndProc() generates messages to itself, WndProc() is said to be a "reentrant." Message handling functions, such as WndProc() are reentrant. A key consideration is to avoid having two parts of the function send each other messages. This can set up an infinite loop of messages, hanging the system. This typically occurs in situations where a scroll bar control changes an integer in an edit control, and changing the integer in the edit control adjusts the same scroll bar. You can make this work, but it requires designing the functions so that messages are not sent after the first adjustment.

Message Hook Functions

Windows provides an almost ultimately powerful set of functions that allow setting message "hooks." Hooks allow a module (running program or DLL) to intercept messages going to other applications. The messages can be acted on, modified, or even stopped. A typical example of a use for a hook function would be to remap the keyboard. Every keyboard message could be intercepted, and then modified to reflect a different keyboard layout. More sophisticated uses are to modify the behavior of specific applications. For example, you could write a hook function that intercepts WM_SIZE and WM_MOVE messages for a program, forcing the application to always be located at one spot and one size on the screen. Still another use is to record and playback Windows messages, for recording repeated actions (macros). There are seven different types of hook functions defined, each with its own special purpose. The SetWindowsHook() installs the hook function into Windows, while UnhookWindowsHook() removes it. The DefHookProc() function is provided to pass messages not acted on by the hook function back on to their next destination. Hook functions can be chained in series. This allows a series of modifications to various messages to be carried out at one time.

Hook types require that the hook function be in a dynamic link library (DLL). DLLs are not covered in this book until Chapter 28, *Dynamic Link Libraries*. However, they are simple to create, and the examples in this chapter show the changes need to be made in the C, NMAKE, and .DEF definition files to create DLLs.

When writing the DLL for a message hook, you will generally write four functions. LibMain() is the standard entry point for a DLL, just like WinMain() for an application program. Write a "SetHook()" function to install the message hook in Windows. Add a "FreeHook()" function to remove the hook. It is inside these two functions that the Windows SDK functions SetWindowsHook() and UnhookWindowsHook() are called. Finally, write the actual message filter function that acts on the message, or just passes it on to DefHookProc(). The example under the SetWindowsHook() function description provides a complete listing. Hook functions are so powerful that extreme care must be taken in using them. Use should be restricted to utility functions and custom modifications of existing applications where the source code is not available. In normal Windows programming, you will have direct control of the message processing logic and will have little need for message hooks.

Cautions

Any time GetMessage(), PeekMessage(), or WaitMessage() is called, Windows has the option of passing control to another application. This will cause local variables and stored far memory addresses to become invalid. More on this in Chapter 14 on memory management.

Message Function Summary

Table 8-1 summarizes the Windows message processing functions. The detailed function descriptions follow immediately after the table.

Function	Purpose	⊠
CallMsgFilter	Activate a message filter (hook) function.	
CallWindowProc	Pass message parameters to a message processing function.	
DefHookProc	Provide default message processing for message hook functions.	
DefWindowProc	Provide the default processing for Windows messages.	
DispatchMessage	Send a Windows message to the program's WndProc() function.	
ExitWindows	Exit the Windows environment to DOS.	
FreeProcInstance	Decouple a procedure instance from a data segment.	
GetMessage	Retrieve a message from Windows, or give control to another application if no messages are waiting for the window currently receiving messages.	
GetMessagePos	Retrieve the X,Y position of the cursor when a message was sent.	
GetMessageTime	Retrieves the time value when a message was sent.	
InSendMessage	Determine if the current message being processed was sent by SendMessage().	
MakeProcInstance	Provide a procedure-instance address for a function.	
PeekMessage	Check the message queue for a message.	
PostAppMessage	Put a message in the application program's message queue.	
PostMessage	Put a message on a windows message queue.	
PostQuitMessage	Shutdown an application.	
RegisterWindowMessage	Create a new, unique Windows message number.	
ReplyMessage	Free the application sending a message to continue to execute.	
SendMessage	Send a Windows message directly to a window's message function.	
SetMessageQueue	Change the size of an application's message queue.	
SetWindowsHook	Install a Window's message filter function. Installs a Window's message filter function.	
TranslateMessage	Generate WM_CHAR, WM_SYSCHAR, WM_DEADCHAR, and WM_SYSDEADCHAR messages when a virtual key code is received.	
UnhookWindowsHook	Remove a message hook function from the system.	
WaitMessage	Yield control to any other application when a message is received.	

Table 8-1. Message Processing Function Summary.

CALLMSGFILTER ■ Win 2.0   ■ Win 3.0   ■ Win 3.1

Purpose	Activates a message filter function.
Syntax	BOOL **CallMsgFilter**(LPMSG *lpMsg*, int *nCode*);
Description	This function passes a message to a message function. The message function must be of the type WH_MSGFILTER, loaded with SetWindowsHook(). The *nCode* parameter allows the calling program to change the type of processing done within the filter depending on the value of *nCode*.
Uses	Modifying the messages intercepted, or doing an operation from within the hook function as messages are received.
Returns	BOOL. TRUE if the message should be processed further, FALSE otherwise.
See Also	SetWindowsHook(), UnhookWindowsHook()
Parameters	
lpMsg	LPMSG: A pointer to a MSG data structure. This is the message that will be filtered by the filter function.
nCode	int: Specifies a code value to control what the filter does. The values between –2 and 8 are defined in WINDOWS.H for special purposes. A good practice is to use values of WM_USER and integer values above it (WM_USER + 1, etc.).
Related Messages	Only messages processed by a WH_MSGFILTER type of filter function will be passed. This includes WM_PAINT messages and messages from menus, dialog boxes and message boxes. See SetWindowsHook() for details on the hook function.
Example	This example sets a hook function from within WinMain(). The hook is activated only if the user clicks the "Do It!" menu item. The hook function is called from within the program's message loop using CallMsgFilter(). The hook function is defined below (in a DLL). The hook is coded so action is taken only if the *nCode* parameter is set to WM_USER. This assures that the hook only works when the CallMsgFilter() requests it. The following code constitutes the main program.

```
/* generic.c */

#include <windows.h>
#include "generic.h"

BOOL    bFilterIt = FALSE;              /* globals */
BOOL    bHooked = FALSE ;

int PASCAL WinMain (HANDLE hInstance, HANDLE hPrevInstance, LPSTR lpszCmdLine, int nCmdShow)
{
        HWND            hWnd ;
        MSG             msg ;
        WNDCLASS        wndclass ;

        ghInstance = hInstance ;        /* store instance handle as global var. */

        if (!hPrevInstance)             /* load data into window class struct. */
        {
                wndclass.style          = CS_HREDRAW | CS_VREDRAW ;
                wndclass.lpfnWndProc    = WndProc ;
                wndclass.cbClsExtra     = 0 ;
                wndclass.cbWndExtra     = 0 ;
                wndclass.hInstance      = hInstance ;
                wndclass.hIcon          = LoadIcon (hInstance, gszAppName) ;
                wndclass.hCursor        = LoadCursor (NULL, IDC_ARROW) ;
                wndclass.hbrBackground  = GetStockObject (WHITE_BRUSH) ;
                wndclass.lpszMenuName   = gszAppName ;
                wndclass.lpszClassName  = gszAppName ;
                                        /* register the window class */
                if (!RegisterClass (&wndclass))
                        return FALSE ;
        }
```

```
        hWnd = CreateWindow (              /* create the program's window here */
                gszAppName,                /* class name */
                gszAppName,                /* window name */
                WS_OVERLAPPEDWINDOW,       /* window style */
                CW_USEDEFAULT,             /* x position on screen */
                CW_USEDEFAULT,             /* y position on screen */
                CW_USEDEFAULT,             /* width of window */
                CW_USEDEFAULT,             /* height of window */
                NULL,                      /* parent window handle (null = none) */
                NULL,                      /* menu handle (null = use class menu) */
                hInstance,                 /* instance handle */
                NULL) ;                    /* lpstr (null = not used) */
        ShowWindow (hWnd, nCmdShow) ;
        UpdateWindow (hWnd) ;              /* send first WM_PAINT message */

        if (SetHook ("MsgFilterFunc", WH_MSGFILTER))
                bHooked = TRUE ;

        while (GetMessage (&msg, NULL, 0, 0))          /* the message loop */
        {
                if (bHooked & bFilterIt)               /* if desired... */
                        CallMsgFilter (&msg, WM_USER) ; /* filter messages */
                TranslateMessage (&msg) ;
                DispatchMessage (&msg) ;
        }
        FreeHook ("msgFilterFunc", WH_MSGFILTER) ;
        return msg.wParam ;
}


long FAR PASCAL WndProc (HWND hWnd, unsigned iMessage, WORD wParam, LONG lParam)
{

        switch (iMessage)                              /* process windows messages */
        {
        case WM_COMMAND:                               /* process menu items */
                switch (wParam)
                {
                case IDM_DOIT:
                        if (bFilterIt)
                        {
                                bFilterIt = FALSE ;
                                MessageBox (hWnd, "Hooked function not active.",
                                        "Message", MB_OK) ;
                        }
                        else
                        {
                                bFilterIt = TRUE ;
                                MessageBox (hWnd, "Hooked function Active.",
                                        "Message", MB_OK) ;
                        }
                        break ;
                case IDM_QUIT:          /* send end of application message */
                        DestroyWindow (hWnd) ;
                        break ;
                }
                break ;
        case WM_DESTROY:                /* stop application */
                PostQuitMessage (0) ;
                break ;
        default:                /* default windows message processing */
                return DefWindowProc (hWnd, iMessage, wParam, lParam) ;
        }
        return (0L) ;
}
```

Note that the hook function is created in a dynamic link library (DLL). Creation of DLLs requires special compiler settings and changes to the .DEF definition files. See the Set-WindowsHook() example for a complete listing. Note in this case that the hook function simply makes the computer beep every time a WM_PAINT message is received. More complex operations could be done in processing the message.

```c
/* msgdll.c  library of message filters */
/* */

#include <windows.h>

HANDLE          hInstanceDll ;
FARPROC lpOldHook ;

int FAR PASCAL LibMain (HANDLE hInstance, WORD wDataSeg, WORD wHeapSize,
        LPSTR lpszCmdLine)
{
        if (wHeapSize > 0)
                UnlockData (0) ;
        hInstanceDll = hInstance ;
        return (1) ;
}

BOOL FAR PASCAL SetHook (LPSTR lpsHookName, int nHookType)
{
        FARPROC         lpHook ;

        lpHook = GetProcAddress (hInstanceDll, lpsHookName) ;
        if (lpHook)
        {
                lpOldHook = SetWindowsHook (nHookType, lpHook) ;
                return (TRUE) ;
        }
        else
                return (FALSE) ;

}

BOOL FAR PASCAL FreeHook (LPSTR lpsHookName, int nHookType)
{
        FARPROC         lpHook ;

        lpHook = GetProcAddress (hInstanceDll, lpsHookName) ;
        return (UnhookWindowsHook (nHookType, lpHook)) ;
}

int FAR PASCAL MsgFilterFunc (int nCode, WORD wParam, DWORD lParam)
{
        LPMSG                   msg ;

        if (nCode != WM_USER)
                DefHookProc (nCode, wParam, lParam, &lpOldHook) ;
        else
        {
                msg = (LPMSG) lParam;    /* lParam holds message address */
                if (msg->message == WM_PAINT)
                {
                        MessageBeep (0) ;
                        return (TRUE) ;
                }
        }
        return (FALSE) ;
}
```

CALLWINDOWPROC

■ Win 2.0   ■ Win 3.0   ■ Win 3.1

Purpose	Passes message parameters to a message processing function.
Syntax	LONG **CallWindowProc**(FARPROC *lpPrevWndFunc*, HWND *hWnd*, WORD *wMsg*, WORD *wParam*, LONG *lParam*);

Description   This function is used commonly within a window subclassing function. Subclassing is used to add new message processing logic to a given window, usually a predefined window type such as BUTTON or SCROLLBAR. CallWindowProc() is called at the end of the new message processing function to pass the message parameter data (*wParam*, etc.) on to the original message function for normal processing.

Uses   Frequently used to add a keyboard interface to the predefined Windows styles. You also can customize the functioning of default styles such as buttons and scroll bars, as shown in the example below.

Returns   LONG. The value depends on the message being processed. Return this value from within your subclassing function.

See Also   SetWindowLong(), GetWindowLong()

Parameters

lpPrevWndFunc   FARPROC: A pointer to the original message processing function for the window. You can use GetWindowLong() to retrieve this value. Store the value in a static or global variable, so that it is accessible to your subclassing function.

hWnd   HWND: The window handle for the window receiving the message.

wMsg   WORD: The message (WM_PAINT, etc.).

wParam   WORD: The *wParam* data that accompanies the message.

lParam   DWORD: The *lParam* data that accompanies the message.

Related Messages   All messages potentially pass through this function. You can act on as many as you need, and then let the original window message function (called with CallWindowProc()) handle the rest.

Comments   Don't forget to add your subclass function to the EXPORTS part of the .DEF definition file.

Example   This example subclasses a button window with a new procedure defined at the bottom of the listing. NewButtonProc() changes the button's text if the button is pressed or released. After that, the default Windows button operations are called with CallWindowProc(). A global variable *lpfnOldProc* is used to save a pointer to the old window procedure.

```
FARPROC lpfnOldProc ;           /* global for old button procedure pointer */

Long FAR PASCAL WndProc (HWND hWnd, unsigned iMessage, WORD wParam, LONG lParam)
{
        static          HWND    hButton ;
        FARPROC                 lpfnNewProc ;

        switch (iMessage)                               /* process windows messages */
        {
            case WM_CREATE:
                hButton = CreateWindow ("BUTTON", "Button",
                        WS_CHILD | WS_VISIBLE ,
                        10, 10, 100, 60, hWnd, NULL, ghInstance, NULL) ;
                ShowWindow (hButton, SW_SHOW) ;
                        /* subclass the scroll bar to a new procedure */
                lpfnNewProc = MakeProcInstance ((FARPROC) NewButtonProc,
                        ghInstance) ;
                lpfnOldProc = (FARPROC) GetWindowLong (hButton, GWL_WNDPROC) ;
                SetWindowLong (hButton, GWL_WNDPROC, (LONG) lpfnNewProc) ;
                break ;
            case WM_SETFOCUS:
                SetFocus (hButton) ;        /* keep input focus on button */
                break ;
            case WM_COMMAND:                    /* process menu items */
                switch (wParam)
                {
                case IDM_DOIT:  /* User hit the "Do it" menu item */
```

```
                        MessageBox (hWnd, "Press Return!", "Message", MB_OK) ;
                        SetFocus (hButton) ;
                        break ;
                case IDM_QUIT:  /* send end of application message */
                        DestroyWindow (hWnd) ;
                        break ;
                }
                break ;
        case WM_DESTROY:          /* stop application */
                PostQuitMessage (0) ;
                break ;
        default:                  /* default windows message processing */
                return DefWindowProc (hWnd, iMessage, wParam, lParam) ;
        }
    return OL ;
}


Long FAR PASCAL NewButtonProc (HWND hWnd, WORD mess, WORD wParam, LONG lParam)
{
        switch (mess)
        {
        case WM_KEYDOWN:
                SetWindowText (hWnd, "Pressed!") ;
                break ;
        case WM_KEYUP:
                SetWindowText (hWnd, "Released!") ;
                break ;
        }
        return CallWindowProc (lpfnOldProc, hWnd, mess, wParam, lParam) ;
}
```

DEFHOOKPROC   ■ Win 2.0   ■ Win 3.0   ■ Win 3.1

Purpose	Provides default message processing for message hook functions.
Syntax	DWORD **DefHookProc**(int *nCode*, WORD *wParam*, DWORD *lParam*, FARPROC FAR * *lplpfnNextHook*);
Description	Used inside of the message hook function, installed with SetWindowsHook(). Used by Windows to reset the pointer to the next hook function pointed to by *lplpfnNextHook*.
Uses	Hook functions are used to change Windows messages before they are sent to applications. There are several different types of hook functions, all of which are explained in the section on the SetWindowsHook() function. In most cases, the hook function must reside in a dynamic link library module (DLL).
Returns	DWORD. Returns the message being processed if *nCode* == HC_ACTION (which equals 0). Returns a pointer to the next hook function if *nCode* == HC_LPFNNEXT (which equals −1). The latter is the case when UnhookWindowsHook() is called.
See Also	SetWindowsHook(), UnhookWindowsHook()
Parameters	
nCode	int: Specifies the action the hook function (message filter) should take. *nCode* will be 0 for normal processing of messages. *nCode* will be HC_LPFNNEXT for the last call to the hook function, after UnhookWindowsHook() has been called.
wParam	WORD: This is the *wParam* parameter of the message being processed.
lParam	DWORD: This is the *lParam* parameter of the message being processed.
lplpfnNextHook	FARPROC FAR *: A pointer to a memory location to hold a FARPROC data. Save this in a static variable. Windows will change this value on the last call to the hook procedure (when *nCode* == HC_LPFNNEXT after the program calls UnhookWindowsHook()).

Related Messages All Windows messages.

Example This example (courtesy of Don Stegall of Playroom Software) shows a DLL that sets a keyboard hook. Only WM_KEYDOWN and WM_KEYUP messages are processed by this hook function. When activated, the function improves the operation of the (SHIFT) and (CAPS LOCK) keys. If the (CAPS LOCK) is on, and the user presses the shift key and an A-Z letter, the hook function shuts off the (CAPS LOCK). This imitates the way most typewriters function. See the SetWindowsHook() function description for a full code listing including definition files for use of the dynamic link library (DLL) hook functions.

```
/* msgdll.c message filter */
/* Courtesy of Don Stegall - Playroom Software */


#include <windows.h>

HANDLE  hInstanceDll ;
FARPROC lpOldHook ;


int FAR PASCAL LibMain (HANDLE hInstance, WORD wDataSeg, WORD wHeapSize,
        LPSTR lpszCmdLine)
{
        if (wHeapSize > 0)
                UnlockData (0) ;
        hInstanceDll = hInstance ;
        return (1) ;
}
                                /* turns on hook function */
void FAR PASCAL SetHook (LPSTR lpsHookName, int nHookType)
{
        FARPROC         lpHook ;

        lpHook = GetProcAddress (hInstanceDll, lpsHookName) ;
        lpOldHook = SetWindowsHook (nHookType, lpHook) ;
}
                                /* turns off hook function */
void FAR PASCAL FreeHook (LPSTR lpsHookName, int nHookType)
{
        FARPROC         lpHook ;

        lpHook = GetProcAddress (hInstanceDll, lpsHookName) ;
        UnhookWindowsHook (nHookType, lpHook) ;
}
                                /* hook function */
DWORD FAR PASCAL MsgKeyboardFunc (int nCode, WORD wParam, DWORD lParam)
{
        char    cKeys [256] ;

        if (nCode != HC_ACTION)
                return (DefHookProc (nCode, wParam, lParam, &lpOldHook)) ;
        else
        {                               /* check if caps-lock, caps and A-Z at once */
            if (wParam >= 'A' & wParam <= 'Z' &
                ((GetKeyState (VK_SHIFT) & 0x80) != 0) &
                (GetKeyState (VK_CAPITAL) & 0x01) != 0)
            {
                GetKeyboardState (cKeys) ;      /* if so, shut off caps lock */
                cKeys [VK_CAPITAL] = cKeys [VK_CAPITAL] & 0xFE ;
                SetKeyboardState (cKeys) ;
            }
        }
        return (0) ;
}
```

DEFWINDOWPROC
■ Win 2.0   ■ Win 3.0   ■ Win 3.1

Purpose	Provides the default processing for Windows messages.
Syntax	LONG **DefWindowProc**(HWND *hWnd*, WORD *wMsg*, WORD *wParam*, LONG *lParam*);
Description	Programs typically only act on a fraction of the messages that Windows sends. The remainder are passed on to the default message processing logic. The default logic handles all of the more mundane tasks, such as making sure that the cursor remains visible.
Uses	Your WndProc() function should always have this function as the default message handling operation.
Returns	LONG. The value depends on the message being processed. Return this value from your WndProc() function.
See Also	DefDlgProc(). The source code for the default message processing logic is provided with the Software Development Kit in a file called DEFWND.C. It is remarkably short and worth reviewing.
Parameters	
hWnd	HWND: The handle to the window receiving the message.
wMsg	WORD: The message (WM_SIZE, etc.). This value, and the following three, will be received by your WndProc() function when a message is sent from Windows to your program.
wParam	WORD: The *wParam* data passed with the message.
lParam	DWORD: The *lParam* data passed with the message.
Related Messages	All messages can be handled by the default message processing logic. In many cases, no action is taken.
Example	This is a minimal WndProc() function, showing how messages that are not acted on by the program's logic default to DefWindowProc().

```
long FAR PASCAL WndProc (HWND hWnd, unsigned iMessage, WORD wParam, LONG lParam)
{
        switch (iMessage)                       /* process windows messages */
        {
                case WM_CREATE:
                        /* etc. */
                        break ;
                case WM_DESTROY:                /* stop application */
                        PostQuitMessage (0) ;
                        break ;
                default:                        /* default windows message processing */
                        return DefWindowProc (hWnd, iMessage, wParam, lParam) ;
        }
        return (0L) ;
}
```

DISPATCHMESSAGE
■ Win 2.0   ■ Win 3.0   ■ Win 3.1

Purpose	Sends a Windows message to the window's WndProc() function.
Syntax	LONG **DispatchMessage**(LPMSG *lpMsg*);
Description	This function is used within the program's message loop. Messages are usually fetched from Windows with the GetMessage() function. After any needed processing (TranslateMessage() function), the message is sent on to the program's WndProc() function for action.
Uses	Used in every program's WinMain() function message loop.
Returns	LONG. The value depends on the message processed, but is generally ignored.
See Also	GetMessage(), TranslateMessage()

Parameters

lpMsg　　　　　　LPMSG: A pointer to a MSG structure. This is generally defined at the top of WinMain().

Related Messages　All Windows messages pass through this function.

Example　　　　This is a typical WinMain() function, including the message loop at the bottom.

```
/* example WinMain() function */

#include         <windows.h>
HANDLE          ghInstance ;

int PASCAL WinMain (HANDLE hInstance, HANDLE hPrevInstance, LPSTR lpszCmdLine,
        int nCmdShow)
{

        HWND            hWnd ;
        MSG             msg ;
        WNDCLASS        wndclass ;

        ghInstance = hInstance ;             /* store instance handle as global var. */
        if (!hPrevInstance)
        {
                wndclass.style          = CS_HREDRAW | CS_VREDRAW ;
                wndclass.lpfnWndProc    = WndProc ;
                wndclass.cbClsExtra     = 0 ;
                wndclass.cbWndExtra     = 0 ;
                wndclass.hInstance      = hInstance ;
                wndclass.hIcon          = LoadIcon (hInstance, gszAppName) ;
                wndclass.hCursor        = LoadCursor (NULL, IDC_ARROW) ;
                wndclass.hbrBackground  = GetStockObject (WHITE_BRUSH) ;
                wndclass.lpszMenuName   = gszAppName ;
                wndclass.lpszClassName  = gszAppName ;
                                                /* register the window class */
                if (!RegisterClass (&wndclass))
                        return FALSE ;
        }
        hWnd = CreateWindow (           /* create the program's window here */
                gszAppName,             /* class name */
                gszAppName,             /* window name */
                WS_OVERLAPPEDWINDOW,    /* window style */
                CW_USEDEFAULT,          /* x position on screen */
                CW_USEDEFAULT,          /* y position on screen */
                CW_USEDEFAULT,          /* width of window */
                CW_USEDEFAULT,          /* height of window */
                NULL,                   /* parent window handle (null = none) */
                NULL,                   /* menu handle (null = use class menu) */
                hInstance,              /* instance handle */
                NULL) ;                 /* lpstr (null = not used) */
        ShowWindow (hWnd, nCmdShow) ;
        UpdateWindow (hWnd) ;

        while (GetMessage (&msg, NULL, 0, 0))    /* the message loop */
        {
                TranslateMessage (&msg) ;
                DispatchMessage (&msg) ;
        }
        return msg.wParam ;
}
```

EXITWINDOWS
□ Win 2.0　■ Win 3.0　■ Win 3.1

Purpose　　　Exits the Windows environment to DOS.

Syntax　　　BOOL **ExitWindows**(DWORD *dwReserved*, WORD *wReturnCode*);

Description　Starts an orderly shutdown sequence for Windows. First, the WM_QUERYENDSESSION message is sent to all applications. If any application returns zero to this message, Windows continues to operate. If all windows agree to exit (all return a nonzero value), a WM_ENDSESSION message is sent to each window. When all of the windows have stopped operations, Windows exits to DOS with the DOS return code specified in *wReturnCode*.

Uses   Used in creating new program manager applications, as a way to exit the Windows environment at the end of a session.

Returns   BOOL. TRUE if all applications agree to quit, FALSE otherwise.

Parameters

dwReserved   DWORD: A reserved value. Set equal to zero.

wReturnCode   WORD: The DOS return code. Normal exits should return a 0 value. Can be set to EW_RESTARTWINDOWS under Windows versions 3.0 and above. This restarts Windows.

Related Messages WM_QUERYENDSESSION, WM_ENDSESSION

Example   If the user clicks the "Do It!" menu item, an attempt is made to exit Windows. However, as the WM_QUERYENDSESSION message results in the program returning 0, this window refuses to exit, so Windows continues to operate. If you change the return value after WM_QUERY-ENDSESSION to 1, and no other applications refuse to exit (such as programs that have unsaved data), Windows will exit to DOS.

```
long FAR PASCAL WndProc (HWND hWnd, unsigned iMessage, WORD wParam, LONG lParam)
{
        BOOL    bExitOK ;

        switch (iMessage)                       /* process windows messages */
        {
                case WM_COMMAND:                /* process menu items */
                        switch (wParam)
                        {
                        case IDM_DOIT:                  /* User hit the "Do it" menu item */
                                bExitOK = ExitWindows (NULL, 0) ;
                                if (!bExitOK)
                                        MessageBox (hWnd,
                                                "An application refuses to Quit!",
                                                "Message", MB_OK) ;
                                break ;

                        case IDM_QUIT:                  /* send end of application message */
                                DestroyWindow (hWnd) ;
                                break ;
                        }
                        break ;
                case WM_QUERYENDSESSION:
                        return (0) ;                    /* refuse to quit! */
                case WM_DESTROY:                        /* stop application */
                        PostQuitMessage (0) ;
                        break ;
                default:                                /* default windows message processing */
                        return DefWindowProc (hWnd, iMessage, wParam, lParam) ;
        }
        return (0L) ;
}
```

FREEPROCINSTANCE   ■ Win 2.0   ■ Win 3.0   ■ Win 3.1

Purpose   Decouples a procedure instance from a data segment.

Syntax   void **FreeProcInstance**(FARPROC *lpProc*);

Description   MakeProcInstance() is used to bind a function to a data segment so that it can be called or passed as a parameter to a function external to the program (such as a Windows function). FreeProcInstance() eliminates the binding of the data segment to the function.

Uses   FreeProcInstance() should be used when the need to call the function is eliminated (such as the end of a dialog box operation). A small amount of memory is consumed by each procedure instance, but released when FreeProcInstance() is called.

Returns   No returned value (void).

See Also   MakeProcInstance()

Parameters
lpProc   FARPROC: The procedure-instance address of the function to be freed. This address is created by MakeProcInstance().

Comments   Don't forget to add the function name to the EXPORTS part of the program's .DEF definition file if you are going to pass the function using MakeProcInstance().

Example   This example displays a simple dialog box when the "Do It!" menu item is clicked. The dialog box function is at the end of the listing. The dialog box function must be passed to the DialogBox() function, which is external to the program (part of Windows). MakeProcInstance() is used to get a procedure-instance address for the dialog box function. After the dialog box is finished, the procedure-instance address is released with FreeProcInstance(). Note that the procedure-instance address is stored in a static variable. The stack will be changed by the activities in the dialog box function.

```
long FAR PASCAL WndProc (HWND hWnd, unsigned iMessage, WORD wParam, LONG lParam)
{
        static FARPROC lpfnDlgProc ;

        switch (iMessage)               /* process windows messages */
        {
                case WM_COMMAND:        /* process menu items */
                        switch (wParam)
                        {
                        case IDM_DOIT:  /* run dialog box */
                                lpfnDlgProc = MakeProcInstance
                                        (DialogProc, ghInstance) ;
                                DialogBox (ghInstance, "ExampleDialog", hWnd,
                                        lpfnDlgProc) ;
                                FreeProcInstance (lpfnDlgProc) ;
                                break ;
                        case IDM_QUIT:
                                DestroyWindow (hWnd) ;
                                break ;
                        }
                        break ;
                case WM_DESTROY:        /* stop application */
                        PostQuitMessage (0) ;
                        break ;
                default:                        /* default windows message processing */
                        return DefWindowProc (hWnd, iMessage, wParam, lParam) ;
        }
        return (0L) ;
}

BOOL FAR PASCAL DialogProc (HWND hDlg, WORD wMess, WORD wParam, LONG lParam)
{
        switch (wMess)
        {
                case WM_INITDIALOG:
                        return TRUE ;
                case WM_COMMAND:        /* there is only one command - quits */
                case WM_DESTROY:
                        EndDialog (hDlg, 0) ;
                        return TRUE ;
        }
        return FALSE ;
}
```

Remember to add the exported function name to the .DEF file:

```
NAME          GENERIC
DESCRIPTION   'generic windows program'
EXETYPE       WINDOWS
STUB          'WINSTUB.EXE'
CODE          PRELOAD MOVEABLE
DATA          PRELOAD MOVEABLE MULTIPLE
HEAPSIZE      1024
STACKSIZE     4096
EXPORTS       WndProc
              DialogProc
```

GetMessage   ■ Win 2.0   ■ Win 3.0   ■ Win 3.1

Purpose   Retrieves a message from Windows or gives control to another application if no messages are waiting for the window currently receiving messages.

Syntax   BOOL **GetMessage**(LPMSG *lpMsg*, HWND *hWnd*, WORD wMsgFilterMin, WORD *wMsgFilterMax*);

Description   GetMessage() pulls the next waiting message from Windows into the MSG structure pointed to by *lpMsg*. If no messages are waiting, control is given by Windows to another window if one has waiting messages.

Uses   Used in a program's message loop to retrieve messages. Only messages for the window are retrieved. Windows programs must use either GetMessage(), PeekMessage(), or WaitMessage() to relinquish control from the running programs.

Returns   BOOL. TRUE if any message other than WM_QUIT is received, FALSE for WM_QUIT. This return value is important because the message loop will quit looping when GetMessage() processes a WM_QUIT, ending the program.

See Also   PeekMessage(), WaitMessage()

Parameters

lpMsg   LPMSG: A pointer to a MSG message structure. The structure is loaded with the data from the message. The MSG structure contains the following fields (defined in WINDOWS.H):

```
typedef struct tagMSG
{
        HWND          hwnd;              /* window handle */
        WORD          message;          /* message ID */
        WORD          wParam;           /* wParam value */
        LONG          lParam;           /* lParam value */
        DWORD         time;             /* msec since startup */
        POINT         pt;               /* mouse location, screen coord */
} MSG;
typedef MSG           *PMSG;
typedef MSG NEAR      *NPMSG;
typedef MSG FAR       *LPMSG;
```

hWnd   HWND: A handle to the window receiving the messages. Set to NULL to receive all messages for a window and its child and popup windows (the normal case). Set to the window's handle (from CreateWindow()) to receive only messages for the parent window.

wMsgFilterMin   WORD: The lowest value message to receive. Normally set to 0.

wMsgFilterMax   WORD: The highest value message to receive. If both *wMsgFilterMin* and *wMsgFilterMax* are set to 0, all messages are processed. *wMsgFilterMax* can be set to WM_USER-1 to process only internally defined messages. Normally it is set to 0.

Related Messages All Windows messages are processed.

Notes   Anytime control is yielded to another program by GetMessage(), PeekMessage(), or WaitMessage(), local variables and pointers to far memory may be invalid when control is returned to the program.

Example   This is a typical message loop, at the end of the WinMain() function.

```
while (GetMessage (&msg, NULL, 0, 0))
{
        TranslateMessage (&msg) ;
        DispatchMessage (&msg) ;
}
```

GETMESSAGEPOS   ■ Win 2.0   ■ Win 3.0   ■ Win 3.1

Purpose   Retrieves the *X,Y* position in screen coordinates of the cursor when a message was sent.

Syntax   DWORD **GetMessagePos**(void);

Description   Every message sent by Windows includes a point structure that contains the position of the mouse
                       cursor when the message was sent. GetMessagePos() extracts that value.

Uses   If messages are stacking up on the message queue, the mouse may have moved since the message
                       being processed was sent. Use this function to retrieve the position where the mouse was when a
                       message was sent.

Returns   DWORD. The *X* position is in the low-order word, and the *Y* position in the high-order word. Use
                       the MAKEPOINT macro to convert the DWORD value to a point structure.
                           Note that the *X,Y* position is in screen coordinates, as are all mouse cursor coordinates. Use
                       ScreenToClient() to convert to client coordinates (see example).

See Also   ScreenToClient(), GetCursorPos()

Parameters   None (void).

Related Messages   WM_MOUSEMOVE

Example   After the user clicks the "Do It!" menu item, the program starts drawing a small line in the client
                       area at the location every message is received. This provides a visual indication as to how often
                       Windows sends messages.

```
Long FAR PASCAL WndProc (HWND hWnd, unsigned iMessage, WORD wParam, LONG lParam)
{
        static  BOOL    bTraceOn = FALSE ;
        HDC             hDC ;
        DWORD           dwMesPos ;
        POINT           pPoint ;

        if (bTraceOn)    /* mark where the cursor was when msg. recvd */
        {
                hDC = GetDC (hWnd) ;
                dwMesPos = GetMessagePos () ;             /* get position */
                pPoint = MAKEPOINT (dwMesPos) ;          /* convert to point struct. */
                ScreenToClient (hWnd, &pPoint) ;          /* convert to client coord. */
                MoveTo (hDC, pPoint.x, pPoint.y) ;        /* draw a small line there */
                LineTo (hDC, pPoint.x + 2, pPoint.y) ;
                ReleaseDC (hWnd, hDC) ;
        }

        switch (iMessage)                        /* process windows messages */
        {
                case WM_COMMAND:                  /* process menu items */
                        switch (wParam)
                        case IDM_DOIT:            /* toggle message marking on/off */
                                if (bTraceOn)
                                        bTraceOn = FALSE ;
                                else
                                        bTraceOn = TRUE ;
                                break ;
                        case IDM_QUIT:            /* send end of application message */
                                DestroyWindow (hWnd) ;
                                break ;
                        }
```

```
                               break ;
               case WM_DESTROY:                    /* stop application */
                       PostQuitMessage (0) ;
                               break ;
               default:                            /* default windows message processing */
                       return DefWindowProc (hWnd, iMessage, wParam, lParam) ;
       }
       return (OL) ;
}
```

GetMessageTime   ■ Win 2.0   ■ Win 3.0   ■ Win 3.1

Purpose   Retrieves the time value when a message was sent.

Syntax   DWORD **GetMessageTime**(void);

Description   All Windows messages include a time value, which is the number of milliseconds since Windows
                      was started. This value "wraps around" back to 0 when the long integer value exceeds the avail-
                      able bit precision.

Uses   Normally used to find out how long a message has been in the message queue. Compare the value
                      to that of GetCurrentTime().

Returns   DWORD, the time at which the message was sent, in milliseconds since Windows started up.

See Also   GetCurrentTime()

Parameters   None (void).

Related Messages All messages are time stamped.

Example   This example displays the longest time between messages in the last 100 received. Messages are
                      received only when the mouse is in the program's client area, so moving the mouse outside for a
                      few seconds will result in a long delay between messages. Also, doing nothing (no mouse move-
                      ments, etc.) will result in no messages being sent to the window until an action is taken.

```
long FAR PASCAL WndProc (HWND hWnd, unsigned iMessage, WORD wParam, LONG lParam)
{
       static    BOOL    bTraceOn = FALSE ;
       HDC                hDC ;
       DWORD              dwMesTime, dwCurrentTime ;
       int                nElapsed ;
       char               cBuf [15] ;
       static    int      nLargest = 0, nCount = 0 ;

       if (bTraceOn)    /* show longest message wait in the last 100 msgs. */
       {
               dwMesTime = GetMessageTime () ;   /* get message time value */
               dwCurrentTime = GetCurrentTime () ;       /* get current time */
               nElapsed = (int) (dwCurrentTime - dwMesTime) ;
               if (nElapsed > nLargest)
               {
                       hDC = GetDC (hWnd) ;
                       SetBkMode (hDC, OPAQUE) ;/* number background opaque */
                       nLargest = nElapsed ;
                       itoa (nElapsed, cBuf, 10) ;
                       strcat (cBuf, "   ") ;
                       TextOut (hDC, 20, 50, cBuf, strlen (cBuf)) ;/* show diff */
               }
               ReleaseDC (hWnd, hDC) ;
               if (nCount++ > 100)                       /* reset counter */
                       nLargest = nCount = 0 ;
       }

       switch (iMessage)                        /* process windows messages */
       {
               case WM_COMMAND:                  /* process menu items */
                       switch (wParam)
```

```
                    {
                    case IDM_DOIT:              /* toggle message marking on/off */
                            if (bTraceOn)
                                    bTraceOn = FALSE ;
                            else
                            {
                                    bTraceOn = TRUE ;
                                    hDC = GetDC (hWnd) ;
                                    TextOut (hDC, 10, 10,
                                            "Elapsed ms. for message:", 24) ;
                                    ReleaseDC (hWnd, hDC) ;
                            }
                            break ;
                    case IDM_QUIT:              /* send end of application message */
                            DestroyWindow (hWnd) ;
                            break ;
                    }
                    break ;
            case WM_DESTROY:                    /* stop application */
                    PostQuitMessage (0) ;
                    break ;
            default:                            /* default windows message processing */
                    return DefWindowProc (hWnd, iMessage, wParam, lParam) ;
        }
        return (0L) ;
}
```

INSENDMESSAGE
■ Win 2.0   ■ Win 3.0   ■ Win 3.1

Purpose	Determines if the current message being processed was sent by SendMessage().
Syntax	BOOL **InSendMessage**(void);
Description	This function distinguishes between messages that originate from normal Windows delivery of messages, and messages sent by other running programs. InSendMessage() will not detect messages sent from within a program, or from a child or popup window's separate message function. Only messages sent from other programs result in detection.
Uses	Handy when you have separate programs which interact.
Returns	BOOL. TRUE if the message was sent from another application, FALSE if not.
See Also	SendMessage(), PostMessage(), PostAppMessage(), RegisterWindowMessage()
Parameters	None (void).
Related Messages	All messages are potentially transmittable via SendMessage().
Example	This example involves two programs. The first program looks for another running program with the title "generic" when the user clicks the "Do It!" menu item. If found, the program sends generic a WM_USER message. If not found, a message box warning is placed on the screen. The second time the "Do It!" menu item is clicked, the input focus is shifted to generic, so that it is active when the WM_USER message is received.

The second program has the title "generic." When it receives a WM_USER message, it checks to see if the message was delivered with a SendMessage() call and if "generic" is the currently active window. If these conditions are met, the window's title is changed to "Got a WM_USER message." If the conditions are not met (usually because the window is inactive), a message box warning is placed on the screen. This example is for demonstration purposes only. See Chapter 30 on DDE for a description of how to correctly exchange data and commands between running applications. Here is the WndProc() function for the message sending program.

```
Long FAR PASCAL WndProc (HWND hWnd, unsigned iMessage, WORD wParam, LONG lParam)
{
        HWND                    hWindow ;
        char                    cBuf [25] ;
```

```
        static          BOOL    bFirstTry = TRUE ;

    switch (iMessage)                       /* process windows messages */
    {
            case WM_COMMAND:                /* process menu items */
                    switch (wParam)
                    {
                    case IDM_DOIT:          /* send generic a WM_USER message */
                            hWindow = hWnd ;        /* start looking with this window */
                            while (hWindow = GetWindow (hWindow, GW_HWNDNEXT))
                            {
                                    GetWindowText (hWindow, cBuf, 24) ;
                                    if (strcmpi (cBuf, "generic") == 0)
                                            break ; /* quit if title = generic */
                            }
                            if (hWindow)
                            {       /* on second try, set focus to generic */
                                    if (!bFirstTry)
                                            SetFocus (hWindow) ;
                                    SendMessage (hWindow, WM_USER, 0, 0L) ;
                            }
                            else
                                    MessageBox (hWnd, "Did not find Generic.",
                                            "Message", MB_OK) ;
                            bFirstTry = FALSE ;
                            break ;
                    case IDM_QUIT:
                            DestroyWindow (hWnd) ;
                            break ;
                    }
                    break ;
            case WM_DESTROY:                /* stop application */
                    PostQuitMessage (0) ;
                    break ;
            default:                        /* default windows message processing */
                    return DefWindowProc (hWnd, iMessage, wParam, lParam) ;
    }
    return (0L) ;
}
```

The following listing is the WndProc() function for GENERIC.C, the program receiving the message.

```
long FAR PASCAL WndProc (HWND hWnd, unsigned iMessage, WORD wParam, LONG lParam)
{

    switch (iMessage)                       /* process windows messages */
    {
            case WM_USER:
                    if (InSendMessage ())
                    {
                            if (hWnd != GetActiveWindow())
                            {
                                    MessageBox (hWnd,
                                            "Got message, but child not active.",
                                            "Warning", MB_ICONHAND | MB_OK) ;
                            }
                            else
                                    SetWindowText (hWnd, "Got a WM_USER message") ;
                    }
                    break ;
            case WM_COMMAND:                /* process menu items */
                    switch (wParam)
                    {
                    case IDM_DOIT:
                            SetWindowText (hWnd, "Parent") ;
                            break ;
                    case IDM_QUIT:          /* send end of application message */
```

```
                              DestroyWindow (hWnd) ;
                              break ;
                    }
                    break ;
            case WM_DESTROY:                    /* stop application */
                    PostQuitMessage (0) ;
                    break ;
            default:                            /* default windows message processing */
                    return DefWindowProc (hWnd, iMessage, wParam, lParam) ;
        }
        return (0L) ;
}
```

Note that the sending function uses GENERIC's window title to determine which application is called "generic." FindWindow() could also have been used. Because GENERIC changes its window title after the first time it gets a WM_USER message and is active, the sending function will not be able to find "GENERIC" a second time. A better way of locating another application is with EnumWindows().

This example could be improved by using the RegisterWindowMessage() function to create a new unique message number for both programs to exchange. WM_USER is safe only if messages are kept within an application and its children.

MAKEPROCINSTANCE   ■ Win 2.0   ■ Win 3.0   ■ Win 3.1

Purpose	Provides a procedure-instance address for a function.
Syntax	FARPROC **MakeProcInstance**(FARPROC *lpProc*, HANDLE *hInstance*);
Description	If you need to call or pass a function address outside of the program, you will need to use MakeProcInstance() to obtain a procedure-instance handle. This binds the function to the data segment. Use FreeProcInstance() to decouple the function and data segment after use. Windows uses procedure-instance addresses so that Windows can move code and data in memory. Creating a procedure-instance address sets up a small section of code that resets the registers to the current address of the stack and local heap when the function is called.
Uses	Any time you need to pass a function address within Windows. The procedure-instance is passed instead of the function's address. This is commonly used in passing dialog box function names, in enumeration functions, and in callback functions.
Returns	FARPROC, the procedure-instance handle for the function.
See Also	FreeProcInstance()
Parameters	
lpProc	FARPROC: The function's real address when MakeProcInstance() is called. This is the function name.
hInstance	HANDLE: The program's instance handle. This handle is importrant, because each instance of the program will link a separate data segment to the function when MakeProcInstance() is called.
Comments	Don't forget to list the function name in the EXPORTS part of the program's .DEF definition file.
Example	See the example under the FreeProcInstance() function description.

PEEKMESSAGE   ■ Win 2.0   ■ Win 3.0   ■ Win 3.1

Purpose	Checks the message queue for a message.
Syntax	BOOL **PeekMessage**(LPMSG *lpMsg*, HWND *hWnd*, WORD *wMsgFilterMin*, WORD *wMsgFilterMax*, WORD *wRemoveMsg*);
Description	PeekMessage() is similar to GetMessage(), but more passive. PeekMessage() does not wait for a message to be placed in the application queue before returning. PeekMessage() yields control to

other applications. Unlike GetMessage(), PeekMessage() does not wait for a message to be placed in the message queue before returning.

Uses PeekMessage() can be used within the body of a program to do background operations until it is interrupted by a message. This is commonly used in printing operations to allow a printing task to be interrupted by a keypress or mouse click. PeekMessage() can also be used in place of Get-Message() in the program's message loop to allow a window to execute some function continuously, but still yield control to other applications. The structure of this special type of message loop should be as follows:

```
while (TRUE)
{
        if (PeekMessage (&msg, NULL, 0, 0, PM_REMOVE))
        {
                if (msg.message == WM_QUIT)
                        break ;
                else
                {
                        TranslateMessage (&msg) ;
                        DispatchMessage (&msg) ;
                }
        }
        else
        {
                /* do some function, like draw on client area */
        }
}
```

Returns BOOL. TRUE if a message is available, FALSE if not.

See Also GetMessage(), WaitMessage()

Parameters

lpMsg LPMSG: A pointer to a message structure. PeekMessage() fills in the message data when a message is found.

hWnd HWND: A handle to the window receiving the messages. PeekMessage() will only find messages in the program's message queue, not messages for other programs. If *hWnd* is set to –1, only messages posted by PostAppMessage() using a *hWnd* value of NULL will be retrieved.

wMsgFilterMin WORD: The lowest value message to be retrieved. You can use the WM_MOUSEFIRST and WM_KEYFIRST message numbers to specify the lower limit to all client area mouse messages and keystrokes respectively.

wMsgFilterMax WORD: The lowest value message to be retrieved. You can use the WM_MOUSELAST and WM_KEYFIRST message numbers to specify the upper limit to all client area mouse messages and keystrokes, respectively. If both *wMsgFilterMin* and *wMsgFilterMax* are both 0, all messages are retrieved.

wRemoveMsg WORD: Specifies how the function responds to a message. The values may be any of the ones listed in Table 8-2.

Value	Meaning
PM_NOREMOVE	Messages peeked by PeekMessage() are left in the application's message queue.
PM_NOYIELD	The current application does not stop and yield to other applications.
PM_REMOVE	Messages are removed from the message queue. This value is typically used when PeekMessage() is used in place of GetMessage() in the program's message loop. Will not remove WM_PAINT messages, which are removed with BeginPaint() and EndPaint() in the message processing function.

Table 8-2. PeekMessage( ) Flags.

PM_NOYIELD can be combined with either PM_NOREMOVE or PM_REMOVE with the C language binary OR operator (|).

Related Messages All messages can be processed by PeekMessage().

Notes Any time control is yielded to another program by GetMessage(), PeekMessage(), or Wait-Message(), local variables and far pointers to memory may be invalid when control is returned to the program.

Example At the bottom of the listing is a function called NoMessages() that paints randomly colored pages of asterisk (*) characters on the client area. When the user clicks the "Do It!" menu item, a loop is entered. The loop is exited when PeekMessage() finds a client area mouse message in the window's message queue. If there are no messages, PeekMessage() calls NoMessages() to paint another astersik and then loops back to check for messages again. Note that this example has two message loops. The normal GetMessage() loop in WinMain() is not shown (identical to GENERIC.C from Chapter 1). The PeekMessage() loop operates independently from the application's main message loop, allowing a separate process to go on.

```
long FAR PASCAL WndProc (HWND hWnd, unsigned iMessage, WORD wParam, LONG lParam)
{
        MSG     msg ;

        switch (iMessage)
        {
                case WM_COMMAND:         /* process menu items */
                        switch (wParam)
                        {
                        case IDM_DOIT:
                                while (!PeekMessage (&msg, hWnd, WM_MOUSEFIRST,
                                        WM_MOUSELAST, PM_NOREMOVE))
                                {
                                        NoMessages (hWnd) ;
                                }
                                break ;
                        case IDM_QUIT:  /* send end of application message */
                                DestroyWindow (hWnd) ;
                                break ;
                        }
                        break ;
                case WM_DESTROY:
                        PostQuitMessage (0) ;
                        return (0) ;
        }
        return (DefWindowProc (hWnd, iMessage, wParam, lParam)) ;
}

void NoMessages (HWND hWnd)      /* paint random "*" chars in client area */
{
        HDC             hDC ;
        static int      nX = 0, nY = 0, nRed = 255, nBlue = 0, nGreen = 0 ;

        hDC = GetDC (hWnd) ;
        SetTextColor (hDC, RGB (nRed, nGreen, nBlue)) ;
        TextOut (hDC, nX, nY, "*", 1) ;             /* show an "*" */
        nX += 10 ;
        if (nX > 200)
        {
                nY += 10 ;
                nX = 0 ;
        }
        if (nY > 200)           /* alter colors when screen area is full */
        {
                nY = 0 ;
                nRed += 23 ;
                if (nRed > 255)
```

```
                        nRed = 0 ;
                nBlue -= 37 ;
                if (nBlue < 0)
                        nBlue = 255 ;
        }
        ReleaseDC (hWnd, hDC) ;
}
```

POSTAPPMESSAGE

■ Win 2.0   ■ Win 3.0   ■ Win 3.1

Purpose	Puts a message in the application's message queue.
Syntax	BOOL **PostAppMessage**(HANDLE *hTask*, WORD *wMsg*, WORD *wParam*, LONG *lParam*);
Description	PostAppMessage() is similar to PostMessage() except that the message is sent to a task instead of a window. A task is a running application (not a DLL).
Uses	Used for communication between different tasks. This function is used less frequently than PostMessage().
Returns	BOOL. TRUE if the message was posted, FALSE on error.
See Also	SendMessage(), PostMessage(), GetCurrentTask(), EnumTaskWindows()
Parameters	
hTask	HANDLE: A handle to the current task. Use GetCurrentTask() and EnumTaskWindows() to fetch task handles.
wMsg	WORD: The message to send (such as WM_MOVE).
wParam	WORD: The *wParam* value to be passed with the message. See Chapter 9, *Windows Messages*, for a full list of messages and their parameter values.
lParam	DWORD: The *lParam* value to be passed with the message.
Related Messages	All Windows messages may be passed with this function.
Note	The message received by GetMessage() or PeekMessage() will have a *hwnd* parameter value of NULL if the message was sent using PostAppMessage().
Example	In this case, when the user clicks the "Do It!" menu item, a WM_USER message is sent to the application's message queue. PeekMessage() is used in the message loop to pull in the message. If the detected message is found to be equal to WM_USER, the function StarMessages() listed at the bottom is called to paint an astersik on the window's client area. This is certainly a round-about method of painting on the screen. The example was designed to illustrate how messages can be generated from within an application and end up being acted upon via the message loop.

```
/* generic.c    example of creating a child window with message processing */
/* */

#include <windows.h>
#include "generic.h"

int PASCAL WinMain (HANDLE hInstance, HANDLE hPrevInstance, LPSTR lpszCmdLine,
        int nCmdShow)
{

        HWND            hWnd ;
        MSG             msg ;
        WNDCLASS        wndclass ;

        ghInstance = hInstance ;        /* store instance handle as global var. */
        if (!hPrevInstance)     /* load data into window class struct. */
        {
                wndclass.style          = CS_HREDRAW | CS_VREDRAW ;
                wndclass.lpfnWndProc    = WndProc ;
                wndclass.cbClsExtra     = 0 ;
                wndclass.cbWndExtra     = 0 ;
```

```
                wndclass.hInstance      = hInstance ;
                wndclass.hIcon          = LoadIcon (hInstance, gszAppName) ;
                wndclass.hCursor        = LoadCursor (NULL, IDC_ARROW) ;
                wndclass.hbrBackground  = GetStockObject (WHITE_BRUSH) ;
                wndclass.lpszMenuName   = gszAppName ;
                wndclass.lpszClassName  = gszAppName ;
                                        /* register the window class */
        if (!RegisterClass (&wndclass))
                return FALSE ;
        }
        hWnd = CreateWindow (                /* create the program's window here */
                gszAppName,                  /* class name */
                gszAppName,                  /* window name */
                WS_OVERLAPPEDWINDOW,         /* window style */
                CW_USEDEFAULT,               /* x position on screen */
                CW_USEDEFAULT,               /* y position on screen */
                CW_USEDEFAULT,               /* width of window */
                CW_USEDEFAULT,               /* height of window */
                NULL,                        /* parent window handle (null = none) */
                NULL,                        /* menu handle (null = use class menu) */
                hInstance,                   /* instance handle */
                NULL) ;                      /* lpstr (null = not used) */
        ShowWindow (hWnd, nCmdShow) ;
        UpdateWindow (hWnd) ;
        while (TRUE)                              /* the program's message loop */
        {
                if (PeekMessage (&msg, NULL, 0, 0, PM_REMOVE))
                {
                        if (msg.message == WM_QUIT)
                                break ;
                        else if (msg.message == WM_USER)
                                StarMessages (hWnd) ;
                        else
                        {
                                TranslateMessage (&msg) ;
                                DispatchMessage (&msg) ;
                        }
                }
        }
        return msg.wParam ;
}


long FAR PASCAL WndProc (HWND hWnd, unsigned iMessage, WORD wParam, LONG lParam)
{
        switch (iMessage)
        {
                case WM_COMMAND:                 /* process menu items */
                        switch (wParam)
                        {
                        case IDM_DOIT:           /* send a WM_USER message */
                                PostAppMessage
                                        (GetCurrentTask(), WM_USER, 0, 0L) ;
                                break ;
                        case IDM_QUIT:
                                DestroyWindow (hWnd) ;
                                break ;
                        }
                        break ;

                case WM_DESTROY:
                        PostQuitMessage (0) ;
                        return (0) ;
        }
        return (DefWindowProc (hWnd, iMessage, wParam, lParam)) ;
}

void StarMessages (HWND hWnd)     /* paint "*" characters in client area */
{
```

```
        HDC               hDC ;
        static        int     nX = 0, nY = 0, nRed = 255, nBlue = 0, nGreen = 0 ;

        hDC = GetDC (hWnd) ;
        SetTextColor (hDC, RGB (nRed, nGreen, nBlue)) ;
        TextOut (hDC, nX, nY, "*", 1) ;          /* show an "*" */
        nX += 10 ;
        if (nX > 200)
        {
                nY += 10 ;
                nX = 0 ;
        }
        if (nY > 200)    /* alter colors when screen area is full */
        {
                nY = 0 ;
                nRed += 23 ;
                if (nRed > 255)
                        nRed = 0 ;
                nBlue -= 37 ;
                if (nBlue < 0)
                        nBlue = 255 ;
        }
        ReleaseDC (hWnd, hDC) ;
}
```

POSTMESSAGE   ■ Win 2.0   ■ Win 3.0   ■ Win 3.1

Purpose	Puts a message on a window's message queue.
Syntax	BOOL **PostMessage**(HWND *hWnd*, WORD *wMsg*, WORD *wParam*, LONG *lParam*);
Description	PostMessage() places a message on a window's message queue and then returns. The posted message can be recovered by using either GetMessage() or PeekMessage() in the program's message loop. PostMessage() returns immediately, without waiting for the message to be processed. PostMessage() cannot be used to send a message to a control (such as a button or list box) where a returned value is expected.
Uses	PostMessage() can be used in place of *goto:* commands to cause another section of the program's logic to be executed, but only after the current message has been processed. The function has the ability to send a message to all running programs at one time.
Returns	BOOL. TRUE if the message was posted, FALSE on error.
See Also	SendMessage(), PostAppMessage()
Parameters	
hWnd	HWND: A handle to the window receiving the posted message. If set to 0xFFFF (–1), all top-level windows will receive this message. Child and popup windows do not receive the message.
wMsg	WORD: The message to send (like WM_MOVE).
wParam	WORD: The *wParam* value to be passed with the message. See Chapter 9, *Windows Messages*, for a full list of messages and their parameter values.
lParam	DWORD: The *lParam* value to be passed with the message.
Related Messages	All Windows messages can be posted with this function.
Example	When the user clicks the "Do It!" menu item, the program posts a WM_USER message to all applications. The window's message function (WndProc()) responds to WM_USER messages by printing a message on the client area. If more than one instance of this program is run, all of them will print the message if any one of the instances posts the WM_USER message. This example could be improved by using RegisterWindowMessage() to create a new, unique message. WM_USER is safe only if messages are confined to within one application program and its children.

```
long FAR PASCAL WndProc (HWND hWnd, unsigned iMessage, WORD wParam, LONG lParam)
{
        HDC     hDC ;

        switch (iMessage)                        /* process windows messages */
        {
                case WM_USER:
                        hDC = GetDC (hWnd) ;
                        TextOut (hDC, 10, 10, "Got WM_USER message.", 20) ;
                        ReleaseDC (hWnd, hDC) ;
                        break ;
                case WM_COMMAND:                 /* process menu items */
                        switch (wParam)
                        {
                        case IDM_DOIT:           /* send popup window a fake keypress */
                                PostMessage (0xFFFF, WM_USER, 0, 0L) ;
                                break ;
                        case IDM_QUIT:           /* send end of application message */
                                DestroyWindow (hWnd) ;
                                break ;
                        }
                        break ;
                case WM_DESTROY:                 /* stop application */
                        PostQuitMessage (0) ;
                        break ;
                default:                         /* default windows message processing */
                        return DefWindowProc (hWnd, iMessage, wParam, lParam) ;
        }
        return 0L ;
}
```

PostQuitMessage

■ Win 2.0   ■ Win 3.0   ■ Win 3.1

Purpose	Terminates an application.
Syntax	void **PostQuitMessage**(int *nExitCode*);
Description	PostQuitMessage() posts a WM_QUIT message to the application. The program's message loop should be constructed so that when this message is received, the program exits.
Uses	Normally used to process WM_DESTROY messages and menu items that force exiting the program. Use DestroyWindow() elsewhere in the application to start the application shutdown process.
Returns	No returned value (void).
See Also	PostMessage(). PostQuitMessage() is functionally equivalent to PostMessage (hWnd, WM_QUIT, nExitCode, 0L)
Parameters	
nExitCode	int: This code will be passed as the *wParam* parameter when the WM_QUIT message is pulled off the message queue.
Related Messages	WM_DESTROY, WM_QUIT
Example	This WndProc() example shows the typical placement of DestroyWindow() and PostQuit-Message(). The DestroyWindow() is in response to the user clicking the "Quit" menu item. Windows responds by sending a WM_DESTROY message. This is also sent in response to the user double-clicking the system message button (at the upper left corner of the application window), or clicking the system message button and then selecting "Close" from the system menu.

```
long FAR PASCAL WndProc (HWND hWnd, unsigned iMessage, WORD wParam, LONG lParam)
{
        switch (iMessage)                        /* process windows messages */
        {
                case WM_COMMAND:                 /* process menu items */
                        switch (wParam)
                        {
```

```
                        case IDM_DOIT:          /* send popup window a fake keypress */
                                /* some action done here */
                                break ;
                        case IDM_QUIT:          /* send end of application message */
                                DestroyWindow (hWnd);
                                break ;
                        }
                        break ;
                case WM_DESTROY:                /* stop application */
                        PostQuitMessage (0) ;
                        break ;
                default:                        /* default windows message processing */
                        return DefWindowProc (hWnd, iMessage, wParam, lParam) ;
        }
        return (0L) ;
}
```

REGISTERWINDOWMESSAGE   ■ Win 2.0   ■ Win 3.0   ■ Win 3.1

Purpose   Creates a new, unique Windows message number.

Syntax   WORD **RegisterWindowMessage**(LPSTR *lpString*);

Description   When two separate programs communicate by sending and receiving messages, it is not safe to use the normal WM_USER, WM_USER + 1, etc. message numbers for special messages. This is because another, unrelated application might use the same message for a different purpose.

Uses   Communication between different applications.

Returns   WORD, the new message value. It will be between 0xC000 and 0xFFFF. Returns NULL on error.

See Also   SendMessage(), PostMessage(), FindWindow()

Parameters

lpString   LPSTR: A pointer to the string name to be registered. If the same string name is used by two different applications calling RegisterWindowMessage(), the same message value will be returned for both applications.

Example   This example shows two program WndProc() functions. The first is a message sender. A unique message is created using RegisterWindowMessage() when the program is started.. If the user clicks the "Do It!" menu item, the program gets a handle to the program called "GENERIC" and sends it the unique message. The second time "Do It!" is clicked, "GENERIC" is made the active window before the unique message is sent by calling SetFocus(). See Chapter 30, *Dynamic Data Exchange*, on DDE, for better ways to exchange data between applications.

```
long FAR PASCAL WndProc (HWND hWnd, unsigned iMessage, WORD wParam, LONG lParam)
{
        HWND                    hWindow ;
        static          BOOL    bFirstTry = TRUE ;
        static          WORD    wNewMessage = WM_NULL ;

        switch (iMessage)                       /* process windows messages */
        {
                case WM_CREATE:
                        wNewMessage = RegisterWindowMessage ("NEWONE") ;
                        break ;
                case WM_COMMAND:                /* process menu items */
                        switch (wParam)
                        {
                        case IDM_DOIT:          /* send generic a new message */
                                hWindow = FindWindow ("generic", "generic") ;
                                if (hWindow)
                                {
                                        if (!bFirstTry) /* on second try, set focus to */
                                                SetFocus (hWindow) ;/* generic, so awake */
```

```
                                      SendMessage (hWindow, wNewMessage, 0, 0L) ;
                        }
                        else
                                MessageBox (hWnd, "Did not find Generic.",
                                        "Message", MB_OK) ;
                        bFirstTry = FALSE ;
                        break ;
                case IDM_QUIT:
                        DestroyWindow (hWnd) ;
                        break ;
                }
                break ;
        case WM_DESTROY:                        /* stop application */
                PostQuitMessage (0) ;
                break ;
        default:                                /* default windows message processing */
                return DefWindowProc (hWnd, iMessage, wParam, lParam) ;
        }
        return (0L) ;
}
```

The listing below shows the WndProc() function for the second program. This program receives a message sent by the program shown on the previous listing. On startup (WM_CREATE), the same unique message is created in this application. The message number will correspond to the number retrieved from RegisterWindowMessage() in the sending program (above) as both calls to RegisterWindowMessage() use the same string constant "NEWONE." If the window receives the unique message, a response is generated. If the window is active when it gets the message, the window's title is changed to "Got a unique message." Otherwise, the window is not active, and a message box is generated.

```
long FAR PASCAL WndProc (HWND hWnd, unsigned iMessage, WORD wParam, LONG lParam)
{
        static  WORD wNewMessage = WM_NULL ;

        if (iMessage == wNewMessage)
        {
                ReplyMessage (NULL) ;
                if (hWnd != GetActiveWindow())
                {
                        MessageBox (hWnd, "Got message, but child not active.",
                                "Warning", MB_ICONHAND | MB_OK) ;
                }
                else
                        SetWindowText (hWnd, "Got a unique message") ;
        }

        switch (iMessage)                       /* process windows messages */
        {
                case WM_CREATE:
                        wNewMessage = RegisterWindowMessage ("NEWONE") ;
                        break ;
                case WM_COMMAND:                /* process menu items */
                        switch (wParam)
                        {
                        case IDM_DOIT:
                                SetWindowText (hWnd, "Parent") ;
                                break ;
                        case IDM_QUIT:
                                DestroyWindow (hWnd) ;
                                break ;
                        }
                        break ;
                case WM_DESTROY:               /* stop application */
                        PostQuitMessage (0) ;
                        break ;
```

```
                default:                    /* default windows message processing */
                        return DefWindowProc (hWnd, iMessage, wParam, lParam) ;
        }
        return (0L) ;
}
```

REPLYMESSAGE   ■ Win 2.0   ■ Win 3.0   ■ Win 3.1

Purpose	Frees the application sending a message to continue to execute.
Syntax	void **ReplyMessage**(LONG *lReply*);
Description	This function is used to respond to messages sent from another window or application calling SendMessage(). The *lReply* value ultimately becomes the returned value from SendMessage() in the sending application. It is not necessary (or possible) to respond with ReplyMessage() if the message was posted with PostMessage().
Uses	Used to return a value to another window which sent the message. Returns control to the sending window.
Returns	No returned value (void).
See Also	SendMessage(), RegisterWindowMessage()
Parameters	
lReply	LONG: The return value for the message sent. The application which sent the message will receive this value as the returned value from SendMessage().
Related Messages	User defined messages, created with RegisterWindowMessage().
Note	In situations where an application receiving a message calls a dialog box or message box, the system can become frozen while both the sending and receiving applications wait for action. ReplyMessage() frees the sending application to continue execution, even if the receiving application has not completed processing the message.
Example	The example illustrated in Figure 8-3 shows the WndProc() functions for both a message sending application, and a message receiving application. Both applications obtain the same unique message number by calling RegisterWindowMessage(). The first sending application transmits this message to the application titled "GENERIC" using SendMessage(). The

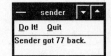 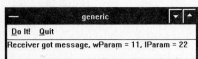

Figure 8-3. ReplyMessage( ) Example.

message is sent with the *wParam* value set to 11, and the *lParam* value set to 22. When the second (GENERIC) application receives the message, it replies with a value of 77. The receiving application displays the *lParam* and *wParam* values it obtained from the message, while the sending application displays the reply value.

⇨ **WndProc( ) Function for the Sending Application (SENDER.C)**

```
long FAR PASCAL WndProc (HWND hWnd, unsigned iMessage, WORD wParam, LONG lParam)
{
        static          WORD    wNewMessage ;
        HWND                    hWindow ;
        int                     nReturned ;
        HDC                     hDC ;
        char                    cBuf [128] ;

        switch (iMessage)                           /* process windows messages */
        {
                case WM_CREATE:
                        wNewMessage = RegisterWindowMessage ("NEWONE") ;
```

```
                        break ;
        case WM_COMMAND:                      /* process menu items */
                switch (wParam)
                {
                case IDM_DOIT:                       /* User hit the "Do it" menu item */
                        hWindow = FindWindow ("generic", "generic") ;
                        if (hWindow)
                        {
                                nReturned = SendMessage (hWindow,
                                        wNewMessage, 11, 22L) ;
                                hDC = GetDC (hWnd) ;
                                TextOut (hDC, 0, 0, cBuf, wsprintf (cBuf,
                                        "Sender got %d back.", nReturned)) ;
                                ReleaseDC (hWnd, hDC) ;
                        }
                        break ;
                case IDM_QUIT:                /* send end of application message */
                        DestroyWindow (hWnd) ;
                        break ;
                }
                break ;
        case WM_DESTROY:              /* stop application */
                PostQuitMessage (0) ;
                break ;
        default:                                /* default windows message processing */
                return DefWindowProc (hWnd, iMessage, wParam, lParam) ;
        }
        return (0L) ;
}
```

⇨ WndProc( ) Function for the Receiving Application (GENERIC.C)

```
long FAR PASCAL WndProc (HWND hWnd, unsigned iMessage, WORD wParam, LONG lParam)
{
        static   WORD    wNewMessage = WM_NULL ;
        HDC              hDC ;
        char             cBuf [128] ;

        if (iMessage == wNewMessage)
        {

                ReplyMessage (77L) ;
                hDC = GetDC (hWnd) ;
                TextOut (hDC, 0, 0, cBuf, wsprintf (cBuf,
                        "Receiver got message, wParam = %u, lParam = %lu",
                                wParam, lParam)) ;
                ReleaseDC (hWnd, hDC) ;
        }
        switch (iMessage)              /* process windows messages */
        {
                case WM_CREATE:
                        wNewMessage = RegisterWindowMessage ("NEWONE") ;
                        break ;
                case WM_COMMAND:           /* process menu items */
                        switch (wParam)
                        {
                                case IDM_QUIT:
                                        DestroyWindow (hWnd) ;
                                        break ;
                        }
                        break ;
                case WM_DESTROY:              /* stop application */
                        PostQuitMessage (0) ;
                        break ;
                default:                        /* default windows message processing */
                        return DefWindowProc (hWnd, iMessage, wParam, lParam) ;
        }
        return (0L) ;
}
```

SendMessage

■ Win 2.0   ■ Win 3.0   ■ Win 3.1

Purpose	Sends a Windows message directly to a window's message function.
Syntax	DWORD **SendMessage**(HWND *hWnd*, WORD *wMsg*, WORD *wParam*, LONG *lParam*);
Description	Can be used to send any window a message. The message is acted on immediately, as it bypasses the receiving window's message queue.

Uses   Used most often to communicate with control windows, such as buttons and list boxes. Used in cases where a program has a series of child windows that each have separate message processing functions. Any window can send any other window a message. The sending window does not restart processing until the message is processed by the receiving window. Reply-Message() is used to return control and a value back to the sender. SendMessage() can also be used within one window to reduce duplicate code. SendMessage() provides an alternative to *goto:* statements in message-based programming.

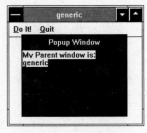

Figure 8-4. SendMessage( ) Example.

Returns	DWORD. Normally the returned value is not used. The returned value depends on which of the Windows messages was sent.
See Also	ReplyMessage(), PostMessage(), SendDlgItemMessage(), RegisterWindowMessage(), InSend-Message()

Parameters

hWnd	HWND: The handle of the window to receive the message. Set to 0xFFFF (−1) to pass a message to all parent and popup windows (not child windows).
wMsg	WORD: The message to be sent (such as WM_PAINT).
wParam	WORD: The *wParam* data to be sent with the message. See Chapter 9, *Windows Messages*, for a full list of the Windows messages and the related *wParam* and *lParam* values.
lParam	DWORD: The *lParam* data to be sent with the message.

Related Messages   All Windows messages can be sent using this function. A useful trick here is to create special messages, specific to your program. Windows defines WM_USER as the lowest message value that you can safely use. You can define your own custom messages as WM_USER + 1, WM_USER + 2, etc. This is an elegant way to allow separate message functions for child and popup windows to communicate.

Example   See the previous example under ReplyMessage() for an example of communication between two applications. In this example, the parent window creates a child popup window. The parent sends the child window a WM_USER message when the user clicks the "Do It!" menu item. The WM_USER message has the parent's window handle set as *wParam*, so that the popup window can print out the parent's name.

```
long FAR PASCAL WndProc (HWND hWnd, unsigned iMessage, WORD wParam, LONG lParam)
{
        HDC                     hDC ;
        static WNDCLASS         wndclass ;
        static HWND             hPopup, hParent ;

        switch (iMessage)                       /* process windows messages */
        {
                case WM_CREATE:         /* build the child window when program starts */

                        wndclass.style          = CS_HREDRAW | CS_VREDRAW | CS_PARENTDC;
                        wndclass.lpfnWndProc    = ChildProc ;
                        wndclass.cbClsExtra     = 0 ;
```

```
                        wndclass.cbWndExtra       = 0 ;
                        wndclass.hInstance        = ghInstance ;
                        wndclass.hIcon            = NULL ;
                        wndclass.hCursor          = LoadCursor (NULL, IDC_ARROW) ;
                        wndclass.hbrBackground    = GetStockObject (LTGRAY_BRUSH) ;
                        wndclass.lpszMenuName     = NULL ;
                        wndclass.lpszClassName    = "SecondClass" ;
                                                  /* register the window class */
                        if(RegisterClass (&wndclass))
                        {
                                hPopup = CreateWindow ("SecondClass", "Popup Window",
                                        WS_POPUP | WS_VISIBLE | WS_BORDER | WS_CAPTION,
                                        10, 50, 200, 150, hWnd, NULL, ghInstance, NULL) ;
                                ShowWindow (hPopup, SW_SHOW) ;
                        }
                        break ;
                case WM_COMMAND:          /* process menu items */
                        switch (wParam)
                        {
                        case IDM_DOIT:   /* User hit the "Do it" menu item */
                                hParent = GetParent (hPopup) ;
                                        /* Tell popup window its parentage */
                                SendMessage (hPopup, WM_USER, hParent, 0L) ;
                                break ;

                        case IDM_QUIT:   /* send end of application message */
                                DestroyWindow (hWnd) ;
                                break ;
                        }
                        break ;

                case WM_DESTROY:          /* stop application */
                        PostQuitMessage (0) ;
                        break ;

                default:        /* default windows message processing */
                        return DefWindowProc (hWnd, iMessage, wParam, lParam) ;
        }
        return (0L) ;
}


/* Here is a separate message processing procedure for the child window */

long FAR PASCAL ChildProc (HWND hWnd, unsigned iMessage, WORD wParam, LONG lParam)
{
        HDC             hDC ;
        HWND            hParent ;
        char            cBuf [25] ;

        switch (iMessage)               /* process windows messages */
        {
                case WM_USER:    /* message from parent - wParam is parent handle */
                        hDC = GetDC (hWnd) ;
                        TextOut (hDC, 1, 1, "My Parent window is:", 21) ;
                        GetWindowText ((HWND) wParam, cBuf, 24) ;
                        TextOut (hDC, 1, 15, cBuf, strlen (cBuf)) ;
                        ReleaseDC (hWnd, hDC) ;
                        break ;
                case WM_DESTROY:                /* stop the application */
                        PostQuitMessage (0) ;
                        break ;
                default:                /* default windows message processing */
                        return DefWindowProc (hWnd, iMessage, wParam, lParam) ;
        }
        return (0L) ;
}
```

SetMessageQueue
■ Win 2.0 ■ Win 3.0 ■ Win 3.1

Purpose	Changes the size of an application's message queue.
Syntax	BOOL **SetMessageQueue**(int *nMsg*);
Description	Windows defaults to a message queue size of eight messages. This is adequate for most applications, but it may be too small for an application that needs to track a series of mouse movements, or other repetitive activities involving messages.
Uses	Used in the program's WinMain() function to set the message queue size before any windows are created and before any messages are sent.
Returns	BOOL. TRUE if the message queue size was set, FALSE if not. If FALSE is returned, the program should try setting the queue size again with a smaller *nMsg* value. Otherwise ,the program will not have a message queue.
Parameters	
nMsg	int: The new queue size. This is the maximum number of messages the application's queue can contain.
Related Messages	Most messages go through the application's message queue. Exceptions are messages transmitted with SendMessage() and UpdateWindow().
Example	This is an example WinMain() function that sets the message queue size for the application equal to 256 messages (a very large value). If this proves too large for the available memory space, SetMessageQueue() is continually tried with message queue sizes repeatedly divided by 2 (right shift by one digit is the same as division by two).

```
int PASCAL WinMain (HANDLE hInstance, HANDLE hPrevInstance, LPSTR lpszCmdLine,
        int nCmdShow)
{
        HWND            hWnd ;                  /* a handle to a message */
        MSG             msg ;                   /* a message */
        WNDCLASS        wndclass ;              /* the window class */
        int             nMsgNumber ;            /* message queue size */

        ghInstance = hInstance ;                /* store instance handle as global var. */

        nMsgNumber = 512 ;                      /* twice desired # messages in queue size*/
        do
        {
                nMsgNumber >>= 1 ;              /* divided by 2 */
        }while (!SetMessageQueue (nMsgNumber))
```
[Other program lines]

SetWindowsHook
■ Win 2.0 ■ Win 3.0 ■ Win 3.1

Purpose	Installs a Windows message filter function.
Syntax	FARPROC **SetWindowsHook**(int *nFilterType*, FARPROC *lpFilterFunc*);
Description	There are several different types of filter functions, specified with the *nFilterType* parameter. Multiple filters can be installed at the same time, forming a chain of message processing functions. In all but one filter type, the filtering function must reside in a dynamic link library (DLL).
Uses	Hook functions can monitor, act on, or change Windows' messages before they are sent to application programs. Hook functions can be used to customize Windows' behavior on a system-wide basis. For example, keyboard messages can be remapped for all WM_KEYDOWN and WM_KEYUP messages to specify an alternate keyboard layout when the hook function is set.
Returns	FARPROC, the procedure-instance address of the previously installed filter function. NULL if this is the first filter installed. The calling program should save this value in a static variable. This value is passed to the DefHookProc() function as the fourth argument.

See Also   UnhookWindowsHook(), DefHookProc()

Parameters

nFilterType   int: Specifies the type of filtering function and what type of messages will be diverted to the filter
                       before being sent to an application. The choices are listed in Table 8-3.

Value	Meaning	⊠
WH_CALLWNDPROC	Filter processes only messages sent by SendMessage(). The hook function must be in a DLL. Primarily for debugging purposes.	
WH_GETMESSAGE	Filter processes messages immediately after the GetMessage() or PeekMessage() function is called in a program's message loop. All messages are passed to the filter. The hook function must be in a DLL.	
WH_JOURNALPLAYBACK	Used with WH_JOURNALRECORD. The filter function plays back an event message recorded with WH_JOURNALRECORD when an event is requested by the system message queue. The hook function must be in a DLL.	
WH_JOURNALRECORD	Used with WH_JOURNALPLAYBACK. The filter function records all messages processed in the system message queue. The stored messages can be played back by a WH_JOURNAL-PLAYBACK hook. The hook function must be in a DLL.	
WH_KEYBOARD	Filter processes WM_KEYDOWN and WM_KEYUP messages received by GetMessage() or PeekMessage(). The hook function must be in a DLL.	
WH_MSGFILTER	Filter processes messages for an application's menu, message boxes, and dialog boxes. This is the only application-specific hook. The hook function does not have to be in a DLL, and can it be part of the program.	
WH_SYSMSGFILTER	Filter processes messages for all menus, message boxes, and dialog boxes. Similar to WH_MSGFILTER, but applies system-wide. The hook function must be in a DLL.	

Table 8-3. Hook Function Types.

lpFilterFunc   FARPROC: The procedure-instance address of the filter function.

Related Messages   All messages processed by the hook function.

**Hook Function
Prototypes**   Each type of message hook expects a different kind of filter function. Each of the function types
                       is described below. With the exception of WH_MSGFILTER, all filter functions must be in dy-
                       namic link libraries (DLLs). The filter function can have any name. "FilterFunc" is shown in the
                       examples. The calling program must use MakeProcInstance() to get the procedure-instance ad-
                       dress of the function before it is passed to SetWindowsHook(). The hook function must also be
                       referenced in the EXPORTS section of the library's .DEF definition file.

WH_CALLWNDPROC
                       void FAR PASCAL **FilterFunc**(int *nCode*, WORD *wParam*, DWORD *lParam*) ;

nCode   int: A code that the filter function should examine before processing a message. If *nCode* is less
                       than zero, the function should pass the message to DefHookProc() without further actions.

wParam   WORD: TRUE (nonzero) if the message was sent by the current task. FALSE if not.

lParam   DWORD: A pointer to five WORDs of data containing the following information. (The data struc-
                       ture is not defined in WINDOWS.H, so no default names are available for references. You can use
                       the names provided in parentheses for a consistent set of structure item names if you want to
                       create your own structure.)

WORD1 (*hlParam*) - The high-order word of the *lParam* message received by the filter function.

WORD2 (*llParam*) - The low-order word of the *lParam* message received by the filter function.

WORD3 (*wParam*) - The *wParam* parameter passed with the message.

WORD4 (*wMsg*) - The message received by the filter.

WORD5 (*hWnd*) - The window handle of the window that will receive the message.

This filter processes only messages sent by SendMessage().

Returns   No returned value (void). This type of filter processes only messages sent by SendMessage(). The hook function must be in a DLL.

WH_GETMESSAGE

void FAR PASCAL **FilterFunc**(int *nCode*, WORD *wParam*, DWORD *lParam*) ;

nCode   int: A code that the filter function should examine before processing a message. If *nCode* is less than zero, the function should pass the message to DefHookProc() without further actions.

wParam   WORD: Always NULL.

lParam   DWORD: A pointer to a message structure.

Returns   No returned value (void). This filter processes messages immediately after the GetMessage() function is called in a program's message loop. All messages are passed to the filter. The message is returned to GetMessage() after any changes made by the hook function.

WH_JOURNALPLAYBACK

DWORD FAR PASCAL **FilterFunc**(int *nCode*, WORD *wParam*, DWORD *lParam*) ;

nCode   int: A code that the filter function should examine before processing a message. If *nCode* is less than zero, the function should pass the message to DefHookProc() without further actions. If *nCode* equals HC_SKIP, the function should wait until the next call to return its next recorded message data.

wParam   WORD: Always NULL.

lParam   DWORD: A pointer to a message structure. This function copies the event data saved by the WH_JOURNALRECORD message filter back to the location pointed to by the *lParam* parameter. The data should not be modified. The function should return the amount of time (in clock ticks) that Windows should wait before processing the message. Return 0L for immediate processing.

Returns   The amount of time (in clock ticks) the system should wait before processing the message. This type of hook is used with WH_JOURNALRECORD. The filter function plays back an event message recorded with WH_JOURNALRECORD when an event is requested by the system message queue. The hook function must be in a DLL.

WH_JOURNALRECORD

void FAR PASCAL **FilterFunc**(int *nCode*, WORD *wParam*, DWORD *lParam*) ;

nCode   int: A code that the filter function should examine before processing a message. If *nCode* is less than zero, the function should pass the message to DefHookProc() without further actions

wParam   WORD: Always NULL.

lParam   DWORD: A pointer to a message structure. If *nCode* is greater or equal to zero, the filter function should save a copy of the message data pointed to by *lParam*. This message will then be sent on to the program's message function (after the specified delay) when the WM_JOURNAL-PLAYBACK filter function is called.

Returns   No returned value (void). This filter type is used to record messages, for future playback by a WM_JOURNALPLAYBACK hook. This type of hook is used with WH_JOURNALPLAYBACK. The filter function records all messages processed in the system message queue. The stored messages can be played back by a WH_JOURNALPLAYBACK hook. The hook function must be in a DLL.

WH_KEYBOARD   DWORD FAR PASCAL **FilterFunc**(int *nCode*, WORD *wParam*, DWORD *lParam*) ;

nCode   int: A code that the filter function should examine before processing a message. If *nCode* is less than zero, the function should pass the message to DefHookProc() without further actions. If the value is HC_NOREMOVE, the application used PeekMessage() with the PM_NOREMOVE option. The message will not be pulled from the system message queue.

wParam   WORD: The virtual key code exactly like *wParam* in WM_KEYDOWN and WM_KEYUP messages.

lParam   DWORD: The key scan code, repeat count, etc. Exactly like *lParam* in WM_KEYDOWN and WM_KEYUP messages. The filter processes only WM_KEYDOWN and WM_KEYUP messages received by either GetMessage() or PeekMessage(). The function should return 0 if Windows is to process the message, 1 if the message should be discarded. This can be a rapid way of removing specified keyboard messages.

Returns   Should return the value returned by DefHookProc() if *nCode* == HC_LPFNNEXT (== -1). Otherwise return NULL.

Comments   An example of a keyboard hook function is shown in the example code under DefHookProc() in this chapter. Although the *wParam* and *lParam* values received by this type of hook match those received by your program on a WM_KEYDOWN or WM_KEYUP message, changing *wParam* or *lParam* within the hook function will not Affect the values passed to the main program's message loop and message processing function. To modify these parameters within the hook function, use the WH_GETMESSAGE type of hook, and change the *wParam* and *lParam* values within the *msg* structure pointed to by the hook function's *lParam* value. The changes within the hook will happen before the message is sent to the program's message processing function.

WH_MSGFILTER   int FAR PASCAL **FilterFunc**(int *nCode*, WORD *wParam*, DWORD *lParam*) ;

nCode   int: Must be one of the values listed in Table 8-4.

Value	Meaning	⊠
MSGF_DIALOGBOX	The message being processed is from a dialog box.	
MSGF_MESSAGEBOX	The message being processed is from a message box.	
MSGF_MENU	The message being processed is mouse or keyboard input from a menu.	
MSGF_MOVE	A MOVE message is being processed.	
MSGF_SIZE	A SIZE message is being processed.	
MSGF_SCROLLBAR	A SCROLLBAR message is being processed.	
MSGF_NEXTWINDOW	A window is gaining the input focus.	

Table 8-4. WH_MSGFILTER nCode Values.

wParam   WORD: Always NULL.

lParam   DWORD: A pointer to a message structure.

Returns   The function should return TRUE (nonzero) if the hook function processed the message, FALSE if no action was taken. This is the only application specific hook function. The hook function can be within the program, and does not have to be in a DLL.

WM_SYSMSGFILTER

                   int FAR PASCAL **FilterFunc**(int *nCode*, WORD *wParam*, DWORD *lParam*) ;

nCode   int: Must be one of the values listed in Table 8-5.

Value	Meaning	⊠
MSGF_DIALOGBOX	The message being processed is from a dialog box.	
MSGF_MENU	The message being processed is mouse or keyboard input from a menu.	
MSGF_MESSAGEBOX	The message being processed is from a message box.	

Table 8-5. WM_SYSMSGFILTER nCode Values.

wParam	WORD: Always NULL.
lParam	DWORD: A pointer to a message structure. Filter processes messages for all menus, message boxes, and dialog boxes. Similar to WH_MSGFILTER, but applies system-wide. The hook function must be in a DLL.
Returns	The filter function should return TRUE (nonzero) if the message was processed, FALSE (zero) otherwise.
	This type of filter processes messages for all menus, message boxes, and dialog boxes. Similar to WH_MSGFILTER, but applies system-wide. The hook function must be in a DLL.
Example	This example sets a hook function when the user clicks the "Do It!" menu item. The hook function intercepts Windows' WM_PAINT messages to *every* application running on the system. Any window receiving a WM_PAINT message has its client area outlined with a red line by the hook function. This is usually repainted by the window's own painting logic, although the outline may persist in windows that do not repaint the entire client area every time a WM_PAINT message is received. The outlining will continue until the "Do It!" menu item is clicked a second time and the hook function is removed. The hook function is placed in a dynamic link library (DLL) called MSGDLL.DLL. The definition file specifies "LIBRARY" rather than "NAME." No stack size is given, as DLLs use the calling program's stack. The DATA segment is set as "SINGLE" as there will never be multiple instances of a DLL. Finally, the hook function is listed as an exported function.The following code is the DLL Definition file, MSGDLL.DEF

```
LIBRARY         MSGDLL
DESCRIPTION     'dll of message hooks'
EXETYPE         WINDOWS
STUB            'WINSTUB.EXE'
CODE            PRELOAD MOVEABLE DISCARDABLE
DATA            PRELOAD MOVEABLE SINGLE
HEAPSIZE        1024
EXPORTS         SetHook
                FreeHook
                MsgFilterFunc
```

To compile the DLL, a separate NMAKE file is created. The key difference is that the compiler switch -ASw is set to check that the stack segment and data segments to be assumed different. This example also shows the debugging switches set. The CodeView for Windows application will allow DLLs to be viewed and debugged in the same manner as conventional Windows programs.

```
# make file for msgdll library
ALL: msgdll.dll
CFLAGS=-c -D LINT_ARGS -ASw -Zip -Od -Gsw -W2
LFLAGS=/NOD /co /align:16

msgdll.obj:             msgdll.c
        $(CC) $(CFLAGS) msgdll.c

msgdll.dll:             msgdll.obj msgdll.def
        link $(LFLAGS) msgdll libentry, msgdll.dll, NUL, libw sdllcew, msgdll
        rc msgdll.dll
```

The hook function is defined in the MSGDLL.C file. The mandatory DLL LibMain() function just unlocks the data segment of the library and returns. The hook function called MsgFilterfunc() waits until a WM_PAINT message is intercepted, and then paints the client area. The window handle for the window to receive the WM_PAINT message is retrieved from the *msg* structure. A pointer to this message structure data is passed in the *lParam* parameter when the hook function is called.

```c
/* msgdll.c  message filter dll */

#include <windows.h>

HANDLE          hInstanceDll ;
FARPROC         lpOldHook ;

int FAR PASCAL LibMain (HANDLE hInstance, WORD wDataSeg, WORD wHeapSize,
      LPSTR lpszCmdLine)
{
        if (wHeapSize > 0)
                UnlockData (0) ;
        hInstanceDll = hInstance ;
        return (1) ;
}

void FAR PASCAL SetHook (LPSTR lpsHookName, int nHookType)
{
        FARPROC         lpHook ;

        lpHook = GetProcAddress (hInstanceDll, lpsHookName) ;
        lpOldHook = SetWindowsHook (nHookType, lpHook) ;
}

void FAR PASCAL FreeHook (LPSTR lpsHookName, int nHookType)
{
        FARPROC         lpHook ;

        lpHook = GetProcAddress (hInstanceDll, lpsHookName) ;
        UnhookWindowsHook (nHookType, lpHook) ;
}

void FAR PASCAL MsgFilterFunc (int nCode, WORD wParam, DWORD lParam)
{
        LPMSG           msg ;
        HDC             hDC ;
        HPEN            hRedPen ;
        RECT            rClient ;
        static  FARPROC lpHook ;
        DWORD           dwTest ;

        if (nCode != HC_ACTION)
                DefHookProc (nCode, wParam, lParam, &lpOldHook) ;
        else if (nCode >= 0)            /* nCode negative, then no action */
        {
                msg = (LPMSG) lParam;    /* lParam holds message address */
                if (msg->message == WM_PAINT)
                {
                        hDC = GetDC (msg->hwnd) ;        /* Outline the client area */
                        GetClientRect (msg->hwnd, &rClient) ;
                        hRedPen = CreatePen (PS_SOLID, 3, RGB (255, 0, 0)) ;
                        SelectObject (hDC, hRedPen) ;
                        MoveTo (hDC, 0, 0) ;
                        LineTo (hDC, rClient.right - 2, 0) ;
                        LineTo (hDC, rClient.right - 2, rClient.bottom - 2) ;
                        LineTo (hDC, 0, rClient.bottom - 2) ;
                        LineTo (hDC, 0, 0) ;
                        DeleteObject (hRedPen) ;
                        ReleaseDC (msg->hwnd, hDC) ;
```

```
                }
        }
        return ;
}
```

The C program calling the hook function must reference the function's name in the definition file as "imported" from the DLL. The hooking and unhooking functions are also referenced.

```
NAME            GENERIC
DESCRIPTION     'generic windows program'
EXETYPE         WINDOWS
STUB            'WINSTUB.EXE'
CODE            PRELOAD MOVEABLE
DATA            PRELOAD MOVEABLE MULTIPLE
HEAPSIZE        1024
STACKSIZE       4096
EXPORTS         WndProc
IMPORTS         MSGDLL.MsgFilterFunc
                MSGDLL.SetHook
                MSGDLL.FreeHook
```

The C program's make file, header file, and resource file are all standard. No reference to the DLL containing the hook function is needed in these files. The following code is the Make file for the C program.

```
ALL: generic.exe
CFLAGS=-c -D LINT_ARGS -Zi -Od -Gsw -W2
LFLAGS=/NOD /co

generic.obj : generic.c generic.h
    $(CC) $(CFLAGS) generic.c

generic.res: generic.rc generic.ico
    rc -r generic.rc

generic.exe : generic.obj generic.def generic.res
    link $(LFLAGS) generic, , ,libw slibcew, generic
    rc generic.res
```

The following code is the resource file.

```
/* generic.rc           */
#include <windows.h>
#include "generic.h"
generic         ICON    generic.ico
generic         MENU
BEGIN
    MENUITEM "&Do It!"          IDM_DOIT
    MENUITEM "&Quit",           IDM_QUIT
END
```

The following code is the header file.

```
/* generic.h   */
#define IDM_DOIT    1                       /* menu item id values */
#define IDM_QUIT    2
        /* global variables */
int     ghInstance ;
char    gszAppName [] = "generic" ;
        /* function prototypes */
long FAR PASCAL WndProc (HWND, unsigned, WORD, LONG) ;
```

The C program sets the message hook function when the "Do It!" menu item is clicked. The hook function is unhooked the second time the menu item is selected, or when the program exits, if it is still active. Note that no changes are required to the message loop to pass messages to the hook function. Windows takes care of this reference when the SetWindowsHook() function is called, and removes it when the UnhookWindowsHook() function is called.

```
long FAR PASCAL WndProc (HWND hWnd, unsigned iMessage, WORD wParam, LONG lParam)
{
        static  BOOL    bHooked = FALSE ;

        switch (iMessage)                                /* process windows messages */
        {
                case WM_COMMAND:                         /* process menu items */
                        switch (wParam)
                        {
                        case IDM_DOIT:
                                if (bHooked)
                                {
                                        FreeHook ("msgFilterFunc", WH_GETMESSAGE) ;
                                        bHooked = FALSE ;
                                        MessageBox (hWnd, "No hook function now.",
                                                "Unhooked",     MB_OK) ;
                                }
                                else
                                {
                                        SetHook ("MsgFilterFunc", WH_GETMESSAGE) ;
                                        bHooked = TRUE ;
                                        MessageBox (hWnd, "A hook function installed.",
                                                "Hooked", MB_OK) ;
                                }
                                break ;
                        case IDM_QUIT:
                                DestroyWindow (hWnd) ;
                                break ;
                        }
                        break ;
                case WM_DESTROY:        /* stop application */
                        if (bHooked)
                                FreeHook ("msgKeyboardFunc", WH_KEYBOARD) ;
                        PostQuitMessage (0) ;
                        break ;
                default:                        /* default windows message processing */
                        return DefWindowProc (hWnd, iMessage, wParam, lParam) ;
        }
        return (0L) ;
}
```

TRANSLATEMESSAGE   ■ Win 2.0   ■ Win 3.0   ■ Win 3.1

Purpose	Generates WM_CHAR, WM_SYSCHAR, WM_DEADCHAR, and WM_SYSDEADCHAR messages when a virtual key code is received.
Syntax	BOOL **TranslateMessage**(LPMSG *lpMsg*);
Description	The low-level Windows drivers generate virtual key messages (VK_TAB, etc.) when a key is pressed. TranslateMessage() posts the corresponding WM_CHAR code on the applications message queue when a virtual key code is received.
Uses	Normally, part of the program's message loop. If you do not use the WM_CHAR messages, you can leave this function out of the message loop.
Returns	BOOL. TRUE if the message was translated. FALSE if not.
See Also	DispatchMessage(), GetMessage(), PeekMessage()
Parameters	
lpMsg	LPMSG: A pointer to a MSG message structure. This is the message data fetched from the application's message queue by GetMessage() or PeekMessage. The message data is not altered by TranslateMessage(). The new WM_CHAR messages are placed on the message queue for separate processing.
Related Messages	The virtual key codes, WM_CHAR, WM_SYSCHAR, WM_DEADCHAR, and WM_SYSDEADCHAR.
Example	This is a typical message loop from the end of a program's WinMain() function.

```
while (GetMessage (&msg, NULL, 0, 0))
{
        TranslateMessage (&msg) ;
        DispatchMessage (&msg) ;
}
```

UNHOOKWINDOWSHOOK   ■ Win 2.0   ■ Win 3.0   ■ Win 3.1

Purpose	Removes a message hook function from the system.
Syntax	BOOL **UnhookWindowsHook**(int *nHook*, FARPROC *lpfnHook*);
Description	There can be any number of message hook functions installed of any one type. UnhookWindowsHook() removes one message from the chain.
Uses	Used within the DLL (dynamic link library) that sets the hook function.
Returns	BOOL. TRUE if the function was removed, FALSE on error.
See Also	SetWindowsHook() has the complete descriptions of the different types of hook functions and a complete program example.

Parameters

nHook   int: Specifies the type of filtering function, and what type of messages will be diverted to the filter before being sent to an application. The choices are lsited in Table 8-6.

Value	Meaning ⊠
WH_CALLWNDPROC	Filter processes only messages sent by SendMessage(). The hook function must be in a DLL.
WH_GETMESSAGE	Filter processes messages immediately after the GetMessage() or PeekMessage() function is called in a program's message loop. All messages are passed to the filter. The hook function must be in a DLL.
WH_JOURNALPLAYBACK	Used with WH_JOURNALRECORD. The filter function plays back an event message recorded with WH_JOURNALRECORD when an event is requested by the system message queue. The hook function must be in a DLL.
WH_JOURNALRECORD	Used with WH_JOURNALPLAYBACK. The filter function records all messages processed in the system message queue. The stored messages can be played back by a WH_JOURNAL-PLAYBACK hook. The hook function must be in a DLL.
WH_KEYBOARD	Filter processes WM_KEYDOWN and WM_KEYUP messages received by GetMessage() or PeekMessage(). The hook function must be in a DLL.
WH_MSGFILTER	Filter processes messages for an application's menu, message boxes, and dialog boxes. This is the only application-specific hook. The hook function does not have to be in a DLL and can be part of the program.
WH_SYSMSGFILTER	Filter processes messages for all menus, message boxes, and dialog boxes. Similar to WH_MSGFILTER, but applies system-wide. The hook function must be in a DLL.

Table 8-6. UnhookWindowsHook( ) Hook Types.

lpfnHook	FARPROC: The procedure-instance address of the hook function.
Related Messages	All Windows messages.
Example	See the examples under the DefHookProc() and SetWindowsHook() function descriptions.

WAITMESSAGE
■ Win 2.0 ■ Win 3.0 ■ Win 3.1

Purpose   Yields control to any other application.

Syntax   void **WaitMessage**(void);

Description   WaitMessage() tells Windows to switch control to another application. Messages to other applications are then processed. This is the most passive of the three functions Windows provides to switch control between running programs. The other two are GetMessage() and PeekMessage().

Uses   Useful in small utility programs where it is desirable to give up control as often as possible to minimize the slowdown of the system due to having the utility program running. You can also use the function to wait for a specific message, such as a mouse movement.

Returns   No returned value (void).

See Also   GetMessage(), PeekMessage().

Parameters   None (void).

Related Messages Any message received by the application calling WaitMessage() will resume message processing.

Notes   Any time control is yielded to another program by GetMessage(), PeekMessage(), or WaitMessage(), the stack and memory segments are subject to being moved in memory. Local variables and pointers to memory may be invalid when control is returned to the program.

Example   When the user clicks the "Do It!" menu item, PeekMessage() is used to clear any waiting messages from the application's message queue. The application then just sits there, waiting for any message (WaitMessage() call). If any key is pressed, or the mouse is moved, the text "Got a message!" appears in the window's client area and execution continues.

```
Long FAR PASCAL WndProc (HWND hWnd, unsigned iMessage, WORD wParam, LONG lParam)
{
        static          HDC       hDC ;
        MSG                       msg ;
        char                      cBuf [128] ;

        switch (iMessage)                       /* process windows messages */
        {
                case WM_COMMAND:                /* process menu items */
                        switch (wParam)
                        {
                        case IDM_DOIT:          /* User hit the "Do it" menu item */
                                while (PeekMessage (&msg, hWnd, 0, 0, PM_REMOVE))
                                        ;       /* clear any waiting messages */
                                WaitMessage () ;        /* now wait for one */
                                hDC = GetDC (hWnd) ;
                                TextOut (hDC, 0, 0, "Got a message!", 14) ;
                                ReleaseDC (hWnd, hDC) ;
                                break ;
                        case IDM_QUIT:
                                DestroyWindow (hWnd) ;
                                break ;
                        }
                        break ;
                case WM_DESTROY:                /* stop application */
                        PostQuitMessage (0) ;
                        break ;
                default:                /* default windows message processing */
                        return DefWindowProc (hWnd, iMessage, wParam, lParam) ;
        }
        return (0L) ;
}
```

Windows Messages

Windows uses a lot of messages. These messages range from common ones, like WM_CREATE that are used in most applications, to obscure messages that you may never use. This chapter documents all of them (except for the DDE messages explained in Chapter 30) with example programs at the start of each group of related messages. If you are beginning to learn Windows, you may want to spend some time just reading the *Purpose* sections for each of the messages. They will give you an idea of what the different types of messages can do. Later, when you need a message, you can look up the right one and its exact syntax.

Transmitted Messages

Windows messages are categorized into ten groups. Each group has a different prefix, such as BM_ for button message. Table 9-1 gives each of the message prefixes and the message type that corresponds.

MESSAGE Prefix	Meaning
BM_	Button message. Sent to a child window button control to do some action, such as change the button's text string.
BN_	Button notification code. Received by the application's WndProc() function from a child window button control. An example is BN_CLICKED, which means the button was clicked.
CB_	Combo box message. Sent to a combo box control to cause some action, such as adding an item.
CBN_	Combo box notification code. Received by the application's WndProc() function from a combo box control as notification that some action occurred, such as the selection was changed.
DM_	Dialog box message. There are only two of these, both dealing with the default pushbutton control. Dialog boxes and their child windows send and receive normal window messages for most actions.
EM_	Edit control message. Sent to a child window edit control to cause some action, such as changing the text string.
EN_	Edit control notification code. Received by the application's WndProc() function as notification that some action occurred to an edit control (for example, if the edit control was scrolled or text was added).
LB_	List box message. Sent to a list box control to cause some action, such as deleting an item.
LBN_	List box notification code. Received by the application's WndProc() function as notification that some action occurred to the list box control, such as the user selected an item.
WM_	All other Windows messages. This includes the WM_DDE messages for dynamic data exchange (Chapter 30, defined in DDE.H) and the WM_MDI messages for the multiple document interface. The MDI messages are documented in this chapter, but discussed more fully in Chapter 29.

Table 9-1. Windows Message Types.

Messages can be either sent or received. Most messages tend to be either sent in a SendMessage() function call or received in a message processing function, such as WndProc(). The message descriptions that follow show the most common situations. You can choose either to send the message to the application's message queue with Post-

Message() or send it directly to the application's message processing function with SendMessage(). SendMessage() is required if you send a message to a control, such as a button.

Transmitted Button Message Summary

Windows provides five messages that you can send to a button control either to change the button's status (checked, unchecked, etc.) or to find the current status. Table 9-2 gives a summary of the messages.

Message	Meaning	
BM_GETCHECK	Find out if a radio button or check box is checked.	
BM_GETSTATE	Find out if a button is highlighted (by a mouse click or spacebar action).	
BM_SETCHECK	Change a radio button or check box to/from checked/unchecked.	
BM_SETSTATE	Highlight or remove highlighting from a button.	
BM_SETSTYLE	Change the style of a button control.	

Table 9-2. Transmitted Button Messages.

A button's text string is usually changed with the SetWindowText() function, not by transmitting a WM_SETTEXT message to the button control. Listing 9-1 gives an example WndProc() function that uses three of the BM_ messages to change a button's style, set the button to a checked state, and confirm that the button is checked using BM_GETSTATE. SendMessage() is used to transmit the messages to the button control.

▷ **Listing 9-1. Example Using Transmitted Button Messages**

```
long FAR PASCAL WndProc (HWND hWnd, unsigned iMessage, WORD wParam, LONG lParam)
{
        static  HWND    hButton ;
        HDC             hDC ;
        int             nButtonState ;

        switch (iMessage)                       /* process windows messages */
        {
                case WM_CREATE:
                        hButton = CreateWindow ("BUTTON", "Button Text",
                                WS_CHILD | WS_VISIBLE | BS_RADIOBUTTON,
                                10, 10, 100, 40, hWnd, 101, ghInstance, NULL) ;
                        ShowWindow (hButton, SW_SHOW) ;
                        break ;
                case WM_COMMAND:                /* process menu items */
                        switch (wParam)
                        {
                        case IDM_DOIT:          /* User hit the "Do it" menu item */
                                SendMessage (hButton, BM_SETSTYLE,
                                        (WORD) BS_CHECKBOX, 1L) ;
                                SendMessage (hButton, BM_SETCHECK, 1, OL) ;
                                nButtonState = SendMessage (hButton,
                                        BM_GETSTATE, 0, OL) ;
                                hDC = GetDC (hWnd) ;
                                if (nButtonState)
                                        TextOut (hDC, 10, 120,
                                                "Button is highlighted.", 22) ;
                                else
                                        TextOut (hDC, 10, 120,
                                                "Button is Not highlighted.", 26) ;
                                ReleaseDC (hWnd, hDC) ;
                                break ;
                        case IDM_QUIT:
                                DestroyWindow (hWnd) ;
                                break ;
                        }
                        break ;
                case WM_DESTROY:                /* stop application */
```

```
                    PostQuitMessage (O) ;
                    break ;
          default:                /* default windows message processing */
                    return DefWindowProc (hWnd, iMessage, wParam, lParam) ;
     }
     return (OL) ;
}
```

Figure 9-1 shows the example program after the user clicked the "Do It!" menu item. Note that the radio button has been changed to a check box style, showing a square check box in place of the radio button circle. The check box has an "X" in the center, because a BM_SETCHECK message was sent.

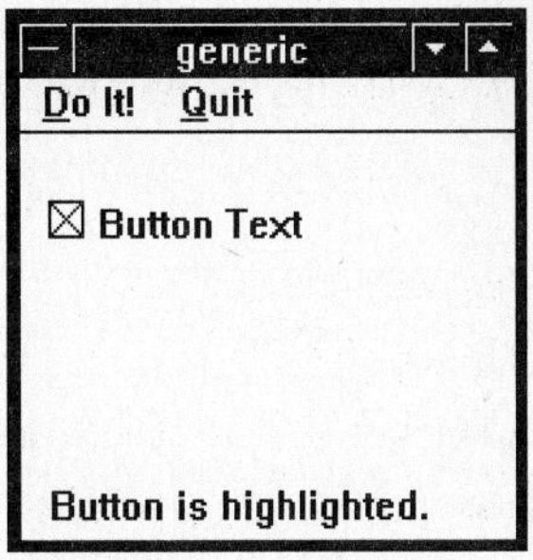

BM_GETCHECK
■ Win 2.0   ■ Win 3.0   ■ Win 3.1

Purpose	Determines if a radio button or check box control is checked.
Syntax	dwReturned = SendMessage (HWND hControl, **BM_GET-CHECK**, WORD wParam, DWORD lParam);
Returns	DWORD. Nonzero if the control is checked, zero if checked. Always returns zero if a pushbutton control is tested (no check box).

Figure 9-1. Sending a Message to a Child Window Control.

Parameters

hControl	HWND: The window handle of the button control.
wParam	WORD: Not used. Set equal to 0.
lParam	DWORD: Not used. Set equal to 0L.
Related Messages	BM_SETCHECK

BM_GETSTATE
■ Win 2.0   ■ Win 3.0   ■ Win 3.1

Purpose	Determines if a button control has been highlighted. Highlighting occurs when the user clicks the button with the mouse, or presses the spacebar when a button has the input focus.
Syntax	dwReturned = SendMessage (HWND hControl, **BM_GETSTATE**, WORD wParam, DWORD lParam)
Returns	DWORD, nonzero if the button is highlighted, zero if not.

Parameters

hControl	HWND: The window handle of the button control.
wParam	WORD: Not used. Set equal to 0.
lParam	DWORD: Not used. Set equal to 0L.

BM_SETCHECK
■ Win 2.0   ■ Win 3.0   ■ Win 3.1

Purpose	Checks or removes a checkmark from a radio button or check box control. Has no effect on push-buttons.
Syntax	SendMessage (HWND hControl, **BM_SETCHECK**, WORD wParam, DWORD lParam)
Returns	DWORD. Is not used.

Parameters

hControl	HWND: The window handle of the button control.
wParam	WORD: 0 to remove a checkmark. 1 to place a checkmark. 2 to gray a button control created with the BS_AUTO3STATE or BS_3STATE style.
lParam	DWORD: Not used. Set equal to 0L.

BM_SETSTATE
■ Win 2.0   ■ Win 3.0   ■ Win 3.1

Purpose	Changes a button control to/from the highlighted state.
Syntax	SendMessage (HWND *hControl*, **BM_SETSTATE**, WORD *wParam*, DWORD *lParam*)
Returns	DWORD. Not used.
Parameters	
hControl	HWND: The window handle of the button control.
wParam	WORD: 0 to remove highlighting. 1 to highlight the button control.
lParam	DWORD: Not used. Set equal to 0L.

BM_SETSTYLE
■ Win 2.0   ■ Win 3.0   ■ Win 3.1

Purpose	Changes the style of a button control.
Syntax	SendMessage (HWND *hControl*, **BM_SETSTYLE**, WORD *wParam*, DWORD *lParam*)
Returns	DWORD. Not used.
Parameters	
hControl	HWND: The window handle of the button control.
wParam	WORD: The button control style to use. *wParam* can be set to any of the values listed in Table 9-3.

Value	Meaning
BS_AUTOCHECKBOX	Small rectangular button with text to the right. The rectangle can be either open or checked. This style toggles automatically between checked and open.
BS_AUTORADIOBUTTON	Small circular button with text to the right. The circle can be either filled or open. This style toggles automatically between checked and open.
BS_AUTO3STATE	Small rectangular button with text to the right. The button can be filled, grayed, or open. This style toggles automatically between checked, grayed, and open.
BS_CHECKBOX	Small rectangular button with text to the right. The rectangle can either be open or checked.
BS_DEFPUSHBUTTON	Button with text in the center and with a defined (dark) border.
BS_GROUPBOX	A box with text at the upper left. Used to group other buttons.
BS_LEFTTEXT	Causes text to be on the left side of the button using the language library OR operator?
BS_OWNERDRAW	Designates a button that will be drawn by the program. Windows sends messages to request paint, invert, and disable. Use this style for custom button controls.
BS_PUSHBUTTON	Button with text in the center.
BS_RADIOBUTTON	Small circular button with text to the right. The circle can be either filled or open.
BS_3STATE	Small rectangular button with text to the right. The button can be filled, grayed, or open.

Table 9-3. Button Styles.

lParam	DWORD: Specifies whether or not the button control should be redrawn. Set to 1L to redraw the control (normal case), or set to 0L to not redraw until the next WM_PAINT cycle.

Button Notification Codes

When a button sends a WM_COMMAND message to its parent, it places the button ID value in the *wParam* value of the message. The ID value of the button is initially set in the CreateWindow() call by setting the *hMenu* parameter equal to the control's ID value. Note that *hMenu* is poorly named. Only parent and popup windows use this parameter to refer to a menu. The button ID values are usually defined in the program's header file. The numbers should be different from any of the menu item ID values because both buttons and menu items interact with the program via

WM_COMMAND messages. When the user clicks a button control, Windows sends a WM_COMMAND message. The button's ID value is passed as the *wParam* parameter, while *lParam* contains the button control's window handle in the low-order word and a notification code like BN_DOUBLECLICKED in the high-order word.

Listing 9-2 shows the WndProc() function of a program with two controls, a pushbutton, and a radio button. The text in the controls is changed when they are clicked with the mouse. The result, after double-clicking both controls, is shown in Figure 9-2. Windows also sends WM_COMMAND messages for button controls when they are enabled, about to be painted, highlighted, or loose highlighting. You can intercept these messages for painting custom button images in place of the usual text and highlighting defaults.

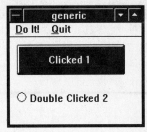

Figure 9-2. Window Controls Responding to Mouse Clicks.

☞ Listing 9-2. Button Notification Codes

```
Long FAR PASCAL WndProc (HWND hWnd, unsigned iMessage, WORD wParam, LONG lParam)
{
        HWND    hButton, hRadioButton, hPickedButton ;

        switch (iMessage)                        /* process windows messages */
        {
                case WM_CREATE:
                        hButton = CreateWindow ("BUTTON", "Button Text",
                                WS_CHILD | WS_VISIBLE | BS_PUSHBUTTON,
                                10, 10, 150, 40, hWnd, 100, ghInstance, NULL) ;
                        ShowWindow (hButton, SW_SHOW) ;
                        hRadioButton = CreateWindow ("BUTTON", "Button Text",
                                WS_CHILD | WS_VISIBLE | BS_RADIOBUTTON,
                                10, 60, 150, 40, hWnd, 101, ghInstance, NULL) ;
                        ShowWindow (hRadioButton, SW_SHOW) ;
                        break ;
                case WM_COMMAND:                 /* process menu items and buttons */
                        switch (wParam)
                        {
                        case 100:                /* push button's id value */
                                hPickedButton = LOWORD (lParam) ;
                                if (HIWORD (lParam) == BN_CLICKED)
                                        SetWindowText (hPickedButton, "Clicked 1") ;
                                break ;
                        case 101:                /* radio button's id value */
                                hPickedButton = LOWORD (lParam) ;
                                if (HIWORD (lParam) == BN_CLICKED)
                                        SetWindowText (hPickedButton, "Clicked 2") ;
                                else if (HIWORD (lParam) == BN_DOUBLECLICKED)
                                        SetWindowText (hPickedButton,
                                                "Double Clicked 2") ;
                                break ;
                        case IDM_QUIT:
                                DestroyWindow (hWnd) ;
                                break ;
                        }
                        break ;
                case WM_DESTROY:                 /* stop application */
                        PostQuitMessage (0) ;
                        break ;
                default:                         /* default windows message processing */
                        return DefWindowProc (hWnd, iMessage, wParam, lParam) ;
        }
        return (0L) ;
}
```

Button Notification Code Summary

Table 9-4 summarizes the button notification codes. These are transmitted with WM_COMMAND messages. The notification code is sent as the high-order word of the *lParam* value sent with WM_COMMAND. The detailed descriptions of the notification codes follow immediately after the table.

Notification Code	Purpose	⊠
BN_CLICKED	Notification that a button control was clicked by the mouse, or the spacebar was pressed when the control had the input focus.	
BN_DISABLE	Notification that a button control was disabled.	
BN_DOUBLECLICKED	Notification that a button control was double-clicked with the mouse.	
BN_HILITE	Notification that a button control will be highlighted.	
BN_PAINT	Notification that a button control is about to be painted.	
BN_UNHILITE	Notification that a button control will loose its highlighting.	

Table 9-4. Button Notification Codes.

Button Notification Code Descriptions

BN_CLICKED
■ Win 2.0   ■ Win 3.0   ■ Win 3.1

Purpose   Notification that a button control was clicked by the mouse, or the spacebar was pressed when the control had the input focus.

Syntax   Returned as part of a WM_COMMAND message, processed by the program's message processing function (WndProc()).

Parameters

wParam   WORD: Contains the ID value for the control. This is the integer value set for the *hMenu* parameter when CreateWindow() was called.

lParam   DWORD: The low-order word contains the handle of the button control. The high-order word contains BN_CLICKED.

BN_DISABLE
■ Win 2.0   ■ Win 3.0   ■ Win 3.1

Purpose   Notification that a button control was disabled. Button controls can be enabled and disabled with the EnableWindow() function.

Syntax   Returned as part of a WM_COMMAND message, processed by the program's message processing function (WndProc()).

Parameters

wParam   WORD: Contains the ID value for the control. This is the integer value set for the *hMenu* parameter when CreateWindow() was called.

lParam   DWORD: The low-order word contains the handle of the button control. The high-order word contains BN_DISABLE.

BN_DOUBLECLICKED
■ Win 2.0   ■ Win 3.0   ■ Win 3.1

Purpose   Notification that a button control was double-clicked with the mouse.

Syntax   Returned as part of a WM_COMMAND message, processed by the program's message processing function (WndProc()).

Parameters

wParam   WORD: Contains the ID value for the control. This is the integer value set for the *hMenu* parameter when CreateWindow() was called.

lParam   DWORD: The low-order word contains the handle of the button control. The high-order word contains BN_DOUBLECLICKED.

BN_HILITE
■ Win 2.0　■ Win 3.0　■ Win 3.1

Purpose　Notification that a button control will be highlighted. This can be used for custom buttons to allow painting of a highlight image or bitmap. Custom buttons are created with the BS_OWNER-DRAW style when calling CreateWindow().

Syntax　Returned as part of a WM_COMMAND message, processed by the program's message processing function (WndProc()).

Parameters
wParam　WORD: Contains the ID value for the control. This is the integer value set for the *hMenu* parameter when CreateWindow() was called.

lParam　DWORD: The low-order word contains the handle of the button control. The high-order word contains BN_HILITE.

BN_PAINT
■ Win 2.0　■ Win 3.0　■ Win 3.1

Purpose　Notification that a button control is about to be painted. Custom buttons are created with the BS_OWNERDRAW style when calling CreateWindow(). See the example of owner-drawn menu items at the begining of Chapter 4, *Menus*, for the similar example.

Syntax　Returned as part of a WM_COMMAND message, processed by the program's message processing function (WndProc()).

Parameters
wParam　WORD: Contains the ID value for the control. This is the integer value set for the *hMenu* parameter when CreateWindow() was called.

lParam　DWORD: The low-order word contains the handle of the button control. The high-order word contains BN_PAINT.

BN_UNHILITE
■ Win 2.0　■ Win 3.0　■ Win 3.1

Purpose　Notification that a button control will lose its highlighting. This can be used by custom button controls to signal repainting of the button's client area with the normal image. Custom buttons are created with the BS_OWNERDRAW style when calling CreateWindow().

Syntax　Returned as part of a WM_COMMAND message, processed by the program's message processing function (WndProc()).

Parameters
wParam　WORD: Contains the ID value for the control. This is the integer value set for the *hMenu* parameter when CreateWindow() was called.

lParam　DWORD: The low-order word contains the handle of the button control. The high-order word contains BN_UNHILITE.

Combo Box Messages

Combo boxes were added with the 3.0 version of Windows. Combo boxes combine an edit control at the top with a list box underneath it. The list box can be either visible all of the time (CBS_SIMPLE style) or visible only when the user clicks a button on the right side of the edit control (CBS_DROPDOWN style). A full description of all of the style possibilities is given in the CreateWindow() function description in Chapter 2, *Creating Windows*.

　　Once created, a program communicates with a combo box by sending and receiving messages. Most of these messages parallel similar messages for list boxes. The additional messages deal with the edit control at the top, which is used to display the most recent selection or allow editing of an entry in the list. Listing 9-3 provides a rudimentary example of creating and dealing with a combo box. When the user clicks the "Do It!" menu item, the list box is filled with four text items. If an item from the list is selected, it is displayed in the combo box edit field at the top (this is automatic), and is also displayed at the bottom of the window. Figure 9-3 shows what the program's window looks like after the second item in the list box is selected.

Note in the listing that the combo box style includes the WS_VSCROLL style, which adds a vertical scroll bar to the right side of the list box area. Also note that the combo box is given an ID value of 100, which is used in processing WM_COMMAND messages to identify which control sent the message. Normally, these ID values are defined in the program's header file and have separate numbers from any menu item.

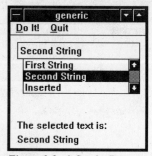

Figure 9-3. A Combo Box Control.

▷ **Listing 9-3. Sending and Receiving Messages from a Combo Box Control**

```
long FAR PASCAL WndProc (HWND hWnd, unsigned iMessage, WORD wParam, LONG lParam)
{
        static HWND     hComboBox ;
        HDC             hDC ;
        int             nSel ;
        char            cBuf [30] ;
        switch (iMessage)                    /* process windows messages */
        {
        case WM_CREATE:
                hComboBox = CreateWindow ("COMBOBOX", "Combo Text",
                        WS_CHILD | WS_VISIBLE | CBS_SIMPLE | CBS_HASSTRINGS
                                | WS_VSCROLL,
                        10, 10, 180, 80, hWnd, 100, ghInstance, NULL) ;
                ShowWindow (hComboBox, SW_SHOW) ;
                break ;
        case WM_COMMAND:                      /* process menu items and buttons */
                switch (wParam)
                {
                case 100:               /* Combo box id value */
                        if (HIWORD (lParam) == CBN_SELCHANGE)
                        {
                                hDC = GetDC (hWnd) ;
                                nSel = (WORD) SendMessage (hComboBox,
                                        CB_GETCURSEL, 0, 0L) ;
                                SendMessage (hComboBox, CB_GETLBTEXT,
                                        nSel, (DWORD) (LPSTR) cBuf) ;
                                TextOut (hDC, 10, 120,
                                        "The selected text is:", 21) ;
                                TextOut (hDC, 10, 140, cBuf, lstrlen (cBuf)) ;
                                ReleaseDC (hWnd, hDC) ;

                        }
                        break ;
                case IDM_DOIT:
                        SendMessage (hComboBox, CB_RESETCONTENT, 0, 0L) ;
                        SendMessage (hComboBox, CB_ADDSTRING, 0,
                                (DWORD) (LPSTR) "First String") ;
                        SendMessage (hComboBox, CB_ADDSTRING, 0,
                                (DWORD) (LPSTR) "Second String") ;
                        SendMessage (hComboBox, CB_ADDSTRING, 0,
                                (DWORD) (LPSTR) "Last String") ;
                        SendMessage (hComboBox, CB_INSERTSTRING, 2,
                                (DWORD) (LPSTR) "Inserted") ;
                        SendMessage (hComboBox, CB_SHOWDROPDOWN, TRUE, 0L) ;
                        break ;
                case IDM_QUIT:          /* send end of application message */
                        DestroyWindow (hWnd) ;
                        break ;
                }
```

```
                    break ;
          case WM_DESTROY:                    /* stop application */
                    PostQuitMessage (0) ;
                    break ;
          default:                            /* default windows message processing */
                    return DefWindowProc (hWnd, iMessage, wParam, lParam) ;
        }
        return (0L) ;
}
```

Owner-Redrawn Combo Boxes

Most combo boxes keep their own copies of the strings used in the list box if the CBS_HASSTRINGS style is used in creating the combo box. If this style is not selected, the combo box has the OWNERREDRAW style, which means that the calling program is responsible for painting every item in the combo box. This is ideal for selecting colors from a palette (showing color bars for the entries in the combo box's list box) or graphic object selection. Combo boxes that are OWNERREDRAW store only a 32-bit value for each element of the combo box. This value can have any meaning desired by the programmer. Common uses are RGB color values and handles to bitmaps. When Windows needs to paint one of the owner-redrawn items, Windows sends a WM_DRAWITEM message. The *lParam* value passed with the message contains a pointer to a DRAWITEMSTRUCT structure. The 32-bit value for the combo box item ends up in the *itemData* element of the structure.

```
/* DRAWITEMSTRUCT for ownerdraw */
typedef struct tagDRAWITEMSTRUCT
  {
  WORD CtlType;                /* ODT_MENU, ODT_LISTBOX, ODT_COMBOBOX, or ODT_BUTTON */
  WORD CtlID;                  /* the control id for the list box, combo box, button */
  WORD itemID;                 /* the item's id number in the list or combo box */
  WORD itemAction;             /* ODA_DRAWITEM, ODA_SELECT, or ODA_FOCUS */
  WORD itemState;              /* ODS_SELECTED, ODS_GRAYED, ODS_DISABLED, ODS_CHECKED */
  HWND hwndItem;               /* the item's handle */                 /* or ODS_FOCUS */
  HDC  hDC;                    /* the item's device context */
  RECT rcItem;                 /* the bounding rectangle of the item */
  DWORD       itemData;        /* 32-bit data goes here */
  } DRAWITEMSTRUCT;
typedef DRAWITEMSTRUCT NEAR *PDRAWITEMSTRUCT;
typedef DRAWITEMSTRUCT FAR  *LPDRAWITEMSTRUCT;
```

The structure also contains the size of the item as a rectangle, the device context, and coded information as to what type of paint operation to do. These options are in the *itemAction* and *itemState* elements of the structure. There are other similar structures defined in WINDOWS.H for passing information on sizing items, deleting items, and sorting them in the list box. These structures are used less frequently. The other structures are shown with their corresponding messages later in this section.

Windows sends WM_DRAWITEM messages for each combo box item that needs to be updated. If the items are to be sorted, WM_COMPAREITEM messages will be sent to add a new item, as simple ASCII sort order cannot be used. WM_DELETEITEM messages are sent to the program if items are to be removed. Finally, if the CBS_OWNER-DRAWVARIABLE style is used, the items in the combo box do not have to be all the same height. WM_MEASURE-ITEM messages will be sent when an item is inserted to set the item's size. Figure 9-4 shows an owner-redrawn combo box that allows the selection of one of four colors. This is a drop down combo box, so that only the selected color is normally visible. The list box showing all of the colors is hidden until the down arrow on the right side of the selection box is clicked.

The trick behind this application is that the color of each of the selection items can be stored as a 32-bit value. When Windows needs to paint one of the list box items, or the top selection box, it sends a WM_DRAWITEM message. The WndProc() function intercepts these and finds the pointer to a DRAWITEMSTRUCT as the *lParam* value. The 32-bit coded value for the RGB color is found in the *itemData* element. All the WndProc() function has to do is paint the given rectangle with the color specified by the RGB value.

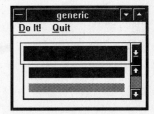

Figure 9-4. An Owner-Redrawn Combo Box.

Listing 9-4 shows the WndProc() function that creates and updates the owner-redrawn combo box. As an added example, when the user clicks the "Do It!" menu item, one of the color values is changed to a new RGB value, matching yellow. Note that WM_MEASUREITEM messages are also processed. This is Windows' way of finding out the vertical size of an item, measured in pixels. In processing either WM_DRAWITEM or WM_MEASUREITEM messages, an item number of −1 refers to the top edit control of the combo box.

▷ **Listing 9-4. Combo Box Example**

```
long FAR PASCAL WndProc (HWND hWnd, unsigned iMessage, WORD wParam, LONG lParam)
{
        static HWND             hComboBox ;
        LPDRAWITEMSTRUCT        lpDIS ;
        LPMEASUREITEMSTRUCT     lpMIS ;
        HBRUSH                  hBrush ;
        RECT                    rcSmaller ;

        switch (iMessage)                       /* process windows messages */
        {
        case WM_CREATE:
                hComboBox = CreateWindow ("COMBOBOX", "Combo Text",
                        WS_CHILD | WS_VISIBLE | CBS_OWNERDRAWFIXED |
                        CBS_DROPDOWNLIST | WS_VSCROLL,
                        10, 10, 180, 80, hWnd, 100, ghInstance, NULL) ;
                ShowWindow (hComboBox, SW_SHOW) ;
        /* add in all of the items, setting the 32 values = RGB color */
                SendMessage (hComboBox, CB_RESETCONTENT, 0, OL) ;
                SendMessage (hComboBox, CB_ADDSTRING, 0,
                        RGB (0, 0, 0)) ;
                SendMessage (hComboBox, CB_ADDSTRING, 0,
                        RGB (255, 0, 0)) ;
                SendMessage (hComboBox, CB_ADDSTRING, 0,
                        RGB (0, 255, 0)) ;
                SendMessage (hComboBox, CB_INSERTSTRING, 2,
                        RGB (0, 0, 255)) ;
                SendMessage (hComboBox, CB_SETCURSEL, 2, OL) ;
                break ;
        case WM_COMMAND:        /* process menu items and buttons */
                switch (wParam)
                {
                case IDM_DOIT:          /* change an item's 32 bit value (color)*/
                        SendMessage (hComboBox, CB_SETITEMDATA, 2,
                                RGB(255, 255, 0)) ;
                        break ;
                case IDM_QUIT:          /* send end of application message */
                        DestroyWindow (hWnd) ;
                        break ;
                }
                break ;
        case WM_DRAWITEM:
                lpDIS = (LPDRAWITEMSTRUCT) lParam ;      /* get pointer to DIS */
                switch (lpDIS->itemAction)
                {
                        case ODA_DRAWENTIRE:    /* get RGB value */
                                hBrush = CreateSolidBrush (lpDIS->itemData) ;
                                CopyRect ((LPRECT) &rcSmaller,
                                        (LPRECT) &lpDIS->rcItem) ;
                                                /* leave room for border */
                                InflateRect ((LPRECT) &rcSmaller, -2, -2) ;
                                                /* paint the item */
                                FillRect (lpDIS->hDC, (LPRECT) &rcSmaller,
                                        hBrush) ;
                                DeleteObject (hBrush) ;
                                break ;
                        case ODA_SELECT:
                                if (lpDIS->itemState & ODS_SELECTED)
                                        hBrush = GetStockObject (BLACK_BRUSH) ;
                                else            /* eraser */
                                        hBrush = GetStockObject (WHITE_BRUSH) ;
                                FrameRect (lpDIS->hDC, (LPRECT) &lpDIS->rcItem,
```

```
                                                    hBrush) ;
                                    DeleteObject (hBrush) ;
                                    break ;
                        }
                        break ;
            case WM_MEASUREITEM:
                        lpMIS = (LPMEASUREITEMSTRUCT) lParam ;
                        if (lpMIS->itemID == -1)            /* if the top edit control */
                                lpMIS->itemHeight = 25 ;
                        else                                /* item in the list box */
                                lpMIS->itemHeight = 20 ;
                        break ;
            case WM_DESTROY:                                /* stop application */
                        PostQuitMessage (0) ;
                        break ;
            default:                     /* default windows message processing */
                        return DefWindowProc (hWnd, iMessage, wParam, lParam) ;
        }
        return (0L) ;
}
```

Combo Box Message Summary

Table 9-5 summarizes the combo box messages. The detailed message descriptions follow immediately after the table.

Message	Purpose	⊠
CB_ADDSTRING	Adds a string to a combo box.	
CB_DELETESTRING	Deletes a string from the combo box.	
CB_DIR	Fills the combo box with file names from a directory search.	
CB_FINDSTRING	Locates the first string in the list box of the combo box that matches a given set of starting characters.	
CB_GETCOUNT	Returns the number of items in the list box of a combo box.	
CB_GETCURSEL	Finds the index number of the currently selected item in the list box of a combo box.	
CB_GETDROPPED-CONTROLRECT	Retrieves the screen coordinates of the list box of a combo box in dropped-down position. (Win 3.1)	
CB_GETEDITSEL	Returns the range of characters selected within the edit control of the combo box.	
CB_GETEXTENDEDUI	Determines if a combo box has the default or extended user interface. (Win 3.1)	
CB_GETITEMDATA	Retrieves the 32-bit value associated with an item in an owner-redrawn combo box.	
CB_GETITEMHEIGHT	Determines the height of an item in a combo box control. (Win 3.1)	
CB_GETLBTEXT	Retrieves the string held in an item in the list box of a combo box.	
CB_GETLBTEXTLEN	Finds the number of characters in a string in the list box of a combo box.	
CB_INSERTSTRING	Adds a new string or 32-bit item to the list box of a combo box.	
CB_LIMITTEXT	Sets the maximum number of characters that a user can enter in the edit control of the combo box.	
CB_RESETCONTENT	Removes all elements from the list box of a combo box and frees memory associated with the items.	
CB_SELECTSTRING	Finds a matching string in the combo box list, and displays it in the edit control of the combo box.	
CB_SETCURSEL	Selects and highlights an item in the list box of a combo box.	
CB_SETEDITSEL	Selects a range of characters in the edit control of a combo box.	
CB_SETEXTENDEDUI	Selects either the default or extended user interface for a combo box. (Win 3.1)	
CB_SETITEMDATA	Changes the 32-bit value associated with a list box item of a combo box created with the owner-redrawn style.	
CB_SETITEMHEIGHT	Sets the height of either the top edit control or list box items in a combo box control. (Win 3.1)	

Table 9-5. Combo Box Message Summary.

One other message worth knowing about is WM_SETREDRAW, which allows the combo box to be temporarily inhibited from redrawing the contents as additions and subtractions are made. WM_SETREDRAW speeds up the redrawing of the contents and reduces the distracting "flicker" of different items showing up one at a time. WM_SETREDRAW is documented at the end of this chapter, due to the WM prefix.

Combo Box Message Descriptions

CB_ADDSTRING
☐ Win 2.0 ■ Win 3.0 ■ Win 3.1

Purpose	Adds a string to a combo box. If the combo box has the CBS_SORT style, the string is placed in the list and the list is re-sorted. Otherwise, the string is added to the end of the list.
Syntax	*dwReturned* = SendMessage (HWND *hControl*, **CB_ADDSTRING**, WORD *wParam*, DWORD *lParam*)
Returns	DWORD. The returned value is the index of the new entry in the combo box. Returns CB_ERRSPACE if there is not enough memory to store the value. Returns CB_ERR on any other error.
Parameters	
hControl	HWND: The window handle of the combo box control.
wParam	WORD: Not used. Set to 0.
lParam	DWORD: For combo boxes with the CBS_HASSTRING style, *lParam* contains a pointer to a null-terminated string for a text item. For other styles, *lParam* encodes a 32-bit value for the item. This can be retrieved when processing WM_DRAWITEM messages as the *itemData* element of the DRAWITEMSTRUCT structure passed with the message.

CB_DELETESTRING
☐ Win 2.0 ■ Win 3.0 ■ Win 3.1

Purpose	Deletes an item from the combo box.
Syntax	*dwReturned* = SendMessage (HWND *hControl*, **CB_DELETESTRING**, WORD *wParam*, DWORD *lParam*)
Returns	DWORD. The number of items remaining in the list. Returns CB_ERR if *wParam* is not a valid list element index.
Parameters	
hControl	HWND: The window handle of the combo box control.
wParam	WORD: Contains the index to the list element. 0 for the first item.
lParam	DWORD: Not used. Set to 0L.
	For combo boxes with the CBS_HASSTRINGS style, this message will free memory associated with the deleted item.

CB_DIR
☐ Win 2.0 ■ Win 3.0 ■ Win 3.1

Purpose	Fills the combo box with file names from a directory search.
Syntax	dwReturned = SendMessage (HWND *hControl*, **CB_DIR**, WORD *wParam*, DWORD *lParam*)
Returns	DWORD. The number of items displayed minus 1. Returns CB_ERRSPACE if there is not enough memory for the list. Returns CB_ERR for any other error.
Parameters	
hControl	HWND: The window handle of the combo box control.
wParam	WORD: Contains the DOS file attribute value. The values can be combined by using the C language binary OR operator (|). The attributes are listed in Table 9-6.

Value	Meaning	⊠
0x0000	Read/write data files with no other attributes set (normal files).	
0x0001	Read only files.	
0x0002	Hidden files.	
0x0004	System files.	
0x0010	Subdirectories.	
0x0020	Archived files.	
0x2000	LB_DIR flag. Places messages associated with filling the list box on the applications message queue, rather than sending them directly.	
0x4000	Drives.	
0x8000	Exclusive bit. If this is set, only the specified file attribute type is recovered. If not set, normal files are displayed in addition to the types listed.	

Table 9-6. File Attribute Flags.

lParam   DWORD: A pointer to a file search specification string (like "*.*" or "*.TXT"). This can be a full directory specification. See the example under the DlgDirListComboBox() function description in Chapter 20, *MS-DOS and Disk File Access.*

CB_FINDSTRING
☐ Win 2.0   ■ Win 3.0   ■ Win 3.1

Purpose   Locates the first string in the list box that matches a given set of starting characters.

Syntax   *dwReturned* = SendMessage (HWND *hControl*, **CB_FINDSTRING**, WORD *wParam*, DWORD *lParam*)

Returns   DWORD. The index of the first string in the list box that starts with the characters in the string pointed to by *lParam*. 0 for the first item, 1 for the second, etc. Returns CB_ERR (−1) if the search did not find a match. For owner-drawn combo boxes without the CBS_HASSTRINGS style, the message returns the index of the item that has a matching 32-bit value to the one specified in *lParam*.

Parameters

hControl   HWND: The window handle of the combo box control.

wParam   WORD: The index of the list box item *before* the first item to start the search. The search will wrap around if the end of the list is passed without a match. Set *wParam* = −1 to search the entire list. You can find multiple occurrences of a matching string by repeatedly sending this message, each time starting from the previous match. The search will loop from the bottom to the top of the list until the entire list has been searched.

lParam   DWORD: A pointer to a null-terminated string. In order to have a match, the characters in this string must all be matched by the beginning characters of an item in the list.

CB_GETCOUNT
☐ Win 2.0   ■ Win 3.0   ■ Win 3.1

Purpose   Returns the number of items in the list box of a combo box.

Syntax   *dwReturned* = SendMessage (HWND *hControl*, **CB_GETCOUNT**, WORD *wParam*, DWORD *lParam*)

Returns   DWORD. The number of items in the list box. Returns CB_ERR on error.

Parameters

hControl   HWND: The window handle of the combo box control.

| *wParam* | WORD: Not used. Set equal to 0. |
| *lParam* | DWORD: Not used. Set equal to 0L. |

CB_GETCURSEL

□ Win 2.0 ■ Win 3.0 ■ Win 3.1

Purpose Finds the index number of the currently selected item in the list box of a combo box.

Syntax *dwReturned* = SendMessage (HWND *hControl*, **CB_GETCURSEL**, WORD *wParam*, DWORD *lParam*)

Returns DWORD. The index of the currently selected item in the list box. Returns CB_ERR if no item is selected.

Parameters
hControl HWND: The window handle of the combo box control.

wParam WORD: Not used. Set equal to 0.

lParam DWORD: Not used. Set equal to 0L.

CB_GETDROPPEDCONTROLRECT

□ Win 2.0 □ Win 3.0 ■ Win 3.1

Purpose Retrieves the screen coordinates of the list box of a combo box in the dropped-down position.

Syntax *dwReturned* = SendMessage (HWND *hControl*, **CB_GETDROPPEDCONTROLRECT**, WORD *wParam*, DWORD *lParam*)

Returns DWORD, always equal to CB_OKAY.

Parameters
hControl HWND: The window handle of the combo box control.

wParam WORD: Not used. Set equal to 0.

lParam DWORD: A pointer to a RECT data structure that will hold the screen coordinates of the combo box drop-down list box when SendMessage() returns.

Related Messages CB_GETITEMHEIGHT

CB_GETEDITSEL

□ Win 2.0 ■ Win 3.0 ■ Win 3.1

Purpose Returns the range of characters selected within the edit control of the combo box.

Syntax *dwReturned* = SendMessage (HWND *hControl*, **CB_GETEDITSEL**, WORD *wParam*, DWORD *lParam*)

Returns DWORD. The low-order word contains the starting position and the high-order word has the ending position of the characters selected. Returns CB_ERR on error.

Parameters
hControl HWND: The window handle of the combo box control.

wParam WORD: Not used. Set equal to 0.

lParam DWORD: Not used. Set equal to 0L.

CB_GETEXTENDEDUI

□ Win 2.0 □ Win 3.0 ■ Win 3.1

Purpose Determines if a combo box has the default or extended user interface.

Syntax *dwReturned* = SendMessage (HWND *hControl*, **CB_GETEXTENDEDUI**, WORD *wParam*, DWORD *lParam*)

Returns DWORD. TRUE if the combo box has an extended user interface, FALSE if not.

Parameters

hControl   HWND: The window handle of the combo box control.

wParam   WORD: Not used. Set equal to 0.

lParam   DWORD: Not used. Set equal to 0L.

Related Messages   CB_SETEXTENDEDUI

Comments   The extended user interface for a combo box is set by sending the CB_SETEXTENDEDUI message to the combo box control. The control must have either the CBS_DROPDOWN or CBS_DROPDOWNLIST style. The extended style has the following effects:

Clicking the static text field at the top causes the list box to be displayed (CBS_DROPDOWNLIST style only).

Pressing the (PGDN) key displays the list box.

The top static text field cannot be scrolled if the list box is not visible.

CB_GETITEMDATA   □ Win 2.0   ■ Win 3.0   ■ Win 3.1

Purpose   Retrieves the 32-bit value associated with an item in an owner-redrawn combo box.

Syntax   *dwReturned* = SendMessage (HWND *hControl*, **CB_GETITEMDATA**, WORD *wParam*, DWORD *lParam*)

Returns   DWORD, the 32 bit value. Returns CB_ERR on error.

Parameters

hControl   HWND: The window handle of the combo box control.

wParam   WORD: The index of the item. The first item is 0.

lParam   DWORD: Not used. Set equal to 0L.

CB_GETITEMHEIGHT   □ Win 2.0   □ Win 3.0   ■ Win 3.1

Purpose   Determines the height of an item in a combo box control.

Syntax   *dwReturned* = SendMessage (HWND *hControl*, **CB_GETITEMHEIGHT**, WORD *wParam*, DWORD *lParam*)

Returns   DWORD, the height of the item in pixels.

Parameters

hControl   HWND: The window handle of the combo box control.

wParam   WORD: Set to –1 to determine the height of the top edit (or static text) control at the top of the combo box. Set to 0 if the combo box does not have the CBS_OWNERDRAWVARIABLE style. The height of items in the list box will be returned.

                If the list box has the CBS_OWNERDRAWVARIABLE style, set *wParam* to the index of the item for which the height should be determined. This will normally be repeated for several items in the list box.

lParam   DWORD: Not used. Set equal to 0L.

Related Messages   CB_SETITEMHEIGHT, WM_DRAWITEM

CB_GETLBTEXT   □ Win 2.0   ■ Win 3.0   ■ Win 3.1

Purpose   Retrieves the string held in an item in the list box of a combo box.

Syntax   *dwReturned* = SendMessage (HWND *hControl*, **CB_GETLBTEXT**, WORD *wParam*, DWORD *lParam*)

Returns   DWORD, the length of the string in bytes. Returns CB_ERR on error.

If the combo box is owner-redrawn, but it does not have the CBS_HASSTRINGS style, the buffer pointed to by *lParam* will receive the 32- bit value associated with the item.

Parameters

hControl HWND: The window handle of the combo box control.

wParam WORD: Contains the index of the list box item. The first item is 0.

lParam DWORD: A pointer to a character buffer to hold the string retrieved. Use CB_GETLBTEXTLEN to retrieve the length of the string. Be sure to include an extra character in the buffer for the terminating NULL character.

CB_GETLBTEXTLEN ☐ Win 2.0 ■ Win 3.0 ■ Win 3.1

Purpose Finds the number of characters in a string in the list box of a combo box.

Syntax *dwReturned* = SendMessage (HWND *hControl*, **CB_GETLBTEXTLEN**, WORD *wParam*, DWORD *lParam*)

Returns DWORD, the length of the string in bytes. Returns CB_ERR on error.

Parameters

hControl HWND: The window handle of the combo box control.

wParam WORD: Contains the index of the string. The first item is 0.

lParam DWORD: Not used. Set equal to 0L.

CB_INSERTSTRING ☐ Win 2.0 ■ Win 3.0 ■ Win 3.1

Purpose Adds a new string or 32-bit item to the list box of a combo box.

Syntax *dwReturned* = SendMessage (HWND *hControl*, **CB_INSERTSTRING**, WORD *wParam*, DWORD *lParam*)

Returns DWORD, the index of the inserted item. Returns CB_ERRSPACE if there is not enough memory for the item. Returns CB_ERR for all other errors.

Parameters

hControl HWND: The window handle of the combo box control.

wParam WORD: Contains the index position to insert the string. 0 for the first item, 1 for the second, etc. Use −1 for the last. All items below the insertion point will have new index values, one greater than their index prior to the insertion.

lParam DWORD: A pointer to a null-terminated character string to be added. If the combo box has the owner-redrawn style, *lParam* holds the 32-bit value to set for the item.

CB_LIMITTEXT ☐ Win 2.0 ■ Win 3.0 ■ Win 3.1

Purpose Sets the maximum number of characters that a user can enter in the edit control of the combo box.

Syntax *dwReturned* = SendMessage (HWND *hControl*, **CB_LIMITTEXT**, WORD *wParam*, DWORD *lParam*)

Returns DWORD, nonzero if the limit was set, zero if not.

Parameters

hControl HWND: The window handle of the combo box control.

wParam WORD: The maximum number of characters for the edit control.

lParam DWORD: Not used. Set equal to 0L.

CB_RESETCONTENT

Purpose	Removes all elements from the list box of a combo box, and frees memory associated with the items.
Syntax	*dwReturned* = SendMessage (HWND *hControl*, **CB_RESETCONTENT**, WORD *wParam*, DWORD *lParam*)
Returns	DWORD, not used.
Parameters	
hControl	HWND: The window handle of the combo box control.
wParam	WORD: Not Used. Set equal to 0.
lParam	DWORD: Not Used. Set equal to 0L.

If the combo box is owner-redrawn, but does not have the CBS_HASSTRINGS style, the owner of the combo box will receive a WM_DELETEITEM message for each item in the combo box.

CB_SELECTSTRING

Purpose	Finds a matching string in the combo box list and displays it in the edit control of the combo box. If the combo box has the owner-redrawn style, the match is based on comparing 32-bit values.
Syntax	*dwReturned* = SendMessage (HWND *hControl*, **CB_SELECTSTRING**, WORD *wParam*, DWORD *lParam*)
Returns	DWORD, the index of the string found. Returns CB_ERR if no match was found. In this case, the edit control is not changed.
Parameters	
hControl	HWND: The window handle of the combo box control.
wParam	WORD: The list box item number *before* the first item to be searched. The search wraps around to the beginning if no match is found between the starting point and the end of the list. You can find duplicate entries in the list by repeatedly using the last index as the starting point for the next search.
lParam	DWORD: A pointer to the character string to match. The string in the list box of the combo box can be longer, as long as the first characters match the string pointed to by *lParam*. If the combo box has the owner-redrawn style, *lParam* contains the 32-bit value to match.

CB_SETCURSEL

Purpose	Selects and highlights an item in the list box of a combo box. If the item is not visible, the list is scrolled into view. The edit control of the combo box is changed to reflect the selection. Any highlighting of the previous selection is removed.
Syntax	*dwReturned* = SendMessage (HWND *hControl*, **CB_SETCURSEL**, WORD *wParam*, DWORD *lParam*)
Returns	DWORD. Normally not used. Set to CB_ERR on error, such as an out of range *wParam* value.
Parameters	
hControl	HWND: The window handle of the combo box control.
wParam	WORD: The index of the item to select. Set *wParam* to –1 to deselect all items.
lParam	DWORD: Not used. Set equal to 0L.

CB_SETEDITSEL ☐ Win 2.0 ■ Win 3.0 ■ Win 3.1

Purpose	Selects a range of characters in the edit control of a combo box.
Syntax	*dwReturned* = SendMessage (HWND *hControl*, **CB_SETEDITSEL**, WORD *wParam*, DWORD *lParam*)
Returns	DWORD, TRUE if successful, FALSE if not.
Parameters	
hControl	HWND: The window handle of the combo box control.
wParam	WORD: Not used. Set equal to 0.
lParam	DWORD: The low-order word contains the starting character position. The high-order word contains the ending position.

CB_SETEXTENDEDUI ☐ Win 2.0 ☐ Win 3.0 ■ Win 3.1

Purpose	Selects either the default or extended user interface for a combo box.
Syntax	*dwReturned* = SendMessage (HWND *hControl*, **CB_SETEXTENDEDUI**, WORD *wParam*, DWORD *lParam*)
Returns	DWORD, CB_OK if successful, CB_ERR on error.
Parameters	
hControl	HWND: The window handle of the combo box control.
wParam	WORD: Set to TRUE to use the extended user interface. Set to FALSE to use the default user interface.
lParam	DWORD: Not used. Set equal to 0L.
Related Messages	CB_GETEXTENDEDUI
Comments	The extended user interface for a combo box is set by sending the CB_SETEXTENDEDUI message to the combo box control. The control must have either the CBS_DROPDOWN or CBS_DROPDOWNLIST style. The extended style has the following effects:

Clicking the static text field at the top causes the list box to be displayed (CBS_DROPDOWNLIST style only).

Pressing the (PGDN) key displays the list box.

The top static text field cannot be scrolled if the list box is not visible.

CB_SETITEMDATA ☐ Win 2.0 ■ Win 3.0 ■ Win 3.1

Purpose	Changes the 32-bit value associated with a list box item of a combo box created with the owner-redrawn style.
Syntax	*dwReturned* = SendMessage (HWND *hControl*, **CB_SETITEMDATA**, WORD *wParam*, DWORD *lParam*)
Returns	DWORD. Normally not used. CB_ERR on error.
Parameters	
hControl	HWND: The window handle of the combo box control.
wParam	WORD: The index number of the item in the list box.
lParam	DWORD: The new 32-bit value to set.

CB_SETITEMHEIGHT

☐ Win 2.0   ☐ Win 3.0   ■ Win 3.1

Purpose	Sets the height of either the top edit control or list box items in a combo box control.
Syntax	*dwReturned* = SendMessage (HWND *hControl*, **CB_SETITEMHEIGHT**, WORD *wParam*, DWORD *lParam*)
Returns	DWORD, CB_ERR on error.
Parameters	
hControl	HWND: The window handle of the combo box control.
wParam	WORD: Set to –1 to change the height of the top edit (or static text) control at the top of the combo box. Set to 0 if the combo box does not have the CBS_OWNERDRAWVARIABLE style. The height of every item in the list box will be changed. If the list box has the CBS_OWNERDRAWVARIABLE style, set *wParam* to the index of the item for which the height should be changed. The first item has an index of zero.
lParam	DWORD: Set equal to the height in pixels for the item to be changed.
Related Messages	CB_GETITEMHEIGHT, CB_SETITEMDATA, WM_DRAWITEM

CB_SHOWDROPDOWN

☐ Win 2.0   ■ Win 3.0   ■ Win 3.1

Purpose	Shows or hides the drop-down list box of a combo box created with the CBS_DROPDOWN or CBS_DROPDOWNLIST style.
Syntax	SendMessage (HWND *hControl*, **CB_SHOWDROPDOWN**, WORD *wParam*, DWORD *lParam*)
Parameters	
hControl	HWND: The window handle of the combo box control.
wParam	WORD: TRUE to display the list box, FALSE to hide it.
lParam	DWORD: Not used. Set equal to 0L.

Combo Box Notification Codes Summary

When the user makes a selection within a combo box or edits the top edit window, Windows notifies the parent window with a WM_COMMAND message. The combo box ID is passed as *wParam*, while the combo box handle is the low-order word of *lParam*. The specific notification code, such as CBN_DBLCLK, is the high-order word of *lParam*. Table 9-7 summarizes the notification codes.

Notification Code	Purpose ☒
CBN_DBLCLK	Notification that the user has double-clicked an item in the list box of the combo box.
CBN_DROPDOWN	Notification that the list box portion of a combo box is about to be made visible.
CBN_EDITCHANGE	The string in the edit control of the combo box has been changed.
CBN_EDITUPDATE	Notification that Windows is about to change the text in the edit control of a combo box.
CBN_ERRSPACE	Notification that Windows has run out of memory room to add another item to a combo box.
CBN_KILLFOCUS	Notification that the combo box has lost the input focus.
CBN_SELCHANGE	Notification that the current selection in the list box part of the combo box has changed.
CBN_SETFOCUS	Notification that a combo box has the input focus.

Table 9-7. Combo Box Notification Codes.

Combo Box Notification Codes Descriptions

CBN_DBLCLK
☐ Win 2.0 ■ Win 3.0 ■ Win 3.1

Purpose	Notification that the user has double-clicked an item in the list box of the combo box. Use CB_GETCURSEL to determine which item was selected. This message will only be sent if the list box of the combo box is always visible(CBS_SIMPLE style). For drop-down list boxes, the first mouse click causes the selection to be made and causes the list box to be pulled up.
Syntax	Returned as part of a WM_COMMAND message, processed by the program's message processing function (WndProc()).
Parameters	
wParam	WORD: Contains the ID value for the combo box. This is the integer value set for the *hMenu* parameter when CreateWindow() was called.
lParam	DWORD: The low-order word contains the window handle of the combo box. The high-order word contains CBN_DBLCLK.

CBN_DROPDOWN
☐ Win 2.0 ■ Win 3.0 ■ Win 3.1

Purpose	Notification that the list box portion of a combo box is about to be made visible. This will not occur if the combo box was created with the CBS_SIMPLE style which always shows the list box.
Syntax	Returned as part of a WM_COMMAND message, processed by the program's message processing function (WndProc()).
Parameters	
wParam	WORD: Contains the ID value for the combo box. This is the integer value set for the *hMenu* parameter when CreateWindow() was called.
lParam	DWORD: The low-order word contains the window handle of the combo box. The high-order word contains CBN_DROPDOWN.

CBN_EDITCHANGE
☐ Win 2.0 ■ Win 3.0 ■ Win 3.1

Purpose	Notification that the string in the edit control of the combo box has been changed. This message is received after the change has been made.
Syntax	Returned as part of a WM_COMMAND message, processed by the program's message processing function (WndProc()).
Parameters	
wParam	WORD: Contains the ID value for the combo box. This is the integer value set for the *hMenu* parameter when CreateWindow() was called.
lParam	DWORD: The low-order word contains the window handle of the combo box. The high-order word contains CBN_EDITCHANGE.

CBN_EDITUPDATE
☐ Win 2.0 ■ Win 3.0 ■ Win 3.1

Purpose	Notification that Windows is about to change the text in the edit control of a combo box.
Syntax	Returned as part of a WM_COMMAND message, processed by the program's message processing function (WndProc()).
Parameters	
wParam	WORD: Contains the ID value for the combo box. This is the integer value set for the *hMenu* parameter when CreateWindow() was called.

lParam	DWORD: The low-order word contains the window handle of the combo box. The high-order word contains CBN_EDITUPDATE.

CBN_ERRSPACE   □ Win 2.0   ■ Win 3.0   ■ Win 3.1

Purpose	Notification that Windows has run out of memory to add another item to a combo box.
Syntax	Returned as part of a WM_COMMAND message, processed by the program's message processing function (WndProc()).
Parameters	
wParam	WORD: Contains the ID value for the combo box. This is the integer value set for the *hMenu* parameter when CreateWindow() was called.
lParam	DWORD: The low-order word contains the window handle of the combo box. The high-order word contains CBN_ERRSPACE.

CBN_KILLFOCUS   □ Win 2.0   ■ Win 3.0   ■ Win 3.1

Purpose	Notification that the combo box has lost the input focus.
Syntax	Returned as part of a WM_COMMAND message, processed by the program's message processing function (WndProc()).
Parameters	
wParam	WORD: Contains the ID value for the combo box. This is the integer value set for the *hMenu* parameter when CreateWindow() was called.
lParam	DWORD: The low-order word contains the window handle of the combo box. The high-order word contains CBN_KILLFOCUS.

CBN_SELCHANGE   □ Win 2.0   ■ Win 3.0   ■ Win 3.1

Purpose	Notification that the current selection in the list box part of the combo box has changed. This can be due to either selecting a new item in the list box or through typing text in the edit control.
Syntax	Returned as part of a WM_COMMAND message, processed by the program's message processing function (WndProc()).
Parameters	
wParam	WORD: Contains the ID value for the combo box. This is the integer value set for the *hMenu* parameter when CreateWindow() was called.
lParam	DWORD: The low-order word contains the window handle of the combo box. The high-order word contains CBN_SELCHANGE.

CBN_SETFOCUS   □ Win 2.0   ■ Win 3.0   ■ Win 3.1

Purpose	Notification that a combo box has the input focus. Keyboard input will show up in the edit control.
Syntax	Returned as part of a WM_COMMAND message, processed by the program's message processing function (WndProc()).
Parameters	
wParam	WORD: Contains the ID value for the combo box. This is the integer value set for the *hMenu* parameter when CreateWindow() was called.
lParam	DWORD: The low-order word contains the window handle of the combo box. The high-order word contains CBN_SETFOCUS.

Dialog Box Window Messages

The only two messages that are specific to the dialog box window itself are DM_GETDEFID and DM_SETDEFID. These functions get and change the push button ID number for the default pushbutton. This is the pushbutton that will be activated if the user hits the (ENTER) key. The WM_NEXTDLGCTL message allows the default pushbutton control to be changed. This message is sent with PostMessage(), not SendMessage(), to avoid having the change occur while other messages are being processed. (WM_NEXTDLGCTL is documented in the last section of this chapter, due to the WM prefix.)

The controls in a dialog box, such as buttons and list boxes, are all child window controls. They can be manipulated by sending the control messages. The SendDlgItemMessage() function is usually more convenient than SendMessage() for dealing with dialog box controls. Chapter 13, *Dialog Boxes*, has a full discussion of dialog box controls.

DM_GETDEFID
■ Win 2.0   ■ Win 3.0   ■ Win 3.1

Purpose	Retrieves the ID value of the default pushbutton in a dialog box. The default pushbutton is the button that will be pressed if the user hits the (ENTER) key right after the dialog box appears.
Syntax	*dwReturned* = SendMessage (HWND *hControl*, **DM_GETDEFID**, WORD *wParam*, DWORD *lParam*)
Returns	DWORD. The low-order word contains the button's ID value. The high-order word contains DM_GETDEFID. Returns NULL on error.
Parameters	
hControl	HWND: The window handle of the dialog box.
wParam	WORD: Not used. Set equal to 0.
lParam	DWORD: Not used. Set equal to 0L.

DM_SETDEFID
■ Win 2.0   ■ Win 3.0   ■ Win 3.1

Purpose	Changes the ID value of the default pushbutton control in a dialog box. The default pushbutton is the button that will be pressed if the user hits the (ENTER) key right after the dialog box appears.
Syntax	*dwReturned* = SendMessage (HWND *hControl*, **DM_SETDEFID**, WORD *wParam*, DWORD *lParam*)
Returns	DWORD, not used.
Parameters	
hControl	HWND: The window handle of the dialog box.
wParam	WORD: The ID value of the default pushbutton.
lParam	DWORD: Not used. Set equal to 0L.

Edit Control Messages

Edit controls are most frequently used for single lines of input. Typically, the user is given a place to enter a file name, or some other short character string. These uses just scratch the surface as to what is possible with edit controls. Windows has a lot of basic word processing functions built into edit controls. Any time your program uses an edit control, you automatically get editing functions such as the ability to select text using the mouse, delete selected text with the (DEL) key, use the cursor keys and the (BACKSPACE) key, etc. Edit controls can be as big as the entire client area of a window, and they can be combined with scroll bars to produce scrollable editing areas.

You will probably find that edit controls give you all the power you need for text input in your programs. Edit controls do not allow text formatting, as is needed in word processing, and they can become cumbersome if you need to add a lot of new functionality. However, you may find that the edit controls allow you to prototype a program quickly.

Figure 9-5 shows a multiline edit control placed as a child window in an application. The edit control style includes the WS_VSCROLL style, which adds a vertical scroll bar to the edit control. After several lines of text are typed, the user can scroll through the text using the scroll bar. Typing in the edit area automatically wraps to the next line when a word exceeds the width of the edit area, and automatically scrolls up when the bottom is reached.

In this example, when the user clicks the "Do It!" menu item, the program logic recovers the string data entered and shows it at the bottom of the screen. This is a bit more complex than it might be, as Windows does not automatically keep the entered text as a null-terminated string (no null at the end is maintained). The program

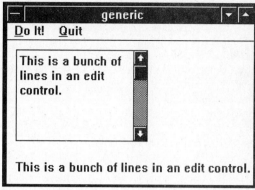

Figure 9-5. A Multiline Edit Control.

must add the length of each of the lines to find the end of the string. This is a small nuisance, considering how much "instant word processing" the program gains by just using an edit control.

Listing 9-5 shows the WndProc() function of the program that creates the edit control. The edit control is built when the program receives the WM_CREATE message. The example allocates a separate local memory area to store the string data. Windows automatically enlarges this area to make room for added text. Note that PostMessage() is used with the EM_SETHANDLE message to establish the link between the string memory area and the edit control. SendMessage() also could have been used to transmit the message to Windows.

Allocating a separate memory area for the edit control's string data is not always necessary. Windows will maintain a default text area if the edit control is inside a dialog box created with the DS_LOCALEDIT style. This is convenient with dialog boxes, as the program can also use the SetDlgItemText(), SetDlgItemInt(), GetDlgItemText(), and GetDlgItemInt() functions for quick ways to fetch and set the text string inside of edit controls. These functions are explained in Chapter 13, *Dialog Boxes*. This technique is not used in the example in Listing 9-5, as the edit control is a child window and is not in a dialog box.

Retrieving the text from the memory buffer is simply a matter of obtaining the handle to the memory area. The program must determine the length of the complete string, including all of the lines in the multiline edit control. This requires adding the length of each line's string. When the total length is known, the program adds the terminating NULL character and displays the string at the bottom of the screen.

⇨ **Listing 9-5. Creating a Multiline Edit Control**

```
long FAR PASCAL WndProc (HWND hWnd, unsigned iMessage, WORD wParam, LONG lParam)
{
        static  HWND            hEdit ;
        HDC                     hDC ;
        static  HANDLE          hEditText ;
        PSTR                    ptzText ;
        int                     i, nTextLen, nTotalLen, nLines, nIndex ;

        switch (iMessage)                               /* process windows messages */
        {
                case WM_CREATE:
                        hEdit = CreateWindow ("EDIT", "",
                                WS_CHILD | WS_VISIBLE | ES_AUTOVSCROLL | ES_MULTILINE
                                | ES_LEFT | ES_NOHIDESEL | WS_BORDER | WS_VSCROLL,
                                10, 10, 150, 100, hWnd, NULL, ghInstance, NULL) ;
                        ShowWindow (hEdit, SW_SHOW) ;
                        hEditText = LocalAlloc (LMEM_MOVEABLE, 30) ;     /* edit buffer */
                        ptzText = LocalLock (hEditText) ;/* null byte for first char */
                        *ptzText = 0 ;                        /* in edit buffer to begin */
                        LocalFree (hEditText) ;
                                               /* attach edit buffer to edit control */
                        PostMessage (hEdit, EM_SETHANDLE, hEditText, 0L) ;
```

```
                            break ;
            case WM_COMMAND:                 /* process menu items */
                switch (wParam)
                {
                case IDM_DOIT:              /* pull the text out and display it */
                    ptzText = LocalLock (hEditText) ;
                    nLines = SendMessage (hEdit, EM_GETLINECOUNT, 0, OL) ;
                    nTotalLen = 0 ;
                    for (i = 0 ; i < nLines ; i++)      /* find string length */
                    {
                            nIndex = SendMessage (hEdit, EM_LINEINDEX,
                                i, OL) ;
                            nTextLen = SendMessage (hEdit, EM_LINELENGTH,
                                    nIndex, OL) ;
                            nTotalLen += nTextLen ;
                    }
                    *(ptzText + nTotalLen) = 0 ;       /* null terminate string */
                    hDC = GetDC (hWnd) ;
                    TextOut (hDC, 10, 130, ptzText, lstrlen (ptzText)) ;
                    ReleaseDC (hWnd, hDC) ;
                    LocalUnlock (hEditText) ;
                    break ;
                case IDM_QUIT:              /* send end of application message */
                    DestroyWindow (hWnd) ;
                    break ;
                }
                break ;
            case WM_DESTROY:                    /* stop application */
                LocalFree (hEditText) ;
                PostQuitMessage (0) ;
                break ;
            default:                            /* default windows message processing */
                return DefWindowProc (hWnd, iMessage, wParam, lParam) ;
        }
        return (OL) ;
}
```

Windows has several undocumented messages, including EM_GETTHUMB and EM_SETFRONT, that are defined in the WINDOWS.H file that deal with edit controls. The adventurous reader can experiment with these at his or her own risk. There is no guarantee that undocumented messages will be continued in future versions of Windows.

Edit Control Message Summary

Table 9-8 summarizes the edit control messages. The detailed message descriptions are in the next section.

Message	Purpose
EM_CANUNDO	Determines if an edit control can correctly process EM_UNDO messages to undo the effect of a change.
EM_EMPTYUNDOBUFFER	Clears the undo buffer that Windows installs for an edit control to handle WM_UNDO messages.
EM_FMTLINES	Used with multiline edit controls to add or remove CR LF character sequences at the end of each line.
EM_GETHANDLE	Returns a handle to the memory area the edit control is using to store the string data.
EM_GETLINE	Copies a line from the edit control into a memory buffer. This message is only processed by multiline edit controls.
EM_GETLINECOUNT	Determines the number of text lines in a multiline edit control.
EM_GETMODIFY	Determines if the text in the edit control has been changed by the user.
EM_GETRECT	Returns the bounding rectangle for the formatting area of an edit control.
EM_GETSEL	Returns the starting and ending character positions of the edit text selected by the user.
EM_LIMITTEXT	Restricts the length of the text string a user may enter into an edit control.

EM_LINEFROMCHAR	Returns the line number of the selected text or of a given character position in an edit control.
EM_LINEINDEX	Returns the character position in the complete string contained in a multiline edit control for the start of a line.
EM_LINELENGTH	Returns the number of characters in a line of a multiine edit control.
EM_LINESCROLL	Scrolls an edit control horizontally or vertically.
EM_REPLACESEL	Replaces the currently selected text with new text.
EM_SETHANDLE	Links the edit control to a memory buffer to hold the edit text.
EM_SETMODIFY	Sets the modify flag for the edit control.
EM_SETPASSWORDCHAR	Allows you to change from an asterisk (*) to any desired character placeholder for the password style.
EM_SETRECT	Sets the inner formatting rectangle of the edit control. The text is repainted.
EM_SETRECTNP	Sets the inner formatting rectangle of the edit control. The text is not repainted.
EM_SETSEL	Selects all of the characters in a given range.
EM_SETTABSTOPS	Sets the positions of the tab stops in a multiline edit control.
EM_SETWORDBREAK	This message sets a new word break function.
EM_UNDO	Copies the text from the delete buffer back into the edit control at the insertion point (the caret location).

Table 9-8. Edit Control Message Summary.

In addition to the EM edit control messages, there are four messages that deal with cut and paste operations for selected text within the edit control area. The messages allow to be copied the selected text between the edit control and the clipboard. These messages are summarized in Table 9-9. The full documentation of these messages is in the last part of this chapter in the Windows messages section, as these messages start with the WM prefix.

Message	Purpose	⊠
WM_CLEAR	Deletes the selected text in an edit control without copying it to the clipboard.	
WM_COPY	Copies selected text within an edit control to the clipboard.	
WM_CUT	Copies the current selected text from an edit control to the clipboard.	
WM_PASTE	Copies the text from the clipboard into an edit control.	

Table 9-9. Additional Edit Control Messages.

Edit Control Message Descriptions

EM_CANUNDO
■ Win 2.0 ■ Win 3.0 ■ Win 3.1

Purpose	Determines if an edit control can correctly process EM_UNDO messages to undo the effect of a change. If the undo buffer size was exceeded, the change cannot be correctly undone.
Syntax	*dwReturned* = SendMessage (HWND *hControl*, **EM_CANUNDO**, WORD *wParam*, DWORD *lParam*)
Returns	DWORD. TRUE if the edit control can undo changes, FALSE if not.
Parameters	
hControl	HWND: The window handle of the child window edit control.
wParam	WORD: Not used. Set equal to 0.
lParam	DWORD: Not used. Set equal to 0L.

EM_EMPTYUNDOBUFFER

☐ Win 2.0 ■ Win 3.0 ■ Win 3.1

Purpose

Clears the undo buffer that Windows installs for an edit control to handle WM_UNDO messages. The edit buffer is automatically emptied if the edit control receives a WM_SETTEXT or EM_SETHANDLE message.

Syntax

SendMessage (HWND *hControl*, **EM_EMPTYUNDOBUFFER**, WORD *wParam*, DWORD *lParam*)

Parameters

hControl   HWND: The window handle of the child window edit control.

wParam   WORD: Not used. Set equal to 0.

lParam   DWORD: Not used. Set equal to 0L.

EM_FMTLINES

■ Win 2.0 ■ Win 3.0 ■ Win 3.1

Purpose

Used with multiine edit controls to add or remove CR CR LF character sequences a the end of each line (0x0D, 0x0D, 0x0A hexadecimal). The line ends where the string word wraps can be marked with these three bytes, which is different from a "hard return," when the user has pressed the (ENTER) key. Normally, multiline edit controls are stored as one long string, without control characters where the string wordwraps. An exception is text in which the user has hit the (ENTER) key. This will add two bytes, CR and LF, to the string. These CR LF pairs are not affected by the EM_FMTLINES message. Note that the string size will change. Use EM_LINELENGTH to find the new length of each line.

Syntax

dwReturned = SendMessage (HWND *hControl*, **EM_FMTLINES**, WORD *wParam*, DWORD *lParam*)

Returns

DWORD. Nonzero if formatting occurs, otherwise zero.

Parameters

hControl   HWND: The window handle of the child window edit control.

wParam   WORD: Nonzero to place CR CR LF character sequences at the end of each wordwrapped line. Zero to remove them.

lParam   DWORD: Not used. Set equal to 0L.

EM_GETHANDLE

■ Win 2.0 ■ Win 3.0 ■ Win 3.1

Purpose

Returns a handle to the memory area the edit control is using to store the string data. Use EM_SETHANDLE to link a memory handle to an edit control.

Syntax

dwReturned = SendMessage (HWND *hControl*, **EM_GETHANDLE**, WORD *wParam*, DWORD *lParam*)

Returns

DWORD, the data handle of the memory buffer that holds the edit string.

Parameters

hControl   HWND: The window handle of the child window edit control.

wParam   WORD: Not used. Set equal to 0.

lParam   DWORD: Not used. Set equal to 0L.

Comments

Allocating a separate memory area for the edit control's string data is not always necessary. Windows will maintain a default text area if the edit control is inside a dialog box created with the DS_LOCALEDIT style. This is convenient with dialog boxes, as the program can also use the SetDlgItemText(), SetDlgItemInt(), GetDlgItemText(), and GetDlgItemInt() functions for quick ways to fetch and set the text string inside of edit controls. These functions are explained in Chapter 13, *Dialog Boxes*.

EM_GETLINE
■ Win 2.0   ■ Win 3.0   ■ Win 3.1

Purpose	Copies a line from the edit control into a memory buffer. This message is only processed by multiline edit controls. Use EM_GETHANDLE to retrieve a handle to the memory area used to store the string of a single line edit control, or for the entire contents of a multiline edit control.
Syntax	*dwReturned* = SendMessage (HWND *hControl*, **EM_GETLINE**, WORD *wParam*, DWORD *lParam*)
Returns	DWORD, the number of characters copied.
Parameters	
hControl	HWND: The window handle of the child window edit control.
wParam	WORD: The line number to copy. 0 is the first line.
lParam	DWORD: A pointer to the memory buffer that will contain the copied string. Set the first WORD of the buffer equal to the maximum number of characters to copy (as an integer). This value will be read before the copy operation begins to ensure that the buffer size is not exceeded. The copied line is not null-terminated. The text copied to the buffer pointed to by *lParam* will not automatically be null-terminated.

EM_GETLINECOUNT
■ Win 2.0   ■ Win 3.0   ■ Win 3.1

Purpose	Finds out the number of text lines in a multiline edit control. Single line edit controls do not respond to this message.
Syntax	*dwReturned* = SendMessage (HWND *hControl*, **EM_GETLINECOUNT**, WORD *wParam*, DWORD *lParam*)
Returns	DWORD. The number of lines in the multiline edit control.
Parameters	
hControl	HWND: The window handle of the child window edit control.
wParam	WORD: Not used. Set equal to 0.
lParam	DWORD: Not used. Set equal to 0L.

EM_GETMODIFY
■ Win 2.0   ■ Win 3.0   ■ Win 3.1

Purpose	Determines whether or not the text in the edit control has been changed by the user.
Syntax	*dwReturned* = SendMessage (HWND *hControl*, **EM_GETMODIFY**, WORD *wParam*, DWORD *lParam*)
Returns	DWORD, nonzero if the edit text has been changed, zero if not.
Parameters	
hControl	HWND: The window handle of the child edit window control.
wParam	WORD: Not used. Set equal to 0.
lParam	DWORD: Not used. Set equal to 0L.

EM_GETRECT
□ Win 2.0   ■ Win 3.0   ■ Win 3.1

Purpose	Returns the bounding rectangle for the formatting area of an edit control. The size of this rectangle can be changed with the EM_SETRECT command.
Syntax	SendMessage (HWND *hControl*, **EM_GETRECT**, WORD *wParam*, DWORD *lParam*)
Parameters	
hControl	HWND: The window handle of the child window edit control.
wParam	WORD: Not used. Set equal to 0.

lParam	DWORD: A pointer to a RECT data structure. The four elements of this structure will be set after the message has been processed. Client coordinates are used.

EM_GETSEL

Purpose	Returns the starting and ending character positions of the edit text selected by the user. Text is selected within the edit control by dragging the mouse pointer over one or more characters. The selected text is highlighted automatically.
Syntax	*dwReturned* = SendMessage (HWND *hControl*, **EM_GETSEL**, WORD *wParam*, DWORD *lParam*)
Returns	DWORD. The low-order word contains the first selected character position. The high-order word contains the position of the first character *after* the selection.
Parameters	
hControl	HWND: The window handle of the child window edit control.
wParam	WORD: Not used. Set equal to 0.
lParam	DWORD: Not used. Set equal to 0L.

EM_LIMITTEXT

Purpose	Restricts the length of the text string a user may enter into an edit control. If the user attempts to exceed this limit, the system beep and no additional characters can be added to the edit area until some are deleted. EM_LIMITTEXT does not limit the length of text that can be inserted using EM_SETHANDLE. It does not affect the size of the memory buffer used to store the characters.
Syntax	SendMessage (HWND *hControl*, **EM_LIMITTEXT**, WORD *wParam*, DWORD *lParam*)
Parameters	
hControl	HWND: The window handle of the child window edit control.
wParam	WORD: The maximum number of characters to allow in the edit control. Set to 0 to remove any limit (other than available memory).
lParam	DWORD: Not used. Set equal to 0L.

EM_LINEFROMCHAR

Purpose	Returns the line number of the selected text or of a given character position in an edit control.
Syntax	*dwReturned* = SendMessage (HWND *hControl*, **EM_LINEFROMCHAR**, WORD *wParam*, DWORD *lParam*)
Returns	DWORD, the line number.
Parameters	
hControl	HWND: The window handle of the child window edit control.
wParam	WORD: Set either to –1 to retrieve the line number of the start of the text block the user has selected, or set to a positive integer to specify a character position in the complete edit string.
lParam	DWORD: Not used. Set equal to 0L.

EM_LINEINDEX

Purpose	Returns the character position in the complete string contained in a multiline edit control for the start of a line. This is the number of characters in the edit control's memory buffer *before* the start of the line. This value is used in processing EM_LINELENGTH messages. The message can also be used to find the location of the edit caret within the edit control. The edit caret is acti-

vated when the user clicks the mouse within the edit area. It can be moved using the mouse, arrow keys, or (BACKSPACE) key.

Syntax	*dwReturned* = SendMessage (HWND *hControl*, **BM_LINEINDEX**, WORD *wParam*, DWORD *lParam*)
Returns	DWORD, the number of characters in the edit control's memory buffer before the start of the given line.
Parameters	
hControl	HWND: The window handle of the child window edit control.
wParam	WORD: The line number. Alternatively, if set equal to –1, the message returns the index of the character position of the edit caret within the edit control.
lParam	DWORD: Not used. Set equal to 0L.

EM_LINELENGTH
■ Win 2.0   ■ Win 3.0   ■ Win 3.1

Purpose	Returns the number of characters (bytes) in a line of a multiline edit control.
Syntax	*dwReturned* = SendMessage (HWND *hControl*, **EM_LINELENGTH**, WORD *wParam*, DWORD *lParam*)
Returns	DWORD, the length of the line.
Parameters	
hControl	HWND: The window handle of the child window edit control.
wParam	WORD: Specifies the character position of the start of the line. Use EM_LINEINDEX to find this value for a given line number. If *wParam* is set equal to –1, the position of the edit caret is returned. If *wParam* is set equal to –1 and a group of characters has been selected (highlighted in the edit control), the returned value is the character number of the first character in the first line of the selection.
lParam	DWORD: Not used. Set equal to 0L.

EM_LINESCROLL
■ Win 2.0   ■ Win 3.0   ■ Win 3.1

Purpose	Scrolls an edit control horizontally or vertically. None of the text is lost, even though a portion may be obscured after the scrolling operation.
Syntax	SendMessage (HWND *hControl*, **EM_LINESCROLL**, WORD *wParam*, DWORD *lParam*)
Parameters	
hControl	HWND: The window handle of the child window edit control.
wParam	WORD: Not used. Set equal to 0.
lParam	DWORD: Set the low-order word equal to the number of lines to scroll vertically, and set the high-order word equal to the number of character positions to scroll horizontally. Positive values scroll down and right, negative values scroll up and left.

EM_REPLACESEL
■ Win 2.0   ■ Win 3.0   ■ Win 3.1

Purpose	Replaces the currently selected text with new text. The selected text is highlighted in the edit area by dragging the mouse cursor over a range of characters.
Syntax	SendMessage (HWND *hControl*, **EM_REPLACESEL**, WORD *wParam*, DWORD *lParam*)
Parameters	
hControl	HWND: The window handle of the child window edit control.
wParam	WORD: Not used. Set equal to 0.

lParam	DWORD: A pointer to a null-terminated string containing the new string to replace the selected text. The edit control string length may change after this replacement.

EM_SETHANDLE ■ Win 2.0 ■ Win 3.0 ■ Win 3.1

Purpose	Links the edit control to a memory buffer to hold the edit text. The buffer must be a local handle (data in the application's data segment). This buffer is automatically resized as needed to hold new input text.
Syntax	SendMessage (HWND *hControl*, **EM_SETHANDLE**, WORD *wParam*, DWORD *lParam*)
Parameters	
hControl	HWND: The window handle of the child window edit control.
wParam	WORD: Contains the handle to the memory buffer. Use LocalAlloc() to create the memory area.
lParam	DWORD: Not used. Set equal to 0L.
Notes:	More than one buffer can be linked to one edit control at different times. This is a way to switch between different default strings, without destroying either buffer when the switch is made. If the edit control is in a dialog box, this message can only be accepted if the dialog box was created with the DS_LOCALEDIT style. Otherwise, the dialog box uses its own memory area for the edit string.

EM_SETMODIFY ■ Win 2.0 ■ Win 3.0 ■ Win 3.1

Purpose	Sets the modify flag for the edit control. This message is handy if you need to repaint the text, and the program uses the EM_GETMODIFY message to check if painting is necessary.
Syntax	SendMessage (HWND *hControl*, **EM_SETMODIFY**, WORD *wParam*, DWORD *lParam*)
Parameters	
hControl	HWND: The window handle of the child window control.
wParam	WORD: TRUE for modified, FALSE for not.
lParam	DWORD: Not used. Set equal to 0L.

EM_SETPASSWORDCHAR □ Win 2.0 ■ Win 3.0 ■ Win 3.1

Purpose	The abilities to have an edit control with the ES_PASSWORD style is new with the 3.0 version of Windows. By default, a password edit control shows every typed letter as an asterisk (*), even though the edit control's buffer contains the characters as typed. EM_SETPASSWORDCHAR allows you to change from the asterisk to any desired character placeholder.
Syntax	SendMessage (HWND *hControl*, **EM_SETPASSWORDCHAR**, WORD *wParam*, DWORD *lParam*)
Parameters	
hControl	HWND: The window handle of the child window edit control.
wParam	WORD: The character to be displayed in place of the input letters. If *hControl* is NULL, the typed letters are displayed as is, removing the password style effects.
lParam	DWORD: Not used. Set equal to 0L.

EM_SETRECT ■ Win 2.0 ■ Win 3.0 ■ Win 3.1

Purpose	Sets the inner formatting rectangle of the edit control. Any text in the edit control is reformatted and repainted to fit within the bounds of the rectangle. This message will not work for single line edit controls.
Syntax	SendMessage (HWND *hControl*, **EM_SETRECT**, WORD *wParam*, DWORD *lParam*)
Parameters	
hControl	HWND: The window handle of the child window edit control.

wParam	WORD: Not used. Set equal to 0.
lParam	DWORD: A pointer to a RECT data structure holding the dimensions of the formatting rectangle in client coordinates.

EM_SETRECTNP ■ Win 2.0 ■ Win 3.0 ■ Win 3.1

Purpose	Sets the inner formatting rectangle of the edit control. Any text in the edit control is reformatted to fit within the bounds of the rectangle. The text is not automatically repainted. Otherwise, it is the same as EM_SETRECT. This message will not work for single line edit controls.
Syntax	SendMessage (HWND *hControl*, **BM_SETRECTNP**, WORD *wParam*, DWORD *lParam*)
Parameters	
hControl	HWND: The window handle of the child window control.
wParam	WORD: Not used. Set equal to 0.
lParam	DWORD: A pointer to a RECT data structure holding the dimensions of the formatting rectangle in client coordinates.

EM_SETSEL ■ Win 2.0 ■ Win 3.0 ■ Win 3.1

Purpose	Selects all of the characters in a given range. The selected characters are highlighted in reverse video.
Syntax	SendMessage (HWND *hControl*, **EM_SETSEL**, WORD *wParam*, DWORD *lParam*)
Parameters	
hControl	HWND: The window handle of the child window edit control.
wParam	WORD: Not used. Set equal to 0.
lParam	DWORD: The starting character position in the low-order word and the ending character position in the high-order word. These positions are in the complete edit string, not in an individual line. Selecting a position beyond the end of the string selects the character up to, and including the last character in the string. You can use the MAKELONG macro to specify a range for *lParam*. For example, MAKELONG(20,3) would specify the characters from position 3 to 20 in the edit string.

EM_SETTABSTOPS ☐ Win 2.0 ■ Win 3.0 ■ Win 3.1

Purpose	Sets the positions of the tab stops in a multiline edit control.
Syntax	*dwReturned* = SendMessage (HWND *hControl*, **EM_SETTABSTOPS**, WORD *wParam*, DWORD *lParam*)
Returns	DWORD. Nonzero if the tabs were set, zero on error.
Parameters	
hControl	HWND: The window handle of the child window control.
wParam	WORD: The number of tab stops that will be set.
lParam	DWORD: A pointer to an integer array containing the tab stops. The tab stops are measured in dialog units (1/4 of a character width). The tab stops must be in ascending order, as illustrated here.

```
int nTab [3] = {20, 40, 68} ;
```

Notes	If *wParam* is zero and *lParam* is NULL, the tab stops default to every 32 dialog units (8 characters). If *wParam* is one, then the tab stops will be uniformly spaced at a distance specified in the *lParam* value.

EM_SETWORDBREAK
■ Win 2.0   ■ Win 3.0   ■ Win 3.1

Purpose	Sets a new word break function. Word break functions determine how a string should be split when it does not fit on one line of a multiline edit control. The default word break function breaks lines at space characters.
Syntax	SendMessage (HWND *hControl*, **EM_SETWORDBREAK**, WORD *wParam*, DWORD *lParam*)
Parameters	
hControl	HWND: The window handle of the child window control.
wParam	WORD: Not used. Set equal to 0.
lParam	DWORD: The procedure-instance address of the word break function. Use MakeProcInstance() to create the procedure-instance. The word break function must be listed in the EXPORTS section of the program's .DEF definition file. The callback function for doing word breaks should have the following format:
	LPSTR FAR PASCAL **WordBreakFunc** (LPSTR *lpchEditText*, short *ichCurrentWord*, short *cchEditText*) ;
lpchEditText	LPSTR: A pointer to the text in the edit control.
ichCurrentWord	short: The point at which the function should start checking for needed word wrapping.
cchEditText	short: The number of character positions in the edit text.
Returns	The function should return a pointer to the first letter of the next word in the edit buffer. If the current word is the last word in the text, the return value should point to the first byte after the last word.

EM_UNDO
■ Win 2.0   ■ Win 3.0   ■ Win 3.1

Purpose	Windows maintains a character buffer to hold the last group of characters selected, deleted, and changed. The buffer expands to hold the selection, limited only by the capacity of the local segment storage. This command copies the text from the delete buffer back into the edit control at the insertion point (the caret location).
Syntax	*dwReturned* = SendMessage (HWND *hControl*, **BM_UNDO**, WORD *wParam*, DWORD *lParam*)
Returns	DWORD. Nonzero if successful, zero on error.
Parameters	
hControl	HWND: The window handle of the child window edit control.
wParam	WORD: Not used. Set equal to 0.
lParam	DWORD: Not used. Set equal to 0L.

Edit Control Notification Messages

Normally, you will not need to process EN_ notification messages (see the list in Table 9-10) in your program. The editing functions in the edit control are so complete that little intervention is needed. If you want to change the default behavior of the edit control, you can intercept the notification messages. For example, you might want to increase the size of an edit control to fit added text. The EN_CHANGE and EN_UPDATE messages provide warning that text has been or will be modified. Edit notification messages are sent to the parent window of the edit control as WM_COMMAND messages. The edit control's ID value is passed as the *wParam* value with WM_COMMAND. The edit control's window handle is the low-order word of *lParam*, while the specific notification code is the high-order word.

Message	Purpose	
EN_CHANGE	Notification that the user has changed text within the edit control.	
EN_ERRSPACE	Notification that the edit control has run out of memory space in the local memory area.	

EN_HSCROLL	Notification that the user has clicked an edit control's horizontal scroll bar.
EN_KILLFOCUS	Notification that the edit control has lost the input focus.
EN_MAXTEXT	Notification that the user has attempted to insert more characters than will fit in an edit control.
EN_SETFOCUS	Notification that an edit control has obtained the input focus.
EN_UPDATE	Notification that an edit control is about to display text changed by the user.
EN_VSCROLL	Notification that the user has clicked the vertical scroll bar of a multiline edit control.

Table 9-10. Edit Control Notification Message Summary.

Edit Control Message Descriptions

EN_CHANGE
■ Win 2.0   ■ Win 3.0   ■ Win 3.1

Purpose   Notification that the user has changed text within the edit control. This message is sent after the display is updated. Use EN_UPDATE to receive notification before the change is shown on the display.

Syntax   Returned as part of a WM_COMMAND message, processed by the program's message processing function (WndProc()).

Parameters

wParam   WORD: Contains the ID value for the edit control. This is the integer value set for the *hMenu* parameter when CreateWindow() was called.

lParam   DWORD: Contains the window handle for the edit control in the low-order word. Contains EN_CHANGE in the high-order word.

EN_ERRSPACE
■ Win 2.0   ■ Win 3.0   ■ Win 3.1

Purpose   Notification that the edit control has run out of memory space in the local memory area.

Syntax   Returned as part of a WM_COMMAND message, processed by the program's message processing function (WndProc()).

Parameters

wParam   WORD: Contains the ID value for the edit control. This is the integer value set for the *hMenu* parameter when CreateWindow() was called.

lParam   DWORD: Contains the window handle for the edit control in the low-order word. Contains EN_ERRSPACE in the high-order word.

EN_HSCROLL
■ Win 2.0   ■ Win 3.0   ■ Win 3.1

Purpose   Notification that the user has clicked the edit control's horizontal scroll bar. This is only possible if the edit control was created with the WS_HSCROLL style.

Syntax   Returned as part of a WM_COMMAND message, processed by the program's message processing function (WndProc()).

Parameters

wParam   WORD: Contains the ID value for the edit control. This is the integer value set for the *hMenu* parameter when CreateWindow() was called.

lParam   DWORD: Contains the window handle for the edit control in the low-order word. Contains EN_HSCROLL in the high-order word.

EN_KILLFOCUS
■ Win 2.0 ■ Win 3.0 ■ Win 3.1

Purpose
Notification that the edit control has lost the input focus. If some input is necessary before continuing, you may want to intercept this code, show a warning, and then use SetFocus() to return the focus to the edit control. If you use this type of logic, always provide the user an escape route, such as hitting the (ESC) key.

Syntax
Returned as part of a WM_COMMAND message, processed by the program's message processing function (WndProc()).

Parameters
wParam
WORD: Contains the ID value for the edit control. This is the integer value set for the *hMenu* parameter when CreateWindow() was called.

lParam
DWORD: Contains the window handle for the edit control in the low-order word. Contains EN_KILLFOCUS in the high-order word.

EN_MAXTEXT
□ Win 2.0 ■ Win 3.0 ■ Win 3.1

Purpose
Notification that the user attempted to insert more characters than will fit in an edit control. Notification code will only be sent if the edit control was created without the ES_AUTOHSCROLL style.

Syntax
Returned as part of a WM_COMMAND message, processed by the program's message processing function (WndProc()).

Parameters
wParam
WORD: Contains the ID value for the edit control. This is the integer value set for the *hMenu* parameter when CreateWindow() was called.

lParam
DWORD: Contains the window handle for the edit control in the low-order word. Contains EN_MAXTEXT in the high-order word.

EN_SETFOCUS
■ Win 2.0 ■ Win 3.0 ■ Win 3.1

Purpose
Notification that an edit control has obtained the input focus. Keyboard input will then show up inside the edit control.

Syntax
Returned as part of a WM_COMMAND message, processed by the program's message processing function (WndProc()).

Parameters
wParam
WORD: Contains the ID value for the edit control. This is the integer value set for the *hMenu* parameter when CreateWindow() was called.

lParam
DWORD: Contains the window handle for the edit control in the low-order word. Contains EN_SETFOCUS in the high-order word.

EN_UPDATE
■ Win 2.0 ■ Win 3.0 ■ Win 3.1

Purpose
Notification that an edit control is about to display text changed by the user. This is sent after the changes have been made to the character data in the edit control's memory buffer, but before the changes are displayed. A common use of this message is to allow resizing of an edit control if necessary to fit added text.

Syntax
Returned as part of a WM_COMMAND message, processed by the program's message processing function (WndProc()).

Parameters
wParam
WORD: Contains the ID value for the edit control. This is the integer value set for the *hMenu* parameter when CreateWindow() was called.

lParam	DWORD: Contains the window handle for the edit control in the low-order word. Contains EN_UPDATE in the high-order word.

EN_VSCROLL   ■ Win 2.0   ■ Win 3.0   ■ Win 3.1

Purpose   Notification that the user has clicked the vertical scroll bar of an edit control. This will only occur if the edit control was created with the WS_VSCROLL style. An example of this style of edit control is given in this chapter at the beginning of the discussion on edit control messages.

Syntax   Returned as part of a WM_COMMAND message, processed by the program's message processing function (WndProc()).

Parameters

wParam   WORD: Contains the ID value for the edit control. This is the integer value set for the *hMenu* parameter when CreateWindow() was called.

lParam   DWORD: Contains the window handle for the edit control in the low-order word. Contains EN_VSCROLL in the high-order word.

List Box Messages

List boxes can be thought of as a subset of combo boxes. Most of the functions are the same, although list boxes have a few more formatting options. List boxes lack the edit control at the top and do not "drop down." That is, list boxes are always visible. When designing an application, you will want to use list boxes in situations where the user will usually select an item. If the user will most often leave the selection as is, but needs to be reminded of which item is selected, a combo box is more appropriate. Combo boxes take up less space in their "rolled up" form, so you can make a complex dialog box or child window look less cluttered with combo boxes.

Figure 9-6. A List Box Control.

     Figure 9-6 shows an example of a list box. This one is unusual, as it was created with a title bar using the WS_CAPTION style. This means that the list box can be moved around on the screen like a typical child window. If you want a title, but do not want a moveable list box, surround a normal list box (without the WS_CAPTION style) with a button group control. Group controls have titles, but are not moveable.

     Note that the list box includes a scroll bar on the right side. The standard list box style LBS_STANDARD is the combination of LBS_NOTIFY | LBS_SORT | WS_VSCROLL | WS_BORDER. The vertical scroll bar is visible only if the number of items in the scroll bar exceeds the size of the formatting area. The notify style is critical, as it instructs the list box to send a WM_COMMAND message when the user selects an item. Another interesting thing about the list box in Figure 9-6 is that the text inside includes tab characters. List boxes can have tab stops set at any location, accurate to within a quarter of a character width. This can be a convenient way to display small database tables.

     Listing 9-6 shows the WndProc() function that creates the list box in Figure 9-6. Note that the LBS_HASSTRINGS style is used, so that the control uses its default near memory buffer to hold the strings. The LBS_USETABSTOPS style is also specified. The list box has the text items added to it when the user clicks the "Do It!" menu item. Three tab stops are set using the LB_SETTABSTOPS message. LB_SETTABS STOPS transmits a pointer to the array *nTabs[ ]* that contains the tab positions as integers. The tab positions are computed based on dialog box units, one quarter of a character width per unit.

     Because the LBS_NOTIFY style was set (as part of LBS_STANDARD), the scroll bar sends a WM_COMMAND message, with *wParam* set to the list box ID value, when the user selects a list item with the mouse. In this example, the program retrieves the text from the list box and displays it below the list box using the TabbedTextOut() function. TabbedTextOut() has the nice feature of using the same convention for tab stops as the list box, so the output text looks right.

▷ Listing 9-6. List Box Control

```
Long FAR PASCAL WndProc (HWND hWnd, unsigned iMessage, WORD wParam, LONG lParam)
{
        static HWND     hListBox ;
        HDC             hDC ;
        int             nSel ;
        char            cBuf [30] ;
        static int      nTabs [3] = {32, 56, 72} ;
        switch (iMessage)                       /* process windows messages */
        {
                case WM_CREATE:
                        hListBox = CreateWindow ("LISTBOX", "List Box",
                                WS_CHILD | WS_VISIBLE | LBS_HASSTRINGS | LBS_STANDARD
                                | LBS_USETABSTOPS | WS_CAPTION,
                                10, 10, 180, 80, hWnd, 100, ghInstance, NULL) ;
                        ShowWindow (hListBox, SW_SHOW) ;
                        break ;
                case WM_COMMAND:                /* process menu items and controls */

                        switch (wParam)
                        {
                        case 100:               /* List box id value */
                                if (HIWORD (lParam) == LBN_SELCHANGE)
                                {
                                        hDC = GetDC (hWnd) ;
                                        nSel = (WORD) SendMessage (hListBox,
                                                LB_GETCURSEL, 0, 0L) ;
                                        SendMessage (hListBox, LB_GETTEXT, nSel,
                                                (DWORD) (LPSTR) cBuf) ;
                                        TextOut (hDC, 10, 120,
                                                "The selected text is:", 21) ;
                                        TabbedTextOut (hDC, 10, 140, cBuf,
                                                strlen (cBuf), 3,          (LPINT) nTabs, 0) ;
                                        ReleaseDC (hWnd, hDC) ;


                                }
                                break ;
                        case IDM_DOIT:
                                SendMessage (hListBox, LB_RESETCONTENT, 0, 0L) ;
                                SendMessage (hListBox, LB_SETTABSTOPS, 3,
                                        (DWORD)(LPINT) nTabs) ;
                                SendMessage (hListBox, LB_ADDSTRING, 0,
                                        (DWORD) (LPSTR) "First \tString") ;
                                SendMessage (hListBox, LB_ADDSTRING, 0,
                                        (DWORD) (LPSTR) "Second \tString") ;
                                SendMessage (hListBox, LB_ADDSTRING, 0,
                                        (DWORD) (LPSTR) "Last \tString") ;
                                SendMessage (hListBox, LB_INSERTSTRING, 2,
                                        (DWORD) (LPSTR) "Inserted \tText") ;
                                SendMessage (hListBox, LB_INSERTSTRING, 2,
                                        (DWORD) (LPSTR) "More \tInserted \tText") ;
                                break ;
                        case IDM_QUIT:          /* send end of application message */

                                DestroyWindow (hWnd) ;
                                break ;
                        }
                        break ;
                case WM_DESTROY:                /* stop application */
                        PostQuitMessage (0) ;

                        break ;
                default:                        /* default windows message processing */
```

```
                          return DefWindowProc (hWnd, iMessage, wParam, lParam) ;
          }
      return (OL) ;
}
```

List boxes can also use owner-redrawn list entries. Using them is handy for selecting a color or bitmap pattern from a list. The methods and messages used exactly match those used for owner-redrawn combo box items. Review the section on combo boxes for an example that uses these powerful features.

Table 9-11 summarizes the list box messages. The detailed message descriptions are in the following section.

Message	Purpose	⊠
LB_ADDSTRING	Adds an item to a list box.	
LB_DELETESTRING	Deletes an item from the list box.	
LB_DIR	Fills the list box with file names from a directory search.	
LB_FINDSTRING	Locates the first string in the list box that matches a given set of starting characters.	
LB_GETCARETINDEX	Determines which item in a list box has the focus. (Win 3.1)	
LB_GETCOUNT	Returns the number of items in the list box.	
LB_GETCURSEL	Finds the index number of the currently selected item in the list box.	
LB_GETHORIZONTALEXTENT	Finds the width in pixels that a scroll bar can be scrolled horizontally.	
LB_GETITEMDATA	Retrieves the 32-bit value associated with an item in an owner-redrawn list box.	
LB_GETITEMHEIGHT	Determines the height of an item in a list box. (Win 3.1)	
LB_GETITEMRECT	Retrieves the dimensions of the rectangle that bounds an item as currently displayed in a list box.	
LB_GETSEL	Finds out if an item in a list box has been selected.	
LB_GETSELCOUNT	Returns the total number of items selected in multiple-selection list box.	
LB_GETSELITEMS	Fills an array of integers with the item numbers of the selections in a multiple-selection list box.	
LB_GETTEXT	Retrieves the string held in an item in the list box.	
LB_GETTEXTLEN	Finds the number of characters in a string in the list box.	
LB_GETTOPINDEX	Returns the index number of the top visible item in a list box.	
LB_INSERTSTRING	Adds a new string or 32-bit item to the list box.	
LB_RESETCONTENT	Removes all elements from the list box and frees memory associated with the items.	
LB_SELECTSTRING	Finds a matching string in the list box and highlights it.	
LB_SELITEMRANGE	Selects or deselects one or more consecutive items from a multiple selection list box.	
LB_SETCARETINDEX	Sets which item in a multiple-selection list box has the focus rectangle. (Win 3.1)	
LB_SETCOLUMNWIDTH	Sets the width in pixels for the columns in a multi-column list box.	
LB_SETCURSEL	Selects and highlights an item in a list box.	
LB_SETHORIZONTALEXTENT	Sets the width in pixels that a list box can be scrolled horizontally.	
LB_SETITEMDATA	Changes the 32-bit value associated with a list box created with the owner-redrawn style.	
LB_SETITEMHEIGHT	Changes the height of items in an owner-redrawn list box. (Win 3.1)	
LB_SETSEL	Selects an item in a multiple-selection list box.	
LB_SETTABSTOPS	Sets the position of the tab stops to use when displaying items inside of the list box.	
LB_SETTOPINDEX	Scrolls a list box so as to make a specified item the top visible item.	

Table 9-11. List Box Message Summary.

List Box Message Summary

One other message worth knowing about is WM_SETREDRAW. This message allows the list box to be temporarily inhibited from redrawing the contents as additions and subtractions are made. WM_SETREDRAW speeds up the redrawing of the contents and reduces the distracting "flicker" of different items being displayed one at a time. (WM_SETREDRAW is documented at the end of this chapter because of its WM prefix.)

List Box Message Descriptions

LB_ADDSTRING　　　　　　　　　　　　　　■ Win 2.0　　■ Win 3.0　　■ Win 3.1

Purpose	Adds an item (usually a character string) to a list box. If the list box has the LBS_SORT style, the string is placed in the list and the list re-sorted. Otherwise, the string is added to the end of the list. If the list box is owner-redrawn, but it was created without the LBS_HASSTRINGS style, the inserted item is a 32-bit value.
Syntax	*dwReturned* = SendMessage (HWND *hControl*, **LB_ADDSTRING**, WORD *wParam*, DWORD *lParam*)
Returns	DWORD. The returned value is the index of the new entry in the list box. Returns LB_ERRSPACE if there is not enough memory to store the value. Returns LB_ERR on any other error.
Parameters	
hControl	HWND: The window handle of the list box control.
wParam	WORD: Not used. Set to 0.
lParam	DWORD: For list boxes with the LBS_HASSTRING style, *lParam* contains a pointer to a null-terminated string for a text item. For other styles, *lParam* encodes a 32-bit value for the item. This value can be retrieved when processing WM_DRAWITEM messages as the *itemData* element of the DRAWITEMSTRUCT structure passed with the message. See the example in the section on owner-redrawn combo boxes for more details.

LB_DELETESTRING　　　　　　　　　　　　　■ Win 2.0　　■ Win 3.0　　■ Win 3.1

Purpose	Deletes an item from the list box.
Syntax	*dwReturned* = SendMessage (HWND *hControl*, **LB_DELETESTRING**, WORD *wParam*, DWORD *lParam*)
Returns	DWORD. The number of items remaining in the list. Returns LB_ERR if *wParam* is not a valid list element index.
Parameters	
hControl	HWND: The window handle of the list box control.
wParam	WORD: Contains the index to the list element. 0 for the first item.
lParam	DWORD: Not used. Set to 0L.

LB_DIR　　　　　　　　　　　　　　　　　　■ Win 2.0　　■ Win 3.0　　■ Win 3.1

Purpose	Fills the list box with file names from a directory search.
Syntax	*dwReturned* = SendMessage (HWND *hControl*, **LB_DIR**, WORD *wParam*, DWORD *lParam*)
Returns	DWORD. The number of items displayed minus 1. Returns LB_ERRSPACE if there is not enough memory for the list. Returns LB_ERR for any other error.
Parameters	
hControl	HWND: The window handle of the list box control.

wParam　　　　WORD: Contains the DOS file attribute value. The values can be combined by using the C language binary OR operator (|). The attributes are listed in Table 9-12.

Value	Meaning	⊠
0x0000	Read/write data files with no other attributes set (normal files).	
0x0001	Read-only files.	
0x0002	Hidden files.	
0x0004	System files.	
0x0010	Subdirectories.	
0x0020	Archived files.	
0x2000	LB_DIR flag. Places messages associated with filling the list box on the applications message queue, rather than sending them directly.	
0x4000	Drives.	
0x8000	Exclusive bit. If this is set, only the specified file attribute type is recovered. If not set, normal files are displayed in addition to the types listed.	

Table 9-12. File Attribute Flags.

lParam　　　　DWORD: A pointer to a file search specification string (like "*.*" or "*.TXT"). The string can contain a full pathname specification.

LB_FINDSTRING　　　　　　　☐ Win 2.0　　■ Win 3.0　　■ Win 3.1

Purpose　　　Locates the first string in the list box that matches a given set of starting characters. Alternatively, finds the list box item matching a 32-bit value for an owner-drawn list box.

Syntax　　　*dwReturned* = SendMessage (HWND *hControl*, **LB_FINDSTRING**, WORD *wParam*, DWORD *lParam*)

Returns　　　DWORD. The index of the first string in the list box that starts with the characters in the string pointed to by *lParam*. Returns LB_ERR (–1) if the search did not find a match.

Parameters
hControl　　　HWND: The window handle of the list box control.

wParam　　　WORD: The index of the list box item *before* the first item to start the search. The search will wrap around if the end of the list is passed without a match. Set *wParam* = –1 to search the entire list. You can find multiple occurrences of a matching string by repeatedly using this message and each time starting from the previous match.

lParam　　　DWORD: A pointer to a null-terminated string. The characters in this string must all be matched by the beginning of an item in the list to have a match.

Note:　　　This message will also match 32-bit values if the list box is an owner-drawn control, created without the LBS_HASSTRINGS style. In this case, *lParam* holds the 32-bit value to match.

LB_GETCARETINDEX　　　　　　☐ Win 2.0　　☐ Win 3.0　　■ Win 3.1

Purpose　　　Determines which item in a list box has the focus.

Syntax　　　*dwReturned* = SendMessage (HWND *hControl*, **LB_GETCARETINDEX**, WORD *wParam*, DWORD *lParam*)

Returns　　　DWORD, the index of the item that has the focus. In a single-selection list box, this is the selected item. In a multiple-selection list box, this is the selection that has the focus rectangle.

Parameters

hControl   HWND: The window handle of the list box control.

wParam   WORD: Not used. Set equal to 0.

lParam   DWORD: Not used. Set equal to 0L.

Related Messages LB_SETCARETINDEX, LB_GETCURSEL

LB_GETCOUNT   ■ Win 2.0   ■ Win 3.0   ■ Win 3.1

Purpose   Returns the number of items in the list box.

Syntax   *dwReturned* = SendMessage (HWND *hControl*, **LB_GETCOUNT**, WORD *wParam*, DWORD *lParam*)

Returns   DWORD. The number of items in the list box. Returns LB_ERR on error.

Parameters

hControl   HWND: The window handle of the list box control.

wParam   WORD: Not used. Set equal to 0.

lParam   DWORD: Not used. Set equal to 0L.

LB_GETCURSEL   ■ Win 2.0   ■ Win 3.0   ■ Win 3.1

Purpose   Finds the index number of the currently selected item in the list box.

Syntax   *dwReturned* = SendMessage (HWND *hControl*, **LB_GETCURSEL**, WORD *wParam*, DWORD *lParam*)

Returns   DWORD. The index of the currently selected item in the list box. Returns LB_ERR if no item is selected.

Parameters

hControl   HWND: The window handle of the list box control.

wParam   WORD: Not used. Set equal to 0.

lParam   DWORD: Not used. Set equal to 0L.

LB_GETHORIZONTALEXTENT   □ Win 2.0   ■ Win 3.0   ■ Win 3.1

Purpose   Finds the width in pixels that a scroll bar can be scrolled horizontally. The list box must have been defined with the WS_HSCROLL style to respond to this message.

Syntax   *dwReturned* = SendMessage (HWND *hControl*, **LB_GETHORIZONTALEXTENT**, WORD *wParam*, DWORD *lParam*)

Returns   DWORD. The scrollable width of the list box, measured in pixels.

Parameters

hControl   HWND: The window handle of the list box control.

wParam   WORD: Not used. Set equal to 0.

lParam   DWORD: Not used. Set equal to 0L.

LB_GETITEMDATA   □ Win 2.0   ■ Win 3.0   ■ Win 3.1

Purpose   Retrieves the 32-bit value associated with an item in an owner-redrawn list box.

Syntax   *dwReturned* = SendMessage (HWND *hControl*, **LB_GETITEMDATA**, WORD *wParam*, DWORD *lParam*)

Returns   DWORD, the 32-bit value. Returns LB_ERR on error.

Parameters

hControl   HWND: The window handle of the list box control.

wParam   WORD: The index of the item. The first item is 0.

lParam   DWORD: Not used. Set equal to 0L.

LB_GETITEMHEIGHT   □ Win 2.0   □ Win 3.0   ■ Win 3.1

Purpose   Determines the height of an item in a list box.

Syntax   *dwReturned* = SendMessage (HWND *hControl*, **LB_GETITEMHEIGHT**, WORD *wParam*, DWORD *lParam*)

Returns   DWORD, the item's height in pixels. Returns LB_ERR on error.

Parameters

hControl   HWND: The window handle of the list box control.

wParam   WORD: Set equal to the index of an element in the list box if the list box has the LBS_OWNER-DRAWVARIABLE style. The first item has an index of zero. Otherwise set it equal to zero, as all elements will have the same height.

lParam   DWORD: Not used. Set equal to 0L.

Related Messages LB_SETITEMHEIGHT, LB_SETITEMDATA, WM_DRAWITEM

LB_GETITEMRECT   □ Win 2.0   ■ Win 3.0   ■ Win 3.1

Purpose   Retrieves the dimensions of the rectangle that bounds an item currently displayed in a list box. This is used with owner-redrawn list boxes with the LBS_OWNERDRAWVARIABLE style.

Syntax   *dwReturned* = SendMessage (HWND *hControl*, **LB_GETITEMRECT**, WORD *wParam*, DWORD *lParam*)

Returns   DWORD, normally ignored. Returns LB_ERR on error.

Parameters

hControl   HWND: The window handle of the list box control.

wParam   WORD: The index of the item. The first item is 0.

lParam   DWORD: Contains a far pointer to a RECT structure. The structure receives the bounding rectangle data after the message is processed. Client coordinates are used.

LB_GETSEL ,   ■ Win 2.0   ■ Win 3.0   ■ Win 3.1

Purpose   Finds out if an item in a list box has been selected.

Syntax   *dwReturned* = SendMessage (HWND *hControl*, **LB_GETSEL**, WORD *wParam*, DWORD *lParam*)

Returns   DWORD, greater than zero if selected, zero if not selected. Returns LB_ERR on error.

Parameters

hControl   HWND: The window handle of the list box control.

wParam   WORD: The index of the item. The first item is 0.

lParam   DWORD: Not used. Set equal to 0L.

LB_GETSELCOUNT   □ Win 2.0   ■ Win 3.0   ■ Win 3.1

Purpose   Returns the total number of items selected in a multiple-selection list box. The list box must have been created with the LBS_MUTIPLESEL style to have more than one item selected.

Syntax   *dwReturned* = SendMessage (HWND *hControl*, **LB_GETSELCOUNT**, WORD *wParam*, DWORD *lParam*)

| Returns | DWORD, the number of selected items. Returns LB_ERR on error (for example, sending this message to a list box without the LBS_MULTIPLESEL style). |

Parameters

hControl	HWND: The window handle of the list box control.
wParam	WORD: Not used. Set equal to 0.
lParam	DWORD: Not used. Set equal to 0L.

LB_GETSELITEMS
☐ Win 2.0　■ Win 3.0　■ Win 3.1

Purpose	Fills an array of integers with the item numbers of the selections in a multiple-selection list box. The list box must have been created with the LBS_MUTIPLESEL style to have more than one item selected.
Syntax	*dwReturned* = SendMessage (HWND *hControl*, **LB_GETSELITEMS**, WORD *wParam*, DWORD *lParam*)
Returns	DWORD, the number of items put in the array. Returns LB_ERR on error, (for example sending this message to a list box without the LBS_MULTIPLESEL style).

Parameters

hControl	HWND: The window handle of the list box control.
wParam	WORD: The maximum number of selection items that will fit into the integer array.
lParam	DWORD: A far pointer to an array of integers. Make sure that there are at least as many elements in the array as the maximum specified by *wParam* to avoid overwriting past the end of the array memory area.

LB_GETTEXT
■ Win 2.0　■ Win 3.0　■ Win 3.1

Purpose	Retrieves the string held in an item in the list box.
Syntax	*dwReturned* = SendMessage (HWND *hControl*, **LB_GETTEXT**, WORD *wParam*, DWORD *lParam*)
Returns	DWORD, the length of the string in bytes. Returns LB_ERR on error.

Parameters

hControl	HWND: The window handle of the list box control.
wParam	WORD: Contains the index of the list box item. The first item is 0.
lParam	DWORD: A pointer to a character buffer that holds the string retrieved. Use LB_GETTEXTLEN to retrieve the length of the string. Add one to this value for the terminating NULL character.
Note:	This message will also retrieve the 32-bit value associated with an item in an owner-redrawn list box.

LB_GETTEXTLEN
■ Win 2.0　■ Win 3.0　■ Win 3.1

Purpose	Finds the number of characters in a string in the list box.
Syntax	*dwReturned* = SendMessage (HWND *hControl*, **LB_GETTEXTLEN**, WORD *wParam*, DWORD *lParam*)
Returns	DWORD, the length of the string in bytes, excluding the terminating NULL character. Returns LB_ERR on error.

Parameters

| *hControl* | HWND: The window handle of the list box control. |

wParam	WORD: Contains the index of the string. The first item is 0.
lParam	DWORD: Not used. Set equal to 0L.

LB_GETTOPINDEX
☐ Win 2.0 ■ Win 3.0 ■ Win 3.1

Purpose	Returns the index number of the top visible item in a list box. This will be greater than 0 if the list box has been scrolled.
Syntax	*dwReturned* = SendMessage (HWND *hControl*, **LB_GETTOPINDEX**, WORD *wParam*, DWORD *lParam*)
Returns	DWORD, normally ignored. Returns LB_ERR on error.
Parameters	
hControl	HWND: The window handle of the list box control.
wParam	WORD: Not used. Set equal to 0.
lParam	DWORD: Not used. Set equal to 0L.

LB_INSERTSTRING
■ Win 2.0 ■ Win 3.0 ■ Win 3.1

Purpose	Adds a new string or 32-bit item to the list box.
Syntax	*dwReturned* = SendMessage (HWND *hControl*, **LB_INSERTSTRING**, WORD *wParam*, DWORD *lParam*)
Returns	DWORD, the index of the inserted item. Returns LB_ERRSPACE if there is not enough memory for the item. Returns LB_ERR for all other errors.
Parameters	
hControl	HWND: The window handle of the list box control.
wParam	WORD: Contains the index position of the location to insert the string. 0 for the first item, 1 for the second, etc. Use –1 for the last. All items below the insertion point will have new index values.
lParam	DWORD: A pointer to a null-terminated character string to be added. If the list box has the owner-redrawn style, *lParam* holds the 32-bit value to set for the item.

LB_RESETCONTENT
■ Win 2.0 ■ Win 3.0 ■ Win 3.1

Purpose	Removes all elements from the list box and frees the memory associated with the items.
Syntax	*dwReturned* = SendMessage (HWND *hControl*, **LB_RESETCONTENT**, WORD *wParam*, DWORD *lParam*)
Parameters	
hControl	HWND: The window handle of the list box control.
wParam	WORD: Not used. Set equal to 0.
lParam	DWORD: Not used. Set equal to 0L.

LB_SELECTSTRING
■ Win 2.0 ■ Win 3.0 ■ Win 3.1

Purpose	Finds a matching string in the list box and highlights it. If the list box has the owner- redrawn style, the match is based on comparing 32-bit values.
Syntax	*dwReturned* = SendMessage (HWND *hControl*, **LB_SELECTSTRING**, WORD *wParam*, DWORD *lParam*)
Returns	DWORD, the index of the string found. Returns LB_ERR if no match was found.

Parameters

hControl   HWND: The window handle of the list box control.

wParam   WORD: The list box item number *before* the first item to be searched. The search wraps around to the beginning if no match is found between the starting point and the end of the list. You can find duplicate entries in the list by repeatedly using the last index as the starting point for the next search.

lParam   DWORD: A pointer to the character string to match. The string in the list box can be longer, as long as the first characters match the string pointed to by *lParam*. If the list box has the owner-redrawn style, but it does not have the LBS_HASSTRINGS style, *lParam* contains the 32-bit value to match.

LB_SELITEMRANGE   □ Win 2.0   ■ Win 3.0   ■ Win 3.1

Purpose   Selects or deselects one or more consecutive items from a multiple-selection list box. The list box must have been created with the LBS_MUTIPLESEL style to have more than one item selected.

Syntax   *dwReturned* = SendMessage (HWND *hControl*, **LB_SELITEMRANGE**, WORD *wParam*, DWORD *lParam*)

Parameters

hControl   HWND: The window handle of the list box control.

wParam   WORD: TRUE to select items, FALSE to deselect them.

lParam   DWORD: The low-order word contains the index of the first item to select. The high-order word contains the index of the last item to select. If both values are the same, only one item is selected.

LB_SETCARETINDEX   □ Win 2.0   □ Win 3.0   ■ Win 3.1

Purpose   Sets which item in a multiple-selection list box has the focus rectangle. If the item is not visible, it is scrolled into view.

Syntax   *dwReturned* = SendMessage (HWND *hControl*, **LB_SETCARETINDEX**, WORD *wParam*, DWORD *lParam*)

Returns   DWORD, returns LB_ERR on error.

Parameters

hControl   HWND: The window handle of the list box control.

wParam   WORD: The index of the list box item which should receive the focus. Zero for the first item.

lParam   DWORD: Not used. Set equal to 0L.

Related Messages LB_GETCARETINDEX, LB_SETCURSEL

LB_SETCOLUMNWIDTH   □ Win 2.0   ■ Win 3.0   ■ Win 3.1

Purpose   Sets the width, in pixels, for the columns in a multicolumn list box. The list box must have been created with the LBS_MULTICOLUMN style to use this message.

Syntax   *dwReturned* = SendMessage (HWND *hControl*, **LB_SETCOLUMNWIDTH**, WORD *wParam*, DWORD *lParam*)

Parameters

hControl   HWND: The window handle of the list box control.

wParam   WORD: The width, in pixels, to set every column. All columns must have the same width.

lParam   DWORD: Not used. Set equal to 0L.

LB_SETCURSEL   ■ Win 2.0   ■ Win 3.0   ■ Win 3.1

Purpose   Selects and highlights an item in a list box. If the item is not visible, the list is scrolled into view. Any highlighting of the previous selection is removed. This message should be used with single-selection list boxes (the standard style), not multiple-selection ones. For the latter, use LB_SELITEMRANGE.

Syntax   *dwReturned* = SendMessage (HWND *hControl*, **LB_SETCURSEL**, WORD *wParam*, DWORD *lParam*)

Returns   DWORD. Normally not used. Set to LB_ERR on error (for example, an out of range *wParam* value).

Parameters
hControl   HWND: The window handle of the list box control.

wParam   WORD: The index of the item to select. Set *wParam* to −1 to deselect all items.

lParam   DWORD: Not used. Set equal to 0L.

LB_SETHORIZONTALEXTENT   □ Win 2.0   ■ Win 3.0   ■ Win 3.1

Purpose   Sets the width, in pixels, that a list box can be scrolled horizontally. If this value is smaller than the list box horizontal size, scrolling is disabled. The list box must have been created with the WS_HSCROLL style to apply this message.

Syntax   SendMessage (HWND *hControl*, **LB_SETHORIZONTALEXTENT**, WORD *wParam*, DWORD *lParam*)

Parameters
hControl   HWND: The window handle of the list box control.

wParam   WORD: The width in pixels that the list box can be scrolled horizontally.

lParam   DWORD: Not used. Set equal to 0L.

LB_SETITEMDATA   □ Win 2.0   ■ Win 3.0   ■ Win 3.1

Purpose   Changes the 32-bit value associated with a list box created with the owner-redrawn style.

Syntax   *dwReturned* = SendMessage (HWND *hControl*, **LB_SETITEMDATA**, WORD *wParam*, DWORD *lParam*)

Returns   DWORD. Normally not used. LB_ERR on error.

Parameters
hControl   HWND: The window handle of the list box control.

wParam   WORD: The index number of the item in the list box.

lParam   DWORD: The new 32-bit value to set.

LB_SETITEMHEIGHT   □ Win 2.0   □ Win 3.0   ■ Win 3.1

Purpose   Changes the height of items in an owner-redrawn list box.

Syntax   *dwReturned* = SendMessage (HWND *hControl*, **LB_SETITEMHEIGHT**, WORD *wParam*, DWORD *lParam*)

Returns   DWORD. Returns LB_ERR on error.

Parameters
hControl   HWND: The window handle of the list box control.

wParam	WORD: For a list box with the LBS_OWNERDRAWVARIABLE style, set *wParam* equal to the index of the element which will change height. Otherwise, set *wParam* equal to zero. All elements of the list box will have their height changed.
lParam	DWORD: Set equal to the new height in pixels.
Related Messages	LB_GETITEMHEIGHT, LB_SETITEMDATA, WM_DRAWITEM

LB_SETSEL ■ Win 2.0 ■ Win 3.0 ■ Win 3.1

Purpose	Selects a string in a multiple-selection list box. The list box must have been created with the LBS_MUTIPLESEL style.
Syntax	*dwReturned* = SendMessage (HWND *hControl*, **LB_SETSEL**, WORD *wParam*, DWORD *lParam*)
Returns	DWORD, normally not used. Returns LB_ERR on error.
Parameters	
hControl	HWND: The window handle of the list box control.
wParam	WORD: TRUE to select and highlight the selection. FALSE to deselect and remove highlighting.
lParam	DWORD: The index of the list box item to be set is put in the low-order word. 0 is the index of the first item. If *lParam* is equal to –1, all of the items in the list box are affected. This allows you to select or deselect every item in one operation.

LB_SETTABSTOPS □ Win 2.0 ■ Win 3.0 ■ Win 3.1

Purpose	Sets the position of the tab stops to use when displaying items inside of the list box. The unit of measurement is the dialog unit, one quarter of the width of a character. The list box must have been created using the LBS_USETABSTOPS style to respond to this message.
Syntax	*dwReturned* = SendMessage (HWND *hControl*, **LB_SETTABSTOPS**, WORD *wParam*, DWORD *lParam*)
Returns	DWORD. TRUE if all tab stops were set, FALSE if not.
Parameters	
hControl	HWND: The window handle of the list box control.
wParam	WORD: The number of tab stops to set. If *wParam* is set to zero and *lParam* is set to NULL, tab stops are set every two dialog units. If *wParam* is 1, the tab stops are set evenly at a distance specified by a single value in *lParam*.
lParam	DWORD: A pointer to an integer array containing the tab stop position measured in dialog units (one-quarter of a character width). The tab stops must be listed in ascending order. Use GetDialogBaseUnits() to find out the width of a dialog unit in pixels.

LB_SETTOPINDEX □ Win 2.0 ■ Win 3.0 ■ Win 3.1

Purpose	Scrolls a list box so that a specified item becomes the top visible item.
Syntax	*dwReturned* = SendMessage (HWND *hControl*, **LB_SETTOPINDEX**, WORD *wParam*, DWORD *lParam*)
Returns	DWORD, normally not used. Returns LB_ERR on error.
Parameters	
hControl	HWND: The window handle of the list box control.
wParam	WORD: The index of the item to be shown at the top of the list box. 0 for the first item.
lParam	DWORD: Not used. Set equal to 0L.

List Box Notification Codes

If the user interacts with a list box, Windows sends a WM_COMMAND message to the parent window of the list box control. The *wParam* value passed with WM_COMMAND will be the ID value of the list box control. The window handle of the list box is passed as the low-order word in the *lParam* value. The notification code (see Table 9-13) is in the high-order word.

Notification Code	Meaning	⊠
LBN_DBLCLK	Notification that the user double-clicked an item in a list box.	
LBN_KILLFOCUS	Notification that a list box has lost the input focus.	
LBN_SELCHANGE	Notification that the user has selected or deselected an item in a list box.	
LBN_SETFOCUS	Notification that a list box has received the input focus.	

Table 9-13. List Box Notification Code Summary.

In addition to the LBN messages, Windows will also send a WM_CHARTOITEM message to the owner of the list box if the user presses a key while the list box is active. This will happen only if the LBS_WANTKEYBOARDINPUT style was used to create the list box. The WM_CHARTOITEM message allows the application to provide a shortcut, jumping straight to the first entry in the list box that begins with the given character. WM_CHARTOITEM is documented in the last part of this chapter, as the name starts with the WM prefix.

List Box Notification Code Descriptions

LBN_DBLCLK
■ Win 2.0   ■ Win 3.0   ■ Win 3.1

Purpose   Notification that the user double-clicked an item in a list box.

Syntax   Returned as part of a WM_COMMAND message, processed by the program's message processing function (WndProc()).

Parameters
wParam   WORD: Contains the ID value for the list box control. This is the integer value set for the *hMenu* parameter when CreateWindow() was called.

lParam   DWORD: Contains the window handle of the list box in the low-order word. Contains LBN_DBLCLK in the high-order word.

LBN_KILLFOCUS
☐ Win 2.0   ■ Win 3.0   ■ Win 3.1

Purpose   Notification that a list box has lost the input focus.

Syntax   Returned as part of a WM_COMMAND message, processed by the program's message processing function (WndProc()).

Parameters
wParam   WORD: Contains the ID value for the list box control. This is the integer value set for the *hMenu* parameter when CreateWindow() was called.

lParam   DWORD: Contains the window handle of the list box in the low-order word. Contains LBN_KILL-FOCUS in the high-order word.

LBN_SELCHANGE
■ Win 2.0   ■ Win 3.0   ■ Win 3.1

Purpose   Notification that the user has selected or deselected an item in a list box. The list box must have been created with the LBS_NOTIFY style for these messages to be received. LBS_NOTIFY is part of the LBS_STANDARD style.

Syntax	Returned as part of a WM_COMMAND message, processed by the program's message processing function (WndProc()).
Parameters	
wParam	WORD: Contains the ID value for the list box control. This is the integer value set for the *hMenu* parameter when CreateWindow() was called.
lParam	DWORD: Contains the window handle of the list box in the low-order word. Contains LBN_SELCHANGE in the high-order word.

LBN_SETFOCUS   □ Win 2.0   ■ Win 3.0   ■ Win 3.1

Purpose	Notification that a list box has received the input focus.
Syntax	Returned as part of a WM_COMMAND message, processed by the program's message processing function (WndProc()).
Parameters	
wParam	WORD: Contains the ID value for the list box control. This is the integer value set for the *hMenu* parameter when CreateWindow() was called.
lParam	DWORD: Contains the window handle of the list box in the low-order word. Contains LBN_SETFOCUS in the high-order word.

Static Control Messages

Windows 3.1 has two new messages for working with static controls within a dialog box. STM_GETICON retrieves the handle of the icon in an icon control. STM_SETICON changes the icon control to a new icon.

STM_GETICON   □ Win 2.0   □ Win 3.0   ■ Win 3.1

Purpose	Retrieves the handle of an icon control.
Syntax	*dwReturned* = SendDlgItemMessage (HWND *hControl*, WORD *wIdIcon*, **STM_GETICON**, WORD *wParam*, DWORD *lParam*);
Returns	DWORD. The handle of the icon is in the low-order word of the returned value. Returns NULL on error.
Parameters	
hControl	HWND: The window handle of the dialog box.
wIdIcon	WORD: The control ID number of the icon control.
wParam	WORD: Not used. Set equal to 0.
lParam	DWORD: Not used. Set equal to 0L.
Related Messages	STM_SETICON

STM_SETICON   □ Win 2.0   □ Win 3.0   ■ Win 3.1

Purpose	Changes the icon shown in an icon control of a dialog box.
Syntax	*dwReturned* = SendDlgItemMessage (HWND *hControl*, WORD *wIdIcon*, **STM_GETICON**, WORD *wParam*, DWORD *lParam*);
Returns	DWORD. The previous icon's handle is in the low-order word of the returned value. Returns zero on error.

Parameters

hControl	HWND: The window handle of the dialog box.
wIdIcon	WORD: The control ID number of the icon control.
wParam	WORD: The handle of the icon to show in the control. Use LoadIcon() to retrieve this value.
lParam	DWORD: Not used. Set equal to 0L.

Related Messages STM_GETICON

Window Messages

All Windows messages are retrieved by GetMessage() or PeekMessage() in the program's message loop, and they are ultimately sent to the program's message processing function, WndProc(). These messages control the operation of your program. You can think of a Windows program as an obedient slave. The program just sits there waiting for a message. When it receives a message, the program does some task and then goes back to just sitting there. This is completely different from a DOS program. DOS programs have an active "mentality." "First I will do this, then I will do that, etc."

When GetMessage() sends a message to the program's WndProc() function, four of the elements of the MSG structure are turned into parameters. These end up being the *hWnd*, *iMessage*, *wParam*, and *lParam* parameters that WndProc() processes. The other elements of the MSG structure, the message time and mouse cursor location, are not sent. They can be retrieved if needed by using GetMessageTime() and GetMessagePos(), described in the previous chapter. The *iMessage* parameter holds the message number. Messages all have coded numbers defined in the WINDOWS.H header file. Depending on the message, the *wParam* and *lParam* values will have different meanings. Listing 9-7 shows an outline of a typical WndProc() function. The function uses the *iMessage* parameter to switch to the right set of program logic.

▷ **Listing 9-7. Outline of a WindProc() Function**

```
Long FAR PASCAL WndProc (HWND hWnd, unsigned iMessage, WORD wParam, LONG lParam)
{
        switch (iMessage)                         /* process windows messages */
        {
            case WM_CREATE:
                    /* program initialization activities here */
                    break ;
            case WM_COMMAND:                       /* process menu items and child controls */
                switch (wParam)
                {
                case ITEM_ONE:
    /* program logic for action based on a menu item or child window control */
                break ;
            case WM_   .. Other window messages ....

            case WM_DESTROY:          /* stop application */
                    DestroyWindow (hWnd) ;
                    break ;
            default:                  /* default windows message processing */
                    return DefWindowProc (hWnd, iMessage, wParam, lParam) ;
        }
        return (0L) ;
}
```

There are about 120 different window messages. Fortunately, you normally will use only a handful of these in most programs. The most common ones are shown with an asterisk following the message name in Table 9-14.

Message	Meaning
WM_ACTIVATE	Notification that a window has become active or inactive.
WM_ACTIVATEAPP	Notification that the window being activated belongs to another application program.
WM_ASKCBFORMATNAME	Windows is requesting that the name of a custom clipboard format be copied into a character string buffer.
WM_CANCELMODE	Notification that the system has cancelled a mode it was in.
WM_CHANGECBCHAIN	Notification that a window in the clipboard-viewer chain of applications is being removed from the chain.
WM_CHAR *	Transmits the ASCII value of a character key pressed on the keyboard.
WM_CHARTOITEM	Sends the message when the list box receives a WM_CHAR message.
WM_CHILDACTIVATE	Sent to a child window's parent when a child window is moved.
WM_CLEAR	Deletes the selection in an edit control without copying it to the clipboard.
WM_CLOSE *	Notification that a window will be closed.
WM_COMMAND *	Notification that the user has selected a menu item or child window control.
WM_COMPACTING	Notification that the system is running low on memory.
WM_COMPAREITEM	Notification that a new item is being added: an owner-redrawn list box or combo box.
WM_COPY	Copies selected text within an edit control to the clipboard.
WM_CREATE *	Notification that a window is being created.
WM_CTLCOLOR	Notification that a child window control is about to be drawn.
WM_CUT	Copies the current selected text from an edit control to the clipboard.
WM_DEADCHAR	Notification that the user has selected a non-English language accent or special character that will change the value of the next character typed.
WM_DELETEITEM	Notification to the parent of an owner-redrawn combo or list box that an item has been removed.
WM_DESTROY *	Notification that a window is being destroyed.
WM_DESTROYCLIPBOARD	Notification to the clipboard owner that the clipboard has been emptied by a call to EmptyClipboard( ).
WM_DEVMODECHANGE	Sent to all top-level windows when the user changes the name of a device in the WIN.INI file.
WM_DRAWCLIPBOARD	Sent automatically by Windows to the first window of the clipboard viewer chain when the contents of the clipboard change.
WM_DRAWITEM	Notification to the owner of a owner-drawn button, list box, or combo box, that one of the items in the list has changed.
WM_DROPFILES	Sent when the left mouse button is released over an application which is registered as a recipient of dropped files. (Win 3.1)
WM_ENABLE	Notification that a window has been enabled or disabled.
WM_ENDSESSION	Final notification that the Windows session is being stopped.
WM_ENTERIDLE	Notification that a modal dialog box or menu has been activated, but has no messages to process.
WM_ERASEBKGND	Notification that the background of a window's client area needs to be repainted.
WM_FONTCHANGE	Notification that the number of fonts available to applications has changed.
WM_GETDLGCODE	Notification that the user is using the direction arrow keys or the (TAB) key from within a dialog box.

WM_GETFONT	Retrieves the font currently being used by a child window control.
WM_GETMINMAXINFO	Notifies the application that Windows is checking the size for the window when minimized or maximized.
WM_GETTEXT	Used to copy text from a child window control into a character buffer.
WM_GETTEXTLENGTH	Used to determine the number of characters in a child window control.
WM_HSCROLL *	Notification that the user has adjusted a horizontal scroll bar.
WM_HSCROLLCLIPBOARD	Indicates that the clipboard viewer horizontal scroll bar has been used.
WM_ICONERASEBKGND	Notification that a minimized (iconic) window needs to have the background painted.
WM_INITDIALOG	Notification that a dialog box is about to be displayed.
WM_INITMENU	Notification that the user has clicked a main menu item.
WM_INITMENUPOPUP	Notification that the window is about to display a popup menu.
WM_KEYDOWN *	Notification that a key was pressed.
WM_KEYUP	Notification that a key was released.
WM_KILLFOCUS	Notification that a window is about to loose the input focus.
WM_LBUTTONDBLCLK	Notification that the user has double-clicked the left mouse button.
WM_LBUTTONDOWN *	Notification that the user has pressed the left mouse button.
WM_LBUTTONUP	Notification that the user has released the left mouse button.
WM_MBUTTONDBLCLK	Notification that the user has double-clicked the center mouse button.
WM_MBUTTONDOWN	Notification that the user has pressed the center mouse button.
WM_MBUTTONUP	Notification that the user has released the center mouse button.
WM_MDIACTIVATE	Used to activate and deactivate child windows within a Multiple Document Interface (MDI) window.
WM_MDICASCADE	Arranges all of the child windows within the MDI client window in "cascade" format.
WM_MDICREATE	Creates an MDI child window.
WM_MDIDESTROY	Destroys (removes) an MDI child window.
WM_MDIGETACTIVE	Obtains the handle of the currently active MDI child window.
WM_MDIICONARRANGE	Causes the MDI client window to arrange all minimized MDI child windows at the bottom of the client area.
WM_MDIMAXIMIZE	Causes an MDI child window to be maximized.
WM_MDINEXT	Activates the next MDI child window.
WM_MDIRESTORE	Restores a MDI child window to its previous size.
WM_MDISETMENU	Links a menu to the MDI frame window.
WM_MDITILE	Causes an MDI client window to arrange all of its children in tile format.
WM_MEASUREITEM	Allows owner-drawn buttons, list boxes, and combo boxes to be sized.
WM_MENUCHAR	Informs the application that the user attempted to use a keyboard shortcut for a menu selection that did not match any menu item.
WM_MENUSELECT	Notification that the user has selected a menu item.
WM_MOUSEACTIVATE	Notification that the cursor is in an inactive window and the user clicked a mouse button.
WM_MOUSEMOVE	Notification that the user has moved the mouse.
WM_MOVE *	Notification that a window has been moved.
WM_NCACTIVATE	Notification that the nonclient area of a window needs to be changed to reflect an active or inactive state.

Table 9-14. continued

Message	Meaning	☒
WM_NCCALCSIZE	Sent when the size of a window, including the title, border, and caption areas, needs to be recalculated.	
WM_NCCREATE	Notification that Windows is about to create the nonclient area of the window.	
WM_NCDESTROY	Informs a window that its nonclient area is being destroyed. This message is sent after WM_DESTROY.	
WM_NCHITTEST	Sent to the window that has the mouse, or that used GetCapture() to capture all mouse input.	
WM_NCLBUTTONDBLCLK	Notification that the user double-clicked the left mouse button while the mouse cursor was in the nonclient area of the window.	
WM_NCLBUTTONDOWN	Notification that the user pressed the left mouse button while the mouse cursor was in the nonclient area of the window.	
WM_NCLBUTTONUP	Notification that the user released the left mouse button while the mouse cursor was in the nonclient area of the window.	
WM_NCMBUTTONDBLCLK	Notification that the user double-clicked the center mouse button while the mouse cursor was in the nonclient area of the window.	
WM_NCMBUTTONDOWN	Notification that the user has pressed the center mouse button while the mouse cursor was in the nonclient area of the window.	
WM_NCMBUTTONUP	Notification that the user released the center mouse button while the mouse cursor was in the nonclient area of the window.	
WM_NCMOUSEMOVE	Notification that the mouse has been moved in the nonclient area of the window.	
WM_NCPAINT	Notification that the nonclient area of a window needs to be repainted.	
WM_NCRBUTTONDBLCLK	Notification that the user double-clicked the right mouse button while the mouse cursor was in the nonclient area of the window.	
WM_NCRBUTTONDOWN	Notification that the user pressed the right mouse button while the mouse cursor was in the nonclient area of the window.	
WM_NCRBUTTONUP	Notification that the user released the right mouse button while the mouse cursor was in the nonclient area of the window.	
WM_NEXTDLGCTL	Moves the input focus to another child window control within a dialog box.	
WM_OTHERWINDOW-CREATED	Sent to all overlapped and popup windows running in the system when a new top-level window is created. (Win 3.1)	
WM_OTHERWINDOW-DESTROYED	Sent to all overlapped and popup windows running in the system when a new top-level window is destroyed. (Win 3.1)	
WM_NULL	No action is taken.	
WM_PAINT *	Notification that the client area of a window needs to be repainted.	
WM_PAINTCLIPBOARD	Used by clipboard viewer applications as notification that the viewer data should be repainted.	
WM_PAINTICON	Notification that a minimized (iconic) window needs to be repainted.	
WM_PALETTECHANGED	Notification that the system color palette has changed.	
WM_PARENTNOTIFY	Notification to the parent window that a child window is being created, destroyed, or is being clicked with the mouse.	
WM_PASTE	Copies the text from the clipboard into an edit control.	
WM_QUERYDRAGICON	Notification that the user is about to move a minimized window.	

WM_QUERYENDSESSION	Notification that the Windows session is about to be ended.
WM_QUERYNEWPALETTE	Notification that an application is about to receive the input focus.
WM_QUERYOPEN	Notification that a minimized window is about to be restored.
WM_QUIT	This is the final message processed by an application.
WM_RBUTTONDBLCLK	Notification that the user double-clicked the right mouse button.
WM_RBUTTONDOWN	Notification that the user pressed the right mouse button.
WM_RBUTTONUP	Notification that the user released the right mouse button.
WM_RENDERALLFORMATS	Notification to the owner of one or more clipboard formats that the application program is exiting.
WM_RENDERFORMAT	Notification to the owner of the clipboard that data should be put into the clipboard in the specified format.
WM_SETCURSOR	Notification that the mouse cursor is moving within a window.
WM_SETFOCUS *	Notification that a window has gained the input focus.
WM_SETFONT	Used to change the font used in dialog box controls.
WM_SETREDRAW	Sent to list box and combo box controls prior to adding or deleting a number of items.
WM_SETTEXT *	Used to change the title or text of a window.
WM_SHOWWINDOW	Notification that a window is to be hidden or shown.
WM_SIZE *	Notification that the size of a window has changed.
WM_SIZECLIPBOARD	Notification that the clipboard viewer application has changed size.
WM_SPOOLERSTATUS	Notification from the Print Manager that a job has been added or subtracted from the printer queue.
WM_SYSCHAR	Generated by TranslateMessage() in the application's message loop when a WM_SYSKEYUP or WM_SYSKEYDOWN message is processed.
WM_SYSCOLORCHANGE	Notification that one or more of the system colors has changed.
WM_SYSCOMMAND	Notification that the user selected a system menu command.
WM_SYSDEADCHAR	Notification of a system dead character.
WM_SYSKEYDOWN	Notification that the user pressed a key while holding down the ⒜ℒⓉ key.
WM_SYSKEYUP	Notification that the user released a key while holding down the ⒜ℒⓉ key.
WM_TIMECHANGE	Notification that the system clock has been changed.
WM_TIMER *	Notification that one of the timers set with the SetTimer() function has passed its time interval.
WM_UNDO	Copies the text from the clipboard to the edit control's client area.
WM_USER	Programmer-defined messages are from WM_USER to 0x7FFF.
WM_VKEYTOITEM	Notification that the user pressed a key while a list box had the input focus.
WM_VSCROLL *	Notification that the user adjusted a vertical scroll bar.
WM_VSCROLLCLIPBOARD	Indicates that the clipboard viewer vertical scroll bar has been used.
WM_WININICHANGE	Notification that the WIN.INI file has been changed.

* Most frequently used messages.

Table 9-14. Window Message Summary. WM_WINDOWPOSCHANGED
WM_WINDOWPOSCHANGING

Window Message Descriptions

WM_ACTIVATE ■ Win 2.0 ■ Win 3.0 ■ Win 3.1

Purpose   Notification that a window has become active or inactive. The active window receives all keyboard input and will have a highlighted caption area or dialog frame (for dialog boxes).

Parameters
wParam   WORD: 0 if the window is inactive. 1 if the window became active via keyboard input or a SetActiveWindow() function call. 2 if the window became active via mouse input. Usually, it is not important how a window becomes active, so the program can just check for *wParam* to be nonzero for active status.

lParam   DWORD: The high-order word is nonzero if the window is minimized, zero if not. The low-order word is a handle to the window becoming active if *wParam* is 0, or a handle to the window becoming inactive if *wParam* is nonzero. In the latter case, the low-order word may be NULL, if no prior window was active.

WM_ACTIVATEAPP ■ Win 2.0 ■ Win 3.0 ■ Win 3.1

Purpose   Notification that the window being activated belongs to another application program. This message is sent to both the window becoming active and the window becoming inactive.

Parameters
wParam   WORD: Nonzero if the window is becoming active, zero if the window will become inactive.

lParam   DWORD: The task handle for the application program. If *wParam* is zero, the low-order word of *lParam* contains the task handle of the application that owns the window being deactivated. If *wParam* is nonzero, the low-order word of *lParam* contains the task handle of the application that owns the window being activated. The task handles for all running programs can be found using the EnumTasks() function.

WM_ASKCBFORMATNAME ■ Win 2.0 ■ Win 3.0 ■ Win 3.1

Purpose   Requests that the name of a custom clipboard format be copied into a character string buffer. This message is used with the CF_OWNERDISPLAY format of clipboard data.

Parameters
wParam   WORD: Specifies the maximum number of bytes to copy.

lParam   DWORD: A far pointer to the buffer which will hold the clipboard data format name. Your program should save the clipboard format name in this buffer when the WM_ASKCBFORMATNAME message is received.

WM_CANCELMODE ■ Win 2.0 ■ Win 3.0 ■ Win 3.1

Purpose   Notification that the system has cancelled a mode it was in. For example, this message is sent when a message box or system modal dialog box is displayed, or when a scroll bar is used, or when a window is moved.

Parameters
wParam   WORD: Not used.

lParam   DWORD: Not used.

WM_CHANGECBCHAIN ■ Win 2.0 ■ Win 3.0 ■ Win 3.1

Purpose   Notification that a window in the clipboard viewer chain of applications is being removed from the chain. Each window receiving this message should use SendMessage() to pass the message on to the next window in the chain. See Chapter 17 for details.

Parameters

wParam WORD: The handle of the window being removed from the clipboard viewer chain.

lParam DWORD: Contains the handle of the next window in the clipboard viewer chain. If the window being removed is the next window in the chain, clipboard messages will be passed to the window who's handle is specified in *lParam*.

WM_CHAR ■ Win 2.0 ■ Win 3.0 ■ Win 3.1

Purpose Transmits the ASCII value of a character key pressed on the keyboard. This message is generated by the TranslateMessage() function in the program's message loop.

Parameters

wParam WORD: The ASCII value of the key pressed.

lParam DWORD: Contains coded data about the key pressed, as shown in Table 9-15. Usually, this data is ignored.

Bits	Meaning	⊠
0-15 (low order word)	The repeat count. This is the number of times the character was repeated because the user held down a key.	
16-23	The keyboard scan code.	
24	1 if an extended key, such as a function key or a key on the numeric keypad.	
25-28	Not available.	
29	1 if the (ALT) key was held down when the key was pressed, 0 if not.	
30	1 if the key is down before the message was sent, 0 if not.	
31	1 if the key is being released, 0 if the key is being pressed.	

Table 9-15. WM_CHAR lParam Coding.

WM_CHARTOITEM □ Win 2.0 ■ Win 3.0 ■ Win 3.1

Purpose This message is sent by a child window list box control to its parent. The list box must have been created with the LBS_WANTKEYBOARDINPUT style to generate this message. The message is sent when the list box receives a WM_CHAR message. The message allows a keyboard shortcut to be added for quick selection of the first list box item that starts with the given character. The window processing function should return a value in response to receiving this message. A returned value of zero or greater specifies the index of a selected item in the list box. A returned value of –1 specifies that the list box should do its default processing of keyboard input (usually ignored). A returned value of –2 specifies that no action should be taken by the list box.

Parameters

wParam WORD: The ASCII value of the key the user pressed.

lParam DWORD: Contains the current caret position in the high-order word and the window handle of the list box in the low-order word.

WM_CHILDACTIVATE ■ Win 2.0 ■ Win 3.0 ■ Win 3.1

Purpose Sent to a child window's parent when a child window is moved or activated. For example, after SetWindowPos() is used to move a child window.

Parameters

wParam WORD: Not used.

lParam DWORD: Not used.

WM_CLEAR

■ Win 2.0　■ Win 3.0　■ Win 3.1

Purpose　Notification that the user is deleting the current selection in an edit control without copying it to the clipboard.

Syntax　SendMessage (HWND *hControl*, **WM_CLEAR**, WORD *wParam*, DWORD *lParam*)

Parameters

hControl　HWND: The edit control's window handle.

wParam　WORD: Not used. Set to 0.

lParam　DWORD: Not used. Set to 0L.

WM_CLOSE

■ Win 2.0　■ Win 3.0　■ Win 3.1

Purpose　Notification that a window will be closed in response to the user pressing (ALT)-(F4) or selecting "close" from the system menu. Passing this message to DefWindowProc() calls the Destroy-Window() function. Intercepting the message prevents the window from being destroyed (closed).

Parameters

wParam　WORD: Not used.

lParam　DWORD: Not used.

WM_COMMAND

■ Win 2.0　■ Win 3.0　■ Win 3.1

Purpose　Notification that the user has selected a menu item or child window control, or has used an accelerator key.

Parameters

wParam　WORD: Contains the menu item or child window control ID value. For child window controls, the ID value is specified as the *hMenu* parameter when CreateWindow() is called.

lParam　DWORD: The low-order word is zero if the message is from a menu item selection. The high-order word is one if the message is from an accelerator keystroke. If the message is from a child window control, the high-order word is the notification code (such as BN_CLICKED), and the low-order word is the window handle of the control.

WM_COMPACTING

☐ Win 2.0　■ Win 3.0　■ Win 3.1

Purpose　Notification that the system is running low on memory. Windows determines when to send this message by calculating how much time is spent compacting memory. When more than 12.5% of the processing time is going into memory compacting, WM_COMPACTING is sent to all active applications. Applications receiving this message should free as much memory as possible.

Parameters

wParam　WORD: Specifies how much CPU time is going into compacting memory. 0xFFFF is 100%, 0x0000 is 0%.

lParam　DWORD: Not used.

WM_COMPAREITEM

■ Win 2.0　■ Win 3.0　■ Win 3.1

Purpose　Notification that a new item is being added into an owner-redrawn list box or combo box created with the LBS_SORT or CBS_SORT styles. Windows uses the COMPAREITEMSTRUCT data structure to facilitate comparison of items. This structure is defined in WINDOWS.H as follows:

```
/* COMPAREITEMSTRUCT for ownerdraw sorting */
typedef struct tagCOMPAREITEMSTRUCT
```

```
  {
    WORD          CtlType;        /* ODT_LISTBOX, or ODT_COMBOBOX*/
    WORD          CtlID;          /* control id number for the list box, or combo box */
    HWND          hwndItem;       /* control window handle */
    WORD          itemID1;        /* item id 1 */
    DWORD         itemData1;      /* item 1s 32-bit value */
    WORD          itemID2;        /* item id 2 */
    DWORD         itemData2;      /* item 2s 32-bit value */
  } COMPAREITEMSTRUCT;
typedef COMPAREITEMSTRUCT NEAR *PCOMPAREITEMSTRUCT;
typedef COMPAREITEMSTRUCT FAR  *LPCOMPAREITEMSTRUCT;
```

When the program owning the list or combo box receives this message, it should return a value specifying the relative ordering of the two items referenced in the COMPAREITEMSTRUCT as follows:

−1 Item 1 comes before item 2.

0 Item 1 and 2 sort the same.

1 Item 2 comes before item 1.

Typically, the program owning the list or combo box will receive this message a number of times, until the position of the new item can be completely determined. See the example owner-redrawn combo box in the combo box section of this chapter.

Parameters

wParam   WORD: Not used.

lParam   DWORD: Contains a far pointer to a COMPAREITEMSTRUCT.

WM_COPY   ■ Win 2.0   ■ Win 3.0   ■ Win 3.1

Purpose   Copies selected text within an edit control to the clipboard. The text is stored in CF_TEXT format in the clipboard.

Syntax   SendMessage (HWND *hControl*, **WM_COPY**, WORD *wParam*, DWORD *lParam*)

Parameters

hControl   HWND: The edit control's window handle.

wParam   WORD: Not used. Set to 0.

lParam   DWORD: Not used. Set to 0L.

WM_CREATE   ■ Win 2.0   ■ Win 3.0   ■ Win 3.1

Purpose   Notification that a window is being created. This is a good place to do program data initialization and startup routines. This message is processed before CreateWindow() returns and before the window is made visible.

Parameters

wParam   WORD: Not used.

lParam   DWORD: A far pointer to a CREATESTRUCT data structure. This structure is defined in WINDOWS.H as follows:

```
typedef struct tagCREATESTRUCT
  {
    LPSTR               lpCreateParams;
    HANDLE              hInstance;
    HANDLE              hMenu;
    HWND                hwndParent;
    int                 cy;
    int                 cx;
    int                 y;
    int                 x;
```

```
    LONG              style;
    LPSTR             lpszName;
    LPSTR             lpszClass;
    DWORD             dwExStyle;
 } CREATESTRUCT;
typedef CREATESTRUCT FAR   *LPCREATESTRUCT;
```

WM_CTLCOLOR   ■ Win 2.0   ■ Win 3.0   ■ Win 3.1

Purpose   Notification that a child window control is about to be drawn. This gives the parent program a chance to change the default colors for the text and background used. The WndProc() function receiving this message can load a brush to paint the background and return the handle to the brush. If the brush uses a pattern, call UnrealizeObject() to align the brush with the upper left corner of the object before returning the handle to the brush.

Parameters

wParam   WORD: The display context for the child window control. Equivalent to the returned value from GetDC().

lParam   DWORD: The low-order word contains a handle to the child window control. The high-order word contains one of the values listed in Table 9-16.

Value	Meaning	
CTLCOLOR_BTN	Button control.	
CTLCOLOR_DLG	A dialog box.	
CTLCOLOR_EDIT	An edit control.	
CTLCOLOR_LISTBOX	A list box control.	
CTLCOLOR_MSGBOX	A message box.	
CTLCOLOR_SCROLLBAR	A scroll bar control.	
CTLCOLOR_STATIC	A static text control.	

Table 9-16. WM_CTLCOLOR Values.

Warning   If the application program processes the WM_CTLCOLOR message, it must return a handle to the brush to use in painting the background of the window. Otherwise, the system will crash.

WM_CUT   ■ Win 2.0   ■ Win 3.0   ■ Win 3.1

Purpose   Copies the current selected text from an edit control to the clipboard, and then deletes the text from the edit control's client area.

Syntax   SendMessage (HWND *hControl*, **WM_CUT**, WORD *wParam*, DWORD *lParam*)

Parameters

hControl   HWND: The window handle of the edit control.

wParam   WORD: Not used.

lParam   DWORD: Not used.

WM_DDE_ACK to WM_DDE_UNADVISE
These messages are covered in Chapter 30, *Dynamic Data Exchange*, and are defined in the DDE.H header file.

WM_DEADCHAR   ■ Win 2.0   ■ Win 3.0   ■ Win 3.1

Purpose   Notification that the user selected a non-English language accent or special character that will change the value of the next character typed. This occurs when WM_KEYUP and WM_KEYDOWN messages for special characters are sent. The character following the dead character is the accent or special character. For example, if the system is using German as the default language (determined by the Setup program during installation of Windows), the sequence dead key, umlaut, and the O key will be sent to create an umlauted O.

Parameters

wParam   WORD: The repeat count (the number of times the key was repeated as a result of the key being held down).

lParam   DWORD: Contains coded data about the key pressed. Usually this data is ignored. (See Table 9-17 for information.)

Bits	Meaning	⊠
0-15 (low order word)	The repeat count. This is the number of times the character was repeated because the user held down a key.	
16-23	The keyboard scan code.	
24	1 if an extended key, such as a function key or a key on the numeric keypad.	
25-28	Not available.	
29	1 if the (ALT) key was held down when the key was pressed, 0 if not.	
30	1 if the key was down before the message was sent, 0 if not.	
31	1 if the key is being released, 0 if the key is being pressed.	

Table 9-17. WM_DEADCHAR lParam Coding.

WM_DELETEITEM

☐ Win 2.0   ■ Win 3.0   ■ Win 3.1

Purpose   Notification to the parent of an owner-redrawn combo or list box that an item has been removed. This is sent when a single item is removed or the entire box has had its contents reset, or when the list or combo box is destroyed. The message includes a pointer to a DELETEITEMSTRUCT structure, defined in WINDOWS.H as

```
/* DELETEITEMSTRUCT for ownerdraw */
typedef struct tagDELETEITEMSTRUCT
{
   WORD        CtlType;       /* ODT_LISTBOX, or ODT_COMBOBOX */
   WORD        CtlID;         /* control id number for the list box, or combo box */
   WORD        itemID;        /* the item's id number in the list or combo box */
   HWND        hwndItem;      /* control window handle */
   DWORD       itemData;      /* item's 32-bit data */
} DELETEITEMSTRUCT;
typedef DELETEITEMSTRUCT NEAR *PDELETEITEMSTRUCT;
typedef DELETEITEMSTRUCT FAR  *LPDELETEITEMSTRUCT;
```

You can use this message to free any memory associated with bitmapped images or similar objects if they are no longer needed by the list or combo box. The message may be received more than once if several items are being deleted.

Parameters

wParam   WORD: Not used.

lParam   DWORD: A far pointer to a DELETEITEMSTRUCT structure for the item being deleted.

WM_DESTROY

■ Win 2.0   ■ Win 3.0   ■ Win 3.1

Purpose   Notification that a window is being destroyed after it has been removed from the screen. This message is sent to the window after the window image is removed from the screen. WM_DESTROY is sent to the parent window before any of the children are destroyed. If the window being destroyed is part of the clipboard viewer chain, the window must remove itself from the chain by calling ChangeClipboardChain(). If the window being destroyed is the last application window, without a parent, it should call PostQuitMessage() in response to this message.

Parameters

wParam   WORD: Not used.

lParam   DWORD: Not used.

WM_DESTROYCLIPBOARD   ■ Win 2.0   ■ Win 3.0   ■ Win 3.1

Purpose   Notification to the clipboard owner that the clipboard has been emptied by a call to EmptyClipboard().

Parameters

wParam   WORD: Not used.

lParam   DWORD: Not used.

WM_DEVMODECHANGE   ■ Win 2.0   ■ Win 3.0   ■ Win 3.1

Purpose   Sent to all top-level windows when the user changes the name of a device in the WIN.INI file.

Parameters

wParam   WORD: Not used.

lParam   DWORD: A pointer to a character string containing the name of the device changed in WIN.INI.

WM_DRAWCLIPBOARD   ■ Win 2.0   ■ Win 3.0   ■ Win 3.1

Purpose   Windows automatically sends this message to the first window of the clipboard viewer chain when the contents of the clipboard change. Each window in the chain should send the message on to the next window in the viewer chain. A handle to the next window in the chain can be obtained with SetClipboardViewer().

Parameters

wParam   WORD: Not used.

lParam   DWORD: Not used.

WM_DRAWITEM   □ Win 2.0   ■ Win 3.0   ■ Win 3.1

Purpose   Notification to the owner of an owner-drawn button, list box, or combo box that one of the items in the list has changed. The message passes a pointer to a DRAWITEMSTRUCT structure, defined in Windows as

```
/* DRAWITEMSTRUCT for ownerdraw */
typedef struct tagDRAWITEMSTRUCT{
    WORD        CtlType;        /* ODT_MENU, ODT_LISTBOX, ODT_COMBOBOX, or ODT_BUTTON */
    WORD        CtlID;          /* control id number for the list box, combo box or button */
    WORD        itemID;         /* the item's id number in the list or combo box */
    WORD        itemAction;     /* ODA_DRAWENTIRE, ODA_SELECT, or ODA_FOCUS */
    WORD        itemState;      /* ODS_SELECTED, ODS_GRAYED, ODS_DISABLED, ODS_CHECKED */
    HWND        hwndItem;       /* the item's handle */              /* or ODS_FOCUS */
    HDC         hDC;            /* the item's device context */
    RECT        rcItem;         /* the bounding rectangle of the item */
    DWORD       itemData;       /* here is where the 32-bit data goes */
} DRAWITEMSTRUCT;
typedef DRAWITEMSTRUCT NEAR *PDRAWITEMSTRUCT;
typedef DRAWITEMSTRUCT FAR  *LPDRAWITEMSTRUCT;
```

The *itemAction* element of the structure determines if the element is to be drawn, shown as selected, or shown as having the focus. Be sure to release any objects used to draw the item before returning from processing this message. An example of an owner-drawn combo box appears in the combo box section of this chapter.

Parameters

wParam   WORD: Not used.

lParam   DWORD: A far pointer to the DRAWITEMSTRUCT structure for the item.

WM_DROPFILES   □ Win 2.0   □ Win 3.0   ■ Win 3.1

Purpose   Sent when the left mouse button is released over an application which is registered as a recipient of dropped files.

Parameters

wParam   WORD: Contains a handle to an internal data structure describing the dropped files. The new Windows 3.1 registration functions are used to create these data structures.

lParam   DWORD: Not used.

WM_ENABLE   ■ Win 2.0   ■ Win 3.0   ■ Win 3.1

Purpose   Notification that a window has been enabled or disabled. Disabling is used to stop a child window button control from functioning. The text inside of the button is grayed. The EnableWindow() function is used to change a window's status to/from enabled or disabled.

Parameters

wParam   WORD: Nonzero if enabled, zero if disabled.

lParam   DWORD: Not used.

WM_ENDSESSION   ■ Win 2.0   ■ Win 3.0   ■ Win 3.1

Purpose   Final notification that the Windows session is being stopped. This message follows WM_QUERY-ENDSESSION, if all windows returned a nonzero response to that message.

Parameters

wParam   WORD: Nonzero if the Windows session is being ended, zero if not. If a nonzero value is sent, Windows can terminate at any time. The application should save any data in preparation for termination.

lParam   DWORD: Not used.

WM_ENTERIDLE   ■ Win 2.0   ■ Win 3.0   ■ Win 3.1

Purpose   Notification that a modal dialog box or menu has been activated, but has no messages to process. This is a good point to set a timer if the dialog or message block should be removed automatically.

Parameters

wParam   WORD: Contains MSGF_DIALOGBOX or MSGF_MENU if the system is idle due to a dialog box or menu, respectively.

lParam   DWORD: The low-order word contains the handle of the dialog box or the window containing the menu. The high-order word is not used.

WM_ERASEBKGND   ■ Win 2.0   ■ Win 3.0   ■ Win 3.1

Purpose   Notification that the background of a window's client area needs to be repainted. Normally, the background is repainted using the brush specified in the window's class definition. If no background brush was specified in the class definition (*hbrbackground* = NULL), the application should process WM_ERASEBKGND messages. If the background brush contains a pattern, use

UnrealizeObject() to align the brush with the window's top left corner. Be sure the window's device context is in the default MM_TEXT mapping mode before using this function to avoid painting only a portion of the client area.

Parameters

wParam   WORD: Contains the device context handle for the background.

lParam   DWORD: Not used.

Returns   The function processing this message should return nonzero if the background was erased, zero if not.

WM_FONTCHANGE   ■ Win 2.0   ■ Win 3.0   ■ Win 3.1

Purpose   Notification that the number of fonts available to applications has changed, probably because an application used the AddFontResource() or RemoveFontResource() function. Any application that changes the fonts on the system should send this message to all running applications. (Using PostMessage() with *hWnd* set equal to 0xFFFF, sends a message to all applications.)

Parameters

wParam   WORD: Not used.

lParam   DWORD: Not used.

WM_GETDLGCODE   ■ Win 2.0   ■ Win 3.0   ■ Win 3.1

Purpose   Windows sends this message to a control's input procedure. This allows the control to specify to what type of keyboard input the control will respond. Generally used in creating custom controls.

Parameters

wParam   WORD: Not used.

lParam   DWORD: Not used.

Returns   The application receiving this message should return one or more of the following values, combined using the C language binary OR operator (|). This will establish which types of messages are, as listed in Table 9-18, processed by the program, skipping Windows' default keyboard handling.

Value	Meaning	⊠
DLGC_ARROWS	The direction keys.	
DLGC_DEFPUSHBUTTON	Default pushbutton.	
DLGC_HASSETSEL	EM_SETSEL messages.	
DLGC_PUSHBUTTON	All pushbuttons.	
DLGC_RADIOBUTTON	All radio buttons.	
DLGC_WANTALLKEYS	All keyboard input.	
DLGC_WANTCHARS	WM_CHAR messages.	
DLGC_WANTMESSAGE	All keyboard input (the application passes this message to the control).	
DLGC_WANTTAB	The tab key.	

Table 9-18. WM_GETDLGCODE Return Flags.

WM_GETFONT   □ Win 2.0   ■ Win 3.0   ■ Win 3.1

Purpose   Retrieves the font currently being used by a child window control (edit, static text, list box, etc.).

Syntax	*dwFont* = SendMessage (HWND *hControl*, **WM_GETFONT**, WORD *wParam*, DWORD *lParam*)
Returns	DWORD, the handle to the font. NULL is the system font.
Parameters	
hControl	HWND: The window handle of the child window control.
wParam	WORD: Not used.
lParam	DWORD: Not used.

WM_GETMINMAXINFO
■ Win 2.0　　■ Win 3.0　　■ Win 3.1

Purpose　Notifies the application that Windows is checking the size of the window when minimized or maximized, giving the application a chance to change the default values. This message is sent by CreateWindow() before CreateWindow() returns. Use the GetSystemMetrics() function to retrieve the size of the screen, window borders, menu bar, etc. as needed to calculate the size of window your application needs.

Parameters
wParam　WORD: Not used.

lParam　DWORD: A far pointer to an array of five POINT structures. Each point holds the *X* and *Y* dimensions in pixels for the window in one of several states. The point array values are listed in Table 9-19.

Point	Used For	⊠
rgpt[0]	Used internally by Windows.	
rgpt[1]	The maximized size. Defaults to the screen size.	
rgpt[2]	The position of the upper left corner when the window is maximized. The default values are SM_CXFRAME, SM_CYFRAME for *X,Y*.	
rgpt[3]	The smallest tracking size. The minimum tracking size is the smallest size obtainable by using the borders to adjust the window size. The default minimum is equal to the icon size.	
rgpt[4]	The maximum tracking size. Defaults to the screen size. The maximum tracking size is the largest size obtainable by using the borders to adjust the window size.	

Table 9-19. WM_GETMINMAXINFO Point Array Values.

The array of five points is initialized to the default values when the message is transmitted by Windows. The application can change any of the values in the array before returning control to Windows. The modified values are then used by Windows to size the application's window.

WM_GETTEXT
■ Win 2.0　　■ Win 3.0　　■ Win 3.1

Purpose　Used to copy text from a child window control into a character buffer. For edit and combo box controls, the text to be copied is the contents of the edit box. For buttons, it is the button text. For list boxes, the text is the currently selected item. For other windows (child windows, popups), the text is the window's caption. Sending this message is equivalent to calling the GetWindowText() function.

Syntax　*dwReturned* = SendMessage (HWND *hControl*, **BM_GETTEXT**, WORD *wParam*, DWORD *lParam*)

Returns　DWORD, the number of characters copied. It is LB_ERR or CB_ERR if the control is a list or combo box, but no selection has been made.

Parameters
hControl　HWND: The window handle of the child window control.

| *wParam* | WORD: The maximum number of characters to copy. |
| *lParam* | DWORD: A far pointer to a character buffer that will receive the string. |

WM_GETTEXTLENGTH ■ Win 2.0   ■ Win 3.0   ■ Win 3.1

Purpose	Used to determine the number of characters in a child window control. For edit and combo box controls, the text is the contents of the edit box. For buttons, it is the button text. For list boxes, the text is the currently selected item. For other windows (child windows, popups), the text is the window's caption. Sending this message is equivalent to calling the GetWindowTextLength() function.
Syntax	*dwReturned* = SendMessage (HWND *hControl*, **BM_GETTEXTLENGTH**, WORD *wParam*, DWORD *lParam*)
Returns	DWORD, the number of characters in the control.
Parameters	
hControl	HWND: The window handle of the child window control.
wParam	WORD: Not used.
lParam	DWORD: Not used.

WM_HSCROLL ■ Win 2.0   ■ Win 3.0   ■ Win 3.1

Purpose	Notification that the user has adjusted a horizontal scroll bar.
Parameters	
wParam	WORD: One of the codes in Table 9-20.

Value	Meaning
SB_BOTTOM	Generated if the scroll bar has the input focus and the (END) key is pressed. Not generated by mouse actions.
SB_ENDSCROLL	Sent when the scroll activity stops.
SB_LINEDOWN	Clicked the arrow on the left.
SB_LINEUP	Clicked the arrow on the right.
SB_PAGEDOWN	Clicked the area of the scroll bar between the left arrow and the thumb.
SB_PAGEUP	Clicked the area of the scroll bar between the right arrow and the thumb.
SB_THUMBPOSITION	The message passes the position of the thumb as the low-order word of *lParam*.
SB_THUMBTRACK	The thumb is being dragged. The current position is passed as the low-order word of *lParam*.
SB_TOP	Generated if the scroll bar has the input focus and the (HOME) key is pressed. Not generated by mouse actions.

Table 9-20. Scroll Bar Codes.

| *lParam* | DWORD: The high-order word contains the window handle of the scroll bar. If the scroll bar is attached to a the boundary of a popup window, the high-order value is not used. The low-order word contains the thumb position if either the SB_THUMBPOSITION or SB_THUMBTRACK value for *wParam* is passed. |

WM_HSCROLLCLIPBOARD ■ Win 2.0   ■ Win 3.0   ■ Win 3.1

| **Purpose** | Used with the CF_OWNERDISPLAY format of data type for the clipboard used by clipboard viewer programs. The message indicates that the clipboard viewer horizontal scroll bar has been used. |

Parameters

wParam	WORD: Contains a handle to the clipboard viewer program.
lParam	DWORD: The low-order word contains one of the scroll bar codes shown in Table 9-20, used in WM_SCROLL messages. The high-order word contains the thumb position if the SB_THUMB-POSITION or SB_THUMBTRACK value is passed in the low-order word. Otherwise, the high-order word is not used.

WM_ICONERASEBKGND ☐ Win 2.0 ■ Win 3.0 ■ Win 3.1

Purpose Notification that a minimized (iconic) window needs to have the background painted. This message is received if a class icon is defined for the window. If there is no class icon defined (see RegisterClass()), WM_ERASEBKGND is sent instead. If this message is processed by the default Windows message processing logic in DefWindowProc(), the background of the minimized window is painted with the desktop window's class background brush.

Parameters

wParam	WORD: Contains the iconic window's device context.
lParam	DWORD: Not used.

WM_INITDIALOG ■ Win 2.0 ■ Win 3.0 ■ Win 3.1

Purpose Notification that a dialog box is about to be displayed. This is similar to WM_CREATE messages in the main WndProc() function. WM_INITDIALOG is sent every time the dialog is displayed, not just when the program starts. WM_INITDIALOG messages offer a good opportunity to initialize any data associated with the dialog box.

Parameters

wParam	WORD: The ID value of the first control to have the input focus when the dialog box starts. This is usually the first item with the WS_TABSTOP style.
lParam	DWORD: If the dialog box was created with either CreateDialogIndirectParam(), CreateDialog-Param(), DialogBoxIndirectParam(), or DialogBoxParam(), this value will hold the *dwInit-Param* data passed when the dialog box was created. Otherwise (with the normal dialog box definition in the resource .RC file), the *lParam* value is not used.

WM_INITMENU ■ Win 2.0 ■ Win 3.0 ■ Win 3.1

Purpose Notification that the user has clicked a main menu item. This message is sent before the menu is accessed. Only one WM_INITMENU message is generated per access to the menu, no matter how many items the mouse may click. It can be used as a reminder to change menu items (grayed, checked, etc.) before the menu selections are activated.

Parameters

wParam	WORD: Contains the menu handle.
lParam	DWORD: Not used.

WM_INITMENUPOPUP ■ Win 2.0 ■ Win 3.0 ■ Win 3.1

Purpose Notification that the window is about to display a popup menu. This can be used as a reminder to change popup menu items (grayed, checked, etc.) before the menu selections are activated.

Parameters

wParam	WORD: The handle of the popup menu.
lParam	DWORD: The low-order word contains the index of the popup menu in the main menu. The high-order word is nonzero if the popup menu is the system menu, zero otherwise.

WM_KEYDOWN ■ Win 2.0 ■ Win 3.0 ■ Win 3.1

Purpose   Notification that a key was pressed. This notification is sent to the window with the input focus as long as the (ALT) key was not depressed at the time of the keypress. WM_SYSKEYDOWN messages are sent if the (ALT) key is down, or if no window has the input focus. SYSKEY messages also cover the system functions such as switching between windows ((ALT)-(TAB), (ALT)-(ESC), etc.).

Parameters

wParam   WORD: The virtual key code of the key. See Chapter 7, *Keyboard Support,* for a list of virtual key codes.

lParam   DWORD: The contents are encoded as shown in Table 9-21.

Bits	Meaning	⊠
0-15 (low order word)	The repeat count. This is the number of times the character was repeated because the user held down a key.	
16-23	The keyboard scan code.	
24	1 if an extended key, such as a function key or a key on the numeric keypad.	
25-28	Not available	
29	1 if the (ALT) key was held down when the key was pressed, 0 if not. Always 0 in this case.	
30	1 if the key is down before the message was sent, 0 if not.	
31	1 if the key is being released, 0 if the key is being pressed.	

Table 9-21. The 32-Bit Keyboard Data For WM_KEYUP, WM_KEYDOWN.

WM_KEYUP ■ Win 2.0 ■ Win 3.0 ■ Win 3.1

Purpose   Notification that a key was released. This notification is sent to the window with the input focus as long as the (ALT) key was not depressed at the time of the keypress. WM_SYSKEYUP messages are sent if the (ALT) key is down, or if no window has the input focus. SYSKEY messages also cover the system functions such as switching between windows ((ALT)-(TAB), (ALT)-(ESC), etc.).

Parameters

wParam   WORD: The virtual key code of the key. See Chapter 7, *Keyboard Support*, for a list of virtual key codes.

lParam   DWORD: The contents are encoded, as shown in Table 9-21 in the WM_KEYDOWN description.

WM_KILLFOCUS ■ Win 2.0 ■ Win 3.0 ■ Win 3.1

Purpose   Notification that a window is about to lose the input focus. If the application is displaying a caret, it should be destroyed at this point.

Parameters

wParam   WORD: Contains the handle of the window that is about to receive the input focus. May be NULL.

lParam   DWORD: Not used.

WM_LBUTTONDBLCLK ■ Win 2.0 ■ Win 3.0 ■ Win 3.1

Purpose   Notification that the user has double-clicked the left mouse button. Only windows that have a class structure that includes the CS_DBLCLKS style will receive these messages. Note that the single mouse click message always precedes a double-click message.

Parameters

wParam   WORD: Contains a value reflecting whether several keys were down at the time the message was sent. This can by any combination of the binary flags listed in Table 9-22.

Value	Meaning	⊠
MK_CONTROL	The CONTROL key is down.	
MK_LBUTTON	The left mouse button is down.	
MK_MBUTTON	The center mouse button (if any) is down.	
MK_RBUTTON	The right mouse button (if any) is down.	
MK_SHIFT	The SHIFT key is down.	

Table 9-22. Mouse Key Flags.

lParam   DWORD: The low-order word contains the X position of the cursor when the button was pressed. The Y position is in the high-order word. The coordinates are in pixels, relative to the upper left corner of the window.

WM_LBUTTONDOWN   ■ Win 2.0   ■ Win 3.0   ■ Win 3.1

Purpose   Notification that the user has pressed the left mouse button.

Parameters

wParam   WORD: Contains a value reflecting whether several keys were down at the time the message was sent. This can by any combination of the binary flags listed in Table 9-23.

Value	Meaning	⊠
MK_CONTROL	The CONTROL key is down.	
MK_LBUTTON	The left mouse button is down.	
MK_MBUTTON	The center mouse button (if any) is down.	
MK_RBUTTON	The right mouse button (if any) is down.	
MK_SHIFT	The SHIFT key is down.	

Table 9-23. Mouse Key Flags.

lParam   DWORD: The low-order word contains the X position of the cursor when the button was pressed. The Y position is in the high-order word. The coordinates are in pixels, relative to the upper left corner of the window.

WM_LBUTTONUP   ■ Win 2.0   ■ Win 3.0   ■ Win 3.1

Purpose   Notification that the user has released the left mouse button.

Parameters

wParam   WORD: Contains a value reflecting whether or not several keys were down at the time the message was sent. This can by any combination of the binary flags listed in Table 9-24.

Value	Meaning	⊠
MK_CONTROL	The CONTROL key is down.	
MK_LBUTTON	The left mouse button is down.	
MK_MBUTTON	The center mouse button (if any) is down.	
MK_RBUTTON	The right mouse button (if any) is down.	
MK_SHIFT	The SHIFT key is down.	

Table 9-24. Mouse Key Flags.

lParam   DWORD: The low-order word contains the *X* position of the cursor when the button was pressed. The *Y* position is in the high-order word. The coordinates are in pixels, relative to the upper left corner of the window.

WM_MBUTTONDBLCLK   ■ Win 2.0   ■ Win 3.0   ■ Win 3.1

Purpose   Notification that the user double-clicked the center mouse button. Only windows that have a class structure that includes the CS_DBLCLKS style will receive these messages. Note that the single mouse click message always precedes a double-click message.

Parameters

wParam   WORD: Contains a value reflecting whether several keys were down at the time the message was sent. This can by any combination of the binary flags in Table 9-25.

Value	Meaning	⊠
MK_CONTROL	The CONTROL key is down.	
MK_LBUTTON	The left mouse button is down.	
MK_MBUTTON	The center mouse button (if any) is down.	
MK_RBUTTON	The right mouse button (if any) is down.	
MK_SHIFT	The SHIFT key is down.	

Table 9-25. Mouse Key Flags.

lParam   DWORD: The low-order word contains the *X* position of the cursor when the button was pressed. The *Y* position is in the high-order word. The coordinates are in pixels, relative to the upper left corner of the window.

WM_MBUTTONDOWN   ■ Win 2.0   ■ Win 3.0   ■ Win 3.1

Purpose   Notification that the user has pressed the center mouse button.

Parameters

wParam   WORD: Contains a value reflecting whether or not several keys were down at the time the message was sent. This can by any combination of the binary flags listed in Table 9-26.

Value	Meaning	⊠
MK_CONTROL	The CONTROL key is down.	
MK_LBUTTON	The left mouse button is down.	
MK_MBUTTON	The center mouse button (if any) is down.	
MK_RBUTTON	The right mouse button (if any) is down.	
MK_SHIFT	The SHIFT key is down.	

Table 9-26. Mouse Key Flags.

lParam   DWORD: The low-order word contains the *X* position of the cursor when the button was pressed. The *Y* position is in the high-order word. The coordinates are in pixels, relative to the upper left corner of the window.

WM_MBUTTONUP   ■ Win 2.0   ■ Win 3.0   ■ Win 3.1

Purpose   Notification that the user has released the center mouse button.

Parameters

wParam WORD: Contains a value reflecting whether several keys were down at the time the message was sent. This can by any combination of the binary flags listed in Table 9-27.

Value	Meaning	⊠
MK_CONTROL	The CONTROL key is down.	
MK_LBUTTON	The left mouse button is down.	
MK_MBUTTON	The center mouse button (if any) is down.	
MK_RBUTTON	The right mouse button (if any) is down.	
MK_SHIFT	The SHIFT key is down.	

Table 9-27. Mouse Key Flags.

lParam DWORD: The low-order word contains the *X* position of the cursor when the button was pressed. The *Y* position is in the high-order word. The coordinates are in pixels, relative to the upper left corner of the window.

WM_MDIACTIVATE
☐ Win 2.0 ■ Win 3.0 ■ Win 3.1

Purpose Used to activate and deactivate child windows within a Multiple Document Interface (MDI) window. Activation of a MDI child window is similar to a window gaining the input focus. Once activated, the child window's border is highlighted, and all keyboard input is directed to the child. When receiving this message, an MDI child frequently changes the frame window menu using the WM_MDISETMENU message.

Syntax SendMessage (HWND *hClient*, **WM_MDIACTIVATE**, WORD *wParam*, DWORD *lParam*)

Parameters

hClient HWND: The window handle of the MDI client or child window.

wParam WORD: If the application is sending the message to the MDI client window, *wParam* contains the handle of the child window to activate. If the MDI client window is sending this to an MDI child window, *wParam* contains nonzero to activate the child window and zero to deactivate it.

lParam DWORD: NULL if the application is sending the message to the MDI client window. If the MDI client window message processing function is sending the message to an MDI child window, the high-order word contains the handle of the child window being deactivated, and the low-order word contains the handle of the child being activated.

WM_MDICASCADE
☐ Win 2.0 ■ Win 3.0 ■ Win 3.1

Purpose Arranges all of the child windows within the MDI client window in "cascade" format. This arrangement makes all of the window titles visible. If the frame window is too small, some of the child windows may not be visible after cascading.

Syntax SendMessage (HWND *hClient*, **WM_MDICASCADE**, WORD *wParam*, DWORD *lParam*)

Parameters

hClient HWND: The window handle of the MDI client window.

wParam WORD: The cascade flag. No flags are defined under Windows 3.0. Under Windows 3.1, the MDITILE_SKIPDISABLED flag prevents disabled MDI child windows from being tiled. Otherwise, set to 0.

lParam DWORD: Not used. Set equal to 0L.

WM_MDICREATE

☐ Win 2.0   ■ Win 3.0   ■ Win 3.1

Purpose   Creates an MDI child window. This message is sent to the client window to create a new child window. The title of the child window name is added to the window menu of the frame window.

Syntax   *dwReturned* = SendMessage (HWND *hClient*, **WM_MDICREATE**, WORD *wParam*, DWORD *lParam*)

Returns   DWORD. The MDI child window handle is in the low-order word. The high-order word is NULL.

Parameters

hClient   HWND: The window handle of the MDI client window.

wParam   WORD: Not used. Set equal to 0.

lParam   DWORD: A far pointer to a MDICREATESTRUCT structure. This is defined in WINDOWS.H as

```
typedef struct tagMDICREATESTRUCT
  {
  LPSTR     szClass;      /* class previously registered with RegisterClass() */
  LPSTR     szTitle;      /* title string */
  HANDLE    hOwner;       /* instance handle of the owner */
  int       x,y;          /* the X,Y position of the upper left corner */
  int       cx,cy;        /* the X, Y window size */
  LONG      style;        /* the style, usually 0 for MDI child windows */
  LONG      lParam;       /* app-defined stuff */
  } MDICREATESTRUCT;
typedef MDICREATESTRUCT FAR * LPMDICREATESTRUCT;
```

If another MDI child window is maximized, it will be restored before the new child window is created. The child window receives a WM_CREATE message, with the *lpCreateParams* field of the CREATESTRUCT containing a pointer to the MDICREATESTRUCT data structure data.

WM_MDIDESTROY

☐ Win 2.0   ■ Win 3.0   ■ Win 3.1

Purpose   Destroys (removes) an MDI child window. The child window title is removed from the window menu of the frame window.

Syntax   SendMessage (HWND *hClient*, **WM_MDIDESTROY**, WORD *wParam*, DWORD lParam)

Parameters

hClient   HWND: The window handle of the MDI client window.

wParam   WORD: The window handle of the MDI child window to destroy.

lParam   DWORD: Not used. Set equal to 0L.

WM_MDIGETACTIVE

☐ Win 2.0   ■ Win 3.0   ■ Win 3.1

Purpose   Obtains the handle of the currently active MDI child window.

Syntax   *dwReturned* = SendMessage (HWND *hClient*, **WM_MDIGETACTIVE**, WORD *wParam*, DWORD *lParam*)

Returns   DWORD. The low-order word contains the handle to the active MDI child window. The high-order word contains 1 if the MDI child is maximized, otherwise it contains 0.

Parameters

hClient   HWND: The window handle of the MDI client window.

wParam   WORD: Not used. Set equal to 0.

lParam   DWORD: Not used. Set equal to 0L.

WM_MDIICONARRANGE
☐ Win 2.0   ■ Win 3.0   ■ Win 3.1

Purpose   Causes the MDI client window to arrange all minimized MDI child windows at the bottom of the client area. This message has no effect on MDI child windows that are not minimized.

Syntax   SendMessage (HWND *hClient*, **WM_MDIICONARRANGE**, WORD *wParam*, DWORD *lParam*)

Parameters
hClient   HWND: The window handle of the MDI client window.

wParam   WORD: Not used. Set equal to 0.

lParam   DWORD: Not used. Set equal to 0L.

WM_MDIMAXIMIZE
☐ Win 2.0   ■ Win 3.0   ■ Win 3.1

Purpose   Causes an MDI child window to be maximized. This makes the child window exactly fill the client area of the client (frame) window. Windows automatically places the child window's system menu in the frame's menu bar and adds the child window's title to the frame window title.

   If a child window hidden behind the maximized window is activated, the maximized window is restored to its previous size, and the newly active window is maximized in its place.

Syntax   SendMessage (HWND *hClient*, **WM_MDIMAXIMIZE**, WORD *wParam*, DWORD *lParam*)

Parameters
hClient   HWND: The window handle of the MDI client window.

wParam   WORD: The MDI child window handle to be maximized.

lParam   DWORD: Not used. Set equal to 0L.

WM_MDINEXT
☐ Win 2.0   ■ Win 3.0   ■ Win 3.1

Purpose   Activates the next MDI child window. The next window is the one immediately behind the currently active window. The currently active window is placed behind all other MDI child windows after this message is processed. If the active MDI child window is maximized, the previously active window is restored in size, and the newly active window is maximized in its place.

Syntax   SendMessage (HWND *hClient*, **WM_MDINEXT**, WORD *wParam*, DWORD *lParam*)

Parameters
hClient   HWND: The window handle of the MDI client window.

wParam   WORD: Not used. Set equal to 0.

lParam   DWORD: Not used. Set equal to 0L.

WM_MDIRESTORE
☐ Win 2.0   ■ Win 3.0   ■ Win 3.1

Purpose   Restores an MDI child window to its previous size. This message is used after a child window has been either minimized or maximized.

Syntax   SendMessage (HWND *hClient*, **WM_MDIRESTORE**, WORD *wParam*, DWORD *lParam*)

Parameters
hClient   HWND: The window handle of the MDI client window.

wParam   WORD: The handle of the MDI child window to restore.

lParam   DWORD: Not used. Set equal to 0L.

WM_MDISETMENU

Purpose	Links a menu to the MDI frame window. The MDI child window list is maintained after the new menu is installed. (The MDI child window list is a popup menu, maintained by the MDICLIENT window as child windows are created and destroyed.)
Syntax	*dwReturned* = SendMessage (HWND hClient, **WM_MDISETMENU**, WORD *wParam*, DWORD *lParam*)
Returns	DWORD, contains a handle (HMENU) to the previous client window menu that was replaced.
Parameters	
hClient	HWND: The window handle of the MDI client window.
wParam	WORD: Not used. Set equal to 0.
lParam	DWORD: The low-order word contains the handle to the new client window menu, or NULL if there is to be no change in the client menu. The high-order word contains the handle to the new Windows popup menu, or NULL if there is to be no change in that menu.
Note	If more than one menu is in use, the MDI application will need to destroy menus before exiting to avoid having the menu resource data remain in memory after the application terminates. The application should call DrawMenuBar() after any change to a menu.

WM_MDITILE

Purpose	Causes an MDI client window to arrange all of its children in tile format. For two or three child windows, this is side-by-side, for four child windows, each child occupies one corner of the client area, etc.
Syntax	SendMessage (HWND *hClient*, **WM_MDITILE**, WORD *wParam*, DWORD *lParam*)
Parameters	
hClient	HWND: The window handle of the MDI client window.
wParam	WORD: The cascade flag. This is composed of one or two of the values in Table 9-28.

Value	Meaning	⊠
MDITILE_HORIZONTAL	Arranges the MDI child windows in a horizontal sequence.	
MDITILE_SKIPDISABLED (Win 3.1)	Disabled MDI child windows are not tiled.	
MDITILE_VERTICAL	Arranges the MDI child windows in a vertical sequence.	

Table 9-28. WM_MDITILE Flags.

MDITILE_SKIPDISABLED can be combined with either of the other flags using the C language binary OR operator (|).

lParam	DWORD: Not used. Set equal to 0L.

WM_MEASUREITEM

Purpose	Sent to the owner of an owner-redrawn button, list box, combo box, or menu item when the item is created. The owner function should fill in the MEASUREITEM data structure pointed to by *lParam* and return. For list boxes and combo boxes, the message is sent once for each item in the list.
wParam	WORD: Not used.
lParam	DWORD: A pointer to a MEASUREITEMSTRUCT structure. This is defined in WINDOWS. H as

```
/* MEASUREITEMSTRUCT for ownerdraw */
typedef struct tagMEASUREITEMSTRUCT

  {
  WORD        CtlType;        /* ODT_MENU, ODT_LISTBOX, ODT_COMBOBOX, or ODT_BUTTON */
  WORD        CtlID;          /* control id number for list box, combo box or button */
  WORD        itemID;         /* the item's id number in the list or combo box */
  WORD        itemWidth;      /* these are the values that need to */
  WORD        itemHeight;     /* be set to specify the size of the control */
  DWORD       itemData;       /* the 32-bit data goes here */
  } MEASUREITEMSTRUCT;
typedef MEASUREITEMSTRUCT NEAR *PMEASUREITEMSTRUCT;
typedef MEASUREITEMSTRUCT FAR  *LPMEASUREITEMSTRUCT;
```

The *itemWidth* and *itemHeight* elements should be set by the owner function before returning.

WM_MENUCHAR   ■ Win 2.0   ■ Win 3.0   · Win 3.1

Purpose   Informs the application that the user attempted to use a keyboard shortcut for a menu selection that did not match any menu item. This provides a way to give more than one keyboard shortcut to a single menu item.

Parameters

wParam   WORD: The ASCII character that the user pressed.

lParam   DWORD: The high-order word contains the menu handle. The low-order word contains either MF_POPUP if the menu is a popup menu, or MF_SYSMENU if the menu is the system menu.

Returns   The WndProc() processing this message can return a value to specify what action Windows should take. The value is returned in the high-order word of the value returned by WndProc(). This can be 0 to ignore the keystroke (default), 1 to tell Windows to close the menu, or 2 to make a different selection. In the last case, the low-order word of the return value should be the menu item number to select.

WM_MENUSELECT   ■ Win 2.0   ■ Win 3.0   ■ Win 3.1

Purpose   Notification that the user has selected a menu item.

Parameters

wParam   WORD: The menu item ID for the selection. If the user selected the caption of a popup menu, *wParam* contains the popup menu ID. The latter is normally ignored.

lParam   DWORD: The low-order word contains a combination of the binary flags listed in Table 9-29.

Value		Meaning
MF_BITMAP	0x0004	The item is a bitmap.
MF_CHECKED	0x0008	The item is checked.
MF_DISABLED	0x0002	The item is disabled.
MF_GRAYED	0x0001	The item is grayed.
MF_MOUSESELECT	0x8000	The item was selected with the mouse.
MF_OWNERDRAW	0x0100	The item is an owner-redrawn menu item.
MF_POPUP	0x0010	The item contains a popup submenu.
MF_SYSMENU	0x2000	The item is in the System menu. In this case, the high-order word is the handle of the menu.

Table 9-29. WM_MENUSELECT Flags.

WM_MOUSEACTIVATE ■ Win 2.0   ■ Win 3.0   ■ Win 3.1

Purpose Notification that the cursor is in an inactive window and the user clicked a mouse button. A parent window will receive this message unless the child window intercepts the message. Normally, the child window will pass the message on to DefWindowProc(), which in turn sends it to the parent window. The parent window can stop the message processing by returning TRUE when the message is received, rather than sending it on via DefWindowProc(). This will stop the child from being activated. The default action is to activate the child window that was clicked.

Parameters

wParam WORD: Contains a handle to the parent window.

lParam DWORD: The mouse message (such as WM_LBUTTONDOWN) is in the high-order word. The low-order word contains the mouse hit test. See Appendix B, *Useful Macros from Windows*, for a list of all the hit test codes.

Returns The receiving application can pass this message on to the DefWindowProc() function, or return a specific value. The returned value must be one of the codes in Table 9-30.

Value	Meaning	☒
MA_ACTIVATE	Activate the window.	
MA_NOACTIVATE	Do not activate the window.	
MA_ACTIVATEANDEAT	Activate the window, and discard the mouse event.	
MA_NOACTIVATEANDEAT (Win 3.1)	Do not activate the window, and discard the mouse event.	

Table 9-30. WM_MOUSEACTIVATE Return Codes.

If a child window passes the message on to DefWindowProc(), the message is sent on to the child's parent window without action or modification.

WM_MOUSEMOVE ■ Win 2.0   ■ Win 3.0   ■ Win 3.1

Purpose Notification that the user moved the mouse.

Parameters

wParam WORD: Contains a value reflecting whether several keys were down at the time the message was sent. This can be any combination of the binary flags in Table 9-31.

Value	Meaning	☒
MK_CONTROL	The CONTROL key is down.	
MK_LBUTTON	The left mouse button is down.	
MK_MBUTTON	The center mouse button (if any) is down.	
MK_RBUTTON	The right mouse button (if any) is down.	
MK_SHIFT	The SHIFT key as down.	

Table 9-31. Mouse Key Flags.

lParam DWORD: The low-order word contains the *X* position of the cursor when the button was pressed. The *Y* position is in the high-order word. The positions are measured in pixels, from the upper left corner of the window.

WM_MOVE
■ Win 2.0   ■ Win 3.0   ■ Win 3.1

Purpose   Notification that a window has been moved.

Parameters

wParam   WORD: Not used.

lParam   DWORD: The low-order word contains the *X* position of the upper left corner of the client area of the window. The *Y* position is in the high-order word. The location is given in screen coordinates, relative to the upper left corner of the screen.

WM_NCACTIVATE
■ Win 2.0   ■ Win 3.0   ■ Win 3.1

Purpose   Notification that the nonclient area of a window needs to be changed to reflect an active or inactive state. The default actions (performed by the DefWindowProc() function) draw a gray caption bar for an inactive window and a black caption bar for an active one.

Parameters

wParam   WORD: Nonzero if the icon or caption is active, zero if inactive.

lParam   DWORD: Not used.

WM_NCCALCSIZE
■ Win 2.0   ■ Win 3.0   ■ Win 3.1

Purpose   Sent when the size of a window, including the title, border, and caption areas, needs to be recalculated. Normally, this message is passed to DefWindowProc(), which fills in the needed data in the RECT data structure. The application program can intercept the message and fill in different values. This message is used in applications that draw their own nonclient areas or applications that control the sizing of the main window.

Parameters

wParam   WORD: Not used.

lParam   DWORD: A far pointer to a RECT data structure. The RECT data contains the screen coordinates of the window's outer rectangle. The application can fill in different values to control the nonclient area sizing.

WM_NCCREATE
■ Win 2.0   ■ Win 3.0   ■ Win 3.1

Purpose   Notification that Windows is about to create the nonclient area of the window. This message is sent prior to WM_CREATE. The default actions of allocating internal memory, initializing scroll bars, and setting the window's text are almost always desirable, so this message is usually passed to DefWindowProc().

Parameters

wParam   WORD: The window handle of the window being created.

lParam   DWORD: A far pointer to a CREATESTRUCT data structure. See WM_CREATE for the structure details.

WM_NCDESTROY
■ Win 2.0   ■ Win 3.0   ■ Win 3.1

Purpose   Informs a window that its nonclient area is being destroyed. This message is sent after WM_DESTROY. The message triggers the release of memory allocated internally for the window when it is passed to DefWindowProc().

Parameters

wParam   WORD: Not used.

lParam   DWORD: Not used.

WM_NCHITTEST
■ Win 2.0　　■ Win 3.0　　■ Win 3.1

Purpose　　Sent to the window that used GetCapture() to capture all mouse input. The message is sent every time the mouse is moved.

Parameters

wParam　　WORD: Not used.

lParam　　DWORD: The low-order word contains the X position of the cursor. The Y position is in the high-order word. Screen coordinates are used.

Note:　　DefWindowProc() returns the mouse hit test code when processing this message. The hit test codes are listed in Appendix 2, *Mouse Hit Test Codes*.

c, Pg. 940

WM_NCLBUTTONDBLCLK
■ Win 2.0　　■ Win 3.0　　■ Win 3.1

Purpose　　Notification that the user double-clicked the left mouse button while the mouse cursor was in the nonclient area of the window.

Parameters

wParam　　WORD: Contains the hit test code. See Appendix 2, *Mouse Hit Test Codes,* for a list.

lParam　　DWORD: Contains a POINT data structure, which gives the mouse cursor position when the mouse button was double-clicked. Mouse cursor locations are always in screen coordinates, with 0,0 in the upper left corner.

WM_NCLBUTTONDOWN
■ Win 2.0　　■ Win 3.0　　■ Win 3.1

Purpose　　Notification that the user pressed the left mouse button while the mouse cursor was in the non client area of the window.

Parameters

wParam　　WORD: Contains the hit test code. See Appendix 2, *Mouse Hit Test Codes*, for the list.

lParam　　DWORD: Contains a POINT data structure, which gives the mouse cursor position when the mouse button was pressed. Mouse cursor locations are always in screen coordinates, with 0,0 being in the upper left corner.

WM_NCLBUTTONUP
■ Win 2.0　　■ Win 3.0　　■ Win 3.1

Purpose　　Notification that the user released the left mouse button while the mouse cursor was in the nonclient area of the window.

Parameters

wParam　　WORD: Contains the hit test code. See Appendix 2, *Mouse Hit Test Codes*, for the list.

lParam　　DWORD: Contains a POINT data structure, which gives the mouse cursor position when the mouse button was released. Mouse cursor locations are always in screen coordinates, with 0,0 being in the upper left corner.

WM_NCMBUTTONDBLCLK
■ Win 2.0　　■ Win 3.0　　■ Win 3.1

Purpose　　Notification that the user double-clicked the center mouse button while the mouse cursor was in the nonclient area of the window.

Parameters

wParam　　WORD: Contains the hit test code. See Appendix 2, *Mouse Hit Test Codes*, for the list.

lParam　　DWORD: Contains a POINT data structure, which gives the mouse cursor position when the mouse button was double-clicked. Mouse cursor locations are always in screen coordinates, with 0,0 in the upper left corner.

WM_NCMBUTTONDOWN

Purpose	Notification that the user has pressed the center mouse button while the mouse cursor was in the nonclient area of the window.
Parameters	
wParam	WORD: Contains the hit test code. See Appendix 2, *Mouse Hit Test Codes*, for the list.
lParam	DWORD: Contains a POINT data structure, which gives the mouse cursor position when the mouse button was pressed. Mouse cursor locations are always in screen coordinates, with 0,0 in the upper left corner.

WM_NCMBUTTONUP

Purpose	Notification that the user released the center mouse button while the mouse cursor was in the nonclient area of the window.
Parameters	
wParam	WORD: Contains the hit test code. See Appendix 2, *Mouse Hit Test Codes,* for a list.
lParam	DWORD: Contains a POINT data structure, which gives the mouse cursor position when the mouse button was released. Mouse cursor locations are always in screen coordinates, with 0,0 in the upper left corner.

WM_NCMOUSEMOVE

Purpose	Notification that the mouse has been moved in the nonclient area of the window.
Parameters	c (p. 940)
wParam	WORD: Contains the hit test code. See Appendix 2, *Mouse Hit Test Codes*, for the list.
lParam	DWORD: Contains a POINT data structure, which gives the mouse cursor position. Mouse cursor locations are always in screen coordinates, with 0,0 in the upper left corner.

WM_NCPAINT

Purpose	Notification that the nonclient area of a window needs to be repainted. Most applications just pass this on to the DefWindowProc() function, which paints the nonclient area. Custom frames and caption areas can be created by intercepting this message and painting the area from within the application code.
Parameters	
wParam	WORD: Not used.
lParam	DWORD: Not used.

WM_NCRBUTTONDBLCLK

Purpose	Notification that the user double-clicked the right mouse button while the mouse cursor was in the nonclient area of the window.
Parameters	
wParam	WORD: Contains the hit test code. See Appendix 2, *Mouse Hit Test Codes*, for the list.
lParam	DWORD: Contains a POINT data structure, which gives the mouse cursor position when the mouse button was double-clicked. Mouse cursor locations are always in screen coordinates, with 0,0 in the upper left corner.

WM_NCRBUTTONDOWN
■ Win 2.0　■ Win 3.0　■ Win 3.1

Purpose　Notification that the user pressed the right mouse button while the mouse cursor was in the nonclient area of the window.

Parameters

wParam　WORD: Contains the hit test code. See Appendix 2, *Mouse Hit Test Codes*, for the list.

lParam　DWORD: Contains a POINT data structure, giving the mouse cursor position when the mouse button was pressed. Mouse cursor locations are always in screen coordinates, with 0,0 in the upper left corner.

WM_NCRBUTTONUP
■ Win 2.0　■ Win 3.0　■ Win 3.1

Purpose　Notification that the user released the right mouse button while the mouse cursor was in the nonclient area of the window.

Parameters

wParam　WORD: Contains the hit test code. See Appendix 2, *Mouse Hit Test Codes*, for the list.

lParam　DWORD: Contains a POINT data structure, which gives the mouse cursor position when the mouse button was released. Mouse cursor locations are always in screen coordinates, with 0,0 in the upper left corner.

WM_NEXTDLGCTL
■ Win 2.0　■ Win 3.0　■ Win 3.1

Purpose　Moves the input focus to another child window control within a dialog box. This message should be sent with PostMessage(), rather than SendMessage(), to avoid having the input focus shift while the dialog box processes other messages.

Syntax　PostMessage (HWND *hDlg*, **WM_NEXTDLGCTL**, WORD *wParam*, DWORD *lParam*)

Parameters

hDlg　HWND: The handle of the dialog box.

wParam　WORD

lParam　DWORD: The *lParam* and *wParam* values work together to specify the action, as shown in Table 9-32.

wParam	lParam	Action	⊠
hControl	TRUE	hControl (handle to a child window control) gets the input focus and gets a dark border.	
FALSE	FALSE	Next control with the WS_TABSTOP style gets the input focus and gets a dark border.	
TRUE	FALSE	Previous control with the WS_TABSTOP style gets the input focus and gets a dark border.	

Table 9-32. WM_NEXTDLGCTL Settings.

WM_NULL
■ Win 2.0　■ Win 3.0　■ Win 3.1

Purpose　No action is taken if this is sent or processed by DefWindowProc(). WM_NULL can be used in hook functions to eliminate the action of a message without eliminating the message itself.

Parameters

wParam　WORD: Not used.

lParam　DWORD: Not used.

WM_OTHERWINDOWCREATED

☐ Win 2.0   ■ Win 3.0   ☐ Win 3.1

Purpose   Sent to all overlapped and popup windows running in the system when a new top-level window (a window unowned by any other window) is created .

Parameters

wParam   WORD: The handle of the window being created.

lParam   DWORD: Not used.

Related Messages   WM_OTHERWINDOWDESTROYED, WM_CREATE

WM_OTHERWINDOWDESTROYED

☐ Win 2.0   ■ Win 3.0   ☐ Win 3.1

Purpose   Sent to all overlapped and popup windows running in the system when a top-level window (a window unowned by any other window) is destroyed.

Parameters

wParam   WORD: The handle of the window being destroyed.

lParam   DWORD: Not used.

Related Messages   WM_OTHERWINDOWCREATED, WM_DESTROY

WM_PAINT

■ Win 2.0   ■ Win 3.0   ■ Win 3.1

Purpose   Notification that the client area of a window needs to be repainted. This message can be forced by calling the UpdateWindow() function. It is automatically generated by Windows if the application window is resized or uncovered from beneath other windows. The update region is reset by calling BeginPaint().

Parameters

wParam   WORD: Not used.

lParam   DWORD: Not used.

WM_PAINTCLIPBOARD

■ Win 2.0   ■ Win 3.0   ■ Win 3.1

Purpose   This message is used by clipboard viewer applications to notify that the viewer data should be repainted. The clipboard data must be in the CF_OWNERDISPLAY format for this to occur.

Parameters

wParam   WORD: Contains the window handle of the clipboard viewer window.

lParam   DWORD: Contains a pointer to a PAINTSTRUCT data structure. This is defined in WINDOWS.H as

```
typedef struct tagPAINTSTRUCT
  {
  HDC          hdc;              /* device context */
  BOOL         fErase;
  RECT         rcPaint;          /* repaint rectangle */
  BOOL         fRestore;
  BOOL         fIncUpdate;
  BYTE         rgbReserved[16];
  } PAINTSTRUCT;
typedef PAINTSTRUCT             *PPAINTSTRUCT;
typedef PAINTSTRUCT NEAR        *NPPAINTSTRUCT;
typedef PAINTSTRUCT FAR         *LPPAINTSTRUCT;
```

The *rcPaint* element contains a RECT data structure that holds the dimensions of the area that needs to be repainted. This can be compared with the most resent dimensions obtained when processing a WM_SIZECLIPBOARD message. The application processing this message will need to use GlobalLock() to fix the location of the PAINTSTRUCT data while reading the data and will need to use GlobalUnlock() to release the data.

WM_PAINTICON
☐ Win 2.0   ■ Win 3.0   ☐ Win 3.1

Purpose   Notification that a minimized (iconic) window needs to be repainted. This message will only be received if the window was created based on a window class containing a class icon. If no class icon is defined, the minimized window receives WM_PAINT messages. DefWindowProc() paints the icon with the class icon. By intercepting this message, the application program can paint directly on the iconized window client area.

Parameters

wParam   WORD: Not used.

lParam   DWORD: Not used.

WM_PALETTECHANGED
☐ Win 2.0   ■ Win 3.0   ■ Win 3.1

Purpose   Notification that the system color palette has changed. This message is sent to all applications when the active window calls the RealizePalette() function. Inactive windows should call RealizePalette() when they receive this message. RealizePalette() minimizes the number of color changes shown on inactive windows when the system palette changes.

Parameters

wParam   WORD: The window handle of the application that changed the system palette. The function calling RealizePalette() can compare this value with its own window handle to avoid an infinite loop of RealizePalette() and WM_PALETTECHANGED messages.

lParam   DWORD: Not used.

WM_PARENTNOTIFY
☐ Win 2.0   ■ Win 3.0   ■ Win 3.1

Purpose   Notification to the parent window that a child window is being created, destroyed, or clicked with the mouse. This message is received only if the child window was created with the WM_PARENTNOTIFY style. If the application has children of children, etc., all of the predecessor windows receive this message if all children have the WM_PARENTNOTIFY style. By default, child window controls inside dialog boxes do not notify their parent windows.

Parameters

wParam   WORD: The type of notification may be any one of the codes in Table 9-33.

Value	Meaning	⊠
WM_CREATE	The child window is about to be created.	
WM_DESTROY	The child window is about to be destroyed.	
WM_LBUTTONDOWN	The user clicked the left mouse button over the child window.	
WM_MBUTTONDOWN	The user clicked the center mouse button over the child window.	
WM_RBUTTONDOWN	The user clicked the right mouse button over the child window.	

Table 9-33. WM_PARENTNOTIFY Codes.

lParam   DWORD: The low-order word contains the handle of the child window. The high-order word contains the child window ID value, which was specified as the *hMenu* parameter when CreateWindow() was called.

WM_PASTE
■ Win 2.0   ■ Win 3.0   ■ Win 3.1

Purpose	Copies the text from the clipboard into an edit control. The text is inserted at the current caret position within the edit control. The text in the clipboard is assumed to be in CF_TEXT format.
Syntax	SendMessage (HWND *hControl*, **WM_PASTE**, WORD *wParam*, DWORD *lParam*)
Parameters	
hControl	HWND: The window handle of the edit control.
wParam	WORD: Not used.
lParam	DWORD: Not used.

WM_QUERYDRAGICON
☐ Win 2.0   ■ Win 3.0   ■ Win 3.1

Purpose	Notification that the user is about to drag (move) a minimized (iconic) window. This message is sent only if the window was created with a class structure that does not have a default icon defined. Windows will display the default icon cursor when moving a minimized window that does not have a class icon. This display has the effect of suddenly changing the icon image, which may not be desirable. The application can intercept this message and return a handle to a monochrome cursor to specify the cursor shape to display. Use LoadCursor() to obtain the cursor handle. Return the handle in the low-order word. Return NULL to use the default icon cursor.
Parameters	
wParam	WORD: Not used.
lParam	DWORD: Not used.

WM_QUERYENDSESSION
■ Win 2.0   ■ Win 3.0   ■ Win 3.1

Purpose	Notification that the Windows session is about to be ended. This gives applications a chance to save data files before the Windows session is over. The application should return a nonzero value if the application can be shut down, zero if not. The DefWindowProc() returns a nonzero value, allowing shutdown to continue.
Parameters	
wParam	WORD: Not used.
lParam	DWORD: Not used.

WM_QUERYNEWPALETTE
☐ Win 2.0   ■ Win 3.0   ■ Win 3.1

Purpose	Notification that an application is about to receive the input focus. If the application needs to realize its logical color palette when it receives the input focus, the window should return a nonzero value to this message. The default return value from DefWindowProc() is zero.
Parameters	
wParam	WORD: Not used.
lParam	DWORD: Not used.

WM_QUERYOPEN
■ Win 2.0   ■ Win 3.0   ■ Win 3.1

Purpose	Notification that a minimized (iconic) window is about to be restored. This provides a chance for the application to refuse to restore the window. This may be appropriate for a small utility, such as a clock program, that should always be minimized. The application should return a nonzero value if the window can be restored, zero if not. The default returned value from DefWindowProc() is nonzero.

Parameters

wParam   WORD: Not used.

lParam   DWORD: Not used.

WM_QUIT   ■ Win 2.0   ■ Win 3.0   ■ Win 3.1

Purpose   This is the final message processed by an application. It is generated when the application calls
                      PostQuitMessage(). When GetMessage() receives this value in the program's message loop, it
                      returns zero, causing the message loop to be exited and the program to exit.

Parameters

wParam   WORD: Contains the exit code given in the PostQuitMessage() function call.

lParam   DWORD: Not used.

WM_RBUTTONDBLCLK   ■ Win 2.0   ■ Win 3.0   ■ Win 3.1

Purpose   Notification that the user has double-clicked the right mouse button. Only windows that have a
                      class structure that includes the CS_DBLCLKS style will receive these messages. Note that the
                      single mouse click messages always precede a double-click message.

Parameters

wParam   WORD: Contains a value reflecting whether several keys were down at the time the message was
                      sent. This can by any combination of the binary flags in Table 9-34.

Value	Meaning	☒
MK_CONTROL	The CONTROL key is down.	
MK_LBUTTON	The left mouse button is down.	
MK_MBUTTON	The center mouse button (if any) is down.	
MK_RBUTTON	The right mouse button is down.	
MK_SHIFT	The SHIFT key is down.	

Table 9-34. Mouse Flags.

lParam   DWORD: The low-order word contains the *X* position of the cursor when the button was pressed.
                      The *Y* position is in the high-order word. The positions are in pixels, from the upper left corner of
                      the window.

WM_RBUTTONDOWN   ■ Win 2.0   ■ Win 3.0   ■ Win 3.1

Purpose   Notification that the user pressed the right mouse button.

Parameters

wParam   WORD: Contains a value reflecting whether several keys were down at the time the message was
                      sent. This can by any combination of the binary flags in Table 9-35.

Value	Meaning	☒
MK_CONTROL	The CONTROL key is down.	
MK_LBUTTON	The left mouse button is down.	
MK_MBUTTON	The center mouse button (if any) is down.	
MK_SHIFT	The SHIFT key is down.	

Table 9-35. Mouse Flags.

lParam	DWORD: The low-order word contains the *X* position of the cursor when the button was pressed. The *Y* position is in the high-order word. The positions are in pixels, from the upper left corner of the window.

WM_RBUTTONUP
■ Win 2.0   ■ Win 3.0   ■ Win 3.1

Purpose	Notification that the user released the right mouse button.
Parameters	
wParam	WORD: Contains a value reflecting whether several keys were down at the time the message was sent. This can by any combination of the binary flags listed in Table 9-36.

Value	Meaning	⊠
MK_CONTROL	The CONTROL key is down.	
MK_LBUTTON	The left mouse button is down.	
MK_MBUTTON	The center mouse button (if any) is down.	
MK_SHIFT	The SHIFT key is down.	

Table 9-36. Mouse Flags.

lParam	DWORD: The low-order word contains the *X* position of the cursor when the button was pressed. The *Y* position is in the high-order word. The positions are in pixels, from the upper left corner of the window.

WM_RENDERALLFORMATS
■ Win 2.0   ■ Win 3.0   ■ Win 3.1

Purpose	Notification to the owner of one or more clipboard formats that the application program is exiting. This message is received if the application uses delayed rendering of clipboard data (waiting until the data is needed to add it to the clipboard). The application receiving this message should put the appropriate data in allocated global memory blocks and call SetClipboardData() for each format of clipboard. See Chapter 17, *The Clipboard*, for details.
Parameters	
wParam	WORD: Not used.
lParam	DWORD: Not used.

WM_RENDERFORMAT
■ Win 2.0   ■ Win 3.0   ■ Win 3.1

Purpose	Notification to the owner of the clipboard that data should be put in the clipboard in the specified format. This message is received if the application uses delayed rendering of clipboard data (waiting until the data is needed to add it to the clipboard). See Chapter 17, *The Clipboard*, for details.
Parameters	
wParam	WORD: The format of the clipboard requesting data. The clipboard formats are listed in Chapter 17, *The Clipboard*, and in the SetClipboardData() function description.
lParam	DWORD: Not used.

WM_SETCURSOR
■ Win 2.0   ■ Win 3.0   ■ Win 3.1

Purpose	Notification that the mouse cursor is moving within a window. This message provides a chance to change the mouse shape depending on where it is. If the cursor is over a child window, DefWindowProc() passes the WM_SETCURSOR message on to the parent window's message pro-

cessing function before acting on it. This gives the parent window's message processing function a chance to determine all the cursor shapes for the application. If the parent also passes the message to DefWindowProc(), the default actions are to change the cursor shape back to the normal arrow cursor when the cursor leaves the client area of the window. This causes a change in cursor shape if the window was created based on a class structure with a cursor shape other than the standard arrow.

Parameters

wParam   WORD: The handle of the window that contains the cursor.

lParam   DWORD: The moue hit test code is in the low-order word, and the mouse message (such as WM_LBUTTONDOWN) is in the high-order word. See Appendix 2, *Mouse Hit Test Codes*, for the list of all mouse hit test codes.

WM_SETFOCUS   ■ Win 2.0   ■ Win 3.0   ■ Win 3.1

Purpose   Notification that a window has gained the input focus. At this point, all keyboard input will start going to the window. If the window uses a caret, this is a good point to display the caret so that the user will know where the next keyboard input will show up.

Parameters

wParam   WORD: Not used.

lParam   DWORD: Not used.

WM_SETFONT   □ Win 2.0   ■ Win 3.0   ■ Win 3.1

Purpose   Used to change the font used in dialog box controls. This message should be sent to each control that changes fonts when the dialog box function receives a WM_INITDIALOG message.

Syntax   SendMessage (HWND *hControl*, **WM_SETFONT**, WORD *wParam*, DWORD *lParam*)

Parameters

hControl   HWND: The window handle of the child window control (button, list box, etc.).

wParam   WORD: A handle to the font. NULL for the system (default) font.

lParam   DWORD: TRUE if the control should be redrawn immediately, FALSE if not. Use *lParam* equal to TRUE if you are changing the font during the execution of the dialog box. Setting the *lParam* value FALSE (zero) saves time if the dialog box function is processing a WM_INITDIALOG message.

Comments   Windows will send the WM_SETFONT message to the dialog box message function if the dialog box was created with the DS_SETFONT style. This is only possible if the CreateDialogIndirect(), CreateDialogIndirectParam(), DialogBoxIndirect(), or DialogBoxIndirectParam() functions were used to create the dialog box.

WM_SETREDRAW   ■ Win 2.0   ■ Win 3.0   ■ Win 3.1

Purpose   Sent to a list box and to combo box controls prior to adding or deleting a number of items. By turning redrawing off during the changes, the changes occur faster and without a lot of distracting action within the list box area of the control. The redraw status is then set back to the normal ON state at the end of the changes.

Syntax   SendMessage (HWND *hControl*, **WM_SETREDRAW**, WORD *wParam*, DWORD *lParam*)

Parameters

hControl   HWND: The window handle of the child window control (list box, combo box).

wParam	WORD: Nonzero to turn on redrawing in the control. Zero to turn off redrawing in the control.
lParam	DWORD: Not used.

WM_SETTEXT
■ Win 2.0   ■ Win 3.0   ■ Win 3.1

Purpose Used to change the title or text of a window. For button controls, this changes the button's text. For edit controls and combo boxes, it changes the edit control text. For parent, child, and popup windows, the window caption is changed. Sending this message is equivalent to calling the SetWindowText() function.

Syntax *dwReturned* = SendMessage (HWND *hControl*, **WM_SETTEXT**, WORD *wParam*, DWORD *lParam*)

Returns DWORD, normally ignored. Returns CB_ERRSPACE if there is not enough room in the edit control of the combo box to hold the string. Returns CB_ERR if the combo box does not have an edit control.

Parameters
hControl	HWND: The window handle of the child window control (button, combo box, etc.).
wParam	WORD: Not used.
lParam	DWORD: A pointer to a null-terminated string containing the new text.

WM_SHOWWINDOW
■ Win 2.0   ■ Win 3.0   ■ Win 3.1

Purpose Notification that a window is to be either hidden or shown. This message occurs when the ShowWindow() function is called, or when an overlapped or popup window is maximized, restored, minimized, or opened. The DefWindowProc() function hides or shows the window when it processes this message.

Parameters
wParam	WORD: Nonzero if the window is being shown, zero if it is being hidden.
lParam	DWORD: Zero if a call to ShowWindow() was the reason for the message. SW_PARENTCLOSING if a parent window is closing, or a popup window is being hidden. SW_PARENTOPENING if a parent window is being displayed, or a popup window is being shown.

WM_SIZE
■ Win 2.0   ■ Win 3.0   ■ Win 3.1

Purpose Notification that the size of a window has changed. Applications usually process this message to keep track of how big the client area of the window is.

Parameters
wParam	WORD: Contains one of the values in Table 9-37.

Value	Meaning
SIZEFULLSCREEN	The window has been maximized.
SIZEICONIC	The window has been minimized (made iconic).
SIZENORMAL	The window has been resized.
SIZEZOOMHIDE	Sent to all popup windows when another window has been maximized.
SIZEZOOMSHOW	Sent to all popup windows when another window has been restored to its previous size.

Table 9-37. WM_SIZE Codes.

lParam	DWORD: The low-order word contains the width of the window's client area. The high-order word contains the height. Both are in pixels.

WM_SIZECLIPBOARD ■ Win 2.0 ■ Win 3.0 ■ Win 3.1

Purpose Notification that the clipboard viewer application has changed size. This will occur only if the clipboard contains a data handle for the CF_OWNERDISPLAY format. This message will be sent with a null rectangle (values 0,0,0,0) when the clipboard viewer is about to be destroyed.

Parameters
wParam WORD: The window handle of the clipboard viewer.

lParam DWORD: A pointer to a RECT data structure that contains the area the clipboard viewer should paint.

WM_SPOOLERSTATUS □ Win 2.0 ■ Win 3.0 ■ Win 3.1

Purpose Notification from the Print Manager that a job has been added or subtracted from the printer queue.

Parameters
wParam WORD: Equal to SP_JOBSTATUS.

lParam DWORD: The low-order word contains the number of jobs in the printer queue. The high-order word is not used.

WM_SYSCHAR ■ Win 2.0 ■ Win 3.0 ■ Win 3.1

Purpose This is the equivalent of a WM_CHAR message, except that it is generated by TranslateMessage() in the application's message loop when a WM_SYSKEYUP or WM_SYSKEYDOWN message is processed. SYSKEY messages are sent if the (ALT) key is down or if no window has the input focus. SYSKEY messages also cover the system functions such as switching between windows ((ALT)-(TAB), (ALT)-(ESC), etc).

Parameters
wParam WORD: The ASCII value of the key pressed.

lParam DWORD: The 32-bit keyboard data for the key, coded as shown in Table 9-38.

Bits	Meaning
0-15 (low order word)	The repeat count. This is the number of times the character was repeated because the user held a key down.
16-23	The keyboard scan code.
24	1 if an extended key, such as a function key or a key on the numeric keypad.
25-28	Not available.
29	1 if the (ALT) key was held down when the key was pressed, 0 if not. This is called the "context code."
30	1 if the key is down before the message was sent, 0 if not.
31	1 if the key is being released, 0 if the key is being pressed.

Table 9-38. 32-Bit Coded Keyboard Data.

Note If bit 29 is zero, the message can be passed to TranslateAccelerator() within the application's message loop. This allows the accelerator keys to be used with the active window even if it does not have the input focus.

WM_SYSCOLORCHANGE
■ Win 2.0   ■ Win 3.0   ■ Win 3.1

Purpose   Notification that one or more of the system colors has changed. This message is sent to all top-level windows when a system color is changed. Applications that use the system colors to create objects (pens, brushes, etc.) should delete those items and create new ones using the current system colors. This message is followed by a WM_PAINT message.

Parameters

wParam   WORD: Not used.

lParam   DWORD: Not used.

WM_SYSCOMMAND
■ Win 2.0   ■ Win 3.0   ■ Win 3.1

Purpose   Notification that the user has selected a system menu command (the menu that appears if the button at the top left corner of a window is clicked), or that the minimize or maximize buttons in the upper right corner of the window are pressed. Note that the system menu can be modified by the application. Menu items added to the system menu generate WM_SYSCOMMAND messages, not WM_COMMAND. Do not pass added menu options on the system menu to DefWindowProc(). Just return after the processing of the message is complete.

Parameters

wParam   WORD: One of the values listed in Table 9-39.

Value	Meaning	
SC_CLOSE	Close the window.	*F060*
SC_HOTKEY (Win 3.1)	Activates a window associated with the application-specified hot key. The low-order word of *lParam* contains the window handle of the window to activate.	
SC_HSCROLL	Scroll horizontally.	*F080*
SC_KEYMENU	Menu retrieved via a keystroke.	*F100*
SC_MAXIMIZE (or SC_ZOOM)	Maximize the window.	*F030*
SC_MINIMIZE (or SC_ICON)	Minimize the window.	*F020*
SC_MOUSEMENU	Menu retrieved via a mouse click.	*F090*
SC_MOVE	Move the window.	*F010*
SC_NEXTWINDOW	Move to the next window.	*F040*
SC_PREVWINDOW	Move to the previous window.	*F050*
SC_RESTORE	Restore the window to its previous size.	*F120*
SC_SCREENSAVE (Win 3.1)	Executes the screen-save application specified in the desktop section of the Windows 3.1 Control Panel.	
SC_SIZE	Resize the window.	*x F000*
SC_TASKLIST (Win 3.1)	Executes or activates the Windows task manager application. *(Ctrl + ESC)*	*F130*
SC_VSCROLL	Scroll the window vertically.	*F070*

Table 9-39. WM_SYSCOMMAND Values.

lParam   DWORD: If the mouse was used to select a system menu command, the low-order word contains the mouse *X* position, and the high-order word contains the *Y* position. Otherwise, *lParam* is not used.

Notes   All the SC_ values are defined in WINDOWS.H all be above 0x000F in value. This is because Windows uses the lower four bits internally. Be sure to AND (&) the *wParam* value with 0xFFF0 before testing the value to see which SC_ option was selected.

WM_SYSDEADCHAR   ■ Win 2.0   ■ Win 3.0   ■ Win 3.1

Purpose   Notification of a system dead character. This occurs when a WM_SYSKEYDOWN or WM_SYSKEYUP message is processed by TranslateMessage() in the window message loop, for a system keystroke on a non-English keyboard that is using an accented character.

Parameters

wParam   WORD: Contains the dead-key value, per the keyboard language definition in use.

lParam   DWORD: The low-order word contains the repeat count. The high-order word contains the auto-repeat count. These values usually can be ignored.

WM_SYSKEYDOWN   ■ Win 2.0   ■ Win 3.0   ■ Win 3.1

Purpose   Notification that the user pressed a key while holding down the (ALT) key. It also occurs when no window has the input focus. WM_SYSKEYDOWN is then sent to the active window. Bit 29 of *lParam* can be used to distinguish between these two cases. This message is processed by TranslateMessage() in the application's message loop, which generates a WM_SYSCHAR message.

Parameters

wParam   WORD: The virtual key code of the key pressed..

lParam   DWORD: The 32-bit encoded data for the keypress. See Table 9-38 under WM_SYSCHAR for the meaning of each bit.

Note   If bit 29 is zero, the message can be passed to TranslateAccelerator() within the application's message loop. This allows accelerator keys to be used with the active window even if it does not have the input focus.

WM_SYSKEYUP   ■ Win 2.0   ■ Win 3.0   ■ Win 3.1

Purpose   Notification that the user released a key while holding down the (ALT) key. It also occurs when no window has the input focus. WM_SYSKEYDOWN is then sent to the active window. Bit 29 of *lParam* can be used to distinguish between these two cases. This message is processed by TranslateMessage() in the application's message loop, which generates a WM_SYSCHAR message.

Parameters

wParam   WORD: The virtual key code of the key pressed.

lParam   DWORD: The 32-bit encoded data for the keypress. See Table 9-38 under WM_SYSCHAR for the meaning of each bit.

Note   If bit 29 is zero, the message can be passed to TranslateAccelerator() within the application's message loop. This allows accelerator keys to be used with the active window even if it does not have the input focus.

WM_TIMECHANGE   ■ Win 2.0   ■ Win 3.0   ■ Win 3.1

Purpose   Notification that the system clock has been changed. This message should be sent to all top-level windows if the application changes the clock.

Syntax   *dwReturned* = SendMessage (0xFFFF, **WM_TIMECHANGE**, 0, 0L) ;

Parameters   The parameters should be set as shown, so that the message is sent to all top-level windows (*hWnd* == 0xFFFF does this).

WM_TIMER

■ Win 2.0　　■ Win 3.0　　■ Win 3.1

Purpose　　Notification that one of the timers set with the SetTimer() function has passed its time interval.

Parameters

wParam　　WORD: The timer ID value, used as the *nIDEvent* parameter when SetTimer() was called.

lParam　　DWORD: Normally NULL. If the value is nonzero, *lParam* is a procedure-instance handle to a function set as the *lpTimerFunc* parameter when SetTimer() was called. In this case, Windows executes the timer function directly, rather than sending the WM_TIMER message to the window's message processing function.

WM_UNDO

■ Win 2.0　　■ Win 3.0　　■ Win 3.1

Purpose　　Copies the text from the clipboard to the edit control's client area. This eliminates the effect of a WM_CUT message. The clipboard contents are assumed to be in CF_TEXT format.

Syntax　　SendMessage (HWND *hControl*, **WM_UNDO**, WORD *wParam*, DWORD *lParam*)

Parameters

hControl　　HWND: The window handle of the edit control.

wParam　　WORD: Not used. Set equal to 0.

lParam　　DWORD: Not used. Set equal to 0L.

WM_USER

■ Win 2.0　　■ Win 3.0　　■ Win 3.1

Purpose　　Values of WM_USER and above, up to 0x7FFF, can be used by an application for messages defined by the application. This is a convenient way for the independent window processing functions of the different child and popup windows to communicate. Most programmers define the new messages for their application in the application's header file:

```
#define NEWMESSAGE          (WM_USER + 1)
#define SECONDMESSAGE       (WM_USER + 2)
```

If messages are being sent between different applications, WM_USER message coding is not saved, as different programs can use the same code for different meanings. Instead, generate a system-wide unique message using RegisterWindowMessage(). Note that Windows defines a number of child window control messages as WM_USER + a value. If you need to use WM_USER + messages with a child window control (perhaps a subclassed control), be sure the added value is large enough that it does not overlap those defined in WINDOWS.H. WM_USER + 200, etc. should be fine.

Parameters

wParam　　WORD: Can have any meaning useful to the application, limited to 16-bits.

lParam　　DWORD: Can have any meaning useful to the application, limited to 32-bits.

WM_VKEYTOITEM

■ Win 2.0　　■ Win 3.0　　■ Win 3.1

Purpose　　Notification that the user pressed a key while a list box had the input focus. The list box must have been created with the LBS_WANTKEYBOARDINPUT style to receive this message. This message allows the application to provide keyboard shortcuts to select list box items.

Parameters

wParam　　WORD: Contains the virtual key code for the key pressed. See Chapter 7, *Keyboard Support*, for a list of all virtual key codes.

lParam	DWORD: The low-order window contains the window handle of the list box. The high-order word contains the current selection index.
Returns	The message processing function should return the index of the item to select. Return 0 for the first item. To let the list box process the keystroke in the default manner, return –1. To stop all processing of the keyboard input to the list box, return –2.

WM_VSCROLL   ■ Win 2.0   ■ Win 3.0   ■ Win 3.1

Purpose	Notification that the user has adjusted a vertical scroll bar.
Parameters	
wParam	WORD: One of the codes in Table 9-40.

Value	Meaning
SB_BOTTOM	Generated if the scroll bar has the input focus and the (END) key is pressed. Not generated by mouse actions.
SB_ENDSCROLL	Sent when the scroll activity stops.
SB_LINEDOWN	Clicked the arrow on the ~~left.~~ *bottom*
SB_LINEUP	Clicked the arrow on the ~~right.~~ *top*
SB_PAGEDOWN	Clicked the area of the scroll bar between the ~~left~~ *bottom* arrow and the thumb.
SB_PAGEUP	Clicked the area of the scroll bar between the ~~right~~ *top* arrow and the thumb.
SB_THUMBPOSITION	The message passes the position of the thumb as the low-order word of *lParam*.
SB_THUMBTRACK	The thumb is being dragged. The current position is passed as the low-order word of *lParam*.
SB_TOP	Generated if the scroll bar has the input focus and the (HOME) key is pressed. Not generated by mouse actions.

Table 9-40. Scroll Bar Codes.

	Windows documentation suggests that SB_BOTTOM and SB_TOP values are also sent. These values are not detected with child window scroll bar controls.
lParam	DWORD: The high-order word contains the window handle of the scroll bar. If the scroll bar is attached to the boundary of a popup window, the high-order value is not used. The low-order word contains the thumb position if either the SB_THUMBPOSITION or SB_THUMBTRACK value for *wParam* is passed.

WM_VSCROLLCLIPBOARD   ■ Win 2.0   ■ Win 3.0   ■ Win 3.1

Purpose	Used with the CF_OWNERDISPLAY format of data type for the clipboard, used by clipboard viewer programs. The message indicates that the clipboard viewer vertical scroll bar has been used.
Parameters	
wParam	WORD: Contains a handle to the clipboard viewer program.
lParam	DWORD: The low-order word contains one of the scroll bar codes shown in Table 9-40, as used in WM_VSCROLL messages. The high-order word contains the thumb position if the SB_THUMB-POSITION or SB_THUMBTRACK value is passed in the low-order word. Otherwise, the high-order word is not used.

WM_WININICHANGE
■ Win 2.0　　■ Win 3.0　　■ Win 3.1

Purpose　　　Notification that the WIN.INI file has been changed. Any program that modifies WIN.INI should send this message to all top-level windows, per the syntax example. The *hWnd* parameter is set equal to 0xFFFF to send a message to all top-level windows. Any program receiving this message can check whether the section changed (*lParam* value) applies to the operation of the program. If so, the application can re-initialize after reading that section from WIN.INI.

Syntax　　　SendMessage (0xFFFF, **WM_WININICHANGE**, WORD *wParam*, DWORD *lParam*)

Parameters

wParam　　　WORD: Not used. Set equal to 0.

lParam　　　DWORD: A pointer to a null-terminated character string that contains the WIN.INI section name that has been changed. The square brackets used in WIN.INI to show section names should NOT be included in this string. Although not officially supported, some applications will send this message with *lParam* set equal to NULL. In this case, the receiving application has no choice but to check every relevant section of WIN.INI and re-initialize.

10

Device Contexts, Text Output, and Printing

In the past, programmers had to continually modify and add to their programs as new printers, video displays, and other hardware entered the market. In most cases, these updates distracted from the goal of improving the real functionality of the software. One of the major advantages to using the Windows environment is that Windows deals with the hardware for you. A well-designed Windows program will continue to function exactly as intended when new computer and printer hardware are introduced.

The Device Context

The basic tool that Windows uses to insulate your program from the "real-world" hardware is called a device context, or DC. The DC amounts to about 800 bytes of information that Windows maintains about an output device, such as a video screen or a printer. Instead of sending output directly to the hardware, your program sends it to the DC, and then Windows sends it to the hardware. As an example, consider the steps necessary to output a string to the client area of a window. First, declare a variable to hold a handle to the device context. This is just an unsigned integer that Windows uses to keep track of which DC is active. (The HDC data type is defined in WINDOWS.H.)

```
HDC            hDC ;            /* a handle to the device context */
```

Second, retrieve a handle to the client area's device context with the GetDC( ) function.

```
hDC = GetDC (hWnd) ;            /* get a handle to the window's client area DC */
```

Finally, output the text to the device context, and release the device context. Releasing the DC is important, as Windows will not allow access to the device context by another program until it is released.

```
TextOut (hDC, 0, 0, "Text Output To Client Area.", 25) ;
ReleaseDC (hWnd, hDC) ;
```

This is not too complicated, but there is more going on here than you might expect. We did not specify the character font to use, what color to draw the text, how big to make the letters, etc. All of these parameters were based on the default values stored in the device context. To expand on this example, let's output the same string again. This time we will pick a different font and make the color of the text bright red. The code now looks like

```
HDC            hDC ;

hDC = GetDC (hWnd) ;
SelectObject (hDC, GetStockObject (ANSI_VAR_FONT)) ;
SetTextColor (hDC,  RGB (255, 0, 0)) ;
TextOut (hDC, 0, 0, "Text Output To Client Area.", 25) ;
ReleaseDC (hWnd, hDC) ;
```

Two new lines were added. SelectObject() was used to select a new font into the device context. In this case, one of the six stock fonts was loaded. The SetTextColor() function modified one of the device context settings, changing the text color to red. A handy macro RGB() defined in WINDOWS.H was used to create the 32-bit color value needed for SetTextColor() by specifying the red, green, and blue elements of the color. The result of these changes is that this time TextOut() writes the output with red letters, using the ANSI_VAR_FONT character font. A wide range of other changes are possible for a device context. You can select different pens, brushes, fonts, and colors. You can also scale the device context in different ways to increase the hardware independence of your program.

Handling WM_PAINT Messages

You will not use the GetDC() and ReleaseDC() functions to retrieve and release the window's client area DC when you process WM_PAINT messages. Windows provides two specialized functions to handle this situation: BeginPaint() and EndPaint(). Windows assumes that you will want to speed up your program's screen refresh logic by only painting the areas that need repainting. Windows updates a PAINTSTRUCT data structure when the WM_PAINT message is sent. The PAINTSTRUCT structure is defined in WINDOWS.H as follows:

```
typedef struct tagPAINTSTRUCT.i.PAINTSTRUCT;
  {
    HDC   hdc;
    BOOL  fErase;
    RECT  rcPaint;
    BOOL  fRestore;
    BOOL  fIncUpdate;
    BYTE  rgbReserved[16];
  } PAINTSTRUCT;
typedef PAINTSTRUCT                *PPAINTSTRUCT;
typedef PAINTSTRUCT NEAR           *NPPAINTSTRUCT;
typedef PAINTSTRUCT FAR            *LPPAINTSTRUCT;
```

The rcPaint element of the structure contains the rectangle that defines the smallest rectangle that covers all of the client area that needs to be repainted. You can also use the hdc element of the PAINTSTRUCT as a quick way to get the client area DC. You do not have to be efficient in repainting just the rectangle that needs updating. You can repaint the whole client area when you get a WM_PAINT message. Most programs do this to simplify their painting logic. Only the parts of the client area that are in the refresh rectangle will actually be repainted, even though the output functions may specify painting in the entire area. If the screen updates become too slow, put some more logic into the processing of WM_PAINT messages to reduce the amount of repainting that needs to be done. This subject will be covered in the next Chapter, *Painting the Screen.*

Selecting Objects into a Device Context

At any given time, a device context will have one pen to draw lines with, one brush to fill areas with, one font to type letters in, and a series of other values to control how the device context behaves. If you want to use a different font, you need to select it into the device context. This makes it available the next time you want to do some text output. Selecting a new font does not redraw text on the window's client area. New text appears only if you select the new font, and then use it to output text with a function like TextOut(). The following example switches from one font to another for the output of two separate lines.

```
HDC              hDC ;

hDC = GetDC (hWnd) ;
SelectObject (hDC, GetStockObject (OEM_FIXED_FONT)) ;
TextOut (hDC, 0, 0, "Text Output With OEM Font.", 24) ;
SelectObject (hDC, GetStockObject (ANSI_VAR_FONT)) ;
TextOut (hDC, 0, 20, "Text Output With ANSI Font". 26) ;
ReleaseDC (hWnd, hDC) ;
```

The first line is typed using the OEM_FIXED_FONT, while the second one is typed with the ANSI_VAR_FONT. Both lines will be visible in the client area when this code fragment is executed. So far, we have used only stock objects, that are always available in Windows. Stock objects are not deleted after use. Most of the time you will need to create new pens, brushes, and fonts. These objects take up memory and need to be deleted when not needed.

Here are a few rules in dealing with device contexts:

1. Only five device contexts can be open at any one time.

2. Do not attempt to delete stock objects. They are the objects listed under the GetStockObject() function, such as OEM_FIXED_FONT.

3. Do not delete objects that are selected into the device context. Always select a new object, or a stock object, into the device context to displace the object you created. Then delete it, when the object is no longer tied to the device context, delete it.

Another way to assure that you do not delete an object that is selected into the device context is to release the device context before deleting the objects it has been using.

Private Device Contexts

In the previous examples, the handle to the window's client area device context was retrieved right before it was needed and released right after its use. This is the normal case. Using this type of logic makes the program as memory efficient as possible, by only tying up the device context during the periods when the program is generating output. The cost of this memory efficiency is program speed. Every time the program wants to output, it must fetch the device context handle, modify the default DC settings as needed, do the output, and finally release the DC. All of this takes time.

An alternative way for a program to deal with the client area device context is to keep its own private copy. This is done by specifying the CS_OWNDC class style in the class definition for the window. The top of the WinMain() function will include a line like

```
wndclass.style = CS_HREDRAW | CS_VREDRAW | CS_OWNDC;
```

With this class style, the device context exists for the life of the window. The program still uses GetDC() to retrieve a handle to the device context. There is no need to call ReleaseDC() after the device context is used (ReleaseDC() will not do anything in this case.) Having a private device context is also convenient for programs that make changes to the device context settings. Changes such as new text colors, pens, and brushes, remain in effect until they are changed again or the program exits.

You should choose between private and public device contexts based on the type of application you are writing. If the program only makes limited use of the device contex or seldom changes the default settings, use a public device context to save memory. If the program makes heavy use of the device context, use a private DC to speed up execution and simplify the program.

Saving a Device Context

In some applications, you may find yourself repeatedly switching between two or three common sets of device context settings. For example, you may be using a combination of one font, color, background mode, etc. to paint the fixed part of the client area and using another combination of font and colors for the parts the user can change. A convenient way to code applications like this is to create separate device contexts and save them with the SaveDC() function. SaveDC() saves the settings in a "context stack," where they can be recovered at any time by calling RestoreDC(). Calling RestoreDC() does not remove the saved copy of the DC from the stack, so you can switch to these settings any number of times. The saved device contexts will be removed with the stack when the application terminates.

Mapping Modes

One of the default assumptions a device context starts with is the coordinate system for mapping points on the device. The default coordinates put the origin (the point with $X = 0$ and $Y = 0$) at the top left corner. X values increase to the right, and Y values increase downward. The measurement units are pixels. A pixel is one dot on the screen, or one dot on the printer.

The default coordinates are acceptable if you only write to the screen. If you also want to write to the printer, you have problems. One pixel on a laser printer is a lot smaller than one pixel on the screen. The result is that the output that fills up the window on the screen ends up the size of a postage stamp when printed. We want Windows to take care of hardware dependencies, so something better has to be done. The answer lies in using a better coordinate system than just pixels. Windows calls changing the coordinate system "setting a mapping mode." The SetMapMode() function does the work. The default mapping mode is called MM_TEXT. There are five other mapping modes that scale output. Size can be measured in English, metric, or printer's units (twips). Table 10-1 lists the fixed size mapping modes.

Mapping Mode	Meaning	⊠
MM_HIENGLISH	Each logical unit is 0.001 inch. *X* increases to the right. *Y* increases upward.	
MM_HIMETRIC	Each logical unit is 0.01 millimeter. *X* increases to the right. *Y* increases upward.	
MM_LOENGLISH	Each logical unit is 0.01 inch. *X* increases to the right. *Y* increases upward.	
MM_LOMETRIC	Each logical unit is 0.1 millimeter. *X* increases to the right. *Y* increases upward.	
MM_TEXT	This is the default mapping mode. Each unit equals one pixel. *X* increases to the right. *Y* increases downward.	
MM_TWIPS	Each logical unit is 1/20 point, or 1/1440 of an inch. *X* increases to the right. *Y* increases upward.	

Table 10-1. Fixed Size Mapping Modes.

The coordinate system units are referred to as "logical units," as they have meaning only with respect to the mapping mode in use. After you have changed the mapping mode, measurements within the device context are based on the new system of units. For example, calling TextOut() with the coordinates 10,10 puts the string at the top left corner of the client area using the default MM_TEXT mapping mode. If you switch to MM_LOMETRIC, the 10, 10 point is 1 mm to the right and 1 mm above the bottom left corner. The text will end up hidden under the window's border! Windows does its best to make the logical units match real measurements in inches and millimeteres. It does a good job with printers, but can be significantly off with video displays. This discrepancy is because Windows has no way of knowing what size monitor you are using.

Another use of a coordinate system is to allow you to shrink or expand graphics by changing the coordinate system, rather than by changing the graphics logic. Windows provides two mapping modes for this purpose, MM_ISO-TROPIC and MM_ANISOTROPIC. Table 10-2 lists the modes that can be scaled.

Mapping Mode	Meaning	⊠
MM_ISOTROPIC	Arbitrary scaling of the axes, but the *X* and *Y* scaling must be the same. Use SetWindowExt( ) and SetViewportExt( ) to set the orientation and scaling.	
MM_ANISOTROPIC	This is the most flexible system of units. Either axis can have any scaling factor. Use SetWindowExt( ) and SetViewportExt( ) to set the orientation and scaling.	

Table 10-2. Mapping Modes that Can Be Scaled.

The MM_ANISOTROPIC mode generally is used for programs that want to distort the graphics displayed in the client area to always match the size of the window. MM_ISOTROPIC is used to shrink and expand graphics, without distorting the image. Windows uses a rather obscure method to scale these two coordinate systems. Rather than use floating point numbers to describe how much to ratio the logical units to the device's pixels, Windows uses two sets of integers. One set is called the "window extent," and the other set is called the "viewport extent." For example, to scale the logical coordinates to be twice the pixel (or "device") units, you would use the following two function calls:

```
SetWindowExt (hDC, 1, 1) ;
SetViewportExt (hDC, 2, 2) ;
```

You can also reverse the direction of either of the axes by making the signs of the scaling integers different. For example, to scale the logical coordinates to be 1/10 pixel and have the *Y* axis increase upward, use

```
SetWindowExt (hDC, 10, 10) ;
SetViewportExt (hDC, 1, -1) ;
```

You can use scaleable coordinates in programs that output to the printer. You will need to adjust the scaling of the printer's device context depending on the resolution of the printer. The function GetDeviceCaps() is handy here, as you can use it to find out the horizontal and vertical resolution of the printer. One final bit of flexibility with logical coordinate systems is the ability to move the origin. This is a good way to implement scrolling of a graphics display. Instead of recalculating where everything should be after the image is scrolled, just change the location of the origin and repaint. Windows overkills on this, by giving you two different ways to move the origin. Normally, you will use either SetViewportOrg() or SetWindowOrg(). If you use both, be aware that the "viewport" origin is an offset from the "window" origin. You can end up with some complex offsets-from-offsets if you use both functions to move the origin.

Fonts

Windows provides six stock fonts that are always available. Figure 10-1 shows what they look like on a VGA display. The stock fonts can be fetched at any time using the GetStockObject() function, and then SelectObject() to add the font to the device context.

Windows also supports importing new fonts. Fonts are defined in files with the .FON extension. Some are provided with Windows, and additional fonts can be pur-

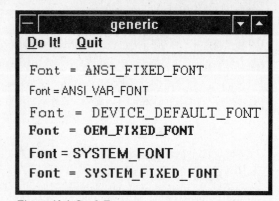

Figure 10-1. Stock Fonts.

chased from third parties. The .FON files typically define a font at certain sizes and with a limited number of styles (italics, bold, underline, etc.). A problem you may run into is that the printer supports a particular font, but it is not defined for the screen device context. Windows provides the powerful CreateFont() function to interpolate new fonts based on the information in a font file. These estimated fonts are called "logical fonts." Windows will synthesize a new font size or an italic style, even if the size or style is not included in the .FON file. These synthesized fonts tend to be lower quality than fonts explicitly defined in the font file.

When scaling fonts, you will need to understand the system of measurements used to describe a character. Figure 10-2 shows the names of each measurement. The GetTextMetrics() function returns a pointer to a structure that contains all of these values for the current font of a device context.

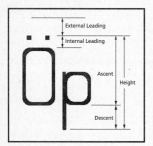

Figure 10-2. Text Dimension (Metrics).

It should be no surprise that Windows provides a wide range of related support for formatting text. Justification of text to fit a space, adding space between characters, changing the background color, and graying the characters are all directly supported.

Printer Support

Sending output to the printer is almost identical to sending it to the screen. The program must get a handle to the printer's device context. Output is then sent to that DC, rather than to the screen's DC. All of the normal output functions, such as TextOut() and LineTo(), work for output to a printer, assuming that the printer supports graphics. Of course, the mapping mode needs to be considered if you want to avoid having all of the graphics squished into the upper left corner of the page. There are a few differences between printer output and screen output. To get the handle to the printer's device context, use the CreateDC() function instead of GetDC(). Before you can use CreateDC(), you will need to find the name of the printer driver currently active in Windows. Windows writes a line in the WIN.INI file something like

```
device=PCL / HP LaserJet,HPPCL,LPT1:
```

when a printer is selected with the Install or Control Panel applications. The GetProfileString() function provides a quick way to read in this string and pass the parameters to CreateDC().

When you have the printer's device context, there are a few extra commands (such as form feeds) for printers that have no equivalent with video displays. Windows provides the Escape() function to send these specialized messages. A minimal program fragment for sending a text string to the printer is shown in Listing 10-1.

▷ **Listing 10-1. Minimal Printer Support**
```
HDC        hDC ;
char       szPrinter [64], *szDriver, *szDevice, *szOutput ;
```

```
GetProfileString ("Windows", "device", "", szPrinter, 64) ;
szDevice = strtok (szPrinter, ",") ;
szDriver = strtok (NULL, ",") ;
szOutput = strtok (NULL, ",") ;
hDC = CreateDC (szDriver, szDevice, szOutput, NULL) ;
if (Escape (hDC, STARTDOC, 4, "Test", NULL) > 0)
{
        TextOut (hDC, 10, 10, "Output is on the printer.", 25) ;
        Escape (hDC, NEWFRAME, NULL, NULL, NULL) ;
        Escape (hDC, ENDDOC, NULL, NULL, NULL) ;
}
DeleteDC (hDC) ;
```

The handy C compiler library function strtok() (string token) is used to divide the device data found in WIN.INI to match the fields expected by CreateDC(). The Escape() function sends the STARTDOC message to start printing and the ENDDOC message to end printing. The NEWFRAME message causes the page to be ejected. Printer output automatically invokes the printer spooler application if the spooler has been selected when the printer was installed. If the user has chosen not to use the spooler, the commands and data are sent directly to the printer.

The simple example shown in Listing 10-1 is suitable only for small print jobs. For larger jobs, you will want to provide a way for the user to stop a print job that is in progress. It is also nice to put a dialog box up on the screen to show that printing is going on and to provide the "cancel" button. These fairly basic printer support items can become a little involved. Remember that Windows programs take control of the system until they choose to release control, usually via the GetMessage() function. For our printer abort function, we want Windows to simultaneously send data to the printer and monitor a dialog box to see if the user has clicked the cancel button. As you may have guessed, this takes some working with Windows message processing logic.

The heart of the printer "abort" logic is a special call to the Escape() function called SETABORTPROC. This function informs Windows of the procedure-instance address of a little message processing function that you build into the program. Windows periodically sends messages to the "abort" procedure during printing. This gives the program a chance to stop printing when one of these messages is being processed. To give you an example of how this is done, we will expand the previous printing example to include a dialog box with a button for cancelling the print job, and an "abort" procedure for processing messages during printing and possibly cancelling the print job. The program's definition file (see Listing 10-2) includes two extra exported functions, the "abort" procedure name and the dialog box procedure.

▷ Listing 10-2. Printing Example Including an Abort Procedure

```
NAME                    generic
DESCRIPTION             'windows printing example'
EXETYPE         WINDOWS
STUB                    'WINSTUB.EXE'
CODE                    PRELOAD MOVEABLE
DATA                    PRELOAD MOVEABLE MULTIPLE
HEAPSIZE                1024
STACKSIZE               5010
EXPORTS                 WndProc
                        PrintStopDlg
                        PrintAbort
```

The header file contains the function prototypes for these functions.

```
/* generic.h         */
#define IDM_DOIT    1               /* menu item id values */
#define IDM_QUIT    2
                /* global variables */
int     ghInstance ;
char    gszAppName [] = "generic" ;
                /* function prototypes */
long FAR PASCAL WndProc (HWND, unsigned, WORD, LONG) ;
BOOL FAR PASCAL PrintStopDlg (HWND hDlg, unsigned iMessage, WORD wParam,
        LONG lParam) ;
BOOL FAR PASCAL PrintAbort (HDC hdcPrinter, int nCode) ;
```

The resource .RC file includes the definition of the dialog box that will be displayed while printing is occurring.

```
/* generic.r          */
#include <windows.h>
#include "generic.h"
generic ICON   generic.ico
generic MENU
BEGIN
    MENUITEM "&Do It!"    IDM_DOIT
    MENUITEM "&Quit",     IDM_QUIT
END

PrintStop       DIALOG  50, 50, 110, 50
STYLE WS_POPUP | WS_VISIBLE | WS_CAPTION | DS_MODALFRAME
FONT 10, "Helv"
CAPTION "Printer Active"
BEGIN
      CTEXT                 "Click Button To Stop", -1, 0, 10, 110, 12
      DEFPUSHBUTTON         "Cancel",        IDCANCEL, 30, 30, 40, 12, WS_GROUP
END
```

The WinMain() function for this example is identical to the GENERIC application in Chapter 1, and is not reprinted. The rest of the C program is as follows:

```
HWND    ghDlgPrintAbort ;                  /* global variables */
BOOL    gbPrintAbort ;

long FAR PASCAL WndProc (HWND hWnd, unsigned iMessage, WORD wParam,      LONG lParam)
{
        HDC                 hDC ;
        char                szPrinter [64], *szDriver, *szDevice, *szOutput ;
        FARPROC             lpfnPrintDlg, lpfnAbortPrint ;
        int                 i ;

        switch (iMessage)          /* process windows messages */
        {
              case WM_COMMAND:          /* process menu items */
                      switch (wParam)
                      {
                      case IDM_DOIT:  /* User hit the "Do it" menu item */
                              GetProfileString ("Windows", "device", "",
                                      szPrinter, 64) ;
                              szDevice = strtok (szPrinter, ",") ;
                              szDriver = strtok (NULL, ",") ;
                              szOutput = strtok (NULL, ",") ;
                              hDC = CreateDC (szDriver, szDevice, szOutput, NULL) ;

                              EnableWindow (hWnd, FALSE) ;    /* disable main window */
                              gbPrintAbort = FALSE ;
                                                      /* show the dialog box */
                              lpfnPrintDlg = MakeProcInstance (PrintStopDlg,
                                      ghInstance) ;
                              ghDlgPrintAbort = CreateDialog (ghInstance,
                                      "PrintStop",     hWnd, lpfnPrintDlg) ;
                                                      /* turn on the abort proc */
                              lpfnAbortPrint = MakeProcInstance (PrintAbort,
                                      ghInstance) ;
                              Escape (hDC, SETABORTPROC, 0,
                                      (LPSTR) lpfnAbortPrint, NULL) ;

                              if (Escape (hDC, STARTDOC, 4, "Test", NULL) > 0)
                              {
                                      TextOut (hDC, 10, 10,
                                              "Output is on the printer.", 25) ;
                                      Escape (hDC, NEWFRAME, NULL, NULL, NULL) ;
                                      Escape (hDC, ENDDOC, NULL, NULL, NULL) ;
                              }
                              else            /* print error of some sort */
```

```
                              {
                                        Escape (hDC, ENDDOC, NULL, NULL, NULL) ;
                                        MessageBox (hWnd, "Could not activate printer",
                                                "Printer Error", MB_ICONHAND | MB_OK) ;
                              }
                              DestroyWindow (ghDlgPrintAbort) ;/* kill dialog box */
                              EnableWindow (hWnd, TRUE) ;        /* enable main window */
                              SetFocus (hWnd) ;
                              FreeProcInstance (lpfnPrintDlg) ;
                              FreeProcInstance (lpfnAbortPrint) ;
                              DeleteDC (hDC) ;
                              break
                   case IDM_QUIT:             /* send end of application message */
                              DestroyWindow (hWnd) ;
                              break ;
                   }
                   break ;
          case WM_DESTROY:                    /* stop application */
                   PostQuitMessage (0) ;
                   break ;
          default:                            /* default windows message processing */
                   return DefWindowProc (hWnd, iMessage, wParam, lParam) ;
          }
          return (0L) ;
}


BOOL FAR PASCAL PrintStopDlg (HWND hDlg, unsigned iMessage, WORD wParam,
       LONG lParam)
{
       if (iMessage == WM_COMMAND)
       {
                gbPrintAbort = TRUE ;
                return (TRUE) ;
       }
       else
                return (FALSE) ;
}


BOOL FAR PASCAL PrintAbort (HDC hdcPrinter, int nCode)
{
       MSG      msg ;

       while (!gbPrintAbort && PeekMessage (&msg, NULL, 0, 0, PM_REMOVE))
       {
                if (!IsDialogMessage (ghDlgPrintAbort, &msg))
                {
                         TranslateMessage (&msg) ;
                         DispatchMessage (&msg) ;
                }
       }
       return (!gbPrintAbort) ;
}
```

Note that the "abort" procedure is basically a message loop. Messages from any window, including the dialog box window displayed while printing is going on, pass through this loop. The key to aborting the printing job is the global variable *gbPrintAbort*. It is set to FALSE before printing starts. If the button in the dialog box is activated, *gbPrintAbort* is set to TRUE. This setting is detected the next time a message passes through the "abort" procedure, and the printing job is cancelled.

The Printer Device Driver

Although Windows shields you from needing to deal directly with the printer hardware, there are a few situations where it is necessary. For example, you may need to determine the size of the paper or the number of paper bins, the printer is using to switch from portrait mode to landscape mode.

When you install a printer under the Windows Control Panel application, a file with the extension .DRV is added to the Windows system directory. This file is called a "driver." Drivers are actually small DLLs (dynamic link libraries, explained in Chapter 28). The printer supplier generally writes the driver program, based on the guidelines provided by Microsoft. The driver contains all of the code needed to translate the Windows output data into printer-specific commands. The driver will also contain the code needed to generate a printer setup dialog box. This is where those dialog boxes come from that allow you to change from portrait to landscape mode, pick paper sizes, etc.

Prior to Windows 3.1, the primary way to deal with the device driver was via the Escape() function. A long series of commands were supported using Escape() to change and determine printer information. With Windows 3.1, most of the Escape() functions are no longer supported, or are at least discouraged. Several more elegant functions that make dealing with the device driver considerably simpler replaced them.

The key function for working with a printer device driver under Windows 3.1 is ExtDeviceMode(). This function is not defined in WINDOWS.H, although a prototype is included in the DRIVINIT.H file which is included with the Windows SDK. ExtDeviceMode() does not show up in WINDOWS.H because it is not part of Windows—it is part of the printer driver. To access ExtDeviceMode() you must load the driver file using LoadLibrary(), and obtain the ExtDeviceMode() function's address using GetProcAddress(). These are DLL functions, and they are explained more fully in Chapter 28, *Dynamic Link Libraries*. ExtDeviceMode() is the function that an application calls to cause the driver to produce the printer setup dialog box.i.printer setup dialog box.

ExtDeviceMode() uses a specialized data structure called DEVMODE to store printer-specific data. This structure is also defined in the DRIVINIT.H file. ExtDeviceMode() will determine the current printer settings and write the data to the DEVMODE structure. This data can be modified to change the printer device context during a print job. The ResetDC() function passes the changes in the DEVMODE structure to the driver. The DeviceCapabilities() function is also provided as a quick way to determine which features a printer supports.

Text and Device Context Function Summary

Table 10-3 summarizes the device context and text output functions. The detailed function descriptions are in the next section.

Function	Purpose
AddFontResource	Loads a font resource from a file into the system.
CreateDC	Creates a device context to a physical device, such as a printer.
CreateFont	Creates a logical font, ready to be used in text output.
CreateFontIndirect	Identical to CreateFont( ), except that the parameter data is passed to the function via a LOGFONT data structure.
CreateIC	Retrieves a device context for a physical device, but only for information purposes.
DeleteDC	Deletes a device context created with CreateDC( ), CompatibleDC( ), or CreateIC( ).
DeviceCapabilities	Determines the capabilities of a device, such as a printer. (Win 3.1)
DPtoLP	Converts from device points to logical points.
DrawText	Formats a text string to fit within the bounds of a rectangle.
EnumFonts	Finds (enumerates) all of the fonts available on a given device.
Escape	Sends special information to a device, such as a printer.
ExtDeviceMode	Determines or modifies the initialization data for a printer. Displays a dialog box for modifying the printer settings. (Win 3.1)
ExtTextOut	Output of text within a rectangular area, with separate control over the spacing between each character.
GetBkColor	Determines the current background color for a device context.

GetBkMode	Determines the current background painting mode for a device context.
GetCharWidth	Determines the width of one or more characters in a font.
GetDC	Retrieves a handle to the device context for the client area of a window.
GetDCOrg	Determines the screen coordinates for the logical origin of the device context.
GetDeviceCaps	Determines the capabilities of a device.
GetMapMode	Determines the mapping mode in use by a device context.
GetSystemMetrics	Retrieves the dimensions of different window items on the video display.
GetTabbedTextExtent	Determines the logical dimensions of a string containing tab characters.
GetTextAlign	Determines the text alignment settings of a device context.
GetTextCharacterExtra	Determines the amount of extra character spacing defined for a device context.
GetTextColor	Retrieves the text color setting for a device context.
GetTextExtent	Determines the length of a string when output to a device context.
GetTextFace	Retrieves the name of the current typeface.
GetTextMetrics	Retrieves basic data about the font currently selected for a device context.
GetViewportExt	Used with GetWindowExt( ) to determine the scaling of the device context.
GetViewportOrg	Used with GetWindowOrg( ) to determine the location of the origin of the logical coordinate system of a device context.
GetWindowDC	Retrieves the device context for the entire window.
GetWindowExt	Used with GetViewportExt( ) to determine the scaling of the device context.
GetWindowOrg	Used with GetViewportOrg( ) to determine the location of the origin of the logical coordinate system of a device context.
GrayString	Draws grayed text or a grayed bitmap at the given location.
LPtoDP	Converts a point from logical coordinates to device coordinates.
OffsetViewportOrg	Changes the X,Y offset of the logical coordinate system origin.
ReleaseDC	Frees the device context.
RemoveFontResource	Removes a font from the system and frees all memory associated with the font.
ResetDC	Updates a printer device context. (Win 3.1)
RestoreDC	Restores an old device context saved with SaveDC( ).
SaveDC	Saves a device context for future use.
ScaleViewportExt	Changes the scaling of the logical coordinate system for a device context.
ScaleWindowExt	Changes the scaling of the logical coordinate system for a device context.
SetBkColor	Sets the color of the background surrounding each character, dashed line, or hatched brush.
SetBkMode	Changes the background painting mode.
SetMapMode	Changes the mapping mode for a device context.
SetMapperFlags	Adjusts how CreateFont( ) and CreateFontIndirect( ) adjust for font dimensions outside of those specified in the font data.
SetTextAlign	Changes the text alignment for a device context.
SetTextCharacterExtra	Adds additional space between characters of a device context.
SetTextColor	Changes the text color for a device context.
SetTextJustification	Justifies a string prior to using TextOut( ) for output.

Table 10-3. continued

Function	Purpose	⊠
SetViewportExt	Used with SetWindowExt( ) to set the scaling of the logical coordinate system with the MM_ISOTROPIC and MM_ANISOTROPIC mapping modes.	
SetViewportOrg	Changes the origin of the coordinate system used for text and graphics locations on a device.	
SetWindowExt	Used with SetViewportExt( ) to set the scaling of the logical coordinate system with the MM_ISOTROPIC and MM_ANISOTROPIC mapping modes.	
SetWindowOrg	Changes the location of the origin of the device context.	
TabbedTextOut	Outputs a text string, expanding all tab characters.	
TextOut	Outputs a character string at a location on the selected device context.	
wsprintf	Formats text output to a character buffer.	
wvsprintf	Formats text output to a character buffer.	

Table 10-3. Text and Device Context Function Summary.

Text and Device Context Function Descriptions

ADDFONTRESOURCE   ■ Win 2.0   ■ Win 3.0   ■ Win 3.1

Purpose   Loads a font resource from a file into the system.

Syntax   int AddFontResource(LPSTR *lpFilename*);

Description   The function normally is used to load a font directly from a disk file. It can also be used to load a font referenced in the program's resource .RC file.

Uses   Once loaded, the font is available to all applications. It is not necessary to use this function to load the system fonts provided with Windows, unless they have been moved to a directory that Windows does not search on startup.

Returns   The number of fonts loaded. Returns zero if no fonts were loaded, usually meaning that the font file or resource was not found.

See Also   RemoveFontResource(), FindResource()

Parameters
lpFilename   LPSTR: A far pointer to a null-terminated character string containing the font file name. This should be a complete DOS file name including the directory path and the ".FON" file extension. Alternatively, *lpFilename* can contain a handle to a font resource loaded as part of the resource .RC file. The resource file should include a line like

```
        number          FONT           script.fon
```

The FindResource() function is then used to obtain the handle to the font. The handle becomes the low-order word of *lpFilename*. The high-order word must be zero.

Related Messages WM_FONTCHANGE should be sent to all top-level windows after a font is loaded or removed. This makes the new font's availability known to all programs running on the system.

Example   This example shows a font file called "script.fon" being loaded at the start of the program and removed at the end. SendMessage() is used to notify all other top-level programs of the font's presence. By setting the first parameter in SendMessage() equal to -1, all top-level windows receive the message.

```
long FAR PASCAL WndProc (HWND hWnd, unsigned iMessage, WORD wParam, LONG lParam)
{
        int             nFontLoad ;

        switch (iMessage)                               /* process windows messages */
        {
```

```
        case WM_CREATE:                    /* bring in the font file */
                nFontLoad = AddFontResource ((LPSTR) "script.fon") ;
                if (!nFontLoad)
                        MessageBox (hWnd, "Could not load font.", "Warning",
                                MB_ICONHAND | MB_OK) ;
                else                               /* tell other apps */
                        SendMessage (-1, WM_FONTCHANGE, 0, 0L) ;
                break ;
        case WM_COMMAND:                   /* process menu items */
/* other program lines here */
                break ;
        case WM_DESTROY:                   /* stop application */
                RemoveFontResource ((LPSTR) "script.fon") ;       /* remove font */
                SendMessage (-1, WM_FONTCHANGE, 0, 0L) ;          /* tell apps */
                PostQuitMessage (0) ;
                break ;
        default:                       /* default windows message processing */
                return DefWindowProc (hWnd, iMessage, wParam, lParam) ;
        }
        return (0L) ;
}
```

CREATEDC
■ Win 2.0   ■ Win 3.0   ■ Win 3.1

Purpose	Creates a device context to a physical device, such as a printer.
Include File	<drivinit.h>
Syntax	HDC **CreateDC**(LPSTR *lpDriverName*, LPSTR *lpDeviceName*, LPSTR *lpOutput*, LPSTR *lpInitData*);
Description	This is the first step in preparing to send the device graphics data such as text or graphics objects.
Uses	Normally used to create a device context for a printer. In this case, the parameters for the printer are fetched from the WIN.INI file using GetProfileString(). The function is also used to get the device context of the screen (the hardware screen, not a window's client area). To do this, set *lpDriverName* equal to "DISPLAY," and the other parameters equal to NULL. This function should be used carefully, as it allows an application to draw anywhere on the screen, not just within the window's boundaries. Normally, you will use GetDC() and BeginPaint() to get a device context to a window on the screen.
Returns	HDC, a device context for the device. Returns NULL on error.
See Also	DeleteDC(), GetProfileString(), ExtDeviceMode(), DeviceCapabilities()
Parameters	
lpDriverName	LPSTR: A pointer to a null-terminated string containing the DOS file name of the printer driver. The driver file is loaded when a new printer is installed under Windows. Example: "PCL / HP LaserJet." This is the first parameter on the WIN.INI line that starts with "device=."
lpDeviceName	LPSTR: A pointer to a null-terminated string containing the device name. Example: "HPPCL." This is the second parameter on the WIN.INI line that starts with "device=." The parameters are separated by commas.
lpOutput	LPSTR: A pointer to a null-terminated string containing the output file or device. Example: "LPT1:." This is the third parameter on the WIN.INI line that starts with "device=." The parameters are separated by commas.
lpInitData	LPDEVMODE: A pointer to a DEVMODE data structure. This structure can be initialized by calling the ExtDeviceMode() function. Set to NULL to use the default initialization data for the device specified by the user in the Control Panel application. The DEVMODE structure is defined in DRIVINIT.H as follows:

```
/* size of a device name string */
```

```
#define CCHDEVICENAME 32

typedef struct _devicemode {
    char dmDeviceName[CCHDEVICENAME];   /* device name string */
    WORD dmSpecVersion;                 /* driver specification ver. eg. 0x300 */
    WORD dmDriverVersion;               /* OEM dirver version number */
    WORD dmSize;                        /* size of DEVMODE structure */
    WORD dmDriverExtra;                 /* number of bytes following DEVMODE data */
    DWORD dmFields;                     /* bitfield for which of the following dm */
                                        /* values are supported.  Bit 0 is one if */
                                        /* dmOrientation is supported, etc. */
    short dmOrientation;                /* DMORIENT_PORTRAIT or DMORIENT_LANDSCAPE */
    short dmPaperSize;                  /* DMPAPER_LETTER, DM_PAPER_LEGAL, DM_PAPER_A4 */
                /* DMPAPER_CSCHEET, DMPAPER_DSCHEET, DMPAPER_ESHEET, DMPAPER_ENV_9 */
                /* DMPAPER_ENV_10, DMPAPER_ENV_11, DMPAPER_ENV_12, DMPAPER_ENV_14 */
    short dmPaperLength;                /* overrides dmPaperSize, in mm/10 */
    short dmPaperWidth;                 /* overrides dmPaperSize, in mm/10 */
    short dmScale;                      /* page is scaled by dmScale/100 */
    short dmCopies;                     /* number of copies supported */
    short dmDefaultSource;              /* Default paper bin */
    short dmPrintQuality;               /* DMRES_HIGH, DMRES_MEDIUM, DMRES_LOW, */
                                        /* or DMRES_DRAFT */
    short dmColor;                      /* DMCOLOR_COLOR or DMCOLOR_MONOCHROME */
    short dmDuplex;                     /* DMDUP_SIMPLEX, DMDUP_HORIZONTAL, */
                                        /* or DMDUP_VERTICAL */
    BYTE  dmDriverData [dmDriverExtra] ; /* 0 or more bytes of extra data */
} DEVMODE;

typedef DEVMODE * PDEVMODE, NEAR * NPDEVMODE, FAR * LPDEVMODE;
```

Example   Here the program writes a single line of text to the printer when the user clicks the "Do It!" menu
item. The printer information is pulled from WIN.INI using GetProfileString(). The string is
parsed with the compiler library function strtok(), to break out the device name, driver name,
and output device name. CreateDC() is used to create the device context for the printer. The
Escape() function is used to send the minimal printer codes necessary to start and stop a print
job.

```
long FAR PASCAL WndProc (HWND hWnd, unsigned iMessage, WORD wParam, LONG lParam)
{
        HDC     hDC ;
        char    szPrinter [64], *szDriver, *szDevice, *szOutput ;

        switch (iMessage)             /* process windows messages */
        {
        case WM_COMMAND:              /* process menu items */
                switch (wParam)
                {
                case IDM_DOIT:  /* User hit the "Do it" menu item */
                        GetProfileString ("Windows", "device", "",
                                szPrinter, 64) ;
                        szDevice = strtok (szPrinter, ",") ;
                        szDriver = strtok (NULL, ",") ;
                        szOutput = strtok (NULL, ",") ;
                        hDC = CreateDC (szDriver, szDevice,
                                szOutput, NULL) ;
                        if (Escape (hDC, STARTDOC, 4, "Test", NULL))
                        {
                                TextOut (hDC, 10, 10,
                                        "Output is on the printer.", 25) ;
                                Escape (hDC, NEWFRAME, NULL, NULL, NULL) ;
                                Escape (hDC, ENDDOC, NULL, NULL, NULL) ;
                        }
                        DeleteDC (hDC) ;
                        break ;
                case IDM_QUIT:  /* send end of application message */
                        DestroyWindow (hWnd) ;
                        break ;
```

```
                    }
                    break ;
        case WM_DESTROY:         /* stop application */
                    PostQuitMessage (0) ;
                    break ;
        default:          /* default windows message processing */
                    return DefWindowProc (hWnd, iMessage, wParam, lParam) ;
        }
    return (0L) ;
}
```

CREATEFONT
■ Win 2.0   ■ Win 3.0   ■ Win 3.1

Purpose	Creates a logical font, ready to be used in text output. The font is the closest match to the given parameters and the font data available.
Syntax	HFONT **CreateFont**(int *nHeight*, int *nWidth*, int *nEscapement*, int *nOrientation*, int *nWeight*, BYTE *cItalic*, BYTE *cUnderline*, BYTE *cStrikeOut*, BYTE *cCharSet*, BYTE *cOutputPrecision*, BYTE *cClipPrecision*, BYTE *cQuality*, BYTE *cPitchAndFamily*, LPSTR *lpFacename*);
Description	Logical fonts are interpolations between existing font data to create new fonts that approximate the font requested. This allows a font to be displayed on the screen with sizes and bold or italic characteristics that may be supported by the printer, but not defined in a .FON file. CreateFont() makes the best use it can of loaded font resources before creating a logical font. Any missing data is interpolated between existing fonts. Because of this, you can create fonts with sizes and styles that do not exist as font resources. The quality of the font will deteriorate as you get farther from the resource data.
Uses	Generally used when a program has only one font to create. CreateFont() has more parameters than any other function in Windows. In many cases, the CreateFontIndirect() function is easier to use because you load the data ahead of time in a LOGFONT structure and have only the pointer to the structure to pass to the function. Both CreateFont() and CreateFontIndirect() can be used to do "tricks" with fonts, such as upside-down characters, characters that print upwards or to the left, etc.
Returns	HFONT, a handle to the font created. This is the handle you use with SelectObject() to make the font available for output onto the device context with functions such as TextOut().
See Also	CreateFontIndirect(), SelectObject(), TextOut(), AddFontResource()
Parameters	
nHeight	int: The desired height of the characters, including internal leading and excluding external leading. Set equal to zero for the default size. To set the ascent size, rather than the total height, make this value negative. The absolute value will then be used to set the ascent size. See Figure 10-2 for a diagram of the ascent size of a character.
nWidth	int: The desired width of the characters. Normally set to 0, which allows Windows to match the width to the height. Positive values force a width, changing the character's aspect ratio.
nEscapement	int: Specifies the orientation of the next character output relative to the previous one in tenths of a degree. Normally, set to 0. Set to 900 to have all the characters go upward from the first character, 1800 to write backwards, or 2700 to write each character from the top down.
nOrientation	int: Specifies how much the character should be rotated when output in tenths of a degree. Set to 900 to have all the characters lying on their backs, 1800 for upside-down writing, etc.
nWeight	int: Sets the line thickness of each character. Only two values are supported in Windows 3.0. FW_NORMAL == 400 for normal characters and FW_BOLD == 700 for boldface. WINDOWS.H has eight other sizes defined, but these end up rounded to either the 400 or 700 weight.
cItalic	BYTE: TRUE to specify italic characters, FALSE (zero) for normal.

cUnderline	BYTE: TRUE to specify underlined characters, FALSE (zero) for normal.
cStrikeOut	BYTE: TRUE to specify characters with a line through the center, FALSE (zero) for normal.
cCharSet	BYTE: The character set of the font. This can be either ANSI_CHARSET, SYMBOL_CHARSET, OEM_CHARSET, or (with Japanese versions of Windows) SHIFTJIS_CHARSET.
cOutputPrecision	BYTE: This field is not yet implemented in the 3.0 version of Windows. Set equal to OUT_DEFAULT_PRECIS for now to be compatible with future releases of Windows.
cClipPrecision	BYTE: This field is not yet implemented in the 3.0 version of Windows. Set equal to CLIP_DEFAULT_PRECIS for now to be compatible with future releases of Windows.
cQuality	BYTE: Can be either DRAFT_QUALITY, PROOF_QUALITY, or DEFAULT QUALITY. PROOF_QUALITY forces the closest match to the loaded font data, which may change the font size if the specified size is not available.
cPitchAndFamily	BYTE: Two values combined with the C language binary OR operator (|). The two low-order bytes specify the font pitch. This can be

DEFAULT_PITCH, FIXED_PITCH or VARIABLE_PITCH

The four high-order bytes specify the font family. This can be any of the following:

FF_DECORATIVE, FF_DONTCARE, FF_MODERN, FF_SCRIPT, or FF_SWISS.

lpFacename	LPSTR: A pointer to a null-terminated string that specifies the name of the typeface. The maximum length of the name is LF_FACESIZE, which is defined in WINDOWS.H as 32. EnumFonts() can be used within the program to find the names of all available fonts.

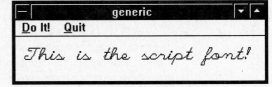

Example	This example, which is illustrated in Figure 10-3, creates a script font 24 by 16 units in size and uses it to print some text on the window's client area.

Figure 10-3. CreateFont() Example.

```
Long FAR PASCAL WndProc (HWND hWnd, unsigned iMessage, WORD wParam, LONG lParam)
{
        HDC             hDC ;
        HFONT           hFont ;

        switch (iMessage)               /* process windows messages */
        {
                case WM_COMMAND:        /* process menu items */
                        switch (wParam)
                        {
                        case IDM_DOIT:  /* User hit the "Do it" menu item */
                                hDC = GetDC (hWnd) ;
                                hFont = CreateFont (24, 16, 0, 0, 400, 0, 0, 0,
                                        OEM_CHARSET,    OUT_DEFAULT_PRECIS,
                                        CLIP_DEFAULT_PRECIS, DEFAULT_QUALITY,
                                        DEFAULT_PITCH | FF_SCRIPT, "script") ;
                                SelectObject (hDC, hFont) ;
                                TextOut (hDC, 10, 10, "This is the script font!", 24) ;
                                ReleaseDC (hWnd, hDC) ;
                                DeleteObject (hFont) ;
                                break ;
                        case IDM_QUIT:  /* send end of application message */
                                DestroyWindow (hWnd) ;
                                break ;
                        }
                        break ;
                case WM_DESTROY:        /* stop application */
                        PostQuitMessage (0) ;
                        break ;
                default:        /* default windows message processing */
```

```
                        return DefWindowProc (hWnd, iMessage, wParam, lParam) ;
            }
        return (OL) ;
}
```

CREATEFONTINDIRECT   ■ Win 2.0   ■ Win 3.0   ■ Win 3.1

Purpose   Creates a logical font.

Syntax   HFONT **CreateFontIndirect**(LOGFONT FAR *lpLogFont*);

Description   The LOGFONT structure is defined in WINDOWS.H as

```
#define LF_FACESIZE        32

typedef struct tagLOGFONT
  {
    int      lfHeight;
    int      lfWidth;
    int      lfEscapement;
    int      lfOrientation;
    int      lfWeight;
    BYTE     lfItalic;
    BYTE     lfUnderline;
    BYTE     lfStrikeOut;
    BYTE     lfCharSet;
    BYTE     lfOutPrecision;
    BYTE     lfClipPrecision;
    BYTE     lfQuality;
    BYTE     lfPitchAndFamily;
    BYTE     lfFaceName[LF_FACESIZE];
  } LOGFONT;
typedef LOGFONT                    *PLOGFONT;
typedef LOGFONT NEAR               *NPLOGFONT;
typedef LOGFONT FAR                *LPLOGFONT;
```

Each of the elements of the LOGFONT structure has the meaning described in the CreateFont() function description.

Uses   CreateFont() is convenient if one font is being used. For more than one, CreateFontIndirect() is more convenient as many of the parameters are repeated for all fonts.

Returns   HFONT, a handle to the font created. This is the handle you use with SelectObject() to make the font available for output onto the device context with functions such as TextOut(). Returns NULL on error.

See Also   CreateFontIndirect(), SelectObject(), TextOut(), AddFontResource()

Parameters

lpLogFont   LPLOGFONT: A pointer to a LOGFONT structure.

Example

```
Long FAR PASCAL WndProc (HWND hWnd, unsigned iMessage, WORD wParam, LONG lParam)
{
        HDC             hDC ;
        HFONT           hFont ;
        LOGFONT         lf ;

        switch (iMessage)                        /* process windows messages */
        {
            case WM_COMMAND:                     /* process menu items */
                switch (wParam)
                {
                case IDM_DOIT:                   /* User hit the "Do it" menu item */
                        hDC = GetDC (hWnd) ;
                        lf.lfHeight = 20 ;
                        lf.lfWidth = lf.lfEscapement = lf.lfOrientation = 0 ;
```

```
                              lf.lfWeight = FW_NORMAL ;
                              lf.lfItalic = lf.lfUnderline = lf.lfStrikeOut = 0 ;
                              lf.lfCharSet = OEM_CHARSET ;
                              lf.lfOutPrecision = OUT_DEFAULT_PRECIS ;
                              lf.lfClipPrecision = CLIP_DEFAULT_PRECIS ;
                              lf.lfQuality = DEFAULT_QUALITY ;
                              lf.lfPitchAndFamily = DEFAULT_PITCH | FF_DONTCARE ;
                              strcpy (lf.lfFaceName, "Helv") ;
                              hFont = CreateFontIndirect (&lf) ;
                              SelectObject (hDC, hFont) ;
                              TextOut (hDC, 10, 10, "This is the font!", 17) ;
                              ReleaseDC (hWnd, hDC) ;
                              DeleteObject (hFont) ;
                              break ;
                     case IDM_QUIT:          /* send end of application message */
                              DestroyWindow (hWnd) ;
                              break ;
                     }
                     break ;
            case WM_DESTROY:                 /* stop application */
                     PostQuitMessage (0) ;
                     break ;
            default:                         /* default windows message processing */
                     return DefWindowProc (hWnd, iMessage, wParam, lParam) ;
     }
     return (0L) ;
}
```

CREATEIC   ■ Win 2.0   ■ Win 3.0   ■ Win 3.1

Purpose	Retrieves a device context for a physical device, but only for information purposes. Output cannot be sent to the device.
Syntax	HDC **CreateIC**(LPSTR *lpDriverName*, LPSTR *lpDeviceName*, LPSTR *lpOutput*, LPSTR *lpInitData*);
Description	This function is identical to CreateDC(), except that the device context is not set up for output.
Uses	Frequently used with GetDeviceCaps() to retrieve information about a printer or screen device. Also used in setting up memory areas to be compatible with the device context of the screen with CreateCompatibleDC().
Returns	HDC, a device context for the device. Returns NULL on error.
See Also	DeleteDC(), GetProfileString(), GetDeviceCaps(), CreateCompatibleDC()
Parameters	
lpDriverName	LPSTR: A pointer to a null-terminated string containing the DOS file name of the printer driver. The driver file is loaded when a new printer is installed under Windows. Example: "PCL/HP LaserJet." This is the first parameter on the WIN.INI line that starts with "device=."
lpDeviceName	LPSTR: A pointer to a null-terminated string containing the device name. Example: "HPPCL." This is the second parameter on the WIN.INI line that starts with "device=." The parameters are separated by commas. Set to NULL for a screen device.
lpOutput	LPSTR: A pointer to a null-terminated string containing the output file or device. Example: "LPT1:." This is the third parameter on the WIN.INI line that starts with "device=." The parameters are separated by commas. Set to NULL for a screen device.
lpInitData	LPDEVMODE: A pointer to a DEVMODE data structure. This structure can be initialized by calling the ExtDeviceMode() function. Set to NULL to use the default initialization data for the device specified by the user in the Control Panel application. The DEVMODE structure is defined in DRIVINIT.H as follows:

```
/* size of a device name string */
#define CCHDEVICENAME 32
```

```
typedef struct _devicemode {
   char dmDeviceName[CCHDEVICENAME];    /* device name string */
   WORD dmSpecVersion;                  /* driver specification ver. eg. 0x300 */
   WORD dmDriverVersion;                /* OEM dirver version number */
   WORD dmSize;                         /* size of DEVMODE structure */
   WORD dmDriverExtra;                  /* number of bytes following DEVMODE data */
   DWORD dmFields;                      /* bitfield for which of the following dm */
                                        /* values are supported.  Bit 0 is one if */
                                        /* dmOrientation is supported, etc. */
   short dmOrientation;                 /* DMORIENT_PORTRAIT or DMORIENT_LANDSCAPE */
   short dmPaperSize;                   /* DMPAPER_LETTER, DM_PAPER_LEGAL, DM_PAPER_A4 */
                /* DMPAPER_CSCHEET, DMPAPER_DSCHEET, DMPAPER_ESHEET, DMPAPER_ENV_9 */
                /* DMPAPER_ENV_10, DMPAPER_ENV_11, DMPAPER_ENV_12, DMPAPER_ENV_14 */
   short dmPaperLength;                 /* overrides dmPaperSize, in mm/10 */
   short dmPaperWidth;                  /* overrides dmPaperSize, in mm/10 */
   short dmScale;                       /* page is scaled by dmScale/100 */
   short dmCopies;                      /* number of copies supported */
   short dmDefaultSource;               /* Default paper bin */
   short dmPrintQuality;                /* DMRES_HIGH, DMRES_MEDIUM, DMRES_LOW, */
                                        /* or DMRES_DRAFT */
   short dmColor;                       /* DMCOLOR_COLOR or DMCOLOR_MONOCHROME */
   short dmDuplex;                      /* DMDUP_SIMPLEX, DMDUP_HORIZONTAL, */
                                        /* or DMDUP_VERTICAL */
   BYTE  dmDriverData [dmDriverExtra] ; /* 0 or more bytes of extra data */
} DEVMODE;

typedef DEVMODE * PDEVMODE, NEAR * NPDEVMODE, FAR * LPDEVMODE;
```

Example   This is a fragment of a WndProc() function that uses CreateIC() to get an information context for the screen. Using the context, the program finds the number of bits per pixel and the number of color planes for the display. For a VGA screen, this will show 1 bit and 4 color planes.

```
long FAR PASCAL WndProc (HWND hWnd, unsigned iMessage, WORD wParam, LONG lParam)
{
        HDC                     hDC ;
        char                    cBuf [10] ;
        int                     nBits, nColorPlanes ;

        switch (iMessage)               /* process windows messages */
        {
                case WM_COMMAND:        /* process menu items */
                        switch (wParam)
                        {
                        case IDM_DOIT:  /* User hit the "Do it" menu item */
                                hDC = CreateIC ("DISPLAY", NULL, NULL, NULL) ;
                                nBits = GetDeviceCaps (hDC, BITSPIXEL) ;
                                nColorPlanes = GetDeviceCaps (hDC, PLANES) ;
                                DeleteDC (hDC) ;
                                hDC = GetDC (hWnd) ;
                                TextOut (hDC, 10, 10, "Color per pixel =", 17) ;
                                itoa (nBits, cBuf, 10) ;
                                TextOut (hDC, 10, 30, cBuf, strlen (cBuf)) ;
                                TextOut (hDC, 10, 50, "Color planes =", 14) ;
                                itoa (nColorPlanes, cBuf, 10) ;
                                TextOut (hDC, 10, 70, cBuf, strlen (cBuf)) ;
                                ReleaseDC (hWnd, hDC) ;
                                break ;
```

[Other program lines]

DELETEDC   ■ Win 2.0   ■ Win 3.0   ■ Win 3.1

Purpose   Deletes a device context created with CreateDC(), CreateCompatibleDC(), or CreateIC().

Syntax   BOOL **DeleteDC**(HDC *hDC*);

Description   Device contexts take up memory in the system. Use this function to free the device context as soon as possible after use.

Uses	Used any time CreateDC(), CreateCompatibleDC(), or CreateIC() was used to create a device context. Do not use it if GetDC() was used to create a device context for a window. In that case, use ReleaseDC().
Returns	BOOL. TRUE if the device context was deleted, FALSE on error.
See Also	CreateDC(), CreateIC(), CreateCompatibleDC()
Parameters	
hDC	HDC: A handle to the device context created with CreateDC(), CreateCompatibleDC(), or CreateIC().
Example	The previous example, shown under CreateIC(), shows the device context being deleted after use. Note how GetDC() is used afterwards to obtain a separate device context for output to the window's client area.

DEVICECAPABILITIES   ☐ Win 2.0   ■ Win 3.0   ■ Win 3.1

Purpose	Determines the capabilities of a device, such as a printer.
Syntax	DWORD **DeviceCapabilities** (LPSTR *lpDeviceName*, LPSTR *lpPort*, WORD *nIndex*, LPSTR *lpOutput*, LPDEVMODE *lpDevMode*);
Include File	<drivinit.h>, <print.h> (3.1)
Description	Physical devices, such as printers, are accessed by calling functions within a device driver file. The file, with the extension .DRV, will reside in the Windows system directory. Drivers are specialized DLLs (dynamic link libraries). Functions within these DLLs can be accessed to determine the capabilities of the physical device. See Chapter 28 for more details on DLLs.
	DeviceCapabilities() is a function that is expected to be supported within the driver file. The function is called indirectly by first loading the driver file with LoadLibrary(), and then obtaining the DeviceCapabilities() function address within the driver with GetProcAddress(). The DRIVINIT.H header file includes the following two typedef statements for use with GetProcAddress() to reference the DeviceCapabilities() function within the driver file.

```
typedef DWORD FAR PASCAL FNDEVCAPS(LPSTR, LPSTR, WORD, LPSTR, LPDEVMODE);
typedef FNDEVCAPS FAR * LPFNDEVCAPS;
```

Uses	Determining the paper sizes, paper bins, etc. that a printer supports.
Returns	DWORD. The returned value depends on the *nIndex* value specified. Returns 1 on error.
See Also	CreateDC(), ExtDeviceMode(), LoadLibrary(), GetProcAddress(), GetProfileString(), GetSystemDirectory()
Parameters	
lpDeviceName	LPSTR: A pointer to a null-terminated character string containing the printer device name, such as "PCL/HP LaserJet." Use GetProfileString() to obtain this string from the WIN.INI file.
lpPort	LPSTR: A pointer to a null-terminated character string containing the name of the port to which the device is connected, such as "LPT1:." This string can also be obtained from WIN.INI.
nIndex	WORD: Specifies which value to obtain from the device. It can be any of the indices listed in Table 10-4 and defined in DRIVINIT.H.

Value	Meaning	
DC_BINNAMES	If the printer driver does not support multiple bins, DeviceCapabilities( ) returns 0. If multiple bins are supported, DeviceCapabilities( ) returns the number of bins. *lpOutput* should then point to a memory buffer to hold data on the bins. The data consists of an array of integers, each containing the bin ID number (one for each bin). This is followed by the bin names, each 24 characters long.	

	Set *lpOutput* to NULL to simply return the number of bins supported. This is usually done to determine the number of bytes to allocate for the bin numbers and names (26 bytes per bin).
DC_BINS	If *lpOutput* is set to NULL, DeviceCapabilities( ) returns the number of paper bins the printer supports. If *lpOuput* is not NULL, it should contain a pointer to a memory buffer. The buffer will receive an array of WORD values, each containing a bin number.
DC_COPIES (Win 3.1)	DeviceCapabilities( ) returns the maximum number of copies that the printer can produce.
DC_DRIVER	DeviceCapabilities( ) returns the printer driver version number.
DC_DUPLEX	Returns 1 if the printer supports duplex printing, 0 if not.
DC_ENUMRESOLUTIONS (Win 3.1)	If *lpOutput* is set to NULL, DeviceCapabilities( ) returns the number output resolutions the printer supports. If *lpOuput* is not NULL, it should contain a pointer to a memory buffer. The buffer will receive an array of groups of two LONG integer values, each containing the horizontal and vertical resolution supported.
DC_EXTRA	Returns the number of bytes of device specific data at the end of the DEVMODE structure for the printer driver.
DC_FIELDS	Returns the bit-field value which specifies which features are supported by the printer driver. This is the same as the *dmFields* element of the DEVMODE structure.
DC_FILEDEPENDENCIES (Win 3.1)	If *lpOutput* is set to NULL, DeviceCapabilities( ) returns the number of files which need to be loaded to make the printer work. If *lpOuput* is not NULL, it should contain a pointer to a memory buffer. The buffer will receive an array of 64 character long file names, each containing the file name of a file that must be loaded to support the printer.
DC_MAXEXTENT	Returns a POINT structure containing the maximum paper size that the printer can support. These are the largest values that can be placed in the *dmPaperLength* and *dmPaperWidth* elements of the DEVMODE structure.
DC_MINEXTENT	Returns a POINT structure containing the minimum paper size that the printer can support. These are the smallest values that can be placed in the *dmPaperLength* and *dmPaperWidth* elements of the DEVMODE structure.
DC_PAPERS	If *lpOutput* is set to NULL, DeviceCapabilities( ) returns the number of supported paper sizes. This is the normal use of this flag. If *lpOuput* is not NULL, it should contain a pointer to a memory buffer. The buffer will receive an array of WORD values, each containing a supported paper size.
DC_PAPERSIZE	*lpOutput* should contain a pointer to a memory buffer. The buffer will receive an array of POINT values, each containing the horizontal and vertical size in 1/10 mm for supported paper sizes. Use DC_PAPERS first to determine the size of the data buffer needed to contain the POINT data.
DC_SIZE	DeviceCapabilities( ) returns the size of the DEVMODE data structure, not including any driver-specific data following the structure. This is the same as the *dmSize* element of the DEVMODE data structure.
DC_VERSION	DeviceCapabilities( ) returns the Microsoft driver specification number to which the driver conforms.

Table 10-4. DeviceCapabilities( ) Index Values.

lpOutput	LPSTR: A pointer to a memory buffer. The data received in the buffer will depend on the *nIndex* value, as described above.
lpDevMode	LPDEVMODE: Normally, set to NULL. In this case, DeviceCapabilities() returns the current initialization values for the specified driver. If *lpDevMode* is not NULL, it should contain a

pointer to a DEVMODE data structure containing the values to be read by DeviceCapabilities().
DEVMODE is defined in DRIVINIT.H as follows:

```
/* size of a device name string */
#define CCHDEVICENAME 32

typedef struct _devicemode {
   char dmDeviceName[CCHDEVICENAME];                /* device name string */
   WORD dmSpecVersion;                /* driver specification ver. eg. 0x300 */
   WORD dmDriverVersion;              /* OEM dirver version number */
   WORD dmSize;                       /* size of DEVMODE structure */
   WORD dmDriverExtra;                /* number of bytes following DEVMODE data */
   DWORD dmFields;                    /* bit-field for which of the following dm */
                                      /* values are supported.  Bit 0 is one if */
                                      /* dmOrientation is supported, etc. */
   short dmOrientation;               /* DMORIENT_PORTRAIT or DMORIENT_LANDSCAPE */
   short dmPaperSize;                 /* DMPAPER_LETTER, DM_PAPER_LEGAL, DM_PAPER_A4 */
              /* DMPAPER_CSCHEET, DMPAPER_DSCHEET, DMPAPER_ESHEET, DMPAPER_ENV_9 */
              /* DMPAPER_ENV_10, DMPAPER_ENV_11, DMPAPER_ENV_12, DMPAPER_ENV_14 */
   short dmPaperLength;               /* overrides dmPaperSize, in mm/10 */
   short dmPaperWidth;                /* overrides dmPaperSize, in mm/10 */
   short dmScale;                     /* page is scaled by dmScale/100 */
   short dmCopies;                    /* number of copies supported */
   short dmDefaultSource;             /* Default paper bin */
   short dmPrintQuality;              /* DMRES_HIGH, DMRES_MEDIUM, DMRES_LOW, */
                                      /* or DMRES_DRAFT */
   short dmColor;                     /* DMCOLOR_COLOR or DMCOLOR_MONOCHROME */
   short dmDuplex;                    /* DMDUP_SIMPLEX, DMDUP_HORIZONTAL, */
                                      /* or DMDUP_VERTICAL */
   BYTE  dmDriverData [dmDriverExtra] ;  /* 0 or more bytes of extra data */
} DEVMODE;

typedef DEVMODE * PDEVMODE, NEAR * NPDEVMODE, FAR * LPDEVMODE;
```

Example
This example, which is illustrated in Figure 10-4, displays the
printer driver name, OEM driver number, and the paper sizes
supported when the user clicks the "Do It!" menu item. The
driver name is determined by parsing the WIN.INI file entry
"device=." The driver file is in the Windows system directory.
The directory name is determined by calling GetSystemDirectory().
When the full directory/file name string for the dirver file has
been assembled, the driver is loaded with LoadLibrary().
GetProcAddress() is used to obtain the address of the De-
viceCapabilities() function within the driver file. This is executed twice to determine the driver number and supported
paper sizes.

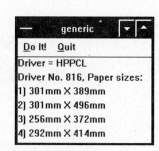

*Figure 10-4. Device-
Capabilities() Example.*

```
long FAR PASCAL WndProc (HWND hWnd, unsigned iMessage, WORD wParam, LONG lParam)
{
        char            szPrinter [64], szSysDir [128], szFullDriver [256],
                                *szDriver, *szDevice, *szOutput, cBuf [128] ;
        HANDLE          hDriver ;
        LPFNDEVCAPS     lpDeviceCaps ;
        DWORD           dwVersion, dwNumPapersize ;
        POINT           PointArray [20] ;
        HDC             hDC ;
        int             i ;

        switch (iMessage)             /* process windows messages */
        {
                case WM_COMMAND:      /* process menu items */
                        switch (wParam)
                        {
                        case IDM_DOIT:  /* get driver name from WIN.INI */
```

```
                        GetProfileString ("windows", "device", "", szPrinter, 64) ;
                        szDevice = strtok (szPrinter, ",") ;
                        szDriver = strtok (NULL, ",") ;
                        szOutput = strtok (NULL, ",") ;
                                /* build full driver path/file spec */
                        GetSystemDirectory (szSysDir, 128) ;
                        lstrcpy (szFullDriver, szSysDir) ;
                        lstrcat (szFullDriver, "\\") ;
                        lstrcat (szFullDriver, szDriver) ;
                        lstrcat (szFullDriver, ".DRV") ;
                                /* get handle to driver */
                        hDriver = LoadLibrary (szFullDriver) ;
                        if (hDriver > 31)
                        {       /* get address of DeviceCaps func. */
                                lpDeviceCaps =
                                        (LPFNDEVCAPS) GetProcAddress (hDriver,
                                        "DeviceCapabilities") ;
                                if (lpDeviceCaps)        /* use DeviceCaps func. */
                                {
                                        dwVersion = (* lpDeviceCaps) (szPrinter,
                                                szOutput, DC_DRIVER, NULL, NULL) ;
                                        dwNumPapersize =
                                                (* lpDeviceCaps) (szPrinter,
                                                szOutput, DC_PAPERSIZE,
                                                (LPSTR) PointArray, NULL) ;
                                                /* output results */
                                        hDC = GetDC (hWnd) ;
                                        TextOut (hDC, 0, 0, cBuf, wsprintf (cBuf,
                                                "Driver = %s", (LPSTR) szDriver)) ;
                                        TextOut (hDC, 0, 20, cBuf, wsprintf (cBuf,
                                                "Driver No. %d, Paper sizes:",
                                                dwVersion)) ;
                                        for (i = 0 ; i < dwNumPapersize ; i++)
                                                TextOut (hDC, 0, 40 + (i * 20), cBuf,
                                                wsprintf (cBuf, "%d) %dmm X %dmm",
                                                        i + 1, PointArray[i].x / 10,
                                                        PointArray[i].y / 10)) ;
                                        ReleaseDC (hWnd, hDC) ;
                                }
                        }
                        else
                                MessageBox (hWnd, "Could not load driver file.",
                                "Message", MB_OK) ;
                        break ;
```

[Other program lines]

DPtoLP   ■ Win 2.0   ■ Win 3.0   ■ Win 3.1

Purpose	Converts from device points to logical points.
Syntax	BOOL **DPtoLP**(HDC *hDC*, LPPOINT *lpPoints*, int *nCount*);
Description	When a window's client area device context is first captured, the MM_TEXT mapping mode is set. This means that the measurement units for locations in the client area are in pixels, measured from the top left corner. As soon as a different mapping mode is set, or the origin is moved, the measurements of a point's location switch to logical units. DPtoLP() allows you to convert one or more points from device coordinates to logical coordinates.
Uses	Used after the mapping mode or origin has been changed, usually to plot items relative to the boundary of the window.
Returns	BOOL. TRUE if the points were converted, FALSE on error.
See Also	SetViewportOrg(), SetWindowOrg(), SetMapMode(), LPtoDP()
Parameters	
hDC	HDC: The device context.

lpPoints	LPPOINT: A pointer to an array of one or more POINT structures.
nCount	int: The number of POINTs in the *lpPoints* array.
Related Messages	WM_SIZE
Example	This example, as shown in Figure 10-5, draws an X from corner to corner of the client area after the mapping mode has been changed. This requires converting the coordinates of the corners of the client area into logical coordinates before the lines are drawn.

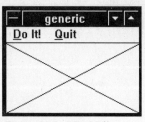

Figure 10-5. DPtoLP( ) Example.

```
long FAR PASCAL WndProc (HWND hWnd, unsigned iMessage, WORD wParam, LONG lParam)
{
        HDC                     hDC ;
        static                  POINT   ptClientSize, ptCenter ;
        POINT                   ptCorners [4] ;

        switch (iMessage)                       /* process windows messages */
        {
                case WM_SIZE:                   /* get client area size */
                        ptClientSize.x = LOWORD (lParam) ;
                        ptClientSize.y = HIWORD (lParam) ;
                        break ;
                case WM_COMMAND:                /* process menu items */
                        switch (wParam)
                        {
                        case IDM_DOIT:          /* User hit the "Do it" menu item */
                                hDC = GetDC (hWnd) ;
                                SetMapMode (hDC, MM_LOMETRIC) ;
                                ptCenter.x = ptClientSize.x / 2 ;/* calc center in */
                                ptCenter.y = ptClientSize.y / 2 ;/* device units */
                                SetViewportOrg (hDC, ptCenter.x, ptCenter.y) ;
                                ptCorners [0].x = 0 ;           /* window corners in */
                                ptCorners [0].y = 0 ;           /* device units */
                                ptCorners [1].x = ptClientSize.x ;
                                ptCorners [1].y = 0 ;
                                ptCorners [2].x = ptClientSize.x ;
                                ptCorners [2].y = ptClientSize.y ;
                                ptCorners [3].x = 0 ;
                                ptCorners [3].y = ptClientSize.y ;
                                                /* now convert to logical coordinates */
                                DPtoLP (hDC, (LPPOINT) &ptCorners, 4) ;
                                MoveTo (hDC, ptCorners [0].x, ptCorners [0].y) ;
                                LineTo (hDC, ptCorners [2].x, ptCorners [2].y) ;
                                MoveTo (hDC, ptCorners [1].x, ptCorners [1].y) ;
                                LineTo (hDC, ptCorners [3].x, ptCorners [3].y) ;
                                ReleaseDC (hWnd, hDC) ;
                                break ;
```

[Other program lines]

DRAWTEXT
■ Win 2.0   ■ Win 3.0   ■ Win 3.1

Purpose	Formats a text string to fit within the bounds of a rectangle.
Syntax	int DrawText(HDC *hDC*, LPSTR *lpString*, int *nCount*, LPRECT *lpRect*, WORD *wFormat*);
Description	DrawText() uses the currently selected text font, color, and background to draw the text. Lines are wrapped to fit within the bounds of the rectangle.
Uses	Used in place of TextOut() when the output string may be too long to fit in one line. Unless the DT_NOCLIP format is used, the text will be clipped if the line(s) cannot be fit into the rectangle.

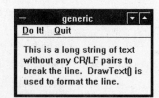

Figure 10-6. DrawText( ) Example.

Returns	int, the height of the output text in device units.
See Also	TextOut()
Parameters	
hDC	HDC: The handle to the device context. Use GetDC() to retrieve a device context for the window, or BeginPaint() if processing a WM_PAINT message.
lpString	LPSTR: A pointer to a string. If the string is null-terminated, the *nCount* parameter can be set to –1. Otherwise, the string length will need to be specified.
nCount	int: The number of characters to output. Set to -1 if the string is null-terminated and you wish to output the entire string.
lpRect	LPRECT: A pointer to the rectangle that will contain the text. Logical coordinates are used. Use GetClientRect() to obtain the client area rectangle. Use DPtoLP() to convert from device units to logical units if the mapping mode has been changed.
wFormat	WORD: One of the values listed in Table 10-5. These values can be combined with the C language binary OR operator (|).

Value	Meaning	⊠
DT_CALCRECT	Calculates the size of the rectangle necessary to hold the text. If the DT_SINGLELINE style is used, the width is adjusted to fit the text. Otherwise, the width is specified in the *lpRect* parameter and the bottom is extended to fit the text.	
DT_CENTER	Centers the text horizontally.	
DT_EXPANDTABS	Expands tab characters. The default tab stops are set at eight character widths. See DT_TABSTOP.	
DT_EXTERNALLEADING	Includes the font's external leading size in computing line spacing. Normally, the external leading dimension is not added to the character height in computing line spacing.	
DT_LEFT	Left justification.	
DT_NOCLIP	Draws the text without clipping. This is faster, but does not assure that the text will be within the bounds of the rectangle.	
DT_NOPREFIX	Normally, "&" characters are used to underline the following letter, and "&&" is used to print a single "&." By specifying DT_NOPREFIX, "&" characters have no special meaning and are printed as is.	
DT_RIGHT	Right justification.	
DT_SINGLELINE	Specifies a single line of text.	
DT_TABSTOP	Sets the tab stops. The high-order byte of *wFormat* should be used to set the number of characters per tab stop.	
DT_TOP	Top justification. Must be used with DT_SINGLELINE.	
DT_VCENTER	Vertically centered justification. Must be used with DT_SINGLELINE.	
DT_WORDBREAK	Specifies that spaces between words will be used to break lines that would otherwise exceed the size of the rectangle. CR/LF pairs also break the line.	

Table 10-5. DrawText( ) Flags.

Example	This is a WndProc() program fragment showing DrawText() being used to format a long line of text. The result is as shown in Figure 10-6.

```
Long FAR PASCAL WndProc (HWND hWnd, unsigned iMessage, WORD wParam, LONG lParam)
{
        HDC             hDC ;
```

```
        RECT           rTextRect ;
        static char    cBuf [] = "This is a long string of text without any CR/LF \\
                                  pairs to break the line.  DrawText() is used to \\
                                  format the line." ;

    switch (iMessage)                       /* process windows messages */
    {
        case WM_COMMAND:                    /* process menu items */
            switch (wParam)
            {
            case IDM_DOIT:                  /* User hit the "Do it" menu item */
                SetRect (&rTextRect, 10, 10, 200, 400) ;
                hDC = GetDC (hWnd) ;
                DrawText (hDC, cBuf, -1, &rTextRect,
                        DT_LEFT | DT_WORDBREAK) ;
                ReleaseDC (hWnd, hDC) ;
                break ;
```

[Other program lines]

ENUMFONTS   ■ Win 2.0   ■ Win 3.0   ■ Win 3.1

Purpose	Finds (enumerates) all of the fonts available on a given device. All of the data in the LOGFONT and TEXTMETRIC structure types is available for examination on each font enumerated.
Syntax	int **EnumFonts**(HDC *hDC*, LPSTR *lpFacename*, FARPROC *lpFontFunc*, LPSTR *lpData*);
Description	EnumFonts() works by using a callback function. You define the callback function in your program, and pass it to the enumeration function as a procedure-instance address *lpFontFunc*. The enumeration function is called once for every font found. This gives the enumeration function a chance to examine and store data from each font as desired. Both the LOGFONT and TEXTMETRIC data associated with a font is available on each pass of the enumeration function.
Uses	Ideal for filling a list box with the fonts available on the system when the program is started.
Returns	The last returned value by the callback function. This is determined by how you program the callback function. Normally, the returned value is not used.
See Also	AddFontResource(), CreateFont(), CreateFontIndirect(), GetDC()
Parameters	
hDC	HDC: The device context of the device that contains the fonts.
lpFacename	LPSTR: A long pointer to a typeface name. Set to NULL to enumerate each type of font. Set *lpFacename* pointing to a character buffer containing a typeface name to enumerate each size or type for a given typeface.
lpFontFunc	FARPROC: The procedure-instance address of the enumeration function. Use MakeProcInstance() to create this value. The function name must also be listed in the EXPORTS section of the .DEF definition file.
lpData	LPSTR: A 32-bit value passed to the enumeration function. This is usually a memory handle to the beginning of a memory buffer that will hold the data captured by the enumeration function. The enumeration function should enlarge the memory buffer each time it needs to add a new item.

Enumeration (Callback) Function

int FAR PASCAL **FontFunc** (LPLOGFONT *lpLogFont*, LPTEXTMETRICS *lpTextMetrics*, short *nFontType*, LPSTR *lpData*)

The enumeration function will be called once for each font found. The enumeration function should return a nonzero value to continue enumeration, zero to stop enumeration. Zero is typically returned on error, such as not being able to allocate more memory.

Parameters

lpLogFont LPLOGFONT: A pointer to a logical font structure. The elements of the structure will be set to a different font's values on each call to the enumeration function. See the CreateFont-Indirect() function description for a listing of this structure.

lpTextMetrics LPTEXTMETRICS: A pointer to a TEXTMETRIC structure. The elements of the structure will be set to a different font's values on each call to the enumeration function. See the GetText-Metrics() function description for a listing of this structure.

nFontType short: Specifies the type of font found. This is a combination of RASTER_FONTTYPE or DEVICE_FONTTYPE. If *nFontType* | RASTER_FONTTYPE is TRUE, then the font is a raster font. Otherwise, it is a vector font. If *nFontType* | DEVICE_FONT-TYPE is TRUE the font is a device font. Otherwise, it is a GDI font.

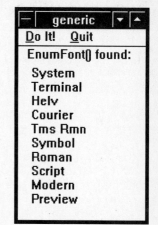

Figure 10-7. EnumFonts() Example.

Example This example, illustrated in Figure 10-7, lists the names of every font type available to the system. In this case, only the font name is extracted from the logical font structure.

The program's header file includes the structure definition for the ENUMER type. This is a handy structure to use in enumeration functions, as it keeps the number of items found and the memory handle together in one structure. The enumeration function prototype is at the end of the header file.

```
/* generic.h   */

#define IDM_DOIT   1              /* menu item id values */
#define IDM_QUIT   2
           /* definitions */
#define TITLEWIDE      20

typedef struct
{
        GLOBALHANDLE          hGMem ;
        int                   nCount ;
} ENUMER ;
           /* global variables */
int      ghInstance ;
char     gszAppName [] = "generic" ;
           /* function prototypes */
long FAR PASCAL WndProc (HWND, unsigned, WORD, LONG) ;
BOOL FAR PASCAL FontEnumFunc (LPLOGFONT lf, LPTEXTMETRIC tm, short nFontType,
        ENUMER FAR *enumer) ;
```

The enumeration function name must also be listed in the EXPORTS section of the program's .DEF definition file. The WndProc() function of the program is shown in the following program. The enumeration function is called when the user hits the "Do It!" menu item. The font names are then shown on the screen. Note that the font names end up one-after-the-next in the ENUMER data structure's data pointed to by GMem.

```
long FAR PASCAL WndProc (HWND hWnd, unsigned iMessage, WORD wParam, LONG lParam)
{
        static  FARPROC lpfnEnumProc ;
        static  ENUMER  enumer ;
        LPSTR           lpFontName ;
        HDC             hDC ;
        int             i ;
```

```
        switch (iMessage)                       /* process windows messages */
        {
                case WM_CREATE:
                        lpfnEnumProc = MakeProcInstance (FontEnumFunc, ghInstance) ;
                        break ;
                case WM_COMMAND:                 /* process menu items */
                        switch (wParam)
                        {
                        case IDM_DOIT:           /* User hit the "Do it" menu item */
                                if (enumer.hGMem)       /* if not first time tried */
                                        GlobalFree (enumer.hGMem) ;/* free the memory */
                                enumer.hGMem = GlobalAlloc (GMEM_MOVEABLE |
                                        GMEM_ZEROINIT, 1L) ;
                                enumer.nCount = 0 ;
                                hDC = GetDC (hWnd) ;
                                        /* let Windows run callback func. */
                                EnumFonts (hDC, NULL, lpfnEnumProc,
                                        (LPSTR) &enumer) ;
                                lpFontName = GlobalLock (enumer.hGMem) ; /* lock mem */
                                TextOut (hDC, 10, 0, "EnumFont() found:", 17) ;
                                for (i = 0 ; i < enumer.nCount ; i++)/* disp font names */
                                {
                                        TextOut (hDC, 15, 20 + (15 * i),
                                                (LPSTR) (lpFontName + (i * LF_FACESIZE)),
                                                lstrlen (lpFontName + (i * LF_FACESIZE))) ;
                                }
                                GlobalUnlock (enumer.hGMem) ;           /* unlock memory */
                                ReleaseDC (hWnd, hDC) ;
                                break ;
                        case IDM_QUIT:
                                DestroyWindow (hWnd) ;
                                break ;
                        }
                        break ;
                case WM_DESTROY:                 /* stop application */
                        GlobalFree (enumer.hGMem) ;      /* release all memory */
                        FreeProcInstance (lpfnEnumProc) ;
                        PostQuitMessage (0) ;
                        break ;
                default:                         /* default windows message processing */
                        return DefWindowProc (hWnd, iMessage, wParam, lParam) ;
        }
        return (0L) ;
}


int FAR PASCAL FontEnumFunc (LPLOGFONT lf, LPTEXTMETRIC tm, short nFontType,
        ENUMER FAR *enumer)
{
        LPSTR   lpFontFace ;

        if (!GlobalReAlloc (enumer->hGMem,
                (DWORD) LF_FACESIZE * (enumer->nCount + 1),
                GMEM_MOVEABLE))                  /* make room for 1 more */
                return (0) ;                     /* quit if can't make room */

        lpFontFace = GlobalLock (enumer->hGMem) ;        /* lock the memory area */
                                                 /* put next name at end */
        lstrcpy (lpFontFace + ((enumer->nCount) * LF_FACESIZE),
                (LPSTR) lf->lfFaceName) ;
        GlobalUnlock (enumer->hGMem) ;           /* unlock the memory area */
        enumer->nCount++ ;                       /* keep track of how many */
        return (1) ;
}
```

EXTDEVICEMODE

Purpose Determines or modifies the initialization data for a printer driver. Displays a dialog box for modifying the driver settings.

Include File <drivinit.h>, <print.h> (3.1)

Syntax int **ExtDeviceMode** (HWND *hWnd*, HANDLE *hDriver*, LPDEVMODE *lpDevModeOutput,* LPSTR *lpDeviceName,* LPSTR *lpPort,* LPDEVMODE *lpDevModeInput,* LPSTR *lpProfile,* WORD *wMode*);

Description Physical devices, such as printers, are accessed by calling functions within a device driver file. The file, with the extension .DRV, will reside in the Windows system directory. Drivers are specialized DLL (dynamic link library) files. Functions within these DLLs can be accessed to determine the capabilities of the physical device. See Chapter 28 for more details on DLLs.

ExtDeviceMode() is a function that is expected to be supported within the driver file. The function is called indirectly by first loading the driver file with LoadLibrary(), and then obtaining the DeviceCapabilities() function address within the driver with GetProcAddress(). The driver file contains the dialog box definition for modifying the driver settings. The DRIVINIT.H header file includes the following two typedef statements for use with GetProcAddress() to reference the DeviceCapabilities() function within the driver file.

```
typedef WORD FAR PASCAL FNDEVMODE(HWND, HANDLE, LPDEVMODE, LPSTR,
            LPSTR, LPDEVMODE, LPSTR, WORD);
typedef FNDEVMODE FAR * LPFNDEVMODE;
```

Uses Used to display the printer dialog box so that the user can modify the printer settings. Also used to fill a DEVMODE structure for use by the CreateDC() and DeviceCapabilities() functions.

Returns int. Returns the size of the DEVMODE data structure for the printer driver if *wMode* is NULL. Returns IDOK or IDCANCEL if a dialog box was presented to the user. Returns a negative value if an error occurred.

See Also CreateDC(), DeviceCapabilities(), GetProfileString(), LoadLibrary(), GetProcAddress()

Parameters

hWnd HWND: A window handle. If a printer setup dialog box is displayed, *hWnd* will be the parent window.

hDriver HANDLE: The handle of the device-driver module. This value is obtained by calling LoadLibrary() or GetModuleHandle().

lpDevModeOutput LPDEVMODE: A pointer to a DEVMODE data structure. The data structure will be filled when ExtDeviceMode() returns. If initialization data is supplied in *lp DevModeInput*, this will be copied to the structure pointed to by *lpDevModeOutput* before any changes are made.

lpDeviceName LPSTR: A pointer to a null-terminated character string containing the name of the printer device such as "PCL/HP LaserJet." This value can be obtained by reading the WIN.INI file using GetProfileString(). See the following example.

lpPort LPSTR: A pointer to a null-terminated character string containing the name of the port to which the printer is attached. This value can also be obtained by reading the WIN.INI file using GetProfileString().

lpDevModeInput LPDEVMODE: A pointer to a DEVMODE data structure that contains initialization data for the printer device. The data will be copied to the buffer pointed to by *lpDevModeOutput* before any modification occurs. Set to NULL to use the default initialization data based on the Windows Control Panel application.

wMode WORD: Specifies the action ExtDeviceMode() should take. It should be one or more of the following values, combined with the C language binary OR operator (|).

Value	Meaning
Zero (0)	ExtDeviceMode( ) returns the size of the memory buffer in bytes needed to hold the DEVMODE data for the printer. This includes the printer-specific data at the end of the DEVMODE structure. *lpDevModeOutput* can be set to NULL for this use of ExtDeviceMode( ).
DM_COPY	Writes the current printer initialization data to the DEVMODE data structure pointed to by *lpDevModeOutput*. This is done in advance of calling CreateDC( ).
DM_MODIFY	The data in the *lpDevModeInput* DEVMODE structure is copied to *lpDevModeOutput* before any modifications to the setup data begin. This is useful if application-specific printer setups are stored, preferably in a private initialization file. If this flag is not used, *lpDevModeOutput* can be set to NULL.
DM_PROMPT	Presents the printer driver Printer Setup dialog box, and allows the user to change values. The dialog box is defined in the driver file.
DM_UPDATE	The printer driver settings are copied to the WIN.INI file when ExtDeviceMode( ) exits.

Table 10-6. ExtDeviceMode( ) Flags.

The DEVMODE data structure is defined in DRIVINIT.H as follows:

```
/* size of a device name string */
#define CCHDEVICENAME 32

typedef struct _devicemode {
    char dmDeviceName[CCHDEVICENAME];    /* device name string */
    WORD dmSpecVersion;                  /* driver specification ver. eg. 0x300 */
    WORD dmDriverVersion;                /* OEM dirver version number */
    WORD dmSize;                         /* size of DEVMODE structure */
    WORD dmDriverExtra;                  /* number of bytes following DEVMODE data */
    DWORD dmFields;                      /* bit-field for which of the following dm */
                                         /* values are supported.  Bit 0 is one if */
                                         /* dmOrientation is supported, etc. */
    short dmOrientation;                 /* DMORIENT_PORTRAIT or DMORIENT_LANDSCAPE */
    short dmPaperSize;                   /* DMPAPER_LETTER, DM_PAPER_LEGAL, DM_PAPER_A4 */
              /* DMPAPER_CSCHEET, DMPAPER_DSCHEET, DMPAPER_ESHEET, DMPAPER_ENV_9 */
              /* DMPAPER_ENV_10, DMPAPER_ENV_11, DMPAPER_ENV_12, DMPAPER_ENV_14 */
    short dmPaperLength;                 /* overrides dmPaperSize, in mm/10 */
    short dmPaperWidth;                   * overrides dmPaperSize, in mm/10 */
    short dmScale;                       /* page is scaled by dmScale/100 */
    short dmCopies;                      /* number of copies supported */
    short dmDefaultSource;               /* Default paper bin */
    short dmPrintQuality;                /* DMRES_HIGH, DMRES_MEDIUM, DMRES_LOW, */
                                         /* or DMRES_DRAFT */
    short dmColor;                       /* DMCOLOR_COLOR or DMCOLOR_MONOCHROME */
    short dmDuplex;                      /* DMDUP_SIMPLEX, DMDUP_HORIZONTAL, */
                                         /* or DMDUP_VERTICAL */
    BYTE  dmDriverData [dmDriverExtra] ; /* 0 or more bytes of extra data */
} DEVMODE;

typedef DEVMODE * PDEVMODE, NEAR * NPDEVMODE, FAR * LPDEVMODE;
```

Example

This example demonstrates a typical call to the Printer Setup dialog box. The printer driver file name is retrieved from the WIN.INI file using GetProfileString(). The ExtDeviceMode() function is accessed indirectly from within the driver file by loading the diver, and obtaining the procedure-instance address of the ExtDeviceMode() function within the driver. The dialog box will depend on the driver installed. Figure 10-8 shows a typical example for the HP LaserJet printer driver.

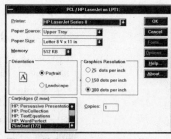

Figure 10-8. ExtDeviceMode( ) Example.

```
long FAR PASCAL WndProc (HWND hWnd, unsigned iMessage, WORD wParam, LONG lParam)
{
        char            szPrinter [64], szSysDir [128], szFullDriver [256],
                                *szDriver, *szDevice, *szOutput ;
        HANDLE          hDriver ;
        DEVMODE         DevMode ;
        LPFNDEVMODE     lpDeviceMode ;

        switch (iMessage)                    /* process windows messages */
        {
                case WM_COMMAND:             /* process menu items */
                        switch (wParam)
                        {
                        case IDM_DOIT:  /* get driver name from WIN.INI */
                                GetProfileString ("windows", "device", "",
                                        szPrinter, 64) ;
                                szDevice = strtok (szPrinter, ",") ;
                                szDriver = strtok (NULL, ",") ;
                                szOutput = strtok (NULL, ",") ;
                                        /* build full driver path/file spec */
                                GetSystemDirectory (szSysDir, 128) ;
                                lstrcpy (szFullDriver, szSysDir) ;
                                lstrcat (szFullDriver, "\\") ;
                                lstrcat (szFullDriver, szDriver) ;
                                lstrcat (szFullDriver, ".DRV") ;
                                        /* get handle to driver */
                                hDriver = LoadLibrary (szFullDriver) ;
                                if (hDriver > 31)
                                {       /* call ExtDeviceMode() indirectly */
                                        lpDeviceMode = (LPFNDEVMODE)
                                                GetProcAddress (hDriver,"ExtDeviceMode") ;
                                        if (lpDeviceMode)
                                                (* lpDeviceMode) (hWnd, hDriver, &DevMode,
                                                        szDevice, szOutput, NULL, NULL,
                                                        DM_PROMPT) ;
                                }
                                else
                                        MessageBox (hWnd, "Could not load driver file.",
                                                "Message", MB_OK) ;
                                break ;
                        case IDM_QUIT:
                                DestroyWindow (hWnd) ;
                                break ;
                        }
                        break ;
                case WM_DESTROY:
                        PostQuitMessage (0) ;
                        break ;
                default:
                        return DefWindowProc (hWnd, iMessage, wParam, lParam) ;
        }
        return (0L) ;
}
```

ESCAPE

■ Win 2.0   ■ Win 3.0 ■ Win 3.1.1

Purpose	Sends special information to a device, such as a printer.
Syntax	int **Escape**(HDC *hDC*, int *nEscape*, int *nCount*, LPSTR *lpInData*, LPSTR *lpOutData*);
Description	The name "Escape" comes from the fact that many printers accept special sequences of data starting with the ASCII ESC character to signal special functions like form feeds and boldface printing. Windows has made this a general function, which can send a wide variety of messages to a device. Many of the Escape() functions supported under Windows versions 2.0 and 3.0 are not supported under versions 3.1 and later. Instead, the DeviceCapabilities(), GetDeviceCaps(), and ResetDC() functions have been added to provide a better way to deal with the printer driver.

Uses   Most commonly used to communicate with a printer.

Returns   int. The meaning depends on the *nEscape* message sent to the device. The value will be positive if the function was successful. The most common negative (error) values are listed in Table 10-7.

Value	Meaning	☒
SP_ERROR	General error.	
SP_OUTOFDISK	The print spooler ran out of disk space.	
SP_OUTOFMEMORY	The print spooler ran out of memory.	
SP_USERABORT	The user killed the print job from the Print Manager window.	

Table 10-7. Escape( ) Return Codes.

See Also   GetDeviceCaps(), GetProfileString(), DeviceCapabilities(), GetDeviceCaps(), ResetDC()

Parameters

hDC   HDC: The device context handle for the device to receive the message.

nEscape   int: One of the escape messages. See Table 10-8.

nCount   int: The number of bytes of data in the buffer pointed to by *lpInData*.

lpInData   LPSTR: A pointer to the data buffer containing the information to send to the device.

lpOutData   LPSTR: A pointer to the data structure to receive data returned by the Escape() function call. Set to NULL if no data is returned.

Common Escape Commands

Escape (*hDC*, STARTDOC, *nCount*, *lpDocName*, NULL) ;

This starts a printing job. *lpDocName* is a pointer to a string that contains the name that will show up in the Print Manager window for the job. The length of the string pointed to by *lpDocName* is given in *nCount*.

Escape (*hDC*, NEWFRAME, NULL, NULL, NULL) ;

Ejects a page.

Escape (*hDC*, ENDDOC, NULL, NULL, NULL) ;

Ends a print job.

Escape (*hDC*, ABORTDOC, NULL, NULL, NULL) ;

Aborts the current printing job, erasing all pending data.

Escape (*hDC*, SETABORTPROC, NULL, *lpAbortFunc*, NULL) ;

Sets an abort procedure. *lpAbortFunc* is the procedure-instance address of the abort procedure. An example abort procedure is given in the introductory part of this chapter.

Note   Windows version 3.1 provides enhanced versions of these common escape functions. The equivalent functions under Windows versions 2.0 and 3.0 are listed in Table 10-8.

Windows Versions 2.0 and 3.0	Windows Version 3.1	☒
ABORTDOC	AbortDoc	
ENDDOC	EndDoc	
NEWFRAME	EndPage	
SETABORTPROC	SetAbortProc	
STARTDOC	StartDoc	

Table 10-8. Escape Function Version Reference.

The Windows 3.1 functions are used in the same manner as their predecessors.

Example   This example shows the minimum code necessary to output a line of text to the printer. A more complete example, including an abort procedure to stop printing, is included at the beginning of this chapter. The printer driver information is retrieved from the WIN.INI file using Get-ProfileString(). This information is used to create the printer device context. The Escape() function is used to start the print job, eject a page, and end the print job. TextOut() is used to output the text string to the printer device context.

```
long FAR PASCAL WndProc (HWND hWnd, unsigned iMessage, WORD wParam, LONG lParam)
{
        HDC                     hDC ;
        char                    szPrinter [64], *szDriver, *szDevice, *szOutput ;

        switch (iMessage)               /* process windows messages */
        {
                case WM_COMMAND:        /* process menu items */
                        switch (wParam)
                        {
                        case IDM_DOIT:  /* User hit the "Do it" menu item */
                                GetProfileString ("Windows", "device", "",
                                        szPrinter, 64) ;
                                szDevice = strtok (szPrinter, ",") ;
                                szDriver = strtok (NULL, ",") ;
                                szOutput = strtok (NULL, ",") ;
                                hDC = CreateDC (szDriver, szDevice, szOutput, NULL) ;
                                if (Escape (hDC, STARTDOC, 4, "Test", NULL)
                                        > 0)
                                {
                                        TextOut (hDC, 10, 10,
                                                "Output is on the printer.", 25) ;
                                        Escape (hDC, NEWFRAME, NULL, NULL, NULL) ;
                                        Escape (hDC, ENDDOC, NULL, NULL, NULL) ;
                                }
                                DeleteDC (hDC) ;
                                break ;
```
[Other program lines]

EXTTEXTOUT   ■ Win 2.0   ■ Win 3.0   ■ Win 3.1

Purpose   Controls text output within a rectangular area, with separate control over the spacing between each character.

Syntax   BOOL **ExtTextOut**(HDC *hDC*, int *X*, int *Y*, WORD *wOptions*, LPRECT *lpRect*, LPSTR *lpString*, WORD *nCount*, LPINT *lpDx*);

Description   Similar to DrawText(), except that the character spacing can be set individually for the space between each character.

Uses   Most often used with large titles or typefaces. If used with the SetTextAlign() function with *wFlags* set to TA_UPDATECP, the *X* and *Y* parameters will be ignored. Instead, Windows will keep track of the ending location (current position) for each call to ExtTextOut() and start the next output there.

Returns   BOOL. TRUE if the function outputs the string, FALSE on error.

See Also   TextOut(), DrawText(), SetTextAlign()

Parameters
hDC   HDC: The output device context. Retrieved with GetDC() or BeginPaint().

X   int: The logical *X* coordinate of the first character in the string.

Y   int: The logical *Y* coordinate of the first character in the string.

Value	Meaning	
ETO_CLIPPED	The text is clipped to fit within the specified rectangle.	
ETO_OPAQUE	The background of each character is opaque, covering up any graphics data underneath the character.	

wOptions WORD: A combination of zero and one or two of the options in Table 10-9, combined with the C language binary OR operator (|):

Table 10-9. ExtTextOut( ) Flags.

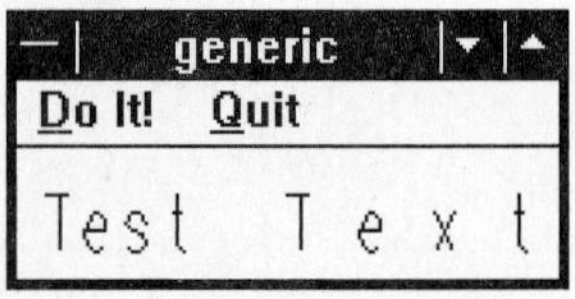

lpRect LPRECT: A pointer to a rectangle RECT structure. The rectangle contains the dimensions of the clipping rectangle. Set to NULL if the ETO_CLIPPED style is not used.

lpString LPSTR: A pointer to a string, containing the characters that will be output.

Figure 10-9. ExtTextOut( ) Example.

nCount int: The number of characters in the string.

lpDx LPINT: A pointer to an array of integers. Each element of the array sets the amount of space between successive characters in the string. *lpDx* is the space between the i and i+1 characters.

Example This example, as shown in Figure 10-9, shows the use of ExtTextOut() to print a series of characters with increasing amounts of space between each character. The character spacing is defined in an array of integers, *nSpace[]*.

```
Long FAR PASCAL WndProc (HWND hWnd, unsigned iMessage, WORD wParam, LONG lParam)
{
        HDC             hDC ;
        HFONT           hFont ;
        RECT            rTextRect ;
        int             nSpace [] = {10, 12, 14, 16, 18, 20, 22, 24, 26, 28} ;
        static char     cBuf [] = "Test Text" ;

        switch (iMessage)                       /* process windows messages */
        {
        case WM_COMMAND:                        /* process menu items */
                switch (wParam)
                {
                case IDM_DOIT:                  /* User hit the "Do it" menu item */
                        SetRect (&rTextRect, 10, 10, 200, 400) ;
                        hDC = GetDC (hWnd) ;
                        hFont = CreateFont (24, 0, 0, 0, 400, 0, 0, 0, OEM_CHARSET,
                                OUT_DEFAULT_PRECIS, CLIP_DEFAULT_PRECIS,
                        DEFAULT_QUALITY, DEFAULT_PITCH | FF_MODERN,
                         "modern") ;
                        SelectObject (hDC, hFont) ;
                        ExtTextOut (hDC, 10, 10, ETO_CLIPPED | ETO_OPAQUE,
                                &rTextRect, cBuf, strlen (cBuf),
                                (LPINT) &nSpace) ;
                        ReleaseDC (hWnd, hDC) ;
                        DeleteObject (hFont) ;
                        break ;
```

[Other program lines]

GETBKCOLOR

■ Win 2.0   ■ Win 3.0   ■ Win 3.1

Purpose Determines the current background color for a device context.

Syntax DWORD **GetBkColor**(HDC *hDC*);

Description Windows can change the background color using SetBkColor(). GetBkColor() allows you to find out the current background color.

Uses	Most often used with windows using the CS_OWNDC class style.
Returns	DWORD, a 32-bit color value. Use the GetRValue(), GetG-Value() and GetBValue() macros to find the individual colors.
See Also	GetBkMode(), SetBkColor(), SetBkMode()
Parameters	
hDC	HDC: The device context handle.

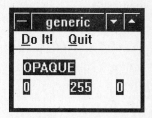

Figure 10-10. GetBkColor() Example.

Example   The example shown in Figure 10-10 creates a window with its own, private device context. The device context character color, background mode, and background color are all set when the program starts running (WM_CREATE received). When the user clicks the "Do It!" menu item, the current background mode and Red, Green, and Blue color values are displayed.

The class definition in the WinMain() function specifies a private device context for the window with the line

```
wndclass.style = CS_HREDRAW | CS_VREDRAW | CS_OWNDC;
```

Here is the top part of the WndProc() function. Because the window has a private device context, the device context settings are "remembered." The changes made when processing the WM_CREATE messages will apply until another change is made, or until the application terminates.

```
long FAR PASCAL WndProc (HWND hWnd, unsigned iMessage, WORD wParam, LONG lParam)
{
        HDC             hDC ;
        int             nBkMode ;
        DWORD           dwBkColor ;
        char            cBuf [10] ;

        switch (iMessage)                       /* process windows messages */
        {
                case WM_CREATE:
                        hDC = GetDC (hWnd) ;    /* owns DC - no need to release */
                        SetBkMode (hDC, OPAQUE) ;          /* opaque background */
                        SetBkColor (hDC, RGB (0, 255, 0)) ;      /* green background */
                        SetTextColor (hDC, RGB (255, 255, 255)) ;      /* white letters */
                        break ;
                case WM_COMMAND:                        /* process menu items */
                        switch (wParam)
                        {
                        case IDM_DOIT:                  /* User hit the "Do it" menu item */
                                hDC = GetDC (hWnd) ;
                                nBkMode = GetBkMode (hDC) ;
                                if (nBkMode == TRANSPARENT)
                                        TextOut (hDC, 10, 10, "TRANSPARENT", 11) ;
                                else
                                        TextOut (hDC, 10, 10, "OPAQUE", 6) ;
                                dwBkColor = GetBkColor (hDC) ;
                                itoa (GetRValue (dwBkColor), cBuf, 10) ;
                                TextOut (hDC, 10, 30, cBuf, strlen (cBuf)) ;
                                itoa (GetGValue (dwBkColor), cBuf, 10) ;
                                TextOut (hDC, 60, 30, cBuf, strlen (cBuf)) ;
                                itoa (GetBValue (dwBkColor), cBuf, 10) ;
                                TextOut (hDC, 110, 30, cBuf, strlen (cBuf)) ;
                                break ;
```

[Other program lines]

GETBKMODE   ■ Win 2.0   ■ Win 3.0   ■ Win 3.1

Purpose	Determines the current background painting mode for a device context.
Syntax	int **GetBkMode**(HDC *hDC*);

Description	The background between characters, dashed lines, or hatched brushes can be either transparent or opaque. The default mode for a device context is transparent. The background painting mode is changed with SetBkMode(). Windows that have their own private device context can change the background painting mode anywhere in the program. This function allows you to find out the current background mode.
Uses	Most often used with windows using the CS_OWNDC class style.
Returns	int, either OPAQUE or TRANSPARENT.
See Also	SetBkColor(), SetBkMode(), GetBkColor()
Parameters	
hDC	HDC: The device context.
Example	See the previous example under GetBkColor().

GETCHARWIDTH   ■ Win 2.0   ■ Win 3.0   ■ Win 3.1

Purpose	Determines the width of one or more characters in a font.
Syntax	BOOL GetCharWidth(HDC *hDC*, WORD *wFirstChar*, WORD *wLastChar*, LPINT *lpBuffer*);
Description	This function finds the width of characters in the font currently selected into the device context. Normally, a range of characters is written at one time into an array, so that the function only has to be called once.
Uses	Not often used. The GetTextExtent() function is more useful in determining the size of strings.
Returns	BOOL. TRUE if the character widths were determined, FALSE on error.
See Also	GetTextExtent()
Parameters	
hDC	HDC: The device context handle for the DC containing the current font. Use SelectObject() to add a font to the device context prior to calling GetCharWidth().
wFirstChar	WORD: The ASCII value of the first character in the font sequence.
wLastChar	WORD: The ASCII value of the last character in the font sequence.
lpBuffer	LPINT: A pointer to an array of integers that will contain the character widths of all of the characters between *wFirstChar* and *wLastChar*, inclusively. Be sure the array is large enough to hold all of the elements.
Example	This example creates a Modern font 24-logical units high. The size of all of the capital letters is placed in an array of integers *nSpace[]* by using the GetCharWidth() function. In this example an "I" is eight units wide, while an "M" is 12 units wide.

```
long FAR PASCAL WndProc (HWND hWnd, unsigned iMessage, WORD wParam, LONG lParam)
{
        HDC             hDC ;
        HFONT           hFont ;
        int             nSpace [26] ;
        char            cBuf [10] ;

        switch (iMessage)               /* process windows messages */
        {
        case WM_COMMAND:                /* process menu items */
                switch (wParam)
                {
                case IDM_DOIT:  /* User hit the "Do it" menu item */
                        hDC = GetDC (hWnd) ;
                        hFont = CreateFont (24, 0, 0, 0, 400, 0, 0, 0,
                                OEM_CHARSET,      OUT_DEFAULT_PRECIS,
                                CLIP_DEFAULT_PRECIS, DEFAULT_QUALITY,
                                DEFAULT_PITCH | FF_MODERN,
```

```
                                     "modern") ;
                    SelectObject (hDC, hFont) ;
                    GetCharWidth (hDC, 'A', 'Z', (LPINT) &nSpace) ;
                    TextOut (hDC, 10, 10, "I width = ", 9) ;
                    itoa ('I' - 'A', cBuf, 10) ;
                    TextOut (hDC, 80, 10, cBuf, strlen (cBuf)) ;
                    TextOut (hDC, 10, 30, "M width = ", 9) ;
                    itoa ('M' - 'A', cBuf, 10) ;
                    TextOut (hDC, 80, 30, cBuf, strlen (cBuf)) ;
                    ReleaseDC (hWnd, hDC) ;
                    DeleteObject (hFont) ;
                    break ;
```

[Other program lines]

GETDC
■ Win 2.0   ■ Win 3.0   ■ Win 3.1

Purpose	Retrieves a handle to the device context for the client area of a window.
Syntax	HDC **GetDC**(HWND *hWnd*);
Description	The attributes of the device context retrieved depend on the class upon which the window was based. For the common display context, GetDC() will use default values for the fonts, colors, etc. each time GetDC() is called. For class and private device contexts, the previous settings for the device context are not changed.
Uses	Used prior to calling a GDI output function. GetDC() is used anywhere within a program except in processing WM_PAINT messages. Use BeginPaint() to retrieve the device context when painting. When the GDI output is finished, use ReleaseDC() to free the device context so that it can be retrieved again by another part of the program. This is not necessary for class or private device contexts.
Returns	HDC, a handle to the device context of the window's client area.
See Also	BeginPaint(), ReleaseDC(), RegisterClass()
Parameters	
hWnd	HWND: A handle to the window containing the client area.
Note	A maximum of five device contexts can be open at one time.
Example	This program fragment uses GetDC() to retrieve the client area device context prior to printing text. A new font is created and selected into the device context, rather than using the default font. After the output is complete, both the font and device context are released.

```
Long FAR PASCAL WndProc (HWND hWnd, unsigned iMessage, WORD wParam, LONG lParam)
{
        HDC             hDC ;
        HFONT           hFont ;

        switch (iMessage)               /* process windows messages */
        {
                case WM_COMMAND:        /* process menu items */
                        switch (wParam)
                        {
                        case IDM_DOIT:  /* User hit the "Do it" menu item */
                                hDC = GetDC (hWnd) ;
                                hFont = CreateFont (48, 0, 0, 0, 400, 0, 0, 0,
                                        OEM_CHARSET,     OUT_DEFAULT_PRECIS,
                                        CLIP_DEFAULT_PRECIS, DEFAULT_QUALITY,
                                        DEFAULT_PITCH | FF_ROMAN,
                                        "roman") ;
                                SelectObject (hDC, hFont) ;
                                TextOut (hDC, 10, 10, "Text Output", 11) ;
                                ReleaseDC (hWnd, hDC) ;
                                DeleteObject (hFont) ;
                                break ;
```

[Other program lines]

GetDCOrg

■ Win 2.0   ■ Win 3.0   ■ Win 3.1

Purpose	Determines the screen coordinates for the logical origin of the device context.
Syntax	DWORD **GetDCOrg**(HDC *hDC*);
Description	GetDCOrg() determines the screen coordinates of the origin (0,0 point) of a device context. This function is equivalent to calling LPtoDP() for point 0,0 followed by ClientToScreen().
Uses	Mouse coordinates are frequently given in screen coordinates. This function allows you to compute where the mouse is relative to a window.
Returns	DWORD. The low-order word contains the *X* position. The high-order word contains the *Y* position.
See Also	LPtoDP(), ClientToScreen(), GetCursorPos()

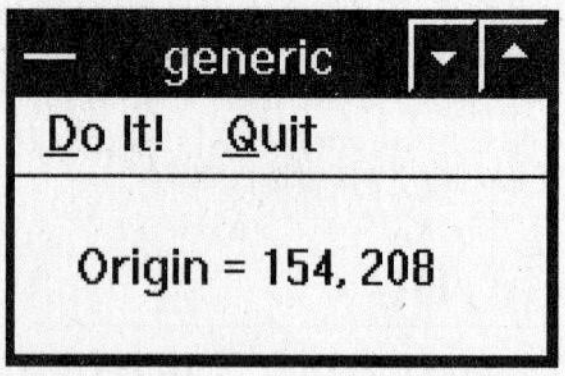

Parameters

hDC   HDC: A handle to the window client area device context. Use GetDC() to retrieve this value, unless the program is processing a WM_PAINT message. If so, use BeginPaint() to retrieve the *hDC* value.

Figure 10-11. GetDCOrg() Example.

Related Messages WM_MOUSEMOVE, WM_LBUTTONDOWN, etc.

Example   The example shown in Figure 10-11 outputs the *X,Y* position of the origin of the window's client area when the user clicks the "Do It!" menu item. The origin of the window's device context is displaced by 20 units in both directions prior to getting the location of the origin in screen coordinates. The offset of the origin results in the TextOut() function's output to logical coordinates 0,0 to show up in client coordinates 20,20.

```
Long FAR PASCAL WndProc (HWND hWnd, unsigned iMessage, WORD wParam, LONG lParam)
{
        HDC             hDC ;
        DWORD           dwOffset ;
        char            cBuf [128] ;

        switch (iMessage)               /* process windows messages */
        {
                case WM_COMMAND:        /* process menu items */
                        switch (wParam)
                        {
                        case IDM_DOIT:  /* User hit the "Do it" menu item */
                                hDC = GetDC (hWnd) ;
                                SetWindowOrg (hDC, -20, -20) ;
                                dwOffset = GetDCOrg (hDC) ;
                                TextOut (hDC, 0, 0, cBuf, wsprintf (cBuf,
                                        "Origin = %d, %d", LOWORD (dwOffset),
                                                HIWORD (dwOffset))) ;
                                ReleaseDC (hWnd, hDC) ;
                                break ;
```

[Other program lines]

GetDeviceCaps

■ Win 2.0   ■ Win 3.0   ■ Win 3.1

Purpose	Determines the capabilities of a device.
Syntax	int **GetDeviceCaps**(HDC *hDC*, int *nIndex*);
Description	Although Windows provides a good deal of device independence, it is sometimes necessary to determine the capabilities of the hardware Windows is using. GetDeviceCaps() can provide a wide range of information for any device that has a device context handle assigned to it.
Uses	Determining if a printer can display graphics, if the screen is monochrome or color, etc.

Returns	int, the value of the device parameter specified by *nIndex*.
See Also	CreateDC(), GetProfileString(), DeleteDC()
Parameters	
hDC	HDC: The device context handle. This can be to a printer, plotter, video, or memory device context. Retrieve this value with GetDC(), CreateIC(), CreateDC(), etc.
nIndex	int: Specifies which value GetDeviceCaps is to obtain for the device. It can be any of the values listed in Table 10-10.

Index	Meaning	☒
DRIVERVERSION	The driver version number, 0x100 for version 1.0, 0x101 for version 1.01, etc.	
TECHNOLOGY	Returns one of the following values:	
	DT_PLOTTER — Vector plotter.	
	DT_RASDISPLAY — Raster display.	
	DT_RASPRINTER — Raster printer.	
	DT_RASCAMERA — Raster camera.	
	DT_CHARSTREAM — Character stream.	
	DT_METAFILE — Metafile.	
	DT_DISPFILE — Display file.	
HORZSIZE	The approximate width of the display in millimeters.	
VERTSIZE	The approximate height of the display in millimeters	
HORZRES	The number of pixels horizontally.	
VERTRES	The number of pixels vertically.	
LOGPIXELSX	The number of pixels per logical inch horizontally.	
LOGPIXELSY	The number of pixels per logical inch vertically.	
BITSPIXEL	The number of color bits per pixel.	
PLANES	The number of color planes per pixel.	
NUMBRUSHES	The number of device brushes.	
NUMPENS	The number of device pens.	
NUMFONTS	The number of device fonts.	
NUMCOLORS	The number of colors the device supports.	
ASPECTX	The relative width of a pixel as used for line drawing.	
ASPECTY	The relative height of a pixel as used for line drawing.	
ASPECTXY	The diagonal width of a pixel as used for line drawing.	
PDEVICESIZE	The size of the PDEVICE internal data structure.	
CLIPCAPS	Determines if the device can clip to a rectangular region. Returns 1 if clipping can be done, 0 if not.	
SIZEPALETTE	The number of entries in the system palette.	
NUMRESERVED	The number of reserved entries in the system palette.	
COLORRES	The number of bits of color information per pixel.	

[handwritten annotation: { = 120 (both) ⟹ Large font / 96 (both) ⟹ small font and / 640×480]

Table 10-10. continued

Index	Meaning	
RASTERCAPS	The raster capabilities of the device. The returned value may contain any of the following binary values:	
	RC_BANDING	Requires that the output be banded (for example: dot matrix printers).
	RC_BITBLT	Can transfer bitmaps.
	RC_BITMAP64	Can transfer bitmaps larger than 64K bytes.
	RC_DI_BITMAP	Can support SetDIBits( ) and GetDiBits( ) functions.
	RC_DIBTODEV	Can support SetDIBitsToDevice( ) function.
	RC_FLOODFILL	Can do flood fills.
	RC_GD120_OUTPUT	Can support Windows 2.0.
	RC_PALETTE	Palette-based device.
	RC_SCALING	Can do scaling.
	RC_STRETCHBLT	Can do StretchBlt( ) function.
	RC_STRETCHDIB	Can do StretchDIBits( ) function.
CURVECAPS	Returns a bit-coded value. Each bit is 1 if TRUE, 0 if FALSE. The bits have the following meanings:	
	Bit 0	Can do circles.
	Bit 1	Can do pie wedges.
	Bit 2	Can do chord arcs.
	Bit 3	Can do ellipses.
	Bit 4	Can do wide borders.
	Bit 5	Can do styled borders.
	Bit 6	Can do wide/styled borders.
	Bit 7	Can do interiors.
LINECAPS	Returns a bit-coded value. Each bit is 1 if TRUE, 0 if FALSE. The bits have the following meanings:	
	Bit 0	Reserved.
	Bit 1	Can do polyline.
	Bit 2	Reserved.
	Bit 3	Reserved.
	Bit 4	Can do wide lines.
	Bit 5	Can do styled lines.
	Bit 6	Can do wide + styled lines.
	Bit 7	Can do interiors.
POLYGONALCAPS	Returns a bit-coded value. Each bit is 1 if TRUE, 0 if FALSE. The bits have the following meanings:	
	Bit 0	Can do alternate fill polygons.
	Bit 1	Can do a rectangle.
	Bit 2	Can do winding number filled polygons.

Bit 3	Can do scan lines.
Bit 4	Can do wide borders.
Bit 5	Can do styled borders.
Bit 6	Can do wide + styled borders.
Bit 7	Can do interiors.

TEXTCAPS — Returns a bit-coded value. Each bit is 1 if TRUE, 0 if FALSE. The bits have the following meanings:

Bit 0	Can do character output precision.
Bit 1	Can do a stroke output precision.
Bit 2	Can do stroke clip precision.
Bit 3	Can do 90-degree character rotation.
Bit 4	Can do any character rotation.
Bit 5	Can do scaling independent of X and Y.
Bit 6	Can do doubled character for scaling.
Bit 7	Can do integer multiples of scaling.
Bit 8	Can do any multiples for exact scaling.
Bit 9	Can do double-weight characters.
Bit 10	Can do italicizing.
Bit 11	Can do underlining.
Bit 12	Can do strikeouts.
Bit 13	Can do raster fonts.
Bit 14	Can do vector fonts.
Bit 15	Reserved. Must be returned zero.

Table 10-10. GetDeviceCaps( ) Index Values.

Example

This example, shown in Figure 10-12, determines the number of fonts and the horizontal resolution of the printer. The printer device name is determined with GetProfile-String(), which reads the WIN.INI file. A device context for the printer is created, and then GetDevice-Caps() determines the printer's capabilities.

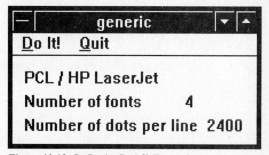

Figure 10-12. GetDeviceCaps( ) Example.

```
long FAR PASCAL WndProc (HWND hWnd, unsigned iMessage, WORD wParam, LONG lParam)
{
        HDC     hDC ;
        char    szPrinter [64], *szDriver, *szDevice, *szOutput, cBuf [10] ;
        int     nFonts, nXPixels ;

        switch (iMessage)                   /* process windows messages */
        {
                case WM_COMMAND:            /* process menu items */
                        switch (wParam)
                        {
```

```
                    case IDM_DOIT:   /* User hit the "Do it" menu item */
                            GetProfileString ("Windows", "device",
                                    "", szPrinter, 64) ;
                            szDevice = strtok (szPrinter, ",") ;
                            szDriver = strtok (NULL, ",") ;
                            szOutput = strtok (NULL, ",") ;
                            hDC = CreateDC (szDriver, szDevice, szOutput, NULL) ;
                            nFonts = GetDeviceCaps (hDC, NUMFONTS) ;
                            nXPixels = GetDeviceCaps (hDC, HORZRES) ;
                            DeleteDC (hDC) ;
                            hDC = GetDC (hWnd) ;
                            TextOut (hDC, 10, 10, szPrinter, lstrlen (szPrinter)) ;
                            itoa (nFonts, cBuf, 10) ;
                            TextOut (hDC, 10, 30, "Number of fonts =", 16) ;
                            TextOut (hDC, 150, 30, cBuf, lstrlen (cBuf)) ;
                            itoa (nXPixels, cBuf, 10) ;
                            TextOut (hDC, 10, 50,
                                    "Number of dots per line =", 24) ;
                            TextOut (hDC, 170, 50, cBuf, lstrlen (cBuf)) ;
                            ReleaseDC (hWnd, hDC) ;
                            break ;
```

[Other program lines]

GetMapMode   ■ Win 2.0   ■ Win 3.0   ■ Win 3.1

Purpose	Determines the mapping mode being used by a device context.
Syntax	int **GetMapMode**(HDC *hDC*);
Description	This function finds out which of the mapping modes is in effect for the given device context. Mapping modes are changed by SetMapMode().
Uses	Normally used with windows including the CS_OWNDC style. This allows the window to keep track of changes to the device context in its own private storage area for the DC.
Returns	The mapping mode. This can be: MM_ANISOTROPIC, MM_HIENGLISH, MM_HIMETRIC, MM_ISOTROPIC, MM_LOENGLISH, MM_LOMETRIC, MM_TEXT, or MM_TWIPS.
See Also	SetMapMode() contains explanations of the meaning of the different mapping modes.
Parameters	
hDC	HDC: The device context.
Example	This example checks the mapping mode of the device context every time a WM_PAINT message is received. The window's class style must include the CS_OWNDC flag, so that changes to the device context are not forgotten every time the DC is released. In WinMain(),

```
wndclass.style = CS_HREDRAW | CS_VREDRAW | CS_OWNDC;
```

In this simple example, clicking the "Do It!" menu item switches the device context to the MM_LOMETRIC mode, but does nothing else.

```
long FAR PASCAL WndProc (HWND hWnd, unsigned iMessage, WORD wParam, LONG lParam)
{
        HDC             hDC ;
        PAINTSTRUCT     ps ;
        int             nMapMode ;
        POINT           ptTextLoc ;

        switch (iMessage)                               /* process windows messages */
        {
                case WM_PAINT:
                        BeginPaint (hWnd, &ps) ;
                        nMapMode = GetMapMode (ps.hdc) ;
                        if (nMapMode == MM_TEXT)
                                TextOut (ps.hdc, 10, 10, "MM_TEXT mode.", 13) ;
                        else if (nMapMode == MM_LOMETRIC)
                        {
```

```
                                ptTextLoc.x = 10 ;
                                ptTextLoc.y = 10 ;
                                DPtoLP (ps.hdc, (LPPOINT) &ptTextLoc, 1) ;
                                TextOut (ps.hdc, ptTextLoc.x, ptTextLoc.y,
                                        "MM_LOMETRIC mode.", 17) ;
                        }
                        EndPaint (hWnd, &ps) ;
                        break ;
                case WM_COMMAND:                /* process menu items */
                        switch (wParam)
                        {
                        case IDM_DOIT:          /* User hit the "Do it" menu item */
                                hDC = GetDC (hWnd) ;
                                SetMapMode (hDC, MM_LOMETRIC) ;
                                ReleaseDC (hWnd, hDC) ;
                                InvalidateRect (hWnd, NULL, TRUE) ;   /* force WM_PAINT */
                                UpdateWindow (hWnd) ;
                                break ;
                        case IDM_QUIT:          /* send end of application message */
                                DestroyWindow (hWnd) ;
                                break ;
                        }
                        break ;
                case WM_DESTROY:                /* stop application */
                        PostQuitMessage (0) ;
                        break ;
                default:                /* default windows message processing */
                        return DefWindowProc (hWnd, iMessage, wParam, lParam) ;
        }
        return (0L) ;
}
```

GetSystemMetrics ■ Win 2.0   ■ Win 3.0   ■ Win 3.1

Purpose	Retrieves the dimensions of different window items on the video display.
Syntax	int **GetSystemMetrics**(int *nIndex*);
Description	Depending on the type of computer and video hardware Windows is running on, different objects will have different sizes and capabilities. GetSystemMetrics() allows your application program to find out the values currently in use on the system.
Uses	In many cases, you can base the sizing of objects you will add to the client area in proportion to a value retrieved by GetSystemMetrics(). For example, if you are adding a scroll bar control, it will look best if the size matches the system metrics scroll bar dimensions. Window borders (SM_CXBORDER) also provide a good basis for the minimum line thickness that will be easily visible.
Returns	int, the value requested.
Parameters	
nIndex	int: Specifies which value GetSystemMetrics() is to retrieve. It can be any one of the values listed in Table 10-11. All screen-related sizes are given in device units (pixels).

Value	Meaning ⊠
SM_CXDOUBLECLK (Win 3.1)	The second mouse click of a double-click sequence must fall within this range horizontally. The width is measured in pixels around the location of the first mouse click.
SM_CYDOUBLECLK (Win 3.1)	The second mouse click of a double-click sequence must fall within this range vertically. The width is measured in pixels around the location of the first mouse click.
SM_CXICONSPACING (Win 3.1)	The width of the rectangles that Windows uses to position tiled icons.
SM_CYICONSPACING (Win 3.1)	The height of the rectangles that Windows uses to position tiled icons.
SM_CXSCREEN	The width of the screen.

Table 10-11. continued

Value	Meaning	
SM_CYSCREEN	The height of the screen.	
SM_CXFRAME	The width of a window frame that can be sized.	
SM_CYFRAME	The height of a window frame that can be sized.	
SM_CXVSCROLL	The width of the arrow bitmap on a vertical scroll bar.	
SM_CYVSCROLL	The height of the arrow bitmap on a vertical scroll bar.	
SM_CXHSCROLL	The width of the arrow bitmap on a horizontal scroll bar.	
SM_CYHSCROLL	The height of the arrow bitmap on a horzontal scroll bar.	
SM_CYCAPTION	The height of the window caption.	
SM_CXBORDER	The width of a window border that cannot be sized.	
SM_CYBORDER	The height of a window border that cannot be sized.	
SM_CXDLGFRAME	The width of a window frame for a window that has the WS_DLGFRAME style.	
SM_CYDLGFRAME	The height of a window frame for a window that has the WS_DLGFRAME style.	
SM_CXHTHUMB	The width of the thumb bitmap on a horizontal scroll bar.	
SM_CYVTHUMB	The height of the thumb bitmap on a vertical scroll bar.	
SM_CXICON	The width of an icon.	
SM_CYICON	The height of an icon.	
SM_CXCURSOR	The width of a cursor.	
SM_CYCURSOR	The height of a cursor.	
SM_CYMENU	The height of a single-line menu bar.	
SM_CXFULLSCREEN	The width of a window client area when the window is maximized.	
SM_CYFULLSCREEN	The height of a window client area when the window is maximized.	
SM_CYKANJIWINDOW	The height of a Kanji window (Japanese character set).	
SM_CXMINTRACK	The minimum tracking width of a window.	
SM_CYMINTRACK	The minimum tracking height of a window.	
SM_CXMIN	The minimum width of a window.	
SM_CYMIN	The minimum height of a window.	
SM_CXSIZE	The width of the bitmaps in the window title bar (minimize, etc.).	
SM_CYSIZE	The height of the bitmaps in the window title bar (minimize, etc.).	
SM_MENUDROPALIGNMENT (Win 3.1)	The alignment of popup menus. A value of zero means that the left side of a popup menu is aligned with the left side of the menu-bar item. A nonzero value means that the left side of the popup menu is aligned with the right side of the corresponding menu-bar item.	
SM_MOUSEPRESENT	TRUE if a mouse is present, FALSE (zero) if not.	
SM_DEBUG	TRUE if the debug version of Windows is running, FALSE if not.	
SM_SWAPBUTTON	TRUE if the left and right mouse buttons have been switched, FALSE if not.	

Table 10-11. GetSystemMetrics( ) nIndex Values.

Example   This example puts a red border (line) in the center of the client area every time a WM_PAINT message is received. The size of the line is computed equal to the width of a window border. This assures that the size will be reasonable on a wide range of video equipment.

```
Long FAR PASCAL WndProc (HWND hWnd, unsigned iMessage, WORD wParam, LONG lParam)
{
        PAINTSTRUCT             ps ;
        HPEN                    hPen ;
        int                     nFrameWide ;
        RECT                    rClient ;

        switch (iMessage)                       /* process windows messages */
        {
                case WM_PAINT:
                        BeginPaint (hWnd, &ps) ;
                        nFrameWide = GetSystemMetrics (SM_CXFRAME) ;
                        hPen = CreatePen (PS_SOLID, nFrameWide, RGB (255, 0, 0)) ;
                        SelectObject (ps.hdc, hPen) ;
                        GetWindowRect (hWnd, &rClient) ;
                        MoveTo (ps.hdc, 0, nFrameWide/2) ;
                        LineTo (ps.hdc, rClient.right, nFrameWide/2) ;
                        DeleteObject (hPen) ;
                        EndPaint (hWnd, &ps) ;
                        break ;
```
[Other program lines]

GETTABBEDTEXTEXTENT   ☐ Win 2.0 ■ Win 3.0 ■ Win 3.1

Purpose	Determines the logical dimensions of a string containing tab characters.
Syntax	DWORD **GetTabbedTextExtent**(HDC *hDC*, LPSTR *lpString*, int *nCount*, int *nTabPositions*, LPINT *lpnTabStopPositions*);
Description	Similar to GetTextExtent(), except that it will correctly expand tab stops.
Uses	Sizing objects on the screen to match a tabbed text string. Used in conjunction with Tabbed-TextOut(). Some devices do not put characters in regular sized character cells. These devices do "kerning" to optimize character spacing. GetTabbedTextExtent() will not return the correct text extend on devices that do kerning.
Returns	DWORD. The low-order word contains the width of the string in logical units. The high-order word contains the height of the string in logical units.
See Also	TabbedTextOut(), GetTextExtent()
Parameters	
hDC	HDC: The device context.
lpString	LPSTR: A pointer to a character string that will be output.
nCount	int: The number of characters, including tab characters, in the string.
nTabPositions	int: The number of tab positions specified in *lpnTabStopPositions*. If set to 0 and *lpnTabStopPositions* is NULL, tabs are expanded to an even eight average character widths. If set to 1, tabs are expanded to an even spacing specified by the first element of the *lpnTabStopPositions* array.
lpnTabStopPositions	LPINT: A pointer to an array of integers, holding the tab stop positions. The tab positions are measured in device units (pixels) and must be in ascending order.
Example	This example WndProc() fragment outputs a tabbed text string, and then underlines the string with a red line. The dimensions and location of the line are calculated based on the text dimensions. GetTabbedTextExtent() is not strictly necessary in this example, as TabbedTextOut() returns the same height and width values.

```
Long FAR PASCAL WndProc (HWND hWnd, unsigned iMessage, WORD wParam, LONG lParam)
{
        HDC             hDC ;
        static  char    cBuf [] = {"First - Field 1\tField 2\tLast Field"} ;
        static  int     nTabs [] = {30, 45, 60} ;
```

```
        DWORD           dwTextSize ;
        HPEN            hPen ;

        switch (iMessage)                       /* process windows messages */
        {
                case WM_COMMAND:                /* process menu items */
                        switch (wParam)
                        {
                        case IDM_DOIT:          /* User hit the "Do it" menu item */
                                hDC = GetDC (hWnd) ;
                                TabbedTextOut (hDC, 10, 10, cBuf, strlen (cBuf), 3,
                                        (LPINT) &nTabs, 10) ;
                                dwTextSize = GetTabbedTextExtent (hDC, cBuf,
                                        strlen (cBuf), 3, (LPINT) &nTabs) ;
                                hPen = CreatePen (PS_SOLID, HIWORD (dwTextSize) / 2,
                                        RGB (255, 0, 0)) ;
                                SelectObject (hDC, hPen) ;
                                MoveTo (hDC, 10, 10 + (2 * HIWORD (dwTextSize))) ;
                                LineTo (hDC, 10 + LOWORD (dwTextSize),
                                        10 + (2 * HIWORD (dwTextSize))) ;
                                DeleteObject (hPen) ;
                                ReleaseDC (hWnd, hDC) ;
                                break ;
```

[Other program lines]

GETTEXTALIGN   ■ Win 2.0   ■ Win 3.0   ■ Win 3.1

Purpose	Determines the text alignment settings of a device context.
Syntax	WORD **GetTextAlign**(HDC *hDC*);
Description	The text alignment settings are set with the SetTextAlign() function. These settings determine how the *X,Y* parameters passed with the TextOut() and ExtTextOut() functions are interpreted.
Uses	Used with windows created with a private device context. The text alignment settings are then "remembered" by the device context.
Returns	One or more of the flags in Table 10-12.

Value	Meaning	⊠
TA_BASELINE	The baseline of the first character is used to specify the string position.	
TA_BOTTOM	The bottom of the first character is used to specify the string position.	
TA_CENTER	The center of the first character is used to specify the string position.	
TA_LEFT	The left side of the first character is used to specify the string position.	
TA_NOUPDATECP	The location at the end of the last text output is not saved.	
TA_RIGHT	The right side of the first character is used to specify the string position.	
TA_TOP	The top of the first character is used to specify the string position.	
TA_UPDATECP	The position at the end of the last text output is saved. The next call to TextOut( ) or ExtTextOut( ) will start from this location, ignoring the *X,Y* data in the output function parameters.	

Table 10-12. GetTextAlign( ) Flags.

Note	The default values for a device context are TA_LEFT, TA_TOP, and TA_NOUPDATECP. The TA_ flags are not defined in WINDOWS.H as unique binary values. It is necessary to break the three types of flags into groups, and then compare each group with the flag values. The example shows how this is done.
See Also	SetTextAlign(), TextOut(), ExtTextOut()

Parameters

hDC   HDC: The device context.

Example   This example shows how to process the returned value from GetTextAlign(). This function is
useful only when a window is created with its own private device context. This means that the
class definition will include the CS_OWNDC style in the WinMain() function.

```
wndclass.style = CS_HREDRAW | CS_VREDRAW | CS_OWNDC ;
```

In this excerpt from a WndProc() function, the text alignment is set when the program first
starts (WM_CREATE message received). When the user clicks the "Do It!" menu item, the text
alignment values are determined via a series of switch statements and output to the device context.

```
long FAR PASCAL WndProc (HWND hWnd, unsigned iMessage, WORD wParam, LONG lParam)
{
        HDC     hDC ;
        WORD    wAlign ;

        switch (iMessage)                                /* process windows messages */
        {
                case WM_CREATE:
                        hDC = GetDC (hWnd) ;             /* owns DC, no need to release */
                        SetTextAlign (hDC, TA_BOTTOM | TA_LEFT) ;
                        break ;
                case WM_COMMAND:                         /* process menu items */
                        switch (wParam)
                        {
                        case IDM_DOIT:                   /* User hit the "Do it" menu item */
                                hDC = GetDC (hWnd) ;
                                wAlign = GetTextAlign (hDC) ;
                                switch (wAlign & (TA_LEFT | TA_CENTER | TA_RIGHT))
                                {
                                        case TA_LEFT:
                                                TextOut (hDC, 10, 20, "LEFT", 4) ;
                                                break ;
                                        case TA_CENTER:
                                                TextOut (hDC, 10, 20, "CENTER", 6) ;
                                                break ;
                                        default:
                                                TextOut (hDC, 10, 20, "RIGHT", 5) ;
                                                break;
                                }
                                switch (wAlign & (TA_TOP | TA_BOTTOM | TA_BASELINE))
                                {
                                        case TA_TOP:
                                                TextOut (hDC, 10, 40, "TOP", 3) ;
                                                break ;
                                        case TA_CENTER:
                                                TextOut (hDC, 10, 40, "BOTTOM", 6) ;
                                                break ;
                                        default:
                                                TextOut (hDC, 10, 40, "BASELINE", 8) ;
                                                break ;
                                }
                                switch (wAlign & TA_UPDATECP)
                                {
                                        case TA_UPDATECP:
                                                TextOut (hDC, 10, 60, "UPDATECP", 8) ;
                                                break ;
                                        default:
                                                TextOut (hDC, 10, 60, "NO UPDATECP", 11) ;
                                                break ;
                                }
                                break ;
```

[Other program lines]

GetTextCharacterExtra
■ Win 2.0   ■ Win 3.0   ■ Win 3.1

Purpose   Determines the amount of extra character spacing defined for a device context.

Syntax   int **GetTextCharacterExtra**(HDC *hDC*);

Description   The SetTextCharacterExtra() function is used to add extra space between letters output by TextOut() and ExtTextOut(). GetTextCharacterExtra() is used to find out how much extra space is defined for a device context.

Uses   Use with windows that have a private device context defined as part of their class definition.

Returns   int, the amount of extra space between characters, measured in logical units.

See Also   SetTextCharacterExtra(), TextOut(), ExtTextOut(), GetMapMode()

Parameters

hDC   HDC: The device context handle.

Example   This function is useful only if the window has its own private device context. This means that the CS_OWNDC style will be part of the window's class definition in the WinMain() function.

```
wndclass.style = CS_HREDRAW | CS_VREDRAW | CS_OWNDC ;
```

This example sets 10 extra units of space between characters when the program starts (receives a WM_CREATE message). Because the default mapping mode MM_TEXT is used, the space equates to 10 pixel widths. When the user clicks the "Do It!" menu item, the program checks whether the extra space is still defined. Because this window has its own private device context, the response will always be "Extra spacing."

```
Long FAR PASCAL WndProc (HWND hWnd, unsigned iMessage, WORD wParam, LONG lParam)
{
        HDC             hDC ;
        int             nSpaceExtra ;

        switch (iMessage)                       /* process windows messages */
        {
                case WM_CREATE:
                        hDC = GetDC (hWnd) ;    /* owns DC, no need to release */
                        SetTextCharacterExtra (hDC, 10) ;
                        break ;
                case WM_COMMAND:                /* process menu items */
                        switch (wParam)
                        {
                        case IDM_DOIT:          /* User hit the "Do it" menu item */
                                hDC = GetDC (hWnd) ;
                                nSpaceExtra = GetTextCharacterExtra (hDC) ;
                                if (nSpaceExtra == 0)
                                        TextOut (hDC, 10, 10, "Normal spacing.", 15) ;
                                else
                                        TextOut (hDC, 10, 10, "Extra spacing.", 14) ;
                                break ;
```

[Other program lines]

GetTextColor
■ Win 2.0   ■ Win 3.0   ■ Win 3.1

Purpose   Retrieves the text color setting for a device context.

Syntax   DWORD **GetTextColor**(HDC *hDC*);

Description   The default text color for a device context is black. This can be changed with SetTextColor(). The color remains effective until a call to SetTextColor() changes the value. GetTextColor() allows the program to determine the current text color.

Uses   Use with windows that have their own private device context.

Returns   The 32-bit color value for the current text color.

See Also   SetTextColor(), SetBkColor(), GetBkColor(), SetBkMode(), GetRValue(), GetGValue(), GetBValue()

Parameters

hDC   HDC: The device context handle.

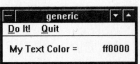

Example   The example in Figure 10-13 has a window with a private device context. When the program starts (WM_CREATE message received), the text color is set to blue. When the user clicks the "Do It!" menu item, the current color value is output in hexadecimal.

Figure 10-13. SetTextColor() and GetTextColor() Example.

The window's class definition in WinMain() includes the CS_OWNDC style, giving the window its own private device context:

```
wndclass.style = CS_HREDRAW | CS_VREDRAW | CS_OWNDC ;
```

Note that the RGB macro parameters are in the opposite order of the storage order inside the 32-bit coded color value (compare RGB (0,0,255) with the output value of 0xFF0000).

```
Long FAR PASCAL WndProc (HWND hWnd, unsigned iMessage, WORD wParam, LONG lParam)
{
        HDC             hDC ;
        DWORD           dwTextColor ;
        char            cBuf [10] ;

        switch (iMessage)                       /* process windows messages */
        {
                case WM_CREATE:
                        hDC = GetDC (hWnd) ;            /* owns DC, no need to release */
                        SetTextColor (hDC, RGB (0, 0, 255)) ;     /* blue letters */
                        break ;
                case WM_COMMAND:                /* process menu items */
                        switch (wParam)
                        {
                        case IDM_DOIT:          /* User hit the "Do it" menu item */
                                hDC = GetDC (hWnd) ;
                                dwTextColor = GetTextColor (hDC) ;
                                ltoa (dwTextColor, cBuf, 16) ;   /* convert to hex */
                                TextOut (hDC, 10, 10, "My Text Color =", 15) ;
                                TextOut (hDC, 150, 10, cBuf, lstrlen (cBuf)) ;
                                break ;
```

[Other program lines]

GETTEXTEXTENT   ■ Win 2.0   ■ Win 3.0   ■ Win 3.1

Purpose   Determines the length of a string when it is output to a device context.

Syntax   DWORD **GetTextExtent**(HDC *hDC*, LPSTR *lpString*, int *nCount*);

Description   The text extent is the width of a string. The width is computed using the currently selected font. In the default MM_TEXT mapping mode, the width is in device units (pixels). If another mapping mode has been set with SetMapMode(), the width will be determined in logical units. Some devices do not put characters in regular sized character cells. These devices do "kerning" to optimize character spacing. GetTabbedTextExtent() will not return the correct text extend on devices that do kerning.

Uses   This function is a direct way to calculate the size of a string prior to output. It also works directly with SetTextJustification() to justify string output (see example).

Returns   DWORD. The low-order word contains the width. The high-order word contains the length.

See Also   SetTextJustification(), GetTabbedTextExtent()

Parameters

hDC   HDC: The device context handle.

lpString	LPSTRING: A pointer to a character string.
nCount	int: The number of characters in the string pointed to by *lpString*.

Example
This example justifies a three-word string to fit exactly within the bounds of a 200 pixel wide rectangle, see Figure 10-14. GetTextExtent() is used to calculate the size of the string prior to justification. SetTextJustification() then adds enough space to expand the string to the full 200 unit size. The next call to TextOut() uses the justification during output to space the words.

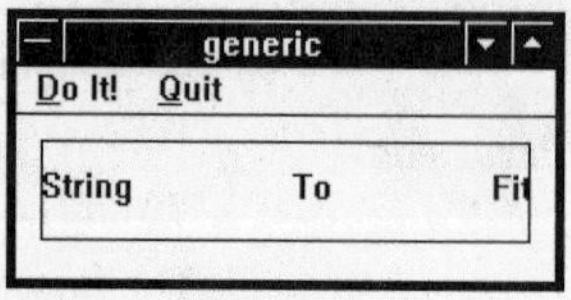

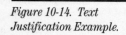

Figure 10-14. Text Justification Example.

With this simple example, the number of spaces in the string (two) is known. Normally, you would have to check the number of spaces (break characters) in the string before calling SetTextJustification().

```
Long FAR PASCAL WndProc (HWND hWnd, unsigned iMessage, WORD wParam, LONG lParam)
{
        HDC             hDC ;
        HPEN            hPen ;
        DWORD           dwExtent ;
        char            cBuf [] = {"String To Fit"} ;

        switch (iMessage)                  /* process windows messages */
        {
                case WM_COMMAND:           /* process menu items */
                        switch (wParam)
                        {
                        case IDM_DOIT:  /* User hit the "Do it" menu item */
                                hDC = GetDC (hWnd) ;
                                SetBkMode (hDC, TRANSPARENT) ;
                                hPen = GetStockObject (BLACK_PEN) ;
                                SelectObject (hDC, hPen) ;
                                Rectangle (hDC, 10, 10, 210, 50) ;
                                dwExtent = GetTextExtent (hDC, cBuf,
                                        lstrlen (cBuf)) ;
                                SetTextJustification (hDC, 200 -
                                        LOWORD(dwExtent), 2) ;
                                TextOut (hDC, 10, 20, cBuf, lstrlen (cBuf)) ;
                                ReleaseDC (hWnd, hDC) ;
                                break ;
```
[Other program lines]

GETTEXTFACE
■ Win 2.0   ■ Win 3.0   ■ Win 3.1

Purpose	Retrieves the name of the current typeface.
Syntax	int **GetTextFace**(HDC *hDC*, int *nCount*, LPSTR *lpFacename*);
Description	The default typeface for a device context is the system font. If another font is selected, GetTextFace() will retrieve its name as a null-terminated string.
Returns	int. The number of characters copied to the *lpFacename* buffer.
See Also	EnumFonts(), CreateFont(), CreateFontIndirect()
Parameters	
hDC	HDC: The device context handle.
nCount	int: The maximum number of characters to copy to the *lpFacename* buffer.
lpFacename	LPSTR: A pointer to a character buffer to hold the typeface name.
Example	This example outputs the name of the current typeface to the window's client area when the user clicks the "Do It!" menu item. Because no other font has been selected, the program will display "system," for the default system font.

```
long FAR PASCAL WndProc (HWND hWnd, unsigned iMessage, WORD wParam, LONG lParam)
{
        HDC     hDC ;
        char    cBuf [30] ;

        switch (iMessage)                  /* process windows messages */
        {
                case WM_COMMAND:           /* process menu items */
                        switch (wParam)
                        {
                        case IDM_DOIT:   /* User hit the "Do it" menu item */
                                hDC = GetDC (hWnd) ;
                                GetTextFace (hDC, 29, cBuf) ;
                                TextOut (hDC, 10, 10, cBuf, lstrlen (cBuf)) ;
                                ReleaseDC (hWnd, hDC) ;
                                break ;
```

[Other program lines]

GetTextMetrics   ■ Win 2.0   ■ Win 3.0   ■ Win 3.1

Purpose	Retrieves basic data about the font currently selected for a device context.
Syntax	BOOL **GetTextMetrics**(HDC *hDC*, LPTEXTMETRIC *lpMetrics*);
Description	Retrieves data on a font by filling a TEXTMETRIC data structure. WINDOWS.H includes the following definition of the TEXTMETRIC data structure

```
typedef struct tagTEXTMETRIC
  {
  int   tmHeight;
  int   tmAscent;
  int   tmDescent;
  int   tmInternalLeading;
  int   tmExternalLeading;
  int   tmAveCharWidth;
  int   tmMaxCharWidth;
  int   tmWeight;
  BYTE  tmItalic;
  BYTE  tmUnderlined;
  BYTE  tmStruckOut;
  BYTE  tmFirstChar;
  BYTE  tmLastChar;
  BYTE  tmDefaultChar;
  BYTE  tmBreakChar;
  BYTE  tmPitchAndFamily;
  BYTE  tmCharSet;
  int   tmOverhang;
  int   tmDigitizedAspectX;
  int   tmDigitizedAspectY;
  } TEXTMETRIC;
typedef TEXTMETRIC          *PTEXTMETRIC;
typedef TEXTMETRIC NEAR         *NPTEXTMETRIC;
typedef TEXTMETRIC FAR      *LPTEXTMETRIC;
```

	GetTextMetrics() fills in all of these values into a memory area pointed to by *lpMetrics*.
Uses	Most commonly used to determine the height of the font. Sum the *tmHeight* and *tmExternal* leading elements to determine the total height of a font.
Returns	BOOL. Nonzero if the function was successful, zero on error.
See Also	GetTextExtent().
Parameters	
hDC	HDC: The device context handle.
lpMetrics	LPTEXTMETRIC: A pointer to a TEXTMETRIC data structure.

Example   This example shows the most common use of GetTextMetrics(). The *tmHeight* and *tmExternal* leading elements total to the height of the font. The font height is used to set the line spacing.

```
long FAR PASCAL WndProc (HWND hWnd, unsigned iMessage, WORD wParam, LONG lParam)
{
        HDC                     hDC ;
        TEXTMETRIC              tm ;
        HFONT                   hFont ;
        int                     nLineSpace ;

        switch (iMessage)               /* process windows messages */
        {
                case WM_COMMAND:        /* process menu items */
                        switch (wParam)
                        {
                        case IDM_DOIT:  /* User hit the "Do it" menu item */
                                hDC = GetDC (hWnd) ;
                                hFont = CreateFont (24, 16, 0, 0, 700, 0, 0, 0,
                                        OEM_CHARSET,    OUT_DEFAULT_PRECIS,
                                        CLIP_DEFAULT_PRECIS, DEFAULT_QUALITY,
                                        DEFAULT_PITCH | FF_MODERN, "modern") ;
                                SelectObject (hDC, hFont) ;
                                GetTextMetrics (hDC, &tm) ;
                                nLineSpace = tm.tmHeight +
                                        tm.tmExternalLeading ;
                                TextOut (hDC, 0, nLineSpace,
                                        "These lines are", 15) ;
                                TextOut (hDC, 0, 2 * nLineSpace,
                                        "evenly spaced.", 14) ;
                                DeleteObject (hFont) ;
                                ReleaseDC (hWnd, hDC) ;
                                break ;
```
[Other program lines]

GETVIEWPORTEXT   ■ Win 2.0   ■ Win 3.0   ■ Win 3.1

Purpose   Used with GetWindowExt() to determine the scale of the device context.

Syntax   DWORD **GetViewportExt**(HDC *hDC*);

Description   The MM_ISOTROPIC and MM_ANISOTROPIC mapping modes allow the logical coordinate system of a device context to be any arbitrary scaled ratio to the physical device. GetViewportExt() and GetWindowExt() are used together to determine the current scaling. The scaling factor is the ratio of the viewport extent divided by the window extent. For example, if the viewport X extent is three, and the window X extent is one, the logical coordinate system expands all horizontal dimensions by a factor of three. If the signs of the viewport and window extents match, the coordinate orientation is unchanged. If one of the signs is negative and the other positive, the orientation is reversed. Reversing one sign is commonly used to make the Y values increase upward, rather than the default system where Y values increase downward.

Uses   Used with windows created with the CS_OWNDC class style that maintain a private copy of their device context.

Returns   DWORD, the viewport extent. The low-order word contains the X value. The high-order word contains the Y value.

See Also   GetWindowExt(), SetViewportExt(), SetMapMode(), SetViewportOrg()

Parameters
hDC   HDC: The device context handle.

Example   This example creates a window with its own private device context. This means that the class style CS_OWNDC is specified in the WinMain() function.

```
wndclass.style = CS_HREDRAW | CS_VREDRAW | CS_OWNDC ;
```

The program sets up the MM_ISOTROPIC mapping mode during startup (when the WM_CREATE message is received). The scaling is fixed at two logical units to one device unit by the SetWindowExt() and SetViewportExt() function calls. The *Y* axis orientation is reversed, so that *Y* values increase upwards by specifying a negative *Y* value in SetViewportExt(), while the *Y* value in SetWindowExt() is positive. When the user clicks the "Do It!" menu item, the current *Y* axis scaling is determined by comparing the values returned by GetViewportExt() and GetWindowExt(). The settings are displayed on the window's client area using TextOut(). Note that the *Y* values for TextOut() are set negative to make the text visible. This is because the logical origin has not been changed from the default upper left corner of the client area, and *Y* values now increase upward.

```
long FAR PASCAL WndProc (HWND hWnd, unsigned iMessage, WORD wParam, LONG lParam)
{
        HDC             hDC ;
        DWORD           dwViewExt, dwWindExt ;

        switch (iMessage)               /* process windows messages */
        {
        case WM_CREATE:
                hDC = GetDC (hWnd) ;
                SetMapMode (hDC, MM_ISOTROPIC) ;
                SetWindowExt (hDC, 1, 1) ;
                SetViewportExt (hDC, 2, -2) ;
                break ;
        case WM_COMMAND:                /* process menu items */
                switch (wParam)
                {
                case IDM_DOIT:  /* User hit the "Do it" menu item */
                        hDC = GetDC (hWnd) ;
                        dwViewExt = GetViewportExt (hDC) ;
                        dwWindExt = GetWindowExt (hDC) ;
                        if (abs (HIWORD (dwViewExt)) ==
                                abs (HIWORD (dwWindExt)))
                        {
                                TextOut (hDC, 10, -10,
                                        "Device Y = Logical Y size", 25) ;
                        }
                        else if (abs (HIWORD (dwViewExt)) <
                                abs (HIWORD (dwWindExt)))
                        {
                                TextOut (hDC, 10, -10,
                                        "Logical Y < Device Y size", 25) ;
                        }
                        else
                        {
                                TextOut (hDC, 10, -10,
                                        "Logical Y > Device Y size", 25) ;
                        }
                        if (((int) HIWORD (dwViewExt) < 0 &&
                                        (int) HIWORD (dwWindExt) > 0) ||
                                ((int) HIWORD (dwViewExt) > 0 &&
                                        (int) HIWORD (dwWindExt) < 0))
                        {
                                TextOut (hDC, 10, -30,
                                        "Y axis increases upward.", 24) ;
                        }
                        else
                        {
                                TextOut (hDC, 10, -30,
                                        "Y axis increases downward.", 26) ;
                        }
                        break ;
```

[Other program lines]

GETVIEWPORTORG
■ Win 2.0   ■ Win 3.0   ■ Win 3.1

Purpose   Used with GetWindowOrg() to determine the location of the origin of the logical coordinate system of a device context.

Syntax   DWORD **GetViewportOrg**(HDC *hDC*);

Description Windows allows two offsets to be applied to the origin (0,0 location) of the logical coordinate system. SetWindowOrg() sets up the first offset, called the "window origin." SetViewportOrg() sets up the second offset, called the "viewport origin." The viewport origin is relative to the window origin, so you can think of the viewport origin as an offset from another offset.

Uses   Used with windows that maintain their own private device context.

Returns   DWORD. The low-order word contains the *X* offset. The high-order word contains the *Y* offset.

See Also   GetWindowOrg(), SetViewportOrg(), SetWindowOrg(), SetMapMode(), SetViewportExt(), SetWindowExt()

Parameters
hDC   HDC: The device context handle.

Note   The scaling (GetViewportExt(), GetWindowExt()) and origin (GetViewportOrg(), GetWindowOrg()) of a device context determine the difference between device coordinates and logical coordinates. The following formulas relate device points (DP) and logical points (LP):

DP = Scale * (LP - WindOrg) + ViewOrg ;

LP = (1/Scale) * (DP - ViewOrg) + WindOrg ;

Where:

Scale = ViewportExtent / WindowExtent ;

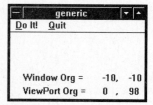

Example   The example shown in Figure 10-15 creates a window with its own private device context. Every time a WM_SIZE message is received, the program resets the logical device scaling and origins. The MM_ISOTROPIC mapping mode is used. The scaling doubles the logical vertical size and reverses the *Y* direction so that *Y* values increase upward on the client area. The *viewport* origin is set equal to the lower left corner of the window. The size of the client area is found by looking at the HIWORD of the *lParam* value passed

Figure 10-15. GetWindow-Org() and GetViewportOrg Example.

with the WM_SIZE message. Because the *window* origin is always offset by 10 units in both the *X* and *Y* directions using SetWindowOrg(), the *viewport* origin appears at a location 10 units above and to the right of the lower left corner. (The viewport origin is always relative to the window origin.)

The upper left corner of the letter V on the bottom line is the logical location 0,0 in the device context coordinate system. The upper left corner of the capital W on the upper text line is at logical location 0,10. The private device context for the window is established in the WinMain() function as part of the class definition.

```
wndclass.style = CS_HREDRAW | CS_VREDRAW | CS_OWNDC ;
```

The output of the window and viewport offset values occurs when the user clicks the "Do It!" menu item.

```
long FAR PASCAL WndProc (HWND hWnd, unsigned iMessage, WORD wParam, LONG lParam)
{
        HDC             hDC ;
        DWORD           dwViewOrg, dwWindOrg ;
        char            cBuf [10] ;

        switch (iMessage)                      /* process windows messages */
```

```
{
          case WM_SIZE:
                  hDC = GetDC (hWnd) ;        /* owns DC, no need to release */
                  SetMapMode (hDC, MM_ISOTROPIC) ;
                  SetWindowExt (hDC, 1, 1) ;
                  SetViewportExt (hDC, 2, -2) ;
                  SetWindowOrg (hDC, -10, -10) ;
                  SetViewportOrg (hDC, 0, HIWORD (lParam)) ;
                  break ;
          case WM_COMMAND:                    /* process menu items */
                  switch (wParam)
                  {
                  case IDM_DOIT:              /* User hit the "Do it" menu item */
                          hDC = GetDC (hWnd) ;
                          dwViewOrg = GetViewportOrg (hDC) ;
                          dwWindOrg = GetWindowOrg (hDC) ;
                          TextOut (hDC, 0, 0, "ViewPort Org =", 14) ;
                          itoa (LOWORD (dwViewOrg), cBuf, 10) ;
                          TextOut (hDC, 60, 0, cBuf, lstrlen (cBuf)) ;
                          TextOut (hDC, 70, 0, ",", 1) ;
                          itoa (HIWORD (dwViewOrg), cBuf, 10) ;
                          TextOut (hDC, 80, 0, cBuf, lstrlen (cBuf)) ;
                          TextOut (hDC, 0, 10, "Window Org =", 12) ;
                          itoa (LOWORD (dwWindOrg), cBuf, 10) ;
                          TextOut (hDC, 60, 10, cBuf, lstrlen (cBuf)) ;
                          TextOut (hDC, 70, 10, ",", 1) ;
                          itoa (HIWORD (dwWindOrg), cBuf, 10) ;
                          TextOut (hDC, 80, 10, cBuf, lstrlen (cBuf)) ;
                          break ;
```

[Other program lines]

GETWINDOWDC ■ Win 2.0　■ Win 3.0　■ Win 3.1

Purpose	Retrieves the device context for the entire window, including the nonclient areas like the caption bar, scroll bars, borders, system menu button, etc.
Syntax	HDC **GetWindowDC**(HWND *hWnd*);
Description	This function allows a program to paint on the nonclient areas of a window. This is normally not necessary or desirable, as Windows automatically maintains the client area as part of the DefWindowProc() function operations.
Uses	Use of this function is generally discouraged. You can use it to create custom window types, but they will not conform to normal Windows conventions.
Returns	HDC, the device context for the window.
See Also	GetDC(), BeginPaint()
Parameters	
hWnd	HWND: The window handle.
Related Messages	WM_NCPAINT, WM_PAINT, WM_NCACTIVATE

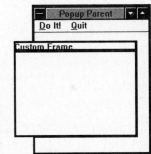

Figure 10-16.
GetWindowDC() Example.

Example　The example shown in Figure 10-16 is one of the most complex in the book. The main window creates a new popup window which has a separate class and a separate message processing function. The popup window intercepts WM_NCPAINT messages in order to paint its own frame. The frame is drawn in red, with a fixed caption "Custom Frame." WM_NCACTIVATE and WM_PAINT messages must also be processed to avoid interference with the custom frame during the default windows processing.

The ChildProc() message processing function must be listed in the EXPORTS section of the program's .DEF definition file. A function prototype must also be included in the program's header file.

```
Long FAR PASCAL WndProc (HWND hWnd, unsigned iMessage, WORD wParam, LONG lParam)
{
        HDC                     hDC ;
        static WNDCLASS         wndclass ;         /* the window class */
        static HWND             hPopup, hParent ;

        switch (iMessage)                          /* process windows messages */
        {
                case WM_CREATE:         /* build the child window when program starts */
                        wndclass.style              = CS_HREDRAW | CS_VREDRAW |
                                                                    CS_PARENTDC ;
                        wndclass.lpfnWndProc        = ChildProc ;
                        wndclass.cbClsExtra         = 0 ;
                        wndclass.cbWndExtra         = 0 ;
                        wndclass.hInstance          = ghInstance ;
                        wndclass.hIcon              = NULL ;
                        wndclass.hCursor            = LoadCursor (NULL, IDC_ARROW) ;
                        wndclass.hbrBackground      = GetStockObject (WHITE_BRUSH) ;
                        wndclass.lpszMenuName       = NULL ;
                        wndclass.lpszClassName      = "SecondClass" ;
                                        /* register the window class */
                        if(RegisterClass (&wndclass))
                        {
                                hPopup = CreateWindow ("SecondClass", "",
                                        WS_POPUP | WS_VISIBLE | WS_BORDER |
                                                WS_CAPTION,
                                        10, 50, 200, 150, hWnd, NULL, ghInstance, NULL) ;
                                ShowWindow (hPopup, SW_SHOW) ;
                        }
                        break ;
                case WM_COMMAND:         /* process menu items */
                        switch (wParam)
                        {
                        case IDM_DOIT:   /* User hit the "Do it" menu item */
                                hParent = GetParent (hPopup) ;
                                SendMessage (hPopup, WM_USER, hParent, OL) ;
                                break ;
                        case IDM_QUIT:   /* send end of application message */
                                DestroyWindow (hWnd) ;
                                break ;
                        }
                        break ;
                case WM_DESTROY:         /* stop application */
                        PostQuitMessage (0) ;
                        break ;
                default:                 /* default windows message processing */
                        return DefWindowProc (hWnd, iMessage, wParam, lParam) ;
        }
        return (OL) ;
}

/* Here is a separate message processing procedure for the popup window */

Long FAR PASCAL ChildProc (HWND hPopup, unsigned iMessage, WORD wParam, LONG lParam)
{
        HDC             hDC ;
        HPEN            hPen ;
        RECT            rBorder, rClient ;

        switch (iMessage)                          /* process windows messages */
        {
                case WM_NCPAINT:                   /* nonclient area needs painting */
                        hDC = GetWindowDC (hPopup) ;
                        GetWindowRect (hPopup, (LPRECT) &rBorder) ;
                        SelectObject (hDC, GetStockObject (WHITE_BRUSH)) ;
                        Rectangle (hDC, 0, 0, rBorder.right - rBorder.left,
```

```
                                   rBorder.bottom - rBorder.top) ;
                        hPen = CreatePen (PS_SOLID, 5, RGB (255, 0, 0)) ;
                        SelectObject (hDC, hPen) ;
                        MoveTo (hDC, 0, 0) ;
                        LineTo (hDC, rBorder.right - rBorder.left - 2, 0) ;
                        LineTo (hDC, rBorder.right - rBorder.left - 2,
                                   rBorder.bottom - rBorder.top - 2) ;
                        LineTo (hDC, 0, rBorder.bottom - rBorder.top - 2) ;
                        LineTo (hDC, 0, 0) ;
                        MoveTo (hDC, 0, 15) ;
                        LineTo (hDC, rBorder.right - rBorder.left, 15) ;
                        SetBkMode (hDC, TRANSPARENT) ;
                        TextOut (hDC, 1, 1, "Custom Frame", 12) ;
                        DeleteObject (hPen) ;
                        ReleaseDC (hPopup, hDC) ;
                        return (0L) ;
            case WM_PAINT:                  /* bypass client area painting */
                        GetClientRect (hPopup, (LPRECT) &rClient) ;
                        ValidateRect (hPopup, (LPRECT) &rClient) ;
                        return (0L) ;
            case WM_USER:                   /* message from parent - just beep */
                        MessageBeep (0) ;
                        break ;
            case WM_DESTROY:                /* stop the popup window */
                        PostQuitMessage (0) ;
                        break ;
            case WM_NCACTIVATE:             /* falls through to DefWindowProc() */
                        PostMessage (hPopup, WM_NCPAINT, 0, 0L) ;
            default:                        /* default windows message processing */
                        return DefWindowProc (hPopup, iMessage, wParam, lParam) ;
      }
      return (0L) ;
}
```

GetWindowExt   ■ Win 2.0   ■ Win 3.0   ■ Win 3.1

Purpose	Used with GetViewportExt() to determine the scale the device context.
Syntax	DWORD **GetWindowExt**(HDC *hDC*);
Description	The MM_ISOTROPIC and MM_ANISOTROPIC mapping modes allow the logical coordinate system of a device context to be scaled to any arbitrary ratio to the physical device. GetViewportExt() and GetWindowExt() are used together to determine the current scaling. The scaling factor is the ratio of the viewport extent divided by the window extent. For example, if the viewport X extent is three and the window X extent is one, the logical coordinate system expands all horizontal dimensions by a factor of three. If the signs of the viewport and window extents match, the coordinate orientation is unchanged. If one of the signs is negative and the other positive, the orientation is reversed. This is commonly used to make the Y values increase upward, rather than the default system where Y values increase downward.
Uses	Used with windows created with the CS_OWNDC class style, that maintain a private copy of their device context.
Returns	DWORD, the window extent. The low-order word contains the X value. The high-order word contains the Y value.
See Also	GetViewportExt(), SetWindowExt(), SetMapMode(), SetWindowOrg()
Parameters	
hDC	HDC: The device context handle.
Example	See the example under the GetViewportExt() function description.

GetWindowOrg

■ Win 2.0   ■ Win 3.0   ■ Win 3.1

Purpose	Used with GetViewportOrg() to determine the location of the origin of the logical coordinate system of a device context.
Syntax	DWORD **GetWindowOrg**(HDC *hDC*);
Description	Windows allows two offsets to be applied to the origin (0,0 location) of the logical coordinate system. SetWindowOrg() sets up the first offset, called the "window origin." SetViewportOrg() sets up the second offset, called the "viewport origin." The viewport origin is relative to the window origin, so you can think of the viewport origin as an offset from another offset.
Uses	Used with windows that maintain their own private device context.
Returns	DWORD. The low-order word contains the *X* offset. The high-order word contains the *Y* offset.
See Also	GetViewportOrg(), SetViewportOrg(), SetWindowOrg(), SetMapMode(), SetViewportExt(), SetWindowExt()
Parameters	
hDC	HDC: The device context handle.
Example	See the example under the GetViewportOrg() function description.

GrayString

■ Win 2.0   ■ Win 3.0   ■ Win 3.1

Purpose	Draws grayed text or a grayed bitmap at the given location.
Syntax	BOOL **GrayString**(HDC *hDC*, HBRUSH *hBrush*, FARPROC *lpOutputFunc*, DWORD *lpData*, int *nCount*, int *X*, int *Y*, int *nWidth*, int *nHeight*);
Description	The graying is accomplished by combining the selected brush and the text string or bitmap. For black text characters, this has the effect of eliminating pixels where the brush bitmap is white and changing the remaining pixels to the brush color. This function is a holdover from the 2.0 version of Windows, which used this technique to gray menu items.
Uses	Can be used to provide different degrees of "graying" of a string or to gray a bitmap.
Returns	BOOL. TRUE is the function was successful, FALSE on error.
See Also	GetStockObject(). SetTextColor() can be used to paint characters with a gray color, but without the elimination of selected pixels.
Parameters	
hDC	HDC: The device context handle.
hBrush	HBRUSH: A handle to the brush to use for graying. Normally, GetStockObject() is used to retrieve one of the three stock gray brushes (see the following example).
lpOutputFunc	FARPROC: NULL if TextOut() is to be used for output. *lpOutputFunc* can also be the procedure-instance address of a special output function that you add as part of the program. Use MakeProcInstance() to create a procedure-instance address for the function. The function format is shown below.
lpData	DWORD: If *lpOutputFunc* is NULL, *lpData* is a pointer to the character string to be output. Otherwise, *lpData* is a long pointer to the data to be passed to the output function described below.
nCount	int: The amount of data to be output. If *nCount* is NULL, *lpData* is assumed to be a null-terminated character string.
X	int: The logical *X* position to start output.

Y	int: The logical *Y* position to start output.
nWidth	int: The width of the output rectangle in logical units. Set to NULL if *lpData* points to a character string.
nHeight	int: The height of the output rectangle in logical units. Set to NULL if *lpData* points to a character string.

Custom Output Function

The program can provide its own specialized output function. The function must have the following format:

BOOL FAR PASCAL **OutputFunc** (HDC *hDC*, DWORD *lpData*, int *nCount*)

Where:

hDC is a memory device context containing a bitmap *nWidth* wide and *nHeight* tall. The output function writes to this device context.

lpData is the pointer to the data passed by GrayString().

nCount is the number of data bytes passed by GrayString().

Like all callback functions, the output function must be declared in the EXPORTS section of the program's .DEF definition file. The output function should return nonzero on success, zero on error. The MM_TEXT mapping mode must be in effect prior to calling GrayString().

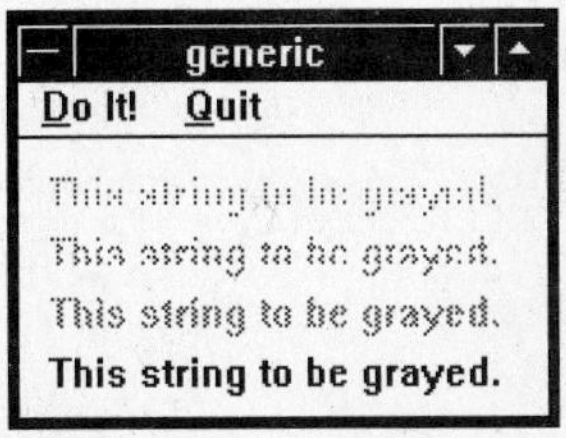

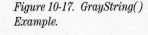

Example   This example outputs the same text with four different levels of graying. The image on a VGA screen is significantly better than that of the illustration in Figure 10-17, as the graying logic changes both the bitmap and the gray color used to display the letters. Only the bitmap effects are visible in this black and white illustration.

Figure 10-17. GrayString( ) Example.

Note that the last text string is created using TextOut(), so no graying of the text occurs.

```
Long FAR PASCAL WndProc (HWND hWnd, unsigned iMessage, WORD wParam, LONG lParam)
{
        HDC             hDC ;
        HBRUSH          hBrush ;
        char            cBuf [] = {"This string to be grayed."} ;

        switch (iMessage)                       /* process windows messages */
        {
                case WM_COMMAND:                /* process menu items */
                        switch (wParam)
                        {
                        case IDM_DOIT:          /* User hit the "Do it" menu item */
                                hDC = GetDC (hWnd) ;
                                hBrush = GetStockObject (LTGRAY_BRUSH) ;
                                GrayString (hDC, hBrush, NULL, (DWORD)(LPSTR) cBuf,
                                        NULL, 10, 10, NULL, NULL) ;
                                hBrush = GetStockObject (GRAY_BRUSH) ;
                                GrayString (hDC, hBrush, NULL, (DWORD)(LPSTR) cBuf,
                                        NULL, 10, 30, NULL, NULL) ;
                                hBrush = GetStockObject (DKGRAY_BRUSH) ;
                                GrayString (hDC, hBrush, NULL, (DWORD)(LPSTR) cBuf,
                                        NULL, 10, 50, NULL, NULL) ;
                                TextOut (hDC, 10, 70, cBuf, lstrlen (cBuf)) ;
                                ReleaseDC (hWnd, hDC) ;
                                break ;
```

[Other program lines]

LPTODP
■ Win 2.0　■ Win 3.0　■ Win 3.1

Purpose	Converts a point from logical coordinates to device coordinates.
Syntax	BOOL **LPtoDP**(HDC *hDC*, LPPOINT *lpPoints*, int *nCount*);
Description	One or more points in an array pointed to by *lpPoints* can be converted in one call to this function.
Uses	Used with the alternate mapping modes when there is a need to relate a point in the client area to an external element such as the mouse position.
Returns	BOOL. TRUE if all points were converted, FALSE on error.
See Also	DPtoLP(), SetMapMode()
Parameters	
hDC	HDC: The device context handle.
lpPoints	LPPOINT: A pointer to a point, or the first element in an array of POINT structures.
nCount	int: The number of points to convert.
Note	The scaling of a device context determines the difference between device coordinates and logical coordinates. The following formulas relate device points (DP) and logical points (LP):

$$DP = Scale * (LP - WindOrg) + ViewOrg ;$$

$$LP = (1/Scale) * (DP - ViewOrg) + WindOrg ;$$

Where:

$$Scale = ViewportExtent / WindowExtent ;$$

Example	This example sets an alternative mapping mode, MM_LOMETRIC. The cursor arrow is moved to the origin of the logical coordinates. This example requires two transformations: LPtoDP() to convert from the logical coordinates to the device coordinates and ClientToScreen() to convert from the device coordinates to the screen coordinates used in positioning the mouse cursor. The cursor moves to the upper left corner of the client area, as changing the mapping mode does not automatically change the origin.

```
Long FAR PASCAL WndProc (HWND hWnd, unsigned iMessage, WORD wParam, LONG lParam)
{
        HDC             hDC ;
        POINT           ptPoint ;

        switch (iMessage)               /* process windows messages */
        {
        case WM_COMMAND:                /* process menu items */
                switch (wParam)
                {
                case IDM_DOIT:  /* User hit the "Do it" menu item */
                        hDC = GetDC (hWnd) ;
                        SetMapMode (hDC, MM_LOMETRIC) ;
                        ptPoint.x = ptPoint.y = 0 ;
                        LPtoDP (hDC, &ptPoint, 1) ;
                        ClientToScreen (hWnd, &ptPoint) ;
                        SetCursorPos (ptPoint.x, ptPoint.y) ;
                        ReleaseDC (hWnd, hDC) ;
                        break ;
```

[Other program lines]

OFFSETVIEWPORTORG
■ Win 2.0　■ Win 3.0　■ Win 3.1

Purpose	Changes the *X,Y* offset of the logical coordinate system origin.
Syntax	DWORD **OffsetViewportOrg**(HDC *hDC*, int *X*, int *Y*);

Description   SetViewportOrg() is used to establish the offset in both the X and Y directions of the origin of the logical coordinate system. OffsetViewportOrg() allows the offset to be changed by increments. Calling OffsetViewportOrg() is equivalent to calling SetViewportOrg() with X and Y values equal to the old values plus the offsets.

Uses   Used with windows that have their own private device context. Offsetting the origin can be a convenient way to scroll a graphics image.

Returns   DWORD, the previous viewport offset. The low-order word contains the X coordinate offset. The high-order word contains the Y coordinate offset.

See Also   The function descriptions for SetViewportOrg() and GetViewportOrg() contain more complete descriptions of offsets.

Parameters

hDC   HDC: The device context handle.

X   int: The number of device units (pixels) to add to the horizontal offset.

Y   int: The number of device units (pixels) to add to the vertical offset.

Example   This example creates a window with its own private device context. When the program starts or is resized (WM_SIZE message received), the mapping mode is set to MM_ISOTROPIC and the vertical scale expanded by a factor of two. The vertical scale is reversed (negative Y value with SetViewportExt()), so that increasing Y values point upward on the windows client area. The viewport origin is set equal to the bottom left corner of the screen using SetViewportOrg(). This offset is in turn affected by offsetting the window origin by 10 units in both the X and Y directions using SetWindowOrg(). The result of these transformations is that the logical 0,0 point on the screen is 10 pixels to the right and 20 pixels above the bottom left corner of the window's client area.

When the user clicks the "Do It!" menu item, the window X offset is eliminated (10 added to the old offset of -10). The viewport origin is also offset by five in both the X and Y directions. The combined effect of these two offsets shifts the origin to the right 15 pixels and down 5. Repeatedly clicking the "Do It!" menu item will continue to shift the image to the left and down by 15 pixels horizontally and 5 pixels vertically. The origin is reset if the window is sized.

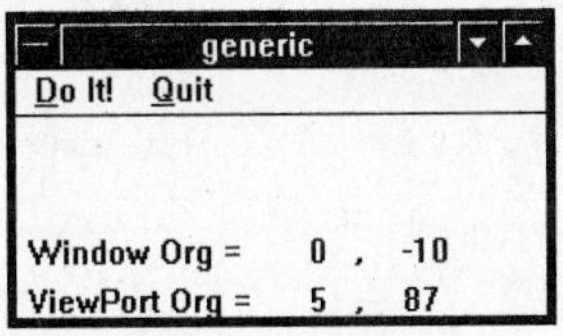

Figure 10-18. OffsetViewportOrg() and OffsetWindowOrg() Example.

The WinMain() function includes the CS_OWNDC class style as part of the window's class definition. This provides the window with its own private device context.

```
wndclass.style = CS_HREDRAW | CS_VREDRAW | CS_OWNDC ;
```

Note in processing the WM_SIZE message that the client area vertical size is passed as the high-order word in the *lParam* parameter. This is convenient for setting the viewport origin at the bottom of the client area.

```
Long FAR PASCAL WndProc (HWND hWnd, unsigned iMessage, WORD wParam, LONG lParam)
{
        HDC             hDC ;
        DWORD           dwViewOrg, dwWindOrg ;
        char            cBuf [10] ;

        switch (iMessage)                       /* process windows messages */
        {
                case WM_SIZE:
                        hDC = GetDC (hWnd) ;       /* owns DC, no need to release */
                        SetMapMode (hDC, MM_ISOTROPIC) ;
                        SetWindowExt (hDC, 1, 1) ;
```

```
                        SetViewportExt (hDC, 2, -2) ;
                        SetWindowOrg (hDC, -10, -10) ;
                        SetViewportOrg (hDC, 0, HIWORD (lParam)) ;
                        break ;
              case WM_COMMAND:                  /* process menu items */
                        switch (wParam)
                        {
                        case IDM_DOIT:          /* User hit the "Do it" menu item */
                                hDC = GetDC (hWnd) ;
                                OffsetWindowOrg (hDC, 10, 0) ;
                                OffsetViewportOrg (hDC, 5, 5) ;
                                dwViewOrg = GetViewportOrg (hDC) ;
                                dwWindOrg = GetWindowOrg (hDC) ;
                                TextOut (hDC, 0, 0, "ViewPort Org =", 14) ;
                                itoa (LOWORD (dwViewOrg), cBuf, 10) ;
                                TextOut (hDC, 60, 0, cBuf, lstrlen (cBuf)) ;
                                TextOut (hDC, 70, 0, ",", 1) ;
                                itoa (HIWORD (dwViewOrg), cBuf, 10) ;
                                TextOut (hDC, 80, 0, cBuf, lstrlen (cBuf)) ;
                                TextOut (hDC, 0, 10, "Window Org =", 12) ;
                                itoa (LOWORD (dwWindOrg), cBuf, 10) ;
                                TextOut (hDC, 60, 10, cBuf, lstrlen (cBuf)) ;
                                TextOut (hDC, 70, 10, ",", 1) ;
                                itoa (HIWORD (dwWindOrg), cBuf, 10) ;
                                TextOut (hDC, 80, 10, cBuf, lstrlen (cBuf)) ;
                                break ;
```

[Other program lines]

OFFSETWINDOWORG
■ Win 2.0   ■ Win 3.0   ■ Win 3.1

Purpose	Changes the X,Y offset of the logical coordinate system origin.
Syntax	DWORD **OffsetWindowOrg**(HDC hDC, int X, int Y);
Description	SetWindowOrg() is used to establish the offset in both the X and Y directions of the origin of the logical coordinate system. OffsetWindowOrg() allows the offset to be changed by increments. Calling OffsetWindowOrg() is equivalent to calling SetWindowOrg() with X and Y values equal to the old values plus the offsets.
Uses	Used with windows that have their own private device context. Offsetting the origin can be a convenient way to scroll a graphics image.
Returns	DWORD, the previous window offset. The low-order word contains the X coordinate offset. The high-order word contains the Y coordinate offset.
See Also	The function descriptions for SetWindowOrg() and GetWindowOrg() contain more complete descriptions of offsets.
Parameters	
hDC	HDC: The device context handle.
X	int: The number of device units (pixels) to add to the horizontal offset.
Y	int: The number of device units (pixels) to add to the vertical offset.
Example	See the previous example under OffsetViewportOrg().

RELEASEDC
■ Win 2.0   ■ Win 3.0   ■ Win 3.1

Purpose	Frees the device context.
Syntax	int **ReleaseDC**(HWND $hWnd$, HDC hDC);
Description	This function is used to free the device context after output is completed. Windows allows a maximum of five device contexts to be open at one time, but only one for a given device. Releasing the DC is necessary unless the window class was created with the CS_OWNDC style.

Uses	It is good practice to use ReleaseDC() immediately after output is completed. Use EndPaint() to release the device context retrieved by BeginPaint() in processing a WM_PAINT message.
Returns	int. Returns nonzero if the device context was released, zero on error.
See Also	GetDC()

Parameters

hWnd	HWND: The handle of the window.
hDC	HDC: The device context to be released. This is the value returned by GetDC() before output was started.
Example	This example outputs the string "This is a character string." when the user hits the "Do It!" menu item. The device context is released immediately after use.

```
long FAR PASCAL WndProc (HWND hWnd, unsigned iMessage, WORD wParam, LONG lParam)
{
        HDC     hDC ;
        char    cBuf [] = {"This is a character string."} ;

        switch (iMessage)                               /* process windows messages */
        {
                case WM_COMMAND:                        /* process menu items */
                        switch (wParam)
                        {
                        case IDM_DOIT:                  /* User hit the "Do it" menu item */
                                hDC = GetDC (hWnd) ;
                                TextOut (hDC, 10, 10, cBuf, lstrlen (cBuf)) ;
                                ReleaseDC (hWnd, hDC) ;
                                break ;
```
[Other program lines]

REMOVEFONTRESOURCE   ■ Win 2.0   ■ Win 3.0   ■ Win 3.1

Purpose	Removes a font from the system and frees all memory associated with the font.
Syntax	BOOL **RemoveFontResource**(LPSTR *lpFilename*);
Description	Fonts take up memory space. It is good practice to remove custom fonts loaded by an application when the application is terminated. Other top-level windows should be notified that the font has been removed from the system by sending a WM_FONTCHANGE message.
Uses	Usually used when processing the WM_DESTROY message to remove added font resources. Do not remove the normal Windows system fonts, or any other font that was not loaded by the application.
Returns	BOOL. TRUE if the font was removed, FALSE on error.
See Also	AddFontResource(), FindResource()

Parameters

lpFilename	LPSTR: A far pointer to a null-terminated character string containing the font file name. This should be a complete DOS file name including the directory path and the ".FON" file extension. Alternatively, *lpFilename* can contain a handle to a font resource loaded as part of the resource .RC file. The resource file should include a line like

```
        1       FONT              script.fon
```

The FindResource() function is then used to obtain the handle to the font. The handle becomes the low-order word of lpFilename. The high-order word must be zero.

Related Messages	WM_FONTCHANGE should be sent to all top-level windows after a font is loaded or removed. This makes the new font's availability known to all programs running on the system.

Example   This example shows a font file called "script.fon" being loaded at the start of the program and removed at the end. SendMessage() is used to notify all other top-level programs of the font's presence. By setting the first parameter in SendMessage() equal to -1, all top-level windows receive the message.

```
long FAR PASCAL WndProc (HWND hWnd, unsigned iMessage, WORD wParam, LONG lParam)
{
        int     nFontLoad ;

        switch (iMessage)               /* process windows messages */
        {
                case WM_CREATE:         /* bring in the font file */
                        nFontLoad = AddFontResource ((LPSTR) "script.fon") ;
                        if (!nFontLoad)
                                MessageBox (hWnd, "Could not load font.", "Warning",
                                    MB_ICONHAND | MB_OK) ;
                        else
                                SendMessage (-1, WM_FONTCHANGE, 0, OL) ;
                        break ;
                case WM_COMMAND:        /* process menu items */
        /* other program lines here */
                        break ;
                case WM_DESTROY:                /* stop application */
                        RemoveFontResource ((LPSTR) "script.fon") ;
                        SendMessage (-1, WM_FONTCHANGE, 0, OL) ;
                        PostQuitMessage (0) ;
                        break ;
                default:                /* default windows message processing */
                        return DefWindowProc (hWnd, iMessage, wParam, lParam) ;
        }
        return (OL) ;
}
```

RESETDC   ☐ Win 2.0   ☐ Win 3.0   ■ Win 3.1

Purpose   Updates a printer device context.

Include File <drivinit.h>, <print.h> (3.1)

Syntax   HDC **ResetDC** (HDC hDC, LPDEVMODE *lpInitData*);

Description   The printer device context, created by CreateDC(), can be updated at any time using ResetDC(). The update is based on data in a DEVMODE data structure, passed to the function. The DEVMODE data is typically initialized using ExtDeviceMode(). Changes to the DEVMODE data can include any value except the driver name, device name, or output port.

Uses   ResetDC() can be used in the middle of a printing job to change printer settings, such as paper orientation or printing resolution. This supersedes a number of Escape() function calls that were used to change printer settings under Windows versions 2.0 to 3.0.

Returns   HDC, the original device context handle. Returns NULL on error.

See Also   CreateDC(), ExtDeviceMode(), Escape()

Parameters

hDC   HDC: The handle to the printer device context. This is the value returned by CreateDC().

lpInitData   LPDEVMODE: A pointer to a DEVMODE data structure containing the new settings for the printer. This data structure typically is initialized using ExtDeviceMode() prior to making changes to the data. The DEVMODE data structure is defined in DRIVINIT.H as follows:

```
/* size of a device name string */
#define CCHDEVICENAME 32

typedef struct _devicemode {
   char dmDeviceName[CCHDEVICENAME];    /* device name string */
   WORD dmSpecVersion;                  /* driver specification ver. eg. 0x300 */
```

```
        WORD dmDriverVersion;                  /* OEM dirver version number */
        WORD dmSize;                           /* size of DEVMODE structure */
        WORD dmDriverExtra;                    /* number of bytes following DEVMODE data */
        DWORD dmFields;                        /* bit-field for which of the following dm */
                                               /* values are supported.  Bit 0 is one if */
                                               /* dmOrientation is supported, etc. */
        short dmOrientation;                   /* DMORIENT_PORTRAIT or DMORIENT_LANDSCAPE */
        short dmPaperSize;                     /* DMPAPER_LETTER, DM_PAPER_LEGAL, DM_PAPER_A4 */
                   /* DMPAPER_CSCHEET, DMPAPER_DSCHEET, DMPAPER_ESHEET, DMPAPER_ENV_9 */
                   /* DMPAPER_ENV_10, DMPAPER_ENV_11, DMPAPER_ENV_12, DMPAPER_ENV_14 */
        short dmPaperLength;                   /* overrides dmPaperSize, in mm/10 */
        short dmPaperWidth;                    /* overrides dmPaperSize, in mm/10 */
        short dmScale;                         /* page is scaled by dmScale/100 */
        short dmCopies;                        /* number of copies supported */
        short dmDefaultSource;                 /* Default paper bin */
        short dmPrintQuality;                  /* DMRES_HIGH, DMRES_MEDIUM, DMRES_LOW, */
                                               /* or DMRES_DRAFT */
        short dmColor;                         /* DMCOLOR_COLOR or DMCOLOR_MONOCHROME */
        short dmDuplex;                        /* DMDUP_SIMPLEX, DMDUP_HORIZONTAL, */
                                               /* or DMDUP_VERTICAL */
        BYTE  dmDriverData [dmDriverExtra] ;          /* 0 or more bytes of extra data */
} DEVMODE;

typedef DEVMODE * PDEVMODE, NEAR * NPDEVMODE, FAR * LPDEVMODE;
```

Related Messages   WM_DEVMODECHANGE

Example   This example illustrates several advanced techniques in dealing with a printer device driver. When the user clicks the "Do It!" menu item, WIN.INI is parsed to obtain the driver name and output port name. The driver is then loaded, and the address of the driver's ExtDeviceMode() function is determined. ExtDeviceMode() is called three times. The first call determines the size of the memory block needed to contain the driver's DEVMODE data structure. A global memory block of this size is then allocated. The second call to ExtDeviceMode(), with the DM_COPY flag set, copies the device data to the global memory block. The third call to ExtDeviceMode(), with the DM_PROMPT flag set, executes the driver's setup dialog box. If the user does not click the cancel button within the dialog box, the WM_DEVMODECHANGE message is sent to all running applications to alert them that the printer settings may have been altered.

Next, the program outputs two lines of text to the printer. The first is output in the printer's default paper orientation mode, assumed to be portrait. ResetDC() is then called to change the printer device context to landscape mode. The second line of text is then output. ResetDC() is called a final time to return the printer to portrait mode. Note that error checking on the memory allocation functions was omitted in this example for clarity. See the example under the GlobalAlloc() function description for a more complete example of memory allocation.

```
long FAR PASCAL WndProc (HWND hWnd, unsigned iMessage, WORD wParam, LONG lParam)
{
        char                szPrinter [64], szSysDir [128], szFullDriver [256],
                                *szDriver, *szDevice, *szOutput ;
        HANDLE              hDriver ;
        LPFNDEVMODE         lpfnDeviceMode ;
        LPDEVMODE           lpDevMode ;
        HDC                 hDCPrinter ;
        int                 nReturned, nBytes ;
        HANDLE              hMem ;

        switch (iMessage)                      /* process windows messages */
        {
                case WM_COMMAND:               /* process menu items */
                        switch (wParam)
                        {
                        case IDM_DOIT:         /* get driver name from WIN.INI */
                                GetProfileString ("windows", "device", "",
                                        szPrinter, 64) ;
```

```
szDevice = strtok (szPrinter, ",") ;
szDriver = strtok (NULL, ",") ;
szOutput = strtok (NULL, ",") ;
                /* build full driver path/file spec */
GetSystemDirectory (szSysDir, 128) ;
lstrcpy (szFullDriver, szSysDir) ;
lstrcat (szFullDriver, "\\") ;
lstrcat (szFullDriver, szDriver) ;
lstrcat (szFullDriver, ".DRV") ;
                /* get handle to driver */
hDriver = LoadLibrary (szFullDriver) ;
if (hDriver > 31)
{
        lpfnDeviceMode = (LPFNDEVMODE) GetProcAddress
                (hDriver, "ExtDeviceMode") ;
        if (lpfnDeviceMode)
        {               /* find size of DEVMODE structure */
                nBytes = (* lpfnDeviceMode) (hWnd, hDriver,
                        lpDevMode, szDevice, szOutput,
                        NULL, NULL, NULL) ;
                hMem = GlobalAlloc
                (GMEM_MOVEABLE | GMEM_ZEROINIT, nBytes) ;
                lpDevMode = (LPDEVMODE) GlobalLock (hMem) ;
                        /* initialize DEVMODE data */
                (* lpfnDeviceMode)
                (hWnd, hDriver, lpDevMode,
                szDevice, szOutput, NULL, NULL, DM_COPY) ;
                        /* call printer dialog box */
        nReturned = (* lpfnDeviceMode) (hWnd, hDriver,
                lpDevMode, szDevice, szOutput, NULL,
                        NULL, DM_PROMPT) ;
                if (nReturned != IDCANCEL)
                PostMessage (-1, WM_DEVMODECHANGE, 0,
                        (DWORD) (LPSTR) szDevice) ;

                hDCPrinter = CreateDC (szDriver, szDevice,
                        szOutput, (LPSTR) lpDevMode) ;
                        /* output in default mode */
        Escape (hDCPrinter, STARTDOC, 4, "Test", NULL) ;
                TextOut (hDCPrinter, 10, 10,
                "Text Output Appears Portrait Mode.", 34) ;
        Escape (hDCPrinter, NEWFRAME, NULL, NULL, NULL) ;
        Escape (hDCPrinter, ENDDOC, NULL, NULL, NULL) ;
                        /* switch printer to landscape */
        lpDevMode->dmOrientation = DMORIENT_LANDSCAPE ;
                if (ResetDC (hDCPrinter, lpDevMode))
                {
                        /* output in landscape mode */
        Escape (hDCPrinter, STARTDOC, 5, "Test2",
                                NULL) ;
                TextOut (hDCPrinter, 10, 10,
                Text Output Appears Landscape Mode.",
                                35) ;
        Escape (hDCPrinter, NEWFRAME,
                                NULL, NULL, NULL) ;

                lpDevMode->dmOrientation =
                                DMORIENT_PORTRAIT ;
                        ResetDC (hDCPrinter, lpDevMode) ;
                }
                else
                        MessageBox (hWnd,
                        "Could not change printer DC.",
                                "Message", MB_OK) ;
                GlobalUnlock (hMem) ;
                GlobalFree (hMem) ;
        }
}
else
```

```
                                MessageBox (hWnd, "Could not load driver file.",
                                        "Message", MB_OK) ;
                        break ;
                case IDM_QUIT:
                        DestroyWindow (hWnd) ;
                        break ;
                }
                break ;
        case WM_DEVMODECHANGE:
                MessageBox (hWnd,
                        "Notification that printer settings were altered.",
                        (LPSTR) lParam, MB_OK) ;
                break ;
        case WM_DESTROY:
                PostQuitMessage (0) ;
                break ;
        default:
                return DefWindowProc (hWnd, iMessage, wParam, lParam) ;
        }
        return (0L) ;
}
```

RESTOREDC
■ Win 2.0   ■ Win 3.0   ■ Win 3.1

Purpose	Restores an old device context saved with SaveDC().
Syntax	BOOL **RestoreDC**(HDC *hDC*, int *nSavedDC*);
Description	The current device context can be saved at any time with SaveDC(). Each call to SaveDC() places a copy of the current device context settings in a stack, above the last saved DC. Calling RestoreDC() returns the device context to the state when it was saved. If more than one device context is saved before RestoreDC() is called, the RestoreDC() calls are normally done in the reverse order to the order of the SaveDC() calls. If a DC below the last saved DC is restored, the ones above it in the stack are destroyed, as shown in Figure 10-19.

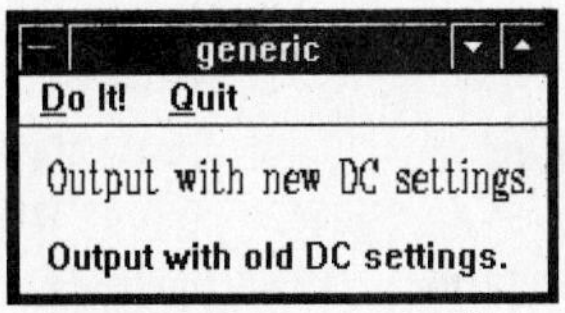

Figure 10-19. RestoreDC() Example.

Uses	Handy if you are changing pen colors, fonts, etc. within a graphics intensive part of the program. Avoids having to continually reload old pens, fonts, etc. to keep the device context current.
Returns	BOOL. TRUE if the device context was restored, FALSE on error.
See Also	SaveDC(), GetDC(), BeginPaint()
Parameters	
hDC	HDC: The device context handle.
nSavedDC	int: The value returned by SaveDC() when the device context was saved. Set to –1 to return the most recently saved DC.
Related Messages	WM_PAINT
Example	This example saves the device context before changing to a new font. After the font is used, the old device context is restored to output the bottom line using the system font.

```
Long FAR PASCAL WndProc (HWND hWnd, unsigned iMessage, WORD wParam, LONG lParam)
{
        HDC             hDC ;
        HFONT           hFont ;
        int             nOldDC ;

        switch (iMessage)                       /* process windows messages */
        {
                case WM_COMMAND:                /* process menu items */
                        switch (wParam)
                        {
                        case IDM_DOIT:          /* User hit the "Do it" menu item */
```

```
hDC = GetDC (hWnd) ;
nOldDC = SaveDC (hDC) ;
hFont = CreateFont (18, 0, 0, 0, 400, 0, 0, 0,
        OEM_CHARSET,     OUT_DEFAULT_PRECIS,
        CLIP_DEFAULT_PRECIS, DEFAULT_QUALITY,
        DEFAULT_PITCH | FF_ROMAN, "roman") ;
SelectObject (hDC, hFont) ;
TextOut (hDC, 10, 10,
        "Output with new DC settings.", 28) ;
RestoreDC (hDC, nOldDC) ;
TextOut (hDC, 10, 40,
        "Output with old DC settings.", 28) ;
ReleaseDC (hWnd, hDC) ;
break ;
```

[Other program lines]

SaveDC

■ Win 2.0   ■ Win 3.0   ■ Win 3.1

Purpose	Saves a device context for future use.
Syntax	int **SaveDC**(HDC *hDC*);
Description	The current device context can be saved at any time with SaveDC(). Each call to SaveDC() places a copy of the current device context settings in a stack, above the last saved DC. Calling RestoreDC() returns the device context to the state when it was saved. The saved DC will be removed from memory when the program terminates.
Uses	Handy if you are changing pen colors, fonts, etc. within a graphics intensive part of the program. Avoids having to continually reload old pens, fonts, etc. to keep the device context current.
Returns	int, the number of the saved device context. Zero on error.
See Also	RestoreDC(), ReleaseDC(), EndPaint()
Parameters	
hDC	HDC: The device context handle.
Related Messages	WM_PAINT
Example	See the previous example under RestoreDC().

ScaleViewportExt

■ Win 2.0   ■ Win 3.0   ■ Win 3.1

Purpose	Changes the scale of the logical coordinate system for a device context.
Syntax	DWORD **ScaleViewportExt**(HDC *hDC*, int *Xnum*, int *Xdenom*, int *Ynum*, int *Ydenom*);
Description	The existing viewport extents (scaling) is a ratio based on the following formulas to come up with the new scaling:

$$xNewVE = (xOldVE * Xnum) / Xdenom ;$$

$$yNewVE = (yOldVE * Ynum) / Ydenom ;$$

Uses	This is a convenient way to change the scaling of the a coordinate system. Only the MM_ISOTOPIC and MM_ANISOTROPIC mapping modes can be scaled.
Returns	The previous viewport extents (scaling). The low-order word contains the X value, while the high-order word contains the Y value.
See Also	ScaleWindowExt(), SetMapMode(), GetViewportExt(), SetViewportExt()
Parameters	
hDC	HDC: The device context handle.
Xnum	int: The multiplier for the current X extent.

Xdenom	int: The divisor for the current *X* extent.
Ynum	int: The multiplier for the current *Y* extent.
Ydenom	int: The divisor for the current *Y* extent.

Example

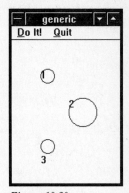

In the example shown in Figure 10-20, three circles, 20 logical units in diameter, are drawn at the logical coordinates 40,40. The three circles end up in different places, and different sizes, due to the scaling of the logical coordinates. To begin, the MM_ISOTROPIC mapping mode is set up with one logical unit equal to one device unit (pixel) in both the *X* and *Y* direction. Because the origin is not changed, the default origin at the upper left corner remains in effect. Circle 1 is drawn at 40,40 and ends up being 20 pixels in diameter.

Before circle 2 is drawn, both the *X* and *Y* extents are scaled up by a factor of two. This results in circle two being drawn twice as far away from the origin, and twice as big (measured in pixels). For circle 3, the scaling is returned to one logical unit equals one pixel, but the origin is relocated to the lower right corner. The *Y* axis is also inverted, so that increasing *Y* values refer to higher positions on the

Figure 10-20.
ScaleViewportExt( ) and
ScaleWindowExt( )
Examples.

client area. These changes result in circle 3 being drawn at location 40,40 relative to the bottom left corner, instead of relative to the top left corner.

```
long FAR PASCAL WndProc (HWND hWnd, unsigned iMessage, WORD wParam, LONG lParam)
{
        HDC             hDC ;
        RECT            rClient ;

        switch (iMessage)               /* process windows messages */
        {
                case WM_COMMAND:        /* process menu items */
                        switch (wParam)
                        {
                        case IDM_DOIT:  /* User hit the "Do it" menu item */
                                hDC = GetDC (hWnd) ;
                                SelectObject (hDC, GetStockObject (BLACK_PEN)) ;
                                SetBkMode (hDC, TRANSPARENT) ;
                                SetMapMode (hDC, MM_ISOTROPIC) ;
                                SetWindowExt (hDC, 1, 1) ;
                                /* first create a map mode where logical unit = pixel */
                                SetViewportExt (hDC, 1, 1) ;
                                Ellipse (hDC, 40, 40, 60, 60) ;
                                TextOut (hDC, 40, 40, "1", 1) ;
                                /* now create a map mode where logical unit = 2 pixels */
                                        /* map mode = 2 * default */
                                ScaleViewportExt (hDC, 2, 1, 2, 1) ;
                                Ellipse (hDC, 40, 40, 60, 60) ;
                                TextOut (hDC, 40, 40, "2", 1) ;
                                        /* undo the last scaling */
                                ScaleViewportExt (hDC, 1, 2, 1, 2) ;
                                /* now create a map mode where the origin is at the */
                                /* lower left corner, and Y values increase upwards. */
                                ScaleWindowExt (hDC, 1, 1, 1, -1) ;
                                GetClientRect (hWnd, (LPRECT) &rClient) ;
                                SetViewportOrg (hDC, rClient.left, rClient.bottom) ;
                                Ellipse (hDC, 40, 40, 60, 60) ;
                                TextOut (hDC, 40, 40, "3", 1) ;
                                ReleaseDC (hWnd, hDC) ;
                                break ;
```

[Other program lines]

ScaleWindowExt
■ Win 2.0   ■ Win 3.0   ■ Win 3.1

Purpose	Changes the scale of the logical coordinate system for a device context.
Syntax	DWORD **ScaleWindowExt**(HDC *hDC*, int *Xnum*, int *Xdenom*, int *Ynum*, int *Ydenom*);
Description	The existing window extents (scaling) is a ratio based on the following formulas to come up with the new scaling:

$$xNewWE = (xOldWE * Xnum) / Xdenom ;$$

$$yNewWE = (yOldWE * Ynum) / Ydenom ;$$

Uses	This is a convenient way to change the scaling of a coordinate system. Only the MM_ISOTOPIC and MM_ANISOTROPIC mapping modes can be scaled.
Returns	The previous window extents (scaling). The low-order word contains the *X* value, while the high-order word contains the *Y* value.
See Also	ScaleViewportExt(), SetMapMode(), GetWindowExt(), SetWindowExt()
Parameters	
hDC	HDC: The device context handle.
Xnum	int: The multiplier for the current *X* extent.
Xdenom	int: The divisor for the current *X* extent.
Ynum	int: The multiplier for the current *Y* extent.
Ydenom	int: The divisor for the current *Y* extent.
Example	The the previous example under ScaleViewportExt().

SetBkColor
■ Win 2.0   ■ Win 3.0   ■ Win 3.1

Purpose	Sets the color of the background surrounding each character, dashed line, or hatched brush.
Syntax	DWORD **SetBkColor**(HDC *hDC*, DWORD *crColor*);
Description	The background color is used to fill in the spaces around characters, dashed lines, and between the lines of hatched brushes. The default background color is white. SetBkColor() allows you to change the background color used by the device context.
Uses	Necessary when text, lines or brushes are painted against a color other than white.
Returns	The previous background color as an RGB color value. Returns 0x80000000 on error. See Chapter 11, *Painting the Screen*, for a discussion of the RGB color model.
See Also	SetBkMode(), CreateHatchBrush(), CreatePen(), TextOut(), GetBkColor(), GetBkMode()
Parameters	
hDC	HDC: The device context handle.
crColor	DWORD: A 32-bit color value. Use the RGB() macro to create a new color value.
Related Messages	WM_PAINT
Example	This program fragment demonstrates output of a character string with a fixed color background. In this case, the text is magenta and the background is green (an awful color combination!).

```
long FAR PASCAL WndProc (HWND hWnd, unsigned iMessage, WORD wParam, LONG lParam)
{
        HDC             hDC ;
        char            cBuf [] = {"This is a character string."} ;

        switch (iMessage)                       /* process windows messages */
        {
                case WM_COMMAND:                /* process menu items */
```

```
switch (wParam)
{
case IDM_DOIT:              /* User hit the "Do it" menu item */
        hDC = GetDC (hWnd) ;
        SetBkMode (hDC, OPAQUE) ;
        SetBkColor (hDC, RGB (0, 255, 0)) ;
        SetTextColor (hDC, RGB (255, 0, 255)) ;
        TextOut (hDC, 10, 10, cBuf, strlen (cBuf)) ;
        ReleaseDC (hWnd, hDC) ;
        break ;
```

[Other program lines]

SETBKMODE   ■ Win 2.0   ■ Win 3.0   ■ Win 3.1

Purpose	Changes the background painting mode.
Syntax	int **SetBkMode**(HDC *hDC*, int *nBkMode*);
Description	Sets the background painting mode. OPAQUE means that the spaces around the characters, dashed lines, and hatched brushes will be filled in with the background color. Selecting a TRANSPARENT mode keeps the rectangular area around each character from "blocking out" the background.
Uses	Frequently used to make the new text "blot out" the old text.
Returns	int, the previous background mode.
See Also	SetBkColor(), TextOut(), GetBkColor(), GetBkMode()
Parameters	
hDC	HDC: The device context handle.
nBkMode	int: The background painting mode. It can be either OPAQUE or TRANSPARENT.
Related Messages	WM_PAINT
Example	See the previous example with SetBkColor().

SETMAPMODE   ■ Win 2.0   ■ Win 3.0   ■ Win 3.1

Purpose	Changes the mapping mode for a device context.
Syntax	int **SetMapMode**(HDC *hDC*, int *nMapMode*);
Description	When a device context is first created, it uses the default set of units for measuring locations on the client area. The default units are in pixels, measured from the top left corner of the screen. These units are used to locate characters and graphics for functions like TextOut() and LineTo().
	The alternate mapping modes allow you to use inches or millimeteres to measure locations. These are not exact sizes, as Windows does not know the precise size of the equipment being used. These modes will provide much more consistent sizing in converting between devices than if the default MM_TEXT mapping mode is used. Two of the mapping modes allow the creation of custom systems of units. These mapping modes are typically used to scale graphics to fit a defined area without having to recalculate the positions of each location.
Uses	The inch and millimeter mapping modes assure you that the output will continue to be reasonably sized on different video and printer systems.
Returns	int, the previous mapping mode.
See Also	SetWindowExt(), SetViewportExt(), SetViewportOrg()
Parameters	
hDC	HDC: The device context handle.
nMapMode	int: One of the mapping modes in Table 10-13.

Value	Meaning
MM_ANISOTROPIC	This is the most flexible system of units. Either axis can have any scaling factor. Use SetWindowExt( ) and SetViewportExt( ) to set the scaling.
MM_HIENGLISH	Each logical unit is 0.001 inch. *X* increases to the right. *Y* increases upward.
MM_HIMETRIC	Each logical unit is 0.01 millimeter. *X* increases to the right. *Y* increases upward.
MM_ISOTROPIC	Arbitrary scaling of the axes, but the *X* and *Y* scaling must be the same. Use SetWindowExt( ) and SetViewportExt( ) to set the orientation and scaling.
MM_LOENGLISH	Each logical unit is 0.01 inch. *X* increases to the right. *Y* increases upward.
MM_LOMETRIC	Each logical unit is 0.1 millimeter. *X* increases to the right. *Y* increases upward.
MM_TEXT	This is the default mapping mode. Each unit equals one pixel. *X* increases to the right. *Y* increases downward.
MM_TWIPS	Each logical unit is 1/20 point, or 1/1440 of an inch. *X* increases to the right. *Y* increases upward.

Table 10-13. Device Context Mapping Modes.

Example

The example shown in Figure 10-21 shows how to change both the mapping mode and the viewport origin. When the device context is created, it has the default MM_TEXT mapping mode. 0,0 is in the upper left corner. Following the first text output, the mapping mode is switched to MM_LOMETRIC and the origin moved to 50,50. The MM_LOMETRIC system has *Y* values increasing upward, so the 100,100 location is above and to the right of the new origin.

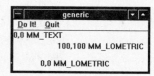

Figure 10-21. SetMapMode( ) Example.

```
Long FAR PASCAL WndProc (HWND hWnd, unsigned iMessage, WORD wParam, LONG lParam)
{
        HDC      hDC ;

        switch (iMessage)                    /* process windows messages */
        {
                case WM_COMMAND:             /* process menu items */
                        switch (wParam)
                        {
                        case IDM_DOIT:   /* User hit the "Do it" menu item */
                                hDC = GetDC (hWnd) ;
                                TextOut (hDC, 0, 0, "0,0 MM_TEXT", 11) ;
                                SetMapMode (hDC, MM_LOMETRIC) ;
                                SetViewportOrg (hDC, 50, 50) ;
                                TextOut (hDC, 0, 0, "0,0 MM_LOMETRIC", 15) ;
                                TextOut (hDC, 100, 100, "100, 100 MM_LOMETRIC", 19) ;
                                ReleaseDC (hWnd, hDC) ;
                                break ;
```

[Other program lines]

SETMAPPERFLAGS
■ Win 2.0 ■ Win 3.0 ■ Win 3.1

Purpose Adjusts the way CreateFont() and CreateFontIndirect() adjust for font dimensions outside of those specified in the font data.

Syntax DWORD **SetMapperFlags**(HDC *hDC*, DWORD *dwFlag*);

Description CreateFont() and CreateFontIndirect() will normally interpolate to achieve specified font sizes and aspect ratios not described in the font data. Use SetMapperFlags() to force the use of the nearest matching font or to allow interpolation.

Returns The previous mapper flag value; 1 for exact matching, 0 if interpolation was allowed.

See Also	CreateFont(), CreateFontIndirect()

Parameters

hDC   HDC: The device context handle.

dwFlag   DWORD: If the low-order bit is 1, exact matching is forced. If the low-order bit is 0, interpolation is allowed.

Example

```
Long FAR PASCAL WndProc (HWND hWnd, unsigned iMessage, WORD wParam, LONG lParam)
{
        HDC             hDC ;
        HFONT           hFont ;

        switch (iMessage)                       /* process windows messages */
        {
                case WM_COMMAND:                /* process menu items */
                        switch (wParam)
                        {
                        case IDM_DOIT:          /* User hit the "Do it" menu item */
                                hDC = GetDC (hWnd) ;
                                SetMapperFlags (hDC, 0L) ;
                                hFont = CreateFont (30, 8, 0, 0, 400, 0, 0, 0,
                                        OEM_CHARSET,    OUT_DEFAULT_PRECIS,
                                        CLIP_DEFAULT_PRECIS, DEFAULT_QUALITY,
                                        DEFAULT_PITCH | FF_SWISS, "swiss") ;
                                SelectObject (hDC, hFont) ;
                                TextOut (hDC, 10, 10, "Mapper flag not now set.", 24) ;
                                SetMapperFlags (hDC, 1L) ;
                                hFont = CreateFont (30, 8, 0, 0, 400, 0, 0, 0,
                                        OEM_CHARSET,    OUT_DEFAULT_PRECIS,
                                        CLIP_DEFAULT_PRECIS, DEFAULT_QUALITY,
                                        DEFAULT_PITCH | FF_SWISS, "swiss") ;
                                SelectObject (hDC, hFont) ;
                                TextOut (hDC, 10, 50, "Mapper flag now set to 1", 24) ;
                                ReleaseDC (hWnd, hDC) ;
                                DeleteObject (hFont) ;
                                break ;
```

[Other program lines]

SETTEXTALIGN   ■ Win 2.0   ■ Win 3.0   ■ Win 3.1

Purpose	Changes the text alignment for a device context.
Syntax	WORD **SetTextAlign**(HDC *hDC*, WORD *wFlags*);
Description	Both TextOut() and ExtTextOut() specify where the output string should start based on a logical *X,Y* position. By default, the device context uses the upper left corner of the first character as the X,Y location. SetTextAlign() allows you to change this alignment location to other locations on the first character.
	There is also a special flag labeled TA_UPDATECP which allows TextOut() and ExtTextOut() to keep track of where the end of the output string ended up on the device context. This allows you to use multiple calls to the output functions, with each successive string ending up at the end of the last one.
Uses	Frequently used to center text if you use the TA_CENTER style.
Returns	int, the previous text alignment. The low-order word contains the horizontal alignment. The high-order word contains the vertical alignment.
See Also	TextOut(), ExtTextOut(), GetTextAlign()

Parameters

hDC   HDC: The device context handle.

wFlags	WORD: One or more of the flags listed in Table 10-14. A vertical, horizontal, and update flag can all be combined using the C language binary OR operator (|).

Value	Meaning	
TA_BASELINE	The baseline of the first character is used to specify the string position.	
TA_BOTTOM	The bottom of the first character is used to specify the string position.	
TA_CENTER	The center of the first character is used to specify the string position.	
TA_LEFT	The left side of the first character is used to specify the string position.	
TA_NOUPDATECP	The location at the end of the last text output is not saved.	
TA_RIGHT	The right side of the first character is used to specify the string position.	
TA_TOP	The top of the first character is used to specify the string position.	
TA_UPDATECP	The position at the end of the last text output is saved. The next call to TextOut( ) or ExtTextOut( ) will start from this location, ignoring the *X,Y* data in the output function parameters.	

Table 10-14. SetTextAlign( ) Flags.

Note	The default values for a device context are TA_LEFT, TA_TOP, and TA_NOUPDATECP.
Example	The example shown in Figure 10-22 demonstrates several uses of SetTextAlign(). The character strings "Top" and "Bottom" are both output with a vertical position (*Y*) value of 50. The second string ends up above the first as the text alignment is changed so that the *Y* value refers to the bottom of the character, instead of the top. The character string "Second Line In Two Parts" is output using two calls to TextOut(). As the text alignment is set to TA_UPDATECP before calling TextOut(), the character position data is ignored. Each character location follows the end of the last call to TextOut().

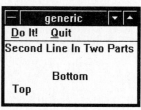

Figure 10-22. SetTextAlign( ) Examples.

```
Long FAR PASCAL WndProc (HWND hWnd, unsigned iMessage, WORD wParam, LONG lParam)
{
        HDC     hDC ;

        switch (iMessage)                /* process windows messages */
        {
                case WM_COMMAND:         /* process menu items */
                        switch (wParam)
                        {
                        case IDM_DOIT:   /* User hit the "Do it" menu item */
                                hDC = GetDC (hWnd) ;
                                SetTextAlign (hDC, TA_TOP) ;
                                TextOut (hDC, 10, 50, "Top", 3) ;
                                SetTextAlign (hDC, TA_BOTTOM) ;
                                TextOut (hDC, 60, 50, "Bottom", 6) ;
                                SetTextAlign (hDC, TA_TOP | TA_UPDATECP) ;
                                TextOut (hDC, 10, 0, "Second Line", 11) ;
                                TextOut (hDC, 0, 0, " In Two Parts", 13) ;
                                ReleaseDC (hWnd, hDC) ;
                                break ;
```

[Other program lines]

SETTEXTCHARACTEREXTRA   ■ Win 2.0   ■ Win 3.0   ■ Win 3.1

Purpose	Adds additional space between characters of a device context.
Syntax	int **SetTextCharacterExtra**(HDC *hDC*, int *nCharExtra*);

Description	This function allows you to add extra space between the letters of the currently selected font of a device context. The extra space is added between the characters output by TextOut() and ExtTextOut(). There is no way to reduce character spacing below the amount specified in the font description.

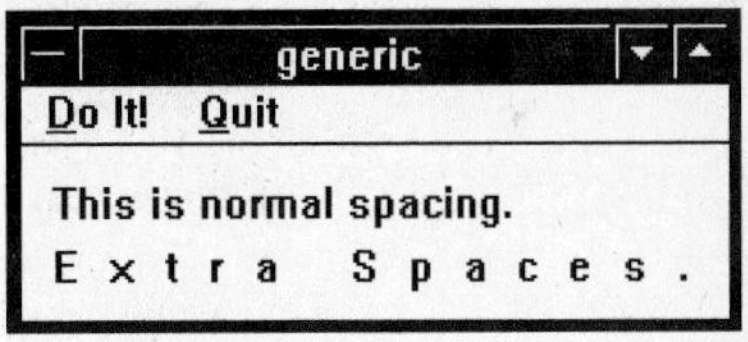

Figure 10-23.
SetTextCharacterExtra( ) Example.

Uses	Handy for making text "fit" in predefined areas.
Returns	int, the previous extra character spacing (usually zero).
See Also	GetTextCharacterExtra(), SetMapMode(), TextOut(), ExtTextOut()
Parameters	
hDC	HDC: The device context handle.
nCharExtra	int: The number of extra logical units of space to add between characters. For the default MM_TEXT mode, this is the extra number of pixels. For the other mapping modes, the extra logical units are rounded to the nearest pixel.
Example	Figure 10-23 shows the effect of adding extra spaces between characters.

```
Long FAR PASCAL WndProc (HWND hWnd, unsigned iMessage, WORD wParam, LONG lParam)
{
        HDC      hDC ;

        switch (iMessage)                          /* process windows messages */
        {
        case WM_COMMAND:           /* process menu items */
                switch (wParam)
                {
                case IDM_DOIT:   /* User hit the "Do it" menu item */
                        hDC = GetDC (hWnd) ;
                        TextOut (hDC, 10, 10, "This is normal spacing.", 23) ;
                        SetTextCharacterExtra (hDC, 10) ;
                        TextOut (hDC, 10, 30, "Extra Spaces.", 13) ;
                        ReleaseDC (hWnd, hDC) ;
                        break ;
```
[Other program lines]

SETTEXTCOLOR ■ Win 2.0 ■ Win 3.0 ■ Win 3.1

Purpose	Changes the text color for a device context.
Syntax	DWORD **SetTextColor**(HDC *hDC*, DWORD *crColor*);
Description	The default text color for a device context is black. This function allows any RGB color to be set for text output with TextOut(), ExtTextOut(), etc. The color stays in effect until the device context is released, or another text color is set. See Chapter 11, *Painting the Screen*, for an explanation of RGB color values.
Uses	Colored text output.
Returns	The 32-bit color value for the previous text color.
See Also	GetTextColor(), SetBkColor()
Parameters	
hDC	HDC: The device context handle.
crColor	COLORREF: The 32-bit color value for the text. This can be set with the RGB macro (see the example).

Example

The example in Figure 10-24 has a window with a private device context. When the program starts (WM_CREATE message received), the text color is set to blue. When the user clicks the "Do It!" menu item, the current color value is output in hexadecimal.

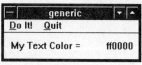

The window's class definition in WinMain() includes the CS_OWNDC style, giving the window its own private device context.

Figure 10-24. SetTextColor()
and GetTextColor() Example.

```
wndclass.style = CS_HREDRAW | CS_VREDRAW | CS_OWNDC ;
```

Note that the RGB macro parameters are in the opposite order of the storage order inside the 32-bit coded color value (compare RGB (0,0,255) with the output value of 0xFF0000).

```
long FAR PASCAL WndProc (HWND hWnd, unsigned iMessage, WORD wParam, LONG lParam)
{
        HDC             hDC ;
        DWORD           dwTextColor ;
        char            cBuf [10] ;

        switch (iMessage)                        /* process windows messages */
        {
                case WM_CREATE:
                        hDC = GetDC (hWnd) ;     /* owns DC, no need to release */
                        SetTextColor (hDC, RGB (0, 0, 255)) ;    /* blue letters */
                        break ;
                case WM_COMMAND:                 /* process menu items */
                        switch (wParam)
                        {
                        case IDM_DOIT:           /* User hit the "Do it" menu item */
                                hDC = GetDC (hWnd) ;
                                dwTextColor = GetTextColor (hDC) ;
                                ltoa (dwTextColor, cBuf, 16) ;    /* convert to hex */
                                TextOut (hDC, 10, 10, "My Text Color =", 15) ;
                                TextOut (hDC, 150, 10, cBuf, lstrlen (cBuf)) ;
                                break ;
```

[Other program lines]

SET TEXT JUSTIFICATION   ■ Win 2.0   ■ Win 3.0   ■ Win 3.1

Purpose   Justifies a string prior to using TextOut() for output.

Syntax   int **SetTextJustification**(HDC *hDC*, int *nBreakExtra*, int *nBreakCount*);

Description   Justification is the process of adding spaces between words to make a text string exactly fit a given space. SetTextJustification() works with the GetTextExtent() and TextOut() functions to accomplish this. GetTextExtent() is used to compute the length of the string before justification. SetTextJustification() then computes the amount of added space needed to match the space available. The next call to TextOut() uses this value to add spaces between words during output.

Normally, the ASCII space character (number 32) is the break character. The break characters are where the extra spaces will be added. Some fonts may use another character as a break character. Use GetTextMetrics() to determine the font's break character. If a line contains multiple fonts, justify and output each group of characters, one font-type at a time. SetTextJustification() accumulates the round-off errors on each call in order to average the errors over the length of a line. Call SetTextJustification() with an *nBreakExtra* value of zero to clear the round-off error at the start of each new line.

Uses   Justification of text.

Returns   int. TRUE (1) if successful, FALSE (0) on error.

See Also   GetTextExtent(), TextOut(), ExtTextOut(), TabbedTextOut()

Parameters

hDC   HDC: The device context handle.

nBreakExtra   int: The total amount of extra space (in logical units) to be added to the line of text when output. In the default MM_TEXT mapping mode, the extra space is measured in pixels.

nBreakCount   int: The total number of break characters in the string. For most fonts, this is the number of space characters ("", or ASCII 32). SetTextJustification() will add additional room at each of these locations to expand the text.

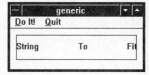

Figure 10-25. Text Justification Example.

Example   The example in Figure 10-25 justifies a three word string to fit exactly within the bounds of a 200 pixel wide rectangle. GetTextExtent() is used to calculate the size of the string prior to justification. SetText-Justification() then adds enough space to expand the string to the full 200 unit size. The next call to TextOut() uses the justification during output to space the words.

With this simple example, the number of spaces in the string (two) is known. Normally, you would have to check the number of spaces (break characters) in the string before calling SetTextJustification().

```
Long FAR PASCAL WndProc (HWND hWnd, unsigned iMessage, WORD wParam, LONG lParam)
{
        HDC             hDC ;
        HPEN            hPen ;
        DWORD           dwExtent ;
        char            cBuf [] = {"String To Fit"} ;

        switch (iMessage)               /* process windows messages */
        {
        case WM_COMMAND:                /* process menu items */
                switch (wParam)
                {
                case IDM_DOIT:  /* User hit the "Do it" menu item */
                        hDC = GetDC (hWnd) ;
                        SetBkMode (hDC, TRANSPARENT) ;
                        hPen = GetStockObject (BLACK_PEN) ;
                        SelectObject (hDC, hPen) ;
                        Rectangle (hDC, 10, 10, 210, 50) ;
                        dwExtent = GetTextExtent (hDC, cBuf,
                                strlen (cBuf)) ;
                        SetTextJustification (hDC,
                                200 - LOWORD(dwExtent), 2) ;
                        TextOut (hDC, 10, 20, cBuf, strlen (cBuf)) ;
                        ReleaseDC (hWnd, hDC) ;
                        break ;
```

[Other program lines]

SETVIEWPORTEXT   ■ Win 2.0   ■ Win 3.0   ■ Win 3.1

Purpose   Used with SetWindowExt() to set the scale of the logical coordinate system with the MM_ISOTROPIC and MM_ANISOTROPIC mapping modes.

Syntax   DWORD **SetViewportExt**(HDC *hDC*, int *X,* int *Y*);

Description   The MM_ISOTROPIC and MM_ANISOTROPIC mapping modes allow you to scale the logical co-ordinates system for a device context with ratio to the physical device coordinates (pixel based). MM_ISOTROPIC keeps both axes scaled equally, and MM_ANISOTROPIC allows both axes to be scaled independently.

In order to allow fractional scaling without using floating point numbers, Windows uses two functions with two sets of integer values to scale the coordinates. SetWindowExt() can be thought of as setting the physical coordinates, and SetViewportExt() sets the logical coordinates. It is the ratio of the two sets of values that determines the scaling. If the signs for the X and Y values are opposite, the orientation of the axes is reversed. This is usually used to make the Y axis increase upward, instead of the default system where Y values increase downward.

Uses
The MM_ISOTROPIC system is ideal for scaling drawings, without having to change any of the dimensions used in the GDI function calls. The MM_ANISOTROPIC system can be used to scale the graphics in the client area to always fit within a sized window. The image will be distorted if the X and Y sizes are not changed equally (MM_ISOTROPIC preserves the image proportions).

Returns
DWORD, the previous viewport extents. The low-order word contains the X extent. The high-order word contains the Y extent. Returns zero on error.

See Also
SetWindowExt(), SetMapMode(), SetViewportOrg(), SetWindowOrg()

Parameters

hDC
HDC: The device context handle.

X
int: The X axis extent. The X axis scaling is the ratio of this value divided by the X parameter in SetWindowExt(). If the signs of the X parameters in SetWindowExt() and SetViewportExt() are opposite, X values will increase to the left. If the signs match, X values will increase to the right.

Y
int: The Y axis extent. The Y axis scaling is the ratio of this value divided by the Y parameter in SetWindowExt(). If the signs of the Y parameters in SetWindowExt() and SetViewportExt() are opposite, Y values will increase upward. If the signs match, Y values will increase downward.

Example
See the example under the ScaleViewportExt() function description.

SETVIEWPORTORG
■ Win 2.0   ■ Win 3.0   ■ Win 3.1

Purpose
Changes the origin of the coordinate system used for text and graphics locations on a device.

Syntax
DWORD **SetViewportOrg**(HDC *hDC*, int *X*, int *Y*);

Description
The origin of the coordinate system is the point that has location 0,0 for X and Y. SetViewportOrg() allows you to place the origin anywhere in the client area. Note that the location of the origin is measured in device units. This is number of pixels measured from the upper left corner of the device's client area.

Uses
In graphics routines, it is frequently more convenient to have the origin at the middle or bottom left of the client area's rectangle. You can also move graphics on the screen by relocating the origin and then repainting. This is a way to scroll graphics images without recalculating where the points will be after scrolling.

Returns
DWORD, the previous origin measured in device units. The X coordinate is in the low-order word, the Y coordinate is in the high-order word.

See Also
SetWindowOrg(), SetMapMode()

Parameters

hDC
HDC: The device context handle.

X
int: The new X location of the origin, measured in device units (pixels from the right side).

Y
int: The new Y location of the origin, measured in device units (pixels from the top, increasing downward).

Related Messages WM_SIZE

Example
In Figure 10-26 a mapping mode is set with the origin at the lower left corner of the window's client area. The WM_SIZE messages are intercepted to find the size of the client area to

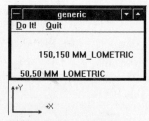

Figure 10-26. SetViewport-Org() Example.

set the *Y* axis origin equal to the bottom of the client area. Because of the MM_LOMETRIC mapping mode, *Y* increases upward. Note that by default the text locations are measured from the upper left corner of the first character of the string. That is why 50 logical units (5 mm) of vertical offset are needed to make the bottom line appear above the border.

```
long FAR PASCAL WndProc (HWND hWnd, unsigned iMessage, WORD wParam, LONG lParam)
{
        HDC                     hDC ;
        static  POINT           ptClientSize ;

        switch (iMessage)                       /* process windows messages */
        {
                case WM_SIZE:                   /* get client area size */
                        ptClientSize.x = LOWORD (lParam) ;
                        ptClientSize.y = HIWORD (lParam) ;
                        break ;
                case WM_COMMAND:                /* process menu items */
                        switch (wParam)
                        {
                        case IDM_DOIT:          /* User hit the "Do it" menu item */
                                hDC = GetDC (hWnd) ;
                                SetMapMode (hDC, MM_LOMETRIC) ;
                                SetViewportOrg (hDC, 0, ptClientSize.y) ;
                                TextOut (hDC, 50, 50, "50,50 MM_LOMETRIC", 17) ;
                                TextOut (hDC, 150, 150, "150,150 MM_LOMETRIC", 19) ;
                                ReleaseDC (hWnd, hDC) ;
                                break ;
```

[Other program lines]

SETWINDOWEXT   ■ Win 2.0   ■ Win 3.0   ■ Win 3.1

Purpose   Used with SetViewportExt() to set the scale of the logical coordinate system with the MM_ISOTROPIC and MM_ANISOTROPIC mapping modes.

Syntax   DWORD **SetWindowExt**(HDC *hDC*, int *X*, int *Y*);

Description   The MM_ISOTROPIC and MM_ANISOTROPIC mapping modes allow you to scale the logical coordinates system for a device context with ratio to the physical device coordinates (pixel based). MM_ISOTROPIC keeps both axes scaled equally, and MM_ANISOTROPIC allows both axes to be scaled independently.

In order to allow fractional scaling without using floating point numbers, Windows uses two functions with two sets of integer values, to scale the coordinates. SetWindowExt() can be thought of as setting the physical coordinates, while SetViewportExt() sets the logical coordinates. It is just the ratio of the two sets of values that determines the scaling. If the signs for the *X* and *Y* values are opposite, the orientation of the axes is reversed. Reversing one axis is usually used to make the *Y* axis increase upward, instead of the default system where *Y* values increase downward.

Uses   The MM_ISOTROPIC system is ideal for scaling drawings, without having to change any of the dimensions used in the GDI function calls. The MM_ANISOTROPIC system can be used to scale the graphics in the client area to always fit within a sized window. The image will be distorted if the *X* and *Y* sizes are not changed equally (MM_ISOTROPIC preserves the image proportions).

Returns   DWORD, the previous window extents. The low-order word contains the *X* extent. The high-order word contains the *Y* extent. Returns zero on error.

See Also   SetViewportExt(), SetMapMode(), SetViewportOrg(), SetWindowOrg()

Parameters
hDC   HDC: The device context handle.

X	int: The X axis extent. The X axis scaling is the ratio of the X parameter in SetWindowExt() divided by this value. If the signs of the X parameters in SetWindowExt() and SetViewportExt() are opposite, X values will increase to the left. If the signs match, X values will increase to the right.
Y	int: The Y axis extent. The Y axis scaling is the ratio of the Y parameter in SetWindowExt() divided by this value. If the signs of the Y parameters in SetWindowExt() and SetViewportExt() are opposite, Y values will increase upward. If the signs match, Y values will increase downward.
Example	See the example under ScaleViewportExt().

SETWINDOWORG   ■ Win 2.0   ■ Win 3.0   ■ Win 3.1

Purpose	Changes the location of the origin of the device context.
Syntax	DWORD **SetWindowOrg**(HDC *hDC*, int *X*, int *Y*);
Description	This is similar to SetViewportOrg(), except that logical units (not device units or pixels) are used. The point set is the logical offset of the upper left corner of the window's client area, measured in logical units.
Uses	Not used as often as SetViewportOrg().
Returns	DWORD, the previous origin of the window. The low-order word contains the X value, the high-order word contains the Y value.
See Also	SetMapMode(), SetViewportOrg()
Parameters	
hDC	HDC: The device context handle.
X	int: The new X location of the origin, measured in logical units.
Y	int: The new Y location of the origin, measured in logical units.
Example	This example sets the logical origin in the center of the window's client area. This is complicated slightly because SetWindowOrg() uses logical units to set the origin, not device units (pixels). The size of the client area returned when a WM_SIZE message is processed in device units, which are converted to logical units using the DPtoLP() function. Finally, the window origin is set using SetWindowOrg(). The origin dimensions are both negative because we are setting the logical value of the upper left corner of the window, measured in the MM_LOMETRIC units of .1 mm.

```
long FAR PASCAL WndProc (HWND hWnd, unsigned iMessage, WORD wParam, LONG lParam)
{
        HDC                     hDC ;
        static   POINT          ptClientSize, ptCenter ;

        switch (iMessage)                       /* process windows messages */
        {
                case WM_SIZE:                   /* get client area size */
                        ptClientSize.x = LOWORD (lParam) ;
                        ptClientSize.y = HIWORD (lParam) ;
                        break ;
                case WM_COMMAND:                /* process menu items */
                        switch (wParam)
                        {
                        case IDM_DOIT:          /* User hit the "Do it" menu item */
                                hDC = GetDC (hWnd) ;
                                SetMapMode (hDC, MM_LOMETRIC) ;
                                ptCenter.x = ptClientSize.x / 2 ;/* calc center in */
                                ptCenter.y = ptClientSize.y / 2 ;/* device units */
                                DPtoLP (hDC, &ptCenter, 1) ;     /* convert to log units */
                                SetWindowOrg (hDC, -ptCenter.x, -ptCenter.y) ;
                                TextOut (hDC, 0, 0, "0,0 MM_LOMETRIC", 15) ;
                                TextOut (hDC, 150, 150, "150,150 MM_LOMETRIC", 19) ;
                                ReleaseDC (hWnd, hDC) ;
                                break ;
```

[Other program lines]

TABBEDTEXTOUT

□ Win 2.0   ■ Win 3.0   ■ Win 3.1

Purpose	Outputs a text string, expanding all tab characters.
Syntax	long **TabbedTextOut**(HDC *hDC*, int *X*, int *Y*, LPSTR *lpString*, int *nCount*, int *nTabPositions*, LPINT *lpnTabStopPositions*, int *nTabOrigin*);
Description	This is an extension of the TextOut() function that adds the ability to expand tab characters to any set of tab positions.
Uses	Text output when the text string contains tab characters. Tabs are used to align text in columns.
Returns	long, the logical dimensions of the string output. The low-order word contains the width, the high-order word contains the height.
See Also	TextOut(), GetTabbedTextExtent(), SetTextAlign(), SetBkMode(), SetTextColor()

Parameters

hDC   HDC: The device context handle.

X   int: The logical *X* coordinate to start the string.

Y   int: The logical *Y* coordinate to start the string.

lpString   LPSTR: A pointer to a character string that will be output.

nCount   int: The number of characters, including tab characters, in the string.

nTabPositions int: The number of tab positions specified in *lpnTabStopPositions*.

lpnTabStopPositions LPINT: A pointer to an array of integers that holds the tab stop positions. The tab positions are measured in device units (pixels), and must be in ascending order.

nTabOrigin   int: The logical *X* coordinate to start tab expansions. You can use TabbedTextOut() several times on one line by changing the *nTabOrigin* parameter to start the tab expansion from different *X* locations.

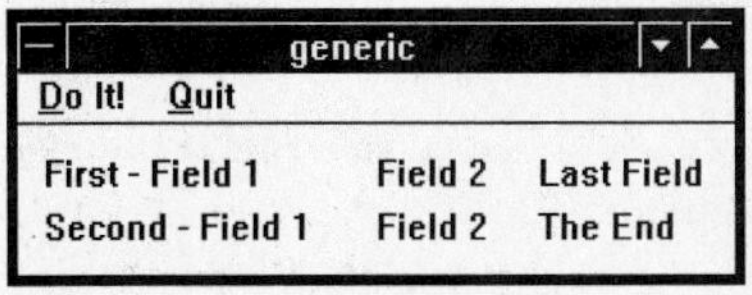

Figure 10-27. TabbedTextOut() Example.

Related Messages WM_PAINT

Example   The example in Figure 10-27 outputs two lines of text and expands the tab characters in the strings.

```
Long FAR PASCAL WndProc (HWND hWnd, unsigned iMessage, WORD wParam, LONG lParam)
{
        HDC             hDC ;
        static  char    cBuf1 [] = {"First - Field 1\tField 2\tLast Field"} ;
        static  char    cBuf2 [] = {"Second - Field 1\tField 2\tThe End"} ;
        static  int     nTabs [] = {30, 45, 60} ;

        switch (iMessage)                       /* process windows messages */
        {
                case WM_COMMAND:                /* process menu items */
                        switch (wParam)
                        {
                        case IDM_DOIT:          /* User hit the "Do it" menu item */
                                hDC = GetDC (hWnd) ;
                                TabbedTextOut (hDC, 10, 10, cBuf1,
                                        lstrlen (cBuf1), 3,
                                        (LPINT) &nTabs, 10) ;
                                TabbedTextOut (hDC, 10, 30, cBuf2,
                                        lstrlen (cBuf2), 3,
                                        (LPINT) &nTabs, 10) ;
                                ReleaseDC (hWnd, hDC) ;
                                break ;
```

[Other program lines]

TextOut
■ Win 2.0   ■ Win 3.0   ■ Win 3.1

Purpose	Outputs a character string at a location on the selected device context.
Syntax	BOOL **TextOut**(HDC *hDC*, int *X*, int *Y*, LPSTR *lpString*, int *nCount*);
Description	This is the standard text output function. The text is output with the currently selected font, pen color, and background color.
Uses	Used for text output where the character string does not contain tab characters. Use TabbedTextOut() if the tabs need to be expanded.
Returns	BOOL. TRUE if the string was output, FALSE on error.
See Also	SetTextAlign(), TabbedTextOut(), SetBkMode(), SetTextColor(), SetTextCharacterExtra(), SetTextJustification()

Parameters

hDC	HDC: The device context handle.
X	int: The logical *X* coordinate to start the string.
Y	int: The logical *Y* coordinate to start the string.
lpString	LPSTR: A pointer to a character string that will be output.
nCount	int: The number of characters in the string. Use the lstrlen() function to determine this value for null-terminated strings.

Related Messages WM_PAINT

Example This example outputs the string "This is a character string." when the user hits the "Do It!" menu item.

```
Long FAR PASCAL WndProc (HWND hWnd, unsigned iMessage, WORD wParam, LONG lParam)
{
        HDC     hDC ;
        char    cBuf [] = {"This is a character string."} ;

        switch (iMessage)              /* process windows messages */
        {
                case WM_COMMAND:       /* process menu items */
                        switch (wParam)
                        {
                        case IDM_DOIT:  /* User hit the "Do it" menu item */
                                hDC = GetDC (hWnd) ;
                                TextOut (hDC, 10, 10, cBuf, lstrlen (cBuf)) ;
                                ReleaseDC (hWnd, hDC) ;
                                break ;
```

[Other program lines]

WSPRINTF
□ Win 2.0   ■ Win 3.0   ■ Win 3.1

Purpose	Formats text output to a character buffer.
Syntax	int **wsprintf**(LPSTR *lpOutput*, LPSTR *lpFormat*[, *argument*]...);
Description	This is the Windows version of the standard C library sprintf() function. The format string defines what the output should look like, and includes special characters as placeholders for numbers and characters that are passed to the function as arguments. Because wsprintf() will accept a variable number of arguments, it does not use the standard Windows function calling convention of PASCAL.
Uses	Formatting text output, especially text containing numbers.
Returns	int, the number of characters output to *lpOutput*.
See Also	wvsprintf(), TextOut(), TabbedTextOut(), ExtTextOut()

Parameters

lpOutput   LPSTR: A pointer to a character buffer to hold the output.

lpFormat   LPSTR: A pointer to a null-terminated character string that contains the format. This can include the special characters listed below.

argument   (variable type): One or more optional arguments. The number and type of these arguments is specified by the special characters used in lpFormat.

Format Characters A typical format string is

A number = %d, a name %s.

The %d is a code for decimal integer, the %s for string. The arguments following the format string would then include the number and a pointer to a character. These values would be inserted into the format string in place of the %d and %s as the string is formatted into the *lpOutput* character buffer. The list of character codes appears in Table 10-15.

Value	Meaning
%s	Insert a character string at the location. The argument corresponding to this location must be passed as a long pointer to a string (LPSTR). Be sure to cast strings as LPSTR when using this type.
%c	Insert a signed character at the location.
%d, %i	Insert a signed integer at the location.
%ld, %li	Insert a signed long integer at the location.
%u	Insert an unsigned integer at the location.
%lu	Insert an unsigned long integer at the location.
%x, %X	Insert an unsigned hexadecimal integer at the location. The uppercase X results in uppercase A-F digits as part of the hexadecimal output.
%lx, %lX	Insert a long unsigned hexadecimal integer at the location. The uppercase X results in uppercase A-F digits as part of the hexadecimal output.

Table 10-15. wsprintf( ) Format Codes.

Additional formatting information can be included between the % and the format letter(s). For example, the format code "%06d" specifies that the field is to have six digits and leading zeros are to be added to fill up the six spaces. The list of these extra formatting characters appears in Table 10-16.

Value	Meaning
-	Justify to the left. Normally, justification is to the right side.
#	Put 0x or 0X in front of hexadecimal numbers.
0	Pad the output with zeros instead of blanks.
A number	The number of digits or characters to display. If no value is given, the field is expanded to make room for the number or string passed as an argument.

Table 10-16. wsprintf( ) Extra Formatting Codes.

Example   This example uses wsprintf() to format a string containing two integers: the height and width of the client region when the user clicked the "Do It!" menu item. The formatted text is stored in the cBuf[] buffer, and then output to the screen with TextOut().

```
Long FAR PASCAL WndProc (HWND hWnd, unsigned iMessage, WORD wParam, LONG lParam)
{
        HDC             hDC ;
```

```
        RECT            rClient ;
        char            cBuf [128] ;

        switch (iMessage)                   /* process windows messages */
        {
                case WM_COMMAND:            /* process menu items */
                        switch (wParam)
                        {
                        case IDM_DOIT: /* User hit the "Do it" menu item */
                                hDC = GetDC (hWnd) ;
                                GetClientRect (hWnd, (LPRECT) &rClient) ;
                                wsprintf (cBuf,
                                        "The client rectangle is %d wide by %d tall.",
                                        rClient.right - rClient.left,
                                        rClient.bottom - rClient.top) ;
                                TextOut (hDC, 10, 10, cBuf, lstrlen (cBuf)) ;
                                ReleaseDC (hWnd, hDC) ;
                                break ;
```

[Other program lines]

WVSPRINTF

Purpose	Formats text output to a character buffer.
Syntax	int **wvsprintf**(LPSTR *lpOutput*, LPSTR *lpFormat*, LPSTR *lpArglist*);
Description	This is the Windows version of the standard C library vsprintf() function. The format string defines what the output should look like, and includes special characters as placeholders for numbers and characters that are passed to the function as arguments. vwsprintf() uses a pointer to an argument list to avoid having a variable number of arguments. It uses the standard Windows function calling convention of PASCAL.
Uses	Formatting text output, especially text containing numbers.
Returns	int, the number of characters output to *lpOutput*.
See Also	wsprintf(), TextOut(), TabbedTextOut(), ExtTextOut()
Parameters	
lpOutput	LPSTR: A pointer to a character buffer to hold the output.
lpFormat	LPSTR: A pointer to a null-terminated character string that contains the format. This can include the special characters listed previously under the wsprintf() function description.
lpArglist	LPSTR: A pointer to an array of WORD values. Each WORD either specifies a numeric value or contains a pointer to a character string. Long values and character pointers require two words of storage. For long values, the low-order word is first in the array, followed by the high-order word. For character pointers, the segment is first in the array, followed by the offset.
Format Characters	See the list under the function description for wsprintf().
Example	This example uses wvsprintf() to format a string with two arguments, an integer and a character string.

```
long FAR PASCAL WndProc (HWND hWnd, unsigned iMessage, WORD wParam, LONG lParam)
{
        HDC             hDC ;
        static  int     nData    = 666 ;
        static  char    cString [] = "Argument Data" ;
        WORD            wArgs [3] ;
        char            cBuf [128] ;

        switch (iMessage)                   /* process windows messages */
        {
                case WM_COMMAND:            /* process menu items */
                        switch (wParam)
                        {
```

```
case IDM_DOIT:   /* User hit the "Do it" menu item */
        hDC = GetDC (hWnd) ;
        wArgs [0] = nData ;
        wArgs [1] = (WORD) cString ;
        wArgs [2] = HIWORD ((LPSTR) cString) ;
        wvsprintf (cBuf,
                "The number = %d, the string = %s",
                (LPSTR) wArgs) ;
        TextOut (hDC, 10, 10, cBuf, lstrlen (cBuf)) ;
        ReleaseDC (hWnd, hDC) ;
        break ;
```

[Other program lines]

Painting the Screen

Windows provides a wide range of functions to simplify the task of painting objects on a device context. In the last chapter, we examined the functions for creating and displaying text characters and fonts. This chapter includes the remaining painting functions for rectangles, lines, ellipses, polygons, and regions, which are all elements of the Windows GDI (Graphics Device Interface). Windows provides a rich collection of functions for painting shapes. In many cases, there is more than one way to paint a given shape. This can be a little confusing when you start programming in Windows. Don't be intimidated by all of these functions. In most cases, you will need only a handful of them for any one application. Only graphics-intensive programs, such as CAD/CAM and paint programs, will put a majority of these functions to work.

The WM_PAINT Message

We briefly looked at the WM_PAINT message in the last chapter under the discussion of device contexts. This section goes into more details on handling this important message. When any part of a window's client area needs to be repainted, Windows sends the application a WM_PAINT message. The program logic for painting the window's client area normally will be in response to WM_PAINT.

Unlike most Windows messages, WM_PAINT messages do not encode any information in the *lParam* or *wParam* parameters that are passed with the message. Instead, Windows provides two functions that are always used in processing WM_PAINT messages, BeginPaint() and EndPaint(). All programs processing WM_PAINT messages will use these two functions in sequence, as shown in Listing 11-1.

▷ **Listing 11-1. Typical WM_PAINT Logic**

```
long FAR PASCAL WndProc (HWND hWnd, unsigned iMessage, WORD wParam, LONG lParam)
{
        PAINTSTRUCT      ps ;

        switch (iMessage)                       /* process windows messages */
        {
                case WM_PAINT:
                        BeginPaint (hWnd, &ps) ;
                        /* the painting logic goes in here */
                        EndPaint (hWnd, &ps) ;
                        break ;
        /* the rest of the WndProc() function */
}
```

BeginPaint() fills the values in a PAINTSTRUCT data structure, which is defined in WINDOWS.H as

```
typedef struct tagPAINTSTRUCT
{
  HDC  hdc;                      /* device context handle */
  BOOL fErase;                   /* background redrawn? TRUE/FALSE */
  RECT rcPaint;                  /* RECT of client area update rect. */
  BOOL fRestore;                 /* reserved */
  BOOL fIncUpdate;               /* reserved */
  BYTE rgbReserved[16];          /* reserved */
} PAINTSTRUCT;
typedef PAINTSTRUCT     *PPAINTSTRUCT;
```

```
typedef PAINTSTRUCT NEAR *NPPAINTSTRUCT;
typedef PAINTSTRUCT FAR  *LPPAINTSTRUCT;
```

Only the first three elements in the PAINTSTRUCT data structure are used by the application program. The remainder are reserved by Windows. The *hdc* element is the device context for the window's client area. The *fErase* element is a flag which is TRUE if the background of the window has been redrawn, FALSE if it has not been. The *rcPaint* element is a pointer to a rectangle that contains the part of the client area that will be repainted, which is called the "invalid" area of the window.

Invalid Rectangle

The invalid part of a window is an important concept. Consider a case where the application scrolls the client area of the window upward by 10 pixels. Only the bottom ten pixels need to be painted to keep the client area up-to-date. The rest of the client area is the same, just repositioned upward.

For efficiency in repainting, Windows keeps track of the size of the smallest rectangle on the client area that includes all of the area that must be repainted. That rectangle's size is put into the *rcPaint* rectangle passed with the PAINTSTRUCT element. The BeginPaint() function fills in the *rcPaint* values. When an application processes WM_PAINT messages and paints in the client area, only the invalid part of the client area is repainted. This is true even if the painting commands for lines, rectangles, etc. have areas outside of the invalid region. Windows just ignores the parts of the lines, etc. that fall outside of the invalid rectangle.

You do not have to concern yourself with the size of the invalid rectangle when writing your application. Most programs have logic that repaints the entire client area every time a WM_PAINT message is received. The fact that only the invalid part of the client area is physically changed is of little consequence. However, you might want to evaluate the invalid rectangle if painting the client area is taking too much time. In this case, you can repaint portions of the client area separately, painting only the parts that are invalidated. This is a good way to speed up scrolling operations. Other situations will not be improved by evaluating the invalid rectangle. For example, when a window is resized, the WM_PAINT message is passed with the entire client area invalidated.

Another way to speed up a program is to inhibit Windows from sending WM_PAINT messages when they are not needed. For example, if you scroll the client area, the area will become invalid. Windows will put a WM_PAINT message on the application's message queue to update the invalid region. To stop this from happening, use ValidateRect() or ValidateRgn() to validate the area. This technique only works outside of the WM_PAINT part of the application's logic. BeginPaint() automatically validates the invalid rectangle.

The opposite situation occurs when you want to force Windows to send a WM_PAINT message. InvalidateRect() and InvalidateRgn() can be used to invalidate some or all of the client area. Used alone, these functions result in a WM_PAINT message being placed on the application's message queue. You can force an immediate WM_PAINT message by following the functions with a call to UpdateWindow(). UpdateWindow() sends the WM_PAINT message directly to the application, bypassing the message queue.

The Device Context

All painting to a device context requires the device context handle. We have been using GetDC() and ReleaseDC() to retrieve the handle outside of the WM_PAINT logic. BeginPaint() and EndPaint() do the same function inside the WM_PAINT processing part of the program. There are two ways to get the device context handle when processing WM_PAINT messages. One way is to make use of the *hdc* element of the PAINTSTRUCT data structure that is updated by BeginPaint(). This typically looks something like Listing 11-2.

▷ **Listing 11-2.   Using the BeginPaint( ) Device Context Handle**

```
long FAR PASCAL WndProc (HWND hWnd, unsigned iMessage, WORD wParam, LONG lParam)
{
        PAINTSTRUCT     ps ;

        switch (iMessage)                    /* process windows messages */
        {
                case WM_PAINT:
                        BeginPaint (hWnd, &ps) ;
                        TextOut (ps.hdc, 10, 10, "Hi There!", 9) ;
```

```
                        EndPaint (hWnd, &ps) ;
                        break ;
        /* the rest of the WndProc() function */
}
```

This style is used in the examples in this chapter. The other way to get the device context handle is to take advantage of the fact that BeginPaint() returns this value. That style of programming looks like the code in Listing 11-3.

▷ **Listing 11-3. Using the BeginPaint() Device Context Handle**

```
long FAR PASCAL WndProc (HWND hWnd, unsigned iMessage, WORD wParam, LONG lParam)
{
        PAINTSTRUCT      ps ;
        HDC              hDC ;

        switch (iMessage)                       /* process windows messages */
        {
                case WM_PAINT:
                        hDC = BeginPaint (hWnd, &ps) ;
                        TextOut (hDC, 10, 10, "Hi There!", 9) ;
                        EndPaint (hWnd, &ps) ;
                        break ;
        /* the rest of the WndProc() function */
}
```

Both methods have the same effect. Note that you do not call ReleaseDC() after BeginPaint(). EndPaint() takes care of releasing the device context.

Selecting Objects into the Device Context

Up to this point, we have used the device context as a means to draw text on the screen. It turns out that the device context can hold much more information than just text attributes. At any one time, a device context will contain a font, pen, and brush. It may also contain a region and a color palette. When you draw a line using a device context, the color, size, and type of line are all determined by what type of line you have "selected into" the device context. Selecting an object, such as a pen, makes that pen available to every drawing function that uses a pen. The selected pen will be used for lines and for the borders on rectangles, ellipses, and polygons.

At any one time, a device context can have only one type of each object (pen, brush, font, region, palette) selected. If you select a new object, the old one of the same type is bumped out. You must avoid deleting objects in an active device context. Always keep one of each object selected at all times. The objects do not physically reside in the device context. Objects are created and stored in

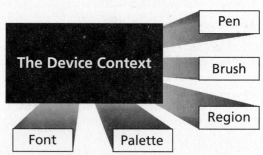

Figure 11-1. Objects Selected into a Device Context.

separate memory areas. Selecting an object passes the pointer to the device context so that Windows' GDI functions can make use of the object. (See Figure 11-1).

To use an object with a device context, you must create the object and then select it. For example, to draw a rectangle with a blue border (pen) and a red hatched pattern interior, the program logic would look something like Listing 11-4, which is illustrated in Figure 11-2.

▷ **Listing 11-4. Selecting a Pen and a Brush into the Device Context**

```
long FAR PASCAL WndProc (HWND hWnd, unsigned iMessage, WORD wParam, LONG lParam)
{
        PAINTSTRUCT      ps ;
        HPEN             hPen, hOldPen;
        HBRUSH           hBrush, hOldBrush ;
```

```
        switch (iMessage)                        /* process windows messages */
        {
              case WM_PAINT:
                      BeginPaint (hWnd, &ps) ;
                      hPen = CreatePen (PS_SOLID, 3, RGB (0, 0, 255)) ;
                      hBrush = CreateHatchBrush (HS_DIAGCROSS,
                            RGB (255, 0, 0)) ;
                      hOldPen = SelectObject (ps.hdc, hPen) ;
                      hOldBrush = SelectObject (ps.hdc, hBrush) ;
                      Rectangle (ps.hdc, 20, 20, 100, 70) ;
                      SelectObject (ps.hdc, hOldPen) ;
                      SelectObject (ps.hdc, hOldBrush) ;
                      DeleteObject (hPen) ;
                      DeleteObject (hBrush) ;
                      EndPaint (hWnd, &ps) ;
                      break ;
```

Note that the pen and brush are deleted after use to avoid filling up system memory. The memory associated with GDI objects will continue to be occupied even if the application program is terminated, so always be sure to delete pens, brushes, fonts, regions, and palettes after use. Objects cannot be deleted if they are attached to a device context. Either delete them after the device context is released (EndPaint() called) or select a stock object into the device context first to displace the object you wish to delete.

Figure 11-2. Example Use of a Pen and Brush Object.

The example in Listing 11-4 demonstrates a foolproof way to make sure that objects are not deleted from an active device context. When an object is selected into the device context, SelectObject() returns a handle to the object that is being displaced. This "old" object handle can be saved, and then selected back into the device context when you are through with the "new" object. Selecting the "old" object again makes it safe to delete the "new" object. This type of logic is usually used when the window maintains its own private device context.

Default and Stock Objects

When you first get a handle to a device context, it will contain handles to predefined objects that are always available, which are called "stock objects." The default pen is a solid black line, one pixel wide. The default brush is a solid white brush. The default font is a black system font. These default objects have allowed us to use the TextOut() function without specifying the color or font to use. The default values for the device context were applied. You can also use GDI functions, such as Rectangle(), without selecting a line or brush style. By default, the rectangle will be painted with a thin black outline and filled on the interior with the default white brush. You can get a handle to the stock objects by using GetStockObject(). Don't try to delete these objects after use—they are part of the Windows GDI.

A good reason for selecting a stock object is to displace another similar object out of the device context. Remember that a device context will contain at most one of each type of object. If you want to get rid of a special pen, but still use the device context, use a function call such as

```
        hOldPen = SelectObject (ps.hdc, GetStockObject (BLACK_PEN)) ;
```

Selecting the stock black pen displaces whatever pen was in the device context before. The value returned by SelectObject() is a handle to the previous object, in this case the previously selected pen. This returned value can be used to delete the object (pen), if it is no longer needed and is not a stock object. Remember that once an object is selected, it is used by every painting function that uses the device context. For example, selecting a brush will result in that brush being used to fill all rectangles, ellipses, polygons, and regions until a new brush is selected.

The device context "forgets" which objects were selected after the device context is released. You will have to select pens, etc. every time a device context handle is obtained with either BeginPaint() or GetDC(). Alternatively, you can save one or more device contexts with SaveDC() in a "context stack." This technique is described in Chapter

10, *Device Contexts, Text Output, and Printing*. You can also maintain a private device context for the window or window class by defining either the CS_OWNDC or CS_CLASSDC styles in the RegisterClass() function call. This is described in Chapter 2, *Creating Windows*.

Colors

Windows encodes colors using three values. The values correspond to the intensity of the Red, Green, and Blue elements that make up any color. This coding is called

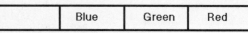

	Blue	Green	Red

Figure 11-3. COLORREF RGB Color Values.

"RGB" color. Windows limits the color values to between 0 and 255 for each of the three colors. RGB colors are encoded into a 32-bit value, called a COLORREF. The red, green, and blue values are stored in the lower three bytes of the 32 bits as shown in Figure 11-3. The most significant byte is used only with palette colors, which are discussed in the subject of the next chapter.

Windows provides several macros for manipulating these 32-bit color values. The RGB macro is the most frequently used. It takes the three color values for red, green, and blue intensity as parameters and combines them into a single 32-bit value. For example, to create a pure blue pen, use

```
COLORREF crColor ;
crColor = RGB (255, 0, 0) ;
```

The opposite conversion extracts a single color value from the combined 32-bit color by using the GetBColor(), GetGColor(), and GetRColor() macros for the blue, green, and red color elements, respectively. These macros are included in the function descriptions in this chapter.

In practice, most displays can show a limited number of pure colors. A typical VGA display can show only 16 pure colors at one time. Windows partially gets around this limit by "dithering", the process of mixing the pixels to get an average color close to the pure color requested. For example, the creation of a brush with the following function call will result in a dithered brush pattern with a blue-green average color.

```
HBRUSH          hBrush ;
hBrush = CreateSolidBrush (RGB (20, 117, 55)) ;
```

If you will be supporting more advanced video equipment, such as the IBM 8514 or a Super VGA adapter, Windows provides support for specifying pure colors. This support is implemented by selecting a palette into the device context and using the colors defined by the program for the palette. This subject is covered in the next chapter, *Color Pallete Control*.

Regions

A powerful element of the Windows GDI is the concept of a "region." Regions are areas on the device that can be used as boundaries to painting. Regions can have any shape. Complex regions can be built by combining small areas made of elliptical regions, rectangular regions, and polygon regions. A single, logical region can contain several areas that do not touch. Consider the task of creating a picture like the one shown in Figure 11-4. The brute force method of painting this type of figure would be to calculate the length of a series of black lines that would be used to build up the shapes. This would end up being a slow process.

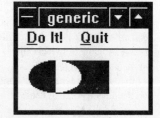

Figure 11-4. A Complex Region.

The elegant way of creating this shape is to create a region, called a "clipping region," that defines the areas that will be painted and excludes the rest of the client area. All painting operations are "clipped" so that only the part of the painted object within the clipping region is painted.

In this case, the region is created by logically combining an elliptical region and a rectangular region. The CombineRgn() function does the work. Once the region is created, it is set up as the clipping region for the device context with SelectClipRgn(). All painting after that is restricted to the interior of the region. For more details on regions, look at the explanations for the CreateRectRgn(), CreateEllipticRgn(), CombineRgn(), and SelectClipRgn() functions.

Painting Function Summary

Function	Purpose
Arc	Draws an elliptical arc using the selected pen.
BeginPaint	Prepares the window's client area for painting.
Chord	Draws a chord segment with the selected pen, and fills the interior with the selected brush.
CombineRgn	Logically combines two regions into one region.
CopyRect	Copies the coordinates of one rectangle into another.
CreateBrushIndirect	Creates a brush from a bitmap or stock brush shape.
CreateEllipticRgn	Creates an elliptically shaped region.
CreateEllipticRgnIndirect	Creates an elliptical region based on the bounding rectangle described in a RECT data structure.
CreateHatchBrush	Creates a brush based on a predefined pattern.
CreatePatternBrush	Creates a brush based on a bitmap.
CreatePen	Creates a custom pen.
CreatePenIndirect	Creates a pen based on LOGPEN data.
CreatePolygonRgn	Creates an arbitrary shaped polygonal region.
CreatePolyPolygonRgn	Creates a region composed of multiple polygons in a single function call.
CreateRectRgn	Creates a rectangular region.
CreateRectRgnIndirect	Creates a rectangular region based on the data in a RECT data structure.
CreateRoundRectRgn	Creates a rectangular region with rounded corners.
CreateSolidBrush	Creates a brush with a solid color.
DeleteObject	Removes pens, brushes, fonts, bitmaps, regions, and palettes from memory.
DrawFocusRect	Draws or removes a dashed line around a rectangle.
Ellipse	Draws an ellipse.
EndPaint	Ends the painting cycle started by BeginPaint( ).
EnumObjects	Enumerates all of the pens or brushes available on a device context.
EqualRect	Checks if two rectangles are equal.
EqualRgn	Checks if two regions are equally sized.
ExcludeClipRect	Removes a rectangular area from a clipping region.
ExcludeUpdateRgn	Prevents drawing in invalid areas of the client area.
ExtFloodFill	Fills an area by replacing a color with the currently selected brush.
FillRect	Fills a rectangular area with a brush pattern and color.
FillRgn	Fills a region with a brush color and pattern.
FloodFill	Fills an area with the currently selected brush.
FrameRect	Draws a frame around a rectangle using a brush.
FrameRgn	Draws a frame around a region using a brush pattern.
GetBrushOrg	Finds the brush origin of a device context.
GetRValue	Retrieves the red color value from a 32-bit color value.
GetClipBox	Gets the dimensions of the smallest rectangle that will enclose the clipping region.

Table 11-1. continued

Function	Purpose
GetCurrentPosition	Determines the current logical position in a device context.
GetNearestColor	Determines the closest solid color a device can display.
GetObject	Retrieves information about an object.
GetPixel	Determines the color of a pixel.
GetPolyFillMode	Determines the current polygon filling mode for a device context.
GetRgnBox	Determines the bounding rectangle of a region.
GetROP2	Determines the current raster drawing mode for a device context.
GetStockObject	Retrieves a handle to one of the predefined objects that are always available to Windows applications.
GetSysColor	Retrieves one of the system colors.
GetUpdateRect	Retrieves the dimensions of the invalid rectangle in the window's client area.
GetUpdateRgn	Copies the update region of a window's client area to another region.
InflateRect	Increases or decreases the size of a rectangle.
IntersectClipRect	Creates a new clipping region by combining the existing rectangle and a rectangular region.
IntersectRect	Computes the rectangle of the intersection of two other rectangles.
InvalidateRect	Adds a rectangular area to a window's update region.
InvalidateRgn	Adds a region to a window's update region.
InvertRect	Inverts the color of every pixel within a rectangular area.
InvertRgn	Inverts the color of every pixel within a region.
IsRectEmpty	Determines if a rectangle has a height or width of zero.
LineDDA	Draws a line with a custom drawing procedure.
LineTo	Draws a line from the current location to a new point.
MAKEPOINT	Converts from a DWORD value to a POINT structure.
MoveTo	Moves the current position to a new location, ready to draw a line.
OffsetClipRgn	Moves the clipping region.
OffsetRect	Shifts a rectangle in the X and Y directions.
OffsetRgn	Moves a region.
PaintRgn	Paints a region with the currently selected brush.
Pie	Draws a pie-shaped wedge.
Polygon	Draws a polygon.
Polyline	Draws a line with multiple segments.
PolyPolygon	Draws one or more polygons.
PtInRect	Determines if a point is within a rectangular area.
PtInRegion	Determines if a point is within a region.
PtVisible	Checks if a point is within the clipping region.
Rectangle	Draws a rectangle.
RectInRegion	Checks if a rectangle is within a region.

RectVisible	Checks if a rectangle has points within the current clipping region.
RGB	Creates a 32-bit color value given the three primary color elements.
RoundRect	Draws a rectangle with rounded corners.
SelectClipRgn	Uses a region to clip output to a device context.
SelectObject	Selects an object into a device context.
SetBrushOrg	Changes the origin used by the device context to line up pattern brushes.
SetPixel	Changes to color of a single point on the device context.
SetPolyFillMode	Changes the polygon filling mode of a device context.
SetRect	Enters all four values for a RECT data structure.
SetRectEmpty	Sets all of the elements of a RECT data structure to zero.
SetRectRgn	Changes the bounds of a rectangular region.
SetROP2	Changes the raster drawing mode of a device context.
SetSysColors	Changes the color values Windows uses to paint background and nonclient areas of the screen and windows.
UnionRect	Sets the size of a rectangle equal to the smallest rectangle that will enclose two other rectangles.
UnrealizeObject	Resets a brush origin, or a palette.
UpdateWindow	Forces an immediate WM_PAINT message, updating the window.
ValidateRect	Removes a rectangular area from the window's update region.
ValidateRgn	Removes a region from the window's update region.

Table 11-1. Painting Function Summary.

Painting Function Descriptions

This section contains the detailed function descriptions of functions used in painting a device context.

ARC
■ Win 2.0   ■ Win 3.0   ■ Win 3.1

Purpose	Draws an elliptical arc using the selected pen.
Syntax	BOOL **Arc**(HDC *hDC*, int *X1*, int *Y1*, int *X2*, int *Y2*, int *X3*, int *Y3*, int *X4* , int *Y4*);
Description	An elliptical arc is a section from an ellipse. The Arc() function specifies the *X,Y* coordinates of the bounding rectangle and two other points that define the start and end points of the arc. The start and end points (*X3,Y3* and *X4,Y4*) do not have to fall on the arc. Windows computes the start of the arc by calculating a line from the specified start point to the center of the bounding rectangle. The intercept of this calculated line and the arc's line is used for the start point. The same logic is used to calculate the end point of the arc.
Uses	Sections of an ellipse can be used as a general way to draw lines with changing curvature.
Returns	BOOL. TRUE if the arc was drawn, FALSE on error.
See Also	SelectObject(), DeleteObject, CreatePen(), BeginPaint(), EndPaint()
Parameters	
hDC	HDC: The device context handle.
X1	int: The logical *X* coordinate of the upper left corner of the bounding rectangle.
Y1	int: The logical *Y* coordinate of the upper left corner of the bounding rectangle.

X2	int: The logical *X* coordinate of the lower right corner of the bounding rectangle.
Y2	int: The logical *Y* coordinate of the lower right corner of the bounding rectangle.
X3	int: The logical *X* coordinate of the starting point of the arc.
Y3	int: The logical *Y* coordinate of the starting point of the arc.
X4	int: The logical *X* coordinate of the ending point of the arc.
Y4	int: The logical *Y* coordinate of the ending point of the arc.

Related Messages WM_PAINT

Example

Figure 11-5. Arc( ) Example.

This example, as shown in Figure 11-5, paints the client area with a red arc. The bounding rectangle is also shown as a thin line, just to clarify how the Arc() function works. The start and end points of the arc are specified as the lower left corner of the rectangle and the top center. Note that the lower left corner does not fall on the arc's line.

```
Long FAR PASCAL WndProc (HWND hWnd, unsigned iMessage, WORD wParam, LONG lParam)
{
        PAINTSTRUCT      ps ;
        HPEN             hPen ;

        switch (iMessage)                              /* process windows messages */
        {
                case WM_PAINT:
                        BeginPaint (hWnd, &ps) ;
                        SelectObject (ps.hdc, GetStockObject (BLACK_PEN)) ;
                        Rectangle (ps.hdc, 10, 10, 110, 110) ; /* bounding rect */
                        hPen = CreatePen (PS_SOLID, 4, RGB (255, 0, 0)) ;
                        SelectObject (ps.hdc, hPen) ;     /* select a thick red pen */
                        Arc (ps.hdc, 10, 10, 110, 110, 10, 110, 60, 10) ;
                        EndPaint (hWnd, &ps) ;
                        DeleteObject (hPen) ;
                        break ;
```
[Other program lines]

BEGINPAINT   ■ Win 2.0   ■ Win 3.0   ■ Win 3.1

Purpose   Prepares the window's client area for painting.

Syntax   HDC **BeginPaint**(HWND *hWnd*, LPPAINTSTRUCT *lpPaint*);

Description   BeginPaint() is used to retrieve the device context handle for the window's client area when processing a WM_PAINT message. This is the only time BeginPaint() is used for this purpose. GetDC() is used anywhere else in the program to get the *hDC* device context handle. Begin-Paint() fills in the data in a PAINTSTRUCT data structure. This is defined in WINDOWS.H as follows:

```
typedef struct tagPAINTSTRUCT
  {
  HDC   hdc;                          /* device context to paint */
  BOOL  fErase;                       /* TRUE if background has been redrawn */
  RECT  rcPaint;                      /* update rectangle */
  BOOL  fRestore;                     /* reserved */
  BOOL  fIncUpdate;                   /* reserved */
  BYTE  rgbReserved[16];              /* reserved */
  } PAINTSTRUCT;
typedef PAINTSTRUCT                   *PPAINTSTRUCT;
typedef PAINTSTRUCT NEAR              *NPPAINTSTRUCT;
typedef PAINTSTRUCT FAR               *LPPAINTSTRUCT;
```

You can either use the returned value from BeginPaint() as the client area device context handle, or use the *hdc* element of the paint structure. Both handles are the same. The *fErase* element is TRUE if the window has redrawn the client area background with the class brush, FALSE if the window does not redraw the background. The *rcPaint* element is a pointer to a RECT rectangle data structure, holding the bounds of the smallest rectangle that encloses the update region of the client area.

Uses   Used anytime a program processes WM_PAINT messages.

Returns   HDC, a handle to the window's client area device context.

See Also   EndPaint(), GetDC(), GetWindowDC()

Parameters

hWnd   HWND: The window's handle.

lpPaint   LPPAINTSTRUCT: A pointer to a PAINTSTRUCT data structure that BeginPaint() will fill.

Related Messages WM_PAINT

Example   This example paints the update region of the client area gray when a WM_PAINT message is received. This only occurs if the "Do It!" menu item has been clicked. The simplest way to generate a WM_PAINT message is to resize the window, which results in the entire client area being the update region.

```
Long FAR PASCAL WndProc (HWND hWnd, unsigned iMessage, WORD wParam, LONG lParam)
{
        PAINTSTRUCT                   ps ;
        static          BOOL          bDoPaint = FALSE ;

        switch (iMessage)                     /* process windows messages */
        {
                case WM_PAINT:
                        if (bDoPaint)
                        {
                                BeginPaint (hWnd, &ps) ;
                                SelectObject (ps.hdc, GetStockObject (LTGRAY_BRUSH)) ;
                                Rectangle (ps.hdc, ps.rcPaint.left, ps.rcPaint.top,
                                        ps.rcPaint.right, ps.rcPaint.bottom) ;
                                EndPaint (hWnd, &ps) ;
                        }
                        else
                                ValidateRect (hWnd, NULL) ;
                        bDoPaint = FALSE ;
                        break ;
                case WM_COMMAND:              /* process menu items */
                        switch (wParam)
                        {
                        case IDM_DOIT:          /* User hit the "Do it" menu item */
                                bDoPaint = TRUE ;
                                break ;
```

[Other program lines]

CHORD   ■ Win 2.0   ■ Win 3.0   ■ Win 3.1

Purpose   Draws a chord segment with the selected pen, and fills the interior with the selected brush.

Syntax   BOOL **Chord**(HDC *hDC*, int *X1*, int *Y1*, int *X2*, int *Y2*, int *X3*, int *Y3*, int *X4* , int *Y4*);

Description   A chord is an elliptical curve, bounded by a line through the ellipse. The elliptical curve is defined by the bounding rectangle *X1,Y1* to *X2,Y2*. The line through the ellipse is defined by *X3,Y3* to *X4,Y4*. The currently selected pen and brush for the device context are used to draw the chord's exterior lines and fill the interior. The line segment defined by *X3,Y3* to *X4,Y4* can be outside of the bounds of the ellipse. Only the portion within the ellipse will be drawn.

Uses	This is the filled equivalent to using the Arc() function.
Returns	BOOL. TRUE if the chord was drawn, FALSE on error.
See Also	Arc(), BeginPaint(), SelectObject()
Parameters	
hDC	HDC: The device context handle.
X1	int: The logical *X* coordinate of the upper left corner of the bounding rectangle.
Y1	int: The logical *Y* coordinate of the upper left corner of the bounding rectangle.
X2	int: The logical *X* coordinate of the lower right corner of the bounding rectangle.
Y2	int: The logical *Y* coordinate of the lower right corner of the bounding rectangle.
X3	int: The logical *X* coordinate of the starting point of the line segment of the chord.
Y3	int: The logical *Y* coordinate of the starting point of the line segment of the chord.
X4	int: The logical *X* coordinate of the ending point of the line segment of the chord.
Y4	int: The logical *Y* coordinate of the ending point of the line segment of the chord.

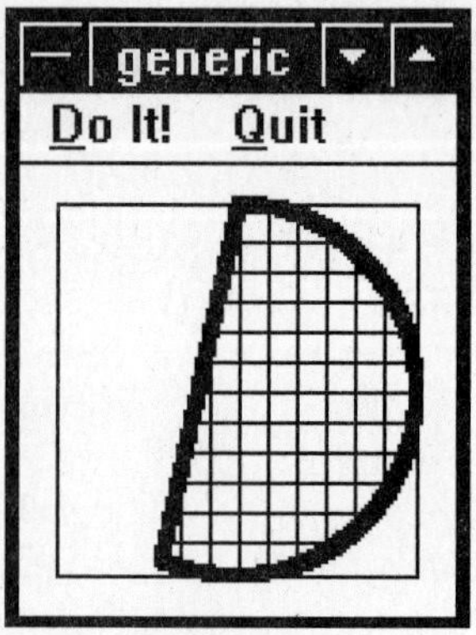

Figure 11-6. Chord() Example.

Example This example, illustrated in Figure 11-6, draws a red chord outline filled with a blue crossed interior. The bounding rectangle is also shown for reference.

```
long FAR PASCAL WndProc (HWND hWnd, unsigned iMessage, WORD wParam, LONG lParam)
{
        PAINTSTRUCT      ps ;
        HPEN             hPen ;
        HBRUSH           hBrush ;
        switch (iMessage)                        /* process windows messages */
        {
                case WM_PAINT:
                        BeginPaint (hWnd, &ps) ;
                        SelectObject (ps.hdc, GetStockObject (BLACK_PEN)) ;
                        Rectangle (ps.hdc, 10, 10, 110, 110) ;    /* show bounding rect */
                        hPen = CreatePen (PS_SOLID, 4, RGB (255, 0, 0)) ;
                        SelectObject (ps.hdc, hPen) ;              /* select a thick red pen */
                        hBrush = CreateHatchBrush (HS_CROSS, RGB (0, 0, 255)) ;
                        SelectObject (ps.hdc, hBrush) ;           /* select a blue brush */
                        Chord (ps.hdc, 10, 10, 110, 110, 0, 200, 60, 10) ;
                        EndPaint (hWnd, &ps) ;
                        DeleteObject (hPen) ;
                        DeleteObject (hBrush) ;
                        break ;
```

[Other program lines]

COMBINERGN   ■ Win 2.0   ■ Win 3.0   ■ Win 3.1

Purpose	Logically combines two regions into one region.
Syntax	int **CombineRgn**(HRGN *hDestRgn*, HRGN *hSrcRgn1*, HRGN *hSrcRgn2*, int *nCombineMode*);
Description	CombineRgn() builds a new region by joining two other regions. The regions do not have to be touching. If they are touching, several logical operations can be used to combine areas that overlap, do not overlap, etc. The destination region must be allocated before the function is started. This can be done by creating a region of arbitrary size (using CreateRectRgn() for example).

Uses	CombineRgn() can be used many times to build up complex regions made of more basic shapes. The combined region can then be used as a mask (clipping region) to limit where painting operations are visible.
Returns	int, the result of the function. This can be any of the values listed in Table 11-2.

Value	Meaning	☒
COMPLEXREGION	The new region has overlapping borders.	
ERROR	No new region was created.	
NULLREGION	The new region is empty.	
SIMPLEREGION	The new region does not have overlapping borders.	

Table 11-2 Region Types.

See Also	SelectClipRgn(), CreateRectRgn(), CreateEllipticRgn()	
Parameters		
hDestRgn	HRGN: A handle to an existing region that will be replaced by the new, combined region.	
hSrcRgn1	HRGN: A handle to an existing region.	
hSrcRgn2	HRGN: A handle to another existing region.	
nCombineMode	int: Specifies how *hSrcRgn1* and *hSrcRgn2* are to be combined. This can be any of the values listed in Table 11-3.	

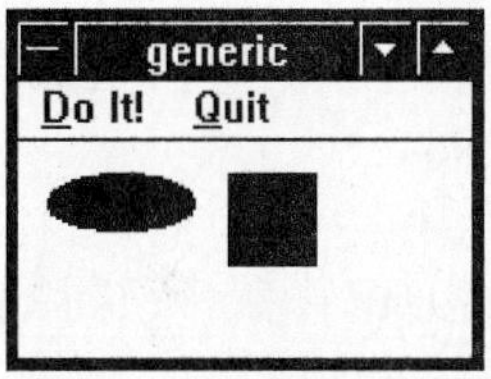

Figure 11-7. Combine-Rgn( ) Example.

Value	Meaning	☒
RGN_AND	Uses the intersection of the two regions (overlapping area).	
RGN_COPY	Creates a copy of the region pointed to by *hSrcRgn1*.	
RGN_DIFF	Copies all of the region pointed to by *hSrcRgn1* except for that overlapped by the region pointed to by *hSrcRgn2*.	
RGN_OR	Combines the two regions.	
RGN_XOR	Combines the two regions, but eliminates the area that overlaps.	

Table 11-3. CombineRgn( ) Modes.

Example   This example, which is illustrated in Figure 11-7, creates two regions, an elliptical one and a rectangular one. The two regions are then combined into one logical region. The combined region is used as a clipping region for painting a large gray area. Only the areas within the region are painted. Note that the "combined" region still consists of two distinct areas that do not connect.

```
long FAR PASCAL WndProc (HWND hWnd, unsigned iMessage, WORD wParam, LONG lParam)
{
        PAINTSTRUCT      ps ;
        HRGN             hRgn1, hRgn2, hRgnComb ;

        switch (iMessage)                               /* process windows messages */
        {
                case WM_PAINT:
                        BeginPaint (hWnd, &ps) ;
                        hRgn1 = CreateEllipticRgn (10, 10, 60, 30) ;
                        hRgn2 = CreateRectRgn (70, 10, 100, 40) ;
                        hRgnComb = CreateRectRgn (1, 1, 2, 2) ;/* initialize */
                        CombineRgn (hRgnComb, hRgn1, hRgn2, RGN_OR) ;
```

```
                        DeleteObject (hRgn1) ;
                        DeleteObject (hRgn2) ;

                        SelectClipRgn (ps.hdc, hRgnComb) ;
                        SelectObject (ps.hdc, GetStockObject (LTGRAY_BRUSH)) ;
                        Rectangle (ps.hdc, 5, 5, 500, 500) ;
                        EndPaint (hWnd, &ps) ;
                        DeleteObject (hRgnComb) ;
                        break ;
```

[Other program lines]

COPYRECT   ■ Win 2.0   ■ Win 3.0   ■ Win 3.1

Purpose	Copies the coordinates of one rectangle into another.
Syntax	int **CopyRect**(LPRECT *lpDestRect*, LPRECT *lpSourceRect*);
Description	RECT data structures hold the coordinates of the upper left and lower right corners of a rectangle. This function copies the coordinates from *lpSouceRect* to *lpDestRect*.
Uses	Commonly used prior to OffsetRect() or InflateRect().
Returns	int, the value has no meaning.
See Also	OffsetRect(), InflateRect()

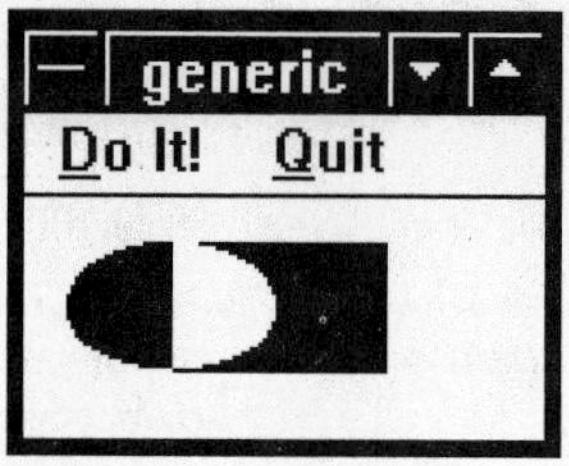

Parameters

lpDestRect   LPRECT: A pointer to a RECT data structure that will contain the copied coordinates.

lpSourceRect   LPRECT: A pointer to a RECT data structure that contains the source data to copy.

Figure 11-8. CopyRect( ) Example.

Example   In the example in Figure 11-8, a complex region is created by combining two regions using the logical RGN_XOR operation. The two regions are both based on the same rectangular size. In the first step, elliptical region *hRgn1* is made from the rectangle's dimensions. A second rectangle is created by copying the first, and then offsetting the rectangle's coordinates to the right 25 logical units. The two regions are combined using CombineRgn() and then used as the clipping region. Only the areas within the clipping region end up painted when a large, gray rectangle is drawn.

```
long FAR PASCAL WndProc (HWND hWnd, unsigned iMessage, WORD wParam, LONG lParam)
{
        PAINTSTRUCT    ps ;
        HRGN           hRgn1, hRgn2, hRgnComb ;
        RECT           rRect1, rRect2 ;

        switch (iMessage)                        /* process windows messages */
        {
                case WM_PAINT:
                        BeginPaint (hWnd, &ps) ;
                        SetRect (&rRect1, 10, 10, 60, 40) ;
                        CopyRect (&rRect2, &rRect1) ;
                        OffsetRect (&rRect2, 25, 0) ;
                        hRgn1 = CreateEllipticRgnIndirect (&rRect1) ;
                        hRgn2 = CreateRectRgnIndirect (&rRect2) ;
                        hRgnComb = CreateRectRgn (1, 1, 2, 2) ;/* initialize */
                        CombineRgn (hRgnComb, hRgn1, hRgn2, RGN_XOR) ;
                        DeleteObject (hRgn1) ;
                        DeleteObject (hRgn2) ;

                        SelectClipRgn (ps.hdc, hRgnComb) ;
                        SelectObject (ps.hdc, GetStockObject (LTGRAY_BRUSH)) ;
                        Rectangle (ps.hdc, 5, 5, 500, 500) ;
                        EndPaint (hWnd, &ps) ;
                        DeleteObject (hRgnComb) ;
                        break ;
```

[Other program lines]

CREATEBRUSHINDIRECT   ■ Win 2.0   ■ Win 3.0   ■ Win 3.1

Purpose	Creates a brush from a bitmap or stock brush shape.
Syntax	HBRUSH **CreateBrushIndirect**(LOGBRUSH FAR *lpLogBrush*);
Description	The LOGBRUSH data type is defined in WINDOWS.H as

```
typedef struct tagLOGBRUSH
  {
  WORD        lbStyle;                   /* BS_DIBPATTERN, BS_HATCHED, BS_HOLLOW */
                                         /* BS_PATTERN, or BS_SOLID */
  DWORD       lbColor;                   /* DIB_PAL_COLORS, or DIB_RGB_COLORS */
  int         lbHatch;                   /* HS_BDIAGONAL, HS_CROSS, HS_DIAGCROSS */
                                         /* HS_FDIAGONAL, HS_HORIZONTAL, or HS_VERTICAL */
  } LOGBRUSH;
typedef LOGBRUSH              *PLOGBRUSH;
typedef LOGBRUSH NEAR         *NPLOGBRUSH;
typedef LOGBRUSH FAR          *LPLOGBRUSH;

typedef LOGBRUSH    PATTERN;
```

The three data elements of the LOGBRUSH structure are filled to define the brush. Logical brushes, like logical fonts, provide a degree of device independence. If an exact match is not found with the physical device being used, Windows will approximate the brush.

Uses	Used to create specialized brush patterns for filling regions.
Returns	HBRUSH, a handle to the brush created. Returns NULL on error.
See Also	SelectObject(), DeleteObject(), CreateHatchBrush(), CreateSolidBrush(), CreatePattern-Brush(), UnrealizeObject()
Parameters	
lpLogBrush	LOGBRUSH FAR *: A pointer to a LOGBRUSH data structure. The elements of the data structure are defined as follows:
lbStyle	WORD: The style of the brush to be created, can be any of the ones listed in Table 11-4.

Value	Meaning	⊠
BS_DIBPATTERN	The brush will be defined by a DIB (device independent bitmap).	
BS_HATCHED	The brush will be a hatched brush based on one of the standard hatch patterns listed in Table 11-6.	
BS_HOLLOW	The brush will be hollow(not visible).	
BS_PATTERN	The brush will be based on a bitmap.	
BS_SOLID	The brush will be a solid color.	

Table 11-4. Logical Brush Types.

lbColor	COLORREF: Specifies the color of the brush for the BS_HATCHED or BS_SOLID styles. Use the RGB macro to set a specific color. *lbColor* is ignored for the BS_HOLLOW or BS_PATTERN style. For the BS_DIBPATTERN style, the *lbColor* parameter can have one of the two values listed in Table 11-5.

Value	Meaning	⊠
DIB_PAL_COLORS	The DIB colors are based on the currently realized logical palette.	
DIB_RGB_COLORS	The DIB colors are literal RGB values.	

Table 11-5. Logical Brush Color Types.

lbHatch   int: For the BS_HATCHED style, *lbHatch* contains one of the values listed in Table 11-6.

Value	Meaning
HS_BDIAGONAL	45-degree lines climbing from left to right.
HS_CROSS	A horizontal and vertical crosshatch.
HS_DIAGCROSS	A 45-degree crosshatch.
HS_FDIAGONAL	45-degree lines climbing from right to left.
HS_HORIZONTAL	Horizontal lines.
HS_VERTICAL	Vertical lines.

Table 11-6. Hatch Brush Patterns.

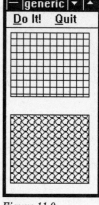

If the style is BS_SOLID or BS_HOLLOW, *lbHatch* is ignored. If the style is BS_PATTERN, *lbHatch* contains a handle to a bitmap. If the style is BS_DIBPATTERN, *lbHatch* contains a handle to a DIB bitmap.

Example   This example uses CreateBrushIndirect() twice to create two different brushes. (See Figure 11-9.) The first is a hatched brush that uses the standard HS_CROSS pattern to paint the top rectangle. The second is a custom brush, based on an 8 by 8 bitmap pattern. The bitmap is referenced with the line

```
brushmap                BITMAP          brush.bmp
```

in the program's .RC resource file. In this case, the bitmap was created using the SDKPaint application.

Figure 11-9.
CreateBrush
Indirect( ) Example.

```
Long FAR PASCAL WndProc (HWND hWnd, unsigned iMessage, WORD wParam, LONG lParam)
{
        PAINTSTRUCT             ps ;
        HBRUSH                  hBrush, hOldBrush ;
        LOGBRUSH                lbBrush ;
        HBITMAP                 hBitmap ;

        switch (iMessage)                       /* process windows messages */
        {
                case WM_PAINT:
                        BeginPaint (hWnd, &ps) ;
                        lbBrush.lbStyle = BS_HATCHED ;
                        lbBrush.lbColor = RGB (0, 255, 0) ;
                        lbBrush.lbHatch = HS_CROSS ;
                        hBrush = CreateBrushIndirect (&lbBrush) ;
                        hOldBrush = SelectObject (ps.hdc, hBrush) ;
                        Rectangle (ps.hdc, 5, 5, 100, 80) ;
                        SelectObject (ps.hdc, hOldBrush) ;
                        DeleteObject (hBrush) ;
                        hBitmap = LoadBitmap (ghInstance, "brushmap") ;
                        lbBrush.lbStyle = BS_PATTERN ;
                        lbBrush.lbColor = NULL ;
                        lbBrush.lbHatch = hBitmap ;
                        hBrush = CreateBrushIndirect (&lbBrush) ;
                        hOldBrush = SelectObject (ps.hdc, hBrush) ;
                        Rectangle (ps.hdc, 5, 100, 100, 180) ;
                        SelectObject (ps.hdc, hOldBrush) ;
                        DeleteObject (hBrush) ;
                        DeleteObject (hBitmap) ;
                        EndPaint (hWnd, &ps) ;
                        break ;
```

[Other program lines]

CREATEELLIPTICRGN
■ Win 2.0   ■ Win 3.0   ■ Win 3.1

Purpose	Creates an elliptically shaped region.
Syntax	HRGN **CreateEllipticRgn**(int *X1*, int *Y1*, int *X2*, int *Y2*);
Description	The region is an ellipse, bounded by the rectangle described by the *X,Y* positions of the upper left and lower right corners.
Uses	Used to create clipping regions.
Returns	HRGN, the handle to the region created. NULL on error.
See Also	SelectObject(), DeleteObject(), SelectClipRgn(), CreateRectRgn(), CreateElliptic RgnIndirect()

Parameters

X1   int: The logical *X* coordinate of the upper left corner of the bounding rectangle.

Y1   int: The logical *Y* coordinate of the upper left corner of the bounding rectangle.

X2   int: The logical *X* coordinate of the lower right corner of the bounding rectangle.

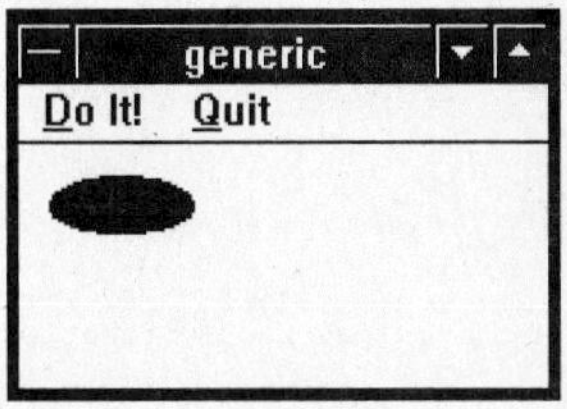

Figure 11-10. Create EllipticRgn() Example.

Y2   int: The logical *Y* coordinate of the lower right corner of the bounding rectangle.

Example   The example in Figure 11-10 sets a small elliptical clipping region, and then paints a large rectangle with a gray brush. Only the part of the rectangle that falls within the clipping region is painted. This results in drawing a filled ellipse.

```
Long FAR PASCAL WndProc (HWND hWnd, unsigned iMessage, WORD wParam, LONG lParam)
{
        PAINTSTRUCT             ps ;
        HRGN                    hRgn ;

        switch (iMessage)                       /* process windows messages */
        {
                case WM_PAINT:
                        BeginPaint (hWnd, &ps) ;
                        hRgn = CreateEllipticRgn (10, 10, 60, 30) ;
                        SelectClipRgn (ps.hdc, hRgn) ;
                        SelectObject (ps.hdc, GetStockObject (LTGRAY_BRUSH)) ;
                        Rectangle (ps.hdc, 5, 5, 500, 500) ;
                        EndPaint (hWnd, &ps) ;
                        DeleteObject (hRgn) ;
                        break ;
```
[Other program lines]

CREATEELLIPTICRGNINDIRECT
■ Win 2.0   ■ Win 3.0   ■ Win 3.1

Purpose	Creates an elliptical region based on the bounding rectangle described in a RECT data structure.
Syntax	HRGN **CreateEllipticRgnIndirect**(LPRECT *lpRect*);
Description	Identical to CreateEllipticRgn(), except that a RECT data structure is used to hold the bounding rectangle for the ellipse.
Uses	A RECT data structure is more convenient if you will be doing operations on the rectangle to create new regions. The following example uses InflateRect() to create another region, smaller than the first.
Returns	HRGN, a handle to the region created. NULL on error.
See Also	CreateEllipticRgn()

Parameters

lpRect   LPRECT: A pointer to a RECT data structure holding the bounding rectangle for the ellipse.

Example   The example shown in Figure 11-11 creates two elliptical regions, one inside the other. The regions are combined using the logical RGN_DIFF operator to create a new region consisting of the parts of the larger ellipse that are not in the smaller one. A large area in the client area is then grayed, but only the logical region is painted.

Figure 11-11. Create-EllipticRgnIndirect( ) Example.

```
Long FAR PASCAL WndProc (HWND hWnd, unsigned iMessage, WORD wParam, LONG lParam)
{
        PAINTSTRUCT         ps ;
        HRGN                hRgn1, hRgn2, hRgnComb ;
        RECT                rRectangle ;

        switch (iMessage)                        /* process windows messages */
        {
                case WM_PAINT:
                        BeginPaint (hWnd, &ps) ;
                        SetRect (&rRectangle, 30, 30, 100, 80) ;
                        hRgn1 = CreateEllipticRgnIndirect (&rRectangle) ;
                        InflateRect (&rRectangle, -10, -10) ;
                        hRgn2 = CreateEllipticRgnIndirect (&rRectangle) ;
                        hRgnComb = CreateRectRgn (1, 1, 2, 2) ;/* initialize */
                        CombineRgn (hRgnComb, hRgn1, hRgn2, RGN_DIFF) ;
                        DeleteObject (hRgn1) ;
                        DeleteObject (hRgn2) ;

                        SelectClipRgn (ps.hdc, hRgnComb) ;
                        SelectObject (ps.hdc, GetStockObject (LTGRAY_BRUSH)) ;
                        Rectangle (ps.hdc, 5, 5, 500, 500) ;
                        EndPaint (hWnd, &ps) ;
                        DeleteObject (hRgnComb) ;
                        break ;
```
[Other program lines]

CREATEHATCHBRUSH   ■ Win 2.0 ■ Win 3.0 ■ Win 3.1

Purpose   Creates a logical brush based on a predefined pattern.

Syntax   HBRUSH **CreateHatchBrush**(int *nIndex*,DWORD *crColor*);

Description   This function is used to create brushes with standard patterns. For creating custom brushes, use CreateBrushIndirect() or CreatePatternBrush().

Uses   Creating brushes to use for filling rectangles, chords, ellipses, etc.

Returns   HBRUSH, a handle to the brush created. NULL on error.

See Also   CreateBrushIndirect(), CreatePatternBrush(), CreateSolidBrush(), UnrealizeObject()

Parameters

nIndex   int: Specifies the hatch style. This can be any of the patterns listed in Table 11-7.

Value	Meaning	
HS_BDIAGONAL	45-degree lines climbing from left to right.	
HS_CROSS	A horizontal and vertical crosshatch.	
HS_DIAGCROSS	A 45-degree crosshatch.	
HS_FDIAGONAL	45-degree lines climbing from right to left.	
HS_HORIZONTAL	Horizontal lines.	
HS_VERTICAL	Vertical lines.	

Table 11-7. Hatch Brush Patterns.

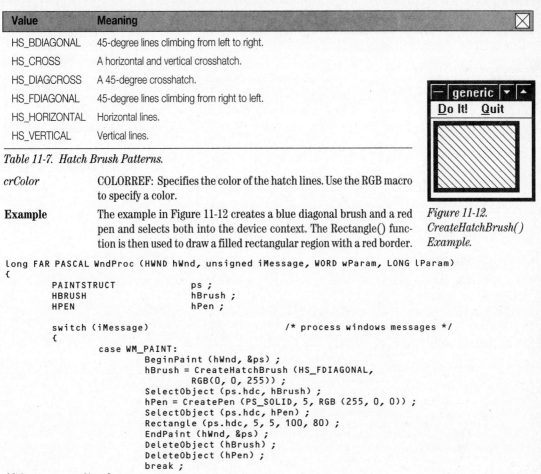

crColor   COLORREF: Specifies the color of the hatch lines. Use the RGB macro to specify a color.

Example   The example in Figure 11-12 creates a blue diagonal brush and a red pen and selects both into the device context. The Rectangle() function is then used to draw a filled rectangular region with a red border.

Figure 11-12. CreateHatchBrush() Example.

```
Long FAR PASCAL WndProc (HWND hWnd, unsigned iMessage, WORD wParam, LONG lParam)
{
        PAINTSTRUCT             ps ;
        HBRUSH                  hBrush ;
        HPEN                    hPen ;

        switch (iMessage)                        /* process windows messages */
        {
                case WM_PAINT:
                        BeginPaint (hWnd, &ps) ;
                        hBrush = CreateHatchBrush (HS_FDIAGONAL,
                                RGB(0, 0, 255)) ;
                        SelectObject (ps.hdc, hBrush) ;
                        hPen = CreatePen (PS_SOLID, 5, RGB (255, 0, 0)) ;
                        SelectObject (ps.hdc, hPen) ;
                        Rectangle (ps.hdc, 5, 5, 100, 80) ;
                        EndPaint (hWnd, &ps) ;
                        DeleteObject (hBrush) ;
                        DeleteObject (hPen) ;
                        break ;
```
[Other program lines]

CREATEPATTERNBRUSH   ■ Win 2.0   ■ Win 3.0   ■ Win 3.1

Purpose   Creates a brush based on a bitmap.

Syntax   HBRUSH **CreatePatternBrush**(HBITMAP *hBitmap*);

Description   This is a handy way to create a custom brush for filling objects like rectangles, ellipses, and chords.

Uses   Used along with LoadBitmap(), CreateBitmap(), CreateBitmapIndirect() or CreateCompatibleBitmap().

Returns   HBRUSH, the handle of the brush created. NULL on error.

See Also   LoadBitmap(), SelectObject(), DeleteObject(), CreateBrushIndirect(), CreateHatchBrush(), CreateSolidBrush(), UnrealizeObject()

Parameters

hBitmap   HBITMAP: The handle of the bitmap to use as a brush. This should be an 8 by 8 bitmap. If the bitmap is larger, only the upper left, 8 by 8 pixel area will be used.

Example   In this case, both a pen and pattern brush are selected into the device context before drawing the rectangle. (See Figure 11-13). The custom brush pattern is an 8 by 8 pixel bitmap created with the Windows SDKPaint application. The program's .RC resource file contains the line

Figure 11-13.
CreatePattern Brush()
Example.

```
brushbitmap              BITMAP              brush.bmp
```

Here is the top of the WndProc() function:

```
long FAR PASCAL WndProc (HWND hWnd, unsigned iMessage, WORD wParam, LONG lParam)
{
        PAINTSTRUCT           ps ;
        HBRUSH                hBrush ;
        HPEN                  hPen ;
        HBITMAP               hBitmap ;

        switch (iMessage)                          /* process windows messages */
        {
                case WM_PAINT:
                        BeginPaint (hWnd, &ps) ;
                        hBitmap = LoadBitmap (ghInstance, "brushbitmap") ;
                        hBrush = CreatePatternBrush (hBitmap) ;
                        SelectObject (ps.hdc, hBrush) ;
                        hPen = CreatePen (PS_SOLID, 5, RGB (255, 0, 0)) ;
                        SelectObject (ps.hdc, hPen) ;
                        Rectangle (ps.hdc, 5, 5, 100, 80) ;
                        EndPaint (hWnd, &ps) ;
                        DeleteObject (hBitmap) ;
                        DeleteObject (hBrush) ;
                        DeleteObject (hPen) ;
                        break ;
```

[Other program lines]

CREATEPEN   ■ Win 2.0   ■ Win 3.0   ■ Win 3.1

Purpose   Creates a logical pen.

Syntax   HPEN **CreatePen**(int *nPenStyle*, int *nWidth*, DWORD *crColor*);

Description   The only two stock pens are a black line and a white line, both one pixel thick. Use CreatePen() to create all other line types.

Uses   Creating a pen prior to selecting the pen into the device context.

Returns   HPEN, the handle of the pen produced.

See Also   CreatePenIndirect(), SelectObject(), DeleteObject()

Figure 11-14.
CreatePen() Example.

Parameters

nPenStyle   int: The pen style. This can be either PS_SOLID, PS_DASH, PS_DOT, PS_DASHDOT, PS_DASHDOTDOT, PS_NULL, or PS_INSIDEFRAME. The latter is used to draw the border of all objects other than polygons and polylines.

nWidth   int: The pen's width in logical units.

crColor   COLORREF: The color of the line. Use the RGB macro to specify an exact color.

Example   The rectangle, shown in Figure 11-14, is drawn with a red pen, created five units wide. Because no brush was selected, the default white brush is used to fill the rectangle.

```
long FAR PASCAL WndProc (HWND hWnd, unsigned iMessage, WORD wParam, LONG lParam)
{
        PAINTSTRUCT             ps ;
        HPEN                    hPen ;

        switch (iMessage)                       /* process windows messages */
        {
                case WM_PAINT:
                        BeginPaint (hWnd, &ps) ;
                        hPen = CreatePen (PS_SOLID, 5, RGB (255, 0, 0)) ;
                        SelectObject (ps.hdc, hPen) ;
                        Rectangle (ps.hdc, 5, 5, 100, 80) ;
                        EndPaint (hWnd, &ps) ;
                        DeleteObject (hPen) ;
                        break ;
```
[Other program lines]

CreatePenIndirect   ■ Win 2.0   ■ Win 3.0   ■ Win 3.1

Purpose   Creates a logical pen based on LOGPEN data.

Syntax   HPEN **CreatePenIndirect**(LOGPEN FAR * *lpLogPen*);

Description   This function is identical to CreatePen(), except the data for the pen is passed in a LOGPEN data structure rather than as parameters. LOGPEN is defined in WINDOWS.H as follows:

```
typedef struct tagLOGPEN
  {
   WORD                 lopnStyle;
   POINT                lopnWidth;
   DWORD                lopnColor;
  } LOGPEN;
typedef LOGPEN          *PLOGPEN;
typedef LOGPEN NEAR     *NPLOGPEN;
typedef LOGPEN FAR      *LPLOGPEN;
```

Uses   More convenient than CreatePen() if you have a number of similar pens to create.

Returns   HPEN, a handle to the pen created. NULL on error.

See Also   CreatePen(), SelectObject(), DeleteObject()

Parameters

lpLogPen   LOGPEN FAR *: A pointer to a LOGPEN data structure. The elements of the data structure are as follows.

lopnStyle   WORD: The pen style. This can be either PS_SOLID, PS_DASH, PS_DOT, PS_DASHDOT, PS_DASHDOTDOT, PS_NULL, or PS_INSIDEFRAME. The latter is used for drawing the border of all objects other than polygons and polylines.

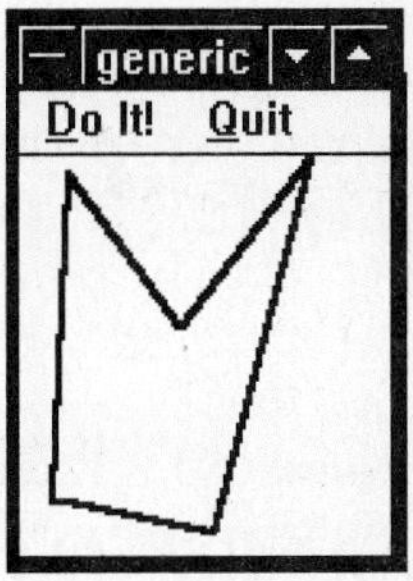

lopnWidth   POINT: A POINT structure. The x element of the POINT structure defines the pen's width. Only the x element of the structure is used.

lopnColor   COLORREF: The 32-bit color value to use for the pen. Use the RGB macro to specify a color.

Example   Here a polygon is drawn, see Figure 11-15, using a pen created with CreatePenIndirect().

Figure 11-15. CreatePenIndirect() Example.

```
long FAR PASCAL WndProc (HWND hWnd, unsigned iMessage, WORD wParam, LONG lParam)
{
        PAINTSTRUCT             ps ;
        HPEN                    hPen ;
```

```
        LOGPEN                  lp ;
        POINT                   pPenWidth ;
        POINT                   pArray [] = {10, 100, 15, 5, 50, 50, 90, 0, 60, 110} ;

        switch (iMessage)                       /* process windows messages */
        {
                case WM_PAINT:
                        BeginPaint (hWnd, &ps) ;
                        pPenWidth.x = 2 ;
                        lp.lopnStyle = PS_DASH ;
                        lp.lopnWidth = pPenWidth ;
                        lp.lopnColor = RGB (0, 40, 50) ;
                        hPen = CreatePenIndirect (&lp) ;
                        SelectObject (ps.hdc, hPen) ;
                        Polygon (ps.hdc, pArray, 5) ;
                        EndPaint (hWnd, &ps) ;
                        DeleteObject (hPen) ;
                        break ;
```

[Other program lines]

CREATEPOLYGONRGN   ■ Win 2.0   ■ Win 3.0   ■ Win 3.1

Purpose	Creates an arbitrary, shaped polygonal region.
Syntax	HRGN **CreatePolygonRgn**(LPPOINT *lpPoints*, int *nCount*, int *nPolyFillMode*);
Description	This function is ideal for creating clipping modes that have complex shapes. Any number of points can be specified.
Uses	Complex clipping modes.
Returns	HRGN, a handle to the region created. NULL on error.
See Also	CreatePolyPolygonRgn()

Parameters

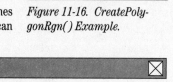

lpPoints   LPPOINT: A pointer to an array of POINT structures containing at least *nCount* points.

nCount   int: The number of points to use in drawing the polygon.

nPolyFillMode   int: The polygon filling mode. This is important only if the lines of the polygon cross each other, creating areas. The mode can be either of the two modes listed in Table 11-8.

Figure 11-16. CreatePolygonRgn( ) Example.

Value	Meaning
ALTERNATE	The GDI fills in areas between sides 1&2, sides 3&4, etc.
WINDING	The GDI fills in the complete area defined by the outermost lines.

Table 11-8. Polygon Filling Modes.

See GetPolyFillMode() or SetPolyFillMode() for more details on the polygon filling modes.

Example   Here a five sided polygon, see Figure 11-16, is used as a clipping region.

```
Long FAR PASCAL WndProc (HWND hWnd, unsigned iMessage, WORD wParam, LONG lParam)
{
        PAINTSTRUCT     ps ;
        HRGN            hRgn ;
        POINT           pArray [5] = {10, 10, 50, 40, 90, 20, 60, 0, 40, 20} ;

        switch (iMessage)                              /* process windows messages */
        {
                case WM_PAINT:
                        BeginPaint (hWnd, &ps) ;
                        hRgn = CreatePolygonRgn (pArray, 5, WINDING) ;
```

```
SelectClipRgn (ps.hdc, hRgn) ;
SelectObject (ps.hdc, GetStockObject (LTGRAY_BRUSH)) ;
Rectangle (ps.hdc, 0, 0, 500, 500) ;      /* paint gray */
EndPaint (hWnd, &ps) ;
DeleteObject (hRgn) ;
break ;
```

[Other program lines]

CREATEPOLYPOLYGONRGN   □ Win 2.0   ■ Win 3.0   ■ Win 3.1

Purpose	Creates a region composed of multiple polygons in a single function call.
Syntax	HRGN **CreatePolyPolygonRgn**(LPPOINT *lpPoints*, LPINT *lpPolyCounts*, int *nCount*, int *nPolyFillMode*);
Description	This function can save time in making and combining regions by providing the ability to create a region of any complexity in a single function call. This is accomplished by passing two arrays to the function, an array of all of the points, and a second array containing an array of integers. The integer array defines how the points are to be grouped. For example, the first four points might define the first shape, the second six the second shape, etc.
Uses	Creating complex clipping regions without having to combine multiple small regions. The individual regions defined in the array of points do not have to be touching.
Returns	HRGN, a handle to the region created. NULL on error.
See Also	CreatePolygonRgn(), CombineRgn()

Parameters

lpPoints   LPPOINT: A pointer to an array of POINT structures containing the location of every point in every polygon that will be defined. The points must be sorted so that all of the points defining the first polygon are together, followed by the points defining the second polygon, etc.

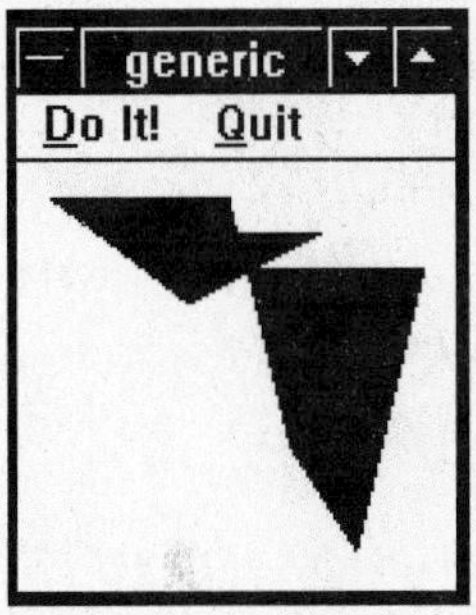

Figure 11-17. Create-PolyPolygonRgn() Example.

lpPolyCounts   LPINT: A pointer to an array of integers. The elements of the array describe how many points belong to each of the polygons.

nCount   int: The number of integers in the *lpPolyCounts* array. This is also the number of polygons that will be defined.

nPolyFillMode   int: The polygon filling mode. This is important only if the lines of the polygon cross each other, creating areas. The mode can be either of the modes listed in Table 11-9.

Value	Meaning	⊠
ALTERNATE	The GDI fills in areas between sides 1&2, sides 3&4, etc.	
WINDING	The GDI fills in the complete area defined by the outermost lines.	

Table 11-9. Polygon Filling Modes.

Example   The clipping region shown in Figure 11-17 is created by defining a triangular and a four-sided polygon in the same call to CreatePolyPolygonRgn().

```
Long FAR PASCAL WndProc (HWND hWnd, unsigned iMessage, WORD wParam, LONG lParam)
{
        PAINTSTRUCT     ps ;
        HRGN            hRgn ;
        POINT           pArray [7] = {10, 10, 50, 40, 90, 20, 60, 0, 80, 80,
                                        100, 110, 120, 30} ;
        int             nPolyCount [] = {3, 4} ;
```

```
        switch (iMessage)                      /* process windows messages */
        {
                case WM_PAINT:
                        BeginPaint (hWnd, &ps) ;
                        hRgn = CreatePolyPolygonRgn (pArray, nPolyCount, 2,
                                WINDING) ;
                        SelectClipRgn (ps.hdc, hRgn) ;
                        SelectObject (ps.hdc, GetStockObject (LTGRAY_BRUSH)) ;
                        Rectangle (ps.hdc, 0, 0, 500, 500) ;      /* paint gray */
                        EndPaint (hWnd, &ps) ;
                        DeleteObject (hRgn) ;
                        break ;
```
[Other program lines]

CREATERECTREGN   ■ Win 2.0   ■ Win 3.0   ■ Win 3.1

Purpose	Creates a rectangular region.
Syntax	HRGN **CreateRectRgn**(int *X1*, int *Y1*, int *X2*, int *Y2*);
Description	The region created is a rectangle, bounded by the *X1,Y1* at the upper left and *X2,Y2* at the lower right.
Uses	Used to create clipping regions or regions to be filled.
Returns	HRGN, the handle to the region created. NULL on error.
See Also	SelectObject(), DeleteObject(), SelectClipRgn(), FillRgn()

Parameters

X1   int: The logical *X* coordinate of the upper left corner of the rectangle.

Y1   int: The logical *Y* coordinate of the upper left corner of the rectangle.

X2   int: The logical *X* coordinate of the lower right corner of the rectangle.

Y2   int: The logical *Y* coordinate of the lower right corner of the rectangle.

Figure 11-18. Create-RectRgn( ) Example.

Example   This example creates a rectangular region, and uses it as a clipping region. When a much larger rectangle is drawn, only the part within the region ends up visible. (See Figure 11-18.)

```
Long FAR PASCAL WndProc (HWND hWnd, unsigned iMessage, WORD wParam, LONG lParam)
{
        PAINTSTRUCT    ps ;
        HRGN           hRgn ;

        switch (iMessage)                              /* process windows messages */
        {
                case WM_PAINT:
                        BeginPaint (hWnd, &ps) ;
                        hRgn = CreateRectRgn (10, 10, 90, 70) ;
                        SelectClipRgn (ps.hdc, hRgn) ;
                        SelectObject (ps.hdc, GetStockObject (LTGRAY_BRUSH)) ;
                        Rectangle (ps.hdc, 5, 5, 500, 500) ;/* paint gray */
                        EndPaint (hWnd, &ps) ;
                        DeleteObject (hRgn) ;
                        break ;
```
[Other program lines]

CREATERECTRGNINDIRECT
■ Win 2.0   ■ Win 3.0   ■ Win 3.1

Purpose Creates a rectangular region based on the data in a RECT data structure.

Syntax HRGN **CreateRectRgnIndirect**(LPRECT *lpRect*);

Description This is identical to CreateRectRgn(), except the rectangle data is passed as the elements of a RECT data structure.

Uses Convenient if the rectangle data will be manipulated. The following example shows the RECT data being used to create a new region, offset from the first.

Returns HRGN, a handle to the region created. NULL on error.

See Also CreateRectRgn()

Parameters

lpRect LPRECT: A pointer to a RECT data structure holding the dimensions of the rectangle.

Example This example creates two rectangular regions, one offset from the other. The regions are combined with the logical RGN_XOR operation. When the entire area is grayed (see Figure 11-19), only the parts of the regions not overlapping end up painted.

Figure 11-19. CreateRectRgnIndirect( ) Example.

```
Long FAR PASCAL WndProc (HWND hWnd, unsigned iMessage, WORD wParam, LONG lParam)
{
        PAINTSTRUCT     ps ;
        HRGN            hRgn1, hRgn2, hRgnComb ;
        RECT            rRectangle1, rRectangle2 ;

        switch (iMessage)                       /* process windows messages */
        {
                case WM_PAINT:
                        BeginPaint (hWnd, &ps) ;
                        SetRect (&rRectangle1, 30, 30, 60, 80) ;
                        hRgn1 = CreateRectRgnIndirect (&rRectangle1) ;
                        CopyRect (&rRectangle2, &rRectangle1) ;
                        OffsetRect (&rRectangle2, 20, 20) ;
                        hRgn2 = CreateRectRgnIndirect (&rRectangle2) ;
                        hRgnComb = CreateRectRgn (1, 1, 2, 2) ;/* initialize */
                        CombineRgn (hRgnComb, hRgn1, hRgn2, RGN_XOR) ;
                        DeleteObject (hRgn1) ;
                        DeleteObject (hRgn2) ;

                        SelectClipRgn (ps.hdc, hRgnComb) ;
                        SelectObject (ps.hdc, GetStockObject (LTGRAY_BRUSH)) ;
                        Rectangle (ps.hdc, 5, 5, 500, 500) ;
                        EndPaint (hWnd, &ps) ;
                        DeleteObject (hRgnComb) ;
                        break ;
```

[Other program lines]

CREATEROUNDRECTRGN
□ Win 2.0   ■ Win 3.0   ■ Win 3.1

Purpose Creates a rectangular region with rounded corners.

Syntax HRGN **CreateRoundRectRgn**(int *X1*, int *Y1*, int *X2*, int *Y2*, int *X3*, int *Y3*);

Description The region created is a rectangle, bounded by *X1,Y1* at the upper left and *X2,Y2* at the lower right. *X3* and *Y3* provide the width and height of the ellipses used to round the corners.

Uses	Used to create clipping regions.
Returns	HRGN, the handle to the region created. NULL on error.
See Also	SelectObject(), DeleteObject(), SelectClipRgn()
Parameters	
X1	int: The logical *X* coordinate of the upper left corner of the bounding rectangle.
Y1 •	int: The logical *Y* coordinate of the upper left corner of the bounding rectangle.
X2	int: The logical *X* coordinate of the lower right corner of the bounding rectangle.
Y2	int: The logical *Y* coordinate of the lower right corner of the bounding rectangle.
X3	int: The logical width of the ellipse used to round the corners.
Y3	int: The logical height of the ellipse used to round the corners.

Figure 11-20. Create-RoundRectRgn() Example.

Example This example creates a rectangular region with rounded corners and uses it as a clipping region. When a much larger rectangle is drawn with a gray brush, only the interior of the region ends up painted, as shown in Figure 11-20.

```
Long FAR PASCAL WndProc (HWND hWnd, unsigned iMessage, WORD wParam, LONG lParam)
{
        PAINTSTRUCT     ps ;
        HRGN            hRgn ;

        switch (iMessage)                               /* process windows messages */
        {
        case WM_PAINT:
                BeginPaint (hWnd, &ps) ;
                hRgn = CreateRoundRectRgn (10, 10, 90, 70, 20, 20) ;
                SelectClipRgn (ps.hdc, hRgn) ;
                SelectObject (ps.hdc, GetStockObject (LTGRAY_BRUSH)) ;
                Rectangle (ps.hdc, 5, 5, 500, 500) ;/* paint gray */
                EndPaint (hWnd, &ps) ;
                DeleteObject (hRgn) ;
                break ;
```

[Other program lines]

CREATESOLIDBRUSH ■ Win 2.0 ■ Win 3.0 ■ Win 3.1

Purpose	Creates a brush with a solid color.
Syntax	HBRUSH **CreateSolidBrush**(DWORD *crColor*);
Description	CreateSolidBrush() allows you to create a solid color brush for filling areas. Before an object like a rectangle or ellipse can have its interior painted, the program must select a brush of the desired color into the device context using SelectObject(). Call DeleteObject() to free the created brush from memory after it is used.

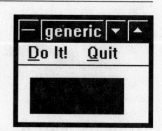

Figure 11-21. CreateSolid-Brush() Example.

Uses	Solid color brushes. Use CreateHatchBrush(), CreatePatternBrush(), and CreateBrushIndirect() to create pattern brushes.
Returns	HBRUSH, a handle for the brush created. NULL on error.
See Also	SelectObject(), DeleteObject(), CreateHatchBrush(), CreatePatternBrush(), CreateBrushIndirect(), Unrealize Object()

Parameters

crColor   DWORD: The 32-bit color value to use for the brush color. Use the RGB macro to specify this value.

Example   This example creates a blue/red brush and uses it to fill a rectangle, as shown in Figure 11-21. The brush is deleted immediately after the rectangle is painted.

```
long FAR PASCAL WndProc (HWND hWnd, unsigned iMessage, WORD wParam, LONG lParam)
{
        PAINTSTRUCT             ps ;
        HBRUSH                  hBrush ;

        switch (iMessage)                       /* process windows messages */
        {
                case WM_PAINT:
                        BeginPaint (hWnd, &ps) ;
                        hBrush = CreateSolidBrush (RGB (10, 0, 50)) ;
                        SelectObject (ps.hdc, hBrush) ;
                        Rectangle (ps.hdc, 10, 10, 90, 40) ;
                        EndPaint (hWnd, &ps) ;
                        DeleteObject (hBrush) ;
                        break ;
```
[Other program lines]

DELETEOBJECT   ■ Win 2.0   ■ Win 3.0   ■ Win 3.1

Purpose   Removes pens, brushes, fonts, bitmaps, regions, and palettes from memory.

Syntax   BOOL **DeleteObject**(HANDLE *hObject*);

Description   GDI objects must be deleted to free the memory they occupy. Otherwise, they will continue to exist in memory after the program exits. Use DeleteObject() to free the memory and eliminate the object. Do not delete stock objects (obtained with GetStockObject()). If a bitmap is used to create a brush, you will have to delete the brush and the bitmap separately. Do not attempt to delete an object that is selected to a device context. Either delete the object after the device context is released (after ReleaseDC() or EndPaint() is called), or displace the object out of the device context by selecting another object of the same type, such as a stock object.

Uses   Generally used immediately after the object is used. Some programs create a series of GDI objects when the program starts (WM_CREATE), and then delete them all right before the program exits (WM_DESTROY).

Returns   BOOL. TRUE if the object was deleted, FALSE on error. Normally, a FALSE return value means that the handle was not valid.

See Also   CreatePen(), CreateSolidBrush(), CreateRectRgn(), LoadBitmap(),

Parameters

hObject   HANDLE: The handle of the pen, bitmap, brush, font, region, or palette to be deleted.

Example   The previous example under CreateSolidBrush() shows a typical cycle of creating a brush, using it, and then deleting it. Also see the discussion at the beginning of this chapter.

DRAWFOCUSRECT   □ Win 2.0   ■ Win 3.0   ■ Win 3.1

Purpose   Draws or removes a dashed line around a rectangle.

Syntax   void **DrawFocusRect**(HDC *hDC*, LPRECT *lpRect*);

Description   The dashed line is drawn with the XOR style, so drawing the focus rectangle a second time at the same location erases the line.

Uses   To highlight an area temporarily.

Returns	No returned value (void).
See Also	Rectangle(), InflateRect()

Parameters

hDC   HDC: The device context handle.

lpRect   LPRECT: A pointer to a RECT structure holding the size of the rectangle to paint.

Example   This example creates a pseudo button, shown in Figure 11-22. The button background and text are created with RoundRect() and DrawText(). The exterior is outlined in a dashed line, or has the dashed line removed, when the user clicks the "Do It!" menu item.

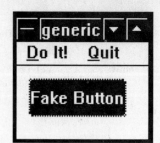

Figure 11-22. Draw-FocusRect( ) Example.

```
long FAR PASCAL WndProc (HWND hWnd, unsigned iMessage, WORD wParam, LONG lParam)
{
        PAINTSTRUCT             ps ;
        HBRUSH                  hBrush ;
        static RECT             rRect ;
        HDC                     hDC ;

        switch (iMessage)                       /* process windows messages */
        {
                case WM_PAINT:
                        BeginPaint (hWnd, &ps) ;
                        hBrush = CreateSolidBrush (RGB (120, 120, 120)) ;
                        SelectObject (ps.hdc, hBrush) ;
                        SetRect (&rRect, 10, 10, 90, 40) ;
                        RoundRect (ps.hdc, 10, 10, 90, 40, 10, 10) ;
                        SetBkMode (ps.hdc, TRANSPARENT) ;
                        SetTextColor (ps.hdc, RGB (255, 255, 255)) ;
                        DrawText (ps.hdc, "Fake Button", 11, &rRect,
                                DT_CENTER | DT_VCENTER | DT_SINGLELINE) ;
                        EndPaint (hWnd, &ps) ;
                        DeleteObject (hBrush) ;
                        break ;
                case WM_COMMAND:                /* process menu items */
                        switch (wParam)
                        {
                        case IDM_DOIT:          /* User hit the "Do it" menu item */
                                hDC = GetDC (hWnd) ;
                                DrawFocusRect (hDC, &rRect) ;
                                ReleaseDC (hWnd, hDC) ;
                                break ;
```

[Other program lines]

ELLIPSE   ■ Win 2.0   ■ Win 3.0   ■ Win 3.1

Purpose	Draws an ellipse.
Syntax	BOOL **Ellipse**(HDC *hDC*, int *X1*, int *Y1*, int *X2*, int *Y2*);
Description	The ellipse is drawn with the currently selected pen and filled with the current brush.
Uses	A circle can be drawn by defining the bounding rectangle to be a square.
Returns	BOOL. TRUE if the ellipse was drawn, FALSE on error.
See Also	Rectangle()

Parameters

X1   int: The logical *X* coordinate of the upper left corner of the bounding rectangle.

Y1   int: The logical *Y* coordinate of the upper left corner of the bounding rectangle.

X2   int: The logical *X* coordinate of the lower right corner of the bounding rectangle.

Y2 int: The logical *Y* coordinate of the lower right corner of the bounding rectangle.

Example The example shown in Figure 11-23 draws two overlapping ellipses in the window's client area. Note that the specification of the TRANSPARENT drawing style allows both of the ellipse lines to be visible in the overlapping region. This does not affect the hatched brush pattern. Only one brush pattern is visible in the overlapping region. Only lines and text are affected by the setting of TRANSPARENT or OPAQUE drawing modes.

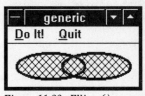

Figure 11-23. Ellipse()
Example.

```
long FAR PASCAL WndProc (HWND hWnd, unsigned iMessage, WORD wParam, LONG lParam)
{
        PAINTSTRUCT      ps ;
        HBRUSH           hBrush ;
        HPEN             hPen ;

        switch (iMessage)                           /* process windows messages */
        {
                case WM_PAINT:
                        BeginPaint (hWnd, &ps) ;
                        hBrush = CreateHatchBrush (HS_DIAGCROSS,
                                                   RGB (120, 0, 120)) ;
                        SelectObject (ps.hdc, hBrush) ;
                        hPen = CreatePen (PS_SOLID, 3, RGB (10, 50, 255)) ;
                        SelectObject (ps.hdc, hPen) ;
                        SetBkMode (ps.hdc, TRANSPARENT) ;
                        Ellipse (ps.hdc, 10, 10, 90, 40) ;
                        Ellipse (ps.hdc, 62, 10, 142, 40) ;
                        EndPaint (hWnd, &ps) ;
                        DeleteObject (hPen) ;
                        DeleteObject (hBrush) ;
                        break ;
```
[Other program lines]

ENDPAINT
■ Win 2.0   ■ Win 3.0   ■ Win 3.1

Purpose Ends the painting cycle started by BeginPaint().

Syntax void **EndPaint**(HWND *hWnd*, LPPAINTSTRUCT *lpPaint*);

Description When processing WM_PAINT messages, BeginPaint() is used to get the device context and load the PAINTSTRUCT data. EndPaint() is used at the end of the painting cycle to release the device context. Use ReleaseDC() to free a device context created with GetDC(), for doing output outside of the WM_PAINT processing section of the program. EndPaint() will restore a caret if the caret was hidden by a call to BeginPaint().

Uses Client area updates while processing WM_PAINT messages.

Returns No returned value (void).

See Also BeginPaint(), ReleaseDC(), GetDC()

Parameters

hWnd HWND: The handle of the window to be repainted.

lpPaint LPPAINTSTRUCT: A pointer to a PAINTSTRUCT data structure that was used by the Begin-Paint() function. See the BeginPaint() function description for the structure definition.

Related Messages WM_PAINT

Example The previous example under Ellipse() shows a typical cycle of using BeginPaint(), GDI functions, and EndPaint() while processing a WM_PAINT message.

ENUMOBJECTS

■ Win 2.0 ■ Win 3.0 ■ Win 3.1

Purpose   Enumerates all of the physical pens or brushes available on a device context.

Syntax   int **EnumObjects**(HDC *hDC*, int *nObjectType*, FARPROC *lpObjectFunct*, LPSTR *lpData*);

Description   EnumObjects() calls a callback function for every pen or brush possible on the device context. The callback function can store this data for later use.

Uses   Determines the number and type of physical pensor brushes that can be attached to the device context. You can use the data to create one or more logical pens that match the exact physical pens/brushes available. Logical pens/brushes that do not have an exact match will end up using the closest physical item.

Returns   int, the last value returned by the callback function. Normally, not used.

See Also   EnumFonts()

Parameters

hDC   HDC: The device context handle.

nObjectType   int: The type of object to enumerate. This can be either OBJ_BRUSH or OBJ_PEN.

lpObjectFunct   FARPROC: The procedure-instance address of the callback function. This function name must be listed in the EXPORTS section of the program's .DEF definition file. The procedure-instance address should be obtained with MakeProc-Instance().

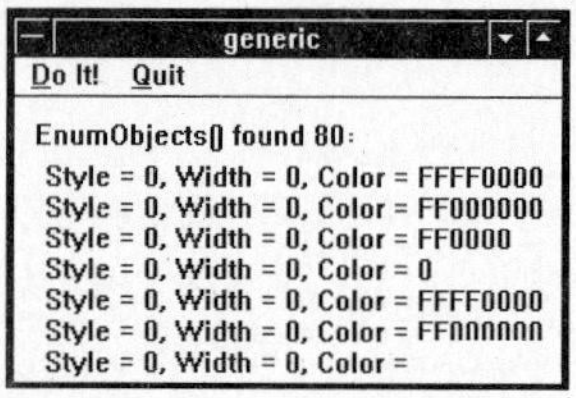

Figure 11-24. EnumObjects() Example.

lpData   LPSTR: A pointer to the data structure that the callback function should use. Normally the callback function will reallocate this memory block to enlarge it every time a new piece of data is to be stored.

Example   This program lists all of the pens possible with the client area's device context, as shown in Figure 11-24. The list goes past the end of the screen. Note that a width of zero draws a one pixel wide line regardless of the mapping mode.

　　　　　　　　The program's header file includes the definition of the ENUMER data type used in the enumeration of the pens. The enumeration function prototype is also in the header file.

```
/* generic.h */
#define IDM_DOIT    1                   /* menu item id values */
#define IDM_QUIT    2
        /* definitions */
typedef struct
{
        GLOBALHANDLE            hGMem ;
        int                     nCount ;
} ENUMER ;

        /* global variables */
int     ghInstance ;
char    gszAppName [] = "generic" ;

        /* function prototypes */
long FAR PASCAL WndProc (HWND, unsigned, WORD, LONG) ;
BOOL FAR PASCAL PenEnumFunc (char FAR *lpLogObject,
        ENUMER FAR *enumer) ;
```

　　　　　　　　The enumeration function name must also be listed in the EXPORTS section of the program's .DEF definition file.

```
Long FAR PASCAL WndProc (HWND hWnd, unsigned iMessage, WORD wParam, LONG lParam)
{
        static          FARPROC         lpfnEnumProc ;
        static          ENUMER          enumer ;
```

```
        LPLOGPEN                        lpLogPen ;
        char            FAR             *fp ;
        HDC                             hDC ;
        int                             i ;
        char                            cBuf [128] ;
        switch (iMessage)                       /* process windows messages */
        {
                case WM_CREATE:
                        lpfnEnumProc =
                                MakeProcInstance (PenEnumFunc, ghInstance) ;
                        break ;
                case WM_COMMAND:                        /* process menu items */
                        switch (wParam)
                        {
                        case IDM_DOIT:                  /* User hit the "Do it" menu item */
                                if (enumer.hGMem)       /* if not first time tried */
                                        GlobalFree (enumer.hGMem) ;
                                                        /* initialize storage area */
                                enumer.hGMem = GlobalAlloc (GMEM_MOVEABLE |
                                                GMEM_ZEROINIT, 1L) ;
                                enumer.nCount = 0 ;
                                hDC = GetDC (hWnd) ;
                                                        /* let Windows run callback func. */
                                EnumObjects (hDC, OBJ_PEN, lpfnEnumProc,
                                        (LPSTR) &enumer) ;
                                lpLogPen = (LPLOGPEN) GlobalLock (enumer.hGMem) ;
                                TextOut (hDC, 10, 10, cBuf, wsprintf (cBuf,
                                        "EnumObjects() found %d:",
                                        enumer.nCount)) ;
                                fp = (char far *) lpLogPen ;
                                for (i = 0 ; i < enumer.nCount ; i++)
                                        {                       /* display each pen found */
                                        TextOut (hDC, 15, 30 + (15 * i),
                                                cBuf, wsprintf (cBuf,
                                                "Style = %d, Width = %d, Color = %0lX",
                                                lpLogPen->lopnStyle,
                                                lpLogPen->lopnWidth,
                                                lpLogPen->lopnColor )) ;
                                        fp += sizeof (LOGPEN) ;
                                        lpLogPen = (LPLOGPEN) fp ;
                                        }
                                GlobalUnlock (enumer.hGMem) ; /* unlock memory */
                                ReleaseDC (hWnd, hDC) ;
                                break ;
                        case IDM_QUIT:          /* send end of application message */
                                DestroyWindow (hWnd) ;
                                break ;
                        }
                        break ;
                case WM_DESTROY:                        /* stop application */
                        GlobalFree (enumer.hGMem) ;     /* release all memory */
                        FreeProcInstance (lpfnEnumProc) ;
                        PostQuitMessage (0) ;
                        break ;
                default:                        /* default windows message processing */
                        return DefWindowProc (hWnd, iMessage, wParam, lParam) ;
        }
        return (0L) ;
}


BOOL FAR PASCAL PenEnumFunc (char FAR *lpLogObject, ENUMER FAR *enumer)
{
        LPLOGPEN                lpLogPen ;
        static          int     i ;
        char            FAR     *fp ;

        if (!GlobalReAlloc (enumer->hGMem,
                        (DWORD) sizeof (LOGPEN) * (enumer->nCount + 1),
```

```
                        GMEM_MOVEABLE))
            return (0) ;                /* quit if can't make room */

        lpLogPen = (LPLOGPEN) GlobalLock (enumer->hGMem) ;
        fp = (char far *) lpLogPen ;
        fp += enumer->nCount * sizeof (LOGPEN) ;
        for (i = 0 ; i < sizeof (LOGPEN); i++)     /* copy pen to buffer */
                *fp++ = *lpLogObject++ ;
        GlobalUnlock (enumer->hGMem) ;      /* unlock the memory area */
        enumer->nCount++ ;                  /* keep track of how many */
        return (1) ;
}
```

EqualRect   ■ Win 2.0   ■ Win 3.0   ■ Win 3.1

Purpose	Checks whether two rectangles are equal.
Syntax	BOOL **EqualRect**(LPRECT *lpRect1*, LPRECT *lpRect2*);
Uses	Normally used to avoid unnecessary painting.
Returns	BOOL. TRUE if the rectangles are equal, FALSE if not.
See Also	EqualRgn()

Parameters

lpRect1   LPRECT: A pointer to the first RECT data structure.

lpRect2   LPRECT: A pointer to the second RECT data structure.

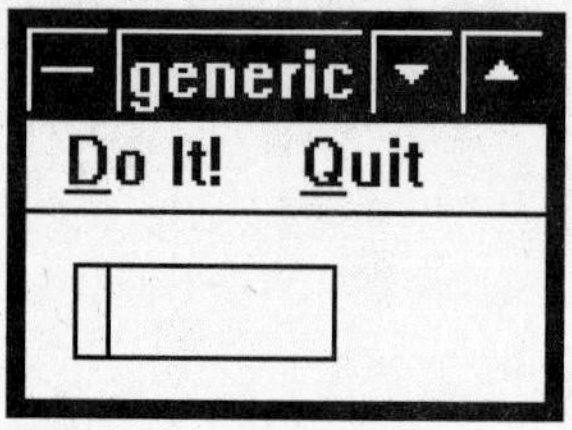

*Figure 11-25. EqualRect()
Example after Several
WM_PAINT Messages.*

Example   This example creates two rectangles every time a WM_PAINT
message is received. If the two are not equal, both are drawn.
The second rectangle is offset to the right every time a WM_PAINT message is processed. (See
Figure 11-25.)

```
Long FAR PASCAL WndProc (HWND hWnd, unsigned iMessage, WORD wParam, LONG lParam)
{
        PAINTSTRUCT             ps ;
        RECT                    rRect1, rRect2 ;
        static          int     nPaintCount = 0 ;

        switch (iMessage)                       /* process windows messages */
        {
                case WM_PAINT:
                        BeginPaint (hWnd, &ps) ;
                        SetRect (&rRect1, 10, 10, 60, 30) ;
                        SetRect (&rRect2, 10 + nPaintCount, 10,
                                60 + nPaintCount++, 30) ;
                        SelectObject (ps.hdc, GetStockObject (BLACK_PEN)) ;
                        Rectangle (ps.hdc, rRect1.left, rRect1.top, rRect1.right,
                                rRect1.bottom) ;
                        if (!EqualRect (&rRect1, &rRect2))
                                Rectangle (ps.hdc, rRect2.left, rRect2.top,
                                        rRect2.right, rRect2.bottom) ;
                        EndPaint (hWnd, &ps) ;
                        break ;
```
[Other program lines]

EqualRgn   ■ Win 2.0   ■ Win 3.0   ■ Win 3.1

Purpose	Checks to see if two regions are equally sized.
Syntax	BOOL **EqualRgn**(HRGN *hSrcRgn1*, HRGN *hSrcRgn2*);
Uses	If two regions are equally sized, there is no reason to combine them.
Returns	BOOL. TRUE if the regions are equal, FALSE if not.

See Also	EqualRect()
Parameters	
hSrcRgn1	HRGN: The first region's handle.
hSrcRgn2	HRGN: The second region's handle.
Example	Here two elliptical regions are created. If they are not identical, they are combined to create a clipping region. Every time a WM_PAINT message is received, one of the bounding rectangles is offset to the right one logical unit (pixel). (See Figure 11-26.)

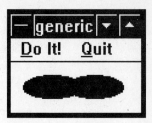

Figure 11-26. EqualRgn() Example after Several WM_PAINT Messages.

```
Long FAR PASCAL WndProc (HWND hWnd, unsigned iMessage, WORD wParam, LONG lParam)
{
        PAINTSTRUCT          ps ;
        HRGN                 hRgn1, hRgn2, hRgnComb ;
        static      int      nPaintCount = 0 ;

        switch (iMessage)                        /* process windows messages */
        {
        case WM_PAINT:
                BeginPaint (hWnd, &ps) ;
                hRgn1 = CreateEllipticRgn (10, 10, 60, 30) ;
                hRgn2 = CreateEllipticRgn (10 + nPaintCount, 10,
                        60 + nPaintCount++, 30) ;
                hRgnComb = CreateRectRgn (1, 1, 2, 2) ;
                if (!EqualRgn (hRgn1, hRgn2))
                        CombineRgn (hRgnComb, hRgn1, hRgn2, RGN_OR) ;
                else
                        CombineRgn (hRgnComb, hRgn1, NULL, RGN_COPY) ;
                DeleteObject (hRgn1) ;
                DeleteObject (hRgn2) ;

                SelectClipRgn (ps.hdc, hRgnComb) ;
                SelectObject (ps.hdc, GetStockObject (LTGRAY_BRUSH)) ;
                Rectangle (ps.hdc, 5, 5, 500, 500) ;
                EndPaint (hWnd, &ps) ;
                DeleteObject (hRgnComb) ;
                break ;
```

[Other program lines]

EXCLUDECLIPRECT
■ Win 2.0　■ Win 3.0　■ Win 3.1

Purpose	Removes a rectangular area from a clipping region.
Syntax	int **ExcludeClipRect**(HDC *hDC*, int *X1*, int *Y1*, int *X2*, int *Y2*);
Description	Hollow clipping regions can be created by first creating a clipping region, and then excluding a central portion with this function.
Uses	Creating clipping regions that limit where on the device context painting will occur.
Returns	int, the type of region created. This can be any of the types listed in Table 11-10.

Value	Meaning	⊠
COMPLEXREGION	The new region has overlapping borders.	
ERROR	No new region was created.	
NULLREGION	The new region is empty.	
SIMPLEREGION	The new region does not have overlapping borders.	

Table 11-10. Region Types.

See Also   ExcludeUpdateRgn(), SelectClipRgn()

Parameters

hDC   HDC: The device context handle.

X1   int: The logical *X* coordinate of the upper left corner of the bounding rectangle.

Y1   int: The logical *Y* coordinate of the upper left corner of the bounding rectangle.

X2   int: The logical *X* coordinate of the lower right corner of the bounding rectangle.

Y2   int: The logical *Y* coordinate of the lower right corner of the bounding rectangle.

Figure 11-27.
ExcludeClipRect( )
Example.

Example   As shown in Figure 11-27, a rectangular clipping region is created. The center of the clipping region is eliminated using ExcludeClipRect(). A large area is painted with a gray brush, but only the clipping area is affected.

```
Long FAR PASCAL WndProc (HWND hWnd, unsigned iMessage, WORD wParam, LONG lParam)
{
        PAINTSTRUCT     ps ;
        HRGN            hRgn ;

        switch (iMessage)                       /* process windows messages */
        {
                case WM_PAINT:
                        BeginPaint (hWnd, &ps) ;
                        hRgn = CreateRectRgn (10, 10, 100, 100) ;
                        SelectClipRgn (ps.hdc, hRgn) ;
                        ExcludeClipRect (ps.hdc, 30, 30, 80, 80) ;
                        SelectObject (ps.hdc, GetStockObject (LTGRAY_BRUSH)) ;
                        Rectangle (ps.hdc, 0, 0, 500, 500) ;      /* paint area */
                        EndPaint (hWnd, &ps) ;
                        DeleteObject (hRgn) ;
                        break ;
```

[Other program lines]

EXCLUDEUPDATERGN   ■ Win 2.0   ■ Win 3.0   ■ Win 3.1

Purpose   Prevents drawing in invalid areas of the client area.

Syntax   int **ExcludeUpdateRgn**(HDC *hDC*, HWND *hWnd*);

Description   If program logic outside of the processing of WM_PAINT messages causes parts of the client area to become invalid (need repainting), these areas will be repainted on the next WM_PAINT cycle. ExcludeUpdateRgn() keeps GDI operations from painting in the invalidated areas.

Uses   Commonly used with programs that scroll the window's client area.

Returns   int, the type of region created. This can be any of the types listed in Table 11-11.

Value	Meaning	
COMPLEXREGION	The new region has overlapping borders.	
ERROR	No new region was created.	
NULLREGION	The new region is empty.	
SIMPLEREGION	The new region does not have overlapping borders.	

Table 11-11. Region Types.

See Also   ExcludeClipRect()

Parameters

hDC   HDC: The device context handle for the window.

hWnd   HWND: The window's handle.

Related Messages WM_PAINT

Example   This example scrolls down the client area of the window when the user clicks the "Do It!" menu item. This invalidates the upper 10 pixel rows. (See Figure 11-28.) Before the WM_PAINT message is processed, the program paints a dark rectangle. The ExcludeUpdateRgn() function keeps the rectangle from being painted in the update region (the region uncovered by scrolling the window's client area down 10 pixels). The WM_PAINT logic is set up to paint alternating gray and white bands as the window's client area is scrolled down.

Figure 11-28. Exclude-UpdateRgn() Example.

```
long FAR PASCAL WndProc (HWND hWnd, unsigned iMessage, WORD wParam, LONG lParam)
{
        PAINTSTRUCT             ps ;
        HDC                     hDC ;
        static          BOOL    bToggle = FALSE ;

        switch (iMessage)                               /* process windows messages */
        {
                case WM_PAINT:
                        BeginPaint (hWnd, &ps) ;
                        if (bToggle)
                        {
                                SelectObject (ps.hdc,
                                        GetStockObject (LTGRAY_BRUSH)) ;
                                bToggle = FALSE ;
                        }
                        else
                        {
                                SelectObject (ps.hdc,
                                        GetStockObject (WHITE_BRUSH)) ;
                                bToggle = TRUE ;
                        }
                        Rectangle (ps.hdc, 0, 0, 500, 500) ;    /* paint area */
                        EndPaint (hWnd, &ps) ;
                        break ;
                case WM_COMMAND:                                /* process menu items */
                        switch (wParam)
                        {
                        case IDM_DOIT:                          /* User hit the "Do it" menu item */
                                ScrollWindow (hWnd, 0, 10, NULL, NULL) ;
                                hDC = GetDC (hWnd) ;
                                ExcludeUpdateRgn (hDC, hWnd) ;
                                SelectObject (hDC, GetStockObject (DKGRAY_BRUSH)) ;
                                Rectangle (hDC, 10, 0, 50, 60) ;
                                ReleaseDC (hWnd, hDC) ;
                                break ;
```

[Other program lines]

EXTFLOODFILL   □ Win 2.0 ■ Win 3.0 ■ Win 3.1

Purpose   Fills an area by replacing a color with the currently selected brush.

Syntax   BOOL **ExtFloodFill**(HDC *hDC*, int *X*, int *Y*, DWORD *crColor*, WORD *wFillType*);

Description This function is similar to FloodFill(). Both functions fill in an area with a color. ExtFloodFill() has the ability to fill in an area based on replacing one color with the currently selected brush of the device context.

Uses	Used in painting programs.
Returns	BOOL. TRUE if the function was successful, FALSE on error. FALSE will be returned if the point is outside the clipping region, falls on a point that has the border color, or falls on a point that does not have the color specified by *crColor* if the FLOODFILLSURFACE style is used. The painting expands from the selected point in all directions until either the boundary color is found (FLOODFILLBORDER style), or until no other touching areas containing the specified color are located (FLOODFILLSURFACE style).

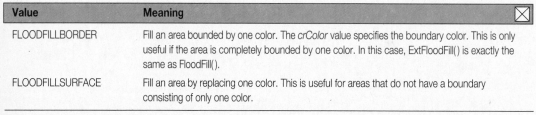

Figure 11-29. ExtFloodFill( ) Example.

See Also	FloodFill()
Parameters	
hDC	HDC: The device context handle.
X	int: The logical *X* coordinate to start the painting process.
Y	int: The logical *Y* coordinate to start the painting process.
crColor	COLORREF: The 32-bit color value specifying either the boundary color or the color of the area to replace.
wFillType	WORD: Specifies which type of filling operation is to be performed. It can be one of the types listed in Table 11-12.

Value	Meaning
FLOODFILLBORDER	Fill an area bounded by one color. The *crColor* value specifies the boundary color. This is only useful if the area is completely bounded by one color. In this case, ExtFloodFill( ) is exactly the same as FloodFill( ).
FLOODFILLSURFACE	Fill an area by replacing one color. This is useful for areas that do not have a boundary consisting of only one color.

Table 11-12. Flood Fill Types.

Example   This example paints a blue rectangle in the client area. When the user clicks the "Do It!" menu item, the square is filled with a solid red brush. (See Figure 11-29.)

```
long FAR PASCAL WndProc (HWND hWnd, unsigned iMessage, WORD wParam, LONG lParam)
{
        PAINTSTRUCT             ps ;
        HDC                     hDC ;
        HBRUSH                  hBrush ;

        switch (iMessage)                        /* process windows messages */
        {
                case WM_PAINT:
                        BeginPaint (hWnd, &ps) ;
                        hBrush = CreateSolidBrush (RGB (0, 0, 255)) ;
                        SelectObject (ps.hdc, hBrush) ;
                        Rectangle (ps.hdc, 10, 10, 50, 50) ;        /* paint area */
                        EndPaint (hWnd, &ps) ;
                        DeleteObject (hBrush) ;
                        break ;
                case WM_COMMAND:                                 /* process menu items */
                        switch (wParam)
                        {
                                case IDM_DOIT:                   /* User hit the "Do it" menu item */
                                        hDC = GetDC (hWnd) ;
                                        hBrush = CreateSolidBrush (RGB (255, 0, 0)) ;
                                        SelectObject (hDC, hBrush) ;
                                        ExtFloodFill (hDC, 20, 20, RGB (0, 0, 255),
                                                FLOODFILLSURFACE) ;
```

```
                          ReleaseDC (hWnd, hDC) ;
                          DeleteObject (hBrush) ;
                          break ;
```
[Other program lines]

FILLRECT

Purpose	Fills a rectangular area with a brush pattern and color.
Syntax	int **FillRect**(HDC *hDC*, LPRECT *lpRect*, HBRUSH *hBrush*);
Description	This function is similar to Rectangle(), except the borders of the rectangle are not drawn and the brush does not have to be selected into the device context before use.
Uses	Coloring rectangular areas.
Returns	int, not used.
See Also	Rectangle(), FillRgn()
Parameters	
hDC	HDC: The device context handle.
lpRect	LPRECT: A pointer to a RECT data structure that holds the dimensions of the rectangle to paint.
hBrush	HBRUSH: A handle to the brush to use in painting the rectangular area.
Example	The example shown in Figure 11-30 uses FillRect() to draw a square area without a border.

Figure 11-30. FillRect() Example.

```
long FAR PASCAL WndProc (HWND hWnd, unsigned iMessage, WORD wParam, LONG lParam)
{
        PAINTSTRUCT     ps ;
        RECT            rRect ;
        HBRUSH          hBrush ;

        switch (iMessage)                       /* process windows messages */
        {
                case WM_PAINT:
                        BeginPaint (hWnd, &ps) ;
                        hBrush = CreateHatchBrush (HS_DIAGCROSS,
                                RGB (0, 0, 255)) ;
                        SetRect (&rRect, 10, 10, 50, 50) ;
                        FillRect (ps.hdc, &rRect, hBrush) ;
                        EndPaint (hWnd, &ps) ;
                        DeleteObject (hBrush) ;
                        break ;
```
[Other program lines]

FILLRGN

Purpose	Fills a region with a brush color and pattern.
Syntax	BOOL **FillRgn**(HDC *hDC*, HRGN *hRgn*, HBRUSH *hBrush*);
Description	This is a powerful function for filling areas. Regions of any complexity can be created by combining smaller regions using CombineRgn(). Once constructed, these regions can be filled with any pattern or brush using FillRgn().
Uses	Filling areas with a color or pattern.
Returns	BOOL. TRUE if the region was filled, FALSE on error.
See Also	FillRect(), CombineRgn(), CreatePatternBrush(), CreateSolidBrush(), CreateHatchBrush()
Parameters	
hDC	HDC: The device context handle.
hRgn	HRGN: The region handle.

hBrush   HBRUSH: The handle of the brush to use in filling the region.

Example   The example in Figure 11-31 creates an elliptical region and fills it with a hatched brush.

```
Long FAR PASCAL WndProc (HWND hWnd, unsigned iMessage, WORD wParam, LONG lParam)
{
        PAINTSTRUCT     ps ;
        HRGN            hRgn ;
        RECT            rRect ;
        HBRUSH          hBrush ;

        switch (iMessage)                               /* process windows messages */
        {
                case WM_PAINT:
                        BeginPaint (hWnd, &ps) ;
                        hBrush = CreateHatchBrush (HS_DIAGCROSS,
                                RGB (0, 0, 255)) ;
                        SetRect (&rRect, 10, 10, 80, 60) ;
                        hRgn = CreateEllipticRgnIndirect (&rRect) ;
                        FillRgn (ps.hdc, hRgn, hBrush) ;
                        EndPaint (hWnd, &ps) ;
                        DeleteObject (hBrush) ;
                        DeleteObject (hRgn) ;
                        break ;
```

[Other program lines]

FLOODFILL   ■ Win 2.0   ■ Win 3.0   ■ Win 3.1

Purpose   Fills an area with the currently selected brush.

Syntax   BOOL **FloodFill**(HDC *hDC*, int *X*, int *Y*, DWORD *crColor*);

Description   FloodFill() demands that the area to be filled be bounded by one color. The area is filled with the currently selected brush, starting from *X,Y* and expanding in all directions until the *crColor* is encountered.

Uses   Used in painting applications for filling irregular shapes with color.

Returns   BOOL. TRUE if the area was filled, FALSE on error. An error will occur if *X,Y* specifies a point outside of the clipping region, or a point that has the same color as *crColor*.

See Also   ExtFloodFill()

Parameters

hDC   HDC: The device context handle.

X   int: The logical *X* coordinate to start the painting process.

Y   int: The logical *Y* coordinate to start the painting process.

crColor   COLORREF: The 32-bit color value of the boundary color. Use the RGB macro to specify a color.

Figure 11-31. FillRgn() Example.

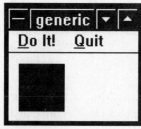

Figure 11-32. FloodFill() Example.

Figure 11-33. FrameRect() Example.

Example

The program illustrated in Figure 11-32 paints a blue rectangle in the client area. When the user clicks the "Do It!" menu item, the square is filled with red.

```
Long FAR PASCAL WndProc (HWND hWnd, unsigned iMessage, WORD wParam, LONG lParam)
{
        PAINTSTRUCT            ps ;
        HDC                    hDC ;
        HBRUSH                 hBrush ;
        HPEN                   hPen ;

        switch (iMessage)                          /* process windows messages */
                {
                case WM_PAINT:
                        BeginPaint (hWnd, &ps) ;
                        hBrush = CreateSolidBrush (RGB (0, 0, 255)) ;
                        SelectObject (ps.hdc, hBrush) ;
                        hPen = CreatePen (PS_SOLID, 2, RGB (0, 0, 0)) ;
                        SelectObject (ps.hdc, hPen) ;
                        Rectangle (ps.hdc, 10, 10, 50, 50) ;
                        EndPaint (hWnd, &ps) ;
                        DeleteObject (hPen) ;
                        DeleteObject (hBrush) ;
                        break ;
                case WM_COMMAND:          /* process menu items */
                        switch (wParam)
                        {
                        case IDM_DOIT:   /* User hit the "Do it" menu item */
                                hDC = GetDC (hWnd) ;
                                hBrush = CreateSolidBrush (RGB (255, 0, 0)) ;
                                SelectObject (hDC, hBrush) ;
                                FloodFill (hDC, 20, 20, RGB (0, 0, 0)) ;
                                ReleaseDC (hWnd, hDC) ;
                                DeleteObject (hBrush) ;
                                break ;
```

[Other program lines]

FRAMERECT

■ Win 2.0   ■ Win 3.0   ■ Win 3.1

Purpose	Draws a frame around a rectangle by using a brush.
Syntax	int **FrameRect**(HDC *hDC*, LPRECT *lpRect*, HBRUSH *hBrush*);
Description	This function draws a frame 1 pixel wide around a rectangle. The brush pattern is used to do the painting.
Uses	Not often used. Multiple calls to FrameRect() and InflateRect() can be used to create borders with a visible pattern (see the example).
Returns	int, not used.
See Also	FrameRgn()
Parameters	
hDC	HDC: The device context handle.
lpRect	LPRECT: A pointer to a RECT data structure that contains the dimensions of the rectangle to frame.
hBrush	HBRUSH: A handle to a brush to use in painting the border.
Example	This example, illustrated in Figure 11-33, creates an extended frame for a rectangle by repeatedly painting and then expanding the rectangle. This gets around FrameRect()'s limitation of only painting borders one pixel wide.

```
Long FAR PASCAL WndProc (HWND hWnd, unsigned iMessage, WORD wParam, LONG lParam)
{
        PAINTSTRUCT            ps ;
        RECT                   rRect ;
```

```
        HBRUSH                  hBrush ;
        int                     i ;

        switch (iMessage)                       /* process windows messages */
        {
                case WM_PAINT:
                        BeginPaint (hWnd, &ps) ;
                        hBrush = CreateHatchBrush (HS_DIAGCROSS,
                                RGB (0, 0, 255)) ;
                        SetRect (&rRect, 10, 10, 80, 60) ;
                        for (i = 0 ; i < 5 ; i++)
                        {
                                FrameRect (ps.hdc, &rRect, hBrush) ;
                                InflateRect (&rRect, 1, 1) ;
                        }
                        EndPaint (hWnd, &ps) ;
                        DeleteObject (hBrush) ;
                        break ;
```

[Other program lines]

FRAMERGN

■ Win 2.0   ■ Win 3.0   ■ Win 3.1

Purpose	Draws a frame around a region using a brush pattern.
Syntax	BOOL **FrameRgn**(HDC *hDC*, HRGN *hRgn*, HBRUSH *hBrush*, int *nWidth*, int *nHeight*);
Description	This function allows you to outline the border of a region using a brush pattern.
Uses	Used with FillRgn() to paint regions.
Returns	BOOL. TRUE if the region was painted, FALSE on error.
See Also	FillRgn(), CreateSolidBrush(), CreatePatternBrush(), CreateHatchBrush(), CombineRgn()

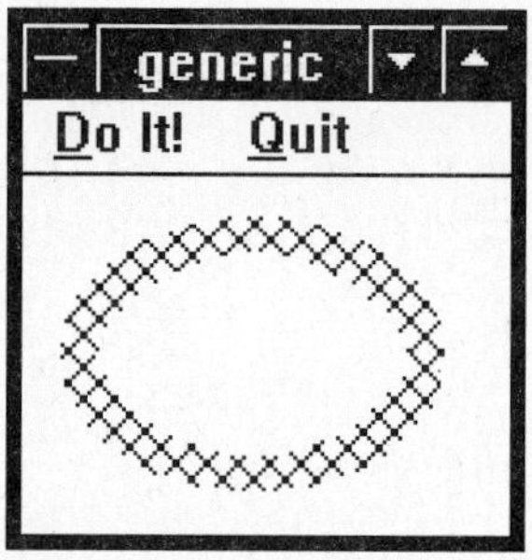

Figure 11-34. FrameRgn() Example.

Parameters

hDC	HDC: The device context handle.
hRgn	HANDLE: The handle of the region to be painted.
hBrush	HBRUSH: The handle of the brush to use in painting the border. Use CreateSolidBrush(), CreatePatternBrush(), etc to create this object.
nWidth	int: The width of the border in logical units.
nHeight	int: The height of the border in logical units.
Example	The example shown in Figure 11-34 frames an elliptical region using a hatched brush. The frame is set to a width of 8 pixels.

```
Long FAR PASCAL WndProc (HWND hWnd, unsigned iMessage, WORD wParam, LONG lParam)
{
        PAINTSTRUCT             ps ;
        HRGN                    hRgn ;
        RECT                    rRect ;
        HBRUSH                  hBrush ;

        switch (iMessage)                       /* process windows messages */
        {
                case WM_PAINT:
                        BeginPaint (hWnd, &ps) ;
                        hBrush = CreateHatchBrush (HS_DIAGCROSS,
                                RGB (0, 0, 255)) ;
                        SetRect (&rRect, 10, 10, 110, 80) ;
                        hRgn = CreateEllipticRgnIndirect (&rRect) ;
                        FrameRgn (ps.hdc, hRgn, hBrush, 8, 8) ;
                        EndPaint (hWnd, &ps) ;
```

```
        DeleteObject (hBrush) ;
        DeleteObject (hRgn) ;
        break ;
```

[Other program lines]

GetBrushOrg   ■ Win 2.0   ■ Win 3.0   ■ Win 3.1

Purpose	Finds the brush origin of a device context.
Syntax	DWORD **GetBrushOrg**(HDC *hDC*);

Description In order to smoothly match brush patterns, Windows maintains a logical origin as the basis for each brush painting. This origin can be moved using SetBrushOrg() and retrieved with GetBrushOrg(). The origin only affects brushes that are being created. Changing the origin after a brush has been created does not affect how the pattern is positioned, unless UnrealizeObject() is called first.

Uses Setting brush patterns so that they do not exactly overlap areas next to each other.

Returns DWORD. The low-order word contains the *X* coordinate. The high-order word contains the *Y* coordinate. Both use device coordinates.

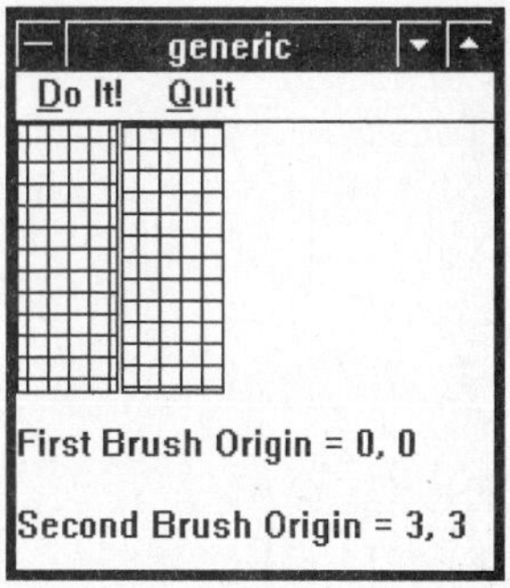

Figure 11-35. GetBrushOrg() and SetBrushOrg() Example.

See Also CreateHatchBrush(), SetBrushOrg(), UnrealizeObject()

Parameters

hDC HDC: The device context handle.

Example This example paints two rectangles with hatched brushes. The first brush is created with 0,0 as the brush origin. The second with 3,3 as the brush origin. This results in the two patterns being offset by three pixels. (See Figure 11-35.) This type of offset can be desirable when it is important to show a separation between two areas, such as to bars on a black and white bar chart.

```
Long FAR PASCAL WndProc (HWND hWnd, unsigned iMessage, WORD wParam, LONG lParam)
{
        PAINTSTRUCT             ps ;
        HBRUSH                  hBrush ;
        char                    cBuf [128] ;
        DWORD                   dwBrushOrg ;

        switch (iMessage)                       /* process windows messages */
        {
                case WM_PAINT:
                        BeginPaint (hWnd, &ps) ;
                        SetBrushOrg (ps.hdc, 0, 0) ;
                        hBrush = CreateHatchBrush (HS_CROSS, RGB (0, 0, 255)) ;
                        SelectObject (ps.hdc, hBrush) ;
                        Rectangle (ps.hdc, 0, 0, 40, 100) ;
                        dwBrushOrg = GetBrushOrg (ps.hdc) ;
                        TextOut (ps.hdc, 0, 110, cBuf, wsprintf (cBuf,
                                "First Brush Origin = %d, %d",
                                        LOWORD (dwBrushOrg), HIWORD (dwBrushOrg))) ;
                        SelectObject (ps.hdc, GetStockObject (WHITE_BRUSH)) ;
                        DeleteObject (hBrush) ;
                        SetBrushOrg (ps.hdc, 3, 3) ;
                        hBrush = CreateHatchBrush (HS_CROSS, RGB (0, 0, 255)) ;
                        SelectObject (ps.hdc, hBrush) ;
                        Rectangle (ps.hdc, 41, 0, 80, 100) ;
                        dwBrushOrg = GetBrushOrg (ps.hdc) ;
                        TextOut (ps.hdc, 0, 140, cBuf, wsprintf (cBuf,
                                "Second Brush Origin = %d, %d",
                                        LOWORD (dwBrushOrg), HIWORD (dwBrushOrg))) ;
```

```
                          EndPaint (hWnd, &ps) ;
                          DeleteObject (hBrush) ;
                          break ;
[Other program lines]
```

GetBValue - GetGValue - GetRValue
■ Win 2.0   ■ Win 3.0   ■ Win 3.1

Purpose	Retrieves a single color value from a 32-bit color value.
Syntax	BYTE **GetBValue**(DWORD *rgbColor*)
Description	Windows uses 32-bit values for colors. The 32-bit value consists of three bytes of information, corresponding to the intensity of the **B**lue, **G**reen, and **R**ed elements of color. Windows uses this color coding scheme even when the physical device can display only a limited number of colors. Missing colors are approximated on most video displays by mixing different colored pixels in the same area (dithering).
Uses	Retrieving an individual color value is frequently useful when creating matching colors.

Returns BYTE, the color value specified.

See Also RGB(), GetSysColor(), SetSysColors()

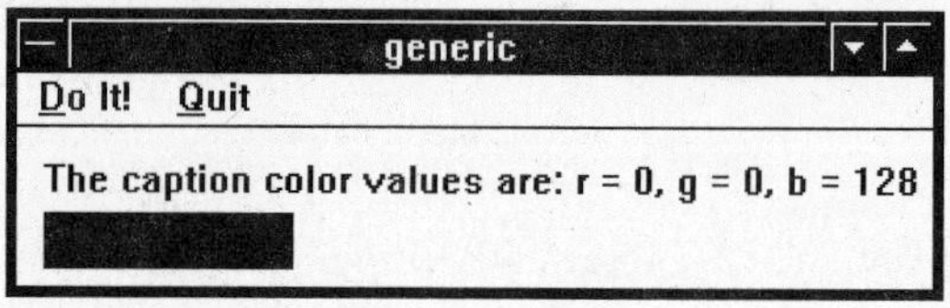

Figure 11-36. GetBValue( ), GetGValue( ), GetRValue( ) Example.

Parameters

rgbColor DWORD: The 32-bit color value.

Example The example (shown in Figure 11-36) displays the blue, green and red color values of the caption bar, and also uses the caption color to draw a small rectangle. In this example the caption color is the default focus color of medium blue.

```
Long FAR PASCAL WndProc (HWND hWnd, unsigned iMessage, WORD wParam, LONG lParam)
{
        PAINTSTRUCT             ps ;
        char                    cBuf [128] ;
        DWORD                   dwColor ;
        HBRUSH                  hBrush ;

        switch (iMessage)                               /* process windows messages */
        {
                case WM_PAINT:
                        BeginPaint (hWnd, &ps) ;
                        dwColor = GetSysColor (COLOR_ACTIVECAPTION) ;
                        TextOut (ps.hdc, 10, 10, cBuf, wsprintf (cBuf,
                        "The caption color values are: r = %d, g = %d, b = %d",
                                GetRValue (dwColor), GetGValue (dwColor),
                                GetBValue (dwColor))) ;
                        hBrush = CreateSolidBrush (dwColor) ;    /* same color */
                        SelectObject (ps.hdc, hBrush) ;
                        Rectangle (ps.hdc, 10, 30, 100, 50) ;
                        EndPaint (hWnd, &ps) ;
                        DeleteObject (hBrush) ;
                        break ;
[Other program lines]
```

GetClipBox
■ Win 2.0   ■ Win 3.0   ■ Win 3.1

Purpose	Gets the dimensions of the smallest rectangle that will enclose the clipping region.
Syntax	int **GetClipBox**(HDC *hDC*, LPRECT *lpRect*);
Description	Clipping regions can have any shape. This function determines the smallest rectangle that will fully enclose the clipping area.

Uses   Used when clipping regions are created. There is no need to call this function to find the update region when processing WM_PAINT messages, as the update rectangle is stored in the PAINTSTRUCTURE initialized by BeginPaint().

Returns   int, the type of clipping region. This can be any of the region types in Table 11-13.

Value	Meaning
COMPLEXREGION	The new region has overlapping borders.
ERROR	No new region was created.
NULLREGION	The new region is empty.
SIMPLEREGION	The new region does not have overlapping borders.

Table 11-13. Region Types.

Parameters

hDC   HDC: The device context handle.

lpRect   LPRECT: A pointer to the RECT data structure that will hold the dimensions of the bounding rectangle.

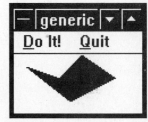

Figure 11-37. GetClipBox() Example.

Example   This example fills in an irregular clipping region with a gray brush. The dimensions of the bounding rectangle of the clipping region are retrieved with GetClipBox() before the area is painted. (See Figure 11-37.) This results in the smallest possible painting area to completely fill the clipping region when painted.

```
Long FAR PASCAL WndProc (HWND hWnd, unsigned iMessage, WORD wParam, LONG lParam)
{
        PAINTSTRUCT     ps ;
        HRGN            hRgn ;
        POINT           pArray [5] = {10, 10, 50, 40, 90, 20, 60, 0,
                                      40, 20} ;
        RECT            rRect ;

        switch (iMessage)                       /* process windows messages */
        {
                case WM_PAINT:
                        BeginPaint (hWnd, &ps) ;
                        hRgn = CreatePolygonRgn (pArray, 5, WINDING) ;
                        SelectClipRgn (ps.hdc, hRgn) ;
                        SelectObject (ps.hdc, GetStockObject (LTGRAY_BRUSH)) ;
                        GetClipBox (ps.hdc, &rRect) ;
                        Rectangle (ps.hdc, rRect.left, rRect.top, rRect.right,
                                rRect.bottom) ;                 /* paint gray */
                        EndPaint (hWnd, &ps) ;
                        DeleteObject (hRgn) ;
                        break ;
[Other program lines]
```

GETCURRENTPOSITION   ■ Win 2.0 ■ Win 3.0 ■ Win 3.1

Purpose   Determines the current logical position in a device context.

Syntax   DWORD **GetCurrentPosition**(HDC *hDC*);

Description   Windows keeps track of the location of a logical point set by calls to MoveTo() and LineTo() so that connected lines can be drawn by specifying only the next point. GetCurrentPosition() determines the current location, which will be the starting point for the next line drawn with LineTo().

Uses   Useful if the user can reposition a line end in a paint program using the mouse cursor.

Returns   DWORD, the current position in logical coordinates. The low-order word contains the *X* coordinate. The high-order word contains the *Y* coordinate.

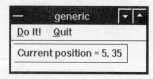

See Also   MoveTo(), LineTo(), MAKEPOINT()

Parameters

hDC   HDC: The device context handle.

Example   The example shown in Figure 11-38 draws a line with three segments, and then displays the current logical position. This is the position of the last call to MoveTo() or LineTo().

Figure 11-38. GetCurrent-Position( ) Example.

```
Long FAR PASCAL WndProc (HWND hWnd, unsigned iMessage, WORD wParam, LONG lParam)
{
        PAINTSTRUCT             ps ;
        DWORD                   dwCurPos ;
        POINT                   pCurPos ;
        char                    cBuf [128] ;

        switch (iMessage)                               /* process windows messages */
        {
                case WM_PAINT:
                        BeginPaint (hWnd, &ps) ;
                        MoveTo (ps.hdc, 5, 5) ;
                        LineTo (ps.hdc, 200, 5) ;
                        LineTo (ps.hdc, 200, 35) ;
                        LineTo (ps.hdc, 5, 35) ;
                        dwCurPos = GetCurrentPosition (ps.hdc) ;
                        pCurPos = MAKEPOINT (dwCurPos) ;
                        TextOut (ps.hdc, 10, 10, cBuf, wsprintf (cBuf,
                                "Current position = %d, %d", pCurPos.x, pCurPos.y)) ;
                        EndPaint (hWnd, &ps) ;
                        break ;
```
[Other program lines]

GETGVALUE (See the GetBValue description in this chapter.)   ■ Win 2.0   ■ Win 3.0   ■ Win 3.1

GETNEARESTCOLOR   ■ Win 2.0   ■ Win 3.0   ■ Win 3.1

Purpose   Determines the most approximate solid color a device can display.

Syntax   DWORD **GetNearestColor**(HDC *hDC*, DWORD *crColor*);

Description The 32-bit color values that Windows uses to specify display colors can generally encode more colors (256 * 256 * 256 combinations) than a physical device can display. Windows approximates colors that cannot be displayed as pure colors by dithering, a process of blending different colored pixels to achieve the desired average color when viewed at a distance. Get-NearestColor() allows the application to determine the nearest pure color that a device can display. In some cases, it may be desirable to use the nearest pure color instead of the dithered approximation.

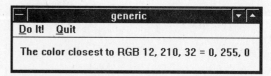

Figure 11-39. GetNearestColor( ) on a 16-Color VGA System.

Uses   The nearest pure color can be used to create solid colored borders, which avoids having FloodFill() color filling "leak" through the borders.

Returns   DWORD, the nearest 32-bit color value to *crColor* that the device can display.

See Also   GetNearestPaletteIndex(), RGB()

Parameters

hDC   HDC: The device context handle.

crColor   COLORREF: The 32-bit color value to check. Normally the RGB macro is used to specify this value.

Example   The example illustrated in Figure 11-39 shows how Windows matches a requested RGB color on a device with limited capabilities. In this case, a 16-color VGA card was in use. The requested color is displayed as a dithered area if used in creating a brush or pen. The nearest pure color the display can produce is pure green.

```
Long FAR PASCAL WndProc (HWND hWnd, unsigned iMessage, WORD wParam, LONG lParam)
{
        PAINTSTRUCT             ps ;
        DWORD                   dwColor ;
        char                    cBuf [128] ;

        switch (iMessage)                       /* process windows messages */
        {
                case WM_PAINT:
                        BeginPaint (hWnd, &ps) ;
                        dwColor = GetNearestColor (ps.hdc, RGB (12, 210, 32)) ;
                        TextOut (ps.hdc, 10, 10, cBuf, wsprintf (cBuf,
                                "The color closest to RGB 12, 210, 32 = %d, %d, %d",
                                GetRValue (dwColor), GetGValue (dwColor),
                                GetBValue (dwColor))) ;
                        EndPaint (hWnd, &ps) ;
                        break ;
```

[Other program lines]

GetObject
      ■ Win 2.0   ■ Win 3.0   ■ Win 3.1

Purpose   Retrieves information about a logical object.

Syntax   int **GetObject**(HANDLE *hObject*, int *nCount*, LPSTR *lpObject*);

Description   This function retrieves information about logical pens, brushes, fonts, bitmaps, and palettes. The information is stored in a data structure pointed to by *lpObject*. This can either be a LOGPEN, LOGBRUSH, LOGFONT, BITMAP, or LOGPALETTE data structure. These structures are defined in WINDOWS.H as follows:

```
typedef struct tagLOGPEN
  {
  WORD                  lopnStyle;
  POINT                 lopnWidth;
  DWORD                 lopnColor;
  } LOGPEN;

typedef struct tagLOGBRUSH
  {
  WORD                  lbStyle;
  DWORD                 lbColor;
  int                   lbHatch;
  } LOGBRUSH;

typedef struct tagLOGFONT
  {
  int           lfHeight;
  int           lfWidth;
  int           lfEscapement;
  int           lfOrientation;
  int           lfWeight;
  BYTE          lfItalic;
  BYTE          lfUnderline;
```

```
        BYTE            lfStrikeOut;
        BYTE            lfCharSet;
        BYTE            lfOutPrecision;
        BYTE            lfClipPrecision;
        BYTE            lfQuality;
        BYTE            lfPitchAndFamily;
        BYTE            lfFaceName[LF_FACESIZE];
     } LOGFONT;

typedef struct tagBITMAP
     {
        int             bmType;
        int             bmWidth;
        int             bmHeight;
        int             bmWidthBytes;
        BYTE            bmPlanes;
        BYTE            bmBitsPixel;
        LPSTR           bmBits;
     } BITMAP;

typedef struct tagLOGPALETTE {
        WORD            palVersion;
        WORD            palNumEntries;
        PALETTEENTRY    palPalEntry[1];
     } LOGPALETTE;
```

Uses   Commonly used to determine the size of bitmaps and the attributes of stock drawing objects.

Returns   int, the number of bytes retrieved. NULL on error.

See Also   GetStockObject()

Parameters

hObject   HANDLE: The pen, brush, font, bit-map, or palette handle.

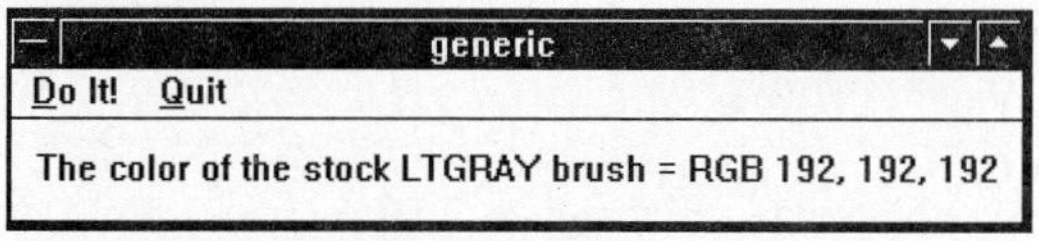

nCount   int: The number of bytes to retrieve. Use the sizeof() operator to specify this for each of the data structures involved (see the following example).

Figure 11-40. GetObject( ) Example.

lpObject   LPSTR: A pointer to the memory area that will contain the desired data. Be sure that this area is at least *nCount* bytes in size.

Example   In the example shown in Figure 11-40, the color of the stock LTGRAY brush is retrieved and displayed in the window's client area.

```
long FAR PASCAL WndProc (HWND hWnd, unsigned iMessage, WORD wParam, LONG lParam)
{
        PAINTSTRUCT         ps ;
        char                cBuf [128] ;
        HBRUSH              hBrush ;
        LOGBRUSH            lbBrush ;

        switch (iMessage)                         /* process windows messages */
        {
                case WM_PAINT:
                        BeginPaint (hWnd, &ps) ;
                        hBrush = GetStockObject (LTGRAY_BRUSH) ;
                        GetObject (hBrush, sizeof (LOGBRUSH), (LPSTR) &lbBrush) ;
                        TextOut (ps.hdc, 10, 10, cBuf, wsprintf (cBuf,
                        "The color of the stock LTGRAY brush = RGB %d, %d, %d",
                                GetRValue (lbBrush.lbColor),
                                GetGValue (lbBrush.lbColor),
                                GetBValue (lbBrush.lbColor))) ;
                        EndPaint (hWnd, &ps) ;
                        break ;
```
[Other program lines]

GetPixel
■ Win 2.0　■ Win 3.0　■ Win 3.1

Purpose	Determines the color of a pixel.
Syntax	DWORD **GetPixel**(HDC *hDC*, int *X*, int *Y*);
Description	This function determines the RGB color value of a point on the device context.
Uses	Used in painting programs to determine existing colors on the client area. Also used to determine if a point is within the clipping region.
Returns	DWORD, the 32-bit color value of the pixel. Returns −1 if the point is outside of the current clipping region.
See Also	SetPixel(), SelectClipRgn()

Parameters

hDC	HDC: The device context handle.
X	int: The logical coordinate of the *X* position to check.
Y	int: The logical coordinate of the *Y* position to check.
Example	This example shows a shaded rectangle being painted, one pixel at a time. The starting pixel color is first retrieved using GetPixel(). This color is then incremented and used to set the new color of the pixel with SetPixel(). This method of drawing is unacceptably slow.

```
long FAR PASCAL WndProc (HWND hWnd, unsigned iMessage, WORD wParam,  LONG lParam)
{
        PAINTSTRUCT             ps ;
        DWORD                   dwColor ;
        int                     nRed, nBlue, nGreen, i, j ;

        switch (iMessage)                       /* process windows messages */
        {
        case WM_PAINT:
                BeginPaint (hWnd, &ps) ;
                for (i = 0 ; i < 10 ; i++)
                {
                        for (j = 0 ; j < 256 ; j++)
                        {
                                dwColor = GetPixel (ps.hdc, j, i) ;
                                nRed = (GetRValue (dwColor) + j) % 256 ;
                                nBlue = (GetBValue (dwColor) + j) % 256 ;
                                nGreen = (GetGValue (dwColor) + j) % 256 ;
                                SetPixel (ps.hdc, j, i,
                                        RGB (nRed, nGreen, nBlue)) ;
                        }
                }
                EndPaint (hWnd, &ps) ;
                break ;
```
[Other program lines]

GetPolyFillMode
■ Win 2.0　■ Win 3.0　■ Win 3.1

Purpose	Determines the current polygon filling mode for a device context.
Syntax	int **GetPolyFillMode**(HDC *hDC*);
Description	The polygon filling mode determines how areas of intersection within the polygon are painted. This is only a factor if the lines defining the polygon intersect.
Uses	Used with SetPolyFillMode() to determine and change the filling mode.
Returns	int, the current polygon filling mode. This can be either mode listed in Table 11-14.

Value	Meaning	
ALTERNATE	The GDI fills in areas between sides 1&2, sides 3&4, etc.	
WINDING	The GDI fills in the complete area defined by the outermost lines. This will normally fill the entire interior of the polygon, except in cases where more than one intersection of areas defined by the polygon's lines occurs (see the example).	

Table 11-14. Polygon Filling Modes.

See Also   SetPolyFillMode(), CreatePolygonRgn()

Parameters
hDC   HDC: The device context handle.

Example   This example draws the same complex polygon twice, but with two different polygon filling modes. (See Figure 11-41.) More of the intersected areas are painted with the WINDING mode, but some areas will still be missed. Use clipping regions to assure that all internal areas inside complex areas are painted.

Figure 11-41. GetPoly-FillMode( ) and SetPolyFill-Mode( ) Example.

```
long FAR PASCAL WndProc (HWND hWnd, unsigned iMessage, WORD wParam, LONG lParam)
{
        PAINTSTRUCT          ps ;
        POINT                pArray [] = {10, 10, 50, 40, 90, 20, 5, 110,
                                                  60, 0, 80, 90, 0, 70, 110, 60} ;
        int                  i, nPolyMode ;

        switch (iMessage)                /* process windows messages */
        {
                case WM_PAINT:
                        BeginPaint (hWnd, &ps) ;
                        SelectObject (ps.hdc, GetStockObject (LTGRAY_BRUSH)) ;
                        Polygon (ps.hdc, pArray, 8) ;
                        for (i = 0 ; i < 8 ; i++)
                                pArray [i].x += 80 ;       /* offset polygon */

                        nPolyMode = GetPolyFillMode (ps.hdc) ;
                        if (nPolyMode == ALTERNATE)
                        {
                                TextOut (ps.hdc, 0, 120, "ALTERNATE", 9) ;
                                TextOut (ps.hdc, 100, 120, "WINDING", 7) ;
                                SetPolyFillMode (ps.hdc, WINDING) ;
                        }
                        else
                        {
                                TextOut (ps.hdc, 100, 120, "ALTERNATE", 9) ;
                                TextOut (ps.hdc, 0, 120, "WINDING", 7) ;
                                SetPolyFillMode (ps.hdc, ALTERNATE) ;
                        }
                        Polygon (ps.hdc, pArray, 8) ;
                        EndPaint (hWnd, &ps) ;
                        break ;
```

[Other program lines]

GetRgnBox
☐ Win 2.0   ■ Win 3.0   ■ Win 3.1

Purpose   Determines the bounding rectangle of a region.

Syntax   int **GetRgnBox**(HRGN *hRgn*, LPRECT *lpRect*);

Description Regions can have any arbitrary shape. This function calculates the minimum size rectangle that will fully enclose a region.

Uses	Handy for computing the minimum size rectangle to paint in order to entirely fill a region. Also handy for computing the rectangle size to invalidate in order to force painting of part of the window's client area.
Returns	int, the region's type. This can be any of the types listed in Table 11-15.

Value	Meaning
COMPLEXREGION	The region has overlapping borders.
ERROR	No new region was created.
NULLREGION	The region is empty.
SIMPLEREGION	The region does not have overlapping borders.

Table 11-15. Region Types.

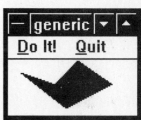

Returns NULL if *hRgn* is not a handle of a valid region.

See Also GetClipBox(), InvalidateRgn()

Parameters

hRgn HRGN: The region's handle.

lpRect LPRECT: A pointer to a RECT data structure that will hold the dimensions of the bounding rectangle.

Example The polygonal area shown in Figure 11-42 is painted by setting the region as a clipping area and painting the minimum sized rectangle that encloses the region with a gray brush.

Figure 11-42. GetRgnBox( ) Example.

```
long FAR PASCAL WndProc (HWND hWnd, unsigned iMessage, WORD wParam, LONG lParam)
{
        PAINTSTRUCT             ps ;
        HRGN                    hRgn ;
        POINT                   pArray [5] = {10, 10, 50, 40, 90, 20, 60, 0,
                                        40, 20} ;
        RECT                    rRect ;

        switch (iMessage)                           /* process windows messages */
        {
        case WM_PAINT:
                BeginPaint (hWnd, &ps) ;
                hRgn = CreatePolygonRgn (pArray, 5, WINDING) ;
                SelectClipRgn (ps.hdc, hRgn) ;
                SelectObject (ps.hdc, GetStockObject (LTGRAY_BRUSH)) ;
                GetRgnBox (hRgn, &rRect) ;
                Rectangle (ps.hdc, rRect.left, rRect.top, rRect.right,
                        rRect.bottom) ;                    /* paint area */
                EndPaint (hWnd, &ps) ;
                DeleteObject (hRgn) ;
                break ;
```

[Other program lines]

GetROP2
■ Win 2.0   ■ Win 3.0   ■ Win 3.1

Purpose	Determines the current raster drawing mode for a device context.
Syntax	int **GetROP2**(HDC *hDC*);
Description	The default R2_COPYPEN paints the pen color regardless of the underlying colors. With the other drawing modes, the pen is drawn on the device context after comparing the pen color to the existing color at each *X,Y* position being drawn. With color devices, each of the three primary colors is dealt with separately, using the same binary logic. The blue element of the pen color is compared to the blue element of the pixel, etc.

Uses   Only a few of the ROP2 operations are typically used. The common ones are R2_NOT, which makes the pen always visible, and R2_XORPEN, which makes the pen line disappear if the same line is drawn twice.

Returns   int, the current drawing mode. This value is one of the 16 values shown in Table 11-16. In the Boolean Operation column, the "P" stands for the pen color value, and the "D" stands for the display color value. For simplicity, the explanations are in terms of a black and white display. For color displays, the same logic is applied to each color element (red, blue, green).

Value	Boolean Operation	Comments
R2_BLACK	0	Always black.
R2_WHITE	1	Always white
R2_NOP	D	No affect on display.
R2_NOT	~D	Invert display under line.
R2_COPYPEN	P	Pen color painted regardless of display.
R2_NOTCOPYPEN	~P	Pen color inverted regardless of display.
R2_MERGEPENNOT	P | ~D	
R2_MASKPENNOT	P & ~D	
R2_MERGENOTPEN	~P | D	
R2_MASKNOTPEN	~P & D	
R2_MERGEPEN	P | D	
R2_NOTMERGEPEN	~(P | D)	
R2_MASKPEN	P & D	
R2_NOTMASKPEN	~(P & D)	
R2_XORPEN	P ^ D	A black pen inverts the device pixels. Drawing twice at the same location erases the line.
R2_NOTXORPEN	~ (P ^ D)	

Table 11-16. Raster Operation Codes.

See Also   The SetROP2() example shows all 16 modes contrasted on a black and white background.

Parameters
hDC   HDC: The device context handle.

Example   This example, as shown in Figure 11-43, paints the client area with a blue hatched brush. When the user clicks the "Do It!" menu item, the ROP drawing mode is checked. If the device context for the client area is not already set to the R2_XORPEN mode, that mode is selected and a line drawn diagonally. Repeatedly clicking the "Do It!" menu item draws and then erases the line, leaving the background intact.

Figure 11-43. GetROP2() Example.

```
long FAR PASCAL WndProc (HWND hWnd, unsigned iMessage, WORD wParam, LONG lParam)
{
        PAINTSTRUCT             ps ;
        HPEN                    hPen ;
        HBRUSH                  hBrush ;
        HDC                     hDC ;
```

```
        RECT                  rClient ;

    switch (iMessage)                /* process windows messages */
    {
        case WM_PAINT:
                BeginPaint (hWnd, &ps) ;
                SelectObject (ps.hdc, GetStockObject (BLACK_PEN)) ;
                hBrush = CreateHatchBrush (HS_CROSS, RGB (0, 0, 255)) ;
                SelectObject (ps.hdc, hBrush) ;  /* select blue brush */
                GetClientRect (hWnd, &rClient) ;
                Rectangle (ps.hdc, rClient.left, rClient.top,
                        rClient.right, rClient.bottom) ;
                EndPaint (hWnd, &ps) ;
                DeleteObject (hBrush) ;
                break ;
        case WM_COMMAND:                  /* process menu items */
                switch (wParam)
                {
                case IDM_DOIT:           /* User hit the "Do it" menu item */
                        hDC = GetDC (hWnd) ;
                        hPen = CreatePen (PS_SOLID, 4, RGB (255, 0, 0)) ;
                        SelectObject (hDC, hPen) ;
                        if (GetROP2 (hDC) != R2_XORPEN)
                                SetROP2 (hDC, R2_XORPEN) ;
                        MoveTo (hDC, 0, 0) ;
                        LineTo (hDC, 100, 100) ;
                        ReleaseDC (hWnd, hDC) ;
                        DeleteObject (hPen) ;
                        break ;
```

[Other program lines]

GETRVALUE (See the GetBValue section in this chapter.)   ■ Win 2.0   ■ Win 3.0   ■ Win 3.1

GETSTOCKOBJECT   ■ Win 2.0   ■ Win 3.0   ■ Win 3.1

Purpose	Retrieves a handle to one of the predefined objects that are always available to Windows applications.
Syntax	HANDLE **GetStockObject**(int *nIndex*);
Description	Windows maintains a small set of stock drawing objects, which can be used without creating the object by just retrieving a handle to the stock object with GetStockObject(). The default objects are the BLACK_PEN, WHITE_BRUSH, and SYSTEM_FONT.
Uses	Using stock objects saves time and memory.
Returns	HANDLE, the object handle. NULL on error.
See Also	GetSysColor(), GetSystemMetrics(), SelectObject()
Parameters	
nIndex	int: An index to one of the stock objects, which can be any of the values listed in Table 11-17.

Value	Meaning	⊠
BLACK_BRUSH	A solid black brush.	
DKGRAY_BRUSH	A dark gray brush.	
GRAY_BRUSH	A gray brush.	
HOLLOW_BRUSH	No painting is done inside of an object, such as a rectangle, if this style is chosen. Handy for creating borders.	
LTGRAY_BRUSH	A light gray brush.	
NULL_BRUSH	Same as HOLLOW_BRUSH.	

Table 11-17. continued

Value	Meaning	
WHITE_BRUSH	A white brush. This paints solid white, instead of not painting the interior with a HOLLOW_BRUSH. This is the default brush.	
BLACK_PEN	A single pixel wide black pen. This is the default pen.	
NULL_PEN	No pen drawing is done. This is a way to eliminate borders drawn with objects such as rectangles.	
WHITE_PEN	A white pen one pixel wide.	
ANSI_FIXED_FONT	ANSI fixed pitch font.	
ANSI_VAR_FONT	ANSI variable pitch font.	
DEVICE_DEFAULT_FONT	The default font for a device. This is important for some printers that have a built-in font that is faster than graphics fonts.	
OEM_FIXED_FONT	A device supplied font.	
SYSTEM_FONT	The system font. This is the default font used by Windows for captions and menus.	
SYSTEM_FIXED_FONT	The old Windows 2.0 fixed font.	
DEFAULT_PALETTE	The default color palette.	

Table 11-17. Stock Objects.

Cautions   Do not attempt to delete stock objects. Be sure the CS_HRE-DRAW and CS_VREDRAW class styles are specified in the window's class definition before using stock brushes. Stock brush origins cannot be changed (see SetBrushOrg() for details on brush origins).

Example   This example, shown in Figure 11-44, uses three stock objects to paint the client area: a stock pen, a stock brush, and a stock font. All of them are selected into the client area device context. The text color is changed to equal the window caption color. The transparent drawing mode is also selected.

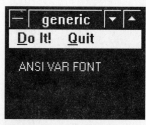

Figure 11-44. GetStock-Object() Example.

```
long FAR PASCAL WndProc (HWND hWnd, unsigned iMessage, WORD wParam, LONG lParam)
{
        PAINTSTRUCT             ps ;
        RECT                    rClient ;

        switch (iMessage)                               /* process windows messages */
        {
            case WM_PAINT:
                    BeginPaint (hWnd, &ps) ;
                    SelectObject (ps.hdc, GetStockObject (BLACK_PEN)) ;
                    SelectObject (ps.hdc, GetStockObject (LTGRAY_BRUSH)) ;
                    SelectObject (ps.hdc, GetStockObject (ANSI_VAR_FONT)) ;
                    SetTextColor (ps.hdc, GetSysColor (COLOR_CAPTIONTEXT)) ;
                    SetBkMode (ps.hdc, TRANSPARENT) ;
                    GetClientRect (hWnd, &rClient) ;
                    Rectangle (ps.hdc, rClient.left, rClient.top,
                            rClient.right, rClient.bottom) ;
                    TextOut (ps.hdc, 10, 10, "ANSI VAR FONT", 13) ;
                    EndPaint (hWnd, &ps) ;
                    break ;
```

[Other program lines]

GetSysColor

Purpose	Retrieves one of the system colors.
Syntax	DWORD **GetSysColor**(int *nIndex*);
Description	The system colors are the colors of the objects Windows paints, such as window caption bars, scroll bars and the desktop surface. These colors can be modified by the user using the Windows Control Panel application. The system colors are shared by all applications running on the system.

Uses The system colors are frequently good choices for use in painting a window's client area. Their choice assures that the colors are consistent with the way the user has set up his or her color choices.

Returns DWORD, the 32-bit color value extracted.

See Also SetSysColors()

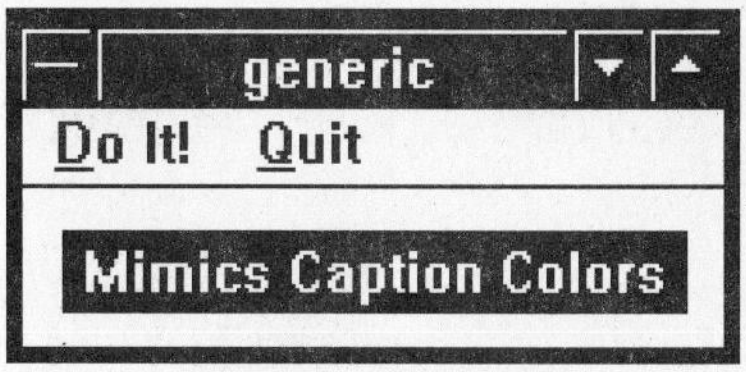

Figure 11-45. GetSysColor( ) Example.

Parameters

nIndex int: One of the values in Table 11-18.

Value	Meaning
COLOR_ACTIVEBORDER	The active window border.
COLOR_ACTIVECAPTION	The active window caption.
COLOR_APPWORKSPACE	The background color for MDI (multiple document interface) applications.
COLOR_BACKGROUND	The desktop (background on which all programs and icons are painted).
COLOR_BTNFACE	Button face color.
COLOR_BTNSHADOW	Button edge color.
COLOR_BTNTEXT	Button text color.
COLOR_CAPTIONTEXT	The caption text color.
COLOR_GRAYTEXT	Grayed (disabled) menu item text color. The returned color is set to zero if the display does not support a solid gray color.
COLOR_HIGHLIGHT	Selected item color in a control.
COLOR_HIGHLIGHTTEXT	Text color in a selected control.
COLOR_INACTIVEBORDER	Color of an inactive window border.
COLOR_INACTIVECAPTION	Color of an inactive window caption.
COLOR_MENU	The menu background color.
COLOR_MENUTEXT	The menu text color.
COLOR_SCROLLBAR	The scroll-bar gray area.
COLOR_WINDOW	The window background color.
COLOR_WINDOWFRAME	The window frame color.
COLOR_WINDOWTEXT	The color of text in a window.

Table 11-18. System Colors.

Example This program, illustrated in Figure 11-45, writes text in a colored rectangle. The rectangle brush color and the text color are both set to match that of the caption, assuring that the color combination will have visible letters. Note how GetTextExtent() is used to size the rectangle to match the length of the text string.

```
long FAR PASCAL WndProc (HWND hWnd, unsigned iMessage, WORD wParam, LONG lParam)
{
        PAINTSTRUCT             ps ;
        char                    cBuf [] = {"Mimics Caption Colors"} ;
        DWORD                   dwColor ;
        HBRUSH                  hBrush ;

        switch (iMessage)                       /* process windows messages */
        {
                case WM_PAINT:
                        BeginPaint (hWnd, &ps) ;
                        dwColor = GetSysColor (COLOR_ACTIVECAPTION) ;
                        hBrush = CreateSolidBrush (dwColor) ;     /* same color */
                        SelectObject (ps.hdc, hBrush) ;
                        Rectangle (ps.hdc, 10, 10,
                                20 + (int) GetTextExtent (ps.hdc, cBuf,
                                        strlen (cBuf)), 30) ;
                        SetTextColor (ps.hdc, GetSysColor (COLOR_CAPTIONTEXT)) ;
                        SetBkMode (ps.hdc, TRANSPARENT) ;
                        TextOut (ps.hdc, 15, 12, cBuf, strlen (cBuf)) ;
                        EndPaint (hWnd, &ps) ;
                        DeleteObject (hBrush) ;
                        break ;
```

[Other program lines]

GetUpdateRect ■ Win 2.0　■ Win 3.0　■ Win 3.1

Purpose	Retrieves the dimensions of the invalid rectangle in the window's client area.
Syntax	BOOL **GetUpdateRect**(HWND *hWnd*, LPRECT *lpRect*, BOOL *bErase*);
Description	The invalid rectangle is the area that will be painted the next time a WM_PAINT message is processed.
Uses	This function is used outside of the WM_PAINT message processing logic of the program. Within the WM_PAINT logic, the PAINTSTRUCT data structure filled by BeginPaint() provides the dimensions of the update rectangle. (BeginPaint()validates the update region, so GetUpdateRect() will always return an empty rectangle if used after BeginPaint()). The usual reason for retrieving the update region is to validate it, so that Windows does not paint the region. This technique can be useful if a number of separated graphics operations are to be performed. The entire painting operation can be done at the end by invalidating the client area with InvalidateRect().

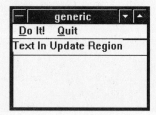

Figure 11-46. GetUpdate-Rect() Example.

Returns	BOOL. TRUE if the update rectangle is not empty, FALSE if it is empty, meaning that none of the client area is invalid.
See Also	ValidateRect(), GetUpdateRgn(), ValidateRgn(), BeginPaint()
Parameters	
hWnd	HWND: The window's handle.
lpRect	LPRECT: A pointer to a RECT data structure that will hold the invalid rectangle dimensions. If the window was created with the CS_OWNDC style, the units are logical coordinates. Otherwise, the units are device coordinates.
bErase	BOOL: Set to TRUE to erase the background of the invalid rectangle, FALSE to not erase the background. Erase the background by sending a WM_ERASEBKGND message.

Related Messages   WM_PAINT, WM_ERASEBKGND

Example   This example, illustrated in Figure 11-46, scrolls the window down and paints text in the update region at the top of the client area when the user clicks the "Do It!" menu item. Scrolling adds the exposed region to the update region, which would normally mean that the text would be painted over immediately by the next processing of a WM_PAINT message. However, the update rectangle is retrieved and validated. This keeps Windows from sending a WM_PAINT message, so the text remains visible.

```
long FAR PASCAL WndProc (HWND hWnd, unsigned iMessage, WORD wParam, LONG lParam)
{
        HDC             hDC ;
        RECT            rUpdate ;

        switch (iMessage)       /* process windows messages */
        {
                case WM_COMMAND:        /* process menu items */
                        switch (wParam)
                        {
                        case IDM_DOIT:  /* User hit the "Do it" menu item */
                                ScrollWindow (hWnd, 0, 20, NULL, NULL) ;
                                hDC = GetDC (hWnd) ;
                                TextOut (hDC, 0, 0, "Text In Update Region", 21) ;
                                GetUpdateRect (hWnd, &rUpdate, FALSE) ;
                                ValidateRect (hWnd, &rUpdate) ;
                                ReleaseDC (hWnd, hDC) ;
                                break ;
```
[Other program lines]

GETUPDATERGN   ■ Win 2.0   ■ Win 3.0   ■ Win 3.1

Purpose   Copies the update region of a window's client area to *hRgn*.

Syntax   int **GetUpdateRgn**(HWND *hWnd*, HRGN *hRgn*, BOOL *bErase*);

Description   This function is similar to GetUpdateRect(), except the invalid area of the window's client area is passed as a region instead of a rectangle. Invalid parts of the client area are caused by scrolling, resizing, or uncovering parts of the window that were under other windows or dialog boxes.

Uses   The update region can be passed to ValidateRgn() to avoid having the region repainted. This only works outside of the WM_PAINT logic section of the program, as BeginPaint() automatically validates the client area in preparation for repainting.

Returns   int, the type of region returned. This can be any of the region types listed in Table 11-19.

Value	Meaning	⊠
COMPLEXREGION	The region has overlapping borders.	
ERROR	No region was created.	
NULLREGION	The region is empty.	
SIMPLEREGION	The region does not have overlapping borders.	

Table 11-19. Region Types.

See Also   ValidateRgn(), GetUpdateRect(), ValidateRect()

Parameters

hWnd   HWND: The window handle.

hRgn   HRGN: The handle of the region that will hold the update region. The region must exist prior to calling GetUpdateRgn(). Use CreateRectRgn() to create a region prior to calling this function (see the example).

bErase	BOOL: TRUE if the background should be erased, FALSE if not.
Related Messages	WM_PAINT

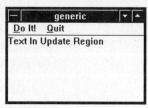

Example   This example, which is shown in Figure 11-47, scrolls the client area down, and then writes in the client area when the user clicks the "Do It!" menu item. Normally, the text would be erased immediately by repainting the invalidated region, which was uncovered by scrolling. In this case, the invalid region is validated before a WM_PAINT message is generated, which keeps the text from being erased.

Figure 11-47. GetUpdate-Rgn( ) and ValidateRgn( ) Example.

```
long FAR PASCAL WndProc (HWND hWnd, unsigned iMessage, WORD wParam, LONG lParam)
{
        HDC             hDC ;
        HRGN            hRgn ;

        switch (iMessage)               /* process windows messages */
        {
                case WM_COMMAND:        /* process menu items */
                        switch (wParam)
                        {
                        case IDM_DOIT:  /* User hit the "Do it" menu item */
                                ScrollWindow (hWnd, 0, 20, NULL, NULL) ;
                                hDC = GetDC (hWnd) ;
                                TextOut (hDC, 0, 0, "Text In Update Region", 21) ;
                                hRgn = CreateRectRgn (0, 0, 1, 1) ; /* initialize */
                                GetUpdateRgn (hWnd, hRgn, FALSE) ;
                                ValidateRgn (hWnd, hRgn) ;
                                ReleaseDC (hWnd, hDC) ;
                                break ;
```

[Other program lines]

INFLATERECT   ■ Win 2.0   ■ Win 3.0   ■ Win 3.1

Purpose	Increases or decreases the size of a rectangle.
Syntax	void **InflateRect**(LPRECT *lpRect*, int *X*, int *Y*);
Description	Rectangles are used not only as drawing objects, but also to define the borders of ellipses, chords, arcs, etc. InflateRect() allows expansion or contraction of a rectangle in a single function call.

Uses	A fairly common need in graphics programs is to create a border containing multiple lines. InflateRect() allows consistent changes to the dimensions of a rectangle without needing to deal with each of the rectangle's four elements.
Returns	No returned value (void).
See Also	SetRect(), Rectangle()
Parameters	
lpRect	LPRECT: A pointer to a RECT data structure that holds the rectangle that is to have its size changed.

Figure 11-48. InflateRect( ) Example.

X	int: The amount to change the horizontal size. Positive values increase, negative values decrease. The size is changed by this amount on both the left and right sides.
Y	int: The amount to change the vertical size. Positive values increase, negative values decrease. The size is changed by this amount on both the top and bottom dimensions.
Example	As shown in Figure 11-48, five concentric rectangles are drawn by repeatedly calling Inflate-Rect() to enlarge the rectangle. Note that the stock object NULL_BRUSH is used for the rectangle filling brush to avoid painting over the internal rectangles.

```
Long FAR PASCAL WndProc (HWND hWnd, unsigned iMessage, WORD wParam, LONG lParam)
{
        PAINTSTRUCT             ps ;
        RECT                    rRect ;
        int                     i ;

        switch (iMessage)                               /* process windows messages */
        {
        case WM_PAINT:
                BeginPaint (hWnd, &ps) ;
                SelectObject (ps.hdc, GetStockObject (NULL_BRUSH)) ;
                SelectObject (ps.hdc, GetStockObject (BLACK_PEN)) ;
                SetRect (&rRect, 30, 30, 90, 90) ;
                for (i = 0 ; i < 5 ; i++)
                {
                        Rectangle (ps.hdc, rRect.left, rRect.top,
                                rRect.right, rRect.bottom) ;
                        InflateRect (&rRect, 4, 4) ;
                }
                EndPaint (hWnd, &ps) ;
                break ;
```
[Other program lines]

INTERSECTCLIPRECT   ■ Win 2.0   ■ Win 3.0   ■ Win 3.1

Purpose	Creates a new clipping region by combining the existing rectangle and a rectangular region. Only the overlapping region common to the two areas remains within the clipping region.
Syntax	int **IntersectClipRect**(HDC *hDC*, int *X1*, int *Y1*, int *X2*, int *Y2*);
Description	This is identical to using CombineRgn() with the RGN_AND clipping style, with one of the regions being rectangular. Limiting a clipping region to a rectangular portion of the client area is such a common need, that this specialized function is provided.
Uses	Restricting painting to a rectangular area on the screen, in addition to the restrictions of the existing clipping region.
Returns	int, the result of the function. This can be any of the region types in Table 11-20.

Value	Meaning	⊠
COMPLEXREGION	The new region has overlapping borders.	
ERROR	No new region was created.	
NULLREGION	The new region is empty.	
SIMPLEREGION	The new region does not have overlapping borders.	

Table 11-20. Region Types.

See Also	CombineRgn(), CreateRectRgn()

Parameters

hDC	HDC: The device context handle.
X1	int: The logical *X* coordinate of the upper left corner of the bounding rectangle.
Y1	int: The logical *Y* coordinate of the upper left corner of the bounding rectangle.
X2	int: The logical *X* coordinate of the lower right corner of the bounding rectangle.
Y2	int: The logical *Y* coordinate of the lower right corner of the bounding rectangle.

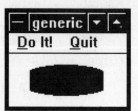

Figure 11-49. Intersect-ClipRect( ) Example.

Example   The example, which is shown in Figure 11-49, creates a clipping region from the intersection of an elliptical region and a slightly smaller rectangle. A larger area is painted with a gray brush, but only the area within the clipping region is painted.

```
Long FAR PASCAL WndProc (HWND hWnd, unsigned iMessage, WORD wParam, LONG lParam)
{
        PAINTSTRUCT          ps ;
        HRGN                 hRgn ;

        switch (iMessage)                         /* process windows messages */
        {
                case WM_PAINT:
                        BeginPaint (hWnd, &ps) ;
                        hRgn = CreateEllipticRgn (10, 10, 100, 40) ;
                        SelectClipRgn (ps.hdc, hRgn) ;
                        IntersectClipRect (ps.hdc, 20, 10, 90, 40) ;
                        SelectObject (ps.hdc, GetStockObject (LTGRAY_BRUSH)) ;
                        Rectangle (ps.hdc, 5, 5, 500, 500) ;
                        EndPaint (hWnd, &ps) ;
                        DeleteObject (hRgn) ;
                        break ;
[Other program lines]
```

INTERSECTRECT   ■ Win 2.0   ■ Win 3.0   ■ Win 3.1

Purpose	Computes the rectangle of intersection of two other rectangles.
Syntax	int **IntersectRect**(LPRECT *lpDestRect*, LPRECT *lpSrc1Rect*, LPRECT *lpSrc2Rect*);
Description	When two rectangles overlap, the area of overlap is always rectangular. IntersectRect() computes the rectangle of the overlap area.
Uses	Useful for clipping rectangles, and for shading.
Returns	int. TRUE if there is an area of intersection, FALSE if the two rectangles do not overlap.
See Also	CombineRgn()

Parameters

lpDestRect   LPRECT: A pointer to the RECT data structure that will hold the dimensions of the rectangle of overlap. If there is no overlap, the rectangle will be empty (all zeros).

Figure 11-50. IntersectRect( ) Example.

lpSrc1Rect   LPRECT: A pointer to a RECT data structure holding the dimensions of a source rectangle.

lpSrc2Rect   LPRECT: A pointer to a RECT data structure holding the dimensions of the second source rectangle.

Example   This example creates a third rectangle from the intersection of two others. The third rectangle is painted with a hatched brush, as shown in Figure 11-50.

```
long FAR PASCAL WndProc (HWND hWnd, unsigned iMessage, WORD wParam, LONG lParam)
{
        PAINTSTRUCT             ps ;
        RECT                    r1, r2, r3 ;
        HBRUSH                  hBrush ;

        switch (iMessage)                       /* process windows messages */
        {
                case WM_PAINT:
                        BeginPaint (hWnd, &ps) ;
                        SetRect (&r1, 10, 10, 70, 80) ;
                        SetRect (&r2, 50, 50, 100, 100) ;
                        IntersectRect (&r3, &r1, &r2) ;
                        SelectObject (ps.hdc, GetStockObject (GRAY_BRUSH)) ;
                        SelectObject (ps.hdc, GetStockObject (BLACK_PEN)) ;
                        Rectangle (ps.hdc, r1.left, r1.top, r1.right,
                                r1.bottom) ;
                        Rectangle (ps.hdc, r2.left, r2.top, r2.right,
                                r2.bottom) ;
                        hBrush = CreateHatchBrush (HS_DIAGCROSS,
                                RGB (0, 0, 255)) ;
                        SelectObject (ps.hdc, hBrush) ;
                        Rectangle (ps.hdc, r3.left, r3.top, r3.right.
                                r3.bottom);
                        EndPaint (hWnd, &ps) ;
                        DeleteObject (hBrush) ;
                        break ;
```

[Other program lines]

INVALIDATERECT   ■ Win 2.0   ■ Win 3.0   ■ Win 3.1

Purpose   Adds a rectangular area to a window's update region, so that it is repainted on the next WM_PAINT cycle.

Syntax   void **InvalidateRect**(HWND *hWnd*, LPRECT *lpRect*, BOOL *bErase*) ;

Description   Invalidating a rectangular region forces Windows to send a WM_PAINT message to the application. The invalidated area is the only part painted.

Uses   Frequently used to force a repainting of the entire client area. Also useful in programs which have "smart" WM_PAINT processing logic, which only repaints areas that are invalid. Invalidating all or part of the client area is a quick way to activate the painting logic from another part of the program.

Returns   No returned value (void).

See Also   InvalidateRgn(). UpdateWindow() can be used to force an immediate WM_PAINT message, rather than waiting for the message to be processed via the system message queue.

Parameters
hWnd   HWND: The window handle.

lpRect	LPRECT: A pointer to a RECT data structure containing the dimensions of the rectangle to invalidate. Set to NULL to invalidate the entire client area.
bErase	BOOL: TRUE if the background should be erased during repainting, FALSE if not. This becomes the *fErase* element of the PAINTSTRUCT data structure filled by BeginPaint().

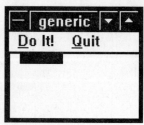

Figure 11-51. Invalidate-Rect() Example.

Related Messages WM_PAINT

Example This example shows graphically, see Figure 11-51, that only the update region gets painted when a WM_PAINT message is processed. When the user clicks the "Do It!" menu item, a rectangular region at the top left of the client area is invalidated, forcing a WM_PAINT message. The logic for handling WM_PAINT messages alternately paints a large area gray or white. Only the update rectangle ends up painted.

```
Long FAR PASCAL WndProc (HWND hWnd, unsigned iMessage, WORD wParam, LONG lParam)
{
        PAINTSTRUCT             ps ;
        HDC                     hDC ;
        static          BOOL    bToggle = FALSE ;
        RECT                    rUpdate ;


        HRGN                    hRgn ;

        switch (iMessage)                               /* process windows messages */
        {
                case WM_PAINT:
                        BeginPaint (hWnd, &ps) ;
                        if (bToggle)
                        {
                                SelectObject (ps.hdc,
                                        GetStockObject (LTGRAY_BRUSH)) ;
                                bToggle = FALSE ;
                        }
                        else
                        {
                                SelectObject (ps.hdc,
                                        GetStockObject (WHITE_BRUSH)) ;
                                bToggle = TRUE ;
                        }
                        Rectangle (ps.hdc, 0, 0, 500, 500) ;
                        EndPaint (hWnd, &ps) ;
                        break ;
                case WM_COMMAND:        /* process menu items */
                        switch (wParam)
                        {
                        case IDM_DOIT:          /* User hit the "Do it" menu item */
                                hRgn = CreateRectRgn (0, 30, 50, 60) ;
                                InvalidateRgn (hWnd, hRgn, TRUE) ;
                                DeleteObject (hRgn) ;
                                break ;
```

[Other program lines]

INVALIDATERGN ■ Win 2.0   ■ Win 3.0   ■ Win 3.1

Purpose	Adds a region to a window's update region, so that it is repainted on the next WM_PAINT cycle.
Syntax	void **InvalidateRgn**(HWND *hWnd*, HRGN *hRgn*, BOOL *bErase*);
Description	Invalidating a rectangular region forces Windows to send a WM_PAINT message to the application. The invalidated area is the only part painted.
Uses	Similar to InvalidateRect(), except that a region is used to pass the dimensions of the invalid area rather than a rectangle. Regions can be of any arbitrary shape and complexity. When the

WM_PAINT message is processed, the invalid area will be the smallest rectangle that encompasses the region.

Returns	No returned value (void).
See Also	ValidateRgn(), InvalidateRect()
Parameters	
hWnd	HWND: The window handle.
hRgn	HRGN: The handle of the region to pass as the invalid part of the client area.
bErase	BOOL: TRUE if the background should be erased during repainting, FALSE if not. This becomes the *fErase* element of the PAINTSTRUCT data structure filled by BeginPaint().
Related Messages	WM_PAINT
Example	When the user clicks the "Do It!" menu item, a small rectangular region is invalidated on the client area. Windows, therefore, sends a WM_PAINT message to the application's message queue. The WM_PAINT logic is set to paint a large area alternately gray or white, switching each time the message is received. Only the invalidated area is ultimately painted.

```
Long FAR PASCAL WndProc (HWND hWnd, unsigned iMessage, WORD wParam, LONG lParam)
{
        PAINTSTRUCT             ps ;
        HDC                     hDC ;
        static          BOOL    bToggle = FALSE ;
                                Rectangle (ps.hdc, r3.left, r3.top, r3.right,
                                    r3.bottom) ;
                        EndPaint (hWnd, &ps) ;
                        DeleteObject (hBrush) ;
                        break ;
```
[Other program lines]

INVERTRECT   ■ Win 2.0   ■ Win 3.0   ■ Win 3.1

Purpose	Inverts the color of every pixel within a rectangular area.
Syntax	void **InvertRect**(HDC *hDC*, LPRECT *lpRect*);
Description	The colors are inverted by applying a logical NOT operation to each RGB element of each pixel within the rectangle. For example, white becomes black and black becomes white. This inversion makes the rectangle visible over the background, including colored backgrounds. Inverting a second time restores the area.

Uses	Inverting an area is a way to show a mouse selection.
Returns	No returned value (void).
See Also	InvertRgn()
Parameters	
hDC	HDC: The device context handle
lpRect	LPRECT: A pointer to a RECT data structure containing the dimensions of the rectangle to invert, in logical coordinates.
Example	When the user clicks the "Do It!" menu item, a rectangular region is inverted, as shown in Figure 11-52. Clicking a second time restores the client area to its previous state.

Figure 11-52. InvertRect() Example.

```
Long FAR PASCAL WndProc (HWND hWnd, unsigned iMessage, WORD wParam, LONG lParam)
{
        PAINTSTRUCT             ps ;
        HDC                     hDC ;
        RECT                    rClient, rInv ;
        HBRUSH                  hBrush ;

        switch (iMessage)                       /* process windows messages */
```

```
        {
                case WM_PAINT:
                        BeginPaint (hWnd, &ps) ;
                        hBrush = CreateHatchBrush (HS_DIAGCROSS, RGB (0, 0, 0)) ;
                        SelectObject (ps.hdc, hBrush) ;
                        GetClientRect (hWnd, &rClient) ;
                        Rectangle (ps.hdc, rClient.left, rClient.top,
                                rClient.right, rClient.bottom) ;
                        EndPaint (hWnd, &ps) ;
                        DeleteObject (hBrush) ;
                        break ;
                case WM_COMMAND:                /* process menu items */
                        switch (wParam)
                        {
                        case IDM_DOIT:          /* User hit the "Do it" menu item */
                                hDC = GetDC (hWnd) ;
                                SetRect (&rInv, 20, 20, 70, 50) ;
                                InvertRect (hDC, &rInv) ;
                                ReleaseDC (hWnd, hDC) ;
                                break ;
```

[Other program lines]

INVERTRGN   ■ Win 2.0   ■ Win 3.0   ■ Win 3.1

Purpose   Inverts the color of every pixel within a region.

Syntax   BOOL **InvertRgn**(HDC *hDC*, HRGN *hRgn*);

Description   The colors are inverted by applying a logical NOT operation to each RGB element of each pixel within the region. For example, white becomes black and black becomes white. This inversion makes the region visible over the background, including colored backgrounds. Inverting a second time restores the area.

Uses   Makes a region visible on the screen in a way that is easy to undo.

Returns   BOOL. TRUE if the region was inverted, FALSE on error.

See Also   InvertRect()

Parameters
hDC   HDC: The device context handle.

hRgn   HRGN: The handle of the region to be inverted.

Figure 11-53. InvertRgn() Example.

Example   The example shown in Figure 11-53 inverts an elliptical region when the user clicks the "Do It!" menu item. Clicking the menu item a second time restores the client area.

```
Long FAR PASCAL WndProc (HWND hWnd, unsigned iMessage, WORD wParam, LONG lParam)
{
        PAINTSTRUCT             ps ;
        HDC                     hDC ;
        RECT                    rClient ;
        HRGN                    hRgn ;
        HBRUSH                  hBrush ;

        switch (iMessage)                       /* process windows messages */
        {
                case WM_PAINT:
                        BeginPaint (hWnd, &ps) ;
                        hBrush = CreateHatchBrush (HS_DIAGCROSS, RGB (0, 0, 0)) ;
                        SelectObject (ps.hdc, hBrush) ;
                        GetClientRect (hWnd, &rClient) ;
                        Rectangle (ps.hdc, rClient.left, rClient.top,
                                rClient.right, rClient.bottom) ;
                        EndPaint (hWnd, &ps) ;
                        DeleteObject (hBrush) ;
                        break ;
                case WM_COMMAND:                /* process menu items */
```

```
            switch (wParam)
            {
            case IDM_DOIT:              /* User hit the "Do it" menu item */
                    hDC = GetDC (hWnd) ;
                    hRgn = CreateEllipticRgn (20, 30, 80, 50) ;
                    InvertRgn (hDC, hRgn) ;
                    ReleaseDC (hWnd, hDC) ;
                    DeleteObject (hRgn) ;
                    break ;
```

[Other program lines]

IsRectEmpty
■ Win 2.0　■ Win 3.0　■ Win 3.1

Purpose	Determines if a rectangle has a height or width of zero.
Syntax	BOOL **IsRectEmpty**(LPRECT *lpRect*);
Description	A rectangle is empty if either the height or the width is zero.
Uses	Useful in determining if the intersection of two rectangles defines a rectangle (if they overlap), or if the current update rectangle is empty.
Returns	BOOL. TRUE if the rectangle is empty, FALSE if not.
See Also	GetUpdateRect(), IntersectRect()
Parameters	
lpRect	LPRECT: A pointer to a RECT data structure.
Example	Each time the "Do It!" menu item is clicked, an elliptical region is drawn on the screen, decreasing in size with each repetition. When either dimension of the rectangle defining the elliptical region becomes zero, the size is reset back to the initial state. (See Figure 11-54.)

Figure 11-54. IsRect-Empty( ) Example.

```
Long FAR PASCAL WndProc (HWND hWnd, unsigned iMessage, WORD wParam, LONG lParam)
{
        HDC             hDC ;
        static RECT     rRect ;
        static int      nSize ;
        HRGN            hRgn ;

        switch (iMessage)                       /* process windows messages */
        {
        case WM_CREATE:
                nSize = 50 ;
                SetRect (&rRect, 10, 10, 10 + nSize, 10 + nSize * 2) ;
                break ;
        case WM_COMMAND:                /* process menu items */
                switch (wParam)
                {
                case IDM_DOIT:                  /* User hit the "Do it" menu item */
                        InvalidateRect (hWnd, NULL, TRUE) ;
                        UpdateWindow (hWnd) ;           /* erase client area */
                        hDC = GetDC (hWnd) ;
                        hRgn = CreateEllipticRgnIndirect (&rRect) ;
                        FillRgn (hDC, hRgn, GetStockObject (BLACK_BRUSH)) ;
                        ReleaseDC (hWnd, hDC) ;
                        DeleteObject (hRgn) ;

                        nSize -= 10 ;           /* shrink rectangle */
                        SetRect (&rRect, 10, 10, 10 + nSize,
                                10 + nSize * 2) ;
                        if (IsRectEmpty (&rRect))
                        {
                                nSize = 50 ;
                                SetRect (&rRect, 10, 10, 10 + nSize,
```

```
                                            10 + nSize * 2) ;
                          }
                          break ;
```

[Other program lines]

LINEDDA
■ Win 2.0　■ Win 3.0　■ Win 3.1

Purpose　　　　Draws a line with a custom drawing procedure.

Syntax　　　　void **LineDDA**(int *X1*, int *Y1*, int *X2*, int *Y2*, FARPROC *lpLineFunc*, LPSTR *lpData*);

Description　　LineDDA() calls a user-defined callback function for every point on a line between *X1,Y1* and *X2,Y2*. The callback function can perform any calculation for each of these points. Normally, the calculation is performed to define the color of each point on the line.

Uses　　　　　Custom line styles.

Returns　　　No returned value.

See Also　　MoveTo(), LineTo()

Parameters

X1　　　　　　int: The starting *X* position in logical coordinates.

Y1　　　　　　int: The starting *Y* position in logical coordinates.

X2　　　　　　int: The ending *X* position in logical coordinates.

Y2　　　　　　int: The ending *Y* position in logical coordinates.

lpLineFunc　　FARPROC: A procedure-instance address for the callback function. This value is obtained with MakeProcInstance(). The callback function name must also be listed in the EXPORTS section of the program's .DEF definition file.

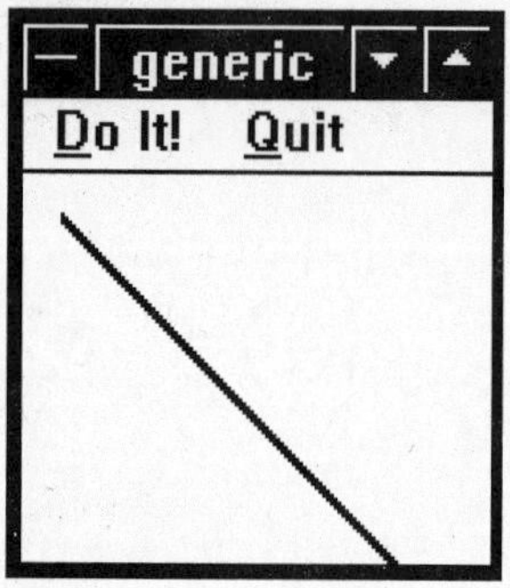

Figure 11-55. LineDDA() Example.

lpData　　　　LPSTR: A pointer to any data that should be passed to the callback function. This pointer is usually used to pass the device context handle.

Callback Function

The callback function must be defined in the following format:

void FAR PASCAL **LineFunc** (int *X*, int *Y*, LPSTR *lpData*) ;

The callback function is called for every point on the line each time the *X* and *Y* position on the line and the *lpData* value are passed to the callback function. No line is drawn unless points are drawn from within the callback function.

Example　　　This program draws a line when the user clicks the "Do It!" menu item, as shown in Figure 11-55. The line is drawn with a custom DDA function that changes the color of the line as a function of the coordinates of each point. Although not visible in the figure, this line changes from blue to brown from top left to bottom right when it is viewed on screen.

　　　　　　　The example code only shows the WndProc() and DDA functions. In addition, the program must include a function declaration in the header file, and list the "LineProc" function name in the EXPORTS section of the .DEF definition file.

```
Long FAR PASCAL WndProc (HWND hWnd, unsigned iMessage, WORD wParam, LONG lParam)
{
        HDC             hDC ;
        FARPROC         lpfnLine ;

        switch (iMessage)                       /* process windows messages */
        {
                case WM_COMMAND:                /* process menu items */
                        switch (wParam)
                        {
                        case IDM_DOIT:                      /* User hit the "Do it" menu item */
                                InvalidateRect (hWnd, NULL, TRUE) ;
                                UpdateWindow (hWnd) ;           /* erase client area */
                                hDC = GetDC (hWnd) ;
```

```
                              lpfnLine = MakeProcInstance (LineProc, ghInstance) ;
                              LineDDA (10, 10, 150, 150, lpfnLine,
                                      (LPSTR) (DWORD) hDC) ;
                              FreeProcInstance (lpfnLine) ;
                              ReleaseDC (hWnd, hDC) ;
                              break ;
                   case IDM_QUIT:
                              DestroyWindow (hWnd) ;
                              break ;
                   }
                   break ;
         case WM_DESTROY:/* stop application */
                   PostQuitMessage (0) ;
                   break ;
         default:                        /* default windows message processing */
                   return DefWindowProc (hWnd, iMessage, wParam, lParam) ;
      }
      return (0L) ;
}

/* callback function */

void FAR PASCAL LineProc (int X, int Y, LPSTR lpData)
{
      SetPixel ((HANDLE) (DWORD) lpData, X, Y,
            RGB (X % 255, Y % 255, (X + Y) % 255)) ;
      SetPixel ((HANDLE) (DWORD) lpData, X, Y + 1,
            RGB (X % 255, Y % 255, (X + Y) % 255)) ;
      SetPixel ((HANDLE) (DWORD) lpData, X, Y + 2,
            RGB (X % 255, Y % 255, (X + Y) % 255)) ;
}
```

LINETO   ■ Win 2.0   ■ Win 3.0   ■ Win 3.1

Purpose	Draws a line from the current location to a new point.
Syntax	BOOL **LineTo**(HDC *hDC*, int *X*, int *Y*);
Description	Used with MoveTo() to draw lines. MoveTo() moves the starting point for the next line to a new location without drawing. LineTo() draws a line to *X,Y* using the currently selected pen.
Uses	LineTo() is convenient when a series of connected lines are to be drawn. Windows does not provide a single function for drawing isolated lines such as *Line (hDC, X1, Y1, X2, Y2)*. You can create such a function by combining MoveTo() and LineTo(). See the example under MoveTo().
Returns	BOOL. TRUE if the line was drawn, FALSE on error.
See Also	MoveTo(), GetCurrentPosition(), CreatePen(), SelectObject(), Polyline()

Figure 11-56. LineTo()
Example.

Parameters

hDC   HDC: The device context handle.

X   int: The logical *X* coordinate for the end of the line. The start of the line is either the end position from the last LineTo() call or the position obtained by calling MoveTo().

Y   int: The logical *Y* coordinate for the end of the line.

Example   This example paints two connected blue lines in the client area, as shown in Figure 11-56.

```
long FAR PASCAL WndProc (HWND hWnd, unsigned iMessage, WORD wParam, LONG lParam)
{
      PAINTSTRUCT        ps ;
      HPEN               hPen ;

      switch (iMessage)                         /* process windows messages */
      {
```

```
        case WM_PAINT:
                BeginPaint (hWnd, &ps) ;
                hPen = CreatePen (PS_DASHDOT, 2, RGB (0, 0, 255)) ;
                SelectObject (ps.hdc, hPen) ;
                MoveTo (ps.hdc, 10, 100) ;
                LineTo (ps.hdc, 40, 10) ;
                LineTo (ps.hdc, 70, 100) ;
                EndPaint (hWnd, &ps) ;
                DeleteObject (hPen) ;
                break ;
```

[Other program lines]

MAKEPOINT
■ Win 2.0   ■ Win 3.0   ■ Win 3.1

Purpose   Converts from a DWORD value to a POINT structure.

Syntax   POINT **MAKEPOINT**(DWORD *dwInteger*);

Description Windows functions frequently encode position values in 32-bit DWORDs. MAKEPOINT() is a macro that converts from the DWORD format to a POINT structure. The macro and point structure are defined in WINDOWS.H as follows:

```
#define MAKEPOINT(l)         (*((POINT FAR *)&(l)))

typedef struct tagPOINT
  {
    int  x;
    int  y;
  } POINT;
typedef POINT          *PPOINT;
typedef POINT NEAR     *NPPOINT;
typedef POINT FAR      *LPPOINT;
```

Uses   The point structure is simpler to work with if you need to extract either the *X* or *Y* value separately.

Returns   A pointer to a POINT data structure.

See Also   MoveTo(), LineTo(), MAKEPOINT()

Parameters

dwInteger   DWORD: A 32-bit value with the low-order word containing the *X* coordinate value, and the high-order word containing the *Y* coordinate value.

Example   See the example under the GetCurrentPosition() function description.

MOVETO
■ Win 2.0   ■ Win 3.0   ■ Win 3.1

Purpose   Moves the current position to a new location, ready to draw a line.

Syntax   DWORD **MoveTo**(HDC *hDC*, int *X*, int *Y*);

Description Used with LineTo() to draw lines. MoveTo() moves the starting point for the next line to a new location without drawing. LineTo() draws a line to *X,Y* using the currently selected pen.

Uses   In order to position the start of the next line, MoveTo() is used before line drawing begins. The following example shows the creation of a typical line drawing function that combines MoveTo() and LineTo.

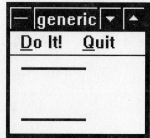

Returns   DWORD, the previous logical position. The low-order word contains the *X* position. The high-order word contains the *Y* position.

See Also   LineTo(), CreatePen(), SelectObject(), Polyline()

Parameters

hDC   HDC: The device context handle.

X   int: The logical *X* coordinate.

Figure 11-57. MoveTo()
Example.

Y	int: The logical *Y* coordinate.
Example	This example, which is illustrated in Figure 11-57, creates a a function called Line() that draws lines using the currently selected pen and allows both the starting point and ending point of the line to be specified in one function call. The function is called twice to draw two blue lines on the client area.

The header file must also include the function declaration for the Line() function.

```
long FAR PASCAL WndProc (HWND hWnd, unsigned iMessage, WORD wParam, LONG lParam)
{
        PAINTSTRUCT             ps ;
        HPEN                    hPen ;

        switch (iMessage)                       /* process windows messages */
        {
                case WM_PAINT:
                        BeginPaint (hWnd, &ps) ;
                        hPen = CreatePen (PS_DASHDOT, 2, RGB (0, 0, 255)) ;
                        SelectObject (ps.hdc, hPen) ;
                        Line (ps.hdc, 10, 10, 60, 10) ;
                        Line (ps.hdc, 10, 50, 60, 50) ;
                        EndPaint (hWnd, &ps) ;
                        DeleteObject (hPen) ;
                        break ;
                case WM_COMMAND:                /* process menu items */
                        switch (wParam)
                        {
                        case IDM_QUIT:          /* send end of application message */
                                DestroyWindow (hWnd) ;
                                break ;
                        }
                        break ;
                case WM_DESTROY:                /* stop application */
                        PostQuitMessage (0) ;
                        break ;
                default:                        /* default windows message processing */
                        return DefWindowProc (hWnd, iMessage, wParam, lParam) ;
        }
        return (0L) ;
}
void Line (HDC hDC, int X1, int Y1, int X2, int Y2)
{
        MoveTo (hDC, X1, Y1) ;
        LineTo (hDC, X2, Y2) ;
}
```

OFFSETCLIPRGN   ■ Win 2.0   ■ Win 3.0   ■ Win 3.1

Purpose	Moves the clipping region.
Syntax	int **OffsetClipRgn**(HDC *hDC*, int *X*, int *Y*);
Description	The clipping region limits the area on the device that will be painted by GDI function calls, such as LineTo() and Rectangle(). OffsetClipRgn() allows an existing clipping region to be moved to a new location on the device context.
Uses	Useful in scrolling operations with graphics images.
Returns	int, the type of region created. This can be any of the region types in Table 11-21.

Value	Meaning	⊠
COMPLEXREGION	The new region has overlapping borders.	
ERROR	No new region was created.	
NULLREGION	The new region is empty.	
SIMPLEREGION	The new region does not have overlapping borders.	

Table 11-21. Region Types.

See Also	SelectClipRgn()

Parameters

hDC HDC: The device context handle.

X int: The amount to offset the region in the *X* direction, measured in logical units.

Y int: The amount to offset the region in the *Y* direction, measured in logical units.

Example This example creates a rectangular clipping region, as shown in Figure 11-59. The clipping region limits the area that is painted when the Rectangle() function is called. OffsetClip-Rgn() is used to move the clipping region down and to the

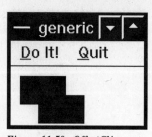

Figure 11-59. OffsetClip-Rgn() Example.

right. The second call to Rectangle() is limited by this new, repositioned clipping region.

```
Long FAR PASCAL WndProc (HWND hWnd, unsigned iMessage, WORD wParam, LONG lParam)
{
        PAINTSTRUCT             ps ;
        HRGN                    hRgn ;

        switch (iMessage)                       /* process windows messages */
        {
                case WM_PAINT:
                        BeginPaint (hWnd, &ps) ;
                        hRgn = CreateRectRgn (10, 10, 60, 40) ;
                        SelectClipRgn (ps.hdc, hRgn) ;
                        SelectObject (ps.hdc, GetStockObject (BLACK_BRUSH)) ;
                        Rectangle (ps.hdc, 5, 5, 500, 500) ;
                        OffsetClipRgn (ps.hdc, 20, 20) ;
                        Rectangle (ps.hdc, 5, 5, 500, 500) ;
                        EndPaint (hWnd, &ps) ;
                        DeleteObject (hRgn) ;
                        break ;
```
[Other program lines]

OFFSETRECT

■ Win 2.0   ■ Win 3.0   ■ Win 3.1

Purpose	Shifts a rectangle in the *X* and *Y* directions.
Syntax	void **OffsetRect**(LPRECT *lpRect*, int *X*, int *Y*);
Description	This is a convenient function for changing the location of a rectangle without changing its size. InflateRect() changes the size without changing the location.
Uses	Frequently used in creating clipping regions.
Returns	No returned value (void).
See Also	SelectClipRgn(), CreateRectRgn(), CreateEllipticRgn(), InflateRect()

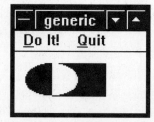

Figure 11-60. OffsetRect() Example.

Parameters

lpRect LPRECT: A pointer to a RECT data structure holding the dimensions of the rectangle to offset.

X int: The amount to offset the rectangle's position horizontally.

Y int: The amount to offset the rectangle's position vertically.

Example In the example shown in Figure 11-60, a complex region is created by combining two regions using the logical RGN_XOR operation. The two regions are both based on the same rectangular size. In the first case, an elliptical region *hRgn1* is made from the rectangle's dimensions. A second rectangle is created by copying the first, and then offsetting the rectangle's coordinates to the right 25 logical units. The two regions are combined using CombineRgn(), and then used as the clipping region. Only the areas within the clipping region are painted when a large, gray rectangle is drawn.

```
long FAR PASCAL WndProc (HWND hWnd, unsigned iMessage, WORD wParam, LONG lParam)
{
        PAINTSTRUCT             ps ;
        HRGN                    hRgn1, hRgn2, hRgnComb ;
        RECT                    rRect1, rRect2 ;

        switch (iMessage)                        /* process windows messages */
        {
                case WM_PAINT:
                        BeginPaint (hWnd, &ps) ;
                        SetRect (&rRect1, 10, 10, 60, 40) ;
                        CopyRect (&rRect2, &rRect1) ;
                        OffsetRect (&rRect2, 25, 0) ;
                        hRgn1 = CreateEllipticRgnIndirect (&rRect1) ;
                        hRgn2 = CreateRectRgnIndirect (&rRect2) ;
                        hRgnComb = CreateRectRgn (1, 1, 2, 2) ;/* initialize */
                        CombineRgn (hRgnComb, hRgn1, hRgn2, RGN_XOR) ;
                        DeleteObject (hRgn1) ;
                        DeleteObject (hRgn2) ;

                        SelectClipRgn (ps.hdc, hRgnComb) ;
                        SelectObject (ps.hdc, GetStockObject (LTGRAY_BRUSH)) ;
                        Rectangle (ps.hdc, 5, 5, 500, 500) ;
                        EndPaint (hWnd, &ps) ;
                        DeleteObject (hRgnComb) ;
                        break ;
```

[Other program lines]

OffsetRgn   ■ Win 2.0   ■ Win 3.0   ■ Win 3.1

Purpose	Moves a region.
Syntax	int **OffsetRgn**(HRGN *hRgn*, int *X*, int *Y*);
Description	This is identical to OffsetRect(), except a region is offset instead of a rectangle.
Uses	Used in creating clipping regions composed of similar shaped objects at different locations.
Returns	int, the type of region created. This can be any of the region types listed in Table 11-22.

Value	Meaning
COMPLEXREGION	The new region has overlapping borders.
ERROR	No new region was created.
NULLREGION	The new region is empty.
SIMPLEREGION	The new region does not have overlapping borders.

Table 11-22. Region Types.

See Also	CreateEllipticRgn(), CreateRectRgn(), CombineRgn()

Parameters

hRgn	HRGN: The handle of the region to offset.
X	int: The amount to offset the region's position horizontally.
Y	int: The amount to offset the region's position vertically.
Example	This example creates a complex clipping region by combining two elliptical regions using the logical RGN_XOR operation. (See Figure 11-61.) The second region is created by copying the first, and then offsetting it to the right by 25 logical units.

Figure 11-61. OffsetRgn() Example.

```
long FAR PASCAL WndProc (HWND hWnd, unsigned iMessage, WORD wParam, LONG lParam)
{
        PAINTSTRUCT             ps ;
```

```
        HRGN                        hRgn1, hRgn2, hRgnComb ;
        RECT                        rRect ;

        switch (iMessage)                       /* process windows messages */
        {
                case WM_PAINT:
                        BeginPaint (hWnd, &ps) ;
                        SetRect (&rRect, 10, 10, 60, 40) ;
                        hRgn1 = CreateEllipticRgnIndirect (&rRect) ;
                        hRgn2 = CreateRectRgn (1, 1, 2, 2) ;       /* initialize */
                        CombineRgn (hRgn2, hRgn1, NULL, RGN_COPY) ;        /* copy */
                        OffsetRgn (hRgn2, 25, 0) ;        /* move rgn 2 to right */
                        hRgnComb = CreateRectRgn (1, 1, 2, 2) ;/* initialize */
                        CombineRgn (hRgnComb, hRgn1, hRgn2, RGN_XOR) ;
                        DeleteObject (hRgn1) ;
                        DeleteObject (hRgn2) ;

                        SelectClipRgn (ps.hdc, hRgnComb) ;
                        SelectObject (ps.hdc, GetStockObject (LTGRAY_BRUSH)) ;
                        Rectangle (ps.hdc, 5, 5, 500, 500) ;
                        EndPaint (hWnd, &ps) ;
                        DeleteObject (hRgnComb) ;
                        break ;
```

[Other program lines]

PaintRgn
■ Win 2.0   ■ Win 3.0   ■ Win 3.1

Purpose	Paints a region with the currently selected brush.
Syntax	BOOL **PaintRgn**(HDC *hDC*, HRGN *hRgn*);
Description	This function is similar to FillRgn(), except the currently selected brush of the device context is used to paint the region, rather than specifying the brush handle in the function call.
Uses	Painting irregular areas.
Returns	BOOL. TRUE if the region is painted, FALSE on error.
See Also	FillRgn()
Parameters	
hDC	HDC: The device context handle. The currently selected brush of the device context is used to paint the region.
hRgn	HRGN: The region to paint.
Example	This example creates a region by combining two elliptical regions. The region is then painted with a hatched brush, as shown in Figure 11-62.

Figure 11-62. PaintRgn() Example.

```
long FAR PASCAL WndProc (HWND hWnd, unsigned iMessage, WORD wParam, LONG lParam)
{
        PAINTSTRUCT                 ps ;
        HRGN                        hRgn1, hRgn2, hRgnComb ;
        HBRUSH                      hBrush ;

        switch (iMessage)                       /* process windows messages */
        {
                case WM_PAINT:
                        BeginPaint (hWnd, &ps) ;
                        hRgn1 = CreateEllipticRgn (10, 40, 90, 70) ;
                        hRgn2 = CreateEllipticRgn (40, 0, 70, 100) ;
                        hRgnComb = CreateRectRgn (1, 1, 2, 2) ;/* initialize */
                        CombineRgn (hRgnComb, hRgn1, hRgn2, RGN_OR) ;
                        DeleteObject (hRgn1) ;
                        DeleteObject (hRgn2) ;

                        SelectClipRgn (ps.hdc, hRgnComb) ;
                        hBrush = CreateHatchBrush (HS_DIAGCROSS,
                                RGB (0, 0, 255)) ;
                        SelectObject (ps.hdc, hBrush) ;
```

```
                    PaintRgn (ps.hdc, hRgnComb) ;
                    EndPaint (hWnd, &ps) ;
                    DeleteObject (hBrush) ;
                    DeleteObject (hRgnComb) ;
                    break ;
```

[Other program lines]

PIE

■ Win 2.0   ■ Win 3.0   ■ Win 3.1

Purpose	Draws a pie-shaped wedge.
Syntax	BOOL **Pie**(HDC *hDC*, int *X1*, int *Y1*, int *X2*, int *Y2*, int *X3*, int *Y3*, int *X4*, int *Y4*);
Description	The pie-shaped wedge is drawn with the currently selected pen and filled with the currently selected brush. The outer circle of the pie is defined by the bounding rectangle of an ellipse. The starting and ending points are defined by lines from points *X3,Y3* and *X4,Y4*, to the center to the bounding rectangle. The height and width must be smaller than 32,767 logical units.
Uses	Making pie charts.
Returns	BOOL. TRUE if the shape was drawn, FALSE on error.
See Also	Chord(), Arc()

Figure 11-63. Pie( ) Example.

Parameters

hDC	HDC: The device context handle.
X1	int: The logical *X* coordinate of the upper left corner of the bounding rectangle.
Y1	int: The logical *Y* coordinate of the upper left corner of the bounding rectangle.
X2	int: The logical *X* coordinate of the lower right corner of the bounding rectangle.
Y2	int: The logical *Y* coordinate of the lower right corner of the bounding rectangle.
X3	int: The logical *X* coordinate of the starting point of the pie slice.
Y3	int: The logical *Y* coordinate of the starting point of the pie slice.
X4	int: The logical *X* coordinate of the ending point of the pie slice.
Y4	int: The logical *Y* coordinate of the ending point of the slice.

Example   This example, which is shown in Figure 11-63, paints a pie-shaped slice with the Pie() function. In addition, the bounding rectangle is painted, and the locations of the four points that define the pie are numbered.

```
Long FAR PASCAL WndProc (HWND hWnd, unsigned iMessage, WORD wParam, LONG lParam)
{
        PAINTSTRUCT             ps ;
        HBRUSH                  hBrush ;
        HPEN                    hPen ;

        switch (iMessage)                       /* process windows messages */
        {
                case WM_PAINT:
                        BeginPaint (hWnd, &ps) ;
                        hBrush = CreateHatchBrush (HS_DIAGCROSS,
                                RGB (0, 0, 255)) ;
                        SelectObject (ps.hdc, hBrush) ;
                        hPen = CreatePen (PS_SOLID, 3, RGB (255, 0, 0)) ;
                        SelectObject (ps.hdc, hPen) ;
                        SetBkMode (ps.hdc, TRANSPARENT) ;
                        Pie (ps.hdc, 10, 10, 100, 100, 0, 70, 70, 0) ;
                        TextOut (ps.hdc, 10, 10, "1", 1) ;
                        TextOut (ps.hdc, 100, 100, "2", 1) ;
                        TextOut (ps.hdc, 0, 70, "3", 1) ;
```

```
                    TextOut (ps.hdc, 70, 0, "4", 1) ;
                    SelectObject (ps.hdc, GetStockObject (NULL_BRUSH)) ;
                    SelectObject (ps.hdc, GetStockObject (BLACK_PEN)) ;
                    DeleteObject (hBrush) ;
                    DeleteObject (hPen) ;
                    Rectangle (ps.hdc, 10, 10, 100, 100) ;
                    EndPaint (hWnd, &ps) ;
                    break ;
```

[Other program lines]

POLYGON   ■ Win 2.0   ■ Win 3.0   ■ Win 3.1

Purpose	Draws a polygon.
Syntax	BOOL **Polygon**(HDC *hDC*, LPPOINT *lpPoints*, int *nCount*);
Description	A polygon is a closed figure composed of three or more straight lines. The polygon is drawn on the device context using the currently selected pen and brush and the current polygon filling mode.
Uses	Creating complex drawings.
Returns	BOOL. TRUE if the function drew the polygon, FALSE on error.
See Also	PolyPolygon(), SelectObject(), DeleteObject(), SetPolyFillMode()

Parameters

hDC HDC: The device context handle.

lpPoints LPPOINT: A pointer to an array of *nCount* or more points that will define the polygon. If the first and last points do not coincide, the function will draw a line between them to close the polygon. The polygon lines may cross, creating a complex polygon. See SetPolyFillMode() to define how these objects are filled.

nCount int: The number of points in the *lpPoints* array to read.

Example In this example, shown in Figure 11-64, a polygon is drawn using a pen created with CreatePenIndirect().

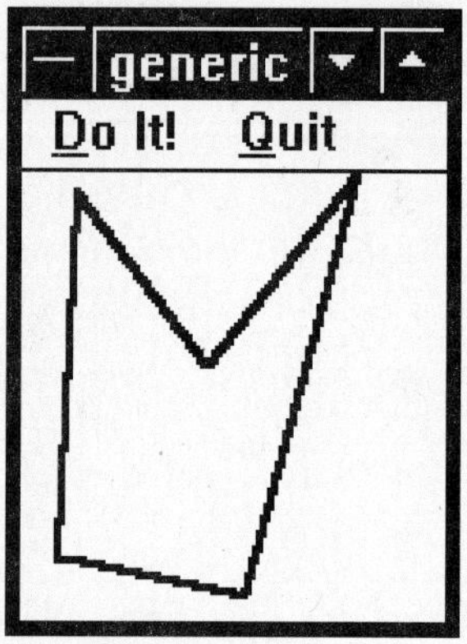

Figure 11-64. Polygon() Example.

```
long FAR PASCAL WndProc (HWND hWnd, unsigned iMessage, WORD wParam, LONG lParam)
{
        PAINTSTRUCT         ps ;
        HPEN                hPen ;
        LOGPEN              LP ;
        POINT               pPenWidth ;
        POINT               pArray [] = {10, 100, 15, 5, 50, 50, 90, 0,
                                         60, 110} ;

        switch (iMessage)                        /* process windows messages */
        {
            case WM_PAINT:
                    BeginPaint (hWnd, &ps) ;
                    pPenWidth.x = 2 ;
                    LP.lopnStyle = PS_DASH ;
                    LP.lopnWidth = pPenWidth ;
                    LP.lopnColor = RGB (0, 40, 50) ;
                    hPen = CreatePenIndirect (&LP) ;
                    SelectObject (ps.hdc, hPen) ;
                    Polygon (ps.hdc, pArray, 5) ;
                    EndPaint (hWnd, &ps) ;
                    DeleteObject (hPen) ;
                    break ;
```

[Other program lines]

POLYLINE   ■ Win 2.0   ■ Win 3.0   ■ Win 3.1

Purpose	Draws a line with multiple segments.
Syntax	BOOL **Polyline**(HDC *hDC*, LPPOINT *lpPoints*, int *nCount*);

Description	This function is equivalent to calling MoveTo(), followed by a series of one or more calls to LineTo(). Each of the line segments drawn is connected to the last. The line is drawn with the currently selected pen.
Uses	Drawing irregular lines which are connected.
Returns	BOOL. TRUE if the line was drawn, FALSE on error.
See Also	MoveTo(), LineTo(), CreatePen(), SelectObject()

Figure 11-65. Polyline( ) Example.

Parameters

hDC	HDC: The device context handle.
lpPoints	LPPOINT: An array of at least *nCount* POINT data structures defining the line to be drawn.
nCount	int: The number of points in the *lpPoints* array. Must be two or more points.
Example	This example, which is shown in Figure 11-65, uses Polyline() to efficiently draw a line with three segments on the client area.

```
Long FAR PASCAL WndProc (HWND hWnd, unsigned iMessage, WORD wParam, LONG lParam)
{
        PAINTSTRUCT              ps ;
        POINT                    pLine [] = {10, 10, 30, 90, 50, 30, 70, 100} ;
        HPEN                     hPen ;

        switch (iMessage)                            /* process windows messages */
        {
                case WM_PAINT:
                        BeginPaint (hWnd, &ps) ;
                        hPen = CreatePen (PS_SOLID, 3, RGB (0, 0, 255)) ;
                        SelectObject (ps.hdc, hPen) ;
                        Polyline (ps.hdc, pLine, 4) ;
                        EndPaint (hWnd, &ps) ;
                        DeleteObject (hPen) ;
                        break ;
```

[Other program lines]

POLYPOLYGON   □ Win 2.0   ■ Win 3.0   ■ Win 3.1

Purpose	Draws one or more polygons.
Syntax	BOOL **PolyPolygon**(HDC *hDC*, LPPOINT *lpPoints*, LPINT *lpPolyCounts*, int *nCount*);
Description	This function allows any number of polygons to be drawn with one function call. The polygons are drawn with the currently selected pen and brush. If the lines of the polygons cross, interior regions are drawn based on the current polygon filling mode.
Uses	An efficient way to draw a series of enclosed areas.
Returns	BOOL. TRUE if the polygons were drawn, FALSE on error.
See Also	Polygon(), SetPolyFillMode()

Parameters

hDC	HDC: The device context handle.
lpPoints	LPPOINT: A pointer to an array of POINT data structures that contain the vertices of the polygons. There must be at least as many points as specified by the *lpPolyCounts* array. The points for each independent polygon must be together in the array.
lpPolyCounts	LPINT: An array of integers that contains the number of points in *lpPoints* to assign to each successive polygon.
nCount	int: The number of elements in the *lpPolyCounts* array (not the number of total points).

Example This example, as shown in Figure 11-66, paints two polygons in one call to PolyPolygon(). The first is a triangle, defined by four points. The first and last points of the four are the same, so the region is closed. The second polygon is defined by five points, but the first and last points are not the same. PolyPolygon() does not close the region automatically.

```
Long FAR PASCAL WndProc (HWND hWnd, unsigned iMessage, WORD wParam, LONG lParam)
{
        PAINTSTRUCT     ps ;
        POINT           pLine [] = {10, 10, 30, 90, 50, 30, 10, 10,
                                    70, 0, 60, 50, 100, 100, 90, 25, 70, 120} ;
        int             pPolygons [] = {4, 5} ;
        HPEN            hPen ;
        HBRUSH          hBrush ;

        switch (iMessage)                       /* process windows messages */
        {
                case WM_PAINT:
                        BeginPaint (hWnd, &ps) ;
                        hPen = CreatePen (PS_SOLID, 3, RGB (0, 0, 255)) ;
                        hBrush = CreateHatchBrush (HS_DIAGCROSS,
                                RGB (255, 0, 0)) ;
                        SelectObject (ps.hdc, hPen) ;
                        SelectObject (ps.hdc, hBrush) ;
                        PolyPolygon (ps.hdc, pLine, pPolygons, 2) ;
                        EndPaint (hWnd, &ps) ;
                        DeleteObject (hPen) ;
                        DeleteObject (hBrush) ;
                        break ;
```

[Other program lines]

PtInRect ■ Win 2.0   ■ Win 3.0   ■ Win 3.1

Purpose	Determines if a point is within a rectangular area.
Syntax	BOOL **PtInRect**(LPRECT *lpRect*, POINT *Point*);
Description	This function typically is used to determine if the mouse cursor is within a certain area on the client region.
Uses	Used in paint programs, and other programs that track the mouse location.
Returns	BOOL. TRUE if the point is within the rectangle, FALSE if not.
See Also	PtInRegion(), PtVisible()

Figure 11-66. PolyPolygon() Example.

Figure 11-67. PtInRect() Example.

Figure 11-68. PtInRegion() Example.

Parameters

lpRect   LPRECT: A pointer to a RECT data structure holding the dimensions of the rectangle to check.

Point   POINT: A POINT data structure.

Example   This example paints a rectangle in the client area, see Figure 11-67. If the user clicks the left mouse button within the rectangle, "In Rect" is flashed. Clicking outside of the rectangle results in "Not Inside" being flashed. The screen is painted when the user releases the mouse button, erasing the message as the rectangle is repainted.

```
Long FAR PASCAL WndProc (HWND hWnd, unsigned iMessage, WORD wParam, LONG lParam)
{
        PAINTSTRUCT             ps ;
        HDC                     hDC ;
        static RECT             rRect ;
        POINT                   pCursor ;

        switch (iMessage)                       /* process windows messages */
        {
                case WM_CREATE :
                        SetRect (&rRect, 10, 10, 100, 100) ;
                        break ;
                case WM_PAINT:
                        BeginPaint (hWnd, &ps) ;
                        SelectObject (ps.hdc, GetStockObject (LTGRAY_BRUSH)) ;
                        Rectangle (ps.hdc, rRect.left, rRect.top, rRect.right,
                                rRect.bottom) ;
                        EndPaint (hWnd, &ps) ;
                        break ;
                case WM_LBUTTONDOWN:
                        pCursor = MAKEPOINT (lParam) ;
                        hDC = GetDC (hWnd) ;
                        if (PtInRect (&rRect, pCursor))
                                TextOut (hDC, 10, 50, "In Rect", 7) ;
                        else
                                TextOut (hDC, 10, 50, "Not Inside", 10) ;
                        ReleaseDC (hWnd, hDC) ;
                        break ;
                case WM_LBUTTONUP:
                        InvalidateRect (hWnd, NULL, TRUE) ;
                        UpdateWindow (hWnd) ;
                        break ;
```

[Other program lines]

PTINREGION   ■ Win 2.0   ■ Win 3.0   ■ Win 3.1

Purpose   Determines if a point is within a region.

Syntax   BOOL **PtInRegion**(HRGN *hRgn*, int *X*, int *Y*);

Description   This function is similar to PtInRect(), except a region is used in place of a rectangle. It is typically used in conjunction with the mouse cursor to determine if the location of the cursor is within a region.

Uses   Used in painting programs. For example, if the cursor is within a region, a flood fill operation may be possible.

Returns   BOOL. TRUE if the point is within the region, FALSE if not.

See Also   PtInRect(), PtVisible()

Parameters

hRgn   HRGN: A handle to a region.

X   int: The logical X coordinate of the point.

Y   int: The logical Y coordinate of the point.

Example   This example paints an irregular shape using a clipping region, as illustrated in Figure 11-68.

When the user clicks the left mouse button inside the client region (WM_LBUTTONDOWN message), the program checks whether the mouse cursor is within the region. If so, it shows the message "In Region" until the mouse button is released.

```
long FAR PASCAL WndProc (HWND hWnd, unsigned iMessage, WORD wParam, LONG lParam)
{
        PAINTSTRUCT             ps ;
        HDC                     hDC ;
        static HRGN             hRgn ;
        POINT                   pArray [5] = {10, 10, 50, 40, 90, 20, 60, 0,
                                             40, 20} ;
        POINT                   pCursor ;

        switch (iMessage)                       /* process windows messages */
        {
        case WM_CREATE :
                hRgn = CreatePolygonRgn (pArray, 5, WINDING) ;
                break ;
        case WM_PAINT:
                BeginPaint (hWnd, &ps) ;
                SelectClipRgn (ps.hdc, hRgn) ;
                SelectObject (ps.hdc, GetStockObject (LTGRAY_BRUSH)) ;
                Rectangle (ps.hdc, 0, 0, 500, 500) ;      /* paint gray */
                EndPaint (hWnd, &ps) ;
                break ;
        case WM_LBUTTONDOWN:
                pCursor = MAKEPOINT (lParam) ;
                hDC = GetDC (hWnd) ;
                if (PtInRegion (hRgn, pCursor.x, pCursor.y))
                        TextOut (hDC, 10, 50, "In Region", 9) ;
                else
                        TextOut (hDC, 10, 50, "Not Inside", 10) ;
                ReleaseDC (hWnd, hDC) ;
                break ;
        case WM_LBUTTONUP:
                InvalidateRect (hWnd, NULL, TRUE) ;
                UpdateWindow (hWnd) ;
                break ;
        case WM_COMMAND:                /* process menu items */
                switch (wParam)
                {
                case IDM_QUIT:          /* send end of application message */
                        DestroyWindow (hWnd) ;
                        break ;
                }
                break ;
        case WM_DESTROY:                /* stop application */
                DeleteObject (hRgn) ;
                PostQuitMessage (0) ;
                break ;
        default:                        /* default windows message processing */
                return DefWindowProc (hWnd, iMessage, wParam, lParam) ;
        }
        return (0L) ;
}
```

PtVisible

■ Win 2.0   ■ Win 3.0   ■ Win 3.1

Purpose	Checks whether a point is within the clipping region.
Syntax	BOOL **PtVisible**(HDC *hDC*, int *X*, int *Y*);
Description	This function checks whether the given point is within the clipping region set for the device context.
Uses	Used most frequently to check if the mouse pointer or caret position is within the area that will ultimately become painted.
Returns	BOOL. TRUE if the point is within the clipping region, FALSE if not.
See Also	PtInRegion(), PtInRect(), SelectClipRgn()

Parameters

hDC   HDC: The device context handle that has a clipping region selected.

X   int: The logical *X* coordinate of the point to check.

Y   int: The logical *Y* coordinate of the point to check.

Example   This example, which is illustrated in Figure 11-69, paints an elliptical area by setting an elliptical clipping region, and then painting over it with a gray brush. If the user clicks the left mouse button within the clipping region, the word "Visible" appears inside the ellipse. Otherwise "Not Visible" appears. The printing must be within the ellipse, as this is the clipping area and text outside of it would not be printed.

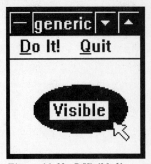

Figure 11-69. PtVisible( ) Example.

Note that the clipping area must be specified every time the device context handle is fetched. In this example, setting the clipping region within the WM_PAINT logic is effective only until the EndPaint() function is called.

```
long FAR PASCAL WndProc (HWND hWnd, unsigned iMessage, WORD wParam, LONG lParam)
{
        PAINTSTRUCT             ps ;
        HDC                     hDC ;
        static HRGN             hRgn ;
        POINT                   pCursor ;

        switch (iMessage)                       /* process windows messages */
        {
                case WM_CREATE :
                        hRgn = CreateEllipticRgn (20, 20, 100, 60) ;
                        break ;
                case WM_PAINT:
                        BeginPaint (hWnd, &ps) ;
                        SelectClipRgn (ps.hdc, hRgn) ;
                        SelectObject (ps.hdc, GetStockObject (LTGRAY_BRUSH)) ;
                        Rectangle (ps.hdc, 0, 0, 100, 100) ;
                        EndPaint (hWnd, &ps) ;
                        break ;
                case WM_LBUTTONDOWN:
                        pCursor = MAKEPOINT (lParam) ;
                        hDC = GetDC (hWnd) ;
                        SelectClipRgn (hDC, hRgn) ;
                        if (PtVisible (hDC, pCursor.x, pCursor.y))
                                TextOut (hDC, 30, 30, "Visible", 7) ;
                        else
                                TextOut (hDC, 30, 30, "Not Visible", 11) ;
                        ReleaseDC (hWnd, hDC) ;
                        break ;
                case WM_LBUTTONUP:
                        InvalidateRect (hWnd, NULL, TRUE) ;
                        UpdateWindow (hWnd) ;
                        break ;
                case WM_COMMAND:                /* process menu items */
                        switch (wParam)
                        {
                        case IDM_QUIT:          /* send end of application message */
                                DestroyWindow (hWnd) ;
                                break ;
                        }
                        break ;
                case WM_DESTROY:                /* stop application */
                        DeleteObject (hRgn) ;
                        PostQuitMessage (0) ;
                        break ;
                default:                        /* default windows message processing */
                        return DefWindowProc (hWnd, iMessage, wParam, lParam) ;
        }
        return (0L) ;
}
```

RECTANGLE

■ Win 2.0　■ Win 3.0　■ Win 3.1

Purpose	Draws a rectangle.
Syntax	BOOL **Rectangle**(HDC *hDC*, int *X1*, int *Y1*, int *X2*, int *Y2*);
Description	The rectangle is drawn with the currently selected pen for the border, and filled with the current brush. The width and height must not exceed 32,767 units.
Uses	Painting rectangular areas. To draw the outline, select the stock object NULL_BRUSH. To fill the area, but not draw the border, select the stock NULL_PEN.
Returns	BOOL. TRUE if the rectangle was drawn, FALSE on error.
See Also	SelectObject()
Parameters	
hDC	HDC: The device context handle.
X1	int: The logical *X* coordinate of the upper left corner of the rectangle.
Y1	int: The logical *Y* coordinate of the upper left corner of the rectangle.
X2	int: The logical *X* coordinate of the lower right corner of the rectangle.
Y2	int: The logical *Y* coordinate of the lower right corner of the rectangle.
Example	This example paints a rectangle in the client area with a hatched brush, as shown in Figure 11-70.

```
long FAR PASCAL WndProc (HWND hWnd, unsigned iMessage, WORD wParam, LONG lParam)
{
        PAINTSTRUCT     ps ;
        HPEN            hPen ;
        HBRUSH          hBrush ;

        switch (iMessage)                       /* process windows messages */
        {
                case WM_PAINT:
                        BeginPaint (hWnd, &ps) ;
                        hPen = CreatePen (PS_SOLID, 3, RGB (0, 0, 255)) ;
                        hBrush = CreateHatchBrush (HS_DIAGCROSS,
                                RGB (255, 0, 0)) ;
                        SelectObject (ps.hdc, hPen) ;
                        SelectObject (ps.hdc, hBrush) ;
                        Rectangle (ps.hdc, 20, 20, 100, 70) ;
                        EndPaint (hWnd, &ps) ;
                        DeleteObject (hPen) ;
                        DeleteObject (hBrush) ;
                        break ;
```

[Other program lines]

RECTINREGION

□ Win 2.0　■ Win 3.0　■ Win 3.1

Purpose	Checks whether a rectangle is within a region.
Syntax	BOOL **RectInRegion**(HRGN *hRgn*, LPRECT *lpRect*);
Description	The rectangle is considered to be within the region if any point falls within the bounds of the region.
Uses	Used to determine if there is any reason to draw a rectangle, as it may fall outside of the clipping region.
Returns	BOOL. TRUE if any part of the rectangle falls inside of the region, FALSE if not.
See Also	RectVisible()
Parameters	
hRgn	HRGN: A handle for a region.
lpRect	LPRECT: A pointer to a RECT data structure holding the dimensions of the rectangle.
Example	This example checks to see if the rectangle is within the clipping region before drawing it. The clipping region is elliptical and ultimately eliminates all but the upper left corner of the rectangle. (See Figure 11-71.)

```
long FAR PASCAL WndProc (HWND hWnd, unsigned iMessage, WORD wParam, LONG lParam)
{
        PAINTSTRUCT          ps ;
        HRGN                 hRgn ;
        RECT                 rRect ;

        switch (iMessage)                        /* process windows messages */
        {
                case WM_PAINT:
                        BeginPaint (hWnd, &ps) ;
                        hRgn = CreateEllipticRgn (10, 10, 100, 80) ;
                        SelectClipRgn (ps.hdc, hRgn) ;
                        SelectObject (ps.hdc, GetStockObject (LTGRAY_BRUSH)) ;
                        SetRect (&rRect, 50, 50, 100, 100) ;
                        if (RectInRegion (hRgn, &rRect))
                                Rectangle (ps.hdc, rRect.left, rRect.top,
                                        rRect.right, rRect.bottom) ;
                        EndPaint (hWnd, &ps) ;
                        DeleteObject (hRgn) ;
                        break ;
```
[Other program lines]

RECTVISIBLE   ■ Win 2.0   ■ Win 3.0   ■ Win 3.1

Purpose	Checks to see if a rectangle has points within the current clipping region.
Syntax	BOOL **RectVisible**(HDC *hDC*, LPRECT *lpRect*);
Description	Clipping regions are created with SelectClipRgn(). Once set, only points within the clipping region are painted. RectVisible() checks that at least one point on a rectangle falls within the clipping region.
Uses	Checking whether the rectangle is visible can save time on screen refresh cycles where the clipping region or rectangle change location. There is no point in painting the rectangle, or shape bounded by a rectangle (arc, chord, pie, ellipse), if all of the shape falls outside of the current clipping region.
Returns	BOOL. TRUE if part of the rectangle falls within the clipping region, FALSE if not.
See Also	RectInRegion(), SelectClipRgn()
Parameters	
hDC	HDC: The device context handle.
lpRect	LPRECT: A pointer to a RECT data structure containing the dimensions of the rectangle. This can also be the bounding rectangle used to paint a chord, arc, pie, or ellipse.
Example	This example, which is shown in Figure 11-72, creates a rectangular clipping region. Before painting a filled ellipse, the program checks that the bounding rectangle of the ellipse will be visible (within the clipping region).

Figure 11-70. Rectangle() Example.

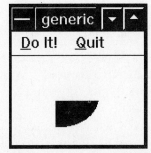

Figure 11-71. RectInRegion() Example.

Figure 11-72. RectVisible() Example.

```
Long FAR PASCAL WndProc (HWND hWnd, unsigned iMessage, WORD wParam, LONG lParam)
{
        PAINTSTRUCT      ps ;
        HRGN             hRgn ;
        RECT             rRect ;
        HBRUSH           hBrush ;

        switch (iMessage)                        /* process windows messages */
        {
                case WM_PAINT:
                        BeginPaint (hWnd, &ps) ;
                        hRgn = CreateRectRgn (10, 10, 100, 80) ;
                        SelectClipRgn (ps.hdc, hRgn) ;
                        hBrush = CreateHatchBrush (HS_DIAGCROSS,
                                RGB (0, 0, 255)) ;
                        SelectObject (ps.hdc, hBrush) ;
                        SetRect (&rRect, 30, 0, 80, 90) ;
                        if (RectVisible (ps.hdc, &rRect))
                                Ellipse (ps.hdc, rRect.left, rRect.top,
                                        rRect.right,    rRect.bottom) ;
                        EndPaint (hWnd, &ps) ;
                        DeleteObject (hBrush) ;
                        DeleteObject (hRgn) ;
                        break ;
```

[Other program lines]

RGB   ■ Win 2.0   ■ Win 3.0   ■ Win 3.1

Purpose   Creates a 32-bit color value when given the three primary color elements.

Syntax   COLORREF **RGB** (BYTE *cRed*, BYTE *cGreen*, BYTE *cBlue*) ;

Description   Windows uses 32-bit values to specify colors when creating pens and brushes. The 32-bit values encode three primary color contributions, the red, green, and blue elements that make up a color. If all of the elements are zero, the color is black (no intensity). If all of the elements are equal to 255, the maximum value for a color element, the color is white. Other combinations give colors which are determined by the mixing of the

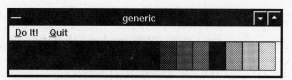

Figure 11-73. RGB() Example.

primary values. Windows achieves colors which are not on the system palette by dithering, the process of mixing pixels of different colors to achieve an area average color similar to the pure color specified. Systems with advanced displays (better than 16-color VGA) can use the palette functions to achieve other pure colors. The RGB() macro will always result in the dithered color being used. RGB() and the Get_Color() macros are defined in WINDOWS.H as

```
#define RGB(r,g,b)  ((DWORD)(((BYTE)(r)|((WORD)(g)<<8))|(((DWORD)(BYTE)(b))<<16)))

#define GetRValue(rgb)        ((BYTE)(rgb))
#define GetGValue(rgb)        ((BYTE)(((WORD)(rgb)) >> 8))
#define GetBValue(rgb)        ((BYTE)((rgb)>>16))
```

Uses   Specifying a color of a pen or brush.

Returns   COLORREF, the 32-bit (DWORD) color value.

See Also   CreatePalette(), PALETTERGB(), PALETTEINDEX()

Parameters

cRed   BYTE: The red component of the color, 0 to 255.

cGreen   BYTE: The green component of the color, 0 to 255.

cBlue   BYTE: The blue component of the color, 0 to 255.

Example

This example uses a series of sixteen brushes to paint sixteen rectangles on the screen. They show a smooth gradation in gray scale from the left to right when displayed on the screen. The reproduction in Figure 11-73 does not fully capture the gray tones. Intermediate colors are represented by dithered patterns if the colors are not available on the system palette.

```
long FAR PASCAL WndProc (HWND hWnd, unsigned iMessage, WORD wParam, LONG lParam)
{
        PAINTSTRUCT             ps ;
        HBRUSH                  hBrush ;
        int                     i ;

        switch (iMessage)                       /* process windows messages */
        {
                case WM_PAINT:
                        BeginPaint (hWnd, &ps) ;
                        for (i = 0 ; i < 16 ; i++)
                        {
                                hBrush = CreateSolidBrush (
                                        RGB (i * 16, i * 16, i * 16)) ;
                                SelectObject (ps.hdc, hBrush) ;
                                Rectangle (ps.hdc, i * 30, 0, (i + 1) * 30, 50) ;
                                SelectObject (ps.hdc, GetStockObject (WHITE_BRUSH)) ;
                                DeleteObject (hBrush) ;
                        }
                        EndPaint (hWnd, &ps) ;
                        break ;
```

[Other program lines]

ROUNDRECT

■ Win 2.0   ■ Win 3.0   ■ Win 3.1

Purpose	Draws a rectangle with rounded corners.
Syntax	BOOL **RoundRect**(HDC *hDC*, int *X1*, int *Y1*, int *X2*, int *Y3*, int *X3*, int *Y3*);
Description	The rectangle is drawn with the selected pen and filled with the selected brush.
Uses	This shape can be used to draw custom buttons.
Returns	BOOL. TRUE if the shape was drawn, FALSE on error.
See Also	CreateRoundRectRgn()

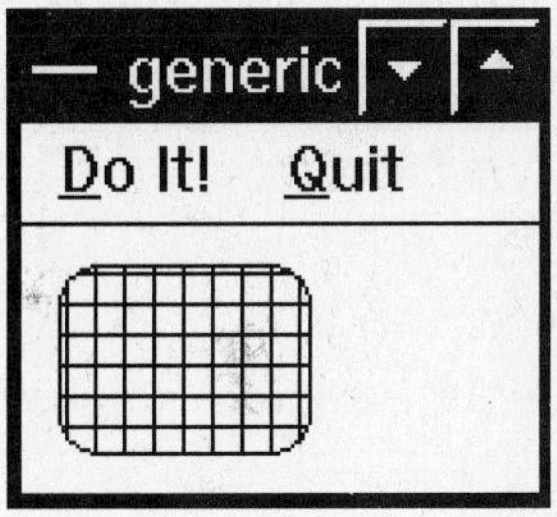

Figure 11-74. RoundRect( ) Example.

Parameters

hDC   HDC: The device context handle.

X1   int: The logical *X* coordinate of the upper left corner of the bounding rectangle.

Y1   int: The logical *Y* coordinate of the upper left corner of the bounding rectangle.

X2   int: The logical *X* coordinate of the lower right corner of the bounding rectangle.

Y2   int: The logical *Y* coordinate of the lower right corner of the bounding rectangle.

X3   int: The logical width of the ellipse used to round the corners.

Y3   int: The logical height of the ellipse used to round the corners.

Example

This example paints a rounded rectangle using a hatched brush and the default black pen, as shown in Figure 11-74.

```
long FAR PASCAL WndProc (HWND hWnd, unsigned iMessage, WORD wParam, LONG lParam)
{
        PAINTSTRUCT             ps ;
        HBRUSH                  hBrush ;

        switch (iMessage)                       /* process windows messages */
        {
                case WM_PAINT:
                        BeginPaint (hWnd, &ps) ;
```

```
hBrush = CreateHatchBrush (HS_CROSS, RGB (0, 0, 255)) ;
SelectObject (ps.hdc, hBrush) ;
RoundRect (ps.hdc, 10, 10, 80, 60, 25, 20) ;
EndPaint (hWnd, &ps) ;
DeleteObject (hBrush) ;
break ;
```

[Other program lines]

SELECTCLIPRGN ■ Win 2.0 ■ Win 3.0 ■ Win 3.1

Purpose Uses a region to clip output to a device context.

Syntax int **SelectClipRgn**(HDC *hDC*, HRGN *hRgn*);

Description Before this function can be used, a region must be created. The region is then selected into the device context as the clipping boundary with SelectClipRgn(). All subsequent output to the device context is only painted if it falls within the clipping region.

Uses Clipping regions are frequently efficient ways to draw complex shapes. For example, consider the example in Figure 11-75. A direct algorithm drawing all of the lines that make up the inner circle to the right length would be slow and difficult to code. Using a clipping region allows the area to be filled with a simple call to Rectangle().

Figure 11-75. SelectClip-Rgn( ) Example.

Returns int, the type of region selected. This can be any of the region types in Table 11-23.

Value	Meaning
COMPLEXREGION	The new region has overlapping borders.
ERROR	No new region was created.
NULLREGION	The new region is empty.
SIMPLEREGION	The new region does not have overlapping borders.

Table 11-23. Region Types.

See Also CreateEllipticRgn(), CreateRectRgn(), CombineRgn()

Parameters

hDC HDC: The device context handle.

hRgn HRGN: The handle of the region to use as the clipping region.

Example In this example, the same rectangle is drawn twice. The first time, there is no selected clipping region. The rectangle is drawn with a NULL brush, so only the border is displayed. An elliptical clipping region is then set up with the same bounding rectangle dimensions. The second time the rectangle is drawn, a hatched brush is used. Only the portion of the rectangle within the elliptical clipping region is drawn. (See Figure 11-75.)

```
Long FAR PASCAL WndProc (HWND hWnd, unsigned iMessage, WORD wParam, LONG lParam)
{
        PAINTSTRUCT             ps ;
        HBRUSH                  hBrush, hOldBrush ;
        HRGN                    hRgn ;

        switch (iMessage)                               /* process windows messages */
        {
        case WM_PAINT:
                BeginPaint (hWnd, &ps) ;
                SelectObject (ps.hdc, GetStockObject (NULL_BRUSH)) ;
```

```
SelectObject (ps.hdc, GetStockObject (BLACK_PEN)) ;
Rectangle (ps.hdc, 10, 10, 100, 100) ;

hBrush = CreateHatchBrush (HS_DIAGCROSS,
        RGB (0, 0, 255)) ;
hOldBrush = SelectObject (ps.hdc, hBrush) ;
hRgn = CreateEllipticRgn (10, 10, 100, 100) ;
SelectClipRgn (ps.hdc, hRgn) ;
Rectangle (ps.hdc, 10, 10, 100, 100) ;
SelectObject (ps.hdc, hOldBrush) ;
DeleteObject (hBrush) ;
EndPaint (hWnd, &ps) ;
DeleteObject (hRgn) ;
break ;
```

[Other program lines]

SELECTOBJECT   ■ Win 2.0   ■ Win 3.0   ■ Win 3.1

Purpose	Selects an object into a device context.
Syntax	HANDLE **SelectObject**(HDC *hDC*, HANDLE *hObject*);
Description	Before an object like a pen, font, brush, or region can be used in painting operations, it must be selected into the device context. If the same type of object was already selected, it is displaced by the new object selected.
Uses	Selecting pens, fonts, brushes, and regions into a device context. Bitmaps can be selected into memory device contexts only. Logical color palettes are selected using the SelectPalette() function, not SelectObject(). Use DeleteObject() to delete every object created after it is no longer needed. Do not delete stock objects. Do not delete objects currently selected into a device context.
Returns	The handle of the object being replaced. This is convenient, as it is frequently desirable to delete the previous object once it is displaced from the device context.
See Also	DeleteObject(), CreatePen(), CreateSolidBrush(), CreateHatchBrush(), CreateRectRgn(), CreateEllipticRgn(), CombineRgn(), CreateFont()
Parameters	
hDC	HDC: The device context handle.
hObject	HANDLE: The handle of the brush, font, pen, or region to select into the device context. It can be the handle of a bitmap if *hDC* is the handle of a memory device context (see Chapter 15, *Bitmaps*).
Example	The previous example under SelectClipRgn() shows SelectObject() initially being used to select two stock objects. They are used to paint a rectangle's border. Later the function is used again to select a hatched brush, prior to painting a second rectangle which is clipped by an elliptical region. The previous brush handle is saved as *hOldBrush*, allowing the old brush to be selected again into the device context prior to deleting the custom brush. Objects that are selected into a device context should not be deleted until they are displaced by another call to SelectObject().

SETBRUSHORG   ■ Win 2.0   ■ Win 3.0   ■ Win 3.1

Purpose	Changes the origin used by the device context to line up pattern brushes.
Syntax	DWORD **SetBrushOrg**(HDC *hDC*, int *X*, int *Y*);
Description	Windows maintains a logical origin in order to calculate how to align pattern and hatched brushes. SetBrushOrg() allows you to change this value. Setting the origin only affects a brush if the origin is changed before the brush is created, or after a call to UnrealizeObject().
Uses	Used to keep patterns from merging into nearby objects, such as with neighboring bars on a bar chart.

Returns 　　　DWORD, the brush origin. The low-order word contains the X position. The high-order word contains the Y position.

See Also 　　　GetBrushOrg(), CreateHatchBrush(), CreatePatternBrush(), UnrealizeObject()

Parameters

hDC 　　　HDC: The device context handle.

X 　　　int: The new brush X origin. Its value must be between 0 and 7.

Y 　　　int: The new brush Y origin. Its value must be between 0 and 7.

Example 　　　This example paints two rectangles with hatched brushes. (See Figure 11-76.) The first brush is created with 0,0 as the brush origin. The second with 3,3 as the brush origin. The result is that the two patterns are offset by three pixels. This type of offset can be desirable when it is important to show a separation between two areas, such as bars on a black and white bar chart.

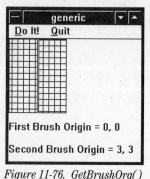

*Figure 11-76. GetBrushOrg()
and SetBrushOrg() Example.*

```
Long FAR PASCAL WndProc (HWND hWnd, unsigned iMessage, WORD wParam, LONG lParam)
{
        PAINTSTRUCT             ps ;
        HBRUSH                  hBrush ;
        char                    cBuf [128] ;
        DWORD                   dwBrushOrg ;

        switch (iMessage)                       /* process windows messages */
        {
                case WM_PAINT:
                        BeginPaint (hWnd, &ps) ;
                        SetBrushOrg (ps.hdc, 0, 0) ;
                        hBrush = CreateHatchBrush (HS_CROSS, RGB (0, 0, 255)) ;
                        SelectObject (ps.hdc, hBrush) ;
                        Rectangle (ps.hdc, 0, 0, 40, 100) ;
                        dwBrushOrg = GetBrushOrg (ps.hdc) ;
                        TextOut (ps.hdc, 0, 110, cBuf, wsprintf (cBuf,
                                "First Brush Origin = %d, %d",
                                        LOWORD (dwBrushOrg), HIWORD (dwBrushOrg))) ;
                        SelectObject (ps.hdc, GetStockObject (WHITE_BRUSH)) ;
                        DeleteObject (hBrush) ;
                        SetBrushOrg (ps.hdc, 3, 3) ;
                        hBrush = CreateHatchBrush (HS_CROSS, RGB (0, 0, 255)) ;
                        SelectObject (ps.hdc, hBrush) ;
                        Rectangle (ps.hdc, 41, 0, 80, 100) ;
                        dwBrushOrg = GetBrushOrg (ps.hdc) ;
                        TextOut (ps.hdc, 0, 140, cBuf, wsprintf (cBuf,
                                "Second Brush Origin = %d, %d",
                                        LOWORD (dwBrushOrg), HIWORD (dwBrushOrg))) ;
                        EndPaint (hWnd, &ps) ;
                        DeleteObject (hBrush) ;
                        break ;
```

[Other program lines]

SETPIXEL 　　　　　　　　　　　　　　　■ Win 2.0　　■ Win 3.0　　■ Win 3.1

Purpose 　　　Changes to the color of a single point on the device context.

Syntax 　　　DWORD **SetPixel**(HDC *hDC*, int *X*, int *Y*, DWORD *crColor*);

Description 　　　This function sets the color of one point on the device context. The color will be the closest color to that specified by *crColor* possible within the limitations of the device.

Uses 　　　Only used in specialized point-by-point drawing operations such as drawing fractal images. Normally, this function is avoided because the time needed to fill a region on the device is unacceptably long.

Returns 　　　DWORD, the 32-bit color value that actually was painted. This value will only be equal to *crColor* if the device can display the exact color.

See Also	GetPixel()
Parameters	
hDC	HDC: The device context handle.
X	int: The logical *X* coordinate of the point to change color.
Y	int: The logical *Y* coordinate of the point to change color.
crColor	DWORD: The 32-bit color value desired. Use the RGB macro to create a color value.
Example	This example shows a shaded rectangle being painted, one pixel at a time. The starting pixel color is first retrieved using GetPixel(). This color is then incremented and used to set the new color of the pixel with SetPixel(). This method of drawing is unacceptably slow.

```
Long FAR PASCAL WndProc (HWND hWnd, unsigned iMessage, WORD wParam, LONG lParam)
{
        PAINTSTRUCT             ps ;
        DWORD                   dwColor ;
        int                     nRed, nBlue, nGreen, i, j ;

        switch (iMessage)                       /* process windows messages */
        {
                case WM_PAINT:
                        BeginPaint (hWnd, &ps) ;
                        for (i = 0 ; i < 10 ; i++)
                        {
                                for (j = 0 ; j < 256 ; j++)
                                {
                                        dwColor = GetPixel (ps.hdc, j, i) ;
                                        nRed = (GetRValue (dwColor) + j) % 256 ;
                                        nBlue = (GetBValue (dwColor) + j) % 256 ;
                                        nGreen = (GetGValue (dwColor) + j) % 256 ;
                                        SetPixel (ps.hdc, j, i,
                                                RGB (nRed, nGreen, nBlue)) ;
                                }
                        }
                        EndPaint (hWnd, &ps) ;
                        break ;
```

[Other program lines]

SETPOLYFILLMODE
■ Win 2.0   ■ Win 3.0   ■ Win 3.1

Purpose	Changes the polygon filling mode of a device context.
Syntax	int **SetPolyFillMode**(HDC *hDC*, int *nPolyFillMode*);
Description	The polygon filling mode determines how areas of intersection within the polygon are painted. This is only a factor if the lines defining the polygon cross.
Uses	Used with GetPolyFillMode() to determine and change the filling mode.
Returns	int, the previous filling mode. NULL on error.
See Also	GetPolyFillMode()
Parameters	
hDC	HDC: The device context handle.
nPolyFillMode	int: The desired polygon filling mode. This can be either of the modes in Table 11-24.

Value	Meaning	⊠
ALTERNATE	The GDI fills in areas between sides 1&2, sides 3&4, etc.	
WINDING	The GDI fills in the total area defined by the outermost lines. This will normally fill the entire interior of the polygon, except in cases where more than one intersection of areas defined by the polygon's lines occurs (see the example).	

Table 11-24. Polygon Filling Modes.

Example	See the example under GetPolyFillMode().

SETRECT

■ Win 2.0 ■ Win 3.0 ■ Win 3.1

Purpose	Enters all four values for a RECT data structure.
Syntax	void **SetRect**(LPRECT *lpRect*, int *X1*, int *Y1*, int *X2*, int *Y2*);
Description	The RECT data structure is defined in WINDOWS.H as follows:

```
typedef struct tagRECT
  {
    int    left;
    int    top;
    int    right;
    int    bottom;
  } RECT;
```

SetRect() allows all four elements of the structure to be set with one function call.

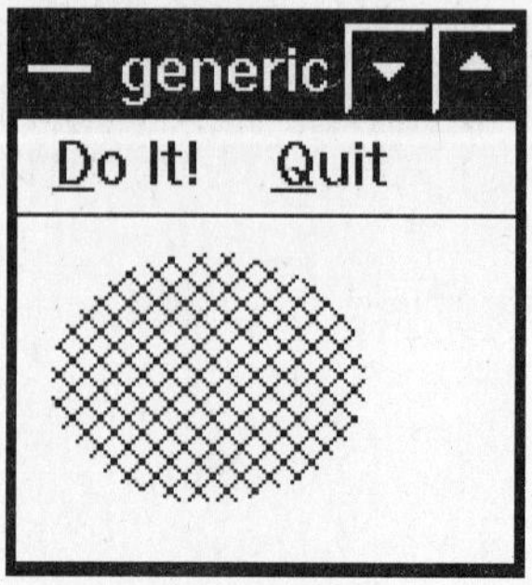

Returns	No returned value (void).

Figure 11-77. SetRect() Example.

Parameters

lpRect	LPRECT: A pointer to a RECT data structure.
X1	int: The *X* coordinate of the upper left corner of the rectangle.
Y1	int: The *Y* coordinate of the upper left corner of the rectangle.
X2	int: The *X* coordinate of the lower right corner of the rectangle.
Y2	int: The *Y* coordinate of the lower right corner of the rectangle.
Example	In this example, SetRect() is used to fill in the values for a rectangle that is then used to define the bounding rectangle of an elliptical region. (See Figure 11-77.)

```
long FAR PASCAL WndProc (HWND hWnd, unsigned iMessage, WORD wParam, LONG lParam)
{
        PAINTSTRUCT            ps ;
        HBRUSH                 hBrush ;
        HRGN                   hRgn ;
        RECT                   rRect ;

        switch (iMessage)                           /* process windows messages */
        {
            case WM_PAINT:
                    BeginPaint (hWnd, &ps) ;
                    hBrush = CreateHatchBrush (HS_DIAGCROSS,
                            RGB (0, 0, 255)) ;
                    SetRect (&rRect, 10, 10, 100, 80) ;
                    hRgn = CreateEllipticRgnIndirect (&rRect) ;
                    FillRgn (ps.hdc, hRgn, hBrush) ;
                    EndPaint (hWnd, &ps) ;
                    DeleteObject (hBrush) ;
                    DeleteObject (hRgn) ;
                    break ;
```

[Other program lines]

SETRECTEMPTY

■ Win 2.0 ■ Win 3.0 ■ Win 3.1

Purpose	Sets all the elements of a RECT data structure to zero.
Syntax	void **SetRectEmpty**(LPRECT *lpRect*);
Description	This is a shortcut method to zero all of the values in a RECT data structure. See SetRect() for the definition of RECT.
Returns	No returned value (void).
See Also	IsRectEmpty(), SetRect()

Parameters

lpRect	LPRECT: A pointer to a RECT data structure.

Example

In this case, a rectangle is defined when the program starts (WM_CREATE message received). The rectangle is used to define a clipping region, which is used to paint an ellipse on the client area. When the user clicks the "Do It!" menu item, the rectangle is set to empty. The next WM_PAINT message clears the client area.

```
long FAR PASCAL WndProc (HWND hWnd, unsigned iMessage, WORD wParam, LONG lParam)
{
        PAINTSTRUCT             ps ;
        HBRUSH                  hBrush ;
        HRGN                    hRgn ;
        static RECT             rRect ;

        switch (iMessage)                         /* process windows messages */
        {
        case WM_CREATE:
                SetRect (&rRect, 10, 10, 80, 120) ;
                break ;
        case WM_PAINT:
                BeginPaint (hWnd, &ps) ;
                if (!IsRectEmpty (&rRect))
                {
                        hBrush = CreateHatchBrush (HS_DIAGCROSS,
                                RGB (0, 0, 255)) ;
                        hRgn = CreateEllipticRgnIndirect (&rRect) ;
                        FillRgn (ps.hdc, hRgn, hBrush) ;
                        SelectObject (ps.hdc, GetStockObject (WHITE_BRUSH)) ;
                        DeleteObject (hBrush) ;
                        DeleteObject (hRgn) ;
                }
                EndPaint (hWnd, &ps) ;
                break ;
        case WM_COMMAND:              /* process menu items */
                switch (wParam)
                {
                case IDM_DOIT:   /* User hit the "Do it" menu item */
                        SetRectEmpty (&rRect) ;
                        InvalidateRect (hWnd, NULL, TRUE) ;
                        break ;
```

[Other program lines]

SETRECTRGN

■ Win 2.0   ■ Win 3.0   ■ Win 3.1

Purpose	Changes the bounds of a rectangular region.
Syntax	void **SetRectRgn**(HRGN *hRgn*, int *X1*, int *Y1*, int *X2*, int *Y2*);
Description	This is an efficient way to change the size of a rectangular region. The region must already exist, with memory allocated in the local heap by a previous call to CreateRectRgn().
Uses	Handy, when there is a series of rectangular regions used in sequence. See the following example. The application must delete the region before the program exits to return all memory to the system.
Returns	No returned value (void).
See Also	CreateRectRgn()

Figure 11-78. SetRectRgn() Example.

Parameters

hRgn   HRGN: A handle to the rectangular region to resize. The region must have been allocated by a previous call to CreateRectRgn().

X1   int: The logical X coordinate of the upper left corner of the rectangle.

Y1   int: The logical Y coordinate of the upper left corner of the rectangle.

X2   int: The logical X coordinate of the lower right corner of the rectangle.

Y2   int: The logical Y coordinate of the lower right corner of the rectangle.

Example   This example efficiently draws a series of progressively smaller regions. The same region is re-used (not destroyed and then created) each time. SetRectRgn() establishes the region's size before each painting. (See Figure 11-78.) Note that memory for the region is allocated when the program starts (WM_CREATE message received). The region is destroyed as the program exits, freeing the memory associated with the region.

```
Long FAR PASCAL WndProc (HWND hWnd, unsigned iMessage, WORD wParam, LONG lParam)
{
        PAINTSTRUCT           ps ;
        HBRUSH                hBrush ;
        static HRGN           hRgn ;
        int                   i ;
        RECT                  rRect ;

        switch (iMessage)                          /* process windows messages */
        {
            case WM_CREATE:
                    hRgn = CreateRectRgn (0, 1, 2, 3) ;        /* arbitrary size */
                    break ;
            case WM_PAINT:
                    BeginPaint (hWnd, &ps) ;
                    SetRect (&rRect, 10, 10, 100, 100) ;
                    for (i = 0 ; i < 8 ; i++)
                    {
                            SelectObject (ps.hdc,
                                    GetStockObject (BLACK_BRUSH)) ;
                            SetRectRgn (hRgn,rRect.left, rRect.top,
                                    rRect.right,    rRect.bottom) ;
                            PaintRgn (ps.hdc, hRgn) ;
                            InflateRect (&rRect, -5, -5) ;
                            SelectObject (ps.hdc,
                                    GetStockObject (WHITE_BRUSH)) ;
                            SetRectRgn (hRgn,rRect.left, rRect.top,
                                    rRect.right,    rRect.bottom) ;
                            PaintRgn (ps.hdc, hRgn) ;
                            InflateRect (&rRect, -5, -5) ;
                    }
                    EndPaint (hWnd, &ps) ;
                    break ;
            case WM_COMMAND:         /* process menu items */
                    switch (wParam)
                    {
                    case IDM_DOIT:   /* User hit the "Do it" menu item */
                            InvalidateRect (hWnd, NULL, TRUE) ;
                            break ;
                    case IDM_QUIT:   /* send end of application message */
                            DestroyWindow (hWnd) ;
                            break ;
                    }
                    break ;
            case WM_DESTROY:         /* stop application */
                    DeleteObject (hRgn) ;
                    PostQuitMessage (0) ;
                    break ;
            default:                 /* default windows message processing */
                    return DefWindowProc (hWnd, iMessage, wParam, lParam) ;
        }
        return (0L) ;
}
```

SetROP2   ■ Win 2.0   ■ Win 3.0   ■ Win 3.1

Purpose   Changes the raster drawing mode of a device context.

Syntax   int **SetROP2**(HDC *hDC*, int *nDrawMode*);

Description   The default, R2_COPYPEN, paints the pen color regardless of the underlying colors. With the other drawing modes, the pen is drawn on the device context after comparing the pen color to the existing color at each *X,Y* position being drawn. With color devices, each of the three primary colors is dealt with separately, using the same binary logic. The blue element of the pen color is compared to the blue element of the pixel, etc.

Uses

Only a few of the ROP2 operations typically are used. The common ones are R2_NOT, which makes the pen always visible and R2_XORPEN which makes the pen line disappear if the same line is drawn twice.

Returns

int, the previous drawing mode. This is one of the 16 values shown in Table 11-25.

See Also

GetROP2

Parameters

hDC

HDC: The device context handle.

nDrawMode

int: One of the following drawing modes. In the Boolean operation column, the "P" stands for the pen color value and the "D"

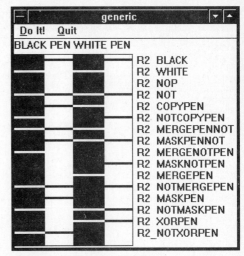

Figure 11-79. SetROP2( ) Example.

stands for the display color value. For simplicity, the explanations are in terms of a black and white display. For color displays, the same logic is applied to each color element (red, blue, green).

Value	Boolian Operation	Comments
R2_BLACK	0	Always black.
R2_WHITE	1	Always white
R2_NOP	D	No effect on display.
R2_NOT	~D	Invert display under line.
R2_COPYPEN	P	Pen color painted regardless of display.
R2_NOTCOPYPEN	~P	Pen color inverted regardless of display.
R2_MERGEPENNOT	P | ~D	
R2_MASKPENNOT	P & ~D	
R2_MERGENOTPEN	~P | D	
R2_MASKNOTPEN	~P & D	
R2_MERGEPEN	P | D	
R2_NOTMERGEPEN	~(P | D)	
R2_MASKPEN	P & D	
R2_NOTMASKPEN	~(P & D)	
R2_XORPEN	P ^ D	A black pen inverts the device pixels. Drawing twice at the same location erases the line.
R2_NOTXORPEN	~ (P ^ D)	

Table 11-25. Raster Drawing Modes.

Example

This example (see Figure 11-79) demonstrates all 16 ROP modes by painting a black and white line against black and white backgrounds with each of the ROP2 modes. (Credit should be given to Peter Norton and Paul Yau for this clever way of displaying the drawing modes.)

```
Long FAR PASCAL WndProc (HWND hWnd, unsigned iMessage, WORD wParam, LONG lParam)
{
        PAINTSTRUCT             ps ;
        HPEN                    hPenWhite, hPenBlack ;
        int                     i ;
        int                     nROPModes [16] = {R2_BLACK, R2_WHITE, R2_NOP,
                R2_NOT, R2_COPYPEN, R2_NOTCOPYPEN, R2_MERGEPENNOT,
                R2_MASKPENNOT, R2_MERGENOTPEN, R2_MASKNOTPEN, R2_MERGEPEN,
                R2_NOTMERGEPEN, R2_MASKPEN, R2_NOTMASKPEN, R2_XORPEN,
                R2_NOTXORPEN} ;
        char                    *cROPModeNames [16] = {"R2_BLACK", "R2_WHITE",
                "R2_NOP", "R2_NOT", "R2_COPYPEN", "R2_NOTCOPYPEN",
                "R2_MERGEPENNOT", "R2_MASKPENNOT", "R2_MERGENOTPEN",
                "R2_MASKNOTPEN", "R2_MERGEPEN", "R2_NOTMERGEPEN",
                "R2_MASKPEN", "R2_NOTMASKPEN", "R2_XORPEN",
                "R2_NOTXORPEN"} ;

        switch (iMessage)                               /* process windows messages */
        {
        case WM_PAINT:
                BeginPaint (hWnd, &ps) ;
                TextOut (ps.hdc, 0, 0, "BLACK PEN", 9) ;
                TextOut (ps.hdc, 80, 0, "WHITE PEN", 9) ;
                SelectObject (ps.hdc, GetStockObject (BLACK_BRUSH)) ;
                Rectangle (ps.hdc, 0, 20, 40, 270) ;
                SelectObject (ps.hdc, GetStockObject (WHITE_BRUSH)) ;
                Rectangle (ps.hdc, 40, 20, 80, 270) ;
                SelectObject (ps.hdc, GetStockObject (BLACK_BRUSH)) ;
                Rectangle (ps.hdc, 80, 20, 120, 270) ;
                SelectObject (ps.hdc, GetStockObject (WHITE_BRUSH)) ;
                Rectangle (ps.hdc, 120, 20, 160, 270) ;
                hPenWhite = CreatePen (PS_SOLID, 3,
                        RGB (255, 255, 255)) ;
                hPenBlack = CreatePen (PS_SOLID, 3, 0L) ;
                for (i = 0 ; i < 16 ; i++)
                {
                        SetROP2 (ps.hdc, nROPModes [i]) ;
                        SelectObject (ps.hdc, hPenBlack) ;
                        MoveTo (ps.hdc, 0, (i * 15) + 27) ;
                        LineTo (ps.hdc, 77, (i * 15) + 27) ;
                        SelectObject (ps.hdc, hPenWhite) ;
                        MoveTo (ps.hdc, 80, (i * 15) + 27) ;
                        LineTo (ps.hdc, 157, (i * 15) + 27) ;
                        TextOut (ps.hdc, 165, (i * 15) + 20,
                                cROPModeNames [i],
                                strlen (cROPModeNames [i])) ;
                }
                EndPaint (hWnd, &ps) ;
                DeleteObject (hPenBlack) ;
                DeleteObject (hPenWhite) ;
                break ;
```

[Other program lines]

SetSysColors   ■ Win 2.0   ■ Win 3.0   ■ Win 3.1

Purpose	Changes the color values that Windows uses to paint background and nonclient areas of the screen and windows.
Syntax	void **SetSysColors**(int *nChanges*, LPINT *lpSysColor*, DWORD FAR **lpColorValues*);
Description	Windows maintains a table of 20-color values that are used to specify what color to paint the borders, buttons, etc. This function allows you to change those values temporarily. The changes remain in effect for the duration of the Windows session. The changes are not permanent, as the WIN.INI file is not modified.
Uses	Temporary changes to the system colors.
Returns	No returned value (void).
See Also	GetSysColor()

Parameters

nChanges   int: The number of system color values that will be changed.

lpSysColor   LPINT: A pointer to an array of at least *nChanges* integers. The value in each array element determines which color will be changed. This value can be any of the colors listed in Table 11-26.

Value	Meaning	☒
COLOR_ACTIVEBORDER	The active window border.	
COLOR_ACTIVECAPTION	The active window caption.	
COLOR_APPWORKSPACE	The background color for MDI (multiple document interface) applications.	
COLOR_BACKGROUND	The desktop (background on which all programs and icons are painted).	
COLOR_BTNFACE	Button face color.	
COLOR_BTNSHADOW	Button edge color.	
COLOR_BTNTEXT	Button text color.	
COLOR_CAPTIONTEXT	The caption text color.	
COLOR_GRAYTEXT	Grayed (disabled) menu item text color. The returned color is set to zero if the display does not support a solid gray color.	
COLOR_HIGHLIGHT	Selected item color in a control.	
COLOR_HIGHLIGHTTEXT	Text color in a selected control.	
COLOR_INACTIVEBORDER	Color of an inactive window border.	
COLOR_INACTIVECAPTION	Color of an inactive window caption.	
COLOR_MENU	The menu background color.	
COLOR_MENUTEXT	The menu text color.	
COLOR_SCROLLBAR	The scroll bar gray area.	
COLOR_WINDOW	The window background color.	
COLOR_WINDOWFRAME	The window frame color.	
COLOR_WINDOWTEXT	The color of text in a window.	

Table 11-26. System Colors.

lpColorValues   DWORD FAR *: A pointer to an array of DWORD values that contain the 32-bit color values to use for each color specified by the *lpSysColor* elements. There must be at least *nChanges* elements in the array.

Related Messages   WM_SYSCOLORCHANGE should be sent after the function is called. This message notifies all applications that the system colors have been modified.

Example   When the user clicks the "Do It!" menu item, the system color for the active caption is changed to bright red, and the system color for button text is changed to blue. Windows automatically repaints the nonclient areas of the windows to accommodate these changes. The changes remain in effect until the Windows session is ended. No change is made to the WIN.INI file settings, so the changes do not appear the next time Windows is started.

```
long FAR PASCAL WndProc (HWND hWnd, unsigned iMessage, WORD wParam, LONG lParam)
{
        int             nColorIndex [2] ;
        DWORD           nColorValue [2] ;

        switch (iMessage)                       /* process windows messages */
        {
                case WM_COMMAND:        /* process menu items */
                        switch (wParam)
                        {
```

```
                    case IDM_DOIT:   /* User hit the "Do it" menu item */
                            nColorIndex [0] = COLOR_ACTIVECAPTION ;
                            nColorValue [0] = RGB (255, 0, 0) ;
                            nColorIndex [1] = COLOR_BTNTEXT ;
                            nColorValue [1] = RGB (0, 0, 255) ;
                            SetSysColors (2, nColorIndex, nColorValue) ;
                            PostMessage (-1, WM_SYSCOLORCHANGE, 0, 0L) ;
                            break ;
```

[Other program lines]

UNIONRECT ■ Win 2.0 ■ Win 3.0 ■ Win 3.1

Purpose   Sets the size of a rectangle equal to the smallest rectangle that will enclose two other rectangles.

Syntax   int **UnionRect**(LPRECT *lpDestRect*, LPRECT *lpSrc1Rect*, LPRECT *lpSrc2Rect*);

Description The union of two rectangles is a third rectangle that encloses the other two. The source rectangles can be either separate or overlapping.

Uses   The union is the smallest area that can be painted to cover the two source rectangles.

Returns   int. Zero if the union is empty, nonzero if the union is not an empty rectangle.

See Also   Rectangle(), IntersectRect(), IsRectEmpty()

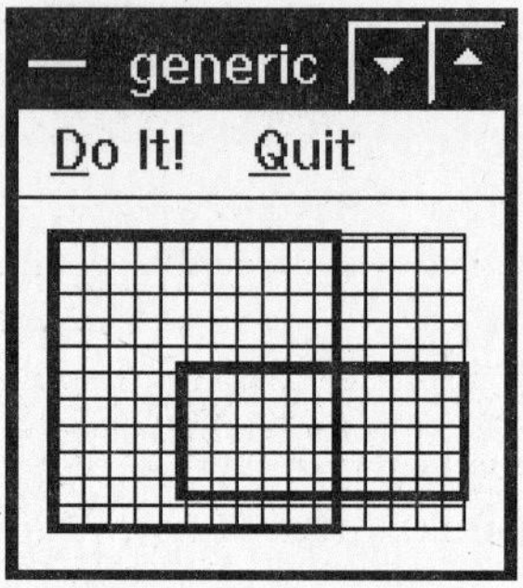

Parameters

Figure 11-80. UnionRect() Example.

lpDestRect   LPRECT: A pointer to a RECT data structure that will hold the union rectangle.

lpSrc1Rect   LPRECT: A pointer to a RECT data structure containing the first source rectangle.

lpSrc2Rect   LPRECT: A pointer to a RECT data structure containing the second source rectangle.

Example   This example creates two rectangles of fixed size, and then creates a third which is the union of the first two. The union is shown as the hatched area, the smallest rectangle that encloses both of the other two. (See Figure 11-80.)

```
long FAR PASCAL WndProc (HWND hWnd, unsigned iMessage, WORD wParam, LONG lParam)
{
        PAINTSTRUCT             ps ;
        RECT                    r1, r2, r3 ;
        HBRUSH                  hBrush ;
        HPEN                    hPen ;

        switch (iMessage)                       /* process windows messages */
        {
            case WM_PAINT:
                    BeginPaint (hWnd, &ps) ;
                    SetRect (&r1, 10, 10, 100, 100) ;
                    SetRect (&r2, 50, 50, 140, 90) ;
                    UnionRect (&r3, &r1, &r2) ;
                    hBrush = CreateHatchBrush (HS_CROSS, RGB (0, 0, 255)) ;
                    SelectObject (ps.hdc, hBrush) ;
                    Rectangle (ps.hdc, r3.left, r3.top, r3.right, r3.bottom) ;
                    SelectObject (ps.hdc, GetStockObject (NULL_BRUSH)) ;
                    DeleteObject (hBrush) ;
                    hPen = CreatePen (PS_SOLID, 3, RGB (255, 0, 0)) ;
                    SelectObject (ps.hdc, hPen) ;
                    Rectangle (ps.hdc, r1.left, r1.top, r1.right, r1.bottom) ;
                    Rectangle (ps.hdc, r2.left, r2.top, r2.right, r2.bottom) ;
                    EndPaint (hWnd, &ps) ;
                    DeleteObject (hPen) ;
```

[Other program lines]

UNREALIZEOBJECT

■ Win 2.0   ■ Win 3.0   ■ Win 3.1

Purpose	Used to reset a brush origin or a palette.
Syntax	BOOL **UnrealizeObject**(HBRUSH *hObject*);
Description	This function resets a device context so that it does not "realize" the brush origin or palette, which allows a new brush origin or palette to be selected into the device context. Do not attempt to reset the origin of a stock brush.

Uses   Used to make sure rectangles filled with hatched brush patterns do not "run into" each other.

Returns   BOOL. TRUE if the function unrealized the object, FALSE on error.

See Also   SetBrushOrg()

Parameters

hObject   HBRUSH: A handle to a brush or a logical palette. If *hObject* is a brush handle, it cannot be currently selected into a display context.

Figure 11-81. Unrealize-Object() Example.

Related Messages WM_CTLCOLOR

Example   This example shows two cases where rectangles are drawn with a hatched brush pattern. In the uppercase, both are drawn with the same brush and the patterns align. In the lowercase, the same brush is used, but the origin of the brush is reset before painting. Resetting the origin allows the brush origin to be moved, resulting in mismatched patterns. Note that it is necessary to remove the brush from the device context to change the brush origin. Selecting a stock object does this without creating additional memory demands.

```
long FAR PASCAL WndProc (HWND hWnd, unsigned iMessage, WORD wParam, LONG lParam)
{
        PAINTSTRUCT             ps ;
        RECT                    r1, r2 ;
        HBRUSH                  hBrush ;

        switch (iMessage)                       /* process windows messages */
        {
                case WM_PAINT:
                        BeginPaint (hWnd, &ps) ;
                        SetRect (&r1, 10, 10, 50, 50) ;
                        SetRect (&r2, 50, 10, 90, 50) ;
                        hBrush = CreateHatchBrush (HS_CROSS, RGB (0, 0, 255)) ;
                        SelectObject (ps.hdc, hBrush) ;
                        Rectangle (ps.hdc, r1.left, r1.top, r1.right, r1.bottom) ;
                        Rectangle (ps.hdc, r2.left, r2.top, r2.right, r2.bottom) ;
                        OffsetRect (&r1, 0, 60) ;
                        OffsetRect (&r2, 0, 60) ;
                        SelectObject (ps.hdc, GetStockObject (WHITE_BRUSH)) ;
                        UnrealizeObject (hBrush) ;
                        SetBrushOrg (ps.hdc, 0, 0) ;
                        SelectObject (ps.hdc, hBrush) ;
                        Rectangle (ps.hdc, r1.left, r1.top, r1.right, r1.bottom) ;
                        SelectObject (ps.hdc, GetStockObject (WHITE_BRUSH)) ;
                        UnrealizeObject (hBrush) ;
                        SetBrushOrg (ps.hdc, 5, 3) ;
                        SelectObject (ps.hdc, hBrush) ;
                        Rectangle (ps.hdc, r2.left, r2.top, r2.right, r2.bottom) ;
                        EndPaint (hWnd, &ps) ;
                        DeleteObject (hBrush) ;
                        break ;
```

[Other program lines]

UpdateWindow
■ Win 2.0　　■ Win 3.0　　■ Win 3.1

Purpose	Forces an immediate WM_PAINT message, which updates the window.
Syntax	void **UpdateWindow**(HWND *hWnd*);
Description	The WM_PAINT message is sent directly to the window's message processing function, bypassing the message queue. This allows a program to repaint the client area before other messages (mouse movements, etc.) are processed. WM_PAINT is sent only if there is an update region for the window that requires repainting. Use InvalidateRect() to create an update region if none exists. To put a WM_PAINT message on the application's message queue, simply call InvalidateRect().
Uses	Rapid repainting of a window after some change to the client area was made.
Returns	No returned value (void).
See Also	InvalidateRect(), InvalidateRgn(), BeginPaint(), EndPaint()
Parameters	
hWnd	HWND: The HANDLE to the window needing repainting.
Related Messages	WM_PAINT
Example	In this example, ten lines of text are written to the client area. To erase them, the client area is invalidated, and UpdateWindow() called. This repaints the client area background, erasing the text.

```
Long FAR PASCAL WndProc (HWND hWnd, unsigned iMessage, WORD wParam, LONG lParam)
{
        HDC             hDC ;
        RECT            rClient ;
        int             i ;

        switch (iMessage)                        /* process windows messages */
        {
        case WM_COMMAND:                         /* process menu items */
                switch (wParam)
                {
                case IDM_DOIT:                   /* User hit the "Do it" menu item */
                        hDC = GetDC (hWnd) ;
                        for (i = 0 ; i < 10 ; i++)
                        {
                                TextOut (hDC, 10, 10 + (i*15),
                                        "This text will be erased.", 25) ;
                        }
                        ReleaseDC (hWnd, hDC) ;
                        GetClientRect (hWnd, &rClient) ;
                        InvalidateRect (hWnd, &rClient, TRUE) ;
                        UpdateWindow (hWnd) ;
                        break ;
```

[Other program lines]

ValidateRect
■ Win 2.0　　■ Win 3.0　　■ Win 3.1

Purpose	Removes a rectangular area from the window's update region. This is done to avoid having WM_PAINT messages generated to repaint invalid parts of the client area.
Syntax	void **ValidateRect**(HWND *hWnd*, LPRECT *lpRect*);
Description	Windows keeps track of parts of a window's client area that have become invalid due to scrolling, resizing, or uncovering parts of the client area from beneath other windows. These areas are called "invalid." Windows will send a WM_PAINT message to a window that contains invalid regions to allow repainting. To temporarily avoid repainting, an application can validate regions. Use GetUpdateRect() to determine the size of the invalid rectangle, and use ValidateRect() to validate it. Once validated, the region will not cause WM_PAINT messages.

Uses	Most often used with windows that scroll the client area. It may be more efficient to repaint the area uncovered by scrolling in the part of the program that scrolls the window, rather than passing the job to the WM_PAINT handling logic. In processing WM_PAINT messages, the update rectangle is part of the PAINTSTRUCT data structure filled by BeginPaint() at the start of the WM_PAINT logic.
Returns	No returned value (void).
See Also	GetUpdateRect(), BeginPaint()
Parameters	
hWnd	HWND: The window handle.
lpRect	LPRECT: A pointer to a RECT data structure that contains the rectangle to validate on the client area. Use GetUpdateRect() to retrieve this value. If the value is within the WM_PAINT processing logic, the update rectangle is part of the PAINTSTRUCT data filled by BeginPaint().
Related Messages	WM_PAINT
Example	See the example under the GetUpdateRect() function description.

VALIDATERGN   ■ Win 2.0   ■ Win 3.0   ■ Win 3.1

Purpose	Removes a region from the window's update region. This is done to avoid having WM_PAINT messages generated to repaint invalid parts of the client area.
Syntax	void **ValidateRgn**(HWND *hWnd*, HRGN *hRgn*);
Description	This is similar to ValidateRect(), except the area to be validated is passed as a region instead of a rectangle. Windows keeps track of parts of a window's client area that have become invalid due to scrolling, resizing, or uncovering parts of the client area from beneath other windows. These areas are called "invalid." Windows will send a WM_PAINT message to a window that contains invalid regions to allow repainting. To temporarily avoid repainting, an application can validate regions. Use GetUpdateRgn() to determine the size of the invalid rectangle, and use Validate Rgn() to validate it. Once validated, the region will not prompt WM_PAINT messages.
Uses	Most often used with windows that scroll the client area. It may be more efficient to repaint the area uncovered by scrolling in the part of the program that scrolls the window, rather than passing the job to the WM_PAINT handling logic.
Returns	No returned value (void).
See Also	GetUpdateRgn(), ValidateRect(), GetUpdateRect()
Parameters	
hWnd	HWND: The window handle.
hRgn	HRGN: The handle of the region containing the update area to validate.
Related Messages	WM_PAINT
Example	See the example under the GetUpdateRgn() function description.

Color Palette Control

In the last chapter, the standard Windows RGB color model was used to create colored brushes and pens. Except for 20 pure tones (less on some systems), most colors that are displayed using objects created from RGB colors are painted with a "dithered" brush. This technique mixes the different colored pixels that average to the desired color. With the versions of Windows prior to 3.0, the RGB color model was the only tool available. Windows 3.0 has the added ability to work with color displays and other devices which can display more than 16 colors at one time. The IBM 8514/A and Super VGA video boards are becoming increasingly common, and many displays are now able to show 256 colors from a selection of many million. Windows uses color palettes to control these powerful display systems.

Hardware Palettes

Only high-cost video systems are able to simultaneously display every possible color at every location on the screen. Most video boards display a limited number of colors. The EGA standard was limited to eight simultaneous colors; VGA started with 16; and Super VGA and IBM 8514/A boards show between 64 and 256 colors at once. About a megabyte of video memory is needed to support 256 colors on a VGA or Super VGA resolution screen. With the limited number of colors that can be shown at one time, video boards must keep track of which colors to use. Using a Super VGA board as an example, the 256 colors that can be shown at one time are selected from a range of 256 * 256 * 256 = 16,777,216 possibilities. That range of colors is determined by the video board's use of three bytes of information to specify the red, green, and blue elements of a color.

To show a color on the screen, the video board first sets the RGB (Red, Green, Blue) values for all of the colors that can be shown at one time. These settings are called the "hardware color palette." When a pixel is to be displayed, the color of the pixel is set to the RGB value of one of the hardware color palette values. Changing the color of a pixel only requires that a different hardware palette entry be referenced. If the RGB value of a palette entry is changed, then every pixel displaying that palette color will be immediately changed on the screen. Figure 12-1 shows the mapping of the hardware palette to the screen.

Hardware palettes are used on video systems for speed and memory conservation. The ability to specify every pixel's RGB value individually would take about three megabytes of memory. Limiting the choices to 256 colors in the palette at one time cuts the memory needed down to one megabyte. In addition, the color of a pixel can be changed by just specifying one byte of information, the new palette entry number. This is faster than specifying three bytes for the RGB value of each pixel. Speed is a big issue on video equipment, especially with the video resolution expanding to 1,024 wide by 768 high pixel resolution and beyond.

Color Palettes in Windows

Windows runs into problems when trying to support hardware color palettes. If Windows were to allow any program to change the RGB color settings in the video display hardware palette, every application running on the system would be affected. For example, if the hardware palette color for black were changed to blue, then every black pixel in every visible window would instantly change to blue. This violates the basic principle that

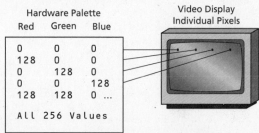

Figure 12-1. A 256-Color Super VGA Hardware Palette.

528

Windows applications run as separate windows that do not interfer with each other. Another problem is that Windows programs can run on any system, many of which will not display as many colors as a Super VGA system.

Windows gets around these problems with two concepts: the "system default palette" and the "logical palette." They are both ways to deal with the actual display equipment's "hardware palette." The system default palette is a group of 20 reserved colors that Windows uses to paint menus, buttons, the screen desktop background, and dithered brushes. If the display equipment supports less than 20 simultaneous colors, some of the 20 entries will be the same. This is normally not a problem, as the text color inside a button can be the same as the text color for menu items, etc. Normally, application programs will not change the system colors. If you have a burning desire to change the system default palette, there are support functions, such as SetSysColors(). With modern display adapters there are usually plenty of extra color choices to use without modifying the system default palette.

The Logical Palette

The logical palette (See Figure 12-2) is a memory area that mimics the hardware palette in the video board. Each entry in the logical palette contains an RGB value that Windows applications can use for creating colored pens, fonts, brushes, and bitmaps. The logical palette can contain more entries than the hardware device actually supports. In this case, the "extra" logical palette entries are mapped to the closest hardware palette color. If the logical palette contains fewer entries than the hardware palette, some of the hardware colors are not used.

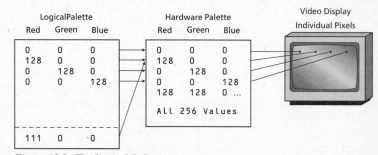

The logical palette gets around the problem of how to deal with systems with small hardware palettes. This still leaves the issue of different ap-

Figure 12-2. The Logical Palette.

plications running at the same time, demanding different colors. There is no escaping the fact that Windows runs on real hardware with only one video card and only one hardware palette. If two different applications are running at the same time and both want to use extended color palettes, the programs will interfere with each other.

Windows minimizes the damage caused when several programs use the logical palette by giving the active window priority in specifying colors for the logical palette. Inactive windows make due with whatever colors are left. Inactive windows use any remaining unused entries in the logical palette, and then use the closest matching colors for any remaining requests on the palette. This is not as much of a problem as it might seem because most programs use only the system colors, which are normally reserved. Windows will allow you to play dangerously, by letting the logical palette change the system palette. The SetSystemPaletteUse() function is provided for this purpose.

Creating a Logical Palette

Activating a logical palette is a three step process.

1. The color settings for every entry in the palette that the application will use are written to an array, and then turned into a palette using the CreatePalette() function. CreatePalette() returns a handle to the palette, which is normally stored as a static variable for use later in the program.

2. The palette is selected into the device context using SelectPalette(), which is similar to the SelectObject() function described in the last chapter for selecting pens, brushes, and fonts. The difference is that selecting a palette does not immediately change the colors because the video hardware palette entries are not changed until the palette is "realized."

3. The palette is "realized" using RealizePalette(), which writes the logical palette settings to the hardware palette, changing the color settings in use. As mentioned previously, the active window is given priority for the hardware

color settings. Any leftover hardware palette entries can be used by inactive windows. Palette entries beyond the limits of the video hardware are mapped to the closest color available.

In processing WM_PAINT messages, it is necessary to select and realize the logical palette every time the message is processed. When the program exits, the logical palette is freed from memory with DeleteObject(). The logical palette can be resized and have entries changed without making a new palette by using the ResizePalette() and SetPaletteEntries() functions. You can use rapid changes in the palette colors to create the illusion that an object is moving on the screen by using AnimatePalette(). To use palette entries for animation, a number of the logical palette entries will need to be the same color, but used to paint different parts of the screen.

Windows Color Palette Messages

Because of the interactions between active and inactive windows using color palettes, communication between applications is needed. Windows sends a WM_QUERYNEWPALETTE message to an application that realizes a logical palette when it is about to get the input focus. This message offers the chance to again realize the palette, regaining colors that may have been lost to other applications while the window was inactive.

The WM_PALETTECHANGED message is sent to all windows when any application realizes its logical palette. For inactive windows, this is notification that colors may be lost to the window with the input focus. The UpdateColors() function is provided to efficiently respond to the new palette choices. The example in this chapter with UpdateColors() shows normal processing logic for handling WM_PALETTECHANGED and WM_QUERYNEWPALETTE messages. Windows sends a WM_SYSCOLORCHANGE message to all windows if an application changes the system palette. The best approach for an application receiving this message is to delete any static brushes and pens and redraw them using the new system colors.

Caution: The array used in CreatePalette() to define all of the colors for the logical palette can exceed the stack space if it is stored as a local variable. It is best to allocate memory for the array.

The colors displayed with the palette functions do not match those produced by the dithering process used by the RGB color model. In general, the palette entries are much darker. Simply converting an application that used RGB colors to comparable palette colors may not result in an acceptable image.

Check the capabilities of the physical hardware before using the palette functions. The GetDeviceCaps() function provides considerable information about what the hardware device can and cannot do. In particular, check the RASTERCAPS index value RC_PALETTE to see if palette changes are supported. The NUMCOLORS index allows the number of colors that can simultaneously be displayed.

Palette Function Summary

Table 12-1 summarizes the Windows functions that provide support for color palettes.

Function	Purpose	
AnimatePalette	Rapidly changes the color of objects painted with colors from a logical palette.	
CreatePalette	Creates a logical palette.	
GetPaletteEntries	Determines the color values for a range of entries in a logical palette.	
GetNearestPaletteIndex	Finds the palette entry number that most closely matches a given RGB value.	
GetSystemPaletteEntries	Determines the colors of each of the system palette items.	
GetSystemPaletteUse	Determines if an application can change the system palette.	
PALETTEINDEX	Specifies a logical palette color directly.	
PALETTERGB	Retrieves the color which is closest to the desired RGB color from the logical palette.	
RealizePalette	Maps the logical palette selected into a device context to the hardware palette.	
ResizePalette	Changes the size of a logical palette.	
SelectPalette	Selects a color palette into a device context.	

SetPaletteEntries	Changes the color values in a logical palette.
SetSysColors	Changes the system colors used to paint window objects.
SetSystemPaletteUse	Allows modifications to the system color palette.
UpdateColors	Redraws the client area when the application does not have the input focus, but has realized a logical palette.

Table 12-1. Palette Function Summary.

Palette Function Descriptions

This section contains the detailed descriptions of the color palette functions.

ANIMATEPALETTE

☐ Win 2.0   ■ Win 3.0   ■ Win 3.1

Purpose	Rapidly changes the color of objects painted with colors from a logical palette.
Syntax	void **AnimatePalette**(HPALETTE *hPalette*, WORD *wStartIndex*, WORD *wNumEntries*, LPPALETTEENTRY *lpPaletteColors*);
Description	Colors can be switched rapidly on the screen by changing the hardware color palette. AnimatePalette() does this for items in a logical palette that have the PC_RESERVED flag (see CreatePalette() for the description of the LOGPALETTE data structure).
Uses	Moving objects on the screen can be simulated by prepainting the objects in the background color (usually white), and then cycling through each object from white, to color, to white.
Returns	No returned value (void).
See Also	CreatePalette()
Parameters	
hPalette	HPALETTE: A handle to the logical palette returned by CreatePalette().
wStartIndex	WORD: The number of the first entry in the logical palette to change.
wNumEntries	WORD: The number of entries in the logical palette to change.
lpPaletteColors	LPPALETTEENTRY: A pointer to an array of PALETTEENTRY data structures containing the new color values to use. See CreatePalette() for the structure definition of PALETTEENTRY.
Example	This example creates a rapidly moving red bar. The bar starts at the left side of the client area (see Figure 12-3). When the user clicks the "Do It!" menu item, the bar appears to move from the

right to the left of the client area in less than one second. This example will only work on a system that supports over 128 simultaneous colors. The movement is caused by rapidly changing the color of a series of 128 rectangles placed ahead of time in the client area. To begin, only the

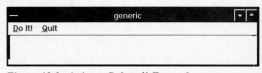

Figure 12-3. AnimatePalette() Example.

leftmost rectangle is colored red. The rest are colored white, so they are not visible. The color of each successive rectangle is changed to red using AnimatePalette(). This is much faster than painting each rectangle using the Rectangle() function.

In the source code, the WM_CREATE section creates the logical palette. The 128 colors are all initialized to white, except for the first one, which is red. The WM_PAINT section paints all 128 rectangles on the client area, even though only the first one is initially visible. This technique allows AnimatePalette() to change the color of each rectangle without the delay of painting.

```
long FAR PASCAL WndProc (HWND hWnd, unsigned iMessage, WORD wParam, LONG lParam)
{
        PAINTSTRUCT                            ps ;
        static         HPALETTE                hPal ;
        HDC                                    hDC ;
        HBRUSH                                 hBrush ;
        static         LOCALHANDLE             hLocPal ;
        static         PLOGPALETTE             pLogPal ;
        int                                    i ;
        static         int                     nNumColor ;

        switch (iMessage)                      /* process windows messages */
        {
                case WM_CREATE:
                        nNumColor = 128 ;
                        hLocPal = LocalAlloc (LMEM_MOVEABLE, sizeof (LOGPALETTE) *
                                nNumColor * sizeof (PALETTEENTRY)) ;
                        pLogPal = (PLOGPALETTE) LocalLock (hLocPal) ;
                        pLogPal->palVersion = 0x300 ;            /* for windows 3.0 */
                        pLogPal->palNumEntries = nNumColor ;
                        for (i = 0 ; i < nNumColor ; i++)
                        {
                                pLogPal->palPalEntry [i].peRed = 255 ;
                                pLogPal->palPalEntry [i].peGreen = (i == 0 ? 0 : 255);
                                pLogPal->palPalEntry [i].peBlue = (i == 0 ? 0 : 255) ;
                                pLogPal->palPalEntry [i].peFlags = PC_RESERVED ;
                        }
                        hPal = CreatePalette (pLogPal) ;
                        LocalUnlock (hLocPal) ;
                        break ;
                case WM_PAINT:
                        BeginPaint (hWnd, &ps) ;
                        SelectPalette (ps.hdc, hPal, FALSE) ;
                        RealizePalette (ps.hdc) ;
                        SelectObject (ps.hdc, GetStockObject (NULL_PEN)) ;

                        for (i = 0 ; i < nNumColor ; i++)
                        {
                                hBrush = CreateSolidBrush (PALETTEINDEX (i)) ;
                                SelectObject (ps.hdc, hBrush) ;
                                Rectangle (ps.hdc, i * 4, 0, (i * 4) + 25, 50) ;
                                SelectObject (ps.hdc, GetStockObject (WHITE_BRUSH)) ;
                                DeleteObject (hBrush) ;
                        }
                        EndPaint (hWnd, &ps) ;
                        break ;
                case WM_COMMAND:                /* process menu items */
                        switch (wParam)
                        {
                        case IDM_DOIT:          /* User hit the "Do it" menu item */
                                pLogPal = (PLOGPALETTE) LocalLock (hLocPal) ;
                                for (i = 0 ; i < nNumColor ; i++)
                                {
                                        pLogPal->palPalEntry [i].peGreen = 255 ;
                                        pLogPal->palPalEntry [i].peBlue = 255 ;
                                        if (i < nNumColor - 1)
                                        {
                                                pLogPal->palPalEntry [i + 1].peGreen = 0 ;
                                                pLogPal->palPalEntry [i + 1].peBlue = 0 ;
                                        }
                                        else
                                        {
                                                pLogPal->palPalEntry [0].peGreen = 0 ;
                                                pLogPal->palPalEntry [0].peBlue = 0 ;
                                        }
                                        AnimatePalette (hPal, 0, nNumColor,
                                                pLogPal->palPalEntry) ;
                                }
                                LocalUnlock (hLocPal) ;
```

```
                                        break ;
                        case IDM_QUIT:                /* send end of application message */
                                DestroyWindow (hWnd) ;
                                break ;
                        }
                        break ;
                case WM_DESTROY:                  /* stop application */
                        LocalUnlock (hLocPal) ;
                        LocalFree (hLocPal) ;
                        DeleteObject (hPal) ;
                        PostQuitMessage (0) ;
                        break ;
                default:                          /* default windows message processing */
                        return DefWindowProc (hWnd, iMessage, wParam, lParam) ;
        }
        return (0L) ;
}
```

CREATEPALETTE

Purpose   Creates a logical palette.

Syntax   HPALETTE **CreatePalette** (LPLOGPALETTE *lpLogPalette*);

Description This function reads the data in the *lpLogPalette* data structure and creates a color palette based on those values. The LOGPALETTE data structure is defined in WINDOWS.H as

```
/* Logical Palette */
typedef struct tagLOGPALETTE_XE "LOGPALETTE"_ {
    WORD                palVersion;
    WORD                palNumEntries;
    PALETTEENTRY        palPalEntry[1];
} LOGPALETTE;
typedef LOGPALETTE                *PLOGPALETTE;
typedef LOGPALETTE NEAR           *NPLOGPALETTE;
typedef LOGPALETTE FAR            *LPLOGPALETTE;
```

The *palVersion* element specifies the Windows version number. 0x300 is used for version 3.0. *palNumEntries* specifies how many entries there are in the palette. Each entry is a PALETTEENTRY data structure, also defined in WINDOWS.H.

```
typedef struct tagPALETTEENTRY_XE "PALETTEENTRY"_ {
    BYTE        peRed;
    BYTE        peGreen;
    BYTE        peBlue;
    BYTE        peFlags;
} PALETTEENTRY;
typedef PALETTEENTRY FAR *LPPALETTEENTRY;
```

The color name elements are allowed to range from 0 to 255. The *peFlags* element is normally set to zero, but can contain one of the values listed in Table 12-2.

Value	Meaning	⊠
PC_EXPLICIT	Specifies that the low-order word is a direct index to the hardware palette.	
PC_NOCOLLAPSE	The color will be placed in available system palette locations, but not matched to an existing color in the system default palette. If the system default palette is full, the color is matched normally.	
PC_RESERVED	Specifies that the palette element will be used for palette animation. This prevents other windows from matching colors using this entry. Only unused palette entries will be filled with this flag set. If all palette entries are taken, the entry will not be available for animation.	

Table12-2. PALETTEENTRY Flags.

Uses   Used to create color palettes. Before the palette can be used, it must be selected into the device context with SelectPalette() and mapped to the hardware palette using RealizePalette().

Returns   HPALETTE, a handle to the palette created. The returned value normally is stored as a static variable.

See Also   DeleteObject(), SelectPalette(), RealizePalette()

Parameters

lpLogPalette   LPLOGPALETTE: A pointer to a LOGPALETTE data structure defining the palette. A memory area large enough to hold the LOGPALETTE data structure and all of the PALETTEENTRY structures for each color must be allocated and initialized before CreatePalette() is called. Once CreatePalette() has been used to register the new palette, the memory for the LOGPALETTE data structure and PALETTEENTRY items can be freed to the system.

Related Messages WM_QUERYNEWPALETTE, WM_PALETTECHANGED

Example   This example shows the creation of a logical palette. The number of available colors is determined with two calls to GetDeviceCaps(). Temporary local memory is allocated to hold the palette during creation using LocalAlloc(). The color values for each palette entry are distributed to cover the size of the palette. The handle to the palette created is stored in a static variable *hPal*. Once the palette is created, the memory used to build the palette can be released.

When a WM_PAINT message is received, the program displays all of the colors by using the palette to create colored brushes that fill the rectangles drawn. Note that each brush created must be removed from the device context before it can be deleted. It is removed by selecting a stock brush into the device context, displacing the colored brush out of the device context. The palette is deleted when the program exits.

```
Long FAR PASCAL WndProc (HWND hWnd, unsigned iMessage, WORD wParam, LONG lParam)
{
        PAINTSTRUCT             ps ;
        HDC                     hDC ;
        static   HPALETTE       hPal ;
        HBRUSH                  hBrush ;
        LOCALHANDLE             hLocPal ;
        PLOGPALETTE             pLogPal ;
        int                     i, j, k, nNumCol, nNumRes, nBlue, nGreen, nRed ;
        static int              nFreeCol ;

        switch (iMessage)                       /* process windows messages */
        {
                case WM_CREATE:
                        hDC = GetDC (hWnd) ;
                        nNumCol = GetDeviceCaps (hDC, SIZEPALETTE) ;
                        nNumRes = GetDeviceCaps (hDC, NUMRESERVED) ;
                        nFreeCol = nNumCol - nNumRes ;
                        ReleaseDC (hWnd, hDC) ;
                        if (nFreeCol >= 216)            /* 216 = 6 cubed */
                                nRed = nGreen = nBlue = 6 ;
                        else if (nFreeCol >= 16)
                        {
                                nRed = nGreen = 2 ;
                                nBlue = 4 ;
                        }
                        else
                                nRed = nGreen = nBlue = 2 ;

                        hLocPal = LocalAlloc (LMEM_MOVEABLE, sizeof (LOGPALETTE) *
                                nFreeCol * sizeof (PALETTEENTRY)) ;
                        pLogPal = (PLOGPALETTE) LocalLock (hLocPal) ;
                        pLogPal->palVersion = 0x300 ;    /* for windows 3.0 */
                        pLogPal->palNumEntries = nFreeCol ;
                        for (i = 0 ; i < nRed ; i++)
                        {
```

```
                        for (j = 0 ; j < nGreen ; j++)
                        {
                                for (k = 0 ; k < nBlue ; k++)
                                {
                                        pLogPal->palPalEntry [i].peRed =
                                                i * (256 / nRed) ;
                                        pLogPal->palPalEntry [i].peGreen =
                                                j * (256 / nGreen) ;
                                        pLogPal->palPalEntry [i].peBlue =
                                                k * (256 / nBlue) ;
                                        pLogPal->palPalEntry [i].peFlags = 0 ;
                                }
                        }
                }
                hPal = CreatePalette (pLogPal) ;
                LocalUnlock (hLocPal) ;
                LocalFree (hLocPal) ;
                break ;
        case WM_PAINT:
                BeginPaint (hWnd, &ps) ;
                SelectPalette (ps.hdc, hPal, FALSE) ;
                RealizePalette (ps.hdc) ;
                for (i = 0 ; i < nFreeCol ; i++)
                {
                        hBrush = CreateSolidBrush (PALETTEINDEX (i)) ;
                        SelectObject (ps.hdc, hBrush) ;
                        Rectangle (ps.hdc, i * 5, 0, (i * 5) + 5, 100) ;
                        SelectObject (ps.hdc, GetStockObject (BLACK_BRUSH)) ;
                        DeleteObject (hBrush) ;
                }
                EndPaint (hWnd, &ps) ;
                break ;
        case WM_COMMAND:                    /* process menu items */
                switch (wParam)
                {
                case IDM_QUIT:                      /* send end of application message */
                        DestroyWindow (hWnd) ;
                        break ;
                }
                break ;
        case WM_DESTROY:            /* stop application */
                DeleteObject (hPal) ;
                PostQuitMessage (0) ;
                break ;
        default:                            /* default windows message processing */
                return DefWindowProc (hWnd, iMessage, wParam, lParam) ;
        }
        return (0L) ;
}
```

GetNearestPaletteIndex   □ Win 2.0   ■ Win 3.0   ■ Win 3.1

Purpose	Finds the palette entry number that most closely matches a given RGB value.
Syntax	WORD **GetNearestPaletteIndex**(HPALETTE *hPalette*, DWORD *crColor*);
Description	In many cases, the system palette will not have an exact match to a given RGB color. This function returns the palette item which most closely matches the color. This palette item may be far removed from the desired color value, if the palette was created with a narrow range of colors.
Uses	Determining if colors in the logical palette need to be changed.
Returns	WORD, the palette item number that is the closest match to the desired RGB value.
See Also	GetNearestColor(), PALETTEINDEX(), PALETTERGB(), SetPaletteEntries()
Parameters	
hPalette	HPALETTE: The handle to the logical palette returned by CreatePalette().

crColor	COLORREF: The desired 32-bit color value. Use the RGB() macro to specify this value.
Example	See the example under PALETTEINDEX().

GETPALETTEENTRIES

☐ Win 2.0   ■ Win 3.0   ■ Win 3.1

Purpose	Determines the color values for a range of entries in a logical palette.
Syntax	WORD **GetPaletteEntries**(HPALETTE *hPalette*, WORD *wStartIndex*, WORD *wNumEntries*, LPPALETTEENTRY *lpPaletteEntries*);
Description	This function will retrieve the RGB color values and flag value for each entry in a color palette.
Uses	Determining the color of a specific index value in the color palette.
Returns	WORD, the number of entries retrieved.
See Also	PALETTEINDEX(), PALETTERGB(), GetSystemPaletteEntries()

Parameters

hPalette	HPALETTE: The handle to the palette, returned by CreatePalette().
wStartIndex	WORD: The number of the first palette entry to start with, 0 for the first.
wNumEntries	WORD: The number of entries to read.

lpPaletteEntries   LPPALETTEENTRY: The address of an array of at least *wNumEntries* PALETTEENTRY data structures. See CreatePalette() for the structure definition of PALETTEENTRY. If you use a local variable array to hold this data, make sure the stack is sized large enough to hold the data.

Figure 12-4. GetPaletteEntries() Example.

Related Messages   WM_QUERYNEWPALETTE, WM_PALETTECHANGED

Example   This example creates a palette with 216 entries, and then displays both the numerical values and a colored rectangle for each. (See Figure 12-4.) Painting occurs well beyond the end of the client area, so only part of the palette is visible. On the screen, the rectangles to the right of the numeric values show the specified colors.

```
long FAR PASCAL WndProc (HWND hWnd, unsigned iMessage, WORD wParam, LONG lParam)
{
        PAINTSTRUCT                     ps ;
        static HPALETTE                 hPal ;
        HBRUSH                          hBrush ;
        LOCALHANDLE                     hLocPal ;
        PLOGPALETTE                     pLogPal ;
        int                             i, j ;
        static   int                    nFreeCol ;
        static PALETTEENTRY             peEntry [256] ;
        char                            cBuf [128] ;

        switch (iMessage)                       /* process windows messages */
        {
             case WM_CREATE:
                     nFreeCol = 216 ;
                     hLocPal = LocalAlloc (LMEM_MOVEABLE, sizeof (LOGPALETTE) +
                             nFreeCol * sizeof (PALETTEENTRY)) ;
```

```
                pLogPal = (PLOGPALETTE) LocalLock (hLocPal) ;
                pLogPal->palVersion = 0x300 ;    /* for windows 3.0 */
                pLogPal->palNumEntries = nFreeCol ;
                for (i = 0 ; i < nFreeCol ; i++)
                {
                        pLogPal->palPalEntry [i].peRed = i ;
                        pLogPal->palPalEntry [i].peGreen = (i * 4) % 256 ;
                        pLogPal->palPalEntry [i].peBlue = (i * 8) % 256 ;
                        pLogPal->palPalEntry [i].peFlags = 0 ;
                }
                hPal = CreatePalette (pLogPal) ;
                LocalUnlock (hLocPal) ;
                LocalFree (hLocPal) ;
                break ;
        case WM_PAINT:
                BeginPaint (hWnd, &ps) ;
                SelectPalette (ps.hdc, hPal, FALSE) ;
                RealizePalette (ps.hdc) ;
                j = GetPaletteEntries (hPal, 0, nFreeCol, peEntry) ;
                for (i = 0 ; i < j ; i++)
                {
                        TextOut (ps.hdc, 10, 17 * i, cBuf, wsprintf (cBuf,
                                "Entry %d = Red %d, Green %d, Blue %d",
                                i, peEntry[i].peRed, peEntry[i].peGreen,
                                peEntry[i].peBlue)) ;
                        hBrush = CreateSolidBrush (PALETTEINDEX (i)) ;
                        SelectObject (ps.hdc, hBrush) ;
                        Rectangle (ps.hdc, 330, (i * 17) + 1, 360,
                                (i * 17) + 16) ;
                        SelectObject (ps.hdc, GetStockObject (WHITE_BRUSH)) ;
                        DeleteObject (hBrush) ;
                }
                EndPaint (hWnd, &ps) ;
                break ;
        case WM_COMMAND:                        /* process menu items */
                switch (wParam)
                {
                case IDM_QUIT:          /* send end of application message */
                        DestroyWindow (hWnd) ;
                        break ;
                }
                break ;
        case WM_DESTROY:        /* stop application */
                DeleteObject (hPal) ;
                PostQuitMessage (0) ;
                break ;
        default:                        /* default windows message processing */
                return DefWindowProc (hWnd, iMessage, wParam, lParam) ;
    }
    return (0L) ;
}
```

GetSystemPaletteEntries   □ Win 2.0   ■ Win 3.0   ■ Win 3.1

Purpose	Determines the colors of each of the system palette items.
Syntax	WORD **GetSystemPaletteEntries**(HDC *hDC*, WORD *wStartIndex*, WORD *wNumEntries*, LPPALETTEENTRY *lpPaletteEntries*);
Description	The system palette is a group of 20 colors that Windows uses for the default color scheme. All applications share the system palette. Entries in the system palette can be changed by calling SetSysColors(). All applications are notified of the change by a WM_SYSCOLORCHANGE message. They can then use GetSystemPaletteEntries() to determine the new system palette colors.
Uses	Processing WM_SYSCOLORCHANGE messages, and determining the system palette entries for painting with pure colors.

Returns	WORD, the number of system palette entries retrieved.
See Also	GetPaletteEntries(), SetSysColors()
Parameters	
hDC	HDC: The device context handle.
wStartIndex	WORD: The first palette entry to read. Zero for the first one.
wNumEntries	WORD: The number of entries to read.
lpPaletteEntries	LPPALETTEENTRY: A pointer to an array of at least *wNumEntries* PALETTEENTRY structures that will hold the data read from the system palette. See CreatePalette() for the structure definition for PALETTEENTRY.
Related Messages	WM_SYSCOLORCHANGE
Example	This example, which is shown in Figure 12-5, demonstrates how to dump the RGB content of each color in the system palette. These colors are the same ones that show up as pure colors in the Windows Control Panel Color application.

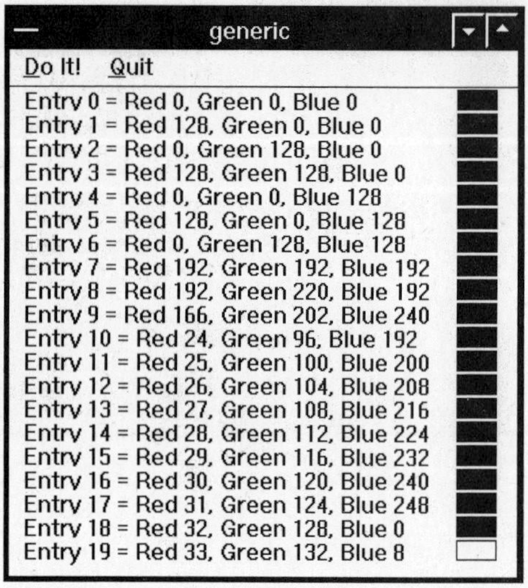

Figure 12-5. GetSystemPaletteEntries() Example.

```
long FAR PASCAL WndProc (HWND hWnd, unsigned iMessage, WORD wParam, LONG lParam)
{
        PAINTSTRUCT                       ps ;
        HBRUSH                            hBrush ;
        int                               i, j ;
        static PALETTEENTRY               peEntry [20] ;
        char                              cBuf [128] ;

        switch (iMessage)                         /* process windows messages */
        {
        case WM_PAINT:
                BeginPaint (hWnd, &ps) ;
                j = GetSystemPaletteEntries (ps.hdc, 0, 20, peEntry) ;
                for (i = 0 ; i < j ; i++)
                {
                        TextOut (ps.hdc, 10, 17 * i, cBuf, wsprintf (cBuf,
                                "Entry %d = Red %d, Green %d, Blue %d",
                                i, peEntry[i].peRed, peEntry[i].peGreen,
                                peEntry[i].peBlue)) ;
                        hBrush = CreateSolidBrush (PALETTEINDEX (i)) ;
                        SelectObject (ps.hdc, hBrush) ;
                        Rectangle (ps.hdc, 330, (i * 17) + 1, 360,
                                (i * 17) + 16) ;
                        SelectObject (ps.hdc, GetStockObject (WHITE_BRUSH)) ;
                        DeleteObject (hBrush) ;
                }
                EndPaint (hWnd, &ps) ;
                break ;
```
[Other program lines]

GetSystemPaletteUse
☐ Win 2.0 ■ Win 3.0 ■ Win 3.1

Purpose	Determines if an application can change the system palette.
Syntax	WORD **GetSystemPaletteUse**(HDC *hDC*, WORD *wUndoc*);

Description   The system palette contains 20 color entries that Windows uses to draw objects, including dithered color brushes. Normally, these entries are not changed if a logical palette is realized. GetSystemPaletteUse() will determine if the values can be changed.

Uses   Used prior to changing the system palette.

Returns   WORD, one of the values in Table 12-3.

Value	Meaning	☒
SYSPAL_NOSTATIC	The system palette contains no static colors.	
SYSPAL_STATIC	The system palette contains static colors which will not change when an application calls RealizePalette().	

Table 12-3. GetSystemPaletteUse() Flags.

See Also   SetSystemPaletteUse()

Parameters
hDC   HDC: The device context handle.

wUndoc   WORD: An undocumented word value. Set this value to SYSPAL_NOSTATIC.

Related Messages WM_SYSCOLORCHANGE

PALETTEINDEX
☐ Win 2.0   ■ Win 3.0   ■ Win 3.1

Purpose   Directly specifies a logical palette color .

Syntax   COLORREF **PALETTEINDEX** (int *nPaletteIndex*);

Description   This macro returns the 32-bit color value for a specific entry in the logical palette. The macro is defined in WINDOWS.H as follows:

```
#define PALETTEINDEX(i)     ((DWORD)(0x01000000 | (WORD)(i)))
```

Note that the 32-bit color value for indexed colors includes a 1 in the high-order byte.

Uses   Directly specifying the use of a palette color in creating a brush, pen, or text color.

Returns   COLORREF, the 32-bit color value.

See Also   PALETTERGB(), RGB()

Parameters
nPaletteIndex   int: The number of the entry in the logical palette. Zero for the first item, etc.

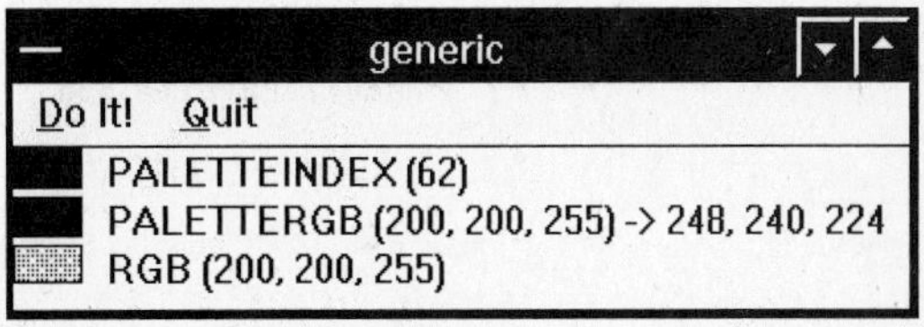

Example   This example (see Figure 12-6) creates a custom palette when the program starts. When a WM_PAINT message is received, three colored rectangles are drawn using three different ways to specify a color. The first one is drawn by specifying a palette index using PALETTEINDEX(). The second one is drawn with PALETTERGB(), which picks the closest palette color to the requested RGB value. In this case, there is not a good match. The actual RGB value for the palette selection is extracted with GetNearestPaletteIndex() and displayed to the far right in the figure. The last rectangle is drawn with a color value specified with the RGB() macro, which creates a hatched brush that simulates the desired color by dithering.

Figure 12-6. PALETTEINDEX() and PALETTERGB() Examples.

Note in the example code that the previous brush is deleted by deleting the returned value from SelectObject(). SelectObject() returns a handle to the last similar object selected. This is a convenient technique because it is not possible to remove the object from memory until it is selected out of the device context. Selecting the new object pushes the old one out, ready to be deleted.

```
long FAR PASCAL WndProc (HWND hWnd, unsigned iMessage, WORD wParam, LONG lParam)
{
        PAINTSTRUCT             ps ;
        static HPALETTE         hPal ;
        HDC                     hDC ;
        HBRUSH                  hBrush ;
        LOCALHANDLE             hLocPal ;
        PLOGPALETTE             pLogPal ;
        int                     i, nNumCol, nNumRes, nColor ;
        static  int             nFreeCol ;
        DWORD                   dwColor ;
        char                    cBuf [128] ;

        switch (iMessage)                       /* process windows messages */
        {
            case WM_CREATE:
                hDC = GetDC (hWnd) ;
                nNumCol = GetDeviceCaps (hDC, SIZEPALETTE) ;
                nNumRes = GetDeviceCaps (hDC, NUMRESERVED) ;
                nFreeCol = nNumCol - nNumRes ;
                ReleaseDC (hWnd, hDC) ;

                hLocPal = LocalAlloc (LMEM_MOVEABLE, sizeof (LOGPALETTE) *
                        nFreeCol * sizeof (PALETTEENTRY)) ;
                pLogPal = (PLOGPALETTE) LocalLock (hLocPal) ;
                pLogPal->palVersion = 0x300 ;     /* for windows 3.0 */
                pLogPal->palNumEntries = nFreeCol ;
                for (i = 0 ; i < nFreeCol ; i++)
                {
                        pLogPal->palPalEntry [i].peRed = (i * 4) % 256 ;
                        pLogPal->palPalEntry [i].peGreen = (i * 8) % 256 ;
                        pLogPal->palPalEntry [i].peBlue = (i * 16) % 256 ;
                        pLogPal->palPalEntry [i].peFlags = 0 ;
                }
                hPal = CreatePalette (pLogPal) ;
                LocalUnlock (hLocPal) ;
                LocalFree (hLocPal) ;
                break ;
            case WM_PAINT:
                BeginPaint (hWnd, &ps) ;
                SelectPalette (ps.hdc, hPal, FALSE) ;
                RealizePalette (ps.hdc) ;

                i = GetNearestPaletteIndex (hPal,
                        RGB (200, 200, 255)) ;
                hBrush = CreateSolidBrush (PALETTEINDEX (i));
                SelectObject (ps.hdc, hBrush) ;
                Rectangle (ps.hdc, 0, 0, 30, 17) ;
                TextOut (ps.hdc, 40, 0, cBuf, wsprintf (cBuf,
                        "PALETTEINDEX (%d)", i)) ;

                hBrush = CreateSolidBrush (
                        PALETTERGB (200, 200, 255)) ;
                DeleteObject (SelectObject (ps.hdc, hBrush)) ;
                Rectangle (ps.hdc, 0, 20, 30, 37) ;
                dwColor = GetNearestColor (ps.hdc,
                        PALETTERGB (200, 200, 255)) ;
                TextOut (ps.hdc, 40, 20, cBuf, wsprintf (cBuf,
                        "PALETTERGB (200, 200, 255) -> %d, %d, %d",
                        GetRValue (dwColor), GetGValue (dwColor),
                        GetBValue (dwColor))) ;
```

```
                        hBrush = CreateSolidBrush (RGB (200, 200, 255)) ;
                        DeleteObject (SelectObject (ps.hdc, hBrush)) ;
                        Rectangle (ps.hdc, 0, 40, 30, 56) ;
                        TextOut (ps.hdc, 40, 40, "RGB (200, 200, 255)", 19) ;
                        EndPaint (hWnd, &ps) ;
                        DeleteObject (hBrush) ;
                        break ;
             case WM_COMMAND:                   /* process menu items */
                        switch (wParam)
                        {
                        case IDM_DOIT:           /* User hit the "Do it" menu item */
                                InvalidateRect (hWnd, NULL, TRUE) ;
                                break ;
                        case IDM_QUIT:           /* send end of application message */
                                DestroyWindow (hWnd) ;
                                break ;
                        }
                        break ;
             case WM_DESTROY:                   /* stop application */
                        DeleteObject (hPal) ;
                        PostQuitMessage (0) ;
                        break ;
             default:                           /* default windows message processing */
                        return DefWindowProc (hWnd, iMessage, wParam, lParam) ;
        }
        return (0L) ;
}
```

PALETTERGB

☐ Win 2.0   ■ Win 3.0   ■ Win 3.1

Purpose	Retrieves the color closest to the desired RGB color from the logical palette.
Syntax	COLORREF **PALETTERGB** (BYTE *cRed*, BYTE *cGreen*, BYTE *cBlue*);
Description	This macro retrieves the logical palette color closest to the desired RGB color. The macro is defined in WINDOWS.H as follows:

```
#define PALETTERGB(r,g,b)  (0x02000000 | RGB(r,g,b))
```

	Note that the high-order byte is set to a value of two.
Uses	Used with devices that support a large number of colors. In these cases, it becomes difficult to keep track of the individual palette index values. PALETTERGB() also has the advantage of behaving similarly to the RGB() macro that defines dithered colors.
Returns	COLORREF, the 32-bit color value.
See Also	PALETTEINDEX(), RGB()
Parameters	
cRed	BYTE: The red element of the color, 0 to 255.
cGreen	BYTE: The green element of the color, 0 to 255.
cBlue	BYTE: The blue element of the color, 0 to 255.
Example	See the previous example under PALETTEINDEX().

REALIZEPALETTE

☐ Win 2.0   ■ Win 3.0   ■ Win 3.1

Purpose	Maps the logical palette selected into a device context to the hardware palette.
Syntax	int **RealizePalette** (HDC *hDC*) ;
Description	Before palette colors can be used, the palette must be created with CreatePalette(), selected into the device context with SelectPalette(), and "realized" using RealizePalette(). RealizePalette() sets the hardware palette entries to the values specified in the palette selected

into the device context. Realizing a palette has system-wide effects, as all windows are painted using the palette entries. Priority is given to the active window for use of the palette colors. Inactive windows can use remaining free palette entries. Any additional colors that are needed will be matched to the closest palette entry available.

Windows sends all applications running on the system a WM_PALETTECHANGED message after RealizePalette() is called. This allows applications that do not have the input focus to realize their logical palettes using the new system palette values.

Uses	This function must be used before attempting to paint with the palette colors. The function also is called when the application receives a WM_QUERYNEWPALETTE message.
Returns	int, the number of entries in the logical palette that were changed.
See Also	CreatePalette(), SelectPalette(), DeleteObject(), UnrealizeObject()
Parameters	
hDC	HDC: The device context handle.
Related Messages	WM_QUERYNEWPALETTE, WM_PALETTECHANGED
Example	See the example under CreatePalette().

RESIZEPALETTE   □ Win 2.0   ■ Win 3.0   ■ Win 3.1

Purpose	Changes the size of a logical palette.
Syntax	BOOL **ResizePalette**(HPALETTE *hPalette*, WORD *nNumEntries*);
Description	This function allows the size of a logical palette to be changed after the palette has been created. If the palette is reduced in size, the remaining entries are not affected. If the palette is increased in size, the new entries are all set to zero.
Uses	Eliminates the need to create a new palette if the number of entries changes as the program runs.
Returns	BOOL. TRUE if the palette was resized, FALSE on error.
See Also	SetPaletteEntries(), CreatePalette()
Parameters	
hPalette	HPALETTE: The palette handle returned by CreatePalette().
nNumEntries	WORD: The new number of elements in the palette.
Related Messages	WM_PALETTECHANGED
Example	In this example, the starting palette is as large as possible. Every time the user clicks the "Do It!" menu item, the palette is reduced in size by 50%.

```
long FAR PASCAL WndProc (HWND hWnd, unsigned iMessage, WORD wParam, LONG lParam)
{
        PAINTSTRUCT                     ps ;
        HDC                             hDC ;
        static   HPALETTE               hPal ;
        HBRUSH                          hBrush ;
        LOCALHANDLE                     hLocPal ;
        PLOGPALETTE                     pLogPal ;
        int                             i, nNumCol, nNumRes ;
        static   int                    nFreeCol ;

        switch (iMessage)                       /* process windows messages */
        {
                case WM_CREATE:
                        hDC = GetDC (hWnd) ;
                        nNumCol = GetDeviceCaps (hDC, SIZEPALETTE) ;
                        nNumRes = GetDeviceCaps (hDC, NUMRESERVED) ;
```

```
                nFreeCol = nNumCol - nNumRes ;
                ReleaseDC (hWnd, hDC) ;

                hLocPal = LocalAlloc (LMEM_MOVEABLE, sizeof (LOGPALETTE) *
                        nFreeCol * sizeof (PALETTEENTRY)) ;
                pLogPal = (PLOGPALETTE) LocalLock (hLocPal) ;
                pLogPal->palVersion = 0x300 ;     /* for windows 3.0 */
                pLogPal->palNumEntries = nFreeCol ;
                for (i = 0 ; i < nFreeCol ; i++)
                {
                        pLogPal->palPalEntry [i].peRed = 0 ;
                        pLogPal->palPalEntry [i].peGreen = 0 ;
                        pLogPal->palPalEntry [i].peBlue = i * (256 / nFreeCol) ;
                        pLogPal->palPalEntry [i].peFlags = 0 ;
                }
                hPal = CreatePalette (pLogPal) ;
                LocalUnlock (hLocPal) ;
                LocalFree (hLocPal) ;
                break ;
        case WM_PAINT:
                BeginPaint (hWnd, &ps) ;
                SelectPalette (ps.hdc, hPal, FALSE) ;
                RealizePalette (ps.hdc) ;
                for (i = 0 ; i < nFreeCol ; i++)
                {
                        hBrush = CreateSolidBrush (PALETTEINDEX (i)) ;
                        SelectObject (ps.hdc, hBrush) ;
                        Rectangle (ps.hdc, i * 5, 0, (i * 5) + 5, 100) ;
                        SelectObject (ps.hdc, GetStockObject (BLACK_BRUSH)) ;
                        DeleteObject (hBrush) ;
                }
                EndPaint (hWnd, &ps) ;
                break ;
        case WM_COMMAND:                   /* process menu items */
                switch (wParam)
                {
                case IDM_DOIT:             /* User hit the "Do it" menu item */
                        nFreeCol /= 2 ;  /* cut num colors in half */
                        ResizePalette (hPal, nFreeCol) ;
                        InvalidateRect (hWnd, NULL, TRUE) ;
                        break ;
                case IDM_QUIT:             /* send end of application message */
                        DestroyWindow (hWnd) ;
                        break ;
                }
                break ;
        case WM_DESTROY:                   /* stop application */
                DeleteObject (hPal) ;
                PostQuitMessage (0) ;
                break ;
        default:                   /* default windows message processing */
                return DefWindowProc (hWnd, iMessage, wParam, lParam) ;
        }
        return (0L) ;
}
```

SELECTPALETTE   □ Win 2.0   ■ Win 3.0   ■ Win 3.1

Purpose	Selects a color palette into a device context.
Syntax	HPALETTE **SelectPalette** (HDC *hDC*,HPALETTE *hPalette*, BOOL *bForceBackground*) ;
Description	This function is the analog to SelectObject(), except that it only works for palettes. The *hPalette* parameter is the handle returned when the palette was created with CreatePalette(). Selecting a palette into the device context does not immediately make the colors available. RealizePalette() must be called to map the selected palette to the hardware so that the colors are available.
Uses	Used in WM_PAINT logic that uses the color palette to define colors.

Returns	HPALETTE, the old logical palette displaced from the device context. NULL on error.
See Also	CreatePalette(), RealizePalette(), DeleteObject(), UnrealizeObject()
Parameters	
hDC	HDC: The device context handle.
hPalette	HPALETTE: The handle of the logical palette returned by CreatePalette().
bForceBackground	BOOL: Specifies if the logical palette is to be in effect if the window does not have the input focus. TRUE if it is to be in effect, FALSE (the normal case) if not.
Related Messages	WM_QUERYNEWPALETTE, WM_PALETTECHANGED
Example	See the example under CreatePalette().

SETPALETTEENTRIES

□ Win 2.0   ■ Win 3.0   ■ Win 3.1

Purpose	Changes the color values in a logical palette.
Syntax	WORD **SetPaletteEntries**(HPALETTE *hPalette*, WORD *wStartIndex*, WORD *wNumEntries*, LPPALETTEENTRY *lpPaletteEntries*);
Description	This function is useful after a palette has been created. It allows the palette colors and flag values for entries in the palette to be changed without creating a new palette. The changes take effect once the palette is realized with RealizePalette().
Uses	This is the most efficient way to change a color palette while an application is running.
Returns	WORD, the number of entries set in the logical palette, zero on error.
See Also	CreatePalette(), RealizePalette(), SelectPalette(), DeleteObject()
Parameters	
hPalette	HPALETTE: The handle to the palette returned by CreatePalette().
wStartIndex	WORD: The number of the first palette entry to change.
wNumEntries	WORD: The number of entries to change.
lpPaletteEntries	LPPALETTEENTRY: A pointer to an array of PALETTEENTRY data structures. See CreatePalette() for the structure definition for PALETTEENTRY. There must be at least *wNumEntries* array elements.
Related Messages	WM_QUERYNEWPALETTE, WM_PALETTECHANGED
Example	This program initially creates a palette of blue shades and paints them across the top of the client area. The number of colors is set to use every free color, excluding those dedicated to the system palette. When the user clicks the "Do It!" menu item, the palette is changed to shades of red. This change is not instantly visible because the palette is not realized until the next WM_PAINT message is processed.

```
long FAR PASCAL WndProc (HWND hWnd, unsigned iMessage, WORD wParam, LONG lParam)
{
        PAINTSTRUCT                     ps ;
        HDC                             hDC ;
        static   HPALETTE               hPal ;
        HBRUSH                          hBrush ;
        LOCALHANDLE                     hLocPal ;
        PLOGPALETTE                     pLogPal ;
        int                             i, nNumCol, nNumRes ;
        static   int                    nFreeCol ;
        static PALETTEENTRY             pePalEnt [256] ;

        switch (iMessage)                       /* process windows messages */
        {
                case WM_CREATE:
                        hDC = GetDC (hWnd) ;
```

```
                        nNumCol = GetDeviceCaps (hDC, SIZEPALETTE) ;
                        nNumRes = GetDeviceCaps (hDC, NUMRESERVED) ;
                        nFreeCol = nNumCol - nNumRes ;
                        ReleaseDC (hWnd, hDC) ;

                        hLocPal = LocalAlloc (LMEM_MOVEABLE, sizeof (LOGPALETTE) *
                                nFreeCol * sizeof (PALETTEENTRY)) ;
                        pLogPal = (PLOGPALETTE) LocalLock (hLocPal) ;
                        pLogPal->palVersion = 0x300 ;     /* for windows 3.0 */
                        pLogPal->palNumEntries = nFreeCol ;
                        for (i = 0 ; i < nFreeCol ; i++)
                        {
                                pLogPal->palPalEntry [i].peRed = 0 ;
                                pLogPal->palPalEntry [i].peGreen = 0 ;
                                pLogPal->palPalEntry [i].peBlue = i * (256 / nFreeCol) ;
                                pLogPal->palPalEntry [i].peFlags = 0 ;
                        }
                        hPal = CreatePalette (pLogPal) ;
                        LocalUnlock (hLocPal) ;
                        LocalFree (hLocPal) ;
                        break ;
                case WM_PAINT:
                        BeginPaint (hWnd, &ps) ;
                        SelectPalette (ps.hdc, hPal, FALSE) ;
                        RealizePalette (ps.hdc) ;
                        for (i = 0 ; i < nFreeCol ; i++)
                        {
                                hBrush = CreateSolidBrush (PALETTEINDEX (i)) ;
                                SelectObject (ps.hdc, hBrush) ;
                                Rectangle (ps.hdc, i * 5, 0, (i * 5) + 5, 100) ;
                                SelectObject (ps.hdc, GetStockObject (BLACK_BRUSH)) ;
                                DeleteObject (hBrush) ;
                        }
                        EndPaint (hWnd, &ps) ;
                        break ;
                case WM_COMMAND:                   /* process menu items */
                        switch (wParam)
                        {
                        case IDM_DOIT:           /* User hit the "Do it" menu item */
                                for (i = 0 ; i < nFreeCol ; i++)
                                {
                                        pePalEnt [i].peRed = i * (256 / nFreeCol) ;
                                        pePalEnt [i].peGreen = 0 ;
                                        pePalEnt [i].peBlue = 0 ;
                                        pePalEnt [i].peFlags = 0 ;
                                }
                                SetPaletteEntries (hPal, 0, nFreeCol, pePalEnt) ;
                                InvalidateRect (hWnd, NULL, TRUE) ;
                                break ;
                        case IDM_QUIT:           /* send end of application message */
                                DeleteObject (hPal) ;
                                DestroyWindow (hWnd) ;
                                break ;
                        }
                        break ;
                case WM_DESTROY:                   /* stop application */
                        PostQuitMessage (0) ;
                        break ;
                default:                           /* default windows message processing */
                        return DefWindowProc (hWnd, iMessage, wParam, lParam) ;
        }
        return (0L) ;
}
```

SetSysColors   ■ Win 2.0   ■ Win 3.0   ■ Win 3.1

Purpose   Changes the system colors used to paint window objects.

Syntax   void **SetSysColors** (int *nChanges*, LPINT *lpSysColor*, DWORD FAR **lpColorValues*);

Description   The system colors define what colors Windows uses to paint objects like borders and buttons. Windows reads these values from the WIN.INI file on startup. The values can be changed using the Windows Control Panel Color application. The values can be temporarily changed during a Windows session by calling SetSysColors(). Use WriteProfileString() for permanent changes to the WIN.INI file.

Uses   Not often used. Allows an application to change the colors of various Windows objects during the session, without changing the default values. This affects every running application.

Returns   No returned value.

See Also   GetSysColors(), GetProfileInt(), GetProfileString(), WriteProfileString()

Parameters

nChanges   int: The number of color items to change.

lpSysColor   LPINT: A pointer to an array of at least *nChanges* int values. Each element of the array should be one of the values in Table 12-4.

Value	Meaning	
COLOR_ACTIVEBORDER	The active window border.	
COLOR_ACTIVECAPTION	The active window caption.	
COLOR_APPWORKSPACE	The background color for MDI windows.	
COLOR_BACKGROUND	The desktop color.	
COLOR_BTNFACE	The button face.	
COLOR_BTNSHADOW	The edge of a button.	
COLOR_BTNTEXT	The button text.	
COLOR_CAPTIONTEXT	The text inside the caption bar.	
COLOR_GRAYTEXT	The color of grayed text, as used in disabled menu items. Set to 0 if the display does not support pure gray colors.	
COLOR_HIGHLIGHT	The highlighted control color.	
COLOR_HIGHLIGHTTEXT	The text color of a highlighted item in a control.	
COLOR_INACTIVEBORDER	The color of an inactive window border.	
COLOR_INACTIVECAPTION	The color of an inactive window caption.	
COLOR_INACTIVECAPTION TEXT (Win 3.1)	Color of the text in an inactive caption.	
COLOR_MENU	The background color for window menus.	
COLOR_MENUTEXT	The text color for menus.	
COLOR_SCROLLBAR	The scroll bar gray area.	
COLOR_WINDOW	The background color for windows.	
COLOR_WINDOWFRAME	The window frame.	
COLOR_WINDOWTEXT	The color of text in windows.	

Table 12-4. System Colors.

lpColorValues   DWORD FAR *: A pointer to an array of DWORD values containing the RGB values used to set each of the items specified in the *lpSysColor* array.

Related Messages   WM_SYSCOLORCHANGE

Example   When the user clicks the "Do It!" menu item, two of the system colors are changed, the window background and the work space background colors. The changes are immediately shown on the screen when Windows updates all applications.

```
Long FAR PASCAL WndProc (HWND hWnd, unsigned iMessage, WORD wParam, LONG lParam)
{
        HDC             hDC ;
        int             nSysIndex [2] = {COLOR_WINDOW, COLOR_BACKGROUND} ;
        DWORD           dwColors [2] = {RGB (240, 240, 255),
                                              RGB (200, 210, 255)} ;

        switch (iMessage)                       /* process windows messages */
        {
                case WM_COMMAND:                /* process menu items */
                        switch (wParam)
                        {
                        case IDM_DOIT:           /* User hit the "Do it" menu item */
                                hDC = GetDC (hWnd) ;
                                SetSysColors (2, nSysIndex, dwColors) ;
                                ReleaseDC (hWnd, hDC) ;
                                break ;
```
[Other program lines]

SETSYSTEMPALETTEUSE   □ Win 2.0   ■ Win 3.0   ■ Win 3.1

Purpose   Allows modifications to the system color palette.

Syntax   WORD **SetSystemPaletteUse**(HDC *hDC*, WORD *wUsage*);

Description   Normally, Windows reserves 20 color values for use by all windows. This is called the system palette. SetSystemPaletteUse() allows an application program to change the system palette, or set the status back to the normal, fixed status.

Uses   Changing the system palette may be a desirable way to extend color options when using a device that has between 16 and 64 colors. Above 64 colors, there are enough free colors that it is simpler to leave the system colors unchanged and add other colors as needed.

Returns   WORD, the previous system palette state, either PAL_NOSTATIC or PAL_STATIC. See the definition of these values in Table 12-5.

See Also   SetSysColors()

Parameters

hDC   HDC: The device context handle.

wUsage   WORD: One of the two values in Table 12-5.

Value	Meaning	⊠
SYSPAL_NOSTATIC	The system palette is not static and will change when the program realizes a logical palette with RealizePalette(). A pure black and pure white value are always retained.	
SYSPAL_STATIC	The system palette is static and will not be affected by realizing a logical palette with RealizePalette().	

Table 12-5. SetSystemPaletteUse( ) Flags.

Related Messages WM_SYSCOLORCHANGE

Example   This example changes the system palette when the user clicks the "Do It!" menu item. Before the changes are made, the existing palette is saved into an array *dwOldColors[]*. When the user clicks the "Quit" menu item, the old palette is restored. Note that UnrealizeObject() is used to make sure that the palette changes are processed as if it were the first palette read into the system. Also note that WM_SYSCOLORCHANGE messages are sent to all applications for both changes as notification that the system palette has changed.

```
#define NUMPALCOL        20

long FAR PASCAL WndProc (HWND hWnd, unsigned iMessage, WORD wParam, LONG lParam)
{
        PAINTSTRUCT                     ps ;
        HDC                             hDC ;
        static   HPALETTE               hPal ;
        LOCALHANDLE                     hLocPal ;
        PLOGPALETTE                     pLogPal ;
        int                             i ;
        static int                      nColorIndex [NUMPALCOL] ;
        static DWORD                    dwOldColors [NUMPALCOL] ;

        switch (iMessage)                       /* process windows messages */
        {
                case WM_CREATE:
                        hLocPal = LocalAlloc (LMEM_MOVEABLE, sizeof (LOGPALETTE) *
                                NUMPALCOL * sizeof (PALETTEENTRY)) ;
                        pLogPal = (PLOGPALETTE) LocalLock (hLocPal) ;
                        pLogPal->palVersion = 0x300 ;    /* for windows 3.0 */
                        pLogPal->palNumEntries = NUMPALCOL ;
                        for (i = 0 ; i < NUMPALCOL ; i++)
                        {
                                pLogPal->palPalEntry [i].peRed = (i * 128) % 256 ;
                                pLogPal->palPalEntry [i].peGreen = (i * 64) % 256 ;
                                pLogPal->palPalEntry [i].peBlue = (i * 32) % 256 ;
                                pLogPal->palPalEntry [i].peFlags = 0 ;
                        }
                        hPal = CreatePalette (pLogPal) ;
                        LocalUnlock (hLocPal) ;
                        LocalFree (hLocPal) ;
                        break ;
                case WM_COMMAND:                 /* process menu items */
                        switch (wParam)
                        {
                        case IDM_DOIT:           /* User hit the "Do it" menu item */
                                hDC = GetDC (hWnd) ;
                                for (i = 0 ; i < NUMPALCOL ; i++)
                                {
                                        nColorIndex [i] = i ;
                                        dwOldColors [i] = GetSysColor (i) ;
                                }
                                SetSystemPaletteUse (hDC, SYSPAL_NOSTATIC) ;
                                UnrealizeObject (hPal) ;
                                SelectPalette (hDC, hPal, FALSE) ;
                                RealizePalette (hDC) ;
                                PostMessage (-1, WM_SYSCOLORCHANGE, 0, 0L) ;
                                ReleaseDC (hWnd, hDC) ;
                                break ;
                        case IDM_QUIT:           /* send end of application message */
                                DestroyWindow (hWnd) ;
                                break ;
                        }
                        break ;
                case WM_DESTROY:                 /* stop application */
                        hDC = GetDC (hWnd) ;
                        UnrealizeObject (hPal) ;
                        SelectPalette (hDC, hPal, FALSE) ;
                        RealizePalette (hDC) ;
                        SetSysColors (NUMPALCOL, nColorIndex, dwOldColors) ;
                        SetSystemPaletteUse (hDC, SYSPAL_STATIC) ;
                        PostMessage (-1, WM_SYSCOLORCHANGE, 0, 0L) ;
                        DeleteObject (hPal) ;
                        ReleaseDC (hWnd, hDC) ;
                        PostQuitMessage (0) ;
                        return (0L) ;
```

```
            default:                    /* default windows message processing */
                    return DefWindowProc (hWnd, iMessage, wParam, lParam) ;
        }
        return (0L) ;
}
```

UPDATECOLORS   ☐ Win 2.0   ■ Win 3.0   ■ Win 3.1

Purpose   Redraws the client area when the application does not have the input focus, but has realized a logical palette.

Syntax   int **UpdateColors** (HDC *hDC*) ;

Description   Windows gives preference to the active window when assigning colors from the logical palette. An active window realizing its logical palette may take previously used colors to draw in the client area of an inactive window.

UpdateColors() is provided for rapid updating of colors in windows that do not have the input focus. The function is only useful if the application has already realized its logical palette.

Uses   Processing WM_PALETTECHANGED messages (see example below).

Returns   int, not used.

See Also   CreatePalette(), SelectPalette(), RealizePalette(), DeleteObject()

Parameters

hDC   HDC: The device context handle for the window.

Related Messages WM_PALETTECHANGED

Example   This example is most effective if two instances of the same program are run at the same time. The program is set to display a series of narrow rectangles, each with a different palette color. Figure 12-7 gives a rough idea of the appearance of the

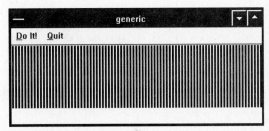

Figure 12-7. UpdateColors() Example.

program's window, when viewing in black and white. Clicking the "Do It!" menu item changes the color palette and causes the screen to be redrawn with the new colors. With two or more versions running on a system that supports 256 colors or less, changing the color palette on one copy of the program will rob colors from the other. The program handles this by processing WM_PALETTECHANGED messages. When a WM_PALETTE-CHANGED message is received, the program calls UpdateColors() to make the best use possible of the remaining colors available.

The program also processes WM_QUERYNEWPALETTE messages. They are received right before the application receives the input focus, giving the program a chance to realize the logical palette and regain colors lost to other applications when the program was inactive. This example shows a standard response to WM_QUERYNEWPALETTE. This is a little redundant, as the program realizes the palette every time a WM_PAINT message is received. The response to WM_QUERYNEWPALETTE could be cut down to just doing the WM_PAINT logic.

```
Long FAR PASCAL WndProc (HWND hWnd, unsigned iMessage, WORD wParam, LONG lParam)
{
        PAINTSTRUCT                     ps ;
        HDC                             hDC ;
        static    HPALETTE              hPal ;
        HBRUSH                          hBrush ;
        LOCALHANDLE                     hLocPal ;
        PLOGPALETTE                     pLogPal ;
        int                             i, nNumCol, nNumRes ;
        static    int                   nFreeCol, nColorChange = 0 ;
```

```
        static PALETTEENTRY                pePalEnt [256] ;

    switch (iMessage)                        /* process windows messages */
    {
        case WM_CREATE:
                hDC = GetDC (hWnd) ;
                nNumCol = GetDeviceCaps (hDC, SIZEPALETTE) ;
                nNumRes = GetDeviceCaps (hDC, NUMRESERVED) ;
                nFreeCol = nNumCol - nNumRes ;
                ReleaseDC (hWnd, hDC) ;

                hLocPal = LocalAlloc (LMEM_MOVEABLE, sizeof (LOGPALETTE) *
                        nFreeCol * sizeof (PALETTEENTRY)) ;
                pLogPal = (PLOGPALETTE) LocalLock (hLocPal) ;
                pLogPal->palVersion = 0x300 ;    /* for windows 3.0 */
                pLogPal->palNumEntries = nFreeCol ;
                for (i = 0 ; i < nFreeCol ; i++)
                {
                        pLogPal->palPalEntry [i].peRed = 0 ;
                        pLogPal->palPalEntry [i].peGreen = 0 ;
                        pLogPal->palPalEntry [i].peBlue = i * (256 / nFreeCol) ;
                        pLogPal->palPalEntry [i].peFlags = 0 ;
                }
                hPal = CreatePalette (pLogPal) ;
                LocalUnlock (hLocPal) ;
                LocalFree (hLocPal) ;
                break ;
        case WM_PAINT:
                BeginPaint (hWnd, &ps) ;
                SelectPalette (ps.hdc, hPal, FALSE) ;
                RealizePalette (ps.hdc) ;
                SelectObject (ps.hdc, GetStockObject (WHITE_PEN)) ;
                for (i = 0 ; i < nFreeCol ; i++)
                {
                        hBrush = CreateSolidBrush (PALETTEINDEX (i)) ;
                        SelectObject (ps.hdc, hBrush) ;
                        Rectangle (ps.hdc, i * 5, 0, (i * 5) + 5, 100) ;
                        SelectObject (ps.hdc, GetStockObject (BLACK_BRUSH)) ;
                        DeleteObject (hBrush) ;
                }
                EndPaint (hWnd, &ps) ;
                break ;
        case WM_COMMAND:                /* process menu items */
                switch (wParam)
                {
                case IDM_DOIT:          /* User hit the "Do it" menu item */
                        nColorChange++ ;
                        for (i = 0 ; i < nFreeCol ; i++)
                        {
                                pePalEnt [i].peRed = i * (256 / nFreeCol) ;
                                pePalEnt [i].peGreen = nColorChange ;
                                pePalEnt [i].peBlue =
                                        (nColorChange & 1 ? 0 : 255) ;
                                pePalEnt [i].peFlags = 0 ;
                        }
                        SetPaletteEntries (hPal, 0, nFreeCol, pePalEnt) ;
                        InvalidateRect (hWnd, NULL, TRUE) ;
                        break ;
                case IDM_QUIT:          /* send end of application message */
                        DestroyWindow (hWnd) ;
                        break ;
                }
                break ;
        case WM_QUERYNEWPALETTE:        /* about to get focus */
                hDC = GetDC (hWnd) ;
                SelectPalette (hDC, hPal, 0) ;
```

```
                if (RealizePalette (hDC))
                        InvalidateRect (hWnd, NULL, TRUE) ;
                ReleaseDC (hWnd, hDC) ;
                break ;
        case WM_PALETTECHANGED:          /* another application changed pal */
                if (wParam != hWnd)
                {
                        hDC = GetDC (hWnd) ;
                        SelectPalette (hDC, hPal, 0) ;
                        if (RealizePalette (hDC))
                                UpdateColors (hDC) ;
                        ReleaseDC (hWnd, hDC) ;
                }
                break ;
        case WM_DESTROY:                 /* stop application */
                DeleteObject (hPal) ;
                PostQuitMessage (0) ;
                break ;
        default:
                return DefWindowProc (hWnd, iMessage, wParam, lParam) ;
        }
        return (0L) ;
}
```

13

Dialog Boxes

Dialog boxes are similar to popup windows. They are frequently used to get input from the user for some specific task, such as to obtain a file name or to obtain a character string for a search activity. The main difference between dialog boxes and popup windows is that the Windows Software Development Kit (SDK) provides a dialog box editor that simplifies the task of positioning the buttons and other controls that make up a dialog box. The dialog box editor does not provide the program logic to process the messages from the dialog box. That task remains up to the programmer.

There are functional differences between the behavior of a popup window and a dialog box. Dialog box functions use a special default message processing function. This function interprets keystrokes such as the arrow keys, (TAB) and (SHIFT)-(TAB) to allow selection of controls in the dialog box using the keyboard. Any activity that can be performed in a dialog box can also be performed in a child or popup window. Dialog boxes are more convenient for simple popup windows that make use of normal control items like buttons and list boxes. Popup and child windows are better if you will be doing extensive painting on the window, or will be modifying the standard behavior of the window.

An Example Dialog Box

To get started, let's modify the GENERIC application we created in Chapter 1 to show a dialog box window. The dialog box will appear as shown in Figure 13-1. It is similar to the dialog box style used by most programs for an "About Box," although this one has two pushbuttons to illustrate how control messages are processed.

Figure 13-1. A Dialog Box.

The first step is to run the SDK Dialog Box Editor application to create the rough dialog box template. The DBEditor will generate two files, a dialog box template file and a header file. It is best to use a separate header file to store the ID values for the dialog box controls. The DBEditor will allow you to update and add to this file for new controls and new dialog boxes as they are added to the application. The DBEditor generates a dialog box template file like the one shown in Listing 13-1. Most people give their dialog box template files the extension ".DLG." In this case, the dialog box is given the name "EXAMPLEDIALOG." We will discuss the meaning of all of the items in the dialog box definition later in this chapter.

▷ **Listing 13-1. GENERIC.DLG The Dialog Box Template File Created with the DBEditor**

```
EXAMPLEDIALOG DIALOG LOADONCALL MOVEABLE DISCARDABLE 20, 34, 160, 67
CAPTION "Example Dialog Box"
FONT 10, "Helv"
STYLE WS_BORDER | WS_CAPTION | WS_DLGFRAME | DS_MODALFRAME | WS_POPUP
BEGIN
    CONTROL "generic Example", -1, "static",
                SS_CENTER | WS_GROUP | WS_CHILD, 42, 12, 81, 10
    CONTROL "This dialog box does nothing.", -1, "static",
                SS_CENTER | WS_GROUP | WS_CHILD, 28, 30, 115, 10
    CONTROL "generic", -1, "static",
                SS_ICON | WS_CHILD, 10, 10, 0, 0
    CONTROL "OK", DLI_OK, "button",
                BS_DEFPUSHBUTTON | WS_TABSTOP | WS_CHILD, 30, 50, 40, 14
    CONTROL "Not OK", DLI_NOTOK, "button",
                BS_PUSHBUTTON | WS_TABSTOP | WS_CHILD, 100, 50, 40, 14
```

```
         CONTROL "generic", -1, "static",
                   SS_ICON | WS_CHILD, 5, 13, 16, 16
END
```

The dialog box template file is a normal ASCII file and can be edited. With the Windows 2.0 version of the DBEditor, it was frequently necessary to go in and edit the dialog box template to add captions, change fonts, etc. These features have all been added to the Windows 3.0 version of the DBEditor, so there is seldom a reason to manually change values. The header file that contains the ID values for all of the controls in every dialog box the application uses can be maintained completely from within the DBEditor. For the simple example shown in Listing 13-2, there are only the two pushbutton controls that need ID values. All of the static items, such as the text strings and the icon, are given ID values of –1. These items are never selected.

▷ **Listing 13-2. GENERICD.H. The Dialog Box ID Header File**

```
#define DLI_OK               101
#define DLI_NOTOK            102
```

It is best to use a numbering convention to keep menu item IDs, dialog box control IDs, and child window control IDs separate. A good system is to number menu items between 1 and 99, dialog box IDs between 100 and 999, and child window control IDs above 1000. The DBEditor will create ID values starting at 100 by default, so this is convenient.

The dialog box template must be compiled to make a binary resource file (.RES) by the resource compiler (RC.EXE) to make the data useful to the application program. The dialog box template file can be either separately compiled or included in the program's resource file, as shown in Listing 13-3. Don't forget to include the header file containing the dialog box ID values.

▷ **Listing 13-3. GENERIC.RC The Resource Script File**

```
/* generic.rc */

#include <windows.h>
#include "generic.h"
#include "genericd.h"
#include "generic.dlg"

generic         ICON    generic.ico

generic         MENU
BEGIN
    MENUITEM "&Do It!"          IDM_DOIT
    MENUITEM "&Quit",           IDM_QUIT
END
```

Note that the resource script file includes the ICON statement. The "generic" icon is also used in the dialog box. Windows does not provide an automated way to process messages from the controls in a dialog box. You will have to create a message processing function for every dialog box in the program. These functions are called "Dialog Box Functions." They are similar to the separate message processing functions we explored in Chapter 3, *Windows Support Functions,* for child and popup windows. Listing 13-4 is a typical example, which processes messages for the simple dialog box previously defined.

▷ **Listing 13-4. A Dialog Box Function**

```
BOOL FAR PASCAL DialogProc (HWND hDlg, WORD wMess, WORD wParam, LONG lParam)
{
        switch (wMess)
        {
            case WM_INITDIALOG:
                                        /* initialization functions go here */
                    return TRUE ;
            case WM_COMMAND:        /* One of the controls was activated */
                    switch (wParam)
                    {
                        case DLI_OK:
                                EndDialog (hDlg, 0) ;
                                return TRUE ;
                        case DLI_NOTOK:
```

```
                                                MessageBeep (0) ;
                                                return TRUE ;
                                }
                                return TRUE ;
                        case WM_DESTROY:
                                EndDialog (hDlg, 0) ;
                                return TRUE ;
                }
                return FALSE ;
        }
```

In this case, the dialog box quits if the user clicks the "OK" button, and just beeps if the "Not OK" button is clicked. Although the dialog box function looks a lot like a child window message processing function, there are differences.

1. Windows sends a WM_INITDIALOG message to the function before the dialog box is made visible. This message replaces the WM_CREATE message that is sent to child windows.

2. Dialog box functions do not pass messages on to DefWindowProc(). Instead, Windows automatically passes messages to a special default message processing logic used only for the dialog boxes. Normally, this is done automatically, so you will not reference the DefDlgProc() function at the bottom of the dialog box function. The only exception is a special case where the dialog box has its own window class. See the DefDlgProc() function description tion for an example.

3. Dialog box functions should return TRUE if the message was processed within the function, and return FALSE if the message was not processed.

4. Dialog box functions end the dialog box's existence by calling EndDialog().

The dialog box function must be included in the EXPORTS section of the program's .DEF definition file, as shown in Listing 13-5.

▷ **Listing 13-5. GENERIC.DEF Definition File**

```
NAME            GENERIC
DESCRIPTION     'generic windows program'
EXETYPE WINDOWS
STUB            'WINSTUB.EXE'
CODE            PRELOAD MOVEABLE
DATA            PRELOAD MOVEABLE MULTIPLE
HEAPSIZE        1024
STACKSIZE       4096
EXPORTS WndProc
                DialogProc
```

The dialog box function prototype, as shown in Listing 13-6, must also be included in the program's header file for the source code to compile properly.

▷ **Listing 13-6. GENERIC.H Header File**

```
/* generic.h */
#define IDM_DOIT   1                          /* menu item id values */
#define IDM_QUIT   2
        /* global variables */
int     ghInstance ;
char    gszAppName [] = "generic" ;
        /* function prototypes */
long FAR PASCAL WndProc (HWND, unsigned, WORD, LONG) ;
BOOL FAR PASCAL DialogProc (HWND, WORD, WORD, LONG) ;
```

Finally we get to the point that we can actually call the dialog box from within the program. Listing 13-7 shows a typical calling sequence.

▷ **Listing 13-7. GENERIC.C Excerpt**

```
long FAR PASCAL WndProc (HWND hWnd, unsigned iMessage, WORD wParam, LONG lParam)
{
        FARPROC lpfnDlgProc ;
```

```
switch (iMessage)                                    /* process windows messages */
{
        case WM_COMMAND:                             /* process menu items */
            switch (wParam)
            {
            case IDM_DOIT:                           /* run dialog box */
                lpfnDlgProc = MakeProcInstance (DialogProc, ghInstance) ;
                DialogBox (ghInstance, "ExampleDialog", hWnd,
                        lpfnDlgProc) ;
                FreeProcInstance (lpfnDlgProc) ;
                break ;
```

[Other program lines]

The DialogBox() function creates and runs the dialog box. DialogBox() requires the procedure-instance address of the dialog box function. MakeProcInstance() is used to obtain this value, and FreeProcInstance() is used to release it from memory. This probably looks like a lot of work for so simple a task. The saving grace is that, like WndProc() functions, dialog box functions all tend to be similar. Once you have created one, all of the rest are a matter of modification. The DBEditor is a big help in taking the guesswork out of creating nice looking dialog boxes.

Types of Dialog Boxes

The most common type of dialog box is a "modal dialog box." When a modal dialog box is on the screen, the user cannot switch to another part of the program. By default, they limit access to the other visible windows of the program that called the dialog box. The user can still switch to other programs while the modal dialog box is displayed.

You can make a system modal dialog box by specifying the WS_SYSMODAL style in the dialog box template. System modal dialog boxes can also be created by calling the SetSysModalWindow() function. System modal dialog boxes take over the whole screen. They are only appropriate if there is a serious problem that the user cannot ignore, such as having the system run out of memory.

Modal dialog boxes and system modal dialog boxes are created with the DialogBox() function. (Actually, there are several versions of DialogBox() that we will discuss in a moment.) When you use DialogBox(), all of the window's messages are sent to the dialog box function while the dialog box is on the screen. The rest of the program just sits there until EndDialog() is called from within the dialog box function to close the dialog box.

Less common, but sometimes handy, are "modeless" dialog boxes. They are basically popup windows. Modeless dialog boxes hang around on the screen, and they can obtain and lose the input focus. They are frequently used for small windows containing lists of tools, or for popup windows that display a continually updated set of values like the cursor *X,Y* position. Modeless dialog boxes are created with CreateDialog(). Again, there are several versions of CreateDialog(), but they all accomplish the same basic task of displaying and initializing a modeless dialog box. Because the modeless dialog box remains on the screen, it must share messages with the application's WndProc() function. This requires a modification to the program's message loop if the modeless dialog box is to respond to keyboard selections using the ⁅TAB⁆ and arrow keys. A typical message loop for an application containing one or more modeless dialog boxes is as follows:

```
while (GetMessage (&msg, NULL, 0, 0))                /* the message loop */
{
        if (hDlgModeless == NULL || !IsDialogMessage (hDlgModeless, &msg))
        {
                TranslateMessage (&msg) ;
                DispatchMessage (&msg) ;
        }
}
```

hDlgModeless is a HWND handle for the dialog box. This global variable is set to NULL if the modeless dialog box is not displayed, and set to the dialog box handle if the modeless dialog box is currently on the screen.

The IsDialogMessage() function determines if a message from Windows is meant for the dialog box. If so, the message is sent to the dialog box function and should not be processed by the normal TranslateMessage() and DispatchMessage() functions.

Indirect and Parameter Dialog Box Functions

DialogBox() and CreateDialog() are the basic functions for creating modal and modeless dialog boxes, respectively. There are actually five versions of each of these functions. I'll use the modal dialog box functions as an example, but the same comments apply to the modeless dialog box functions related to CreateDialog(). As previously mentioned, the dialog box template file is compiled using the resource compiler to make a binary .RES resource file. The compiled resource information is linked into the program when RC.EXE is called a second time at the end of the compile/link cycle. When you call DialogBox(), the resource data is loaded into memory and executed. This is how Windows knows how to display the dialog box image. When the dialog box is closed (EndDialog() is called to do this), the resource data is released. Sometimes it is desirable to control when the dialog box template data is loaded or unloaded from memory. To do this, load and lock the resource data for the dialog box in advance, and then call DialogBoxIndirect(). DialogBoxIndirect() takes a handle to the locked resource data in memory and runs the dialog box. The dialog box resource data is not removed from memory when the dialog box exits. Do this manually by using UnlockResource() and FreeResource(). Examples of using these functions are included with the DialogBoxIndirect() function description. More detail is included in Chapter 25, *Resources*.

Indirect loading of dialog box template data also makes it possible to modify the dialog box definition as the application runs. (This subject is discussed later in this chapter under the heading *Dynamic Dialog Boxes*.)

The DialogBox() function has another limitation. There is no clean way to pass dialog box information, such as variable names and constants. Prior to Windows 3.0, programmers were forced to pass data by using global variables. This is not a good practice, as it makes the dialog box functions less portable. With Windows 3.0, several new functions have been added that include data passing between the calling function and the dialog box function. These are the "Param" versions of DialogBox() and CreateDialog(). DialogBoxParam() is a typical example. This function allows a 32-bit value to be passed to the dialog box function. Normally, 32 bits is not enough room to pass all of the data the dialog box function will need. In this case, the 32-bit value can be used to pass a handle to a memory area that contains the data. The memory block is allocated outside of the dialog box function. The dialog box function uses the handle to lock the memory area, read and change values, and then unlock the memory block. See the example under DialogBoxParam() for a typical application.

Communicating with Dialog Box Controls

The controls within a dialog box, such as buttons, list boxes, and static text, are all child windows. The dialog box receives WM_COMMAND messages from the controls when they are activated, and it can send messages to the controls using SendMessage(). Usually, it is easier to use the specialized SendDlgItemMessage() function from within a dialog box, as it uses the control's ID value rather than the control's window handle.

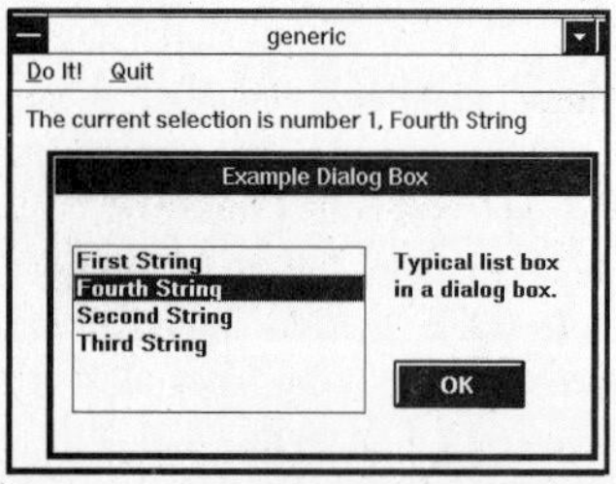

To see how messages are handled from within a dialog box function, we will use a list box control. List boxes are child window controls that allow the user to select an item from among a number of choices. Although list box controls can

Figure 13-2. A List Box Control in a Dialog Box.

be attached to any window or child window, they are most often part of dialog boxes. Common uses are to select a file from a group of files in a subdirectory, to select a tool from a list of tools, etc.

The Windows SDK does not provide a series of specialized functions to deal with list boxes. Instead, the application communicates with the list box with a series of Windows messages. The list box communicates with the application by sending WM_COMMAND messages, with the specific message encoded in the *wParam* and *lParam* parameters. The messages are described in Chapter 9, *Windows Messages*. To see how this works in a dialog box, consider the simple example shown in Figure 13-2. The dialog box contains one list box, which contains four character strings. The user selects one of the items using the mouse, and then clicks the "OK" button. The selected value is then displayed on the application's client area.

The dialog box was defined using the SDK DBEditor application. The resulting dialog box template file is as follows:

⇨ **Listing 13-8. Dialog Box Definition Containing a List Box**

```
EXAMPLEDIALOG DIALOG LOADONCALL MOVEABLE DISCARDABLE 20, 36, 162, 75
CAPTION "Example Dialog Box"
FONT 10, "Helv"
STYLE WS_BORDER | WS_CAPTION | WS_DLGFRAME | DS_MODALFRAME | WS_POPUP
BEGIN
    CONTROL "OK", DLI_OK, "button",
        BS_DEFPUSHBUTTON | WS_TABSTOP | WS_CHILD, 102, 48, 40, 14
    CONTROL "", DLI_LISTBOX, "listbox",
        LBS_NOTIFY | LBS_SORT | LBS_STANDARD | LBS_HASSTRINGS
        | WS_BORDER | WS_VSCROLL | WS_CHILD, 6, 15, 87, 49
    CONTROL "Typical list box in a dialog box.", -1, "static",
        SS_LEFT | WS_CHILD, 102, 15, 54, 27
END
```

The list box control definition contains several flags. The key ones are LBS_SORT, which causes the items to be sorted in ASCII sequence, and LBS_HASSTRINGS, which tells the list box control to store the list box items in its own memory area. The LBS_NOTIFY style is also critical, as without it the list box will not send WM_COMMAND messages to the application when the user clicks or double-clicks an item.

The processing logic for the dialog box function is fairly simple. The list box items are added to the list box when the dialog box is first created. Once the dialog box is displayed, clicking an item in the list box results in a WM_COMMAND message being sent to the dialog box function. The dialog box function logic extracts the current selection number and the string that selection contains, and stores the values in the global variables *nSelection* and *cSelection*.

⇨ **Listing 13-9. Dialog Box Procedure for the List Box Example**

```
BOOL FAR PASCAL DialogProc (HWND hDlg, WORD wMess, WORD wParam, LONG lParam)
{
        switch (wMess)
        {
                case WM_INITDIALOG:
                        SendDlgItemMessage (hDlg, DLI_LISTBOX, WM_SETREDRAW,
                                FALSE, OL) ;
                        SendDlgItemMessage (hDlg, DLI_LISTBOX, LB_ADDSTRING, O,
                                (DWORD)(LPSTR) "First String") ;
                        SendDlgItemMessage (hDlg, DLI_LISTBOX, LB_ADDSTRING, O,
                                (DWORD)(LPSTR) "Second String") ;
                        SendDlgItemMessage (hDlg, DLI_LISTBOX, LB_ADDSTRING, O,
                                (DWORD)(LPSTR) "Third String") ;
                        SendDlgItemMessage (hDlg, DLI_LISTBOX, LB_ADDSTRING, O,
                                (DWORD)(LPSTR) "Fourth String") ;
                        SendDlgItemMessage (hDlg, DLI_LISTBOX, WM_SETREDRAW,
                                TRUE, OL) ;
                        return TRUE ;
                case WM_COMMAND:         /* One of the controls was activated */
                        switch (wParam)
                        {
                                case DLI_OK:
                                        EndDialog (hDlg, O) ;
                                        return TRUE ;
                                case DLI_LISTBOX:
                                        if (HIWORD (lParam) == LBN_SELCHANGE)
                                        {
                                                nSelection = SendDlgItem Message (hDlg,
                                                        DLI_LISTBOX, LB_GETCURSEL, O, OL) ;
                                                SendDlgItemMessage (hDlg, DLI_LISTBOX,
                                                        LB_GETTEXT, nSelection,
                                                        (LONG)(LPSTR) cSelection) ;
                                        }
                        }
                        return TRUE ;
                case WM_DESTROY:
```

```
                    EndDialog (hDlg, 0) ;
                    return TRUE ;
        }
        return FALSE ;
}
```

Review Chapter 9, *Windows Messages*, for the full list of messages concerning dialog boxes and combo boxes. There are other examples in those sections, including creating list boxes with the owner-redrawn style. Owner-redrawn list boxes and combo boxes allow selection from groups of bitmaps, colors, etc. Windows includes direct support for filling a list with a selected group of file names.

The Dialog Box Keyboard Interface

The built-in logic Windows provides for dialog boxes includes provisions for a keyboard alternative to selecting items with the mouse. Three sets of keyboard logic can be provided: keyboard "hot keys" for selecting items using (ALT)-letter key combinations; response to the (TAB) key for big movements; and response to the keyboard arrow keys for smaller movements.

The (ALT)-letter key selection logic is done the same way for dialog boxes as for menu items. If you procede a letter in the control's text string with an ampersand (&), the letter following the & is underlined. The & characters are not displayed. For example, the following definition for a DEFPUSHBUTTON control would use (ALT)-D for a hot key to activate the "Done" button.

```
CONTROL "&Done", DLI_DONE, "button",
        BS_DEFPUSHBUTTON | WS_TABSTOP | WS_CHILD, 45, 66, 48, 12
```

Using the (TAB) and arrow keys is sometimes a convenient alternative to the mouse, and critical for users who are not using a mouse. To take advantage of this logic, you set certain elements in the dialog box template with the WS_TABSTOP and/or WS_GROUP style. Here is an example

```
EXMPDLG DIALOG LOADONCALL MOVEABLE DISCARDABLE 10, 18, 145, 80
STYLE WS_DLGFRAME | WS_VISIBLE | WS_POPUP
BEGIN
    CONTROL "", DLI_CHECK1, "button",
        BS_CHECKBOX | WS_TABSTOP | WS_GROUP | WS_CHILD, 12, 20, 48, 12
    CONTROL "", DLI_CHECK2, "button",
        BS_CHECKBOX | WS_CHILD, 12, 39, 48, 12
    CONTROL "", DLI_CHECK3, "button",
        BS_CHECKBOX | WS_TABSTOP | WS_GROUP | WS_CHILD, 84, 21, 45, 12
    CONTROL "", DLI_CHECK4, "button",
        BS_CHECKBOX | WS_CHILD, 84, 39, 45, 12
    CONTROL "Done", DLI_DONE, "button",
        BS_DEFPUSHBUTTON | WS_TABSTOP | WS_CHILD, 45, 66, 48, 12
END
```

The WS_TABSTOP style marks each item that will receive the input focus when the user presses (TAB) or (SHIFT)-(TAB). In this case, three items have this style. The WS_GROUP style marks the beginning of a group. All of the items up until the next WS_GROUP item are part of the same group. The user can use the arrow keys to move between items in a group, but not outside of the group. The (ENTER) key will select or deselect a pushbutton, check box, or radio button item that has the input focus. This procedure has the same effect as selection with the left mouse button.

The default keyboard interface works fine if your dialog box template is in a logical order. You will probably find that this is not the case when you first create the dialog box template using the DBEditor. Go in with a text editor and edit the template as soon as it is done, moving the items until they are in the right order for the WS_TABSTOP and WS_GROUP style markers to work properly. The order of the lines in the dialog box template also determines the order in which the items are displayed on the screen as the dialog box is painted. Having the screen painted in a reasonable order is more aesthetic than having the controls appear randomly over the screen.

Dynamic Dialog Boxes

Some applications require that the dialog box be altered as the program operates. For example, a database application would need to add and subtract fields from a data-entry dialog box to match the structure of the underlying database. This is a complex subject, so you may wish to skip to the next section if you do not need this information right away. For simple changes, the child window controls in the dialog box can be manipulated directly. For example, MoveWindow() can be called to relocate a control. For complete control over a dialog box during run time, the application can modify the dialog box definition in memory. This is not a simple matter, as the definition of a dialog box contains three separate data structures, each with variable length fields.

The CreateDialogIndirect(), CreateDialogIndirectParam(), DialogBoxIndirect(), and DialogBoxIndirectParam() functions read the data in memory in a specified format and create a dialog box. The simplest way to create data in the right format is to define the dialog box with the DBEditor, add it to the application's resources, and load it into memory with LoadResource() and LockResource(). The data will be in the format defined below. You will have to create the data format from scratch in an allocated memory block if your dialog box is to be truly "dynamic."

The overall structure of a dialog box definition in memory is as follows:

DLGTEMPLATE   The header information for the dialog box.

FONTINFO   The data structure for the font data.

DLGITEMTEMPLATE   The data structure for *each* control in the dialog box.

These data structures are placed one after the other in memory. The data structures are not defined in WINDOWS.H. Here are their definitions:

▷ **Listing 13-10. Dialog Box Data Structures**

```
typedef struct {                        /* only one of these structs per dial. box */
        long    dtStyle ;               /* Any of the DS_ styles (CreateWindow()) */
        BYTE    dtItemCount ;           /* number of controls, 255 max */
        int     dtX ;                   /* X pos. of upper left of the dialog box */
        int     dtY ;                   /* Y pos. of upper left of the dialog box */
        int     dtCX ;                  /* width of the dialog box */
        int     dtCY ;                  /* height of the dialog box */
        char    dtMenuName [1] ;        /* menu name, null term. string, NULL=none */
        char    dtClassName [1] ;       /* class, null term. string, NULL=standard */
        char    dtCaptionText [1] ;     /* dialog box caption, null term. string */
} DLGTEMPLATE ;

typedef struct {                        /* only one of these strucs per dial. box */
        short   int     PointSize ;     /* point size of font */
        char            szTypeFace [1] ; /* typeface name, null term. string */
} FONTINFO ;

typedef struct {                    /* one of these for each control */
        int     dtilX ;             /* X pos. of upper left of the control */
        int     dtilY ;             /* Y pos. of upper left of the control */
        int     dtilCX ;            /* width of the control */
        int     dtilCY ;            /* Y pos. of upper left of the control */
        int     dtilID ;            /* control id value */
        long    dtilStyle ;         /* control child window syle */
        char    dtilClass [1] ;     /* null term. string "BUTTON", "EDIT", etc. */
        char    dtilText [1] ;      /* control text, null term. string */
        BYTE    dtilInfo ;          /* number of bytes of data that follow */
        PTR     dtilData ;          /* the extra data bytes go here */
} DLGITEMTEMPLATE ;
```

The size and location of the dialog box and all controls are given in dialog box base units. These are relative to the size of the font in use. Vertical dimensions are in eighths of the font height, and horizontal dimensions are in fourths of the font width.

All of the character elements in the structures are variable-length arrays. The minimum size will be one byte, for a NULL character. Normally, there will be a series of ASCII characters, followed by a terminating NULL. Windows parses the memory block, using the terminating NULL character to mark the end of the field.

A full demonstration of the use of dynamic dialog boxes is beyond the scope of this book. If you are interested in more information, refer to Chapter 3 of Jeffrey Richter's excellent book *Windows 3: A Developer's Guide* (1991, M&T Books) for a complete example.

Dialog Template Statement Description

This section contains a full list of the statements that you can include in the dialog box template. Normally, you will use the SDK DBEditor to do all of the additions and changes to the dialog box template file. Sometimes it is easier to just go in and edit a specific value in the resource script file for small changes. One of the peculiarities of dialog box templates is the system of units. Instead of measuring locations in terms of pixels, or logical units, dialog boxes use "dialog base units." These units are fractions of the dialog box character font size. The horizontal direction is measured in fourths of a character width, and the vertical direction is measured in eighths of a character height. The effect of this system of units is to properly scale the dialog box, regardless of the screen resolution in use. Typically high-resolution monitors will use more pixels per character, so the character size remains about the same as on a low-resolution monitor. A side effect of this system is that you can change the size of a dialog box by simply picking a different font. The FONT statement is provided for this purpose.

DIALOG
■ Win 2.0　■ Win 3.0　■ Win 3.1

Purpose	Starts the dialog box template definition.
Syntax	*nameID* **DIALOG** [*load-option*] [*mem-option*] *x,y, width, height,* [*option-statements*]
Example	EXMPDLG DIALOG LOADONCALL MOVEABLE DISCARDABLE 10, 18, 145, 80

BEGIN

　　　　(dialog box items defined here)

END

Description	This statement starts the dialog box template definition. All statements from BEGIN until the END statement is reached are part of the dialog box template.

The *nameID* string is the name of the dialog box. This is the character string that is used with DialogBox() to specify which dialog box should be loaded and executed.

The *load-option* can be either PRELOAD or LOADONCALL. PRELOAD specifies that the dialog box resource data be loaded when the application starts. Doing so takes up memory, but makes the dialog box appear quickly. LOADONCALL is the normal (default) option, where the dialog box resource data is not loaded into memory until needed.

The *mem-option* is a combination of FIXED, MOVEABLE, and DISCARDABLE. Normally, both the MOVEABLE and DISCARDABLE styles are chosen. FIXED should be avoided, as this freezes the dialog box resource data in memory, making it much more difficult for Windows to optimize memory use.

x,y, width, height specifies the position and size of the dialog box. Dialog base units are used for all dimensions. The *x,y* location is relative to the upper left corner of the window which called the dialog box.

The *option-statements* include STYLE, CAPTION, MENU, CLASS, and FONT. All statements after DIALOG, up to the BEGIN statement in the dialog box definition, are assumed to be option statements.

STYLE
■ Win 2.0　■ Win 3.0　■ Win 3.1

Purpose	Specifies the window style to use for the dialog box.
Syntax	**STYLE** *style*
Example	STYLE WS_DLGFRAME I WS_VISIBLE I WS_POPUP
Description	All of the styles described in Chapter 2, *Creating Windows*, under CreateWindow() that start with WS_ or DS_ can be used in the dialog box style. If you are creating a modeless dialog box with CreateDialog(), be sure to include the WS_VISIBLE style in order to avoid using Show-Window() to make the dialog box visible. Dialog boxes cannot use the WM_MINIMIZEBOX and WM_MAXIMIZEBOX styles.

CAPTION
■ Win 2.0   ■ Win 3.0   ■ Win 3.1

Purpose	Specifies the text used in the dialog box caption bar.
Syntax	**CAPTION** *captiontext*
Example	CAPTION "Dialog Box Title Here"
Description	Used with dialog boxes that have the WS_CAPTION style. This is a good idea, as it allows the user to move the dialog box on the screen. The caption is also a visual reminder of what activity is taking place.

CLASS
■ Win 2.0   ■ Win 3.0   ■ Win 3.1

Purpose	Specifies that the dialog box is to have its own window class.
Syntax	**CLASS** *classname*
Example	CLASS "separate"
Description	Normally, a dialog box shares the window class of the parent. This statement causes a separate class to be used for the dialog box. The class must be registered in advance with RegisterClass(). The class must be registered with the *cbWndExtra* element set to DLGWINDOWEXTRA. Dialog box functions for windows with their own class must specify a separate default message processing function. See the example under DefDlgProc() to see how this is done.

FONT
■ Win 2.0   ■ Win 3.0   ■ Win 3.1

Purpose	Specifies the font to use inside the dialog box for all controls.
Syntax	**FONT** *pointsize, typeface*
Example	FONT 10, "Helv"
Description	As previously mentioned, the font determines not only the typeface, but also the sizing of every control and the dialog box itself. This is because dialog box dimensions use dialog base units, computed as fractions of the font character size. The 10-point "Helv" font is a good choice for most dialog boxes, as it matches the font used in the dialog boxes of the applications supplied with Windows 3.0.

Dialog Box Control Statements

Windows provides two equivalent ways to specify a child window control in a dialog box template. One way is to use an explicit statement like COMBOBOX. The other way is to use the CONTROL statement, which will then include the "combobox" style as a parameter. The DBEditor always uses the CONTROL statement. The explicit statements are leftovers from the days before the DBEditor was available, when programmers coded dialog boxes by hand. As an example, the following two examples produce the same control.

```
CONTROL "Push Me", DLI_BUTTON1, "button",
        BS_DEFPUSHBUTTON | WS_TABSTOP | WS_CHILD, 45, 66, 48, 12

DEFPUSHBUTTON "Push Me", DLI_BUTTON1, 45, 66, 48, 12, WS_TABSTOP
```

A number of the statements include the position and size of the control. In the descriptions that follow, they will be labeled "*x, y, width, height.*" Keep in mind that all values are integers, and all use dialog base units.

The ID values for each control are normally defined in a separate header file. By convention, dialog box control items are normally given names starting with "DLI_" for "DiaLog Item." For the controls with the optional *style* parameter, the choices include the WS_TABSTOP and/or WS_GROUP styles. These control the default keyboard interface, as described above. The two styles can be combined with the C language binary OR operator (|).

CHECKBOX

■ Win 2.0 ■ Win 3.0 ■ Win 3.1

Purpose	Defines a check box control.
Syntax	**CHECKBOX** *text, id, x, y, width, height* [*style*]
Example	CHECKBOX "Autosave On/Off", DLI_CHECKBOX, 3, 10, 35, 15
Description	Check boxes belong to the "button" window class. They are ideal for specifying binary choices, such as if an autosave feature is on or off.

COMBOBOX

■ Win 2.0 ■ Win 3.0 ■ Win 3.1

Purpose	Defines a combo box control.
Syntax	**COMBOBOX** *id, x, y, width, height,* [*style*]
Example	COMBOBOX DLI_COMBO, 40, 10, 60, 90, WS_VSCROLL
Description	Combo boxes are a new addition with Windows 3.0. They include an edit control at the top, combined with a drop-down list box at the bottom for making a selection. The optional *style* parameter can include any combination of WS_TABSTOP, WS_GROUP, WS_DISABLED, and WS_VSCROLL. Examples using combo boxes are included in Chapter 9, *Windows Messages*, in the combo box message section.

CONTROL

■ Win 2.0 ■ Win 3.0 ■ Win 3.1

Purpose	Specifies all forms of child window control within a dialog box.
Syntax	**CONTROL** *text, id, class, style, x, y, width, height*
Example	CONTROL "Push Me", DLI_BUTTON1, "button", BS_DEFPUSHBUTTON	WS_TABSTOP	WS_CHILD, 45, 66, 48, 12
Description	This is the general-purpose statement for specifying all types of controls used in dialog box templates. The DBEditor uses this form when it creates a template file. The *text* field specifies the character string that will appear in the control. This is not always displayed. For example, list box controls do not display a string until the string is added to the body of the list box using the LB_ADDTEXT message.
	The *class* parameter can be either BUTTON, COMBOBOX, EDIT, LISTBOX, SCROLLBAR, or STATIC. See the descriptions in Chapter 2, Table 2-2 under CreateWindow() for the full details. The child window *style* is also identical to the styles used in CreateWindow(). Table 2-3 contains a complete list of these values.

CTEXT

■ Win 2.0 ■ Win 3.0 ■ Win 3.1

Purpose	Defines a centered static text control.
Syntax	**CTEXT** *text, id, x, y, width, height,* [*style*]
Example	CTEXT "Centered Text," −1, 10, 10, 100, 15
Description	This control places static text in a dialog box. The text is centered within the bounds of the rectangle specified by *x, y, width, height*. Normally, static text controls are given an ID value of −1, as they are never selected. An exception is where the dialog box function changes the text content as the dialog box operates.

DEFPUSHBUTTON

■ Win 2.0 ■ Win 3.0 ■ Win 3.1

Purpose	Defines the default pushbutton for a dialog box.
Syntax	**DEFPUSHBUTTON** *text, id, x, y, width, height,* [*style*]

Example	DEFPUSHBUTTON "Cancel", DLI_CANCEL, 40, 10, 40, 15, WS_TABSTOP
Description	The default pushbutton is the button that will be activated if the user presses (ENTER) when the dialog box first starts operation. There can be only one DEFPUSHBUTTON control in a dialog box definition. It will be displayed on the screen with a bold border. The other buttons should have the PUSHBUTTON style.

EDITTEXT

■ Win 2.0   ■ Win 3.0   ■ Win 3.1

Purpose	Defines an editable text control in a dialog box.
Syntax	**EDITTEXT** *id, x, y, width, height, [style]*
Example	EDITTEXT DLI_EDIT, 10, 20, 45, 15, WS_HSCROLL
Description	Edit controls are the standard method for getting user input for typed text or numbers. Windows includes a lot of built-in logic in edit controls, including selection of groups of characters by clicking and dragging the mouse cursor, deletion and insertion of characters, cursor (arrow) key support, etc. Edit controls can be one line of text, or multiple lines, including both horizontal and vertical scrolling of the client area of the edit control. Chapter 9, *Windows Messages*, includes an example of a multiline edit control in the section on Edit Control Messages.
	The *style* parameter can include any combination of the following styles: WS_TABSTOP, WS_GROUP, WS_VSCROLL (vertical scroll bar), WS_HSCROLL (horizontal scroll bar), WS_BORDER, and WS_DISABLED. Text is aligned based on ES_LEFT, ES_RIGHT, or ES_CENTER. See Table 2-3 for additional details on edit styles.

GROUPBOX

■ Win 2.0   ■ Win 3.0   ■ Win 3.1

Purpose	Draws a rectangle with a title at the top left around a group of other controls.
Syntax	**GROUPBOX** *text, id, x, y, width, height, [style]*
Example	GROUPBOX "Filetype Choices:", −1, 10, 10, 65, 100
Description	Check boxes or radio buttons frequently deal with related options, or choices from a narrow set of possibilities. Surrounding the related options with a group box makes it clear that the controls belong to related functions. The WS_TABSTOP and WS_GROUP styles can be applied to the group control, but normally it is better to have the first item within the group receive the input focus.

ICON

■ Win 2.0   ■ Win 3.0   ■ Win 3.1

Purpose	Places an icon within a dialog box.
Syntax	**ICON** *text, id, x, y, [style]*
Description	ICON "generic", DLI_ICON, 40, 40
Example	Icons belong to the "static" class of controls. The *text* parameter is the name of the icon, specified elsewhere in the program's resource .RC file with an ICON statement such as

```
generic        ICON    generic.ico
```

The *x,y* parameters specify the upper left corner of the icon in dialog units. The size of the icon is fixed, so there are no height or width parameters. The only allowed style is SS_ICON.

LISTBOX

■ Win 2.0   ■ Win 3.0   ■ Win 3.1

Purpose	Defines a list box control within a dialog box.
Syntax	**LISTBOX** *id, x, y, width, height, [style]*
Example	LISTBOX DLI_LIST, 10, 10, 50, 100, LBS_NOTIFY, WS_VSCROLL, WS_BORDER

Description	List box controls are the most common means of allowing users to select an item from a list of possibilities. More than one selection is possible if the list box includes the LBS_MULTIPLESEL style. The complete list of style possibilities is given in Table 2-3 under the CreateWindow() function description. An example program with a list box control is included at the beginning of this chapter. Additional examples are given in Chapter 8, *Message Processing Functions*, in the list box messages section.

LTEXT
■ Win 2.0   ■ Win 3.0   ■ Win 3.1

Purpose	Defines a left-justified static text control.
Syntax	**LTEXT** *text, id, x, y, width, height,* [*style*]
Example	LTEXT "Left Justified Text", –1, 10, 10, 150, 15
Description	This control places static text in a dialog box. The text is justified to the left border within the bounds of the rectangle specified by *x, y, width, height*. Normally, static text controls are given an ID value of –1 because they are never selected. An exception is when the dialog box function changes the text content as the dialog box operates.

MENU
■ Win 2.0   ■ Win 3.0   ■ Win 3.1

Purpose	Specifies a menu to be attached to the dialog box.
Syntax	**MENU** *menuname*
Example	MENU testmenu
Description	Used with dialog boxes that have menus. This is unusual, but possible. The menu must be defined elsewhere, such as in the program's .RC resource script file.

PUSHBUTTON
■ Win 2.0   ■ Win 3.0   ■ Win 3.1

Purpose	Defines a pushbutton for a dialog box.
Syntax	**PUSHBUTTON** *text, id, x, y, width, height,* [*style*]
Example	PUSHBUTTON "Done", DLI_DONE, 40, 10, 40, 15, WS_TABSTOP
Description	Dialog boxes usually have at least one PUSHBUTTON (or DEFPUSHBUTTON) control to allow the user to exit the dialog box. The allowed styles are WS_TABSTOP, WS_DISABLED, and WS_GROUP.

RADIOBUTTON
■ Win 2.0   ■ Win 3.0   ■ Win 3.1

Purpose	Defines a radio button control in a dialog box.
Syntax	**RADIOBUTTON** *text, id, x, y, width, height,* [*style*]
Example	RADIOBUTTON "Select Option ON", DLI_RADIO1, 10, 10, 40, 15
Description	Radio buttons are usually used in groups to specify selection of one out of a limited number of choices. Radio buttons belong to the "button" window class. See the CheckRadioButton() function description later in this chapter for an example.

RTEXT
■ Win 2.0   ■ Win 3.0   ■ Win 3.1

Syntax	**RTEXT** *text, id, x, y, width, height,* [*style*]
Example	RTEXT "Right Justified Text", –1, 10, 10, 150, 15

Description   This control places static text in a dialog box. The text is justified to the right border within the bounds of the rectangle specified by *x, y, width, height*. Normally, static text controls are given an ID value of –1, as they are never selected. An exception is when the dialog box function changes the text content as the dialog box operates.

SCROLLBAR   ■ Win 2.0   ■ Win 3.0   ■ Win 3.1

Purpose	Defines a scroll bar control within a dialog box.
Syntax	**SCROLLBAR** *id, x, y width, height,* [*style*]
Example	SCROLLBAR DLI_SCROLL, 50, 10, 8, 50, SBS_VERT
Description	Scroll bar controls are excellent ways of getting user input for scaleable items, such as integers. Scroll bars can also be used to scroll the client area of a window, but this is unlikely with a dialog box. The most common styles are SBS_VERT for vertical scroll bars, and SBS_HORZ for horizontal ones. See Table 2-3 under the CreateWindow() function description for a full list of scroll bar styles.

Dialog Box Function Summaries

Table 13-1 summarizes the dialog box functions. The detailed function descriptions are in the next section.

Function	Purpose
CheckDlgButton	Checks or removes a check from a dialog box control.
CheckRadioButton	Changes the selected item from a group of radio buttons.
CreateDialog	Creates a modeless dialog box.
CreateDialogIndirect	Creates a modeless dialog box.
CreateDialogIndirectParam	Creates a modeless dialog box, and passes a 32-bit value to the dialog box function when it starts processing messages.
CreateDialogParam	Creates a modeless dialog box, and passes a 32-bit value to the dialog box function when it starts processing messages.
DefDlgProc	Provides default message processing logic for dialog boxes created with their own, separate window class.
DialogBox	Creates a modal dialog box.
DialogBoxIndirect	Creates a modal dialog box.
DialogBoxIndirectParam	Creates a modal dialog box, and passes a 32-bit data item to the dialog box as it is created.
DialogBoxParam	Creates a modal dialog box, and passes a 32-bit data item to the dialog box as it is created.
EndDialog	Closes a modal dialog box, and returns control to the calling function.
GetDialogBaseUnits	Determines the size of the dialog base units used to create dialog boxes and position controls.
GetDlgCtrlID	Retrieves a dialog box control's ID values given the control's window handle.
GetDlgItem	Retrieves the window handle for a dialog box control, given the control's ID number.
GetDlgItemInt	Retrieves an integer value from a control in a dialog box.
GetDlgItemText	Retrieves a character string from an edit control in a dialog box.
GetNextDlgGroupItem	Finds the next (or previous) window handle of the dialog box control that will receive the input focus if the user presses the arrow keys.

Table 13-1. continued

Function	Purpose	
GetNextDlgTabItem	Finds the next (or previous) window handle of the dialog box control that will receive the input focus if the user presses the (TAB) key.	
IsDialogMessage	Determines if a message is meant for a dialog box.	
IsDlgButtonChecked	Determines if a check box or radio button control is checked.	
MapDialogRect	Converts from dialog base units to screen units (pixels).	
MessageBox	Creates and displays a small window containing a message.	
SendDlgItemMessage	Sends a dialog box control a message.	
SetDlgItemInt	Changes the text in a dialog box control to an integer value.	
SetDlgItemText	Changes the text in a dialog box control.	

Table 13-1. Dialog Box Function Summaries.

Dialog Box Function Descriptions

This section combines the detailed descriptions for the dialog box functions.

CHECKDLGBUTTON   ■ Win 2.0   ■ Win 3.0   ■ Win 3.1

Purpose	Checks or removes a check from a dialog box control.
Syntax	void **CheckDlgButton**(HWND *hDlg*, int *nIdButton*, WORD *wCheck*);
Description	This is a shortcut method for inserting and removing checks from dialog box controls. It is used with the BS_CHECKBOX and BS_3STATE types of buttons. Using CheckDlgButton() is equivalent to sending a BM_SETCHECK message to the dialog box control .
Uses	Used with check boxes and three-state buttons to insert and remove the checkmark from the control.
Returns	No returned value (void).
See Also	CheckRadioButton(), CheckMenuItem()
Parameters	
hDlg	HWND: The dialog box window's handle.
nIdButton	int: The control ID for the check box or three-state button. Control ID values are normally defined in a header file.
wCheck	WORD: Set to 0 to remove the checkmark. Set to 1 to set the checkmark. For three-state buttons, set to 2 to gray the check box. Settings of 0 and 1 have the same effect on check boxes and three-state buttons.
Related Messages	BM_SETCHECK

Example   This example, which is illustrated in Figure 13-3, displays a
modal dialog box when the user clicks the "Do It!" menu item.
The dialog box contains a check box and a set of two radio buttons. Both controls provide a way to show a selection. The
check box is best used for an on/off choice. Groups of radio
buttons are better for selections from a set of mutually exclusive choices.

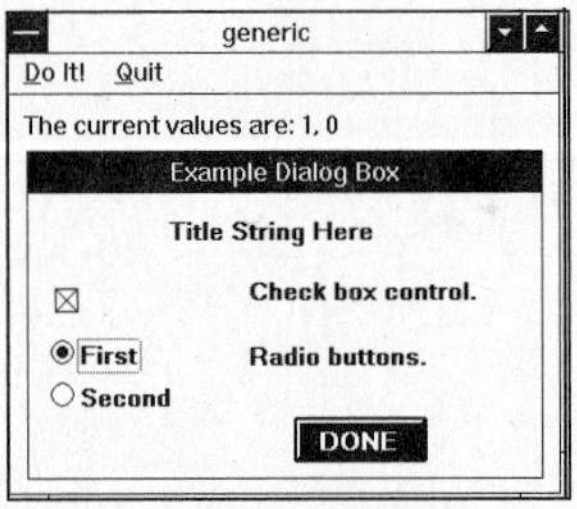

Figure 13-3. CheckDlg-Button( ) and CheckRadio-Button( ) Example.

The dialog box is defined in a .DLG file created with the SDK Dialog Box Editor.

⇨ GENERIC.DLG Dialog Box Definition File

```
EXMPDLG DIALOG LOADONCALL MOVEABLE DISCARDABLE 10, 18, 139, 75
CAPTION "Example Dialog Box"
FONT 10, "Helv"
STYLE WS_BORDER | WS_CAPTION | WS_DLGFRAME | WS_POPUP
BEGIN
    CONTROL "Title String Here", -1, "static",
                    SS_CENTER | WS_CHILD, 27, 6, 78, 9
    CONTROL "Check box control.", -1, "static",
                    SS_LEFT | WS_CHILD, 60, 22, 67, 9
    CONTROL "Radio buttons.", -1, "static",
                    SS_LEFT | WS_CHILD, 60, 39, 73, 10
    CONTROL "DONE", DLI_DONE, "button",
                    BS_DEFPUSHBUTTON | WS_TABSTOP | WS_CHILD, 72, 59, 36, 12
    CONTROL "", DLI_CHECKBOX, "button",
                    BS_CHECKBOX | WS_TABSTOP | WS_CHILD, 7, 24, 16, 9
    CONTROL "First", DLI_RADIO1, "button",
                    BS_RADIOBUTTON | WS_TABSTOP | WS_CHILD, 6, 36, 28, 12
    CONTROL "Second", DLI_RADIO2, "button",
                    BS_RADIOBUTTON | WS_TABSTOP | WS_CHILD, 6, 47, 44, 12
END
```

In addition to the .DLG file, a header file containing the definitions of the dialog control IDs (DLI_DONE, etc.) and a standard header file containing the function declarations are needed. This file can be created from within the Dialog Box Editor.

⇨ GENERIC.HD Dialog Box Item Defines

```
#define DLI_CHECKBOX   101
#define DLI_DONE       102
#define DLI_RADIO1     103
#define DLI_RADIO2     104
```

The program's resource file includes the dialog box definition file (.DLG file) and the header file containing the dialog box ID value (.HD file).

⇨ GENERIC.RC Resource Definition File

```
/* generic.rc    */

#include <windows.h>
#include "generic.h"
#include "generic.hd"
#include "generic.dlg"

generic         ICON    generic.ico

generic         MENU
BEGIN
    MENUITEM "&Do It!"            IDM_DOIT
    MENUITEM "&Quit",            IDM_QUIT
END
```

The dialog box function DialogProcedure() at the end of the listing shows typical program logic for handling check boxes and radio buttons. The current status of each of the button groups is held in two global variables, *nCheckOne* and *nRadioOne*. Use of global variables allows the WndProc() function to keep track of the button status. A function prototype for DialogProcedure() must be included in the program's header file and listed in the EXPORTS section of the program's .DEF definition file.

```
int nCheckOne = 0 ;
int nRadioOne = 0 ;

long FAR PASCAL WndProc (HWND hWnd, unsigned iMessage, WORD wParam, LONG lParam)
{
```

```
                PAINTSTRUCT                     ps ;
                static          FARPROC         lpfnDialogProc ;
                static          char            cBuf [256] ;

                switch (iMessage)                       /* process windows messages */
                {
                        case WM_PAINT:
                                BeginPaint (hWnd, &ps) ;
                                TextOut (ps.hdc, 10, 10, cBuf, wsprintf (cBuf,
                                        "The current values are: %d, %d",
                                        nCheckOne, nRadioOne)) ;
                                EndPaint (hWnd, &ps) ;
                                break ;
                        case WM_COMMAND:                /* process menu items */
                                switch (wParam)
                                {
                                case IDM_DOIT:          /* User hit the "Do it" menu item */
                                        lpfnDialogProc = MakeProcInstance
                                                (DialogProcedure,         ghInstance) ;
                                        DialogBox (ghInstance, "exmpdlg", hWnd,
                                                lpfnDialogProc) ;
                                        FreeProcInstance (lpfnDialogProc) ;
                                        InvalidateRect (hWnd, NULL, TRUE) ; /* force paint */
                                        break ;
                                case IDM_QUIT:
                                        DestroyWindow (hWnd) ;
                                        break ;
                                }
                                break ;
                        case WM_DESTROY:                /* stop application */
                                PostQuitMessage (0) ;
                                break ;
                        default:                        /* default windows message processing */
                                return DefWindowProc (hWnd, iMessage, wParam, lParam) ;
                }
        return (0L) ;
}


BOOL FAR PASCAL DialogProcedure (HWND hDlg, unsigned iMessage, WORD wParam, LONG lParam)
{
        BOOL    bBool ;

        switch (iMessage)
        {
        case WM_INITDIALOG:
                if (nCheckOne)
                        CheckDlgButton (hDlg, DLI_CHECKBOX, MF_CHECKED) ;
                else
                        CheckDlgButton (hDlg, DLI_CHECKBOX, MF_UNCHECKED) ;

                if (nRadioOne)
                        CheckRadioButton (hDlg, DLI_RADIO1, DLI_RADIO2,
                                DLI_RADIO2) ;
                else
                        CheckRadioButton (hDlg, DLI_RADIO1, DLI_RADIO2,
                                DLI_RADIO1) ;
                break ;
        case WM_COMMAND:
                switch (wParam)
                {
                case DLI_CHECKBOX:
                        if (nCheckOne)
                        {
                                nCheckOne = 0 ;
                                CheckDlgButton (hDlg, DLI_CHECKBOX,
                                        MF_UNCHECKED) ;
                        }
                        else
```

```
                        {
                            nCheckOne = 1 ;
                            CheckDlgButton (hDlg, DLI_CHECKBOX,
                                    MF_CHECKED) ;
                        }
                        return (TRUE) ;
                case DLI_RADIO1:
                        nRadioOne = 0 ;
                        CheckRadioButton (hDlg, DLI_RADIO1, DLI_RADIO2,
                                DLI_RADIO1) ;
                        return (TRUE) ;
                case DLI_RADIO2:
                        nRadioOne = 1 ;
                        CheckRadioButton (hDlg, DLI_RADIO1, DLI_RADIO2,
                                DLI_RADIO2) ;
                        return (TRUE) ;
                case DLI_DONE:
                        EndDialog (hDlg, NULL) ;
                        return (TRUE) ;
                }
                break ;
        default:
                return (FALSE) ;
        }
        return (FALSE) ;
}
```

CHECKRADIOBUTTON   ■ Win 2.0   ■ Win 3.0   ■ Win 3.1

Purpose	Changes the selected item from a group of radio buttons.
Syntax	void **CheckRadioButton**(HWND *hDlg*, int *nIDFirstButton*, int *nIDLastButton*, int *nIDCheckButton*);
Description	Radio buttons are used in groups to show a selection from a group of mutually exclusive choices. CheckRadioButton() works best if all of the related radio buttons are given ID values in sequential order. CheckRadioButton() will update the group of buttons in one function call to show a new selection. This function is equivalent to sending each of the buttons a BM_SETCHECK message.
Uses	Changing a group of radio buttons to reflect a selection.
Returns	No returned value (void).
See Also	CheckDlgButton(), CheckMenuItem()
Parameters	
hDlg	HWND: The dialog box window's handle.
nIDFirstButton	int: The ID value for the first radio button control of the group. The group of related radio buttons is assumed to be numberd in sequential order.
nIDLastButton	int: The ID value for the last radio button control of the group.
nIDCheckButton	int: The ID value for the radio button control that should show a checkmark. All of the other radio buttons in the group will have their checkmarks removed.
Related Messages	WM_SETCHECK
Example	See the previous example under CheckDlgButton().

CREATEDIALOG   ■ Win 2.0   ■ Win 3.0   ■ Win 3.1

Purpose	Creates a modeless dialog box.
Syntax	HWND **CreateDialog**(HANDLE *hInstance*, LPSTR *lpTemplateName*, HWND *hWndParent*, FARPROC *lpDialogFunc*);

Description A modeless dialog box behaves like a popup window. The user can switch the focus to the parent window, or another application, while the modeless dialog box is still visible. The dialog box template file should contain the WS_VISIBLE style. If not, the ShowWindow() function will be needed to make the modeless dialog box visible. Unlike DialogBox(), CreateDialog() returns immediately, returning the handle of the dialog box window created. Modeless dialog boxes are ended by calling DestroyWindow() within the dialog box function. The application's message loop needs to be modified for modeless dialog boxes, so that keyboard input to the dialog box is properly processed. See the example below for the proper use of the IsDialogMessage() function.

Uses Modeless dialog boxes are convenient for tool windows that may remain on the screen for an extended period of time.

Returns HWND, the handle to the modeless dialog box created.

See Also CreateDialogIndirect(), CreateDialogParam(), DestroyWindow(), IsDialogMessage(), SetFocus(), DialogBox()

Parameters

hInstance HANDLE: The program's instance handle.

lpTemplateName LPSTR: A pointer to a character string containing the name of the dialog box template in the application's resource file. Dialog box templates are normally created with the SDK Dialog Box Editor.

hWndParent HWND: The parent window's handle. Destroying the parent window will automatically destroy the modeless dialog box.

lpDialogFunc FARPROC: The procedure-instance address of the dialog box function. This address is created with MakeProcInstance(). The dialog box function processes messages for the dialog box. This function must be declared in the EXPORTS section of the program's .DEF definition file, and it must have the following format:

BOOL FAR PASCAL **DialogFunc**(HWND *hDlg*, WORD *wMsg*, WORD *wParam*, DWORD *lParam*);

The parameters passed to the dialog box function have the following meanings.

hDlg HWND: This is the window handle for the modeless dialog box window. This handle can be used just like any other window handle for setting colors, changing the caption, etc.

wMsg WORD: The message being passed to the dialog function. For example, WM_INITDIALOG is sent to the dialog function right before the window is made visible.

wParam WORD: The WORD data associated with the message.

lParam DWORD: The 32-bit data associated with the message.

    The dialog box function should return TRUE if the function processes the message, and FALSE if the message is not acted on. The exception is processing a WM_INITDIALOG message. In this case, the function should return TRUE only if the SetFocus() function is not called, FALSE if SetFocus() is called. SetFocus() is used to establish which control will have the input focus when the dialog box is first made visible. If SetFocus() is not used, the first control in the dialog box definition receives the input focus.

Related Messages WM_INITDIALOG

Example This example creates the same dialog box shown in the example under CheckDlgButton(), except that the dialog box is a modeless dialog box. This means that the dialog box behaves like a popup window. The focus can be switched from the dialog box to the main window or other windows on the screen. The dialog box definition is identical to the one for a normal (modal) dialog box, except that the window style includes WS_VISIBLE. This avoids having to call the ShowWindow() function to make the modeless dialog box visible.

```
EXMPDLG DIALOG LOADONCALL MOVEABLE DISCARDABLE 0, 0, 139, 75
FONT 10, "Helv"
CAPTION "Modeless Dialog box"
STYLE WS_BORDER | WS_DLGFRAME | WS_CAPTION | WS_POPUP | WS_VISIBLE
BEGIN
    CONTROL "Title String Here", -1, "static",
                SS_CENTER | WS_CHILD, 27, 6, 78, 9
    CONTROL "Check box control.", -1, "static",
                SS_LEFT | WS_CHILD, 60, 22, 67, 9
    CONTROL "Radio buttons.", -1, "static",
                SS_LEFT | WS_CHILD, 60, 39, 73, 10
    CONTROL "DONE", DLI_DONE, "button",
                BS_DEFPUSHBUTTON | WS_TABSTOP | WS_CHILD, 72, 59, 36, 12
    CONTROL "", DLI_CHECKBOX, "button",
                BS_CHECKBOX | WS_TABSTOP | WS_CHILD, 7, 24, 16, 9
    CONTROL "First", DLI_RADIO1, "button",
                BS_RADIOBUTTON | WS_TABSTOP | WS_CHILD, 6, 36, 28, 12
    CONTROL "Second", DLI_RADIO2, "button",
                BS_RADIOBUTTON | WS_TABSTOP | WS_CHILD, 6, 47, 44, 12
END
```

The C program uses CreateDialog() to start the modeless dialog box when the user clicks the "Do It!" menu item. The logic shown is incomplete, as this program allows any number of modeless dialog boxes to be created by repeatedly clicking the menu item. Note that the handle for the dialog box *hDlgModeless* is defined as a global variable at the top of the listing. This handle is used in the window's message loop to check whether the dialog box is present. If it is, IsDialogMessage() is used to screen keyboard input and translate it as necessary for the dialog box to process. Dialog box messages are not sent to the window's WndProc() function with DispatchMessage().

In the dialog box function at the bottom of the listing, note that DestroyWindow() is used to end the dialog box. Also note that the *hDlgModeless* handle is set back to zero, shutting down the dialog box message interception in the application's message loop.

```
/* generic.c */

#include <windows.h>            /* window's header file - always included */
#include "generic.h"            /* the application's header file */
#include "generic.hd"

int         nCheckOne = 0 ;            /* globals */
int         nRadioOne = 0 ;
HWND        hDlgModeless = 0 ;

int PASCAL WinMain (HANDLE hInstance, HANDLE hPrevInstance, LPSTR lpszCmdLine, int nCmdShow)
{                                   /* variable types defined in windows.h */

        HWND            hWnd ;          /* a handle to a message */
        MSG             msg ;           /* a message */
        WNDCLASS        wndclass ;      /* the window class */

        ghInstance = hInstance ;        /* store instance handle as global var. */
        if (!hPrevInstance)             /* load data into window class struct. */
        {
                wndclass.style          = CS_HREDRAW | CS_VREDRAW ;
                wndclass.lpfnWndProc    = WndProc ;
                wndclass.cbClsExtra     = 0 ;
                wndclass.cbWndExtra     = 0 ;
                wndclass.hInstance      = hInstance ;
                wndclass.hIcon          = LoadIcon (hInstance, gszAppName) ;
                wndclass.hCursor              = LoadCursor (NULL, IDC_ARROW) ;
                wndclass.hbrBackground = GetStockObject (WHITE_BRUSH) ;
                wndclass.lpszMenuName  = gszAppName ;
                wndclass.lpszClassName = gszAppName ;
                                                /* register the window class */
                if (!RegisterClass (&wndclass))
                        return FALSE ;
        }
```

```
        hWnd = CreateWindow (                    /* create the program's window here */
                gszAppName,                      /* class name */
                gszAppName,                      /* window name */
                WS_OVERLAPPEDWINDOW,             /* window style */
                CW_USEDEFAULT,                   /* x position on screen */
                CW_USEDEFAULT,                   /* y position on screen */
                CW_USEDEFAULT,                   /* width of window */
                CW_USEDEFAULT,                   /* height of window */
                NULL,                            /* parent window handle (null = none) */
                NULL,                            /* menu handle (null = use class menu) */
                hInstance,                       /* instance handle */
                NULL) ;                          /* lpstr (null = not used) */

        ShowWindow (hWnd, nCmdShow) ;
        UpdateWindow (hWnd) ;                    /* send first WM_PAINT message */

        while (GetMessage (&msg, NULL, 0, 0))    /* the message loop */
        {
                if (hDlgModeless == NULL ||
                        !IsDialogMessage (hDlgModeless, &msg))
                {
                        TranslateMessage (&msg) ;
                        DispatchMessage (&msg) ;
                }
        }
        return msg.wParam ;
}

long FAR PASCAL WndProc (HWND hWnd, unsigned iMessage, WORD wParam, LONG lParam)
{
        PAINTSTRUCT             ps ;
        static          FARPROC lpfnDialogProc ;
        static          char    cBuf [256] ;

        switch (iMessage)                        /* process windows messages */
        {
                case WM_PAINT:
                        BeginPaint (hWnd, &ps) ;
                        TextOut (ps.hdc, 10, 10, cBuf, wsprintf (cBuf,
                                "The current values are: %d, %d",
                                nCheckOne, nRadioOne)) ;
                        EndPaint (hWnd, &ps) ;
                        break ;
                case WM_COMMAND:                 /* process menu items */
                        switch (wParam)
                        {
                        case IDM_DOIT:           /* User hit the "Do it" menu item */
                                lpfnDialogProc = MakeProcInstance (DialogProcedure,
                                        ghInstance) ;
                                hDlgModeless = CreateDialog (ghInstance, "exmpdlg",
                                        hWnd,   lpfnDialogProc) ;
                                break ;
                        case IDM_QUIT:
                                DestroyWindow (hWnd) ;
                                break ;
                        }
                        break ;
                case WM_DESTROY:        /* stop application */
                        FreeProcInstance (lpfnDialogProc) ;
                        PostQuitMessage (0) ;
                        break ;
                default:                /* default windows message processing */
                        return DefWindowProc (hWnd, iMessage, wParam, lParam) ;
        }
        return (0L) ;
}

BOOL FAR PASCAL DialogProcedure (HWND hDlg, unsigned iMessage, WORD wParam, LONG lParam)
{
```

```
        BOOL    bBool ;

        switch (iMessage)
        {
        case WM_INITDIALOG:
                if (nCheckOne)
                        CheckDlgButton (hDlg, DLI_CHECKBOX, MF_CHECKED) ;
                else
                        CheckDlgButton (hDlg, DLI_CHECKBOX, MF_UNCHECKED) ;

                if (nRadioOne)
                        CheckRadioButton (hDlg, DLI_RADIO1, DLI_RADIO2,
                                DLI_RADIO2) ;
                else
                        CheckRadioButton (hDlg, DLI_RADIO1, DLI_RADIO2,
                                DLI_RADIO1) ;
                return (TRUE) ;
        case WM_COMMAND:
                switch (wParam)
                {
                case DLI_CHECKBOX:
                        if (nCheckOne)
                        {
                                nCheckOne = 0 ;
                                CheckDlgButton (hDlg, DLI_CHECKBOX, MF_UNCHECKED) ;
                        }
                        else
                        {
                                nCheckOne = 1 ;
                                CheckDlgButton (hDlg, DLI_CHECKBOX, MF_CHECKED) ;
                        }
                        return (TRUE) ;
                case DLI_RADIO1:
                        nRadioOne = 0 ;
                        CheckRadioButton (hDlg, DLI_RADIO1, DLI_RADIO2,
                                DLI_RADIO1) ;
                        return (TRUE) ;
                case DLI_RADIO2:
                        nRadioOne = 1 ;
                        CheckRadioButton (hDlg, DLI_RADIO1, DLI_RADIO2,
                                DLI_RADIO2) ;
                        return (TRUE) ;
                case DLI_DONE:
                        DestroyWindow (hDlg) ;
                        hDlgModeless = 0 ;
                        return (TRUE) ;
                }
                break ;
        default:
                return (FALSE) ;
        }
        return (FALSE) ;
}
```

CREATEDIALOGINDIRECT   ■ Win 2.0   ■ Win 3.0   ■ Win 3.1

Purpose	Creates a modeless dialog box.
Syntax	HWND **CreateDialogIndirect**(HANDLE *hInstance*, LPSTR *lpDialogTemplate*, HWND *hWnd-Parent*, FARPROC *lpDialogFunc*);
Description	This function is identical to CreateDialog(), except that the dialog template is specified with a pointer to memory containing a dialog box template. The dialog box template can be either created from scratch in memory, or loaded into memory from a dialog box resource. The structure of the dialog box definition in memory is discussed at the beginning of this chapter under the heading *Dynamic Dialog Boxes*.

Uses	This function can be used to create modal dialog boxes that can be modified as the program runs (called "dynamic dialog boxes"). Typical applications are database programs, with which the user can add or subtract fields from the database. Using this function provides greater control over when the program loads and discards the resource data that defines the dialog box. This can be important in applications that use a large number of resources and need to control which ones are preloaded, and which are discarded.
Returns	Modeless dialog boxes are convenient for tool windows that may remain on the screen for an extended period of time.
See Also	CreateDialog(), CreateDialogParam(), DestroyWindow(), IsDialogMessage(), SetFocus(), DialogBox()

Parameters

hInstance	HANDLE: The program's instance handle.
lpDialogTemplate	LPSTR: A pointer to a memory area containing the dialog definition. The definition can be created in a global memory block, and then locked with GlobalLock(). Alternatively, the dialog definition can be loaded from a resource with LoadResource() and locked with LockResource() prior to calling CreateDialogIndirect().
hWndParent	HWND: The parent window's handle. Destroying the parent window will automatically destroy the modeless dialog box.
lpDialogFunc	FARPROC: The procedure-instance address of the dialog box function. This address is created with MakeProcInstance(). The dialog box function processes messages for the dialog box. This function must be declared in the EXPORTS section of the program's .DEF definition file, and must have the following format:

BOOL FAR PASCAL **DialogFunc**(HWND *hDlg*, WORD *wMsg*, WORD *wParam*, DWORD *lParam*);

The parameters passed to the dialog box function have the following meanings.

hDlg	HWND: This is the window handle for the modeless dialog box window. This handle can be used just like any other window handle for setting colors, changing the caption, etc.
wMsg	WORD: The message being passed to the dialog function. For example, WM_INITDIALOG is sent to the dialog function right before the window is made visible.
wParam	WORD: The WORD data associated with the message.
lParam	DWORD: The 32-bit data associated with the message.

The dialog box function should return TRUE if the function processes the message, and FALSE if the message is not acted on. The exception is processing a WM_INITDIALOG message. In this case, the function should return TRUE only if the SetFocus() function is not called, FALSE if SetFocus() is called. SetFocus() is used to establish which control will have the input focus when the dialog box is first made visible. If SetFocus() is not used, the first control in the dialog box definition receives the input focus.

Related Messages	WM_INITDIALOG
Example	This example creates the dialog box definition in memory by loading a dialog box resource. The result is identical to the one shown in more detail under CreateDialog(). The only differences are in the processing of the IDM_DOIT menu item. Because CreateDialogIndirect() is used to create the modeless dialog box, some preparation is required. First, the dialog box information is loaded into memory with LoadResource(). Second, the memory block containing the dialog box information is locked in memory using LockResource(). LockResource() returns a handle to the memory area, needed to call CreateDialogIndirect(). As the dialog box is created, the memory area can be unlocked.

```
Long FAR PASCAL WndProc (HWND hWnd, unsigned iMessage, WORD wParam, LONG lParam)
{
```

```
PAINTSTRUCT                        ps ;
static          FARPROC            lpfnDialogProc ;
char                               cBuf [256] ;
static          HANDLE             hDialog = NULL;
LPSTR                              lpResource ;

switch (iMessage)                              /* process windows messages */
{
        case WM_PAINT:
                BeginPaint (hWnd, &ps) ;
                TextOut (ps.hdc, 10, 10, cBuf, wsprintf (cBuf,
                        "The current values are: %d, %d", nCheckOne, nRadioOne)) ;
                EndPaint (hWnd, &ps) ;
                break ;
        case WM_COMMAND:                       /* process menu items */
                switch (wParam)
                {
                case IDM_DOIT:                 /* User hit the "Do it" menu item */
                        lpfnDialogProc = MakeProcInstance (DialogProcedure,
                                ghInstance) ;
                        hDialog = LoadResource (ghInstance,
                                FindResource (ghInstance, "exmpdlg", RT_DIALOG)) ;
                        lpResource = LockResource (hDialog) ;
                        hDlgModeless = CreateDialogIndirect (ghInstance,
                                lpResource,      hWnd, lpfnDialogProc) ;
                        UnlockResource (hDialog) ;
                        break ;
                case IDM_QUIT:                 /* send end of application message */
                        FreeResource (hDialog) ;
                        FreeProcInstance (lpfnDialogProc) ;
                        DestroyWindow (hWnd) ;
                        break ;
                }
                break ;
```

[Other program lines]

CreateDialogIndirectParam □ Win 2.0 ■ Win 3.0 ■ Win 3.1

Purpose   Creates a modeless dialog box, and passes a 32-bit value to the dialog box function when it starts processing messages.

Syntax   HWND **CreateDialogIndirectParam**(HANDLE *hInstance*, LPSTR *lpDialogTemplate*, HWND *hWndParent*, FARPROC *lpDialogFunc*, LONG *dwInitParam*);

Description This function is identical to CreateDialogParam(), except that the dialog box definition is passed as a pointer to a memory area. Like CreateDialogParam(). This function has the added feature of allowing a 32-bit item (usually a pointer to a data structure) to be passed to the dialog box function on startup.

Uses   This is the most sophisticated of the modeless dialog box functions. The function can be used to create dynamic dialog boxes that can be changed as the program executes. Using a memory pointer for the dialog resource information, instead of just the dialog box template name, gives more control over when the resource data is loaded and discarded. The 32-bit data element allows the dialog box to avoid global variables as a means of communication between the dialog box function and the rest of the application program.

Returns   HWND, the handle to the modeless dialog box created.

See Also   CreateDialog(), CreateDialogIndirect(), DestroyWindow(), IsDialogMessage(), SetFocus()

Parameters

hInstance   HANDLE: The program's instance handle.

lpDialogTemplate LPSTR: A pointer to a memory area containing the dialog definition. The definition can be created in a global memory block, and then locked with GlobalLock(). Alternatively, the dialog definition can be loaded from a resource with LoadResource() and locked with LockResource() prior to calling CreateDialogIndirect().

hWndParent	HWND: The parent window's handle. Destroying the parent window will automatically destroy the modeless dialog box.
lpDialogFunc	FARPROC: The procedure-instance address of the dialog box function. This address is created with MakeProcInstance().
dwInitParam	LONG: The 32-bit value passed to the DialogFunc(). Normally this value is used to pass a handle to a memory block containing data that the dialog box will use or modify.

The dialog box function processes messages for the dialog box. This function must be declared in the EXPORTS section of the program's .DEF definition file, and must have the following format:

BOOL FAR PASCAL **DialogFunc**(HWND *hDlg*, WORD *wMsg*, WORD *wParam*, DWORD *lParam*);

The parameters passed to the dialog box function have the following meanings.

hDlg	HWND: This is the window handle for the modeless dialog box window. This handle can be used just like any other window handle for setting colors, changing the caption, etc.
wMsg	WORD: The message being passed to the dialog function. For example, WM_INITDIALOG is sent to the dialog function right before the window is made visible.
wParam	WORD: The WORD data associated with the message.
lParam	DWORD: The 32-bit data associated with the message. The value will be sent as *dwInitParam* when the WM_INITDIALOG message is processed by the dialog box function.

The dialog box function should return TRUE if the function processes the message, and FALSE if the message is not acted on. The exception is processing a WM_INITDIALOG message. In this case, the function should return TRUE only if the SetFocus() function is not called, FALSE if SetFocus() is called. SetFocus() is used to establish which control will have the input focus when the dialog box is first made visible. If SetFocus() is not used, the first control in the dialog box definition receives the input focus.

Related Messages WM_INITDIALOG

Example This example is identical to the one under CreateDialogParam(), except for the changes needed for CreateDialogIndirectParam(). In both cases the 32-bit value is used to pass the handle to a custom data structure TWODATA that contains the settings for the dialog box buttons. See the example under CreateDialogParam() for further details.

```
typedef struct tagTwoData
{
        int             nOne ;
        int             nTwo ;
} TWODATA ;

long FAR PASCAL WndProc (HWND hWnd, unsigned iMessage, WORD wParam, LONG lParam)
{
        PAINTSTRUCT                     ps ;
        static          FARPROC         lpfnDialogProc ;
        static          HANDLE          hMem ;
        TWODATA                         *ptd ;
        static          HANDLE          hDialog = NULL;
        LPSTR                           lpResource ;

        switch (iMessage)                       /* process windows messages */
        {
                case WM_CREATE:
                        hMem = LocalAlloc (LMEM_MOVEABLE | LMEM_DISCARDABLE,
                                sizeof (TWODATA)) ;
                        ptd = (TWODATA *) LocalLock (hMem) ;
                        ptd->nOne = 1 ;
                        ptd->nTwo = 1 ;
                        LocalUnlock (hMem) ;
```

```
                               break ;
                   case WM_COMMAND:                    /* process menu items */
                          switch (wParam)
                          {
                          case IDM_DOIT:               /* User hit the "Do it" menu item */
                                 lpfnDialogProc = MakeProcInstance (DialogProcedure,
                                        ghInstance) ;
                                 hDialog = LoadResource (ghInstance,
                                        FindResource (ghInstance, "exmpdlg", RT_DIALOG)) ;
                                 lpResource = LockResource (hDialog) ;
                                 hDlgModeless = CreateDialogIndirectParam
                                        (ghInstance,      lpResource, hWnd,
                                        lpfnDialogProc, (DWORD) hMem) ;
                                 UnlockResource (hDialog) ;
                                 break ;
                          case IDM_QUIT:               /* send end of application message */
                                 FreeResource (hDialog) ;
                                 FreeProcInstance (lpfnDialogProc) ;
                                 LocalFree (hMem) ;
                                 DestroyWindow (hWnd) ;
                                 break ;
                          }
                          break ;
```

[Other program lines]

CREATEDIALOGPARAM □ Win 2.0   ■ Win 3.0   ■ Win 3.1

Purpose   Creates a modeless dialog box, and passes a 32-bit value to the dialog box function when it starts processing messages.

Syntax   HWND **CreateDialogParam**(HANDLE *hInstance*, LPSTR *lpTemplateName*, HWND *hWndParent*, FARPROC *lpDialogFunc*, LONG *dwInitParam*);

Description   A modeless dialog box behaves like a popup window. The user can switch the focus to the parent window, or another application, while the modeless dialog box is still visible. This function is identical to CreateDialog(), except that an additional 32-bit value *dwInitParam* has been added. This value is passed to the dialog box function when the WM_INITDIALOG message is processed. The 32-bit value ends up as the *lParam* value when WM_INITDIALOG is received. The advantage of this function is that the 32-bit value can be used to pass a handle to memory containing values that the dialog box will change. This avoids having to use global variables for all values changed within the dialog box. The dialog box template file should contain the WS_VISIBLE style. If not, the ShowWindow() function will be needed to make the modeless dialog box visible.

  Modeless dialog boxes are ended by calling DestroyWindow() within the dialog box function. The application's message loop needs to be modified for modeless dialog boxes, so that keyboard input to the dialog box is properly processed. See the example under CreateDialog() for the proper use of the IsDialogMessage() function.

Uses   Modeless dialog boxes are convenient for tool windows that may remain on the screen for an extended period of time.

Returns   HWND, the handle to the modeless dialog box created.

See Also   CreateDialog(), CreateDialogIndirect(), DestroyWindow(), IsDialogMessage(), SetFocus(), DialogBox()

Parameters

hInstance   HANDLE: The program's instance handle.

lpTemplateName   LPSTR: A pointer to a character string containing the name of the dialog box template in the application's resource file. Dialog box templates are normally created with the SDK Dialog Box Editor.

hWndParent	HWND: The parent window's handle. Destroying the parent window will automatically destroy the modeless dialog box.
lpDialogFunc	FARPROC: The procedure-instance address of the dialog box function. This address is created with MakeProcInstance().
dwInitParam	LONG: The 32-bit value passed to the DialogFunc(). Normally, this value is used to pass a handle to a memory block containing data that the dialog box will use or modify.

The dialog box function processes messages for the dialog box. This function must be declared in the EXPORTS section of the program's .DEF definition file, and it must have the following format:

BOOL FAR PASCAL **DialogFunc**(HWND *hDlg*, WORD *wMsg*, WORD *wParam*, DWORD *lParam*);

The parameters passed to the dialog box function have the following meanings.

hDlg	HWND: This is the window handle for the modeless dialog box window. This handle can be used just like any other window handle for setting colors, changing the caption, etc.
wMsg	WORD: The message being passed to the dialog function. For example, WM_INITDIALOG is sent to the dialog function right before the window is made visible.
wParam	WORD: The WORD data associated with the message.
lParam	DWORD: The 32-bit data associated with the message. The value will be the same as *dwInitParam* with then WM_INITDIALOG message is processed by the dialog box function.

The dialog box function should return TRUE if the function processes the message, and FALSE if the message is not acted on. The exception is processing a WM_INITDIALOG message. In this case, the function should return TRUE only if the SetFocus() function is not called, FALSE if SetFocus() is called. SetFocus() is used to establish which control will have the input focus when the dialog box is first made visible. If SetFocus() is not used, the first control in the dialog box definition receives the input focus.

Related Messages WM_INITDIALOG

Example This example is similar to the one under CreateDialog(), except that CreateDialogParam() has been used to avoid global variables. A custom structure called TWODATA is defined to hold the two integers needed by the dialog box to control the check box and radio button status. A handle to memory containing this data structure is passed to the dialog box function when CreateDialogIndirect() is called. The handle ends up as the *lParam* value passed to DialogProcedure() when that function receives the WM_INITDIALOG message.

In this case, the data passed in the TWODATA structure is so small that all of the information could be passed in the one 32-bit value (*dwInitParam*) passed with CreateDialogParam(). The reservation of a local memory area for the TWODATA structure is shown as the more general case, as usually a dialog box will require a number of fields of data, including character strings. See the CheckDlgButton() function description for a figure showing the appearance of the dialog box and other related program files.

```
typedef struct tagTwoData
{
        int             nOne ;
        int             nTwo ;
} TWODATA ;

long FAR PASCAL WndProc (HWND hWnd, unsigned iMessage, WORD wParam, LONG lParam)
{
        PAINTSTRUCT                     ps ;
        static          FARPROC         lpfnDialogProc ;
        static          HANDLE          hMem ;
        TWODATA                         *ptd ;

        switch (iMessage)                       /* process windows messages */
        {
```

```
                case WM_CREATE:
                        hMem = LocalAlloc (LMEM_MOVEABLE | LMEM_DISCARDABLE,
                                sizeof (TWODATA)) ;
                        ptd = (TWODATA *) LocalLock (hMem) ;
                        ptd->nOne = 1 ;
                        ptd->nTwo = 1 ;
                        LocalUnlock (hMem) ;
                        break ;
                case WM_COMMAND:                    /* process menu items */
                        switch (wParam)
                        {
                        case IDM_DOIT:              /* User hit the "Do it" menu item */
                                lpfnDialogProc = MakeProcInstance (DialogProcedure,
                                        ghInstance) ;
                                hDlgModeless = CreateDialogParam (ghInstance,
                                        "exmpdlg", hWnd, lpfnDialogProc,
                                        (DWORD) hMem) ;
                                break ;
                        case IDM_QUIT:              /* send end of application message */
                                DestroyWindow (hWnd) ;
                                break ;
                        }
                        break ;
                case WM_DESTROY:                    /* stop application */
                        FreeProcInstance (lpfnDialogProc) ;
                        LocalFree (hMem) ;
                        PostQuitMessage (0) ;
                        break ;
                default:                            /* default windows message processing */
                        return DefWindowProc (hWnd, iMessage, wParam, lParam) ;
        }
        return (0L) ;
}


BOOL FAR PASCAL DialogProcedure (HWND hDlg, unsigned iMessage, WORD wParam, LONG lParam)
{
        BOOL                    bBool ;
        static          HANDLE          hMem ;
        TWODATA                 *ptd ;

        switch (iMessage)
        {
        case WM_INITDIALOG:
                hMem = LOWORD (lParam) ;
                ptd = (TWODATA *) LocalLock (hMem) ;
                if (ptd->nOne)
                        CheckDlgButton (hDlg, DLI_CHECKBOX, MF_CHECKED) ;
                else
                        CheckDlgButton (hDlg, DLI_CHECKBOX, MF_UNCHECKED) ;

                if (ptd->nTwo)
                        CheckRadioButton (hDlg, DLI_RADIO1, DLI_RADIO2,
                                DLI_RADIO2) ;
                else
                        CheckRadioButton (hDlg, DLI_RADIO1, DLI_RADIO2,
                                DLI_RADIO1) ;
                LocalUnlock (hMem) ;
                return (TRUE) ;
        case WM_COMMAND:
                ptd = (TWODATA *) LocalLock (hMem) ;
                switch (wParam)
                {
                case DLI_CHECKBOX:
                        if (ptd->nOne)
                        {
                                ptd->nOne = 0 ;
                                CheckDlgButton (hDlg, DLI_CHECKBOX,
                                        MF_UNCHECKED) ;
                        }
                        else
```

```
                                {
                                        ptd->nOne = 1 ;
                                        CheckDlgButton (hDlg, DLI_CHECKBOX,
                                                MF_CHECKED) ;
                                }
                                LocalUnlock (hMem) ;
                                return (TRUE) ;
                        case DLI_RADIO1:
                                ptd->nTwo = 0 ;
                                CheckRadioButton (hDlg, DLI_RADIO1, DLI_RADIO2,
                                        DLI_RADIO1) ;
                                LocalUnlock (hMem) ;
                                return (TRUE) ;
                        case DLI_RADIO2:
                                ptd->nTwo = 1 ;
                                CheckRadioButton (hDlg, DLI_RADIO1, DLI_RADIO2,
                                        DLI_RADIO2) ;
                                LocalUnlock (hMem) ;
                                return (TRUE) ;
                        case DLI_DONE:
                                DestroyWindow (hDlg) ;
                                hDlgModeless = 0 ;
                                LocalUnlock (hMem) ;
                                return (TRUE) ;
                        }
                        break ;
                default:
                        return (FALSE) ;
                }
                return (FALSE) ;
        }
```

DEFDLGPROC
■ Win 2.0 ■ Win 3.0 ■ Win 3.1

Purpose	Provides default message processing logic for dialog boxes created with their own separate window class.
Syntax	LONG **DefDlgProc**(HWND *hDlg*, WORD *wMsg*, WORD *wParam*, LONG *lParam*);
Description	Normally, Windows takes care of processing messages that the dialog box function does not handle. An exception is when a separate window class is used for the dialog box window. To do this, include the CLASS statement in the dialog box definition in the program's resource file.
	The window class must be registered with RegisterClass() before the dialog box is called. The dialog window class must include the DLGWINDOWEXTRA value for the *cbWndExtra* element of the class structure. This provides extra data space in the class definition. Because the class definition includes a pointer to the dialog box function, it is not necessary to specify the procedure-instance address of the dialog box function when calling DialogBox() or the other related functions.
Uses	Only used with dialog boxes that include the CLASS statement to specify a separate window class. This is unusual, and is not encouraged in the Windows SDK documentation.
Returns	LONG, the value returned by DefDlgProc() is returned to Windows after the message is processed (see the usage at the bottom of the example listing).
Parameters	
hDlg	HWND: The dialog box window handle.
wMsg	WORD: The message ID value, such as WM_INITDIALOG. Messages that are not processed by the dialog box function logic are passed to DefDlgProc().
wParam	WORD: The WORD parameter passed to the dialog box function.
lParam	DWORD: The DWORD parameter passed to the dialog box function.

Related Messages All Windows messages that are not processed by the dialog box function should be passed to DefDlgProc() if the dialog box has its own window class.

Example The dialog box resource definition has had the CLASS statement added. In this case, the dialog box will use the "separate" class when the dialog box is created and shown. Otherwise, the dialog box is identical to the one shown in Figure 13-3, under the CheckDlgButton() function description. That description also includes listings of the header files and .DEF definition file.

```
EXMPDLG DIALOG LOADONCALL MOVEABLE DISCARDABLE 10, 18, 139, 75
CAPTION "Example Dialog Box"
FONT 10, "Helv"
STYLE WS_BORDER | WS_CAPTION | WS_DLGFRAME | WS_POPUP | WS_VISIBLE
CLASS "separate"
BEGIN
    CONTROL "Title String Here", -1, "static",
                SS_CENTER | WS_CHILD, 27, 6, 78, 9
    CONTROL "Check box control.", -1, "static",
                SS_LEFT | WS_CHILD, 60, 22, 67, 9
    CONTROL "Radio buttons.", -1, "static",
                SS_LEFT | WS_CHILD, 60, 39, 73, 10
    CONTROL "DONE", DLI_DONE, "button",
                BS_DEFPUSHBUTTON | WS_TABSTOP | WS_CHILD, 72, 59, 36, 12
    CONTROL "", DLI_CHECKBOX, "button",
                BS_CHECKBOX | WS_TABSTOP | WS_CHILD, 7, 24, 16, 9
    CONTROL "First", DLI_RADIO1, "button",
                BS_RADIOBUTTON | WS_TABSTOP | WS_CHILD, 6, 36, 28, 12
    CONTROL "Second", DLI_RADIO2, "button",
                BS_RADIOBUTTON | WS_TABSTOP | WS_CHILD, 6, 47, 44, 12
END
```

Note that the separate class for the dialog box is created in WndProc() when the WM_CREATE message is processed. The class definition specifies the IDC_CROSS cursor shape instead of the normal IDC_ARROW. Note that this change only applies to the dialog box window class, not to the class upon which the dialog box controls are based. The result is that the cursor shape is a cross when the mouse points to an area on the dialog box window, but it switches to an arrow when the mouse points to one of the dialog box controls.

```
/* generic.c */

#include <windows.h>                     /* window's header file - always included */
#include "generic.h"                     /* the application's header file */
#include "generic.hd"

int     nCheckOne = 0 ;                  /* globals */
int     nRadioOne = 0 ;
HWND    hDlgModeless = 0 ;

int PASCAL WinMain (HANDLE hInstance, HANDLE hPrevInstance, LPSTR lpszCmdLine, int nCmdShow)
{                                        /* variable types defined in windows.h */

        HWND            hWnd ;           /* a handle to a message */
        MSG             msg ;            /* a message */
        WNDCLASS        wndclass ;       /* the window class */

        ghInstance = hInstance ;         /* store instance handle as global var. */
        if (!hPrevInstance)              /* load data into window class struct. */
        {
                wndclass.style          = CS_HREDRAW | CS_VREDRAW ;
                wndclass.lpfnWndProc    = WndProc ;
                wndclass.cbClsExtra     = 0 ;
                wndclass.cbWndExtra     = 0 ;
                wndclass.hInstance      = hInstance ;
                wndclass.hIcon          = LoadIcon (hInstance, gszAppName) ;
```

```
                        wndclass.hCursor        = LoadCursor (NULL, IDC_ARROW) ;
                        wndclass.hbrBackground  = GetStockObject (WHITE_BRUSH) ;
                        wndclass.lpszMenuName   = gszAppName ;
                        wndclass.lpszClassName  = gszAppName ;
                                                /* register the window class */
                if (!RegisterClass (&wndclass))
                        return FALSE ;
        }

        hWnd = CreateWindow (                   /* create the program's window here */
                gszAppName,                     /* class name */
                gszAppName,                     /* window name */
                WS_OVERLAPPEDWINDOW,            /* window style */
                CW_USEDEFAULT,                  /* x position on screen */
                CW_USEDEFAULT,                  /* y position on screen */
                CW_USEDEFAULT,                  /* width of window */
                CW_USEDEFAULT,                  /* height of window */
                NULL,                           /* parent window handle (null = none) */
                NULL,                           /* menu handle (null = use class menu) */
                hInstance,                      /* instance handle */
                NULL) ;                         /* lpstr (null = not used) */
        ShowWindow (hWnd, nCmdShow) ;
        UpdateWindow (hWnd) ;                   /* send first WM_PAINT message */

        while (GetMessage (&msg, NULL, 0, 0))       /* the message loop */
        {
                if (hDlgModeless == NULL ||
                        !IsDialogMessage (hDlgModeless, &msg))
                {
                        TranslateMessage (&msg) ;
                        DispatchMessage (&msg) ;
                }
        }
        return msg.wParam ;
}


long FAR PASCAL WndProc (HWND hWnd, unsigned iMessage, WORD wParam, LONG lParam)
{
        PAINTSTRUCT                 ps ;
        char                        cBuf [256] ;
        WNDCLASS                    dlgclass ;

        switch (iMessage)               /* process windows messages */
        {
                case WM_CREATE:
                        dlgclass.style          = CS_HREDRAW | CS_VREDRAW ;
                        dlgclass.lpfnWndProc    = DialogProcedure ;
                        dlgclass.cbClsExtra     = 0 ;
                        dlgclass.cbWndExtra     = DLGWINDOWEXTRA ;
                        dlgclass.hInstance      = ghInstance ;
                        dlgclass.hIcon          = NULL ;
                        dlgclass.hCursor        = LoadCursor (NULL, IDC_CROSS) ;
                        dlgclass.hbrBackground  = GetStockObject (WHITE_BRUSH) ;
                        dlgclass.lpszMenuName   = NULL ;
                        dlgclass.lpszClassName  = "separate" ;

                        RegisterClass (&dlgclass) ;
                        break ;
                case WM_PAINT:
                        BeginPaint (hWnd, &ps) ;
                        TextOut (ps.hdc, 10, 10, cBuf, wsprintf (cBuf,
                                "The current values are: %d, %d",
                                nCheckOne, nRadioOne)) ;
                        EndPaint (hWnd, &ps) ;
                        break ;
                case WM_COMMAND:            /* process menu items */
                        switch (wParam)
                        {
                        case IDM_DOIT:  /* User hit the "Do it" menu item */
```

```
                                DialogBox (ghInstance, "exmpdlg", hWnd,
                                        NULL) ;
                                break ;
                        case IDM_QUIT:   /* send end of application message */
                                DestroyWindow (hWnd) ;
                                break ;
                        }
                        break ;
                case WM_DESTROY:              /* stop application */
                        PostQuitMessage (0) ;
                        break ;
                default:                      /* default windows message processing */
                        return DefWindowProc (hWnd, iMessage, wParam, lParam) ;
        }
        return (0L) ;
}


long FAR PASCAL DialogProcedure (HWND hDlg, unsigned iMessage, WORD wParam, LONG lParam)
{
        BOOL    bBool ;

        switch (iMessage)
        {
        case WM_INITDIALOG:
                if (nCheckOne)
                        CheckDlgButton (hDlg, DLI_CHECKBOX, MF_CHECKED) ;
                else
                        CheckDlgButton (hDlg, DLI_CHECKBOX, MF_UNCHECKED) ;

                if (nRadioOne)
                        CheckRadioButton (hDlg, DLI_RADIO1, DLI_RADIO2,
                                DLI_RADIO2) ;
                else
                        CheckRadioButton (hDlg, DLI_RADIO1, DLI_RADIO2,
                                DLI_RADIO1) ;
                return (TRUE) ;
        case WM_COMMAND:
                switch (wParam)
                {
                case DLI_CHECKBOX:
                        if (nCheckOne)
                        {
                                nCheckOne = 0 ;
                                CheckDlgButton (hDlg, DLI_CHECKBOX, MF_UNCHECKED) ;
                        }
                        else
                        {
                                nCheckOne = 1 ;
                                CheckDlgButton (hDlg, DLI_CHECKBOX, MF_CHECKED) ;
                        }
                        return (TRUE) ;
                case DLI_RADIO1:
                                nRadioOne = 0 ;
                        CheckRadioButton (hDlg, DLI_RADIO1, DLI_RADIO2,
                                DLI_RADIO1) ;
                        return (TRUE) ;
                case DLI_RADIO2:
                                nRadioOne = 1 ;
                        CheckRadioButton (hDlg, DLI_RADIO1, DLI_RADIO2,
                                DLI_RADIO2) ;
                        return (TRUE) ;
                case DLI_DONE:
                        EndDialog (hDlg, 0) ;
                                hDlgModeless = 0 ;
                        return (TRUE) ;
                }
                break ;
        default:
```

```
                              return (DefDlgProc (hDlg, iMessage, wParam, lParam)) ;
        }
        return (FALSE) ;
}
```

DialogBox

Purpose	Creates a modal dialog box.
Syntax	int **DialogBox**(HANDLE *hInstance*, LPSTR *lpTemplateName*, HWND *hWndParent*, FARPROC *lpDialogFunc*);
Description	The dialog box created is application-modal, meaning that the dialog box window retains the input focus for the application until the dialog box is closed. The user can switch to another application, but not to another window of the application that called DialogBox().

This function is the most common way to create a dialog box. The dialog box template is defined in the program's .RC resource file. A dialog box function must be defined to process messages while the dialog box is in operation. Messages pass through this dialog procedure until the procedure calls EndDialog(). The dialog box function must be listed in the EXPORTS section of the program's .DEF definition file. Before DialogBox() can be called, the program must obtain a procedure-instance address for the dialog box function. A typical set of program lines to run a dialog box is as follows:

```
static          FARPROC         lpfnDialogProc ;

lpfnDialogProc = MakeProcInstance (DialogProcedure, ghInstance) ;
DialogBox (ghInstance, "exmpdlg", hWnd, lpfnDialogProc) ;
FreeProcInstance (lpfnDialogProc) ;
```

Uses	Running a dialog box. The dialog box can be made system-modal by calling SetSysModalWindow() during the processing of the WM_INITDIALOG message.
Returns	The returned value is equal to the *nResult* parameter passed when EndDialog() was called. Using return() inside the dialog function does not result in the value being returned to the application. These values are used by Windows. The function returns −1 if the dialog box could not be created.
See Also	DialogBoxIndirect(), DialogBoxIndirectParam(), DialogBoxParam(),
Parameters	
hInstance	HANDLE: The application's procedure-instance handle.
lpTemplateName	LPSTR: This is the name of the dialog box template in the program's .RC resource file.
hWndParent	HWND: The parent window's handle.
lpDialogFunc	FARPROC: The procedure-instance address of the dialog box function. Use MakeProcInstance() to create this value. The dialog box function must have the following style:

int FAR PASCAL **DialogFunc** (HWND *hDlg*, WORD *wMsg*, WORD *wParam*, DWORD *lParam*);

The name "DialogFunc" is replaced by the name of the message processing function to use for a dialog box. Each dialog box will have a separate "DialogFunc" with a different name. The meanings of the parameters are as follows.

hDlg	HWND: The handle to the dialog box window. This handle can be used just like any other window handle: to obtain the device context, to change the caption, etc.
wMsg	WORD: This is the Windows message being passed to the function. For example, *wMsg* will equal WM_INITDIALOG when the dialog box is first started and the first message is sent to the dialog box function.
wParam	WORD: This is the WORD parameter passed with the message. See Chapter 9, *Windows Messages,* for the meaning of the *wParam* and *lParam* values for each message.

lParam	DWORD: This is the DWORD parameter passed with the message.

The dialog box function should return TRUE if the function processes the message, and FALSE if the message is not acted on. The exception is processing a WM_INITDIALOG message. In this case, the function should return TRUE only if the SetFocus() function is not called, FALSE if SetFocus() is called. SetFocus() is used to establish which control will have the input focus when the dialog box is first made visible. If SetFocus() is not used, the first control in the dialog box definition receives the input focus.

Figure13-4. DialogBox( ) Example.

Related Messages Most Windows messages can be processed by a dialog box. WM_CREATE is replaced with WM_INITDIALOG for dialog boxes.

Example This example, shown in Figure 13-4, creates a dialog box for entering two integer values. The values are also displayed on the main window's client area. The dialog box style has been changed to include a caption bar. This allows the dialog box to be moved on the screen. The dialog box font has also been changed to "Helv," to match the dialog box style used by the dialog boxes in the standard Windows applications, such as Paint and Write.

The dialog resource script that creates the dialog box was originally created with the SDK Dialog Box Editor. The .DLG file must be included as part of the program's .RC file.

⇨ GENERIC.DLG

```
EXMPDLG DIALOG LOADONCALL MOVEABLE DISCARDABLE 10, 18, 139, 75
STYLE WS_DLGFRAME | WS_POPUP | WS_CAPTION
CAPTION "Example Dialog Box"
FONT 10, "Helv"
BEGIN
    CONTROL "Title String Here", -1, "static",
        SS_CENTER | WS_CHILD, 27, 6, 78, 9
    CONTROL "", DLI_EDIT1, "edit",
        ES_LEFT | WS_BORDER | WS_TABSTOP | WS_CHILD, 12, 22, 26, 12
    CONTROL "Input field one.", -1, "static",
        SS_LEFT | WS_CHILD, 60, 24, 67, 9
    CONTROL "", DLI_EDIT2, "edit",
        ES_LEFT | WS_BORDER | WS_TABSTOP | WS_CHILD, 12, 37, 26, 12
    CONTROL "Input field two.", -1, "static",
        SS_LEFT | WS_CHILD, 60, 39, 73, 10
    CONTROL "DONE", DLI_DONE, "button",
        BS_DEFPUSHBUTTON | WS_TABSTOP | WS_CHILD, 45, 60, 36, 12
END
```

The dialog box item numbers for the controls are defined in a separate header file, created during the SDK Dialog Box Editor session. This file must be included at the top of the resource script .RC file and at the top of the C program source file.

⇨ GENERIC.HD

```
#define DLI_EDIT1   100
#define DLI_EDIT2   101
#define DLI_DONE    102
```

The program's header file includes both the dialog box definition file and the dialog box ID value file GENERIC.HD. The latter must also be included at the top of the C program file. Note that the dialog box function prototype is included at the end of the header file.

⇨ GENERIC.H.

```
/* generic.h 1 */
#define IDM_DOIT    1                                /* menu item id values */
```

```
#define IDM_QUIT   2
        /* global variables */
int     ghInstance ;
char    gszAppName [] = "generic" ;
        /* function prototypes */
long FAR PASCAL WndProc (HWND, unsigned, WORD, LONG) ;
BOOL FAR PASCAL DialogProcedure (HWND hDlg, unsigned iMessage, WORD wParam, LONG lParam) ;
```

The program's .DEF definition file must list the dialog box function in the EXPORTS section.

```
NAME          generic
DESCRIPTION   'windows enumeration example'
EXETYPE WINDOWS
STUB          'WINSTUB.EXE'
CODE          PRELOAD MOVEABLE
DATA          PRELOAD MOVEABLE MULTIPLE
HEAPSIZE      1024
STACKSIZE     4096
EXPORTS WndProc

        DialogProcedure
```

The WndProc() and DialogProcedure() functions of the C program are shown in the following example. The WinMain() function is identical to the GENERIC.C function in Chapter 1, *Overview of Windows Programming*. Note that the two integer values, which can be changed from within the dialog box, are defined as global variables. This makes their values available to both the WndProc() function and the DialogProcedure() function.

⇨ GENERIC.C Excerpt

```
int nEditOne = 0 ;            /* global variables */
int nEditTwo = 0 ;

long FAR PASCAL WndProc (HWND hWnd, unsigned iMessage, WORD wParam, LONG lParam)
{
        PAINTSTRUCT                   ps ;
        static  FARPROC               lpfnDialogProc ;
        char                          cBuf [128] ;

        switch (iMessage)                     /* process windows messages */
        {
            case WM_PAINT:
                    BeginPaint (hWnd, &ps) ;
                    TextOut (ps.hdc, 10, 10, cBuf, wsprintf (cBuf,
                            "The current values are: %d, %d", nEditOne, nEditTwo)) ;
                    EndPaint (hWnd, &ps) ;
                    break ;
            case WM_COMMAND:              /* process menu items */
                    switch (wParam)
                    {
                    case IDM_DOIT:        /* User hit the "Do it" menu item */
                            lpfnDialogProc = MakeProcInstance (DialogProcedure,
                                    ghInstance) ;
                            DialogBox (ghInstance, "exmpdlg", hWnd,
                                    lpfnDialogProc) ;
                            FreeProcInstance (lpfnDialogProc) ;
                            InvalidateRect (hWnd, NULL, TRUE) ; /* force paint */
                            break ;
                    case IDM_QUIT:        /* send end of application message */
                            DestroyWindow (hWnd) ;
                            break ;
                    }
                    break ;
            case WM_DESTROY:             /* stop application */
                    PostQuitMessage (0) ;
```

```
                             break ;
                 default:                          /* default windows message processing */
                         return DefWindowProc (hWnd, iMessage, wParam, lParam) ;
         }
         return (OL) ;
}


BOOL FAR PASCAL DialogProcedure (HWND hDlg, unsigned iMessage, WORD wParam, LONG lParam)
{
         BOOL    bBool ;

         switch (iMessage)
         {
         case WM_INITDIALOG:
                 SetDlgItemInt (hDlg, DLI_EDIT1, nEditOne, TRUE) ;
                 SetDlgItemInt (hDlg, DLI_EDIT2, nEditTwo, TRUE) ;
                 break ;
         case WM_COMMAND:
                 switch (wParam)
                 {
                 case DLI_EDIT1:
                         nEditOne = GetDlgItemInt (hDlg, DLI_EDIT1, &bBool, TRUE) ;
                         return (TRUE) ;
                 case DLI_EDIT2:
                         nEditTwo = GetDlgItemInt (hDlg, DLI_EDIT2, &bBool, TRUE) ;
                         return (TRUE) ;
                 case DLI_DONE:
                         EndDialog (hDlg, NULL) ;
                         return (TRUE) ;
                 }
                 break ;
         default:
                 return (FALSE) ;
         }
         return (FALSE) ;
}
```

DIALOGBOXINDIRECT   ■ Win 2.0   ■ Win 3.0   ■ Win 3.1

Purpose   Creates a modal dialog box.

Syntax   int **DialogBoxIndirect**(HANDLE *hInstance*, HANDLE *hDialogTemplate*, HWND *hWndParent*, FARPROC *lpDialogFunc*);

Description   This function is identical to DialogBox(), except that the dialog box resource data is specified by a memory handle instead of the resource name. In both cases, the dialog box created is application-modal, meaning that the dialog box window keeps the input focus until it is closed. The focus can be switched to another application, but not to another window of the application that called DialogBoxIndirect().

Uses   The dialog box template in memory can be modified to change the dialog box as the application runs (called a "dynamic dialog box"). Typical applications are database programs. See the discussion at the beginning of this chapter. Specifying the dialog box resource data indirectly allows the program to have more control over when the resource data is loaded and discarded. This can be important in applications that use a large number of resources, or in applications when memory or efficiency is critical.

Returns   int, the *wResult* parameter passed within the dialog box function when EndDialog() was called. This value is not normally used. Windows returns –1 if the dialog box could not be created.

See Also   DialogBox(), for a full description of the dialog box function and the related files. See also DialogBoxParam() and DialogBoxIndirectParam().

Parameters

hInstance   HANDLE: The application's procedure-instance handle.

hDialogTemplate   HANDLE: The handle to the dialog box resource data. The dialog box template can be created in a global memory block and locked with GlobalLock(). Alternatively, the dialog box can be defined as a resource and loaded into memory. This handle to the resource data is obtained with Load-Resource(). The LockResource() function must also be called before using DialogBoxIndirect(). LockResource() physically causes the resource data to be loaded into memory.

hWndParent   HWND: The parent window's handle.

lpDialogFunc   FARPROC: The procedure-instance address of the dialog box function. Use MakeProcInstance() to create this value. The dialog box function must have the following style:

> int FAR PASCAL **DialogFunc** (HWND *hDlg*, WORD *wMsg*, WORD *wParam*, DWORD *lParam*);

The name "DialogFunc" is replaced by the name of the message processing function to use for a dialog box. Each dialog box will have a separate "DialogFunc" with a different name. The meanings of the parameters are as follows.

hDlg   HWND: The handle to the dialog box window. This handle can be used just like any other window handle: to obtain the device context, to change the caption, etc.

wMsg   WORD: This is the Windows message being passed to the function. For example, *wMsg* will equal WM_INITDIALOG when the dialog box is first started and the first message is sent to the dialog box function.

wParam   WORD: This is the WORD parameter passed with the message. See Chapter 9, *Windows Messages*, for the meaning of the *wParam* and *lParam* values for each message.

lParam   DWORD: This is the DWORD parameter passed with the message.

The dialog box function should return TRUE if the function processes the message, and FALSE if the message is not acted on. The exception is processing a WM_INITDIALOG message. In this case, the function should return TRUE only if the SetFocus() function is not called, FALSE if SetFocus() is called. SetFocus() is used to establish which control will have the input focus when the dialog box is first made visible. If SetFocus() is not used, the first control in the dialog box definition receives the input focus.

Related Messages Most Windows messages can be processed by a dialog box. WM_CREATE is replaced with WM_INITDIALOG for dialog boxes.

Example   This example is identical to the example under the DialogBox() function description, except for the changes needed to use the DialogBoxIndirect() function. Note that LockResource() must be called before using the dialog box resource handle *hDialog* because the resource is not loaded into memory until LockResource() is called.

```
long FAR PASCAL WndProc (HWND hWnd, unsigned iMessage, WORD wParam, LONG lParam)
{
        PAINTSTRUCT                 ps ;
        static          FARPROC     lpfnDialogProc ;
        static          char        cBuf [256] ;
        static          HANDLE      hDialog ;

        switch (iMessage)                       /* process windows messages */
        {
                case WM_PAINT:
                        BeginPaint (hWnd, &ps) ;
                        TextOut (ps.hdc, 10, 10, cBuf, wsprintf (cBuf,
                                "The current values are: %d, %s", nEditOne,
                                        (LPSTR) cEditBuf)) ;
                        EndPaint (hWnd, &ps) ;
                        break ;
                case WM_COMMAND:                /* process menu items */
```

```
                        switch (wParam)
                        {
                        case IDM_DOIT:              /* User hit the "Do it" menu item */
                                lpfnDialogProc = MakeProcInstance (DialogProcedure,
                                        ghInstance) ;
                                hDialog = LoadResource (ghInstance,
                                        FindResource (ghInstance, "exmpdlg",
                                                RT_DIALOG)) ;
                                LockResource (hDialog) ;
                                DialogBoxIndirect (ghInstance, hDialog, hWnd,
                                        lpfnDialogProc) ;
                                UnlockResource (hDialog) ;
                                FreeResource (hDialog) ;
                                FreeProcInstance (lpfnDialogProc) ;
                                InvalidateRect (hWnd, NULL, TRUE) ; /* force paint */
                                break ;
```

[Other program lines]

DIALOGBOXINDIRECTPARAM   ☐ Win 2.0   ■ Win 3.0   ■ Win 3.1

Purpose   Creates a modal dialog box, and passes a 32-bit data item to the dialog box as it is created.

Syntax   int **DialogBoxIndirectParam**(HANDLE *hInstance*, HANDLE *hDialogTemplate*, HWND *hWndParent*, FARPROC *lpDialogFunc*, DWORD *dwInitParam*);

Description   This function is identical to DialogBox(), except that the dialog box resource data is specified by a memory handle instead of the resource name, and the function passes a 32-bit data item to the dialog procedure when the dialog box is created.

The dialog box created is application-modal, meaning that the dialog box retains the input focus until the dialog box is closed. The focus can be shifted to another application, but no other window of the application that called DialogBoxIndirectParam() can gain the focus while the dialog box is active.

The 32-bit data item specified by the *dwInitParam* parameter is ultimately passed to the dialog box function as *lParam* when the dialog box function receives the WM_INITDIALOG message. Normally, this value is used to pass a memory handle to the data that the dialog box will use for edit controls, list boxes, and other controls that the user will be changing.

Because the dialog box definition is loaded from a global memory block, the application can change the dialog box definition at run time (called a "dynamic dialog box"). See the discussion at the beginning of this chapter on dynamic dialog boxes for details.

Uses   This is the most sophisticated of the dialog box functions. Indirect loading of the dialog resource data provides the opportunity to control when resource data is loaded and discarded. The dialog box template data in memory can be created or modified as the application runs, allowing the dialog box to be dynamic. The 32-bit parameter data allows data to be passed to and from the dialog function without resorting to global variables.

Returns   int, the *wResult* parameter passed within the dialog box function when EndDialog() was called. This value is not normally used. Windows returns −1 if the dialog box could not be created.

See Also   DialogBox() for a full description of the dialog box function and the related files. See also DialogBoxParam() and DialogBoxIndirect().

Parameters

hInstance   HANDLE: The application's procedure-instance handle.

hDialogTemplate HANDLE: The handle to the dialog box resource data. The dialog box definition can be created in a global memory block and locked with GlobalLock(). Alternatively, this handle is obtained with LoadResource(). The LockResource() function must also be called before using DialogBoxIndirect(). LockResource() physically causes the resource data to be loaded into memory.

hWndParent	HWND: The parent window's handle.
lpDialogFunc	FARPROC: The procedure-instance address of the dialog box function. Use MakeProcInstance() to create this value.
dwInitParam	DWORD: This is a 32-bit data item that is passed to the dialog box function as the *lParam* value when the WM_INITDIALOG message is processed. Frequently used to pass a handle to a memory block containing data that the dialog box function will use and/or modify. The dialog box function must have the following style:

int FAR PASCAL **DialogFunc** (HWND *hDlg*, WORD *wMsg*, WORD *wParam*, DWORD *lParam*);

The name "DialogFunc" is replaced by the name of the message processing function to use for a dialog box. Each dialog box will have a separate "DialogFunc" with a different name. The meanings of the parameters are as follows.

hDlg	HWND: The handle to the dialog box window. This handle can be used just like any other window handle: to obtain the device context, to change the caption, etc.
wMsg	WORD: This is the Windows message being passed to the function. For example, *wMsg* will equal WM_INITDIALOG when the dialog box is first started and the first message is sent to the dialog box function.
wParam	WORD: This is the WORD parameter passed with the message. See Chapter 9, *Windows Messages*, for the meaning of the *wParam* and *lParam* values for each message.
lParam	DWORD: This is the DWORD parameter passed with the message. This value will be the same as *dwInitParam* when the dialog box function processes the WM_INITDIALOG message.

       The dialog box function should return TRUE if the function processes the message, and FALSE if the message is not acted on. The exception is processing a WM_INITDIALOG message. In this case, the function should return TRUE only if the SetFocus() function is not called, FALSE if SetFocus() is called. SetFocus() is used to establish which control will have the input focus when the dialog box is first made visible. If SetFocus() is not used, the first control in the dialog box definition receives the input focus.

Related Messages Most Windows messages can be processed by a dialog box. WM_CREATE is replaced with WM_INITDIALOG for dialog boxes.

Example   This example runs the same dialog box shown in the DialogBox() function example. In this case, the more sophisticated DialogBoxIndirectParam() function is used. This allows the data for the dialog box to be passed in a custom data structure called TWODATA. Because the function uses "indirect" loading of the dialog box resource, the resource data is specified by a memory handle obtained with LoadResource().

       Note in the dialog box procedure that the memory for the TWODATA structure is locked and unlocked before and after each call to SetDlgItemInt() and SetDlgItemText(). This is necessary, as the address of the TWODATA structure may become invalid when Windows processes messages for the dialog box. The dialog box function name "DialogProcedure" must be included in the EXPORTS section of the program's .DEF definition file. The function prototype must also be included in the program's header file.

```
typedef struct tagTwoData                 /* this could be defined in the header file */
{
        int               nOne ;
        char              cBuf [128] ;
} TWODATA ;

long FAR PASCAL WndProc (HWND hWnd, unsigned iMessage, WORD wParam, LONG lParam)
{
        PAINTSTRUCT               ps ;
        static       FARPROC      lpfnDialogProc ;
```

```
        static          char            cBuf [256] ;
        static          HANDLE          hDialog ;
        static          HANDLE          hMem ;
        TWODATA                         *ptd ;

        switch (iMessage)               /* process windows messages */
        {
                case WM_CREATE:         /* allocate memory for TWODATA data */
                        hMem = LocalAlloc (LMEM_MOVEABLE | LMEM_DISCARDABLE,
                                sizeof (TWODATA)) ;
                        ptd = (TWODATA *) LocalLock (hMem) ;
                        ptd->nOne = 1 ;
                        lstrcpy (ptd->cBuf, "Hi Mom!") ;
                        LocalUnlock (hMem) ;
                        break ;
                case WM_PAINT:          /* display current TWODATA contents */
                        BeginPaint (hWnd, &ps) ;
                        ptd = (TWODATA *) LocalLock (hMem) ;
                        TextOut (ps.hdc, 10, 10, cBuf, wsprintf (cBuf,
                                "The current values are: %d, %s", ptd->nOne,
                                        (LPSTR) ptd->cBuf)) ;
                        LocalUnlock (hMem) ;
                        EndPaint (hWnd, &ps) ;
                        break ;
                case WM_COMMAND:        /* process menu items */
                        switch (wParam)
                        {
                        case IDM_DOIT:  /* run dialog box to edit TWODATA data */
                                lpfnDialogProc = MakeProcInstance (DialogProcedure,
                                        ghInstance) ;
                                hDialog = LoadResource (ghInstance,
                                        FindResource (ghInstance, "exmpdlg", RT_DIALOG)) ;
                                LockResource (hDialog) ;
                                DialogBoxIndirectParam (ghInstance, hDialog,
                                        hWnd,   lpfnDialogProc, (DWORD) hMem) ;
                                UnlockResource (hDialog) ;
                                FreeProcInstance (lpfnDialogProc) ;
                                FreeResource (hDialog) ;
                                InvalidateRect (hWnd, NULL, TRUE) ; /* force paint */
                                break ;
                        case IDM_QUIT:
                                DestroyWindow (hWnd) ;
                                break ;
                        }
                        break ;
                case WM_DESTROY:        /* stop application */
                        LocalFree (hMem) ;
                        PostQuitMessage (0) ;
                        break ;
                default:                /* default windows message processing */
                        return DefWindowProc (hWnd, iMessage, wParam, lParam) ;
        }
        return (0L) ;
}


BOOL FAR PASCAL DialogProcedure (HWND hDlg, unsigned iMessage, WORD wParam, LONG lParam)
{
        BOOL                    bBool ;
        static          HANDLE          hMem ;
        TWODATA                 *ptd ;

        switch (iMessage)
        {
        case WM_INITDIALOG:
                hMem = LOWORD (lParam) ;  /* get mem handle from 32 bit data */
                ptd = (TWODATA *) LocalLock (hMem) ;
                SetDlgItemInt (hDlg, DLI_EDIT1, ptd->nOne, TRUE) ;
```

```
                    SetDlgItemText (hDlg, DLI_EDIT2, ptd->cBuf) ;
                    LocalUnlock (hMem) ;
                    return (TRUE) ;
            case WM_COMMAND:
                    switch (wParam)
                    {
                    case DLI_EDIT1:              /* get edited integer data */
                            ptd = (TWODATA *) LocalLock (hMem) ;
                            ptd->nOne = GetDlgItemInt (hDlg, DLI_EDIT1, &bBool, TRUE) ;
                            LocalUnlock (hMem) ;
                            return (TRUE) ;
                    case DLI_EDIT2:              /* get edited string data */
                            ptd = (TWODATA *) LocalLock (hMem) ;
                            GetDlgItemText (hDlg, DLI_EDIT2, ptd->cBuf, 127) ;
                            LocalUnlock (hMem) ;
                            return (TRUE) ;
                    case DLI_DONE:
                            EndDialog (hDlg, NULL) ;
                            return (TRUE) ;
                    }
                    break ;
            default:
                    return (FALSE) ;
            }
            return (FALSE) ;
}
```

DialogBoxParam

Purpose   Creates a modal dialog box, and passes a 32-bit data item to the dialog box as it is created.

Syntax   int **DialogBoxParam**(HANDLE *hInstance*, LPSTR *lpTemplateName*, HWND *hWndParent*, FARPROC *lpDialogFunc*, DWORD *dwInitParam*);

Description   This function is identical to DialogBox(), except that the function passes a 32-bit data item to the dialog procedure when the dialog box is created. The dialog box created is application-modal, meaning that the dialog box retains the input focus until the dialog box is closed. The focus can be shifted to another application, but no other window of the application that called DialogBoxIndirectParam() can gain the focus while the dialog box is active.

The 32-bit data item specified by the *dwInitParam* parameter ends up being passed to the dialog box function as *lParam* when the dialog box function receives the WM_INITDIALOG message. Normally, this value is used to pass a memory handle to the data that the dialog box will be using for edit controls, list boxes, and other controls the user will be changing.

Uses   This is probably the best of the DialogBox() functions for normal dialog boxes. The 32-bit data item allows data to be exchanged between the program's WndProc() function and the dialog box function, without using global variables. DialogBoxParam() is simpler to use than DialogBoxIndirectParam(), in that only the dialog definition name is needed. This function avoids the complexity of separately loading the dialog box resource data, but at the expense of not being able to modify the dialog box template in memory while the application runs.

Returns   int, the *wResult* parameter passed within the dialog box function when EndDialog() was called. This value is not normally used. Windows returns −1 if the dialog box could not be created.

See Also   DialogBox() for a full description of the dialog box function and the related files. See also DialogBoxIndirectParam() and DialogBoxIndirect().

Parameters

hInstance   HANDLE: The application's procedure-instance handle.

lpTemplateName   LPSTR: A pointer to a character string containing the name of the dialog box definition in the resource script file.

hWndParent	HWND: The parent window's handle.
lpDialogFunc	FARPROC: The procedure-instance address of the dialog box function. Use MakeProcInstance() to create this value.
dwInitParam	DWORD: This is a 32-bit data item that is passed to the dialog box function as the *lParam* value when the WM_INITDIALOG message is processed. The dialog box function must have the following style:

int FAR PASCAL **DialogFunc** (HWND *hDlg*, WORD *wMsg*, WORD *wParam*, DWORD *lParam*);

The name "DialogFunc" is replaced by the name of the message processing function to use for a dialog box. Each dialog box will have a separate "DialogFunc" with a different name. The meanings of the parameters are as follows.

hDlg	HWND: The handle to the dialog box window. This handle can be used just like any other window handle: to obtain the device context, to change the caption, etc.
wMsg	WORD: This is the Windows message being passed to the function. For example, *wMsg* will equal WM_INITDIALOG when the dialog box is first started and the first message is sent to the dialog box function.
wParam	WORD: This is the WORD parameter passed with the message. See Chapter 9, *Windows Messages,* for the meaning of the *wParam* and *lParam* values for each message.
lParam	DWORD: This is the DWORD parameter passed with the message. This value will be equal to *dwInitParam* when the WM_INITDIALOG message is processed.

The dialog box function should return TRUE if the function processes the message, and FALSE if the message is not acted on. The exception is processing a WM_INITDIALOG message. In this case, the function should return TRUE only if the SetFocus() function is not called, FALSE if SetFocus() is called. SetFocus() is used to establish which control will have the input focus when the dialog box is first made visible. If SetFocus() is not used, the first control in the dialog box definition receives the input focus.

Related Messages Most Windows messages can be processed by a dialog box. WM_CREATE is replaced with WM_INITDIALOG for dialog boxes.

Example This example runs the same dialog box shown in the DialogBox() function example. In this case, the more sophisticated DialogBoxParam() function is used. This example allows the data for the dialog box to be passed in a custom data structure called TWODATA. The dialog box function name "DialogProcedure" must be included in the EXPORTS section of the program's .DEF definition file. The function prototype must also be included in the program's header file.

```
typedef struct tagTwoData              /* this definition can go in header file */
{
        int             nOne ;
        char            cBuf [128] ;
}                       TWODATA ;

long FAR PASCAL WndProc (HWND hWnd, unsigned iMessage, WORD wParam, LONG lParam)
{
        PAINTSTRUCT                     ps ;
        static          FARPROC         lpfnDialogProc ;
        static          char            cBuf [256] ;
        static          HANDLE          hDialog ;
        static          HANDLE          hMem ;
        TWODATA                         *ptd ;

        switch (iMessage)               /* process windows messages */
        {
                case WM_CREATE:         /* allocate memory for the TWODATA data */
                        hMem = LocalAlloc (LMEM_MOVEABLE | LMEM_DISCARDABLE,
```

```
                                  sizeof (TWODATA)) ;
                      ptd = (TWODATA *) LocalLock (hMem) ;
                      ptd->nOne = 1 ;
                      lstrcpy (ptd->cBuf, "Hi Mom!") ;
                      LocalUnlock (hMem) ;
                      break ;
              case WM_PAINT:          /* display the current TWODATA contents */
                      BeginPaint (hWnd, &ps) ;
                      ptd = (TWODATA *) LocalLock (hMem) ;
                      TextOut (ps.hdc, 10, 10, cBuf, wsprintf (cBuf,
                              "The current values are: %d, %s", ptd->nOne,
                              (LPSTR) ptd->cBuf)) ;
                      LocalUnlock (hMem) ;
                      EndPaint (hWnd, &ps) ;
                      break ;
              case WM_COMMAND:         /* process menu items */
                      switch (wParam)
                      {
                      case IDM_DOIT:   /* User hit the "Do it" menu item */
                              lpfnDialogProc = MakeProcInstance (DialogProcedure,
                                      ghInstance) ;
                              DialogBoxParam (ghInstance, "exmpdlg", hWnd,
                                      lpfnDialogProc, (DWORD) hMem) ;
                              FreeProcInstance (lpfnDialogProc) ;
                              InvalidateRect (hWnd, NULL, TRUE) ; /* force paint */
                              break ;
                      case IDM_QUIT:   /* send end of application message */
                              DestroyWindow (hWnd) ;
                              break ;
                      }
                      break ;
              case WM_DESTROY:          /* stop application */
                      LocalFree (hMem) ;
                      PostQuitMessage (0) ;
                      break ;
              default:                  /* default windows message processing */
                      return DefWindowProc (hWnd, iMessage, wParam, lParam) ;
      }
      return (0L) ;
}


BOOL FAR PASCAL DialogProcedure (HWND hDlg, unsigned iMessage, WORD wParam, LONG lParam)
{
      BOOL                      bBool ;
      static        HANDLE      hMem ;
      TWODATA                   *ptd ;

      switch (iMessage)
      {
      case WM_INITDIALOG:
              hMem = LOWORD (lParam) ;   /* get mem handle from 32 bit data */
              ptd = (TWODATA *) LocalLock (hMem) ;
              SetDlgItemInt (hDlg, DLI_EDIT1, ptd->nOne, TRUE) ;
              SetDlgItemText (hDlg, DLI_EDIT2, ptd->cBuf) ;
              LocalUnlock (hMem) ;
              return (TRUE) ;
      case WM_COMMAND:
              switch (wParam)
              {
              case DLI_EDIT1:           /* edit integer data */
                      ptd = (TWODATA *) LocalLock (hMem) ;
                      ptd->nOne = GetDlgItemInt (hDlg, DLI_EDIT1,
                              &bBool, TRUE) ;
                      LocalUnlock (hMem) ;
                      return (TRUE) ;
              case DLI_EDIT2:           /* edit string data */
                      ptd = (TWODATA *) LocalLock (hMem) ;
                      GetDlgItemText (hDlg, DLI_EDIT2, ptd->cBuf, 127) ;
```

```
                    LocalUnlock (hMem) ;
                    return (TRUE) ;
            case DLI_DONE:
                    EndDialog (hDlg, NULL) ;
                    return (TRUE) ;
            }
            break ;
      default:
            return (FALSE) ;
      }
      return (FALSE) ;
}
```

ENDDIALOG   ■ Win 2.0   ■ Win 3.0   ■ Win 3.1

Purpose	Closes a modal dialog box and returns control to the calling function.
Syntax	void **EndDialog**(HWND *hDlg*, int *nResult*);
Description	This function stops and erases modal dialog boxes displayed with the DialogBox() function. EndDialog() can be called at any point in the dialog box function.
Uses	This is the only way to properly exit a modal dialog box and return control to the calling function. If a dialog box is created from within another dialog box function, calling EndDialog() only deletes the dialog box associated with the active dialog box and dialog box function.
Returns	No returned value (void).
See Also	DialogBox()
Parameters	
hDlg	HWND: The handle of the dialog box window.
nResult	int: The value to be returned when DialogBox() returns the calling function.
Example	See the example under DialogBox().

GETDIALOGBASEUNITS   □ Win 2.0   ■ Win 3.0   ■ Win 3.1

Purpose	Determines the size of the dialog base units used to create dialog boxes and position controls.
Syntax	LONG **GetDialogBaseUnits**(void);
Description	Dialog boxes use measurements based on the size of the font characters. These are called "dialog base units." The X direction is measured in units of one-fourth of the font width. The Y direction is measured in units of one-eighth of the font height. This function allows you to determine the size of the font width in use. Note that the returned values are for the entire font bounding rectangle measured in pixels, not for one-fourth or one-eighth of the size.
Uses	Useful if you want to paint on the dialog box window, but you only know the location of controls as measured with dialog box units. The location of the controls measured in pixels will change on different displays with different resolutions.
Returns	LONG. The low-order word contains the width of the dialog box font, measured in pixels. The high-order word contains the height of the dialog box font, measured in pixels.
See Also	See the discussion of the FONT statement at the beginning of this chapter.
Parameters	None (void).
Related Messages	WM_PAINT
Example	This example, as shown in Figure 13-5, creates a dialog box with only one control. The dialog box function processes WM_PAINT messages and outputs text directly to the dialog

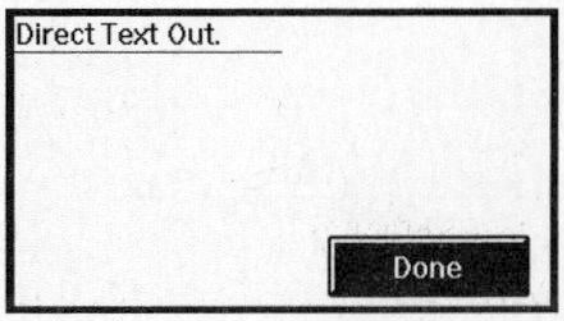

Figure13-5. GetDialog-BaseUnits() Example.

box window. It also draws a line under the text. The line length is computed to be the number of characters times the width of a character. Note that the line ends up longer than the text string, as the system font does not use fixed character spacing. To compute the actual length of the string, the program would need to use GetTextExtent().

The dialog box definition for the resource file is simple. Because the font is not specified with a FONT statement, the system font is used in the dialog box. The dialog control ID DLI_DONE is defined in the program's header file.

```
EXMPDLG DIALOG LOADONCALL MOVEABLE DISCARDABLE 10, 18, 128, 66
STYLE WS_DLGFRAME | WS_POPUP
BEGIN
    CONTROL "Done", DLI_DONE, "button",
                BS_DEFPUSHBUTTON | WS_TABSTOP | WS_CHILD, 75, 50, 48, 14
END
```

Here is the dialog box function. This function would be called using the DialogBox() function and listed in the EXPORTS section of the program's .DEF definition file.

```
BOOL FAR PASCAL DialogProc (HWND hDlg, WORD wMess, WORD wParam, LONG lParam)
{
        PAINTSTRUCT         ps ;
        static      int     nBaseX, nBaseY ;
        LONG                lBaseUnits ;

        switch (wMess)
        {
                case WM_INITDIALOG:
                        lBaseUnits = GetDialogBaseUnits () ;
                        nBaseX = LOWORD (lBaseUnits) ;
                        nBaseY = HIWORD (lBaseUnits) ;
                        return TRUE ;
                case WM_PAINT:
                        BeginPaint (hDlg, &ps) ;
                        TextOut (ps.hdc, 0, 0, "Direct Text Out.", 16) ;
                        MoveTo (ps.hdc, 0, nBaseY) ;
                        LineTo (ps.hdc, nBaseX * 16, nBaseY) ;
                        EndPaint (hDlg, &ps) ;
                        break ;
                case WM_COMMAND:
                        switch (wParam)
                        {
                                case DLI_DONE:
                                        EndDialog (hDlg, 0) ;
                                        return TRUE ;
                                default:
                                        return FALSE ;
                        }
        }
        return FALSE ;
}
```

GetDlgCtrlID

☐ Win 2.0 ■ Win 3.0 ■ Win 3.1

Purpose	Retrieves a dialog box control's ID value, given the control's window handle.
Syntax	int **GetDlgCtrlID**(HWND *hWnd*);
Description	This is the opposite of GetDlgItem(). Given that the program has the window handle of a control, this function will retrieve the control's ID value.
Uses	Not often used. Normally, you will define all of the ID values in a header file, and use them to send messages to the child window controls.
Returns	int, the control ID number for the dialog box control that has a *hWnd* as a window handle. Returns NULL if *hWnd* is not a valid window handle. The return value is undefined if *hWnd* is not a dialog box control window.

See Also   GetDlgItem(), SendDlgItemMessage().

Parameters

hWnd   HWND: The control ID's window handle.

Example   This example, which is shown in Figure 13-6, shows several equivalent ways of sending messages to dialog box controls. When the WM_INITDIALOG message is received, the dialog box control

sets the edit control's text to "First Text." The handle to the edit control's window is also retrieved. When the DLI_SECOND button is pressed, the edit text is changed directly by sending a message to the edit control window. This technique is equivalent to using SetDlgItemText(). When the DLI_THIRD button is pressed, the dialog box ID value for the edit control is obtained from the edit control's window handle using GetDlgCtrlID(). The ID is then used to change the edit control's text, again using SetDlgItemText().

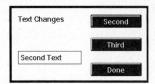

Figure 13-6. GetDlgCtrlID( ) And GetDlgItem( ) Example.

This example only shows the dialog box procedure for the program. See the example under the DialogBox() function description for related program files.

```
BOOL FAR PASCAL DialogProc (HWND hDlg, WORD wMess, WORD wParam, LONG lParam)
{
        static          HWND    hControl ;
        int                     nEditID ;

        switch (wMess)
        {
                case WM_INITDIALOG:
                        SetDlgItemText (hDlg, DLI_EDIT, "First Text") ;
                        hControl = GetDlgItem (hDlg, DLI_EDIT) ;
                        return TRUE ;
                case WM_COMMAND:
                        switch (wParam)
                        {
                                case DLI_SECOND:
                                        SendMessage (hControl, WM_SETTEXT, 0,
                                                (DWORD)(LPSTR) "Second Text") ;
                                        return TRUE ;
                                case DLI_THIRD:
                                        nEditID = GetDlgCtrlID (hControl) ;
                                        SetDlgItemText (hDlg, nEditID, "Third Text") ;
                                        return TRUE ;
                                case DLI_DONE:
                                        EndDialog (hDlg, 0) ;
                                        return TRUE ;
                                default:
                                        return FALSE ;
                        }
        }
        return FALSE ;
}
```

GetDlgItem   ■ Win 2.0   ■ Win 3.0   ■ Win 3.1

Purpose   Retrieves the window handle for a dialog box control, given the control's ID number.

Syntax   HWND **GetDlgItem**(HWND *hWnd*, int *nIDDlgItem*);

Description   All dialog box controls, such as buttons and list boxes, are child windows. Normally, they are dealt with indirectly using a function like SendDlgItemMessage(), which uses the dialog box control ID. An alternative is to deal with the child windows directly by obtaining the window's handle.

Uses   The handle of the dialog box control window can be used to change the behavior of the child window by subclassing. After the window handle is obtained with GetDlgItem(), the application uses SetWindowLong() and CallWindowProc() to subclass the control.

Returns	HWND, the window handle for the dialog box control.
See Also	GetDlgCtrlID(), SetWindowLong(). The CallWindowProc() function description in Chapter 8, *Message Processing Functions*, has an example of subclassing a button control.
Parameters	
hWnd	HWND: The dialog box handle, usually named *hDlg*.
nIDDlgItem	int: The dialog box control ID value.
Example	See the previous example under the GetDlgCtrlID() function description.

GetDlgItemInt
■ Win 2.0   ■ Win 3.0   ■ Win 3.1

Purpose	Retrieves an integer value from a control in a dialog box.
Syntax	WORD **GetDlgItemInt**(HWND *hDlg*, int *nIDDlgItem*, BOOL FAR **lpTranslated*, BOOL *bSigned*);
Description	This is a shortcut method of retrieving an integer value from a control in a dialog box. The function is equivalent to using the WM_GETTEXT message to retrieve the character string from the control, and then using the atoi() C library function to convert the string to an integer. The text characters in the edit control are converted to an integer value starting with the leftmost character. The first nonnumeric character halts the reading process.
Uses	This is the standard way to retrieve an integer value from an edit control.
Returns	The integer value of the text in the edit control. Because zero is a valid integer value, errors are reported with the *lpTranslated* parameter.
See Also	SetDlgItemInt(), GetDlgItemText(), SetDlgItemText()
Parameters	
hDlg	HWND: The dialog box handle.
nIDDlgItem	int: The dialog box edit control ID. Normally, these values are defined in a separate header file.
lpTranslated	BOOL FAR *: The location pointed to by *lpTranslated* is set to TRUE if the edit control was properly converted to an integer. It is set to FALSE if the value overflowed (unsigned greater than 65,535 or signed greater than 32,767), or if nonnumeric characters preceded any digits.
bSigned	BOOL: TRUE if the value to be retrieved is to be a signed integer (int), FALSE if unsigned.
Related Messages	WM_GETTEXT

Figure 13-7.
GetDlgItemInt(),
GetDlgItemText(),
SetDlgItemInt(), and
SetDlgItemText() Example.

Example   This example, which is shown in Figure 13-7, uses a dialog box to allow editing of two global variables, an integer and a character string. The dialog box pops up when the user clicks the "Do It!" menu item. The current values are updated into the edit fields of the dialog box with SetDlgItemInt() and SetDlgItemText(). When the user does any activity involving selection or editing of either edit field, the current value is retrieved using GetDlgItemInt() and GetDlgItemText(). See the example under DialogBox() for details of the other files associated with this example. Only the C source code for the WndProc() and dialog functions are shown in this example.

```
int nEditOne = 0 ;
char cEditBuf [128] = {"Hi There!"} ;

long FAR PASCAL WndProc (HWND hWnd, unsigned iMessage, WORD wParam, LONG lParam)
{
```

```
        PAINTSTRUCT                   ps ;
        static          FARPROC       lpfnDialogProc ;
        char                          cBuf [256] ;

        switch (iMessage)             /* process windows messages */
        {
                case WM_PAINT:
                        BeginPaint (hWnd, &ps) ;
                        TextOut (ps.hdc, 10, 10, cBuf, wsprintf (cBuf,
                                "The current values are: %d, %s", nEditOne,
                                        (LPSTR) cEditBuf)) ;
                        EndPaint (hWnd, &ps) ;
                        break ;
                case WM_COMMAND:        /* process menu items */
                        switch (wParam)
                        {
                        case IDM_DOIT:   /* User hit the "Do it" menu item */
                                lpfnDialogProc = MakeProcInstance (DialogProcedure,
                                        ghInstance) ;
                                DialogBox (ghInstance, "exmpdlg", hWnd, lpfnDialogProc) ;
                                FreeProcInstance (lpfnDialogProc) ;
                                InvalidateRect (hWnd, NULL, TRUE) ; /* force paint */
                                break ;
                        case IDM_QUIT:   /* send end of application message */
                                DestroyWindow (hWnd) ;
                                break ;
                        }
                        break ;
                case WM_DESTROY:        /* stop application */
                        PostQuitMessage (0) ;
                        break ;
                default:                /* default windows message processing */
                        return DefWindowProc (hWnd, iMessage, wParam, lParam) ;
        }
        return (0L) ;
}

BOOL FAR PASCAL DialogProcedure (HWND hDlg, unsigned iMessage, WORD wParam, LONG lParam)
{
        BOOL    bBool ;

        switch (iMessage)
        {
        case WM_INITDIALOG:
                SetDlgItemInt (hDlg, DLI_EDIT1, nEditOne, TRUE) ;
                SetDlgItemText (hDlg, DLI_EDIT2, cEditBuf) ;
                break ;
        case WM_COMMAND:
                switch (wParam)
                {
                case DLI_EDIT1:
                        nEditOne = GetDlgItemInt (hDlg, DLI_EDIT1,
                                &bBool, TRUE) ;
                        return (TRUE) ;
                case DLI_EDIT2:
                        GetDlgItemText (hDlg, DLI_EDIT2, cEditBuf, 127) ;
                        return (TRUE) ;
                case DLI_DONE:
                        EndDialog (hDlg, NULL) ;
                        return (TRUE) ;
                }
                break ;
        default:
                return (FALSE) ;
        }
        return (FALSE) ;
}
```

GetDlgItemText

Purpose	Retrieves a character string from an edit control in a dialog box.
Syntax	int **GetDlgItemText**(HWND *hDlg*, int *nIDDlgItem*, LPSTR *lpString*, int *nMaxCount*);
Description	This is a shortcut method of retrieving the text string from a control in a dialog box. It is equivalent to sending a WM_GETTEXT message to the control.
Uses	Normally used with edit controls to retrieve the current edited value.
Returns	int, the number of characters copied.
See Also	GetDlgItemInt(), SetDlgItemText(), SetDlgItemInt()
Parameters	
hDlg	HWND: The dialog box handle.
nIDDlgItem	int: The dialog box edit control ID. Normally, these values are defined in a separate header file.
lpString	LPSTR: A pointer to a buffer that holds the character string. It must be at least *nMaxCount* characters wide.
nMaxCount	int: The maximum number of characters to copy into the buffer pointed to by *lpString*.
Related Messages	WM_GETTEXT
Example	See the previous example under the GetDlgItemInt() function description.

(handwritten annotation: max string length + 1)

GetNextDlgGroupItem

Purpose	Finds the next (or previous) window handle of the dialog box control, within a group of controls, that will receive the input focus if the user presses one of the arrow keys.
Syntax	HWND **GetNextDlgGroupItem**(HWND *hDlg*, HWND *hCtl*, BOOL *bPrevious*);
Description	Dialog box controls can be placed in groups by starting each group with an item with the WS_GROUP style. The group continues until the next WS_GROUP styled item is encountered. The user can move between items of a group by pressing the arrow keys. The GetNextDlgGroupItem() returns the handle of the control that will be highlighted next within the group.
Uses	Used in building keyboard interfaces for dialog boxes.
Returns	HWND, the handle of the next or previous dialog box control of the group.
See Also	GetDlgItem(), GetNextDlgTabItem()
Parameters	
hDlg	HWND: The handle of the dialog box windows.
hCtl	HWND: The handle of the dialog box control to start from. Retrieve this handle with GetDlgItem().
bPrevious	BOOL: Set to TRUE to find the previous control in the group. This is the item that will have the input focus if the user presses the left or down arrow key. Set to FALSE to find the next control in the group. This is the item that will have the input focus if the user presses the right or up arrow key.

Example

The example illustrated in Figure 13-8 shows a dialog box with four check boxes and a pushbutton. When the dialog box starts, the check box in the upper left has the input focus. The dialog box function processes the WM_INITDIALOG message and changes the names of the controls for the button with the input focus, the next group button (the button that will receive the input focus if the right arrow key is pressed), and the next tab button (the button that will receive the input focus if the tab key is pressed).

Figure 13-8. GetNextDlg-GroupItem() and GetNext-DlgTabItem() Example.

Note in the dialog box definition that the WS_TABSTOP flags are placed at each location where the cursor should jump to if the tab key is pressed. The WS_GROUP flags are placed at the start of each group, and continue until the next WS_GROUP flag. These control the reaction to pressing the arrow keys.

```
EXMPDLG DIALOG LOADONCALL MOVEABLE DISCARDABLE 10, 18, 145, 80
STYLE WS_DLGFRAME | WS_VISIBLE | WS_POPUP
BEGIN
    CONTROL "", DLI_CHECK1, "button",
        BS_CHECKBOX | WS_TABSTOP | WS_GROUP | WS_CHILD, 12, 20, 48, 12
    CONTROL "", DLI_CHECK2, "button",
        BS_CHECKBOX | WS_CHILD, 12, 39, 48, 12
    CONTROL "", DLI_CHECK3, "button",
        BS_CHECKBOX | WS_TABSTOP | WS_GROUP | WS_CHILD, 84, 21, 45, 12
    CONTROL "", DLI_CHECK4, "button",
        BS_CHECKBOX | WS_CHILD, 84, 39, 45, 12
    CONTROL "Done", DLI_DONE, "button",
        BS_DEFPUSHBUTTON | WS_TABSTOP | WS_CHILD, 45, 66, 48, 12
END
```

This listing only shows the dialog box function for the program. The remainder of the program is identical to the CreateDialog() example.

```
BOOL FAR PASCAL DialogProc (HWND hDlg, WORD wMess, WORD wParam, LONG lParam)
{
        HWND      hControl, hFirstGroup ;

        switch (wMess)
        {
                case WM_INITDIALOG:
                        SetDlgItemText (hDlg, DLI_CHECK1, "1") ;
                        SetDlgItemText (hDlg, DLI_CHECK2, "2") ;
                        SetDlgItemText (hDlg, DLI_CHECK3, "3") ;
                        SetDlgItemText (hDlg, DLI_CHECK4, "4") ;
                        hFirstGroup = GetDlgItem (hDlg, DLI_CHECK1) ;
                        SendMessage (hFirstGroup, WM_SETTEXT, 0,
                                (DWORD)(LPSTR) "Focus here") ;
                        hControl = GetNextDlgGroupItem (hDlg, hFirstGroup,
                                FALSE) ;
                        SendMessage (hControl, WM_SETTEXT, 0,
                                (DWORD)(LPSTR) "Next Group") ;
                        hControl = GetNextDlgTabItem (hDlg, hFirstGroup,
                                FALSE) ;
                        SendMessage (hControl, WM_SETTEXT, 0,
                                (DWORD)(LPSTR) "Next Tab") ;
                        return TRUE ;
                case WM_COMMAND:        /* there is only one command - quits */
                        switch (wParam)
                        {
                                case DLI_DONE:
                                        EndDialog (hDlg, 0) ;
                                        hDlgBox = NULL ;
                                        return TRUE ;
                        }
        }
        return FALSE ;
}
```

GetNextDlgTabItem

■ Win 2.0　■ Win 3.0　■ Win 3.1

Purpose	Finds the next (or previous) window handle of the dialog box control that will receive the input focus if the user presses the (TAB) key.
Syntax	HWND **GetNextDlgTabItem**(HWND *hDlg*, HWND *hCtl*, BOOL *bPrevious*);
Description	A keyboard shortcut for moving between dialog box controls can be obtained by placing WS_TABSTOP styles in the definition of each item that the tab key should stop on. Pressing the

(TAB) key moves to the next item with the WS_TABSTOP style. Pressing (SHIFT)-(TAB) moves in the opposite direction. GetNextDlgTabItem() returns the handle of the control that will be highlighted next if the (TAB) key is used.

Uses Used in building keyboard interfaces for dialog boxes.

Returns HWND, the handle of the next or previous dialog box control that will be selected if the (TAB) key is used.

See Also GetDlgItem(), GetNextDlgGroupItem()

Parameters

hDlg HWND: The handle of the dialog box windows.

hCtl HWND: The handle of the dialog box control from which to start. Retrieve this handle with GetDlgItem().

bPrevious BOOL: Set to TRUE to find the previous WS_TABSTOP control in the dialog box. This is the item that will have the input focus if the user presses (SHIFT)-(TAB). Set to FALSE to find the next WS_TABSTOP control. This is the item that will have the input focus if the user presses (TAB).

Example See the previous example under GetNextDlgGroupItem().

IsDialogMessage

■ Win 2.0   ■ Win 3.0   ■ Win 3.1

Purpose Determines whether a message is meant for a dialog box. If so, keyboard translations are performed, and the message is passed to the dialog box function.

Syntax BOOL **IsDialogMessage**(HWND *hDlg*, LPMSG *lpMsg*);

Description Modeless dialog boxes can remain on the screen for the duration of the program. During this period, the message loop must determine whether to send the message to the WndProc() function, or to the dialog box function(s). In addition to diverting messages to the dialog box function, IsDialogMessage() converts some keypress messages. For example, the (TAB) key is interpreted to move the input focus to the next control with the WS_TABSTOP message. DispatchMessage() will also send messages to the dialog box function, but without the character translations.

Uses Necessary in the message loop for all applications containing modeless dialog boxes that use a keyboard interface.

Returns BOOL. TRUE if the message was processed and sent to the dialog box function, FALSE if not. If FALSE is returned, the message should be passed to the TranslateMessage() and DispatchMessage() functions.

See Also GetMessage(), CreateDialog()

Parameters

hDlg HWND: The dialog box handle. This value is returned by CreateDialog() and the other CreateDialog functions. The value should be stored in a global variable to make it available to the message loop within WinMain(). Set *hDlg* to zero before and after the modeless dialog box is active.

lpMsg LPMSG: A pointer to the MSG structure retrieved from Windows by GetMessage() or PeekMessage().

Example This listing shows a typical message loop for an application with one or more modeless dialog boxes. The TranslateMessage() and DispatchMessage() functions only process the message if the dialog box is not currently active or if the message is not for a dialog box. See CreateDialog() for a more complete listing.

```
while (GetMessage (&msg, NULL, 0, 0))
{
    if (hDlgModeless == NULL ||
```

```
                        !IsDialogMessage (hDlgModeless, &msg))
            {
                        TranslateMessage (&msg) ;
                        DispatchMessage (&msg) ;
            }
      }
      return msg.wParam ;
```

IsDlgButtonChecked

Purpose	Determines whether a check box or radio button control is checked, or whether a three-state button control is checked or grayed.
Syntax	WORD **IsDlgButtonChecked**(HWND *hDlg*, int *nIDButton*);
Description	Radio buttons and check boxes can be checked or unchecked. Three-state buttons can be checked or grayed. IsDlgButtonChecked() determines the current state of a dialog box control.
Uses	Normally used with the AUTO button styles that automatically change from unchecked to checked, etc.
Returns	WORD, the current checked state. 0 for unchecked, 1 for checked, 2 for grayed (if the control is a three-state radio button or check box).
See Also	CheckDlgButton(), CheckRadioButton()
Parameters	
hDlg	HWND: The dialog box window handle.
nIDButton	int: The dialog box control ID number for the check box or radio button.
Related Messages	BM_SETCHECK, BM_GETCHECK
Example	This example uses AUTO button styles to accomplish the same logic as demonstrated in the example under the CreateDialog() function description. The dialog box template is modified to use the AUTO button styles.

```
EXMPDLG DIALOG LOADONCALL MOVEABLE DISCARDABLE 10, 18, 139, 75
CAPTION "Example Dialog Box"
FONT 10, "Helv"
STYLE WS_BORDER | WS_CAPTION | WS_DLGFRAME | WS_POPUP | WS_VISIBLE
BEGIN
   CONTROL "Title String Here", -1, "static",
           SS_CENTER | WS_CHILD, 27, 6, 78, 9
   CONTROL "Check box control.", -1, "static",
           SS_LEFT | WS_CHILD, 60, 22, 67, 9
   CONTROL "Radio buttons.", -1, "static",
           SS_LEFT | WS_CHILD, 60, 39, 73, 10
   CONTROL "DONE", DLI_DONE, "button",
           BS_DEFPUSHBUTTON | WS_TABSTOP | WS_CHILD, 72, 59, 36, 12
   CONTROL "", DLI_CHECKBOX, "button",
           BS_AUTOCHECKBOX | WS_TABSTOP | WS_CHILD, 7, 24, 16, 9
   CONTROL "First", DLI_RADIO1, "button",
           BS_AUTORADIOBUTTON | WS_TABSTOP | WS_CHILD, 6, 36, 28, 12
   CONTROL "Second", DLI_RADIO2, "button",
           BS_AUTORADIOBUTTON | WS_TABSTOP | WS_CHILD, 6, 47, 44, 12
END
```

The dialog box function is modified to take advantage of the automatic checking of both the check box and radio buttons. The global variables are updated when the dialog box is closed. The remainder of the program files are identical to the example shown under CreateDialog().

```
BOOL FAR PASCAL DialogProcedure (HWND hDlg, unsigned iMessage, WORD wParam, LONG lParam)
{
        BOOL    bBool ;
```

```
        switch (iMessage)
        {
        case WM_INITDIALOG:
                if (nCheckOne)
                        CheckRadioButton (hDlg, DLI_RADIO1, DLI_RADIO2,
                                DLI_RADIO1) ;
                if (nRadioOne)
                        CheckRadioButton (hDlg, DLI_RADIO1, DLI_RADIO2,
                                DLI_RADIO2) ;
                else
                        CheckRadioButton (hDlg, DLI_RADIO1, DLI_RADIO2,
                                DLI_RADIO1) ;
                return (TRUE) ;
        case WM_COMMAND:
                switch (wParam)
                {
                case DLI_CHECKBOX:
                        if (IsDlgButtonChecked (hDlg, DLI_CHECKBOX))
                                CheckDlgButton (hDlg, DLI_CHECKBOX, MF_CHECKED) ;
                        else
                                CheckDlgButton (hDlg, DLI_CHECKBOX, MF_UNCHECKED) ;
                        return (TRUE) ;
                case DLI_RADIO1:
                case DLI_RADIO2:
                        if (IsDlgButtonChecked (hDlg, DLI_RADIO1))
                                CheckRadioButton (hDlg, DLI_RADIO1, DLI_RADIO2,
                                        DLI_RADIO1) ;
                        else
                                CheckRadioButton (hDlg, DLI_RADIO1, DLI_RADIO2,
                                        DLI_RADIO2) ;
                        return (TRUE) ;
                case DLI_DONE:
                        nCheckOne = IsDlgButtonChecked (hDlg,
                                DLI_CHECKBOX) ;
                        nRadioOne = IsDlgButtonChecked (hDlg,
                                DLI_RADIO2) ;
                        DestroyWindow (hDlg) ;
                        hDlgModeless = 0 ;
                        return (TRUE) ;
                }
                break ;
        default:
                return (FALSE) ;
        }
        return (FALSE) ;
}
```

MapDialogRect   ■ Win 2.0   ■ Win 3.0   ■ Win 3.1

Purpose	Converts from dialog base units to screen units (pixels).
Syntax	void **MapDialogRect**(HWND hDlg, LPRECT *lpRect*);
Description	In the dialog box template file, dimensions are given in dialog base units. These are one-fourth of a character width for *X* coordinates and one-eighth of a character height for *Y* coordinates. MapDialogRect() converts a rectangle from these units to screen units. The screen dimensions are relative to the upper left corner of the dialog box windows.
Uses	This is a convenient way to determine the size of a dialog box control. All controls are rectangular child windows.
Returns	No returned value (void).
See Also	ScreenToClient(), ClientToScreen()
Parameters	
hDlg	HWND: The dialog box window handle.

lpRect	LPRECT: A pointer to a RECT data structure containing the rectangle's dimensions in dialog base units. After MapDialog-Rect() is called, the RECT data will contain the same rectangle converted to screen units.

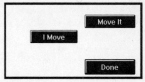

Figure13-9. MapDialog-Rect() Example.

Related Messages   WM_SIZE

Example   This example, which is shown in Figure 13-9, moves a child window control when either the "I Move" or "Move It" pushbutton controls are clicked with the mouse.

The dialog box template defines three pushbuttons. The third pushbutton is the one that will be moved. Note that the sizes are given in dialog units.

```
EXMPDLG DIALOG LOADONCALL MOVEABLE DISCARDABLE 10, 18, 128, 66
STYLE WS_DLGFRAME | WS_POPUP
BEGIN
    CONTROL "Done", DLI_DONE, "button",
                BS_DEFPUSHBUTTON | WS_TABSTOP | WS_CHILD, 75, 50, 48, 14
    CONTROL "Move It", DLI_MOVEIT, "button",
                BS_PUSHBUTTON | WS_TABSTOP | WS_CHILD, 75, 9, 48, 12
    CONTROL "I Move", DLI_MOVED, "button",
                BS_PUSHBUTTON | WS_TABSTOP | WS_CHILD, 9, 9, 45, 12
END
```

The dialog box function takes the size of the third pushbutton and converts it to a RECT data structure. MapDialogRect() then converts the RECT data from dialog units to screen units (pixels). This is an ideal way to move the pushbutton using the MoveWindow() function.

```
BOOL FAR PASCAL DialogProc (HWND hDlg, WORD wMess, WORD wParam, LONG lParam)
{
        RECT            rRect ;
        HWND            hControl ;
        static     BOOL bToggle = 1 ;

        switch (wMess)
        {
                case WM_COMMAND:
                        switch (wParam)
                        {
                        case DLI_MOVED:
                        case DLI_MOVEIT:
                                SetRect (&rRect, 9, 9, 45 + 9, 12 + 9) ;
                                MapDialogRect (hDlg, &rRect) ;
                                if (bToggle)
                                {
                                        OffsetRect (&rRect, 35, 35) ;
                                        bToggle = 0 ;
                                }
                                else
                                        bToggle = 1 ;
                                hControl = GetDlgItem (hDlg, DLI_MOVED) ;
                                MoveWindow (hControl, rRect.left, rRect.top,
                                        rRect.right - rRect.left,
                                        rRect.bottom - rRect.top, TRUE) ;
                                return TRUE ;
                        case DLI_DONE:
                                EndDialog (hDlg, 0) ;
                                return TRUE ;
                        default:
                                return FALSE ;
                        }
        }
        return FALSE ;
}
```

MESSAGEBOX

Purpose	Creates and displays a small window containing a message.
Syntax	int **MessageBox**(HWND *hWndParent*, LPSTR *lpText*, LPSTR *lpCaption*, WORD *wType*);
Description	MessageBox() is one of the most useful functions in Windows. A simple function call provides a complete dialog box, including a limited selection of buttons and icons. The window is automatically sized.
Uses	Most often used for error and warning messages. Also useful as a placeholder in program development. You can put message boxes in for menu items that have not yet been developed, etc.
Returns	int, the button that was pressed to exit the message box. This can be any of the values listed in Table 13-2.

Value	Meaning	⊠
IDABORT	An "Abort" button was pressed.	
IDCANCEL	A "Cancel" button was pressed.	
IDIGNORE	An "Ignore" button was pressed.	
IDNO	A "No" button was pressed.	
IDOK	An "OK" button was pressed.	
IDRETRY	A "Retry" button was pressed.	
IDYES	A "Yes" button was pressed.	

Table 13-2. Message Box Returned Values.

See Also	MessageBeep(), DialogBox()
Parameters	
hWndParent	HWND: The handle of the parent window. This can be a main window, child window, or dialog box handle.
lpText	LPSTR: A pointer to a character string to be placed in the center of the message box.
lpCaption	LPSTR: A pointer to a character string to be placed in the caption bar at the top of the message box.
wType	WORD: One or more of the values in Table 13-3, combined with the C language OR operator (|).

Value	Meaning	⊠
MB_ABORTRETRYIGNORE	The message box contains three buttons: (Abort,) (Retry,) and (Ignore).	
MB_APPLMODAL	The message box is application-modal. The user must click one of the message box buttons before any other part of the application will respond. The user can switch to another program, and then return.	
MB_DEFBUTTON1	The first pushbutton is the default. The default button is the one that will be activated if the user presses the return key. The first button is the default button, unless one of the following two styles is used.	
BM_DEFBUTTON2	The second button is the default button.	
BM_DEFBUTTON3	The third button is the default button.	
MB_ICONASTERISK	An icon with a lowercase "i" in a circle is displayed in the message box.	
MB_ICONEXCLAMATION	An icon containing an exclamation point is displayed in the message box.	
MB_ICONHAND	An icon with a hand (stop symbol) is displayed in the message box.	

MB_ICONINFORMATION	An icon with a lowercase "i" in a circle is displayed in the message box.
MB_ICONQUESTION	An icon containing a question mark is displayed in the message box.
MB_ICONSTOP	An icon containing a stop sign is displayed in the message box. This is normally reserved for drastic situations.
MB_OK	The message box contains one pushbutton: "OK".
MB_OKCANCEL	The message box contains two pushbuttons: "OK" and "Cancel."
MB_RETRYCANCEL	The message box contains two pushbuttons: "Retry" and "Cancel."
MB_SYSTEMMODAL	The message box is system-modal. No other program can gain the input focus until a button in the message box is clicked. If the MB_ICONHAND style is used with this style, Windows messages are immediately stopped to all applications.
MB_TASKMODAL	Similar to MB_APPLMODAL. With this style, *hWndParent* can be set to NULL. This causes all child windows of the parent to be disabled until a pushbutton on the message box window is clicked.
MB_YESNO	The message box contains two buttons: "Yes" and "No."
MB_YESNOCANCEL	The message box contains three buttons: "Yes," "No," and "Cancel."

Table 13-3. Message Box Flags.

Example

This example displays a message box when the user clicks the "Do It!" menu item. The appearance of the message box is shown in Figure 13-10. The MessageBox() returns an integer value that specifies which button was clicked to exit the message box. In this case, the result is displayed on the main window's client area after the message box disappears.

Figure 13-10. MessageBox() Example.

```
long FAR PASCAL WndProc (HWND hWnd, unsigned iMessage, WORD wParam, LONG lParam)
{
        int     nReturned ;
        HDC     hDC ;

        switch (iMessage)                       /* process windows messages */
        {
        case WM_COMMAND:                        /* process menu items */
                switch (wParam)
                {
                case IDM_DOIT:          /* User hit the "Do it" menu item */
                        nReturned = MessageBox (hWnd,
                                "This Message is Of Little Value",
                                "Message Box",
                                MB_ICONEXCLAMATION | MB_OKCANCEL) ;
                        hDC = GetDC (hWnd) ;
                        if (nReturned == IDCANCEL)
                                TextOut (hDC, 10, 10, "Returned Cancel.", 16) ;
                        else
                                TextOut (hDC, 10, 10, "Returned OK.", 12) ;
                        ReleaseDC (hWnd, hDC) ;
                        break ;
```

[Other program lines]

SEND DLG ITEM MESSAGE

■ Win 2.0   ■ Win 3.0   ■ Win 3.1

Purpose   Sends a message to a dialog box control.

Syntax   DWORD **SendDlgItemMessage**(HWND *hDlg*, int *nIDDlgItem*, WORD *wMsg*, WORD *wParam*, LONG *lParam*);

Description　　This is a shortcut method for sending a message to a dialog box control. It is equivalent to calling GetDlgItem() to obtain the control's handle, and then using SendMessage() to send the message. Like SendMessage(), SendDlgItemMessage() sends the message directly to the dialog box function, bypassing the message queue.

Uses　　Used to send nonroutine messages to dialog box controls. The normal activities, such as setting the text in a control, are covered by functions like SetDlgItemText(). Less common activities, such as adding items to a list box control, are best handled with SendDlgItemMessage().

Returns　　DWORD, the value returned after the control processed the message. See the message description in Chapter 8, *Message Processing Functions*, to determine the meaning of this value for a specific message.

See Also　　SendMessage(), GetDlgItem()

Parameters

hDlg　　HWND: The dialog box window handle (not the handle of the control).

nIDDlgItem　　WORD: The ID value of the control that will receive the message.

wMsg　　WORD: The message that the control will receive.

wParam　　WORD: The WORD length data sent with the message. See Chapter 9, *Windows Messages*, for the meaning of *wParam* and *lParam* for a specific message.

lParam　　DWORD: The DWORD length (32-bit) data sent with the message.

Related Messages　　All messages can be sent with this function.

Example　　This example shows a dialog box with an edit control and scroll bar. (See Figure 13-11.) SendDlgItemMessage() is used to send an EM_LIMITTEXT message to the edit control when the dialog box starts, limiting input to three digits. The example is interesting in that the edit control and scroll bar interact. Changing the scroll bar position changes the number in the edit control. Manually editing the number in the edit control changes the scroll bar position. This is an excellent way to provide user input for integers. Note in the program logic that no action is taken if the number has not changed. This is critical to avoid having infinite loops of messages sent to the dialog box function.

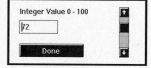

*Figure 13-11. SendDlg-
ItemMessage( ) Example.*

```
EXMPDLG DIALOG LOADONCALL MOVEABLE DISCARDABLE 9, 18, 126, 57
STYLE WS_DLGFRAME | WS_POPUP
BEGIN
    CONTROL "", DLI_SCROLL, "scrollbar",
                SBS_VERT | WS_CHILD, 102, 6, 9, 45
    CONTROL "", DLI_EDIT, "edit",
                ES_LEFT | WS_BORDER | WS_TABSTOP | WS_CHILD, 9, 18, 36, 12
    CONTROL "Integer Value 0 - 100", -1, "static",
                SS_LEFT | WS_CHILD, 9, 6, 75, 12
    CONTROL "Done", DLI_DONE, "button",
                BS_PUSHBUTTON | WS_TABSTOP | WS_CHILD, 9, 39, 60, 12
END
```

Only the dialog box function is shown in the listing. See DialogBox() for other related files and commands.

```
BOOL FAR PASCAL DialogProc (HWND hDlg, WORD wMess, WORD wParam, LONG lParam)
{
        static        HWND       hScroll ;
        int                      nInt ;
        static        int        nOldInt = 0 ;
        BOOL                     bBool ;
```

```
    switch (wMess)
    {
        case WM_INITDIALOG:
            hScroll = GetDlgItem (hDlg, DLI_SCROLL) ;
            SetScrollRange (hScroll, SB_CTL, 0, 100, FALSE) ;
            SetScrollPos (hScroll, SB_CTL, 100, TRUE) ;
            SetDlgItemInt (hDlg, DLI_EDIT, 0, TRUE) ;
            SendDlgItemMessage (hDlg, DLI_EDIT, EM_LIMITTEXT,
                    3, 0L) ;
            return TRUE ;
        case WM_VSCROLL:
            nInt = nOldInt ;
            switch (wParam)
            {
                case SB_LINEUP:
                    nInt += 1 ;
                    break ;
                case SB_PAGEUP:
                    nInt += 10 ;
                    break ;
                case SB_LINEDOWN:
                    nInt -= 1 ;
                    break ;
                case SB_PAGEDOWN:
                    nInt -= 10 ;
                    break ;
                case SB_THUMBPOSITION:
                    nInt = 100 - LOWORD (lParam) ;
                    break ;
            }
            nInt = min (100, max (0, nInt)) ;
            if (nInt != nOldInt)
            {
                nOldInt = nInt ;
                SetScrollPos (hScroll, SB_CTL, 100 - nOldInt, TRUE) ;
                SetDlgItemInt (hDlg, DLI_EDIT, nOldInt, TRUE) ;
            }
            return TRUE ;
        case WM_COMMAND:        /* there is only one command - quits */
            switch (wParam)
            {
                case DLI_EDIT:
                    nInt = GetDlgItemInt (hDlg, DLI_EDIT, &bBool,
                            TRUE) ;
                    if (nInt != nOldInt)
                    {
                        nOldInt = min (100, max (0, nInt)) ;
                        SetScrollPos (hScroll, SB_CTL,
                                100 - nOldInt, TRUE) ;
                    }
                    return TRUE ;
                case DLI_DONE:
                    EndDialog (hDlg, 0) ;
                    return TRUE ;
            }
            return TRUE ;
        case WM_DESTROY:
            EndDialog (hDlg, 0) ;
            return TRUE ;
    }
    return FALSE ;
}
```

SETDLGITEMINT   ■ Win 2.0   ■ Win 3.0   ■ Win 3.1

Purpose	Changes the text in a dialog box control to an integer value.
Syntax	void **SetDlgItemInt**(HWND *hDlg*, int *nIDDlgItem*, WORD *wValue*, BOOL *bSigned*);

Description	This is a shortcut method of changing the text in a control (usually an edit control) to an integer value. It is equivalent to sending the WM_SETTEXT message to the control.
Uses	Normally used to change edit control values.
Returns	No returned value (void).
See Also	GetDlgItemInt(), SetDlgItemText(), GetDlgItemText()
Parameters	
hDlg	HWND: The dialog box handle.
nIDDlgItem	int: The dialog box control ID. Normally, these values are defined in a separate header file.
wValue	WORD: The integer value to be set as text in the control.
bSigned	BOOL: TRUE if the integer is a signed value (int), FALSE if unsigned.
Related Messages	WM_SETTEXT
Example	See the example under GetDlgItemInt().

SETDLGITEMTEXT   ■ Win 2.0   ■ Win 3.0   ■ Win 3.1

Purpose	Changes the text in a dialog box control.
Syntax	void **SetDlgItemText**(HWND *hDlg*, int *nIDDlgItem*, LPSTR *lpString*);
Description	This is a shortcut function for setting the text in one of the controls of a dialog box. It is equivalent to sending the WM_SETTEXT message.
Uses	Normally used to change the text in edit controls.
Returns	No returned value (void).
See Also	GetDlgItemText(), SetDlgItemInt(), GetDlgItemInt()
Parameters	
hDlg	HWND: The dialog box handle.
nIDDlgItem	int: The dialog box control ID. Normally, these values are defined in a separate header file.
lpString	LPSTR: A pointer to a null-terminated string containing the characters to be inserted into the dialog box control.
Related Messages	WM_SETTEXT
Example	See the example under GetDlgItemInt().

Most programmers are apprehensive when they first find out that Windows moves objects around in memory while programs are running. This is completely different from programming in a conventional environment like MS-DOS, where memory objects stay fixed until deleted.

Windows provides ample support for managing moveable memory. Using memory blocks under Windows boils down to following a few simple rules. Once these rules are understood, memory management becomes no more complex under Windows, than in environments like MS-DOS Windows provides the programmer with complete control over the way memory is used. Most applications do not take advantage of all of these features, but they are worth knowing about. This chapter discusses

- Memory organizaton under Windows.

- Allocating memory blocks.

- Using automatic variables.

- Controlling the program's use of memory with the .DEF definition file.

- How C compiler memory models affect memory use.

- Starting and stopping other programs from within an application.

Local and Global Memory

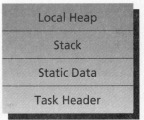

Figure 14-1. The Automatic
Data Segment Organization.

There are two basic kinds of memory under Windows: local memory and global memory. A program can take advantage of either type of memory, depending on its needs. Every program has a private local memory block called the "automatic data segment." The starting size of this area is defined in the program's .DEF definition file, although it can be changed as the program runs. The organization of an application's automatic data segment is shown in Figure 14-1. The maximum size of the segment is limited to 64K. The first section is the task header, a fixed 16 bytes of information that Windows uses. Above that is any static data. Static data is the collection of data, such as strings you define in the program.

```
char      cBuf[] = "This is a static data string." ;        /* static data */
```

Other examples of static data are global variables declared outside of a function definition, and variables within a function whose declarations are prefixed by the word "static."

```
static    int    i, j ;          /* static variables */
```

Above the static data is the program's stack. The C language stores automatic variables (variables declared within a function and without the "static" prefix) in the stack. The stack size is also set in the program's .DEF file, with a minimum size of 5,120 bytes. The local heap is at the top of the automatic data segment.

The local heap is the area where programs can allocate blocks of local memory for their own purposes, and then free the blocks when they are no longer needed. If you are familiar with programming under MS-DOS, you can think of the local heap as similar to the memory area allocated using the C function malloc(). This analogy does not go too far, as we will soon see.

The other kind of memory available to Windows applications is the global heap. This is the rest of the memory on the system. Windows programs typically use the global heap for large blocks of memory (over 256 bytes as a rule of thumb). The local heap is used for smaller blocks, or blocks that will only be used for a short period of time. Again making an analogy to MS-DOS programming, the global memory area is something like the area accessed by _fmalloc().

Segments and Offsets

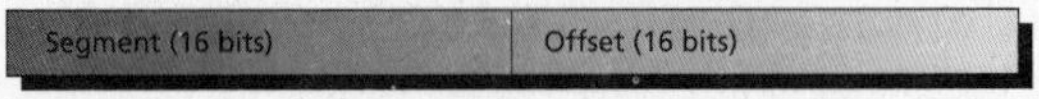

Segment (16 bits)	Offset (16 bits)

Figure 14-2. Windows 32-Bit Address (LPSTR) Values.

Windows uses two types of memory allocation. The two types relate to the architecture of the CPUs (Central Processing Unit) on the computers on which Windows programs run. The 8086 through 80486 chips access memory using two 16-bit values. These values are called the "segment" and the "offset." Windows stores full addresses as 32-bit values consisting of both the segment and offset, as shown in Figure 14-2. These are "long pointers." A typical long pointer is the memory address of a string. Using conventional C notation, this would be a far pointer to a character

```
char far *cp ;
```

These data types are so common that Windows defines an abbreviation in WINDOWS.H as LPSTR (long pointer to a string). In some functions, you will also pass a long address as a double-word (32-bit) value, abbreviated DWORD. Both values are 32 bits long.

▷ **DWORD and LPSTR Definitions in WINDOWS.H**

```
typedef unsigned long    DWORD;
typedef char     far     *LPSTR;
```

In either case, the segment and offset are stored within the 32-bit value as a far address.

For accessing values within an memory area limited to 64K, the segment value does not have to change. All of the memory locations within the 64K region can be addressed by changing the offset. This ability makes it possible to access memory more quickly, as only 16 bits have to be changed, not the full 32 bits. These are called NEAR addresses. The typdefs within WINDOWS.H for these 16-bit data types are as follows.

▷ **PSTR and WORD Definitions in WINDOWS.H**

```
typedef char     near    *PSTR;
typedef unsigned int      WORD;
```

When you use automatic variables, their values are on the stack. The stack is part of the automatic data segment, so they are near memory values with 16-bit addresses. When you allocate memory in the local heap, the addresses are also 16-bit values. Only global memory objects use the full 32-bit memory addressing.

Allocating Memory in the Local Heap

As an example, let's set aside some memory in the local heap (the top part of the automatic data segment) for storing up to 128 characters. We will put the string "Hi there!" into the block using the C library function strcpy(). The bare-bones Windows code for this is

```
static  HANDLE          hMem ;
PSTR                    pStr ;

hMem = LocalAlloc (LMEM_MOVEABLE, 128) ;
pStr = LocalLock (hMem) ;
strcpy (pStr, "Hi there!") ;
LocalUnlock (hMem) ;
```

(Note that Windows has a version of strcpy() called "lstrcpy()." It is preferable to using strcpy(), as it is stored in a DLL and does not add to the size of the application. lstrcpy() and related functions are covered in Chapter 19, *Character Sets and Strings*.)

The LocalAlloc() function reserves 128 bytes of memory in the local heap. The memory is allocated with the LMEM_MOVEABLE attribute, meaning that Windows can move this block when it needs to make room for other memory objects. Note that the returned value is saved in a static variable, *hMem*. This is the handle to the memory block. It is not an address, just a handle. Windows programs use the memory handles to keep track of memory blocks. Before we can copy the string to the memory block, we need to lock the block in memory by using LocalLock(). This function returns the current address of the memory block we allocated. The block is fixed in memory at this point. Windows will not be able to move the block unless LocalUnlock() is called. When the memory block is locked, it is just like fixed memory allocated in an MS-DOS program. The strcpy() function copies a string into the memory area. Once the string is loaded, there is no reason to leave the memory block locked. LocalUnlock() is used to free the block so that Windows can move it if necessary. If the block is moved, it will still contain the same character string, but at a new address. The handle *hMem* remains valid and still refers to the same memory block no matter where it is moved. The *pStr* pointer to the old address is invalid as soon as LocalUnlock() is called.

Later in the program, we might want to output the text string using the TextOut() function. If this is the last time we will need the data, we can free the memory block, returning it to Windows to use for the next memory need. Here is an example

```
pStr = LocalLock (hMem) ;
TextOut (hDC, 10, 10, pStr, strlen (pStr)) ;
LocalUnlock (hMem) ;
LocalFree (hMem) ;
```

Again, the block is locked only for the period of time when the string value in memory is being used. As soon as that activity is over, LocalUnlock() is called to allow the block to be moved. In this case, the memory block was no longer needed. LocalFree() was called to return the memory block to Windows, for use by any other application.

If separate parts of an application can lock the same block of memory, the block can be locked more than once. Windows keeps track of the number of times a block is locked as the "lock count." Calling LocalLock() increases the lock count by one. Calling LocalUnlock() reduces the lock count by one. An equal number of LocalLock() and LocalUnlock() calls is needed before the memory block is free to be moved in memory. These examples have omitted the logic for dealing with situations where Windows did not have room to allocate the needed memory. See the example program under the LocalAlloc() function description for a more complete listing.

Allocating Memory in the Global Heap

As mentioned previously, the local heap is limited to the size of the 64K automatic data segment. For large memory blocks, the global heap provides much larger areas from which to work. Global memory objects use the full 32-bit segmented memory addresses.

The following example below again shows a 128-character buffer being allocated and used to store a string. In this case, the memory is allocated on the global heap.

```
static  HANDLE          hMem ;
LPSTR                   lpStr ;

hMem = GlobalAlloc (GMEM_MOVEABLE, 128) ;
lpStr = GlobalLock (hMem) ;
lstrcpy (lpStr, "Hi there!") ;
GlobalUnlock (hMem) ;
```

Note that the *lpStr* address pointer is now a long pointer to a string (LPSTR), a 32-bit value. A string copy function capable of handling the far pointers like lstrcpy() is also required. Otherwise, the allocation of the global memory block exactly parallels the same activities for a block in the local heap.

A side effect of segmented memory addressing for global memory is that the minimum size of a global memory block is 32 bytes. Windows will round up requests for "uneven" sizes of memory to the nearest 32 bytes. For example, a request for a global memory block of 33 bytes will result in 64 bytes being allocated. Using the global memory block is similar to local memory. We will assume that this is the last time the block is needed, so it is freed after use. If the block will be used again, the GlobalFree() function will not be called until after the last use.

```
lpStr = GlobalLock (hMem) ;
TextOut (hDC, 10, 10, lpStr, lstrlen (lpStr)) ;
GlobalUnlock (hMem) ;
GlobalFree (hMem) ;
```

One thing to notice in these examples is that the handle to the memory object is of the same data type (HANDLE) for both global and local memory objects. Somewhere internal to the system, Windows maintains tables that keep track of where the actual memory objects are located. Some of them may be in the local heap, and some in the global heap. The only time the physical address of the data is known to the program is when LocalLock() or GlobalLock() is called. The rest of the time you just trust Windows to keep track of the data.

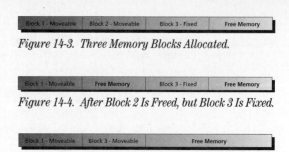

Figure 14-3. Three Memory Blocks Allocated.

Figure 14-4. After Block 2 Is Freed, but Block 3 Is Fixed.

Figure 14-5. After Block 2 Is Freed, Block 3 Is Moveable.

Moveable, Fixed, and Discardable Memory Blocks

The majority of the time you will use moveable memory objects to store data in your programs. Windows provides two other types of memory for both the local and global heaps, ("fixed" and "discardable"). Fixed memory is just what it sounds like, fixed in a certain location in memory. Fixed blocks are allocated with the LMEM_FIXED flag when using LocalAlloc(), or the GMEM_FIXED flag when using GlobalAlloc().

Fixed memory should be thought of like taxes: sometimes necessary, but best avoided. To illustrate why, consider the case where three memory blocks have been allocated in a limited space. Memory Block 3 is fixed, as shown in Figure 14-3. If block 2 is freed (deleted), the free memory is split into two parts, separated by Block 3. The fixed block limits the maximum size of the next block allocated. (See Figure 14-4.)

Now consider the case where all three of the blocks are allocated as moveable. In this case, Windows will be able to move Block 3 to make room the next time memory is requested. This makes a larger memory area available. (See Figure 14-5.) These savings multiply as the number of blocks increases. Conversely, one poorly written application that fixes a few blocks in the global memory area can reduce the performance of every other application running on the system.

The opposite extreme from a fixed memory block is a discardable one. Discardable blocks are allocated with the moveable and discardable flags set, which allows Windows to move the block to make room. If the available room is still not big enough, discardable blocks are reduced in size to zero bytes to make more room. The most recently used discardable blocks are the last to be discarded.

To visualize how this works, consider a case, as illustrated in Figure 14-6, where two discardable and one moveable block are allocated. If a large memory block is requested, Blocks 1 and 2 can be discarded, and Block 3 moved. This makes the maximum amount of space available.

This type of compression can be forced by calling the LocalCompact() and GlobalCompact() functions. Moveable memory blocks are moved before any blocks are discarded. The minimum number of blocks are discarded to make the required memory space available.

Discardable memory blocks are typically used to store data that can be retrieved from disk. Program response is much faster if the data stays in memory. If the system demands it, the data can be shed, and then reloaded when needed. Some typical examples include saving graphics images which are only displayed in certain parts of the application, and database applications. The memory handle for the discarded block remains valid even after the block has been discarded. Memory blocks will not be discarded if they have been locked. Memory blocks can be resized at any time. The LocalReAlloc() and GlobalReAlloc() functions do the work. The existing data is not destroyed if the block size is increased. You can check the size of a block at any time by calling LocalSize() or GlobalSize(). You can also check the status of a block (locked, unlocked, discarded, discardable) using LocalFlags() or GlobalFlags().

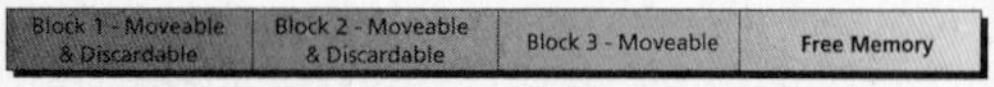

Figure 14-6. Three Memory Blocks Allocated, Two Discardable.

Figure 14-7. Memory after a Request for a Large Allocation.

Traps to Avoid

If your program has just finished processing a Windows message and control passes back to Windows via the program's message loop, Windows has control. If your program is actively processing a message in the WndProc() function, or is in a program function called from within WndProc(), your application has control. Windows will not "jump in" and move memory around. Remember that Windows is a "nonpreemptive multitasking" system. This means that your program has to give Windows control, Windows cannot take control by itself.

The impact of giving Windows control is that the stack will be changed, because an application only has one stack, and it is used by different functions. Listing 14-1 is a simple example showing correct and incorrect uses of automatic (stack) variables.

▷ **Listing 14-1. Automatic Variables**

```
Long FAR PASCAL WndProc (HWND hWnd, unsigned iMessage, WORD wParam, LONG lParam)
{
        int             i, n ;          /* automatic (stack) variables */
        static    int     m ;           /* static variable */

        switch (iMessage)               /* process windows messages */
        {
            case WM_CREATE:
                n = 20 ;                 /* n initialize here to 20 */
                for (i = 0 ; i < n ; i++)
                                         /* do something */
                break ;
            case WM_KEYDOWN:
                for (i = 0 ; i < n ; i++) /* WRONG!,  n is */
                                         /* do something */         /* no longer 20 */
                break ;
        /* rest of program here */
```

This example shows a classic Windows programming error under the WM_KEYDOWN case. The automatic variable n cannot be assumed to be equal to 20, as Windows must have gained control between processing WM_CREATE and processing WM_KEYDOWN. The correct practice here would be to use the static variable m in place of n in both locations. Statics retain their value, even if Windows moves objects in memory. Note that the automatic variable i is used correctly in these examples, as it is initialized to zero within the for() loop for each message processed.

The other situation to be careful of is storing far pointers to moveable memory instead of storing the handle to a memory block. When more memory is allocated, old memory blocks may be moved to make room. The handle to the memory block will remain valid, but not the old pointer to an absolute address. Avoid this problem by using the memory handle to keep track of memory blocks. Only determine the absolute address of the memory block for the short period of time that the block is locked for reading or writing.

Windows Memory Configurations

With Windows versions 3.0 and 3.1, there are three possible memory configurations: Real, Standard, and Enhanced. Real mode is like the old 2.0 version of Windows. Memory is limited to a 640K block. Standard mode allows access to up to 16 megabytes of memory. Enhanced mode allows access to 16 megabytes of memory and automatically swaps data off to the disk if memory runs short. Swapping data makes the "virtual memory" limited only to the size of the hard disk.

For 99% of all applications, you can forget about what kind of computer and/or memory model your end user has. Programs run faster on 386 and 486 machines with a lot of memory. Your program will run on more limited hardware if you follow basic Windows programing practices.

- Keep memory blocks reasonably sized, ideally less than 32K each.

- Use moveable and discardable memory blocks wherever possible.

- Avoid fixed memory blocks if at all possible.

- Keep code segments small, ideally less than 8K each.

You can check the type of memory model and memory hardware in use. GetWinFlags() will determine the CPU type, memory configuration, and Windows operating mode the system is using.

Moveable Program Code

Data is not the only thing being moved around in memory. Windows is also busy moving pieces of your program around. Back in Chapter 1, we saw that a .DEF module definition file was needed to compile the GENERIC.C application. Here is what GENERIC.DEF looks like.

```
NAME            GENERIC
DESCRIPTION     'generic windows program'
EXETYPE         WINDOWS
STUB            'WINSTUB.EXE'
CODE            PRELOAD MOVEABLE
DATA            PRELOAD MOVEABLE MULTIPLE
HEAPSIZE        1024
STACKSIZE       5120
EXPORTS         WndProc
```

A couple of these terms may start to look familiar. The HEAPSIZE statement sets the minimum size of the program's local heap at 1,024 bytes. It will grow if the program uses LocalAlloc() and LocalReAlloc() to demand more than 1,024. STACKSIZE specifies the size of the stack. In this case, the minimum stack size of 5,120 bytes is specified.

Two other critical lines are the CODE and DATA statements. The CODE is specified as PRELOAD MOVEABLE, which means that all of the program is loaded into memory when the program begins. All of the parts of the program's code will be moveable in memory. Similarly, the DATA statement specifies PRELOAD MOVEABLE MULTIPLE. MULTIPLE means that more than one instance of the program can be run, each instance with its own data.

You can get more specific with a program's segments, and set up separate attributes for different segments by using the SEGMENTS statement in the .DEF file. This statement is described later in this chapter in the section on module-definition statements. An example that uses different segment attributes is given under the GetCodeHandle() function description.

The choices for the program's code segments are

FIXED   The program code is fixed in memory. This configuraton should only be used for critical applications, such as interrupt processing functions, that must be located in fixed memory. Keep these parts of the program as small as possible, and load them early.

MOVEABLE   The normal case. The code segments can be moved in memory to make room. The movement has no effect on the way you program most applications.

DISCARDABLE   Always combined with MOVEABLE. This configuration allows Windows to discard segments of the program that have not recently been used if space is needed. The segments will be reloaded if functions within the segment are called. Use this setting for as much of the program as possible, particularly portions containing seldom-used functions. In most cases, you will not make the central WndProc() function DISCARDABLE, as too much time will be taken loading it back from the disk.

In addition, you can specify either PRELOAD or LOADONCALL. LOADONCALL works best for parts of the program that are not needed when the program first starts.

Compiler Memory Models

When you compile a Windows program using the Microsoft C compiler's default *small* memory model, all of the code ends up in one segment. Windows had no choice but to treat the entire segment as a single block. The CODE statement in the .DEF file determines if the code segment is MOVEABLE, PRELOAD, etc.

When you compile a Windows program using the *medium* memory model, each source code file ends up compiled into a separate segment. The startup code and any library functions that are used end up in a segment named _TEXT. Other files are compiled into segments given the file name followed by _TEXT. For example, if two files GENERIC.C and HELPERS.C are compiled and linked to make one application, the application will end up with three segments:

_TEXT, GENERIC_TEXT, and HELPERS_TEXT. Windows keeps each of these parts of the program's code separate, and it can move each segment independently if needed to make room. As you can see, the *medium* memory model is the model of choice for all but the smallest Windows programs.

The other memory models, *compact* and *large*, are seldom used in Windows programs because they require that all data segments be fixed in memory. There is no reason to use the *compact* or *large* model. Windows provides excellent support for allocating blocks of memory in the global heap using GlobalAlloc() and the related functions.

Locked, Fixed, and Page-Locked Memory Blocks

In most situations, you can consider a locked memory block to be stationary in memory. Pointers to locked memory blocks remain valid between messages, memory allocation of other blocks, etc. Normally, this is all you have to worry about. In a few situations, such as when writing device drivers, you may need to know exactly where a memory block is located. You may be in for a shock, as it turns out that locked memory blocks can be moved, without invalidating pointers to the block. There are a couple of reasons for this.

1. In enhanced mode, memory blocks can be temporarily copied off onto the system's hard disk. This technique is called "virtual memory." If data or code within the portions copied to the hard disk is needed, it is copied back into the physical memory. Pointers to the memory block remain valid, regardless of whether the data is in "real memory" or on the disk.

2. The built-in memory management logic in the 80386 and 80486 chips is sophisticated. In the protected-mode memory management scheme that Windows uses, the 80x86 chip maintains tables that translate a logical address called a "selector" into a physical address in memory using lookup tables. The tables (called the Local Descriptor Table and Global Descriptor Table) are maintained by Windows. Because of this translation, it is possible for a logical Windows address (pointer) to point to different physical locations in memory if one of the descriptor tables is changed to make better use of available memory.

As mentioned above, you will normally not have to worry about this low-level management of memory. In fact, the transparency of Windows' handling of real and virtual memory is a major advantage to the developer. If you do need to control the physical memory location of one or more blocks, you can use the GlobalFix() or GlobalPageLock() functions. GlobalFix() assures that a memory block is not moved in linear memory. The block can still be copied off onto the hard disk. GlobalPageLock() really locks the block down. Not only is a page-locked block stationary in physical memory, but it cannot be copied off to the hard disk. Normally, GlobalPageLock() is used with GlobalDosAlloc() to page-lock a memory block that can be accessed by both Windows and DOS applications. This is useful if a DOS device driver or interrupt handler is being used under Windows. Fixed and page-locked memory blocks will limit Windows' ability to optimize memory use. Only use these features when necessary.

Running Other Modules

In Windows, the term "module" is used to describe a running program, including all its associated data and code segments. Windows has a number of functions for working with modules. The most frequently used is LoadModule() which loads and runs another program. A similar function, WinExec(), also loads and runs programs.

Some modules, such as the graphics and sound modules that Windows loads, are used by many applications. Each application that calls the module increases the module's "reference count" by one. In order to remove a module from memory, the FreeModule() function must be called as many times as the current reference count. The reference count can be determined with GetModuleUsage(). You may also find it useful to determine the name and path name of the file that was loaded to create the module. GetModuleFileName() does this. Direct support of loading and running other programs from within your Windows program opens up a lot of possibilities. If you do not like the standard program manager, write your own version!

Module-Definition Statements

There are twelve statements that can be used in an application's .DEF module definition file. The LINK.EXE linker application uses the .DEF statements to control the final linking of the application's code, data, and resources. .DEF files are standard ASCII text files. The statement names must be capitalized, as shown in the following example.

▷ **GENERIC.DEF Definition File**

```
NAME            GENERIC
DESCRIPTION     'generic windows program'
EXETYPE WINDOWS
STUB            'WINSTUB.EXE'
CODE            PRELOAD MOVEABLE
DATA            PRELOAD MOVEABLE MULTIPLE
SEGMENTS        MAINSEG MOVEABLE
                SECOND   LOADONCALL FIXED DISCARDABLE
HEAPSIZE        1024
STACKSIZE       5120
EXPORTS         WndProc
                nStrCopy
```

In the statement descriptions, option choices are surrounded by square brackets. The possible choices are separated by a vertical line (|).

Module-Definiton Statement Descriptions

CODE   ■ Win 2.0   ■ Win 3.0   ■ Win 3.1

Purpose   Defines the attributes of the application's code segment.

Syntax   **CODE** [FIXED | MOVEABLE] [DISCARDABLE] [PRELOAD | LOADONCALL]

Example   CODE PRELOAD MOVEABLE

Description This statement is required. The FIXED option makes the application's code fixed in memory. MOVEABLE is preferred, as it allows Windows to move code segments to make better use of memory. DISCARDABLE is ideal for seldom-used portions of the program, as the discarded portions will be reloaded if a function within the segment is called. Dynamic Link Libraries must use the DISCARDABLE option if the code is to be MOVEABLE.

Specifying PRELOAD causes all of the program's code to be loaded at startup. LOADONCALL allows windows to wait until a portion of the application is needed before loading it into memory. If there are conflicting options on the CODE line, MOVEABLE overrides FIXED, and PRELOAD overrides LOADONCALL.

Individual portions of the application's code can be given different attributes by using the SEGMENTS statement. See its description below.

DATA   ■ Win 2.0   ■ Win 3.0   ■ Win 3.1

Purpose   Defines the attributes of the application's data segment.

Syntax   **DATA** [NONE | SINGLE | MULTIPLE] [FIXED | MOVEABLE]

Example   DATA PRELOAD MOVEABLE MULTIPLE

Description The NONE option causes the application to be linked without a data segment. This must be the only option on the line. This is only applicable to Dynamic Link Libraries (DLL). The SINGLE option also applies to DLLs only. This means that there is only one data segment for the application. MULTIPLE is the standard option for .EXE programs, as each instance of the application has a separate data segment. The FIXED option causes the data segment to stay at a fixed memory location. MOVEABLE is preferable, as it allows Windows to make maximum use of available memory.

DESCRIPTION   ■ Win 2.0   ■ Win 3.0   ■ Win 3.1

Purpose   Embeds a text string in the beginning of the application's code.

Syntax   **DESCRIPTION** 'text'

Example   DESCRIPTION 'Property of XYZ Co. All Rights Reserved'.

Description   This is useful for putting copyright notices into code. The text ends up about 735 bytes from the beginning of the file, as the Windows stub ends up in front of the beginning of the application's code (see STUB below).

EXETYPE

☐ Win 2.0   ■ Win 3.0   ■ Win 3.1

Purpose   Tells the linker if the application is a Windows or an OS/2 program.

Syntax   **EXETYPE** [WINDOWS | OS/2]

Example   EXETYPE WINDOWS

Description   This is a requirement with the 3.x versions of Windows.

EXPORTS

■ Win 2.0   ■ Win 3.0   ■ Win 3.1

Purpose   Defines the names of functions that will be exported to other applications or passed to Windows functions. Also defines the callback functions used by such functions as EnumWindows().

Syntax   **EXPORTS** *exportname* [*@ordinal*] [RESIDENTNAME] [NODATA] [*parameter*]

exportname   The function name of the functions to be exported. You can give the functions an alias to be used by other applications by following the *exportname* with an equal sign and a second name. For example,

ChangeFileName=FileName

allows other applications to use the function name FileName(), even though the source code defines the function as ChangeFileName().

ordinal   Defines an optional ordinal number value. The number must be preceded by an @ character. Ordinal numbers are used by Dynamic Link Libraries as a shortcut way to refer to the functions inside of the DLL. For example,

EXPORTS FileNameFunc @1

sets the FileNameFunc() function as the number 1 function in the library. See Chapter 28, *Dynamic Link Libraries*, for a complete example.

RESIDENTNAME   Specifies that the function's name must be resident at all times (not just the ordinal value).

NODATA   An option that specifies that the function is not bound to a specific data segment. The function uses the current data segment when the function is called.

Parameter   An optional integer that specifies the number of words the function expects to be passed as parameters. Checking that the number of parameters inately is a crude form of type checking.

Example   EXPORTS
        FunctionFirst @1
        FunctionSecond @2
        FunctionThird=AliasThird @3
      See the examples under the GetCodeHandle() function description for more complete examples including DLLs.

Description   Specifying the function name in the EXPORTS section of the program's .DEF definition file is an easy thing to forget, and doing so causes unpredictable program crashes. Dialog box functions and callback functions must be exported. DLL functions must be exported if they are to be called from other applications.

HEAPSIZE

■ Win 2.0   ■ Win 3.0   ■ Win 3.1

Purpose   Specifies the size of an application's local memory heap.

Syntax   **HEAPSIZE** *bytes*

bytes	An integer between 0 and 65,536. The minimum size above zero is 256 bytes.
Example	HEAPSIZE 1024
Description	The default heapsize is zero, so HEAPSIZE must be specified for applications. Some DLLs may not need a heap. The heap will be automatically expanded if the application calls LocalAlloc() or LocalReAlloc(), requesting space larger than the current heap. The heap will stay expanded until LocalShrink() is called.

IMPORTS   ■ Win 2.0   ■ Win 3.0   ■ Win 3.1

Purpose	Specifies the names of the functions that will be imported from Dynamic Link Libraries (DLLs).
Syntax	**IMPORTS** [*internal-name*] *modulename* [*entry*]
internal-name	An optional alias that the application will use for the function. The alias must be followed by an equal sign and the function's name as defined in the DLL. For example,
	IMPORTS Reader=Samlib.FileRead
	specifies that the function name Reader() will be used by the application for a function in SAMLIB.DLL called FileRead().
modulename	The name of the DLL module. This will be the same as the file name of the .DLL file. For example, SAMLIB.DLL will create a module SAMLIB when loaded into memory.
entry	The function to be imported. This can either be the function's name, or the function's ordinal number as specified in the DLL's definition file in the EXPORTS section (see EXPORTS above). The function name or ordinal number must be preceded by a period to separate it from the module name.
Example	IMPORTS FileLib.ReadFile
	FileLib.1
	MyName=FileLib.FuncName
Description	IMPORTS is an optional statement. It is used only if the application uses functions that are defined in a Dynamic Link Library. See Chapter 28, *Dynamic Link Libraries*, for a full description.

LIBRARY   ■ Win 2.0   ■ Win 3.0   ■ Win 3.1

Purpose	Names a Dynamic Link Library (DLL).
Syntax	**LIBRARY** *libraryname*
Example	LIBRARY MyDLL
Description	This statement is similar to the NAME statement, except that LIBRARY is used for DLLs. If *libraryname* is left blank, LINK will use the library file name without the extension.

NAME   ■ Win 2.0   ■ Win 3.0   ■ Win 3.1

Purpose	Defines the name of an application's module.
Syntax	**NAME** *modulename*
Example	NAME generic
Description	The *modulename* must match the executable file name. For example, GENERIC.EXE must have a module name GENERIC. If *modulename* is left blank, LINK will use the file name without the extension. If both NAME and LIBRARY are missing from the .DEF file, LINK will assume that NAME was implied and use the file name to create an executable file.

SEGMENTS

Purpose	Specifies the attributes of code and data segments.
Syntax	**SEGMENTS** *segmentname* [CLASS *'class-name'*] [*minalloc*] [FIXED ǀ MOVEABLE] [DISCARDABLE] [PRELOAD ǀ LOADONCALL]
segmentname	The name of the segment. If default names are used, _TEXT will be the code segment name, and _DATA will be the data segment name. Use the Microsoft C compiler -NT switch to name code segments.
class-name	An optional character string, surrounded in single quotes, specifies the class name. If no class name is specified, LINK uses the name 'CODE' by default.
minalloc	An optional integer that specifies the minimum size to allocate for the segment.
	FIXED specifies that the segment must remain at one location in memory. MOVEABLE is preferred, as it allows Windows to make maximum use of available memory.
	DISCARDABLE specifies that the segment can be discarded if memory space is needed for another use.
	The PRELOAD option causes the segment to be loaded when the application is started. LOADONCALL allows the segment to be left on disk until a function within the segment is called.
Example	See the example under the GetCodeHandle() function description.
Description	The SEGMENTS statement allows individual control over how each segment of the program is set up during linking. Common uses are to set the less frequently used code segments to DISCARDABLE and LOADONCALL. This speeds program startup, and minimizes memory consumption by the remote parts of the program.

STACKSIZE

Purpose	Specifies the size of the program's stack.
Syntax	**STACKSIZE** *bytes*
bytes	An integer value. The minimum size is 5,120.
Example	STACKSIZE 6144
Description	The local stack is where automatic variables are stored. Because Windows programs are reentrant (different parts of the same program may be executed in parallel), a large stack is needed. Dynamic Link Libraries use the calling application's stack. Do not use the STACKSIZE statement with DLLs.

STUB

Purpose	Specifies which "stub" file to append to the front of the application.
Syntax	**STUB** *'filename'*
Example	STUB 'WINSTUB.EXE'
Description	If you try to run a Windows program from MS-DOS, the program will terminate with a warning message that the application needs Windows to run. This action takes place because Windows applications have a small "stub" file placed on their front. The stub file shows the message on the screen, and then terminates the program. The stub file is nothing more than a small MS-DOS application. You can substitute your own stub file if desired.

Memory Function Summary

Table 14-1 summarizes Windows memory manangement functions. The detailed function descriptions are in the next section.

Function	Purpose
FreeModule	Removes a module from memory.
GetCodeHandle	Determines the code segment of a function, and/or loads a code segment into memory.
GetCodeInfo	Determines information about a code segment.
GetCurrentPDB	Returns the segment address of the DOS PDB (PSP).
GlobalDosAlloc	Allocates a memory block that can be accessed by both DOS and Windows.
GlobalDosFree	Releases a block of memory allocated with GlobalDosAlloc( ).
GlobalFix	Stops a memory block from being moved in memory.
GetFreeSpace	Determines the amount of memory left in the global heap.
GetModuleFileName	Determines the full file and pathname for the executable file from which a module was loaded.
GetModuleHandle	Retrieves the handle of a module given the module's name.
GetModuleUsage	Returns the reference count of the given module.
GlobalAlloc	Allocates a block of memory in the global heap.
GlobalCompact	Compacts memory in the global heap, and determines the size of the largest available memory area.
GlobalDiscard	Discards a memory block from the global heap.
GlobalFlags	Determines if a memory block in the global heap is locked, discarded, or potentially discardable.
GlobalFree	Frees a block of memory allocated in the global heap.
GlobalHandle	Returns the handle of a global memory block, given its address.
GlobalLock	Locks an allocated memory block in the global heap.
GlobalLRUNewest	Marks a memory block to be the last one to be discarded in the global heap.
GlobalLRUOldest	Marks a memory block to be the first one to be discarded in the global heap.
GlobalNotify	Installs a notification function, which is called if global memory objects are about to be discarded.
GlobalPageLock	Stops a memory block from being moved in linear memory, or from being written to disk (virtual memory inhibited).
GlobalPageUnlock	Unlocks a memory block locked with GlobalPageLock( ).
GlobalReAlloc	Changes the size and/or attributes of a global memory block.
GlobalSize	Determines the size of a memory block allocated in the global heap.
GlobalUnfix	Frees a memory block fixed by GlobalFix( ).
GlobalUnlock	Unlocks a locked memory block in the global heap.
GlobalUnWire	Unwires a wired (locked) block in the global heap.
GlobalWire	Locks a global memory block in low memory.
LimitEmsPages	Limits the amount of expanded memory that Windows will assign to an application.
LoadModule	Loads and executes a Windows program, or creates a new instance of the program if one or more instances are already running.
LocalAlloc	Allocates a block of memory in the local heap.
LocalCompact	Determines the amount of available memory in the local heap, compacting memory if necessary to increase space.
LocalDiscard	Discards a memory block from the local heap.
LocalFlags	Determines if a memory block in the local heap is locked, discarded, or potentially discardable.

LocalFree	Frees a block of memory allocated in the local heap.
LocalHandle	Retrieves the handle of a memory block, given the address.
LocalLock	Locks an allocated memory block in the local heap.
LocalReAlloc	Changes the size and/or attributes of a local memory block.
LocalShrink	Reduces the size of the local heap.
LocalSize	Determines the size of a memory block allocated in the local heap.
LocalUnlock	Unlocks a locked memory block in the local heap.
LockSegment	Locks a segment in memory.
MulDiv	Computes the result of (a * b) / c, where a, b, and c are short integers.
UnlockSegment	Unlocks a memory segment locked with LockSegment().
WinExec	Loads and executes a Windows program.

Table 14-1. Memory Function Summary.

Memory Function Descriptions

This section contains detailed descriptions of the memory management functions.

FREEMODULE
□ Win 2.0   ■ Win 3.0   ■ Win 3.1

Purpose   Removes a module from memory.

Syntax   void **FreeModule**(HANDLE *hModule*);

Description   A module is a running application. Every time a module is loaded by another program, the module's usage count is increased by one. FreeModule() reduces the usage count by one. It removes the module from memory if the module's usage count is reduced to zero.

Uses   Used to remove modules that do not have visible windows from memory. To remove a module that has a visible window, send the window a WM_DESTROY message with SendMessage(). To remove a DLL (Dynamic Link Library), use FreeLibrary().

Returns   No returned value (void).

See Also   FreeLibrary(), LoadModule(), GetModuleHandle(), GetModuleUsage()

Parameters
hModule   HANDLE: The handle of the module to free. This value can be obtained by calling GetModuleHandle().

Example   This example, as illustrated in Figure 14-8, checks for the "SOUND" module in the global memory area every time a WM_PAINT message is received. The full file name of the file from which the sound driver was loaded is displayed, as well as the

generic	▼ ▲
Do It! Quit	
File C:\WINDOWS\SYSTEM\SOUND.DRV, Useage = 6	

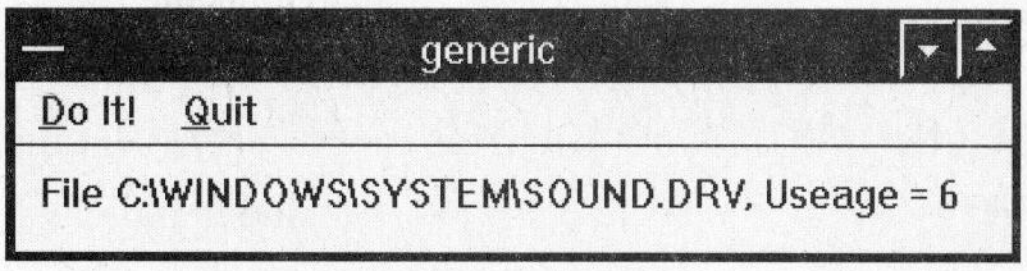

Figure 14-8. FreeModule( ) Example.

number of times the driver has been called by running applications. The usage count will equal the number of running applications on the system, as Windows loads the SOUND driver for all applications. If the user clicks the "Do It!" menu item, the sound driver is freed. FreeModule() is called once for every usage count. The HEAPWALK application that comes with the Microsoft Windows SDK can be used to verify that the SOUND module has been removed from memory.

```
Long FAR PASCAL WndProc (HWND hWnd, unsigned iMessage, WORD wParam, LONG lParam)
{
        PAINTSTRUCT                     ps ;
        static          HANDLE          hModule ;
        char                            cBuf [256], cWindName [64] ;
        int                             nCount, i ;

        switch (iMessage)                       /* process windows messages */
        {
                case WM_PAINT:
                        BeginPaint (hWnd, &ps) ;
                        hModule = GetModuleHandle ("sound") ;
                        nCount = GetModuleUsage (hModule) ;
                        GetModuleFileName (hModule, cWindName, 64) ;
                        TextOut (ps.hdc, 10, 10, cBuf, wsprintf (cBuf,
                                "File %s, Useage = %d", (LPSTR) cWindName, nCount)) ;
                        EndPaint (hWnd, &ps) ;
                        break ;
                case WM_COMMAND:                 /* process menu items */
                        switch (wParam)
                        {
                        case IDM_DOIT:           /* User hit the "Do it" menu item */
                                nCount = GetModuleUsage (hModule) ;
                                for (i = 0 ; i < nCount ; i++)
                                        FreeModule (hModule) ;
                                break ;
                        case IDM_QUIT:           /* send end of application message */
                                DestroyWindow (hWnd) ;
                                break ;
                        }
                        break ;
                case WM_DESTROY:                 /* stop application */
                        PostQuitMessage (0) ;
                        break ;
                default:                         /* default windows message processing */
                        return DefWindowProc (hWnd, iMessage, wParam, lParam) ;
        }
        return (0L) ;
}
```

GetCodeHandle

■ Win 2.0   ■ Win 3.0   ■ Win 3.1

Purpose	Determines the code segment of a function, and/or loads a code segment into memory.
Syntax	HANDLE **GetCodeHandle**(FARPROC *lpProc*);
Description	Normally, applications let Windows load code segments either on startup (PRELOAD attribute in the .DEF file), or when first needed (LOADONCALL attribute). GetCodeHandle() allows an application to control when a segment containing a function is loaded.

Uses   Can be used to load a series of segments in advance, during an idle period. Doing so avoids the delay of waiting for LOAD-ONCALL segments to be loaded.

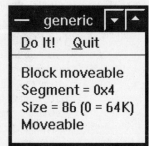

Returns   HANDLE, the code segment containing the function.

See Also   GetCodeInfo(), GetModuleHandle()

Parameters

lpProc   FARPROC: The procedure-instance address of the function to load. Retrieve this value with MakeProcInstance().

Example   This example, which is illustrated in Figure 14-9, demonstrates named code segments, using GetCodeHandle() to load a code segment into memory and using GetCodeInfo() to determine information about the code segment.

Figure 14-9. GetCode-Handle() and GetCodeInfo() Example.

The application's make file specifies the medium memory model and debugging options, and it also uses the Microsoft C compiler-NT switch to name two code segments as "MAINSEG" and "SECOND."

▷ GENERIC.NMAKE File

```
ALL: generic.exe

CFLAGS=-c -D LINT_ARGS -AM -Zi -Od -Gsw -W2
LFLAGS=/NOD /co

generic.obj : generic.c generic.h
    $(CC) $(CFLAGS) -NT MAINSEG generic.c

second.obj : second.c
    $(CC) $(CFLAGS) -NT SECOND second.c

generic.res: generic.rc generic.ico
    rc -r generic.rc

generic.exe : generic.obj second.obj generic.def generic.res
    link $(LFLAGS) generic+second, , ,libw mlibcew, generic
    rc generic.res
```

The definition file specifies separate memory attributes for the two named segments. The segment named SECOND is fixed not loaded until needed, and set as DISCARDABLE, as the nStrCopy() function in this segment will only be used once.

▷ GENERIC.DEF Definition File

```
NAME            GENERIC
DESCRIPTION     'generic windows program'
EXETYPE         WINDOWS
STUB            'WINSTUB.EXE'
CODE            PRELOAD  MOVEABLE
DATA            PRELOAD  MOVEABLE MULTIPLE
SEGMENTS        MAINSEG  MOVEABLE
                SECOND   LOADONCALL FIXED DISCARDABLE
HEAPSIZE        1024
STACKSIZE       5120
EXPORTS         WndProc
                nStrCopy
```

A small function will be in the fixed memory segment. In this case, the function is just a string copy function. This example is purely for demonstration. This simple function does not need to be in a fixed data segment.

▷ SECOND.C Listing

```
/* second.c  a second c program file with a separate segment */
#include <windows.h>

int FAR PASCAL nStrCopy (char *pDest, char *pSource, int nMax)
{
        int i ;

        for (i = 0 ; i < nMax ; i ++)
        {
                if (! (*pDest++ = *pSource++))
                        break ;
        }
        return (i) ;
}
```

When WM_CREATE is received, the application loads the code for the nStrCopy() function by calling GetCodeHandle(). The returned segment value *hCode* is not used in this example. The loaded function is used to copy a string to a local memory block.

When the "Do It!" menu item is clicked, the application uses GetCodeInfo() to retrieve information about the code segment containing the nStrCopy() function. Some of this information is displayed on the application's client area, as shown in Figure 14-9.

▷ GENERIC.C Listing

```
long FAR PASCAL WndProc (HWND hWnd, unsigned iMessage, WORD wParam, LONG lParam)
{
        PAINTSTRUCT                     ps ;
        static          HANDLE          hMem ;
        char                            *pMem ;
        char                            cBuf [128] ;
        FARPROC                         fpProc ;
        HANDLE                          hCode ;
        WORD                            wValue [8] ;
        HDC                             hDC ;

        switch (iMessage)                       /* process windows messages */
        {
                case WM_CREATE:
                        fpProc = MakeProcInstance (nStrCopy, ghInstance) ;
                        hCode = GetCodeHandle (fpProc) ;
                        hMem = LocalAlloc (LMEM_MOVEABLE, 128) ;
                        pMem = LocalLock (hMem) ;
                        nStrCopy (pMem, "Block moveable", 14) ;
                        LocalUnlock (hMem) ;
                        FreeProcInstance (fpProc) ;
                        break ;
                case WM_PAINT:
                        BeginPaint (hWnd, &ps) ; /* note no locking of hMem */
                        pMem = LocalLock (hMem) ;
                        TextOut (ps.hdc, 10, 10, pMem, strlen (pMem)) ;
                        LocalUnlock (hMem) ;
                        EndPaint (hWnd, &ps) ;
                        break ;
                case WM_COMMAND:                /* process menu items */
                        switch (wParam)
                        {
                        case IDM_DOIT:          /* User hit the "Do it" menu item */
                                GetCodeInfo (nStrCopy, (LPVOID) wValue) ;
                                hDC = GetDC (hWnd) ;
                                TextOut (hDC, 10, 30, cBuf, wsprintf (cBuf,
                                        "Segment = 0x%x", wValue [0])) ;
                                TextOut (hDC, 10, 50, cBuf, wsprintf (cBuf,
                                        "Size = %i (0 = 64K)", wValue [1])) ;
                                if (wValue [2] & 0x10)
                                        TextOut (hDC, 10, 70, "Moveable", 8) ;
                                else
                                        TextOut (hDC, 10, 70, "Fixed", 5) ;
                                ReleaseDC (hWnd, hDC) ;
                                break ;
                        case IDM_QUIT:          /* send end of application message */
                                LocalFree (hMem) ;
                                DestroyWindow (hWnd) ;
                                break ;
                        }
                        break ;
                case WM_DESTROY:                        /* stop application */
                        PostQuitMessage (0) ;
                        break ;
                default:                        /* default windows message processing */
                        return DefWindowProc (hWnd, iMessage, wParam, lParam) ;
        }
        return (0L) ;
}
```

GETCODEINFO

Purpose	Determines information about a code segment.
Syntax	void **GetCodeInfo**(FARPROC *lpProc*, LPVOID *lpSegInfo*);
Description	This function copies information about a code segment into an array pointed to by *lpSegInfo*.
Uses	Determining the status of a code segment, such as if it is fixed in memory or moveable.
Returns	No returned value (void).
See Also	GetCodeHandle(), GetModuleHandle()
Parameters	
lpProc	FARPROC: The address of the function in the segment. This is the function name, not the procedure-instance address. The value is passed as segment:offset. The parameter can also be passed as module handle:segment. Use GetModuleHandle() to retrieve the module handle.
lpSegInfo	LPVOID: A pointer to a 16-byte wide array. Information about the code segment is copied to this array when the function is called. The information is coded as shown in Table 14-2.

Byte Offset	Meaning	⊠
0	The offset within the sector of the specified function or data, relative to the beginning of the sector.	
2	The size of the segment in the sector in bytes. Zero = 64K.	
4	Contains flags which specify the attributes of the segment. These are set as follows:	

	Bit	Meaning	⊠
	0-2	Bit 0 is 1 if the segment is a data segment. Otherwise, it is a code segment.	
	3	Set to 1 if the segment is iterated, such as multiple data segments.	
	4	Set to 1 if the segment is moveable; otherwise, the segment is fixed.	
	5-6	Not used.	
	7	If the segment is a code segment and bit 7 is 1, the segment is an execute-only segment. If the segment is a code segment and bit 7 is 1, the segment is a read-only segment.	
	8	If bit 8 is 1, the segment has relocation information.	
	9	If bit 9 is 1, the segment contains debugging information.	
	10-15	Not used.	
6		The amount of memory allocated for the segment. Zero = 64K.	

Table 14-2. GetCodeInfo( ) Data Array.

Example	See the previous example under GetCodeHandle().

GETCURRENTPDB

Purpose	Returns the segment address of the DOS PDB (PSP).
Syntax	WORD **GetCurrentPDB**(void);
Description	Windows is a descendant of the MS-DOS operating system, which is a descendant of the CP/M operating system. Because of the desire to retain CP/M compatibility in the early days of MS-DOS, MS-DOS retained the Program Segment Prefix (PSP) data structure used by CP/M and added to it. The PSP is now referred to as the Program Data Base (PDB).

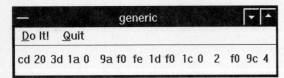

Figure 14-10. GetCurrentPDB() Example.

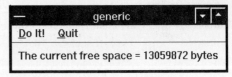

Figure 14-11. GetFreeSpace() Example.

The PDB contains basic information about an application, such as the address to call for MS-DOS file handling, and the address to call for a critical error. These fields are seldom needed from within a Windows program. For more information on this data, refer to the *MS-DOS Encyclopedia* (1988, Microsoft Press).

Uses	Rarely used.
Returns	WORD, the paragraph address (selector) for the current PDB.
See Also	GetCodeInfo(), GetCurrentTask()
Parameters	None (void).
Example	This example, illustrated in Figure 14-10, prints the first 16 bytes of the program segment prefix (PSP) when the user clicks the "Do It!" menu item.

```
long FAR PASCAL WndProc (HWND hWnd, unsigned iMessage, WORD wParam, LONG lParam)
{
        WORD            wPSP ;
        LPSTR           lpStr ;
        char            cBuf [16] ;
        int             i ;
        BYTE FAR        *pcVal ;
        HDC             hDC ;

        switch (iMessage)                       /* process windows messages */
        {
                case WM_COMMAND:                /* process menu items */
                        switch (wParam)
                        {
                        case IDM_DOIT:          /* User hit the "Do it" menu item */
                                wPSP = GetCurrentPDB () ;
                                lpStr = (LPSTR) MAKELONG (0, wPSP) ;
                                hDC = GetDC (hWnd) ;
                                for (i = 0 ; i < 16 ; i++)
                                {
                                        pcVal = (BYTE FAR *) (lpStr + i) ;
                                        TextOut (hDC, i * 25, 10, cBuf, wsprintf (cBuf,
                                                " %x", (int) *pcVal)) ;
                                }
                                ReleaseDC (hWnd, hDC) ;
                                break ;
```

[Other program lines]

GetFreeSpace

☐ Win 2.0 ■ Win 3.0 ■ Win 3.1

Purpose	Determines the amount of memory left in the global heap.
Syntax	DWORD **GetFreeSpace**(WORD *wFlags*);
Description	This function adds all of the unused memory in the global heap. The value reported may not be the size of the largest contiguous block of memory, as fixed memory blocks will break the memory area into smaller pieces. Use GlobalCompact() to find the size of the largest available contiguous piece of memory in the global heap.

Uses	Determining how much memory is left. If the value is getting low, the application may want to shed unneeded data or resources.
Returns	DWORD, the number of free bytes.
See Also	GlobalCompact()

Parameters

wFlags	WORD: Normally set to zero. For systems running with extended (banked) memory systems, the value can be set to GMEM_NOT_BANKED to specify that only the amount of memory below the EMS bank line is returned.

Related Messages	WM_COMPACTING
Example	This example, which is shown in Figure 14-11, displays the number of free bytes of memory when the user clicks the "Do It!" menu item.

```
long FAR PASCAL WndProc (HWND hWnd, unsigned iMessage, WORD wParam, LONG lParam)
{
        WORD            wPSP ;
        char            cBuf [128] ;
        DWORD           dwFree;
        HDC             hDC ;

        switch (iMessage)                       /* process windows messages */
        {
                case WM_COMMAND:                /* process menu items */
                        switch (wParam)
                        {
                        case IDM_DOIT:          /* User hit the "Do it" menu item */
                                dwFree = GetFreeSpace (0) ;
                                hDC = GetDC (hWnd) ;
                                TextOut (hDC, 10, 10, cBuf, wsprintf (cBuf,
                                        (LPSTR) "The current free space = %li bytes",
                                        dwFree)) ;
                                ReleaseDC (hWnd, hDC) ;
                                break ;
```

[Other program lines]

GETMODULEFILENAME ■ Win 2.0 ■ Win 3.0 ■ Win 3.1

Purpose	Determines the full file name and path name for the executable file from which a module was loaded.
Syntax	int **GetModuleFileName**(HANDLE *hModule*, LPSTR *lpFilename*, int *nSize*);
Description	A module is a running application. This function determines the name of the file that was loaded to start the application. The file name will be preceded by the path name, such as "C:\WIN-DOWS\PBRUSH.EXE."
Uses	The returned string can be parsed to find out which application a module handle represents.
Returns	int, the number of characters copied to *lpFilename*.
See Also	GetModuleHandle()

Parameters

hModule	HANDLE: The handle of the module. This is the value returned by LoadModule().
lpFilename	LPSTR: A pointer to a character buffer that will contain the file and path name. The buffer must be at least *nSize* characters wide.
nSize	int: The maximum number of characters to copy.
Example	See the example under LoadModule().

GETMODULEHANDLE

■ Win 2.0　■ Win 3.0　■ Win 3.1

Purpose	Retrieves the handle of a module, given the module's name.
Syntax	HANDLE **GetModuleHandle**(LPSTR *lpModuleName*);
Description	A module is a running application. This function returns the handle of a module.
Uses	The handle is needed to call FreeModule().
Returns	HANDLE, the module's handle. NULL on error.
See Also	LoadModule(), GetModuleUsage(), GetModuleFileName()

Parameters

lpModuleName　LPSTR: A null-terminated character string containing the name of the module. This is the same as the program name, but without the extension.

Example　See the example under LoadModule().

GETMODULEUSAGE

■ Win 2.0　■ Win 3.0　■ Win 3.1**1**

Purpose	Returns the reference count of the given module.
Syntax	int **GetModuleUsage**(HANDLE *hModule*);
Description	A module is a running application.
Returns	int, the reference count. This is the number of other applications that have caused the module to be loaded. Modules are loaded by either calling functions in the module, or by explicitly loading the module with LoadModule().
See Also	GetModuleHandle(), LoadModule()

Parameters

hModule　HANDLE: The handle of the module.

Example　See the example under LoadModule().

GLOBALALLOC

■ Win 2.0　■ Win 3.0　■ Win 3.1

Purpose	Allocates a block of memory in the global heap.
Syntax	HANDLE **GlobalAlloc**(WORD *wFlags*, DWORD *dwBytes*);
Description	This is the first step in allocating and using memory in the global heap. The global heap size is limited only by the size of the system's memory, less the room taken up by DOS, Windows, and the currently running applications. Global memory is allocated in blocks of 32 bytes. If the amount requested is not a multiple of 32, the block size will be rounded upward to the nearest 32 bytes.
Uses	Global memory is ideal for large memory blocks. Access is slightly slower than with memory on the local heap, as the full 32-bit address is used to specify the memory location.
Returns	HANDLE, the handle to the memory block allocated. Returns NULL on error.
See Also	GlobalLock(), GlobalReAlloc(), GlobalFree(), GlobalCompact()

Parameters

wFlags　WORD: One or more of the flags, listed in Table 14-3, combined with the C language binary OR operator (|). Choose either GMEM_FIXED or GMEM_MOVEABLE, and then combine the choice with other options.

Value	Meaning
GMEM_DDESHARE	Allocates memory that can be shared by applications exchanging data using dynamic data exchange (DDE). See Chapter 30 for an explanation of DDE. This type of memory is automatically discarded when the application that allocated the block terminates.
GMEM_DISCARDABLE	Allocates memory that can be discarded if Windows needs to make room. Used only with GMEM_MOVEABLE.
GMEM_FIXED	Allocates fixed memory. Do not use this flag unless necessary. Fixed memory limits Windows' ability to optimize memory use.
GMEM_MOVEABLE	Allocates moveable memory.
GMEM_NOCOMPACT	Memory in the global heap is not compacted or discarded to make room for the new memory block.
GMEM_NODISCARD	Memory in the global heap is not discarded to make room for the new memory block.
GMEM_NOT_BANKED	Allocates memory that cannot be banked (EMS systems only).
GMEM_NOTIFY	The notification routine, set by GlobalNotify(), is called if the memory object is to be discarded.
GMEM_ZEROINIT	Initializes the new allocated memory block contents to zero.

Table 14-3. GlobalAlloc( ) Flags.

Whenever possible, use GMEM_MOVEABLE. WINDOWS.H includes two common combinations:

```
#define GHND        (GMEM_MOVEABLE | GMEM_ZEROINIT)
#define GPTR        (GMEM_FIXED | GMEM_ZEROINIT)
```

dwBytes DWORD: The number of bytes to allocate. The actual number of bytes allocated may be a larger number in order to end the boundary on an address which is a multiple of 32.

If GlobalCompact() was used to determine the maximum *dwBytes* value, GMEM_NO-COMPACT and GMEM_NODISCARD should not be used.

Caution If the program's data segment is defined as moveable in the .DEF file, calling GlobalAlloc() may cause the data segment to move, which will invalidate stored far pointers.

Example This example shows the allocation of memory in the global heap used to store a string. When the program first starts (WM_CREATE received), room for 27 characters is allocated. GlobalAlloc() actually allocates 32. A string is stored in the memory block. This string, along with the block size and several memory status bytes, is displayed on the window's client area every time a WM_PAINT message is received.

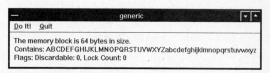

Figure 14-12. GlobalAlloc( ) Example.

When the user clicks the "Do It!" menu item, the memory block is reallocated to make room for another 27 characters. The additional characters are written to the buffer and are displayed when WM_PAINT messages are processed. Repeatedly clicking the "Do It!" menu item does not allocate more room in this case. The block is simply reallocated to the same size, resulting in no change. Figure 14-12 shows the window's appearance after the "Do It!" menu item was clicked.

```
long FAR PASCAL WndProc (HWND hWnd, unsigned iMessage, WORD wParam, LONG lParam)
{
        PAINTSTRUCT                     ps ;
        static          HANDLE          hMem ;
        char            FAR             *pMem ;
        char                            cBuf [128] ;
        int                             i, nSize, nFlags ;

        switch (iMessage)                               /* process windows messages */
        {
                case WM_CREATE:
                        if (hMem = GlobalAlloc (GMEM_MOVEABLE, 27))
                        {
                                if (pMem = GlobalLock (hMem))
                                {
                                        for (i = 0 ; i < 26 ; i++)
                                                *pMem++ = 'A' + i ;
                                        *pMem = 0 ;
                                        GlobalUnlock (hMem) ;
                                }
                                else
                                        MessageBox (hWnd, "Could not lock memory block.",
                                                "Memory Error", MB_ICONHAND | MB_OK) ;
                        }
                        else
                        {
                                MessageBox (hWnd, "Could not allocate memory",
                                        "Memory Error", MB_ICONHAND | MB_OK) ;
                                DestroyWindow (hWnd) ;
                        }
                        break ;
                case WM_PAINT:
                        BeginPaint (hWnd, &ps) ;
                        if (pMem = GlobalLock (hMem))
                        {
                                nSize = GlobalSize (hMem) ;
                                nFlags = GlobalFlags (hMem) ;
                                TextOut (ps.hdc, 10, 10, cBuf, wsprintf (cBuf,
                                        "The memory block is %d bytes in size.",
                                        nSize)) ;
                                TextOut (ps.hdc, 10, 30, cBuf, wsprintf (cBuf,
                                        "Contains: %s", (LPSTR) pMem)) ;
                                TextOut (ps.hdc, 10, 50, cBuf, wsprintf (cBuf,
                                        "Flags: Discardable: %d, Lock Count: %d",
                                        nFlags & GMEM_DISCARDABLE, nFlags &
                                        GMEM_LOCKCOUNT)) ;
                                GlobalUnlock (hMem) ;
                        }
                        EndPaint (hWnd, &ps) ;
                        break ;
                case WM_COMMAND:                /* process menu items */
                        switch (wParam)
                        {
                                case IDM_DOIT:          /* User hit the "Do it" menu item */
                                        if (hMem = GlobalReAlloc (hMem,
                                                (26 * 2) + 1, GMEM_MOVEABLE))
                                        {
                                                if (pMem = GlobalLock (hMem))
                                                {
                                                        for (i = 0 ; i < 26 ; i++)
                                                                *pMem++ ;        /* skip old stuff */
                                                        for (i = 0 ; i < 26 ; i++)
                                                                *pMem++ = 'a' + i ;
                                                        *pMem = 0 ;
                                                        GlobalUnlock (hMem) ;
                                                }
                                                else
                                                        MessageBox (hWnd,
                                                                "Could not lock memory block.",
```

```
                                                "Memory Error",
                                                MB_ICONHAND | MB_OK) ;
                        }
                        else
                                MessageBox (hWnd,
                                        "Could not re-allocate memory",
                                        "Memory Error", MB_ICONHAND | MB_OK) ;
                        InvalidateRect (hWnd, NULL, TRUE) ;        /* force paint */
                        break ;
                case IDM_QUIT:                /* send end of application message */
                        DestroyWindow (hWnd) ;
                        break ;
                }
                break ;
        case WM_DESTROY:                     /* stop application */
                GlobalFree (hMem) ;
                PostQuitMessage (0) ;
                break ;
        default:                             /* default windows message processing */
                return DefWindowProc (hWnd, iMessage, wParam, lParam) ;
        }
        return (0L) ;
}
```

GLOBALCOMPACT   ■ Win 2.0   ■ Win 3.0   ■ Win 3.1

Purpose	Compacts memory in the global heap, and determines the size of the largest available memory area.
Syntax	DWORD **GlobalCompact**(DWORD *dwMinFree*);
Description	GlobalCompact() first compacts the global memory heap by moving all moveable blocks together. If *dwMinFree* bytes of contiguous memory are not available after compacting, GlobalCompact() discards blocks. This continues until either the requested memory space is available, or until no further discardable memory blocks can be found.
Uses	Use this function any time a series of memory blocks is allocated and freed. Use of GlobalCompact assures that the largest possible memory block is made available if needed.
Returns	DWORD, the number of bytes in the largest available block of free memory in the global heap.
See Also	GlobalAlloc(), GlobalReAlloc(), GlobalFree()
Parameters	
dwMinFree	DWORD: The number of bytes of contiguous memory desired in the global heap. If *dwMinFree* is zero, GlobalCompact() returns the size of the largest block of global memory that can be returned if all discardable segments are removed.
Caution	If the returned value is used as the *dwBytes* parameter for GlobalAlloc(), do not use the GMEM_NOCOMPACT or GMEM_NODISCARD flags.
Related Messages	WM_COMPACTING

Example This example, which is illustrated in Figure 14-13, allocates four blocks of global memory, each 1,024 bytes in size. Block 0 is moveable, block 1 is moveable and discardable, block 2 is moveable, and block 3 is fixed. When the user clicks the "Do It!" menu item, the application discards block 1. This does not increase the size of the largest available block of memory because the fixed block number 3 gets in the way.

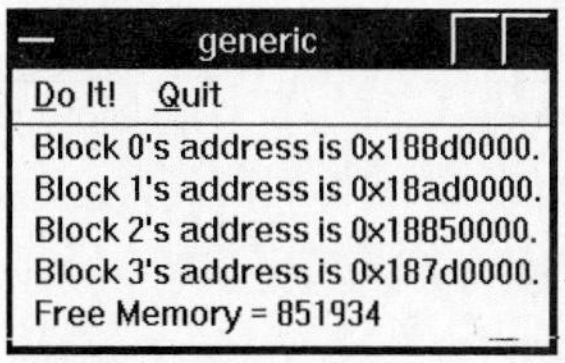

```
┌──────────────── generic ──────────┌─┌─┐
│ Do It!   Quit                        └─└─┘
├─────────────────────────────────────────┤
│ Block 0's address is 0x188d0000.         │
│ Block 1's address is 0x18ad0000.         │
│ Block 2's address is 0x18850000.         │
│ Block 3's address is 0x187d0000.         │
│ Free Memory = 851934                     │
```

Figure 14-13. Global-Compact( ) Example.

```
long FAR PASCAL WndProc (HWND hWnd, unsigned iMessage, WORD wParam, LONG lParam)
{
        PAINTSTRUCT                    ps ;
        static           HANDLE        hMem [4] ;
```

```
        char                            cBuf [128] ;
        LPSTR                           pMem [4] ;
        int                             i ;
        DWORD                           dwFree ;

        switch (iMessage)                       /* process windows messages */
        {
                case WM_CREATE:
                        hMem [0] = GlobalAlloc (GMEM_MOVEABLE, 1024) ;
                        hMem [1] = GlobalAlloc (GMEM_MOVEABLE |
                                GMEM_DISCARDABLE, 1024) ;
                        hMem [2] = GlobalAlloc (GMEM_MOVEABLE, 1024) ;
                        hMem [3] = GlobalAlloc (GMEM_FIXED, 1024) ;
                        break ;
                case WM_PAINT:
                        BeginPaint (hWnd, &ps) ;
                        for (i = 0 ; i < 4 ; i++)
                        {
                                pMem [i] = GlobalLock (hMem [i]) ;
                                TextOut (ps.hdc, 10, 20 * i, cBuf, wsprintf (cBuf,
                                        "Block %d's address is 0x%lx.", i, pMem [i])) ;
                                GlobalUnlock (hMem [i]) ;
                        }
                        dwFree = GlobalCompact (0) ;        /* find free space */
                        TextOut (ps.hdc, 10, 80, cBuf, wsprintf (cBuf,
                                "Free Memory = %li", dwFree)) ;
                        EndPaint (hWnd, &ps) ;
                        break ;
                case WM_COMMAND:                        /* process menu items */
                        switch (wParam)
                        {
                        case IDM_DOIT:                  /* User hit the "Do it" menu item */
                                GlobalDiscard (hMem [1]) ;
                                InvalidateRect (hWnd, NULL, TRUE) ; /* force paint */
                                break ;
                        case IDM_QUIT:                  /* send end of application message */
                                for (i = 0 ; i < 4 ; i ++)
                                        GlobalFree (hMem [i]) ;
                                DestroyWindow (hWnd) ;
                                break ;
                        }
                        break ;
                case WM_DESTROY:                        /* stop application */
                        PostQuitMessage (0) ;
                        break ;
                default:                                /* default windows message processing */
                        return DefWindowProc (hWnd, iMessage, wParam, lParam) ;
        }
        return (0L) ;
}
```

GlobalDosAlloc □ Win 2.0 ■ Win 3.0 ■ Win 3.1

Purpose	Allocates a memory block that can be accessed by both DOS and Windows.
Syntax	DWORD **GlobalDosAlloc** (DWORD *dwBytes*);
Description	The memory block allocated will be in the first megabyte of linear address space.
Uses	Not normally used. Can be used to allocate memory for device drivers that will be accessed by MS-DOS applications. Using this function reduces Windows' ability to optimize memory usage.
Returns	DWORD. The high-order word contains the paragraph segment for the memory block (real-mode memory address). The low-order word contains the selector (protected-mode memory address).
See Also	GlobalAlloc(), LocalAlloc(), GlobalPageLock()
Parameters	
dwBytes	DWORD: The number of bytes to be allocated.

Example

This example (courtesy of Mark Peterson) demonstrates allocating a block of memory that can be accessed by either Windows or DOS. In this case, only Windows uses the block. The block is also page-locked, forcing it to remain in the same physical address and stopping any possible writing of the data to virtual (disk) memory. The address does not change when GlobalCompact() is called (user clicks the "Do It!" menu item). Figure 14-14 shows how the returned value translates into the selector and segment values. A Windows far pointer is the selector value in the high-order word. DOS in real mode (and Windows in real mode) uses the simple segment value to point to the memory block.

Figure 14-14.
GlobalDosAlloc( ) Example.

```
long FAR PASCAL WndProc (HWND hWnd, unsigned iMessage, WORD wParam, LONG lParam)
{
        PAINTSTRUCT             ps ;
        DWORD                   dwValue ;
        static WORD             wSegment, wSelector ;
        static LPSTR            WindowsPtr ;
        LPSTR                   pWind ;
        static void far         *DosPtr ;
        char                    cBuf [128] ;
        int                     i, nLockCount ;

        switch (iMessage)                       /* process windows messages */
        {
        case WM_CREATE:
                dwValue = GlobalDosAlloc (27) ;         /* allocate mem block */
                if (dwValue)            /* demonstrate selector/segment */
                {                       /* show casts of returned value */
                        wSegment = HIWORD (dwValue) ;
                        wSelector = LOWORD (dwValue) ;
                        WindowsPtr = (LPSTR) MAKELONG (0, wSelector) ;
                        DosPtr = (void far *) MAKELONG (0, wSegment) ;
                                                /* page lock it */
                        nLockCount = GlobalPageLock (wSelector) ;
                        if (nLockCount)
                        {
                                pWind = WindowsPtr ;
                                for (i = 0 ; i < 26 ; i++)
                                        *pWind++ = 'A' + i ;
                                *pWind = 0 ;
                        }
                }
                break ;
        case WM_PAINT:
                BeginPaint (hWnd, &ps) ;
                TextOut (ps.hdc, 10, 0, cBuf, wsprintf (cBuf,
                        "Contains: %s", WindowsPtr)) ;
                TextOut (ps.hdc, 10, 20, cBuf, wsprintf (cBuf,
                        "Segment = 0x%x, Selector = 0x%x",
                        wSegment, wSelector)) ;
                TextOut (ps.hdc, 10, 40, cBuf, wsprintf (cBuf,
                        "DosPtr = 0x%lx, WindowsPtr = 0x%lx, ",
                        DosPtr, WindowsPtr)) ;
                EndPaint (hWnd, &ps) ;
                break ;
        case WM_COMMAND:                /* process menu items */
                switch (wParam)
                {
                case IDM_DOIT:          /* User hit the "Do it" menu item */
                        GlobalCompact (0) ;             /* try to budge it */
                        InvalidateRect (hWnd, NULL, TRUE) ;     /* force paint */
                        break ;
                case IDM_QUIT:          /* send end of application message */
                        DestroyWindow (hWnd) ;
                        break ;
```

```
                    }
                    break ;
            case WM_DESTROY:                    /* stop application */
                    nLockCount = GlobalPageUnlock (wSelector) ;
                    wSelector = GlobalDosFree (wSelector) ;
                    if (wSelector)
                            MessageBox (hWnd, "Did not free memory block.",
                                    "GlobalDosFree() Error", MB_OK) ;
                    PostQuitMessage (0) ;
                    break ;
            default:                            /* default windows message processing */
                    return DefWindowProc (hWnd, iMessage, wParam, lParam) ;
        }
        return (0L) ;
}
```

GLOBALDOSFREE

☐ Win 2.0   ■ Win 3.0   ■ Win 3.1

Purpose	Releases a block of memory allocated with GlobalDosAlloc().
Syntax	WORD **GlobalDosFree** (WORD *wSelector*);
Description	Memory blocks allocated with GlobalDosAlloc() inhibit memory optimization by Windows. GlobalDosFree() should be called as soon as possible to release the memory blocks.
Uses	Memory blocks allocated by GlobalDosAlloc() are accessible by both Windows and real-mode DOS applications.
Returns	WORD, NULL if the function was successful. Equal to *wSelector* on error.
See Also	GlobalDosAlloc(), GlobalPageLock(), GlobalAlloc()
Parameters	
wSelector	WORD: The selector returned in the low-order word of the returned DWORD when GlobalDosAlloc() was called. This is the selector value for the memory block.
Example	See the example under the GlobalDosAlloc() function description.

GLOBALDISCARD

■ Win 2.0   ■ Win 3.0   ☐ Win 3.1

Purpose	Discards a memory block from the global heap.
Syntax	HANDLE **GlobalDiscard**(DWORD *hMem*);
Description	Discarding a memory block makes the space available for allocating other blocks of memory. The *hMem* handle remains usable after the block is discarded, although it does not point to active memory. *hMem* can be reused by using GlobalReAlloc() to allocate another block of memory. Only blocks allocated with the GMEM_DISCARDABLE and GMEM_MOVEABLE flags set can be discarded.
Uses	Discarding memory to make room for other blocks. Note that GlobalFree() removes the memory block and invalidates the memory handle. GlobalDiscard() just discards the memory block, but the *hMem* handle remains valid.
Returns	HANDLE. Equal to *hMem* if the function was successful, NULL on error.
See Also	GlobalFree(), GlobalReAlloc()
Parameters	
hMem	HANDLE: The handle to the discardable memory block. This is the value returned by GlobalAlloc() when the block was first allocated.
Example	See the previous example under GlobalCompact().

GLOBALFIX

Purpose	Stops a memory block from being moved in memory.
Syntax	void **GlobalFix** (HANDLE *hMem*);

Description When Windows is operating in Standard or 386 enhanced mode (not real mode), locked memory blocks can be relocated in linear memory. This does not invalidate far pointers to the block used within the program, but will change the physical address of the block in memory. Calling GlobalFix() prevents the global memory block from being moved in linear memory. As shown in Figure 14-15, this does not stop the block from being paged to disk as virtual memory. Use GlobalPageLock() to stop virtual memory writes for a memory block. Each time GlobalFix() is called, the block's lock count is increased by one. An equal number of GlobalUnfix() calls is required to free the block.

Figure 14-15. GlobalFix( ) Example.

Uses Not often used. Used with (old) drivers that assume a fixed-memory address. Fixing a memory block reduces Windows' ability to optimize memory use and should be avoided.

Returns No returned value (void).

See Also GlobalUnfix(), GlobalLock(), GlobalPageLock(), GlobalAlloc()

Parameters

hMem HANDLE: The global memory block's handle. This is the value returned by GlobalAlloc().

Example This example, initially allocates a moveable global memory block big enough to hold 27 bytes. The uppercase alphabet is written to the memory block. The block is then fixed in memory by calling GlobalFix(). Clicking the "Do It!" menu item causes the GlobalCompact() function to be called. This has no effect on the memory block's address, as it is fixed. The memory block is unfixed and deleted when the application terminates.

```
long FAR PASCAL WndProc (HWND hWnd, unsigned iMessage, WORD wParam, LONG lParam)
{
        PAINTSTRUCT             ps ;
        static HANDLE           hMem ;
        static LPSTR            pMem ;
        LPSTR                   pMemTemp ;
        char                    cBuf [128] ;
        int                     i, nSize, nFlags ;

        switch (iMessage)                        /* process windows messages */
        {
                case WM_CREATE:
                        hMem = GlobalAlloc (GMEM_MOVEABLE, 27) ;
                        pMemTemp = pMem = GlobalLock (hMem) ;
                        for (i = 0 ; i < 26 ; i++)
                                *pMemTemp++ = 'A' + i ;
                        *pMemTemp = 0 ;
                        GlobalFix (hMem) ;         /* fix block in memory */
                        break ;
                case WM_PAINT:
                        BeginPaint (hWnd, &ps) ;
                        nSize = GlobalSize (hMem) ;
                        nFlags = GlobalFlags (hMem) ;
                        TextOut (ps.hdc, 10, 10, cBuf, wsprintf (cBuf,
                                "The memory block is %d bytes in size.", nSize)) ;
                        TextOut (ps.hdc, 10, 30, cBuf, wsprintf (cBuf,
                                "Contains: %s", (LPSTR) pMem)) ;
                        TextOut (ps.hdc, 10, 50, cBuf, wsprintf (cBuf,
                                "Flags: Discardable: %d, Lock Count: %d",
```

```
                              nFlags & GMEM_DISCARDABLE, nFlags & GMEM_LOCKCOUNT)) ;
                TextOut (ps.hdc, 10, 70, cBuf, wsprintf (cBuf,
                         "Handle = Ox%x, Address = Ox%lx", hMem, pMem)) ;
                EndPaint (hWnd, &ps) ;
                break ;
        case WM_COMMAND:                    /* process menu items */
                switch (wParam)
                {
                case IDM_DOIT:              /* User hit the "Do it" menu item */
                        GlobalCompact (0) ;        /* try to budge it */
                        InvalidateRect (hWnd, NULL, TRUE) ;       /* force paint */
                        break ;
                case IDM_QUIT:              /* send end of application message */
                        DestroyWindow (hWnd) ;
                        break ;
                }
                break ;
        case WM_DESTROY:                    /* stop application */
                GlobalUnfix (hMem) ;
                GlobalFree (hMem) ;
                PostQuitMessage (0) ;
                break ;
        default:                            /* default windows message processing */
                return DefWindowProc (hWnd, iMessage, wParam, lParam) ;
        }
        return (OL) ;
}
```

GLOBALFLAGS
■ Win 2.0   ■ Win 3.0   ■ Win 3.1

Purpose Determines if a memory block in the global heap is locked, discarded, or potentially discardable.

Syntax WORD **GlobalFlags**(HANDLE *hMem*);

Description This function checks the status of a memory block allocated in the global heap. If a memory block is locked with GlobalLock() more than once without calling GlobalUnlock(), the block's lock count will be more than one. GlobalUnlock() will have to be called as many times as the lock count to unlock the memory area. Memory blocks can be discarded using GlobalDiscard() and still have valid handles. GlobalFlags() will determine if the memory block has been discarded, or if it was allocated using the LMEM_DISCARDABLE flag.

Uses To check the validity of a memory handle, or to check if a memory block has been locked more than once.

Returns WORD. The high-order byte contains one of the flags in Table 14-4.

Value	Meaning
GMEM_DDESHARE	The block can be shared by other applications. This is only used with dynamic data exchange.
GMEM_DISCARDABLE	The block was allocated with the GMEM_DISCARDABLE flag.
GMEM_DISCARDED	The block has been discarded. The GlobalReAlloc() function will need to be called to make the memory area usable.
GMEM_NOT_BANKED	The block cannot be banked. This only applies to EMS memory banking systems.

Table 14-4. GlobalFlags( ) Flags.

The low-order byte contains the lock-count of the memory block. Combine the returned word with GMEM_LOCKCOUNT using the C language binary and ampersand (&) to determine the lock-count.

See Also GlobalAlloc(), GlobalSize(), GlobalLock()

Parameters

hMem   HANDLE: The handle to the global memory block returned by GlobalAlloc().

Example   See the example under GlobalAlloc().

GLOBALFREE
■ Win 2.0   ■ Win 3.0   ■ Win 3.1

Purpose	Frees a block of memory allocated in the global heap.
Syntax	HANDLE **GlobalFree**(HANDLE *hMem*);
Description	Freeing a memory block returns the memory to the system for reuse. All memory blocks allocated within an application should be freed before the application exits to return the memory to Windows.
Uses	There should be a call to GlobalFree() for every call to GlobalAlloc() in a program.
Returns	Returns NULL if the global block was successfully freed from memory. If an error occurred, Global Free() returns a positive value (equal to the block's handle).
See Also	GlobalAlloc(), GlobalDiscard(), GlobalReAlloc()

Parameters

hMem   HANDLE: The handle to the memory block allocated in the local heap with GlobalAlloc().

Example   See the example under GlobalAlloc().

GLOBALHANDLE
■ Win 2.0   ■ Win 3.0   ■ Win 3.1

Purpose	Returns the handle of a global memory block given its address.
Syntax	DWORD **GlobalHandle**(WORD *wMem*);
Description	Returns the handle of the memory block given the segment address (or selector) of a block of memory in the global heap. This is the reverse of the normal procedure of getting the address of a memory block by using GlobalLock() to lock a block using the memory block handle.
Uses	This is useful in cases where locked (fixed) memory blocks are used. With locked blocks, the address does not change, so it is efficient to store only the block's address and not store the handle. GlobalHandle() can be used to retrieve the handle if it is needed to free the block.
Returns	DWORD. The low-order word contains the handle of the global memory block. The high-order word contains the segment address of the memory block. Returns NULL on error.
See Also	GlobalFlags()

Parameters

wMem   WORD: An unsigned integer value. This is the segment address of the global memory block.

Example   See the example under GlobalFix().

GLOBALLOCK
■ Win 2.0   ■ Win 3.0   ■ Win 3.1

Purpose	Locks an allocated memory block in the global heap.
Syntax	LPSTR **GlobalLock**(HANDLE *hMem*);
Description	Moveable memory blocks allocated with GlobalAlloc() must be locked before data can be written or read from the memory area. The block should be unlocked with GlobalUnlock() as soon after use as possible.
Uses	Used to "realize" a memory pointer. This means that the return value is a far pointer to a block of memory. The pointer will remain valid until the block is unlocked with GlobalUnlock().
Returns	LPSTR, a far pointer to the beginning of the memory area.
See Also	GlobalUnlock(), GlobalAlloc()

Parameters

hMem   HANDLE: A handle to the memory area allocated with GlobalAlloc().

Example   See the example under GlobalAlloc().

GLOBALLRUNEWEST   ■ Win 2.0   ■ Win 3.0   ■ Win 3.1

Purpose   Marks a memory block to be the last one to be discarded in the global heap.

Syntax   HANDLE **GlobalLRUNewest**(HANDLE *hMem*);

Description   Windows keeps track of discardable memory blocks. Normally, the most recently used blocks are the last to be discarded if Windows runs short of memory. GlobalLRUNewest() allows the application to specify a memory block that should be the last one discarded if the global heap is compacted. This function is called internally by Windows whenever GlobalLock() or GlobalWire() is called. The LRU position is also used to determine if a memory block should be located in virtual memory (in 386 enhanced mode).

Uses   Used to optimize an application's performance if a number of discardable memory blocks are used. This is the ideal way to keep a memory block available for immediate access without locking it in memory, or using the GMEM_NODISCARD attribute.

Returns   HANDLE. Returns *hMem* if the function was successful, NULL on error.

See Also   GlobalLRUOldest(), GlobalCompact()

Parameters

hMem   HANDLE: The global memory block handle. This is the value returned by GlobalAlloc() or GlobalReAlloc() the last time the memory block was allocated or resized.

Related Messages WM_COMPACTING

Example   This example, which is illustrated in Figure 14-16, allocates two memory blocks on the local heap. Both are moveable and discardable. When the user clicks the "Do It!" menu item, the first block is marked with GlobalLRUNewest(), and the second is marked with GlobalLRU-Oldest(). This makes the second

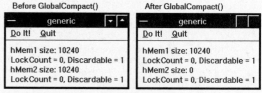

Figure 14-16. GlobalLRUNewest() and Global-LRUOldest() Example.

block the most likely to be discarded. Requesting a contiguous memory space slightly larger than the amount available on the global heap with GlobalCompact() forces a block to be discarded. Only the second memory block ends up discarded. Note that the second memory block's handle and status (flags) remain valid. The block can be restored with GlobalReAlloc().

```
long FAR PASCAL WndProc (HWND hWnd, unsigned iMessage, WORD wParam, LONG lParam)
{
        PAINTSTRUCT                     ps ;
        static          HANDLE          hMem1, hMem2 ;
        char                            cBuf [128] ;
        int                             nFlags1, nFlags2 ;
        DWORD                           dwFree, dwSize1, dwSize2 ;

        switch (iMessage)                       /* process windows messages */
        {
                case WM_CREATE:
                        hMem1 = GlobalAlloc (GMEM_MOVEABLE |
                                GMEM_DISCARDABLE, 10240) ;
                        hMem2 = GlobalAlloc (GMEM_MOVEABLE |
                                GMEM_DISCARDABLE, 10240) ;
                        if (!hMem1 || !hMem2)
```

```
                      {
                              MessageBox (hWnd,
                                      "Could not allocate memory blocks.",
                                      "Memory Error", MB_ICONHAND | MB_OK) ;
                              DestroyWindow (hWnd) ;
                      }
                      break ;
              case WM_PAINT:
                      BeginPaint (hWnd, &ps) ;
                      nFlags1 = GlobalFlags (hMem1) ;
                      nFlags2 = GlobalFlags (hMem2) ;
                      dwSize1 = GlobalSize (hMem1) ;
                      dwSize2 = GlobalSize (hMem2) ;
                      TextOut (ps.hdc, 10, 10, cBuf, wsprintf (cBuf,
                              "hMem1 size: %li", dwSize1)) ;
                      TextOut (ps.hdc, 10, 30, cBuf, wsprintf (cBuf,
                              "LockCount = %d, Discardable = %d",
                              nFlags1 & GMEM_LOCKCOUNT,
                              (nFlags1 & GMEM_DISCARDABLE ? 1 : 0))) ;
                      TextOut (ps.hdc, 10, 50, cBuf, wsprintf (cBuf,
                              "hMem2 size: %li", dwSize2)) ;
                      TextOut (ps.hdc, 10, 70, cBuf, wsprintf (cBuf,
                              "LockCount = %d, Discardable = %d",
                              nFlags2 & GMEM_LOCKCOUNT,
                              (nFlags2 & GMEM_DISCARDABLE ? 1 : 0))) ;
                      EndPaint (hWnd, &ps) ;
                      break ;
              case WM_COMMAND:                  /* process menu items */
                      switch (wParam)
                      {
                      case IDM_DOIT:            /* User hit the "Do it" menu item */
                              GlobalLRUNewest (hMem1) ;       /* only one of these */
                              GlobalLRUOldest (hMem2) ;       /* two calls is needed */
                              dwFree = GlobalCompact (0) ;    /* check free space */
                              GlobalCompact (dwFree + 64) ;   /* force discard */
                              InvalidateRect (hWnd, NULL, TRUE) ;      /* force paint */
                              break ;
                      case IDM_QUIT:            /* send end of application message */
                              DestroyWindow (hWnd) ;
                              break ;
                      }
                      break ;
              case WM_DESTROY:                  /* stop application */
                      GlobalFree (hMem1) ;
                      GlobalFree (hMem2) ;
                      PostQuitMessage (0) ;
                      break ;
              default:                          /* default windows message processing */
                      return DefWindowProc (hWnd, iMessage, wParam, lParam) ;
      }
      return (0L) ;
}
```

GlobalLRUOldest   ■ Win 2.0   ■ Win 3.0   ■ Win 3.1

Purpose	Marks a memory block to be the first one to be discarded in the global heap.
Syntax	HANDLE **GlobalLRUOldest**(HANDLE *hMem*);
Description	Windows keeps track of discardable memory blocks. Normally, the most recently used blocks are the last to be discarded if Windows runs short of memory. GlobalLRUOldest() allows the application to specify a memory block that should be the first one discarded if the global heap is compacted.
Uses	Used to optimize an application's performance if a number of discardable memory blocks are used. This function and GlobalLRUNewest() are the ideal way to prioritize which memory blocks should be available for immediate access without locking it in memory, or using the GMEM_NODISCARD attribute.

Returns	HANDLE. Returns *hMem* if the function was successful, NULL on error.
See Also	GlobalLRUNewest(), GlobalCompact()
Parameters	
hMem	HANDLE: The global memory block handle. This is the value returned by GlobalAlloc() or GlobalReAlloc() the last time the memory block was allocated or resized.
Related Messages	WM_COMPACTING
Example	See the previous example under GlobalLRUNewest().

GLOBALNOTIFY
■ Win 2.0 ■ Win 3.0 ■ Win 3.1

Purpose	Installs a notification function, which is called if global memory objects are about to be discarded.
Syntax	void **GlobalNotify**(HANDLE *lpNotifyProc*);
Description	Memory blocks allocated with the GMEM_DISCARDABLE and GMEM_MOVEABLE flags can be discarded if Windows needs a larger memory space in the global heap than is currently available. Normally, discarding is done on a most-recently-used-last-discarded basis, with no warning to the application that allocated the block. Installing a notification function causes Windows to activate the function before any memory block is discarded. This provides an opportunity for the notification function to free a less critical memory block. Only blocks allocated with the GMEM_DISCARDABLE I GMEM_MOVEABLE I GMEM_NOTIFY flags will result in the notification function being called. The notification function must be part of a DLL (Dynamic Link Library) with a fixed code segment. The DLL cannot use the calling application's stack. Even though the notification must be in a DLL, discarding memory allocated by a DLL does not result in the notification function being called.
Uses	Used in applications that allocate discardable memory blocks.
Returns	No returned value (void).
See Also	GlobalLRUOldest(), GlobalLRUNewest()
Parameters	
lpNotifyProc	HANDLE: The procedure-instance address of the notification function. This is the value returned by GetProcAddress(). The notification function must be defined in a DLL with a fixed-code segment. The notification function must have the following form:

BOOL FAR PASCAL **NotifyProc** (HANDLE *hMem*);

where *hMem* is the handle to the block being discarded. The notification function should return nonzero if Windows should discard the block, zero if the block should not be discarded.

The notification function will continue to be called unless the situation causing Windows to discard the memory block is changed. Typical actions within the notification function include discarding some other block of memory, eliminating the need to discard the block whose handle is *hMem*. The callback function should not call any function which may cause relocation of memory objects (GlobalAlloc(), GlobalReAlloc()).

Related Messages	WM_COMPACTING
Caution	Notification functions cannot be installed while processing the WM_CREATE message. The calling program must be processing messages via the message loop before GlobalNotify() is called. This function can only be called once per application instance.
Example	This example sets up a notification procedure to warn when memory blocks are about to be discarded. All the notification

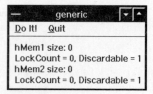

Figure 14-17. GlobalNotify() Example.

procedure does is put a message box on the screen warning that memory is about to be deleted. After the memory has been deleted, the window appears as shown in Figure 14-17.

The notification must reside in a Dynamic Link Library (DLL) with a fixed code segment. The code segment is fixed by specifying the "FIXED" attribute in the DLL's definition file. The two functions called from outside the DLL are listed in the EXPORTS section.

⇨ NOTIFY.DEF Definition File for DLL

```
LIBRARY          NOTIFY
DESCRIPTION      'dll for notification'
EXETYPE          WINDOWS
CODE             PRELOAD FIXED
DATA             PRELOAD FIXED SINGLE
HEAPSIZE         1024
EXPORTS          NotifyFunc
                 SavehWnd
```

The notification function has a standard format (described above). In order to use the MessageBox() function from within the DLL, the DLL must use a second function , SaveWnd(), to just store the calling window's handle.

The notification function NotifyFunc() shown here is only an outline. A useful notification function would take some action to avoid discarding a memory block, such as discarding the least important block. Note that no local variables are used. Notification functions cannot assume the stack segment of the calling program, as they are called from Windows' memory management logic.

⇨ NOTIFY.C C Source Code for Notification Function DLL

```c
/* notify.c  memory discard notification functions */

#include <windows.h>

static          HANDLE          hWindow = NULL ;

int FAR PASCAL LibMain (HANDLE hInstance, WORD wDataSeg, WORD wHeapSize,
        LPSTR lpszCmdLine)
{
        if (wHeapSize > 0)
                UnlockData (0) ;
        return (1) ;
}

void FAR PASCAL SavehWnd (HANDLE hWnd)
{
        hWindow = hWnd ;
}



BOOL FAR PASCAL NotifyFunc (HANDLE hMem)
{
        static int n ;

        if (hWindow == NULL)
                MessageBeep (0) ;          /* forgot to run SavehWnd - just beep */
        else
        {
        n = MessageBox (hWindow, "Memory About To Be Discarded.",
                "Warning", MB_ICONASTERISK | MB_OKCANCEL) ;
        if (n == IDCANCEL)
        {
                /* delete some other block of memory here */
                return (0) ;
        }
        }
        return (1) ;
}
```

The NMAKE file for the DLL file shown here includes the debugging switches. The key difference when compiling DLLs is that the stack segment and data segment are not the same (ASw switch with the Microsoft compile).

▷ **NOTIFY NMAKE File for NOTIFY.DLL**

```
# make file for notify library

ALL: notify.dll

CFLAGS=-c -D LINT_ARGS -ASw -Zip -Od -Gsw -W2
LFLAGS=/NOD /co /align:16

notify.obj:              notify.c
        $(CC) $(CFLAGS) notify.c

notify.dll:             notify.obj notify.def
        link $(LFLAGS) notify libentry, notify.dll, NUL, libw sdllcew, notify
        rc notify.dll
```

The main program's header file (GENERIC.H) must include function prototypes of the two exported functions. The program's definition file must also list them in the IMPORTS section.

▷ **GENERIC.DEF Module-Definition File for GENERIC.C**

```
NAME            GENERIC
DESCRIPTION     'generic windows program'
EXETYPE         WINDOWS
STUB            'WINSTUB.EXE'
CODE            PRELOAD MOVEABLE
DATA            PRELOAD MOVEABLE MULTIPLE
HEAPSIZE        1024
STACKSIZE       5120
EXPORTS         WndProc
IMPORTS         NOTIFY.NotifyFunc
                NOTIFY.SavehWnd
```

The main program sets up two global memory blocks on startup. Both are discardable. When WM_PAINT messages are received, the size and status of the two blocks are written to the window's client area. The notification function is not installed until the user clicks the "Do It!" menu item for the first time. First SavehWnd() is called to give the DLL the main window's handle. Then GlobalNotify() is called to set up the notification procedure. The notification procedure can only be set up once per program instance, so a static Boolean variable, *bSetNotify*, is used to stop GlobalNotify() from being called twice. Discarding global memory is forced by calling GlobalCompact(), requesting a memory block larger than the largest available block. At this point in the program's execution, the notification function is called by Windows. NotifyFunc() displays the message box.

▷ **GENERIC.C Program Extract of Only WndProc() Function**

```
long FAR PASCAL WndProc (HWND hWnd, unsigned iMessage, WORD wParam, LONG lParam)
{
        PAINTSTRUCT                     ps ;
        static          HANDLE          hMem1, hMem2 ;
        char                            cBuf [128] ;
        int                             nFlags1, nFlags2 ;
        DWORD                           dwFree, dwSize1, dwSize2 ;
        static          FARPROC         fpNotify ;
        static          BOOL            bSetNotify = FALSE ;

        switch (iMessage)                       /* process windows messages */
        {
                case WM_CREATE:
                        hMem1 = GlobalAlloc (GMEM_MOVEABLE |
                                GMEM_DISCARDABLE | GMEM_NOTIFY, 10240) ;
```

```
                    hMem2 = GlobalAlloc (GMEM_MOVEABLE |
                            GMEM_DISCARDABLE | GMEM_NOTIFY, 10240) ;
                    if (!hMem1 || !hMem2)
                    {
                            MessageBox (hWnd,
                                    "Could not allocate memory blocks.",
                                    "Memory Error", MB_ICONHAND | MB_OK) ;
                            DestroyWindow (hWnd) ;
                    }
                    break ;
            case WM_PAINT:
                    BeginPaint (hWnd, &ps) ;
                    nFlags1 = GlobalFlags (hMem1) ;
                    nFlags2 = GlobalFlags (hMem2) ;
                    dwSize1 = GlobalSize (hMem1) ;
                    dwSize2 = GlobalSize (hMem2) ;
                    TextOut (ps.hdc, 10, 10, cBuf, wsprintf (cBuf,
                            "hMem1 size: %li", dwSize1)) ;
                    TextOut (ps.hdc, 10, 30, cBuf, wsprintf (cBuf,
                            "LockCount = %d, Discardable = %d",
                            nFlags1 & GMEM_LOCKCOUNT,
                            (nFlags1 & GMEM_DISCARDABLE ? 1 : 0))) ;
                    TextOut (ps.hdc, 10, 50, cBuf, wsprintf (cBuf,
                            "hMem2 size: %li", dwSize2)) ;
                    TextOut (ps.hdc, 10, 70, cBuf, wsprintf (cBuf,
                            "LockCount = %d, Discardable = %d",
                            nFlags2 & GMEM_LOCKCOUNT,
                            (nFlags2 & GMEM_DISCARDABLE ? 1 : 0))) ;
                    EndPaint (hWnd, &ps) ;
                    break ;
            case WM_COMMAND:                 /* process menu items */
                    switch (wParam)
                    {
                    case IDM_DOIT:           /* User hit the "Do it" menu item */
                            if (!bSetNotify)
                            {
                                    bSetNotify = TRUE ;
                                    SavehWnd (hWnd) ;
                                    hModule = GetModuleHandle ("notify") ;
                                    fpNotify = GetProcAddress (hModule,
                                            "NotifyFunc") ;
                                    GlobalNotify (fpNotify) ;
                            }
                            dwFree = GlobalCompact (0) ;      /* check free space */
                            GlobalCompact (dwFree + 64) ;     /* force discard */
                            InvalidateRect (hWnd, NULL, TRUE) ;     /* force paint */
                            break ;
                    case IDM_QUIT:           /* send end of application message */
                            DestroyWindow (hWnd) ;
                            break ;
                    }
                    break ;
            case WM_DESTROY:                 /* stop application */
                    FreeProcInstance (fpNotify) ;
                    GlobalFree (hMem1) ;
                    default:                 /* default windows message processing */
                    return DefWindowProc (hWnd, iMessage, wParam, lParam) ;
    }
    return (0L) ;
}
```

GLOBALPAGELOCK
☐ Win 2.0   ■ Win 3.0   ■ Win 3.1

Purpose	Stops a memory block from being moved in linear memory, or from being written to disk (virtual memory inhibited).
Syntax	WORD **GlobalPageLock** (WORD *wSelector*);

Description   Although pointers to locked memory blocks remain valid, the block may still be moved in physical memory. Locked memory blocks can also be temporarily written to disk as virtual memory storage. Calling GlobalPageLock() physically locks down a memory block. The block will not be moved and will not be written to virtual (disk) space. Each call to GlobalPageLock() increases the memory block's lock-count by one. An equal number of calls to GlobalPageUnlock() is required to unlock the memory block.

Uses   Normally not used. Page-locked memory blocks inhibit Windows' ability to optimize memory use. Page-locked blocks may be needed for device drivers and interrupt driven routines that expect to write to a fixed address in real address space and that need rapid response.

Returns   WORD, the page-lock-count. Returns zero on error.

See Also   GlobalPageUnlock(), GlobalDosAlloc()

Parameters
wSelector   WORD: The selector for the memory block. This is the protected-mode equivalent of an offset.

Example   See the example under the GlobalDosAlloc() function description.

GLOBALPAGEUNLOCK   □ Win 2.0   ■ Win 3.0   ■ Win 3.1

Purpose   Unlocks a memory block locked with GlobalPageLock().

Syntax   WORD **GlobalPageUnlock** (WORD *wSelector*);

Description   Each call to GlobalPageLock() for a given selector increases the page-lock-count by one. Calling GlobalPageUnlock() decreases the page-lock-count by one. An equal number of calls to GlobalPageUnlock() is required to unlock a memory block.

Uses   Unlocking a memory block locked with GlobalPageLock(). Once unlocked, the block can be moved in linear memory and be paged to disk (virtual memory).

Returns   WORD, the page-lock-count after the function operates. Returns zero on error.

See Also   GlobalPageLock(), GlobalDosAlloc()

Parameters
wSelector   WORD: The selector for the memory block. This is the protected-mode equivalent of an offset.

Example   See the example under the GlobalDosAlloc() function description.

GLOBALREALLOC   ■ Win 2.0   ■ Win 3.0   ■ Win 3.1

Purpose   Changes the size and/or attributes of a global memory block.

Syntax   HANDLE **GlobalReAlloc**(HANDLE *hMem*, WORD *wBytes*, WORD *wFlags*);

Description   When a memory block is allocated with GlobalAlloc(), it can be resized using GlobalReAlloc() as needed to fit the program's data needs. Discardable memory blocks use this function to restore the memory size block.

Uses   Usually used to increase the size of a data block as new items are added. It can also be used to change the memory attributes from moveable to fixed, etc.

Returns   HANDLE, the handle of the resized memory block. Returns NULL on error. The returned value will equal *hMem* unless the GMEM_MOVEABLE flag is set, or unless the block was reallocated past a multiple of 64K (64K minus 17 bytes in standard mode).

See Also   GlobalAlloc(), GlobalDiscard()

Parameters
hMem   HANDLE: The handle of the memory block in the local heap, initially allocated with LocalAlloc().
dwBytes   DWORD: The new size of the memory block.

wFlags WORD: The type of memory to reallocate. This should be one or more of the flags listed in Table 14-5, combined with the C language binary OR operator (|). Choose either GMEM_FIXED or GMEM_MOVEABLE, and then combine the choice with other options.

Value	Meaning	⊠
GMEM_DISCARDABLE	Memory that can be discarded if Windows needs to make room. Used only with GMEM_MODIFY.	
GMEM_MODIFY	Specifies that the attributes of the memory block will be changed, not the memory block size. The *dwBytes* parameter will be ignored.	
GMEM_MOVEABLE	Moveable memory. If *wBytes* is zero, this flag causes a previously fixed block to be freed, or a previously moveable object to be discarded. This only occurs if the block has not been locked. If *wBytes* is nonzero and the *hMem* block is fixed, GlobalReAlloc() will move the block to a new fixed location. The means that the returned value will not be the same as *hMem*. Use with GMEM_MODIFY to make a fixed memory block moveable.	
GMEM_NOCOMPACT	Memory in the local heap is not compacted or discarded to make room for the resized memory block. Ignored if GMEM_MODIFY is set.	
GMEM_NODISCARD	Memory in the local heap is not discarded to make room for the resized memory block. Ignored if GMEM_MODIFY is set.	
GMEM_ZEROINIT	Initialize the new part of the allocated memory block to zero. Ignored if GMEM_MODIFY is set.	

Table 14-5. GlobalReAlloc( ) Flags.

Caution If the program's data segment is defined as moveable in the .DEF file, calling LocalAlloc() may cause the data segment to move. This will invalidate any far pointers.

Example See the example under GlobalAlloc().

GLOBALSIZE ■ Win 2.0 ■ Win 3.0 ■ Win 3.1

Purpose Determines the size of a memory block allocated in the global heap.

Syntax DWORD **GlobalSize**(HANDLE *hMem*);

Description This function determines the actual number of bytes allocated in the global heap by GlobalAlloc() and/or GlobalReAlloc(). The number of bytes may be slightly larger than the number requested, as global memory blocks are rounded upward to the nearest 32 bytes.

Returns DWORD, the actual size of the memory block in bytes. NULL if *hMem* is not a valid memory handle. The return value is invalid if the memory block has been discarded.

See Also GlobalFlags, GlobalAlloc()

Parameters
hMem HANDLE: The handle of the global memory block.

Example See the example under GlobalAlloc().

GLOBALUNFIX □ Win 2.0 ■ Win 3.0 ■ Win 3.1

Purpose Frees a memory block fixed by GlobalFix().

Syntax BOOL **GlobalUnfix** (HANDLE *hMem*);

Description Each call to GlobalFix() increases the memory block's lock count by one. GlobalUnfix() reduces the lock-count by one. An equal number of calls to GlobalUnfix() is required to release the fixed memory block.

Uses	Used with GlobalFix() in applications that require a memory block to remain at the same location in linear memory.
Returns	BOOL. Zero if the lock-count decreased to zero (block no longer fixed). Nonzero if the lock-count is above zero.
See Also	GlobalFix(), GlobalAlloc()
Parameters	
hMem	HANDLE: A handle to a global memory block. This is the value returned by GlobalAlloc().
Example	See the example under the GlobalFix() function description.

GLOBALUNLOCK
■ Win 2.0　　■ Win 3.0　　■ Win 3.1

Purpose	Unlocks a locked memory block in the global heap.
Syntax	BOOL **GlobalUnlock**(HANDLE *hMem*);
Description	Unlocks a memory block. Once unlocked, the memory block can be moved by Windows, unless the block with allocated with the GMEM_FIXED flag. Unlocked blocks can also be discarded, if they were allocated with the GMEM_MOVEABLE | GMEM_DISCARDABLE style. If a memory block is locked more than once without being unlocked, the block's reference count will be more than one. GlobalUnlock() will have to be called the number of times specified by the reference count before the block can be moved or discarded.
Uses	Memory blocks should be unlocked as soon after being locked as possible. Doing so makes it possible for Windows to make maximum use of the memory space.
Returns	BOOL. Zero if the block's lock-count is zero (completely unlocked), nonzero if not.
See Also	GlobalLock(), GlobalAlloc()
Parameters	
hMem	HANDLE: The handle of the global memory block to unlock. This is the value initially returned by GlobalAlloc().
Example	See the example under GlobalAlloc().

GLOBALUNWIRE
■ Win 2.0　　■ Win 3.0　　□ Win 3.1

Purpose	Unwires a wired (locked) block in the global heap.
Syntax	BOOL **GlobalUnWire**(HANDLE *hMem*);
Description	This function unlocks a block locked in low memory by GlobalWire(). If more than one call to GlobalWire(), GlobalLock(), or GlobalFix() has been made, the lock-count for the memory block will be greater than one. A matching number of calls to GlobalUnWire(), GlobalUnlock(), and GlobalUnfix() will be needed to unlock the memory block.
Uses	There should be one call to GlobalUnWire() for every call to GlobalWire() in an application.
Returns	BOOL. TRUE if the segment is unlocked, FALSE if not.
See Also	GlobalWire(), GlobalLock(), GlobalFix()
Parameters	
hMem	HANDLE: The handle of the global memory block to unwire. This is the value returned by GlobalAlloc() or GlobalReAlloc() the last time the block was created or resized.
Example	This example, illustrated in Figure 14-18, allocates two blocks of memory in the global heap. When the user clicks the "Do It!"

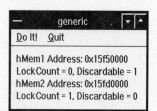

Figure 14-18. GlobalWire() and GlobalUnWire() Example.

menu item, the program "wires" the second block, locking it in low memory. The block is "unwired" when the program exits.

```
long FAR PASCAL WndProc (HWND hWnd, unsigned iMessage, WORD wParam, LONG lParam)
{
        PAINTSTRUCT                     ps ;
        static          HANDLE          hMem1, hMem2 ;
        LPSTR                           pMem1, pMem2 ;
        char                            cBuf [128] ;
        int                             nFlags1, nFlags2 ;

        switch (iMessage)                               /* process windows messages */
        {
                case WM_CREATE:
                        hMem1 = GlobalAlloc (GMEM_MOVEABLE |
                                GMEM_DISCARDABLE, 10240) ;
                        hMem2 = GlobalAlloc (GMEM_MOVEABLE, 10240) ;
                        if (!hMem1 || !hMem2)
                        {
                                MessageBox (hWnd,
                                        "Could not allocate memory blocks.",
                                        "Memory Error", MB_ICONHAND | MB_OK) ;
                                DestroyWindow (hWnd) ;
                        }
                        break ;
                case WM_PAINT:
                        BeginPaint (hWnd, &ps) ;
                        nFlags1 = GlobalFlags (hMem1) ;
                        nFlags2 = GlobalFlags (hMem2) ;
                        if ((pMem1 = GlobalLock (hMem1)) &&
                                (pMem2 = GlobalLock (hMem2)))
                        {
                                TextOut (ps.hdc, 10, 10, cBuf, wsprintf (cBuf,
                                        "hMem1 Address: 0x%lx", pMem1)) ;
                                TextOut (ps.hdc, 10, 30, cBuf, wsprintf (cBuf,
                                        "LockCount = %d, Discardable = %d",
                                        nFlags1 & GMEM_LOCKCOUNT,
                                        (nFlags1 & GMEM_DISCARDABLE ? 1 : 0))) ;
                                TextOut (ps.hdc, 10, 50, cBuf, wsprintf (cBuf,
                                        "hMem2 Address: 0x%lx", pMem2)) ;
                                TextOut (ps.hdc, 10, 70, cBuf, wsprintf (cBuf,
                                        "LockCount = %d, Discardable = %d",
                                        nFlags2 & GMEM_LOCKCOUNT,
                                        (nFlags2 & GMEM_DISCARDABLE ? 1 : 0))) ;
                                GlobalUnlock (hMem1) ;
                                GlobalUnlock (hMem2) ;
                        }
                        EndPaint (hWnd, &ps) ;
                        break ;
                case WM_COMMAND:                /* process menu items */
                        switch (wParam)
                        {
                        case IDM_DOIT:          /* User hit the "Do it" menu item */
                                nFlags2 = GlobalFlags (hMem2) ;
                                if (!(nFlags2 & GMEM_LOCKCOUNT))
                                        GlobalWire (hMem2) ;
                                InvalidateRect (hWnd, NULL, TRUE) ;     /* force paint */
                                break ;
                        case IDM_QUIT:          /* send end of application message */
                                DestroyWindow (hWnd) ;
                                break ;
                        }
                        break ;
                case WM_DESTROY:                /* stop application */
                        GlobalUnWire (hMem2) ;
                        GlobalFree (hMem1) ;
                        GlobalFree (hMem2) ;
                        PostQuitMessage (0) ;
```

```
                        break ;
        default:                            /* default windows message processing */
                return DefWindowProc (hWnd, iMessage, wParam, lParam) ;
        }
        return (OL) ;
}
```

GLOBALWIRE
■ Win 2.0   ■ Win 3.0   □ Win 3.1

Purpose   Locks a global memory block in low memory.

Syntax   LPSTR **GlobalWire**(HANDLE *hMem*);

Description   This is similar to GlobalLock(), except that Windows attempts to move the memory block into low memory before the block is locked. This reduces the impact of having a fixed block in the middle of the global heap.

Uses   GlobalWire() is preferable to GlobalLock() if the application can allow the block to be moved before it is locked. Applications should avoid locking memory, and should unlock locked memory blocks as soon as possible.

Returns   LPSTR, the new segment location. NULL on error.

See Also   GlobalUnWire(), GlobalLock(), GlobalFix()

Parameters
hMem   HANDLE: The handle of the global memory block to unwire. This is the value returned by Global-Alloc() or GlobalReAlloc() the last time the block was created or resized.

Example   See the example above under GlobalUnWire().

LIMITEMSPAGES
■ Win 2.0   ■ Win 3.0   ■ Win 3.1

Purpose   Limits the amount of expanded memory that Windows will assign to an application.

Syntax   void **LimitEmsPages**(DWORD *dwKbytes*);

Description   This function has no effect unless expanded memory is installed and is being used under Windows. It will not affect applications that bypass Windows' memory manager by directly calling INT 67H.

Returns   No returned value (void).

Parameters
dwKbytes   DWORD: The number of kilobytes of expanded memory the application calling this function should be able to access.

Example

```
Long FAR PASCAL WndProc (HWND hWnd, unsigned iMessage, WORD wParam, LONG lParam)
{
        switch (iMessage)                       /* process windows messages */
        {
        case WM_COMMAND:                        /* process menu items */
                switch (wParam)
                {
                case IDM_DOIT:                  /* User hit the "Do it" menu item */
                        LimitEmsPages (10) ;
                        break ;
```
[Other program lines]

LOADMODULE
□ Win 2.0   ■ Win 3.0   ■ Win 3.1

Purpose   Loads and executes a Windows program, or creates a new instance of the program if one or more instances are already running.

Syntax   HANDLE **LoadModule**(LPSTR *lpModuleName*, LPVOID *lpParameterBlock*);

Description	This function allows one Windows application to load and run others. The function can pass the loaded file a command line, like a file name to load on startup.
Uses	Useful for creating master applications that run a series of "slave" programs. Also handy for loading the standard Windows applications like NOTEPAD.
Returns	HANDLE, the instance of the loaded module. LoadModule() returns after the application loaded enters its message loop. If the value returned is less than 32, the module was not loaded. The possible error values are listed in Table 14-6.

Value	Meaning
0	Out of memory.
2	File not found.
3	Path not found.
5	Attempt to dynamically link to a task.
6	Library requires separate data segments for each task.
10	Incorrect Windows version.
11	Non-Windows .EXE file.
12	OS/2 application.
13	DOS 4.0 application.
14	Unknown .EXE type.
15	Attempt to load a .EXE file created for an earlier version of Windows. Only affects standard and 386 enhanced modes.
16	Attempt to load a second .EXE containing multiple, writeable data segments.
17	Attempt to load a second instance linked to a nonshareable DLL.
18	Attempt to load a protected mode-only application in real mode.

Table 14-6. LoadModule() Error Codes.

See Also	WinExec() accomplishes the same purpose, but is somewhat simpler to use.
Parameters	
lpModuleName	LPSTR: A pointer to a null-terminated string containing the name of the application to run. If no extension is included, .EXE is assumed. If *lpModuleName* does not contain a directory path, Windows will search for the file based on the following search order:

1. In the current directory.
2. In the Windows directory. This is the directory containing WIN.COM. Use GetWindowsDirectory() to determine the path name of this directory.
3. In the Windows system directory. Use the GetSystemDirectory() function to determine the path name of this directory.
4. In the directories specified in the PATH environment variable. This is the PATH command that is executed from DOS, before Windows is loaded. Typical systems set their PATH values in the AUTOEXEC.BAT file.
5. In the directories mapped in a network.

lpParameterBlock LPVOID: This is a data structure containing four fields. For some reason, WINDOWS.H does not include this structure. Define the PARAMBLOCK data type as follows:

```
typedef struct tagParamBlock
{
        WORD            wEnvSeg ;              /* usually NULL */
        LPSTR           lpCmdLine ;            /* command line string */
        LPVOID          lpCmdShow ;            /* WORD w[2] */
        DWORD           dwReserved ;           /* always NULL */
} PARAMBLOCK ;
```

The meaning of each of the fields is as follows.

wEnvSeg   WORD: The segment address of the environment under which the module is to run. This is the location of the environment variables like PATH. Set to NULL to use the Windows environment (normal case).

lpCmdLine   LPSTR: A pointer to a null-terminated character string containing the command line. This is typically the file name that the application will run. The first character should be a blank space. Set to a null string ("")if no command line is to be passed.

lpCmdShow   LPVOID: This must point to an array of two WORD values. Set the first one equal to the number two. Set the second equal to one of the ShowWindow() style values in Table 14-7.

Value	Meaning
SW_HIDE	Hides the window. The top window on Windows' list is activated.
SW_MINIMIZE	Minimizes the window. The top window on Windows' list is activated.
SW_RESTORE	Activates and displays the window (same as SW_SHOWNORMAL).
SW_SHOW	Activates and displays the window in its current size and position.
SW_SHOWMAXIMIZED	Activates and maximizes the window.
SW_SHOWMINIMIZED	Activates and minimizes the window.
SW_SHOWMINNOACTIVE	Displays and minimizes the window. The currently active window remains active.
SW_SHOWNA	Displays the window, but does not change which window is active.
SW_SHOWNOACTIVE	Displays the window, but does not change which window is active.
SW_SHOWNORMAL	Activates and displays the window. If the window was minimized or maximized, the window is returned to its previous size and position.

Table 14-7. lpCmdShow ShowWindow( ) Styles.

dwReserved   DWORD: A reserved value. Set equal to NULL.

Example   This program, illustrated in Figure 14-19, creates a window that automatically loads the NOTEPAD.EXE application and loads READ-ME.TXT into NOTEPAD (if the files exist). The program loads NOTE-PAD.EXE while processing its own WM_CREATE message, so NOTEPAD appears before the GENERIC application. GENERIC displays the full file name and reference count of the module it loaded (NOTEPAD). When the user clicks the "Do It!" menu item, the NOTEPAD application is sent a WM_DESTROY message, removing the program from memory.

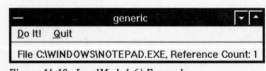

Figure 14-19. LoadModule( ) Example.

```
typedef struct tagParamBlock
{
        WORD            wEnvSeg ;
        LPSTR           lpCmdLine ;
        LPVOID          lpCmdShow ;
        DWORD           dwReserved ;
```

```
} PARAMBLOCK ;

Long FAR PASCAL WndProc (HWND hWnd, unsigned iMessage, WORD wParam, LONG lParam)
{
        PAINTSTRUCT             ps ;
        PARAMBLOCK              pb ;
        char                    cWindName [128] ;
        char                    cBuf [256], cCommandLine [] = " readme.txt" ;
        WORD                    wCmdShow [2] ;
        HANDLE                  hModule ;
        int                     nCount ;
        HWND                    hNotePad ;

        switch (iMessage)                       /* process windows messages */
        {
                case WM_CREATE:
                        pb.wEnvSeg = 0 ;
                        pb.lpCmdLine = (LPSTR) cCommandLine ;
                        wCmdShow [0] = 2 ;
                        wCmdShow [1] = SW_SHOWNORMAL ;
                        pb.lpCmdShow = wCmdShow ;
                        pb.dwReserved = NULL ;
                        LoadModule ("notepad.exe", (LPVOID) &pb) ;
                        break ;
                case WM_PAINT:
                        BeginPaint (hWnd, &ps) ;
                        hModule = GetModuleHandle ("notepad") ;
                        GetModuleFileName (hModule, cWindName, 127) ;
                        nCount = GetModuleUsage (hModule) ;
                        TextOut (ps.hdc, 10, 10, cBuf, wsprintf (cBuf,
                                "File %s, Reference Count: %d",
                                (LPSTR) cWindName, nCount)) ;
                        EndPaint (hWnd, &ps) ;
                        break ;
                case WM_COMMAND:                /* process menu items */
                        switch (wParam)
                        {
                        case IDM_DOIT:          /* User hit the "Do it" menu item */
                                hNotePad = FindWindow (NULL, "Notepad - README.TXT") ;
                                if (hNotePad)
                                        SendMessage (hNotePad, WM_DESTROY, 0, 0L) ;
                                break ;
                        case IDM_QUIT:          /* send end of application message */
                                DestroyWindow (hWnd) ;
                                break ;
                        }
                        break ;
                case WM_DESTROY:                /* stop application */
                        PostQuitMessage (0) ;
                        break ;
                default:                        /* default windows message processing */
                        return DefWindowProc (hWnd, iMessage, wParam, lParam) ;
        }
        return (0L) ;
}
```

LocalAlloc
■ Win 2.0   ■ Win 3.0   ■ Win 3.1

Purpose	Allocates a block of memory in the local heap.
Syntax	HANDLE **LocalAlloc**(WORD *wFlags*, WORD *wBytes*);
Description	This is the first step in allocating and using memory in the local heap. The maximum amount of memory in the local heap is 64K, less the stack and static variable storage sizes.
Uses	Local memory is ideal for small memory items. Access to local memory is faster than to global memory, as only a 16-bit address is needed.
Returns	HANDLE, the handle to the memory block allocated. Returns NULL on error.

See Also   LocalLock(), LocalReAlloc(), LocalFree()

Parameters

wFlags   WORD: One or more of the flags in Table 14-8, combined with the C language binary OR operator (|). Choose either LMEM_FIXED or LMEM_MOVEABLE, and then combine the choice with other options.

Value	Meaning
LMEM_DISCARDABLE	Allocates memory that can be discarded if Windows needs to make room. Used only with LMEM_MOVEABLE.
LMEM_FIXED	Allocates fixed memory. Do not use this unless absolutely necessary. Fixed memory limits Windows' ability to optimize memory use.
LMEM_MOVEABLE	Allocates moveable memory.
LMEM_NOCOMPACT	Memory in the local heap is not compacted or discarded to make room for the new memory block.
LMEM_NODISCARD	Memory in the local heap is not discarded to make room for the new memory block.
LMEM_ZEROINIT	Initialize the new allocated memory block contents to zero.

Table 14-8. LocalAlloc() Flags.

Whenever possible, use LMEM_MOVEABLE. WINDOWS.H includes two common combinations:

```
#define LHND        (LMEM_MOVEABLE | LMEM_ZEROINIT)
#define LPTR        (LMEM_FIXED | LMEM_ZEROINIT)
```

wBytes   WORD: The number of bytes to allocate. The actual number of bytes allocated may be slightly higher, to ensure that the boundary ends on an even-numbered address.

Example   This example shows the allocation of memory on the local heap to store a string. When the program first starts (WM_CREATE received), room for 27 characters is allocated. A string is stored in the memory block. This string, along with the

Figure 14-20. LocalAlloc() Example.

block size and several memory status bytes, is displayed on the window's client area every time a WM_PAINT message is received. When the user clicks the "Do It!" menu item, the memory block is reallocated to make room for another 27 characters. The additional characters are written to the buffer and are displayed when WM_PAINT messages are processed. Repeatedly clicking the "Do It!" menu item does not allocate more room in this case. The block is simply reallocated to the same size, resulting in no change. Figure 14-20 shows the window's appearance after the "Do It!" menu item was clicked.

```
Long FAR PASCAL WndProc (HWND hWnd, unsigned iMessage, WORD wParam, LONG lParam)
{
        PAINTSTRUCT             ps ;
        static   HANDLE         hMem ;
        char                    *pMem, cBuf [128] ;
        int                     i, nSize, nFlags ;

        switch (iMessage)                       /* process windows messages */
        {
                case WM_CREATE:
                        if (hMem = LocalAlloc (LMEM_MOVEABLE, 27))
                        {
                                if (pMem = LocalLock (hMem))
                                {
```

```
                                for (i = 0 ; i < 26 ; i++)
                                        *pMem++ = 'A' + i ;
                                *pMem = 0 ;
                                LocalUnlock (hMem) ;
                        }
                        else
                                MessageBox (hWnd,
                                        "Could not lock memory block.",
                                        "Memory Error", MB_ICONHAND | MB_OK) ;
                }
                else
                {
                        MessageBox (hWnd, "Could not allocate memory",
                                "Memory Error", MB_ICONHAND | MB_OK) ;
                        DestroyWindow (hWnd) ;
                }
                break ;
        case WM_PAINT:
                BeginPaint (hWnd, &ps) ;
                if (pMem = LocalLock (hMem))
                {
                        nSize = LocalSize (hMem) ;
                        nFlags = LocalFlags (hMem) ;
                        TextOut (ps.hdc, 10, 10, cBuf, wsprintf (cBuf,
                                "The memory block is %d bytes in size.",
                                nSize)) ;
                        TextOut (ps.hdc, 10, 30, cBuf, wsprintf (cBuf,
                                "Contains: %s", (LPSTR) pMem)) ;
                        TextOut (ps.hdc, 10, 50, cBuf, wsprintf (cBuf,
                                "Flags: Discardable: %d, Lock Count: %d",
                                nFlags & LMEM_DISCARDABLE,
                                nFlags & LMEM_LOCKCOUNT)) ;
                        LocalUnlock (hMem) ;
                }
                EndPaint (hWnd, &ps) ;
                break ;
        case WM_COMMAND:                        /* process menu items */
                switch (wParam)
                {
                case IDM_DOIT:                  /* User hit the "Do it" menu item */
                        if (hMem = LocalReAlloc (hMem, (26 * 2) + 1,
                                LMEM_MOVEABLE))
                        {
                                if (pMem = LocalLock (hMem))
                                {
                                        for (i = 0 ; i < 26 ; i++)
                                                *pMem++ ;/* skip over old stuff */
                                        for (i = 0 ; i < 26 ; i++)
                                                *pMem++ = 'a' + i ;
                                        *pMem = 0 ;
                                        LocalUnlock (hMem) ;
                                }
                                else
                                        MessageBox (hWnd,
                                        "Could not lock memory block.",
                                        "Memory Error", MB_ICONHAND | MB_OK) ;
                        }
                        else
                                MessageBox (hWnd, "Could not re-allocate memory",
                                        "Memory Error", MB_ICONHAND | MB_OK) ;
                        InvalidateRect (hWnd, NULL, TRUE) ;/* force paint */
                        break ;
                case IDM_QUIT:                  /* send end of application message */
                        LocalFree (hMem) ;
                        DestroyWindow (hWnd) ;
                        break ;
                }
                break ;
        case WM_DESTROY:                        /* stop application */
```

```
                        PostQuitMessage (0) ;
                        break ;
            default:                        /* default windows message processing */
                        return DefWindowProc (hWnd, iMessage, wParam, lParam) ;
        }
        return (0L) ;
}
```

LOCALCOMPACT   ■ Win 2.0   ■ Win 3.0   ■ Win 3.1

Purpose   Determines the amount of available memory in the local heap, compacting memory if necessary to increase space.

Syntax   WORD **LocalCompact**(WORD *wMinFree*);

Description   First, LocalCompact() checks to see if there are *wMinFree* bytes available in one contiguous area of the local heap. If not, LocalCompact() moves all unlocked, moveable blocks to the high memory end of the heap. If this still is not enough room, enough discardable blocks are removed from memory to make room for the requested size, or blocks are removed until there are no more discardable blocks to remove.

Uses   Used to make room in the heap. If an application is creating and discarding memory in the heap constantly, the heap may become fragmented, which limits the size of blocks that can be allocated. LocalCompact() reshuffles the memory blocks to make room available for the next LocalAlloc() or LocalReAlloc() function call.

Returns   WORD, the number of bytes in the largest available block of free memory in the local heap.

See Also   LocalAlloc(), LocalReAlloc(), LocalLock(), LocalUnlock(), LocalFree()

Parameters
wMinFree   WORD: The number of bytes desired. If *wMinFree* is zero, the function returns the amount of memory in the largest contiguous free block of memory, without compacting.

Related Messages WM_COMPACTING

Example   This example, which is illustrated in Figure 14-21, allocates four blocks of memory, each 64 bytes in length. Block 0 is moveable, block 1 is moveable and discardable, block 2 is moveable, and block 3 is fixed. Each block's address is displayed (after locking the blocks) when the application processes a WM_PAINT message. When the user clicks the

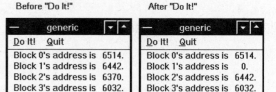

Figure 14-21. LocalCompact( ) and LocalDiscard( ) Example.

"Do It!" menu item, block 1 is discarded. The heap is forced to be compacted by requesting a block of memory larger than the largest available block. After compacting, block 2 is moved into discarded block 1's place. Block 3 remains at the same location because it was given the LMEM_FIXED attribute.

```
Long FAR PASCAL WndProc (HWND hWnd, unsigned iMessage, WORD wParam, LONG lParam)
{
        PAINTSTRUCT             ps ;
        static      HANDLE      hMem [4] ;
        char                    *pMem [4], cBuf [128] ;
        int                     i, nFree ;

        switch (iMessage)                       /* process windows messages */
        {
```

```
            case WM_CREATE:
                    hMem [0] = LocalAlloc (LMEM_MOVEABLE, 64) ;
                    hMem [1] = LocalAlloc (LMEM_MOVEABLE | LMEM_DISCARDABLE, 64) ;
                    hMem [2] = LocalAlloc (LMEM_MOVEABLE, 64) ;
                    hMem [3] = LocalAlloc (LMEM_FIXED, 64) ;
                    break ;
            case WM_PAINT:
                    BeginPaint (hWnd, &ps) ;
                    for (i = 0 ; i < 4 ; i++)
                    {
                            pMem [i] = LocalLock (hMem [i]) ;
                            TextOut (ps.hdc, 10, 20 * i, cBuf, wsprintf (cBuf,
                                    "Block %d's address is %6d.", i, pMem [i])) ;
                            LocalUnlock (hMem [i]) ;
                    }
                    EndPaint (hWnd, &ps) ;
                    break ;
            case WM_COMMAND:                    /* process menu items */
                    switch (wParam)
                    {
                    case IDM_DOIT:              /* User hit the "Do it" menu item */
                            LocalDiscard (hMem [1]) ;
                            nFree = LocalCompact (0) ;          /* find free space */
                            LocalCompact (nFree + 16) ;        /* force compact */
                            InvalidateRect (hWnd, NULL, TRUE) ;        /* force paint */
                            break ;
                    case IDM_QUIT:             /* send end of application message */
                            for (i = 0 ; i < 4 ; i ++)
                                    LocalFree (hMem [i]) ;
                            PostQuitMessage (NULL) ;
                            break ;
                    }
                    break ;
            case WM_DESTROY:                   /* stop application */
                    PostQuitMessage (0) ;
                    break ;
            default:                           /* default windows message processing */
                    return DefWindowProc (hWnd, iMessage, wParam, lParam) ;
        }
        return (0L) ;
}
```

LOCALDISCARD

■ Win 2.0   ■ Win 3.0   □ Win 3.1

Purpose	Discards a memory block from the local heap.
Syntax	HANDLE **LocalDiscard**(HANDLE *hMem*).
Description	Discarding a memory block makes the space available for allocating other blocks of memory. The *hMem* handle remains usable after the block is discarded, although it does not point to active memory. *hMem* can be reused by using LocalReAlloc() to allocate another block of memory. Only blocks allocated with the LMEM_DISCARDABLE and LMEM_MOVEABLE flags set can be discarded.
Uses	Discarding memory to make room for other blocks. Note that LocalFree() removes the memory block and invalidates the memory handle. LocalDiscard() discards the memory block, but the *hMem* handle remains valid.
Returns	HANDLE. Equal to *hMem* if the function was successful, NULL on error.
See Also	LocalFree(), LocalReAlloc()
Parameters	
hMem	HANDLE: The handle to the discardable memory block, returned by LocalAlloc().
Example	See the previous example under LocalCompact().

LOCALFLAGS
■ Win 2.0   ■ Win 3.0   ■ Win 3.1

Purpose	Determines if a memory block in the local heap is locked, discarded, or potentially discardable.
Syntax	WORD **LocalFlags**(HANDLE *hMem*);
Description	This function checks the status of a memory block allocated in the local heap. If a memory block is locked with LocalLock() more than once without calling LocalUnlock(), the block's lock-count will be more than one. LocalUnlock() will have to be called as many times as the lock-count to unlock the memory area. Memory blocks can be discarded using LocalDiscard() and still have valid handles. LocalFlags() will determine if the memory block has been discarded, or if it was allocated using the LMEM_DISCARDABLE flag.
Uses	To check the validity of a memory handle, or to check if a memory block has been locked more than once.
Returns	WORD. The high-order byte contains one of the flags in Table 14-9.

Value	Meaning	⊠
LMEM_DISCARDABLE	The block was allocated with the LMEM_DISCARDABLE flag.	
LMEM_DISCARDED	The block has been discarded. The LocalReAlloc() function will need to be called to make the memory area usable.	

Table 14-9. LocalFlags() Flags.

	The low-order byte contains the lock-count of the memory block. Combine the returned word with LMEM_LOCKCOUNT using the C language binary AND operator (&) to determine the lock-count.
See Also	LocalAlloc(), LocalDiscard(), LocalReAlloc()
Parameters	
hMem	HANDLE: The handle to the memory block allocated in the local heap with LocalAlloc().
Example	See the example under LocalAlloc().

LOCALFREE
■ Win 2.0   ■ Win 3.0   ■ Win 3.1

Purpose	Frees a block of memory allocated in the local heap.
Syntax	HANDLE **LocalFree**(HANDLE *hMem*);
Description	Freeing a memory block returns the memory to the system for reuse. All memory blocks allocated within an application should be freed before the application exits, to return the memory to Windows.
Uses	There should be a call to LocalFree() for every call to LocalAlloc() in a program.
Returns	HANDLE, equal to *hMem* if the memory block was freed. NULL on error.
See Also	LocalAlloc(), LocalDiscard(), LocalReAlloc()
Parameters	
hMem	HANDLE: The handle to the memory block allocated in the local heap with LocalAlloc().
Example	See the example under LocalAlloc() for a complete example. The example below shows a short-cut way to allocate a small block of local memory for a quick purpose, and then immediately delete it. The shortcut takes advantage of the fact that the block is allocated using the LMEM_FIXED attribute. The block does not have to be locked and unlocked. This techinque is only suitable for blocks that are used for a quick purpose and then discarded.

```
long FAR PASCAL WndProc (HWND hWnd, unsigned iMessage, WORD wParam, LONG lParam)
{
        PAINTSTRUCT             ps ;
        PSTR                    pStr, pS2 ;
        int                     i ;

        switch (iMessage)                       /* process windows messages */
        {
                case WM_PAINT:
                        pStr = (char NEAR *) LocalAlloc (LMEM_FIXED | LMEM_ZEROINIT,
                                27) ;
                        pS2 = pStr ;
                        for (i = 0 ; i < 26 ; i++)
                                *pS2++ = 'A' + i ;
                        BeginPaint (hWnd, &ps) ;
                        TextOut (ps.hdc, 10, 10, pStr, 26) ;
                        EndPaint (hWnd, &ps) ;
                        LocalFree ((LOCALHANDLE) pStr) ;
                        break ;
```

[Other program lines]

LOCALHANDLE

■ Win 2.0   ■ Win 3.0   ■ Win 3.1

Purpose	Retrieves the handle of a memory block, given the address.
Syntax	HANDLE **LocalHandle**(WORD *wMem*);
Description	This function returns the handle to a local memory block, given the address of the block.
Uses	Used with fixed memory blocks to retrieve the handle so that the block can be freed using LocalFree().
Returns	HANDLE, the local memory block's handle.
See Also	LocalFree()
Parameters	
wMem	WORD: The address of the local memory block.
Example	This example illustrates a number of bad practices, so use the example as what NOT to do. The program allocates and locks a local memory buffer. The address is saved as the static variable *pMem*, and a text string is copied into the buffer. This string is displayed when a WM_PAINT message is received. Note that the memory buffer is not unlocked (it should be). When the user clicks the "Do It!" menu item, the local memory block is freed. This invalidates the memory block, but the static handle *pMem* remains unchanged. The WM_PAINT messages will start to output garbage, as the memory once used by the text block is used for other purposes by Windows.

```
long FAR PASCAL WndProc (HWND hWnd, unsigned iMessage, WORD wParam, LONG lParam)
{
        PAINTSTRUCT             ps ;
        HANDLE                  hMem ;
        static          char    *pMem ;
        char                    cBuf [128] ;

        switch (iMessage)                       /* process windows messages */
        {
                case WM_CREATE:
                        hMem = LocalAlloc (LMEM_MOVEABLE, 128) ;
                        pMem = LocalLock (hMem) ;
                        lstrcpy (pMem, "This is bad example - fixed memory") ;
                        break ;
                case WM_PAINT:
                        BeginPaint (hWnd, &ps) ;
                        TextOut (ps.hdc, 10, 10, pMem, lstrlen (pMem)) ;
                        EndPaint (hWnd, &ps) ;
                        break ;
```

```
case WM_COMMAND:                /* process menu items */
        switch (wParam)
        {
        case IDM_DOIT:          /* Free the memory block */
                LocalFree (LocalHandle ((WORD) pMem)) ;
                break ;
```

[Other program lines]

LocalLock

Purpose	Locks an allocated memory block in the local heap.
Syntax	PSTR **LocalLock**(HANDLE *hMem*);
Description	Memory blocks allocated with LocalAlloc() must be locked before data can be written to or read from the memory area. The block should be unlocked with LocalUnlock() as soon after use as possible.
Uses	Used to "realize" a memory pointer. This means that the return value is a far pointer to a block of memory.
Returns	PSTR, a near pointer to the beginning of the memory area.
See Also	LocalUnlock(), LocalAlloc()
Parameters	
hMem	HANDLE: A handle to the memory area allocated with LocalAlloc().
Example	See the example under LocalAlloc().

LocalReAlloc

Purpose	Changes the size and/or attributes of a local memory block.
Syntax	HANDLE **LocalReAlloc**(HANDLE *hMem*, WORD *wBytes*, WORD *wFlags*);
Description	Once a memory block is allocated with LocalAlloc(), it can be resized using LocalReAlloc() as needed to fit the program's data needs. Discardable memory blocks use this function to restore the memory block.
Uses	Usually used to increase the size of a data block as new items are added. It can also be used to change the memory attributes from moveable to fixed, etc.
Returns	HANDLE, the handle of the resized memory block. Returns NULL on error. The returned value will equal *hMem* unless the LMEM_MOVEABLE flag is set.
See Also	LocalAlloc(), LocalDiscard()
Parameters	
hMem	HANDLE: The handle of the memory block in the local heap, initially allocated with LocalAlloc().
wBytes	WORD: The new size of the memory block. Local memory blocks are limited to the size of the local heap (64K, less the size of the stack and static variable storage space).
wFlags	WORD: The type of memory to reallocate. This should be one or more of the flags listed in Table 14-10, combined with the C language binary OR operator (|). Choose either LMEM_FIXED or LMEM_MOVEABLE, and then combine the choice with other options.

Value	Meaning	⊠
LMEM_DISCARDABLE	Memory that can be discarded if Windows needs to make room. Used with LMEM_MODIFY.	
LMEM_MODIFY	Specifies that the attributes of the memory block will be changed. The *wBytes* parameter is ignored. Used only with LMEM_DISCARDABLE.	

LMEM_MOVEABLE	Moveable memory. If *wBytes* is zero, this flag causes a previously fixed block to be freed, or a previously moveable object to be discarded. This only occurs if the block has not been locked. If *wBytes* is nonzero and the *hMem* block is fixed, LocalReAlloc() will move the block to a new fixed location. This means that the returned value will not be the same as *hMem*. Cannot be used with LMEM_MODIFY.
LMEM_NOCOMPACT	Memory in the local heap is not compacted or discarded to make room for the resized memory block. Cannot be used with LMEM_MODIFY.
LMEM_NODISCARD	Memory in the local heap is not discarded to make room for the resized memory block. Cannot be used with LMEM_MODIFY.
LMEM_ZEROINIT	Initializes the new part of the allocated memory block to zero. Cannot be used with LMEM_MODIFY.

Table 14-10. LocalReAlloc( ) Flags.

Caution   If the program's data segment is defined as moveable in the .DEF file, calling LocalAlloc() may cause the data segment to move. This will invalidate automatic (stack) variable pointers.

Example   See the example under LocalAlloc().

LOCALSHRINK   ■ Win 2.0   ■ Win 3.0   ■ Win 3.1

Purpose   Reduces the size of the local heap.

Syntax   WORD **LocalShrink**(HANDLE *hSeg*, WORD *wSize*);

Description   The local heap is increased in size as needed to hold new objects allocated with LocalAlloc() and LocalReAlloc(). The heap is not automatically reduced in size, even if objects are freed or discarded. LocalShrink() reduces the heap in size. The minimum size is defined in the application's .DEF definition file as the HEAPSIZE statement.

Uses   Making global memory room available, by reducing the size of an application's local heap. Call in response to a WM_COMPACTING message. LocalShrink() does not affect the size of the stack.

Returns   WORD, the size of the local heap after shrinkage.

See Also   LockData(), UnlockData()

Parameters
hSeg   HANDLE: The handle of the local data heap. This value can be obtained by calling LockData().

wSize   WORD: The desired size of the local heap after shrinkage.

Example   This example allocates four discardable memory blocks on the local heap. When the user clicks the "Do It!" menu item, two of the blocks are discarded, and the local heap is reduced in size. All of the discardable memory blocks end up discarded after the local heap is reduced in size.

```
long FAR PASCAL WndProc (HWND hWnd, unsigned iMessage, WORD wParam, LONG lParam)
{
        PAINTSTRUCT                     ps ;
        static          HANDLE          hMem [4] ;
        HANDLE                          hSegment ;
        char                            *pMem [4], cBuf [128] ;
        int                             i, nFree, nLHeap ;

        switch (iMessage)                       /* process windows messages */
        {
                case WM_CREATE:
                        for (i = 0 ; i < 4 ; i++)
                                hMem [i] = LocalAlloc (LMEM_MOVEABLE|
                                        LMEM_DISCARDABLE, 2048) ;
                        break ;
```

```
            case WM_PAINT:
                    BeginPaint (hWnd, &ps) ;
                    for (i = 0 ; i < 4 ; i++)
                    {
                            pMem [i] = LocalLock (hMem [i]) ;
                            TextOut (ps.hdc, 10, 20 * i, cBuf, wsprintf (cBuf,
                                    "Block %d's address is %6d.", i, pMem [i])) ;
                            LocalUnlock (hMem [i]) ;
                    }
                    EndPaint (hWnd, &ps) ;
                    break ;
            case WM_COMMAND:                    /* process menu items */
                    switch (wParam)
                    {
                    case IDM_DOIT:              /* User hit the "Do it" menu item */
                            LocalDiscard (hMem [1]) ;
                            LocalDiscard (hMem [3]) ;
                            nFree = LocalCompact (16) ;        /* find free space */
                            LocalCompact (nFree + 16) ;        /* force compact */
                            hSegment = LockData (0) ;          /* get segment */
                            UnlockData (0) ;
                            nLHeap = LocalShrink (hSegment, 6144) ;
                            InvalidateRect (hWnd, NULL, TRUE) ;
                            break ;
                    case IDM_QUIT:              /* send end of application message */
                            for (i = 0 ; i < 4 ; i ++)
                                    LocalFree (hMem [i]) ;
                            DestroyWindow (hWnd) ;
                            break ;
                    }
                    break ;
            case WM_DESTROY:                    /* stop application */
                    PostQuitMessage (0) ;
                    break ;
            default:                            /* default windows message processing */
                    return DefWindowProc (hWnd, iMessage, wParam, lParam) ;
    }
    return (0L) ;
}
```

LOCALSIZE   ■ Win 2.0   ■ Win 3.0   ■ Win 3.1

Purpose	Determines the size of a memory block allocated in the local heap.
Syntax	WORD **LocalSize**(HANDLE *hMem*);
Description	This function determines the actual number of bytes allocated in the local heap by LocalAlloc() and/or LocalReAlloc(). The number of bytes may be slightly larger than the number requested, as the allocated block will be sized to end on an even memory address.
Returns	WORD, the actual size of the memory block in bytes. NULL if *hMem* is not a valid memory handle.
See Also	LocalFlags(), LocalAlloc()
Parameters	
hMem	HANDLE: The handle of the local memory block.
Example	See the example under LocalAlloc().

LOCALUNLOCK   ■ Win 2.0   ■ Win 3.0   ■ Win 3.1

Purpose	Unlocks a locked memory block in the local heap.
Syntax	BOOL **LocalUnlock**(HANDLE *hMem*);
Description	Unlocks a memory block. Once unlocked, the memory block can be moved by Windows, unless the block was allocated with the LMEM_FIXED flag. Unlocked blocks can also be discarded, if they were allocated with the LMEM_DISCARDABLE style. If a memory block is locked more than

once without unlocking, the block's reference count will be more than one. LocalUnlock() will have to be called the number of times specified by the reference count before the block can be moved or discarded.

Uses	Memory blocks should be unlocked as soon after being locked as possible. This makes it possible for Windows to make maximum use of the memory space.
Returns	BOOL. Zero if the block's lock-count is zero (completely unlocked), nonzero if not.
See Also	LocalLock(), LocalAlloc()
Parameters	
hMem	HANDLE: The handle of the local memory block to unlock. This is the value initially returned by LocalAlloc().
Example	See the example under LocalAlloc().

LockSegment ■ Win 2.0　■ Win 3.0　■ Win 3.1

Purpose	Locks a segment in memory.
Syntax	HANDLE **LockSegment**(WORD *wSegment*);
Description	Locking a segment in memory is normally not desirable, as it limits Windows' ability to make maximum use of memory. Some programming elements, such as interrupt handlers, require a locked program segment to be efficient. The size of the segment that must be locked should be kept as small as possible and should be unlocked whenever possible.
Uses	Generally used to lock specific program segments. Can also be used to lock the program's data segment, as shown in the example.
Returns	HANDLE, the locked segment's handle, or NULL on error.
See Also	UnlockSegment(), LocalInit()
Parameters	
wSegment	WORD: The segment address of the segment to be locked. If *wSegment* equals –1, the application's data segment is locked.
Example	This example locks the entire data segment while the program is running. As a consequence, the pointer to a memory block allocated within the segment remains valid, even though the block was allocated with the LMEM_MOVEABLE attribute. This is not a good programming practice under normal conditions.

```
long FAR PASCAL WndProc (HWND hWnd, unsigned iMessage, WORD wParam, LONG lParam)
{
        PAINTSTRUCT              ps ;
        static          HANDLE   hMem ;
        static          char     *pMem ;
        char                     cBuf [128] ;

        switch (iMessage)                       /* process windows messages */
        {
                case WM_CREATE:
                        LockSegment (-1) ;
                        hMem = LocalAlloc (LMEM_MOVEABLE, 128) ;
                        pMem = LocalLock (hMem) ;
                        strcpy (pMem,
                                "Block moveable, but segment in fixed memory") ;
                        LocalUnlock (hMem) ;
                        break ;
                case WM_PAINT:
                        BeginPaint (hWnd, &ps) ; /* note no locking of hMem */
                        TextOut (ps.hdc, 10, 10, pMem, lstrlen (pMem)) ;
                        EndPaint (hWnd, &ps) ;
```

```
                        break ;
        case WM_COMMAND:                /* process menu items */
                switch (wParam)
                {
                case IDM_DOIT:          /* User hit the "Do it" menu item */
                        break ;
                case IDM_QUIT:          /* send end of application message */
                        LocalFree (hMem) ;
                        UnlockSegment (-1) ;
                        DestroyWindow (hWnd) ;
                        break ;
                }
                break ;
        case WM_DESTROY:                /* stop application */
                PostQuitMessage (0) ;
                break ;
        default:                        /* default windows message processing */
                return DefWindowProc (hWnd, iMessage, wParam, lParam) ;
        }
        return (0L) ;
}
```

MulDiv

■ Win 2.0   ■ Win 3.0   ■ Win 3.1

Purpose	Computes the result of (a * b) / c, where a, b, and c are short integers.
Syntax	int **MulDiv**(int *nNumber*, int *nNumerator*, int *nDenominator*);
Description	Short integers are limited to 16 bits of precision. This limitation frequently results in truncation problems when doing address arithmetic or graphics calculations. MulDiv() deals internally with the values as 32-bit numbers, reducing truncation errors.
Uses	Address arithmetic and graphics calculations.
Returns	int, the result of (*nNumber* * *nNumerator*) / *nDenominator*.

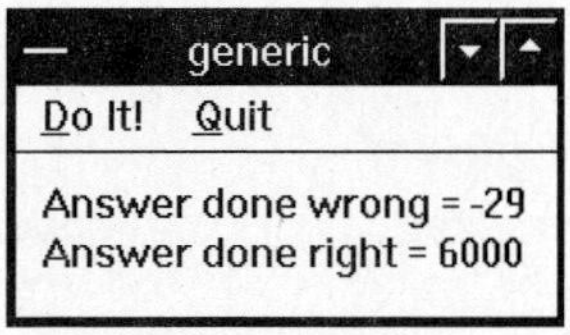

Parameters

nNumber	int: The value a in the formula (a * b) / c.
nNumerator	int: The value b in the formula (a * b) / c.
nDenominator	int: The value c in the formula (a * b) / c.

Figure 14-22. MulDiv( ) Example.

Caution	The result is not guaranteed to be correct! For example the calculation 20000 * 30000 / 10000 will overflow because the multiplication exceeds the 32-bit precision used.
Example	This example shows the calculation (2000 * 3000) / 1000. Done with pure integer math, the values overflow the 16-bit limit of short integer math. Using MulDiv() provides the correct result.

```
Long FAR PASCAL WndProc (HWND hWnd, unsigned iMessage, WORD wParam, LONG lParam)
{
        HDC             hDC ;
        int             n1, n2, n3, nAnswer ;
        char            cBuf [128] ;

        switch (iMessage)                       /* process windows messages */
        {
                case WM_COMMAND:                /* process menu items */
                        switch (wParam)
                        {
                        case IDM_DOIT:          /* User hit the "Do it" menu item */
                                n1 = 2000 ;
                                n2 = 3000 ;
                                n3 = 1000 ;
                                nAnswer = (n1 * n2) / n3 ;              /* wrong! */
                                hDC = GetDC (hWnd) ;
                                TextOut (hDC, 10, 10, cBuf, wsprintf (cBuf,
                                        "Answer done wrong = %d", nAnswer)) ;
```

```
                              nAnswer = MulDiv (n1, n2, n3) ;           /* correct */
                              TextOut (hDC, 10, 30, cBuf, wsprintf (cBuf,
                                      "Answer done right = %d", nAnswer)) ;
                              ReleaseDC (hWnd, hDC) ;
                              break ;
```

[Other program lines]

UNLOCKSEGMENT   ■ Win 2.0   ■ Win 3.0   ■ Win 3.1

Purpose	Unlocks a memory segment locked with LockSegment().
Syntax	BOOL **UnlockSegment**(WORD *wSegment*);
Uses	Locked segments are used for special purposes, such as for interrupt handlers. Any segment locked in memory by LockSegment() should be unlocked before the application terminates.
Returns	BOOL. Zero if the segment is completely unlocked, nonzero if the segment lock-count is not zero. UnlockSegment() may have to be called more than once to unlock the segment if LockSegment() has been called more than once.
See Also	LockSegment()
Parameters	
wSegment	WORD: The segment address of the segment to be unlocked. If *wSegment* equals –1, the segment is the program's data segment.
Example	See the example under LockSegment().

WINEXEC   □ Win 2.0   ■ Win 3.0   ■ Win 3.1

Purpose	Loads and executes a Windows or DOS program, or creates a new instance of the program if one or more instances are already running.
Syntax	WORD **WinExec**(LPSTR *lpCmdLine*, WORD *nCmdShow*);
Description	This function allows one Windows application to load and run others. The function can pass the loaded file a command line, such as a file name to load on startup. Unlike LoadModule(), Win-Exec() will execute a DOS application.
Uses	Useful for creating master applications that run a series of "slave" programs. Also handy for loading the standard Windows applications such as NOTEPAD. NOTEPAD can provide instant editing facilities for applications that need to process simple text files.
Returns	WORD. If the value returned is greater than 32, the function was successful. Otherwise, one of the error codes in Table 14-11 will be returned:

Value	Meaning	⊠
0	Out of memory.	
2	File not found.	
3	Path not found.	
5	Attempt to dynamically link to a task.	
6	Library requires separate data segments for each task.	
10	Incorrect Windows version.	
11	Non-Windows .EXE file.	
12	OS/2 application.	
13	DOS 4.0 application.	
14	Unknown .EXE type.	

Table 14-11. continued

Value	Meaning	
15	Attempt to load an .EXE file created for an earlier version of Windows. Only affects standard and 386 enhanced modes.	☒
16	Attempt to load a second .EXE containing multiple, writeable data segments.	
17	Attempt to load a second instance linked to a nonshareable DLL.	
18	Attempt to load a protected mode-only application in real mode.	

Table 14-11. WinExec( ) Error Codes.

See Also   LoadModule() will accomplish the same purpose.

Parameters

lpCmdLine   LPSTR: A pointer to a null-terminated string containing the name of the application to run. If no extension is included, .EXE is assumed. If *lpCmdLine* does not contain a directory path, Windows will search for the file based on the following search order:

1. In the current directory.

2. In the Windows directory. This is the directory containing WIN.COM. Use GetWindowsDirectory() to determine the path name of this directory.

3. In the Windows system directory. Use the GetSystemDirectory() function to determine the path name of this directory.

4. In the directories specified in the PATH environment variable. This is the PATH command that is executed from DOS before Windows is loaded. Typical systems set their PATH values in the AUTOEXEC.BAT file.

5. In the directories mapped in a network.

nCmdShow   WORD: Set equal to one of the values in Table 14-12 for a Windows application. For a DOS application, the .PIF file (if any) will determine how the application is run.

Value	Meaning	
SW_HIDE	Hides the window. The top window on Windows' list is activated.	☒
SW_MINIMIZE	Minimizes the window. The top window on Windows' list is activated.	
SW_RESTORE	Activates and displays the window (same as SW_SHOWNORMAL).	
SW_SHOW	Activates and displays the window in its current size and position.	
SW_SHOWMAXIMIZED	Activates and maximizes the window.	
SW_SHOWMINIMIZED	Activates and minimizes the window.	
SW_SHOWMINNOACTIVE	Displays and minimizes the window. The currently active window remains active.	
SW_SHOWNA	Displays the window, but does not change which window is active.	
SW_SHOWNOACTIVE	Displays the window, but does not change which window is active.	
SW_SHOWNORMAL	Activates and displays the window. If the window was minimized or maximized, the window is returned to its previous size and position.	

Table 14-12. lpCmdLine ShowWindow( ) Styles.

Related Messages Send a WM_DESTROY message to a running application to remove it from the system.

Example   This example runs the NOTEPAD.EXE application and has it load the README.TXT file when the user clicks the "Do It!" menu item. NOTEPAD is closed (sent a WM_DESTROY message) when the example application's "Quit" menu item is clicked.

```
long FAR PASCAL WndProc (HWND hWnd, unsigned iMessage, WORD wParam,        LONG lParam)
{
        HANDLE          hNotePad ;

        switch (iMessage)                       /* process windows messages */
        {
                case WM_COMMAND:                /* process menu items */
                        switch (wParam)
                        {
                        case IDM_DOIT:          /* User hit the "Do it" menu item */
                                WinExec ("notepad.exe readme.txt",
                                        SW_SHOWNORMAL) ;
                                break ;
                        case IDM_QUIT:          /* send end of application message */
                                hNotePad = FindWindow (NULL, "Notepad - README.TXT") ;
                                if (hNotePad)
                                        SendMessage (hNotePad, WM_DESTROY, 0, 0l) ;
                                DestroyWindow (hWnd) ;
                                break ;
                        }
                        break ;
                case WM_DESTROY:                /* stop application */
                        PostQuitMessage (0) ;
                        break ;
                default:                        /* default windows message processing */
                        return DefWindowProc (hWnd, iMessage, wParam, lParam) ;
        }
        return (0L) ;
}
```

Bitmaps are blocks of pixel data that can be output directly to a device, such as a video display. You can think of them as a way to store the pixel data directly from the screen into a memory buffer. Painting bitmaps onto the screen is fast, much faster than using GDI functions like Rectangle() and LineTo(). The drawback to bitmaps is that they take up a lot of memory and/or disk space. Literally, every pixel has to be saved. Prior to the 3.0 version of Windows, there was only one bitmap format, the device-dependent bitmap (DDB), or "old" bitmap format. Windows 3.0 introduced a second kind of bitmap called a "Device-Independent Bitmap" (DIB). Both formats have their purposes.

DDB Bitmap Format

The simplest bitmap form is the one for a black and white (monochrome) image. In this case, we can use one bit to store each pixel's color, 0 for black and 1 for white. A simple outlined rectangle would be stored as

Binary Bitmap Data	Hexadecimal Equivalent	⊠
0 0 0 0 0 0 0 0 0 0 0 0 0 0 0 0	0x00	
0 1 1 1 1 1 1 1 1 1 1 1 1 1 1 0	0x7E	
0 1 1 1 1 1 1 1 1 1 1 1 1 1 1 0	0x7E	
0 0 0 0 0 0 0 0 0 0 0 0 0 0 0 0	0x00	

This example would encode the 64 black and white pixels with eight bytes of data. If the bitmap is copying a color display, then more than one bit will be required for each pixel. For example, a 16-color VGA display would require four bits to encode the color of each pixel. The same rectangle would require 4 * 64 = 256 bits, or 32 bytes of data to encode the pixels. Typically, bitmaps are not copies of an entire screen or page. Usually, they are small images, such as custom button faces. In order to make sense out of the pixel data, Windows starts the DDB bitmap data with some header information. The BITMAP data type is defined in WINDOWS.H as follows:

⇨ **Bitmap Structure**

```
typedef struct tagBITMAP
  {
       int     bmType;          /* always zero */
       int     bmWidth;         /* width in pixels */
       int     bmHeight;        /* height in pixels */
       int     bmWidthBytes;    /* bytes per line of data */
                                /* must be a multiple of 2 */
       BYTE    bmPlanes;        /* the number of color planes */
       BYTE    bmBitsPixel;     /* the number of bits per pixel */
       LPSTR   bmBits;          /* far pointer to the bitmap data */
  } BITMAP;
typedef BITMAP                  *PBITMAP;
typedef BITMAP NEAR             *NPBITMAP;
typedef BITMAP FAR              *LPBITMAP;
```

The BITMAP structure allows two different ways to specify the number of color bits used in the pixel data. *bmPlanes* is the number of color planes a device, such as a VGA display, may use. If this value is used, then *bmBitsPixel* will be set to one. *bmBitsPixel* is the number of bits per pixel for a device that does not use color planes.

If this value is used, *bmPlanes* will be set to one. The function CreateCompatibleBitmap() will set these color values to match a physical device, so you do not have to know how colors are stored internally by the device. The actual pixel data is stored in a memory buffer pointed to by *bmBits*. This buffer is normally right after the header data in memory, although it can be located separately, as shown in Figure 15-1.

Using DDB Bitmaps

The most common way to use bitmaps in a program is to display bitmaps created with the SDKPaint application. SDKPaint creates bit-

Figure 15-1. The DDB Bitmap Format in Memory.

maps that are stored as disk files. (SDKPaint actually creates DIB bitmaps, which are explained below. This format is converted automatically to the DDB format when LoadBitmap() is called.) Bitmap files created by SDKPaint can be added to a program's .RC resource file with the BITMAP statement

```
pen             BITMAP          pen.bmp
```

This example loads a file called PEN.BMP and gives the bitmap resource the name "pen." This example bitmap was created 60 pixels wide and 60 pixels tall. With the bitmap loaded as part of the application's resources, it is a simple matter to bring a bitmap into memory using LoadBitmap().

```
HBITMAP hBitmap ;
hBitmap = LoadBitmap (hInstance , "pen") ;
```

Pasting the bitmap image on the screen is a little more involved than you might expect. There is no function called PaintBitmap(). Instead, the application loads the bitmap into a memory object called "Memory Device Context," and then paints the memory device context onto the screen. Here is some example code.

```
HDC       hDC, hMemDC ;

hDC = GetDC (hWnd) ;                    /* get screen DC */
hMemDC = CreateCompatibleDC (hDC) ;     /* create memory DC */
SelectObject (hMemDC, hBitmap) ;
BitBlt (hDC, 10, 10, 60, 60, hMemDC, 0, 0, SRCCOPY) ;
DeleteDC (hMemDC) ;
ReleaseDC (hWnd, hDC) ;
```

The function that paints the bitmap onto the screen is BitBlt(). It copies bitmap data from one device context to a second device context. To make the bitmap data available through a device context, we first create a device context in memory that has the same attributes as the display. To do this, use CreateCompatibleDC(). Once we have the memory device context, the bitmap can be selected into it with SelectObject(). Finally, BitBlt() is called to do the actual painting.

Memory Device Contexts

The previous example probably seems a little involved, but there is a payoff. When a bitmap is selected into a memory device context, you can paint on the memory device context just like you paint on the screen or printer's device context. All of the standard GDI functions, like LineTo() and Rectangle(), work just fine painting into the memory device context. As soon as the painting is done, the memory device context can be copied to the real screen with BitBlt().

Why not just paint directly on the screen? You can, but there are a few situations where it is much better to paint to the memory device context, and then copy the memory image to the screen or printer. One use is when repeating patterns. If you have to paint the same object over and over, just paint it once to memory and then copy it to the screen when you need it. BitBlt() and related functions are much faster than using the GDI functions, such as Rectangle(). Another reason to paint on a memory device context is to avoid having the painting operations visible to the user. Although Windows 3.0 paints quickly, it is frequently possible to see different parts of the image being painted, one line or rectangle at a time. Avoid this situation by painting to a memory device context, and then using BitBlt() to copy to the screen.

Stretching and Painting Bitmap Images

In addition to BitBlt(), there are functions for pasting a bitmap onto a device context that allow the bitmap to be stretched or compressed. StretchBlt() does this for the DDB bitmap type. If the bitmap is increased in size, extra bits matching the colors of their neighbors are added to fill in the missing bits. This technique is acceptable for modest enlargements, but will produce ragged edges on diagonal lines if the expansion is too large. When a bitmap is reduced in size, some pixels have to be eliminated. In bitmaps with thin lines, the lines may be eliminated if they happen to fall on a row or column that is deleted. To save their information during compression, you can set the "stretching mode" of the device context using SetStretchBltMode(). Three modes are provided. One preserves white pixels, one preserves black (colored) pixels, and one just deletes pixels.

When painting a bitmap onto a device context, you would normally want to cover up any underlying image data. There are other choices. Windows can do Boolean (binary) logic on both the source and destination pixels, and have each pixel painted as a result of these calculations. For example, instead of painting the bitmap directly, the bitmap pixels can be compared to the destination pixels using an XOR operator. This technique has the advantage of allowing a bitmap to be erased by painting it twice in the same location.

These Boolean comparisons are called "Raster-Operation Codes." There are 256 possible combinations of the source and destination data. They are defined in the Windows SDK documentation in Volume 2, Table 11.3. You probably will never use more that two or three of these possibilities. The most common choices are given names in WINDOWS.H and are listed in Table 15-1, along with their Boolean logic equivalent. For the Boolean codes, "S" is the source bitmap, "D" is the destination bitmap, and "P" is the currently selected brush (called a "pattern"). The Boolean operators follow the C language conventions.

Value	Meaning	☒
BLACKNESS	Turns all output black. (0)	
DSTINVERT	Inverts the destination bitmap. (~D)	
MERGECOPY	The source and destination bitmaps are combined with the Boolean AND operator. (P & S)	
MERGEPAINT	The source and destination bitmaps are combined with the Boolean OR operator. (~S | D)	
NOTSRCCOPY	Inverts the source bitmap, then copies it to the destination. (~S)	
NOTSRCERASE	Inverts the result of combining the source and destination bitmaps using the Boolean OR operator. (~(S | D))	
PATCOPY	Copies the pattern to the destination. (P)	
PATINVERT	Combines the destination bitmap with the pattern using the SetStretchBltMode OR operator. (P ^ D)	
PATPAINT	P	~(S | D)	
SRCAND	Combines the source and destination bitmaps with the Boolean AND operator. (S & D)	
SRCCOPY	Copies the source to the destination. (S)	
SRCERASE	S & ~ D	
SRCINVERT	Combines the source and destination bitmaps using the Boolean XOR operator. (S ^ D)	
SRCPAINT	Combines the source and destination bitmaps using the Boolean OR operator. (S | D)	
WHITENESS	Turns all output white. This is a quick way to blank a device context. (1)	

Table 15-1. Raster-Operation Codes.

Problems with the Old Bitmap Format

The old bitmap format works well for copying parts of the screen into memory and pasting them back onto other locations on the screen. Windows provides extensive support for this type of operation, using memory device contexts. We will examine these later in this chapter.

Problems occur when your program needs to save bitmap data on disk files, and then display it on some other type of device. The old bitmap header does not have a place to store the colors used in creating the bitmap. There is an underlying assumption that the bitmap will be displayed on the same type of device, with the same arrangement of colors on color planes or in color bits. If you display an old bitmap on some other device, the colors may end up completely different. This was not a big issue when EGA and VGA systems were the only devices available. Today, with Super VGA and other expanded color displays becoming widespread, Windows must provide a better way to store bitmaps so that they will be properly displayed on any device.

Device-Independent Bitmaps (DIB)

The device-independent bitmap, called a DIB, is the Windows 3.0 solution to the shortcomings of the old bitmap format. The big difference between DIBs and old bitmaps is that DIBs include a table of the colors the bitmap will use. The header format is also more complex.

One thing to keep in mind is that the DIB format is not a graphics object like a DDB. You cannot select a DIB into a device context. Think of the DIB specification as a data format. It is a standard way

Figure. 15-2 Device-Independent Bitmap (DIB) Format.

of storing bitmap data along with the color data needed to reproduce the bitmap image. The DIB format consists of three sections. The first one is the BITMAPINFOHEADER, shown in Figure 15-2.

```
typedef struct tagBITMAPINFOHEADER{
        DWORD           biSize;           /* size of BITMAPINFOHEADER */
        DWORD           biWidth;          /* width in pixels */
        DWORD           biHeight;         /* height in pixels */
        WORD            biPlanes;         /* always 1 */
        WORD            biBitCount;       /* color bits per pixel */
                                          /* must be 1, 4, 8 or 24 */
        DWORD           biCompression;    /* BI_RGB, BI_RLE8 */
                                          /* or BI_RLE4 */
        DWORD           biSizeImage;      /* total bytes in image */
        DWORD           biXPelsPerMeter;  /* 0, or opt. h res. */
        DWORD           biYPelsPerMeter;  /* 0, or opt. v res. */
        DWORD           biClrUsed;        /* normally 0, can set a */
                        /* lower no. colors than biBitCount */
        DWORD           biClrImportant;   /* normally 0 */
} BITMAPINFOHEADER;

typedef BITMAPINFOHEADER FAR *LPBITMAPINFOHEADER;
typedef BITMAPINFOHEADER *PBITMAPINFOHEADER;
```

Although similar to the BITMAP header structure, BITMAPINFOHEADER contains some added fields. The *biBitCount* element contains the number of color bits per pixel, either 1, 4, 8, or 24 bits. Table 15-2 describes these values.

Color Bits	Number of Colors	⊠
1	A monochrome bitmap. Each bit in the bitmap data will represent one pixel.	
4	A bitmap with 16 colors. Each pixel requires four bits of information in the bitmap data. The four bits represent an index in the color table.	
8	A bitmap with 256 colors. Each pixel requires a byte of information in the bitmap data. The byte value represents an index into the color table.	
24	A bitmap with 224 colors. Each pixel requires three bytes of information, representing the RGB (Red, Green, Blue) color bytes.	

Table 15-2. Color Resolutions.

The *biCompression* element contains a value to define how the bitmap is compressed (to save space) in the memory buffer holding the pixel data. If it is set to BI_RGB, no compression is used. BI_RLE4 is a four bits per pixel run length encoding compression. BI_RLE8 is an eight bits per pixel compression.

biSizeImage is the bitmap size in bytes. Each row of pixels data must terminate on a 32-bit (DWORD) boundary. If a row of pixels, with the specified number of color bits per pixel, does not end at an even 32-bit number, the remainder is padded with zero bits.

The last four values are not usually used. The *biXPelsPerMeter* and *biYPelsPerMeter* values can be used to encode the bitmap resolution in pixels per meter. Set both to zero if these elements are not needed. *biClrUsed* specifies the number of color values in the color table (described below) that are actually used. *biClrUsed* is normally set to zero, meaning that all colors are used. This value must be set to zero if the bitmap is compressed. *biClrImportant* specifies the number of critical colors. *biClrImportant* is normally set to zero, meaning that all of the colors are important.

After the BITMAPINFOHEADER structure, a DIB will contain the color table. This is a set of RGBQUAD data structures, holding the RGB color for each of the colors used in the bitmap. There will be as many RGBQUAD entries as there are color choices in the bitmap. For example, if *biBitCount* is four, there will be 16 color possibilities, requiring 16 RGBQUAD elements to define, taking up 16 * 4 = 64 bytes of space, assuming *biClrUsed* is set to zero. If *biClrUsed* is set to a value above zero, the *biClrUsed* value will be the number of RGBQUAD elements.

```
typedef struct tagRGBQUAD {
        BYTE      rgbBlue;           /* blue intensity, 0 - 255 */
        BYTE      rgbGreen;          /* green intensity, 0 - 255 */
        BYTE      rgbRed;            /* red intensity, 0 - 255 */
        BYTE      rgbReserved;       /* reserved, set to zero */
} RGBQUAD;
```

Windows provides an alternative to specifying the bitmap colors using RGB color values. The color table can be an array of 16-bit unsigned integers, each of which is an index into the currently realized logical palette (see Chapter 12, *Color Palette Control*). Using pallet index values allows bitmap colors to change as the palette is changed. Several of the DIB functions include a *wUsage* parameter that can be set to DIB_PAL_COLORS if the color table contains palette entries. DIB_PAL_COLORS informs Windows not to interpret the values as 32-bit RGB colors. You can use palette colors in a DIB in a memory device context. RGB colors should be used if the bitmap is to be saved to disk, potentially for use by some other type of device which may have a different color resolution.

WINDOWS.H includes two other structure definitions that are useful in manipulating DIBs. The BITMAPINFO structure simply combines the first two parts of a DIB into one structure.

```
typedef struct tagBITMAPINFO {
        BITMAPINFOHEADER        bmiHeader;
        RGBQUAD                 bmiColors[1];
} BITMAPINFO;
typedef BITMAPINFO FAR          *LPBITMAPINFO;
typedef BITMAPINFO              *PBITMAPINFO;
```

Note that the RGBQUAD element *bmiColors* shows only one element. This element is a placeholder, as the number of colors will be greater than one, but it is not fixed for all DIBs. The application using a DIB will allocate a memory block to hold the entire DIB structure, including all of the colors needed.

The last structure is used only when DIBs are stored to disk. The BITMAPFILEHEADER structure is the first part of a bitmap stored as a disk file. This is the way Windows PaintBrush and SDKPaint applications store their outputs.

```
typedef struct tagBITMAPFILEHEADER {
        WORD      bfType;                      /* always equal to 'BM' */
        DWORD     bfSize;                      /* size of file in DWORDs */
        WORD      bfReserved1;                 /* set to zero */
        WORD      bfReserved2;                 /* set to zero */
        DWORD     bfOffBits;                   /* byte offset from BITMAPFILEHEADER to */
                                               /* bitmap pixel data in the file */
} BITMAPFILEHEADER;
typedef BITMAPFILEHEADER FAR            *LPBITMAPFILEHEADER;
typedef BITMAPFILEHEADER                *PBITMAPFILEHEADER;
```

Figure 15-3 shows how the four elements of a complete DIB are arranged in a disk file.

Working with DIBs

As mentioned, the SDKPaint application allows you to create bitmaps and store them to disk. If you examine the

Figure 15-3. Device-Independent Bitmap Formatted as a Disk File.

disk file, you will notice that the bitmaps are stored in DIB format. However, if you include bitmap files created with SDKPaint in an application's resource file, and load them with LoadBitmap(), the resultant bitmap is in the old DDB format in memory. What happened?

To maintain compatibility with applications written under Windows 2.*x* versions, LoadBitmap() was set up to automatically convert DIB bitmap data to the DDB bitmap format. This is convenient, as it means that you can use both old and new bitmap files as resource data in a Windows 3.*x* application.

The problem with LoadBitmap()'s conversion from DIB to DDB format is that you lose the color information stored with the DIB data. If the bitmap was stored with 256 colors, and is to be displayed on a 256 color system, you will still be able to use only the 20 reserved system colors when the bitmap is displayed. The way around color information loss is to load the color information from the bitmap's header separately. LoadBitmap() will not do this for you. Instead, use FindResource(), LoadResource(), and LockResource() to return a handle to a locked memory block containing the BITMAPINFO data structure. As discussed in the previous section, that amounts to a BITMAPINFO-HEADER structure, followed by an array of RGBQUAD data structures that contain the actual colors.

With access to the color data from the BITMAPINFO data header, the application can create a logical palette that matches that specified in the bitmap. The steps involved are

1. Use FindResource(), LoadResource(), and LockResource() to obtain a handle to a memory block containing the DIB data.
2. Examine the *biBitCount* and *biClrUsed* fields to determine the number of colors stored in the DIB data.
3. Retrieve the color entries from the RGBQUAD array.
4. Create a logical palette with the DIB colors by calling CreatePalette().
5. Select the palette into the device context by calling SelectPalette().
6. Realize the palette by calling RealizePalette().
7. Call SetDIBitsToDevice() or StretchDIBits() to transfer the image to the device context.

DIB Example

Listing 15-1 shows an example of loading the color data from a DIB, and then displaying the bitmap. The example assumes that the PEN.BMP DIB bitmap file was made part of the resource script data with a line like

```
pen            BITMAP          pen.bmp
```

The color data from the DIB is read and converted to a logical palette when the WM_CREATE message is processed. This procedure gets a little involved, as the program has to calculate how many color values are stored with the bitmap. Note that although the logical palette is created while processing the WM_CREATE message, it is not realized until the WM_PAINT message is processed.

The SetDIBitsToDevice() function is used to display the bitmap. This function requires a pointer to both the BITMAPINFO data and the DIB bitmap data. The latter is calculated as an offset from the start of the BITMAPINFO data, as the resource data loads the bitmap bits right after the end of the color data.

▷ Listing 15-1. Example Loading a DIB Bitmap

```
long FAR PASCAL WndProc (HWND hWnd, unsigned iMessage, WORD wParam, LONG lParam)
{
        static HANDLE            hRes, hPal ;
        static LPBITMAPINF       lpBitmapInfo ;
        LPLOGPALETTE             lpLogPalette ;
        static HPALETTE          hPalette ;
        LPSTR                    lpBits ;
        int                      i ;
        static int               nColorData ;
        PAINTSTRUCT              ps ;
```

```
        switch (iMessage)              /* process windows messages */
        {
        case WM_CREATE:
                        /* load DIB, and get handle to its locked mem. block */
        hRes = LoadResource (ghInstance,
        FindResource (ghInstance, "pen", RT_BITMAP)) ;
        lpBitmapInfo = (LPBITMAPINFO) LockResource (hRes) ;
                        /* calculate the number of color data entries in DIB */
        if (lpBitmapInfo->bmiHeader.biClrUsed != 0)
        nColorData = lpBitmapInfo->bmiHeader.biClrUsed ;
                else
                {
                        switch (lpBitmapInfo->bmiHeader.biBitCount)
                        {
                                case 1:
                                        nColorData = 2 ; /* monochrome */
                                        break ;
                                case 4:
                                        nColorData = 16 ;         /* typical vga */
                                        break ;
                                case 8:
                                        nColorData = 256 ;        /* 256 colors */
                                        break ;
                                case 24:
                                        nColorData = 0 ;/* rgb encoded for */
                                        break ; /* every pixel in bitmap */
                        }
                }
                        /* allocate memory to hold palette */
                hPal = GlobalAlloc (GMEM_MOVEABLE, sizeof (LOGPALETTE) +
                        (nColorData * sizeof (PALETTEENTRY))) ;
                lpLogPalette = (LPLOGPALETTE) GlobalLock (hPal) ;
                        /* create the logical palette */
                lpLogPalette->palVersion = 0x300 ;         /* Windows 3.0 */
                lpLogPalette->palNumEntries = nColorData ;
                        /* load each color into palette fields */
                for (i = 0 ; i < nColorData ; i++)
                {
                        lpLogPalette->palPalEntry [i].peRed =
                                lpBitmapInfo->bmiColors [i].rgbRed ;
                        lpLogPalette->palPalEntry [i].peGreen =
                                lpBitmapInfo->bmiColors [i].rgbGreen ;
                        lpLogPalette->palPalEntry [i].peBlue =
                                lpBitmapInfo->bmiColors [i].rgbBlue ;

                }       /* create the palette */
                hPalette = CreatePalette (lpLogPalette) ;
                GlobalUnlock (hRes) ;
                GlobalUnlock (hPal) ;
                GlobalFree (hPal) ;
                break ;
        case WM_PAINT:
                BeginPaint (hWnd, &ps) ;
                SelectPalette (ps.hdc, hPalette, FALSE) ;
                RealizePalette (ps.hdc) ;       /* put palette into action */
                        /* get handle to DIB, reloading if necessary */
                hRes = LoadResource (ghInstance,
                FindResource (ghInstance, "pen", RT_BITMAP)) ;
                lpBitmapInfo = (LPBITMAPINFO) LockResource (hRes) ;
                        /* find address of the bitmap data */
                lpBits = (LPSTR) lpBitmapInfo ;
                lpBits += (WORD) lpBitmapInfo->bmiHeader.biSize +
                (WORD) (nColorData * sizeof (RGBQUAD)) ;
                        /* display the bitmap on the window's client area */
                SetDIBitsToDevice (ps.hdc, 10, 10,
                (WORD) lpBitmapInfo->bmiHeader.biWidth,
                (WORD) lpBitmapInfo->bmiHeader.biHeight,
                0, 0,
                0, (WORD) lpBitmapInfo->bmiHeader.biHeight,
                lpBits, lpBitmapInfo, DIB_RGB_COLORS) ;
                GlobalUnlock (hRes) ;
                EndPaint (hWnd, &ps) ;
```

```
                              break ;
                              case WM_COMMAND:           /* process menu items */
                              switch (wParam)
                              {
                              case IDM_QUIT:   /* send end of application message */
                                      DestroyWindow (hWnd) ;
                                      break ;
                              }
                              break ;
              case WM_DESTROY:          /* stop application */
                      DeleteObject (hPalette) ;
                      FreeResource (hRes) ;
                      PostQuitMessage (0) ;
                      break ;
              default:                  /* default windows message processing */
                      return DefWindowProc (hWnd, iMessage, wParam, lParam) ;
      }
      return (OL) ;
}
```

Bitmap Function Summary

Table 15-3 summarizes the bitmap functions. The detailed function descriptions are in the next section.

Function	Purpose
BitBlt	Copies a bitmap from a memory device context to another device context.
Create Bitmap	Creates a DDB bitmap based on an array of color bit values.
CreateBitmapIndirect	Creates a DDB bitmap based on data in a BITMAP data structure.
CreateCompatibleBitmap	Creates a memory bitmap compatible with a device.
CreateDIBitmap	Creates a memory bitmap based on device-independent bitmap (DIB) data.
CreateDIBPatternBrush	Creates a pattern brush based on a device-independent bitmap stored in a global memory block.
CreateDiscardableBitmap	Creates a DDB bitmap compatible with a device. Windows can discard the bitmap data if the bitmap is not selected.
GetBitmapBits	Loads the bitmap data into a memory block.
GetBitmapDimension	Retrieves two values that were associated with the bitmap by a previous call to SetBitmapDimension().
GetDIBits	Fills in BITMAPINFO data for a DIB, and/or writes a DIB's pixel data into a memory buffer.
GetStretchBltMode	Determines the current bitmap stretching mode of a device context.
LoadBitmap	Loads a bitmap resource into memory.
PatBlt	Outputs a pattern brush to a device.
SetBitmapBits	Sets the pixel data for a DDB bitmap.
SetBitmapDimension	Sets two values that are associated with the bitmap. These values can be retrieved later using GetBitmapDimension().
SetDIBits	Sets device-independent bitmap (DIB) pixel data to the data in a memory buffer.
SetDIBitsToDevice	Paints from a device-independent bitmap (DIB) directly on a device context.
SetStretchBltMode	Sets the bitmap stretching mode for the StretchBlt() function.
StretchBlt	Copies a DDB bitmap from one device context to another, stretching or contracting the image to fit the destination rectangle.
StretchDIBits	Paints from a DIB directly on a device context, stretching and/or compressing the image as it is painted.

Table 15-3. Bitmap Function Summary.

Bitmap Function Descriptions

This section contains descriptions for the bitmap functions.

BitBlt

■ Win 2.0   ■ Win 3.0   ■ Win 3.1

Purpose	Copies a bitmap from a memory device context to another device context.
Syntax	BOOL **BitBlt**(HDC *hDC*, int *X*, int *Y*, int *nWidth*, int *nHeight*, HDC *hSrcDC*, int *XSrc*, int *YSrc*, DWORD *dwRop*);
Description	The bitmap must first be selected into a memory device context, created with CreateCompatibleDC(). Normally, the bitmap is copied without modification. The bitmap can be combined with the existing background using any of the raster-operation codes if desired. The source bitmap is stretched or compressed to match the dimensions of the destination. Not all devices support BitBlt(). Use GetDeviceCaps() to check if BitBlt() operations are supported.
Uses	This is the standard function for copying a bitmap to a device.
Returns	BOOL. Nonzero if the function was successful, zero on error.
See Also	PatBlt(), CreateCompatibleDC(), DeleteObject(), LoadBitmap(), SelectObject(), GetDevice-Caps()

Parameters

hDC	HDC: The device context handle to receive the bitmap.
X	int: The logical *X* coordinate of the upper left corner of the destination rectangle.
Y	int: The logical *Y* coordinate of the upper left corner of the destination rectangle.
nWidth	int: The width, in logical units, of the destination rectangle.
nHeight	int: The height, in logical units, of the destination rectangle.
hSrcDC	HDC: The device context from which the bitmap will be copied. This is normally a memory device context created with CreateCompatibleDC(). A bitmap is loaded into the memory device context using SelectObject(). *hSrcDC* must be NULL if the *dwRop* parameter does not require a source bitmap. For example, the BLACKNESS, WHITENESS, and DSTINVERT options operate solely on the background of the destination device context.
XSrc	int: The logical *X* coordinate of the upper left corner in the source bitmap. Normally 0, for the whole bitmap.
YSrc	int: The logical *Y* coordinate of the upper right corner in the source bitmap. Normally 0, for the whole bitmap.
dwRop	DWORD: One of the raster-operation codes. Fifteen of the 256 possibilities have names defined in WINDOWS.H and are listed in Table 15-4. The remainder have hexadecimal codes, specified in Volume 2, Section 11, Table 11.3 of the Microsoft SDK Reference manuals. These codes determine how the colors of the brush are combined with the existing colors of the background. For the Boolean codes, "S" is the source bitmap, "D" is the destination bitmap, and "P" is the currently selected brush (called a "pattern") of the device context. The Boolean operators in Table 15-4 follow the C language conventions.

Value	Meaning	⊠
BLACKNESS	Turns all output black. (0)	
DSTINVERT	Inverts the destination bitmap. (~D)	
MERGECOPY	The source and destination bitmaps are combined with the Boolean AND operator. (D & S)	
MERGEPAINT	The source and destination bitmaps are combined with the Boolean OR operator. (~S | D)	

NOTSRCCOPY	Inverts the source bitmap, then copies it to the destination. (~S)
NOTSRCERASE	Inverts the result of combining the source and destination bitmaps using the Boolean OR operator. (~(S I D))
PATCOPY	Copies the pattern to the destination. (P)
PATINVERT	Combines the destination bitmap with the pattern using the Boolean XOR operator. (P ^ D)
PATPAINT	P I ~(S ID)
SRCAND	Combines the source and destination bitmaps with the Boolean AND operator. (S & D)
SRCCOPY	Copies the source to the destination. (S)
SRCERASE	S & ~ D
SRCINVERT	Combines the source and destination bitmaps using the Boolean XOR operator. (S ^ D)
SRCPAINT	Combines the source and destination bitmaps using the Boolean OR operator. (S I D)
WHITENESS	Turns all output white. This is a quick way to blank a device context. (1)

Table 15-4. Raster-Operation Codes.

Example This example (see Figure 15-4) copies a bitmap to the window's client area when the user clicks the "Do It!" menu item.

The resource script file loads a bitmap file. The PEN.BMP file is a 60 by 60 pixel color bitmap reated with the Windows SDKPaint application.

Figure 15-4. BitBlt() Example.

▷ **GENERIC.RC Resource Script File**

```
/* generic.rc */

#include <windows.h>
#include "generic.h"

generic         ICON            generic.ico
pen             BITMAP          pen.bmp

generic         MENU
BEGIN
        MENUITEM "&Do It!"                      IDM_DOIT
        MENUITEM "&Quit",                       IDM_QUIT
END
```

The "pen" bitmap is loaded into memory when the WM_CREATE message is processed. The bitmap is copied to the client area device context when the user clicks the "Do It!" menu item. Note that the pen is deleted from memory as the application exits (WM_DESTROY message processed).

```
long FAR PASCAL WndProc (HWND hWnd, unsigned iMessage, WORD wParam, LONG lParam)
{
        static          HBITMAP         hBitmap ;
        HDC                             hDC, hMemDC ;

        switch (iMessage)                       /* process windows messages */
        {
                case WM_CREATE:
                        hBitmap = LoadBitmap (ghInstance , "pen") ;
                        break ;
                case WM_COMMAND:                /* process menu items */
                        switch (wParam)
                        {
                        case IDM_DOIT:                  /* User hit the "Do it" menu item */
                                hDC = GetDC (hWnd) ;
```

```
                        hMemDC = CreateCompatibleDC (hDC) ;
                        SelectObject (hMemDC, hBitmap) ;
                        BitBlt (hDC, 10, 10, 60, 60, hMemDC, 0, 0,
                                SRCCOPY) ;
                        DeleteDC (hMemDC) ;
                        ReleaseDC (hWnd, hDC) ;
                        break ;
            case IDM_QUIT:                  /* send end of application message */
                        DestroyWindow (hWnd) ;
                        break ;
                }
            break ;
        case WM_DESTROY:                    /* stop application */
                DeleteObject (hBitmap) ;
                PostQuitMessage (0) ;
                break ;
        default:                    /* default windows message processing */
                return DefWindowProc (hWnd, iMessage, wParam, lParam) ;
    }
    return (0L) ;
}
```

CREATEBITMAP   ■ Win 2.0   ■ Win 3.0   ■ Win 3.1

Purpose	Creates a DDB bitmap based on an array of color bit values.
Syntax	HBITMAP **CreateBitmap**(int *nWidth*, int *nHeight*, BYTE *nPlanes*, BYTE *nBitCount*, LPSTR *lpBits*);
Description	This function creates a bitmap based on the array of color bit data pointed to by *lpBits*.
Uses	Not often used. Normally, bitmaps are created using the SDKPaint application and loaded as part of the application's resource data. See LoadBitmap() for an example.
Returns	HBITMAP, the bitmap handle. NULL on error.
See Also	CreateBitmapIndirect(), SelectObject(), DeleteObject(), SetBitmapBits()

Parameters

nWidth   int: The width, in pixels, of the bitmap.

nHeight   int: The height, in pixels, of the bitmap.

nPlanes   int: The number of color planes in the bitmap. This is used for devices (such as video boards) that specify colors with color planes. Each plane will need *nWidth* * *nHeight* bits.

nBitCount   int: The number of color bits per display pixel. Either *nPlanes* or *nBitCount* will be set to one in all cases. For black and white bitmaps, both are set to one.

lpBits   LPSTR: A pointer to an array of byte values containing the pixel data. For black and white bitmaps, 0 is for black and 1 is for white. For color bitmaps, the colors are device dependent. lpBits can be set to NULL. Use SetBitmapBits() to initialize the bitmap data.

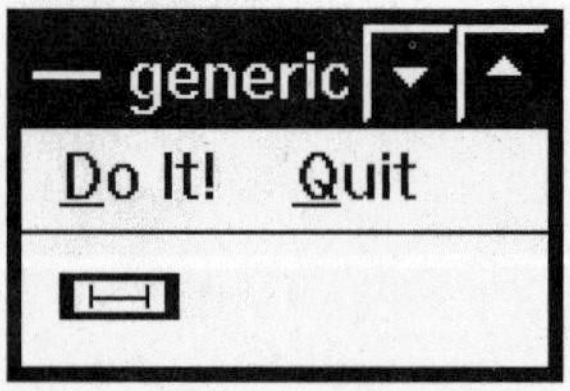

Figure 15-5. CreateBitmap( ) Example.

Example   This example (see Figure 15-5) paints a small bitmap at coordinates 10,10 in the upper left corner of the window's client area when the user clicks the "Do It!" menu item.

```
Long FAR PASCAL WndProc (HWND hWnd, unsigned iMessage, WORD wParam, LONG lParam)
{
        static          HBITMAP         hBitmap ;
        HDC                             hDC, hMemDC ;
        static  BYTE    BitMapBits [] = {              /* define bitmap pattern */
                0x00, 0x00, 0x00, 0x00,
                0x00, 0x00, 0x00, 0x00,
```

```
                      0x0f, 0xff, 0xff, 0xf0,
                      0x0f, 0x7f, 0xfe, 0xf0,
                      0x0f, 0x7f, 0xfe, 0xf0,
                      0x0f, 0x7f, 0xfe, 0xf0,
                      0x0f, 0x00, 0x00, 0xf0,
                      0x0f, 0x7f, 0xfe, 0xf0,
                      0x0f, 0x7f, 0xfe, 0xf0,
                      0x0f, 0xff, 0xff, 0xf0,
                      0x00, 0x00, 0x00, 0x00,
                      0x00, 0x00, 0x00, 0x00 } ;

      switch (iMessage)                 /* process windows messages */
      {
            case WM_CREATE:
                  hBitmap = CreateBitmap (32, 12, 1, 1, BitMapBits) ;
                  break ;
            case WM_COMMAND:            /* process menu items */
                  switch (wParam)
                  {
                  case IDM_DOIT:             /* User hit the "Do it" menu item */
                        hDC = GetDC (hWnd) ;
                        hMemDC = CreateCompatibleDC (hDC) ;
                        SelectObject (hMemDC, hBitmap) ;
                        BitBlt (hDC, 10, 10, 32, 12, hMemDC, 0, 0, SRCCOPY) ;
                        DeleteDC (hMemDC) ;
                        ReleaseDC (hWnd, hDC) ;
                        break ;
                  case IDM_QUIT:             /* send end of application message */
                        DestroyWindow (hWnd) ;
                        break ;
                  }
                  break ;
            case WM_DESTROY:            /* stop application */
                  DeleteObject (hBitmap) ;
                  PostQuitMessage (0) ;
                  break ;
            default:                    /* default windows message processing */
                  return DefWindowProc (hWnd, iMessage, wParam, lParam) ;
      }
      return (0L) ;
}
```

CREATEBITMAPINDIRECT   ■ Win 2.0   ■ Win 3.0   ■ Win 3.1

Purpose   Creates a DDB bitmap based on data in a BITMAP data structure.

Syntax   HBITMAP **CreateBitmapIndirect**(BITMAP FAR * *lpBitmap*);

Description   The BITMAP data structure is defined in WINDOWS.H as

```
typedef struct tagBITMAP
  {
        int             bmType;                 /* set to zero */
        int             bmWidth;                /* pixel width */
        int             bmHeight;               /* pixel height */
        int             bmWidthBytes;           /* no bytes per row */
        BYTE            bmPlanes;               /* no. color plains */
        BYTE            bmBitsPixel;            /* color bits/pixel */
        LPSTR           bmBits;                 /* pointer to bit data */
  } BITMAP;
typedef BITMAP                  *PBITMAP;
typedef BITMAP NEAR             *NPBITMAP;
typedef BITMAP FAR              *LPBITMAP;
```

Fill in this data structure and call CreateBitmapIndirect() as an alternative to calling Create-Bitmap(). The *bmBits* element should be set to point to an array of byte values containing the bitmap data. For black and white bitmaps, zero is black and 1 is white. For color bitmaps, the colors are device dependent.

Uses   Not often used. Normally, bitmaps are created using the SDKPaint application, and loaded as part of the application's resource data. See LoadBitmap() for an example.

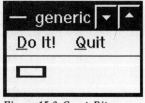

Returns   HBITMAP, the bitmap handle. NULL on error.

See Also   CreateBitmap(), SelectObject(), DeleteObject()

Parameters

lpBitmap   BITMAP FAR *: A far pointer to a bitmap data structure (shown above).

Figure 15-6. CreateBitmap-Indirect( ) Example.

Example   This example, as shown in Figure 15-6, paints a small, rectangular bitmap in the upper left corner of the window's client area when the user clicks the "Do It!" menu item.

```
long FAR PASCAL WndProc (HWND hWnd, unsigned iMessage, WORD wParam, LONG lParam)
{
        static          HBITMAP         hBitmap ;
        HDC                             hDC, hMemDC ;
        BITMAP                          bitmap ;
        static          BYTE    BitMapBits [] = {        /* define bitmap pattern */
        0x00, 0x00, 0x00, 0x00,
        0x00, 0x00, 0x00, 0x00,
        0x0f, 0xff, 0xff, 0xf0,
        0x0f, 0xff, 0xff, 0xf0,
        0x0f, 0xff, 0xff, 0xf0,
        0x0f, 0xff, 0xff, 0xf0,
        0x0f, 0xff, 0xff, 0xf0,
        0x0f, 0xff, 0xff, 0xf0,
        0x0f, 0xff, 0xff, 0xf0,
        0x0f, 0xff, 0xff, 0xf0,
        0x00, 0x00, 0x00, 0x00,
        0x00, 0x00, 0x00, 0x00 } ;

        switch (iMessage)                               /* process windows messages */
        {
        case WM_CREATE:
                bitmap.bmType = 0 ;
                bitmap.bmWidth = 32 ;
                bitmap.bmHeight = 12 ;
                bitmap.bmWidthBytes = 4 ;
                bitmap.bmPlanes = 1 ;
                bitmap.bmBitsPixel = 1 ;
                bitmap.bmBits = (LPSTR) BitMapBits ;
                hBitmap = CreateBitmapIndirect (
                        (BITMAP FAR *) &bitmap) ;
                break ;
        case WM_COMMAND:                        /* process menu items */
                switch (wParam)

                case IDM_DOIT:                  /* User hit the "Do it" menu item */
                        hDC = GetDC (hWnd) ;
                        hMemDC = CreateCompatibleDC (hDC) ;
                        SelectObject (hMemDC, hBitmap) ;
                        BitBlt (hDC, 10, 10, 32, 12, hMemDC, 0, 0,
                                SRCCOPY) ;
                        DeleteDC (hMemDC) ;
                        ReleaseDC (hWnd, hDC) ;
                        break ;
                case IDM_QUIT:                  /* send end of application message */
                        DestroyWindow (hWnd) ;
                        break ;
                }
                break ;
        case WM_DESTROY:                /* stop application */
                DeleteObject (hBitmap) ;
```

```
                            PostQuitMessage (0) ;
                            break ;
                default:                    /* default windows message processing */
                            return DefWindowProc (hWnd, iMessage, wParam, lParam) ;
        }
        return (OL) ;
}
```

CREATECOMPATIBLEBITMAP   ■ Win 2.0   ■ Win 3.0   ■ Win 3.1

Purpose	Creates a memory bitmap that is compatible with a device.
Syntax	HBITMAP **CreateCompatibleBitmap**(HDC *hDC*, int *nWidth*, int *nHeight*);
Description	This function creates a memory bitmap with the same number of color panes and the same number of color bits per pixel as the device specified by *hDC*. Bitmap can then be selected into a memory device context and drawn upon. The bitmap memory area is not initialized when created. It will be filled with random bytes and can be converted to a solid color by using a GDI function, such as Rectangle() or PatBlt(), to paint the memory device context.
Uses	Memory device contexts and compatible bitmaps allow an application to draw a complex figure in memory, and then quickly copy it to a physical device using BitBlt() and similar functions. This technique can be more attractive than letting an image appear in sections on the screen. It is also an efficient way to draw small repeating patterns (see the following example).
Returns	HBITMAP, the handle of the bitmap created. Returns NULL on error.
See Also	CreateCompatibleDC(), CreateDiscardableBitmap()
Parameters	
hDC	HDC: The device context handle for the physical device with which the bitmap is to be compatible. Typically, this is a handle to the window's client area device context, retrieved by either GetDC() or BeginPaint().
nWidth	int: The width, in pixels, to which the bitmap is to be initialized.
nHeight	int: The height, in pixels, to which the bitmap is to be initialized.

Figure 15-7. CreateCompatibleBitmap() Example.

Example   This example, shown in Figure 15-7, draws three identical patterns on the window's client area when the user clicks the "Do It!" menu item. Rather than use the GDI painting functions for each of the drawings, the application draws the pattern to a memory device context containing a bitmap compatible with the screen. As soon as that pattern is painted to the memory device context, the pattern can be copied to the window's client area efficiently using BitBlt(). Note that similar efficiencies could have been obtained using a metafile.

```
long FAR PASCAL WndProc (HWND hWnd, unsigned iMessage, WORD wParam, LONG lParam)
{
        static          HBITMAP         hBitmap ;
        HDC                             hDC, hMemDC ;
        int                             i ;

        switch (iMessage)                               /* process windows messages */
        {
                case WM_COMMAND:                        /* process menu items */
                        switch (wParam)
```

```
                                {
                                case IDM_DOIT:  /* first create a memory dc */
                                        hDC = GetDC (hWnd) ;
                                        hMemDC = CreateCompatibleDC (hDC) ;
                                        hBitmap = CreateCompatibleBitmap (hDC,
                                                50, 50) ;
                                                /* paint on memory device context */
                                        SelectObject (hMemDC, hBitmap) ;
                                        SelectObject (hMemDC, GetStockObject (BLACK_BRUSH)) ;
                                        Rectangle (hMemDC, 0, 0, 50, 50) ;
                                        SelectObject (hMemDC, GetStockObject (WHITE_BRUSH)) ;
                                        Ellipse (hMemDC, 0, 0, 50, 50) ;
                                        Rectangle (hMemDC, 5, 5, 45, 45) ;
                                        Ellipse (hMemDC, 10, 10, 40, 40) ;
                                        SelectObject (hMemDC, GetStockObject (BLACK_BRUSH)) ;
                                        Rectangle (hMemDC, 15, 15, 35, 35) ;
                                                /* now copy the memory device context to screen */
                                        for (i = 0 ; i < 3 ;i++)
                                                BitBlt (hDC, 0, 50 * i, 50, 50 + (50 * i),
                                                        hMemDC, 0, 0, SRCCOPY) ;
                                        DeleteDC (hMemDC) ;
                                        DeleteObject (hBitmap) ;
                                        ReleaseDC (hWnd, hDC) ;
                                        break ;
```

[Other program lines]

CREATEDIBITMAP   □ Win 2.0   ■ Win 3.0   ■ Win 3.1

Purpose   Creates a memory DDB bitmap based on device-independent bitmap (DIB) data.

Syntax   HBITMAP **CreateDIBitmap**(HDC *hDC*, LPBITMAPINFOHEADER *lpInfoHeader*, DWORD *dwUsage*, LPSTR *lpInitBits*, LPBITMAPINFO *lpInitInfo*, WORD *wUsage*);

Description The CreateDIBitmap() function creates a memory DDB bitmap based on data in several data structures. The primary structure is BITMAPINFO, defined in WINDOWS.H as

```
typedef struct tagBITMAPINFO {
        BITMAPINFOHEADER          bmiHeader;
        RGBQUAD                   bmiColors[1];
} BITMAPINFO;
typedef BITMAPINFO FAR *LPBITMAPINFO;
typedef BITMAPINFO *PBITMAPINFO;
```

BITMAPINFO contains two other structures, BITMAPINFOHEADER and RGBQUAD, also defined in WINDOWS.H.

⇨ The BITMAPINFOHEADER Structure

```
typedef struct tagBITMAPINFOHEADER{
        DWORD           biSize;         /* size of BITMAPINFOHEADER */
        DWORD           biWidth;        /* width in pixels */
        DWORD           biHeight;               /* height in pixels */
        WORD            biPlanes;               /* always 1 */
        WORD            biBitCount;             /* color bits per pixel */
                                                /* must be 1, 4, 8 or 24 */
        DWORD           biCompression;                  /* BI_RGB, BI_RLE8 */
                                                        /* or BI_RLE4 */
        DWORD           biSizeImage;            /* total bytes in image */
        DWORD           biXPelsPerMeter;                /* 0, or opt. h res. */
        DWORD           biYPelsPerMeter;                /* 0, or opt. v res. */
        DWORD           biClrUsed;              /* normally 0, can set a */
                                                /* lower no. colors than biBitCount */
        DWORD           biClrImportant;         /* normally 0 */
} BITMAPINFOHEADER;

typedef BITMAPINFOHEADER FAR *LPBITMAPINFOHEADER;
typedef BITMAPINFOHEADER *PBITMAPINFOHEADER;
```

⇨ RGBQuad Structure

```
typedef struct tagRGBQUAD {
        BYTE     rgbBlue;
        BYTE     rgbGreen;
        BYTE     rgbRed;
        BYTE     rgbReserved;
} RGBQUAD;
```

Uses There are two ways to use CreateDIBitmap(). If *dwUsage* is set to NULL, an uninitialized DIB bitmap is created. This is the first step in using the DIB with a memory device context. If *dwUsage* is set to CBM_INIT, CreateDIBitmap() is used to create a complete DDB bitmap. Data is passed to the function for all color values and header settings.

Returns HBITMAP, a handle to the bitmap created. NULL on error.

See Also GetDIBits(), CreateBitmap()

Parameters

hDC HDC: The device context of the physical device to which the bitmap will be mapped. Typically, this is the window's client area device context, retrieved with either GetDC() or BeginPaint().

lpInfoHeader LPBITMAPINFOHEADER: A pointer to a BITMAPINFOHEADER data structure. The values in this structure must be set before CreateDIBitmap() is called. These values determine the size and color resolution of the bitmap.

dwUsage DWORD: Determines if CreateDIBitmap() creates an initialized or uninitialized bitmap. If NULL, the bitmap is created uninitialized, and the following three parameters should be set to NULL. If *dwUsage* equals CBM_INIT, the bitmap is initialized based on the data pointed to by *lpInitBits* and *lpInitInfo*.

lpInitBits LPSTR: A pointer to an array of bitmap pixel color values. The format will depend on the color resolution of the device, as specified in the BITMAPINFO data pointed to by *lpInitInfo*.

lpInitInfo LPBITMAPINFO: A pointer to a BITMAPINFO data structure containing the data format used in *lpInitBits*.

wUsage WORD: Specifies if the *bmiColors[]* fields in the *lpInitInfo* data structure contain explicit RGB values, or if they are 16-bit indexes, to the currently realized logical palette. DIB_PAL_COLORS specifies palette entries. DIB_RGB_COLORS specifies explicit colors.

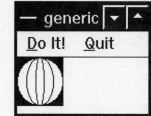

Example This example paints a small globe image on the window's client area when the user clicks the "Do It!" menu item. The image shown in Figure 15-8 is created by painting on a memory device context containing a 50 by 50 pixel DIB bitmap. The bitmap is then copied to the screen using BitBlt().

Figure 15-8. CreateDIBit-map() Example.

```
Long FAR PASCAL WndProc (HWND hWnd, unsigned iMessage, WORD wParam, LONG lParam)
{
        BITMAPINFOHEADER                  bi ;
        BITMAPINFOHEADER FAR              *lpbi ;
        HBITMAP                           hBitmap ;
        HDC                               hDC, hMemDC ;
        HANDLE                            hDIB ;

        switch (iMessage)                         /* process windows messages */
        {
                case WM_COMMAND:                  /* process menu items */
                        switch (wParam)
                        {
                        case IDM_DOIT:
                                hDC = GetDC (hWnd) ;
```

```
                            /* initialize BITMAPINFOHEADER data */
           bi.biSize = sizeof (BITMAPINFOHEADER) ;
           bi.biWidth = 50 ;          /* 50 by 50 bitmap */
           bi.biHeight = 50 ;
           bi.biPlanes = 1 ;
           bi.biBitCount = 4 ;        /* 16 colors on screen */
           bi.biCompression = BI_RGB ;      /* no compression */
           bi.biSizeImage = 0 ;
           bi.biXPelsPerMeter = 0 ;
           bi.biYPelsPerMeter = 0 ;
           bi.biClrUsed = 0 ;
           bi.biClrImportant = 0 ;
                            /* create uninitialized DIB bitmap */
           hBitmap = CreateDIBitmap (hDC, &bi, OL,
                   NULL,   NULL, 0) ;
                            /* allocate memory for BITMAPINFOstruct */
           hDIB = GlobalAlloc (GHND,
                   sizeof (BITMAPINFOHEADER) +
                   16 * sizeof (RGBQUAD)) ;
           lpbi = (BITMAPINFOHEADER FAR *)
                   GlobalLock (hDIB) ;
                            /* copy bi to top of BITMAPINFO */
           *lpbi = bi ;
                            /* use GetDIBits() to init bi struct data */
           GetDIBits (hDC, hBitmap, 0, 50, NULL,
                   (LPBITMAPINFO) lpbi, DIB_RGB_COLORS) ;
           GlobalUnlock (hDIB) ;
                            /* create memory device context */
           hMemDC = CreateCompatibleDC (hDC) ;
                            /* select DIB bitmap into device context */
           SelectObject (hMemDC, hBitmap) ;
                            /* paint on memory device context */
           SelectObject (hMemDC, GetStockObject
                   (BLACK_BRUSH)) ;
           Rectangle (hMemDC, 0, 0, 50, 50) ;
           SelectObject (hMemDC, GetStockObject
                   (WHITE_BRUSH)) ;
           Ellipse (hMemDC, 0, 0, 50, 50) ;
           Ellipse (hMemDC, 10, 0, 40, 50) ;
           Ellipse (hMemDC, 20, 0, 30, 50) ;
                            /* copy the memory dc to screen */
           BitBlt (hDC, 0, 0, 50, 50, hMemDC, 0, 0,
                   SRCCOPY) ;
           DeleteDC (hMemDC) ;
           GlobalFree (hDIB) ;
           ReleaseDC (hWnd, hDC) ;
           break ;
```

[Other program lines]

CREATEDIBPATTERNBRUSH   □ Win 2.0   ■ Win 3.0   ■ Win 3.1

Purpose	Creates a pattern brush based on a device-independent bitmap stored in a global memory block.
Syntax	HBRUSH **CreateDIBPatternBrush**(HANDLE *hPackedDIB*,WORD *wUsage*);
Description	This function works by passing a handle to a memory block containing both the BITMAPINFO structure data and the pixel data for the bitmap. The memory block is read and converted to a brush pattern that can be selected into a device context for painting.
Uses	Using a DIB pattern brush provides a way to ensure that the colors will not end up drastically different when displayed on a different device. See the example program at the beginning of this chapter for how to use the DIB color data to realize a logical palette.
Returns	HBRUSH, a handle to the brush created. NULL on error.
See Also	GetDIBits(), CreateDIBitmap()

Parameters

hPackedDIB   GLOBALHANDLE: The handle of a global memory block (allocated with GlobalAlloc()) that contains the bitmap data. The memory block must contain an initialized BITMAPINFO data structure at the beginning, followed immediately by the bitmap bytes. The size of the bitmap data will depend on the color resolution and the height/width of the bitmap. Each line of the bitmap data must terminate on an even DWORD address (an even 32 bits). This requirement will extend the size of the memory area needed if the bitmap size (width * color bits) does not end on an even 32-bit boundary.

wUsage   WORD: Specifies whether the *bmiColors[]* fields at the end of the BITMAPINFO data structure contain explicit RGB color values, or if they are indexes into the currently realized logical palette. *wUsage* can be either DIB_PAL_COLORS for palette colors, or DIB_RGB_COLORS for explicit RGB colors.

Example   This example, illustrated in Figure 15-9, creates a device-independent bitmap, and uses it as a brush to paint a square area. The DIB is created uninitialized, and then painted in a memory device context. Once painted, the pixel data is copied to the end of the memory buffer containing the BITMAPINFO data. The memory block containing both the BITMAPINFO data followed by the bitmap pixels is read by CreateDIBPattern-Brush() to create the pattern brush. Once the pattern is selected into the device context, painting a rectangle results in the area being filled with the DIB pattern.

Figure 15-9. CreateDIB-PatternBrush() Example.

Note that the ALIGNLONG macro is defined to help compute even DWORD address lengths for the storage of the bitmap data. For simplicity, this example assumes a 16-color device context. This example also omits error checking for memory allocation.

```c
#define ALIGNLONG(i)    ((i+3)/4*4)
#define WIDTH           8
#define HEIGHT          8
#define COLORBITS       4

Long FAR PASCAL WndProc (HWND hWnd, unsigned iMessage, WORD wParam, LONG lParam)
{
        static          BITMAPINFOHEADER                bi ;
        LPBITMAPINFOHEADER                              lpbi ;
        HBITMAP                                         hBitmap ;
        HDC                                             hDC, hMemDC ;
        HANDLE                                          hDIB ;
        HBRUSH                                          hDIBrush ;
        LPSTR                                           lpstBitmap ;

        switch (iMessage)                       /* process windows messages */
        {
                case WM_COMMAND:                /* process menu items */
                        switch (wParam)
                        {
                        case IDM_DOIT:
                                hDC = GetDC (hWnd) ;
                                        /* initialize BITMAPINFOHEADER data */
                                bi.biSize = sizeof (BITMAPINFOHEADER) ;
                                bi.biWidth = WIDTH ;     /* 8 by 8 bitmap */
                                bi.biHeight = HEIGHT ;
                                bi.biPlanes = 1 ;
                                bi.biBitCount = COLORBITS ;      /* 16 colors */
```

```
                        bi.biCompression = BI_RGB ;
                        bi.biSizeImage =
                            (ALIGNLONG((WIDTH * COLORBITS)/8) * HEIGHT);
                        bi.biXPelsPerMeter = 0 ;
                        bi.biYPelsPerMeter = 0 ;
                        bi.biClrUsed = 0 ;
                        bi.biClrImportant = 0 ;
                            /* create uninitialized DIB bitmap */
                        hBitmap = CreateDIBitmap (hDC, &bi, OL, NULL,
                            NULL, O) ;
                            /* allocate memory for BITMAPINFO structure */
                        hDIB = GlobalAlloc (GHND, sizeof (BITMAPINFOHEADER) +
                            16 * sizeof (RGBQUAD) +
                            (ALIGNLONG((WIDTH * COLORBITS)/8) * HEIGHT));
                        lpbi = (BITMAPINFOHEADER FAR *) GlobalLock (hDIB) ;
                            /* tricky way to copy bi to top of BITMAPINFO */
                        *lpbi = bi ;
                            /* use GetDIBits() to init lpbi struct data */
                        GetDIBits (hDC, hBitmap, 0, 50, NULL,
                            (LPBITMAPINFO) lpbi,    DIB_RGB_COLORS) ;

                            /* create memory device context */
                        hMemDC = CreateCompatibleDC (hDC) ;
                            /* select DIB bitmap into device context */
                        SelectObject (hMemDC, hBitmap) ;
                            /* paint on memory device context */
                        SelectObject (hMemDC, GetStockObject (BLACK_BRUSH)) ;
                        Rectangle (hMemDC, O, O, WIDTH, HEIGHT) ;
                        SelectObject (hMemDC, GetStockObject (WHITE_BRUSH)) ;
                        Ellipse (hMemDC, O, O, WIDTH, HEIGHT) ;
                            /* set pointer to bitmap's bit data */
                        lpstBitmap = (LPSTR) lpbi +
                            (WORD) sizeof (BITMAPINFOHEADER) +
                            (16 * sizeof (RGBQUAD)) ;
                        GetDIBits (hDC, hBitmap, O, HEIGHT, lpstBitmap,
                            (LPBITMAPINFO) lpbi, DIB_RGB_COLORS) ;

                            /* now use DIB as pattern brush */
                        hDIBrush = CreateDIBPatternBrush (hDIB,
                            DIB_RGB_COLORS) ;
                        SelectObject (hDC, hDIBrush) ;
                        PatBlt (hDC, O, O, 100, 100, PATCOPY) ;

                        GlobalUnlock (hDIB) ;
                        GlobalFree (hDIB) ;
                        DeleteDC (hMemDC) ;
                        ReleaseDC (hWnd, hDC) ;
                        break ;
```

[Other program lines]

CREATEDISCARDABLEBITMAP   ■ Win 2.0   ■ Win 3.0   ■ Win 3.1

Purpose   Creates a DDB bitmap that is compatible with a device. Windows can discard the bitmap data if the bitmap is not selected.

Syntax   HBITMAP **CreateDiscardableBitmap**(HDC *hDC*, int *nWidth*, int *nHeight*);

Description   This function is identical to CreateCompatibleBitmap(), except that the memory for the bitmap is discardable. CreateDiscardableBitmap() creates a DDB bitmap with the same number of color panes and the same number of color bits per pixel as the device specified by *hDC*. The bitmap can then be selected into a memory device context and drawn upon.

    The bitmap memory area is not initialized when created. It will be filled with random bytes and can be converted to a solid color by using a GDI function, such as Rectangle(), to paint the memory device context.

    Windows will only discard the bitmap data if the bitmap is not selected into a device context. The application can test whether the bitmap has been discarded by determining if SelectObject()

returns NULL when an attempt is made to select the bitmap. In that case, the bitmap handle should be deleted with DeleteObject(), and the bitmap re-created and redrawn.

Uses Memory device contexts and compatible bitmaps allow an application to draw a complex figure in memory, and then quickly copy it to a physical device using BitBlt() and similar functions. This technique can be more attractive than letting an image appear in sections on the screen. It is also an efficient way to draw small repeating patterns (see the following example). Having the memory for the bitmap discardable gives Windows the maximum freedom to use available memory.

Returns HBITMAP, the handle of the bitmap created. Returns NULL on error.

See Also CreateCompatibleDC(), CreateCompatibleBitmap()

Parameters

hDC HDC: The device context handle for the physical device with which the bitmap is to be compatible. Typically, this is a handle to the window's client area device context, retrieved by either GetDC() or BeginPaint().

nWidth int: The width, in pixels, to which the bitmap is to be initialized.

nHeight int: The height, in pixels, to which the bitmap is to be initialized.

Example This example draws nine identical patterns on the window's client area when the user clicks the "Do It!" menu item. (See Figure 15-10.) Rather than use the GDI painting functions for each of the drawings, the application draws the pattern to a memory device context containing a bitmap compatible with the screen. As soon as that pattern is painted to the memory device context, the pattern can be efficiently copied to the window's client area using BitBlt().

This code fragment tests to see if the discardable bitmap is still valid using SelectObject(). In this case, the bitmap is redrawn every time the "Do It!" menu item is selected. A more complex program would draw the bitmap in a separate function. This function would be called at the beginning of the program, and again later if the bitmap was discarded and needed to be re-created and redrawn.

Figure 15-10. CreateDiscardableBitmap() Example.

```
long FAR PASCAL WndProc (HWND hWnd, unsigned iMessage, WORD wParam, LONG lParam)
{
        static          HBITMAP         hBitmap ;
        HDC                             hDC, hMemDC ;
        int                             i, j ;

        switch (iMessage)                       /* process windows messages */
        {
        case WM_CREATE:
                hDC = GetDC (hWnd) ;
                hBitmap = CreateDiscardableBitmap (hDC, 50, 50) ;
                ReleaseDC (hWnd, hDC) ;
                break ;
        case WM_COMMAND:                        /* process menu items */
                switch (wParam)
                {
                case IDM_DOIT:          /* first create a memory dc */
                        hDC = GetDC (hWnd) ;
                        hMemDC = CreateCompatibleDC (hDC) ;
                        if (SelectObject (hMemDC, hBitmap) == NULL)
                        {
                                DeleteObject (hBitmap) ;
```

```
                              hBitmap = CreateDiscardableBitmap
                                     (hDC, 50, 50) ;
                        }
                                     /* paint on memory device context */
                        Rectangle (hMemDC, 0, 0, 50, 50) ;
                        SelectObject (hMemDC, GetStockObject
                               (BLACK_BRUSH)) ;
                        Ellipse (hMemDC, 0, 0, 50, 50) ;
                        SelectObject (hMemDC, GetStockObject
                               (WHITE_BRUSH)) ;
                        Rectangle (hMemDC, 5, 5, 45, 45) ;
                        SelectObject (hMemDC, GetStockObject
                               (BLACK_BRUSH)) ;
                        Ellipse (hMemDC, 10, 10, 40, 40) ;
                        SelectObject (hMemDC, GetStockObject
                               (WHITE_BRUSH)) ;
                        Rectangle (hMemDC, 15, 15, 35, 35) ;
                                     /* now copy the memory dc to screen */
                        for (j = 0 ; j < 3 ; j++)
                        {
                               for (i = 0 ; i < 3 ; i++)
                               {
                                      BitBlt (hDC, 50 * j, 50 * i,
                                             50 + (50 * j),
                                             50 + (50 * i), hMemDC,
                                             0, 0, SRCCOPY) ;
                               }
                        }
                        DeleteDC (hMemDC) ;
                        ReleaseDC (hWnd, hDC) ;
                        break ;
                 case IDM_QUIT:          /* send end of application message */
                        DestroyWindow (hWnd) ;
                        break ;
                 }
                 break ;
          case WM_DESTROY:              /* stop application */
                 DeleteObject (hBitmap) ;
                 PostQuitMessage (0) ;
                 break ;
          default:                      /* default windows message processing */
                 return DefWindowProc (hWnd, iMessage, wParam, lParam) ;
      }
      return (0L) ;
}
```

GETBITMAPBITS   ■ Win 2.0   ■ Win 3.0   ■ Win 3.1

Purpose	Loads the DDB bitmap data into a memory block.
Syntax	DWORD **GetBitmapBits**(HBITMAP *hBitmap*, LONG *dwCount*, LPSTR *lpBits*);
Description	DDB Bitmaps consist of a header of type BITMAP, and a block of data that contains the color data for each pixel in the bitmap. GetObject() is used to retrieve the data in the BITMAP header. GetBitmapBits() is used to retrieve the pixel data. The size of the memory block can be computed from the BITMAP data retrieved with GetObject. Use the formula

$dwCount = $ (DWORD) $bm.bmWidthBytes * bm.bmHeight * bm.bmPlanes$;

Uses	Used in cases where the application needs to selectively change some of the color pixels in the DDB bitmap. For example, a bitmap used as a button can be copied and modified to create a similar bitmap showing the button in a depressed or activated state.
Returns	DWORD, the number of bytes copied. Zero on error.
See Also	SetBitmapBits(), GetObject()
Parameters	
hBitmap	HANDLE: The handle of the bitmap.

dwCount   DWORD: The number of bytes to copy to the *lpBits* buffer. Use the *dwCount* formula to compute this number.

lpBits   LPSTR: A pointer to a memory block to hold the bitmap data. Normally, this block is allocated using GlobalAlloc().

Example   This example loads a bitmap from the application's resource data when the WM_CREATE message is processed. The bitmap's data is loaded into a temporary global memory block. Each byte of the bitmap data is examined. White pixels are converted to black, and black pixels to white. Colored pixels are not changed. The modified bitmap data is then written back to the bitmap, and the global memory block freed. The bitmap is displayed as a stretched image on the window's client area when the user clicks the "Do It!" menu item. Although not visible in Figure 15-11, the colors on the interior of the pen are not changed by the transformation. Note that this example assumes eight color bits per pixel. The program logic would need to be expanded to cover other color resolutions.

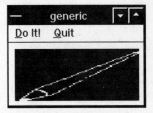

Figure 15-11. GetBitmap-Bits() Example.

```
long FAR PASCAL WndProc (HWND hWnd, unsigned iMessage, WORD wParam, LONG lParam)
{
        static          HBITMAP         hBitmap ;
        HDC                             hDC, hMemDC ;
        int                             nStrMode ;
        BITMAP                          bm ;
        DWORD                           dwBitmapSize, dwCount ;
        HANDLE                          hMem ;
        LPSTR                           lpMem, lpData ;

        switch (iMessage)                       /* process windows messages */
        {
                case WM_CREATE:
                        hBitmap = LoadBitmap (ghInstance , "pen") ;
                        GetObject (hBitmap, sizeof (BITMAP), (LPSTR) &bm) ;
                        dwBitmapSize = (DWORD) bm.bmWidthBytes * bm.bmHeight *
                                bm.bmPlanes ;
                        hMem = GlobalAlloc (GMEM_MOVEABLE, dwBitmapSize) ;
                        lpMem = GlobalLock (hMem) ;
                        GetBitmapBits (hBitmap, dwBitmapSize, lpMem) ;
                        lpData = lpMem ;
                        for (dwCount = 0 ; dwCount < dwBitmapSize ; dwCount++)
                        {
                                if (0xff == (BYTE) *lpData)
                                        *lpData = 0 ;           /* change white to black */
                                else if (0 == (BYTE) *lpData)
                                        *lpData = 0xff ;        /* change black to white */
                                lpData++ ;
                        }
                        SetBitmapBits (hBitmap, dwBitmapSize, lpMem) ;
                        GlobalUnlock (hMem) ;
                        GlobalFree (hMem) ;
                        break ;
                case WM_COMMAND:                        /* process menu items */
                        switch (wParam)
                        {
                        case IDM_DOIT:          /* User hit the "Do it" menu item */
                                hDC = GetDC (hWnd) ;
                                hMemDC = CreateCompatibleDC (hDC) ;
                                SetStretchBltMode (hDC, COLORONCOLOR) ;
                                SelectObject (hMemDC, hBitmap) ;
                                StretchBlt (hDC, 10, 10, 200, 80, hMemDC,
                                        0, 0, 60, 60, SRCCOPY) ;
                                DeleteDC (hMemDC) ;
                                ReleaseDC (hWnd, hDC) ;
```

```
                            break ;
                  case IDM_QUIT:            /* send end of application message */
                        DestroyWindow (hWnd) ;
                        break ;
                  }
                  break ;
            case WM_DESTROY:                /* stop application */
                  DeleteObject (hBitmap) ;
                  PostQuitMessage (0) ;
                  break ;
            default:                  /* default windows message processing */
                  return DefWindowProc (hWnd, iMessage, wParam, lParam) ;
      }
      return (0L) ;
}
```

GetBitmapDimension ■ Win 2.0   ■ Win 3.0   ■ Win 3.1

Purpose	Retrieves two values that were associated with the bitmap by a previous call to SetBitmap-Dimension().
Syntax	DWORD **GetBitmapDimension**(HBITMAP *hBitmap*);
Description	The SetBitmapDimension() function sets two integer values, *X* and *Y*, which are associated with the bitmap. These values do not affect the bitmap. They are provided so that an application can store dimensional data with the bitmap. This is preferable to using static or global variables to store the width and height of the bitmap. The Windows SDK documentation suggests using the MM_LOMETRIC system of units (0.1 mm per unit) to specify the bitmap size. Because the values are not used in painting the bitmap, any system of units (including device units — pixels) can be used.
Uses	Handy if an application uses a number of bitmaps that are different sizes.
Returns	DWORD. The low-order word contains the *X* value. The high-order word contains the *Y* value. If SetBitmapDimension() was not called previously to set these values, zero is returned.
See Also	SetBitmapDimension()

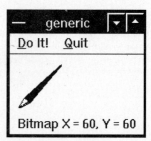

Figure 15-12. GetBit-mapDimension() Example.

Parameters

hBitmap   HBITMAP: The handle of the bitmap.

Example   This example, which is illustrated in Figure 15-12, sets the "dimension" values associated with the bitmap to 60,60 when the bitmap is first loaded from the resource file. When the user clicks the "Do It!" menu item, the bitmap is painted and the "dimension" values are displayed.

```
long FAR PASCAL WndProc (HWND hWnd, unsigned iMessage, WORD wParam, LONG lParam)
{
        static          HBITMAP         hBitmap ;
        HDC                             hDC, hMemDC ;
        DWORD                           dwBmSize ;
        char                            cBuf [128] ;

        switch (iMessage)                       /* process windows messages */
        {
        case WM_CREATE:
                hBitmap = LoadBitmap (ghInstance , "pen") ;
                SetBitmapDimension (hBitmap, 60, 60) ;
                break ;
        case WM_COMMAND:                        /* process menu items */
                switch (wParam)
                {
```

```
                    case IDM_DOIT:          /* User hit the "Do it" menu item */
                        hDC = GetDC (hWnd) ;
                        hMemDC = CreateCompatibleDC (hDC) ;
                        SelectObject (hMemDC, hBitmap) ;
                        BitBlt (hDC, 10, 10, 60, 60, hMemDC, 0, 0,
                            SRCCOPY) ;
                        DeleteDC (hMemDC) ;
                        dwBmSize = GetBitmapDimension (hBitmap) ;
                        TextOut (hDC, 10, 80, cBuf, wsprintf (cBuf,
                            "Bitmap X = %d, Y = %d", LOWORD (dwBmSize),
                            HIWORD (dwBmSize))) ;
                        ReleaseDC (hWnd, hDC) ;
                        break ;
                    case IDM_QUIT:          /* send end of application message */
                        DestroyWindow (hWnd) ;
                        break ;
                    }
                    break ;
            case WM_DESTROY:                /* stop application */
                    DeleteObject (hBitmap) ;
                    PostQuitMessage (0) ;
                    break ;
            default:                        /* default windows message processing */
                    return DefWindowProc (hWnd, iMessage, wParam, lParam) ;
        }
        return (0L) ;
}
```

GetDIBits   □ Win 2.0   ■ Win 3.0   ■ Win 3.1

Purpose	Fills in the BITMAPINFO data for a device-independent bitmap, and/or writes a DIB's pixel data into a memory buffer.
Syntax	int **GetDIBits**(HDC *hDC*, HANDLE *hBitmap*, WORD *nStartScan*, WORD *nNumScans*, LPSTR *lpBits*, LPBITMAPINFO *lpBitsInfo*, WORD *wUsage*);
Description	This function does two related functions. If the *lpBits* parameter is NULL, GetDIBits() fills in the BITMAPINFO data structure to which the *lpBitsInfo* parameter points. This is the normal way to copy device context color values to the *bmiColors* part of the BITMAPINFO data structure.
	If *lpBits* is not NULL, the function copies the pixel values for a bitmap to the memory area pointed to by *lpBits*. In this case, *lpBits* normally points to an address in a global memory block, right after the BITMAPINFO header data. A memory block containing a combination of a BITMAPINFO header, followed by the bitmap bits, is a complete device-independent bitmap. If the bitmap is to be written to a disk file, the data just described should be preceded by a BITMAPFILEHEADER data structure. Note that the origin for DIBs is the bottom left corner of the array instead of the top left corner. This origin makes the bits upside down relative to the default MM_TEXT mapping mode for a device context.
Uses	Used in the creation of device-independent bitmaps. For large bitmaps, the bitmap data can be read as a series of horizontal bands by specifying different *nStartScan* and *nNumScans* values. This technique reduces memory demands.
Returns	int, the number of lines of pixels copied from the bitmap. Zero on error.
See Also	SetDIBits(), SetDIBitsToDevice(), StretchDIBits(). The function description for Create-DIBitmap() includes the BITMAPINFO header definition. See CreateDIBPatternBrush() also.
Parameters	
hDC	HDC: The device context handle for the device to which the DIB is to be mapped. The device context will determine the color values written to the RGBQUAD color table in the BITMAPINFO structure.
hBitmap	HBITMAP: A handle to the bitmap.

nStartScan	WORD: The first pixel line number on which to start in the bitmap. Usually, zero.
nNumScans	WORD: The number of lines of pixels to be copied. Normally, equal to the vertical height of the bitmap in pixels.
lpBits	LPSTR: A pointer to a memory buffer that will contain the bitmap data after the function is called. If set to NULL, only the *lpBitsInfo* data is written, not the bitmap bits. Setting this parameter to NULL is the normal way to write a set of color values to the *bmiColors* data section of the BITMAPINFO structure. The number of colors written will depend on the color resolution of the device. (See Table 15-5.)

Color Bits	Number of Colors	⊠
1	A monochrome bitmap. *bmiColors* will contain two entries. Each bit in the bitmap data will represent one pixel.	
4	A bitmap with 16 colors. *bmiColors* will contain 16 entries. Each pixel requires four bits of information in the bitmap data. The four bits represent an index in the color table.	
8	A bitmap with 256 colors. *bmiColors* will contain 256 entries. Each pixel requires a byte of information in the bitmap data. The byte value represents an index into the color table.	
24	A bitmap with 224 colors. *bmiColors* will contain NULL. Each pixel requires three bytes of information, representing the RGB (Red, Green, Blue) color bytes.	

Table 15-5. Color Resolutions.

lpBitsInfo	LPBITMAPINFO: A pointer to a BITMAPINFO data structure that specifies the size and color format of the bitmap. The pointer can point to the top of the same memory area the bitmap data is being written to if the BITMAPINFO data has been initialized.
wUsage	WORD: Specifies whether the *bmiColors[]* fields at the end of the BITMAPINFO data structure contain explicit RGB color values, or if they are indexes into the currently realized logical palette. *wUsage* can be either DIB_PAL_COLORS for palette colors, or DIB_RGB_COLORS for explicit RGB colors.
Example	The example under CreateDIBPatternBrush() includes both usages of this function.

GETSTRETCHBLTMODE

■ Win 2.0　　■ Win 3.0　　■ Win 3.1

Purpose	Determines the current bitmap stretching mode of a device context.
Syntax	int **GetStretchBltMode**(HDC *hDC*);
Description	The stretching mode determines how pixels are eliminated if a bitmap image is changed in size. Bitmaps that are increased in size end up simply adding more matching pixels between existing ones. The stretching mode becomes a property of the device context, and remains in effect until the device context is deleted or a new stretching mode is set.
Uses	Used to determine if the stretching mode needs to be changed using SetStretchBltMode().
Returns	Returns the current stretching mode which can be any of the modes listed in Table 15-6.

Value	Meaning	⊠
BLACKONWHITE	Preserves black pixels at the expense of white ones.	
COLORONCOLOR	Deletes eliminated lines. No attempt to use the color value information of the eliminated pixels.	
WHITEONBLACK	Preserves white pixels at the expense of black ones.	

Table 15-6. Bitmap Stretching Modes.

See Also	SetStretchBltMode(), StretchBlt()
Parameters	
hDC	HDC: The device context handle.
Example	See the example under StretchBlt().

LOADBITMAP

■ Win 2.0   ■ Win 3.0   ■ Win 3.1

Purpose	Loads a bitmap resource into memory.
Syntax	HBITMAP **LoadBitmap**(HANDLE *hInstance*, LPSTR *lpBitmapName*);
Description	Bitmap images are normally created using the Windows SDKPaint application. The output of SDKPaint is stored in a file with the .BMP extension. To use a bitmap, the application must list the bitmap file in the .RC resource script file, using the BITMAP statement. Within the application's code, LoadBitmap() is used to load the bitmap data from the resource data into memory. After the application is finished using the bitmap, DeleteObject() should be called to free the bitmap from memory.

This function will load either DDB or DIB bitmaps. If a DIB is loaded, it will be converted to a DDB, losing color information. See the discussion on DIBs at the beginning of this chapter for an example using the DIB color data to create a logical palette.

Uses	This is the first step in using a bitmap file within a program.
Returns	HBITMAP, the bitmap handle. Returns NULL on error, usually meaning that the bitmap was not found in the resource data.
See Also	DeleteObject(), PatBlt()
Parameters	
hInstance	HANDLE: The instance handle of the module (running program) which has the bitmap in its resource data. You can use GetWindowWord() to obtain this value. If *hInstance* is NULL, LoadBitmap() accesses one of the predefined bitmaps listed below.

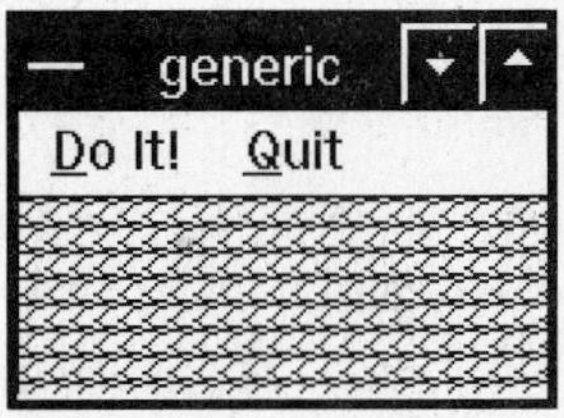

Figure 15-13. LoadBitmap() and PatBlt() Example.

lpBitmapName   LPSTR: A pointer to a null-terminated character string containing the bitmap name. The string is the name to the left of the BITMAP statement in the application's .RC resource script file. For example, the line

```
mybitmap              BITMAP        bitfile.bmp
```

names the bitmap "mybitmap." The bitmap data is loaded from the file BITFILE.BMP.

If *hInstance* is NULL, *lpBitmapName* must be one of the following predefined bitmap names:

OBM_BTNCORNERS, OBM_BTSIZE, OBM_CHECK, OBM_CHECKBOXES, OBM_CLOSE, OBM_COMBO, OBM_DNARROW, OBM_DNARROWD, OBM_DNARROWI, OBM_LFARROW, OBM_LFARROWI, OBM_MNARROW, OBM_OLD_CLOSE, OBM_OLD_DNARROW, OBM_OLD_LFARROW, OBM_OLD_REDUCE, OBM_OLD_RESTORE, OBM_OLD_RGARROW, OBM_OLD_UPARROW, OBM_OLD_ZOOM, OBM_REDUCE, OBM_REDUCED, OBM_RESTORE, OBM_RESTORED, OBM_RGARROW, OBM_RGARROWD, OBM_RGARROWI, OBM_SIZE, OBM_UPARROW, OBM_UPARROWD, OBM_UPARROWI, OBM_ZOOM, OBM_ZOOMD

The values starting with OBM_OLD are bitmaps used by versions of Windows prior to 3.0

Example	This example paints the client area with a bitmap pattern brush, as shown in Figure 15-13. The client area pattern colors are inverted when the user clicks the "Do It!" menu item.

The program's resource file includes a BITMAP statement to load a bitmap file from disk, and add it to the program's resources. The bitmap file BRUSHPAT.BMP is an 8 by 8 pixel bitmap created with the Windows SDKPaint application.

▷ **GENERIC.RC**

```
/* generic.rc */

#include <windows.h>
#include "generic.h"

generic         ICON            generic.ico
brushpat        BITMAP          brushpat.bmp

generic         MENU
BEGIN
        MENUITEM "&Do It!"        IDM_DOIT
        MENUITEM "&Quit",        IDM_QUIT
END
```

The bitmap is loaded into memory when the WM_CREATE message is processed. The client area size is kept current by processing WM_SIZE messages. Because PatBlt() paints using the currently selected brush, the bitmap is used to create a pattern brush using CreatePatternBrush(). PatBlt() paints the entire client area with the bitmap pattern brush every time a WM_PAINT message is received.

PatBlt() is also called when the user clicks the "Do It!" menu item. In this case, the DSTINVERT raster code is specified, inverting the colors of the client area. Clicking the "Do It!" menu item a second time restores the pattern colors to their original state.

▷ **GENERIC.C WndProc( ) Function**

```
Long FAR PASCAL WndProc (HWND hWnd, unsigned iMessage, WORD wParam, LONG lParam)
{
        HBRUSH                          hBrush, hOldBrush ;
        static          HBITMAP         hBitmap ;
        static          int             nXclient, nYclient ;
        PAINTSTRUCT                     ps ;
        HDC                             hDC ;

        switch (iMessage)                       /* process windows messages */
        {
                case WM_CREATE:
                        hBitmap = LoadBitmap (ghInstance , "brushpat") ;
                        break ;
                case WM_SIZE:
                        nXclient = LOWORD (lParam) ;    /* get client size */
                        nYclient = HIWORD (lParam) ;
                        break ;
                case WM_PAINT:
                        BeginPaint (hWnd, &ps) ;
                        hBrush = CreatePatternBrush (hBitmap) ;
                        hOldBrush = SelectObject (hDC, hBrush) ;
                        PatBlt (ps.hdc, 0, 0, nXclient, nYclient,
                                PATCOPY) ;
                        SelectObject (ps.hdc, hOldBrush) ;
                        DeleteObject (hBrush) ;
                        EndPaint (hWnd, &ps) ;
                        break ;
                case WM_COMMAND:                        /* process menu items */
                        switch (wParam)
                        {
                        case IDM_DOIT:                 /* User hit the "Do it" menu item */
                                hDC = GetDC (hWnd) ;
                                PatBlt (hDC, 0, 0, nXclient, nYclient,
```

```
                                    DSTINVERT) ;
                        ReleaseDC (hWnd, hDC) ;
                        break ;
                case IDM_QUIT:            /* send end of application message */
                        DestroyWindow (hWnd) ;
                        break ;
                }
                break ;
        case WM_DESTROY:                    /* stop application */
                DeleteObject (hBitmap) ;
                PostQuitMessage (0) ;
                break ;
        default:                 /* default windows message processing */
                return DefWindowProc (hWnd, iMessage, wParam, lParam) ;
        }
        return (0L) ;
}
```

PATBLT   ■ Win 2.0   ■ Win 3.0   ■ Win 3.1

Purpose	Outputs a pattern brush to a device.
Syntax	BOOL **PatBlt**(HDC *hDC*, int *X*, int *Y*, int *nWidth*, int *nHeight*, DWORD *dwRop*);
Description	The currently selected brush is output to the device referenced by *hDC*. The brush is used to fill the rectangle defined by the *X, Y, nWidth*, and *nHeight* parameters. The brush is combined with the background colors in different ways, depending on the raster-operation code specified in *dwRop*.
Uses	Used to fill regions with a pattern.
Returns	BOOL. Nonzero if the function was successful, zero on error.
See Also	BitBlt(), CreatePatternBrush(), LoadBitmap()
Parameters	
hDC	HDC: The destination device context handle.
X	int: The logical *X* coordinate of the upper left corner of the rectangle that is to be filled with the selected brush.
Y	The logical *Y* coordinate of the upper left corner of the rectangle that is to be filled with the selected brush.
nWidth	int: The width, in logical units, of the rectangle that is to be filled with the selected brush.
nHeight	int: The height, in logical units, of the rectangle that is to be filled with the selected brush.
dwRop	DWORD: One of the raster-operation codes in Table 15-7. These codes determine how the colors of the brush are combined with the existing colors of the background.

Value	Meaning	⊠
PATCOPY	Copies the pattern to the destination.	
PATINVERT	Combines the destination bitmap with the pattern using the Boolean OR operator.	
DSTINVERT	Inverts the destination bitmap.	
BLACKNESS	Turns all output black.	
WHITENESS	Turns all output white. This is a quick way to blank a device context.	

Table 15-7. Raster-Operation Codes that PatBlt( ) Can Use.

Example	See the previous example under LoadBitmap().

SETBITMAPBITS

Purpose	Sets the pixel data for a DDB bitmap.
Syntax	LONG **SetBitmapBits**(HBITMAP *hBitmap*, DWORD *dwCount*, LPSTR *lpBits*);
Description	Normally, the pixel bit data array is set when CreateBitmap() is called. SetBitmapBits() allows the pixel data to be set or changed later.
Uses	Generally, used if the application modifies the pixel data before displaying it.
Returns	LONG, the number of bytes used in setting the bitmap bits. Zero on error.
See Also	CreateBitmap(), CreateBitmapIndirect()
Parameters	
hBitmap	HBITMAP: The handle of the bitmap which will receive the color bit data.
dwCount	DWORD: The number of bytes of data in the array pointed to by *lpBits*.
lpBits	LPSTR: A pointer to an array of bytes containing the color bit data. The array should be at least *dwCount* bytes in size.

Example This example (see Figure 15-14) paints a small bitmap containing an "H" at location 10,10 in the upper left corner of the window's client area when the user clicks the "Do It!" menu item.

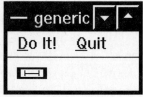

Figure 15-14. SetBitmap-Bits( ) Example.

```
long FAR PASCAL WndProc (HWND hWnd, unsigned iMessage, WORD wParam, LONG lParam)
{
        static          HBITMAP         hBitmap ;
        HDC                             hDC, hMemDC ;
        static  BYTE    BitMapBits [48] = {        /* define bitmap pattern */
                0x00, 0x00, 0x00, 0x00,
                0x00, 0x00, 0x00, 0x00,
                0x0f, 0xff, 0xff, 0xf0,
                0x0f, 0x7f, 0xfe, 0xf0,
                0x0f, 0x7f, 0xfe, 0xf0,
                0x0f, 0x7f, 0xfe, 0xf0,
                0x0f, 0x00, 0x00, 0xf0,
                0x0f, 0x7f, 0xfe, 0xf0,
                0x0f, 0x7f, 0xfe, 0xf0,
                0x0f, 0xff, 0xff, 0xf0,
                0x00, 0x00, 0x00, 0x00,
                0x00, 0x00, 0x00, 0x00 } ;

        switch (iMessage)                       /* process windows messages */
        {
                case WM_CREATE:
                        hBitmap = CreateBitmap (32, 12, 1, 1, NULL) ;
                        SetBitmapBits (hBitmap, 48,
                                (LPSTR) BitMapBits) ;
                        break ;
                case WM_COMMAND:                /* process menu items */
                        switch (wParam)
                        {
                        case IDM_DOIT:          /* User hit the "Do it" menu item */
                                hDC = GetDC (hWnd) ;
                                hMemDC = CreateCompatibleDC (hDC) ;
                                SelectObject (hMemDC, hBitmap) ;
                                BitBlt (hDC, 10, 10, 32, 12, hMemDC, 0, 0,
                                        SRCCOPY) ;
                                DeleteDC (hMemDC) ;
                                ReleaseDC (hWnd, hDC) ;
                                break ;
                        case IDM_QUIT:          /* send end of application message */
                                DestroyWindow (hWnd) ;
                                break ;
```

```
                    }
                    break ;
            case WM_DESTROY:                 /* stop application */
                    DeleteObject (hBitmap) ;
                    PostQuitMessage (0) ;
                    break ;
            default:                    /* default windows message processing */
                    return DefWindowProc (hWnd, iMessage, wParam, lParam) ;
        }
        return (0L) ;
}
```

SETBITMAPDIMENSION

■ Win 2.0   ■ Win 3.0   ■ Win 3.1

Purpose	Sets two values that are associated with the bitmap. These values can be retrieved later using GetBitmapDimension().
Syntax	LONG **SetBitmapDimension**(HBITMAP *hBitmap*, int *X*, int *Y*);
Description	The SetBitmapDimension() function sets two integer values, *X* and *Y*, which are associated with the bitmap. These values do not affect the bitmap. They are provided so that an application can store dimensional data with the bitmap. This is preferable to using static or global variables to store the width and height of the bitmap. The Windows SDK documentation suggests using the MM_LOMETRIC system of units (0.1 mm per unit) to specify the bitmap size. Because the values are not used in painting the bitmap, any system of units (including device units—pixels) can be used.
Uses	Handy if an application uses a number of bitmaps that are different sizes.
Returns	DWORD, the previous bitmap dimensions. The low-order word contains the *X* value. The high-order word contains the *Y* value. If SetBitmapDimension() was not called previously to set these values, zero is returned.
See Also	GetBitmapDimension()
Parameters	
hBitmap	HBITMAP: The handle of the bitmap.
X	int: The *X* value to associate with the bitmap.
Y	int: The *Y* value to associate with the bitmap.
Example	See the example under GetBitmapDimension().

SETDIBITS

□ Win 2.0   ■ Win 3.0   ■ Win 3.1

Purpose	Sets device-independent bitmap (DIB) pixel data to the data in a memory buffer.
Syntax	int **SetDIBits**(HDC *hDC*, HANDLE *hBitmap*, WORD *nStartScan*, WORD *nNumScans*, LPSTR *lpBits*, LPBITMAPINFO *lpBitsInfo*, WORD *wUsage*);
Description	DIBs consist of header information followed by the bitmap data for each pixel of the bitmap (see CreateDIBitmap() for descriptions of the header format). SetDIBits() allows an application to modify the pixel data of the bitmap, changing the image represented. 　　The bitmap must not be selected into a device context at the time SetDIBits() is called. For large bitmaps, the image can be changed in horizontal segments to minimize memory use. Specify a series of *nStartScan* and *nNumScans* values to process bands of the bitmap data.
Uses	Used when the application modifies the pixel data for the DIB bitmap prior to displaying it. One possible use is to change the colors of a button to show selection status.
Returns	int, the number of scan lines changed. Zero on error.
See Also	CreateDIBitmap(), GetDIBits()

Parameters

hDC	HDC: The device context handle.
hBitmap	HBITMAP: A handle to the bitmap. This value is returned by CreateDIBitmap().
nStartScan	WORD: The first pixel line number on which to start in the bitmap. Usually zero, unless the bitmap is being set by several SetDIBits() calls, for horizontal bands of the bitmap image.
nNumScans	WORD: The number of lines of pixels to be copied. Normally, equal to the vertical height of the bitmap in pixels, unless the changes are being made one horizontal band at a time.
lpBits	LPSTR: A pointer to a memory buffer that contains the bitmap data.
lpBitsInfo	LPBITMAPINFO: A pointer to a BITMAPINFO data structure that specifies the size and color format of the bitmap. The pointer can point to the top of the same memory area the bitmap data is being written to if the BITMAPINFO data has been initialized.
wUsage	WORD: Specifies whether the *bmiColors[]* fields at the end of the BITMAPINFO data structure contain explicit RGB color values, or if they are indexes into the currently realized logical palette. *wUsage* can be either DIB_PAL_COLORS for palette colors, or DIB_RGB_COLORS for explicit RGB colors.

Example

This example paints a Device-Independent Bitmap (DIB) on the window's client area. (See Figure 15-15.) Initially, the bitmap is colored black and white. When the user clicks the "Do It!" menu item, the bitmap data is altered so that any two black pixels next to each other (0 value for a byte within a 16-color bitmap) are changed to a blue-black pixel combination.

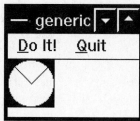

Figure 15-15. SetDIBits() Example.

For simplicity, this example assumes a 16-color bitmap. Sixteen-color bitmaps use four bits per pixel in the bitmap data, so each byte of data encodes two pixels. This example also omits error checking on memory allocation.

```
#define ALIGNLONG(i)    ((i+3)/4*4)
#define WIDTH           50
#define HEIGHT          50
#define COLORBITS       4

long FAR PASCAL WndProc (HWND hWnd, unsigned iMessage, WORD wParam, LONG lParam)
{
        PAINTSTRUCT                             ps ;
        static          BITMAPINFOHEADER        Bi ;
        LPBITMAPINFOHEADER                      lpbi ;
        static          HBITMAP                 hBitmap ;
        HDC                                     hDC, hMemDC ;
        static          HANDLE                  hDIB ;
        HBRUSH                                  hDIBrush ;
        LPSTR                                   lpstBitmap, lpstTemp ;
        int                                     i, nBytes ;

        switch (iMessage)               /* process windows messages */
        {
        case WM_CREATE:
                hDC = GetDC (hWnd) ;
                        /* initialize BITMAPINFOHEADER data */
                Bi.biSize = sizeof (BITMAPINFOHEADER) ;
                Bi.biWidth = WIDTH ;            /* 8 by 8 bitmap */
                Bi.biHeight = HEIGHT ;
                Bi.biPlanes = 1 ;
                Bi.biBitCount = COLORBITS ;        /* 16 colors */
                Bi.biCompression = BI_RGB ;
                Bi.biSizeImage = (ALIGNLONG((WIDTH * COLORBITS)/8)
                        * HEIGHT);
                Bi.biXPelsPerMeter = 0 ;
```

```
            Bi.biYPelsPerMeter = 0 ;
            Bi.biClrUsed = 0 ;
            Bi.biClrImportant = 0 ;
                    /* create uninitialized DIB bitmap */
            hBitmap = CreateDIBitmap (hDC, &Bi, OL, NULL,
                    NULL, O) ;
                    /* allocate memory for BITMAPINFO structure */
            hDIB = GlobalAlloc (GHND, sizeof (BITMAPINFOHEADER) +
                    16 * sizeof (RGBQUAD) +
                    (ALIGNLONG((WIDTH * COLORBITS)/8) * HEIGHT));
            lpbi = (BITMAPINFOHEADER FAR *) GlobalLock (hDIB) ;
                    /* tricky way to copy Bi to top of BITMAPINFO */
            *lpbi = Bi ;
                    /* use GetDIBits() to initialize structure data */
            GetDIBits (hDC, hBitmap, O, 50, NULL,
                    (LPBITMAPINFO) lpbi,    DIB_RGB_COLORS) ;
                    /* create memory device context */
            hMemDC = CreateCompatibleDC (hDC) ;
                    /* select DIB bitmap into device context */
            SelectObject (hMemDC, hBitmap) ;
                    /* paint on memory device context */
            SelectObject (hMemDC, GetStockObject (BLACK_BRUSH)) ;
            Rectangle (hMemDC, O, O, WIDTH, HEIGHT) ;
            SelectObject (hMemDC, GetStockObject (WHITE_BRUSH)) ;
            Ellipse (hMemDC, O, O, WIDTH, HEIGHT) ;
            MoveTo (hMemDC, O, O) ;
            LineTo (hMemDC, WIDTH / 2, HEIGHT / 2) ;
            LineTo (hMemDC, WIDTH, O) ;
                    /* set pointer to bitmap's bit data */
            lpstBitmap = (LPSTR) lpbi +
                    (WORD) sizeof (BITMAPINFOHEADER) +
                    (16 * sizeof (RGBQUAD)) ;
            GetDIBits (hDC, hBitmap, O, HEIGHT, lpstBitmap,
                    (LPBITMAPINFO) lpbi, DIB_RGB_COLORS) ;
            GlobalUnlock (hDIB) ;
            DeleteDC (hMemDC) ;
            ReleaseDC (hWnd, hDC) ;
            break ;
    case WM_PAINT:
            BeginPaint (hWnd, &ps) ;
            hMemDC = CreateCompatibleDC (ps.hdc) ;
            SelectObject (hMemDC, hBitmap) ;
            BitBlt (ps.hdc, O, O, WIDTH, HEIGHT, hMemDC, O,
                    O, SRCCOPY) ;
            DeleteDC (hMemDC) ;
            EndPaint (hWnd, &ps) ;
            break ;
    case WM_COMMAND:                    /* process menu items */
            switch (wParam)
            {
            case IDM_DOIT:
                    hDC = GetDC (hWnd) ;
                    lpbi = (BITMAPINFOHEADER FAR *)
                            GlobalLock (hDIB) ;
                    lpstBitmap = (LPSTR) lpbi +
                            (WORD) sizeof (BITMAPINFOHEADER) +
                            (16 * sizeof (RGBQUAD)) ;
                    nBytes = ALIGNLONG((WIDTH * COLORBITS)/8)
                            * HEIGHT ;
                    lpstTemp = lpstBitmap ;
                            /* change O bytes to Ox2C in bitmap data */
                    for (i = O ; i < nBytes ; i++)
                    {
                            if (O == *lpstTemp)             /* if black */
                                    *lpstTemp = Ox2C ;
                            lpstTemp++ ;
                    }
                    SetDIBits (hDC, hBitmap, O, HEIGHT, lpstBitmap,
                            (LPBITMAPINFO) lpbi, DIB_RGB_COLORS) ;
```

```
                              ReleaseDC (hWnd, hDC) ;
                              GlobalUnlock (hDIB) ;
                              InvalidateRect (hWnd, NULL, TRUE) ;        /* paint */
                              break ;
                      case IDM_QUIT:   /* send end of application message */
                              DestroyWindow (hWnd) ;
                              break ;
                 }
                 break ;
          case WM_DESTROY:          /* stop application */
                 GlobalFree (hDIB) ;
                 PostQuitMessage (0) ;
                 break ;
          default:        /* default windows message processing */
                 return DefWindowProc (hWnd, iMessage, wParam, lParam) ;
     }
     return (0L) ;
}
```

SETDIBITSTODEVICE   □ Win 2.0   ■ Win 3.0   ■ Win 3.1

Purpose   Paints from a device-independent bitmap (DIB) directly to a device context.

Syntax   WORD **SetDIBitsToDevice**(HDC *hDC*, WORD *DestX*, WORD *DestY*, WORD *nWidth*, WORD *nHeight*, WORD *SrcX*, WORD *SrcY*, WORD *nStartScan*, WORD *nNumScans*, LPSTR *lpBits*, LPBITMAPINFO *lpBitsInfo*, WORD *wUsage*) ;

Description   This is the fastest method of painting a DIB to a device, once the DIB is stored in a memory buffer. Normally, the BITMAPINFO data pointed to by *lpBitsInfo* will be right in front of the bitmap pixel data (pointed to by *lpBits*), all in the same memory block.

Unless the BITMAPINFO color data is separately processed to realize a logical palette, the color data will be lost when the DIB is output to the device context. For example, a 256-color bitmap will be mapped to the 20 default system colors when output to a VGA device. Note that the origin for the DIB pixel data is the bottom left corner. The data is upside down relative to the default MM_TEXT mapping mode.

Uses   Outputs a DIB directly to the screen. Parts of a DIB can be output by manipulating the *SrcX*, *SrcY*, *nStartScan*, and *nNumScans* parameters. Memory demands for painting the DIB can be reduced by successively painting horizontal bands out of a DIB bitmap, rather than painting all of the image at once.

You can also use a DIB as an alternative to direct manipulation of the screen pixels with the slow GetPixel() and SetPixel() functions. The changes can be made to the DIB data, and then periodically sent to the screen with SetDIBitsToDevice().

Returns   WORD, the number of scan lines copied to the output device context. Zero on error.

See Also   CreateDIBitmap(), GetDIBits(), SetDIBits(), StretchDIBits()

Parameters

hDC   HDC: The device context on which the DIB will be output.

DestX   WORD: The logical *X* coordinate on the device context to start the bitmap output.

DestY   WORD: The logical *Y* coordinate on the device context to start the bitmap output.

nWidth   WORD: The width, in pixels, of the DIB.

nHeight   WORD: The height, in pixels, of the DIB.

SrcX   WORD: The *X* position in the DIB from which to start reading pixel data for output. Normally 0.

SrcY   WORD: The *Y* position in the DIB from which to start reading pixel data for output. Normally 0.

nStartScan   WORD: The line number of the horizontal line of pixels in the DIB that is the first line in the *lpBits* memory buffer.

nNumScans	WORD: The number of scan lines of the DIB that are contained in the memory buffer pointed to by *lpBits*.
lpBits	LPSTR: A pointer to the memory buffer that contains the pixel data. Normally, this follows the BITMAPINFO header data in a memory buffer. The pixel data can be in a separate buffer.
lpBitsInfo	LPBITMAPINFO: A pointer to an initialized BITMAPINFO data structure. This data describes the size and color data for the bitmap. See CreateDIBitmap() for a description of this data structure.
wUsage	WORD: Specifies whether the *bmiColors[]* fields at the end of the BITMAPINFO data structure contain explicit RGB color values, or if they are indexes into the currently realized logical palette. *wUsage* can be either DIB_PAL_COLORS for palette colors, or DIB_RGB_COLORS for explicit RGB colors.
Caution	This function cannot be used to output to a memory device context.

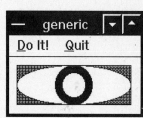

Example   The DIB example at the beginning of this chapter shows how to preserve the color data associated with a DIB by using it to realize a logical palette. This example paints a colored DIB bitmap and saves the bytes in a global memory buffer. The bitmap is painted to the screen when WM_PAINT messages are received using SetDIBitsToDevice(). (See Figure 15-16.)

Figure 15-16. SetDIBits-ToDevice( ) Example.

```
#define ALIGNLONG(i)    ((i+3)/4*4)
#define WIDTH          150
#define HEIGHT         50
#define COLORBITS      4

Long FAR PASCAL WndProc (HWND hWnd, unsigned iMessage, WORD wParam, LONG lParam)
{
        PAINTSTRUCT                                 ps ;
        static        BITMAPINFOHEADER              bi ;
        LPBITMAPINFOHEADER                          lpbi ;
        LPBITMAPINFO                                lpBitInfo ;
        static        HBITMAP                       hBitmap ;
        HDC                                         hDC, hMemDC ;
        static        HANDLE                        hDIB ;
        HBRUSH                                      hBrush ;
        LPSTR                                       lpstBitmap, lpstTemp ;
        int                                         i, nBytes ;

        switch (iMessage)                    /* process windows messages */
        {
                case WM_CREATE:
                        hDC = GetDC (hWnd) ;
                                /* initialize BITMAPINFOHEADER data */
                        bi.biSize = sizeof (BITMAPINFOHEADER) ;
                        bi.biWidth = WIDTH ;          /* 8 by 8 bitmap */
                        bi.biHeight = HEIGHT ;
                        bi.biPlanes = 1 ;
                        bi.biBitCount = COLORBITS ;         /* 16 colors */
                        bi.biCompression = BI_RGB ;
                        bi.biSizeImage = (ALIGNLONG((WIDTH * COLORBITS)/8)
                                * HEIGHT);
                        bi.biXPelsPerMeter = 0 ;
                        bi.biYPelsPerMeter = 0 ;
                        bi.biClrUsed = 0 ;
                        bi.biClrImportant = 0 ;
                                /* create uninitialized DIB bitmap */
                        hBitmap = CreateDIBitmap (hDC, &bi, OL, NULL,
                                NULL, 0) ;
                                /* allocate memory for BITMAPINFO structure */
                        hDIB = GlobalAlloc (GHND, sizeof (BITMAPINFOHEADER) +
```

```
                   16 * sizeof (RGBQUAD) +
                   (ALIGNLONG((WIDTH * COLORBITS)/8) * HEIGHT));
           lpbi = (BITMAPINFOHEADER FAR *) GlobalLock (hDIB) ;
                   /* tricky way to copy bi to top of BITMAPINFO */
           *lpbi = bi ;
                   /* use GetDIBits() to init lpbi struct data */
           GetDIBits (hDC, hBitmap, 0, 50, NULL,
                   (LPBITMAPINFO) lpbi,    DIB_RGB_COLORS) ;

                   /* create memory device context */
           hMemDC = CreateCompatibleDC (hDC) ;
                   /* select DIB bitmap into device context */
           SelectObject (hMemDC, hBitmap) ;
                   /* paint on memory device context */
           hBrush = CreateSolidBrush (RGB (255, 80, 80)) ;
           SelectObject (hMemDC, hBrush) ;
           Rectangle (hMemDC, 0, 0, WIDTH, HEIGHT) ;
           DeleteObject (SelectObject (hMemDC,
                   GetStockObject (WHITE_BRUSH))) ;
           Ellipse (hMemDC, 0, 0, WIDTH, HEIGHT) ;
           hBrush = CreateSolidBrush (RGB (0, 0, 255)) ;
           SelectObject (hMemDC, hBrush) ;
           Ellipse (hMemDC, WIDTH / 3, 0, 2 * WIDTH / 3,
                   HEIGHT) ;
           DeleteObject (SelectObject (hMemDC,
                   GetStockObject (BLACK_BRUSH))) ;
           Ellipse (hMemDC, 2 * WIDTH / 5, HEIGHT / 5,
                   3 * WIDTH / 5,
                   4 * HEIGHT / 5) ;
                   /* set pointer to bitmap's bit data */
           lpstBitmap = (LPSTR) lpbi +
                   (WORD) sizeof (BITMAPINFOHEADER) +
                   (16 * sizeof (RGBQUAD)) ;
           GetDIBits (hDC, hBitmap, 0, HEIGHT, lpstBitmap,
                   (LPBITMAPINFO) lpbi, DIB_RGB_COLORS) ;
           GlobalUnlock (hDIB) ;
           DeleteDC (hMemDC) ;
           ReleaseDC (hWnd, hDC) ;
           break ;
   case WM_PAINT:
           BeginPaint (hWnd, &ps) ;
           lpBitInfo = (LPBITMAPINFO) GlobalLock (hDIB) ;
           lpstBitmap = (LPSTR) lpBitInfo +
                   (WORD) sizeof (BITMAPINFOHEADER) +
                   (16 * sizeof (RGBQUAD)) ;
           SetDIBitsToDevice (ps.hdc, 10, 10, WIDTH, HEIGHT,
                   0, 0,    0, HEIGHT, lpstBitmap, lpBitInfo,
                   DIB_RGB_COLORS) ;
           GlobalUnlock (hDIB) ;
           EndPaint (hWnd, &ps) ;
           break ;
```

[Other program lines]

SETSTRETCHBLTMODE   ■ Win 2.0   ■ Win 3.0   ■ Win 3.1

Purpose	Sets the bitmap stretching mode for the StretchBlt() function.
Syntax	int **SetStretchBltMode**(HDC *hDC*, int *nStretchMode*);
Description	The stretching mode determines how pixels are eliminated if a bitmap image is reduced in size. Bitmaps that are increased in size simply add more matching pixels between existing ones. The stretching mode becomes a property of the device context, and remains in effect until the device context is deleted or a new stretching mode is set.
Uses	The most desirable stretching mode will depend on the bitmap being reduced. Images with a few thin lines will be processed most effectively by BLACKONWHITE. Images with a few fat lines will be processed more effectively by WHITEONBLACK. General color images can use COLORONCOLOR.

Returns	int, the previous stretching mode.
See Also	GetStretchBltMode(), StretchBlt()
Parameters	
hDC	HDC: The device context handle that will have the stretching mode set.
nStretchMode	int: One of the values defined in WINDOWS.H and listed in Table 15-8.

Value	Meaning	⊠
BLACKONWHITE	Preserves black pixels at the expense of white ones.	
COLORONCOLOR	Deletes eliminated lines. No attempt to use the color value information of the eliminated pixels.	
WHITEONBLACK	Preserves white pixels at the expense of black ones.	

Table 15-8. Bitmap Stretching Modes.

Example	See the following example under the StretchBlt() function description.

STRETCHBLT   ■ Win 2.0   ■ Win 3.0   ■ Win 3.1

Purpose	Copies a bitmap from one device context to another, stretching or contracting the image to fit the destination rectangle.
Syntax	BOOL **StretchBlt**(HDC *hDestDC*, int *X*, int *Y*, int *nWidth*, int *nHeight*, HDC *hSrcDC*, int *XSrc*, int *YSrc*, int *nSrcWidth*, int *nSrcHeight*, DWORD *dwRop*);
Description	This function is similar to BitBlt(), except that it has the added ability to stretch or compress the bitmap. The method used to fill in missing pixels (if enlarging), or delete overlapping pixels (if shrinking), is governed by the current stretching mode of the device context. SetStretchBltMode() sets the stretching mode.
	The image can be inverted, or made a mirror image, by changing the signs of either the source or destination bitmap size. If StretchBlt() copies a monochrome bitmap to a color device context, white bits (1) are set to the background color, and black bits (0) are set to the foreground color.
Uses	Allows a bitmap to be sized. This function is convenient for windows that are sizeable, but may need to enlarge or contract bitmap images depending on the size of the window. The tool bars on the left of the Windows Paintbrush application are an excellent example of scaling graphics images to fit the window size. Large expansions of bitmaps will result in jagged edges. Consider using a metafile for large images.
Returns	BOOL. Nonzero if the bitmap was drawn, zero on error.
See Also	SetStretchBltMode(), GetDeviceCaps() to check whether the device supports raster operations. Use the RC_BITBLT flag.
Parameters	
hDestDC	HDC: The destination device context handle.
X	int: The logical X coordinate of the upper left corner of the destination rectangle.
Y	int: The logical Y coordinate of the upper left corner of the destination rectangle.
nWidth	int: The width, in logical units, of the destination rectangle.
nHeight	int: The height, in logical units, of the destination rectangle.
hSrcDC	HDC: The device context from which the bitmap will be copied. This is normally a memory device context created with CreateCompatibleDC(). A bitmap is loaded into the memory device context using SelectObject().
XSrc	int: The logical *X* coordinate of the upper left corner of the source bitmap. Normally, zero.

YSrc	int: The logical *Y* coordinate of the upper right corner of the source bitmap. Normally, zero.	
nSrcWidth	int: The width, in logical units, of the source bitmap. If the default coordinate system is being used for *hSrcDC*, this is the width in pixels.	
nSrcHeight	int: The height, in logical units, of the source bitmap. If the default coordinate system is being used for *hSrcDC*, this is the height in pixels.	
dwRop	DWORD: One of the raster-operation codes. Fifteen of the 256 possibilities have names that are defined in WINDOWS.H and are listed in Table 15-9. The remainder have hexadecimal	*Figure 15-17. StretchBlt() Example.*

codes, specified in Volume 2, Section 11, Table 11.3 of the Microsoft SDK Reference manuals.

These codes determine how the colors of the brush are combined with the existing colors of the background. For the Boolean codes, "S" is the source bitmap, "D" is the destination bitmap, and "P" is the currently selected brush (called a "pattern"). The Boolean operators follow the C language conventions.

Value	Meaning
BLACKNESS	Turns all output black. (0)
DSTINVERT	Inverts the destination bitmap. (~D)
MERGECOPY	The source and destination bitmaps are combined with the Boolean AND operator. (D & S)
MERGEPAINT	The source and destination bitmaps are combined with the Boolean OR operator. (~S | D)
NOTSRCCOPY	Inverts the source bitmap, then copies it to the destination. (~S)
NOTSRCERASE	Inverts the result of combining the source and destination bitmaps using the Boolean XOR opera-tor. (~(S | D))
PATCOPY	Copies the pattern to the destination. (P)
PATINVERT	Combines the destination bitmap with the pattern using the Boolean XOR operator. (P ^ D)
PATPAINT	P	~(S |D)
SRCAND	Combines the source and destination bitmaps with the Boolean AND operator. (S & D)
SRCCOPY	Copies the source to the destination. (S)
SRCERASE	S & ~ D
SRCINVERT	Combines the source and destination bitmaps using the Boolean XOR operator. (S ^ D)
SRCPAINT	Combines the source and destination bitmaps using the Boolean OR operator. (S | D)
WHITENESS	Turns all output white. This is a quick way to blank a device context. (1)

Table 15-9. Raster-Operation Codes.

Example This example, shown in Figure 15-17, uses StretchBlt() four times to draw the same bitmap in four different sizes. The stretching mode is set to COLORONCOLOR prior to using StretchBlt(). GetStretchBltMode() is used at the end of the output session to demonstrate that the stretching mode is still in effect. The current stretching mode is output under the bitmaps.

```
Long FAR PASCAL WndProc (HWND hWnd, unsigned iMessage, WORD wParam, LONG lParam)
{
        static          HBITMAP         hBitmap ;
        HDC                             hDC, hMemDC ;
        int                             nStrMode ;

        switch (iMessage)                       /* process windows messages */
```

```
        {
                case WM_CREATE:
                        hBitmap = LoadBitmap (ghInstance , "pen") ;
                        break ;
                case WM_COMMAND:                    /* process menu items */
                        switch (wParam)
                        {
                        case IDM_DOIT:              /* User hit the "Do it" menu item */
                                hDC = GetDC (hWnd) ;
                                hMemDC = CreateCompatibleDC (hDC) ;
                                SetStretchBltMode (hDC, COLORONCOLOR) ;
                                SelectObject (hMemDC, hBitmap) ;
                                StretchBlt (hDC, 10, 10, 200, 80, hMemDC,
                                        0, 0, 60, 60, SRCCOPY) ;
                                StretchBlt (hDC, 10, 10, 100, 40, hMemDC,
                                        0, 0, 60, 60, SRCCOPY) ;
                                StretchBlt (hDC, 10, 10, 50, 20, hMemDC,
                                        0, 0, 60, 60, SRCCOPY) ;
                                StretchBlt (hDC, 10, 10, 25, 10, hMemDC,
                                        0, 0, 60, 60, SRCCOPY) ;
                                DeleteDC (hMemDC) ;

                                nStrMode = GetStretchBltMode (hDC) ;
                                switch (nStrMode)
                                {
                                        case WHITEONBLACK:
                                                TextOut (hDC, 10, 100,
                                                        "WHITEONBLACK", 12) ;
                                                break ;
                                        case BLACKONWHITE:
                                                TextOut (hDC, 10, 100,
                                                        "BLACKONWHITE", 12) ;
                                                break ;
                                        case COLORONCOLOR:
                                                TextOut (hDC, 10, 100,
                                                        "COLORONCOLOR", 12) ;
                                                break ;
                                }
                                ReleaseDC (hWnd, hDC) ;
                                break ;
                        case IDM_QUIT:              /* send end of application message */
                                DestroyWindow (hWnd) ;
                                break ;
                        }
                        break ;
                case WM_DESTROY:                    /* stop application */
                        DeleteObject (hBitmap) ;
                        PostQuitMessage (0) ;
                        break ;
                default:                    /* default windows message processing */
                        return DefWindowProc (hWnd, iMessage, wParam, lParam) ;
        }
        return (0L) ;
}
```

StretchDIBits

□ Win 2.0 ■ Win 3.0 ■ Win 3.1

Purpose   Paints from a device-independent bitmap (DIB) directly to a device context, stretching and/or compressing the image as it is painted.

Syntax   WORD **StretchDIBits**(HDC *hDC*, WORD *DestX*, WORD *DestY*, WORD *wDestWidth*, WORD *wDestHeight*, WORD *SrcX*, WORD *SrcY*, WORD *wSrcWidth*, WORD *wSrcHeight*, LPSTR *lpBits*, LPBITMAPINFO *lpBitsInfo*, WORD *wUsage*, DWORD *dwRop*) ;

Description   This function is similar to SetDIBitsToDevice(). The bitmap can be stretched and/or compressed as it is painted to the device context. No provision is given for banding the output (painting the bitmap in sections to conserve memory), so the entire bitmap must be output in one call to StretchDIBits().

This function will output to a memory device context, unlike SetDIBitsToDevice(), which only outputs to a physical device context. If the image is compressed, bits will be eliminated from the output. How this is done is controlled by the SetStretchBltMode() function. The image can be reversed or inverted by using unmatched signs (one positive, one negative) for the source and destination width or height parameters.

Like SetDIBitsToDevice(), this function will not preserve the color data in the DIB header. The colors in the DIB will be mapped to the existing color palette. To preserve the color information, the DIB color data must be used to realize a logical palette. There is an example of this in the beginning of this chapter under the section *DIB Example*.

Uses	Convenient if the bitmap image must be scaled to fit a particular space. The images on the left side of the Windows PaintBrush application are good examples. They change size depending on the size of the parent windows.
Returns	The return value is the number of lines of pixels copied. Zero on error.
See Also	CreateDIBitmap(), GetDiBits(), SetDIBitsToDevice()

Parameters

hDC   HDC: The device context on which the DIB will be output. This can be a physical device or a memory device context created with CreateCompatibleDC().

DestX   WORD: The logical *X* coordinate on the device context to start the bitmap output. The logical units equal pixels unless the mapping mode has been changed.

DestY   WORD: The logical *Y* coordinate on the device context to start the bitmap output.

wDestWidth   WORD: The width, in logical units, of the output bitmap.

wDestHeight WORD: The height, in logical units, of the output bitmap.

SrcX   WORD: The *X* position in the DIB from which to start reading pixel data for output. Normally 0.

SrcY   WORD: The *Y* position in the DIB from which to start reading pixel data for output. Normally 0.

wSrcWidth   WORD: The width, in pixels, of the memory bitmap pointed to by *lpBits*.

wSrcHeight   WORD: The height, in pixels, of the memory bitmap pointed to by *lpBits*.

lpBits   LPSTR: A pointer to the memory buffer that contains the pixel data. Normally, this follows the BITMAPINFO header data in a memory buffer. The pixel data can be in a separate buffer.

lpBitsInfo   LPBITMAPINFO: A pointer to an initialized BITMAPINFO data structure. This data describes the size and color data for the bitmap. See CreateDIBitmap() for a description of this data structure.

wUsage   WORD: Specifies whether the *bmiColors[]* fields at the end of the BITMAPINFO data structure contain explicit RGB color values, or if they are indexes into the currently realized logical palette. *wUsage* can be either DIB_PAL_COLORS for palette colors, or DIB_RGB_COLORS for explicit RGB colors.

dwRop   DWORD: One of the raster-operation codes. Fifteen of the 256 possibilities have names that are defined in WINDOWS.H and are listed in Table 15-10. The remainder have hexadecimal codes, specified in Volume 2, Section 11, Table 11.3 of the Microsoft SDK Reference manuals.

These codes determine how the colors of the brush are combined with the existing colors of the background. For the Boolean codes, "S" is the source bitmap, "D" is the destination bitmap, and "P" is the currently selected brush (called a "pattern"). The Boolean operators follow the C language conventions.

Value	Meaning
BLACKNESS	Turns all output black. (0)
DSTINVERT	Inverts the destination bitmap. (~D)
MERGECOPY	The source and destination bitmaps are combined with the Boolean AND operator. (D & S)
MERGEPAINT	The source and destination bitmaps are combined with the Boolean OR operator. (~S I D)
NOTSRCCOPY	Inverts the source bitmap, then copies it to the destination. (~S)
NOTSRCERASE	Inverts the result of combining the source and destination bitmaps using the Boolean OR operator. (~(S I D))
PATCOPY	Copies the pattern to the destination. (P)
PATINVERT	Combines the destination bitmap with the pattern using the Boolean XOR operator. (P ^ D)
PATPAINT	P I ~(S ID)
SRCAND	Combines the source and destination bitmaps with the Boolean AND operator. (S & D)
SRCCOPY	Copies the source to the destination. (S)
SRCERASE	S & ~ D
SRCINVERT	Combines the source and destination bitmaps using the Boolean XOR operator. (S ^ D)
SRCPAINT	Combines the source and destination bitmaps using the Boolean OR operator. (S I D)
WHITENESS	Turns all output white. This is a quick way to blank a device context. (1)

Table 15-10. Raster-Operation Codes.

Example

This example creates a colored DIB in memory when the WM_CREATE message is processed. The image is painted on the window's client area every time a WM_PAINT message is processed. StretchDIBits() paints by compressing the horizontal dimension by two-thirds and expanding the vertical size by a factor of two. Compare this figure with the nonstretched image under the SetDIBitsToDevice() example.

Figure 15-18. Stretch-DIBits( ) Example.

The example code also demonstrates changing the pixel data in the bitmap. In this case, when the user clicks the "Do It!" menu item, any set of two black pixels (color value equals 0xFF with a 16-color bitmap) are changed to two white pixels (color value of 0x00). This is a device-dependent way to change colors, and is unusual. Normally, the bitmap data would be repainted using GDI functions, as demonstrated with the code under the WM_CREATE message.

```
#define ALIGNLONG(i)            ((i+3)/4*4)
#define WIDTH                   150
#define HEIGHT                  50
#define COLORBITS               4

long FAR PASCAL WndProc (HWND hWnd, unsigned iMessage, WORD wParam, LONG lParam)
{
        PAINTSTRUCT                             ps ;
        static          BITMAPINFOHEADER        bi ;
```

```
LPBITMAPINFOHEADER                              lpbi ;
LPBITMAPINFO                                    lpBitInfo ;
static          HBITMAP                         hBitmap ;
HDC                                             hDC, hMemDC ;
static          HANDLE                          hDIB ;
HBRUSH                                          hBrush ;
LPSTR                                           lpstBitmap, lpstTemp ;
int                                             i, nBytes ;

switch (iMessage)                       /* process windows messages */
{
    case WM_CREATE:
        hDC = GetDC (hWnd) ;
                /* initialize BITMAPINFOHEADER data */
        bi.biSize = sizeof (BITMAPINFOHEADER) ;
        bi.biWidth = WIDTH ;            /* 8 by 8 bitmap */
        bi.biHeight = HEIGHT ;
        bi.biPlanes = 1 ;
        bi.biBitCount = COLORBITS ;     /* 16 colors on screen */
        bi.biCompression = BI_RGB ;
        bi.biSizeImage = (ALIGNLONG((WIDTH * COLORBITS)/8)
                * HEIGHT);
        bi.biXPelsPerMeter = 0 ;
        bi.biYPelsPerMeter = 0 ;
        bi.biClrUsed = 0 ;
        bi.biClrImportant = 0 ;
                /* create uninitialized DIB bitmap */
        hBitmap = CreateDIBitmap (hDC, &bi, 0L, NULL,
                NULL, 0) ;
                /* allocate memory for BITMAPINFO structure */
        hDIB = GlobalAlloc (GHND, sizeof (BITMAPINFOHEADER) +
                16 * sizeof (RGBQUAD) +
                (ALIGNLONG((WIDTH * COLORBITS)/8) * HEIGHT));
        lpbi = (BITMAPINFOHEADER FAR *) GlobalLock (hDIB) ;
                /* tricky way to copy bi to top of BITMAPINFO */
        *lpbi = bi ;
                /* use GetDIBits() to init lpbi struct data */
        GetDIBits (hDC, hBitmap, 0, 50, NULL,
                (LPBITMAPINFO) lpbi,    DIB_RGB_COLORS) ;

                /* create memory device context */
        hMemDC = CreateCompatibleDC (hDC) ;
                /* select DIB bitmap into device context */
        SelectObject (hMemDC, hBitmap) ;
                /* paint on memory device context */
        hBrush = CreateSolidBrush (RGB (255, 80, 80)) ;
        SelectObject (hMemDC, hBrush) ;
        Rectangle (hMemDC, 0, 0, WIDTH, HEIGHT) ;
        DeleteObject (SelectObject (hMemDC,
                GetStockObject (WHITE_BRUSH))) ;
        Ellipse (hMemDC, 0, 0, WIDTH, HEIGHT) ;
        hBrush = CreateSolidBrush (RGB (0, 0, 255)) ;
        SelectObject (hMemDC, hBrush) ;
        Ellipse (hMemDC, WIDTH / 3, 0, 2 * WIDTH / 3, HEIGHT) ;
        DeleteObject (SelectObject (hMemDC,
                GetStockObject (BLACK_BRUSH))) ;
        Ellipse (hMemDC, 2 * WIDTH / 5, HEIGHT / 5,
                3 * WIDTH / 5, 4 * HEIGHT / 5) ;
                /* set pointer to bitmap's bit data */
        lpstBitmap = (LPSTR) lpbi +
                (WORD) sizeof (BITMAPINFOHEADER) +
                (16 * sizeof (RGBQUAD)) ;
        GetDIBits (hDC, hBitmap, 0, HEIGHT, lpstBitmap,
                (LPBITMAPINFO) lpbi, DIB_RGB_COLORS) ;
        GlobalUnlock (hDIB) ;
        DeleteDC (hMemDC) ;
        ReleaseDC (hWnd, hDC) ;
        break ;
```

```
            case WM_PAINT:
                    BeginPaint (hWnd, &ps) ;
                    SetStretchBltMode (ps.hdc, COLORONCOLOR) ;
                    lpBitInfo = (LPBITMAPINFO) GlobalLock (hDIB) ;
                    lpstBitmap = (LPSTR) lpBitInfo +
                            (WORD) sizeof (BITMAPINFOHEADER) +
                            (16 * sizeof (RGBQUAD)) ;
                    StretchDIBits (ps.hdc, 10, 10, 2 * WIDTH / 3,
                            HEIGHT * 2, 0, 0, WIDTH, HEIGHT,
                            lpstBitmap, lpBitInfo, DIB_RGB_COLORS,
                            SRCCOPY ) ;
                    GlobalUnlock (hDIB) ;
                    EndPaint (hWnd, &ps) ;
                    break ;
            case WM_COMMAND:                    /* process menu items */
                    switch (wParam)
                    {
                    case IDM_DOIT:   /* change black pixels to white */
                            hDC = GetDC (hWnd) ;
                            lpbi = (BITMAPINFOHEADER FAR *) GlobalLock (hDIB) ;
                            lpstBitmap = (LPSTR) lpbi +
                                    (WORD) sizeof (BITMAPINFOHEADER) +
                                    (16 * sizeof (RGBQUAD)) ;
                            nBytes = ALIGNLONG((WIDTH * COLORBITS)/8) * HEIGHT ;
                                    /* copy bitmap bytes into temp buffer */
                            lpstTemp = lpstBitmap ;
                            for (i = 0 ; i < nBytes ; i++)
                            {
                                    if (0 == *lpstTemp)
                                            *lpstTemp = 0xff ;
                                    lpstTemp++ ;
                            }
                            SetDIBits (hDC, hBitmap, 0, HEIGHT, lpstBitmap,
                                    (LPBITMAPINFO) lpbi, DIB_RGB_COLORS) ;
                            ReleaseDC (hWnd, hDC) ;
                            GlobalUnlock (hDIB) ;
                            InvalidateRect (hWnd, NULL, TRUE) ;      /* paint */
                            break ;
                    case IDM_QUIT:   /* send end of application message */
                            DestroyWindow (hWnd) ;
                            break ;
                    }
                    break ;
            case WM_DESTROY:            /* stop application */
                    GlobalFree (hDIB) ;
                    PostQuitMessage (0) ;
                    break ;
            default:                    /* default windows message processing */
                    return DefWindowProc (hWnd, iMessage, wParam, lParam) ;
    }
    return (0L) ;
}
```

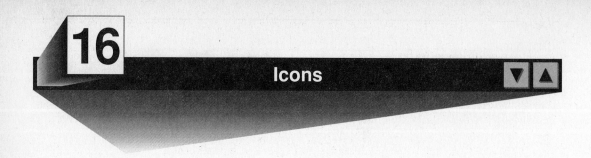

Icons are small bitmaps that Windows uses as visual placeholders for applications. They are the small pictures you see at the bottom left corner of the screen when applications are minimized. Putting some time into an attractive program icon is well worth the effort because the icon is frequently the image that sticks in the user's mind when he or she thinks of the program. Figure 16-1 depicts three typical icons.

Using Icons

Normally, you will create an icon using the Windows SDKPaint application, and add it to the program's resource file. A typical resource file is shown below.

```
/* generic.rc */

#include <windows.h>
#include "generic.h"

generic        ICON        generic.ico
childic        ICON        child.ico

generic        MENU
BEGIN
    MENUITEM "&Do It!"              IDM_DOIT
    MENUITEM "&Quit",              IDM_QUIT
END
```

In this example two icon files are included in the program's resources. Both icons are given names ("generic" and "childic") that are used to reference them when they are loaded. An icon can be associated with a window class. An application normally does this in the WinMain() function.

```
wndclass.hIcon = LoadIcon (hInstance, "generic") ;
```

With an icon loaded as part of the window's class structure, the icon will be painted automatically if the window is minimized. Windows will send WM_PAINT-ICON messages when the icon is about to be painted, rather than WM_PAINT messages. Every window created from the same class will have the same class icon. Note that the program's instance handle (*hInstance*) is needed with the LoadIcon() function because resources, such as icons, are associated with the program's data, not the program's code. Each instance has its own data.

Figure 16-1. Program Icons.

If the window class does not load an icon, the window will not display an icon when it is minimized.

```
wndclass.hIcon = NULL ;
```

In this case, the application can paint on the small bit of window client area that is visible when the application is minimized using the normal GDI painting functions. WM_PAINT messages are sent to the application when the minimized window needs to be painted. The IsIconic() function can be used to determine if the window is minimized.

WM_PAINT messages will not be sent to a minimized window if an icon is specified in the window's class definition (see RegisterClass()).

Applications that use a number of child windows that can be minimized end up with a number of icons. Minimizing a child window causes Windows to display the child window icon at the bottom of the parent window's client area. These icons can be dragged with the mouse within the bounds of the client area. The convenient function ArrangeIconicWindows() is provided to neatly arrange all of the icons at the bottom left corner of the client area.

Creating Icons at Run Time

Windows 3.0 allows icons to be created and modified while the program is running. The CreateIcon() function is similar to CreateCursor(). They both create an image by combining two bitmaps. CreateIcon() has the ability to create icons from a binary array, bitmap data, and device-independent bitmaps. The DestroyIcon() function is provided to delete an icon created with CreateIcon(), freeing memory consumed by the icon's data. Exercise restraint when creating and modifying an icon as the program operates. Users expect icons to remain unchanged. If the application needs to make the minimized window change (small clock applications are an example), it is simpler not to load a class icon, and just paint on the minimized window's client area.

Figure 16-2. Icon Resource Data Format.

Although it is seldom necessary to work with the internals of an icon, its structure is worth knowing. The icon resource file consists of two data structures, a header and one or more icon descriptions. (See the illustration in Figure 16-2.)

Although the structures are not defined in WINDOWS.H, you can define your own to manipulate the icon data. The header has the following format:

```
typedef tagIconHeader;
{
        WORD    icoReserved ;          /* must be zero */
        WORD    icoResourceType ;      /* the type of resource, 1 for icons */
        WORD    icoResourceCount;      /* the number of icons defined in this file */
} IconHeader ;
```

Each icon defined in the file (there will be *iconResourceCount* of them, normally one) will have the following structure:

```
typedef tagIconData;
{
        BYTE    Width ;        /* icon width in pixels, 16, 32, or 64 */
        BYTE    Height ;       /* icon height in pixels, 16, 32, or 64 */
        BYTE    ColorCount ;   /* the number of colors, 2, 8, or 16 */
        BYTE    Reserved1 ;    /* reserved for future use */
        WORD    Reserved2 ;    /* reserved for future use */
        WORD    Reserved3 ;    /* reserved for future use */
        DWORD   icoDIBSize ;   /* the size of the pixel array */
        DWORD   icoDIBOffset ; /* the number of bytes from the beginning of */
                               /* the file to the DIB bitmap for this icon */
} IconData ;
```

The actual bitmap data consists of two parts. The first (called the XOR mask) is the color bitmap for the image. It is followed by a second, monochrome bitmap, called the AND mask. The AND mask is used to mark the transparent and opaque pixels of the icon. Note that the icon bitmap size for both the vertical and horizontal dimensions is limited to one of three values: 16, 32, or 64 pixels. Similarly, the number of colors can be only 2, 8, or 16.

Because the header allows more than one icon to be defined in one resource file, you can build an icon file with three different sizes, or with different color resolutions. Windows will pick the best match of resolution and color capabilities when deciding which icons to load. This approach gives a measure of device-independence to icons.

Icon Function Summary

Table 16-1 summarizes the icon functions. The detailed function descriptions are in the next section.

Function	Purpose	☒
ArrangeIconicWindows	Arranges all minimized child windows in the lower left corner of the parent window's client area.	
CreateIcon	Creates an icon based on two memory blocks containing bit data.	
DestroyIcon	Destroys an icon that was previously created with CreateIcon( )	
DrawIcon	Draws an icon on a device.	
LoadIcon	Retrieves a handle to an icon listed in the program's resource file.	
OpenIcon	Restores a minimized window to its last size and position.	

Table 16-1. Icon Function Summary.

Icon Function Descriptions

This section contains the detail descriptions of the icon functions.

ARRANGEICONICWINDOWS   □ Win 2.0   ■ Win 3.0   ■ Win 3.1

Purpose	Arranges all minimized child windows in the lower left corner of the parent window's client area.
Syntax	WORD **ArrangeIconicWindows**(HWND *hWnd*);
Description	Applications that use a number of child windows that can be minimized or restored run into the problem where some child window icons are covered up by other child windows. ArrangeIconicWindows() puts all iconic windows in a row, starting at the lower left corner of the parent window's client area. If there is not enough room for all of the icons, additional rows of icons are created above the first one. This procedure mimics the behavior of the program manager application's positioning of group boxes and Windows' positioning of program icons on the background.
Uses	Used with applications that have child windows that can be minimized. ArrangeIconicWindows() can also be used to arrange the program icons at the bottom of the screen. Use GetDesktopWindow() to retrieve the desktop window handle.
Returns	WORD, the height of one row of icons, measured in pixels. Zero if there were no icons associated with *hWnd*.
See Also	GetDesktopWindow(), OpenIcon(), Chapter 29 on MDI applications.
Parameters	
hWnd	HWND: The parent window handle.

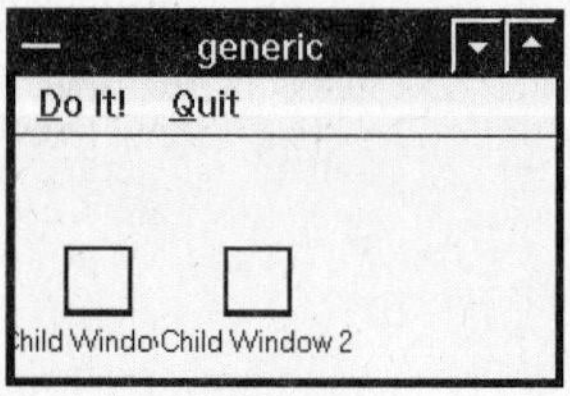

Related Messages WM_SIZE. An application can call ArrangeIconicWindows() for the desktop background (using GetDesktopWindow() to retrieve the background handle) every time a WM_SIZE message passes a SIZEICONIC value. Using this function assures that all program icons, including the application that was just minimized, are arranged at the bottom left of the screen.

Figure 16-3. Arrange-IconicWindows() and OpenIcon() Example.

Example This example creates two child windows that have their own window class, and share the same message processing procedure, ChildProc(). (See Figure 16-3.) The child windows are initially shown minimized, and arranged at the lower left of the parent window's client area. When the user clicks the "Do It!" menu item, one of the child windows is restored to its normal size with OpenIcon(), and the remaining minimized child window is arranged at the lower left corner with Arrange-IconicWindows().

The child window message-processing function "ChildProc" must be listed in the EXPORTS section of the program's .DEF definition file. A function prototype should also be added to the header file.

Note in the listing that the client area of the parent window is repainted before the iconic windows are arranged (InvalidateRect() and SendMessage() function calls). They are repainted because Windows will not erase the lettering under the iconized windows when they are restored to normal size. Repainting the client area before the icons are arranged solves this problem.

```
long FAR PASCAL WndProc (HWND hWnd, unsigned iMessage, WORD wParam, LONG lParam)
{
        HDC                     hDC ;
        WNDCLASS                wndclass ;
        static HWND             hChild1, hChild2 ;

        switch (iMessage)                       /* process windows messages */
        {
                case WM_CREATE:                 /* build the child windows */
                        wndclass.style                  = CS_HREDRAW | CS_VREDRAW |
                                CS_PARENTDC;
                        wndclass.lpfnWndProc            = ChildProc ;
                        wndclass.cbClsExtra             = 0 ;
                        wndclass.cbWndExtra             = 0 ;
                        wndclass.hInstance              = ghInstance ;
                        wndclass.hIcon                  = LoadIcon (NULL,
                                IDI_APPLICATION) ;
                        wndclass.hCursor                = LoadCursor (NULL,
                                IDC_ARROW) ;
                        wndclass.hbrBackground          =
                                GetStockObject (LTGRAY_BRUSH) ;
                        wndclass.lpszMenuName           = gszAppName ;
                        wndclass.lpszClassName          = "SecondClass" ;
                        if(RegisterClass (&wndclass))
                        {
                                hChild1 = CreateWindow ("SecondClass",
                                        "Child Window 1",
                                        WS_CHILD | WS_VISIBLE | WS_CAPTION |
                                        WS_BORDER,      10, 50, 200, 150, hWnd,
                                        NULL, ghInstance, NULL) ;
                                ShowWindow (hChild1, SW_SHOWMINIMIZED) ;
                                hChild2 = CreateWindow ("SecondClass",
                                        "Child Window 2",
                                        WS_CHILD | WS_VISIBLE | WS_CAPTION |
                                        WS_BORDER,      100, 30, 150, 100, hWnd,
                                        NULL, ghInstance, NULL) ;
                                ShowWindow (hChild2, SW_SHOWMINIMIZED) ;
                                ArrangeIconicWindows (hWnd) ;
                        }
                        break ;
                case WM_COMMAND:                /* process menu items */
                        switch (wParam)
                        {
                        case IDM_DOIT:
                                OpenIcon (hChild1) ;
                                InvalidateRect (hWnd, NULL, TRUE) ;
                                SendMessage (hWnd, WM_PAINT, 0, 0L) ;
                                ArrangeIconicWindows (hWnd) ;
                                break ;
                        case IDM_QUIT:          /* send end of application message */
                                DestroyWindow (hWnd) ;
                                break ;
                        }
```

```
                        break ;
           case WM_DESTROY:          /* stop application */
                    PostQuitMessage (0) ;
                    break ;

           default:       /* default windows message processing */
                    return DefWindowProc (hWnd, iMessage, wParam, lParam) ;
     }
     return (0L) ;
}

/* Here is a separate message procedure for the child window */

long FAR PASCAL ChildProc (HWND hWnd, unsigned iMessage, WORD wParam, LONG lParam)
{
     PAINTSTRUCT     ps ;

     switch (iMessage)               /* process windows messages */
     {
           case WM_PAINT:
                    BeginPaint (hWnd, &ps) ;
                    TextOut (ps.hdc, 0, 0, "I'm a child.", 12) ;
                    EndPaint (hWnd, &ps) ;
                    break ;
           default:                         /* default windows message processing */
                    return DefWindowProc (hWnd, iMessage, wParam, lParam) ;
     }
     return (0L) ;
}
```

CREATEICON

☐ Win 2.0   ■ Win 3.0   ■ Win 3.1

Purpose   Creates an icon based on two memory blocks containing bit data.

Syntax   HICON **CreateIcon**(HANDLE *hInstance*, int *nWidth*, int *nHeight*, BYTE *nPlanes*, BYTE *nBitsPixel*, LPSTR *lpANDbits*, LPSTR *lpXORbits*);

Description   Normally, icons are created using the Windows SDKPaint application and added to the program as resources. CreateIcon() provides an alternative, creating icon images dynamically as the program operates. The icon can be created from binary data, a bitmap, or a device-independent bitmap (DIB). The icon is created by combining two bitmaps, the AND mask, and the XOR mask. The AND mask is always a monochrome bitmap, with one bit per pixel. Table 16-2 shows how the two bitmaps are combined.

AND Bit Mask Value	XOR Bit Mask Value	Result Onscreen	⊠
0	0	Black	
0	1	White	
1	0	Transparent	
1	1	Inverted color	

Table 16-2. Monochrome Icon Bit Masks.

If the XOR bit mask is replaced with a bitmap or DIB, set the AND mask to all ones (0xFF bytes).

Uses   Can be used to provide bitmaps that change as an application runs. Users expect icons to retain the same shape, so change bitmaps cautiously. Note that an application can paint on the small amount of window area that shows when the window is iconic, if the window's class definition does not load a class icon. This is the normal way to change the appearance of an iconic window.

Returns   HICON, the handle to the icon created. NULL on error.

See Also   DeleteIcon(), GetSystemMetrics()

Parameters

hInstance	HANDLE: The program's instance handle.
nWidth	int: The width , in pixels, of the icon. Use GetSystemMetrics(SM_CXICON) to retrieve this value.
nHeight	int: The height, in pixels, of the icon. Use GetSystemMetrics(SM_CYICON) to retrieve this value.
nPlanes	int: The number of color planes in the XOR mask for the icon. For example, 1 for monochrome, 4 for 16-color VGA, etc.
nBitsPixel	int: The number of bits per pixel in the XOR mask for the icon. Again, 1 for monochrome, 4 for 16 colors. One or both of *nPlanes* and *nBitsPixel* must be set to 1.
lpANDbits	LPSTR: A pointer to an array of monochrome bits, specifying the AND mask for the icon. The AND mask determines the opaque and transparent portions of the icon. Set to 1 for opaque.
lpXORbits	LPSTR: A pointer to an array of bits specifying the XOR mask for the icon. Alternatively, the pointer can point to a memory block containing a monochrome bitmap or device-dependent color bitmap (DDB).

Example

This example creates a monochrome icon, illustrated in Figure 16-4, by directly specifying the bit values of both the AND mask and the XOR mask of the icon. The icon is created when the WM_CREATE message is processed, and it is painted to the client area when a WM_PAINT message is received. The icon is destroyed as the application terminates.

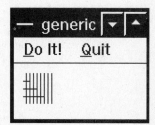

Note in the listing that the data defining the bitmap is freed from memory after the icon is created. The icon will contain valid bitmap data from the time it is created, until DestroyIcon() is called.

Figure 16-4. CreateIcon( ) and DeleteIcon( ) Example.

```
#define EVENBYTE(i)            ((i+7)/8*8)

long FAR PASCAL WndProc (HWND hWnd, unsigned iMessage, WORD wParam, LONG lParam)
{
        PAINTSTRUCT                     ps ;
        static          HANDLE          hANDBits, hXORBits ;
        PSTR                            psAND, psXOR, psA, psX ;
        static          int             nIconWide, nIconTall ;
        int                             i, j, nIconBytes ;
        static          HICON           hIcon ;

        switch (iMessage)                       /* process windows messages */
        {
            case WM_CREATE:
                    nIconWide = GetSystemMetrics (SM_CXICON) ;
                    nIconTall = GetSystemMetrics (SM_CYICON) ;
                    nIconBytes = (EVENBYTE (nIconWide) / 8) * nIconTall ;
                    hANDBits = LocalAlloc (LMEM_MOVEABLE, nIconBytes) ;
                    hXORBits = LocalAlloc (LMEM_MOVEABLE, nIconBytes) ;
                    psA = psAND = LocalLock (hANDBits) ;
                    psX = psXOR = LocalLock (hXORBits) ;
                    for (i = 0 ; i < EVENBYTE (nIconWide) / 8 ; i++)
                    {
                            for (j = 0 ; j < nIconTall ; j++)
                            {
                                    *psA++ = 0xFF ;
                                    if (i > j)
                                            *psX++ = 0xFF ;
                                    else
                                            *psX++ = 0x11 ;
                            }
                    }
```

```
                         hIcon = CreateIcon (ghInstance, nIconWide,
                                 nIconTall, 1, 1, psAND, psXOR) ;
                         LocalUnlock (hANDBits) ;
                         LocalUnlock (hXORBits) ;
                         LocalFree (hANDBits) ;
                         LocalFree (hXORBits) ;
                         break ;
                 case WM_PAINT:
                         BeginPaint (hWnd, &ps) ;
                         DrawIcon (ps.hdc, 10, 10, hIcon) ;
                         EndPaint (hWnd, &ps) ;
                         break ;
                 case WM_COMMAND:                        /* process menu items */
                         switch (wParam)
                         {
                         case IDM_QUIT:         /* send end of application message */
                                 DestroyWindow (hWnd) ;
                                 break ;
                         }
                         break ;
                 case WM_DESTROY:               /* stop application */
                         DestroyIcon (hIcon) ;
                         PostQuitMessage (0) ;
                         break ;
                 default:                   /* default windows message processing */
                         return DefWindowProc (hWnd, iMessage, wParam, lParam) ;
        }
        return (0L) ;
}
```

DESTROYICON   □ Win 2.0   ■ Win 3.0   ■ Win 3.1

Purpose	Destroys an icon that was previously created with CreateIcon().
Syntax	BOOL **DestroyIcon**(HICON *hIcon*);
Description	Destroying an icon removes the icon data from memory. This should only be used for icons created using CreateIcon().
Uses	Used to free memory once the icon is no longer needed. Do not call DestroyIcon() if the icon is in use.
Returns	BOOL. TRUE if the icon was destroyed, FALSE on error.
See Also	CreateIcon()
Parameters	
hIcon	HICON: The handle of the icon, returned by CreateIcon() when the icon was created.
Example	See the previous example under CreateIcon().

DRAWICON   ■ Win 2.0   ■ Win 3.0   ■ Win 3.1

Purpose	Draws an icon on a device.
Syntax	BOOL **DrawIcon**(HDC *hDC*, int *X*, int *Y*, HICON *hIcon*);
Description	This is the only function for painting icons. The icon is normally loaded from the resource data using LoadIcon(). It can also be created using CreateIcon(). The device context must be in the MM_TEXT mapping mode for this function to operate properly.
Uses	Drawing an icon.
Returns	BOOL. TRUE if the icon was drawn, FALSE on error.
See Also	LoadIcon(), CreateIcon()

Parameters

hDC HDC: The device context handle.

X int: The logical *X* coordinate of the upper left corner of the icon.

Y int: The logical *Y* coordinate of the upper left corner of the icon.

hIcon HICON: The handle of the icon. This value is returned either by LoadIcon() or CreateIcon().

Example This example, as shown in Figure 16-5, paints all five stock icons to the screen, and also paints the GENERIC application's icon on the lower left. From left to right, the five stock icons on the top row are named IDI_APPLICATION, IDI_ASTERISK, IDI_EXCLAMATION, IDI_HAND, and IDI_QUESTION. The image and the name of the IDI_ASTERISK and IDI_HAND icons do not match because the icons were a different shape with the 2.0 release of Windows.

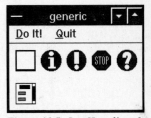

Figure 16-5. LoadIcon( ) and DrawIcon Example.

```
long FAR PASCAL WndProc (HWND hWnd, unsigned iMessage, WORD wParam, LONG lParam)
{
        PAINTSTRUCT             ps ;
        static  HICON           hIcon1, hIcon2, hIcon3, hIcon4, hIcon5, hIcon6 ;

        switch (iMessage)                       /* process windows messages */
        {
                case WM_CREATE:
                        hIcon1 = LoadIcon (NULL, IDI_APPLICATION) ;
                        hIcon2 = LoadIcon (NULL, IDI_ASTERISK) ;
                        hIcon3 = LoadIcon (NULL, IDI_EXCLAMATION) ;
                        hIcon4 = LoadIcon (NULL, IDI_HAND) ;
                        hIcon5 = LoadIcon (NULL, IDI_QUESTION) ;
                        hIcon6 = LoadIcon (ghInstance, "generic") ;
                        break ;
                case WM_PAINT:
                        BeginPaint (hWnd, &ps) ;
                        DrawIcon (ps.hdc, 10, 10, hIcon1) ;
                        DrawIcon (ps.hdc, 50, 10, hIcon2) ;
                        DrawIcon (ps.hdc, 90, 10, hIcon3) ;
                        DrawIcon (ps.hdc, 130, 10, hIcon4) ;
                        DrawIcon (ps.hdc, 170, 10, hIcon5) ;
                        DrawIcon (ps.hdc, 10, 60, hIcon6) ;
                        EndPaint (hWnd, &ps) ;
                        break ;
```

[Other program lines]

LOADICON ■ Win 2.0 ■ Win 3.0 ■ Win 3.1

Purpose Retrieves a handle to an icon listed in the program's resource file.

Syntax HICON **LoadIcon**(HANDLE *hInstance*, LPSTR *lpIconName*);

Description LoadIcon() does two related tasks. It retrieves a handle to an icon referenced in the program's .RC resource script file. It also retrieves stock icon images. If more than one call to LoadIcon() is made for the same icon name, a handle is retrieved to the existing icon data in memory. Normally, icons are created with the Windows SDKPaint application and stored in a disk file. A program can use the icon by including an ICON statement in the .RC resource file.

```
generic          ICON           generic.ico
```

Then, the program can obtain a handle to the icon using the icon's name, "generic" in this case. To load a stock icon, the *hInstance* parameter must be set to NULL.

Uses	Obtaining a handle to an icon, ready to use for DrawIcon().
Returns	HICON, the handle to the icon. NULL on error.
See Also	DrawIcon()
Parameters	
hInstance	HANDLE: The application's instance handle. Use GetWindowWord() to obtain this value if it has not been saved. Set to NULL to load a stock icon.
lpIconName	LPSTR: A pointer to a character string containing the name of the icon. (This is the name on the left side of the ICON statement in the application's .RC resource file.) If *hInstance* is set to NULL, *lpIconName* can be one of the five stock icon names listed in Table 16-3.

Value	Meaning	⊠
IDI_APPLICATION	The default application icon, an open rectangle.	
IDI_ASTERISK	An information icon.	
IDI_EXCLAMATION	An exclamation point icon (for warning messages).	
IDI_HAND	A stop sign icon (for serious warning messages).	
IDI_QUESTION	A question mark.	

Table 16-3. Stock Icons.

Example	See the previous example under DrawIcon().

OpenIcon ■ Win 2.0　■ Win 3.0　■ Win 3.1

Purpose	Restores a minimized window to its last size and position.
Syntax	BOOL **OpenIcon**(HWND *hWnd*);
Description	This is a shortcut method of restoring a window that has been minimized. Windows retains the last size and position of the window before it was minimized. Calling OpenIcon() restores the window to its former position and size. Note that this function has little to do with the application's icon. It is simply a means of restoring a window.
Uses	Used in applications that have child window controls that can be minimized.
Returns	BOOL. TRUE if the window was restored, FALSE on error.
See Also	ArrangeIconicWindows()
Parameters	
hWnd	HWND: The handle of the window to be restored. This value is returned when CreateWindow() is used to create the (child) window.
Related Messages	WM_SIZE
Example	See the example under ArrangeIconicWindows().

17

The Clipboard

Windows provides two methods for applications to exchange information: the clipboard and Dynamic Data Exchange (DDE). The clipboard is used for information that is exchanged on demand by the user. DDE is used when the information needs to be transferred in the background, or as it becomes available from some outside source, such as a modem. Windows applications use the clipboard frequently. Any time you cut or copy text or bitmaps from within the Windows Notepad, PaintBrush, Windows Write, Excel, etc., the data ends up in the clipboard. Because the clipboard is available to all applications, you can cut and paste between different programs. This information exchange is a powerful feature of Windows, and one of the benefits of using Windows as a development platform.

Using the Clipboard

Physically, the clipboard is just a global memory block. When an application gives data to the clipboard, Windows takes ownership of the memory block. Any application can then request a handle to the memory block and read the data. The block remains the property of Windows. To put data in the clipboard, an application allocates a global memory block and fills it with data. The function SetClipboardData() then passes the memory block to Windows. Any application wanting to read the memory block can use GetClipboardData() to obtain a handle to the global memory location containing the data. Figure 17-1 shows this relationship graphically.

A typical program fragment loads a text string into the clipboard in the follwoing code:

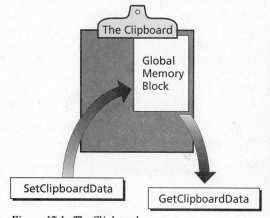

Figure 17-1. The Clipboard.

```
hMem = GlobalAlloc (GHND, 64) ;
lpStr = GlobalLock (hMem) ;
lstrcpy (lpStr, "Text In Clipboard") ;
GlobalUnlock (hMem) ;
if (OpenClipboard (hWnd))
{
        EmptyClipboard () ;
        SetClipboardData (CF_TEXT, hMem) ;
        CloseClipboard () ;
}
```

The program allocates a global block 64 bytes wide and copies some text to it. The block is then unlocked, but not freed. OpenClipboard() alerts Windows that the clipboard is going to be used. If another application has the clipboard open, OpenClipboard() will return zero. Otherwise, EmptyClipboard() clears any data currently in the clipboard and frees the memory block associated with it. SetClipboardData() adds the new block to the clipboard. CloseClipboard() lets Windows know that the clipboard is not needed by this application.

The program code needed to retrieve the text is shown below.

```
if (OpenClipboard (hWnd))
{
```

```
hClipMem = GetClipboardData (CF_TEXT) ;
hMem = GlobalAlloc (GHND, GlobalSize (hClipMem)) ;
lpStr = GlobalLock (hMem) ;
lpClip = GlobalLock (hClipMem) ;
lstrcpy (lpStr, lpClip) ;
GlobalUnlock (hMem) ;
GlobalUnlock (hClipMem) ;
CloseClipboard () ;
}
```

Because the global memory block in the clipboard belongs to Windows, the application cannot use it directly. Instead, the application needs to copy the data to another memory area that is owned by the application. Again, OpenClipboard() alerts Windows that the clipboard will be used, and checks to make sure that no other application has the clipboard open. GetClipboardData() obtains a handle to the clipboard's memory block. The clipboard data is then copied into a separate block allocated with GlobalAlloc(). The clipboard memory block is unlocked (but not freed) to release the block for use by other applications. CloseClipboard() informs Windows that the clipboard is no longer needed.

Clipboard Formats

You may have noticed the CF_TEXT string in the SetClipboardData() and GetClipboardData() function calls. This is one of several predefined clipboard formats available to all applications. Clipboard formats are used to distinguish different types of data that can be exchanged by applications. Without formats, an application might try to read in bitmap data and use it as character data. Formats keep the different types of data separate. Table 17-1 lists all of the predefined clipboard formats.

Value	Meaning
CF_BITMAP	A bitmap handle (HBITMAP).
CF_DIB	A memory block containing a device-independent bitmap (DIB). The block will contain a BITMAPINFO data structure followed by the bitmap bits (see Chapter 15, *Bitmaps*).
CF_DIF	Software Arts' Data Interchange Format.
CF_DISPBITMAP	A private bitmap display format.
CF_DSPMETAFILEPICT	A private metafile display format.
CF_DISPTEXT	A private text display format.
CF_METAFILEPICT	A metafile picture. The memory block will contain a METAFILEPICT data structure (see Chapter 23, *Metafiles*, and the following discussion).
CF_OEMTEXT	A memory block containing only OEM text characters. Each line is ended with a CR-LF pair. A NULL byte marks the end of the text. Windows uses this format to transfer data between non-Windows and Windows applications.
CF_OWNERDISPLAY	The clipboard owner is responsible for painting the clipboard. The clipboard owner should process WM_ASKCBFORMATNAME, WM_HSCROLLCLIPBOARD, WM_PAINTCLIPBOARD, WM_SIZECLIPBOARD, and WM_VSCROLLCLIPBOARD messages.
CF_PALETTE	A handle to a color palette (see Chapter 12, *Color Pallette Control*).
CF_SYLK	Microsoft Symbolic Link (SYLK) format.
CF_TEXT	A memory block containing text characters. Each line is ended with a CR-LF pair. A NULL byte marks the end of the text. This is the standard format for exchanging text between Windows applications.
CF_TIFF	Tag Image File Format.

Table 17-1. Clipboard Data Formats.

The predefined formats cover the most common types of data exchange. Even if your application uses specialized data fields, it should support at least one of the predefined clipboard formats. For example, a spreadsheet might write the selected cell contents to the clipboard using only the CF_TEXT clipboard format. This would lose the formatting and calculations in the complete spreadsheet data field, but at least it would allow another application to read the character data.

Multiple Clipboard Formats

Applications may use specialized data formats to exchange data with the clipboard. Windows supports this with the process of "registering" a special format. The RegisterClipboardFormat() function allows applications to create custom formats.

Using a spreadsheet as an example, let's say that the program needs to cut and paste the complete contents of one or more cells in the spreadsheet. There is a lot of data behind each spreadsheet cell, including the calculation formula and text formatting options. If the data were passed as a standard format, such as CF_TEXT, another application might read all of the formatting data as text, and end up with a lot of strange characters.

The solution is to register a new clipboard format. The format might be called "CELL." The spreadsheet application cuts and pastes cells by copying memory blocks to and from the clipboard using the CELL format. Another application trying to read CF_TEXT format data would not get a handle to this data when it called GetClipboardData (CF_TEXT).

Supporting more than one clipboard format is even more sophisticated than this approach. The clipboard can hold more than one memory handle, and each handle can contain data in a different format. Our spreadsheet can write the full contents of the cells using the CELL format, and also write the cell text using the simple CF_TEXT format. This ability allows a word processor to paste text off of the clipboard, while also allowing the spreadsheet to paste the full cell data.

Word for Windows provides an excellent example of this type of flexibility. When a block of text is cut or copied from within Word for Windows, the clipboard has five separate versions of the text available. They range from the sophisticated "Rich Text Format" special clipboard format, to the lowly CF_OEMTEXT predefined format. A wide range of applications will be able to read the text copied to the clipboard by Word For Windows. The examples under the EnumClipboardFormats() and GetPriorityClipboardFormat() function descriptions provide more details. The latter has an example that provides two clipboard formats at the same time.

Delayed Rendering of Clipboard Data

"Rendering" is an awful word for putting data in the clipboard ("rendering" brings to mind boiling caldrons of fat and lime, but this is a different use of the word). Normally, an application will pass a memory block to the clipboard when SetClipboardData() is called. Windows provides another option. If SetClipboardData() is called with a NULL memory handle, Windows assumes that the application wants to wait to load the memory block into the clipboard. This is called "delayed rendering."

There are a couple of reasons why you may want to use delayed rendering. One is if there is a low probability that the data will be needed. For example, if the user highlights some text and then presses the (DEL) key, he or she probably wants to get rid of the text. Loading the memory block into the clipboard takes time and fills up memory space. Waiting to see if the user wants the data recovered can save memory and speed up the program. You should also use delayed rendering if the clipboard will end up passing a large memory block, or several clipboard formats at once. In either case, the memory area filled by the clipboard block will interfere with the operation of other programs if memory gets tight. It is better to load the data at the moment it is required.

As previously mentioned, the first step in using delayed rendering of clipboard data is to call SetClipboardData(), passing NULL as the memory handle. The clipboard format will be registered with Windows, but no data changes hands. If another application attempts to read the specified clipboard format data from the clipboard, Windows will send a WM_RENDERFORMAT message to the application that called SetClipboardData(). At this point, the application should pass the memory block containing the requested data by calling SetClipboardData(), with a global memory block handle.

Applications that use delayed rendering are also expected to process the WM_RENDERALLFORMATS message. This message is sent to the application when the application is about to exit. The application should pass valid global memory block handles to the clipbaord for all formats that the application supports. Doing so will let other applications paste from the clipboard after the application exits. Examples of delayed rendering of clipboard data are provided under the EnumClipboardFormats() and IsClipboardFormatAvailable() function descriptions.

Bitmap and Metafile Clipboard Formats

The CF_BITMAP format specifies the "old" DDB bitmap format. Bitmaps are transferred to the clipboard by passing a handle to the bitmap in place of a handle to an ordinary memory block. The bitmap handle is returned by the CreateCompatibleBitmap() function, which creates a memory bitmap in global memory. The example under SetClipboardData() provides an example program that captures bitmap images from the screen and copies them to the clipboard.

Device-independent bitmaps (DIBs) are passed to the clipboard as a global memory block. This is the CF_DIB clipboard format. The memory block contains the BITMAPINFO data structure followed by the bitmap bits. Metafiles are transferred to the clipboard using the METAFILEPICT structure, which is defined in WINDOWS.H as

```
typedef struct tagMETAFILEPICT
  {
    int         mm;                /* the mapping mode */
    int         xExt;              /* the metafile X extent (width) */
    int         yExt;              /* the metafile Y extent (height) */
    HANDLE      hMF;               /* a handle to the memory metafile */
  } METAFILEPICT;
typedef METAFILEPICT FAR          *LPMETAFILEPICT;
```

The METAFILEPICT data structure is initialized in a global memory block. The *hMF* element points to a metafile in memory (not a disk metafile). When the handle to the METAFILEPICT data structure memory block is passed to Windows using SetClipboardData(), both that memory block and the memory block containing the metafile (*hMF*) become the property of Windows.

Clipboard Viewer Programs

Windows comes with a clipboard viewer called "Clipboard." This application is put in the Main group when Windows is installed. The application will display whatever data is in the clipboard, and will support most of the predefined clipboard formats (every one that the author tested). Other applications can be clipboard viewers, and more than one clipboard viewer can be active at one time. If more than one application displays the clipboard contents, the applications are said to form a "clipboard viewing chain." The functions SetClipboardViewer() and ChangeClipboardChain() are provided to establish an application as a clipboard viewer, and to remove an application from the viewing chain.

Windows sends clipboard viewers the WM_DRAWCLIPBOARD message when the clipboard data changes. The application can display the data (if it supports the clipboard data format). The viewer has the obligation to pass the message to the next viewer in the chain. When a clipboard viewer is removed from the viewing chain, the WM_CHANGECBCHAIN message is sent by Windows. Again, each application in the viewing chain is responsible for sending this message to the next viewer.

An example of a clipboard viewer that displays both text and bitmap data is given under the ChangeClip-boardChain() function description. Normally, clipboard viewers are only written to view custom clipboard data formats. The Clipboard application supplied with Windows is fine for viewing the standard formats.

Caution: Because Windows owns the memory block associated with the clipboard, applications should not leave this block locked after data has been read. Applications should not allow control to pass back to Windows while the clipboard is open. In other words, the clipboard should be opened and closed while processing a single Windows message. This can be more complicated than it sounds. For example, an application that opens the clipboard may use a dialog box to display an error. If the dialog box is not system-modal, the user can select another application while the dialog box is on the screen. This effectively passes control back to Windows while the clipboard is still open. Avoid this situation by closing the clipboard immediately after use.

Clipboard Function Summary

Table 17-2 summarizes the clipboard functions. The detailed function descriptions are in the next section.

Function	Purpose	⊠
ChangeClipboardChain	Removes a clipboard viewer program from the chain of viewer programs.	
CloseClipboard	Closes the clipboard after it was opened either to add data, or to read data.	
CountClipboardFormats	Determines the number of clipboard formats currently in use.	
EmptyClipboard	Empties the clipboard and frees the data associated with it.	
EnumClipboardFormats	Lists all of the formats available in the clipboard.	
GetClipboardData	Retrieves a handle to the data in the clipboard.	
GetClipboardFormatName	Determines the name of a special clipboard format.	
GetClipboardOwner	Retrieves the handle of the application that owns the clipboard.	
GetClipboardViewer	Retrieves the handle of the first clipboard viewer in the clipboard viewer chain.	
GetOpenClipboardWindow	Determines the handle of the window that most recently opened the clipboard.	
GetPriorityClipboardFormat	Checks the clipboard for availability of desired data formats.	
IsClipboardFormatAvailable	Checks whether the clipboard contains data in a specific format.	
OpenClipboard	Opens the clipboard so that an application can read or set the contents.	
RegisterClipboardFormat	Registers a new clipboard format name with Windows.	
SetClipboardData	Passes a global memory handle to the clipboard. The memory block becomes the clipboard data.	
SetClipboardViewer	Adds a new window to the list of windows in the clipboard viewer chain.	

Table 17-2. Clipboard Function Summary.

Clipboard Function Descriptions

This section contains the detailed descriptions of the clipboard function.

CHANGECLIPBOARDCHAIN   ■ Win 2.0   ■ Win 3.0   ■ Win 3.1

Purpose	Removes a clipboard viewer program from the chain of viewer programs.
Syntax	BOOL **ChangeClipboardChain**(HWND *hWnd*, HWND *hWndNext*);
Description	This function is useful only if SetClipboardViewer() has been called to install a clipboard viewer. Clipboard viewers receive WM_DRAWCLIPBOARD messages, and are expected to display the data currently in the clipboard.
Uses	Used when an application is removed from the clipboard viewing chain.
Returns	BOOL. TRUE if *hWnd* was removed from the clipboard viewer chain, FALSE on error.
See Also	SetClipboardViewer()
Parameters	
hWnd	HWND: The window handle of the window to be removed from the clipboard viewer chain. This handle must have been previously passed to Windows by SetClipboardViewer().
hWndNext	HWND: The window handle of the window that follows *hWnd* in the chain of clipboard viewers. This value is returned by SetClipboardViewer(), and should be saved in a static variable.
Related Messages	WM_DRAWCLIPBOARD, WM_CHANGECBCHAIN

Example   This example creates a clipboard viewer. The application will display the current contents of the clipboard if the clipboard contains either the CF_TEXT or CF_BITMAP data type. Clicking the "Do It!" menu item empties the clipboard. The viewer installs itself in the clipboard viewer chain when the application starts, and removes itself from the chain on exit.

```
Long FAR PASCAL WndProc (HWND hWnd, unsigned iMessage, WORD wParam, LONG lParam)
{
        PAINTSTRUCT             ps ;
        HDC                     hMemDC ;
        HBITMAP                 hBitmap ;
        BITMAP                  bm ;
        RECT                    rClientRect ;
        HANDLE                  hMem ;
        LPSTR                   lpMem ;
        static          HWND    hNextViewer ;

        switch (iMessage)       /* process windows messages */
        {
                case WM_CREATE:
                        hNextViewer = SetClipboardViewer (hWnd) ;
                        break ;
                case WM_PAINT:
                        BeginPaint (hWnd, &ps) ;
                        GetClientRect (hWnd, &rClientRect) ;
                        OpenClipboard (hWnd) ;
                        if (hMem = GetClipboardData (CF_TEXT))
                        {
                                lpMem = GlobalLock (hMem) ;
                                DrawText (ps.hdc, lpMem, -1, &rClientRect,
                                DT_LEFT) ;
                                GlobalUnlock (hMem) ;
                        }
                        else if (hBitmap = GetClipboardData (CF_BITMAP))
                        {
                                hMemDC = CreateCompatibleDC (ps.hdc) ;
                                SelectObject (hMemDC, hBitmap) ;
                                GetObject (hBitmap, sizeof (BITMAP),
                                (LPSTR) &bm) ;
                                BitBlt (ps.hdc, 0, 0, bm.bmWidth, bm.bmHeight,
                                hMemDC, 0, 0, SRCCOPY) ;
                                DeleteDC (hMemDC) ;
                        }
                        CloseClipboard () ;
                        EndPaint (hWnd, &ps) ;
                        break ;
                case WM_DRAWCLIPBOARD:
                        if (hNextViewer)
                        SendMessage (hNextViewer, WM_DRAWCLIPBOARD,
                        wParam, lParam) ;
                        InvalidateRect (hWnd, NULL, TRUE) ;      /* force paint */
                        break ;
                case WM_CHANGECBCHAIN:
                        if (wParam == hNextViewer)
                                hNextViewer = LOWORD (lParam) ;
                        else if (hNextViewer)
                                SendMessage (hNextViewer, WM_CHANGECBCHAIN,
                                        wParam, lParam) ;
                        break ;
                case WM_COMMAND:                    /* process menu items */
                        switch (wParam)
                        {
                        case IDM_DOIT:              /* empty the clipboard */
                                OpenClipboard (hWnd) ;
                                EmptyClipboard () ;
                                CloseClipboard () ;
                                InvalidateRect (hWnd, NULL, TRUE) ;
                                break ;
```

```
                        case IDM_QUIT:
                                DestroyWindow (hWnd) ;
                                break ;
                        }
                        break ;
                case WM_DESTROY:                        /* stop application */
                        ChangeClipboardChain (hWnd, hNextViewer) ;
                        PostQuitMessage (0) ;
                        break ;
                default:              *                 /* default windows message processing */
                        return DefWindowProc (hWnd, iMessage, wParam, lParam) ;
        }
        return (0L) ;
}
```

CLOSECLIPBOARD   ■ Win 2.0   ■ Win 3.0   ■ Win 3.1

Purpose	Closes the clipboard after it was opened either to add data or to read data.
Syntax	BOOL **CloseClipboard**(void);
Description	The clipboard is a global memory block which has been passed to Windows from an application. OpenClipboard() makes the data temporarily available to an application. CloseClipboard() returns control of the memory block to Windows.
Uses	Used after OpenClipboard() to return control of the clipboard data to Windows. Control should not be passed to Windows while the clipboard is open. Open and close the clipboard while processing a single Windows message.
Returns	BOOL. TRUE if the clipboard was closed, FALSE on error.
See Also	OpenClipboard(), EmptyClipboard()
Parameters	None (void).
Example	See the previous example under ChangeClipboardChain() and the example under SetClipboardData().

COUNTCLIPBOARDFORMATS   ■ Win 2.0   ■ Win 3.0   ■ Win 3.1

Purpose	Determines the number of clipboard formats currently in use.
Syntax	int **CountClipboardFormats**(void);
Description	Some applications put more than one format of data in the clipboard. This allows a variety of applications to read the data, even if they do not support all of the formats available.
Uses	Determines if more than one clipboard format is available. EnumClipboardFormats() can then be used to determine which formats are available.
Returns	int, the number of data formats currently in the clipboard.
See Also	EnumClipboardFormats(), GetClipboardFormatName()
Parameters	None (void).
Example	See the example under EnumClipboardFormats().

EMPTYCLIPBOARD   ■ Win 2.0   ■ Win 3.0   ■ Win 3.1

Purpose	Empties the clipboard and frees the data associated with it.
Syntax	BOOL **EmptyClipboard**(void);
Description	This function is used to remove data from the clipboard. It is called after OpenClipboard(), and before CloseClipboard(). Any global memory that was associated with the clipboard by an appli-

cation calling SetClipboardData() is freed. The window calling EmptyClipboard() becomes the current clipboard owner.

Uses	Use this prior to calling SetClipboardData() to make sure that the clipboard is empty. Also used to empty the clipboard so that no data is visible in an open clipboard viewer.
Returns	BOOL. TRUE if the clipboard was emptied, FALSE on error.
See Also	OpenClipboard(), CloseClipboard()
Parameters	None (void).
Related Messages	WM_DRAWCLIPBOARD, WM_CHANGECBCHAIN
Example	See the examples under ChangeClipboardChain() and SetClipboardData().

ENUMCLIPBOARDFORMATS
■ Win 2.0　　■ Win 3.0　　■ Win 3.1

Purpose	Lists all of the formats available in the clipboard.
Syntax	WORD **EnumClipboardFormats**(WORD *wFormat*);
Description	The clipboard can contain data that uses any of the predefined clipboard formats (listed under SetClipboardData()) or a special clipboard format made with RegisterClipboardFormat().

EnumClipboardFormats() is called repeatedly to determine all of the formats. On the first call, *wFormat* is set to zero. EnumClipboardFormats() returns the first format available. On the second and subsequent calls, the last format returned is used for *wFormat* in the next call. This sequence is repeated until the function returns zero, specifying that the last format has been read.

EnumClipboardFormats() lists all of the formats that are currently in use in the clipboard. In most cases, this will be a single format. Some applications set more than one version of the data to the clipboard, so that other applications can read the data if they only support a few formats.

EnumClipboardFormats() lists the formats in the same order that the application that set the clipboard used in loading the data. The first format enumerated should be the most desirable (least data lost). For example, a DIB (device-independent bitmap) would be preferable to a DDB bitmap.

Uses	Used with applications that support more than one means of reading the clipboard. Enumerating the clipboard allows the application to choose which format to use in reading the data.
Returns	WORD, the next known clipboard format number. Returns zero if the last format was read.
See Also	CountClipboardFormats, GetClipboardFormatName()
Parameters	
wFormat	WORD: The format number of the last format read. Set to zero for the first call to EnumClipboardFormats(). Set to the last value returned by the function for all subsequent calls.
Example	This example lists all of the clipboard formats available when the user clicks the "Do It!" menu item. For custom formats (set by applications which call RegisterClipboardFormat()), the name of the format can be retrieved using GetClipboardFormatName(). For predefined clipboard for-

mats, the names are not returned by GetClipboardFormatName(). The listing includes a function called NameClipFormat() that supplies the names of the predefined formats.

Figure 17-2 shows the list of available clipboard formats after Microsoft Word for Windows has

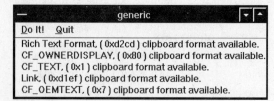

Figure 17-2. EnumClipboardFormats() Example.

been used to copy text to the clipboard (Edit/Copy menu item). This application supplies the clipboard with five clipboard formats. An application reading or viewing the clipboard could use any of these to obtain the text copied.

EnumClipboardFormats() retrieves the formats in the same order that data was added into the clipboard, which should be the priority order. In this case, the most desirable format is a special format called "Rich Text Format." The next most desirable is the CF_OWNERDISPLAY predefined format, which is only suitable for a clipboard viewer. Next is the CF_TEXT format, which includes the text characters, but omits formatting characters. Next is a special format called "Link." The last, and least desirable format, is CF_OEMTEXT which will only have the OEM character set. As you can see, Word for Windows goes to a lot of trouble to make the data in the clipboard useful.

```c
void NameClipFormat (int nFormat, char *cName) ;

long FAR PASCAL WndProc (HWND hWnd, unsigned iMessage, WORD wParam, LONG lParam)
{
        HDC             hDC ;
        int             i, n, nCBFormats, nFormat ;
        char            cBuf [128], cName [64] ;

        switch (iMessage)                       /* process windows messages */
        {
                case WM_COMMAND:                /* process menu items */
                        switch (wParam)
                        {
                        case IDM_DOIT:          /* User hit the "Do it" menu item */
                                hDC = GetDC (hWnd) ;
                                nCBFormats = CountClipboardFormats() ;
                                OpenClipboard (hWnd) ;
                                nFormat = 0 ;
                                for (i = 0 ; i < nCBFormats ; i++)
                                {
                                        nFormat = EnumClipboardFormats
                                                (nFormat) ;
                                        n = GetClipboardFormatName (nFormat,
                                                cName, 63) ;
                                        if (n == 0)
                                                NameClipFormat (nFormat, cName) ;
                                        TextOut (hDC, 10, i * 20, cBuf,
                                                wsprintf (cBuf,
                                        "%s, ( 0x%x ) clipboard format available.",
                                                (LPSTR) cName, nFormat)) ;
                                }
                                CloseClipboard () ;
                                ReleaseDC (hWnd, hDC) ;
                                break ;
                        case IDM_QUIT:
                                DestroyWindow (hWnd) ;
                                break ;
                        }
                        break ;
                case WM_DESTROY:
                        PostQuitMessage (0) ;
                        break ;
                default:
                        return DefWindowProc (hWnd, iMessage, wParam, lParam) ;
        }
        return (0L) ;
}

                /* fills in cName with the name of a predefined clipboard format */

void NameClipFormat (int nFormat, char *cName)
{
        static char *cClipName [9] = {"CF_TEXT", "CF_BITMAP",
                "CF_METAFILEPICT", "CF_SYLK", "CF_DIF", "CF_TIFF",
```

```
              "CF_OEMTEXT", "CF_DIB", "CF_PALETTE" } ;
      static char *cClipName2 [4] = {"CF_OWNERDISPLAY",
              "CF_DSPTEXT", "CF_DSPBITMAP", "CF_DISPMETAFILEPICT"} ;

      if (nFormat <= 9)
              strcpy (cName, cClipName [nFormat - CF_TEXT]) ;
      else if (nFormat <= 0x83)
              strcpy (cName, cClipName2 [nFormat - CF_OWNERDISPLAY]) ;
      else
              strcpy (cName, "<Not named>") ;
}
```

GetClipboardData

■ Win 2.0   ■ Win 3.0   ■ Win 3.1

Purpose	Retrieves a handle to the data in the clipboard.
Syntax	HANDLE **GetClipboardData**(WORD *wFormat*);
Description	This function checks the clipboard to see if the clipboard holds the specified data format. If so, a handle to the clipboard memory block is returned. This function is called after OpenClipboard(), and before CloseClipboard(). The application should copy the memory block immediately after receiving the handle. Otherwise, another application may empty the clipboard, invalidating the handle.
Uses	Retrieving data from the clipboard.
Returns	HANDLE, a handle to a global memory block. NULL on error. Lock the memory block with GlobalLock() before reading the data, and unlock it with GlobalUnlock() as soon as the data is read.
See Also	OpenClipboard(), CloseClipboard(), SetClipboardData()
Parameters	
wFormat	WORD: Specifies what type of data the application would like to read from the clipboard memory block. The format can be any of the ones listed in Table 17-3.

Value	Meaning
CF_BITMAP	A bitmap handle (HBITMAP).
CF_DIB	A memory block containing a device-independent bitmap (DIB). The block will contain a BITMAPINFO data structure followed by the bitmap bits.
CF_DIF	Software Arts' Data Interchange Format.
CF_DISPBITMAP	A private bitmap display format.
CF_DSPMETAFILEPICT	A private metafile display format.
CF_DISPTEXT	A private text display format.
CF_METAFILEPICT	A metafile picture. The memory block will contain a METAFILEPICT data structure.
CF_OEMTEXT	A memory block containing only OEM text characters. Each line ends with a CR-LF pair. A NULL byte marks the end of the text. This is the format Windows uses to transfer data between non-Windows and Windows applications.
CF_OWNERDISPLAY	The clipboard owner is responsible for painting the clipboard. The clipboard owner should process WM_ASKCBFORMATNAME, WM_HSCROLLCLIPBOARD, WM_PAINTCLIPBOARD, WM_SIZECLIPBOARD, and WM_VSCROLLCLIPBOARD messages.
CF_PALETTE	A handle to a color palette.
CF_SYLK	Microsoft Symbolic Link (SYLK) format.
CF_TEXT	A memory block containing text characters. Each line ends with a CR-LF pair. A NULL byte marks the end of the text. This is the standard format for exchanging text between Windows applications.
CF_TIFF	Tag Image File Format.

Table 17-3. Clipboard Data Formats.

In addition, private clipboard formats can have values between CF_PRIVATEFIRST and CF_PRIVATELAST.

Related Messages WM_ASKCBFORMATNAME, WM_HSCROLLCLIPBOARD, WM_PAINTCLIPBOARD, WM_SIZE-CLIPBOARD, WM_VSCROLLCLIPBOARD

Caution The application calling GetClipboardData() should unlock the memory block as soon as it is read. Leaving the clipboard memory block locked while Windows processes messages may cause the system to crash.

Example See the examples under the ChangeClipboardChain() and SetClipboardData() function descriptions.

GETCLIPBOARDFORMATNAME

■ Win 2.0　■ Win 3.0　■ Win 3.1

Purpose Determines the name of a special clipboard format.

Syntax int **GetClipboardFormatName**(WORD *wFormat*, LPSTR *lpFormatName*, int *nMaxCount*);

Description Applications can use RegisterClipboardFormat() to store data in the clipboard under a special format name. GetClipboardFormatName() allows other applications to check the name(s) of the clipboard formats available to see if the data in the clipboard is in the right format to use. Names of predefined clipboard formats are not returned.

The special format name does not imply that the data is coded. The data can be in a standard format such as CF_TEXT. The format name simply gives the clipboard data special meaning. For example, a spreadsheet might cut and paste using the clipboard with a special format registered as "SPREADSHEET." The actual data passed to the clipboard could be the characters in the spreadsheet cell plus formatting characters.

Uses Used with EnumClipboardFormats() to find the names of the formats available. Only special formats registered with RegisterClipboardFormat() have stored names. The standard formats (listed under SetClipboardData()) will not return a name.

Returns int, the number of characters read. Zero on error.

See Also EnumClipboardFormats(), RegisterClipboardFormat()

Parameters

wFormat WORD: The format number. This is a format number returned by EnumClipboardFormats() or RegisterClipboardFormat().

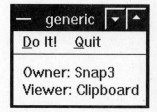

lpFormatName LPSTR: A pointer to a memory buffer that will hold the name of the clipboard format. The buffer should be at least *nMaxCount* bytes wide.

Figure 17-3. GetClipboardOwner( ) and GetClipboardViewer( ) Example.

nMaxCount int: The maximum string size to be read into the *lpFormatName* buffer. If the clipboard format name is longer, it will be truncated.

Example See the example under EnumClipboardFormats().

GETCLIPBOARDOWNER

■ Win 2.0　■ Win 3.0　■ Win 3.1

Purpose Retrieves the handle of the application that owns the clipboard.

Syntax HWND **GetClipboardOwner**(void);

Description The clipboard owner is the last application to call SetClipboardData(). This function returns that application's handle.

Returns HWND, the handle of the application that owns the clipboard. NULL if the clipboard is currently unowned.

See Also   GetClipboardViewer()

Parameters   None (void).

Example   This example displays the current clipboard viewer and owner window names. (See Figure 17-3.)
                      The names are updated when the user clicks the "Do It!" menu item, or when the window is
                      painted for any reason.

```
long FAR PASCAL WndProc (HWND hWnd, unsigned iMessage, WORD wParam, LONG lParam)
{
        PAINTSTRUCT             ps ;
        HWND                    hCBOwner, hCBViewer ;
        char                    cBuf [128], cName [64] ;

        switch (iMessage)
        {
            case WM_PAINT:
                    BeginPaint (hWnd, &ps) ;
                    hCBOwner = GetClipboardOwner () ;
                    if (hCBOwner == NULL)
                            lstrcpy (cName, "<None>") ;
                    else
                            GetWindowText (hCBOwner, cName, 63) ;
                    TextOut (ps.hdc, 10, 10, cBuf, wsprintf (cBuf,
                            "Owner: %s", (LPSTR) cName)) ;
                    hCBViewer = GetClipboardViewer () ;
                    if (hCBViewer == NULL)
                            lstrcpy (cName, "<None>") ;
                    else
                            GetWindowText (hCBViewer, cName, 63) ;
                    TextOut (ps.hdc, 10, 30, cBuf, wsprintf (cBuf,
                            "Viewer: %s", (LPSTR) cName)) ;
                    EndPaint (hWnd, &ps) ;
                    break ;
            case WM_COMMAND:
                    switch (wParam)
                    {
                    case IDM_DOIT:
                            InvalidateRect (hWnd, NULL, TRUE) ;
                            break ;
```

[Other program lines]

GETCLIPBOARDVIEWER   ■ Win 2.0   ■ Win 3.0   ■ Win 3.1

Purpose   Retrieves the handle of the first clipboard viewer in the clipboard viewer chain.

Syntax   HWND **GetClipboardViewer**(void);

Description   The standard clipboard viewer application is supplied with Windows. This is the Clipboard appli-
                      cation that Windows installs in the Main group. Other applications can be added to the clipboard
                      viewer chain. See ChangeClipboardChain() for an example.

Returns   HWND, the handle of the first window in the clipboard viewer chain. NULL if a clipboard viewer
                      is not running.

See Also   GetClipboardOwner()

Parameters   None (void).

Example   See the previous example under the GetClipboardOwner() function description.

GETOPENCLIPBOARDWINDOW   □ Win 2.0   □ Win 3.0   ■ Win 3.1

Purpose   Determines the handle of the window that most recently opened the clipboard.

Syntax   HWND **GetOpenClipboardWindow** (void);

Description   The clipboard is a shared resource. Only one application can have the clipboard open for reading and writing data at any one time. This function returns the window handle of the application that currently has the clipboard open.

Returns   HWND, the window handle of the window which currently has the clipboard open. If the clipboard is not open, the function returns NULL.

See Also   GetClipboardOwner(), GetClipboardViewer(), OpenClipboard()

Parameters   None (void).

Example   This example, as shown in Figure 17-4, displays the current clipboard owner, viewer, and the window which most recently opened the clipboard. The owner is the applica-

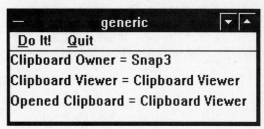

Figure 17-4. GetOpenClipboardWindow() Example.

tion that placed the current data into the clipboard. In this case, SNAP3.EXE placed data in the clipboard. The standard Windows clipboard viewer application was then activated, which becomes both the clipboard viewer and the application that most recently opened the clipboard.

```
Long FAR PASCAL WndProc (HWND hWnd, unsigned iMessage, WORD wParam, LONG lParam)
{
        PAINTSTRUCT             ps ;
        char                    cBuf [128], cWindName [64] ;
        HWND                    hClipWind ;

        switch (iMessage)                       /* process windows messages */
        {
            case WM_PAINT:
                    BeginPaint (hWnd, &ps) ;
                    hClipWind = GetClipboardOwner () ;
                    GetWindowText (hClipWind, cWindName, 63) ;
                    TextOut (ps.hdc, 0, 0, cBuf, wsprintf (cBuf,
                            "Clipboard Owner = %s", (LPSTR) cWindName)) ;
                    hClipWind = GetClipboardViewer () ;
                    GetWindowText (hClipWind, cWindName, 63) ;
                    TextOut (ps.hdc, 0, 20, cBuf, wsprintf (cBuf,
                            "Clipboard Viewer = %s", (LPSTR) cWindName)) ;
                    hClipWind = GetOpenClipboardWindow () ;
                    GetWindowText (hClipWind, cWindName, 63) ;
                    TextOut (ps.hdc, 0, 40, cBuf, wsprintf (cBuf,
                            "Opened Clipboard = %s", (LPSTR) cWindName)) ;
                    EndPaint (hWnd, &ps) ;
                    break ;
            case WM_CHANGECBCHAIN:          /* clipboard view chain changed */
                    InvalidateRect (hWnd, NULL, TRUE) ;     /* force paint */
                    break ;
            case WM_COMMAND:                    /* process menu items */
                    switch (wParam)
                    {
                    case IDM_QUIT:
                            DestroyWindow (hWnd) ;
                            break ;
                    }
                    break ;
            case WM_DESTROY:
                    PostQuitMessage (0) ;
                    break ;
            default:
                    return DefWindowProc (hWnd, iMessage, wParam, lParam) ;
        }
        return (0L) ;
}
```

GetPriorityClipboardFormat
☐ Win 2.0 ■ Win 3.0 ■ Win 3.1

Purpose Checks the clipboard for the availability of desired data formats.

Syntax int **GetPriorityClipboardFormat**(WORD FAR *lpPriorityList*, int *nCount*);

Description Applications can support more than one data format for exchanging data to and from the clipboard. There can be more than one predefined format (see SetClipboardData() for a list), and more than one custom clipboard format (see RegisterClipboardFormat()). Generally, some data formats will be better than others for exchanging data. GetPriorityClipboardFormat() allows the clipboard to be scanned using a list of formats. The first format from the *lpPriorityList* that is available on the clipboard is returned by the function. This will be the best format for the application to read in data from the clipboard using GetClipboardData().

Uses Generally used with applications that use special clipboard formats, registered with RegisterClipboardFormat().

Returns int, the highest priority clipboard format available. If the clipboard is empty, the function returns NULL. If the clipboard contains data, but not in any of the desired formats, the function returns -1.

See Also RegisterClipboardFormat(), IsClipboardFormatAvailable(), EnumClipboardFormats()

Parameters

lpPriorityList WORD FAR *: A pointer to an array of word values. Each element of the array should contain the number of a desired clipboard format. This is either one of the predefined formats such as CF_TEXT, or a special format returned by either RegisterClipboardFormat() or EnumClipboardFormats(). The list should be in priority order, with the most desirable formats first.

nCount int: The number of elements in the array pointed to by *lpPriorityList*.

Example This example demonstrates several advanced uses of the clipboard. When the application is started (WM_CREATE message is processed), a special clipboard format is registered. In addition, the clipboard is set for delayed rendering of two clipboard formats, CF_TEXT and the special format. With delayed rendering, data is not loaded into the clipboard unless an application requests it. In this case, Windows sends the WM_RENDERFORMAT message. The application then loads the data into the clipboard. When a WM_PAINT message is received, the application reads the clipboard. Both clipboard formats are read. The CF_TEXT format is read via standard clipboard protocol. Before reading the special clipboard format, the application uses

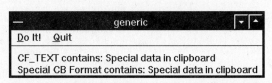

Figure 17-5. GetPriorityClipboardFormat() Example.

GetPriority ClipboardFormat() to check which formats are available. In this case, a list of only two desired formats is checked. If the special format is available, the contents of the clipboard are displayed on the application's client area, as shown in Figure 17-5.

```
long FAR PASCAL WndProc (HWND hWnd, unsigned iMessage, WORD wParam,  LONG lParam)
{
        PAINTSTRUCT             ps ;
        HANDLE                  hMem, hMem2, hClipMem ;
        LPSTR                   lpStr, lpClip ;
        char                    cBuf [128] ;
        static          WORD    wClipFormat ;
        WORD                    wPriorityList [2] ;

        switch (iMessage)                       /* process windows messages */
        {
                case WM_CREATE:
                        wClipFormat = RegisterClipboardFormat
                                (|SPECIAL■) ;
```

```
            OpenClipboard (hWnd) ;    /* set clipboard for delayed */
            EmptyClipboard () ;       /* rendering of CF_TEXT */
            SetClipboardData (CF_TEXT, 0) ;
            if (wClipFormat)
                    SetClipboardData (wClipFormat, 0) ;
            CloseClipboard () ;
            break ;
    case WM_RENDERALLFORMATS:
    case WM_RENDERFORMAT:            /* now put data in clipboard */
            OpenClipboard (hWnd) ;
            EmptyClipboard () ;
            hMem = GlobalAlloc (GHND, 64) ;
            lpStr = GlobalLock (hMem) ;
            lstrcpy (lpStr, "Text In Clipboard") ;
            GlobalUnlock (hMem) ;
            SetClipboardData (CF_TEXT, hMem) ;
            if (wClipFormat)
            {
                    hMem2 = GlobalAlloc (GHND, 64) ;
                    lpStr = GlobalLock (hMem2) ;
                    lstrcpy (lpStr, "Special data in clipboard") ;
                    GlobalUnlock (hMem2) ;
                    SetClipboardData (wClipFormat, hMem2) ;
            }
            CloseClipboard () ;
            break ;
    case WM_PAINT:
            BeginPaint (hWnd, &ps) ;
            OpenClipboard (hWnd) ;
            hClipMem = GetClipboardData (CF_TEXT) ;
            if (hClipMem)
            {
                    lpClip = GlobalLock (hClipMem) ;
                    TextOut (ps.hdc, 10, 10, cBuf, wsprintf (cBuf,
                            "CF_TEXT contains: %s", lpClip)) ;
                    GlobalUnlock (hClipMem) ;
            }
            CloseClipboard () ;

            OpenClipboard (hWnd) ;
            wPriorityList [0] = wClipFormat ;
            wPriorityList [1] = CF_TEXT ;
            if (wClipFormat =
                    GetPriorityClipboardFormat (wPriorityList, 2))
            {
                    hClipMem = GetClipboardData (wClipFormat) ;
                    lpClip = GlobalLock (hClipMem) ;
                    TextOut (ps.hdc, 10, 30, cBuf, wsprintf (cBuf,
                            "Special CB Format contains: %s", lpClip)) ;
                    GlobalUnlock (hClipMem) ;
            }
            CloseClipboard () ;
            EndPaint (hWnd, &ps) ;
            break ;
    case WM_COMMAND:
            switch (wParam)
            {
            case IDM_DOIT:
                    InvalidateRect (hWnd, NULL, TRUE) ;
                    break ;
            case IDM_QUIT:
                    DestroyWindow (hWnd) ;
                    break ;
            }
            break ;
    case WM_DESTROY:                /* stop application */
            PostQuitMessage (0) ;
            break ;
    default:                        /* default windows message processing */
```

```
                    return DefWindowProc (hWnd, iMessage, wParam, lParam) ;
          }
          return (0L) ;
}
```

IsClipboardFormatAvailable   ■ Win 2.0   ■ Win 3.0   ■ Win 3.1

Purpose	Checks whether the clipboard contains data in a specific format.
Syntax	BOOL **IsClipboardFormatAvailable**(WORD *wFormat*);
Description	The clipboard can contain data in any of the predefined data formats (see SetClipboardData() for a list), or in a special format set with RegisterClipboardFormat(). IsClipboardFormat-Available() checks to see if one specific data format is currently loaded on the clipboard.
Uses	This function is appropriate if only one data format is being read. If the application can use several formats, use GetPriorityClipboardFormat() instead.
Returns	BOOL. TRUE if data of the specified format is available in the clipboard, FALSE if not.
See Also	GetPriorityClipboardFormat(), EnumClipboardFormats()
Parameters	
wFormat	WORD: The desired clipboard format. This is either one of the predefined formats, or a special format registered by an application with RegisterClipboardFormat().

Example   This example registers a special clipboard format called "SPECIAL" when the WM_CREATE message is processed. The clipboard is set for delayed rendering of the data. This means that the actual data is not loaded into the clipboard unless ei-

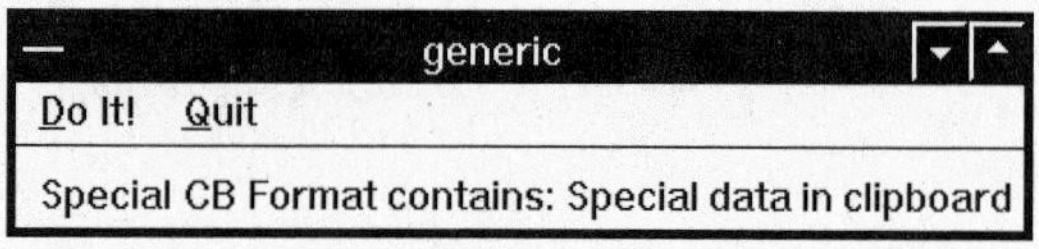

Figure 17-6. IsClipboardFormatAvailable( ) Example.

ther a WM_RENDERFORMAT or WM_RENDERALLFORMATS message is received. When a WM_PAINT message is processed, the application checks whether data in the "SPECIAL" format is available in the clipboard. If so, the data (as a character string) is displayed on the application's client area, as shown in Figure 17-6. If not, nothing is displayed.

```
long FAR PASCAL WndProc (HWND hWnd, unsigned iMessage, WORD wParam, LONG lParam)
{
          PAINTSTRUCT            ps ;
          HANDLE                 hMem, hClipMem ;
          LPSTR                  lpStr, lpClip ;
          char                   cBuf [128] ;
          static       WORD      wClipFormat ;

          switch (iMessage)                          /* process windows messages */
          {
                  case WM_CREATE:
                          wClipFormat = RegisterClipboardFormat
                                  ("SPECIAL") ;
                          OpenClipboard (hWnd) ;   /* set clipboard for delayed */
                          EmptyClipboard () ;         /* rendering */
                          SetClipboardData (wClipFormat, 0) ;
                          CloseClipboard () ;
                          break ;
                  case WM_RENDERALLFORMATS:
                  case WM_RENDERFORMAT:               /* now put data in clipboard */
                          OpenClipboard (hWnd) ;
                          EmptyClipboard () ;
                          hMem = GlobalAlloc (GHND, 64) ;
                          lpStr = GlobalLock (hMem) ;
                          lstrcpy (lpStr, "Special data in clipboard") ;
                          SetClipboardData (wClipFormat, hMem) ;
                          GlobalUnlock (hMem) ;
```

```
                            CloseClipboard () ;
                            break ;
               case WM_PAINT:
                            BeginPaint (hWnd, &ps) ;
                            OpenClipboard (hWnd) ;
                            if (IsClipboardFormatAvailable (wClipFormat))
                            {
                                     hClipMem = GetClipboardData (wClipFormat) ;
                                     hMem = GlobalAlloc (GHND, GlobalSize (hClipMem)) ;
                                     lpStr = GlobalLock (hMem) ;
                                     lpClip = GlobalLock (hClipMem) ;
                                     lstrcpy (lpStr, lpClip) ;
                                     TextOut (ps.hdc, 10, 10, cBuf, wsprintf (cBuf,
                                             "Special CB Format contains: %s", lpStr)) ;
                                     GlobalUnlock (hMem) ;
                                     GlobalFree (hMem) ;
                                     GlobalUnlock (hClipMem) ;
                            }
                            CloseClipboard () ;
                            EndPaint (hWnd, &ps) ;
                            break ;
               case WM_COMMAND:
                            switch (wParam)
                            {
                            case IDM_DOIT:
                                     InvalidateRect (hWnd, NULL, TRUE) ;
                                     break ;
                            case IDM_QUIT:
                                     DestroyWindow (hWnd) ;
                                     break ;
                            }
                            break ;
               case WM_DESTROY:                        /* stop application */
                            PostQuitMessage (0) ;
                            break ;
               default:                                /* default windows message processing */
                            return DefWindowProc (hWnd, iMessage, wParam, lParam) ;
       }
       return (0L) ;
}
```

OPENCLIPBOARD   ■ Win 2.0   ■ Win 3.0   ■ Win 3.1

Purpose	Opens the clipboard so that an application can read or set the contents.
Syntax	BOOL **OpenClipboard**(HWND *hWnd*);
Description	The clipboard is a global memory block maintained by Windows. OpenClipboard() makes the memory block available to the application. GetClipboardData() can then be used to read the data in the memory block, and SetClipboardData() can be used to give the clipboard a new memory block. The clipboard remains open to the application until CloseClipboard() is called. The application should not relinquish control to Windows while the clipboard is open. The clipboard should be opened and closed while the application processes one Windows message.
Uses	Used prior to GetClipboardData() and SetClipboardData(). OpenClipboard() works by changing the memory attributes of the block of memory that the clipboard is currently referencing.
Returns	BOOL. TRUE if the clipboard is opened, FALSE on error (for example, if another application has left the clipboard open).
See Also	CloseClipboard(), GetClipboardData(), SetClipboardData()
Parameters	
hWnd	HWND: The handle of the window that is opening the clipboard.
Example	See the examples under ChangeClipboardChain() and SetClipboardData().

REGISTERCLIPBOARDFORMAT
■ Win 2.0 ■ Win 3.0 ■ Win 3.1

Purpose	Registers a new clipboard format name with Windows.
Syntax	WORD **RegisterClipboardFormat**(LPSTR *lpFormatName*);
Description	Applications can use special clipboard format names to pass data to and from the clipboard. For example, a spreadsheet may want to cut and paste cell contents using a format called "SPREADSHEET." Using a special format name prevents other applications from attempting to read data that will not be correctly interpreted. Applications can simultaneously load more than one data format to the clipboard. By doing so, data is made available to many other applications which may differ in their abilities to read different formats. For example, the spreadsheet could put the complete cell data in the clipboard under the special "SPREADSHEET" format, and put the text contents of the cell using the standard CF_TEXT format.
Uses	Used with applications that need to transfer data using specialized formats.
Returns	WORD, the format number. NULL on error. The format number will be between 0xC000 and 0xFFFF.
See Also	EnumClipboardFormats(), GetClipboardFormatName()
Parameters	
lpFormatName	LPSTR: A pointer to a null-terminated character string containing the new format name.
Example	See the examples under IsClipboardFormatAvailable() and GetPriorityClipboardFormat().

SETCLIPBOARDDATA
■ Win 2.0 ■ Win 3.0 ■ Win 3.1

Purpose	Passes a global memory handle to the clipboard. The memory block becomes the clipboard data.
Syntax	HANDLE **SetClipboardData**(WORD *wFormat*, HANDLE *hMem*);
Description	The clipboard consists of a global memory block that has been registered in Windows as belonging to the clipboard. SetClipboardData() registers the memory block with Windows. When the block of memory has been registered, applications should not free the data or leave the block locked. The memory block should be considered to be owned by the clipboard. Applications using the clipboard should not allow control to pass to Windows while the clipboard is open. In other words, the clipboard should be opened and closed while processing one Windows message.
Uses	This is the only way to set the clipboard data. Prior to calling this function, the application should call OpenClipboard() and EmptyClipboard(). As soon as the memory block is passed to the clipboard with SetClipboardData(), CloseClipboard() should be called and the memory block unlocked (if it has been locked).
Returns	HANDLE, a handle to the data in the clipboard. This value is normally not used.
See Also	OpenClipboard(), GetClipboardData(), EmptyClipboard(), CloseClipboard()
Parameters	
wFormat	WORD: Specifies what type of data the memory block referenced by *hMem* contains. The data type can be any of the those listed in Table 17-4.

Value	Meaning	⊠
CF_BITMAP	A bitmap handle (HBITMAP).	
CF_DIB	A memory block containing a device-independent bitmap (DIB). The block will contain a BITMAPINFO data structure followed by the bitmap bits.	
CF_DIF	Software Arts' Data Interchange Format.	
CF_DISPBITMAP	A private bitmap display format.	
CF_DSPMETAFILEPICT	A private metafile display format.	

CF_DISPTEXT	A private text display format.
CF_METAFILEPICT	A metafile picture. The memory block will contain a METAFILEPICT data structure.
CF_OEMTEXT	A memory block containing only OEM text characters. Each line ends with a CR-LF pair. A NULL byte marks the end of the text. This is the format Windows uses to transfer data between non-Windows and Windows applications.
CF_OWNERDISPLAY	The clipboard owner is responsible for painting the clipboard. The clipboard owner should process WM_ASKCBFORMATNAME, WM_HSCROLLCLIPBOARD, WM_PAINTCLIPBOARD, WM_SIZECLIPBOARD, and WM_VSCROLLCLIPBOARD messages.
CF_PALETTE	A handle to a color palette.
CF_SYLK	Microsoft Symbolic Link (SYLK) format.
CF_TEXT	A memory block containing text characters. Each line ends with a CR-LF pair. A NULL byte marks the end of the text. This is the standard format for exchanging text between Windows applications.
CF_TIFF	Tag Image File Format.

Table 17-4. Clipboard Data Formats.

In addition, private clipboard formats can have values between CF_PRIVATEFIRST and CF_PRIVATELAST.

hMem   HANDLE: A handle to a global memory block that contains the data in the specified format. For delayed rendering of the clipboard, set *hMem* to NULL. This means that the data does not have to be passed to the clipboard until a WM_RENDERFORMAT message is received.

Related Messages   WM_RENDERFORMAT, WM_RENDERALLFORMATS

Example   This example shows the workings of a screen capture program called SNAP3. When the user clicks the "Start Capture" menu item, the mouse changes to a cross hair shape. If the user depresses the left mouse button and drags the mouse, a rectangle appears on the screen. Dragging the mouse increases the size of the rectangle. When the mouse button is released, the area bounded by the rectangle is copied to the clipboard and shown in the application's client area.

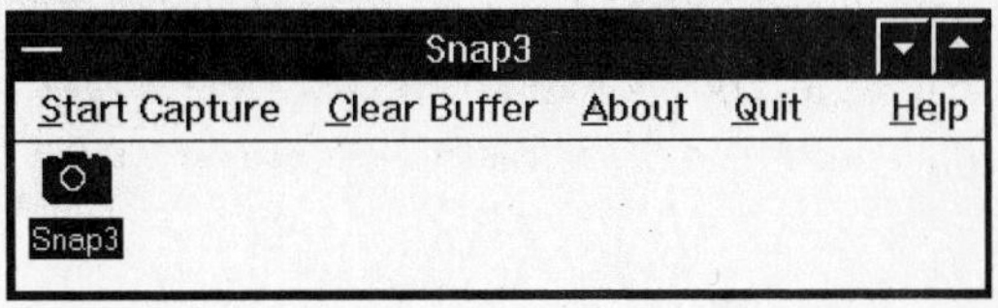

Figure 17-7. SetClipboardData( ) Example SNAP3.

In order to get the program's window out of the way, SNAP3 minimizes itself during the capture process. The window is restored when capturing is completed, so that the captured image is visible inside of SNAP3's window. Clicking the "Clear Buffer" menu item empties the clipboard.

Figure 17-7 shows SNAP3 capturing its own icon's image. This image was created by using one instance of SNAP3 to capture a bitmap of a second instance of SNAP3 (capturing an image of the icon of SNAP3!).

➪ **Resource Script File**

```
/* snap3.rc */
#include "snap3.h"
snap3   ICON     snap3.ico
snap3 MENU
BEGIN
       MENUITEM "&Start Capture"          IDM_START
       MENUITEM "&Clear Buffer",          IDM_CLEAR
       MENUITEM "&About",                 IDM_ABOUT
```

```
        MENUITEM "&Quit",                       IDM_QUIT
        MENUITEM "\a&Help",                      IDM_HELP
END
```

⇨ WndProc() and OutlineBlock() Functions

```
long FAR PASCAL WndProc (HWND hWnd, unsigned iMessage, WORD wParam, LONG lParam)
{
        static BOOL             bCapturing = FALSE, bBlocking = FALSE ;
        static POINT            beg, end, oldend ;
        static short            xSize, ySize ;
        static HANDLE           hInstance ;
        HDC                     hDC, hMemDC ;
        BITMAP                  bm ;
        HBITMAP                 hBitmap ;
        PAINTSTRUCT             ps ;

        switch (iMessage)
        {
                case WM_CREATE:                 /* get program instance */
                        hInstance = GetWindowWord (hWnd, GWW_HINSTANCE) ;
                        break ;
                case WM_COMMAND:/* one of the menu items */
                        switch (wParam)
                        {
                        case IDM_START:         /* the start capture item */
                                bCapturing = TRUE ;
                                bBlocking = FALSE ;
                                SetCapture (hWnd) ;             /* grab mouse */
                                SetCursor (LoadCursor (NULL, IDC_CROSS) ;
                                CloseWindow (hWnd) ;            /* minimize window */
                                break ;
                        case IDM_CLEAR:         /* clears screen and clipboard */
                                OpenClipboard (hWnd) ;
                                EmptyClipboard () ;
                                CloseClipboard () ;
                                InvalidateRect (hWnd, NULL, TRUE) ;
                                break ;
                        case IDM_QUIT:
                                DestroyWindow (hWnd) ;
                                break ;
                        case IDM_ABOUT:         /* show about box */
                                MessageBox (hWnd,
        "Snap3 - Windows screen capture to clipboard.\nJim Conger 1990.",
                                        "Snap3 About", MB_OK) ;
                                break ;
                        case IDM_HELP:
                                MessageBox (hWnd, "After you click the Start Capture
                                        menu item, move the mouse to the upper left of
                                        the area you want to copy to the clipboard.
                                Hold down the left mouse button while you drag the
                                        mouse to the lower right of the area.  Once you
                                        release the mouse button, the area is sent to the
                                        clipboard and shown in Snap3's window.",
                                        "Snap3 Help", MB_OK) ;
                                break ;
                        }
                        break ;
                case WM_LBUTTONDOWN:     /* starting capturing screen */
                        if (bCapturing)
                        {
                                bBlocking = TRUE ;
                                oldend = beg = MAKEPOINT (lParam) ;
                                OutlineBlock (hWnd, beg, oldend) ;
                                SetCursor (LoadCursor (NULL, IDC_CROSS)) ;
                        }
                        break ;
                case WM_MOUSEMOVE:      /* show area as rectangle on screen */
```

```
                    if (bBlocking)
                    {
                    end = MAKEPOINT (lParam) ;
                    OutlineBlock (hWnd, beg, oldend) ;       /* erase outline */
                    OutlineBlock (hWnd, beg, end) ;  /* draw new one */
                            oldend = end ;
                    }
                    break ;
          case WM_LBUTTONUP:                    /* capture and send to clipboard */
                    if (bBlocking)
                    {
                            bBlocking = bCapturing = FALSE ;
                            SetCursor (LoadCursor (NULL, IDC_ARROW)) ;
                            ReleaseCapture () ;              /* free mouse */

                            end = MAKEPOINT (lParam) ;
                            OutlineBlock (hWnd, beg, oldend) ;
                            xSize = abs (beg.x - end.x) ;
                            ySize = abs (beg.y - end.y) ;
                            hDC = GetDC (hWnd) ;
                            hMemDC = CreateCompatibleDC (hDC) ;
                            hBitmap = CreateCompatibleBitmap
                                    (hDC, xSize, ySize) ;
                            if (hBitmap)
                            {
                                    SelectObject (hMemDC, hBitmap) ;
                                    StretchBlt (hMemDC, 0, 0, xSize, ySize,
                                            hDC, beg.x, beg.y, end.x - beg.x,
                                            end.y - beg.y, SRCCOPY) ;
                                    OpenClipboard (hWnd) ;
                                    EmptyClipboard () ;
                                    SetClipboardData (CF_BITMAP, hBitmap) ;
                                    CloseClipboard () ;
                                    InvalidateRect (hWnd, NULL, TRUE) ;
                            }
                            else
                                    MessageBeep (0) ;

                            DeleteDC (hMemDC) ;
                            ReleaseDC (hWnd, hDC) ;

                    }
                    ShowWindow (hWnd, SW_RESTORE) ;  /* un-minimize window */
                    break ;
          case WM_PAINT:          /* display contents of clipboard if bitmap */
                    hDC = BeginPaint (hWnd, &ps) ;
                    OpenClipboard (hWnd) ;
                    if (hBitmap = GetClipboardData (CF_BITMAP))
                    {
                            hMemDC = CreateCompatibleDC (hDC) ;
                            SelectObject (hMemDC, hBitmap) ;
                            GetObject (hBitmap, sizeof (BITMAP), (LPSTR) &bm) ;
                            SetStretchBltMode (hDC, COLORONCOLOR) ;
                            StretchBlt (hDC, 0, 0, xSize, ySize, hMemDC, 0, 0,
                                    bm.bmWidth, bm.bmHeight, SRCCOPY) ;
                            DeleteDC (hMemDC) ;
                    }
                    CloseClipboard () ;
                    EndPaint (hWnd, &ps) ;
                    break ;
          case WM_DESTROY:
                    PostQuitMessage (0) ;
                    break ;
          default:
                    return DefWindowProc (hWnd, iMessage, wParam, lParam) ;
     }
     return (0L) ;
}
```

```
/* OutlineBlock() writes a rectangle on the screen given the two corner */
/* points.      The R2_NOT style is used, so drawing twice on the same location */
/* erases the outline. */

void OutlineBlock (HWND hWnd, POINT beg, POINT end)
{
        HDC   hDC ;

        hDC = CreateDC ("DISPLAY", NULL, NULL, NULL) ;
        ClientToScreen (hWnd, &beg) ;              /* convert to screen units */
        ClientToScreen (hWnd, &end) ;
        SetROP2 (hDC, R2_NOT) ;                    /* use logical NOT pen */
        MoveTo (hDC, beg.x, beg.y) ;               /* draw rectangle */
        LineTo (hDC, end.x, beg.y) ;
        LineTo (hDC, end.x, end.y) ;
        LineTo (hDC, beg.x, end.y) ;
        LineTo (hDC, beg.x, beg.y) ;
        DeleteDC (hDC) ;
}
```

SETCLIPBOARDVIEWER

■ Win 2.0   ■ Win 3.0   ■ Win 3.1

Purpose Adds a new window to the list of windows in the clipboard viewer chain.

Syntax HWND **SetClipboardViewer**(HWND *hWnd*);

Description Windows comes with a default clipboard viewing application called Clipboard. It is added to the Main program group when Windows is first installed. Other applications can be clipboard viewers. SetClipboardViewer() adds a window to the chain of clipboard viewer windows. Windows in the clipboard viewer chain receive WM_DRAWCLIPBOARD messages any time the clipboard data is changed. This is the signal to display the clipboard data, if the data format is known to the viewer program. Viewers must pass WM_CHANGECBCHAIN messages to the next window in the chain. Viewers must also remove themselves from the chain when they are about to terminate (WM_DESTROY message processed). ChangeClipboardChain() does this function.

Uses Adding a window to the clipboard viewer chain.

Returns HWND, the handle of the next window in the clipboard viewer chain. This value should be saved as a static variable, as it will be needed to process WM_DRAWCLIPBOARD, WM_CHANGE-CBCHAIN, and WM_DESTROY messages.

See Also ChangeClipboardChain()

Parameters
hWnd HWND: The window handle for the window to be added to the clipboard viewer chain.

Related Messages WM_DRAWCLIPBOARD, WM_CHANGECBCHAIN

Example See the example under ChangeClipboardChain() for a clipboard viewer listing that handles both text and bitmap clipboard data.

Sound Functions

Windows 3.0 provides 17 functions for sound support. However, all of the functions in this chapter are obsolete in Windows 3.1 and have been supplanted by Windows Multimedia Extensions. Unfortunately, the functions in this chapter require additional hardware to produce reasonable sounding musical notes and sound effects. Sound hardware varies from simple tone generators to compact disk quality external sound devices. Windows 2.0 and 3.0 provided only basic functionality for producing sequences of sounds, and a limited amount of control over the sound types. For more complete control, see coverage of 3.1's Multimedia Extensions in volume 2 of this series.

Sound Sources

The speaker attached to the IBM PC family of computers is a simple device. Sound patterns are generated by the computer's timing chip. The timer sends a series of pulses to the speaker. The faster the pulses, the higher the pitch. Clever programmers have found ways to get more than a beep out of this speaker. For Windows' purposes, we can consider the speaker to be little more than a beeper. You can generate monophonic (one note at a time) music by controlling the speaker under Windows, but it is dreadful to listen to.

The next level up from the PC speaker is to install an internal sound card in the PC. The most popular boards are the Adlib Board, the Sound Blaster Card, and the IBM Music Feature Card. All of these include a sound synthesis chip. The chip can be programmed to provide a wide range of sounds, roughly simulating both musical sounds and sound effects. In addition, the Sound Blaster Card provides input and output of sampled sounds (for example, recording and playing back voices recorded to disk from a microphone). These internal cards use 8-bit sound resolution, which means that the sound waves are recorded and generated by measuring the wave amplitude with 8-bit numbers. The result is acceptable sound for game applications and limited room-size presentations. Eight-bit sound is not acceptable for amplification for use in larger rooms, or in serious musical applications.

Obtaining high quality sound requires 16-bit sound resolution. (The resolution that compact disk (CD) players use to store and replay music). Sixteen-bit resolution sound provides professional quality sound for studio use, and it is completely acceptable for amplification for presentations in large rooms and auditoriums. Roland Corporation markets several internal PC boards that have 16-bit resolution. Most 16-bit sound sources are complete synthesizers that are much too large to fit inside of a PC. These external sound "boxes" are controlled by connecting them to the computer with cables. A standard communication protocol called "MIDI" (Musical Instrument Digital Interface) allows the computer to control the sound sources, and also to record keyboard playing if the sound source has a keyboard.

Microsoft offers MIDI support as part of a Windows Multimedia Developer's Kit. Hopefully, Microsoft will add MIDI support to future releases of Windows. MIDI drivers for Windows can also be purchased from Playroom Software, although their current release only supports Windows' real and standard mode operations (not enhanced mode). For the purposes of this book, we will assume that the reader is either limited to the PC speaker or has an inexpensive internal sound board attached. References for other sound sources are included in the bibliography.

Sound Drivers

The SYSTEM.INI file that Windows uses to initialize devices on startup includes a line specifying the sound driver:

```
sound.drv=sound.drv
```

SOUND.DRV is the default Windows sound driver. This file is loaded into the SYSTEM subdirectory when Windows is installed. The driver includes the low-level functions for controlling the PC speaker.

If another sound device is installed in the PC, Windows will not immediately know how to access it. The sound card manufacturer will (or at least should) supply a specialized driver file for the board. To use the new sound source, edit SYSTEM.INI to include the name of the new driver. For example, for the driver FM.DRV use

```
sound.drv=fm.drv
```

Installing the Windows driver does not immediately provide support for all of the Windows sound functions. Three of the functions are so specialized that many sound boards will not be able to use them. This limitation is because the internal architecture of the sound board's hardware may not match the assumptions that Windows' developers made when they created these three functions. The functions are SetSoundNoise(), SetVoiceEnvelope(), and Set-VoiceSound(). The remaining 14 functions should work regardless of the sound hardware, assuming that the sound driver has been written correctly. (The sound functions were originally developed for the IBM PC Junior, which had a simple sound chip.)

Voices and Voice Queues

The lowly PC speaker can play only one note at a time. Internal sound boards typically allow between eight and 16 sounds to be output at once. Windows refers to each separate sound type as a "voice." To keep track of when to play each note, Windows uses the concept of a note queue. A queue is just a list of notes stored in memory. All of the notes that are to be played for each voice are loaded into a queue in the order that they are to be played. When the play process is started, the notes are read from each queue and played. The queues shrink as the notes are played. The queues are empty (occupy no memory) when all notes have been played. Figure 18-1 illustrates a voice queue.

A minimum program fragment that will load and play a series of notes is shown in Listing 18-1. The OpenSound() function takes control of the system's sound device. Only one device has control of the sound source at a time. The application calling OpenSound() retains control of the sound device until it calls Close-Sound().

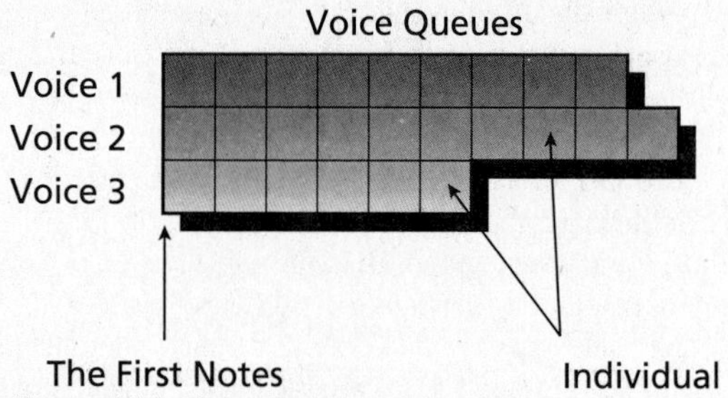

Figure 18-1. Voice Queues.

▷ **Listing 18-1. Playing One Voice**

```
if (OpenSound() > 0)
{
        SetVoiceQueueSize (1, 30) ;
        SetVoiceAccent (1, 120, 128, S_NORMAL, 0) ;
        for (i = 0 ; i < 5 ; i++)
                SetVoiceNote (1, i + 20, 8, 0) ;
        StartSound() ;
}
```

The size of the memory buffer for the note data is set with SetVoiceQueueSize(). In this case, 30 bytes are reserved. This is enough room for six notes. The tempo and volume are set with a call to SetVoiceAccent(). Five notes are added to the voice queue by repeatedly calling SetVoiceNote(). Finally, StartSound() is called to start playing the notes. Windows will play the notes in the background, while continuing to process messages and run other applications. This is convenient for the programmer, as you can "set and forget" the sound functions in most cases.

Elsewhere in the program, the program will need to be able to shut down the sounds, if they are still playing, and release the sound device to Windows for use by other applications. StopSound() stops playback of any voice queues that have been playing. CloseSound() returns control to Windows. (See Listing 18-2.)

▷ **Listing 18-2. Stopping Sound Playback**

```
StopSound () ;
CloseSound () ;
```

These examples have used only one voice and are compatible with programming the PC's speaker using the default SOUND.DRV driver. For more advanced sound sources, you will need to know the number of voices available.

OpenSound() returns this value. OpenSound() will return a negative integer if the sound source is not available, meaning that another application has control of the sound source. If you program more than one voice, be sure to call SyncAllVoices() to keep the playback of each voice synchronized with the others.

When the voices have been played, the memory buffers that held the voice data are emptied. This means that the voice data has to be reloaded each time that the data is to be played. Voice queues occupy locked global memory. These locked blocks of memory will clog up the global heap from the time the voices have been allocated with SetVoiceQueueSize() until the time the play process is over.

You may notice the system performance being degraded by these locked blocks. To minimize the impact of the locked voice queue data, do not load the voice queues until right before the sounds are to be played.

Voice Thresholds

You may want to keep track of when a voice goes beyond a certain note. For example, you might want a graphics image to appear in sync with music in a presentation. Windows allows for this by allowing each voice to have a "threshold" value. This value is the number of notes remaining when an action should occur. For example, if a program needs to display a graphics object when 100 notes remain in voice queue 2, then the threshold for queue 2 would be set to 100.

Threshold values are set for each voice that requires one with the SetVoiceThreshold() function. The status of up to 16 voices can be checked with a call to GetThresholdStatus(). Typically, a Windows program will start the play process, and then check the threshold status for a track at intervals. The system clock can be used to trigger a periodic check of the track threshold status.

Sound Function Error Codes

All of the sound functions that return integer status values use the convention that errors are returned as negative numbers. In most cases, it is not important which error occurred. If you need this information, the error codes are defined in WINDOWS.H as follows:

```
#define S_SERDVNA    (-1)  /* Device not available */
#define S_SEROFM     (-2)  /* Out of memory */
#define S_SERMACT    (-3)  /* Music active       */
#define S_SERQFUL    (-4)  /* Queue full */
#define S_SERBDNT    (-5)  /* Invalid note       */
#define S_SERDLN     (-6)  /* Invalid note length */
#define S_SERDCC     (-7)  /* Invalid note count */
#define S_SERDTP     (-8)  /* Invalid tempo        */
#define S_SERDVL     (-9)  /* Invalid volume     */
#define S_SERDMD     (-10) /* Invalid mode       */
#define S_SERDSH     (-11) /* Invalid shape      */
#define S_SERDPT     (-12) /* Invalid pitch      */
#define S_SERDFQ     (-13) /* Invalid frequency */
#define S_SERDDR     (-14) /* Invalid duration */
#define S_SERDSR     (-15) /* Invalid source     */
#define S_SERDST     (-16) /* Invalid state      */
```

Sound Function Summary

Table 18-1 summarizes the Windows sound functions. The detailed function descriptions are in the next section.

Function	Purpose	
CloseSound	Shuts down the play process.	⊠
CountVoiceNotes	Determines the number of notes in a note queue.	
GetThresholdEvent	Checks all voice queues to see if the threshold value has been surpassed.	
GetThresholdStatus	Checks all voice queues to see if the threshold value has been passed.	
MessageBeep	Beeps the sound device.	
OpenSound	Provides the application with access to the sound device.	
SetSoundNoise	Sets the noise waveform table for a sound device.	
SetVoiceAccent	Sets the tempo, volume, mode, and pitch offset for a voice.	

Table 18-1. continued

Function	Purpose	⊠
SetVoiceEnvelope	Specifies the sound waveform to use for a voice.	
SetVoiceNote	Adds a note to a voice queue.	
SetVoiceQueueSize	Sets the size of the memory buffer to hold the note values for a voice.	
SetVoiceSound	Sets the sound frequency of a voice in a voice queue.	
SetVoiceThreshold	Sets a number of notes in the voice queue that will trip the threshold status.	
StartSound	Starts all voice queues playing.	
StopSound	Stops the play process.	
SyncAllVoices	Synchronizes the timing of playback of notes from several voice queues.	
WaitSoundState	Stops Windows from regaining control until one or more voice queues surpasses a threshold state or is empty.	

Table 18-1. Sound Function Summary.

Sound Function Descriptions

This section contains the detailed description of the Windows sound functions.

CLOSESOUND   ■ Win 2.0   ■ Win 3.0   ☐ Win 3.1

Purpose	Shuts down the play process.
Syntax	void **CloseSound**(void);
Description	This function stops all voice queues currently playing, frees memory associated with the voice data, and releases the sound device for use by other applications.
Uses	Every call to OpenSound() should have a matching call to CloseSound().
Returns	No returned value (void).
See Also	OpenSound()
Parameters	None (void).
Example	This example will play five notes on the PC speaker when the user clicks the "Do It!" menu item. The program displays the number of voices available each time the menu item is clicked. (This number will be 1 for a standard PC without a sound card installed.) If "Do It!" is clicked more than once, a free voices value of –1 will be displayed because the sound source has already been opened. The sound source is not freed until the user clicks the "Quit" menu item. If another sound device and driver have been installed, the notes will be played on that device.

```
long FAR PASCAL WndProc (HWND hWnd, unsigned iMessage, WORD wParam, LONG lParam)
{
        HDC             hDC ;
        int             i, nVoice ;
        char            cBuf [128] ;

        switch (iMessage)                       /* process windows messages */
        {
                case WM_COMMAND:                /* process menu items */
                        switch (wParam)
                        {
                        case IDM_DOIT:          /* User hit the "Do it" menu item */
                                hDC = GetDC (hWnd) ;
                                if ((nVoice = OpenSound()) > 0)
                                {
                                        TextOut (hDC, 10, 10, cBuf, wsprintf (cBuf,
```

```
                                              "%d voices free.", nVoice)) ;
                              SetVoiceQueueSize (1, 30) ;
                              SetVoiceAccent (1, 120, 128, S_NORMAL, 0) ;
                              for (i = 0 ; i < 5 ; i++)
                                      SetVoiceNote (1, i + 20, 8, 0) ;
                              StartSound() ;
                      }
                      ReleaseDC (hWnd, hDC) ;
                      break ;
              case IDM_QUIT:
                      DestroyWindow (hWnd) ;
                      break ;
              }
              break ;
      case WM_DESTROY:                        /* stop application */
              StopSound () ;
              CloseSound () ;
              PostQuitMessage (0) ;
              break ;
      default:                                /* default windows message processing */
              return DefWindowProc (hWnd, iMessage, wParam, lParam) ;
      }
      return (0L) ;
}
```

CountVoiceNotes   ■ Win 2.0   ■ Win 3.0   □ Win 3.1

Purpose	Determines the number of notes in a note queue.
Syntax	int **CountVoiceNotes**(int *nVoice*);

Description   The SetVoiceNote() function is used to add notes to a voice queue. When the StartSound() function has been called, CountVoiceNotes() will return the number of notes left in the queue. The function will return zero if StartSound() has not been called, or if all of the notes have been played.

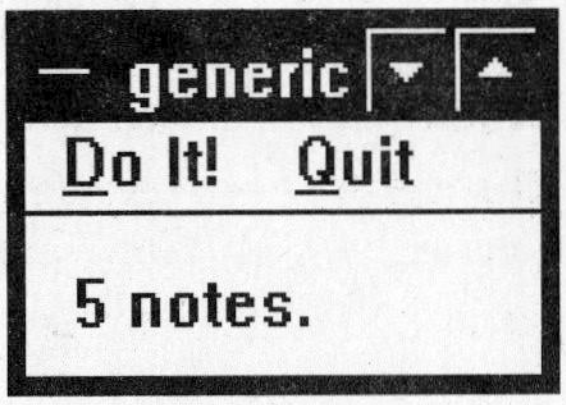

Uses   Determining the position in a song.

Returns   int, the number of notes remaining in the note queue.

See Also   SetVoiceNote()

Figure 18-2. CountVoice-Notes( ) Example.

Parameters

nVoice   int: The voice number. The first voice is numbered 1. OpenSound() returns the number of voices that are available on the sound device.

Example   This example plays five notes when the "Do It!" menu item is clicked, as shown in Figure 18-2. The note count is checked right after StartSound() is called, so all of the notes are in the queue.

```
long FAR PASCAL WndProc (HWND hWnd, unsigned iMessage, WORD wParam, LONG lParam)
{
      HDC             hDC ;
      int             i, nNotes ;
      char            cBuf [128] ;

      switch (iMessage)                       /* process windows messages */
      {
              case WM_COMMAND:                /* process menu items */
                      switch (wParam)
                      {
                      case IDM_DOIT:          /* User hit the "Do it" menu item */
                              hDC = GetDC (hWnd) ;
                              if (OpenSound() > 0)
                              {
                                      SetVoiceQueueSize (1, 30) ;
                                      SetVoiceAccent (1, 120, 128, S_NORMAL, 0) ;
                                      for (i = 0 ; i < 5 ; i++)
```

```
                                        SetVoiceNote (1, i + 20, 8, 0) ;
                                  StartSound() ;
                                  nNotes = CountVoiceNotes (1) ;
                                  TextOut (hDC, 10, 10, cBuf, wsprintf (cBuf,
                                         "%d notes.", nNotes)) ;
                            }
                            ReleaseDC (hWnd, hDC) ;
                            break ;
                  case IDM_QUIT:            /* send end of application message */
                            StopSound () ;
                            CloseSound () ;
                            DestroyWindow (hWnd) ;
                            break ;
```

[Other program lines]

GetThresholdEvent (Requires sound device and sound driver)   ■ Win 2.0   ■ Win 3.0   □ Win 3.1

Purpose   Checks all voice queues to see if the threshold value has been passed.

Syntax   LPINT **GetThresholdEvent**(void);

Description   The SetVoiceThreshold() function is used to set a note count called the "threshold" value. As the play process continues, the number of notes in each note queue decreases. When the number of notes remaining is less than the threshold value, the threshold status is true. The returned value from GetThresholdEvent() is a pointer to an integer that encodes the threshold status of every note queue as a binary number. The bit is set to 1 if the threshold value for the queue has been passed, or to 0 if not. The least significant bit is for track 1.

Uses   This function can be used to synchronize other activities to the sound/music playing. The threshold status can be checked periodically to determine if a threshold value has been passed. If so, some action, such as displaying a graphics image, can be taken.

Returns   LPINT, a far pointer to a memory buffer that contains the 16-bit value, encoding the threshold status of each track.

See Also   SetVoiceThreshold(), GetThresholdStatus()

Parameters   None (void).

Figure 18-3. GetThresholdEvent( ) Example.

Example   This example, which is illustrated in Figure 18-3, is designed for a sound device with nine or more voices. The program sets nine voice queues with five notes each, and sets a threshold value of three notes in each queue. GetThresholdEvent() is used to obtain a pointer to the memory area where Windows stores the threshold flag value. The threshold value is determined to be 0x1ff, showing that all nine queues have tripped their threshold values (0x1ff = 111111111 binary).

```
Long FAR PASCAL WndProc (HWND hWnd, unsigned iMessage, WORD wParam, LONG lParam)
{
        HDC                     hDC ;
        static          int     nVoices ;
        int                     i, nActiveVoice ;
        LPINT                   lpEvent ;
        char                    cBuf [128] ;

        switch (iMessage)                            /* process windows messages */
        {
                case WM_CREATE:
                        nVoices = OpenSound() ;
                        if (nVoices < 0)
                        {
                                MessageBox (hWnd, "Could not open sound device.",
                                        "Error", MB_ICONHAND | MB_OK) ;
                                DestroyWindow (hWnd) ;
                        }
```

```
                        break ;
        case WM_COMMAND:                    /* process menu items */
                switch (wParam)
                {
                case IDM_DOIT:              /* User hit the "Do it" menu item */
                        hDC = GetDC (hWnd) ;
                        for (nActiveVoice = 1 ; nActiveVoice <= nVoices ;
                                nActiveVoice++)
                        {
                                SetVoiceAccent (nActiveVoice, 120, 128,
                                        S_NORMAL, 0) ;
                                SetVoiceEnvelope (nActiveVoice, nActiveVoice,
                                        100) ;
                                SetVoiceQueueSize (nActiveVoice, 256) ;
                                for (i = 0 ; i < 5 ; i++)
                                        SetVoiceNote (nActiveVoice, i + 20,
                                                8, 0) ;
                                SetVoiceThreshold (nActiveVoice, 3) ;
                        }
                        SyncAllVoices () ;
                        StartSound() ;
                        lpEvent = GetThresholdEvent () ;
                        TextOut (hDC, 0, 0, cBuf, wsprintf (cBuf,
                                "The Threshold Flag = 0x%x", *lpEvent)) ;
                        ReleaseDC (hWnd, hDC) ;
                        break ;
                case IDM_QUIT:              /* send end of application message */
                        DestroyWindow (hWnd) ;
                        break ;
                }
                break ;
        case WM_DESTROY:                    /* stop application */
                StopSound () ;
                CloseSound () ;
                PostQuitMessage (0) ;
                break ;
        default:                            /* default windows message processing */
                return DefWindowProc (hWnd, iMessage, wParam, lParam) ;
        }
        return (0L) ;
}
```

GetThresholdStatus (Requires sound device and sound driver)   ■ Win 2.0   ■ Win 3.0   □ Win 3.1

Purpose	Checks the threshold status of all voice queues.
Syntax	**int GetThresholdStatus**(void);
Description	The SetVoiceThreshold() function is used to set a note count called the "threshold" value. As the play process continues, the number of notes in each note queue decreases. When the number of notes remaining is less than the threshold value, the threshold status is true. The returned value encodes the threshold status of every note queue as a binary number. The bit is set to 1 if the threshold value for the queue has been passed, or to 0 if not. The least significant bit is for track 1. This function is similar to GetThresholdEvent(), except that GetThresholdStatus() also clears the event flags.
Uses	This function can be used to synchronize other activities to the sound/music playing. The threshold status can be checked periodically to determine if a threshold value has been passed. If so, some action, such as displaying a graphics image, can be taken.
Returns	int, the bit-coded threshold status for each track. The bits will be one for the tracks which are currently below the threshold value. For example: 101 binary (5 decimal) codes tacks one and three as being below the threshold value.
See Also	SetVoiceThreshold()

Parameters	None (void).
Example	See the example under the SetVoiceThreshold() function description.

MESSAGEBEEP   ■ Win 2.0   ■ Win 3.0   ☐ Win 3.1

Purpose	Beeps the sound device.
Syntax	void **MessageBeep**(WORD *wType*);
Description	This is the easy way to have the PC speaker or installed sound board beep.
Uses	Use to alert the user. Commonly associated with error and warning messages. A good use is to summon the user after a background task, such as a long file transfer, is complete.
Returns	No returned value (void).
See Also	MessageBox()
Parameters	
wType	WORD: This value is not used. Set equal to zero.
Example	This example shows a typical use of MessageBeep(), immediately before MessageBox().

```
long FAR PASCAL WndProc (HWND hWnd, unsigned iMessage, WORD wParam, LONG lParam)
{
        switch (iMessage)                        /* process windows messages */
            {
            case WM_COMMAND:                     /* process menu items */
                    switch (wParam)
                    {
                    case IDM_DOIT:               /* User hit the "Do it" menu item */
                            MessageBeep (0) ;
                            MessageBox (hWnd, "This is a warning message",
                                    "Warning", MB_ICONASTERISK | MB_OK) ;
                            break ;
```
[Other program lines]

OPENSOUND   ■ Win 2.0   ■ Win 3.0   ☐ Win 3.1

Purpose	Provides the application with access to the sound device.
Syntax	int **OpenSound**(void);
Description	Only one application can have access to the sound device at one time. The sound device is controlled via a driver file that is specified in the Windows SYSTEM.INI file with a line like

> `sound.drv=fm.drv.`

OpenSound() returns the number of voices available on the sound device. This is the number of independent sound waveforms that can be played at once. As soon as one application has called OpenSound(), all other applications will receive a negative value from OpenSound() if they attempt to use OpenSound() to access the sound device. The sound device is returned to the system with CloseSound().

Uses	This is the first step in starting the play process.
Returns	int, the number of voices available. For the default SOUND.DRV driver that runs the PC's speaker, this will be 1. Returns a negative value if the sound driver has been opened by another application, or has been opened earlier in the same program without a call to CloseSound().
See Also	CloseSound()
Parameters	None (void).
Example	See the example under the CloseSound() function description.

SETSOUNDNOISE (Requires sound device and sound driver)   ■ Win 2.0   ■ Win 3.0   ☐ Win 3.1

Purpose   Sets the noise waveform table for a sound device.

Syntax   int **SetSoundNoise**(int *nSource*, int *nDuration*);

Description   Some sound drivers allow the sound wave table to be programmed. This function allows one of a number of "noise" wave tables to be specified. Noise waveforms find wide application in sound effects for explosions, engines, etc.

Uses   Used with specialized sound devices. This function will have no effect if the default SOUND.DRV driver is being used to drive the PC speaker.

Returns   int, zero if successful. Returns S_SERDSR if the *nSource* value is not valid.

See Also   SetVoiceEnvelope(), SetVoiceSound()

Parameters

nSource   int: One of the values in Table 18-2.

Value	Meaning	⊠
S_PERIOD512	High-pitch hiss.	
S_PERIOD1024	Hiss.	
S_PERIOD2048	Low-pitch hiss.	
S_PERIODVOICE	Source frequency from voice channel 3 (device dependent).	
S_WHITE512	High-pitch noise.	
S_WHITE1024	Noise.	
S_WHITE2048	Low-pitch noise.	
S_WHITEVOICE	Source frequency from voice channel 3 (device dependent).	

Table 18-2. SetSoundNoise( ) Values.

Example   In this example, SetSoundNoise() is used as part of a play function. The author does not have a sound device that responds to this command. This is only a demonstration.

```
long FAR PASCAL WndProc (HWND hWnd, unsigned iMessage, WORD wParam, LONG lParam)
{
        static   int          nVoices ;
        int                   i, nActiveVoice ;

        switch (iMessage)                       /* process windows messages */
        {
        case WM_CREATE:
                nVoices = OpenSound() ;
                if (nVoices <= 0)
                {
                        MessageBox (hWnd, "Could not open sound device.",
                                "Error", MB_ICONHAND | MB_OK) ;
                        DestroyWindow (hWnd) ;
                }
                break ;
        case WM_COMMAND:                        /* process menu items */
                switch (wParam)
                {
                case IDM_DOIT:                  /* User hit the "Do it" menu item */
                        SetSoundNoise (S_PERIOD1024, 100) ;
                        for (nActiveVoice = 1 ; nActiveVoice <= nVoices ;
                                nActiveVoice++)
                        {
                                SetVoiceAccent (nActiveVoice, 120, 128,
                                        S_NORMAL, 0) ;
```

```
                                    SetVoiceQueueSize (nActiveVoice, 256) ;
                                    for (i = 0 ; i < 5 ; i++)
                                            SetVoiceNote (nActiveVoice, i + 20, 8, 0) ;
                            }
                            SyncAllVoices () ;
                            StartSound() ;
                            break ;
                    case IDM_QUIT:          /* send end of application message */
                            DestroyWindow (hWnd) ;
                            break ;
                    }
                    break ;
            case WM_DESTROY:                /* stop application */
                    StopSound () ;
                    CloseSound () ;
                    PostQuitMessage (0) ;
                    break ;
            default:                        /* default windows message processing */
                    return DefWindowProc (hWnd, iMessage, wParam, lParam) ;
        }
        return (0L) ;
}
```

SETVOICEACCENT   ■ Win 2.0   ■ Win 3.0   □ Win 3.1

Purpose	Sets the tempo, volume, mode, and pitch offset for a voice.
Syntax	int **SetVoiceAccent**(int *nVoice*, int *nTempo*, int *nVolume*, int *nMode*, int *nPitch*);
Description	Accents can be placed at any point in a voice's play pattern. The number of parameters that SetVoiceAccent() will affect depends on the sound driver in use.
Uses	Used to change the volume and tempo of a song. Can also be used to transpose a portion of the song by setting *nPitch* to a nonzero value.
Returns	int, zero if the function was successful. If an error occurs, one of the values in Table 18-3 will be returned.

Value	Meaning	⊠
S_SERDMD	Invalid mode.	
S_SERDTP	Invalid tempo.	
S_SERDVL	Invalid volume.	
S_SERQFUL	Queue full.	

Table 18-3. SetVoiceAccent() Error Codes.

See Also	SetVoiceQueueSize()

Parameters

nVoice	int: The number of the voice that will receive the added note. The first voice is number 1.
nTempo	int: The tempo in beats (quarter notes) per minute. The valid range is from 32 to 255. The default value is 120.
nVolume	int: The voice volume level, 0 to 255. This parameter will not affect the default SOUND.DRV driver for the PC speaker.
nMode	int: Specifies how the notes are to be played. This parameter will not affect the default SOUND.DRV driver for the PC speaker. For other drivers and devices, the value may change the duration of the notes. *nMode* can be set to any of the values in Table 18-4.

Value	Meaning	☒
S_LEGATO	Note duration will continue into the next beat, overlapping the next note, in order to provide a "smooth" musical style.	
S_NORMAL	Note durations will stop at the end of the beat.	
S_STACCATO	Note duration will stop before the end of the beat, leaving an open period between notes, in order to provide a "choppy" musical style.	

Table 18-4. SetVoiceAccent( ) Mode Values.

nPitch	int: The pitch offset to add to the notes. This offset is used to transpose note values. Possible range is 0 to 83.
Example	See the example under the CloseSound() function description.

SETVOICEENVELOPE (Requires sound device and sound driver) ■ Win 2.0 ■ Win 3.0 ☐ Win 3.1

Purpose	Specifies the sound waveform to use for a voice.
Syntax	int **SetVoiceEnvelope**(int *nVoice*, int *nShape*, int *nRepeat*);
Description	This function changes the wave shape used by a sound device to produce a sound. The wave shape change is set to occur at the current location in the note queue. This allows voices to be altered in the course of playback.
Uses	Used with sound devices that have tables of wave shapes. This function will have no effect if the default SOUND.DRV driver is being used to control the PC speaker.
Returns	int, zero if the function was successful. If an error occurs, one of the values in Table 18-5 is returned.

Value	Meaning	☒
S_SERDRC	Invalid repeat count.	
S_SERDSH	Invalid shape.	
S_SERQFUL	Queue full.	

Table 18-5. SetVoiceEnvelope( ) Error Codes.

See Also	SetVoiceSound(), SetSoundNoise()
Parameters	
nVoice	int: The number of the voice that will receive the added note. The first voice is number 1.

```
─        generic       ▼ ▲
Do It!   Quit
Sync value = 0, Voices = 9
```

nShape	int: The index number of a sound device wave shape. This number will depend on the hardware sound device in use.

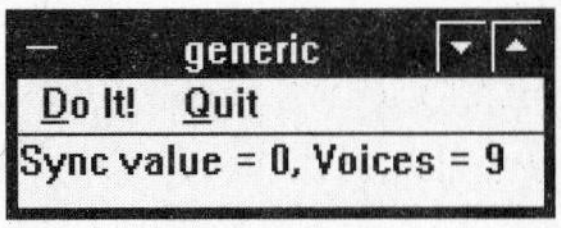

Figure 18-4. SetVoice-Envelope( ) Example.

nRepeat	int: The number of times the wave shape should be repeated during the duration of one note. This number is hardware dependent.
Example	This example plays the same five notes simultaneously on every available voice of the sound device when the user clicks the "Do It!" menu item. As shown in Figure 18-4, the used device has nine voices. The frequency of the waveform used for each voice is set to 440 Hz with SetVoiceSound(). SetVoiceEnvelope() is used to specify the first nine preset sound patterns. SyncAllVoices() is used to make sure the notes are played at the same time on each voice.

```
long FAR PASCAL WndProc (HWND hWnd, unsigned iMessage, WORD wParam, LONG lParam)
{
        HDC                     hDC ;
        static    int           nVoices ;
        int                     i, nActiveVoice, nSync ;
        char                    cBuf [128] ;

        switch (iMessage)                       /* process windows messages */
        {
                case WM_CREATE:
                        nVoices = OpenSound() ;
                        if (nVoices <= 0)
                        {
                                MessageBox (hWnd, "Could not open sound device.",
                                        "Error", MB_ICONHAND | MB_OK) ;
                                DestroyWindow (hWnd) ;
                        }
                        break ;
                case WM_COMMAND:                /* process menu items */
                        switch (wParam)
                        {
                        case IDM_DOIT:          /* User hit the "Do it" menu item */
                                hDC = GetDC (hWnd) ;
                                for (nActiveVoice = 1 ; nActiveVoice <= nVoices ;
                                        nActiveVoice++)
                                {
                                        SetVoiceSound (nActiveVoice,
                                                (LONG) (440 << 16), 100) ;
                                        SetVoiceEnvelope (nActiveVoice,
                                                nActiveVoice, 100) ;
                                        SetVoiceAccent (nActiveVoice, 120, 128,
                                                S_NORMAL, 0) ;
                                        SetVoiceQueueSize (nActiveVoice, 256) ;
                                        for (i = 0 ; i < 5 ; i++)
                                                SetVoiceNote (nActiveVoice, i + 20, 8, 0) ;
                                }
                                nSync = SyncAllVoices () ;
                                TextOut (hDC, 0, 0, cBuf, wsprintf (cBuf,
                                        "Sync value = %d, Voices = %d", nSync, nVoices)) ;
                                StartSound() ;
                                ReleaseDC (hWnd, hDC) ;
                                break ;
                        case IDM_QUIT:
                                DestroyWindow (hWnd) ;
                                break ;
                        }
                        break ;
                case WM_DESTROY:                        /* stop application */
                        StopSound () ;
                        CloseSound () ;
                        PostQuitMessage (0) ;
                        break ;
                default:                                /* default windows message processing */
                        return DefWindowProc (hWnd, iMessage, wParam, lParam) ;
        }
        return (0L) ;
}
```

SETVOICENOTE   ■ Win 2.0   ■ Win 3.0   ☐ Win 3.1

Purpose	Adds a note to a voice queue.
Syntax	int **SetVoiceNote**(int *nVoice*, int *nValue*, int *nLength*, int *nCDots*);
Description	When a voice queue's memory buffer has been allocated with SetVoiceQueueSize(), notes can be added to the queue with this function. Each note is added to the end of the queue. If the number of notes added exceeds the queue size allocated, additional calls to SetVoiceNote() are ignored. The notes will not be played until StartSound() is called.
Uses	Putting a musical pattern into the voice queue, prior to playing the pattern.

Returns   int, zero if the function added the note to the queue. If an error occurs, one of the values in Table 18-6 will be returned.

Value	Meaning	☒
S_SERDCC	Invalid dot count.	
S_SERDLN	Invalid note length.	
S_SERDNT	Invalid note number	
S_SERQFUL	The note queue is full.	

Table 18-6. SetVoiceNote( ) Error Values.

See Also   SetVoiceQueueSize(), StartSound()

Parameters

nVoice   int: The number of the voice that will receive the added note. The first voice is number 1.

nValue   int: The number of the note. Note numbers range from 1 to 84. Zero is used for a rest (time period with no note sounding). The frequency of the note specified will depend on the sound device in use.

nLength   int: The duration of the note. 1 for a whole note (4 beats), 2 for a half note (2 beats), 4 for a quarter note (1 beat), etc.

nCDots   int: The number of half-duration increments to add to the note value. This is not the same as adding musical dots. For example, if *nLength* is 2, the basic note value will be two beats. If *nCDots* is then set to 1, the duration will be three beats. If *nCDots* is set to 2, the duration is four beats.

Example   See the example under the CloseSound() and SetVoiceEnvelope() function descriptions.

SETVOICEQUEUESIZE   ■ Win 2.0   ■ Win 3.0   ☐ Win 3.1

Purpose   Sets the size of the memory buffer to hold the note values for a voice.

Syntax   int **SetVoiceQueueSize**(int *nVoice*, int *nBytes*);

Description Windows stores each voice's note data in a separate memory buffer. The SetVoiceNote() function adds notes to the buffer. Each note occupies six bytes of memory. To make room for the note data, SetVoiceQueueSize() should be called before SetVoiceNote() is used to put notes into the buffer.

Uses   Used to allocate memory for a voice's note data. The memory block is freed when CloseSound() is called.

Returns   int, returns zero if the function was successful. Returns one of the values in Table 18-7 if an error was detected.

Value	Meaning	☒
S_SERMACT	The device is currently playing.	
S_SEROFM	Out of memory.	

Table 18-7. SetVoiceQueueSize( ) Error Codes.

See Also   SetVoiceNote()

Parameters

nVoice   int: The number of the voice. The first voice is number 1.

nBytes   int: The number of bytes to allocate. Each note requires six bytes. The default buffer size is 192 bytes (32 notes).

Example   See the example under the CloseSound() and SetVoiceEnvelope() function descriptions.

SETVOICESOUND (Requires sound device and sound driver)　　■ Win 2.0　■ Win 3.0　□ Win 3.1

Purpose	Sets the sound frequency of a voice in a voice queue.
Syntax	int **SetVoiceSound**(int *nVoice*, LONG *lFrequency*, int *nDuration*);
Description	This function changes the frequency used by a sound device to produce a sound. The wave shape change is set to occur at the current location in the note queue, which allows voices to be altered in the course of playback.
Uses	Used with sound devices that have variable frequency sound generators. This function will have no effect if the default SOUND.DRV driver is being used to control the PC speaker.
Returns	int, zero if the function was successful. If an error occurs, one of the values in Table 18-8 is returned:

Value	Meaning	☒
S_SERDDR	Invalid duration.	
S_SERDFQ	Invalid frequency.	
S_SERDVL	Invalid volume.	
S_SERQFUL	Queue full.	

Table 18-8. SetVoiceSound( ) Error Codes.

See Also	SetVoiceEnvelope(), SetSoundNoise()
Parameters	
nVoice	int: The number of the voice that will receive the added note. The first voice is number 1.
lFrequency	LONG: The frequency to set. The high-order word contains the frequency in cycles per second (Hz). The low-order word contains the fractional frequency (usually zero).
nDuration	int: Sets the duration of the sound in system clock ticks. (This may not impact the sound, depending on the sound hardware in use.)
Example	See the example under the SetVoiceEnvelope() function description.

SETVOICETHRESHOLD (Requires sound device and sound driver)　　■ Win 2.0　■ Win 3.0　□ Win 3.1

Purpose	Sets the number of notes in the voice queue that will trip the threshold status.
Syntax	int **SetVoiceThreshold**(int *nVoice*, int *nNotes*);
Description	The "threshold" is a number of notes in a voice queue. As the voice queue is played, the number of remaining notes declines. When the number of remaining notes falls below the threshold value, the threshold is said to have been passed. The current threshold status on all voices can be checked at any time with GetThresholdStatus(). The WaitSoundState() function will suspend Windows message processing until the threshold number is surpassed on one or more voice queues.
Uses	Normally used in conjunction with GetThresholdStatus(). The application can start music playing, and then periodically check the threshold status (perhaps with a timer, or when any Windows message is received). When the threshold is surpassed, the application can take some action, which will then be synchronized with the music.
Returns	int, zero if the function is successful, 1 if *nNotes* is out of range.
See Also	GetThresholdStatus(), WaitSoundState()
Parameters	
nVoice	int: The number of the voice queue to set the threshold value. The first voice queue is number 1.

nNotes   int: The threshold number of notes for the voice queue. This value must be less than the number of notes in the queue. CountVoiceNotes() can be used to determine the number of notes in a queue.

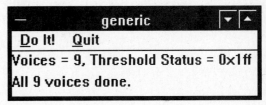

Figure 18-5. SetVoiceThreshold() Example.

Example   This example, which is illustrated in Figure 18-5, was run with a device with nine voices. The program loads all nine voices with a five note song, and sets a threshold value of three notes in each voice queue. The Threshold status value is displayed on the top line. The value of 0x1ff shows that all nine voices have a threshold value set (111111111 binary = 0x1ff). Unlike the normal case of letting the music play while Windows continues to process other messages, this example calls WaitSoundState() to wait until all nine voice queues are empty before returning control to Windows. When the WaitSoundState() returns (voice queues empty), a message is shown on the second line.

```
long FAR PASCAL WndProc (HWND hWnd, unsigned iMessage, WORD wParam, LONG lParam)
{
        HDC                             hDC ;
        static          int             nVoices ;
        int                             i, nActiveVoice, nTStatus ;
        char                            cBuf [128] ;

        switch (iMessage)                       /* process windows messages */
        {
        case WM_CREATE:
                nVoices = OpenSound() ;
                if (nVoices <= 0)
                {
                        MessageBox (hWnd, "Could not open sound device.",
                                "Error", MB_ICONHAND | MB_OK) ;
                        DestroyWindow (hWnd) ;
                }
                break ;
        case WM_COMMAND:                         /* process menu items */
                switch (wParam)
                {
                case IDM_DOIT:                   /* User hit the "Do it" menu item */
                        hDC = GetDC (hWnd) ;
                        for (nActiveVoice = 1 ; nActiveVoice <= nVoices ;
                                nActiveVoice++)
                        {
                                SetVoiceAccent (nActiveVoice, 120, 128,
                                        S_NORMAL, 0) ;
                                SetVoiceEnvelope (nActiveVoice, nActiveVoice,
                                        100) ;
                                SetVoiceQueueSize (nActiveVoice, 256) ;
                                for (i = 0 ; i < 5 ; i++)
                                        SetVoiceNote (nActiveVoice, i + 20, 8, 0) ;
                                SetVoiceThreshold (nActiveVoice, 3) ;
                        }
                        SyncAllVoices () ;
                        StartSound() ;
                        nTStatus = GetThresholdStatus () ;
                        TextOut (hDC, 0, 0, cBuf, wsprintf (cBuf,
                                "Voices = %d, Threshold Status = 0x%x",
                                        nVoices, nTStatus)) ;
                        WaitSoundState (S_QUEUEEMPTY) ;
                        TextOut (hDC, 0, 20, cBuf, wsprintf (cBuf,
                                "All %d voices done.", nVoices)) ;
                        ReleaseDC (hWnd, hDC) ;
```

```
                                    break ;
                        case IDM_QUIT:
                                DestroyWindow (hWnd) ;
                                break ;
                        }
                        break ;
                case WM_DESTROY:                    /* stop application */
                        StopSound () ;
                        CloseSound () ;
                        PostQuitMessage (0) ;
                        break ;
                default:                            /* default windows message processing */
                        return DefWindowProc (hWnd, iMessage, wParam, lParam) ;
        }
        return (0L) ;
}
```

STARTSOUND

Purpose	Starts playing all voice queues.
Syntax	int **StartSound**(void);
Description	This function is called after SetVoiceNote() is used to put notes in one or more voice queues. All voices begin to play and will continue to play until either StopSound() is called, or all queues are out of notes.
Returns	int, not used.
See Also	StopSound(), OpenSound()
Parameters	None (void).
Example	This program fragment shows the typical usage of the StartSound() function. Elsewhere in the listing would be calls to StopSound() and CloseSound(). See the CloseSound() function description for a more complete listing.

```
if (OpenSound() > 0)
{
        SetVoiceQueueSize (1, 30) ;
        SetVoiceAccent (1, 120, 128, S_NORMAL, 0) ;
        for (i = 0 ; i < 5 ; i++)
                SetVoiceNote (1, i + 20, 8, 0) ;
        StartSound() ;
}
```

STOPSOUND

Purpose	Stops the play process.
Syntax	int **StopSound**(void);
Description	Stops all notes playing on all voice queues. The contents of all voice queues are deleted and the sound driver shut down.
Uses	Used to interrupt the playing of a song. Typically, this is called by a user action, such as clicking a button or menu item.
Returns	int, not used.
See Also	StartSound()
Parameters	None (void).
Example	See the example under the CloseSound() function description.

SYNCALLVOICES (Requires sound device and sound driver)   ■ Win 2.0   ■ Win 3.0   ☐ Win 3.1

Purpose	Synchronizes the timing of the playback of notes from several voice queues.
Syntax	int **SyncAllVoices**(void);
Description	Each queue filled with note data by SetVoiceNote() is an independent set of play data. Normally, you will want to force all queues to be played in time by calling SyncAllVoices().
Uses	Used with sound devices that support more than one voice (multitimbral). This function will have no effect if the default SOUND.DRV driver is used to drive the PC speaker.
Returns	int, zero if successful. The function will return S_SERQFUL if one of the voice queue's is full.
See Also	SetVoiceNote(), SetVoiceQueueSize()
Parameters	None (void).
Example	See the example under the SetVoiceEnvelope() function description.

WAITSOUNDSTATE (Requires sound device and sound driver)   ■ Win 2.0   ■ Win 3.0   ☐ Win 3.1

Purpose	Prevents Windows from regaining control until one or more voice queues, passes a threshold state or is empty.
Syntax	int **WaitSoundState**(int *nState*);
Description	Normally, control is passed back to Windows once StartSound() is called. The sound/music continues while other Windows operations proceed normally. WaitSoundState() allows Windows activities to be halted until a specified state has passed, such as a certain number of notes remaining in a voice queue, or all queues are empty.
Uses	Not normally used.
Returns	int, zero if successful, S_SERDST if the *nState* value is invalid.
See Also	SetVoiceThreshold()
Parameters	
nState	int: One of the states listed in Table 18-9.

Value	Meaning	☒
S_ALLTHRESHOLD	Activity stops until all voices have passed their threshold values, set with SetVoiceThreshold().	
S_QUEUEEMPTY	Activity stops until all voice queues are empty (play complete).	
S_THRESHOLD	Activity stops until a voice queue passes its threshold value. In this case, WaitSoundState() should return the voice number (driver dependent).	

Table 18-9. WaitSoundState( ) Values.

Example	See the example under the SetVoiceThreshold() function description.

Character Sets and Strings

Windows uses a different character set than DOS uses. This difference is not a big problem for English-speaking users, but it can be significant for users who work with other languages that use accented characters (French, German, Spanish, etc.). Understanding how Windows deals with the two character sets is the key to writing programs that will be directly portable to other languages. The Windows function library also includes several string manipulation functions. They are convenient and reduce the size of the programs you write because the executable code is stored in Windows' dynamic link libraries.

Character Sets

Windows uses the MS-DOS operating system to do file access. MS-DOS uses a character set which is commonly called the "IBM PC character set." Windows politely refers to the IBM set as the "OEM character set." As shown in Figure 19-1, the OEM character set includes a number of graphic symbols. These symbols date to the early days of the IBM PC, when most applications operated in character mode. The graphics symbols were used to draw lines for boxes and highlight areas. These symbols are unnecessary in a graphical environment like Windows.

To read Figure 19-1, add the index on the top row to the index at the left side. For example, the code for a capital "A" character is 0x41, or 65 decimal.

The internal character set used by Windows is somewhat different. Windows refers to its internal set as the "ANSI character set." ANSI is the American National Standards Institute. ANSI is an advisory board that works to coordinate standards on everything from computer languages (ANSI C) to shipping containers. ANSI works closely with non-USA

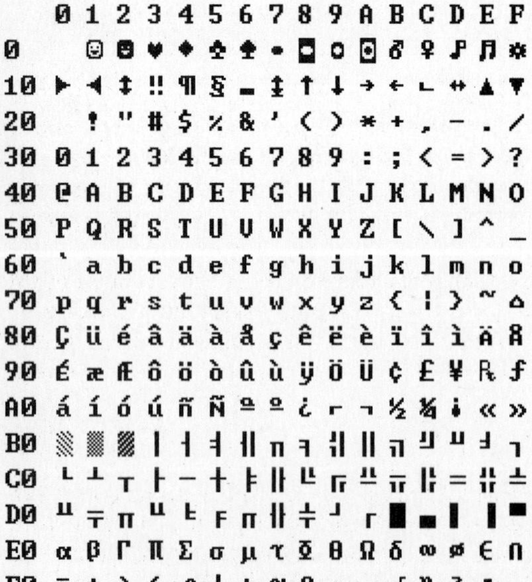

Figure 19-1. OEM Character Set.

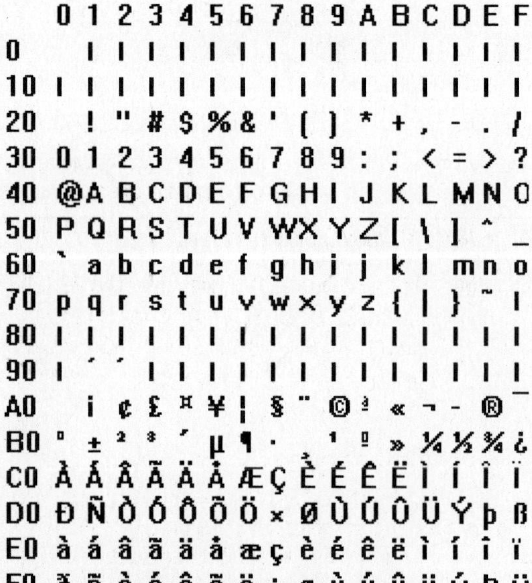

Figure 19-2. ANSI Character Set.

advisory boards, such as ISO (International Standards Organization), to come up with standards that apply internationally. The ANSI character set, which is displayed in Figure 19-2, is designed so that a text file in French transferred to a computer in Singapore will still display with the correct characters.

If you compare the OEM and ANSI character sets, you will notice that the numeric digits and the alphabetical characters without accents have the same codes. The accented characters occupy different locations, and the ANSI character set contains a number of accented characters that are not present in the OEM set. The ANSI set also has a number of undefined character locations that show up as vertical bars when displayed.

The differences between the two character sets becomes a problem when the user attempts to read a file created in DOS into Windows, or if the user runs a DOS program to access a file created by a Windows program. Even the file's name can be a problem. For example, if a French-speaking user creates a file in DOS using the common accented "É" character, the character will not be defined when viewed by a Windows program. This discrepancy occurs because the OEM code for "É" is 0x90, while the ANSI code for the same letter is 0xC9.

Character Set Conversions

To convert between the two character sets, Windows provides the OemToAnsi() and AnsiToOem() functions. These functions convert strings from one set of character codes to the other. AnsiToOem() converts a file name, input by the user of a Windows program, to the equivalent DOS file name. In cases where the OEM character set does not contain the same accented characters, the nearest equivalent OEM character is selected. The presence of accented characters causes some other problems. The standard C library functions, such as toupper() and tolower(), will not work properly under Windows because those functions assume the OEM character set. Windows provides alternatives for the most common character conversion functions. AnsiLower() and AnsiUpper() correctly convert ANSI strings from uppercase to lowercase and vice versa. Accented characters are correctly converted. Avoid the trap of built-in assumptions about the character set in use. For example, the following code fragment completely ignores accented characters.

```
          /* WRONG !!! */
if (c >= 'A' && c <= 'Z' || c >= 'a' && c <= 'z')
          /* do something */
```

The correct alternative to this incorrect example is to use the Windows functions IsCharAlpha() and IsCharAlphaNumeric(). IsCharLower() and IsCharUpper() also process accented characters correctly for the ANSI character set.

Fonts and Character Sets

Although Windows uses the ANSI character set as its default, Windows programs can use different fonts. This font change commonly occurs in word processing applications, when the user has installed a new set of fonts for a printer. Because suppliers of printer fonts must support both Windows and non-Windows programs, the OEM character set is frequently used. This means that the character codes for accented characters within a document will change depending on the font selected. The fonts will display the same character on the screen that is ultimately printed, as the supplier of the printer fonts also supplies the screen font drivers.

When writing a Windows program, use a stock Windows font for user input and file name editing. Normally, the font is set in a dialog box or edit control, so there is no need to support printer fonts for these isolated bits of text. If your application supports multiple fonts, consider making a character assignment table available via a help screen. Doing so will save the user from having to dig up a listing of all of the character assignments for the font when an accented character is used.

String Functions

The Windows function library includes a number of convenient string manipulation functions. The examples in this book frequently use several of these. lstrlen() is used to determine a string's length. lstrcpy() is used to copy a string into a buffer, and lstrcat() to add one string to the end of another. These functions have equivalents in the run-time function libraries supplied with C compilers. There are several reasons why you should use the Windows versions whenever possible.

1. The executable versions of the Windows string functions reside in DLL (dynamic link library) files. If you use these functions in your program, no additional code is added to your .EXE file. Using the compiler's library files adds extra code to the end of your program, enlarging the .EXE file.

2. The Windows versions of the string functions process both short and long addresses. Using these functions avoids problems later if you switch a character string from local memory storage to a global memory block.

3. The string comparison function lstrcmpi() (string comparison ignoring the difference between upper- and lower-case letters) correctly processes accented characters for the ANSI character set. Using the C compiler library functions will cause odd behavior in sorting applications if the data has accented characters.

Character Set and String Function Summary

Table 19-1 summarizes Windows character set and string functions. The detailed function descriptions are in the next section.

Function	Purpose	⊠
AnsiLower	Converts a character string to lowercase.	
AnsiLowerBuff	Converts a character string to lowercase.	
AnsiNext	Moves to the next character in a string.	
AnsiPrev	Moves to the previous character in a string.	
AnsiToOem	Converts a string from the ANSI character set to the OEM character set.	
AnsiToOemBuff	Converts a character string from the ANSI to the OEM character set.	
AnsiUpper	Converts a character string to uppercase.	
AnsiUpperBuff	Converts a character string to uppercase.	
IsCharAlpha	Determines whether an ANSI character is an alphabetical character.	
IsCharAlphaNumeric	Determines whether an ANSI character is an alphabetical or numeric character.	
IsCharLower	Determines whether an ANSI character is lowercase.	
IsCharUpper	Determines whether an ANSI character is an uppercase letter.	
lstrcat	Adds one character string on to the end of another string.	
lstrcmp	Compares two character strings.	
lstrcmpi	Compares two character strings, ignoring the difference between uppercase and lowercase letters.	
lstrcpy	Copies a character string to a memory buffer.	
lstrlen	Determines the length of a character string.	
OemToAnsi	Converts a character string from the OEM character set to the ANSI character set.	
OemToAnsiBuff	Converts a character string from the OEM character set to the ANSI character set.	
ToAscii	Converts from virtual key/scan code data to ANSI characters.	

Table 19-1. Character Set and String Function Summary.

Character Set and String Function Descriptions

This section contains the detailed descriptions of the character set and string functions.

ANSILOWER   ■ Win 2.0   ■ Win 3.0   ■ Win 3.1

Purpose   Converts a string to lowercase.

Syntax   LPSTR **AnsiLower**(LPSTR *lpString*);

Description	This function is the equivalent of the C library tolower() function, except that accented characters are properly converted to lowercase.
Uses	To preserve special characters, this function should be used for case conversion with the default Windows character set.
Returns	LPSTR, a pointer to the converted string. If *lpString* contains a single character, the returned value contains the converted character in the low-order byte.
See Also	AnsiUpper(), AnsiLowerBuff()
Parameters	
lpString	LPSTR: A pointer to a null-terminated character string, or to a single character.
Notes	The MAKEINTRESOURCE macro is convenient if a single character is being converted. For example,

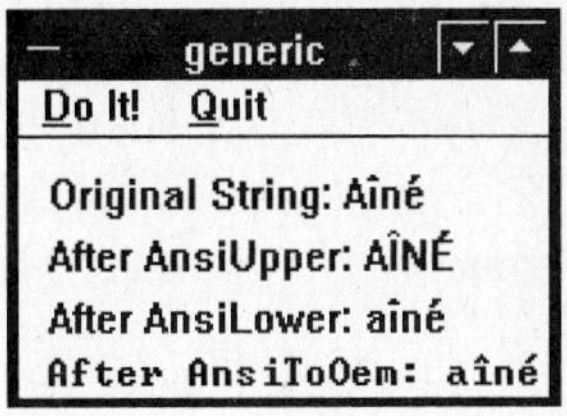

```
char    c ;
c = (char) (DWORD) AnsiLower (MAKEINTRESOURCE ('a')) ;
```

Example	This example, which is illustrated in Figure 19-3, converts the word "AINÉ" (meaning elder in French) to upper- and lowercase. The string is then converted to the OEM character set.

Figure 19-3. AnsiLower( ) Example.

```
Long FAR PASCAL WndProc (HWND hWnd, unsigned iMessage, WORD wParam, LONG lParam)
{
        PAINTSTRUCT         ps ;
        char                cBuf [128], cTemp [15] ;
        static char         cFrench [] = {0x41, 0xee, 0x6e, 0xe9, 0} ;

        switch (iMessage)                               /* process windows messages */
        {
        case WM_PAINT:
                BeginPaint (hWnd, &ps) ;
                lstrcpy (cTemp, cFrench) ;
                TextOut (ps.hdc, 10, 10, cBuf, wsprintf (cBuf,
                        "Original String: %s", (LPSTR) cTemp)) ;
                AnsiUpper (cTemp) ;
                TextOut (ps.hdc, 10, 30, cBuf, wsprintf (cBuf,
                        "After AnsiUpper: %s", (LPSTR) cTemp)) ;
                AnsiLower (cTemp) ;
                TextOut (ps.hdc, 10, 50, cBuf, wsprintf (cBuf,
                        "After AnsiLower: %s", (LPSTR) cTemp)) ;
                AnsiToOem (cTemp, cTemp) ;
                SelectObject (ps.hdc, GetStockObject
                        (OEM_FIXED_FONT)) ;
                TextOut (ps.hdc, 10, 70, cBuf, wsprintf (cBuf,
                        "After AnsiToOem: %s", (LPSTR) cTemp)) ;
                EndPaint (hWnd, &ps) ;
                break ;
```

[Other program lines]

ANSILOWERBUFF   ■ Win 2.0   ■ Win 3.0   ■ Win 3.1

Purpose	Converts a character string to lowercase.
Syntax	WORD **AnsiLowerBuff**(LPSTR *lpString*, WORD *nLength*);
Description	This function correctly converts the characters in a string to lowercase. Accented characters are properly converted to their lowercase equivalents.
Uses	Can be used to eliminate capital letters in all, or part, of a string.
Returns	WORD, the length of the converted string.
See Also	AnsiLower(), AnsiUpperBuff()

Parameters

lpString   LPSTR: A pointer to a character string to be converted to lowercase.

nLength   WORD: The number of characters to convert. If *nLength* is zero, the length is assumed to be 65,536.

Example   This example, which is shown in Figure 19-4, uses AnsiUpperBuff() and AnsiLowerBuff() to convert the case of a character string. The first call capitalizes the entire string. Note that the accented characters are correctly capitalized. Next, AnsiLowerBuff() is used to reduce characters in the center of the string to lowercase. The last line demonstrates a programming error. The non-ANSI character conversion function strlwr(), from the C library, is used to convert all the letters in the string to lowercase. Note that the accented characters are ignored because the accented characters fall in the range of the graphics symbols for the OEM (IBM PC) character set, and they are not correctly processed by strlwr(). Note how lstrlen() is used to pass the string length to AnsiUpperBuff() and AnsiLowerBuff().

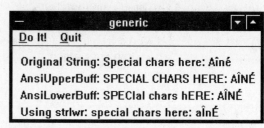

Figure 19-4. AnsiUpperBuff( ) and AnsiLowerBuff( ) Example.

```
long FAR PASCAL WndProc (HWND hWnd, unsigned iMessage, WORD wParam, LONG lParam)
{
        PAINTSTRUCT           ps ;
        char                  cBuf [128], cTemp [64] ;
        static char           cStart [30] = {"Special chars here: "} ;
        static char           cFrench [] = {0x41, 0xee, 0x6e, 0xe9} ;

        switch (iMessage)                         /* process windows messages */
        {
                case WM_PAINT:
                        BeginPaint (hWnd, &ps) ;
                        lstrcpy (cTemp, cStart) ;
                        lstrcat (cTemp, cFrench) ;
                        TextOut (ps.hdc, 10, 10, cBuf, wsprintf (cBuf,
                                "Original String: %s", (LPSTR) cTemp)) ;
                        AnsiUpperBuff (cTemp, lstrlen (cTemp)) ;
                        TextOut (ps.hdc, 10, 30, cBuf, wsprintf (cBuf,
                                "AnsiUpperBuff: %s", (LPSTR) cTemp)) ;
                        AnsiLowerBuff (cTemp + 5, 10) ;
                        TextOut (ps.hdc, 10, 50, cBuf, wsprintf (cBuf,
                                "AnsiLowerBuff: %s", (LPSTR) cTemp)) ;
                        strlwr (cTemp) ; /* wrong !!! */
                        TextOut (ps.hdc, 10, 70, cBuf, wsprintf (cBuf,
                                "Using strlwr: %s", (LPSTR) cTemp)) ;
                        EndPaint (hWnd, &ps) ;
                        break ;
```

[Other program lines]

AnsiNext   ■ Win 2.0   ■ Win 3.0   ■ Win 3.1

Purpose   Moves to the next character in a string.

Syntax   LPSTR AnsiNext(LPSTR *lpCurrentChar*);

Description This function is required only if the application will use character sets that require more than one byte per character (for example, the Japanese character set). AnsiNext() will move to the next character position, regardless of the number of bytes required.

Returns   LPSTR, a pointer to the next character in the string. Returns NULL if the end of the string has
                       been reached.

See Also   AnsiPrev()

Parameters

lpCurrentChar   LPSTR: A pointer to the current
                       character in a character string.

Example   This example, which is shown in
                       Figure 19-5, uses AnsiNext() and
                       AnsiPrev() to move to different lo-
                       cations in a character string. These
                       functions are not required for the
                       character set in Figure 19-5 (the
                       ANSI character set), as only one
                       byte is required per character.

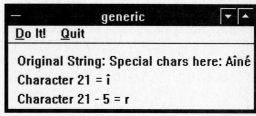

Figure 19-5. *AnsiNext() and AnsiPrev() Example.*

```
Long FAR PASCAL WndProc (HWND hWnd, unsigned iMessage, WORD wParam, LONG lParam)
{
        PAINTSTRUCT             ps ;
        char                    cBuf [128], cTemp [64] ;
        static char             cStart [30] = {"Special chars here: "} ;
        static char             cFrench [] = {0x41, 0xee, 0x6e, 0xe9} ;
        LPSTR                   lpStr ;
        int                     i ;
        char                    c ;

        switch (iMessage)                               /* process windows messages */
        {
        case WM_PAINT:
                BeginPaint (hWnd, &ps) ;
                lstrcpy (cTemp, cStart) ;
                lstrcat (cTemp, cFrench) ;
                lpStr = (LPSTR) cTemp ;
                TextOut (ps.hdc, 10, 10, cBuf, wsprintf (cBuf,
                        "Original String: %s", lpStr)) ;
                for (i = 0 ; i < 21 ; i++)
                        lpStr = AnsiNext (lpStr) ;
                TextOut (ps.hdc, 10, 30, cBuf, wsprintf (cBuf,
                        "Character 21 = %c", *lpStr)) ;
                for (i = 0 ; i < 5 ; i++)
                        lpStr = AnsiPrev (cTemp, lpStr) ;
                TextOut (ps.hdc, 10, 50, cBuf, wsprintf (cBuf,
                        "Character 21 - 5 = %c", *lpStr)) ;
                EndPaint (hWnd, &ps) ;
                break ;
```
[Other program lines]

AnsiPrev   ■ Win 2.0   ■ Win 3.0   ■ Win 3.1

Purpose   Moves to the previous character in a string.

Syntax   LPSTR **AnsiPrev**(LPSTR *lpStart*, LPSTR *lpCurrentChar*);

Description   This function is only required if the application will use character sets that require more than
                       one byte per character (for example, the Japanese character set). AnsiNext() will move to the
                       previous character position, regardless of the number of bytes required.

Returns   LPSTR, a pointer to the previous character in the string. Returns *lpStart* if *lpCurrentChar* points
                       to the start of the string.

See Also   AnsiNext()

Parameters

lpStart   LPSTR: A pointer to the beginning of the character string.

lpCurrentChar   LPSTR: A pointer to the current character in a character string.

Example   See the previous example under AnsiNext().

ANSITOOEM   ■ Win 2.0   ■ Win 3.0   ■ Win 3.1

Purpose	Converts a string from the ANSI character set to the OEM character set.
Syntax	int **AnsiToOem**(LPSTR *lpAnsiStr*, LPSTR *lpOemStr*);
Description	This function does a direct conversion of the characters. If an equivalent character exists in the OEM character set, that character is selected. The string can be longer than 64K.
Returns	int, always −1.
See Also	OemToAnsi()

Parameters

lpAnsiStr   LPSTR: A pointer to a null-terminated ANSI character string to be converted.

lpOemStr   LPSTR: A pointer to a character buffer that will contain the translated characters. The buffer must be at least as long as the string in the buffer pointed to by *lpAnsiStr*. *lpOemStr* can be the same as *lpAnsiStr*. In this case, the string is converted in place.

Example   See the example under the AnsiLower() function description.

ANSITOOEMBUFF   ■ Win 2.0   ■ Win 3.0   ■ Win 3.1

Purpose	Converts a character string from the ANSI to the OEM character set.
Syntax	void **AnsiToOemBuff**(LPSTR *lpAnsiStr*, LPSTR *lpOemStr*, int *nLength*);
Description	This function converts characters from the default Windows ANSI character set to the OEM (IBM PC) characters. Accented characters are converted to the nearest alternative.
Uses	AnsiToOemBuff() is useful for converting strings that are not null-terminated. AnsiToOem() is simpler to use for null-terminated strings.
Returns	No returned value (void).
See Also	AnsiToOem()

Parameters

lpAnsiStr   LPSTR: A pointer to an ANSI character string to be converted. The string does not have to be null-terminated.

lpOemStr   LPSTR: A pointer to a character buffer that will contain the translated characters. The buffer must be at least as long as the string in the buffer pointed to by *lpAnsiStr*. *lpOemStr* can be the same as *lpAnsiStr*. In this case, the string is converted in place.

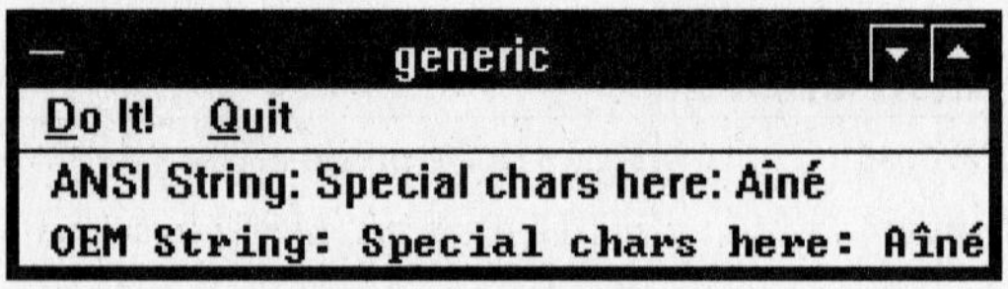

Figure 19-6. AnsiToOemBuff( ) Example.

nLength   WORD: The number of characters to be converted.

Example   This example, which is illustrated in Figure 19-6, converts an ANSI character string to OEM characters, so that the characters are properly displayed when the OEM_FIXED_FONT is selected.

```
Long FAR PASCAL WndProc (HWND hWnd, unsigned iMessage, WORD wParam, LONG lParam)
{
        PAINTSTRUCT             ps ;
        char                    cBuf [128], cANSI [64], cOEM [64] ;
        static char             cStart [30] = {"Special chars here: "} ;
        static char             cFrench [] = {0x41, 0xee, 0x6e, 0xe9} ;

        switch (iMessage)                         /* process windows messages */
        {
                case WM_PAINT:
                        BeginPaint (hWnd, &ps) ;
                        lstrcpy (cANSI, cStart) ;
                        lstrcat (cANSI, cFrench) ;
                        TextOut (ps.hdc, 10, 0, cBuf, wsprintf (cBuf,
                                "ANSI String: %s", (LPSTR) cANSI)) ;
                        AnsiToOemBuff (cANSI, cOEM, 1 + lstrlen (cANSI)) ;
                        SelectObject (ps.hdc, GetStockObject (OEM_FIXED_FONT)) ;
                        TextOut (ps.hdc, 10, 20, cBuf, wsprintf (cBuf,
                                "OEM String: %s", (LPSTR) cOEM)) ;
                        EndPaint (hWnd, &ps) ;
                        break ;
```
[Other program lines]

ANSIUPPER   ■ Win 2.0   ■ Win 3.0   ■ Win 3.1

Purpose	Converts a character string to uppercase.
Syntax	LPSTR **AnsiUpper**(LPSTR *lpString*);
Description	This function is the equivalent of the C library toupper() function, except that accented characters are properly converted to uppercase.
Uses	To preserve special characters, this function should be used for case conversion with the default Windows character set.
Returns	LPSTR, a pointer to the converted string. If *lpString* contains a single character, the returned value contains the converted character in the low-order byte.
See Also	AnsiLower(), AnsiUpperBuff()
Parameters	
lpString	LPSTR: A pointer to a null-terminated character string, or a single character.
Notes	The MAKEINTRESROUCE macro is convenient if a single character is being converted. For example,

```
char    c ;
c = (char) (DWORD) AnsiUpper (MAKEINTRESOURCE ('a')) ;
```

Example	See the example under AnsiLower().

ANSIUPPERBUFF   ■ Win 2.0   ■ Win 3.0   ■ Win 3.1

Purpose	Converts a character string to uppercase.
Syntax	WORD **AnsiUpperBuff**(LPSTR *lpString*, WORD *nLength*);
Description	This function correctly converts the characters in a string to uppercase. Accented characters are properly converted to their uppercase equivalents.
Uses	Can be used to eliminate the lowercase letters in all, or part, of a string.
Returns	WORD, the length of the converted string.
See Also	AnsiUpper(), AnsiLowerBuff()

Parameters

lpString   LPSTR: A pointer to a character string to be converted to uppercase.

nLength   WORD: The number of characters to convert.

Example   See the example under AnsiLowerBuff().

IsCharAlpha   □ Win 2.0   ■ Win 3.0   ■ Win 3.1

Purpose   Determines whether an ANSI character is an alphabetical character.

Syntax   BOOL **IsCharAlpha**(char *cChar*);

Description   This function determines whether *cChar* is alphabetical. Accented characters are correctly processed.

Returns   BOOL. TRUE if the character is alphabetical, FALSE if not.

See Also   IsCharAlphaNumeric()

Parameters

cChar   char: The character to test.

Example   This example examines each character of an ANSI character string, as shown in Figure 19-7. Note that the IsChar... functions correctly process accented characters in both upper- and lowercase.

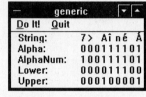

Figure 19-7. IsCharAlpha() Example.

```
long FAR PASCAL WndProc (HWND hWnd, unsigned iMessage, WORD wParam, LONG lParam)
{
        PAINTSTRUCT            ps ;
        char                  cBuf [128] ;
        static char           cFrench [] = {0x37, 0x3e, 0x20, 0x41, 0xee,
                                            0x6e, 0xe9, 0x20, 0xc1, 0} ;
        int                   i ;

        switch (iMessage)                        /* process windows messages */
        {
        case WM_PAINT:
                BeginPaint (hWnd, &ps) ;
                TextOut (ps.hdc, 10, 0, "String:", 7) ;
                TextOut (ps.hdc, 10, 15, "Alpha:", 6) ;
                TextOut (ps.hdc, 10, 30, "AlphaNum:", 9) ;
                TextOut (ps.hdc, 10, 45, "Lower:", 6) ;
                TextOut (ps.hdc, 10, 60, "Upper:", 6) ;
                for (i = 0 ; i < lstrlen (cFrench) ; i++)
                {
                        TextOut (ps.hdc, 100 + (i * 10), 0, cBuf,
                        wsprintf (cBuf, "%c", cFrench [i])) ;
                        TextOut (ps.hdc, 100 + (i * 10), 15, cBuf,
                                wsprintf (cBuf, "%1i",
                                        (IsCharAlpha (cFrench [i])
                                                ? 1 : 0))) ;
                        TextOut (ps.hdc, 100 + (i * 10), 30, cBuf,
                                wsprintf (cBuf, "%1i",
                                        (IsCharAlphaNumeric (cFrench [i])
                                                ? 1 : 0))) ;
                        TextOut (ps.hdc, 100 + (i * 10), 45, cBuf,
                                wsprintf (cBuf, "%1i",
                                        (IsCharLower (cFrench [i])
                                                ? 1 : 0))) ;
                        TextOut (ps.hdc, 100 + (i * 10), 60, cBuf,
                                wsprintf (cBuf, "%1i",
                                        (IsCharUpper (cFrench [i])
                                                ? 1 : 0))) ;
                }
```

```
          EndPaint (hWnd, &ps) ;
          break ;
```
[Other program lines]

IsCharAlphaNumeric   □ Win 2.0   ■ Win 3.0   ■ Win 3.1

Purpose	Determines whether an ANSI character is an alphabetical or numeric character.
Syntax	BOOL **IsCharAlphaNumeric**(char *cChar*);
Description	This function determines whether *cChar* is an alphabetical character or a numerical digit. Accented characters are correctly processed.
Returns	BOOL. TRUE if the character is alphanumeric, FALSE if not.
See Also	IsCharAlpha()
Parameters	
cChar	char: The character to test.
Example	See the example under the IsCharAlpha() function description.

IsCharLower   □ Win 2.0   ■ Win 3.0   ■ Win 3.1

Purpose	Determines whether an ANSI character is lowercase.
Syntax	BOOL **IsCharLower**(char *cChar*);
Description	This function determines whether *cChar* is a lowercase alphabetical character. Accented characters are correctly processed.
Returns	BOOL. TRUE if the character is an uppercase alphabetical character, FALSE if not.
See Also	IsCharUpper()
Parameters	
cChar	char: The character to test.
Example	See the example under the IsCharAlpha() function description.

IsCharUpper   □ Win 2.0   ■ Win 3.0   ■ Win 3.1

Purpose	Determines whether an ANSI character is an uppercase letter.
Syntax	BOOL **IsCharUpper**(char *cChar*);
Description	This function determines whether *cChar* is an uppercase alphabetical character. Accented characters are correctly processed.
Returns	BOOL. TRUE if the character is an uppercase alphabetical character, FALSE if not.
See Also	IsCharLower()
Parameters	
cChar	char: The character to test.
Example	See the example under the IsCharAlpha() function description.

lstrcat   ■ Win 2.0   ■ Win 3.0   ■ Win 3.1

Purpose	Adds one character string to the end of another string.
Syntax	LPSTR **lstrcat**(LPSTR *lpString1*, LPSTR *lpString2*);
Description	The function name is short for "long string concatenation." lstrcat() searches the string pointed to by *lpString1* for the first null character. The string pointed to by *lpString2* is copied into *lpString1* starting at that point. All strings must be less than 64K in length. This function is

equivalent to the standard C library function strcat(), except that it uses far pointers. Near pointers will automatically be converted to far pointers by the compiler.

Uses Frequently used to build composite character strings, such as warning messages that contain a file name, or to add a file name to file path.

Returns LPSTR, a pointer to *lpString1*. This will be the start of the combined string. Returns zero on error.

See Also lstrcpy(), lstrcmp(), lstrcmpi()

Parameters

lpString1 LPSTR: A pointer to the destination character array. The string pointed to by *lpString2* will be copied to the end of *lpString1*, starting at the first null character. The character array or memory buffer pointed to by *lpString1* must be large enough to hold the combined strings. The string in *lpString1* must be null-terminated.

lpString2 LPSTR: A pointer to the character string to be copied to the end of *lpString1*. The string must be null-terminated.

Example This example shows a typical use of the string copying and concatenation functions. Text is copied into a global memory block, allocated with GlobalAlloc(). First, the *cBegin* string is placed in the memory block. Then the *cFrench* string (consisting of some accented characters) is added with lstrcat(). When the text is needed for the WM_PAINT message processing, the block is locked. The address of the memory block is then a far pointer to a string. The memory block is released after use.

```
long FAR PASCAL WndProc (HWND hWnd, unsigned iMessage, WORD wParam, LONG lParam)
{
        PAINTSTRUCT            ps ;
        char                   cBuf [128] ;
        static char            cBegin [] = {"Starting Text. "} ;
        static char            cFrench [] = {0x41, 0xee, 0x6e, 0xe9, 0} ;
        static HANDLE          hMem ;
        LPSTR                  lpMem ;

        switch (iMessage)                          /* process windows messages */
        {
                case WM_CREATE:
                        hMem = GlobalAlloc (GHND, 64) ;
                        lpMem = GlobalLock (hMem) ;
                        lstrcpy (lpMem, cBegin) ;
                        lstrcat (lpMem, cFrench) ;
                        GlobalUnlock (hMem) ;
                        break ;
                case WM_PAINT:
                        BeginPaint (hWnd, &ps) ;
                        lpMem = GlobalLock (hMem) ;
                        TextOut (ps.hdc, 0, 0, lpMem, lstrlen (lpMem)) ;
                        GlobalUnlock (hMem) ;
                        EndPaint (hWnd, &ps) ;
                        break ;
                case WM_COMMAND:                /* process menu items */
                        switch (wParam)
                        {
                        case IDM_QUIT:          /* send end of application message */
                                DestroyWindow (hWnd) ;
                                break ;
                        }
                        break ;
                case WM_DESTROY:                /* stop application */
                        GlobalFree (hMem) ;
                        PostQuitMessage (0) ;
                        break ;
```

```
                    default:                            /* default windows message processing */
                            return DefWindowProc (hWnd, iMessage, wParam, lParam) ;
          }
          return (0L) ;
}
```

LSTRCMP   □ Win 2.0   ■ Win 3.0   ■ Win 3.1

Purpose	Compares two character strings.
Syntax	int **lstrcmp**(LPSTR *lpString1*, LPSTR *lpString2*);
Description	This function determines which of the two strings would come first in the dictionary. The determination is based on the language installed in Windows. The comparison is case sensitive, with capital letters coming before lowercase letters.
	The strings must be smaller than 64K bytes long. The result of the comparison may not be the same as would be returned by the C library function strcmp(), as accented characters are correctly processed only by lstrcmp().
Uses	Used in determining the sort order of strings in database applications. Often used to simply check if two strings are identical.
Returns	int, 0 if the strings are identical. Negative if *lpString1* would come before *lpString2* in the dictionary. Positive if *lpString1* would come after *lpString2*.
See Also	lstrcmpi()
Parameters	
lpString1	LPSTR: A pointer to the first null-terminated character string.
lpString2	LPSTR: A pointer to the second null-terminated character string.
Example	The example shown in Figure 19-8 compares two strings. Both of the strings contain the same letters; although, the second string has a capitalized word. lstrcmp() detects this, and returns 1,

as the lowercase letters in the first string would come after the uppercase letters in the second. lstrcmpi() finds the two strings equal, and returns 0. lstrlen() determines the length of a string. The returned length of 11 characters does not include the terminating NULL character.

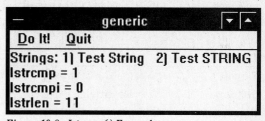

Figure 19-8. lstrcmp() Example.

```
long FAR PASCAL WndProc (HWND hWnd, unsigned iMessage, WORD wParam, LONG lParam)
{
        PAINTSTRUCT             ps ;
        char                    cBuf [128] ;
        static char             cString1 [] = {"Test String"} ;
        static char             cString2 [] = {"Test STRING"} ;
        int                     n ;

        switch (iMessage)                       /* process windows messages */
        {
                case WM_PAINT:
                        BeginPaint (hWnd, &ps) ;
                        TextOut (ps.hdc, 0, 0, cBuf, wsprintf (cBuf,
                                "Strings: 1) %s    2) %s",
                                (LPSTR) cString1, (LPSTR) cString2)) ;
                        n = lstrcmp (cString1, cString2) ;
                        TextOut (ps.hdc, 0, 15, cBuf, wsprintf (cBuf,
                                "lstrcmp = %d", n)) ;
```

```
n = lstrcmpi (cString1, cString2) ;
TextOut (ps.hdc, 0, 30, cBuf, wsprintf (cBuf,
        "lstrcmpi = %d", n)) ;
n = lstrlen (cString1) ;
TextOut (ps.hdc, 0, 45, cBuf, wsprintf (cBuf,
        "lstrlen = %d", n)) ;
EndPaint (hWnd, &ps) ;
break ;
```

[Other program lines]

LSTRCMPI
☐ Win 2.0 ■ Win 3.0 ■ Win 3.1

Purpose	Compares two character strings, ignoring the difference between uppercase and lowercase letters.
Syntax	int **lstrcmpi**(LPSTR *lpString1*, LPSTR *lpString2*);
Description	This function determines which of the two strings would come first in the dictionary. The determination is based on the language installed in Windows. The comparison is not case sensitive. Capital letters are treated the same as lowercase letters. The strings must be smaller than 64K in length. The result of the comparison may not be the same as would be returned by the C library function strcmpi(), as accented characters are correctly processed only by lstrcmp().
Uses	Used in determining the sort order of strings in database applications. Often used to simply check whether two strings of identical upper- and lowercase letters are equivalent (file names).
Returns	int, 0 if the strings are identical. Negative, if *lpString1* would come before *lpString2* in the dictionary. Positive, if *lpString1* would come after *lpString2*.
See Also	lstrcmp(), lstrcat(), lstrcpy(), lstrlen()
Parameters	
lpString1	LPSTR: A pointer to the first null-terminated character string.
lpString2	LPSTR: A pointer to the second null-terminated character string.
Example	See the previous example under the lstrcmp() function description.

LSTRCPY
■ Win 2.0 ■ Win 3.0 ■ Win 3.1

Purpose	Copies a character string to a memory buffer.
Syntax	LPSTR **lstrcpy**(LPSTR *lpString1*, LPSTR *lpString2*);
Description	The function name is short for "long string copy." lstrcpy() copies all of the characters including the terminating NULL character in the buffer pointed to by *lpString2,* into the buffer pointed to by *lpString1*. All strings must be less than 64K in length. This function is equivalent to the standard C library function strcpy(), except that it uses far pointers. Near pointers are automatically converted to far pointers by the compiler.
Uses	Used to put character strings in local and global memory buffers. Frequently used with lstrcat().
Returns	LPSTR, a pointer to *lpString1*. Returns zero on error.
See Also	lstrcat()
Parameters	
lpString1	LPSTR: A pointer to the destination character array. The string pointed to by *lpString2* will be copied to the beginning of *lpString1*. The character array or memory buffer pointed to by *lpString1* must be large enough to hold *lpString2*.
lpString2	LPSTR: A pointer to the character string to be copied to *lpString1*.
Example	See the example under the lstrcat() function description.

LSTRLEN   ■ Win 2.0   ■ Win 3.0   ■ Win 3.1

Purpose	Determines the length of a character string.
Syntax	int **lstrlen** (LPSTR *lpString*);
Description	The length returned does not include the terminating NULL character. Be sure to allocate an extra byte for the NULL character is lstrlen() if being used to size a memory space to hold a null-terminated character string. The string must be smaller than 64K in length.
Uses	Frequently used within other functions to pass the character string length as a parameter. For example, inside TextOut()

```
char cBuf [] = {"Some Text."} ;
TextOut (hDC, 10, 10, cBuf, lstrlen (cBuf)) ;
```

In this case, lstrlen() is used to pass the number of characters in the *cBuf[]* buffer to TextOut().

Returns	int, the number of characters in the buffer pointed to by *lpString*.
Parameters	
lpString	LPSTR: A pointer to a null-terminated character string.
Example	See the examples under the AnsiLowerBuff() and lstrcmp() function descriptions.

OEMTOANSI   ■ Win 2.0   ■ Win 3.0   ■ Win 3.1

Purpose	Converts a string from the OEM character set to the ANSI character set.
Syntax	int **OemToAnsi**(LPSTR *lpOemStr*, LPSTR *lpAnsiStr*);
Description	This function does a direct conversion of the characters from the OEM (IBM PC) character set to the default Windows character set (ANSI). If an equivalent character exists in the ANSI character set, that character is selected. If no equivalent exists (graphics characters), the nearest match is chosen. The string can be longer than 64K.
Uses	This function is needed if strings captured in the DOS environment are to be displayed in Windows using the default ANSI character set.
Returns	int, always –1.
See Also	OemToAnsiBuff(), AnsiToOem()
Parameters	
lpOemStr	LPSTR: A pointer to a null-terminated character string containing OEM characters.
lpAnsiStr	LPSTR: A pointer to a character buffer that will contain the converted characters. *lpAnsiStr* can be the same as *lpOemStr*, which causes the string to be converted in place.
Example	This example, as shown in Figure 19-9, demonstrates two different stock fonts. The upper string is written with the OEM font. The characters must be converted to the ANSI character set before the bottom line can be written using the ANSI fixed-pitch stock font.

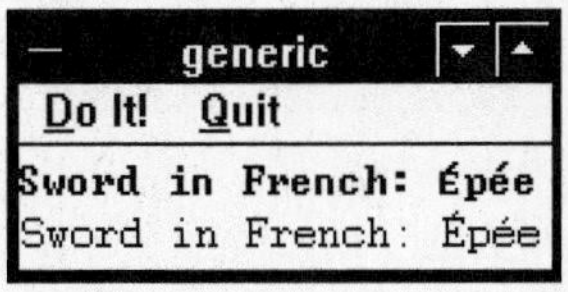

Figure 19-9. OemToAnsi() Example.

```
Long FAR PASCAL WndProc (HWND hWnd, unsigned iMessage, WORD wParam, LONG lParam)
{
        PAINTSTRUCT             ps ;
        char                    cBuf [128] ;
        static char             cString1 [] = {"Sword in French: "} ;
        static char             cString2 [] = {0x90, 0x70, 0x82, 0x65, 0} ;

        switch (iMessage)                               /* process windows messages */
        {
```

```
        case WM_PAINT:
                BeginPaint (hWnd, &ps) ;
                lstrcpy (cBuf, cString1) ;
                lstrcat (cBuf, cString2) ;
                SelectObject (ps.hdc, GetStockObject (OEM_FIXED_FONT)) ;
                TextOut (ps.hdc, 0, 5, cBuf, lstrlen (cBuf)) ;
                OemToAnsi (cBuf, cBuf) ; /* in-place conversion */
                SelectObject (ps.hdc, GetStockObject (ANSI_FIXED_FONT)) ;
                TextOut (ps.hdc, 0, 20, cBuf, lstrlen (cBuf)) ;
                EndPaint (hWnd, &ps) ;
                break ;
```

[Other program lines]

OEMTOANSIBUFF   ■ Win 2.0   ■ Win 3.0   ■ Win 3.1

Purpose	Converts a character string from the OEM character set to the ANSI character set.
Syntax	void **OemToAnsiBuff**(LPSTR *lpOemStr*, LPSTR *lpAnsiStr*, int *nLength*);
Description	This function is identical to OemToAnsi(), except that the number of characters to convert can be specified. OemToAnsiBuff() does a direct conversion of the characters from the OEM (IBM PC) character set to the default Windows character set (ANSI). If an equivalent character exists in the ANSI character set, that character is selected. If no equivalent exists (graphics characters), the nearest match is chosen.
Uses	Used in place of OemToAnsi() when the string to be converted is not null-terminated.
Returns	No returned value (void).
See Also	OemToAnsi(), AnsiToOem()
Parameters	
lpOemStr	LPSTR: A pointer to a character string containing OEM characters.
lpAnsiStr	LPSTR: A pointer to a character buffer that will contain the converted characters. *lpAnsiStr* can be the same as *lpOemStr*, which uses the string to be converted in place.
nLength	int: The number of characters in *lpOemStr* to convert.
Example	This example produces the same results as the previous example under OemToAnsi(). In this case, the conversion to the ANSI character set is accomplished with OemToAnsiBuff().

```
long FAR PASCAL WndProc (HWND hWnd, unsigned iMessage, WORD wParam, LONG lParam)
{
        PAINTSTRUCT             ps ;
        char                    cBuf [128], cBuf2 [128] ;
        static char             cString1 [] = {"Sword in French: "} ;
        static char             cString2 [] = {0x90, 0x70, 0x82, 0x65, 0} ;

        switch (iMessage)                               /* process windows messages */
        {
                case WM_PAINT:
                        BeginPaint (hWnd, &ps) ;
                        lstrcpy (cBuf, cString1) ;
                        lstrcat (cBuf, cString2) ;
                        OemToAnsiBuff (cBuf, cBuf2, lstrlen (cBuf)) ;
                        SelectObject (ps.hdc, GetStockObject (OEM_FIXED_FONT)) ;
                        TextOut (ps.hdc, 0, 5, cBuf, lstrlen (cBuf)) ;
                        SelectObject (ps.hdc, GetStockObject (ANSI_FIXED_FONT)) ;
                        TextOut (ps.hdc, 0, 20, cBuf2, lstrlen (cBuf2)) ;
                        EndPaint (hWnd, &ps) ;
                        break ;
```

[Other program lines]

ToAscii

Purpose   Converts virtual key/scan code data to ANSI characters.

Syntax   int **ToAscii**(WORD *wVirtKey*, WORD *wScanCode*, LPSTR *lpKeyState*, LPVOID *lpChar*, WORD *wFlags*);

Description   Mainly used with international (non-USA) keyboard translations. The function reads the virtual key, scan code, and key state data, and then puts the translated ANSI character equivalent into the buffer pointed to by *lpChar*.

Uses   Useful in processing accent characters.

Returns   int, the number of bytes copied to the *lpChar* buffer. Two for accent or dead-key characters that do not have an ANSI value. One for direct translation to an ANSI character. Zero if no translation was possible.

See Also   OemToAnsi(), AnsiToOem()

Parameters

wVirtKey   WORD: The virtual key code. This is the *wParam* value used when processing a WM_KEYUP or WM_KEYDOWN message.

wScanCode   WORD: This is the OEM scan code. Bytes 16 to 23 of *lParam* contain this value when processing a WM_KEYUP or WM_KEYDOWN message.

lpKeyState   LPSTR: A pointer to a 256-byte array containing the current status of all virtual keys. Use GetKeyboardState() to initialize this array prior to calling ToAscii().

lpChar   LPVOID: A pointer to a 32-bit buffer (DWORD) that will hold the translated character.

wFlags   WORD: The bit 0 flag's setting. Set to NULL.

Related Messages WM_KEYDOWN, WM_KEYUP

Example   This example uses ToAscii() to convert the WM_KEYDOWN parameter data into its ANSI character equivalent. Every time a key is pressed, the number of translated bytes (usually one) and the ANSI character are displayed in the program's client area.

```
long FAR PASCAL WndProc (HWND hWnd, unsigned iMessage, WORD wParam, LONG lParam)
{
        HDC          hDC ;
        char         cKeyBuf [256], cBuf [10] ;
        DWORD        dwAnsiValue ;
        int          nCharResult, nScanCode ;

        switch (iMessage)                       /* process windows messages */
        {
        case WM_KEYDOWN:
                InvalidateRect (hWnd, NULL, TRUE) ;      /* clear client area */
                UpdateWindow (hWnd) ;
                hDC = GetDC (hWnd) ;
                nScanCode = (lParam >> 16) & 0x00ff ;    /* get scan code */
                GetKeyboardState (cKeyBuf) ;     /* read all 256 VK_ values */
                nCharResult = ToAscii (wParam, nScanCode, cKeyBuf,
                                &dwAnsiValue, NULL) ;
                itoa (nCharResult, cBuf, 10) ;
                TextOut (hDC, 10, 10, cBuf, strlen (cBuf)) ;
                TextOut (hDC, 50, 10, "= bytes ToAscii() returned.", 27) ;
                cBuf [0] = (char) (dwAnsiValue & 0x00ff) ;
                TextOut (hDC, 10, 30, cBuf, 1) ;
                TextOut (hDC, 50, 30, "= ASCII char.", 13) ;
                ReleaseDC (hWnd, hDC) ;
                break ;
```

[Other program lines]

Windows uses the MS-DOS disk file functions. Prior to Windows 3.0, the use of MS-DOS was obvious to the Windows programmer as only the OpenFile() function was provided for file access. The MS-DOS file functions from the C compiler's run-time library were used to read and write data. The Windows function library included function calls to the lower-level DOS functions, but these were "undocumented" functions. The function names were preceded by an underscore character to emphasize their temporary nature. With the release of Windows 3.0, the file functions have been legitimized. The Windows function library now includes the previously "undocumented" functions. The underscore characters in front of the function names have been retained for compatibility with previous versions.

You are most likely to run into the differences between the OEM character set used by MS-DOS and the ANSI character set used by Windows when using file functions. All of the file functions available within Windows do the conversion from ANSI to OEM characters for you. If you access the MS-DOS file or path name data directly (perhaps using the OFSTRUCT data filled by the OpenFile() function), keep in mind that the file names and path names will contain OEM characters.

Windows includes excellent support for maintaining initialization files, such as WIN.INI. These files are read on startup, and provide information to the program concerning how the user left the application when it was last run. Typically, they are used to remember window sizes and locations, default file names, and preferred color combinations.

Disk Files

From the point of view of an application program, a disk file is just a series of byte values. There is no automatic structure to the data. An application writes the data to the file in any arbitrary order. This might be a series of integers (two-byte values) followed by string data (one byte per character). When the data is read back from the disk, the application must know the order in which the data was written in order to make sense out of the individual bytes.

Before any action on a disk file can be taken, the file must be opened. Opening the file alerts MS-DOS that the file will see activity. MS-DOS uses an unsigned integer value, called a "file handle," to keep track of the open files. Only a limited number of files can be open at one time (determined by the FILES environment variable in DOS). Files should be closed as soon as possible after use.

Within Windows, the preferred way to open or create a new file is with the OpenFile() function. A typical call to OpenFile() is as follows:

```
int                    hFileHandle ;
OFSTRUCT               of ;

hFileHandle = OpenFile ("MYFILE.TMP", &of, OF_CREATE) ;
```

This example creates a file called MYFILE.TMP on the default directory. Because of the OF_CREATE flag, the file is opened and truncated to zero bytes of data if the file already exists. The file handle is returned by OpenFile(). The file handle is an integer. The file handle is used by all of the data reading and writing functions.

OpenFile() uses a data structure called OFSTRUCT, that is defined in WINDOWS.H as follows:

```
typedef struct tagOFSTRUCT
  {
  BYTE        cBytes;                    /* Length of OFSTRUCT */
```

```
    BYTE         fFixedDisk;                    /* non-zero if fixed drive */
    WORD         nErrCode;                      /* MS DOS error code */
    BYTE         reserved[4];                   /* file date and time */
    BYTE         szPathName[128];               /* full path name and */
                                                /* file name (OEM chars) */
  } OFSTRUCT;
typedef OFSTRUCT                                *POFSTRUCT;
typedef OFSTRUCT NEAR                           *NPOFSTRUCT;
typedef OFSTRUCT FAR                            *LPOFSTRUCT;
```

This data is filled in every time OpenFile() is called.

An alternative to using OpenFile() is to used the lower-level file functions like _lcreat() and _lopen(). They do the specific jobs of creating new files and opening existing ones. OpenFile() is more versatile, and generally preferred. When the file is open, the low-level file access functions _lread(), _lwrite(), and _llseek() are used to read, write, and move to data in the file. These functions are direct calls to their MS-DOS function equivalents. As soon as the need for the file's data is complete, the application must call _lclose() to close the file. Failing to close a file risks losing the file's data after the application terminates.

Lists of File Names

Most applications need to allow the user to select a file from a list of files on a certain directory. This task is so common that Windows provides automatic functions for filling list boxes and combo boxes with a specified directory list. The list box or combo box must be inside a dialog box. DlgDirList() fills a list box with a set of file names specified by an MS-DOS search string like "*.TXT" (show every file on the directory with the TXT extension). DlgDirListComboBox() does the same function for a combo box.

When the list of files is added to the list or combo box, related directory and drive names are included in the list surrounded by square brackets. A typical example is shown in Figure 20-1.

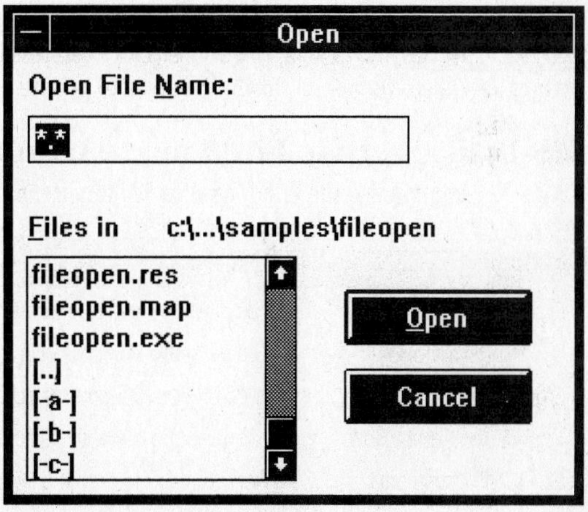

Figure 20-1. Files Listed in a List Box.

The Windows Software Development Kit (SDK) provides an excellent example program called OPENFILE. Figure 20-1 shows the file selection dialog box that this example program creates. Extract the dialog box definition and dialog box function from this file and use it in any application requiring file selection.

Initialization Files

A common problem for many programs is "remembering" settings from the last time a user ran the application. Many applications store the main window's size and location, color selections, most recently opened file names, and other common data for the next session. Prior to Windows 3.0, all of this initialization data was stored in a single file called WIN.INI. WIN.INI includes initialization information used by Windows, and specialized information written and accessed by other applications. The WIN.INI file is located in the Windows subdirectory, the subdirectory that contains WIN.COM. A typical excerpt from WIN.INI is shown below.

```
[Windows Help]
Maximized=0
Xl=59
Yu=54
Xr=666
Yd=683
```

In this case, the Windows Help application stores information about the size and location of the help window the last time Help was called.

Applications can write new entries to WIN.INI using WriteProfileString(). This function will search for an existing entry, such as [Windows Help], and write data below it. If a matching entry does not exist, a new one is written to WIN.INI. The data can be read from WIN.INI with GetProfileString() and GetProfileInt() for character and integer data, respectively.

The problem with always using WIN.INI to store initialization data is that WIN.INI becomes very long. This slows down the Windows startup routines because all of WIN.INI is read every time Windows is started. There is also no provision for deleting entries from WIN.INI when an application has been removed from the system. WIN.INI files tend to collect large numbers of unnecessary entries over time.

With Windows 3.0, support is provided for private initialization files. These files have the same format as WIN.INI, but are specific to one application. The WritePrivateProfileString(), GetPrivateProfileString(), and GetPrivateProfileInt() functions are provided for simple support of these files. Private initialization files should be used for data that is specific to the application. WIN.INI should be used for data that might be used by more than one application, such as preferred color choices.

Because WIN.INI holds initialization data common to all applications, an application that changes WIN.INI should notify all other running applications if a change is made. The application changing WIN.INI should send the WM_WININICHANGE to all applications (call PostMessage() with the *hWnd* parameter set to −1) after WriteProfileString() is called. Do not do this for changes to private initialization files.

MS-DOS and Disk File Function Summary

Table 20-1 summarizes the Windows disk file functions. The detailed function descriptions are in the next section.

Function	Purpose	
DlgDirList	Fills a list box control in a dialog box with a set of file names.	
DlgDirListComboBox	Fills a combo box control in a dialog box with a set of file names.	
DlgDirSelect	Retrieves the currently selected file name from a list box.	
DlgDirSelectComboBox	Retrieves the currently selected file name from a combo box.	
GetDOSEnvironment	Retrieves a pointer to the DOS environment string buffer.	
GetDriveType	Determines if a drive is fixed, removeable, or a network drive.	
GetEnvironment	Retrieves the Windows environment string for a device.	
GetPrivateProfileInt	Retrieves an integer value from an application's private profile (.INI) file.	
GetPrivateProfileString	Retrieves a character string from an application's private profile (.INI) file.	
GetProfileInt	Reads an integer value from the WIN.INI file.	
GetProfileString	Retrieves a character string from the WIN.INI file.	
GetSystemDirectory	Determines the path name of the Windows system directory.	
GetTempDrive	Determines which drive to use for temporary files.	
GetTempFileName	Creates a unique, temporary file name.	
GetWindowsDirectory	Determines the path name of the Windows directory.	
_lclose	Closes a disk file.	
_lcreat	Creates a new disk file.	
_llseek	Moves to a new location in a disk file.	
_lopen	Opens a file for reading or writing data.	
_lread	Reads data from a disk file.	
_lwrite	Writes data to a disk file.	
OpenFile	Creates, opens, or deletes files.	

SetEnvironment	Changes the environment variable settings for a port.
SetErrorMode	Sets whether Windows shows the default critical error message.
SetHandleCount	Changes the number of files an application can have open at once.
WritePrivateProfileString	Copies a character string to an application's private profile (.INI) file.
WriteProfileString	Writes an entry to the WIN.INI file.

Table 20-1. Disk File Function Summary.

MS-DOS and Disk File Function Descriptions

This section contains the detailed descriptions for the disk file functions.

DLGDIRLIST
■ Win 2.0   ■ Win 3.0   ■ Win 3.1

Purpose	Fills a list box control in a dialog box with a set of file names.
Syntax	int **DlgDirList**(HWND *hDlg*, LPSTR *lpPathSpec*, int *nIDListBox*, int *nIDStaticPath*, WORD *wFileType*);
Description	List box controls are ideal for allowing the user to select a file name from a list. This function conveniently fills the list box with a set of file names which match a DOS file search string.
Uses	Used in the File/Save, File/Load dialog boxes for most applications.
Returns	int, nonzero if files were found. Zero if no files were found that matched *lpPathSpec*.
See Also	DlgDirListComboBox(), DlgDirSelect()
Parameters	
hDlg	HWND: The dialog box handle.
lpPathSpec	LPSTR: A pointer to a character string containing the DOS file search string. For example, "C:\DOS*.COM" would list all files in the DOS subdirectory with the .COM extension.
nIDListBox	int: The dialog box ID value for the list box control. Normally the list box will have the LBS_SORT style, so that the files are listed in ASCII sort order.
nIDStaticPath	int: The dialog box ID value for a static text control that will be updated with the current path name.
wFileType	WORD: The DOS file attribute value. (See the list in Table 20-2.) Only files with the selected attributes will be displayed.

Value	Meaning	⊠
0x0000	Read/write data files with no other attributes set (normal files).	
0x0001	Read only files.	
0x0002	Hidden files.	
0x0004	System files.	
0x0010	Subdirectories.	
0x0020	Archived files.	
0x2000	LB_DIR flag. Flag places messages associated with filling the list box on the application's message queue, rather than sending them directly. See the LB_DIR message description in Chapter 9, *Windows Messages*.	
0x4000	Drives (A, B, C, ...).	
0x8000	Exclusive bit. If this is set, only the specified file attribute type is recovered. If not set, normal files are displayed in addition to the types listed.	

Table 20-2. DOS File Attributes.

Related Messages LB_RESETCONTENT, LB_DIR

Example This example, as shown in Figure 20-2, creates a dialog box when the user clicks the "Do It!" menu item. The dialog box contains a list box, showing all of the files in the current directory. The dialog box also displays the directory name and the number of files displayed. When the user selects a file from the list box, the selection number and file name are stored in global variables. This allows the calling WndProc() function to display the current selection at the top of the window's client area when WM_PAINT messages are processed.

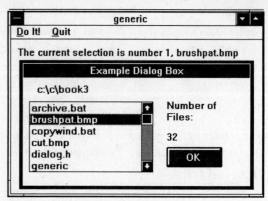

Figure 20-2. DlgDirList() Example.

The dialog box is defined in a resource file created with the dialog box editor.

```
EXAMPLEDIALOG DIALOG LOADONCALL MOVEABLE DISCARDABLE 20, 36, 162, 75
CAPTION "Example Dialog Box"
FONT 10, "Helv"
STYLE WS_BORDER | WS_CAPTION | WS_DLGFRAME | DS_MODALFRAME | WS_POPUP
BEGIN
    CONTROL "OK", DLI_OK, "button", BS_DEFPUSHBUTTON | WS_TABSTOP |
            WS_CHILD, 102, 48, 40, 14
    CONTROL "", DLI_LISTBOX, "listbox", LBS_STANDARD | LBS_HASSTRINGS |
            WS_BORDER | WS_VSCROLL | WS_CHILD, 5, 17, 87, 49
    CONTROL "Number of Files:", -1, "static", SS_LEFT | WS_CHILD,
            102, 15, 54, 18
    CONTROL "", DLI_DIRSTRING, "static", SS_LEFT | WS_CHILD,
            10, 4, 141, 12
    CONTROL "", DLI_NUMFILES, "static", SS_LEFT | WS_CHILD,
            102, 37, 41, 10
END
```

The dialog box control ID numbers are defined in a separate header file, GENERIC.HD.

```
#define DLI_LISTBOX         104
#define DLI_NUMFILES        103
#define DLI_DIRSTRING       102
#define DLI_OK              101
```

The following listing shows the dialog box function at the end. The function must be listed in the EXPORTS section of the application's .DEF definition file, and it must have a function prototype in the header file.

```
int             nSelection = 0 ;                    /* global variables */
char            cSelection [128] ;

long FAR PASCAL WndProc (HWND hWnd, unsigned iMessage, WORD wParam, LONG lParam)
{
        FARPROC             lpfnDlgProc ;
        PAINTSTRUCT         ps ;
        char                cBuf [128] ;

        switch (iMessage)                           /* process windows messages */
        {
                case WM_PAINT:
                        BeginPaint (hWnd, &ps) ;
```

```
                    TextOut (ps.hdc, 10, 10, cBuf, wsprintf (cBuf,
                            "The current selection is number %d, %s",
                            nSelection, (LPSTR) cSelection)) ;
                    EndPaint (hWnd, &ps) ;
                    break ;
            case WM_COMMAND:                /* process menu items */
                    switch (wParam)
                    {
                    case IDM_DOIT:          /* run dialog box */
                            lpfnDlgProc = MakeProcInstance (DialogProc,
                                    ghInstance) ;
                            DialogBox (ghInstance, "ExampleDialog", hWnd,
                                    lpfnDlgProc) ;
                            FreeProcInstance (lpfnDlgProc) ;
                            InvalidateRect (hWnd, NULL, TRUE) ;
                            break ;
                    case IDM_QUIT:
                            DestroyWindow (hWnd) ;
                            break ;
                    }
                    break ;
            case WM_DESTROY:                /* stop application */
                    PostQuitMessage (0) ;
                    break ;
            default:                        /* default windows message processing */
                    return DefWindowProc (hWnd, iMessage, wParam, lParam) ;
        }
        return (0L);
}


BOOL FAR PASCAL DialogProc (HWND hDlg, WORD wMess, WORD wParam, LONG lParam)
{
        int             nFiles ;

        switch (wMess)
        {
            case WM_INITDIALOG:
                    DlgDirList (hDlg, "*.*", DLI_LISTBOX,
                            DLI_DIRSTRING, 0) ;
                    nFiles = SendDlgItemMessage (hDlg, DLI_LISTBOX,
                            LB_GETCOUNT,    0, 0L) ;
                    SetDlgItemInt (hDlg, DLI_NUMFILES, nFiles, TRUE) ;
                    return TRUE ;
            case WM_COMMAND:                /* One of the controls was activated */
                    switch (wParam)
                    {
                            case DLI_OK:
                                    EndDialog (hDlg, 0) ;
                                    return TRUE ;
                            case DLI_LISTBOX:
                                    if (HIWORD (lParam) == LBN_SELCHANGE)
                                    {
                                            nSelection = SendDlgItemMessage (hDlg,
                                            DLI_LISTBOX,    LB_GETCURSEL, 0, 0L) ;
                                            DlgDirSelect (hDlg,
                                                    (LPSTR) cSelection,
                                                    DLI_LISTBOX) ;
                                    }
                    }
                    return TRUE ;
            case WM_DESTROY:
                    EndDialog (hDlg, 0) ;
                    return TRUE ;
        }
        return FALSE ;
}
```

DlgDirListComboBox   □ Win 2.0 ■ Win 3.0 ■ Win 3.1

Purpose	Fills a combo box control in a dialog box with a set of file names.
Syntax	int **DlgDirListComboBox**(HWND *hDlg*, LPSTR *lpPathSpec*, int *nIDListBox*, int *nIDStaticPath*, WORD *wFileType*);
Description	Combo box controls are ideal for allowing the user to select a file name from a list. This function fills the combo box with a set of file names which match a DOS file search string.
Uses	Used in the File/Save, File/Load dialog boxes.
Returns	int, nonzero if files were found. Zero if no files were found matching *lpPathSpec*.
See Also	DlgDirList(), DlgDirSelectComboBox()
Parameters	
hDlg	HWND: The dialog box handle.
lpPathSpec	LPSTR: A pointer to a character string containing the DOS file search string. For example "C:\DOS*.COM" would list all files in the DOS subdirectory with the .COM extension.
nIDListBox	int: The dialog box ID value for the combo box control. Normally the combo box will have the CBS_SORT style, so that the files are listed in ASCII sort order.
nIDStaticPath	int: The dialog box ID value for a static text control that will be updated with the current path name.
wFileType	WORD: The DOS file attribute value. (See the list in Table 20-3.) Only files with the selected attributes will be displayed.

Value	Meaning
0x0000	Read/write data files with no other attributes set (normal files).
0x0001	Read only files.
0x0002	Hidden files.
0x0004	System files.
0x0010	Subdirectories.
0x0020	Archived files.
0x2000	LB_DIR flag. This places messages associated with filling the combo box on the application's message queue, rather than sending them directly. See the LB_DIR message description in Chapter 9, *Windows Messages*.
0x4000	Drives (A, B, C,...).
0x8000	Exclusive bit. If this is set, only the specified file attribute type is recovered. If not set, normal files are displayed in addition to the types listed.

Table 20-3. DOS File Attributes.

Related Messages CB_RESETCONTENT, CB_DIR

Example   This example, as shown in Figure 20-3, is identical to the previous example, except that a combo box is used in place of the list box for showing the list of files. The combo box has the advantage of automatically showing the selected file in the edit control at the top of the combo box.

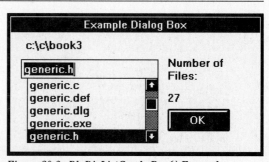

Figure 20-3. DlgDirListComboBox( ) Example.

The SDK Dialog Box Editor is used to create the dialog box definition file. This can either be physically added to the program's .RC resource file or included via an #include statement.

```
EXAMPLEDIALOG DIALOG LOADONCALL MOVEABLE DISCARDABLE 20, 36, 162, 75
CAPTION "Example Dialog Box"
FONT 10, "Helv"
STYLE WS_BORDER | WS_CAPTION | WS_DLGFRAME | DS_MODALFRAME | WS_POPUP
BEGIN
    CONTROL "OK", DLI_OK, "button", BS_DEFPUSHBUTTON | WS_TABSTOP
            | WS_CHILD, 102, 48, 40, 14
    CONTROL "Number of Files:", -1, "static", SS_LEFT | WS_CHILD,
            102, 15, 54, 18
    CONTROL "", DLI_DIRSTRING, "static", SS_LEFT | WS_CHILD,
            10, 4, 141, 12
    CONTROL "", DLI_NUMFILES, "static", SS_LEFT | WS_CHILD,
            102, 37, 41, 10
    CONTROL "", DLI_COMBO, "combobox", CBS_SIMPLE | CBS_SORT |
            WS_VSCROLL | WS_CHILD, 7, 17, 89, 57
END
```

The dialog box control ID numbers are defined in a separate header file, GENERIC.HD.

```
#define DLI_COMBO        104
#define DLI_NUMFILES     103
#define DLI_DIRSTRING    102
#define DLI_OK           101
```

Only the dialog box procedure is shown in the following example. The WndProc() function is identical to the example shown above under the DlgDirList() function description. The dialog box function must be listed in the EXPORTS section of the application's .DEF definition file, and should have a function prototype in the program's header file.

```
BOOL FAR PASCAL DialogProc (HWND hDlg, WORD wMess, WORD wParam, LONG lParam)
{
        int             nFiles ;

        switch (wMess)
        {
                case WM_INITDIALOG:
                        DlgDirListComboBox (hDlg, "*.*", DLI_COMBO,
                                DLI_DIRSTRING, 0) ;
                        nFiles = SendDlgItemMessage (hDlg, DLI_COMBO,
                                CB_GETCOUNT,    0, 0L) ;
                        SetDlgItemInt (hDlg, DLI_NUMFILES, nFiles, TRUE) ;
                        return TRUE ;
                case WM_COMMAND:                 /* One of the controls was activated */
                        switch (wParam)
                        {
                                case DLI_OK:
                                        EndDialog (hDlg, 0) ;
                                        return TRUE ;
                                case DLI_COMBO:
                                        if (HIWORD (lParam) == LBN_SELCHANGE)
                                        {
                                                nSelection = SendDlgItemMessage (hDlg,
                                                DLI_COMBO,        CB_GETCURSEL, 0, 0L) ;
                                                DlgDirSelectComboBox (hDlg,
                                                        (LPSTR) cSelection,
                                                        DLI_COMBO) ;
                                        }
                                }
                                return TRUE ;
                        case WM_DESTROY:
                                EndDialog (hDlg, 0) ;
                                return TRUE ;
                }
                return FALSE ;
}
```

DLGDIRSELECT   ■ Win 2.0   ■ Win 3.0   ■ Win 3.1

Purpose	Retrieves the currently selected file name from a list box.
Syntax	BOOL **DlgDirSelect**(HWND *hDlg*, LPSTR *lpString*, int *nIDListBox*);
Description	This function assumes that the list box in a dialog box was filled with file names using the DlgDirList() function. The currently selected file or directory name is copied to the memory buffer pointed to by *lpString*. This function is equivalent to sending the LB_GETCURSEL and LB_GETTEXT messages to the list box control.
Uses	Used in File/Save and File/Load dialog boxes.
Returns	BOOL. Nonzero if the item selected is a directory name, otherwise zero.
See Also	DlgDirList()
Parameters	
hDlg	HWND: The dialog box handle.
lpString	LPSTR: A pointer to a memory buffer that will hold the name of the file or directory selected. Directories will be displayed with square brackets surrounding the directory name. The brackets are not copied to the memory buffer.
nIDListBox	int: The ID value for the list box control in the dialog box.
Related Messages	LB_GETCURSEL, LB_GETTEXT
Example	See the example under the DlgDirList() function description.

DLGDIRSELECTCOMBOBOX   □ Win 2.0   ■ Win 3.0   ■ Win 3.1

Purpose	Retrieves the currently selected file name from a combo box.
Syntax	BOOL **DlgDirSelectComboBox**(HWND *hDlg*, LPSTR *lpString*, int *nIDComboBox*);
Description	This function assumes that the combo box in a dialog box was filled with file names using the DlgDirListComboBox() function. The currently selected file or directory name is copied to the memory buffer pointed to by *lpString*. This function is equivalent to sending the CB_GETCURSEL and CB_GETLBTEXT messages to the combo box control.
Uses	Used in File/Save and File/Load dialog boxes.
Returns	BOOL. Nonzero if the item selected is a directory name, otherwise zero.
See Also	DlgDirListComboBox()
Parameters	
hDlg	HWND: The dialog box handle.
lpString	LPSTR: A pointer to a memory buffer that will hold the name of the file or directory selected. Directories will be displayed with square brackets surrounding the directory name. The brackets are not copied to the memory buffer.
nIDComboBox	int: The ID value for the combo box control in the dialog box.
Related Messages	CB_GETCURSEL, CB_GETLBTEXT
Example	See the example under the DlgDirListComboBox() function description.

GETDOSENVIRONMENT   □ Win 2.0   ■ Win 3.0   ■ Win 3.1

Purpose	Retrieves a pointer to the DOS environment string buffer.
Syntax	LPSTR **GetDOSEnvironment**(void);
Description	When you issue a PATH or SET command from within MS-DOS, the string is stored in the DOS environment buffer. This memory area is expanded by DOS to hold all of the input strings.

GetDOSEnvironment() retrieves a pointer to this memory area. Each string is separated by a single NULL character. The end of the last environment string is marked by two NULL characters. The environment string is not updated after the application or DLL is loaded. Changes after that point are not reflected in the returned memory area. This function will work within a DLL (dynamic link library).

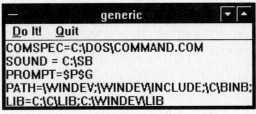

Figure 20-4. GetDOSEnvironment( ) Example.

Uses	Frequently used to find which directories are on the current PATH.
Returns	LPSTR, a pointer to the MS-DOS environment string memory buffer.
See Also	GetEnvironment(), GetWindowsDirectory()
Parameters	None (void) ;
Example	This example displays the current DOS environment variables on the window's client area, as shown in Figure 20-4. Note that the output code must skip over the single NULL characters that separate the environment strings, and must stop when it finds two NULL characters in a row.

```
long FAR PASCAL WndProc (HWND hWnd, unsigned iMessage, WORD wParam, LONG lParam)
{
        PAINTSTRUCT          ps ;
        LPSTR                lpstr ;
        int                  nLine ;

        switch (iMessage)                                /* process windows messages */
        {
        case WM_PAINT:
                BeginPaint (hWnd, &ps) ;
                lpstr = GetDOSEnvironment () ;
                TextOut (ps.hdc, 0, 0, lpstr, lstrlen (lpstr)) ;
                nLine = 1 ;
                do {
                        if (*lpstr == 0 && *(lpstr + 1) != 0 )
                        {
                                lpstr++ ;
                                TextOut (ps.hdc, 0, nLine++ * 15, lpstr,
                                        lstrlen (lpstr)) ;
                        }
                }while (*lpstr++ + *lpstr) ;     /* not two nulls */
                EndPaint (hWnd, &ps) ;
                break ;
```

[Other program lines]

GetDriveType

□ Win 2.0   ■ Win 3.0   ■ Win 3.1

Purpose	Determines if a drive is fixed, removable, or a network drive.
Syntax	WORD **GetDriveType**(int *nDrive*);
Description	Network and removeable disks are much slower than fixed disks. It is frequently desirable to know which disk is the fastest available for writing temporary files, etc.
Returns	WORD, zero if unknown, 1 if the specified drive does not exist. Otherwise, one of the values in Table 20-4 is returned.

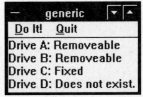

Figure 20-5. GetDriveType( ) Example.

Value	Meaning	
DRIVE_REMOVABLE	Floppy disk.	⊠
DRIVE_FIXED	Hard disk.	
DRIVE_REMOTE	Network drive.	

Table 20-4. GetDriveType() Returned Values.

See Also GetTempDrive()

Parameters

nDrive int: The drive to check. 0 for the A drive, 1 for the B drive, etc.

Example This example displays the drive type of the first four drives when the user clicks the "Do It!" menu item.

```
long FAR PASCAL WndProc (HWND hWnd, unsigned iMessage, WORD wParam, LONG lParam)
{
        HDC             hDC ;
        int             i, nType ;
        char            c, cBuf [128] ;

        switch (iMessage)                       /* process windows messages */
        {
                case WM_COMMAND:                /* process menu items */
                        switch (wParam)
                        {
                        case IDM_DOIT:          /* User hit the "Do it" menu item */
                                hDC = GetDC (hWnd) ;
                                for (i = 0 ; i < 4 ; i++)
                                {
                                        nType = GetDriveType (i) ;
                                        switch (nType)
                                        {
                                                case DRIVE_REMOVABLE:
                                                        TextOut (hDC, 0, 15 * i, cBuf,
                                                                wsprintf (cBuf,
                                                                "Drive %c: %s", 'A' + i,
                                                                (LPSTR) "Removeable")) ;
                                                        break ;
                                                case DRIVE_FIXED:
                                                        TextOut (hDC, 0, 15 * i, cBuf,
                                                                wsprintf (cBuf,
                                                                "Drive %c: %s", 'A' + i,
                                                                (LPSTR) "Fixed")) ;
                                                        break ;
                                                case DRIVE_REMOTE:
                                                        TextOut (hDC, 0, 15 * i, cBuf,
                                                                wsprintf (cBuf,
                                                                "Drive %c: %s", 'A' + i,
                                                                (LPSTR) "Removeable")) ;
                                                        break ;
                                                default:
                                                        TextOut (hDC, 0, 15 * i, cBuf,
                                                                wsprintf (cBuf,
                                                                "Drive %c: %s", 'A' + i,
                                                (LPSTR) "Does not exist.")) ;
                                                        break ;
                                        }
                                }
                                ReleaseDC (hWnd, hDC) ;
                                break ;
```

[Other program lines]

GETENVIRONMENT   ■ Win 2.0   ■ Win 3.0   ■ Win 3.1

Purpose	Retrieves the Windows environment string or a device.
Syntax	int **GetEnvironment**(LPSTR *lpPortName*, LPSTR *lpEnviron*, WORD *nMaxCount*);

Description   The Windows GDI (Graphics Device Interface) maintains a string table for each port. If the port has been initialized via the Windows setup program, the port environment string will be set. Otherwise, the environment string will not exist, and Get-Environment() will return zero. GetEnvironment() will return the length of the environment string if *lpEnviron* is set to NULL.

Uses   A quick way to get the printer name. The *lpPortName* variable will normally be "LPT1" for the printer device.

Figure 20-6. GetEnvironment( ) Example.

Returns	int, the number of characters copied to *lpEnviron*.
See Also	GetDOSEnvironment(), SetEnvironment()

Parameters

lpPortName   LPSTR: A pointer to a null-terminated character string containing the port name. For example "LPT1."

lpEnviron   LPSTR: A pointer to a character buffer that will hold the environment string. If this value is set to NULL, GetEnvironment() will return the length of the environment string.

nMaxCount   int: The maximum number of characters to copy to *lpEnviron*.

Example   This example, as shown in Figure 20-6, displays the GDI environment string associated with the LPT1 port.

```
Long FAR PASCAL WndProc (HWND hWnd, unsigned iMessage, WORD wParam, LONG lParam)
{
        PAINTSTRUCT             ps ;
        char                    cBuf [128] ;

        switch (iMessage)                                       /* process windows messages */
        {
        case WM_PAINT:
                BeginPaint (hWnd, &ps) ;
                GetEnvironment ("lpt1", cBuf, 128) ;
                TextOut (ps.hdc, 0, 0, cBuf, lstrlen (cBuf)) ;
                EndPaint (hWnd, &ps) ;
                break ;
```

[Other program lines]

GETPRIVATEPROFILEINT   □ Win 2.0   ■ Win 3.0   ■ Win 3.1

Purpose	Retrieves an integer value from an application's private profile (.INI) file.
Syntax	WORD **GetPrivateProfileInt**(LPSTR *lpApplicationName*, LPSTR *lpKeyName*, int *nDefault*, LPSTR *lpFileName*);

Description   The best way for a program to "remember" user preferences, such as favored colors and sub-directory names, is to write them to an initialization file. For items that may affect more than one application, this should be the main WIN.INI file. For items that will affect only the application itself, this should be a private .INI file. GetPrivateProfileInt() reads an integer value. The value is assumed to be in a file with the format

```
[application name]
keyname = int value
```

These files are best created and maintained using the WritePrivateProfileString() function.

Uses   Reading in saved values, such as the window size and location when last closed.

Returns   WORD, the value read. If the key name exists, but the value following the equal sign is not a positive integer, the function returns zero. If the key name does not exist, the *nDefault* value is returned.

See Also   WritePrivateProfileString(), GetPrivateProfileString()

Parameters

lpApplicationName LPSTR: A pointer to a character string that contains the application name in the private .INI file. This is the string that appears inside the square brackets.

lpKeyName   LPSTR: A pointer to the key name in the private .INI file. This is the string to the left of the equal sign.

nDefault   int: The default value to return if the *lpKeyName* match is not found.

lpFileName   LPSTR: A pointer to a character string containing the private .INI file name. The file is assumed to be in the Windows subdirectory unless a path name is included with the file name in *lpFileName*.

Example   When started, this example creates a private profile file, GENERIC.INI, in the Windows subdirectory. The file is written with two values under the heading [TestApp]. The first value is an integer with the key name "Value," which is set to 437. The second value is a string with the key name "StringConst," which is set to "This String."

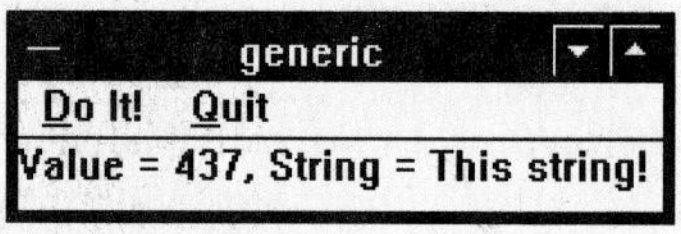

Figure 20-7. GetPrivateProfileInt( ) Example.

When the user clicks the "Do It!" menu item, the private profile string is read, and the two values are extracted. They are written to the window's client area as shown in Figure 20-7.

▷ **GENERIC.INI File Created**

```
[TestApp]
Value=437
StringConst=This string!
```

▷ **GENERIC.C WndProc( ) Function**

```
Long FAR PASCAL WndProc (HWND hWnd, unsigned iMessage, WORD wParam, LONG lParam)
{
        HDC             hDC ;
        char            cBuf [128], szStringVal [32] ;
        int             nValue ;

        switch (iMessage)                       /* process windows messages */
        {
                case WM_CREATE:
                        WritePrivateProfileString ("TestApp", "Value", "437",
                                "GENERIC.INI") ;
                        WritePrivateProfileString ("TestApp", "StringConst",
                                "This string!", "GENERIC.INI") ;
                        break ;
                case WM_COMMAND:                /* process menu items */
                        switch (wParam)
                        {
                        case IDM_DOIT:          /* User hit the "Do it" menu item */
                                hDC = GetDC (hWnd) ;
                                nValue = GetPrivateProfileInt ("TestApp", "Value",
                                        -1, "GENERIC.INI") ;
                                GetPrivateProfileString ("TestApp", "StringConst",
                                        "<none>", szStringVal, 32, "GENERIC.INI") ;
                                TextOut (hDC, 0, 0, cBuf, wsprintf (cBuf,
                                        "Value = %d, String = %s", nValue,
```

```
                              (LPSTR) szStringVal)) ;
            ReleaseDC (hWnd, hDC) ;
            break ;
```

[Other program lines]

GETPRIVATEPROFILESTRING

□ Win 2.0   ■ Win 3.0   ■ Win 3.1

Purpose	Retrieves a character string from an application's private profile (.INI) file.
Syntax	int **GetPrivateProfileString**(LPSTR *lpApplicationName*, LPSTR *lpKeyName*, LPSTR *lpDefault*, LPSTR *lpReturnedString*, int *nSize*, LPSTR *lpFileName*);
Description	The best way for a program to "remember" user preferences, such as subdirectory names, is to write them to an initialization file. For items that may affect more than one application, this should be the main WIN.INI file. For items that will only affect the application itself, this should be a private .INI file. GetPrivateProfileInt() reads a character string. The string is assumed to be in a file with the format

```
[application name]
keyname = string
```

These files are best created and maintained using the WritePrivateProfileString() function.

Uses	Reading saved values, such as the last file(s) read, or the working subdirectory path name.
Returns	int, the number of characters copied to the *lpReturnedString* buffer. If the returned string is truncated to fit the *nSize* parameter, only the number of copied characters is returned.
See Also	GetPrivateProfileInt(), WritePrivateProfileString()
Parameters	
lpApplicationName	LPSTR: A pointer to a character string that contains the application name in the private .INI file. This is the string that appears inside the square brackets.
lpKeyName	LPSTR: A pointer to the key name in the private .INI file. This is the string to the left of the equal sign. If *lpKeyName* is set to NULL, all of the key names are copied to the buffer pointed to by *lpReturnedString*.
lpDefault	LPSTR: The default string to return if the *lpKeyName* match is not found.
lpReturnedString	LPSTR: A pointer to a character buffer to hold the returned string. The buffer must be at least *nSize* bytes long.
nSize	int: The maximum number of characters to copy to *lpReturnedString*.
lpFileName	LPSTR: A pointer to a character string containing the private .INI file name. The file is assumed to be in the Windows subdirectory unless a path name is included with the file name in *lpFileName*.
Example	See the previous example under the GetPrivateProfileInt() function description.

GETPROFILEINT

■ Win 2.0   ■ Win 3.0   ■ Win 3.1

Purpose	Reads an integer value from the WIN.INI file.
Syntax	WORD **GetProfileInt**(LPSTR *lpApplicationName*, LPSTR *lpKeyName*, int *nDefault*);
Description	Windows uses the WIN.INI file to initialize applications. With Windows 3.0, support is provided for both private initialization files and the general file WIN.INI. WIN.INI should be used for programs that have settings that impact more than one application. Private profile files should be used for initialization data that only impacts one application. GetProfileInt() reads an integer value from WIN.INI. The value is assumed to be in a file with the format

```
[application name]
keyname = int value
```

Uses	The integer value can either be associated with a specific program, or one of the parameters Windows reads on startup (for example CursorBlinkRate=460).

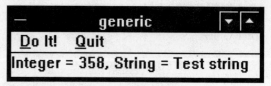

Figure 20-8. GetProfileInt( ) Example.

Returns WORD, the value read. If the key name exists, but the value following the equal sign is not a positive integer, the function returns zero. If the key name does not exist, the *nDefault* value is returned.

See Also WriteProfileString(), GetProfileString(), GetWindowsDirectory()

Parameters

lpApplicationName LPSTR: A pointer to a character string that contains the application name in the WIN.INI file. This is the string that appears inside the square brackets.

lpKeyName LPSTR: A pointer to the key name in the private .INI file. This is the string to the left of the equal sign.

nDefault int: The default value to return if the *lpKeyName* match is not found.

Example This example, illustrated in Figure 20-8, writes an integer and a string constant to the WIN.INI file on startup. When the user clicks the "Do It!" menu item, the values are retrieved from WIN.INI and displayed on the window's client area.

▷ **The Bottom of the WIN.INI File after Running GENERIC.C**

```
[Generic]
IntValue=358
StringConst=Test string
```

▷ **GENERIC.C WndProc( ) Function**

```
long FAR PASCAL WndProc (HWND hWnd, unsigned iMessage, WORD wParam, LONG lParam)
{
        HDC             hDC ;
        char            cBuf [128], szStringVal [32] ;
        int             nValue ;

        switch (iMessage)                       /* process windows messages */
        {
                case WM_CREATE:
                        WriteProfileString ("Generic", "IntValue", "358") ;
                        WriteProfileString ("Generic", "StringConst",
                                "Test string") ;
                        break ;
                case WM_COMMAND:                /* process menu items */
                        switch (wParam)
                        {
                        case IDM_DOIT:          /* User hit the "Do it" menu item */
                                hDC = GetDC (hWnd) ;
                                nValue = GetProfileInt ("Generic", "IntValue", -1) ;
                                GetProfileString ("Generic", "StringConst",
                                        "<none>", szStringVal, 32) ;
                                TextOut (hDC, 0, 0, cBuf, wsprintf (cBuf,
                                        "Integer = %d, String = %s", nValue,
                                                (LPSTR) szStringVal)) ;
                                ReleaseDC (hWnd, hDC) ;
                                break ;
```

[Other program lines]

GetProfileString
■ Win 2.0   ■ Win 3.0   ■ Win 3.1

Purpose   Retrieves a character string from the WIN.INI file.

Syntax   int **GetProfileString**(LPSTR *lpApplicationName*, LPSTR *lpKeyName*, LPSTR *lpDefault*, LPSTR *lpReturnedString*, int *nSize*);

Description   Windows uses the WIN.INI file to initialize applications. With Windows 3.0, support is provided for both private initialization files and the general file WIN.INI. WIN.INI should be used for programs that have settings that impact more than one application. Private profile files should be used for initialization data that only impacts one application. GetProfileString() reads a character string from WIN.INI. The value is assumed to be in a file with the format

```
[application name]
keyname = string
```

Uses   Useful both for reading strings associated with an application and strings that Windows reads on startup (for example, device=PCL / HP LaserJet,HPPCL,LPT1:).

Returns   int, the number of characters copied to the *lpReturnedString* buffer. If the returned string is truncated to fit the *nSize* parameter, only the number of copied characters is returned.

See Also   GetProfileInt(), WriteProfileString(), GetWindowsDirectory()

Parameters

lpApplicationName LPSTR: A pointer to a character string that contains the application name in the WIN.INI file. This is the string that appears inside the square brackets.

lpKeyName   LPSTR: A pointer to the key name in the WIN.INI file. This is the string to the left of the equal sign. If *lpKeyName* is set to NULL, all of the key names are copied to the buffer pointed to by *lpReturnedString*.

lpDefault   LPSTR: The default string to return if the *lpKeyName* match is not found.

lpReturnedString LPSTR: A pointer to a character buffer to hold the returned string. The buffer must be at least *nSize* bytes long.

nSize   int: The maximum number of characters to copy to *lpReturnedString*.

Example   See the previous example under the GetProfileInt() function description.

GetSystemDirectory
□ Win 2.0   ■ Win 3.0   ■ Win 3.1

Purpose   Determines the path name of the Windows system directory.

Syntax   WORD **GetSystemDirectory**(LPSTR *lpBuffer*,WORD *nSize*);

Description   The system directory contains the Windows driver files and the dynamic link libraries that Windows uses to load the GDI and Kernel functions. Depending on how Windows was installed, this directory can be on different drives and can have different names. The full path name of the system directory is copied to the buffer pointed to by *lpBuffer*. The path name will not include the terminating backslash (\) character unless the system directory is the root directory.

Uses   Programs that install drivers should add them to the system subdirectory.

Returns   WORD, the number of characters written to the buffer pointed to by *lpBuffer*.

See Also   GetWindowsDirectory()

Parameters

lpBuffer   LPSTR: A pointer to a character buffer that holds the directory name. This buffer must be at least *nSize* bytes long.

nSize	int: The maximum number of characters to copy to the buffer pointed to by *lpBuffer*.
Example	The system directory is written to the window's client area when the user clicks the "Do It!" menu item, as shown in Figure 20-9.

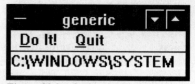

*Figure 20-9. GetSystemDirectory()
Example.*

```
Long FAR PASCAL WndProc (HWND hWnd, unsigned iMessage, WORD wParam, LONG lParam)
{
        HDC             hDC ;
        char            cBuf [128] ;

        switch (iMessage)                       /* process windows messages */
        {
                case WM_COMMAND:                /* process menu items */
                        switch (wParam)
                        {
                        case IDM_DOIT:          /* User hit the "Do it" menu item */
                                hDC = GetDC (hWnd) ;
                                GetSystemDirectory (cBuf, 128) ;
                                TextOut (hDC, 0, 0, cBuf, lstrlen (cBuf)) ;
                                ReleaseDC (hWnd, hDC) ;
                                break ;
```

[Other program lines]

GetTempDrive   ■ Win 2.0   ■ Win 3.0   ■ Win 3.1

Purpose	Determines which drive to use for temporary files.
Syntax	BYTE **GetTempDrive**(BYTE *cDriveLetter*);
Description	This function is used with GetTempFileName() to create temporary files. The drive letter returned is the first hard disk drive letter, if the system has one.
Uses	Temporary files can be used to store memory data if the system becomes low on memory.
Returns	BYTE, the drive letter as an ASCII character.
See Also	GetTempFileName()
Parameters	
cDriveLetter	BYTE: If zero, the function will return the drive letter for the disk drive that Windows is running on (usually the fastest drive). If an ASCII letter, the function will return the next hard disk drive letter, starting with the *cDriveLetter* drive.
Example	This example, which is illustrated in Figure 20-10, creates a temporary file and writes a character string to it. When the user clicks the "Do It!" menu item, the file is read and its contents are displayed on the window's client area.

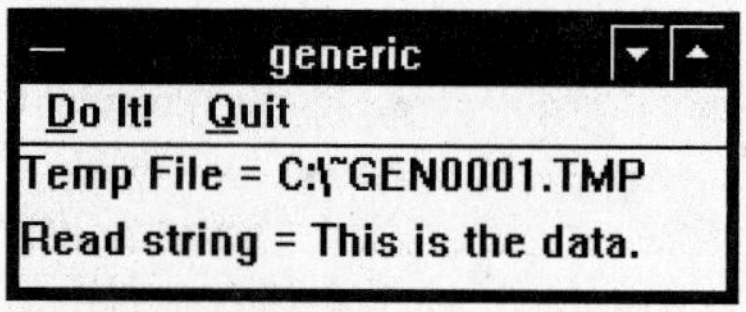

*Figure 20-10. GetTempDrive()
Example.*

```
Long FAR PASCAL WndProc (HWND hWnd, unsigned iMessage, WORD wParam, LONG lParam)
{
        HDC                     hDC ;
        static          char    szTempFile [144], cData [] = {"This is the data."} ;
        char                    cBuf [128], cReadBuf [64] ;
        BYTE                    cDriveLetter ;
        HANDLE                  hFileHandle ;
        int                     nStatus, nFileLong ;

        switch (iMessage)                       /* process windows messages */
```

```
        {
                case WM_CREATE:
                        cDriveLetter = GetTempDrive (O) ;
                        GetTempFileName (cDriveLetter | TF_FORCEDRIVE,
                                "GEN", 1, szTempFile) ;
                        hFileHandle = _lcreat (szTempFile, 0) ;
                        nStatus = _lwrite (hFileHandle, cData, lstrlen (cData)) ;
                        if (nStatus != -1 && hFileHandle != -1)
                                _lclose (hFileHandle) ;
                        else
                                MessageBox (hWnd, "Could not open temp file.",
                                        "File Error", MB_OK) ;
                        break ;
                case WM_COMMAND:                    /* process menu items */
                        switch (wParam)
                        {
                        case IDM_DOIT:              /* User hit the "Do it" menu item */
                                hDC = GetDC (hWnd) ;
                                hFileHandle = _lopen (szTempFile, OF_READ) ;
                                if (hFileHandle != -1)
                                {                       /* find file length */
                                        nFileLong = (int) _llseek (hFileHandle, OL, 2) ;
                                                        /* return to beginning */
                                        _llseek (hFileHandle, OL, 0) ;
                                                        /* read the data into cReadBuf */
                                        _lread (hFileHandle, (LPSTR) cReadBuf,
                                                nFileLong) ;
                                        _lclose (hFileHandle) ;
                                }
                                TextOut (hDC, 0, 0, cBuf, wsprintf (cBuf,
                                        "Temp File = %s", (LPSTR) szTempFile)) ;
                                TextOut (hDC, 0, 20, cBuf, wsprintf (cBuf,
                                        "Read string = %s", (LPSTR) cReadBuf)) ;
                                ReleaseDC (hWnd, hDC) ;
                                break ;
                        case IDM_QUIT:              /* send end of application message */
                                DestroyWindow (hWnd) ;
                                break ;
                        }
                        break ;
                case WM_DESTROY:                    /* stop application */
                        PostQuitMessage (0) ;
                        break ;
                default:                            /* default windows message processing */
                        return DefWindowProc (hWnd, iMessage, wParam, lParam) ;
        }
        return (OL) ;
}
```

GetTempFileName

■ Win 2.0　　■ Win 3.0　　■ Win 3.1

Purpose	Creates a unique, temporary file name.
Syntax	int **GetTempFileName**(BYTE *cDriveLetter*, LPSTR *lpPrefixString*, WORD *wUnique*, LPSTR *lpTempFileName*);
Description	This function generates a unique temporary file name that the application can use to store data. The file name will include the full path name in the form

drive:\path\filename.tmp

The path will either be the root directory (eg. ,C:\) or the path name specified by the TEMP environment variable. Environment variables are created from DOS using the SET command (eg., SET TEMP=C:\TEMP).

Uses	Temporary files can be used to store memory data if the system becomes low on memory.

Returns	int, a unique numeric value used in the temporary file name. If *wUnique* was set to a nonzero value, that value will be returned.
See Also	GetTempDrive()
Parameters	
cDriveLetter	BYTE: The drive letter as an ASCII character. If zero, the default drive is used. Use GetTempDrive() to determine the best drive to use.
	Windows will ignore the *cDriveLetter* drive specification unless there is no hard disk. To force the selection of drive *cDriveLetter*, OR the drive letter with TF_FORCEDRIVE using the C language binary OR operator (|). This sets the high-order bit to one.
lpPrefixString	LPSTR: A pointer to a character string with which to start the temporary file. The characters must be from the OEM character set. Use AnsiToOem() to convert the string if the prefix is based on the default Windows character set (ANSI). Normally, only two or three characters are supplied to leave room for the unique file name numbers.
wUnique	WORD: Specifies an unsigned integer. If nonzero, the function will use *wUnique* to create a file name. If *wUnique* is zero, GetTempFileName() forms a unique file name from the system time. If a file with that name exists, the value is incremented until a unique file name is found. The file is then created and closed. This is the only case where GetTempFileName() creates a file.
lpTempFileName	LPSTR: A pointer to a memory buffer to hold the temporary file name. The buffer should be at least 144 bytes long. The characters written to the buffer will use the OEM character set.
Example	See the previous example under the GetTempDrive() function description.

GETWINDOWSDIRECTORY

☐ Win 2.0 ■ Win 3.0 ■ Win 3.1

Purpose	Determines the path name of the Windows directory.
Syntax	WORD **GetWindowsDirectory**(LPSTR *lpBuffer*,WORD *nSize*);
Description	The Windows subdirectory contains WIN.COM and WIN.INI. Depending on how Windows was installed; this directory can be on different drives and have different names. The full path name of the Windows directory is copied to the buffer pointed to by *lpBuffer*. The path name will not include the terminating backslash (\) character unless the system directory is the root directory.
Uses	The Windows subdirectory is frequently where applications install dynamic link library files (DLLs).
Returns	WORD, the number of characters written to the buffer pointed to by *lpBuffer*.
See Also	GetSystemDirectory()
Parameters	
lpBuffer	LPSTR: A pointer to a character buffer to hold the directory name. This buffer must be at least *nSize* bytes long.
nSize	int: The maximum number of characters to copy to the buffer pointed to by *lpBuff*.
Example	The Windows subdirectory is displayed in the client area when the user clicks the "Do It!" menu item, as shown in Figure 20-11.

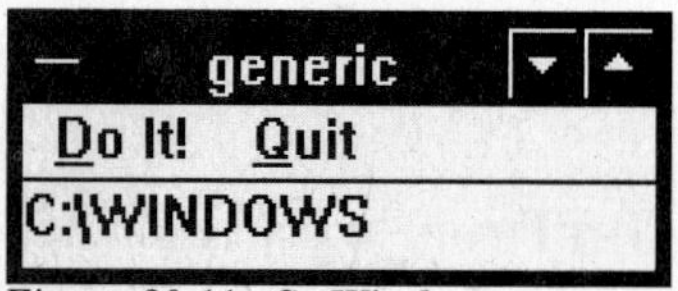

Figure 20-11. GetWindows-Directory() Example.

```
Long FAR PASCAL WndProc (HWND hWnd, unsigned iMessage, WORD wParam, LONG lParam)
{
        HDC             hDC ;
        char            cBuf [128] ;

        switch (iMessage)                               /* process windows messages */
        {
                case WM_COMMAND:                        /* process menu items */
```

```
                        switch (wParam)
                        {
                        case IDM_DOIT:              /* User hit the "Do it" menu item */
                                hDC = GetDC (hWnd) ;
                                GetWindowsDirectory (cBuf, 128) ;
                                TextOut (hDC, 0, 0, cBuf, lstrlen (cBuf)) ;
                                ReleaseDC (hWnd, hDC) ;
                                break ;
```

[Other program lines]

_LCLOSE   ■ Win 2.0   ■ Win 3.0   ■ Win 3.1

Purpose	Closes a disk file.
Syntax	int **_lclose**(int *hFile*);
Description	This function closes a disk file opened with either _lcreat(), _lopen(), or OpenFile(). As soon as it is closed, the file handle becomes invalid. The file cannot be read from or written to until it is reopened.
Uses	Files should be closed as soon as possible after they are created or opened. Doing so avoids having the application terminate without closing the file.
Returns	int, zero if the file was closed, –1 on error.
See Also	_lopen(), _lcreat(), OpenFile()

Parameters

hFile   int: The file handle. This is an integer value that DOS returns when a file is opened or created. The value is obtained by calling either _lopen(), _lcreat(), or OpenFile().

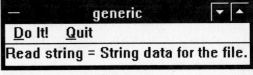

Figure 20-12. _lclose( ) Example.

Example   When the WM_CREATE message is processed, the file MYFILE.TXT is created on the default drive and directory. A character string is written to the file. When the user clicks the "Do It!" menu item, the file is read. The file contents are written to the window's client area, as shown in Figure 20-12.

```
long FAR PASCAL WndProc (HWND hWnd, unsigned iMessage, WORD wParam, LONG lParam)
{
        HDC                     hDC ;
        static          char    cData [] = {"String data for the file."} ;
        char                    cBuf [128], cReadBuf [64] ;
        int                     hFileHandle ;
        int                     nFileLong ;

        switch (iMessage)                       /* process windows messages */
        {
                case WM_CREATE:
                        hFileHandle = _lcreat ("MYFILE.TXT", 0) ;
                        if (hFileHandle != -1)
                        {
                                _lwrite (hFileHandle, cData, lstrlen (cData) + 1) ;
                                _lclose (hFileHandle) ;
                        }
                        else
                                MessageBox (hWnd, "Could not open temp file.",
                                        "File Error", MB_OK) ;
                        break ;
                case WM_COMMAND:                        /* process menu items */
                        switch (wParam)
                        {
                        case IDM_DOIT:              /* User hit the "Do it" menu item */
                                hDC = GetDC (hWnd) ;
```

```
                                        hFileHandle = _lopen ("MYFILE.TXT", OF_READ) ;
                                        if (hFileHandle != -1)
                                        {                   /* find file length */
                                                nFileLong = (int) _llseek (hFileHandle, OL, 2) ;
                                                            /* return to beginning */
                                                _llseek (hFileHandle, OL, 0) ;
                                                            /* read the data into cReadBuf */
                                                _lread (hFileHandle, (LPSTR) cReadBuf,
                                                        nFileLong) ;
                                                _lclose (hFileHandle) ;
                                        }
                                        TextOut (hDC, 0, 0, cBuf, wsprintf (cBuf,
                                                "Read string = %s", (LPSTR) cReadBuf)) ;
                                        ReleaseDC (hWnd, hDC) ;
                                        break ;
                                case IDM_QUIT:
                                        DestroyWindow (hWnd) ;
                                        break ;
                        }
                        break ;
                case WM_DESTROY:                        /* stop application */
                        PostQuitMessage (0) ;
                        break ;
                default:                                /* default windows message processing */
                        return DefWindowProc (hWnd, iMessage, wParam, lParam) ;
        }
        return (OL) ;
}
```

_LCREAT   ■ Win 2.0   ■ Win 3.0   ■ Win 3.1

Purpose	Creates a new disk file.
Syntax	int **_lcreat**(LPSTR *lpPathName*, int *iAttribute*);
Description	This function creates a new file if the specified file name does not already exist. If the file already exists, the file is opened and truncated to zero bytes.
Uses	This is the standard way to create a new disk file. OpenFile() is an alternative, if information about the file (date, full path name) is needed.
Returns	int, the MS-DOS file handle for the file. Returns –1 on error.
See Also	OpenFile(), _lclose()
Parameters	
lpPathName	LPSTR: A pointer to a null-terminated character string containing the file name. The string must contain characters from the ANSI character set (not the OEM/DOS character set).
iAttribute	int: The DOS file attribute. This should be one of the attributes listed in Table 20-5.

Value	Meaning	⊠
0	Normal. Both reading and writing data is allowed.	
1	Read-only. The file cannot be opened for writing data.	
2	Hidden. Not shown on a directory list.	
3	System. Not shown on a directory list.	

Table 20-5. DOS File Attributes.

Example	See the example under the _lclose() function description.

_LLSEEK

Purpose	Moves to a new location in a disk file.
Syntax	LONG _llseek(int *hFile*, long *lOffset*, int *iOrigin*);
Description	_llseek() repositions a pointer in a file that was previously opened with either _lcreat(), _lopen(), or OpenFile(). The pointer marks the position at which the next _lread() and _lwrite() function calls will start.
Uses	This function is the basis for all random-access file operations. The function can also be used to determine the length of a file.
Returns	LONG, the offset in bytes from the beginning of the file to the file position pointer. The pointer points to the location at which the next _lread() and _lwrite() operations will begin.
See Also	_lopen(), _lread(), _lwrite(), _lclose()
Parameters	
hFile	int: The file handle. This is an integer value that DOS returns when a file is opened or created. The value is obtained by calling _lopen(), _lcreat(), or OpenFile().
lOffset	LONG: The number of bytes the pointer is to be moved.
iOrigin	int: The starting position or direction to move the pointer. This can be any of the values listed in Table 20-6.

Value	Meaning ⊠
0	Moves the file pointer *lOffset* bytes from the beginning of the file. Setting both *lOffset* and *iOrigin* to zero moves the pointer to the beginning of the file.
1	Moves the file pointer *lOffset* bytes from the current position in the file.
2	Moves the file pointer *lOffset* bytes from the end of the file.

Table 20-6. _llseek( ) Position Values.

Example	See the example under the _lclose() function description.

_LOPEN

Purpose	Opens a file for reading or writing data.
Syntax	int _lopen(LPSTR *lpPathName*, int *iReadWrite*);
Description	This is the normal function for opening an existing file for reading or writing data. OpenFile() can be used as an alternative if additional information is needed about the file (date created, etc.). Use _lcreat() to create a file for the first time.
Uses	Called before _lread() or _lwrite() can be used to read or write data in the file.
Returns	int, the MS-DOS file handle for the file. Returns –1 on error, such as the file not being found.
See Also	OpenFile(), _lread(), _lwrite()
Parameters	
lpPathName	LPSTR: A pointer to a null-terminated character string containing the file name. The string must contain characters from the ANSI character set (not the OEM/DOS character set).
iReadWrite	int: Specifies how the file is to be accessed. This can be any combination of the values in Table 20-7, combined with the C language binary OR operator (|).

Value	Meaning	⊠
OF_READ	The file is opened for reading only.	
OF_READWRITE	The file is opened for reading and writing.	
OF_SHARE_COMPAT	The file can be opened by any number of applications at the same time. The function will fail (return −1) if the file has been opened previously with a different mode. This is called "compatibility mode."	
OF_SHARE_DENY_NONE	The file can be opened by any number of applications at the same time. The function will fail (return −1) if the file has been opened previously in compatibility mode using OF_SHARE_COMPAT.	
OF_SHARE_DENY_READ	Opens the file and denies other applications read access. The function will fail (return −1) if the file has been opened by another application for read access, or in compatibility mode using OF_SHARE_COMPAT.	
OF_SHARE_DENY_WRITE	Opens the file and denies other applications write access. The function will fail (return −1) if the file has been opened by another application for write access, or in compatibility mode using OF_SHARE_COMPAT.	
OF_SHARE_EXCLUSIVE	Opens the file and denies other applications read or write access. The function will fail (return−1) if the file has been opened by another application or opened previously by the same application.	
OF_WRITE	Opens the file for writing only.	

Table 20-7. _lopen( ) Access Values.

Example   See the example under the _lclose() function description.

_LREAD
■ Win 2.0   ■ Win 3.0   ■ Win 3.1

Purpose   Reads data from a disk file.

Syntax   int **_lread**(int *hFile*, LPSTR *lpBuffer*, int *wBytes*);

Description This function reads data from a disk file starting at the current file position pointer. When a file is initially opened by _lopen() or OpenFile(), the file pointer is set to the beginning of the file. As data is read using _lread(), the pointer moves forward by the number of bytes read. The pointer can be repositioned in the file by calling _llseek().

Returns   int, the number of bytes actually read from the file. Returns −1 on error. The returned value may be less than *wBytes* if the end-of-file is detected during the read process.

See Also   _lopen(), OpenFile(), _lclose()

Parameters

hFile   int: The file handle. This is an integer value that DOS returns when a file is opened or created. The value is obtained by calling _lopen() or OpenFile().

lpBuffer   LPSTR: A pointer to a memory buffer to hold the data read from the disk file. The buffer must be at least *wBytes* in length.

wBytes   WORD: The number of bytes to read from the disk file.

Example   See the example under the _lclose() function description.

_LWRITE
■ Win 2.0   ■ Win 3.0   ■ Win 3.1

Purpose   Writes data to a disk file.

Syntax   int **_lwrite**(int *hFile*, LPSTR *lpBuffer*, int *wBytes*);

Description   This function writes data from a disk file starting at the current file position pointer. When a file is initially opened by _lopen(), _lcreat(), or OpenFile(), the file pointer is set to the beginning of the file. As data is written using _lwrite(), the pointer moves forward by the number of bytes written. The pointer can be repositioned in the file by calling _llseek().

Returns   int, the number of bytes written to the file. Returns −1 on error.

See Also   _lopen(), _lcreat(), OpenFile(), _lclose()

Parameters

hFile   int: The file handle. This is an integer value that DOS returns when a file is opened or created. The value is obtained by calling _lopen(), _lcreat(), or OpenFile().

lpBuffer   LPSTR: A pointer to a memory buffer that contains the data to be written to the disk file.

wBytes   WORD: The number of bytes to write to the disk file.

Example   See the example under the _lclose() function description.

OPENFILE

■ Win 2.0   ■ Win 3.0   ■ Win 3.1

Purpose   Creates, opens, or deletes files.

Syntax   int **OpenFile**(LPSTR *lpFileName*, LPOFSTRUCT *lpReOpenBuf*, WORD *wStyle*);

Description   This function combines a number of more primitive file initiation functions (such as _lcreat() and _lopen()) into a single powerful function. The function uses the OFSTRUCT data structure defined in WINDOWS.H as follows:

```
typedef struct tagOFSTRUCT
  {
   BYTE         cBytes;                    /* Length of OF struct */
   BYTE         fFixedDisk;                /* non-zero if fixed drive */
   WORD         nErrCode;                  /* MS DOS error code */
   BYTE         reserved[4];               /* file date and time */
   BYTE         szPathName[128];           /* full path name and */
                                           /* file name (OEM chars) */

  } OFSTRUCT;
typedef OFSTRUCT                  *POFSTRUCT;
typedef OFSTRUCT NEAR             *NPOFSTRUCT;
typedef OFSTRUCT FAR              *LPOFSTRUCT;
```

    OpenFile() includes options that will create a simple dialog box to display error messages automatically.

Uses   This is the standard way to create and/or open a disk file. It is the only direct way to delete a file from within Windows.

Returns   int, the MS-DOS file handle. Returns −1 on error.

See Also   _lopen(), _lclose(), _lcreat()

Parameters

lpFileName   LPSTR: A pointer to a null-terminated character string that contains the name of the disk file. The characters should be from the ANSI (Windows default) character set. If the file name string contains OEM (MS-DOS) characters, use OemToAnsi() to convert the characters to the ANSI character set before calling OpenFile().

lpReOpenBuf   LPSTR: A pointer to an OFSTRUCT data structure. The data fields in this structure will be filled in after OpenFile() has been called.

wStyle   WORD: A flag to determine what OpenFile() is to do. The flag values listed in Table 20-8 can be combined using the C language binary OR operator (|).

Value	Meaning
OF_CANCEL	Only used with the OF_PROMPT style. Adds a Cancel button to the file-not-found dialog box.
OF_CREATE	Creates a new file. If the file already exists, the file is truncated to zero bytes.
OF_DELETE	Deletes a file.
OF_EXIST	Checks if the file exists. The file is opened, and then immediately closed.
OF_PARSE	Fills in the OFSTRUCT data structure, but does not open or close the file. Useful for determining the full path name or file date/time.
OF_PROMPT	Displays a dialog box if the requested file does not exist. The dialog box requests that the user put a disk in drive A and retry. This is seldom a reasonable action.
OF_READ	The file is opened for reading only.
OF_READWRITE	The file is opened for reading and writing.
OF_REOPEN	Opens the file specified in the *szPathName* field of the OFSTRUCT. This assures that the same file is opened that was originally open when OpenFile() was first called. Otherwise, changing default directories could result in changing which of several files with the same name, but residing in different directories, is opened.
OF_SHARE_COMPACT	The file can be opened by any number of applications at the same time. The function will fail (return –1) if the file has been opened previously with a different mode. This is called "compatibility mode."
OF_SHARE_DENY_NONE	The file can be opened by any number of applications at the same time. The function will fail (return –1) if the file has been opened previously in compatibility mode.
OF_SHARE_DENY_READ	Opens the file and denies other applications read access. The function will fail (return–1) if the file has been opened by another application for read access, or opened in compatibility mode.
OF_SHARE_DENY_WRITE	Opens the file and denies other applications write access. The function will fail (return –1) if the file has been opened by another application for write access, or opened in compatibility mode.
OF_SHARE_EXCLUSIVE	Opens the file and denies other applications read or write access. The function will fail (return –1) if the file has been opened by another application or has been opened previously by the same application.
OF_VERIFY	Verifies that the date and time of the file on the disk are the same as the data in the OFSTRUCT data structure. This assumes that OpenFile() has already been called at least once to fill in the data.
OF_WRITE	Opens the file for writing data only.

Table 20-8. OpenFile( ) Flag Values.

Example

This example uses OpenFile() twice. When the WM_CREATE message is processed, the application creates a file called "MYFILE.TMP" using OpenFile(). Ten integers are written to the file. When the user clicks the "Do It!" menu item, OpenFile() is called again to open the file. The ten integers are read into an array, and displayed on the window's client area, as shown in Figure 20-13. SetHandleCount() is also used in this example to allow the application to open as many as 50 files at one time. This maximum is not taken advantage of in this simple example, which only has one file open at a time.

Figure 20-13. OpenFile( ) Example.

```
long FAR PASCAL WndProc (HWND hWnd, unsigned iMessage, WORD wParam, LONG lParam)
{
        HDC                     hDC ;
        OFSTRUCT                of ;
        char                    cBuf [128], cReadBuf [64] ;
        HANDLE                  hFileHandle ;
        int                     i, nStatus, nFileLong, nData [10] ;

        switch (iMessage)                       /* process windows messages */
        {
                case WM_CREATE:
                        nStatus = SetHandleCount (50) ;
                        if (nStatus != 50)
                                MessageBox (hWnd, "Not able to open 50 files.",
                                        "Warning", MB_OK) ;
                        hFileHandle = OpenFile ("MYFILE.TMP", &of,
                                OF_CREATE) ;
                        if (nStatus != -1 && hFileHandle != -1)
                        {
                                for (i = 0 ; i < 10 ; i++)/* write 10 ints */
                                        _lwrite (hFileHandle, (LPSTR) &i,
                                                sizeof (int)) ;
                                _lclose (hFileHandle) ;
                        }
                        else
                                MessageBox (hWnd, "Could not open file.",
                                        "File Error", MB_OK) ;
                        break ;
                case WM_COMMAND:                /* process menu items */
                        switch (wParam)
                        {
                        case IDM_DOIT:          /* User hit the "Do it" menu item */
                                hDC = GetDC (hWnd) ;
                                hFileHandle = OpenFile ("MYFILE.TMP", &of,
                                        OF_READ) ;
                                if (hFileHandle != -1)
                                {               /* find file length in bytes */
                                        nFileLong = (int) _llseek (hFileHandle, 0L, 2) ;
                                                /* return to beginning */
                                        _llseek (hFileHandle, 0L, 0) ;
                                                /* file length in integers */
                                        nFileLong /= sizeof (int) ;
                                                /* read the data into array */
                                        for (i = 0 ; i < nFileLong ; i++)
                                                _lread (hFileHandle, (LPSTR) &nData [i],
                                                        sizeof (int)) ;
                                        _lclose (hFileHandle) ;
                                }
                                TextOut (hDC, 0, 0, "Data Read From Disk", 19) ;
                                for (i = 0 ; i < nFileLong ; i++)
                                        TextOut (hDC, 15 * i, 20, cBuf, wsprintf (cBuf,
                                                "%d", nData [i])) ;
                                ReleaseDC (hWnd, hDC) ;
                                break ;
                        case IDM_QUIT:          /* send end of application message */
                                DestroyWindow (hWnd) ;
                                break ;
                        }
                        break ;
                case WM_DESTROY:                /* stop application */
                        PostQuitMessage (0) ;
                        break ;
                default:                        /* default windows message processing */
                        return DefWindowProc (hWnd, iMessage, wParam, lParam) ;
        }
        return (0L) ;
}
```

SETENVIRONMENT

■ Win 2.0   ■ Win 3.0   ☐ Win 3.1

Purpose	Changes the environment variable settings for a port.
Syntax	int **SetEnvironment**(LPSTR *lpPortName*, LPSTR *lpEnviron*, WORD *nCount*);
Description	Windows maintains a table of environment settings for each of the ports as a part of the GDI (graphics device interface). These settings control the current port configuration, such as the baud rate and parity settings for a serial port.
Uses	Changing the settings of a port. An application can redirect printer output to a disk file by changing the printer port's environment string to a disk file name.
Returns	int, the number of bytes copied to the environment table. Zero on error, –1 if the environment was deleted.
See Also	GetEnvironment(), CreateDC()

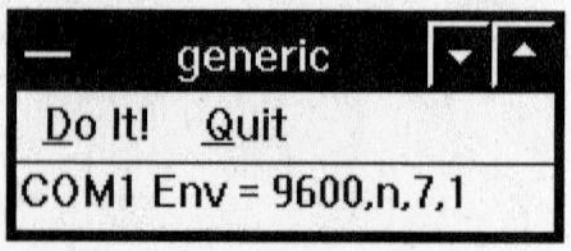

Figure 20-14. SetEnvironment() Example.

Parameters

lpPortName   LPSTR: A pointer to a null-terminated character string containing the port name. Examples are "LPT1" and "COM2."

lpEnviron   LPSTR: A pointer to a null-terminated character string containing the new environment string. The WIN.INI file contains a number of examples of preset values for environment variables.

nCount   WORD: The number of bytes to be copied.

Example   This example, which is illustrated in Figure 20-14, loads and displays the current environment variable settings for the COM1 device when the user clicks the "Do It!" menu item. If none have been set, the port is set to 9600 baud, no parity, 8-bit word length, and one stop bit.

```
Long FAR PASCAL WndProc (HWND hWnd, unsigned iMessage, WORD wParam, LONG lParam)
{
        HDC             hDC ;
        char            cBuf [128], cEnv [64] ;
        int             nEnvChar ;

        switch (iMessage)                       /* process windows messages */
        {
                case WM_COMMAND:                /* process menu items */
                        switch (wParam)
                        {
                        case IDM_DOIT:          /* User hit the "Do it" menu item */
                                nEnvChar = GetEnvironment ("COM1", cEnv, 64) ;
                                hDC = GetDC (hWnd) ;
                                TextOut (hDC, 0, 0, cBuf, wsprintf (cBuf,
                                        "COM1 Env = %s", (LPSTR) cEnv)) ;
                                if (nEnvChar == 0)
                                        SetEnvironment ("COM1", "9600,n,8,1", 10) ;
                                break ;
```

[Other program lines]

SETERRORMODE

■ Win 2.0   ■ Win 3.0   ■ Win 3.1

Purpose	Sets whether or not Windows shows the default critical error message.
Syntax	WORD **SetErrorMode**(WORD *wMode*);
Description	Windows uses MS-DOS for disk functions. DOS sends an INT 24H interrupt when a critical error occurs, such as being unable to read a disk. This is where the dreaded message "Abort, Cancel, Retry?" message comes from under DOS. Windows has its own message box as a default critical error handler. SetErrorMode() allows an application to turn this default message box on and off.
Uses	Usually, the error message box is left on, except when the application is doing file access and has its own error messages.

Returns   WORD, the previous error mode. 0 if Windows was set to display the default critical error message box, 1 if not.

Parameters
wMode   WORD: Set to 1 to shut off the default critical error message box. Set to 0 to turn it on.

Example   This example shuts down the default critical error message box when the WM_CREATE message is processed. When the user clicks the "Do It!" menu item, the application attempts to open a file on the A drive. Assuming that the drive door has been left open, a critical DOS error occurs. The normal Windows warning message box is not shown, so the application can go ahead and show its own error message via the MessageBox() function.

```
Long FAR PASCAL WndProc (HWND hWnd, unsigned iMessage, WORD wParam, LONG lParam)
{
        PAINTSTRUCT              ps ;
        OFSTRUCT                 ofFile ;
        int                      n ;

        switch (iMessage)                       /* process windows messages */
        {
        case WM_CREATE:
                SetErrorMode (1) ;       /* no error message */
                break ;
        case WM_COMMAND:
                switch (wParam)
                {
                case IDM_DOIT:
                        n = OpenFile ("A:Temp", &ofFile, OF_READ) ;
                        if (n == -1)
                                MessageBox (hWnd,
                                        "Could not read file on drive A:",
                                        "File Problem", MB_ICONHAND | MB_OK) ;
                        break ;
```
[Other program lines]

SETHANDLECOUNT   ☐ Win 2.0   ■ Win 3.0   ■ Win 3.1

Purpose   Changes the number of files an application can have open at once.

Syntax   WORD **SetHandleCount**(WORD *wNumber*);

Description   The default number of files an application can have open at one time is 20. SetHandleCount() allows this number to increase to any number up to 255.

Uses   Useful in disk-intensive applications, such as database programs.

Returns   WORD, the number of files that can actually be opened at one time. This may be less than *wNumber* if MS-DOS runs out of file handle space.

See Also   OpenFile()

Parameters
wNumber   WORD: The desired number of files that can be open at one time. The maximum is 255.

Example   See the example under the OpenFile() function description.

WRITEPRIVATEPROFILESTRING   ☐ Win 2.0   ■ Win 3.0   ■ Win 3.1

Purpose   Copies a character string to an application's private profile (.INI) file.

Syntax   BOOL **WritePrivateProfileString**(LPSTR *lpApplicationName*, LPSTR *lpKeyName*, LPSTR *lpString*, LPSTR *lpFileName*);

Description   The best way for a program to "remember" user preferences, such as subdirectory names, is to write them to an initialization file. For items that may affect more than one application, this should be the main WIN.INI file. For items that will affect only the application itself, this should be a private .INI file. WritePrivateProfileString() writes a character string. The string is assumed to be in a file with the format

```
[application name]
keyname = string
```

The file is assumed to be in the Windows subdirectory (the subdirectory containing WIN.EXE). A different subdirectory can be specified by using the full path name for *lpFileName*. If the file is not found, a new one is created. If the application name is not found in the file, *lpApplicationName* is written to the file and enclosed in square brackets. If *lpKeyName* is not found, it is written to the file, followed by an equal sign.

Uses	Writing and updating the application's private .INI file. The values written in the .INI file can be both character strings and numeric values. Integer values are written using the numeric characters as a string (eg., "124").
Returns	BOOL. TRUE if the function is successful, FALSE on error.
See Also	GetPrivateProfileInt(), GetPrivateProfileString()

Parameters

lpApplicationName	LPSTR: A pointer to a character string that contains the application name in the private .INI file. This is the string that appears inside the square brackets.
lpKeyName	LPSTR: A pointer to the key name in the private .INI file. This is the string to the left of the equal sign. If *lpKeyName* is set to NULL, the entire section starting with *lpApplicationName* is deleted. Comment lines (starting with a semicolon) are not deleted.
lpString	LPSTR: The string value to write to the right of the equal sign. If *lpString* is NULL, the entire line starting with *lpKeyName* is deleted.
lpFileName	LPSTR: A pointer to a character string containing the private .INI file name. The file is assumed to be in the Windows subdirectory unless a path name is include with the file name in *lpFileName*.
Example	See the example under the GetPrivateProfileInt() function description.

WRITEPROFILESTRING
■ Win 2.0   ■ Win 3.0   ■ Win 3.1

Purpose	Writes an entry to the WIN.INI file.
Syntax	BOOL **WriteProfileString**(LPSTR *lpApplicationName*, LPSTR *lpKeyName*, LPSTR *lpString*);
Description	The best way for a program to "remember" user preferences, such as subdirectory names, is to write them to an initialization file. For items that may affect more than one application, this should be the main WIN.INI file. For items that will affect only the application itself, this should be a private .INI file. WriteProfileString() writes a character string in WIN.INI. The string is assumed to be written with the format

```
[application name]
keyname = string
```

WIN.INI is assumed to be in the Windows subdirectory (the subdirectory containing WIN.EXE). A different subdirectory can be specified by using the full path name for *lpFileName*. If the application name is not found, *lpApplicationName* is written to the file, and enclosed in square brackets. If *lpKeyName* is not found, it is written to the file, and followed by an equal sign.

Uses	Most often used as an application, to remember user settings, and file names. The value written to the .INI file can be either character strings or numeric values. Integer values are written to WIN.INI by writing the numeric characters in a string (eg., "124").

Returns   BOOL. TRUE if the function is successful, FALSE on error.

See Also   GetProfileInt(), GetProfileString(), GetWindowsDirectory()

Parameters

lpApplicationName LPSTR: A pointer to a character string that contains the application name in the WIN.INI file. This is the string that appears inside the square brackets.

lpKeyName   LPSTR: A pointer to the key name in the WIN.INI file. This is the string to the left of the equal sign. If *lpKeyName* is set to NULL, the entire section starting with *lpApplicationName* is deleted. Comment lines (starting with a semicolon) are not deleted.

lpString   LPSTR: The string value to write to the right of the equal sign. If *lpString* is NULL, the entire line starting with *lpKeyName* is deleted.

Example   See the example under the GetProfileInt() function description.

Windows programs need to be able to communicate with external devices. The most common device is a printer. This specialized requirement is well supported in Windows, as described in Chapter 10, *Device Contexts, Text Output, and Printing*. Other important external devices are communications equipment, such as modems and instrumentation that may be connected to the computer via serial or parallel communications lines. Because of the wide range of external devices that can be connected to a computer, Windows cannot provide high-level support for every piece of equipment. Instead, the function library contains 16 low-level functions that provide the programmer with the basic tools for dealing with any device.

Communications Support

Communications support is not a trivial matter for Windows. Consider the case of a communications program that sends and receives data via a modem attached to the computer's serial port. The data from the modem arrives slowly (relative to the internal clock speed of the computer) and can arrive at any time. If the Windows program simply looped, checking for incoming data bytes, the program would take over the Windows environment. No other application could get the input focus. This violates the basic principle behind the structure of all Windows programs, which must give up control of the environment frequently to allow other programs to run.

To get around this problem, the Windows function library includes interrupt-driven communications support. When the communications device receives an input byte, it generates a hardware interrupt. The interrupt briefly halts whatever application is running and stores the input byte in a memory buffer. Control is then immediately given back to Windows.

The memory buffer is called the "receive data queue." The data bytes accumulate in the queue as they are received. When a Windows communications application wants to read the incoming data, it reads the receive queue data. Data to be transmitted is also stored in a buffer before being sent to the communications device. This buffer is called the "transmit data queue."

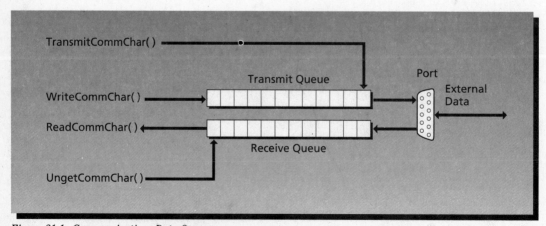

Figure 21-1. Communications Data Queues.

Figure 21-1 shows the organization of communications functions and data queues. The OpenComm() function opens up a communications link to an external device, such as a serial port, and sets up the transmit and receive data queues. Only one application can open a device at one time. The application retains control of the device until CloseComm() is called. The application that has control of the device uses the WriteComm() function to send data to the device, and uses ReadComm() to read data received from the device. In both cases, the data is buffered via the data queues. For example, calling WriteComm() places the data in the transmit queue. Windows will send the data to the device when the device completes sending bytes already in the transmit queue.

Two functions are provided which allow the normal first-in, first-out processing of data in the queues to be by-passed. TransmitCommChar() makes a character become the next character sent, which is useful for sending special control sequences, such as escape sequences. UngetCommChar() puts a character at the beginning of the receive queue. This character will be the next character read. This is convenient for programming applications that have multiple functions for processing incoming data.

Reading Data in the Receive Data Queue

As previously mentioned, the communications program cannot simply loop forever, checking for data in the data queues. The application must continually give up control to Windows so that other applications can run. There are two approaches to checking the data queues from within a Windows program. The simplest way is to use a timer. The Windows timer can be set to generate a WM_TIMER message on a frequency of perhaps ten times per second. Each time the WM_TIMER message is processed by the application, the receive data queue can be checked with ReadComm() to look for data.

Although the timer approach will work, it is not the best way to design a communications program. A better way to write a communications program is to use a PeekMessage() loop for the program's main message loop. Peek-Message() takes control if no other application is requesting it. This approach allows the communications program to continually check the receive data queue in the "gaps" when other Windows applications are not active. The example programs under the function descriptions in this chapter all use the PeekMessage() approach.

Writing a complete communications program requires an understanding of the several protocols in use for transmitting and receiving data. A good source of information is *Practical Digital and Data Communications* by Paul Bates (Prentice-Hall, 1987). This book covers both serial and parallel communications.

Communications Function Summary

Table 21-1 summarizes the Windows communication support functions. The detailed function descriptions are in the next section.

Function	Purpose	⊠
BuildCommDCB	Converts a command string in DOS MODE command format to fill the fields in a Device Control Block (DCB).	
ClearCommBreak	Clears a communications device break state, restoring operation.	
CloseComm	Closes a communications device.	
EscapeCommFunction	Sets a communications device extended function.	
FlushComm	Clears all data in a communications queue.	
GetCommError	Determines the error status of a communications port, and clears the error.	
GetCommEventMask	Determines which communication event has occurred.	
GetCommState	Determines the current settings of a communications device.	
OpenComm	Opens a communications device (port) and allocates memory for the input and output data queues.	
ReadComm	Reads data from an open communications device.	
SetCommBreak	Temporarily suspends operation of a communications device.	
SetCommEventMask	Sets which communications events are enabled.	

Figure 21-1. continued

Function	Purpose	
SetCommState	Changes the settings (baud rate, etc.) for a communications device.	
TransmitCommChar	Sends a character to a communications device immediately, bypassing the transmit data queue.	
UngetCommChar	Places a character at the beginning of the receive data queue, bypassing any other characters already in the queue.	
WriteComm	Sends data to a communications device.	

Table 21-1. Communications Function Summary.

Communications Function Descriptions

This section contains the detailed descriptions of the Windows communication functions.

BUILDCOMMDCB
■ Win 2.0   ■ Win 3.0   ■ Win 3.1

Purpose   Converts a command string in DOS MODE command format to fill the fields in a Device Control Block (DCB).

Syntax   int **BuildCommDCB**(LPSTR *lpDef*, DCB FAR * *lpDCB*);

Description   The SetCommState() function requires that the configuration data for the communications port (baud rate, parity, etc.) be stored in a data structure of type DCB. BuildCommDCB() provides a convenient way to set the DCB elements based on a character string. The character string must be in the format used by the DOS MODE command. The DCB data structure is defined in WINDOWS.H as:

```
typedef struct tagDCB          /* device control block (DCB) */
  {
  BYTE Id;                     /* Internal Device ID    */
  WORD BaudRate;               /* Baudrate at which runing */
  BYTE ByteSize;               /* Number of bits/byte, 4-8    */
  BYTE Parity;                 /* 0-4=None,Odd,Even,Mark,Space */
  BYTE StopBits;               /* 0,1,2 = 1, 1.5, 2    */
  WORD RlsTimeout;             /* Timeout for RLSD to be set */
  WORD CtsTimeout;             /* Timeout for CTS to be set    */
  WORD DsrTimeout;             /* Timeout for DSR to be set    */

  BYTE fBinary: 1;             /* Binary Mode (skip EOF check */
  BYTE fRtsDisable:1;          /* Don't assert RTS at init time */
  BYTE fParity: 1;             /* Enable parity checking */
  BYTE fOutxCtsFlow:1;         /* CTS handshaking on output */
  BYTE fOutxDsrFlow:1;         /* DSR handshaking on output */
  BYTE fDummy: 2;              /* Reserved      */
  BYTE fDtrDisable:1;          /* Don't assert DTR at init time */

  BYTE fOutX: 1;               /* Enable output X-ON/X-OFF    */
  BYTE fInX: 1;                /* Enable input X-ON/X-OFF */
  BYTE fPeChar: 1;             /* Enable Parity Err Replacement */
  BYTE fNull: 1;               /* Enable Null stripping  */
  BYTE fChEvt: 1;              /* Enable Rx character event. */
  BYTE fDtrflow: 1;            /* DTR handshake on input */
  BYTE fRtsflow: 1;            /* RTS handshake on input */
  BYTE fDummy2: 1;

  char XonChar;                /* Tx and Rx X-ON character */
  char XoffChar;               /* Tx and Rx X-OFF character    */
  WORD XonLim;                 /* Transmit X-ON threshold    */
  WORD XoffLim;                /* Transmit X-OFF threshold    */
  char PeChar;                 /* Parity error replacement char */
```

```
   char EofChar;                    /* End of Input character */
   char EvtChar;                    /* Recieved Event character */
   WORD TxDelay;                    /* Amount of time between chars */
 } DCB;
```

Note that two groups of the structure's elements are coded bit values, saving space.

Uses   Used prior to SetCommState() to prepare the DCB data.

Returns   int, zero if the *lpDef* string is translated, negative on error.

See Also   SetCommState()

Parameters

lpDef   LPSTR: A pointer to a character string in DOS MODE format. For example the string "com1:1200,e,7,1" establishes the port at 1200 baud, even parity, 7-bit word length, and one stop bit.

lpDCB   DCB FAR *: A pointer to a DCB structure. The structure's elements will be initialized based on the *lpDef* string. It may be necessary to set additional values by directly initializing the DCB elements after BuildCommDCB() has been called.

Example   This example creates a primitive communications program. When the program first starts, COM1 is opened for 1200 baud, even parity, 7-bit word length, and one stop bit. All of the characters the user types show up on the line marked "Out>." Any characters received from COM1 show up on the line marked "In>," including echoed characters. No formatting is done for the characters. Control characters such as CR/LF show up as vertical lines.

Figure 21-2 shows a typical log-on sequence. A Hayes modem is connected to COM1. The Hayes modem command ATDT is used to dial a phone number. Note that the typed characters are

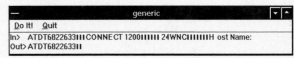

Figure 21-2. Simple Communications Program Example.

echoed on the "In>" line. When a connection is made, the input line begins to show the characters received from the remote computer.

The program uses a PeekMessage() loop for the main program loop. This function allows for periodic checking of the input data queue using ReadComm(). If characters are in the queue, they are copied to the *cInBuf* buffer. A user message numbered WM_USER + 1 is posted to cause the WndProc() function to do the actual output of the received characters.

Within the WndProc() function, the COM1 port is opened when processing the WM_CREATE message. Note that both the input and output data queues are flushed after the port is opened. A combination of BuildCommDCB() and SetCommState() is used to set the port to the desired baud rate, parity, etc. EscapeCommFunction() is demonstrated by sending a reset to the port. This is usually not necessary.

User-typed characters for output to the port are handled by sending each typed character to the port using WriteComm(). The remainder of the logic in WndProc() displays character stings on the window's client area. As soon as 80 characters are collected, the strings are erased and started again. The "Do It!" menu item toggles a temporary break in communications on and off. The communications break state is displayed in the program's window caption. Note that the port is closed by CloseComm() as the program exits.

```
/* generic.c   simple com program example */
#include <windows.h>
#include "generic.h"

static          int       nComID = -1 ;
static          char      cInBuf [256 + 128], cOutBuf [128] ;
```

```
int PASCAL WinMain (HANDLE hInstance, HANDLE hPrevInstance, LPSTR lpszCmdLine, int nCmdShow)
{
        HWND            hWnd ;
        MSG             msg ;
        WNDCLASS        wndclass ;
        COMSTAT         ComStat ;
        char            cBuf [128] ;
        int             i, nReadChars, nStart ;

        ghInstance = hInstance ;
        if (!hPrevInstance)
        {
                wndclass.style          = CS_HREDRAW | CS_VREDRAW ;
                wndclass.lpfnWndProc    = WndProc ;
                wndclass.cbClsExtra     = 0 ;
                wndclass.cbWndExtra     = 0 ;
                wndclass.hInstance      = hInstance ;
                wndclass.hIcon          = LoadIcon (hInstance, gszAppName) ;
                wndclass.hCursor        = LoadCursor (NULL, IDC_ARROW) ;
                wndclass.hbrBackground  = GetStockObject (WHITE_BRUSH) ;
                wndclass.lpszMenuName   = gszAppName ;
                wndclass.lpszClassName  = gszAppName ;

                if (!RegisterClass (&wndclass))
                        return FALSE ;
        }

        hWnd = CreateWindow (                   /* create the program's window here */
                gszAppName,                     /* class name */
                gszAppName,                     /* window name */
                WS_OVERLAPPEDWINDOW,            /* window style */
                CW_USEDEFAULT,                  /* x position on screen */
                CW_USEDEFAULT,                  /* y position on screen */
                CW_USEDEFAULT,                  /* width of window */
                CW_USEDEFAULT,                  /* height of window */
                NULL,                           /* parent window handle (null = none) */
                NULL,                           /* menu handle (null = use class menu) */
                hInstance,                      /* instance handle */
                NULL) ;                         /* lpstr (null = not used) */
        ShowWindow (hWnd, nCmdShow) ;
        UpdateWindow (hWnd) ;

        while (TRUE)                            /* use peek message loop to check com1 */
        {
                if (PeekMessage (&msg, NULL, 0, 0, PM_REMOVE))
                {
                        if (msg.message == WM_QUIT)
                                break ;
                        else
                        {
                                TranslateMessage (&msg) ;
                                DispatchMessage (&msg) ;
                        }
                }
                else if (nComID >= 0)           /* check the com port for data */
                {
                        if ((nReadChars = ReadComm (nComID, cBuf, 128)) > 0)
                        {
                                if ((nStart = lstrlen (cInBuf)) < 80)
                                {                       /* add chars to end of string */
                                        for (i = 0 ; i < nReadChars ; i++)
                                                cInBuf [nStart + i] = cBuf [i] ;
                                        cInBuf [nReadChars + nStart] = 0 ;
                                        PostMessage (msg.hwnd, WM_USER + 1, 0, 0L) ;
                                }
                                else
                                {                       /* start string over */
                                        for (i = 0 ; i < nReadChars ; i++)
```

```
                                        cInBuf [i] = cBuf [i] ;
                                cInBuf [nReadChars] = 0 ;
                                PostMessage (msg.hwnd, WM_USER + 1, 1, OL) ;
                        }
                else
                        GetCommError (nComID, &ComStat) ;
                }
        }
        return msg.wParam ;
}



long FAR PASCAL WndProc (HWND hWnd, unsigned iMessage, WORD wParam, LONG lParam)
{
        PAINTSTRUCT             ps ;
        HDC                     hDC ;
        DCB                     dcb ;
        int                     i, nStatus ;
        char                    cBuf [128] ;
        static          BOOL    bToggle = TRUE ;

        switch (iMessage)
        {
        case WM_CREATE:
                nComID = OpenComm ("COM1", 128, 128) ;
                if (nComID < 0)
                        MessageBox (hWnd, "Could not open COM1", "Warning",
                                MB_OK) ;
                else
                {
                        FlushComm (nComID, 0) ;   /* empty output queue */
                        FlushComm (nComID, 1) ;   /* empty input queue */
                        BuildCommDCB ("com1:1200,e,7,1", &dcb) ;
                        SetCommState (&dcb) ;
                        EscapeCommFunction (nComID, RESETDEV) ;
                        MessageBox (hWnd, "COM1 is open.", "Message",
                                MB_OK) ;
                }
                break ;
        case WM_PAINT:
                BeginPaint (hWnd, &ps) ;
                TextOut (ps.hdc, 0, 0, "In>", 3) ;
                TextOut (ps.hdc, 40, 0, cInBuf, lstrlen (cInBuf)) ;
                TextOut (ps.hdc, 0, 20, "Out>", 4) ;
                TextOut (ps.hdc, 40, 20, cOutBuf, lstrlen (cOutBuf)) ;
                EndPaint (hWnd, &ps) ;
                break ;
        case WM_COMMAND:                /* process menu items */
                switch (wParam)
                {
                case IDM_DOIT:
                        if (bToggle)
                        {
                                bToggle = FALSE ;
                                SetCommBreak (nComID) ;
                                SetWindowText (hWnd, "Comm Break") ;
                        }
                        else
                        {
                                bToggle = TRUE ;
                                ClearCommBreak (nComID) ;
                                SetWindowText (hWnd, "Comm Open") ;
                        }
                        break ;
                case IDM_QUIT:          /* send end of application message */
                        DestroyWindow (hWnd) ;
                        break ;
```

```
                }
                break ;
        case WM_CHAR:                   /* user typed a char */
                if (nComID >= 0)
                {
                        nStatus = WriteComm (nComID,
                                (LPSTR) &wParam, 1) ;
                        if (nStatus < 0)
                                MessageBox (hWnd, "Output comm error.",
                                        "Message", MB_OK) ;
                        else
                        {
                                i = lstrlen (cOutBuf) ;
                                if (i > 80)/* don't overflow line size */
                                {
                                        cOutBuf [0] = (char) wParam ;
                                        cOutBuf [1] = 0 ;
                                        InvalidateRect (hWnd, NULL, TRUE) ;
                                }
                                else    /* added char to end of typed string */
                                {
                                        cOutBuf [i] = (char) wParam ;
                                        cOutBuf [i + 1] = 0 ;
                                        hDC = GetDC (hWnd) ;
                                        TextOut (hDC, 40, 20, cOutBuf,
                                                lstrlen (cOutBuf)) ;
                                        ReleaseDC (hWnd, hDC) ;
                                }

                        }
                }
                else
                        MessageBox (hWnd, "Click Do It! to connect.",
                                "Message", MB_OK) ;
                break ;
        case WM_USER + 1:               /* need to update screen from input */
                switch (wParam)
                {
                        case 0:         /* input chars added to end of string */
                        hDC = GetDC (hWnd) ;
                        TextOut (hDC, 40, 0, cInBuf, lstrlen (cInBuf)) ;
                        ReleaseDC (hWnd, hDC ) ;
                        break ;
                        case 1:         /* started string over from start */
                        InvalidateRect (hWnd, NULL, TRUE) ;
                        break ;
                }
                break ;
        case WM_DESTROY:                /* stop application */
                CloseComm (nComID) ;
                PostQuitMessage (0) ;
                break ;
        default:                        /* default windows message processing */
                return DefWindowProc (hWnd, iMessage, wParam, lParam) ;
        }
        return (0L) ;
}
```

ClearCommBreak   ■ Win 2.0   ■ Win 3.0   ■ Win 3.1

Purpose	Clears a communications device break state, restoring operation.
Syntax	int **ClearCommBreak**(int *nCid*);
Description	Communications devices (parallel and serial ports) can be temporarily turned off by calling SetCommBreak(). ClearCommBreak() clears the break state, restoring the port's operation. Data remaining in the input and output data queues is not affected.
Uses	It is simpler to use SetCommBreak() to temporarily close a communications device than to close

and then reopen the port.

Returns	int, zero if the function was successful, negative on error (such as *nCid* not being a valid device).
See Also	SetCommBreak(), OpenComm()
Parameters	
nCid	int: The communications device ID value. This is the value returned by OpenComm().
Example	See the previous example under the BuildCommDCB() function description.

CLOSECOMM ■ Win 2.0 ■ Win 3.0 ■ Win 3.1

Purpose	Closes a communications device.
Syntax	int **CloseComm**(int *nCid*);
Description	This function closes the communications device previously opened by OpenComm(), and frees the memory associated with the input and output data queues. Any data in the output queue is sent before the device is closed. Only one application can have a port open at any one time.
Uses	Any application that opens a communications device must call CloseComm() to return the port to the system. Failure to do this will cause the port to be inaccessible to other applications.
Returns	int, zero if the communications device (port) is closed, negative on error.
See Also	OpenComm()
Parameters	
nCid	int: The ID of the device to be closed. This is the value returned by OpenComm() when the device was first opened.
Example	See the example under the BuildCommDCB() function description.

ESCAPECOMMFUNCTION ■ Win 2.0 ■ Win 3.0 ■ Win 3.1

Purpose	Sets a communications device extended function.
Syntax	int **EscapeCommFunction**(int *nCid*, int *nFunc*);
Description	This function provides a convenient way to send a communications device a control code, such as DTR, RTS, or XON/OFF.
Uses	DTR and RTS signals are used in establishing communications links between two devices. XON/OFF pairs are used in sending packets of data between two devices.
Returns	int, zero if the function is successful, negative on error.
See Also	OpenComm()
Parameters	
nCid	int: The ID of the device to be closed. This is the value returned by OpenComm() when the device was first opened.
nFunc	int: The function code. This can be any of the codes listed in Table 21-2.

Value	Meaning	⊠
CLRDTR	Clears the data-terminal-ready (DTR) signal.	
CLRRTS	Clears the request-to-send (RTS) signal.	
RESETDEV	Attempts to reset the device.	
SETDTR	Sends the data-terminal-ready (DTR) signal.	
SETRTS	Sends the request-to-send (RTS) signal.	

Table 21-2. continued

Value	Meaning	⊠
SETXOFF	Emulates receipt of an XOFF character.	
SETXON	Emulates receipt of an XON character.	

Table 21-2. Communications Codes.

Example   See the example under the BuildCommDCB() function description.

FLUSHCOMM   ■ Win 2.0   ■ Win 3.0   ■ Win 3.1

Purpose   Clears all data in a communications queue.

Syntax   int **FlushComm**(int *nCid*, int *nQueue*);

Description   Windows uses memory buffers to store incoming and outgoing data for a communications device (port). FlushComm() is used to clear the buffers.

Uses   Used when the communications device is first opened with OpenComm(). It can also be used within the communications program logic if it is desirable to purge the queues.

Returns   int, zero if the queue was cleared, negative on error.

See Also   OpenComm()

Parameters

nCid   int: The communications device ID value. This is the value returned by OpenComm().

nQueue   int: Set to zero to clear the transmit data queue. Set to one to clear the receive data queue.

Example   See the example under the BuildCommDCB() function description.

GETCOMMERROR   ■ Win 2.0   ■ Win 3.0   ■ Win 3.1

Purpose   Determines the error status of a communications port, and clears the error.

Syntax   int **GetCommError**(int *nCid*, COMSTAT FAR **lpStat*);

Description   Windows locks a communications device (port) when an error is detected. The port remains locked until GetCommError() is called. The error data is copied to the COMSTAT data structure. This structure is defined in WINDOWS.H as follows:

```
typedef struct tagCOMSTAT
  {
  BYTE fCtsHold: 1;            /* Transmit is on CTS hold */
  BYTE fDsrHold: 1;            /* Transmit is on DSR hold */
  BYTE fRlsdHold: 1;           /* Transmit is on RLSD hold */
  BYTE fXoffHold: 1;           /* Received handshake */
  BYTE fXoffSent: 1;           /* Issued handshake */
  BYTE fEof: 1;                /* End-of-file character found */
  BYTE fTxim: 1;               /* Character being transmitted */
  WORD cbInQue;                /* count of characters in Rx Queue */
  WORD cbOutQue;               /* count of characters in Tx Queue */
  } COMSTAT;
```

Note that the first seven elements of the COMSTAT data structure are bit values.

Uses   Used to unlock the communications device and determine the error status.

Returns   int, the error code returned by the most recently used communications function. This can be any of the error codes listed in Table 21-3.

Value	Meaning	⊠
CE_BREAK	A break condition was detected.	
CE_CTSTO	Clear-to-send time-out. The amount of time before time-out is set by the *CtsTimeout* element of the DCB data structure passed to SetCommState(). See BuildCommDCB() for the DCB structure definition.	
CE_DNS	Parallel device not selected.	
CE_DSRTO	Data-set-ready time-out. The amount of time before time-out is set by the *DsrTimeout* element of the DCB data structure passed to SetCommState(). See BuildCommDCB() for the DCB structure definition.	
CD_FRAME	Hardware framing error detected.	
CD_IOE	Input/Output error on a parallel device.	
CD_MODE	The requested communications mode is not supported by the device, or *nCid* is not valid.	
CE_OOP	The parallel device is out of paper.	
CE_OVERRUN	A character arrived before the last character could be read. The character is lost.	
CE_PTO	Parallel device time out.	
CE_RLSDTO	Receive-line-signal-detect time-out. The amount of time before time-out is set by the *RlsTimeout* element of the DCB data structure passed to SetCommState(). See Build-CommDCB() for the DCB structure definition.	
CE_RXOVER	The receive queue overflowed. This can also be set by having a character be received after the end-of-file character has been set. The end-of-file character is determined by the *EofChar* element of the DCB data structure passed to SetCommState(). See BuildCommDCB() for the DCB structure definition.	
CE_RXPARITY	A parity error was detected.	
CE_TXFULL	The transmit queue is full.	

Table 21-3. Communications Error Codes.

See Also	BuildCommDCB(), SetCommState()
Parameters	
nCid	int: The communications device ID value. This is the value returned by OpenComm().
lpStat	COMSTAT FAR *: A pointer to a COMSTAT data structure. The structure will be filled with the current device status.
Example	See the example under BuildCommDCB().

GETCOMMEVENTMASK ■ Win 2.0 ■ Win 3.0 ■ Win 3.1

Purpose	Determines which communication event has occurred.
Syntax	WORD **GetCommEventMask**(int *nCid*, int *nEvtMask*);
Description	Events are noncharacter communication data, such as clear-to-send (CTS) line status. The events which will be detected for a device are set with SetCommEventMask(). GetCommEventMask() determines which event has occurred. Each event is coded as a bit flag.
Uses	Used within the message loop (or timer message processing function) to determine the event status of a communications device (port).

Returns   WORD. The event status for each type of event is coded as a bit in the returned WORD. Each of the
                    event flags is given a name in WINDOWS.H as listed in Table 21-4.

Value	Meaning	⊠
EV_BREAK	Break detected on input.	
EV_CTS	Clear-to-send (CTS) signal change detected.	
EV_DSR	Data-set-ready (DSR) signal change detected.	
EV_ERR	Line-status error detected. They are CE_FRAME, CE_OVERRUN, and CE_RXPARITY.	
EV_PERR	Printer error detected. They are CE_NDS, CE_IOE, CE_LOOP, and CE_PTO.	
EV_RING	Ring indicator detected.	
EV_RLSD	Receive-line-signal-detect (RLSD) change detected.	
EV_RXCHAR	Any character placed in the receive queue was detected.	
EV_RXFLAG	The event character was received and placed in the receive queue.	
EV_TXEMPTY	The last character in the transmit queue has been sent.	

Table 21-4. Communications Event Flags.

See Also   SetCommEventMask()

Parameters

nCid   int: The communications device ID value. This is the value returned by OpenComm().

nEvtMask   int: Sets which events are to be monitored after the call to GetCommEventMask(). *nEvtMask*
                    can be any combination of the bit flags in Table 21-4, combined with the C language binary OR
                    operator (|). Set *nEvtMask* to 0xFFFF to monitor all events.

Example   See the example under the SetCommEventMask() function description.

GETCOMMSTATE   ■ Win 2.0   ■ Win 3.0   ■ Win 3.1

Purpose   Determines the current settings of a communications device.

Syntax   int **GetCommState**(int *nCid*, DCB FAR **lpDCB*);

Description   This function copies the current settings for a communications
                    device (serial or parallel port) to a DCB data structure.

Uses   Determining the settings for a communications device, such as
                    the current baud rate.

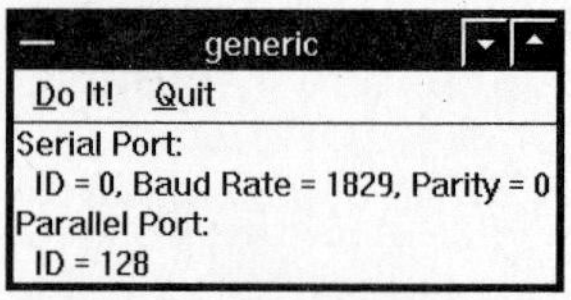

Returns   int, zero if the function was successful, negative on error.

See Also   SetCommState(), BuildCommDCB(), OpenComm()

Figure 21-3. GetComm-State( ) Example.

Parameters

nCid   int: The communications device ID value. This is the value returned by OpenComm().

lpDCB   DCB FAR *: A pointer to a DCB (Device Control Block) data structure. See the BuildCommDCB()
                    function description for the definition of this structure.

Example   This example, which is illustrated in Figure 21-3, opens the COM1 and LPT1 ports and displays
                    the initial settings when the user clicks the "Do It!" menu item.

```
long FAR PASCAL WndProc (HWND hWnd, unsigned iMessage, WORD wParam, LONG lParam)
{
        HDC             hDC ;
        char            cBuf [128] ;
        int             nComm ;
        DCB             dcb ;

        switch (iMessage)                       /* process windows messages */
```

814

```
        {
                case WM_COMMAND:                    /* process menu items */
                        switch (wParam)
                        {
                        case IDM_DOIT:              /* User hit the "Do it" menu item */
                                hDC = GetDC (hWnd) ;
                                nComm = OpenComm ("COM1", 128, 128) ;
                                GetCommState (nComm, &dcb) ;
                                TextOut (hDC, 0, 0, "Serial Port:", 12) ;
                                TextOut (hDC, 10, 20, cBuf, wsprintf (cBuf,
                                        "ID = %d, Baud Rate = %d, Parity = %d",
                                                dcb.Id, dcb.BaudRate, dcb.Parity)) ;
                                CloseComm (nComm) ;
                                nComm = OpenComm ("LPT1", 0, 0) ;
                                GetCommState (nComm, &dcb) ;
                                TextOut (hDC, 0, 40, "Parallel Port:", 14) ;
                                TextOut (hDC, 10, 60, cBuf, wsprintf (cBuf,
                                        "ID = %d",dcb.Id)) ;
                                CloseComm (nComm) ;
                                ReleaseDC (hWnd, hDC) ;
                                break ;
```

[Other program lines]

OPENCOMM
■ Win 2.0   ■ Win 3.0   ■ Win 3.1

Purpose   Opens a communications device (port) and allocates memory for the input and output data queues.

Syntax   int **OpenComm**(LPSTR *lpComName*, WORD *wInQueue*, WORD *wOutQueue*);

Description   Before a communications device can be used, it must be opened. The device will be opened with default settings for baud rate, parity, etc. These settings can be changed by using BuildCommDCB() and SetCommState(). Serial ports use data buffers called "queues" to temporarily store data being sent and received by the port. OpenComm() also allocates memory for the input and output data queues. Parallel ports do not use data buffers. The *wInQueue* and *wOutQueue* values will be ignored if a parallel port is being opened. Only one application can open a communications device at a time. Be sure to call CloseComm() when the device is no longer needed.

Uses   OpenComm() must be called before a communications device, such as a serial or parallel port, can be used.

Returns   int, the ID value of the opened communications device. This value should be saved in a static variable. If an error occurs in opening the device, the function returns one of the negative values listed in Table 21-5.

Value	Meaning	☒
IE_BADID	An invalid device name.	
IE_BAUDRATE	Unsupported baud rate.	
IE_BYTESIZE	Unsupported byte size.	
IE_DEFAULT	Error in the default parameters.	
IE_HARDWARE	Hardware not present.	
IE_MEMORY	Unable to allocate memory for the data queues.	
IE_NOPEN	Not able to open the device.	
IE_OPEN	Device already open.	

Table 21-5. OpenComm() Error Codes.

See Also   CloseComm(), BuildCommDCB(), SetCommState(), WriteComm()

Parameters

lpComName   LPSTR: A pointer to a null-terminated character string containing the device name. Examples are "COM1" and "LPT2." The valid device numbers start with 1, and are limited by the number of devices on the system.

wInQueue   WORD: The size of the receive data queue. For serial devices, this is typically set at 1,024 bytes. For parallel devices, the value is ignored.

wOutQueue   WORD: The size of the transmit data queue. For serial devices, this is typically set at 128 bytes. For parallel devices, the value is ignored.

Example   See the example under BuildCommDCB().

READCOMM   ■ Win 2.0   ■ Win 3.0   ■ Win 3.1

Purpose	Reads data from an open communications device.
Syntax	int **ReadComm**(int *nCid*, LPSTR *lpBuf*, int *nSize*);
Description	With a serial communications device, input data is stored temporarily in a data queue as it is received. ReadComm() reads the data queue and copies the data into a buffer pointed to by *lpBuf*, removing the data from the data queue. With a parallel communications device, only one data byte is available at any one time. This value is read and copied to the buffer pointed to by *lpBuf*.
Uses	Reading data from a communications device previously opened by OpenComm().
Returns	int, the number of characters actually read. This number will be smaller than *nSize* if the data queue contains fewer than *nSize* bytes. If the returned value is equal to *nSize*, more than *nSize* bytes may be in the data queue and the queue should be read again with ReadComm(). If an error occurs, the returned value will be negative. The absolute value of the returned value will be the number of characters read. Use GetCommError() to retrieve the error code. It is a good practice to call GetCommError() every time ReadComm() returns zero to clear any possible errors on a serial device. For parallel devices, the returned value is always zero.
See Also	OpenComm(), GetCommError()

Parameters

nCid   int: The communications device ID value. This is the value returned by OpenComm().

lpBuf   LPSTR: A pointer to the data buffer to receive the data. The buffer must be at least *nSize* bytes long.

nSize   int: The maximum number of bytes to read from the data queue.

Example   See the example under BuildCommDCB().

SETCOMMBREAK   ■ Win 2.0   ■ Win 3.0   ■ Win 3.1

Purpose	Temporarily suspends operation of a communications device.
Syntax	int **SetCommBreak**(int *nCid*);
Description	This function shuts down character transmission to and from a communications device. The device is left in the break state until ClearCommBreak() is called. Data sent to the transmit data queue is stored in the queue, but it is not transmitted until the break state is cleared.
Uses	Setting the communications device in a break state is simpler for temporary interruptions than closing and then reopening the device.
Returns	int, zero if the break state is established, negative on error (such as an invalid *nCid* value).
See Also	ClearCommBreak(), OpenComm()

Parameters

nCid   int: The communications device ID value. This is the value returned by OpenComm().

Example   See the example under the BuildCommDCB() function description.

SETCOMMEVENTMASK   ■ Win 2.0   ■ Win 3.0   ■ Win 3.1

Purpose	Sets which communications events are enabled.
Syntax	WORD FAR ***SetCommEventMask**(int *nCid*, WORD *nEvtMask*);
Description	Events are noncharacter communication data, such as the DSR (Data Set Ready) signal state. This function allows certain events to be screened. Use GetCommEventMask() to retrieve the event status.
Uses	Used in low-level control over a port's signal status.
Returns	WORD FAR *, a pointer to a WORD that contains the bit mask for the event status. The event has occurred if the bit is set to 1.
See Also	GetCommEventMask(), GetCommError()

Parameters

nCid   int: The communications device ID value. This is the value returned by OpenComm().

nEvtMask   int: The bit mask for the events to be enabled. This can be any combination of the values in Table 21-6, combined with the C language binary OR operator (I).

Value	Meaning
EV_BREAK	Breaks are detected on input.
EV_CTS	Clear-to-send (CTS) signal changes are detected.
EV_DSR	Data-set-ready (DSR) signal changes are detected.
EV_ERR	Line-status errors are detected. They are CE_FRAME, CE_OVERRUN, and CE_RXPARITY.
EV_PERR	Printer errors are detected. They are CE_NDS, CE_IOE, CE_LOOP, and CE_PTO.
EV_RING	Ring indicator is detected.
EV_RLSD	Receive-line-signal-detect (RLSD) changes are detected.
EV_RXCHAR	Any character placed in the receive queue is detected.
EV_RXFLAG	The event character is received and placed in the receive queue.
EV_TXEMPTY	The last character in the transmit queue has been sent.

Table 21-6. Communications Event Flags.

Example   This example is similar to the simple communications program under the BuildCommDCB() function description. In this case, Set-CommEventMask() is used to enable both break and CTS signal changes for the communications port. Communications events are detected in the program's message loop. The current event mask is displayed in the window's client area by sending a WM_USER + 1 message to WndProc(). WndProc() intercepts this message, and displays the error mask on the third line, as shown in Figure 21-4.

Figure 21-4. SetCommEventMask( ) Example.

```
/* generic.c   simple serial communications application */

#include <windows.h>
#include "generic.h"

static          int     nComID = -1 ;
static          char    cInBuf [256], cOutBuf [128] ;

int PASCAL WinMain (HANDLE hInstance, HANDLE hPrevInstance, LPSTR lpszCmdLine, int nCmdShow)
{

        HWND            hWnd ;
        MSG             msg ;
        WNDCLASS        wndclass ;
        COMSTAT         ComStat ;
        char            cBuf [128] ;
        WORD            wComError ;
        int             i, nReadChars, nStart ;

        ghInstance = hInstance ;                /* store instance handle as global var. */
        if (!hPrevInstance)
        {
                wndclass.style                  = CS_HREDRAW | CS_VREDRAW ;
                wndclass.lpfnWndProc            = WndProc ;
                wndclass.cbClsExtra             = 0 ;
                wndclass.cbWndExtra             = 0 ;
                wndclass.hInstance              = hInstance ;
                wndclass.hIcon                  = LoadIcon (hInstance, gszAppName) ;
                wndclass.hCursor                = LoadCursor (NULL, IDC_ARROW) ;
                wndclass.hbrBackground          = GetStockObject (WHITE_BRUSH) ;
                wndclass.lpszMenuName           = gszAppName ;
                wndclass.lpszClassName          = gszAppName ;

                if (!RegisterClass (&wndclass))
                        return FALSE ;
        }

        hWnd = CreateWindow (                   /* create the program's window here */
                gszAppName,                     /* class name */
                gszAppName,                     /* window name */
                WS_OVERLAPPEDWINDOW,            /* window style */
                CW_USEDEFAULT,                  /* x position on screen */
                CW_USEDEFAULT,                  /* y position on screen */
                CW_USEDEFAULT,                  /* width of window */
                CW_USEDEFAULT,                  /* height of window */
                NULL,                           /* parent window handle (null = none) */
                NULL,                           /* menu handle (null = use class menu) */
                hInstance,                      /* instance handle */
                NULL) ;                         /* lpstr (null = not used) */

        ShowWindow (hWnd, nCmdShow) ;
        UpdateWindow (hWnd) ;

        while (TRUE)                            /* use peek message loop to check com1 */
        {
                if (PeekMessage (&msg, NULL, 0, 0, PM_REMOVE))
                {
                        if (msg.message == WM_QUIT)
                                break ;
                        else
                        {
                                TranslateMessage (&msg) ;
                                DispatchMessage (&msg) ;
                        }
                }
                else if (nComID >= 0)           /* check the com port for data */
                {
                        if ((nReadChars = ReadComm (nComID, cBuf, 128)) > 0)
                        {
```

```
                           if ((nStart = lstrlen (cInBuf)) < 80)
                           {               /* add to end */
                                   for (i = 0 ; i < nReadChars ; i++)
                                           cInBuf [nStart + i] = cBuf [i] ;
                                   cInBuf [nReadChars + nStart] = 0 ;
                                   PostMessage (msg.hwnd, WM_USER + 1, 0, 0L) ;
                           }
                           else
                           {               /* start string over */
                                   for (i = 0 ; i < nReadChars ; i++)
                                           cInBuf [i] = cBuf [i] ;
                                   cInBuf [nReadChars] = 0 ;
                                   PostMessage (msg.hwnd, WM_USER + 1, 1, 0L) ;
                           }
                   }
                   else    /* clear error, post mesg. to disp. error */
                   {
                           GetCommError (nComID, &ComStat) ;
                           wComError = GetCommEventMask (nComID, 0xFFFF) ;
                           PostMessage (msg.hwnd, WM_USER + 1, 2,
                                   (LONG) wComError) ;
                   }
           }
       }
       return msg.wParam ;
}


long FAR PASCAL WndProc (HWND hWnd, unsigned iMessage, WORD wParam, LONG lParam)
{
       PAINTSTRUCT             ps ;
       HDC                     hDC ;
       DCB                     dcb ;
       int                     i, nStatus ;
       char                    cBuf [128] ;
       static        BOOL      bToggle = TRUE ;

       switch (iMessage)
       {
           case WM_CREATE:
                   nComID = OpenComm ("COM1", 128, 128) ;
                   if (nComID < 0)
                           MessageBox (hWnd, "Could not open COM1", "Warning",
                                   MB_OK) ;
                   else
                   {
                           FlushComm (nComID, 0) ;  /* empty output queue */
                           FlushComm (nComID, 1) ;  /* empty input queue */
                           BuildCommDCB ("com1:1200,e,7,1", &dcb) ;
                           SetCommState (&dcb) ;
                           SetCommEventMask (nComID, EV_BREAK | EV_CTS) ;
                           MessageBox (hWnd, "COM1 is open.", "Message",
                                   MB_OK) ;
                   }
                   break ;
           case WM_PAINT:
                   BeginPaint (hWnd, &ps) ;
                   TextOut (ps.hdc, 0, 0, "In>", 3) ;
                   TextOut (ps.hdc, 40, 0, cInBuf, lstrlen (cInBuf)) ;
                   TextOut (ps.hdc, 0, 20, "Out>", 4) ;
                   TextOut (ps.hdc, 40, 20, cOutBuf, lstrlen (cOutBuf)) ;
                   EndPaint (hWnd, &ps) ;
                   break ;
           case WM_COMMAND:                     /* process menu items */
                   switch (wParam)
                   {
                   case IDM_DOIT:               /* put ESC into receive queue */
                           break ;
                   case IDM_QUIT:               /* send end of application message */
```

```
                                DestroyWindow (hWnd) ;
                                break ;
                        }
                        break ;
        case WM_CHAR:                           /* user typed a char */
                        if (nComID >= 0)
                        {
                                nStatus = WriteComm (nComID, (LPSTR) &wParam, 1) ;
                                if (nStatus < 0)
                                        MessageBox (hWnd, "Output comm error.",
                                                "Message", MB_OK) ;
                                else
                                {
                                        i = lstrlen (cOutBuf) ;
                                        if (i > 80)         /* don't overflow line size */
                                        {
                                                cOutBuf [0] = (char) wParam ;
                                                cOutBuf [1] = 0 ;
                                                InvalidateRect (hWnd, NULL, TRUE) ;
                                        }
                                        else    /* added char to end of typed string */
                                        {
                                                cOutBuf [i] = (char) wParam ;
                                                cOutBuf [i + 1] = 0 ;
                                                hDC = GetDC (hWnd) ;
                                                TextOut (hDC, 40, 20, cOutBuf,
                                                        lstrlen (cOutBuf)) ;
                                                ReleaseDC (hWnd, hDC) ;
                                        }


                                }
                        }
                        break ;
        case WM_USER + 1:                       /* need to update screen from input */
                        switch (wParam)
                        {
                                case 0:         /* input chars added to end of string */
                                        hDC = GetDC (hWnd) ;
                                        TextOut (hDC, 40, 0, cInBuf, lstrlen (cInBuf)) ;
                                        ReleaseDC (hWnd, hDC) ;
                                        break ;
                                case 1:         /* started string over from start */
                                        InvalidateRect (hWnd, NULL, TRUE) ;
                                        break ;
                                case 2:         /* display an error value */
                                        hDC = GetDC (hWnd) ;
                                        TextOut (hDC, 0, 40, cBuf, wsprintf (cBuf,
                                                "Error mask 0x%x", LOWORD (lParam))) ;
                                        ReleaseDC (hWnd, hDC) ;
                                        break ;
                        }
                        break ;
        case WM_DESTROY:                        /* stop application */
                        CloseComm (nComID) ;
                        PostQuitMessage (0) ;
                        break ;
        default:                                /* default windows message processing */
                        return DefWindowProc (hWnd, iMessage, wParam, lParam) ;
        }
        return (0L) ;
}
```

SETCOMMSTATE   ■ Win 2.0   ■ Win 3.0   ■ Win 3.1

Purpose   Changes the settings (baud rate, etc.) for a communications device.

Syntax   int **SetCommState**(DCB FAR *lpDCB);

Description	When a communications device is initially opened with OpenComm(), the default settings for the device are in place. SetCommState() allows these values to be changed. The new values are passed in a data structure of type DCB. This structure is typically initialized using Build-CommDCB(). The port ID value that SetCommState() is determined by is the ID element of the DCB structure. SetCommState() does not affect the input and output data queues.
Uses	Changing the settings for a communications device, such as the baud rate and parity for a serial port.
Returns	int, zero if the settings were changed, negative on error.
See Also	BuildCommDCB()
Parameters	
lpDCB	DCB FAR *: A pointer to a DCB (Device Control Block) data structure that contains the settings to use for the communications device. See the BuildCommDCB() description for a listing of the DCB structure.
Example	See the example under the BuildCommDCB() function description.

TRANSMITCOMMCHAR   ■ Win 2.0   ■ Win 3.0   ■ Win 3.1

Purpose	Sends a character to a communications device immediately, bypassing the transmit data queue.
Syntax	int **TransmitCommChar**(int *nCid*, char *cChar*);
Description	Normally, characters are sent to a communications device (port) by using WriteComm() to copy characters to the transmit data queue, and then having Windows send the characters when the port is available. TransmitCommChar() places a character at the head of the queue, so that it is the next character sent. Only one character can be sent at a time using TransmitCommChar(). The function will return a negative (error) value if the previous character sent by Transmit-CommChar() has not been sent to the device.
Uses	Used to send special characters out of normal transmission sequence. For example, an external device may respond to an ESC or CAN (ASCII 27 or 24) character by resetting or starting a new mode.
Returns	int, zero if the character was sent, negative on error.
See Also	WriteComm()
Parameters	
nCid	int: The communications device ID value. This is the value returned by OpenComm().
cChar	char: The character to be transmitted.
Example	This example creates a primitive communications program. The program is similar to one described under the BuildCommDCB() function description, but it is modified to demonstrate TransmitCommChar() and UngetCommChar(). Communications are to and from the COM1 serial port. When the user clicks the "Do It!" menu item, an ESC character is placed at the end of the receive data queue by a call to UngetCommChar(). The ESC is the next character displayed on the window's client area (displayed as a vertical line).
	When the user presses the key cap key, the ESC character is sent directly to COM1, bypassing any other characters in the transmit data queue. Do this by using TransmitCommChar() to send ESC, rather than using WriteComm() as is used for all other characters. This logic is typical of dealing with an external serial device that used the ESC character to force a reset or change the device state.

```
/* generic.c  generic windows application */
#include <windows.h>
#include "generic.h"
```

```
static          int       nComID = -1 ;
static          char      cInBuf [256 + 128], cOutBuf [128] ;

int PASCAL WinMain (HANDLE hInstance, HANDLE hPrevInstance, LPSTR lpszCmdLine, int nCmdShow)
{
        HWND            hWnd ;
        MSG             msg ;
        WNDCLASS        wndclass ;
        COMSTAT         ComStat ;
        char            cBuf [128] ;
        int             i, nReadChars, nStart ;

        ghInstance = hInstance ;                    /* store instance handle as global var. */
        if (!hPrevInstance)
        {
                wndclass.style              = CS_HREDRAW | CS_VREDRAW ;
                wndclass.lpfnWndProc        = WndProc ;
                wndclass.cbClsExtra         = 0 ;
                wndclass.cbWndExtra         = 0 ;
                wndclass.hInstance          = hInstance ;
                wndclass.hIcon              = LoadIcon (hInstance, gszAppName) ;
                wndclass.hCursor            = LoadCursor (NULL, IDC_ARROW) ;
                wndclass.hbrBackground      = GetStockObject (WHITE_BRUSH) ;
                wndclass.lpszMenuName       = gszAppName ;
                wndclass.lpszClassName      = gszAppName ;

                if (!RegisterClass (&wndclass))
                        return FALSE ;
        }

        hWnd = CreateWindow (                       /* create the program's window here */
                gszAppName,                         /* class name */
                gszAppName,                         /* window name */
                WS_OVERLAPPEDWINDOW,                /* window style */
                CW_USEDEFAULT,                      /* x position on screen */
                CW_USEDEFAULT,                      /* y position on screen */
                CW_USEDEFAULT,                      /* width of window */
                CW_USEDEFAULT,                      /* height of window */
                NULL,                               /* parent window handle (null = none) */
                NULL,                               /* menu handle (null = use class menu) */
                hInstance,                          /* instance handle */
                NULL) ;                             /* lpstr (null = not used) */

        ShowWindow (hWnd, nCmdShow) ;
        UpdateWindow (hWnd) ;

        while (TRUE)                                /* use peek message loop to check com1 */
        {
                if (PeekMessage (&msg, NULL, 0, 0, PM_REMOVE))
                {
                        if (msg.message == WM_QUIT)
                                break ;
                        else
                        {
                                TranslateMessage (&msg) ;
                                DispatchMessage (&msg) ;
                        }
                }
                else if (nComID >= 0)               /* check the com port for data */
                {
                        if ((nReadChars = ReadComm (nComID, cBuf, 128)) > 0)
                        {
                                if ((nStart = lstrlen (cInBuf)) < 80)
                                {                   /* add chars to end of string */
                                        for (i = 0 ; i < nReadChars ; i++)
                                                cInBuf [nStart + i] = cBuf [i] ;
                                        cInBuf [nReadChars + nStart] = 0 ;
                                        PostMessage (msg.hwnd, WM_USER + 1, 0, 0L) ;
```

```
                              }
                              else
                              {                           /* start string over */
                                      for (i = 0 ; i < nReadChars ; i++)
                                              cInBuf [i] = cBuf [i] ;
                                      cInBuf [nReadChars] = 0 ;
                                      PostMessage (msg.hwnd, WM_USER + 1, 1, 0L) ;
                              }
                      }
                      else
                              GetCommError (nComID, &ComStat) ;
              }
      }
      return msg.wParam ;
}

long FAR PASCAL WndProc (HWND hWnd, unsigned iMessage, WORD wParam, LONG lParam)
{
      PAINTSTRUCT           ps ;
      HDC                   hDC ;
      DCB                   dcb ;
      int                   i, nStatus ;
      char                  cBuf [128] ;
      static        BOOL    bToggle = TRUE ;

      switch (iMessage)
      {
              case WM_CREATE:
                      nComID = OpenComm ("COM1", 128, 128) ;
                      if (nComID < 0)
                              MessageBox (hWnd, "Could not open COM1", "Warning",
                                      MB_OK) ;
                      else
                      {
                              FlushComm (nComID, 0) ;  /* empty output queue */
                              FlushComm (nComID, 1) ;  /* empty input queue */
                              BuildCommDCB ("com1:1200,e,7,1", &dcb) ;
                              SetCommState (&dcb) ;
                              EscapeCommFunction (nComID, RESETDEV) ;
                              MessageBox (hWnd, "COM1 is open.", "Message",
                                      MB_OK) ;
                      }
                      break ;
              case WM_PAINT:
                      BeginPaint (hWnd, &ps) ;
                      TextOut (ps.hdc, 0, 0, "In>", 3) ;
                      TextOut (ps.hdc, 40, 0, cInBuf, lstrlen (cInBuf)) ;
                      TextOut (ps.hdc, 0, 20, "Out>", 4) ;
                      TextOut (ps.hdc, 40, 20, cOutBuf, lstrlen (cOutBuf)) ;
                      EndPaint (hWnd, &ps) ;
                      break ;
              case WM_COMMAND:                    /* process menu items */
                      switch (wParam)
                      {
                      case IDM_DOIT:              /* put ESC into receive queue */
                              UngetCommChar (nComID, 27) ;
                              break ;
                      case IDM_QUIT:
                              DestroyWindow (hWnd) ;
                              break ;
                      }
                      break ;
              case WM_CHAR:                       /* user typed a char */
                      if (nComID >= 0)
                      {
                              if (wParam == 27)        /* ESC char - send direct */
                                      nStatus = TransmitCommChar (nComID,
                                          (char) wParam) ;
```

```
                        else          /* all other chars go into queue */
                                nStatus = WriteComm (nComID,
                                        (LPSTR) &wParam, 1) ;
                        if (nStatus < 0)
                                MessageBox (hWnd, "Output comm error.",
                                        "Message", MB_OK) ;
                        else
                        {
                                i = lstrlen (cOutBuf) ;
                                if (i > 80)       /* don't overflow line size */
                                {
                                        cOutBuf [0] = (char) wParam ;
                                        cOutBuf [1] = 0 ;
                                        InvalidateRect (hWnd, NULL, TRUE) ;
                                }
                                else      /* added char to end of typed string */
                                {
                                        cOutBuf [i] = (char) wParam ;
                                        cOutBuf [i + 1] = 0 ;
                                        hDC = GetDC (hWnd) ;
                                        TextOut (hDC, 40, 20, cOutBuf,
                                                lstrlen (cOutBuf)) ;
                                        ReleaseDC (hWnd, hDC) ;
                                }

                        }
                }
                break ;
        case WM_USER + 1:                  /* need to update screen from input */
                switch (wParam)
                {
                        case 0:        /* input chars added to end of string */
                                hDC = GetDC (hWnd) ;
                                TextOut (hDC, 40, 0, cInBuf, lstrlen (cInBuf)) ;
                                ReleaseDC (hWnd, hDC ) ;
                                break ;
                        case 1:        /* started string over from start */
                                InvalidateRect (hWnd, NULL, TRUE) ;
                                break ;
                }
                break ;
        case WM_DESTROY:                   /* stop application */
                CloseComm (nComID) ;
                PostQuitMessage (0) ;
                break ;
        default:                           /* default windows message processing */
                return DefWindowProc (hWnd, iMessage, wParam, lParam) ;
        }
        return (0L) ;
}
```

UNGETCOMMCHAR   ■ Win 2.0   ■ Win 3.0   ■ Win 3.1

Purpose   Places a character at the beginning of the receive data queue, bypassing any other characters already in the queue.

Syntax   int UngetCommChar(int *nCid*, char *cChar*);

Description   Normally, characters are read from the receive data queue in the order that they were received using ReadComm(). UngetCommChar() allows a character to be placed at the beginning of the data queue. This character will be the next character read by ReadComm(). Only one character can be placed at the start of the receive data queue at a time. If the last character placed by UngetCommChar() has not been read, the next call to UngetCommChar() will return a negative (error) value.

Uses	This function is convenient if the program deals with certain characters as special markers. For example, a program might read each character received looking for an ESC character. When the ESC is received, it is put back on the receive queue, and then a separate function within the program is called to deal with the sequence of characters starting with ESC.
Returns	int, zero if the character was placed at the start of the transmit data queue, negative on error.
See Also	ReadComm()
Parameters	
nCid	int: The communications device ID value. This is the value returned by OpenComm().
cChar	char: The character to be placed at the beginning of the receive data queue.
Example	See the previous example under the TransmitCommChar() function description.

WRITECOMM
■ Win 2.0   ■ Win 3.0   ■ Win 3.1

Purpose	Sends data to a communications device.
Syntax	int **WriteComm**(int *nCid*, LPSTR *lpBuf*, int *nSize*);
Description	This function sends a group of characters to a communications device. The data is copied to the transmit data queue, and then sent in the background while Windows processes the data request interrupts from the device. If the number of characters to be sent is larger than the space available in the transmit data queue, data in the transmit queue will be lost. Use GetCommError() to determine the space in the transmit queue.
Uses	Sending data to a communications device, such as a serial port.
Returns	int, the number of characters transmitted. If an error occurs, the value will be negative, and have an absolute value equal to the number of characters sent. Use GetCommError() to determine the error type and clear the device's error status.
See Also	OpenComm()
Parameters	
nCid	int: The communications device ID value. This is the value returned by OpenComm().
lpBuf	LPSTR: A pointer to the buffer containing the data to be transmitted.
nSize	int: The number of characters to be written.
Example	See the example under the BuildCommDCB() function description.

A common programming problem is determining if a character string belongs to a group of strings. For example, a compiler will need to check each word in the source code listing against the set of commands and function names. If a match is found, the compiler knows that the word is part of the language. If not, the compiler must assume that it is a new variable name or constant.

With any reasonably sized program, comparing each word to all of the commands and function names on a character-by-character basis is unacceptably slow. Compilers use hash table techniques to reduce the number of comparisons to a manageable number. Windows provides a similar facility in the form of atom functions. A group of character strings can be loaded into an atom table. Each string is identified with a unique integer value. Because only integer values need to be compared, checking to see if a new string exists in the atom table is quick. Atoms are also useful for exchanging character data between running applications.

Atom Tables

Windows implements two types of atom tables, local atoms and global atoms. Local atoms are stored in the application's local memory block. (This is the 64K memory segment that is private to the application.) Only one local atom table is allowed per application. The table is created using the InitAtomTable() and AddAtom() functions. The table remains in existence until either all of the elements of the table have been deleted using DeleteAtom(), or until the application terminates.

Global atoms are stored in the global memory area. Windows maintains one global atom table at all times. This table is shared by every application running on the system. Any application can add new elements (atoms) to the global atom table using GlobalAddAtom() and can delete them using GlobalDeleteAtom(). There is no equivalent to InitAtomTable() for the global atom table, as the global table is always in existence if Windows is running.

If the same character string is added to an atom table more than once, the string is not duplicated. Instead, a counter called the "reference count" of the atom is incremented. Each time the same string is added, the reference count goes up by one. Every time the same string is deleted, the reference count is reduced by one. When the reference count is reduced to zero, the string (atom) is removed from the atom table.

The FindAtom() and GlobalFindAtom() functions determine if a character string has already been loaded in the atom table. These functions are fast. Of course, the program must load all of the comparison strings into the atom table before the search can be started. Using atom tables for string searches makes sense if the same group of strings will be searched a large number of times.

If the application knows the atom value (the unique integer tag) for the string, the character string can be recovered with GetAtomName() or GlobalGetAtomName(). Because the atom values are integers, they can be passed between parts of a program as parameters in function calls. For example, a program can load all of the error and warning messages into a local atom table. The atom number for the string to display can then be used to pass the string to a message display function.

Atom Data Structure

Normally, you will not deal directly with the atom data. The atom functions provide all the needed functionality for adding, finding, and removing entries. If you need to deal directly with the atom data, the format used internally by Windows is

```
typedef struct tagATOMENTRY
{
        WORD    wReserved ;
        int     nRefCount ;              /* the number of times the string has been added */
        BYTE    cStrLen ;                /* the length of the string in bytes */
        char    cContent [1] ;   /* the string characters (length variable) */
} ATOMENTRY ;
```

This structure is not defined in WINDOWS.H. The number of bytes in the *cContent* element is arbitrary, as it will vary depending on the string stored. The GetAtomHandle() function will retrieve a handle to the memory block containing data in this format.

Data Exchange

A useful property of the global atom table is that it is available to all applications running on the system. This availability allows one program to load a string into the atom table, and another to pull it out. Because the atom's unique value is a 16-bit number, atoms can be transmitted between running applications as the *wParam* part of a Windows message. This transmission requires that both the sending and receiving applications know the same message ID to use to transmit the atom value. The RegisterWindowMessage() takes care of determining a unique message ID value to use. This message ID is then posted with the atom value as *wParam* using PostMessage(), and is received by the second application through the normal message loop and WndProc() function. The receiving application uses the *wParam* value to recover the string from the global atom table using GlobalGetAtomName().

The techniques for exchanging character strings between applications described above are demonstrated in the example program under the GlobalAddAtom() function. These simple techniques work fine if you are writing both the sending and receiving applications. The more general case is when you may want to send data to another programmer's application, or receive data from that application. Working with other applications requires a consistent protocol for sending and receiving data, which is defined in the Dynamic Data Exchange (DDE) protocol, covered in Chapter 30.

Atom Function Summary

Table 22-1 summarizes the atom functins. The detailed function descriptions are in the next section.

Function	Purpose
AddAtom	Adds a character string to the application's local atom table.
DeleteAtom	Deletes an item from the local atom table.
FindAtom	Determines if a character string has been stored in the local atom table.
GetAtomHandle	Retrieves a local memory handle to the memory area containing an atom.
GetAtomName	Retrieves the character string, given the atom's value.
GlobalAddAtom	Adds a character string to the global atom table.
GlobalDeleteAtom	Removes a character string from the global atom table.
GlobalFindAtom	Determines if a character string is stored in the global atom table.
GlobalGetAtomName	Retrieves a character string from the global atom table.
InitAtomTable	Initializes the local, atom table.

Table 22-1. Atom Function Summary.

Atom Function Descriptions

This section contains the detailed descriptions of the atom functions.

ADDATOM

Purpose	Adds a character string to the application's local atom table.
Syntax	ATOM **AddAtom**(LPSTR *lpString*);
Description	This function is used to add entries to the local atom table. Each string is given a unique identifier called an atom. This atom is a 16-bit unsigned integer. If an exact copy of the string pointed to by *lpString* already exists in the atom table, the existing entry's reference count (number of duplicates for the string) is increased by one. Note that atoms are not case-sensitive. The maximum string length is 256 characters.
Uses	Atom tables are a convenient way to store and retrieve character strings.
Returns	ATOM, the string's unique identifier. The returned value will be in the range 0xC000 to 0xFFFF. Returns NULL on error.
See Also	InitAtomTable()
Parameters	
lpString	LPSTR: A pointer to a null-terminated character string that will be added to the local atom table.

Example　This example, which is illustrated in Figure 22-1, loads six character strings into the local atom table when the program first starts (WM_CREATE message processed). Two of the strings are duplicates. The atom values for the six strings are stored in an array of ATOM values. When a WM_PAINT message is processed, the atom table is displayed. The string contents are retrieved from the atom table using the GetAtom Name() function. To retrieve the reference count for each

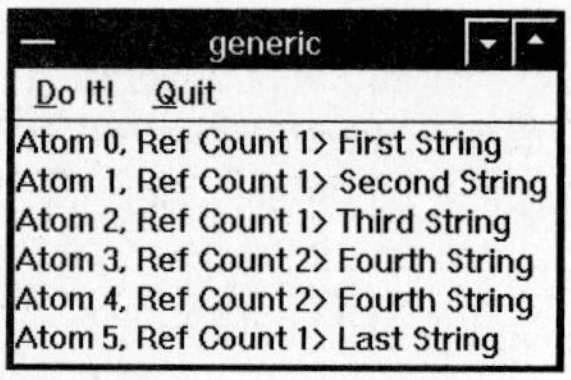

Figure 22-1. AddAtom( ) Example.

string, the local memory area containing the atom is locked. The memory area contains data in the structure ATOMENTRY format. This data structure is defined at the top of the listing.

When the user clicks the "Do It!" menu item, the application deletes atom number 3. As this atom starts with a reference count of two (it was duplicated), the first call to DeleteAtom() simply reduces the atom's reference count by one. The second time the "Do It!" menu item is clicked, the atom is deleted by setting the atom value to zero. Atom 4 remains valid with a reference count of 1.

```
typedef struct tagATOMENTRY
{
        WORD      wReserved ;
        int       nRefCount ;
        BYTE      cStrLen ;
        char      cContent [1] ;
} ATOMENTRY ;

long FAR PASCAL WndProc (HWND hWnd, unsigned iMessage, WORD wParam, LONG lParam)
{
        PAINTSTRUCT               ps ;
        char                      cBuf [128], cAtomContent [32] ;
        char                      *cNames [6] = {"First String", "Second String",
                                      "Third String", "Fourth String", "Fourth String",
                                      "Last String"} ;
        static         ATOM       AtomArray [6] ;
        WORD                      i, wAtom ;
        HANDLE                    hMem ;
        ATOMENTRY                 *AtomEntry ;

        switch (iMessage)                         /* process windows messages */
        {
                case WM_CREATE:
                        InitAtomTable (NULL) ;    /* initialize local atom table */
```

```
                    for (i = 0 ; i < 6 ; i++)
                            AtomArray [i] = AddAtom (cNames [i]) ;
                    break ;
        case WM_PAINT:
                BeginPaint (hWnd, &ps) ;
                for (i = 0 ; i < 6 ; i++)
                {
                        wAtom = GetAtomName (AtomArray [i],
                                cAtomContent, 32) ;
                        if (wAtom)
                        {
                                hMem = GetAtomHandle (AtomArray [i]) ;
                                AtomEntry = (ATOMENTRY *) LocalLock (hMem) ;
                                TextOut (ps.hdc, 0, i*20, cBuf, wsprintf (cBuf,
                                        "Atom %d, Ref Count %d> %s",
                                         AtomEntry->nRefCount,
                                         (LPSTR) cAtomContent)) ;
                                LocalUnlock (hMem) ;
                        }
                        else
                                TextOut (ps.hdc, 0, i*20, cBuf, wsprintf (cBuf,
                                        "Atom %d is no longer valid", i)) ;
                }
                EndPaint (hWnd, &ps) ;
                break ;
        case WM_COMMAND:                    /* process menu items */
                switch (wParam)
                {
                case IDM_DOIT:              /* delete atom #3 */
                        if (AtomArray [3])
                        {
                                hMem = GetAtomHandle (AtomArray [3]) ;
                                AtomEntry = (ATOMENTRY *) LocalLock (hMem) ;
                                if (AtomEntry->nRefCount > 1)
                                        DeleteAtom (AtomArray [3]) ;
                                else
                                        AtomArray [3] = 0 ;
                                LocalUnlock (hMem) ;
                        }
                        InvalidateRect (hWnd, NULL, TRUE) ;        /* force paint */
                        break ;
                case IDM_QUIT:
                        DestroyWindow (hWnd) ;
                        break ;
                }
                break ;
        case WM_DESTROY:
                PostQuitMessage (0) ;
                break ;
        default:
                return DefWindowProc (hWnd, iMessage, wParam, lParam) ;
        }
        return (0L) ;
}
```

DeleteAtom   ■ Win 2.0   ■ Win 3.0   ■ Win 3.1

Purpose	Deletes an item from the local atom table.
Syntax	ATOM **DeleteAtom**(ATOM *nAtom*);
Description	Each time the same character string is added to the atom table using AddAtom(), that entry's reference count is increased by one. DeleteAtom() reduces the reference count by one. When the entry's reference count is reduced to zero, the string is removed from the local atom table.
Uses	Removing strings from the local atom table. The entire local atom table will be removed from memory when the application is terminated, so it is not necessary to delete each atom prior to stopping the program.

Returns	ATOM. NULL if the function was successful. The *nAtom* value is returned on error.
See Also	AddAtom()
Parameters	
nAtom	ATOM: The atom to be deleted. This is the value returned by AddAtom().
Example	See the previous example under the AddAtom() function description.

FINDATOM   ■ Win 2.0   ■ Win 3.0   ■ Win 3.1

Purpose	Determines if a character string has been stored in the local atom table.
Syntax	ATOM **FindAtom**(LPSTR *lpString*);
Description	This function searches the local atom table for a case-insensitive match to the string pointed to by *lpString*. If a match is found, the atom's value is returned as a 16-bit value.
Uses	Locating a string in the atom table.
Returns	ATOM, the 16-bit atom value for the atom containing the requested string. NULL if the string pointed to by *lpString* has not been loaded into the local atom table by AddAtom().
See Also	AddAtom()
Parameters	

lpString   LPSTR: A pointer to a null-terminated character string containing the string to locate in the local atom table.

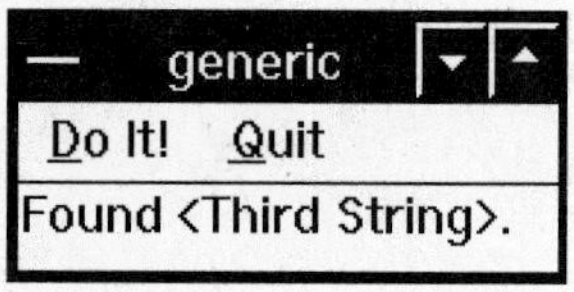

Example   This example loads six character strings into the local atom table when the program starts (WM_CREATE message received). When the user clicks the "Do It!" menu item, the table is searched for the string "Third String." When the string is located, the result is displayed in the window's client area, as shown in Figure 22-2.

```
Long FAR PASCAL WndProc (HWND hWnd, unsigned iMessage, WORD wParam, LONG lParam)
{
        HDC             hDC ;
        char            cBuf [128], cAtomContent [32] ;
        char            *cNames [6] = {"First String", "Second String",
                            "Third String", "Fourth String", "Fourth String",
                            "Last String"} ;
        WORD            i, wAtom ;

        switch (iMessage)                       /* process windows messages */
        {
        case WM_CREATE:
                InitAtomTable (NULL) ;  /* initialize local atom table */
                for (i = 0 ; i < 6 ; i++)
                        AddAtom (cNames [i]) ;
                break ;
        case WM_COMMAND:                        /* process menu items */
                switch (wParam)
                {
                case IDM_DOIT:                  /* delete atom #3 */
                        hDC = GetDC (hWnd) ;
                        wAtom = FindAtom ("Third String") ;
                        if (wAtom)
                                TextOut (hDC, 0, 0,
                                        "Found <Third String>.", 21) ;
                        else
                                TextOut (hDC, 0, 0,
                                        "Did not find <Third String>.", 27) ;
                        ReleaseDC (hWnd, hDC) ;
                        break ;
[Other program lines]
```

Figure 22-2. FindAtom()
Example.

GetAtomHandle

Purpose	Retrieves a local memory handle to the memory area containing an atom.
Syntax	HANDLE **GetAtomHandle**(ATOM *wAtom*);
Description	When a character string is added to the local atom table with AddAtom(), the data is stored in local memory in a data structure with the following format:

```
typedef struct tagATOMENTRY
{
        WORD      wReserved ;
        int       nRefCount ;
        BYTE      cStrLen ;
        char      cContent [1] ;
} ATOMENTRY ;
```

This structure is not defined in WINDOWS.H. The array size of the *cContent* element is arbitrary. The maximum length of an individual atom string is 256 characters. Windows' total atom storage space is limited by the size of the local memory area (64K). GetAtomHandle() returns a handle to the memory area containing the ATOMENTRY data structure. The application can use this structure to determine the reference count of an atom. This is the number of times the same string was added to the local atom table using AddAtom().

Uses	Seldom used. Normally, GetAtomName() is used to retrieve the contents of the atom's string. GetAtomHandle() can be used to determine the reference count of an atom, if atom entries are being added and deleted from the atom table as the application runs.
Returns	HANDLE, a local memory handle. This handle can be used to lock the ATOMENTRY memory block by calling LocalLock().
See Also	GetAtomName(), AddAtom()
Parameters	
wAtom	ATOM: This is the atom number returned by AddAtom().
Example	See the example under the AddAtom() function description.

GetAtomName

Purpose	Retrieves the character string, given the atom's value.
Syntax	WORD **GetAtomName**(ATOM *nAtom*, LPSTR *lpBuffer*, int *nSize*);
Description	This function copies the atom's character string to the *lpBuffer* memory buffer, given the atom's value. The atom's value is the value returned by AddAtom() when the string was added to the local atom table.
Uses	This is the normal way to retrieve an atom's string.
Returns	WORD, the number of characters copied to *lpBuffer*. Returns zero if the atom is not valid.
See Also	GetAtomHandle(), AddAtom()
Parameters	
nAtom	ATOM: This is the 16-bit atom value returned by AddAtom() when the character string was added to the local atom table.
lpBuffer	LPSTR: A pointer to a memory buffer that will receive the character string. The buffer must be at least *nSize* bytes long.
nSize	int: The maximum number of characters to copy to the buffer pointed to by *lpBuffer*.
Example	See the example under the AddAtom() function description.

GLOBALADDATOM

Purpose	Adds a character string to the global atom table.
Syntax	ATOM **GlobalAddAtom**(LPSTR *lpString*);
Description	The global atom table is shared by all running applications. GlobalAddAtom() adds a character string to the table. If the string already exists, the reference count for the atom (number of times the string has been stored) is increased by one. The maximum string length is 256 characters.
Uses	Storing a string in the global atom table makes the string available to any application that has the atom value (the returned value from this function is the atom value). This is a way to exchange character data between applications.
Returns	ATOM, the atom value for the stored string. NULL on error. The atom value will be between 0xC000 and 0xFFFF.
See Also	GlobalGetAtomName(), GlobalDeleteAtom()

Parameters

lpString   LPSTR: A pointer to a character string containing the string to be added to the global atom table.

Example   This example demonstrates using global atoms to exchange string data between running applications. The demonstration is most effective if two or more instances of the program are running at once. When the "Do It!" menu item on any of the program instances is clicked, all of the instances display the string "Got>Transmitted data" at once.

The program uses two important keys to communications between applications: registering a unique message and using the global atom table to store character strings. The Register-WindowMessage() creates a unique message ID value that will be the same for each program that requests the message ID. GlobalAddAtom() loads the character string into the global atom table that is accessible to all applications.

When the user clicks the "Do It!" menu item, the program posts the unique message to all running applications. The *wParam* value is set equal to the atom value returned by GlobalAddAtom(). The –1 for the window handle in the PostMessage() call does the trick of sending the message to every window. Because the message is unique, only applications which called RegisterWindowMessage("generic") will have the message ID value to respond.

When the unique message is received, the application uses the *wParam* value passed with the message to read the string back from the global atom table. GlobalGetAtomName() recovers the string, allowing it to be displayed in the window's client area, as shown in Figure 22-3. Note that the atom is deleted from the global atom table when the program exits. This step is necessary, as the global atom table remains in place after the program terminates.

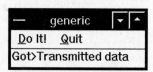

Figure 22-3. GlobalAdd-Atom( ) Example .

```
Long FAR PASCAL WndProc (HWND hWnd, unsigned iMessage, WORD wParam, LONG lParam)
{
        HDC                     hDC ;
        char                    cBuf [128], cAtomContent [32] ;
        static          WORD    wMessageID ;
        static          ATOM    AtomID ;

        switch (iMessage)                       /* process windows messages */
        {
                case WM_CREATE:
                        wMessageID = RegisterWindowMessage ("generic") ;
                        AtomID = GlobalAddAtom ("Transmitted data") ;
                        break ;
                case WM_COMMAND:                /* process menu items */
                        switch (wParam)
                        {
```

```
                        case IDM_DOIT:
                                PostMessage (-1, wMessageID, AtomID, OL) ;
                                break ;
                        case IDM_QUIT:
                                DestroyWindow (hWnd) ;
                                break ;
                        }
                        break ;
                case WM_DESTROY:
                        GlobalDeleteAtom (AtomID) ;
                        PostQuitMessage (O) ;
                        break ;
                default:
                        if (iMessage == wMessageID)        /* registered message? */
                        {
                                hDC = GetDC (hWnd) ;
                                GlobalGetAtomName (wParam, cAtomContent, 32) ;
                                TextOut (hDC, O, O, cBuf, wsprintf (cBuf,
                                        "Got>%s", (LPSTR) cAtomContent)) ;
                                ReleaseDC (hWnd, hDC) ;
                        }
                        else
                                return DefWindowProc (hWnd, iMessage, wParam, lParam) ;
        }
        return (OL) ;
}
```

GLOBALDELETEATOM   ■ Win 2.0   ■ Win 3.0   ■ Win 3.1

Purpose	Removes a character string from the global atom table.
Syntax	ATOM **GlobalDeleteAtom**(ATOM *nAtom*);
Description	If a character string has been added to the global atom table more than once with the Global-AddAtom() function, the atom's reference count will be more than one. Calling Global-DeleteAtom() reduces the reference count by one. When the reference count is reduced to zero, the atom is deleted from the global atom table.
Uses	Atoms added to the global table by an application should be deleted before the application terminates. Otherwise, they will remain in memory for the duration of the Windows session.
Returns	ATOM. NULL if the function was successful. The *nAtom* value will be returned if the function fails, indicating that *nAtom* is not a valid atom.
See Also	GlobalAddAtom()
Parameters	
nAtom	ATOM: The atom value for the string to delete. This is the value returned by GlobalAddAtom().
Example	See the previous example under the GlobalAddAtom() function description.

GLOBALFINDATOM   ■ Win 2.0   ■ Win 3.0   ■ Win 3.1

Purpose	Determines if a character string is stored in the global atom table.
Syntax	ATOM **GlobalFindAtom**(LPSTR *lpString*);
Description	The global atom table is shared by all running applications. GlobalFindAtom() is used to determine if a character string has been loaded into the global atom table. The search is case-insensitive.
Uses	Normally not used. Usually, the atom values are stored and/or exchanged between applications, rather than the character strings.
Returns	ATOM the atom value for the string in the global atom table. NULL if the string is not loaded in the atom table.

See Also   GlobalAddAtom()

Parameters

lpString   LPSTR: A pointer to a character string containing the string to locate in the global atom table.

Example   This example demonstrates the passive exchange of string data between running applications. It
is most effective if two instances of the program run at the
same time. The first time the "Do It!" menu item on any of the
applications is clicked, the atom containing the string "Test
String" is not found. This is because it has not been added to
the global atom table. After the message "Test String Not
Found" is displayed, the string is added to the global atom
table. Any instance of the program that has the "Do It!" menu
item clicked after that point will display the message shown in
Figure 22-4, "Test String Found."

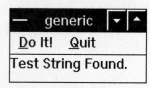

Figure 22-4. GlobalFind Atom() Example.

Note that the program calls GlobalDeleteAtom() as many times as the atom was added to the
global atom table. This is necessary to reduce the atom's reference count to zero, if the "Do It!"
menu item has been clicked more than once. Each running instance of the program ends up
deleting as many reference counts as it added. When the last instance of the program is terminated, the atom is certain to be removed from the global atom table.

```
Long FAR PASCAL WndProc (HWND hWnd, unsigned iMessage, WORD wParam, LONG lParam)
{
        HDC             hDC ;
        char            cBuf [128], cAtomContent [32] ;
        ATOM            Atom ;
        static    int   nCount = 0 ;
        int             i ;

        switch (iMessage)                       /* process windows messages */
        {
        case WM_COMMAND:                        /* process menu items */
                switch (wParam)
                {
                case IDM_DOIT:
                        hDC = GetDC (hWnd) ;
                        Atom = GlobalFindAtom ("Test String") ;
                        if (Atom)
                                TextOut (hDC, 0, 0,
                                        "Test String Found.", 18) ;
                        else
                                TextOut (hDC, 0, 0,
                                        "Test String Not Found.", 22) ;
                        GlobalAddAtom ("Test String") ;
                        nCount++ ;
                        ReleaseDC (hWnd, hDC) ;
                        break ;
                case IDM_QUIT:
                        DestroyWindow (hWnd) ;
                        break ;
                }
                break ;
        case WM_DESTROY:
                Atom = GlobalFindAtom ("Test String") ;
                for (i = 0 ; i < nCount ; i++)
                        GlobalDeleteAtom (Atom) ;
                PostQuitMessage (0) ;
                break ;
        default:
                return DefWindowProc (hWnd, iMessage, wParam, lParam) ;
        }
        return (0L) ;
}
```

GLOBALGETATOMNAME

Purpose	Retrieves a character string from the global atom table.
Syntax	WORD **GlobalGetAtomName**(ATOM *nAtom*, LPSTR *lpBuffer*, int *nSize*);
Description	Any application that has the *nAtom* value for an atom in the global atom table can determine the associated character string by calling this function. The character string is copied to the *lpBuffer* memory buffer.
Uses	Used by applications that exchange character data. The *nAtom* value can be passed as the *wParam* value in a message sent between the two applications.
Returns	WORD, the number of bytes copied to the *lpBuffer* memory buffer. Zero on error.
See Also	GlobalAddAtom()
Parameters	
nAtom	ATOM: The atom value. This is the value returned by GlobalAddAtom().
lpBuffer	LPSTR: A pointer to a memory buffer that will contain the character string. The buffer must be at least *nSize* bytes long.
nSize	int: The maximum number of characters to copy to *lpBuffer*.
Example	See the example under the GlobalAddAtom() function description.

INITATOMTABLE

Purpose	Initializes the local atom table.
Syntax	BOOL **InitAtomTable**(int *nSize*);
Description	Before the local atom table can be used, it must be initialized. InitAtomTable() allows the number of top-level table entries to be specified. The default number (if *nSize* is set to NULL) is 37. This is adequate to efficiently store several hundred character strings. Larger values can be set if a large number of strings are to be stored in the local atom table. Note that the local atom table resides in the limited local memory area. Large amounts of data should be stored in the global atom table.
Uses	This function must be called before the local atom table can be used.
Returns	BOOL. TRUE if the function was successful, FALSE on error.
See Also	AddAtom()
Parameters	
nSize	int: The number of top-level entries to set in the local atom table. This value should be a prime number. Set to NULL for the default number of 37 top-level entries. Larger values result in faster retrieval of strings, but require more memory space.
Example	See the example under the AddAtom() and FindAtom() function descriptions.

Metafiles are coded GDI (Graphics Device Interface) function calls. The GDI functions are described in Chapter 10, *Device Contexts, Text Output, and Printing,* and Chapter 11, *Painting the Screen.* When a metafile is "played," the result is the same as if the GDI functions had been used directly. The difference is that metafiles can be stored in memory or as disk files, reloaded, and played any number of times by different applications. Metafiles are frequently the most compact means of storing graphical data. Most GDI functions require less than 16 bytes of data when encoded in a metafile The exact number of bytes depends on the number of parameters the function uses. Compare metafiles to bitmaps. A 100 by 100 pixel bitmap with 16 colors requires 5,000 bytes of storage. Metafiles are also more device-independent than bitmaps, as the GDI functions are interpreted at run time, based on the output device context.

Creating and Playing a Memory Metafile

Metafiles are created by using GDI functions on a metafile device context. This is a special type of device context that only records the GDI function calls, not the results of the functions. If the GDI function calls are recorded in memory, the metafile is a "memory metafile."

To create a metafile that draws a rectangle filled with a hatched brush pattern, use the following code:

```
static              HANDLE  hMetaFile ;
HBRUSH              hBrush ;
HDC                 hMetaDC, hDC ;

hMetaDC = CreateMetaFile (NULL) ;          /* create memory metafile */
if (hMetaDC != NULL)
{
        hBrush = CreateHatchBrush (HS_DIAGCROSS, RGB (0, 0, 255)) ;
        SelectObject (hMetaDC, hBrush) ;
        Rectangle (hMetaDC, 0, 0, 100, 50) ;
        hMetaFile = CloseMetaFile (hMetaDC) ;      /* stop GDI input */
        DeleteObject (hBrush) ;
        hDC = GetDC (hWnd) ;
        PlayMetaFile (hDC, hMetaFile) ;  /* display metafile to hDC */
        ReleaseDC (hWnd, hDC) ;
}
```

CreateMetaFile() creates the metafile device context. The GDI functions CreateHatchBrush(), SelectObject(), and Rectangle() are recorded into this device context. When all of the graphics functions have been recorded, the metafile device context is closed with CloseMetaFile().

CloseMetaFile() returns a handle to the memory metafile, which is a global memory area containing the encoded GDI function calls. PlayMetaFile() is used to display this data to a physical device, such as the screen or printer. PlayMetaFile() sends each encoded function to the Windows GDI. The results appear just as if the GDI functions were being used directly. If you are going to use the metafile again, you will want to save the metafile handle as a static variable.

Creating and Displaying a Disk Metafile

The GDI functions can be captured in a disk file just as easily as in a memory block. The advantage of using a disk file is that the metafile can be saved and played later without the time required to re-create all of the GDI function calls.

Here is the same example shown previously, but using a disk metafile:

```
HANDLE          hMetaFile ;
HBRUSH          hBrush ;
HDC             hMetaDC, hDC ;

hMetaDC = CreateMetaFile ("mymeta.mf") ; /* create disk metafile */
if (hMetaDC != NULL)
{
        hBrush = CreateHatchBrush (HS_DIAGCROSS, RGB (0, 0, 255)) ;
        SelectObject (hMetaDC, hBrush) ;
        Rectangle (hMetaDC, 0, 0, 100, 50) ;
        CloseMetaFile (hMetaDC) ;
        DeleteObject (hBrush) ;
}
```

[Other program lines]

```
hDC = GetDC (hWnd) ;
hMetaFile = GetMetaFile ("mymeta.mf") ;             /* load metafile */
PlayMetaFile (hDC, hMetaFile) ;                     /* display it on hDC */
ReleaseDC (hWnd, hDC) ;
```

In this example, a file name is passed to CreateMetaFile(). The encoded GDI calls go into this file, rather than into a memory area. Later in the program, the GetMetaFile() function is used to load the disk metafile into memory so that it can be played using PlayMetaFile().

There are two common uses for disk metafiles. One is as a compact method of storing graphics data for use in a program. The metafiles are generated as the program is developed. The final program is distributed with the metafiles on the distribution disks. The program uses the metafile data, without having to generate the metafile each time the program is run. The second use for disk metafiles is as a means of storing graphics data for a painting or design application. Metafiles are ideal if the application uses objects like lines, rectangles, and ellipses for drawing. Metafiles are not useful if the paint program is pixel based, allowing arbitrary changes to any pixel. In this case, a DIB bitmap is the best option. Windows also uses metafiles internally when printing to a printer that only prints one band of pixels at a time (such as a dot matrix printer). The GDI outputs are stored in a metafile before printing begins. The metafile is played once for each band of printer output. A convenient way to keep track of metafiles used by a program is to add them to the .RC resource script file. The line

```
mymeta METAFILE "mymeta.mf"
```

will include the MYMETA.MF disk metafile in the resource data. When it is time to play the metafile, the data can be recovered from the resource pool by using

```
HANDLE          hMetaFile, hResource ;
HDC             hDC ;

hResource = LoadResource (hInstance, FindResource (hInstance, "mymeta", "METAFILE")) ;
LockResource (hResource) ;
hMetaFile = SetMetaFileBits (hResource) ;
GlobalUnlock (hResource) ;

hDC = GetDC (hWnd) ;
PlayMetaFile (hDC, hMetaFile) ;
ReleaseDC (hWnd, hDC) ;
```

SetMetaFileBits() returns a handle that can be passed to PlayMetaFile() to display the metafile data.

Metafile Disk Format

Normally, you will not have to be concerned with the data format used internally by metafiles. If you are curious, read on. Otherwise, skip to the next section. The disk file format for metafiles starts with a METAHEADER structure, defined in WINDOWS.H as follows:

```
typedef struct tagMETAHEADER
{
        WORD            mtType;             /* 1=memory, 2=disk file*/
        WORD            mtHeaderSize;       /* the size of this header */
        WORD            mtVersion;          /* windows version number, 0x300 = ver 3.0 */
        DWORD           mtSize;             /* size of the data */
        WORD            mtNoObjects;        /* number of objects (brush, pen, etc) */
        DWORD           mtMaxRecord;        /* size of the largest record */
        WORD            mtNoParameters      /* reserved */
} METAHEADER
```

After the header, each GDI function is encoded in a METARECORD data structure.

```
typedef struct tagMETARECORD
 {
        DWORD     rdSize;                  /* size of the record */
        WORD      rdFunction;             /* the function id value */
    WORD          rdParm[1];              /* parameter data - may be more than one */
 } METARECORD;
typedef METARECORD                  *PMETARECORD;
typedef METARECORD FAR              *LPMETARECORD;
```

The METARECORD structure is the same structure used to encode the metafile data in memory. The key element in this structure is *rdFunction*, the numeric ID value for the GDI function. The ID values are defined in WINDOWS.H, and they all start with the prefix "META_." For example, the ID value for the LineTo() function is META_LINETO, which is defined as 0x0213. The parameter values follow the GDI function ID values. The number of parameter data words will depend on the parameters in the function.

Altering the Metafile Image

The simplest way to use a metafile is to just play back the GDI data without modification. The metafile will always be displayed in the same location and with the same dimensions, because the function parameters, such as a rectangle's *X* and *Y* corner locations, are written directly into the metafile data. To move the location where a metafile is displayed, you must "trick" the metafile by changing the logical coordinate system. If a metafile is set to output starting at the 0,0 point, but the origin is moved to the center of the window's client area, the metafile picture will be displayed in the center. The SetWindowOrg() function moves the logical origin of a device context.

Metafiles can also be stretched and compressed during playback by changing the scale of the logical coordinate system. The SetMapMode(), SetWindowExt(), and SetViewportExt() functions allow complete flexibility as to the relative scaling. The example program under the CloseMetaFile() function description uses all of these techniques to display one metafile at two different locations, with two different sizes, and scale the images to fit the size of the window's client area.

The ultimate way to modify a metafile is to intercept each GDI function call as the data is pulled from the metafile, and modify the data before it is displayed. The EnumMetaFile() and PlayMetaFileRecord() functions are provided for this purpose. To use EnumMetaFile() requires adding a callback function to your program. EnumMetaFile() calls this function once for each GDI call in the metafile. Within the callback function you can examine and change any of the coded metafile data, prior to displaying it with PlayMetaFileRecord(). The example program under the Enum MetaFile() function description uses this approach to change the pattern brush used to fill in regions.

Metafile Limitations

Not every GDI function can be recorded to a metafile. The simplest way to check whether a function can be used is to see if the function name is defined with a metafile ID number in WINDOWS.H. This is not foolproof, as some GDI IDs apply to more than one function. Here are some general rules covering the functions that cannot be used in metafiles.

1. Metafiles cannot return information about the environment because the metafile data exists independent of any real device. Functions such as PtVisible(), DPtoLP(), GetDeviceCaps(), and GetTextMetrics() will not work in a metafile.

2. Metafiles cannot process bitmap data or align brush patterns. Functions like GrayString(), DrawIcon(), and SetBrushOrg() cannot be used.

3. The metafile device context does not refer a "real" device. Functions like CreateCompatibleDC(), ReleaseDC(), and DeleteDC() should not be used in metafiles.

4. The FillRect() and FrameRect() functions do not work in metafiles because they require handles to brushes.

By design, metafiles do not have default values for pens, brushes, colors, etc. When a metafile is played, it simply executes the GDI function calls given the current status of the device context. This means that you may end up with different results depending on when a metafile is played. For example, a metafile that does not create a pen will draw with whatever pen color is in effect.

The opposite problem occurs when a metafile changes the device context settings for colors, coordinate system scaling, etc. There is no way for a metafile to determine the current settings in order to reset them to their previous state after use. Any changes made to the device context by the metafile will remain in effect after playback has stopped.

There are several ways to handle the device context changes incurred with a metafile. The simplest is to create a new device context after the metafile is played. That way any changes the metafile makes to pens, brushes, etc. will be deleted when the old device context is destroyed.

A more sophisticated way of dealing with the device context changes is to store a copy of the device context before the metafile is played. SaveDC() does this. After the metafile has been played, RestoreDC() is used to recover the old device context settings. You should decide on a general philosophy of either having the metafile use the existing brushes and pens selected into a device context, or always having the metafile create its own pens and brushes. The latter is the preferred approach.

Metafile Function Summary

Table 23-1 summarizes the metafile functions. The detailed function descriptions are in the next section.

Function	Purpose ⊠
CloseMetaFile	Closes the metafile device context, and returns a handle that can be used to play the metafile.
CopyMetaFile	Copies a metafile to either a disk file or a memory metafile.
CreateMetaFile	Creates a metafile device context, ready to receive GDI painting information.
DeleteMetaFile	Frees the system resources associated with a metafile.
EnumMetaFile	Plays a memory metafile back one GDI function at a time, allowing the GDI function parameters to be changed.
GetMetaFile	Loads a disk metafile into memory.
GetMetaFileBits	Returns a handle to the global memory block containing a memory metafile.
PlayMetaFile	Outputs a metafile to a device context.
PlayMetaFileRecord	Displays a single GDI function call to a device from within an enumeration callback function for a metafile.
SetMetaFileBits	Creates a memory metafile from data stored in a global memory block.

Table 23-1. Metafile Function Summary.

Metafile Function Descriptions

This section contains detailed descriptions for the metafile functions.

CLOSEMETAFILE
■ Win 2.0   ■ Win 3.0   ■ Win 3.1

Purpose   Closes the metafile device context and returns a handle that can be used to play the metafile.

Syntax   HANDLE **CloseMetaFile**(HANDLE *hDC*);

Description	When painting operations to the metafile device context opened with CreateMetaFile() are completed, the metafile must be closed for input. CloseMetaFile() returns a handle to the completed memory metafile. This handle is used to play the metafile using the PlayMetaFile() function.
Uses	Used after the painting operations creating the metafile are complete. This function must be used before the metafile can be displayed.
Returns	HANDLE, the metafile handle. Returns NULL on error.
See Also	CreateMetaFile(), PlayMetaFile()

Parameters

hDC

HDC: The metafile device context created with CreateMeta-File(). This device context is invalid after CloseMetaFile() is called.

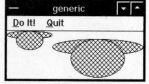

Figure 23-1. CloseMetaFile( ) Example.

Example

This example demonstrates creating and painting a metafile image. The metafile is created when the application processes the WM_CREATE message. WM_SIZE messages are intercepted to save the size of the client area. When a WM_PAINT message is received, the metafile is painted twice. The size of the image the metafile creates is changed by using the MM_ANISOTROPIC mapping mode, to change the logical device scaling. The second time the metafile is painted, the size is doubled, as the logical *X* and *Y* extents are cut in half. If the user clicks the "Do It!" menu item, the metafile is written to a disk file named "twoelips.mf." The memory metafile is deleted as the application exits.

```
long FAR PASCAL WndProc (HWND hWnd, unsigned iMessage, WORD wParam, LONG lParam)
{
        static          HANDLE          hMetaFile ;
        HBRUSH                          hBrush ;
        HDC                             hMetaDC ;
        PAINTSTRUCT                     ps ;
        static          int             xClient, yClient ;

        switch (iMessage)                       /* process windows messages */
        {
        case WM_CREATE:                         /* build memory metafile */
                hMetaDC = CreateMetaFile (NULL) ;
                if (hMetaDC != NULL)
                {
                        hBrush = CreateHatchBrush (HS_DIAGCROSS,
                                RGB (0, 0, 255)) ;
                        SelectObject (hMetaDC, hBrush) ;
                        Ellipse (hMetaDC, 0, 0, 100, 50) ;
                        Ellipse (hMetaDC, 20, 0, 80, 120) ;
                        hMetaFile = CloseMetaFile (hMetaDC) ;
                        DeleteObject (hBrush) ;
                }
                break ;
        case WM_SIZE:
                xClient = LOWORD (lParam) ;
                yClient = HIWORD (lParam) ;
                break ;
        case WM_PAINT:
                BeginPaint (hWnd, &ps) ;
                SetMapMode (ps.hdc, MM_ANISOTROPIC) ;
                SetWindowExt (ps.hdc, 300, 300) ;
                SetViewportExt (ps.hdc, xClient, yClient) ;
                SetWindowOrg (ps.hdc, 0, 0) ;
                PlayMetaFile (ps.hdc, hMetaFile) ;

                SetWindowExt (ps.hdc, 150, 150) ;
                SetViewportExt (ps.hdc, xClient, yClient) ;
```

```
                        SetWindowOrg (ps.hdc, -50, -25) ;
                        PlayMetaFile (ps.hdc, hMetaFile) ;
                        EndPaint (hWnd, &ps) ;
                        break ;
            case WM_COMMAND:                /* process menu items */
                        switch (wParam)
                        {
                        case IDM_DOIT:          /* save the meta file to disk */
                                CopyMetaFile (hMetaFile, "twoelips.mf") ;
                                break ;
                        case IDM_QUIT:
                                DestroyWindow (hWnd) ;
                                break ;
                        }
                        break ;
            case WM_DESTROY:                /* stop application */
                        DeleteMetaFile (hMetaFile) ;
                        PostQuitMessage (0) ;
                        break ;
            default:                        /* default windows message processing */
                        return DefWindowProc (hWnd, iMessage, wParam, lParam) ;
        }
        return (0L) ;
}
```

COPYMETAFILE
■ Win 2.0   ■ Win 3.0   ■ Win 3.1

Purpose	Copies a metafile to either a disk file or a memory metafile.
Syntax	HANDLE **CopyMetaFile**(HANDLE *hSrcMetaFile*, LPSTR *lpFileName*);
Description	This function copies a metafile to a disk file. Disk metafiles are a compact means of storing graphical information. Alternatively, if the *lpFileName* parameter is set to NULL, the source metafile is copied to a memory metafile.
Uses	Normally used to write memory metafile data to a disk file.
Returns	HANDLE, the handle of the new metafile created.
See Also	GetMetaFile()
Parameters	
hSrcMetaFile	HANDLE: The handle of the metafile to copy. This is the value returned by CloseMetaFile() or GetMetaFile().
lpFileName	LPSTR: A pointer to a null-terminated character string containing the disk file name to create. If *lpFileName* is set to NULL, the source metafile is copied to a new memory metafile.
Example	See the previous example under the CloseMetaFile() function description.

CREATEMETAFILE
■ Win 2.0   ■ Win 3.0   ■ Win 3.1

Purpose	Creates a metafile device context, ready to receive GDI painting information.
Syntax	HDC **CreateMetaFile**(LPSTR *lpFilename*);
Description	This function creates a metafile device context. This is not the same as a device context opened with GetDC() or CreateDC(). Metafile device contexts store GDI (Graphics Device Interface) function calls, so that they can be played back later.
Uses	This is the first step in creating a metafile.
Returns	HDC, a handle to the metafile device context created.
See Also	CloseMetaFile(), PlayMetaFile()

Parameters

lpFilename   LPSTR: A pointer to a null-terminated character string containing the name of the disk file that will receive the metafile data. Alternatively, *lpFilename* can be set to NULL, creating a memory metafile device context.

Example   See the example under the CloseMetaFile() function description.

DELETEMETAFILE   ■ Win 2.0   ■ Win 3.0   ■ Win 3.1

Purpose   Frees the system resources associated with a metafile.

Syntax   BOOL **DeleteMetaFile**(HANDLE *hMF*);

Description   This function frees the system resources associated with a metafile. The metafile handle can be retrieved with GetMetaFile(). Disk metafiles are not deleted from disk by this function.

Uses   Used to free the system memory when the metafile is no longer needed by the application.

Returns   BOOL. TRUE if the system resources have been freed, FALSE on error.

See Also   CloseMetaFile(), GetMetaFile(), CopyMetaFile()

Parameters

hMF   HANDLE: The metafile handle. This is the value returned by CloseMetaFile() when the metafile was created, or by GetMetaFile() when a disk metafile was loaded.

Example   See the example under the CloseMetaFile() function description.

ENUMMETAFILE   ■ Win 2.0   ■ Win 3.0   ■ Win 3.1

Purpose   Plays (enumerates) a memory metafile back one GDI function at a time, allowing the GDI function parameters to be changed.

Syntax   BOOL **EnumMetaFile**(HDC *hDC*, LOCALHANDLE *hMF*, FARPROC *lpCallbackFunc*, BYTE FAR **lpClientData*);

Description   Metafiles consist of a series of binary coded GDI (Graphics Device Interface) function calls. EnumMetaFile() calls a callback function once per GDI call. The callback function can examine the GDI data and modify it before using PlayMetaFileRecord() to display the GDI output.

Uses   Modifying a metafile during playback (for example to change the colors, pens, or brush patterns used).

Returns   BOOL. TRUE if the function successfully processed each GDI function call in the metafile. False on error.

See Also   PlayMetaFileRecord()

Parameters

hDC   HDC: The device context handle passed to the callback function with each enumeration.

hMF   LOCALHANDLE: The handle of the memory metafile. This is the value returned by CloseMetaFile() and/or GetMetaFile().

lpCallbackFunc   FARPROC: The procedure-instance address of the callback function. This value is returned by MakeProcInstance(). The callback function must be listed in the EXPORTS section of the program's .DEF definition file, and it must have the format shown below.

lpClientData   BYTE FAR *: A pointer to data to be passed to the callback function. This can be used to pass data, such as colors or pattern numbers, to the callback function.

Callback Function The callback function must be in the following format:

int FAR PASCAL **EnumFunc** (HDC *hDC*, LPHANDLETABLE *lpHTable*, LPMETARECORD *lpMFR*, int *nObj*, BYTE FAR **lpClientData*) ;

The callback function should return 1 to continue displaying the metafile, 0 to stop playback. The callback function parameters are defined as follows.

hDC   HDC: This is the device context handle for the device to receive the metafile output. This value is passed to the callback function by EnumMetaFile().

lpHTable   LPHANDLETABLE: A far pointer to a HANDLETABLE data structure. This is defined in WINDOWS.H as follows:

```
typedef struct tagHANDLETABLE
  {
   HANDLE        objectHandle[1];              /* can be more than one */
  } HANDLETABLE;
typedef HANDLETABLE            *PHANDLETABLE;
typedef HANDLETABLE FAR        *LPHANDLETABLE;
```

lpMFR   LPMETARECORD: A far pointer to a METARECORD data structure. This is defined in WINDOWS.H as follows:

```
typedef struct tagMETARECORD

   {
   DWORD        rdSize;                         /* the size of this record */
   WORD         rdFunction;                     /* the GDI function number */
   WORD         rdParm[1];                      /* the parameter data */
   } METARECORD;
typedef METARECORD            *PMETARECORD;
typedef METARECORD FAR        *LPMETARECORD;
```

The *rdSize* element of this structure is convenient, as the size of each METARECORD entry depends on the number of bytes of parameter data used by the GDI function called. The number of *rdParam[]* elements will depend on the number of parameters the GDI function calls. The function is identified with the *rdFunction* element. Metafile-compatible GDI functions are identified in WINDOWS.H with ID values starting with "MF_."

nObj   int: The number of objects with handles stored in the HANDLE TABLE.

lpClientData BYTE FAR *: The data passed to the callback function by EnumMetaFile().

Example   As shown in Figure 23-2, this example displays the disk metafile TWOELIPS.MF when the user clicks the "Do It!" menu item. During playback, the brush pattern used in the Create HatchBrush() GDI function call is changed to the HS_CROSS style. Compare this figure with Figure 23-1 to see the differences in the brush patterns.

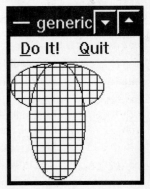

The brush pattern is changed within the metafile enumeration function EnumMF(), shown at the bottom of the listing. This function is called one time for every GDI call in the metafile. EnumMF() checks for the GDI function ID for Create HatchBrush(), and then modifies one of the parameter values before passing the data to PlayMetaFileRecord(). Note that EnumMF() must be listed in the EXPORTS section of the program's .DEF definition file, and it must have a function prototype added to the program's header file.

Figure 23-2. Enum Meta-File() Example.

```
Long FAR PASCAL WndProc (HWND hWnd, unsigned iMessage, WORD wParam, LONG lParam)
{
        static          HANDLE          hMetaFile ;
        HDC                             hDC ;
        FARPROC                         fpEnumFunc ;
```

```
        switch (iMessage)                        /* process windows messages */
        {
                case WM_CREATE:                  /* load metafile */
                        if(!(hMetaFile = GetMetaFile ("twoelips.mf")))
                                MessageBox (hWnd, "Could not load TWOELIPS.MF",
                                        "File Problem", MB_OK) ;
                        break ;
                case WM_COMMAND:                 /* process menu items */
                        switch (wParam)
                        {
                        case IDM_DOIT:
                                hDC = GetDC (hWnd) ;
                                fpEnumFunc = MakeProcInstance (EnumMF, ghInstance) ;
                                EnumMetaFile (hDC, hMetaFile, fpEnumFunc, NULL) ;
                                FreeProcInstance (fpEnumFunc) ;
                                ReleaseDC (hWnd, hDC) ;
                                break ;
                        case IDM_QUIT:           /* send end of application message */
                                DestroyWindow (hWnd) ;
                                break ;
                        }
                        break ;
                case WM_DESTROY:                 /* stop application */
                        DeleteMetaFile (hMetaFile) ;
                        PostQuitMessage (0) ;
                        break ;
                default:                         /* default windows message processing */
                        return DefWindowProc (hWnd, iMessage, wParam, lParam) ;
        }
        return (0L) ;
}


int FAR PASCAL EnumMF (HDC hDC, LPHANDLETABLE lpHTable,
        LPMETARECORD lpMFR, int nObj, BYTE FAR *lpClientData)
{
        /* check for create hatch brush function == MF_CREATEBRUSHINDIRECT */
        if (lpMFR->rdFunction == MF_CREATEBRUSHINDIRECT)
        {
                lpMFR->rdParm [3] = HS_CROSS ;   /* change brush pattern */
        }
        PlayMetaFileRecord (hDC, lpHTable, lpMFR, nObj) ;
        return (1) ;
}
```

GetMetaFile

■ Win 2.0   ■ Win 3.0   ■ Win 3.1

Purpose	Loads a disk metafile into memory.
Syntax	HANDLE **GetMetaFile**(LPSTR *lpFilename*);
Description	This function reads a disk metafile into memory and returns a handle to the metafile. The handle can be used to display the metafile using PlayMetaFile().
Uses	Disk metafiles are a compact way to store graphics data created with GDI function calls. They require much less space than storing the bitmapped image.
Returns	HANDLE, the metafile handle. Returns NULL on error, such as not finding the disk file.
See Also	PlayMetaFile(), CopyMetaFile(), CreateMetaFile()

*Figure 23-3. GetMetaFile()
Example.*

Parameters

lpFilename   LPSTR: A pointer to a null-terminated string containing the DOS file name of the disk metafile. This can be an extended file name, including the full directory name.

Example   This example, which is shown in Figure 23-3, displays the disk metafile "twoelips.mf.". See the CloseMetaFile() function description for an example program that creates the disk metafile.

```
long FAR PASCAL WndProc (HWND hWnd, unsigned iMessage, WORD wParam, LONG lParam)
{
        static          HANDLE          hMetaFile = NULL ;
        PAINTSTRUCT                     ps ;
        HANDLE                          hMem ;
        char                            cBuf [128] ;
        HDC                             hDC ;
        int                             nSize ;

        switch (iMessage)                               /* process windows messages */
        {
        case WM_CREATE:                         /* load metafile */
                if(!(hMetaFile = GetMetaFile ("twoelips.mf")))
                        MessageBox (hWnd, "Could not load TWOELIPS.MF",
                                "File Problem", MB_OK) ;
                break ;
        case WM_PAINT:
                BeginPaint (hWnd, &ps) ;
                if (hMetaFile)
                        PlayMetaFile (ps.hdc, hMetaFile) ;
                EndPaint (hWnd, &ps) ;
                break ;
        case WM_COMMAND:
                switch (wParam)
                {
                case IDM_QUIT:
                        DestroyWindow (hWnd) ;
                        break ;
                }
                break ;
        case WM_DESTROY:
                DeleteMetaFile (hMetaFile) ;
                PostQuitMessage (0) ;
                break ;
        default:
                return DefWindowProc (hWnd, iMessage, wParam, lParam) ;
        }
        return (OL) ;
}
```

GetMetaFileBits   ■ Win 2.0   ■ Win 3.0   ■ Win 3.1

Purpose   Returns a handle to the global memory block containing a memory metafile.

Syntax   HANDLE **GetMetaFileBits**(HANDLE *hMF*);

Description   This function returns a handle to a global memory block containing a metafile. The metafile data consists of binary-coded GDI function calls. This data should not be modified. The *hMF* handle to the metafile is invalid after GetMetaFileBits() returns. SetMetaFileBits() can be used to restore the metafile handle.

Uses   Applications can manipulate the global memory block using the normal memory management functions. This is typically done in order to copy more than one memory metafile into a file or data structure used by a graphics program.

Returns   HANDLE, the global memory handle for the metafile data. NULL on error.

See Also   SetMetaFileBits() is used to restore the metafile handle after GetMetaFileBits() has been called.

Parameters

hMF   HANDLE: The memory metafile handle. This is the value returned by CloseMetaFile() and/or GetMetaFile().

Example   This example creates and paints a metafile. When the user clicks the "Do It!" menu item, the program obtains a global memory handle to the memory block containing the memory metafile. The GlobalSize() function is used to determine the size of the memory block. The metafile requires 128 bytes of storage, which is remarkably compact. For comparison, 128 bytes would store only 32 pixels of a bitmap with a 16-color bitmap. The graphics portion of Figure 23-4 contains 13,000 pixels, or 6,500 bytes if stored as a bitmap.

Figure 23-4. GetMeta-FileBits( ) Example.

```
Long FAR PASCAL WndProc (HWND hWnd, unsigned iMessage, WORD wParam, LONG lParam)
{
        static          HANDLE          hMetaFile = NULL;
        HBRUSH                          hBrush ;
        HDC                             hMetaDC ;
        int                             nSize ;
        PAINTSTRUCT                     ps ;
        HDC                             hDC ;
        HANDLE                          hMem ;
        char                            cBuf [128] ;

        switch (iMessage)                       /* process windows messages */
        {
        case WM_CREATE:                     /* build metafile */
                hMetaDC = CreateMetaFile (NULL) ;
                if (hMetaDC != NULL)
                {
                        hBrush = CreateHatchBrush (HS_DIAGCROSS,
                                RGB (0, 0, 255)) ;
                        SelectObject (hMetaDC, hBrush) ;
                        Rectangle (hMetaDC, 0, 0, 100, 30) ;
                        Pie (hMetaDC, 0, 30, 100, 100, 100, 100, 0, 100) ;
                        MoveTo (hMetaDC, 0, 100) ;
                        LineTo (hMetaDC, 100, 100) ;
                        hMetaFile = CloseMetaFile (hMetaDC) ;
                        DeleteObject (hBrush) ;
                }
                break ;
        case WM_PAINT:
                BeginPaint (hWnd, &ps) ;
                if (hMetaFile)
                        PlayMetaFile (ps.hdc, hMetaFile) ;
                EndPaint (hWnd, &ps) ;
                break ;
        case WM_COMMAND:                    /* process menu items */
                switch (wParam)
                {
                case IDM_DOIT:
                        hDC = GetDC (hWnd) ;
                        hMem = GetMetaFileBits (hMetaFile) ;
                        nSize = GlobalSize (hMem) ;
                        hMetaFile = SetMetaFileBits (hMem) ;
                        TextOut (hDC, 0, 120, cBuf, wsprintf (cBuf,
                                "Metafile size = %d bytes.", nSize)) ;
```

```
                              ReleaseDC (hWnd, hDC) ;
                              break ;
                    case IDM_QUIT:
                              DestroyWindow (hWnd) ;
                              break ;
                    }
                    break ;
          case WM_DESTROY:                    /* stop application */
                    DeleteMetaFile (hMetaFile) ;
                    PostQuitMessage (0) ;
                    break ;
          default:                            /* default windows message processing */
                    return DefWindowProc (hWnd, iMessage, wParam, lParam) ;
          }
     return (0L) ;
}
```

PLAYMETAFILE
■ Win 2.0 ■ Win 3.0 ■ Win 3.1

Purpose	Outputs a metafile to a device context.
Syntax	BOOL **PlayMetaFile**(HDC *hDC*, HANDLE *hMF*);
Description	This function runs the metafile in order to display the graphics output. The metafile GDI (Graphics Device Interface) function calls are played to the *hDC* device context. The size and location of the output can be changed by setting different device context scalings and origin locations for *hDC*.
Uses	Displaying a metafile on a device.
Returns	BOOL. TRUE if the function was successful, FALSE on error.
See Also	CreateMetaFile(), CloseMetaFile, SetWindowExt(), SetWindowOrg()
Parameters	
hDC	HDC: The device context handle for the device that will receive the metafile output.
hMF	HANDLE: The handle of the metafile to play. This is the value returned by CloseMetaFile() or GetMetaFile().
Example	See the example under the CloseMetaFile() function description.

PLAYMETAFILERECORD
■ Win 2.0 ■ Win 3.0 ■ Win 3.1

Purpose	Displays a single GDI function call to a device from within an enumeration callback function for a metafile.
Syntax	void **PlayMetaFileRecord**(HDC *hDC*, LPHANDLETABLE *lpHandletable*, LPMETARECORD *lpMetaRecord*, WORD *nHandles*);
Description	EnumMetaFile() calls a callback function once per GDI function in the metafile. Within the callback function, PlayMetaFileRecord() is used to output the single GDI call to the device. The GDI parameter data can be modified before this function is called.
Uses	Used within the callback function when using EnumMetaFile() to modify a metafile during playback.
Returns	No returned value (void).
See Also	EnumMetaFile()
Parameters	
hDC	HDC: The device context handle for the device to receive the GDI output. This is the HDC passed to the callback function by EnumMetaFile().

lpHandletable   LPHANDLETABLE: A far pointer to a HANDLETABLE data structure, defined in WINDOWS.H as follows:

```
typedef struct tagHANDLETABLE
  {
  HANDLE        objectHandle[1];                /* can be more than one */
  } HANDLETABLE;
typedef HANDLETABLE             *PHANDLETABLE;
typedef HANDLETABLE FAR         *LPHANDLETABLE;
```

lpMetaRecord   LPMETARECORD: A far pointer to a METARECORD data structure, defined in WINDOWS.H as follows:

```
typedef struct tagMETARECORD
  {
  DWORD           rdSize;                 /* the size of this record */
  WORD            rdFunction;             /* the GDI function number */
  WORD            rdParm[1];              /* the parameters */
  } METARECORD;
typedef METARECORD              *PMETARECORD;
typedef METARECORD FAR          *LPMETARECORD;
```

nHandles   WORD: The number of handles in the HANDLETABLE. This value is passed to the callback function as the *nObj* parameter.

Example   See the example under the EnumMetaFile() function description.

SetMetaFileBits

    ■ Win 2.0   ■ Win 3.0   ■ Win 3.1

Purpose	Creates a memory metafile from data stored in a global memory block.
Syntax	HANDLE **SetMetaFileBits**(HANDLE *hMem*);
Description	GetMetaFileBits() is used to obtain a handle to a memory metafile's global memory block. After it is called, SetMetaFileBits() should be used to restore the metafile handle. SetMetaFileBits() returns a valid metafile handle that can be used for PlayMetaFile().
Uses	Used to convert a block of resource data into a memory metafile that can be played using PlayMetaFile().
Returns	HANDLE, a memory metafile handle that can be passed to PlayMetaFile().
See Also	GetMetaFileBits()
Parameters	
hMem	HANDLE: The memory handle of the global memory block containing the metafile. This handle is returned by GetMetaFileBits() or LoadResource().
Example	See the example under the GetMetaFileBits() function description. Also see the discussion of loading a metafile as resource data at the beginning of this chapter.

The Timer

Windows includes the useful ability to set timers. Once set, a timer sends WM_TIMER messages to an application at preset intervals. These messages continue until the timer is shut off. Timers are used more frequently in Windows applications than in programs running in a conventional environment, such as MS-DOS. A DOS program can just loop forever, waiting for some event to occur. This situation would not work under Windows, as the application would take over the system and not allow other applications to run. Timers are a convenient way to periodically initiate some action, without having the application hog the environment.

Using Timers

Windows allows a maximum of 16 timers to be active at once. Each timer has a separate ID value, so that an application can use more than one timer. The timers use the system clock, which limits the minimum time between timer events to 55 milliseconds. Longer time periods, up to about 596 hours, are possible.

The SetTimer() function starts a timer. There are two ways to use this function. The most common way is to call SetTimer() with the fourth parameter set to NULL.

```
static int nTimer ;

if (!(nTimer = SetTimer (hWnd, 1, 1000, NULL)))
        MessageBox (hWnd, "No Timers Left!", "Message",
                MB_OK) ;
```

In this case, the timer will send WM_TIMER messages to the program's WndProc() function every 1,000 milliseconds (once per second). The timer's ID value is returned by SetTimer(). The ID is an integer value that will be passed as the *wParam* value when the WM_TIMER message is received. If more than one timer is set, the timers will have different ID values, so they can be kept apart. Note that the SetTimer() return value is checked to see if it is zero. A zero value means that all 16 timers are being used. This is possible, so be sure to check this value before proceeding.

The other way to call SetTimer() is to pass a procedure-instance address of a callback function to the function. The callback function receives the WM_TIMER messages, not the WndProc() function. A typical program fragment for this usage is

```
static int nTimer ;

fpTimerFunc = MakeProcInstance (TimerFunction, ghInstance) ;
if (!(nTimer = SetTimer (hWnd, 1, 15000, fpTimerFunc)))
        MessageBox (hWnd, "No timers left!", "Message",
                MB_OK) ;
```

The callback function must follow a specific format, and it must be listed in the EXPORTS section of the program's .DEF definition file. See the SetTimer() function description for a complete example.

The WM_TIMER messages will continue until the timer is shut down with the KillTimer() function.

```
KillTimer (hWnd, nTimer) ;
```

Timer Accuracy

Although timers can be set to a frequency of one every 55 milliseconds, the interval between timer events will not be that accurate. This inaccuracy is because the WM_TIMER messages are placed on the application's message queue.

Windows will only place the WM_TIMER message on the queue if the queue is empty (empty of all messages except WM_PAINT). Windows will not put more than one WM_TIMER message on the queue. This keeps the queue from filling up with WM_TIMER messages if a very short time interval is set.

For most applications, exact precision between WM_TIMER messages is not necessary because the applications are not significantly affected if the WM_TIMER message is a bit late. For applications that require greater accuracy, other techniques are required. Applications like music recording/playback and some process control programs require more accurate time keeping. This is generally done by using hardware interrupts, processed by a small program function and data buffer in a page locked memory block. The Windows program can periodically read and write to the memory buffer, leaving the exact timing of transmission/reception to the interrupt driven routine.

Other Time Functions

Windows keeps track of the number of milliseconds since the system was started. This period of time is called "Windows time." The millisecond count is a DWORD value that can be retrieved using GetCurrentTime() or GetTick Count(). Every Windows message is tagged with a time value. You can determine this value by either examining the contents of the MSG data structure in the program's message loop, or by calling the GetMessageTime() function within the body of the program.

Windows does not provide a way to determine the outside world date and time from the system clock. The C compiler run-time library functions time() and ctime() can be used to fetch the current date/time and convert it to a character sting.

Timer Function Summary

Table 24-1 summarizes the Windows timer functions. The detailed function descriptions are in the next section.

Function	Purpose	
GetCurrentTime	Returns the number of milliseconds since the system was booted.	⊠
GetTickCount	Returns the number of milliseconds since the system was booted.	
KillTimer	Stops a timer.	
SetTimer	Starts a Windows timer.	

Table 24-1. Timer Function Summary.

Function Descriptions

This section contains the detailed description of Windows time functions.

GETCURRENTTIME
■ Win 2.0   ■ Win 3.0   ■ Win 3.1

Purpose	Returns the number of milliseconds since the system was booted.
Syntax	DWORD **GetCurrentTime**(void);
Description	Windows keeps an internal clock that starts when the system is booted. Each message is tagged with the clock count when the message is sent (GetMessageTime() retrieves this value). GetCurrentTime() returns the current clock count. The maximum accuracy is about 1/18th of a second.
Uses	Used to determine how long a message has been waiting in the message queue. The difference between GetCurrentTime() and GetMessageTime() is the delay.
Returns	DWORD, the internal clock count in milliseconds.
See Also	GetTickCount()
Parameters	None (void).
Example	This example, which is illustrated in Figure 24-1, sets a one second timer when the user clicks the "Do It!" menu item. When a WM_TIME message is received, both the message time and Windows

current clock value are retrieved. The difference between the two is the length of time the WM_TIME message waited on the application's message queue. Because the WM_TIME messages are sent only if Windows passes control to the application, there will be no time delays if the application is sharing the Windows environment with other Windows applications. However, if Windows is running DOS applications concurrently in 386 enhanced mode, delays will be registered by this program.

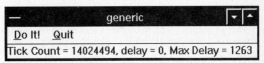

Figure 24-1. GetCurrentTime( ) Example.

```
Long FAR PASCAL WndProc (HWND hWnd, unsigned iMessage, WORD wParam, LONG lParam)
{
        DWORD                   dwTickCount, dwMessageTime, dwDelay ;
        static          DWORD   dwMaxDelay = 0 ;
        char                    cBuf [128] ;
        HDC                     hDC ;
        static          int     nTimer ;

        switch (iMessage)                               /* process windows messages */
        {
                case WM_TIMER:
                        hDC = GetDC (hWnd) ;
                        SetBkMode (hDC, OPAQUE) ;
                        dwTickCount = GetCurrentTime () ;
                        dwMessageTime = GetMessageTime () ;
                        dwDelay = dwTickCount - dwMessageTime ;
                        if (dwDelay > dwMaxDelay)
                                dwMaxDelay = dwDelay ;
                        TextOut (hDC, 0, 0, cBuf, wsprintf (cBuf,
                                "Tick Count = %lu, delay = %lu, Max Delay = %lu ",
                                dwTickCount, dwDelay, dwMaxDelay)) ;
                        ReleaseDC (hWnd, hDC) ;
                        break ;
                case WM_COMMAND:                        /* process menu items */
                        switch (wParam)
                        {
                        case IDM_DOIT:
                                if (!(nTimer = SetTimer (hWnd, 1, 1000, NULL)))
                                        MessageBox (hWnd, "No Timers Left!", "Message",
                                                MB_OK) ;
                                break ;
                        case IDM_QUIT:
                                DestroyWindow (hWnd) ;
                                break ;
                        }
                        break ;
                case WM_DESTROY:                        /* stop application */
                        KillTimer (hWnd, nTimer) ;
                        PostQuitMessage (0) ;
                        break ;
                default:                                /* default windows message processing */
                        return DefWindowProc (hWnd, iMessage, wParam, lParam) ;
        }
        return (0L) ;
}
```

GETTICKCOUNT   ■ Win 2.0   ■ Win 3.0   ■ Win 3.1

Purpose	Returns the number of milliseconds since the system was booted.
Syntax	DWORD **GetTickCount**(void);
Description	This function is identical to GetCurrentTime().
Returns	DWORD, the number of milliseconds since the system was booted.
See Also	GetCurrentTime()

Parameters	None (void).
Example	The previous example can be modified to use GetTickCount() in place of GetCurrentTime() with no change in the operation of the program.

KILLTIMER ■ Win 2.0　　■ Win 3.0　　■ Win 3.1

Purpose	Stops a timer.
Syntax	BOOL **KillTimer**(HWND *hWnd*, int *nIDEvent*);
Description	Timers are created with SetTimer(). Once set, the timer will continue to generate WM_TIMER messages until the KillTimer() function is used to stop the timer's execution. Any pending WM_TIMER messages are removed from the message queue when KillTimer() is executed.
Uses	Shutting down a Windows timer. This is necessary to return the timer to Windows, so that it can be used by another application.
Returns	BOOL. TRUE if the timer was removed, FALSE on error.
See Also	SetTimer()
Parameters	
hWnd	HWND: The handle of the window that owns the timer.
nIDEvent	int: The ID value of the timer to kill. This is the value returned by SetTimer.
Related Messages	WM_TIMER
Example	See the examples under the SetTimer() and GetCurrentTime() function descriptions.

SETTIMER ■ Win 2.0　　■ Win 3.0　　■ Win 3.1

Purpose	Starts a Windows timer.
Syntax	WORD **SetTimer**(HWND *hWnd*, int *nIDEvent*, WORD *wElapse*, FARPROC *lpTimerFunc*);
Description	This function starts a timer. If *lpTimerFunc* is set to NULL, the timer sends WM_TIMER messages to the application at the *wElapse* interval. If *lpTimerFunc* is a procedure-instance address of a callback function, the WM_TIMER messages are sent directly to that function, bypassing the normal WndProc() message processing.
	Because the timer messages are placed on the application's message queue, they will not be received at the exact interval specified by *wElapse*, but they may be delayed by other Windows activities. A maximum of 16 timers are available to all applications running on the system. The application should check the returned value from SetTimer() to verify that a timer was available.
Uses	Any time a periodic interruption is required within a Windows application.
Returns	WORD, the integer ID of the timer. This value is passed to KillTimer() to remove the timer. Returns zero if no timer was available.
See Also	KillTimer()
Parameters	
hWnd	HWND: The handle of the window that will receive the WM_TIMER messages.
nIDEvent	int: The number of the timer. This value will be passed with the WM_TIMER message as the *wParam* value. Timer ID values allow more than one timer to be set within an application, and their WM_TIMER messages to be distinguished.
wElapse	WORD: The number of milliseconds between timer events. The minimum time between events is about 55 milliseconds.
lpTimerFunc	FARPROC: This is set to NULL if the application will receive the WM_TIMER messages directly to the WndProc() function. To send the WM_TIMER messages to a separate callback function,

set *lpTimerFunc* to the procedure-instance address of the callback function. This is the value returned by MakeProcInstance().

Callback Function The timer callback function must be in the following form:

WORD FAR PASCAL **TimerFunc** (HWND *hWnd*, WORD *wMsg*, int *nIDEvent*, DWORD *dwTime*) ;

hWnd   HWND: The window handle of the window owning the timer.

wMsg   WORD: Always WM_TIMER.

nIDEvent   int: The ID number of the timer. This is the returned value set when the SetTimer() function was called.

dwTime   DWORD: The Windows clock value when the callback function is first called. This value is not updated as the callback function is repeatedly called.

Related Messages WM_TIMER

Example This example, which is illustrated in Figure 24-2, sets a timer that calls a callback function directly, rather than issuing WM_TIMER messages. The callback function displays the number of milliseconds since the system was started. The callback function TimerFunction() must be listed in the EXPORTS section of the program's .DEF definition, and a function prototype should be included in the header file. Note that the callback function cannot use the *dwTime* parameter to show the system time. *dwTime* is only valid the first time the callback function is called. (See the example under GetCurrentTime() for an example of setting a timer without a callback function.)

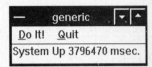

Figure 24-2. SetTimer() Example.

```
Long FAR PASCAL WndProc (HWND hWnd, unsigned iMessage, WORD wParam, LONG lParam)
{
        FARPROC fpTimerFunc ;
        static  int     nTimer ;

        switch (iMessage)                       /* process windows messages */
        {
                case WM_TIMER:
                        break ;
                case WM_COMMAND:                /* process menu items */
                        switch (wParam)
                        {
                        case IDM_DOIT:
                                fpTimerFunc = MakeProcInstance (TimerFunction,
                                        ghInstance) ;
                                if (!(nTimer = SetTimer (hWnd, 1, 1000,
                                        fpTimerFunc)))
                                        MessageBox (hWnd, "No timers left!", "Message",
                                        MB_OK) ;
                                break ;
                        case IDM_QUIT:
                                DestroyWindow (hWnd) ;
                                break ;
                        }
                        break ;
                case WM_DESTROY:                /* stop application */
                        KillTimer (hWnd, nTimer) ;
                        FreeProcInstance (fpTimerFunc) ;
                        PostQuitMessage (0) ;
                        break ;
                default:                        /* default windows message processing */
                        return DefWindowProc (hWnd, iMessage, wParam, lParam) ;
        }
        return (0L) ;
}

WORD FAR PASCAL TimerFunction (HWND hWnd, WORD wMsg, int nIDTimer, DWORD dwTime)
```

```
{
        HDC             hDC ;
        char    cBuf [128] ;
        DWORD   dwCurrentTime ;

        dwCurrentTime = GetCurrentTime () ;
        hDC = GetDC (hWnd) ;
        SetBkMode (hDC, OPAQUE) ;
        TextOut (hDC, 0, 0, cBuf, wsprintf (cBuf,
                "System Up %lu msec.", dwCurrentTime)) ;
        ReleaseDC (hWnd, hDC) ;
}
```

Every example program in this book uses resources. The .RC resource script file of the GENERIC application includes the menu definition and program icon data. Other examples of defining dialog boxes, keyboard accelerators, and menus have been discussed in their respective chapters. Resources are frequently the most convenient way to store raw data needed by the program. Combining the static data needed by the application in the resource file avoids having a number of separate files that the application reads when needed. Resources are also efficient because they are usually loaded into memory only when needed.

The Resource Compiler

The NMAKE file for the GENERIC application includes two calls to the resource compiler RC.EXE (shown here with debugging options set on).

```
ALL: generic.exe

CFLAGS=-c -D LINT_ARGS -Zi -Od -Gsw -W2
LFLAGS=/NOD /co

generic.obj : generic.c generic.h
    $(CC) $(CFLAGS) generic.c

generic.res:  generic.rc generic.ico paragraf.txt
    rc -r generic.rc

generic.exe : generic.obj generic.def generic.res
    link $(LFLAGS) generic, , ,libw slibcew, generic
    rc generic.res
```

The first call to RC has the "-r" switch. This switch just compiles the resource file GENERIC.RC, producing an output file GENERIC.RES. The second call to the RC at the bottom of the listing does not have the "-r" switch. This call adds the compiled resource data to the executable program, creating the finished ready-to-run program. It also marks the program with the Windows version data, even if the program does not have resource data. The version data is detected when Windows version 3.0 or higher starts a program. If an earlier version of Windows is detected, a warning message is put on the screen.

Both the resource compilation and final program assembly can be done with one call to RC. Just drop the first call to RC, and eliminate the ".res" after the resource name on the last line. Combining them this way is not recommended because the compilation is slow relative to final assembly. If there have been no changes to the resource data, there is no reason to recompile the resources every time the program is compiled and linked. There are some other compiler switches that you may find useful. They are listed in Table 25-1.

Value	Meaning
-R	Compile only. Creates a .RES file from a .RC file.
-D	Defines a symbol. This allows conditional compilation of the resource file if you use compiler directives, such as #ifdef in the .RC file (explained later).
-FO	Renames the output .RES file. The character string following this switch will be the output file name.

Table 25-1. continued

Value	Meaning	
-FE	Renames the .EXE file. The character string following this switch will be the .EXE file name.	☒
-I	Specifies a directory to search for include files.	
-V	Verbose compiler messages.	
-X	Prevents searching of directories in the DOS PATH environment variable when the resource compiler is looking for include files.	
-L or -LIM32	Use Lotus/Intel/Microsoft Expanded Memory Specification (EMS).	
-M or -MULTINST	Assigns each program instance to a separate EMS bank (only if the EMS 4.0 memory configuration is active).	
-E	Changes the global memory location for a DLL to above the EMS bank line.	
-P	Creates a private DLL (dynamic link library) that is only accessible to one application.	
-K	Disables load optimization of PRELOAD resources. By default all PRELOAD resource data is grouped together so that it can be loaded quickly.	
-T	Creates an application that will not run in Window's real mode.	
-? or -H	Displays help information on the resource compiler.	

Table 25-1. Resource Compiler Switches.

You can combine more than one letter option after an initial dash. For example

```
RC -T -K -R generic.rc
```

is equivalent to

```
RC -TKR generic.rc
```

Capital and lowercase letters are equivalent.

The Resource Script File

All of the resources used by the program are defined in the resource script file. Here is a typical example.

```
/* generic.rc */
#include <windows.h>
#include "generic.h"

generic         ICON    generic.ico

generic         MENU
BEGIN
    MENUITEM "&Do It!"    IDM_DOIT
    MENUITEM "&Quit",     IDM_QUIT
END
```

This resource script file includes an icon file in the data and defines the program's menu.

There are four single-line resource script statements: BITMAP, CURSOR, FONT, and ICON. Each of these statements loads a data file of the specified type into the resource data. Once included in the resource data, the LoadBitmap(), LoadCursor(), and LoadIcon() functions are provided for direct access to the respective data within a program. AddFontResource() is the normal means of adding font data for use by all applications. There are five multiple-line resource script statements: ACCELERATORS, DIALOG, MENU, RCDATA, and STRINGTABLE. The first three are explained in Chapters 7, 13, and 4, respectively. The RCDATA and STRINGTABLE statements are described later in this chapter.

The resource compiler recognizes a number of directives that can be used to control compilation. The most common one is #include, which allows other files to be included into the resource file during compilation. The header file and any dialog box definition files (created by the dialog box editor) are typically added to the resource file using #include lines.

Different parts of the resource file can be compiled by using conditional compilation directives. They are #elif (else if), #else, #endif, #if, #ifdef, #ifndef, and #undef. These switches are usually used to allow the same resource file to compile both debug and non-debug versions. For example, the a resource file in the format

```
#ifdef DEBUG
        [debug program lines]
#else
        [non-debug program lines]
#endif
```

would only compile the first group of program lines if the variable DEBUG was defined. It could be defined at the top of the resource script file with the #define directive, or defined in the command line for RC using the -D switch.

```
rc -r -d DEBUG generic.rc
```

Using the command line switch is a better approach, as it means that the debugging options can be controlled entirely from the program's NMAKE file.

String Tables

Most programs use a series of character strings in messages and character outputs. The conventional programming practice is to code the character strings right into the program as static data. Windows provides an alternative, called a string table. In this case, the character strings are defined in the resource data and are given an ID value. Here is an example.

```
STRINGTABLE
BEGIN
        S_TITLE                 "Caption From .RC"
        S_STRING                "String Loaded From .RC"
END
```

Each string is given an ID value, which is usually defined in a separate header file.

```
/* generic.h */

#define S_TITLE        16                      /* string table ID values */
#define S_STRING       17
```

When the application needs to use the data, the LoadString() function copies the character data from the resource file into a memory buffer.

```
char    gszTitle [32] ;
char    gszString [64] ;

LoadString              (ghInstance, S_TITLE, gszTitle, sizeof (gszTitle)) ;
LoadString              (ghInstance, S_STRING, gszString, sizeof (gszString)) ;
```

Strings in a string table can contain control characters like tabs and line feeds. They must be encoded as octal constants preceded by a backslash character (\). The octal value is the ASCII code for the control character. Here is an example.

```
STRINGTABLE
BEGIN
        BODYTEXT        "This text contains a \011tab,\012\015and a CR/LF pair"
END
```

There are a number of advantages to using string tables. The main one is the reduction in memory use. The strings are not loaded until they are needed. Windows loads strings into memory in blocks of up to 16 strings, based on the string ID numbers. Strings 0-15 are loaded in one call to LoadString(), 16-31 as another block, etc. Strings that are likely to be used together are best numbered within a group of 16 integers.

By default, strings are loaded into memory that is both moveable and discardable. If the memory containing the string has been discarded, the next call to LoadString() will reload it from the disk data. The memory status for the strings in a string table can be set to either PRELOAD or LOADONCALL. The default is LOADONCALL, which means that the strings are not loaded into memory until LoadString() is called. PRELOAD loads the strings into memory when the program first starts.

The string table can also be set to have the memory block FIXED, MOVEABLE, or DISCARDABLE. The least desirable combinations of options would be a table listed as

```
STRINGTABLE PRELOAD FIXED
BEGIN
        /* strings here *
END
```

You can defeat the whole purpose of using string tables if the string data ends up copied into a static memory buffer. This means that the buffer will take up space, even if the character data has not been loaded into it from the string table. Most applications load the strings into automatic variables, which are temporarily stored on the stack and then discarded.

Another reason to put strings into string tables is for future editing. For example, if the program is marketed in several countries, the resource file can be translated into another language without changing the source code. Because the resource file also contains the menu and dialog box definitions, translating the resource file ends up completely transforming the program into a new language with a minimum of fuss.

Custom Resources

Resource files are also an excellent place to put other types of static data, which can be anything from metafiles to raw binary data. The brute force way to include data is with an RCDATA statement in the resource script file. Here is an example.

```
DataID RCDATA PRELOAD MOVEABLE
BEGIN
        3
        78
        0X444,
        "a string\0"
END
```

Like all resource data types, the RCDATA is given an ID number. The same memory options mentioned under string tables are available for RCDATA. In this case, the data will be preloaded, but not fixed in memory, and not discarded. The data consists of four integers and a character string.

Usually, the best place to store the custom resource data is in an external file during program development. The file's contents are then added to the resource data when the resource file is compiled. A typical set of custom resources is shown here.

```
paragraph       TEXT            "paragraf.txt"
twoelips        METAFILE        "twoelips.mf"
```

These lines define the custom resource types "TEXT" and "METAFILE." The data for these two resources is in two separate files, PARAGRAF.TXT and TWOELIPS.MF. The resource compiler reads in the two files and puts the data right into the resource file for the program. Within the body of the program, it is necessary to locate the start of the resource data before the data can be loaded into memory. FindResource() locates the resource data in the resource file, and LoadResource() loads it into a memory block. These are typically called together.

```
HANDLE          hMFRes ;

hMFRes = LoadResource (ghInstance, FindResource (ghInstance, "paragraph", "TEXT")) ;
```

This example shows the location and loading of the TEXT data. The *hMFRes* returned value is a handle to the global memory block containing the loaded resource data. See the example under the FindResource() function description for a more complete program listing.

Resource Function Summary

Table 25-2 summarizes the resource functions. The detailed function descriptions are in the next section.

Function	Purpose	⊠
AccessResource	Returns a file handle to data in the resource file.	
AllocResource	Allocates global memory to hold a resource.	
FindResource	Locates a resource in the resource file.	
FreeResource	Removes a resource from memory.	
GetInstanceData	Copies data from a previous instance of the same program into a memory buffer.	
LoadResource	Loads a resource into memory.	
LoadString	Loads a string from the resource file string table into a buffer.	
LockResource	Locks a global memory block containing a resource.	
SetResourceHandler	Creates a custom resource loading function, called by LoadResource( ).	
SizeofResource	Determines the size of a resource.	

Table 25-2. Resource Function Summary.

Resource Function Descriptions

This section contains the detailed descriptions of resource functions.

ACCESSRESOURCE   ■ Win 2.0   ■ Win 3.0   ■ Win 3.1

Purpose	Returns a DOS file handle to data in the resource file.
Syntax	int **AccessResource**(HANDLE *hInstance*, HANDLE *hResInfo*);
Description	This function opens the resource file data and moves the file pointer to the beginning of the data specified by *hResInfo*. The file handle can be used with the standard file functions, such as _lread(), and should be closed after use with _lclose(). The file cannot be written to. DOS file handles are a limited resource. Be sure to release the file handle when done by calling _lclose().
Uses	Can be used to allow selective reading of portions of a resource item. To load the entire resource, use LoadResource()
Returns	int, a DOS file handle. Returns –1 on error.
See Also	AllocResource(), SizeofResource()

Parameters

hInstance   HANDLE: The instance handle of the application which has the resource file. This value can be retrieved with GetWindowWord().

hResInfo   HANDLE: A handle to the specific data item in the resource file. Use FindResource() to obtain this value.

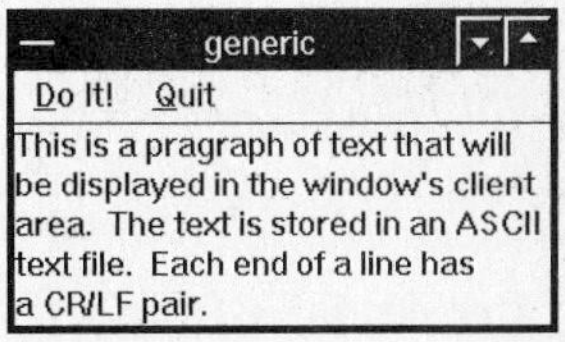

```
┌─────────────────────────────┐
│ ─        generic        ▾│▴│
├─────────────────────────────┤
│ Do It!   Quit               │
├─────────────────────────────┤
│This is a pragraph of text that will│
│be displayed in the window's client │
│area. The text is stored in an ASCII│
│text file. Each end of a line has   │
│a CR/LF pair.                       │
└─────────────────────────────┘
```

Figure 25-1. Access Resource( ) Example.

Example	This example loads and displays a custom resource. In this case, the resource data is just a block of text saved in an ASCII file. The text is displayed in the window's client area when the user clicks the "Do It!" menu item, as shown in Figure 25-1.
Note	This example demonstrates several seldom used resource functions. Considerably simpler methods are available for loading resources. See the example under the FindResource() function description for a more typical example.

    The resource file defines the custom resource type "TEXT" as being loaded from the file PARAGRAF.TXT.

```
/* generic.rc */
#include <windows.h>
#include "generic.h"
generic        ICON     generic.ico
generic        MENU
BEGIN
    MENUITEM "&Do It!"              IDM_DOIT
    MENUITEM "&Quit",              IDM_QUIT
END
paragraph      TEXT     paragraf.txt
```

The PARAGRAF.TXT file was created with a text processor.

```
This is a paragraph of text that will
be displayed in the window's client
area.  The text is stored in an ASCII
text file. Each end of a line has
a CR/LF pair.
```

The custom resource is located in the resource data using FindResource(). AllocResource() allocates a global memory block to hold the data. AccessResource() provides a file handle to the data, so that it can be loaded into memory using _lread().

```
long FAR PASCAL WndProc (HWND hWnd, unsigned iMessage, WORD wParam, LONG lParam)
{
        HDC                         hDC ;
        HANDLE                      hText ;
        static       HANDLE         hMem ;
        WORD                        wResSize ;
        int                         i, nResFile ;
        LPSTR                       lpResData ;
        static       RECT           rClient ;

        switch (iMessage)                       /* process windows messages */
        {
                case WM_CREATE:
                        hText = FindResource (ghInstance, "paragraph", "TEXT") ;
                        wResSize = SizeofResource (ghInstance, hText) ;
                        hMem = AllocResource (ghInstance, hText,
                                (DWORD) wResSize) ;
                        lpResData = GlobalLock (hMem) ;
                        nResFile = AccessResource (ghInstance, hText) ;
                        if (nResFile != -1)
                        {
                                _lread (nResFile, lpResData, wResSize) ;
                        }
                        GlobalUnlock (hMem) ;
                        _lclose (nResFile) ;
                        break ;
                case WM_SIZE:
                        SetRect (&rClient, 0, 0, LOWORD (lParam), HIWORD (lParam)) ;
                        break ;
                case WM_COMMAND:                /* process menu items */
                        switch (wParam)
                        {
                        case IDM_DOIT:
                                hDC = GetDC (hWnd) ;
                                lpResData = GlobalLock (hMem) ;
                                DrawText (hDC, lpResData, lstrlen (lpResData),
                                        &rClient, DT_EXPANDTABS) ;
                                GlobalUnlock (hMem) ;
                                ReleaseDC (hWnd, hDC) ;
                                break ;
                        case IDM_QUIT:
                                DestroyWindow (hWnd) ;
                                break ;
                        }
                        break ;
```

```
            case WM_DESTROY:
                    GlobalFree (hMem) ;
                    PostQuitMessage (0) ;
                    break ;
            default:
                    return DefWindowProc (hWnd, iMessage, wParam, lParam) ;
        }
        return (OL) ;
}
```

ALLOCRESOURCE   ■ Win 2.0   ■ Win 3.0   ■ Win 3.1

Purpose	Allocates global memory to hold a resource.
Syntax	HANDLE **AllocResource**(HANDLE *hInstance*, HANDLE *hResInfo*, DWORD *dwSize*);
Description	This function returns a handle to a global memory block. The function will compute the size of the block to allocate if the *dwSize* parameter is set to NULL.
Uses	AllocResource() is called internally by Windows to process LoadResource() function calls. It is not normally used by itself.
Returns	HANDLE, a handle to a global memory block.
See Also	AccessResource(), SizeofResource()
Parameters	
hInstance	HANDLE: The instance handle of the program containing the resource data. This value can be retrieved with GetWindowWord().
hResInfo	HANDLE: The handle of the specific resource that will be loaded into memory. Use FindResource() to determine this value.
dwSize	DWORD: The number of bytes to allocate. If this value is set to NULL, the minimum size that will hold the resource data will be allocated.
Example	See the example under the AccessResource() function description.

FINDRESOURCE   ■ Win 2.0   ■ Win 3.0   ■ Win 3.1

Purpose	Locates a resource in the resource file.
Syntax	HANDLE **FindResource**(HANDLE *hInstance*, LPSTR *lpName*, LPSTR *lpType*);
Description	Before a resource can be loaded into memory for use, it must be located. FindResource() returns a handle to the resource in the resource file.
Uses	Used in conjunction with LoadResource() to load resources into memory for use.
Returns	HANDLE, the handle of the resource in the resource file. NULL if the resource cannot be located. This handle is not the memory handle of a loaded resource. Use LoadResource() to return a memory handle.
See Also	LoadResource()
Parameters	
hInstance	HANDLE: The program's instance handle. This value can be retrieved by calling GetWindowWord().
lpName	LPSTR: A pointer to a null-terminated character string containing the name of the resource. This is the name specified on the left side of the resource definition line in the .RC resource script file.
lpType	LPSTR: A pointer to a null-terminated character string containing the resource type. For custom resources, this is the string specified in the second field of the resource definition line in the .RC resource script file. For predefined resource types, the *lpType* parameter should be set equal to one of the values in Table 25-3.

Value	Meaning	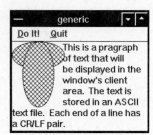
RT_ACCELERATOR	Accelerator table.	
RT_BITMAP	Bitmap.	
RT_DIALOG	Dialog box template.	
RT_FONT	Font.	
RT_FONTDIR	Font directory.	
RT_MENU	Menu definition.	
RT_RCDATA	User-defined resource.	

Table 25-3. Predefined Resource Types.

Example

This example, which is shown in Figure 25-2, loads and displays two custom resources, a metafile and a block of ASCII text.

The program's resource script file includes two custom resource types, "TEXT" and "METAFILE." They used to include the data in the two referenced files into the application's resource data.

```
/* generic.rc */
#include <windows.h>
#include "generic.h"
generic          ICON    generic.ico

generic          MENU
BEGIN
    MENUITEM "&Do It!"              IDM_DOIT
    MENUITEM "&Quit",              IDM_QUIT
END

paragraph        TEXT           "paragraf.txt"
twoelips         METAFILE       "twoelips.mf"
```

*Figure 25-2. FindResource()
Example.*

The text file PARAGRAF.TXT was created with a text editor. The first six lines are tabbed, to make room for a metafile picture.

```
        This is a paragraph
        of text that will
        be displayed in the
        window's client
        area.  The text is
        stored in an ASCII
text file.  Each end of a line has
a CR/LF pair.\
```

The application loads the resource data when the WM_CREATE message is processed. SetMetaFileBits() is used to return a handle to the metafile that can be passed later to PlayMetaFile(). The length of the character string resource is determined by searching for the backslash character (\).

```
long FAR PASCAL WndProc (HWND hWnd, unsigned iMessage, WORD wParam, LONG lParam)
{
        PAINTSTRUCT                ps ;
        static        RECT         rClient ;
        static        HANDLE       hTextRes, hMetaFile ;
        static        int          nTextLong ;
        LPSTR                      lpChar ;
        HANDLE                     hMFRes ;
```

```
        switch (iMessage)                         /* process windows messages */
        {
            case WM_CREATE:
                    hMFRes = LoadResource (ghInstance,
                            FindResource (ghInstance, "twoelips",
                                    "METAFILE")) ;
                    LockResource (hMFRes) ;
                    hMetaFile = SetMetaFileBits (hMFRes) ;
                    GlobalUnlock (hMFRes) ;
                    hTextRes = LoadResource (ghInstance,
                            FindResource (ghInstance, "paragraph", "TEXT")) ;
                    lpChar = LockResource (hTextRes) ;
                    nTextLong = 0 ;
                    while (*lpChar++ != '\\')                /* find text length */
                            nTextLong++ ;                   /* '\' at end */
                    GlobalUnlock (hTextRes) ;
                    break ;
            case WM_SIZE:
                    SetRect (&rClient, 0, 0, LOWORD (lParam), HIWORD (lParam)) ;
                    break ;
            case WM_PAINT:
                    BeginPaint (hWnd, &ps) ;
                    lpChar = LockResource (hTextRes) ;
                    DrawText (ps.hdc, lpChar, nTextLong, &rClient,
                            DT_EXPANDTABS) ;
                    GlobalUnlock (hTextRes) ;
                    PlayMetaFile (ps.hdc, hMetaFile) ;
                    EndPaint (hWnd, &ps) ;
                    break ;
            case WM_COMMAND:                        /* process menu items */
                    switch (wParam)
                    {
                    case IDM_DOIT:                  /* "Do it" menu  item  does  nothing */
                            break ;
                    case IDM_QUIT:                  /* send end of application message */
                            DestroyWindow (hWnd) ;
                            break ;
                    }
                    break ;
            case WM_DESTROY:                        /* stop application */
                    FreeResource (hMetaFile) ;
                    FreeResource (hTextRes) ;
                    PostQuitMessage (0) ;
                    break ;
            default:                                /* default windows message processing */
                    return DefWindowProc (hWnd, iMessage, wParam, lParam) ;
        }
        return (0L) ;
}
```

FreeResource
■ Win 2.0   ■ Win 3.0   ■ Win 3.1

Purpose	Removes a resource from memory.
Syntax	BOOL **FreeResource**(HANDLE *hResData*);
Description	If a resource is loaded more than once, Windows does not load two copies of the data. Instead, the reference count of the resource is increased by one for each time LoadResource() is called. FreeResource() decreases the reference count by one. When the reference count reaches zero, the resource is deleted. Note that the resource data is freed when the program terminates. It is not necessary to call FreeResource() for every resource loaded. Normally, FreeResource() is used within a program to reduce memory consumption for resources that are unlikely to be reused.
Uses	Because of the use of a reference count for each resource, different parts of the same application can both load and delete the same resource without concern about interfering with other uses of the data in the application.

Returns	BOOL. Zero if the function was successful, non-zero on error. Note that this is the opposite of the normal TRUE/FALSE assignment.
See Also	LoadResource(), FindResource()
Parameters	
hResData	HANDLE: The resource handle returned by LoadResource().
Example	See the example under the FindResource() function description.

GetInstanceData
■ Win 2.0   ■ Win 3.0   ■ Win 3.1

Purpose	Copies data from a previous instance of the same program into a memory buffer.
Syntax	int **GetInstanceData**(HANDLE *hInstance*, NPSTR *pData*, int *nCount*);
Description	If more than one copy of a program is run at the same time, each copy shares the same code segments, but separate copies of data segments are maintained. GetInstanceData() allows data to be copied from a previous instance of the program into a subsequent instance's data segment. The data is copied in the order that it occurs in the first instance's data segment. Repeated calls to GetInstanceData() read successive blocks of data, each *nCount* bytes long.
Uses	Used with programs that are likely to have multiple instances loaded, such as terminal emulator programs that allow several sessions to be run at the same time. Reading from a previous instance is faster than reloading the data from disk.
Returns	int, the number of bytes copied.
See Also	LoadResource(), LoadString()
Parameters	
hInstance	HANDLE: The instance handle of the previous instance of the application. This is available as the *hPrevInstance* parameter passed to the WinMain() function.
pData	NPSTR: A pointer to a memory block in the application's own data segment.
nCount	int: The number of bytes to copy.
Example	This example loads two strings from a resource file. One is used for the window's caption. The other is displayed in the client area if the "Do It!" menu item is clicked, as shown in Figure 25-3.

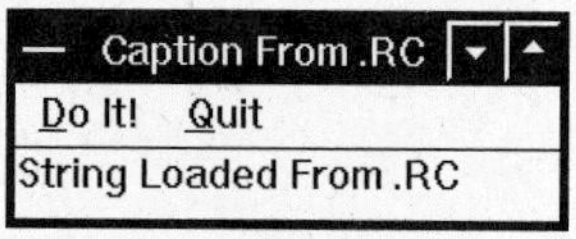

Figure 25-3. GetInstance-Data( ) Example.

The program's .RC resource file includes two strings in a string table.

```
/* generic.rc */
#include <windows.h>
#include "generic.h"
generic         ICON    generic.ico

generic         MENU
BEGIN
   MENUITEM "&Do It!"    IDM_DOIT
   MENUITEM "&Quit",     IDM_QUIT
END

STRINGTABLE
BEGIN
       S_TITLE          "Caption From .RC"
       S_STRING              "String Loaded From .RC"
END
```

The ID values for the strings are defined in the program's header file.

```
/* generic.h    */
#define IDM_DOIT1                               /* menu item id values */
```

```
#define IDM_QUIT 2
#define S_TITLE         16                          /* string table ID values */
#define S_STRING        17
        /* global variables */
int     ghInstance ;
char    gszAppName [] = "generic" ;
        /* function prototypes */
long FAR PASCAL WndProc (HWND, unsigned, WORD, LONG) ;
```

The first time the program is run, the two strings are loaded into memory with LoadString().
If the program is started a second or subsequent time, the first instance of the program uses the
GetInstanceData() function within WinMain() to copy the two strings into global character buff-
ers from the resource data.

```
/* generic.c   generic windows application */

#include <windows.h>
#include "generic.h"


char    gszTitle [32] ;
char    gszString [64] ;

int PASCAL WinMain (HANDLE hInstance, HANDLE hPrevInstance, LPSTR lpszCmdLine, int nCmdShow)
{

        HWND            hWnd ;
        MSG             msg ;
        WNDCLASS        wndclass ;

        ghInstance = hInstance ;                    /* store instance handle as global var. */
        if (!hPrevInstance)
        {
                LoadString (ghInstance, S_TITLE, gszTitle,
                        sizeof (gszTitle)) ;
                LoadString (ghInstance, S_STRING, gszString,
                        sizeof (gszString)) ;
                wndclass.style              = CS_HREDRAW | CS_VREDRAW ;
                wndclass.lpfnWndProc        = WndProc ;
                wndclass.cbClsExtra         = 0 ;
                wndclass.cbWndExtra         = 0 ;
                wndclass.hInstance          = hInstance ;
                wndclass.hIcon              = LoadIcon (hInstance, gszAppName) ;
                wndclass.hCursor            = LoadCursor (NULL, IDC_ARROW) ;
                wndclass.hbrBackground      = GetStockObject (WHITE_BRUSH) ;
                wndclass.lpszMenuName        = gszAppName ;
                wndclass.lpszClassName       = gszAppName ;

                if (!RegisterClass (&wndclass))
                        return FALSE ;
        }
        else
        {
                GetInstanceData (hPrevInstance, gszTitle,
                        sizeof (gszTitle)) ;
                GetInstanceData (hPrevInstance, gszString,
                        sizeof (gszString)) ;
        }

        hWnd = CreateWindow (                       /* create the program's window here */
                gszAppName,                         /* class name */
                gszTitle,                           /* window name */
                WS_OVERLAPPEDWINDOW,                /* window style */
                CW_USEDEFAULT,                      /* x position on screen */
                CW_USEDEFAULT,                      /* y position on screen */
                CW_USEDEFAULT,                      /* width of window */
                CW_USEDEFAULT,                      /* height of window */
                NULL,                               /* parent window handle (null = none) */
```

```
                NULL,                        /* menu handle (null = use class menu) */
                hInstance,                   /* instance handle */
                NULL) ;                      /* lpstr (null = not used) */
        ShowWindow (hWnd, nCmdShow) ;
        UpdateWindow (hWnd) ;
        while (GetMessage (&msg, NULL, 0, 0))    /* the message loop */
        {
                TranslateMessage (&msg) ;
                DispatchMessage (&msg) ;
        }
        return msg.wParam ;
}


long FAR PASCAL WndProc (HWND hWnd, unsigned iMessage, WORD wParam, LONG lParam)
{
        HDC             hDC ;

        switch (iMessage)                    /* process windows messages */
        {
                case WM_COMMAND:             /* process menu items */
                        switch (wParam)
                        {
                        case IDM_DOIT:               /* User hit the "Do it" menu item */
                                hDC = GetDC (hWnd) ;
                                TextOut (hDC, 0, 0, gszString, lstrlen (gszString)) ;
                                ReleaseDC (hWnd, hDC) ;
                                break ;
                        case IDM_QUIT:
                                DestroyWindow (hWnd) ;
                                break ;
                        }
                        break ;
                case WM_DESTROY:             /* stop application */
                        PostQuitMessage (0) ;
                        break ;
                default:                     /* default windows message processing */
                        return DefWindowProc (hWnd, iMessage, wParam, lParam) ;
        }
        return (0L) ;
}
```

LOADRESOURCE   ■ Win 2.0   ■ Win 3.0   ■ Win 3.1

Purpose	Loads a resource into memory.
Syntax	HANDLE **LoadResource**(HANDLE *hInstance*, HANDLE *hResInfo*);
Description	Resource data must be loaded into memory before it can be used. If LoadResource() is called more than once for the same resource, the data is not loaded multiple times. Instead, Windows keeps track of the number of times LoadResource() was called for the given resource as the "reference count" of the resource. The resource is not removed from memory until Free Resource() has been called an equal number of times, or the application is terminated.
	The application can provide a custom resource loading callback function that will be called when the LoadResource() function is called. Use SetResourceHandler() to set the callback function.
Uses	Used with FindResource() to load resources into memory so that they can be used.
Returns	HANDLE, the handle to the global memory block that contains the loaded resource. Returns NULL if the resource could not be loaded.
See Also	FindResource(), FreeResource(), SetResourceHandler()
Parameters	
hInstance	HANDLE: The instance handle of the running program. This value can be retrieved by calling GetWindowWord().

hResInfo	HANDLE: The handle of the resource within the resource data. This value is obtained by calling FindResource().
Example	See the example under the FindResource() function description.

LOADSTRING

Purpose	Loads a string from the resource file string table into a buffer.
Syntax	int **LoadString**(HANDLE *hInstance*, WORD *wID*, LPSTR *lpBuffer*, int *nBufferMax*);
Description	Strings are added to the program's resource file in a string table. Each string is given an ID value, normally defined in the program's header file. LoadString() copies the string from the resource file into a buffer so that it can be manipulated and displayed. To be memory efficient, the *lpBuffer* should either be an automatic variable (stored on the program's stack), a temporary memory block allocated by the program, or a static buffer that can be reused as different strings are loaded. Loading string resources into a series of static buffers is inefficient and defeats the purpose of using resource files to minimize memory consumption.
Uses	The best place to store string constants is in resource files. This method of storage is memory efficient, and it makes edits or translations of the strings much simpler.
Returns	int, the number of characters copied to the buffer. Returns zero on error.
See Also	LoadResource()
Parameters	
hInstance	HANDLE: The instance handle for the program.
wID	WORD: The ID value for the string in the string table. This is the value to the left of the string in the resource file. Normally, it is given a defined name in the program's header file.
lpBuffer	LPSTR: A pointer to a memory buffer to hold the character string. The buffer must be at least *nBufferMax* characters long.
nBufferMax	int: The maximum number of characters to copy to the *lpBuffer* memory buffer.

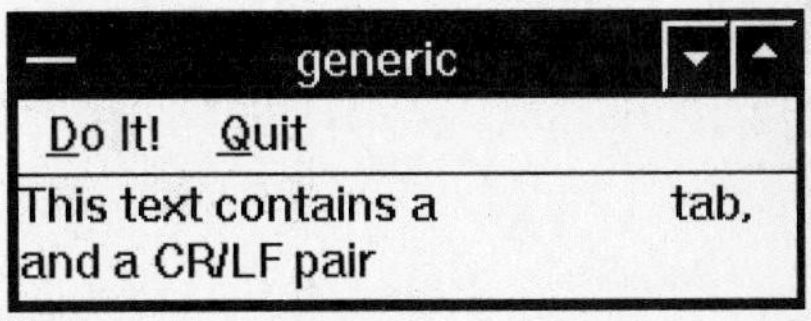

Figure 25-4. LoadString() Example.

Example	This example, which is illustrated in Figure 25-4, includes three character strings in the resource file string table. One string is displayed in the window's client area each time a WM_PAINT message is received. The other two strings are used in message box functions.
	The strings are defined in the program's resource file. Note the octal constants used to code the tab, CR, and LF characters in the first text line.

```
/* generic.rc */

#include <windows.h>
#include "generic.h"

generic         ICON    generic.ico

generic         MENU
BEGIN
   MENUITEM "&Do It!"              IDM_DOIT
   MENUITEM "&Quit",              IDM_QUIT
END

STRINGTABLE
BEGIN
```

```
        BODYTEXT          "This text contains a \011tab,\012\015and a CR/LF pair"
        MESSAGE1          "This is message 1"
        MESSAGE2          "This is message 2"
END
```

The ID values for the strings are defined in the program's header file.

```
/* generic.h   */

#define IDM_DOIT       1                        /* menu item id values */
#define IDM_QUIT       2

#define BODYTEXT       0                        /* number 0 - in first segment */
#define MESSAGE1       16                       /* numbers 16 & 17 will be loaded */
#define MESSAGE2       17                       /* into a different segment together */
        /* global variables */
int     ghInstance ;                            /* these two globals are required */
char    gszAppName [] = "generic" ;             /* if you include winmain.c */
        /* function prototypes */
long FAR PASCAL WndProc (HWND, unsigned, WORD, LONG) ;
```

The program uses the BODYTEXT string when processing WM_PAINT messages. The other two strings are used in message boxes.

```
long FAR PASCAL WndProc (HWND hWnd, unsigned iMessage, WORD wParam, LONG lParam)
{
        PAINTSTRUCT        ps ;
        static RECT        rClient ;
        char               cBuf [128] ;

        switch (iMessage)                       /* process windows messages */
        {
                case WM_SIZE:
                        SetRect (&rClient, 0, 0, LOWORD (lParam), HIWORD (lParam)) ;
                        break ;
                case WM_PAINT:
                        BeginPaint (hWnd, &ps) ;
                        LoadString (ghInstance, BODYTEXT, cBuf, 128) ;
                        DrawText (ps.hdc, cBuf, lstrlen (cBuf), &rClient,
                                DT_EXPANDTABS) ;
                        EndPaint (hWnd, &ps) ;
                        break ;
                case WM_COMMAND:                /* process menu items */
                        switch (wParam)
                        {
                        case IDM_DOIT:
                                LoadString (ghInstance, MESSAGE1, cBuf, 128) ;
                                MessageBox (hWnd, cBuf, "Message", MB_OK) ;
                                break ;
                        case IDM_QUIT:
                                LoadString (ghInstance, MESSAGE2, cBuf, 128) ;
                                MessageBox (hWnd, cBuf, "Message", MB_OK) ;
                                DestroyWindow (hWnd) ;
                                break ;
                        }
                        break ;
                case WM_DESTROY:
                        PostQuitMessage (0) ;
                        break ;
                default:
                        return DefWindowProc (hWnd, iMessage, wParam, lParam) ;
        }
        return (0L) ;
}
```

LOCKRESOURCE ■ Win 2.0 ■ Win 3.0 ■ Win 3.1

Purpose	Locks a global memory block containing a resource.
Syntax	LPSTR **LockResource**(HANDLE *hResData*).
Description	This function locks a resource in global memory and returns a far pointer to the memory block's address. If the resource is locked more than once with LockResource(), an equal number of FreeResource() function calls will be needed before the memory block is freed.
Uses	This is a convenient way to temporarily lock resource data loaded into memory by Load Resource().
Returns	LPSTR, a pointer to the beginning of the memory block containing the resource data. NULL on error.
See Also	LoadResource(), FindResource()
Parameters	
hResData	HANDLE: The handle of the loaded resource data in memory, returned by LoadResource().
Example	See the example under the FindResource() function description.

SETRESOURCEHANDLER ■ Win 2.0 ■ Win 3.0 ■ Win 3.1

Purpose	Creates a custom resource loading function, called by LoadResource().
Syntax	FARPROC **SetResourceHandler**(HANDLE *hInstance*, LPSTR *lpType*, FARPROC *lpLoadFunc*);
Description	This function allows you to define a custom resource loading function that will be called by LoadResource(). This is convenient if you will need to examine or modify the resource data during the loading process.
Uses	Not often used. Can be used with custom resource types, where the data in the resource file needs to be reformatted in memory. For example, appending a null character to the end of character data once it is loaded in memory.
Returns	FARPROC, a pointer to the callback function.
See Also	LoadResource(), FindResource(), AccessResource()
Parameters	
hInstance	HANDLE: The instance handle of the program containing the resource data. You can use Get-WindowWord() to retrieve this value.
lpType	LPSTR: A pointer to a null-terminated character string containing the resource type. This is the second field in the resource script file line that defines the resource.
lpLoadFunc	FARPROC: The procedure-instance address of the loader function. This value is returned by MakeProcInstance().
Callback Function	The callback function must have the following format, and be listed in the EXPORTS section of the program's .DEF definition file:
	FARPROC FAR PASCAL **LoadFunc** (HANDLE *hMem*, HANDLE *hInstance*, HANDLE *hResInfo*)
hMem	HANDLE: A handle to the global memory block that will contain the resource data. If this value is NULL, the callback function should allocate a global memory block big enough to hold the resource. The SizeofResource() function will return the minimum size to allocate.
hInstance	HANDLE: The instance-handle of the program containing the resource data.
hResInfo	HANDLE: The handle of the resource in the resource data file. This value is obtained by FindResource()and passed to the callback function when the LoadResource() function is called.

The callback function should return the memory handle of the global memory block containing the loaded resource data. If *hMem* is not NULL, but an attempt to lock the memory block fails, the block has been discarded. In this case, the callback function should reallocate and reload the resource data.

Example   This example demonstrates the use of a custom resource loading function. The loader LoadStringRes() is shown at the bottom of the listing. It must also be included in the EXPORTS section of the program's .DEF definition file, and a function prototype must be added to the header file. In this case, a custom resource type TEXT is defined in the resource file. This includes a text file PARAGRAF.TXT in the resource data.

```
/* generic.rc */
#include <windows.h>
#include "generic.h"
generic        ICON     generic.ico
generic        MENU
BEGIN
   MENUITEM "&Do It!"    IDM_DOIT
   MENUITEM "&Quit",     IDM_QUIT
END
paragraph      TEXT     paragraf.txt
```

The custom resource loader for the TEXT resource type is set by SetResourceHandler(). Once set, the loader function is called when LoadResource() is used to load this resource type into memory. The callback function returns a handle to the loaded resource data in a global memory block.

```
long FAR PASCAL WndProc (HWND hWnd, unsigned iMessage, WORD wParam,  LONG lParam)
{
        HDC                         hDC ;
        HANDLE                      hText ;
        static      HANDLE          hMem ;
        LPSTR                       lpResData ;
        static      RECT            rClient ;
        FARPROC                     fpLoaderInst ;

        switch (iMessage)                       /* process windows messages */
        {
                case WM_CREATE:
                        hText = FindResource (ghInstance, "paragraph", "TEXT") ;
                        fpLoaderInst = MakeProcInstance ((FARPROC) LoadStringRes,
                                ghInstance) ;
                        SetResourceHandler (ghInstance, "TEXT", fpLoaderInst) ;
                        hMem = LoadResource (ghInstance, hText) ;
                        break ;
                case WM_SIZE:
                        SetRect (&rClient, 0, 0, LOWORD (lParam), HIWORD (lParam)) ;
                        break ;
                case WM_COMMAND:                        /* process menu items */
                        switch (wParam)
                        {
                        case IDM_DOIT:          /* display the resource text */
                                hDC = GetDC (hWnd) ;
                                lpResData = LockResource (hMem) ;
                                DrawText (hDC, lpResData, lstrlen (lpResData),
                                        &rClient, DT_EXPANDTABS) ;
                                GlobalUnlock (hMem) ;
                                ReleaseDC (hWnd, hDC) ;
                                break ;
                        case IDM_QUIT:
                                DestroyWindow (hWnd) ;
                                break ;
                        }
                        break ;
                case WM_DESTROY:
```

```
                        PostQuitMessage (0) ;
                        break ;
                default:
                        return DefWindowProc (hWnd, iMessage, wParam, lParam) ;
        }
        return (OL) ;
}


FARPROC FAR PASCAL LoadStringRes (HANDLE hMem, HANDLE hInstance,  HANDLE hResInfo)
{
        int     wResSize, nResFile ;
        LPSTR   lpResData ;

        if (hMem == NULL)
                hMem = AllocResource (hInstance, hResInfo, (DWORD) wResSize) ;
        wResSize = SizeofResource (ghInstance, hResInfo) ;
        lpResData = GlobalLock (hMem) ;
        nResFile = AccessResource (hInstance, hResInfo) ;
        if (nResFile != -1)
        {
                _lread (nResFile, lpResData, wResSize) ;
                _lclose (nResFile) ;
        }
        GlobalUnlock (hMem) ;
        return ((FARPROC) (DWORD) hMem) ;
}
```

SizeofResource   ■ Win 2.0   ■ Win 3.0   ■ Win 3.1

Purpose	Determines the size of a resource.
Syntax	WORD **SizeofResource**(HANDLE *hInstance*, HANDLE *hResInfo*);
Description	This function returns the minimum size that a resource will occupy when loaded into memory.
Uses	Used with AllocResource() and AccessResource() to size and resource data into a memory area.
Returns	WORD, the size of the resource in bytes. Returns zero on error.
See Also	AccessResource(), AllocResource()
Parameters	
hInstance	HANDLE: The program's instance handle. The value can be retrieved with GetWindowWord().
hResInfo	HANDLE: The resource handle of the specific item in the resource file to size. This value is returned by FindResource().
Example	See the example under the AccessResource() function description.

26

Execution Profiling and Debugging

A new addition to the Software Development Kit (SDK) for Windows 3.0 is the execution profiler. This tool allows you to track which parts of an application are taking the most time. Armed with this knowledge, you can work on speeding up the slowest parts of the program to get the maximum improvement for programming time spent.

The CodeView for Windows debugger is a critical element of the SDK. Besides allowing debugging of Windows programs, the debugger is an excellent way to learn how Windows programs work. Armed with a two-monitor system (VGA and monochrome display on the same computer), the programmer can watch the source code execute line-by-line on the monochrome monitor while seeing the Windows application's progress on the VGA screen. (The Windows 3.1 debugger allows debugging with only one monitor, or two VGA screens.) This chapter documents a few functions that can be used to "hard code" debugging information into the program during development.

How the Profiler Works

The basic idea behind a profiler is simple. When the profiler is on, the program is interrupted at some fixed frequency. Every time the program is interrupted, the profiler checks and stores the name of the part of the program that was executing at that moment. Over time, the parts of the program that are taking the most time tend to get the most "hits." They tend to be the parts of the program that are operating when the interruption occurs. After the program is stopped, the statistics from the profiler are summed and analyzed to determine which parts of the program are taking the most time.

The Windows profiler works on this principle. The profiler stores the hit data in a memory buffer. When the profiler is stopped, or the ProfFlush() function is called, the memory buffer is written to a disk file. A DOS application called SHOWHITS.EXE then summarizes the statistics and outputs the data to the screen. This chain of actions to use the profiler is shown in Figure 26-1.

The profiler reduces the performance of the application being run. The amount of degradation will depend on how often the program is interrupted. Typically, the reduction in performance is not noticeable.

Preparing to Run the Profiler

Assuming that you are running Windows in the 386 enhanced memory mode, the profiler is a Windows device driver. You install the profiler by adding the VPROD.386 driver to the [386Enh] portion of the SYSTEM.INI file and restarting Windows.

```
[386Enh]
DEVICE=VPROD.386
```

The SDK also includes support for profiling applications in the Windows "real" memory mode by running the PROF.COM program before Windows is started. Because commercial realities demand that all Windows programs be able to run in standard and 386 enhanced modes, this option is of little value.

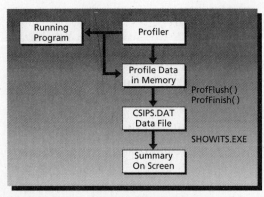

Figure 26-1. Windows Execution Profiler.

The program that will be profiled must be modified slightly to control the profiler. The sample rate and sample buffer size are set at the beginning of the program using the ProfSampRate() and ProfSetup() functions.

```
ProfSampRate (1, 2) ;           /* two milliseconds sample interval*/
ProfSetup (100, 0) ;            /* 100 kbyte buffer in memory */
ProfClear () ;                  /* empty buffer to start*/
```

Specific parts of the program are marked for profiling by surrounding the code with ProfStart() and ProfStop() function calls. The profiler will be active from the point of execution marked with ProfStart() to the point marked with ProfStop(). The range of program lines profiled includes all functions called between ProfStart() and ProfStop() (including Windows functions), and any other parts of the program that may be executed as Windows processes other messages in the time period between these two markers.

```
ProfStart () ;
[Program lines to profile]
ProfStop () ;
```

Any number of ProfStart() and ProfStop() pairs can be placed in the program, isolating sections that will be profiled. At the end of the program, the ProfFinish() function should be called to write the profile memory buffer data to disk. The data is written to the CSIPS.DAT file on the WINDOWS subdirectory.

When compiling the program, add the "-M" linker flag so link will generate a .MAP file for the application. This map file includes the name and segment address of every function called by the program. Run the MAPSYM utility program after the program is compiled and linked. This utility generates a .SYM symbol file that is used by the profile report program to determine the names of the segments that were "hit" during profiling.

With all of this done, you simply run the program. The profiler writes the "hit" data to the memory buffer during execution of the code between the ProfStart() and ProfStop() function calls. When the program is finished, the data will be stored in raw form in the CIPS.DATA file on the WINDOWS subdirectory. To get a readable analysis of this data, run the SHOWHITS.EXE program from DOS. SHOWHITS comes with the Windows SDK. SHOWHITS collects all of the hit data in the file, organizes it, and displays a report on the screen in the following format:

```
C:\WINDOWS>showhits -3
Windows Profiler Data Displayer
Copyright (c) 1988-1990, Microsoft Corp. All Rights Reserved.


Here are the Hits for Unrecognized Segments

      4  Hits on Segment 01AD

Here are the Hits for Known Segments

    586  Hits on GENERIC-1
      6  Hits on KRNL386-0
      1  Hits on USER-0
     49  Hits on USER-15
     76  Hits on GDI-0
    777  Hits on DISPLAY-0
     30  Hits on SYSTEM-0

  1529 TOTAL HITS


Profiler Summary (Top 10 Hits):
```

SHOWHITS.EXE allows several command line switches. They are

SHOWHITS [-r/-3] [-ipath] [csips_file] [seg_file]

-3	386 enhanced mode profiling. Implies that VPROD.386 was installed as a driver in SYSTEM.INI's [386Enh] section.
-r	Real mode profiling. Implies that PROF.COM was run before Windows was started in real mode.

-ipath	Specifies the directory path to locate the .SYM file output by MAPSYM.
csips_file	Specifies the full path name of the CIPS.DAT file. By default, this file is in the WINDOWS subdirectory.
seg_file	Specifies the full path name of the SEGENTRY.DAT file. This file is generated when Windows starts, if the profiler has been installed. By default, this file is located in the WINDOWS subdirectory.

Normally, you will just run SHOWHITS from the WINDOWS subdirectory with the "-3" switch. SHOWHITS will prompt you with a short help screen if you forget to set a switch.

Using the Profiler

Getting meaningful data out of the profiler is not as simple as it might appear. Most Windows applications spend the majority of their time executing Windows functions for output to the display and for other Windows activities. You tend to get a lot of hit data in the segments that Windows loads, such as USER, DISPLAY, and GDI. This information is not very helpful.

If there are specific parts of the program that are calculation intensive, surround these parts with the ProfStart() and ProfStop() functions as closely as possible. Avoid having calls to Windows functions between the profile markers, particularly ones that require user response. For example, if the program calls MessageBox() between ProfStart() and ProfStop(), you know that most of the time will be spent waiting for the user to click the OK button, not in program execution.

In general, you cannot compare the performance of two different but similar Windows functions within one version of the program. For example, you cannot compare the time spent by TextOut() and DrawText() by surrounding each of these calls with a ProfStart() and ProfStop() function. Both of these functions use portions of the same Windows .DLL files and end up contributing hits to the same segments.

To compare Windows function performance, compile the same code section two different times. Each time, surround the function to be analyzed with the ProfStart() and ProfStop() functions. If the profiler sample rate is the same, the absolute number of hits that you collect will reflect the total time the function occupied. Comparing the total hits for the two different versions of the program will tell you which version is faster.

Debugging Functions

A full discussion of the excellent CodeView for Windows (CVW) debugger is beyond the scope of this book. However, the debugging functions are documented. In general, you will not need to use any of these functions when debugging. The debugger allows breakpoints to be set, conditions to be checked, etc., without modification to the code other than compiler switch settings.

A point worth noting is that the CVW debugger will work fine in 386 enhanced mode without installing the WINDEBUG.386 driver in the [386Enh] section of the SYSTEM.INI file. Not having the debugger driver installed will eliminate the possibility of breaking to the debugger with the (CTRL)-(ALT)-(SYSREQ) key combination, and also makes several of the debugging functions inoperative. These functions are not normally needed to debug a program.

Execution Profiling and Debugging Function Summary

Table 26-1 summarizes the Windows profiling and debugging functions. The next section conatins the detailed function descriptions.

Function	Purpose	
DebugBreak	Forces a break to the debugger.	
FatalExit	Forces an immediate termination of the application.	
OutputDebugString	Displays a character string at the bottom of the debug screen.	
ProfClear	Clears all data from the profile sample buffer.	
ProfFinish	Stops the profiler, and copies the data buffer to the disk file CSIPS.DAT.	

ProfFlush	Copies the profiler sample buffer to disk.
ProfInsChk	Checks if the profiler has been installed.
ProfSampRate	Sets the sampling rate of the profiler.
ProfSetup	Initializes the size of the profile data buffer and disk file.
ProfStart	Starts the execution profiler.
ProfStop	Stops the profiler.
ValidateCodeSegments	Enables debugging checking if code segments are overwritten.
ValidateFreeSpaces	Enables checking of memory overwriting of free areas.

Table 26-1. Execution Profiling and Debugging Function Summary.

Execution Profiling and Debugging Function Descriptions

This section contains the detailed descriptions of the Windows profiling and debugging functions.

DEBUGBREAK   □ Win 2.0   ■ Win 3.0   ■ Win 3.1

Purpose	Forces a break to the debugger.
Syntax	void **DebugBreak**(void);
Description	This function codes a debugger break right into the program. It is only used when debugging.
Uses	Not often used. It is usually easier to set breakpoints from within the debugger.
Returns	No returned value (void).
See Also	OutputDebugString()
Parameters	None (void).
Example	This example breaks to the debugger when the "Do It!" menu item is clicked.

```
Long FAR PASCAL WndProc (HWND hWnd, unsigned iMessage, WORD wParam, LONG lParam)
{

        switch (iMessage)                       /* process windows messages */
        {
        case WM_COMMAND:                        /* process menu items */
                switch (wParam)
                {
                case IDM_DOIT:                  /* User hit the |Do it■ menu item */
                        DebugBreak () ;
                        break ;
```

[Other program lines]

FATALEXIT   ■ Win 2.0   ■ Win 3.0   ■ Win 3.1

Purpose	Forces an immediate termination of the application.
Syntax	void **FatalExit**(int *Code*);
Description	This function is only used in debugging. It forces an immediate end to the program's operation, bypassing WM_DESTROY processing logic and the message loop. It should only be called if the application cannot be shut down by any other means.
Uses	Used in debugging as an emergency way to shut down the application, in most cases without forcing Windows to shut down or fail.
Returns	No returned value (void).
See Also	DebugBreak()

Parameters

nCode int: The SDK documentation suggests that FatalExit displays this error code and message in the debugger window. The message is not reliable.

Example

```
Long FAR PASCAL WndProc (HWND hWnd, unsigned iMessage, WORD wParam, LONG lParam)
{

        switch (iMessage)                        /* process windows messages */
        {
            case WM_COMMAND:                     /* process menu items */
                switch (wParam)
                {
                case IDM_DOIT:                   /* User hit the "Do it" menu item */
                    FatalExit (1) ;
                    break ;
```

[Other program lines]

OUTPUTDEBUGSTRING

☐ Win 2.0   ■ Win 3.0   ■ Win 3.1

Purpose	Displays a character string at the bottom of the debug screen.
Syntax	void **OutputDebugString**(LPSTR *lpOutputString*);
Description	This function is only used in debugging. The character string is ultimately added to the bottom of the screen in the debugger. If no debug monitor is installed, the character string is sent to the AUX port (assumed to be connected to a terminal).
Uses	Handy for tracking which parts of a program were executed, and in what order. A series of different messages can be output, each at a different location. This procedure minimizes the disruption to the program, compared to setting breakpoints in the debugger.
Returns	No returned value (void).

Parameters

lpOutputString LPSTR: A pointer to a null-terminated character string that will be displayed at the bottom of the debug monitor screen.

Example This example outputs the string "Testing debug function" at the bottom of the debug screen when the user clicks the "Do It!" menu item.

```
Long FAR PASCAL WndProc (HWND hWnd, unsigned iMessage, WORD wParam, LONG lParam)
{

        switch (iMessage)                        /* process windows messages */
        {
            case WM_COMMAND:                     /* process menu items */
                switch (wParam)
                {
                case IDM_DOIT:                   /* User hit the "Do it" menu item */
                    OutputDebugString ("Testing debug function") ;
                    break ;
```

[Other program lines]

PROFCLEAR

☐ Win 2.0   ■ Win 3.0   ■ Win 3.1

Purpose	Clears all data from the profile sample buffer.
Syntax	void **ProfClear**(void);
Description	The profile copies the hit data to a memory buffer while the profiler is active. This data is written to a disk file when ProfFlush() or ProfFinish() is called. The memory buffer can be emptied by calling ProfClear() in the program being profiled. This does not affect any profile data already written to disk.

Uses	Generally used at the start of a profiling session.
Returns	No returned value (void).
See Also	ProfFlush()
Parameters	None (void).
Example	This example profiles the operation of two functions. The Method1() function uses the TextOut() and wsprintf() functions repeatedly. Method2() just counts integers 10^6 times. To run the profiler, the profile device driver VPROD.386 must be added to the SYSTEM.INI file in the [386Enh] section with the line

```
DEVICE=VPROD.386
```

Windows must be restarted with this change in SYSTEM.INI before profiling begins.

The program must be linked with the linker switch, -m (for map), set on. After the program is compiled and linked, MAPSYM.EXE is run to generate a MAP file. When the program executes, it generates the file CSIPS.DAT in the \WINDOWS subdirectory. Running SHOWHITS.EXE as a DOS application from within the \WINDOWS subdirectory will display the profile information.

```
C:\WINDOWS>showhits -3
Windows Profiler Data Displayer
Copyright (c) 1988-1990, Microsoft Corp. All Rights Reserved.


Here are the Hits for Unrecognized Segments

      4  Hits on Segment 01AD

Here are the Hits for Known Segments

    586  Hits on GENERIC-1
      6  Hits on KRNL386-0
      1  Hits on USER-0
     49  Hits on USER-15
     76  Hits on GDI-0
    777  Hits on DISPLAY-0
     30  Hits on SYSTEM-0

   1529 TOTAL HITS


Profiler Summary (Top 10 Hits):
```

Five hundred and eighty-six hits were within the GENERIC application's segment. The hits were times that the profile timer checked the application and found the current segment to be the application's segment. These hits occurred in the Method2() function, which counts for a long period of time. The majority of the hits were detected in the DISPLAY and GDI segments. They reflect the repeated use of the TextOut() and wsprintf() Windows functions in the Method1() function. The remainder of the hits were in other portions of the Windows environment used to process messages, etc.

The program initializes the profiler for 2 millisecond intervals between checks when the WM_CREATE message is processed. The sample data buffer is set to 100K. The calls to ProfStart() and ProfStop() occur within the functions that are profiled. ProfFlush() is called between the two function calls to copy all of the profile data to disk before the second function is called. This reduces the chance of overflowing the buffer.

```
long FAR PASCAL WndProc (HWND hWnd, unsigned iMessage, WORD wParam, LONG lParam)
{
        int     nProfMode ;

        switch (iMessage)                        /* process windows messages */
```

```
        {
                case WM_CREATE:
                        nProfMode = ProfInsChk () ;
                        if (!nProfMode)
                                MessageBox (hWnd, "Profiler not installed", "Message",
                                        MB_OK) ;
                        else
                        {
                                ProfSampRate (1, 2) ;      /* two milliseconds */
                                ProfSetup (100, 0) ;       /* 100 kbyte buffer */
                                ProfClear () ;             /* empty buffer */
                        }
                case WM_COMMAND:                           /* process menu items */
                        switch (wParam)
                        {
                        case IDM_DOIT:
                                Method1 (hWnd) ;           /* try method1 function */
                                ProfFlush () ;             /* write samples to disk */
                                Method2 (hWnd) ;           /* try method2 function */
                                break ;
                        case IDM_QUIT:
                                ProfFinish () ;
                                DestroyWindow (hWnd) ;
                                break ;
                        }
                        break ;
                case WM_DESTROY:
                        PostQuitMessage (0) ;
                        break ;
                default:
                        return DefWindowProc (hWnd, iMessage, wParam, lParam) ;
        }
        return (0L) ;
}


void Method1 (HWND hWnd)
{
        HDC             hDC ;
        int             i ;
        char            cBuf [128] ;

        ProfStart () ;
        hDC = GetDC (hWnd) ;
        for (i = 0 ; i < 1000 ; i++)
                TextOut (hDC, 0, 0, cBuf, wsprintf (cBuf, "%d", i)) ;
        ReleaseDC (hWnd, hDC) ;
        ProfStop () ;
}


void Method2 (HWND hWnd)
{
        HDC             hDC ;
        int             i, j ;

        ProfStart () ;
        hDC = GetDC (hWnd) ;
        SetBkMode (hDC, OPAQUE) ;
        TextOut (hDC, 0, 0, "Starting", 8) ;
        for (i = 0 ; i < 1000 ; i++)
        {
                for (j = 0 ; j < 1000 ; j++)
                        ;
        }
        TextOut (hDC, 0, 0, "Done Counting", 13) ;
        ReleaseDC (hWnd, hDC) ;
        ProfStop () ;
}
```

PROFFINISH

Purpose	Stops the profiler, and copies the data buffer to the disk file CSIPS.DAT.
Syntax	void **ProfFinish**(void);
Description	While the profiler is running, the hit data is copied to a memory buffer. This function stops the profiler, and copies the data to the file CSIPS.DAT in the WINDOWS subdirectory. This file is part of the input to the SHOWHITS.EXE program that outputs the profiler findings.
Uses	Used at the end of a profile session.
Returns	No returned value (void).
See Also	ProfFlush()
Parameters	None (void).
Example	See the example under the ProfClear() function description.

PROFFLUSH

Purpose	Copies the profiler sample buffer to disk.
Syntax	void **ProfFlush**(void);
Description	While the profiler is running, the hit data is copied to a sample buffer. ProfFlush() copies this data to the file CSIPS.DAT in the WINDOWS subdirectory and empties the memory buffer. This allows more data to be accumulated without fear of overflowing the buffer. It is not necessary to call ProfFlush() if ProfFinish() will be called before the buffer is full. ProfFlush() should not be run when the program may be processing an interrupt.
Uses	Used within the body of the program being profiled to copy the profile data to a disk file.
Returns	No returned value (void).
See Also	ProfFinish()
Parameters	None (void).
Example	See the example under the ProfClear() function description.

PROFINSCHK

Purpose	Checks if the profiler has been installed.
Syntax	int **ProfInsChk**(void);
Description	This function checks to see if the 386 enhanced mode device driver VPROD.386 has been installed, or whether the PROF.COM function was executed before WINDOWS was started.
Uses	Verification that the profiler is available.
Returns	int, 0 if the profiler is not installed, 1 if PROF.COM was installed, 2 if VPROD.386 was installed.
See Also	ProfStart(), ProfSetup()
Parameters	None (void).
Example	See the example under the ProfClear() function description.

PROFSAMPRATE

Purpose	Sets the sampling rate of the profiler.
Syntax	void **ProfSampRate**(int *nRate286*,int *nRate386*);

Description   This function allows the sampling rate that the profiler uses to be set. The sampling rate is the number of times per second that the sampler will check and record the part of the program that is active.

Uses   Used in initializing the profiler.

Returns   No returned value (void).

See Also   Prof Setup()

Parameters

nRate286   int: The sampling rate that the profiler will use in any mode except 386 enhanced mode. If *nRate386* is set, the *nRate386* parameter is ignored. *nRate286* can be any of the values in Table 26-2.

Value	Meaning - Sampling Rate	⊠
1	122.070 microseconds	
2	244.141 microseconds	
3	488.281 microseconds	
4	976.562 microseconds	
5	1.953125 milliseconds	
6	3.90625 milliseconds	
7	7.8125 milliseconds	
8	15.625 milliseconds	
9	31.25 milliseconds	
10	65.2 milliseconds	
11	125 milliseconds	
12	250 milliseconds	
13	500 milliseconds	

Table 26-2. Sampling Rates for Non-386 EnhancedMode Profiling.

nRate386   int: The sampling rate in milliseconds for the application if it is running in 386 enhanced mode. If *nRate286* is set, the *nRate286* parameter is ignored. The *nRate386*value can be between 1 and 1,000.

Example   See the example under the ProfClear() function description.

PROFSETUP   □ Win 2.0   ■ Win 3.0   ■ Win 3.1

Purpose   Initializes the size of the profile data buffer and disk file.

Syntax   void **ProfSetup**(int *nBufferSize*,int *nSamples*);

Description   This function is only effective if Windows is running in 386 enhanced mode. If the function is not called, the sampling buffer defaults to 64K, and the output file size is not limited.

Uses   Setting the sample buffer size and file size. This could be important if the system were running low on memory.

Returns   No returned value (void).

See Also   ProfSampRate()

Parameters

nBufferSize   int: The side of the sample data memory buffer in kilobytes. This value must be between 1 and 1,064.

nSamples   int: Sets a maximum on the number of hits that will be recorded to the disk file. A value of zero allows unlimited sample data.

Example   See the example under the ProfClear() function description.

PROFSTART   □ Win 2.0   ■ Win 3.0   ■ Win 3.1

Purpose   Starts the execution profiler.

Syntax   void **ProfStart**(void);

Description   Once this function is started, the profiler begins checking the application at the time interval specified by ProfSampRate(). The location within the program is recorded as a "hit" in the sample buffer each time it is checked.

Returns   No returned value (void).

See Also   ProfStop()

Parameters   None (void).

Example   See the example under the ProfClear() function description.

PROFSTOP   □ Win 2.0   ■ Win 3.0   ■ Win 3.1

Purpose   Stops the profiler.

Syntax   void **ProfStop**(void);

Description   This function stops the profiler. The data collected in the profile data buffer is not affected. The profiler can be restarted by calling ProfStart(). The new data will be added to the profile data buffer.

Returns   No returned value (void).

See Also   ProfStart()

Parameters   None (void).

Example   See the example under the ProfClear() function description.

VALIDATECODESEGMENTS   □ Win 2.0   ■ Win 3.0   ■ Win 3.1

Purpose   Enables debug checking if code segments are overwritten.

Syntax   void **ValidateCodeSegments**(void);

Description   Enables output of debugging information if memory areas containing code segments are overwritten by program operations.

Uses   Validity checking is enabled by default with the debug version of Windows, so this function is normally not needed. If code segment checking has been turned off by including the line

```
[kernel]
EnableSegmentChecksum=0
```

in the [kernel] section of WIN.INI, then ValidateCodeSegments() will override this switch and enable checking.

Returns   No returned value (void).

See Also   ValidateFreeSpaces()

Parameters None (void).

Example   This example shows an application that has the debugging memory validation functions set when the WM_CREATE message is processed. Calling these functions assures that any program actions that overwrite code or data areas will be trapped by the debugger.

```
long FAR PASCAL WndProc (HWND hWnd, unsigned iMessage, WORD wParam,  LONG lParam)
{

        switch (iMessage)                          /* process windows messages */
        {
        case WM_CREATE:
                ValidateCodeSegments () ;
                ValidateFreeSpaces () ;
                break ;
        case WM_COMMAND:                           /* process menu items */
                switch (wParam)
                {
                case IDM_DOIT:                     /* User hit the "Do it" menu item */
                        GlobalCompact (NULL) ;
                        break ;
```
[Other program lines]

VALIDATEFREESPACES   ■ Win 2.0 ■ Win 3.0 ■ Win 3.1

Purpose   Enables checking of memory overwriting of free areas.

Syntax   LPSTR **ValidateFreeSpaces**(void);

Description This function is only available with the debugging version of Windows. Free memory areas are portions of memory that have not been allocated with GlobalAlloc() and that do not contain code. This function enables checking of these areas when memory access functions are used, to make sure that memory writing operations use only valid memory areas.

       Two lines must be added to WIN.INI in the [kernel] section before using this function.

```
[kernel]
EnableFreeChecking=1
EnableHeapChecking=1
```

       Windows must be restarted if these lines were not in place when the system was started. Once installed, free memory areas will be loaded with the value 0xCC. Global memory operations, such as GlobalAlloc() and GlobalCompact(), will cause memory checking to start, which slows system performance.

Uses   Used only with the debug version of Windows. Use should be limited to tracking down memory errors, as this function slows system performance.

Returns   LPSTR. This value is not used.

See Also   ValidateCodeSegments()

Parameters None (void).

Example   See the previous example under the ValidateCodeSegments() function description.

27 Help File Support

Microsoft added a hypertext help system to Windows 3.0. "Hypertext" refers to the ability to jump from one subject to another while reading a document. The Windows help system has several advantages for the developer.

1. The help system will be installed on any computer running Windows 3.0 or later. The Windows INSTALL program puts the WINHELP.EXE file in the WINDOWS directory.
2. The help system is fully integrated into the Software Development Kit (SDK). Your application can include context-sensitive help, automatically loading the help system when called. "Context-sensitive" means that a different part of the help file is displayed depending on what part of the program is active.
3. Because all of the applications provided with Windows use the help system, users can be expected to have some familiarity with its operation.

This chapter documents the help file support command to Windows 3.0 and 3.1. Version 3.1 additions are not discussed.

Building a Help File

Adding Windows help file support to your application is a three-step process. First, create a *help document* using a text editor. Special characters are used to mark key words, index entries, etc. Second, compile the document using the HC.EXE help compiler provided with the SDK. This creates a *help file* that is ready to use by the WINHELP.EXE program. Last, add calls to the WinHelp() function in your program. This function loads WINHELP.EXE, if it is not already running, and jumps to a specified location in the help file.

Although in theory you can use any text editor to create the help document, in practice you are much better off if you use Microsoft Word for Windows. Besides being an excellent editor, Word for Windows supports all of the special characters needed to create help documents. The help compiler expects to read a file in the rich text format (rtf). Word for Windows will save and read files in this format, although it must be specified in each file save and open operation.

The help document uses several techniques to code the information the help compiler needs to figure out indexes and jump points to other parts of the file. Footnotes are used to label parts of the file with names and index entries. The double-underline character style is used to mark jump points. Jump points are the words that the user can click with the mouse to jump to another part of the help file. Underlined text is used to mark definitions. Clicking a definition word pops up a small box containing the word's meaning. The box disappears when the user releases the mouse button. The hidden text style (a character style supported by Word for Windows) is used to put cross-reference strings into the documents. Cross-reference strings are the names of the labels that the help system will jump to when the user clicks an item.

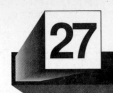

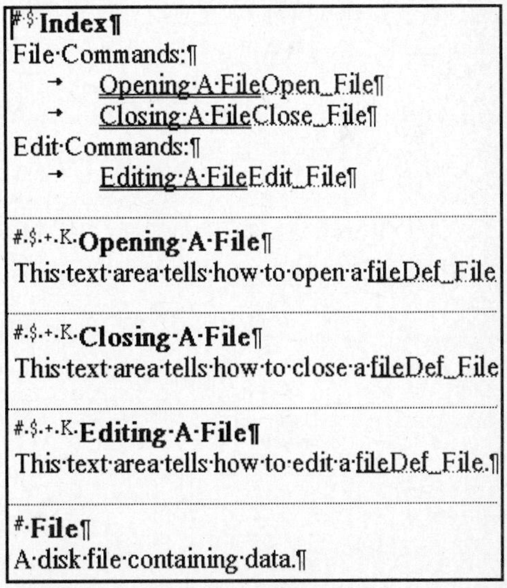
#$ Index¶
File·Commands:¶
→ Opening·A·FileOpen_File¶
→ Closing·A·FileClose_File¶
Edit·Commands:¶
→ Editing·A·FileEdit_File¶

#.$.+.K.Opening·A·File¶
This·text·area·tells·how·to·open·a·fileDef_File

#.$.+.K.Closing·A·File¶
This·text·area·tells·how·to·close·a·fileDef_File

#.$.+.K.Editing·A·File¶
This·text·area·tells·how·to·edit·a·fileDef_File.¶

#.File¶
A·disk·file·containing·data.¶

Figure 27-1. A Help Document.

Figure 27-1 shows a small help document with all of the special characters exposed. The top portion of the file is the index. Below that, separated by page breaks, are three help subjects and a definition of the term "File." Each title is preceded by footnote characters. The footnotes contain the names and labels for each page of the help document.

(Hidden text is exposed and indicated with a dotted underline. Page breaks are indicated by a continuous dotted line between pages. Tab characters are indicated by the arrows to the right.)

The hypertext jump destinations use the "hidden text" style (shown in Figure 27-1 with a dotted underline). For example, if the user clicks the visible "Opening A File" item in the index, the help system will jump to the label "Open_File." "Open_File" is a footnote label for the second page of the help document. If you were to open the footnote entries for editing within Word for Windows, the footnote list would appear as shown in Figure 27-2.

In Word for Windows, footnotes are added by placing the cursor at the location where the footnote is to be added, and then selecting the Insert/Footnote menu item. The footnote dialog box requests a "Footnote Reference Mark." This box is where you enter the $, #, +, or K character. Word for Windows will then open the footnote editing area at the bottom of the screen, so that you can enter the label string for the footnote. The editor keeps the footnotes in the correct order, and it will jump to a footnote if you position the cursor within the text area while the footnote edit area is visible.

```
# Index
$ Index
# Open_File
$ Opening A File
+ File_Commands:10
K File;Open File
# Close_File
$ Closing A File
+ File_Commands:20
K File;Closing Files
# Edit_File
$ Edit File
+ File_Commands:30
K File;Editing Files
# Def_File
```

Figure 27-2. Index Entries for the Help Document.

Help Document Special Characters

When building the help document, you will add footnotes and special character types to structure the hypertext jumps. Table 27-1 contains a list of the special characters. The characters preceding the word "footnote" are the "Footnote Reference Mark" characters used when creating a footnote in the document.

Special Character	Meaning
# footnote	Marks a context string. This is a destination label that the help system can jump to. The point(s) to jump from will be marked with double-underlined text, followed by the same context string in hidden text.
$ footnote	Defines a title string. Title strings are optional.
K footnote	Key word. Key words are used to build the list of search strings that the help system will search for. They are not required, but are highly recommended.
+ footnote	Browse sequence number. In the footnote definition you put a group subject name, a colon, and an integer. Browse sequences mark the order that the subjects will be viewed if the user clicks the browse buttons on the help system window.
Double-underlined text (strike through text has the same effect)	Marks a cross-reference point. The marked characters will be highlighted in color on the help system. Clicking the mouse pointer on the highlighted characters causes a jump to another topic. The destination is named in hidden text immediately following the double-underlined text.
Underlined text	Marks a definition. The underlined characters will be highlighted in underlined color on the help system. Clicking the mouse pointer on the highlighted characters causes a small window containing a definition of the term to appear. The definition is obtained from another topic. The topic is specified in hidden text immediately following the underlined text.
* footnote	Marks a buildtag. Buildtags are used to allow conditional compilation of parts of a help file.

Table 27-1. Help Document Special Characters.

Defining Hypertext Jumps and Index Entries

The critical aspect in creating the help document is marking topics with the # footnotes. They are the context labels that allow that point to be a destination for a hypertext jump. Normally, these labels will be on the first line of a page (following a page break), as shown in the example in Figure 27-1. The footnotes can be placed anywhere in the page if desired.

To allow jumping to the point, you must do two things. First, the text string that will mark the jumping off point is typed using double-underlined characters. This mark is followed by the exact context label for the destination, typed with hidden characters. Once compiled, the footnote markers and hidden characters are not visible in the help window. The double-underlined characters (the jumping off points) are highlighted in color.

Creating an index using these techniques is simple. As shown in Figure 27-1, the top of the help file is normally the index. Each jumping off point is marked with double-underlined characters, followed by the hidden characters defining where to jump. Each of the destination subjects is on a separate page, with the top line of each marked with the # footnote context string. Context strings can be up to 255 characters long, and can contain letters, numbers, periods, and underscore characters. Spaces between words are not allowed. Uppercase and lowercase letters are treated as identical.

Adding Search Strings and Bookmarks

The K footnotes are also important. The help window includes a magnifying glass button marked "search." Topics that have K footnote entries will appear in a list of subjects that can be searched for. The search feature allows the user to quickly locate information in a large file. With the footnotes shown in Figure 27-2, the search list would have four entries: "File," "Open File," "Closing Files," and "Editing Files." Searching for "File" within the help system would reveal three topics to jump to. "Open File," "Closing Files," and "Editing Files" would show single entries.

Key words can be up to 255 characters long, and can contain any ANSI character including spaces. A group of key words can be defined on one footnote line by separating them with a semicolon. Here is an example with four key words defined.

^{K} Files;Opening Files;Disk;Disk Access

Titles are marked with $ footnotes. Titles appear in the help system bookmark list. Bookmarks allow the user to mark a location for future reference. Titles also appear in the "Topics found" section when the user searches for a key word. Titles and key words are usually used together. Titles can be up to 128 characters long, and can contain any ANSI character, including spaces. The entire line in the footnote entry is considered to be one title entry.

Browse sequences, marked with + footnotes, are less critical. They allow the user to jump from one section to the next section in a logical order. In a large file, there will be a number of groups of subjects (pages) that logically fit together. Each can be organized in a separate browse sequence. In the simple example shown in Figures 27-1 and 27-2, there is only one group, labeled "File_Commands," available to browse. Each + footnote is followed by a colon and an integer. The integer order sets the browse sequence. The help system will not allow browsing to go past the first or last entry in a browse sequence. Note that the browse numbers are sorted in character order, not numerical order. To avoid confusion, you can precede the browse sequence numbers by zeros. For example, if you will be using browse numbers up to 999, code the number five as 005.

Adding Bitmap Graphics

The help system will display bitmap graphics in the help window. Bitmap graphics can be useful to clarify subjects, although large bitmaps can take up a lot of disk space.

The simplest way to add a bitmap to a help document is to paste it into a Word for Windows document. The bitmap is saved along with the file. Chapter 15, *Bitmaps*, includes the source code for a program that will "cut" bitmap images from any Windows application, and then allow them to be "pasted" into Word for Windows.

If your word processor does not support direct cut and paste operations with bitmaps, you can still include bitmaps stored as files in your help document. There are three ways to do this, depending on whether you want the bitmap to show up on the left or right of the document, or to be fit in with the character data. Here are the commands.

{**bmc** filename.bmp}	Fits filename.bmp in with the text at this location.
{**bml** filename.bmp}	Puts the bitmap at the far left of the document.
{**bmr** filename.bmp}	Puts the bitmap at the far right of the document.

Note that the bitmap file is the same in all three cases. Only the loction on the help document changes.

Compiling a Help File

The help compiler is called HC.EXE. HC reads a project file with the extension .HPJ that specifies how a help document is to be built. The project file is a normal ASCII text file. Here is an example.

▷ **HELPEX.HPJ Help Project File Listing.**

```
[OPTIONS]
TITLE=Help Example
COMPRESS=true
WARNING=1

[MAP]
Open_File      10
Close_File     20
Edit_File      30

[FILES]
\c\work\helpex.rtf
```

In this example, the help document created by Word for Windows is called HELPEX.RTF. It is referenced in the [FILES] section of the project file. To compile this file and create the file HELPEX.HLP, use the following command line:

```
C:>HC HELPEX.HPJ
```

Note that the project file name, not the help document, is passed to the help compiler. If the help compiler does not find an error during compilation, it outputs the finished help file, HELPEX.HLP. This file can be read into the Windows help program and examined. The help program can also be launched from within another program using the WinHelp() function.

Help Project File Options

The help project file has a large number of options that allow control over the help compiler. The project file is a standard ASCII file, not the RTF format used for the help document itself. The structure of the project file is similar to that of WIN.INI and the other Windows initialization files. There are six possible sections in a help project file: [Files], [Options], [BuildTags], [Alias], [Map], and [Bitmaps]. Only the [Files] section is required, although most project files will include some [Options] and [Map] statements.

Project [Files] Section

The [Files] section is where all of the document files that will be combined to form the complete help system are listed. A typical section is

```
[FILES]
HELPEX.RTF
HELPINDX.RTF
COMMON.RTF
```

The files are assumed to be in the same directory as the project file. The directory can be specified with the ROOT option, described later in this chapter.

Project [Buildtags] Section

The help compiler allows portions of the help document to be included or omitted based on settings in the project file. This ability is useful when you want one version of the help document to allow generation of two or more different help files. This might be the case if you are marketing beginner and advanced versions of the same program.

Implementing buildtags requires additions to both the help document and the project file. Within the help document, each section is preceded with a buildtag footnote. (This is a footnote with the asterisk (*) as the reference mark.) The footnote text can contain one or more strings that are the "buildtags" for the section. For example, the footnote

* Beginner; Advanced

would code a section as being included if either the "Beginner" or "Advanced" option were defined in the BUILD option of the help project file. The footnote

* Advanced

would only add the section if the "Advanced" BUILD option were defined.

All of the buildtags used in the document file should be listed in the help project file under the [Buildtags] section. Finally, you specify which build =tag or tags will be included during compilation with a BUILD command in the [Options] part of the project file.

```
[Options]
BUILD=Advanced

[Buildtags]
Beginner
Advanced
```

Project [Options] Section

The [Options] section of the project file provides information to the help compiler. Here is an example [Options] section using every possible statement.

```
[Options]
BUILD=Advanced | Beginner
COMPRESS=TRUE
WARNING=3
ROOT=C:\C\WORK
INDEX=main_index
TITLE=Help Example
FORECEFONT=Modern
MAPFONTSIZE=8-12:12
MULTIKEY=A
```

The BUILD option controls which of the sections marked with buildtags will be added to the finished help file. Usually, this is just one key word.

```
BUILD=Advanced
```

You can also combine more than one buildtag with the logical operators & (AND), | (OR), and ~ (NOT). Parentheses can be used to group buildtag names.

The COMPRESS option controls whether the final help file is stored in compressed form, or is left uncompressed. Normally, you will set this value to FALSE during the development of the help file to save time. During the final compilation, set the value to TRUE to reduce the disk space taken up by the help file. Decompression is fast, so there is little value in storing the help files uncompressed.

The WARNING option determines the amount of debugging information the help compiler generates. Level 1 is minimal output, 2 is medium, 3 is maximum output. Set this value to 3 during development.

The ROOT option specifies the starting directory for all help compiler operations. Directory names listed in the FILES section are assumed to be subdirectories of the ROOT directory. You can get around this assumption by typing the full path name of a file, starting with the drive letter.

The INDEX option sets which section of the help document contains the index. The name following the INDEX= key word must be a context string (marked with a # footnote). If no INDEX value is specified in the project file, the first topic is assumed to be the index by the compiler. This is usually the best way to organize a help document, so INDEX is not often used.

The TITLE option specifies a character string that will be added to the caption bar of the help window. The string will be followed by "Help - Filename," where Filename is the name of the file that was loaded.

The FORCEFONT option causes the help compiler to convert all characters to the specified font. Because fonts are a Windows resource, the text will not be displayed if the help file references fonts that are not installed on the user's system. In these cases, use FORCEFONT to specify one of the fonts supplied with Windows (Courier, Helv, Modern, Roman, Script, Symbol, and Tms Rmn).

MAPFONTSIZE allows conversions from one font size to another during the help file compilation. This option is generally used with FORCEFONT to pick font sizes appropriate for the font that will be used. MAPFONTSIZE can convert either a single font size to another size, or a range of font sizes to one final size. Here are two examples.

```
[OPTIONS]
MAPFONTSIZE=8:12                  ; Convert all 8 pt to 12 pt
MAPFONTSIZE=10-16:14             ; Convert all 10 to 16 pt to 14 pt
```

MULTIKEY allows the creation of additional key word tables. By default, only the letter K footnotes go into a key word table. MULTIKEY allows other letters to be used, creating additional tables of key words that can be searched. Upper- and lowercase letters are not equivalent. The letters "K" and "k" are reserved.

To use the MULTIKEY option, specify the HELP_MULTIKEY option when calling WinHelp().

Project [Alias] Section

The [Alias] section allows the help compiler to use one context string in place of another. You might use this option as an alternative to changing the footnote names within a help document. For example, to eliminate the "Edit_Info" and "Cut_Info" topics, and have the jump points destinations changed to "General_Edits," use

```
[ALIAS]
Edit_Info=General_Edit
Cut_Info=General_Edit
```

If the [ALIAS] section gets too long, the help document will be difficult to follow, so use this option with discretion.

Project [Map] Section

One of the best features of the Windows help system is the ability to create context-sensitive help systems. Context-sensitive means that the help topic displayed will depend on the portion of the program that is currently active.

To create context-sensitive help files, you must assign numbers to the context strings. Context strings are placed by inserting topics marked with # footnotes. The string in the footnote's text for the # footnote is the context string. For example, the help document shown at the beginning of the chapter, in Figures 27-1 and 27-2, contained several context strings. Each context string can be assigned a number within the project file as follows:

```
[MAP]
Open_File                10
Close_File               20
Edit_File                30
```

The Open_File Context string assigned number 10, Close_File number 20, and Edit_File number 30. These numbers are used when calling the WinHelp() function.

Within the program calling WinHelp() to load the help file, the *dwData* parameter passed to WinHelp() is set equal to the context number. An example of this is shown under the WinHelp() function description. The help system will jump to this numbered topic when WinHelp() is called.

Project [Bitmaps] Section

If bitmap files have been referenced within the help document using the bmc, bml, or bmr commands, the bitmap files must be listed in the help project file under the [Bitmaps] section. Here is an example.

```
[BITMAPS]
bit1.bmp
bit2.bmp
c:\paint\bit3.bmp
```

Using the [Bitmaps] will only be necessary if you are using a text editor that does not support direct pasting of bitmaps into the help document file.

Using the Help System

Although the help system works well, it does not provide any method to debug a help document. In large help files, it is easy to end up with a missing context string footnote, or some other important marker. Missing string errors are noted by the help compiler, but they are not always easy to track down. The best cure for these development problems is prevention. Organize the structure of your help document before you start writing the text. Use a consistent set of naming conventions (such as preceding key words with "k_," topics with "t_," etc.). You can use a Microsoft Excel spreadsheet to keep track of the various labels used.

WINHELP	☐ Win 2.0 ■ Win 3.0 ■ Win 3.1

Purpose	Loads and/or locates an entry in a help file accessed via the Windows help system.
Syntax	BOOL **WinHelp**(HWND *hWnd*, LPSTR *lpHelpFile*, WORD *wCommand*, DWORD *dwData*);
Description	This function allows an application to call the Windows help system. The help file is assumed to have been created by the HC help compiler. If the help system (a Windows program) is not active, it is loaded, and the help file is read. If the help system is already viewing the help file, calling WinHelp() can be used to jump to a new location in the help file, or to close the help system. WinHelp() allows several methods of starting the help system at a specific point in the help file, which allows context-sensitive help systems to be created.
Uses	Used within applications to provide online help documents.
Returns	BOOL. TRUE if the function was successful. FALSE on error.
Parameters	
hWnd	HWND: The handle of the window that is calling the help system.
lpHelpFile	LPSTR: A pointer to a null-terminated character string containing the name of the help file. The file name can include the full directory path if needed. The file is assumed to have been created by compiling a help document with the HC help compiler.
wCommand	WORD: Sets what action WinHelp() is to take. This can be any of the values in Table 27-2.

Value	Meaning ⊠
HELP_CONTEXT	Displays the help file, starting with a context string. In this case, *dwData* is a 32-bit unsigned integer. The integer's value is set to match a number in the [MAP] section of the help project file.
HELP_HELPONHELP	Displays help on the help system. Both *lpHelpFile* and *dwData* are ignored.
HELP_INDEX	Displays the help file, starting with the help file's index. This assumes that there is only one index. For files with more than one index, use HELP_SETINDEX.
HELP_KEY	Displays the help file, starting with a key word in the help file. In this case, *dwData* contains a pointer to a character string containing the name of the key word.
HELP_MULTIKEY	Displays help for a key word in an alternate key word table. This is used with the MULTIKEY option in the help project file. In this case, *dwData* points to a MULTIKEYHELP data structure.
HELP_QUIT	Closes the help file and terminates the help system for this application. Other applications' use of the help system is not affected. *dwData* is ignored.
HELP_SETINDEX	Sets a help index in a file containing more than one index. The index is identified by placing the context string number in *dwData*. The context string number is set in the [MAP] section of the help project file (see the following example). Calling WinHelp() with this option is always followed by calling WinHelp() a second time with the HELP_CONTEXT command.

Table 27-2. WinHelp() Command.

dwData   DWORD: The DWORD value passed to the help system. The value's meaning depends on the *wCommand* option. See Table 27-2 for the description.

For the HELP_MULTIKEY option, *dwData* points to a MULTIKEYHELP data structure, defined in WINDOWS.H as

```
typedef struct tagMULTIKEYHELP

  {
  WORD    mkSize;                         /* size of this structure */
  BYTE    mkKeylist;                      /* table footnote character */
  BYTE    szKeyphrase[1];                 /* key word to start on.  This */
                                          /* string will contain more */
                                          /* than one byte */

  } MULTIKEYHELP;
```

Example   This example shows four uses of the WinHelp() function. When the user clicks the "Do It!" menu item, the HELPEX.HLP file is loaded and displayed starting from the index. If the user presses the (F1) key, the same file is loaded, but it is started from the topic "Editing Files." If the help file has already been loaded, the file jumps to this topic. Similarly, if the user presses the (F2) key, the help file jumps to the context string labeled number 20. The labels are set in the help project file.

▷ HELPEX.HPJ Project File

```
[OPTIONS]
TITLE=Help Example
COMPRESS=true
WARNING=3
FORCEFONT=Modern
MAPFONTSIZE=8-12:10

[MAP]
Open_File       10
Close_File      20
Edit_File       30

[FILES]
c:\c\book3\helpex.rtf
```

Item 20 is mapped to the context string "Close_File." The final use of the WinHelp() function is to close the help system when the application terminates. This does not cause a problem if the help system is not currently loaded, or if two or more applications of the help system are in use. Only an active instance of this application is removed by calling WinHelp() with the HELP_QUIT command.

```
long FAR PASCAL WndProc (HWND hWnd, unsigned iMessage, WORD wParam, LONG lParam)
{

        switch (iMessage)                     /* process windows messages */
        {
        case WM_COMMAND:                      /* process menu items */
                switch (wParam)
                {
                case IDM_DOIT:                /* User hit the "Do it" menu item */
                        WinHelp (hWnd, "helpex.hlp", HELP_INDEX, NULL) ;
                        break ;
                case IDM_QUIT:
                        DestroyWindow (hWnd) ;
                        break ;
                }
                break ;
        case WM_KEYDOWN:
                if (wParam == VK_F1)
                        WinHelp (hWnd, "helpex.hlp", HELP_KEY,
                                (DWORD) (LPSTR) "Editing Files") ;
                else if (wParam == VK_F2)
                        WinHelp (hWnd, "helpex.hlp", HELP_CONTEXT,
```

```
                            (DWORD) 20) ;
                break ;
        case WM_DESTROY:                    /* stop application */
                WinHelp (hWnd, "helpex.hlp", HELP_QUIT, NULL) ;
                PostQuitMessage (0) ;
                break ;
        default:                            /* default windows message processing */
                return DefWindowProc (hWnd, iMessage, wParam, lParam) ;
    }
    return (0L) ;
}
```

Dynamic Link Libraries

Dynamic Link Libraries(DLLs) have a reputation for being difficult to create. This reputation dates from the early days of Windows, when you had to write your own assembly language prolog, and when the unique aspects of programming within a DLL were not well documented.

Today DLLs are simple to write and debug. DLLs offer major advantages to programmers over conventional libraries of functions that are included in the linking process when a program is compiled. DLLs do not have to be recompiled or relinked. Functions in a DLL can be used by another program by just referencing the function names in the IMPORTS section of the program's .DEF definition file. Once loaded, the DLL functions can be used by any running application on the system, without loading another copy of the DLL into memory.

Because of these advantages, DLLs are the preferred way to program functions that are likely to be useful to more than one application. As your experience as a Windows programmer grows, your collection of DLLs will increase. You may find that DLLs are the best way to market libraries of functions.

What Is a DLL?

If you have been programming with the C language for some time, you are probably familiar with object libraries. All of the C library functions, such as printf() and strcat(), are stored in object libraries. You can also create your own object library using the LIB program. During the linking process, the linker copies the functions that are called within a C program from the library file, and adds them to the executable program. This is more efficient than just storing the functions in a compiled .OBJ objective file, as only the functions that are used are copied into the finished .EXE file.

Objective libraries are fine for an operating system like MS-DOS that only allows one program to run at one time (TSRs and other tricks are ignored here). Under Windows, objective libraries are not efficient. Windows programs would be enormous if every one had to have its own functions for output to the screen, message processing, memory management, dialog boxes, etc.

The developers of Windows invented DLLs to allow several programs running at the same time to share a single copy of a group of functions. Almost all of the basic functionality of Windows is stored in DLL files with names like USER, KERNEL, and GDI. You can also create your own DLL files, as described in the next section. DLL files usually have the extension .DLL, although they can be named with the extension .EXE.

The term "dynamic link" describes how DLLs work. With a regular objective library, the linker copies all of the library functions it needs and passes the exact function addresses to the program that calls the functions. With DLLs, the library functions are in a separate DLL file. The DLL file is not involved in the linking process when a Windows program is created. The program that calls a function in a DLL does not find out the address of the function until the program is running and uses that function. Only then does Windows find the function in the DLL and pass its address to the calling program. The result is that DLLs provide the ultimate in reusable code. Once a DLL is created, it never needs to be recompiled or relinked again. Any number of running applications can call functions in a single copy of the DLL loaded into memory.

Creating a DLL

DLLs are simpler to create than a full Windows program. You do not need to create a window, window class, or message loop. You will need to add two short functions, LibMain() and WEP(), that take care of starting and closing the DLL. The LibMain() function is called when a DLL is first loaded into memory. The function must always have the format

```
int FAR PASCAL LibMain (HANDLE hInstance, WORD wDataSeg, WORD wHeapSize,
        LPSTR lpszCmdLine) ;
```

hInstance is the DLL's instance handle. *wDataSeg* is the data segment, if the DLL has a local heap defined in the .DEF file (see below). *wHeapSize* is the size of the local heap. *lpszCmdLine* is a pointer to a null-terminated character string that can contain a command line string. The command line string will only be available if the DLL is loaded with the LoadModule() function. The command line is passed as the *lpCmdShow* element in the *lpParameterBlock* parameter passed to LoadModule().

The only thing LibMain() must do is to call UnlockData() to unlock the DLL's data segment in memory (assuming that there is no special reason why a locked data segment is required). You can also put any initialization functions, such as allocating memory blocks, in LibMain().

The other standard function is WEP(), which is an exit routine called right before Windows removes the DLL from memory. The function must have the following format:

```
void FAR PASCAL WEP (int nParameter) ;
```

The parameter *nParameter* will either have the value WEP_SYSTEMEXIT if Windows is being shut down, or WEP_FREE_DLL if Windows is just removing the DLL from memory. You can code functions, such as freeing allocated memory, into WEP(). A WEP() function is not actually required if there is no cleanup to do, as the DLL is removed from memory. The Windows SDK documentation strongly recommends including a WEP() function in all DLLs, so it is a good idea to put one in even if it is not needed with the current version of Windows.

Besides LibMain() and WEP(), the DLL consists of functions that you create and add to the library. These functions need to be declared as FAR, and they are usually declared as FAR PASCAL following the normal Windows function declarations. Any pointer passed to a DLL function must be a FAR pointer.

Listing 28-1 provides an example of a DLL source code file. Besides the required LibMain() and WEP() functions, the library contains a single function called InStr(). This function locates a string *lszCheck* in the string *lszString* and returns the character position of the match. It returns −1 if there is not a match. Note that the function is declared FAR PASCAL, and it uses only FAR pointers (LPSTR is defined as CHAR FAR * in WINDOWS.H).

▷ Listing 28-1. EXMAPDLL.C

```
/* exmpdll.c   example dynamic link library */

#include <windows.h>

/* dll initiator function */
int FAR PASCAL LibMain (HANDLE hInstance, WORD wDataSeg, WORD wHeapSize,
        LPSTR lpszCmdLine)
{
        if (wHeapSize > 0)
                UnlockData (0) ;
/* any initialization code goes here. return 0 if initialization fails */
        return (1) ;
}

/* check if lszCheck is in lszString, return match pos, -1 if no match */
int FAR PASCAL InStr (LPSTR lszString, LPSTR lszCheck)
{
        LPSTR           lpCheck, lpString ;
        int             nMatch, nPos ;

        nPos = 0 ;
        do {
                lpCheck = lszCheck ;
                lpString = lszString ;
                nMatch = 0 ;
                do {
                        if (*lpCheck == *lpString)
                                nMatch++ ;
                        else
                                break ;
                } while (*lpCheck++ && *lpString++) ;
                if (nMatch == lstrlen (lszCheck))
```

```
                              return (nPos) ;
                  else
                              nPos++ ;
          } while (*lszString++) ;
          return (-1) ;
}

void FAR PASCAL WEP (int nParameter)                /* dll terminator */
{
          return ;
}
```

If you examine the code the InStr() function, you will note that there is nothing special about it. The only special consideration in writing this function in a DLL was to make sure that only FAR pointers were used. Once you have written the DLL source code, you will need to compile and link it. In this case, "linking" does not link the functions into another program. Linking simply creates the executable .DLL file. Like any Windows program, a .DEF definition file is required for linking.

There are several differences between the .DEF file for a DLL and the .DEF file for a Windows application program. Instead of the NAME statement, DLLs use LIBRARY to name the file. DLLs do not have a STACK statement because the DLL will use the stack of any application that calls a function in the DLL. DLLs can have a local heap, so the HEAPSIZE statement is included. Note that SINGLE is added to the DATA statement. Because DLLs only have one data segment. Only one instance of a DLL is ever loaded, unlike Windows applications where multiple instances each have their own data segments.

Listing 28-2 shows a typical>DEF definition file for a DLL.

⇨ Listing 28-2. EXAMPDLL.DEF Definition File

```
LIBRARY         EXAMPDLL

DESCRIPTION             'Example DLL'
EXETYPE                 WINDOWS
STUB                    'WINSTUB.EXE'
CODE                    PRELOAD MOVEABLE DISCARDABLE
DATA                    PRELOAD MOVEABLE SINGLE
HEAPSIZE                1024
EXPORTS                 InStr
```

The EXPORTS statement in the DLL's .DEF file is where the library function namesare listed. Any application calling a function in the DLL will use this name to reference the library function. It is easy to forget to add the function name to the .DEF file after adding a new function to the C program.

The last adjustments needed to compile a DLL are made to the NMAKE file. Listing 28-3 shows the NMAKE file needed to compile EXAMPDLL.C. The C compiler switch "-ASw" is added. The "s" specifies the compiler small memory model. The "w" provides warning messages if the compiler detects the use of a NEAR pointer that assumes that the stack is in the local data segment (more on this later). You will use the "-AM" flag for a medium memory model compilation.

⇨ Listing 28-3. EXAMPDLL NMAKE File

```
# make file for exampdll library

ALL: exampdll.dll

CFLAGS=-c -D LINT_ARGS -ASw -Zp -Ow -Gsw -W2
LFLAGS=/NOD /align:16

exampdll.obj:           exampdll.c
        $(CC) $(CFLAGS) exampdll.c

exampdll.dll:           exampdll.obj exampdll.def
        link $(LFLAGS) exampdll libentry, exampdll.dll, NUL, libw sdllcew, exampdll
        rc exampdll.dll
```

The NMAKE file includes the LIBENTRY.OBJ and the SDLLCEW.LIB files in the linker command line. LIBENTRY is a small assembly language program that starts all DLLs and ultimately calls the LibMain() function in the DLL. A listing of this assembly language program is included in the LocalInit() function description later in this chapter. SDLLCEW.LIB is the standard objective library for all DLL files using the small memory model.

As with Windows applications, the resource compiler RC.EXE is called at the end of the compile/link cycle. This example is so simple that no resource data was included. RC.EXE simply tags the DLL as being a Windows 3.0 version program. DLLs can include all types of resource data if desired.

That is all there is to creating a DLL. When you are done, the file EXAMPDLL.DLL will be created. You can't run this program from the file manager or program manager. It is only useful if the functions included are called by another Windows program.

Using the Functions in a DLL

Continuing with our example, let's say that you want to use the InStr() function in the DLL in a Windows program. The only requirement is that you add the function's name in the IMPORTS section of the calling program's .DEF definition file. Listing 28-4 provides an example of a .DEF file for a program that uses InStr().

▷ **Listing 28-4. GENERIC.DEF**

```
NAME            GENERIC
DESCRIPTION     'generic windows program'
EXETYPE WINDOWS
STUB            'WINSTUB.EXE'
CODE            PRELOAD MOVEABLE
DATA            PRELOAD MOVEABLE MULTIPLE
HEAPSIZE        1024
STACKSIZE       5120
EXPORTS         WndProc
IMPORTS         EXAMPDLL.InStr
```

The only thing special about this .DEF file is the last line. The program IMPORTS the function InStr() from the file EXAMPDLL. This is how you tell Windows where to find the InStr() function when GENERIC.EXE calls it. With InStr() listed in the .DEF file, you can use it within the program like any other library function. Listing 28-5 provides an excerpt from a program calling this function.

▷ **Listing 28-5. Calling the InStr() Function from within a Windows Program**

```
int FAR PASCAL InStr (LPSTR lszString, LPSTR lszCheck) ;

long FAR PASCAL WndProc (HWND hWnd, unsigned iMessage, WORD wParam, LONG lParam)
{
        static char     cBuf1 [] = {"This is a string to check out."} ;
        HDC             hDC ;
        char            cBuf [128] ;

        switch (iMessage)                       /* process windows messages */
        {
        case WM_COMMAND:                        /* process menu items */
                switch (wParam)
                {
                case IDM_DOIT:          /* User hit the "Do it" menu item */
                        hDC = GetDC (hWnd) ;
                        TextOut (hDC, 0, 0, cBuf, wsprintf (cBuf,
                                "String to Check->%s", (LPSTR) cBuf1)) ;
                        TextOut (hDC, 10, 20, cBuf, wsprintf (cBuf,
                                "check is at position %d",
                                        InStr ((LPSTR) cBuf1,
                                                (LPSTR) "check"))) ;
                        TextOut (hDC, 10, 40, cBuf, wsprintf (cBuf,
                                "other is at position %d",
                                        InStr ((LPSTR) cBuf1,
                                                (LPSTR) "other"))) ;
                        ReleaseDC (hWnd, hDC) ;
                        break ;
```

[Other program lines]

With this simple example, the function prototype for the InStr() function is coded right into the calling program. For a larger DLL, the DLL's exported functions would be prototyped in a header file that could be included in any program calling the functions.

InStr() is called twice in the example. Note that the parameters passed to InStr() are cast to long pointers. This explicit calling is not necessay if you use a function protypefor InStr(). This example will produce the output shown in Figure 28-1 when the user clicks the "Do It!" menu item.

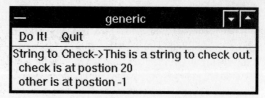

Figure 28-1. Output from Program Calling InStr() DLL Function.

Other Ways to Call DLL Functions

The previous example used the most common method of providing Windows with the function address to use in the DLL: reference by function name. This method works for any number of functions in a DLL. For example, if the DLL has three functions, the EXPORTS section of the DLL's .DEF definition file would look like

```
EXPORTS FirstFunc
        SecondFunc
        ThirdFunc
```

If the DLL file's name is MYDLL.DLL, then any program wanting to use these three functions would include the following in its .DEF definition file:

```
IMPORTS MYDLL.FirstFunc
        MYDLL.SecondFunc
        MYDLL.ThirdFunc
```

A more efficient, but less transparent, method of linking the functions is to give each exported function a number. These numbers, called "ordinal" numbers, are preceded by an ampersand (@) character in the DLL's EXPORT section. Here is an example.

```
EXPORTS FirstFunc            @1
        SecondFunc           @2
        ThirdFunc            @3
```

The program using the DLL's functions can then IMPORT them based on the ordinal value.

```
        IMPORTS FirstFunc        = MYDLL.1
        SecondFunc               = MYDLL.2
        ThirdFunc                = MYDLL.3
```

This produces smaller and faster code than using the function names to define the link. The trade-off is that it is easy to get the ordinal numbers confused when using large DLL files.

One trick that you can use with either the function name or ordinal number methods of linking DLLs is to rename the function within the program's .DEF file. For example, the program calling the three functions could have the following lines in its .DEF definition file:

```
IMPORTS FirstF           = MYDLL.FirstFunc
        SecondF          = MYDLL.SecondFunc
        ThirdF           = MYDLL.ThirdFunc
```

This is called giving the function an "alias." You can do a lot of clever tricks using function alias names, such as replacing standard Windows functions with your own versions. Again, the trade-off is that the code gets more difficult to follow when the same function may have move than one name.

The last way to link a DLL's functions to a program is to explicitly load the library with the LoadLibrary() function, and obtain a function address with GetProcAddress(). This provides precise control of when a DLL is loaded into memory, and when it is removed with FreeLibrary(). Using these functions is more complex than defining the links in the program .DEF files, as you must use indirect function references. An example is provided under the FreeLibrary() function description.

Importing Windows Library Functions

All of the examples used in this book import functions from the Windows DLLs that contain functions like ShowWindow(), TextOut(), etc. You may wonder why we have not had to include a long list of function names in the IMPORTS section of every .DEF file to allow links to the Windows functions.

The answer is that Windows allows you to summarize all of the functions that are exported from a DLL in a small file that the linker can read. This file is called an "import library." The IMPLIB.EXE program creates this type of file. IMPLIB has the following syntax:

IMPLIB *imp-lib-name mod-def-file*

Where *imp-lib-name* is the name of the import library file to create, and *mod-def-file* is the name of the DLL's .DEF definition file. For example, to create an import library for EXAMPDLL.DEF, you would use the following command line from DOS:

```
IMPLIB EXAMPDLL.LIB EXAMPDLL.DEF
```

Once this is done, you can forget about all of those IMPORT statements, and just use the import library in the LINK command line. For example,

```
LINK GENERIC, GENERIC.EXE, , /NOD SLIBCEW LIBW EXAMPDLL, GENERIC.DEF
```

would give the linker the dynamic link function information to link the EXAMPDLL functions into GENERIC.EXE at run time.

You have probably figured it out already, but the SLIBCEW and LIBW import libraries of Windows functions were created this way. We have included them in every LINK command for the examples in this book. That is how the DLL functions for all of the Windows library are referenced into the programs.

All links of Windows programs include the LIBW.LIB import library. The other Windows import library you will include in the LINK command line depends on the memory model, math calculation basis, and whether the program to be created is a Windows application or DLL. Table 28-1 summarizes the import library names.

Memory Model	For an Application Program	For a Dynamic Link Library (DLL)	⊠
Coprocessor Emulation Math Routines			
Small	SLIBCEW.LIB	SDLLCEW.LIB	
Medium	MLIBCEW.LIB	MDLLCEW.LIB	
Compact	CLIBCEW.LIB	CDLLCEW.LIB	
Large	LLIBCEW.LIB	LDLLCEW.LIB	
Alternate Math Routines			
Small	SLIBCAW.LIB	SDLLCAW.LIB	
Medium	MLIBCAW.LIB	MDLLCAW.LIB	
Compact	CLIBCAW.LIB	CDLLCAW.LIB	
Large	LLIBCAW.LIB	LDLLCAW.LIB	

Table 28-1. Windows Import Library Names.

The compact and large memory models are not often used in Windows programs, as they require the program's code to be fixed in memory. If you are not familiar with the memory models or math calculation options, you may want to review your C compiler manual.

Problems with Writing DLLs

We briefly mentioned in the description of creating a DLL that the DLL uses the calling program's stack. The DLL does not have a stack of its own. This is different from a conventional Windows application, where the stack and the local heap share the same data segment. This difference can cause problems if you are not aware of its effects.

(If you have some assembly language background, you may find it simpler to think of the differences between a Windows application and DLL in terms of the CPU's registers. With an application, the stack segment and data segment are the same. That is DS == SS. With a DLL, the stack segment belongs to the calling program, and the data segment belongs to the DLL. DS != SS.)

Some C compiler library functions take shortcuts that make the assumption that the stack and the local heap are in the same segment. These functions will cause the DLL to attempt to write in a protected area of memory and cause the application to fail. You can also fall into the same trap if you use automatic variables inside the DLL for pointers or arrays. Short pointers for automatic variables will point to the stack of the calling program. Short pointers for static variables will point to the local heap. You can get all sorts of incorrect pointers if you are not careful.

There are several simple ways to avoid these problems.

1. Use FAR pointers. FAR pointers code both the segment and the offset for an address. It does not matter if the pointer points to another application's stack, or the DLL's memory heap. The pointers will be valid.

2. Use static variables. Static variables are always stored in the local heap, not in the stack. This rule avoids the DS != SS problem, but may waste memory if the variables are only needed for a short period of time.

3. Use third-party C library functions with caution. The C library that comes with the Microsoft 5.0 and later compilers is safe, but most non-Windows code is suspect.

Static variables have their own set of pitfalls inside DLLs. Remember that any number of applications can call the same DLL functions. Imagine a database application that uses one function call to move to the first record and stores this location in a static variable. While the first application is working on the database, a second application can call the same function and reset the static variable to a new value. The first application will not be alerted to this, but the static value will suddenly be invalid.

Avoiding these types of problems requires careful DLL design. Assume that all DLL functions are potentially reentrant. That is, the function can be called independently at different times by separate applications. If you need to store data specific to one application's use of the DLL, allocate separate memory for each calling application. The application's instance handle is a good choice for a parameter to pass to the DLL's functions so that calling applications can be differentiated.

Debugging DLLs

The CodeView for Windows debugger works perfectly for DLLs. When you initiate the debugger, you will need to enter the name of the application that calls the DLL and the name of the DLL(s). After that, the DLL will behave just like any other file that the debugger processes. You can set breakpoints in the DLL, examine registers, etc.

Use the same -Zi -Od compiler switches to disable optimization and add debugging information when creating a DLL. Here is an example NMAKE file, preparing the EXAMPDLL.C file for debugging.

```
# make file for exampdll library

ALL: exampdll.dll

CFLAGS=-c -D LINT_ARGS -ASw -Zip -Od -Gsw -W2
LFLAGS=/NOD /co /align:16

exampdll.obj:           exampdll.c
        $(CC) $(CFLAGS) exampdll.c

exampdll.dll:           exampdll.obj exampdll.def
        link $(LFLAGS)  exampdll libentry, exampdll.dll, NUL, libw sdllcew, exampdll
        rc exampdll.dll
```

Dynamic Link Library Function Summary

Table 28-2 summarizes the functions that support the DLLs in Windows applications. The next section contains the detailed function descriptions.

Function	Purpose	⊠
FreeLibrary	Removes a DLL library from memory.	
GetProcAddress	Retrieves the address of a function in a DLL.	
LoadLibrary	Loads a DLL into memory.	
LocalInit	Initializes the local memory heap during the startup of a DLL.	

Table 28-2. Dynamic Link Library Function Summary.

Dynamic Link Library Function Descriptions

This section contains the detailed description of the functions that support using DLLs in Windows applications.

FREELIBRARY   ■ Win 2.0   ■ Win 3.0   ■ Win 3.1

Purpose	Removes a DLL library from memory.
Syntax	void **FreeLibrary**(HANDLE *hLibModule*);
Description	LoadLibrary() and FreeLibrary() directly control when a DLL is loaded and removed from memory. DLL library modules are only loaded into memory once. If more than one call to Load-Library() is made, Windows keeps track of the number of loads as the reference count. Each call to FreeLibrary() reduces the reference count by one. When the reference count reaches zero, the DLL module is removed from memory.
Uses	Each call to LoadLibrary() should have a matching call to FreeLibrary() to make sure that the DLL is not left in memory after the user applications are terminated.
Returns	No returned value (void).
See Also	LoadLibrary(), GetProcAddress()
Parameters	
hLibModule	HANDLE: The handle of the DLL library module. This value is returned by LoadLibrary().
Example	This example demonstrates explicitly loading and freeing a dynamic link library. In this case, the InStr() function in the EXAMPDLL.DLL library (discussed at the beginning of the chapter) is used. The program using InStr() does **not** include the library and function name in the IMPORTS section of its .DEF definition file. Instead, LoadLibrary() is used to load the library when the WM_CREATE message is processed. Figure 28-2 shows the example program after the .DEF menu item was selected.

The library file EXAMPDLL.DLL is loaded by calling LoadLibrary(). If the returned handle has a value greater than 31, the library was successfully loaded. GetProcAddress() returns the address of the InStr() function within the library, so that the function can be called.

One trick here is the definition of the pointer to the InStr() function. The top line in the listing shows a typdef of the INSTR data type. INSTR is defined as a function that has the same type and parameters as the InStr() function in the library. This data type is used to create the *lpFuncInStr* static pointer for the InStr() function. This avoids getting compiler warning messages every time the function is called.

The InStr() function is actually used in the processing of the WM_PAINT messages. The function is called indirectly, using the

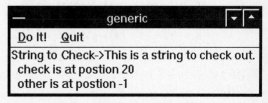

Figure 28-2. FreeLibrary() Example.

lpFuncInStr pointer. This is done twice, checking the occurrence of two strings within the *cBuf1[]* character array. The results are output to the window's client area with a combination of the TextOut() and wsprintf() functions.

When the program terminates, the library is removed from memory with a call to FreeLibrary(). If another running application is using EXAMPDLL.DLL at the same time, FreeLibrary() will just reduce the library's reference count by one. The library will not be removed from memory until all applications using it have terminated, or called FreeLibrary().

```
typedef int (FAR PASCAL *INSTR)(LPSTR, LPSTR) ;

long FAR PASCAL WndProc (HWND hWnd, unsigned iMessage, WORD wParam, LONG lParam)
{
        static char             cBuf1 [] = {"This is a string to check out."} ;
        HDC                     hDC ;
        char                    cBuf [128] ;
        static HANDLE           hLibrary ;
        static INSTR            lpFuncInStr ;

        switch (iMessage)                       /* process windows messages */
        {
                case WM_CREATE:
                        hLibrary = LoadLibrary ("EXAMPDLL.DLL") ;
                        if (hLibrary < 32)
                        {
                                MessageBox (hWnd, "Could not load dll",
                                        "LoadLibrary Error", MB_OK) ;
                                DestroyWindow (hWnd) ;
                        }
                        lpFuncInStr = GetProcAddress (hLibrary, "InStr") ;
                        break ;
                case WM_COMMAND:                /* process menu items */
                        switch (wParam)
                        {
                        case IDM_DOIT:          /* User hit the "Do it" menu item */
                                hDC = GetDC (hWnd) ;
                                TextOut (hDC, 0, 0, cBuf, wsprintf (cBuf,
                                        "String to Check->%s", (LPSTR) cBuf1)) ;
                                TextOut (hDC, 10, 20, cBuf, wsprintf (cBuf,
                                        "check is at position %d",
                                                (*lpFuncInStr) ((LPSTR) cBuf1,
                                                        (LPSTR) "check"))) ;
                                TextOut (hDC, 10, 40, cBuf, wsprintf (cBuf,
                                        "other is at position %d",
                                                (*lpFuncInStr) ((LPSTR) cBuf1,
                                                        (LPSTR) "other"))) ;
                                ReleaseDC (hWnd, hDC) ;
                                break ;
                        case IDM_QUIT:
                                DestroyWindow (hWnd) ;
                                break ;
                        }
                        break ;
                case WM_DESTROY:                /* stop application */
                        FreeLibrary (hLibrary) ;
                        PostQuitMessage (0) ;
                        break ;
                default:                        /* default windows message processing */
                        return DefWindowProc (hWnd, iMessage, wParam, lParam) ;
        }
        return (0L) ;
}
```

GETPROCADDRESS   ■ Win 2.0   ■ Win 3.0   ■ Win 3.1

Purpose   Retrieves the address of a function in a dynamic link library (DLL).

Syntax   FARPROC **GetProcAddress**(HANDLE *hModule*, LPSTR *lpProcName*);

Description	This function returns the address of a function in a DLL. It is equivalent to MakeProcInstance() which returns a function address for a Windows application module. The *lpProcName* function name must be listed in the EXPORTS section of the DLL's .DEF definition file. Normally, *lpProcName* points to a null-terminated character string containing the exported function name. Alternatively, if the function is given an ordinal value in the EXPORTS section,

```
EXPORTS  FunctionName @1
```

the function can be referenced by using the MAKEINTORESOURCE() macro

```
FARPROC fpFuncName ;

fpFuncName = GetProcAddress (hLibrary, MAKEINTORESOURCE (1)) ;
```

Uses	Used with LoadLibrary() to obtain a function address within a loaded DLL, so that the function can be called.
Returns	FARPROC, the function's address (entry point). Returns NULL on error. Note that if an incorrect ordinal value is used to reference the function, GetProcAddress() may still return a non-NULL value.
See Also	MakeProcInstance(), LoadModule()
Parameters	
hModule	HANDLE: The handle of the library module that contains the module. This value is returned by LoadLibrary(). Set *hModule* to NULL to reference the current module (the module that contains the GetProcAddress() function call).
lpProcName	LPSTR: A pointer to a null-terminated character string containing the function name. Alternatively, this can be the ordinal value of the function, as listed in the EXPORTS section of the DLL's .DEF definition file. The spelling of the function name must be identical to that used in the EXPORTS section of the DLL's .DEF definition file.
Example	See the example under the FreeLibrary() function description.

LOADLIBRARY   ■ Win 2.0   ■ Win 3.0   ■ Win 3.1

Purpose	Loads a dynamic link library (DLL) into memory.
Syntax	HANDLE **LoadLibrary**(LPSTR *lpLibFileName*);
Description	This function provides an alternative to simply adding the DLL function names to the IMPORTS section of the .DEF definition file for the program calling the library functions. LoadLibrary() loads the DLL into memory and returns a handle to the DLL. The GetProcAddress() function can then be used to obtain the address of functions within the library.
Uses	Ideal if a DLL will only be used for a small portion of the application. The DLL can be loaded, used, and then freed using FreeLibrary().
Returns	HANDLE, the handle of the library. This value will be over 31. Otherwise, an error has occurred. The type of error is determined by the returned value, which may be any of the codes listed in Table 28-3.

Value	Meaning	⊠
0	Out of memory.	
2	File not found.	
3	Path not found (invalid directory path specified in *lpLibFileName*).	
5	Attempted to load a task, not a DLL.	

Table 28-3. continued

Value	Meaning
6	Library requires separate data segments for each task.
10	Wrong Windows version.
11	Invalid .EXE file (DOS file, or error in program header).
12	OS/2 application.
13	DOS 4.0 application.
14	Unknown .EXE type.
15	Attempt to load an .EXE created for an earlier version of Windows. This error will not occur if Windows is run in real mode.
16	Attempt to load a second instance of an .EXE file containing multiple, writeable data segments.
17	EMS memory error on the second loading of a DLL.
18	Attempt to load a protected-mode-only application while Windows is running in real mode.

Table 28-3. LoadLibrary( ) Error Codes.

See Also FreeLibrary(), GetProcAddress()

Parameters

lpLibFileName LPSTR: A pointer to a null-terminated character string containing the library name. The name can contain the full DOS path name if necessary.

Example See the example under the FreeLibrary() function description.

LOCALINIT

■ Win 2.0   ■ Win 3.0   ■ Win 3.1

Purpose Initializes the local memory heap during the startup of a dynamic link library (DLL).

Syntax BOOL **LocalInit**(WORD *wSegment*, WORD *pStart*, WORD *pEnd*);

Description During the creation of a DLL, the LIBENTRY.OBJ module is linked into the program to add the startup routine for the DLL. LIBENTRY.OBJ is the standard startup routine for DLLs, provided with the Windows Software Development Kit. The source code (shown below) for this file is an assembly language function that does two things:

1. Initializes the local memory heap for the DLL by calling LocalInit().

2. Calls the LibMain() function in the C language source code file for the DLL.

LocalInit() leaves the local heap as a locked memory segment. Normally, this is unlocked in the LibMain() function by calling UnlockData(). The heap can end up moved if either LocalAlloc() or LocalReAlloc() is called. Use LockData() to explicitly lock the heap memory block.

Uses Normally, not called from a C program because the inclusion of LIBENTRY.OBJ in the creation of a DLL takes care of this function call.

Returns BOOL. TRUE if the heap was initialized, FALSE on error.

See Also LockData(), UnlockData()

Parameters

wSegment WORD: The segment address of the segment that will contain the local heap.

pStart PSTR: The address of the start of the local heap within the segment.

pEnd PSTR: The address of the end of the local heap within the segment.

Example   This is the source code for the LIBENTRY.OBJ file that is included during the link step in the creation of a DLL. LIBENTRY calls LocalInit() to create the application's local memory heap, and then calls the LibMain() function within the DLL to allow the DLL to do initialization.

```
PAGE,132
;;;;;;;;;;;;;;;;;;;;;;;;;;;;;;;;;;;;;;;;;;;;;;;;;;;;;;;;;;;;;;;;;;;;;;;;;;;;;;;;
;
;      LIBENTRY.ASM
;
;      Windows dynamic link library entry routine
;
;  This module generates a code segment called INIT_TEXT.
;  It initializes the local heap if one exists and then calls
;  the C routine LibMain() which should have the form:
;  BOOL FAR PASCAL LibMain(HANDLE hInstance,
;                   WORD   wDataSeg,
;                   WORD   cbHeap,
;                   LPSTR  lpszCmdLine);
;
;  The result of the call to LibMain is returned to Windows.
;  The C routine should return TRUE if it completes initialization
;  successfully, FALSE if some error occurs.
;
;;;;;;;;;;;;;;;;;;;;;;;;;;;;;;;;;;;;;;;;;;;;;;;;;;;;;;;;;;;;;;;;;;;;;;;;;;;;;;;;

include cmacros.inc

externFP <LibMain>            ; the C routine to be called

createSeg       INIT_TEXT, INIT_TEXT, BYTE, PUBLIC, CODE
sBegin          INIT_TEXT
assumes CS,INIT_TEXT

?PLM=0                  ; 'C'naming
externA  <_acrtused>            ; ensures that Win DLL startup code is linked

?PLM=1                  ; 'PASCAL' naming
externFP <LocalInit>            ; Windows heap init routine

cProc  LibEntry, <PUBLIC,FAR>  ; entry point into DLL

cBegin
      push    di          ; handle of the module instance
      push    ds          ; library data segment
      push    cx          ; heap size
      push    es          ; command line segment
      push    si          ; command line offset

      ; if we have some heap then initialize it
      jcxz    callc         ; jump if no heap specified

      ; call the Windows function LocalInit() to set up the heap
      ; LocalInit((LPSTR)start, WORD cbHeap);

      xor     ax,ax
      cCall   LocalInit <ds, ax, cx>
      or      ax,ax        ; did it do it ok ?
      jz      error        ; quit if it failed

      ; invoke the C routine to do any special initialization

callc:
      call    LibMain       ; invoke the 'C' routine (result in AX)
      jmp short exit        ; LibMain is responsible for stack clean up

error:
      pop     si                ; clean up stack on a LocalInit error
```

```
        pop    es
        pop    cx
        pop    ds
        pop    di

exit:

cEnd

sEnd    INIT_TEXT
```

Multiple Document Interface (MDI)

Multiple Document Interface (MDI) is a standard way to write applications in which one master window holds a number of child windows. The most popular Windows program that uses this interface is Microsoft Excel, although many other programs also use it. Excel will hold a number of spreadsheets, charts, and macro sheets within the bounds of the Excel main window.

Realizing that this type of program interface could be used for many types of programs, IBM included a description of the proper behavior of an MDI application in the book *Systems Application Architecture, Common User Access, Advanced Interface Design Guide* (IBM, 1989). This book describes how all windowing applications should behave, including complex applications like MDI programs. Microsoft added several functions to Windows 3.0 that make creating MDI applications simpler. These functions, and related MDI messages, are discussed in this chapter.

MDI Frame and Child Windows

Windows 3.0 includes a little-known application called SYSEDIT.EXE. By default, it is loaded in the SYSTEM subdirectory. SYSEDIT allows you to edit the initialization files CONFIG.SYS, AUTOEXEC.BAT, WIN.INI, and SYSTEM.INI. Figure 29-1 shows a typical session. In this case, the child windows are cascaded, so that at least a part of each window is visible and can be activated by a mouse click.

SYSEDIT is a classic MDI application. The outer window, called the "frame" window, contains all of the child windows. Each child is a separate editor application. The child windows can be minimized to an icon, shown within the bounds of the frame. Children can also be maximized to fill the entire frame, covering up all other child windows below them.

MDI applications end up being their own "little world." All the child windows stay within the bounds of the frame window, and all use the same menu. This provides a consistent feel to the elements of an MDI appli-

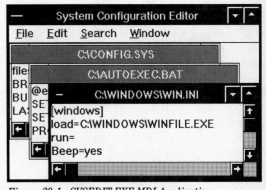

Figure 29-1. SYSEDIT.EXE MDI Application.

cation. The trade-off is that the child windows are limited to the size limits of the frame window. This contrasts with applications that use popup windows that can be placed anywhere on the screen. Popup windows are usually better for relatively independent windows, while MDI child windows are best suited to closely coupled applications.

One interesting aspect of the MDI child windows is that they do not have their own menus. All MDI windows share the same menu line on the outer frame. If there are different modes (such as graphics vs. spreadsheet child windows), the menu items may be different. To minimize confusion for the user, the menus should be as similar as possible.

The Structure of an MDI Application

You can create MDI applications without using special functions. Child windows will minimize to within the bounds of their parent's client areas, and they will display an icon when minimized. Child window extents are automatically limited by the parent window's borders. The advantage of using the new MDI functions and messages is that Windows developers have provided direct implementations of several useful features.

1. The MDI frame menu can automatically keep a list of the names of all active child windows. You can take advantage of this feature to allow the user to select any active child from the menu item, even if the child window is hidden under other children.

2. Special messages are provided which automate the arrangement of the child windows into cascades (as shown in Figure 29-1), or tiled windows to fill the frame window's client area with all of the child windows.

3. If some of the children have been minimized, a single message will arrange the icons at the bottom of the frame window's client area. The program manager (an MDI application) uses this feature to arrange icons at the bottom of the client area.

To implement these features, Windows 3.0 adds the MDICLIENT predefined window class. This class is similar to the definition of BUTTON and LISTBOX classes. You do not have to register predefined classes, they are already defined within Windows.

The MDICLIENT window class runs the client area of the frame window. When starting, the MDI application creates a frame window, then an MDICLIENT window as a child of the frame, and then all child windows as children of the MDICLIENT window. The structure is shown in Figure 29-2.

This arrangement allows the MDICLIENT window to take care of activities like cascading child windows or arranging icons. You will not draw on the MDICLIENT window. Its sole purpose is to control the behavior of the child windows. The child window client areas and the frame window menu are the areas of an MDI application that respond to user actions.

With the tree structure of windows in an MDI application, the most efficient way to communicate between the frame, MDICLIENT, and child windows is via Windows messages. To automate default keyboard actions,

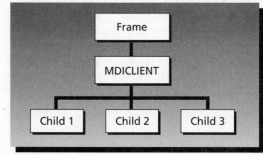

Figure 29-2. Window Structure in an MDI Application.

the TranslateMDISysAccel() function is added to the application's message loop. This function is similar to TranslateAccelerator(), but it is customized to convert keystrokes into equivalent MDI messages.

Windows provides two default message processing functions, DefFrameProc() and DefMDIChildProc(), to process messages for the frame and child windows. They take the place of DefWindowProc() that we have been using at the bottom of every WndProc() function to handle messages not processed by the application. Communication between the frame, client window, and child windows is handled via eleven specialized messages. Table 29-1 provides a summary of each of these messages. The full message description for each is included in Chapter 9, *Windows Messages*.

Message	Meaning	☒
WM_MDIACTIVATE	Used to activate child windows within a Multiple Document Interface (MDI) window. This is similar to a main window gaining the input focus.	
WM_MDICASCADE	Arranges all of the child windows within the MDI client window in "cascade" format.	
WM_MDICREATE	Creates an MDI child window.	
WM_MDIDESTROY	Destroys (removes) an MDI child window.	
WM_MDIGETACTIVE	Obtains the handle of the currently active MDI child window.	
WM_MDIICONARRANGE	Causes the MDI client window to arrange all minimized MDI child windows at the bottom of the client area.	
WM_MDIMAXIMIZE	Causes an MDI child window to be maximized.	
WM_MDINEXT	Activates the next MDI child window.	

WM_MDIRESTORE	Restores an MDI child window to its previous size.
WM_MDISETMENU	Links a new menu to the MDI frame window.
WM_MDITILE	Causes an MDI client window to arrange all of its children in tile format.

Table 29-1. MDI Message Summary.

The example program in this chapter demonstrates the use of these messages.

MDI Interface Bugs

Although the MDI functions work well, there are a few bugs that you may run into. One is that the maximized child windows cannot be closed by double-clicking the child window's close box (upper left corner). You can get around this problem by trapping WM_NCLBUTTONDBLCLK messages and checking if the active child window is maximized. The returned value from sending the WM_MDIGETACTIVE message will be 1 if the active child is maximized. If the child window is maximized and the mouse position is within the close box, you can close the child window directly.

Another bug is that MDI applications tend to not release all of the Windows system resource memory when the MDI application terminates. The loss will only show up if you start and terminate the MID application a number of times. This small loss occurs even if you explicitly remove all child windows and their class definitions before the MDI application exits. The system memory area is a limited resource, with a maximum of 64K available. You can check this value from the program manager Help/About Program Manager menu item. Be sure to explicitly delete any resources (such as unattached menus) before the MDI application exits to minimize the drain on system resources.

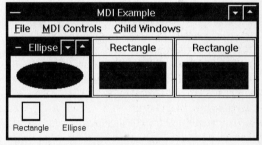

Figure 29-3. MDI Example Program.

MDI Example Program

This example creates a simple MDI application. There are only two child window types. One displays a rectangle, the other an ellipse. In both cases, the object changes size to fit within the child window borders. The MDI frame window supports two similar menus. If one of the children is active, the menu allows the color of the rectangle/ellipse to be changed. If the frame is active, the "MDI Controls" menu item replaces the color selection item. "MDI Controls" demonstrates standard MDI features for tiling and cascading opened child windows, selecting the next child window, and arranging iconized child windows.

Figure 29-3 shows the example with five child windows created. The top three were tiled when the frame window was smaller. After enlarging the frame window, two more children were created and then minimized to icons.

The resource file defines both menus, and the keyboard accelerators. The upper menu is used when the frame window is active. The lower menu applies when a child window is active.

⇨ GENERIC.RC Resource File for MDI

```
/* generic.rc */

#include <windows.h>
#include "generic.h"

generic          ICON    generic.ico

Accel    ACCELERATORS
{
        VK_F2, IDM_CASCADE, VIRTKEY
        VK_F3, IDM_ARRANGE, VIRTKEY
        VK_F4, IDM_TILE,VIRTKEY
        VK_F5, IDM_NEXT,VIRTKEY
}

FrameMenu        MENU
```

```
BEGIN
    POPUP "&File"
        BEGIN
                MENUITEM "New &Rectangle",              IDM_NEWRECT
                MENUITEM "New &Ellipse",                IDM_NEWELIP
                MENUITEM SEPARATOR
                MENUITEM "&Close Child",                IDM_CLOSE
                MENUITEM "&Exit Demo",                  IDM_QUIT
        END
        POPUP "&MDI Controls"
        BEGIN
                MENUITEM "Cascade Windows\tF2",         IDM_CASCADE
                MENUITEM "Arrange Icons\tF3",           IDM_ARRANGE
                MENUITEM "Tile Windows\tF4",            IDM_TILE
                MENUITEM "Next Window\tF5",             IDM_NEXT
        END
        POPUP    "&Child Windows"
        BEGIN
                MENUITEM "Child Window List",    IDM_MDILIST
        END
END

ChildMenu       MENU
BEGIN
        POPUP    "&File"
        BEGIN
                MENUITEM "&Top Menu",                   IDM_TOP
                MENUITEM SEPARATOR
                MENUITEM "&Close Child",                IDM_CLOSE
                MENUITEM "&Exit Demo",                  IDM_QUIT
        END
        POPUP    "&Color"
        BEGIN
                MENUITEM "&Blue"                        IDM_BLUE
                MENUITEM "&Green"                       IDM_GREEN
                MENUITEM "&Red"                         IDM_RED
        END
        POPUP    "&Child Windows"
        BEGIN
                MENUITEM "Child Window List",    IDM_MDILIST
        END
END
```

The header file defines all of the menu item ID numbers and provides function declarations and the standard two global variables used in the examples in this book.

⇨ GENERIC.H Header File

```
/* generic.h    */

#define IDM_MDILIST     1                       /* menu item id values */
#define IDM_QUIT        2
#define IDM_NEWRECT     3
#define IDM_NEWELIP     4
#define IDM_CASCADE     5
#define IDM_ARRANGE     6
#define IDM_CLOSE       7
#define IDM_TOP         8
#define IDM_TILE        9
#define IDM_RED         10
#define IDM_BLUE        11
#define IDM_GREEN       12
#define IDM_NEXT        13

#define FIRST_CHILD     100                     /* child window numbers above menu items */

        /* global variables */
int     ghInstance ;
char    gszAppName [] = "generic" ;
```

```
                /* function prototypes */
long FAR PASCAL FrameWndProc (HWND, unsigned, WORD, LONG) ;
long FAR PASCAL ElipProc (HWND hChild, WORD wMessage, WORD wParam,
      LONG lParam) ;
long FAR PASCAL RectProc (HWND hChild, WORD wMessage, WORD wParam,
      LONG lParam) ;
void SetFrameMenu (void) ;
void SetChildMenu (void) ;
BOOL FAR PASCAL EnumChildDestroy (HWND hWndChild, DWORD lParam) ;
```

The program definition file shows the message processing functions for the frame window and the two types of child windows in the EXPORTS section. In addition, an enumeration function EnumChildDestroy() is listed. This function is used to delete all of the child windows before the MDI application exits.

▷ **GENERIC.DEF Definition File**

```
NAME           GENERIC
DESCRIPTION    'generic mdi program'
EXETYPE        WINDOWS
STUB           'WINSTUB.EXE'
CODE           PRELOAD MOVEABLE DISCARDABLE
DATA           PRELOAD MOVEABLE MULTIPLE
HEAPSIZE       1024
STACKSIZE      8192
EXPORTS        FrameWndProc
               ElipProc
               RectProc
               EnumChildDestroy
```

The NMAKE file is shown with the debug options set on.

▷ **GENERIC.NMAKE File**

```
ALL: generic.exe

CFLAGS=-c -D LINT_ARGS -Zi -Od -Gsw -W2
LFLAGS=/NOD /co

generic.obj : generic.c generic.h
    $(CC) $(CFLAGS) generic.c

generic.res: generic.rc generic.ico
    rc -r generic.rc

generic.exe : generic.obj generic.def generic.res
    link $(LFLAGS) generic, , ,libw slibcew, generic
    rc generic.res
```

The source code creates the frame window inside WinMain(). Creating the frame window causes a WM_CREATE message to be sent to the frame window message processing function FrameWndProc(). The MDI client window is created while processing WM_CREATE.

The two new window classes, "rectangle" and "ellipse," are also registered in the WM_CREATE section. The *cbWndExtra* element of the window class definition is set to hold one global memory handle. This memory area will store the current color of the rectangle or ellipse for each window created. As the data is stored with each window, not with the class, changing the color of one MDI child does not change the color of any other similar child window. Note that the message loop in WinMain() has been modified to include both the TranslateMDISysAccel() and TranslateAccelerator() functions.

The FrameWndProc() function demonstrates several of the MDI messages for controlling tiling and cascading child windows. Note that WM_COMMAND messages not processed by FrameWndProc() are sent on to any active child.

The window functions for the two types of child windows are very similar. Both process WM_COMMAND messages, and change the rectangle or ellipse color if a color menu item has been selected. Note that the memory area for storing the color of the rectangle/ellipse is allocated when the child window processes a WM_CREATE message. The handle is stored in the *cbWndExtra* element of the window's private data. The memory value is changed when the

window color value is altered. The memory value is retrieved before painting the rectangle or ellipse in the WM_PAINT
section of these child window functions.

⇨ GENERIC.C Source Code

```
/* generic.c   generic windows application */
/**/

#include <windows.h>                    /* window's header file - always included */
#include "generic.h"                    /* the application's header file */

HWND    ghWndFrame, ghWndClient ;                   /* globals */

int PASCAL WinMain (HANDLE hInstance, HANDLE hPrevInstance, LPSTR lpszCmdLine, int nCmdShow)
{
        HANDLE          hAccel ;
        MSG                     msg ;
        WNDCLASS        wndclass ;
        HMENU           hMenu ;

        ghInstance = hInstance ;        /* store instance handle as global var. */
        hMenu = LoadMenu (hInstance, "FrameMenu") ;

        if (!hPrevInstance)             /* create frame window class */
        {
                wndclass.style          = CS_HREDRAW | CS_VREDRAW ;
                wndclass.lpfnWndProc    = FrameWndProc ;
                wndclass.cbClsExtra     = 0 ;
                wndclass.cbWndExtra     = 0 ;
                wndclass.hInstance      = hInstance ;
                wndclass.hIcon          = LoadIcon (hInstance, gszAppName) ;
                wndclass.hCursor        = LoadCursor (NULL, IDC_ARROW) ;
                wndclass.hbrBackground  = GetStockObject (WHITE_BRUSH) ;
                        /* aternative:, set background to COLOR_APPWORKSPACE + 1 */
                wndclass.lpszMenuName   = NULL ;
                wndclass.lpszClassName  = "MDIFrame" ;
                                        /* register frame window class */
                if (!RegisterClass (&wndclass))
                        return FALSE ;
        }

        ghWndFrame = CreateWindow (             /* create the frame window */
                "MDIFrame",                     /* class name */
                "MDI Example",                  /* window name */
                WS_OVERLAPPEDWINDOW | WS_CLIPCHILDREN,   /* window style */
                CW_USEDEFAULT,                  /* x position on screen */
                CW_USEDEFAULT,                  /* y position on screen */
                CW_USEDEFAULT,                  /* width of window */
                CW_USEDEFAULT,                  /* height of window */
                NULL,                           /* parent window handle */
                LoadMenu (ghInstance, "FrameMenu"),     /* menu handle */
                hInstance,                      /* instance handle */
                NULL) ;                         /* lpstr (null = not used) */

        ShowWindow (ghWndFrame, nCmdShow) ;
        DrawMenuBar (ghWndFrame) ;
        UpdateWindow (ghWndFrame) ;
        hAccel = LoadAccelerators (hInstance, "Accel") ;


        while (GetMessage (&msg, NULL, 0, 0))                   /* the message loop */
        {
                if (!TranslateMDISysAccel (ghWndClient, &msg) &&
                        !TranslateAccelerator (ghWndFrame, hAccel, &msg))
                {
                        TranslateMessage (&msg) ;
                        DispatchMessage (&msg) ;
```

```
                }
        }
        return msg.wParam ;
}


long FAR PASCAL FrameWndProc (HWND hWnd, unsigned iMessage, WORD wParam, LONG lParam)
{
        HWND                            hChild ;
        CLIENTCREATESTRUCT              ccs ;
        MDICREATESTRUCT                 mcs ;
        WNDCLASS                        wndclass ;
        HMENU                           hMenu ;
        FARPROC                         lpEnumFunc ;

        switch (iMessage)
        {
                case WM_CREATE:             /* create MDI client window here */
                        ccs.idFirstChild = FIRST_CHILD ;
                        hMenu = LoadMenu (ghInstance, "FrameMenu") ;
                        ccs.hWindowMenu = GetSubMenu (hMenu, 0) ;
                        ghWndClient = CreateWindow ("MDICLIENT", NULL,
                                WS_CHILD | WS_CLIPCHILDREN | WS_VISIBLE,
                                0, 0, 0, 0, hWnd, NULL, ghInstance, (LPSTR) &ccs) ;
                        SendMessage (hWnd, WM_MDISETMENU, 0,
                                MAKELONG (ccs.hWindowMenu, hMenu)) ;

                        wndclass.style            = CS_HREDRAW | CS_VREDRAW ;
                        wndclass.lpfnWndProc      = ElipProc ;
                        wndclass.cbClsExtra       = 0 ;
                        wndclass.cbWndExtra       = sizeof (GLOBALHANDLE) ;
                        wndclass.hInstance        = ghInstance ;
                        wndclass.hIcon            = LoadIcon (NULL, IDI_APPLICATION) ;
                        wndclass.hCursor          = LoadCursor (NULL, IDC_CROSS) ;
                        wndclass.hbrBackground    = GetStockObject (WHITE_BRUSH) ;
                        wndclass.lpszMenuName     = NULL ;
                        wndclass.lpszClassName    = "Ellipse" ;
                        RegisterClass (&wndclass) ; /* reg ellipse wind class */

                        wndclass.lpfnWndProc      = RectProc ;
                        wndclass.lpszClassName    = "Rectangle" ;
                        RegisterClass (&wndclass) ; /* reg rectangle wind class */

                        return (0) ;
                case WM_COMMAND:           /* process menu items */
                        switch (wParam)
                        {
                        case IDM_NEWRECT:          /* make a new rectangle child window */
                                mcs.szClass      = "Rectangle" ;
                                mcs.szTitle      = "Rectangle" ;
                                mcs.hOwner       = ghInstance ;
                                mcs.x            = CW_USEDEFAULT ;
                                mcs.y            = CW_USEDEFAULT ;
                                mcs.cx           = CW_USEDEFAULT ;
                                mcs.cy           = CW_USEDEFAULT ;
                                mcs.style        = 0 ;
                                mcs.lParam       = NULL ;
                                SendMessage (ghWndClient, WM_MDICREATE, 0,
                                        (LONG) (LPMDICREATESTRUCT) &mcs) ;
                                break ;
                        case IDM_NEWELIP:          /* make a new ellipse child window */
                                mcs.szClass      = "Ellipse" ;
                                mcs.szTitle      = "Ellipse" ;
                                mcs.hOwner       = ghInstance ;
                                mcs.x            = CW_USEDEFAULT ;
                                mcs.y            = CW_USEDEFAULT ;
                                mcs.cx           = CW_USEDEFAULT ;
                                mcs.cy           = CW_USEDEFAULT ;
                                mcs.style        = 0 ;
```

```
                                        mcs.lParam        = NULL ;
                                        SendMessage (ghWndClient, WM_MDICREATE, 0,
                                               (LONG) (LPMDICREATESTRUCT) &mcs) ;
                                        break ;
                              case IDM_CLOSE:
                                        hChild = LOWORD (SendMessage (ghWndClient,
                                               WM_MDIGETACTIVE, 0, OL)) ;
                                        SendMessage (ghWndClient, WM_MDIDESTROY, hChild, OL) ;
                                        break ;
                              case IDM_ARRANGE:
                                        SendMessage (ghWndClient, WM_MDIICONARRANGE, 0, OL) ;
                                        break ;
                              case IDM_CASCADE:
                                        SendMessage (ghWndClient, WM_MDICASCADE, 0, OL) ;
                                        break ;
                              case IDM_TILE:
                                        SendMessage (ghWndClient, WM_MDITILE, 0, OL) ;
                                        break ;
                              case IDM_NEXT:
                                        SendMessage (ghWndClient, WM_MDINEXT, 0, OL) ;
                                        break ;
                              case IDM_QUIT:   /* destroy children, frame */
                                        lpEnumFunc = MakeProcInstance (EnumChildDestroy,
                                               ghInstance) ;
                                        EnumChildWindows (ghWndClient, lpEnumFunc, OL) ;
                                        FreeProcInstance (lpEnumFunc) ;
                                        DestroyWindow (hWnd) ;
                                        break ;
                              default:          /* pass command to active child */
                                        hChild = LOWORD (SendMessage (ghWndClient,
                                               WM_MDIGETACTIVE, 0, OL)) ;
                                        if (IsWindow (hChild))
                                               SendMessage (hChild, WM_COMMAND, wParam,
                                                      lParam) ;
                                        break ;
                              }
                              break ;
                    case WM_DESTROY:/* free menu data before exit */
                              hMenu = FindResource (ghInstance, "FrameMenu", RT_MENU) ;
                              hMenu = LoadResource (ghInstance, hMenu) ;
                              if (hMenu)
                                        while (FreeResource (hMenu))
                                               ;
                              hMenu = FindResource (ghInstance, "ChildMenu", RT_MENU) ;
                              hMenu = LoadResource (ghInstance, hMenu) ;
                              if (hMenu)
                                        while (FreeResource (hMenu))
                                               ;
                              PostQuitMessage (0) ;
                              break ;
                    default:                          /* default windows message processing */
                              return DefFrameProc (hWnd, ghWndClient, iMessage, wParam, lParam) ;
          }
          return (OL) ;
}

/* child window message processing procedure for ellipse windows */

long FAR PASCAL ElipProc (HWND hChild, WORD wMessage, WORD wParam, LONG lParam)
{
          RECT                    rClient ;
          PAINTSTRUCT             ps ;
          GLOBALHANDLE            hMem ;
          LPSTR                   lpMem ;
          HBRUSH                  hBrush ;

          switch (wMessage)
          {
```

```
        case WM_CREATE: /* put default black color in window data */
                hMem = GlobalAlloc (GHND, sizeof (DWORD)) ;
                SetWindowWord (hChild, O, hMem) ;              /*save handle with window */
                break ; ;
        case WM_MDIACTIVATE:
                if (wParam)
                        SetChildMenu () ;                     /* gained input focus */
                else
                        SetFrameMenu () ;                     /* lost input focus */
                DrawMenuBar (ghWndFrame) ;
                return (0) ;
        case WM_PAINT:
                GetClientRect (hChild, &rClient) ;
                hMem = GetWindowWord (hChild, 0) ;            /* color stored here */
                lpMem = GlobalLock (hMem) ;                   /* get handle to color */
                BeginPaint (hChild, &ps) ;
                hBrush = CreateSolidBrush (RGB (*(lpMem + 1), *(lpMem + 2),
                        *(lpMem + 3))) ;
                GlobalUnlock (hMem) ;
                SelectObject (ps.hdc, hBrush) ;
                Ellipse (ps.hdc, 10, 10, rClient.right - 10,
                        rClient .bottom - 10) ;
                DeleteObject (hBrush) ;
                EndPaint (hChild, &ps) ;
                return (0) ;
        case WM_COMMAND:
                switch (wParam)
                {
                        case IDM_RED:    /* change the color used to paint ellipse */
                        case IDM_BLUE:   /* the color value is stored in global */
                        case IDM_GREEN:  /* memory. Mem handle stored with wind */
                                hMem = GetWindowWord (hChild, 0) ;
                                lpMem = GlobalLock (hMem) ;
                                *(lpMem + 1) = (wParam == IDM_RED ? 255 : 0) ;
                                *(lpMem + 2) = (wParam == IDM_GREEN ? 255 : 0) ;
                                *(lpMem + 3) = (wParam == IDM_BLUE ? 255 : 0) ;
                                GlobalUnlock (hMem) ;
                                InvalidateRect (hChild, NULL, TRUE) ;
                        case IDM_TOP:
                                SetFrameMenu () ;
                                break ;
                }
                return (0) ;
        case WM_DESTROY:
                hMem = GetWindowWord (hChild, 0) ;
                GlobalFree (hMem) ;
                return (0) ;
        }
        return DefMDIChildProc (hChild, wMessage, wParam, lParam) ;
}


/* child window message processing procedure for rectange windows */

long FAR PASCAL RectProc (HWND hChild, WORD wMessage, WORD wParam, LONG lParam)
{
        RECT                    rClient ;
        PAINTSTRUCT             ps ;
        GLOBALHANDLE            hMem ;
        LPSTR                   lpMem ;
        HBRUSH                  hBrush ;

        switch (wMessage)
        {
                case WM_CREATE: /* put default black color in window data */
                        hMem = GlobalAlloc (GHND, sizeof (DWORD)) ;
                        SetWindowWord (hChild, O, hMem) ;              /* save handle with window */
                        break ;
                case WM_MDIACTIVATE:
```

```
                    if (wParam)
                            SetChildMenu () ;                       /* gained input focus */
                    else
                            SetFrameMenu () ;                       /* lost input focus */
                    DrawMenuBar (ghWndFrame) ;
                    return (0) ;
            case WM_PAINT:
                    GetClientRect (hChild, &rClient) ;
                    hMem = GetWindowWord (hChild, 0) ;              /* color stored here */
                    lpMem = GlobalLock (hMem) ;                     /* get handle to color */
                    BeginPaint (hChild, &ps) ;
                    hBrush = CreateSolidBrush (RGB (*(lpMem + 1), *(lpMem + 2),
                            *(lpMem + 3))) ;
                    GlobalUnlock (hMem) ;
                    SelectObject (ps.hdc, hBrush) ;
                    Rectangle (ps.hdc, 10, 10, rClient.right - 10,
                            rClient .bottom - 10) ;
                    DeleteObject (hBrush) ;
                    EndPaint (hChild, &ps) ;
                    return (0) ;
            case WM_COMMAND:
                    switch (wParam)
                    {
                            case IDM_RED:    /* change the color used to paint rect. */
                            case IDM_BLUE:   /* the color value is stored in global */
                            case IDM_GREEN: /* memory. Mem handle stored with wind */
                                    hMem = GetWindowWord (hChild, 0) ;
                                    lpMem = GlobalLock (hMem) ;
                                    *(lpMem + 1) = (wParam == IDM_RED ? 255 : 0) ;
                                    *(lpMem + 2) = (wParam == IDM_GREEN ? 255 : 0) ;
                                    *(lpMem + 3) = (wParam == IDM_BLUE ? 255 : 0) ;
                                    GlobalUnlock (hMem) ;
                                    InvalidateRect (hChild, NULL, TRUE) ;
                            case IDM_TOP:
                                    SetFrameMenu () ;
                                    break ;
                    }
                    return (0) ;
            case WM_DESTROY:
                    hMem = GetWindowWord (hChild, 0) ;
                    GlobalFree (hMem) ;
                    return (0) ;
    }
    return DefMDIChildProc (hChild, wMessage, wParam, lParam) ;
}


void SetFrameMenu (void) /* put the frame menu at top */
{
    static  HMENU     hMenu = NULL ;
    HMENU             hSubMenu ;
    int               nMenuItems ;

    if (!hMenu)
            hMenu = LoadMenu (ghInstance, "FrameMenu") ;
    nMenuItems = GetMenuItemCount (hMenu) ;
    hSubMenu = GetSubMenu (hMenu, nMenuItems - 1) ;
    SendMessage (ghWndClient, WM_MDISETMENU, 0,
            MAKELONG (hMenu, hSubMenu)) ;
    DrawMenuBar (ghWndFrame) ;
}

void SetChildMenu (void) /* put the child window menu at top */
{
    static  HMENU     hMenu = NULL ;
    HMENU             hSubMenu ;
    int               nMenuItems ;

    if (!hMenu)
```

```
        hMenu = LoadMenu (ghInstance, "ChildMenu") ;
    nMenuItems = GetMenuItemCount (hMenu) ;
    hSubMenu = GetSubMenu (hMenu, nMenuItems - 1) ;
    SendMessage (ghWndClient, WM_MDISETMENU, 0,
            MAKELONG (hMenu, hSubMenu)) ;
    DrawMenuBar (ghWndFrame) ;
}

BOOL FAR PASCAL EnumChildDestroy (HWND hWndChild, DWORD lParam)
{
    SendMessage (ghWndClient, WM_MDIDESTROY, hWndChild, 0L) ;
    return (TRUE) ;
}
```

Because the example program uses two menus, only one of the menus is attached to the frame window when the program exits. This means that the menu data for the unattached menu will be left in memory after the application terminates unless it is explicitly removed. The logic in the processing of the WM_DESTROY message in Frame-WndProc() handles removal of the menu resource data. FreeResource() must be called as many times as Load-Resource() was called to actually remove the resource from memory. The EnumChildDestroy() function at the bottom of the listing demonstrates a simple technique for sending a message to all of the child windows. In this case, it is the WM_MDIDESTROY message. The same technique can be used to send any message, including user messages.

This example shows two separate functions for processing rectangular and elliptical child windows. This approach was used to demonstrate passing control to separate message processing functions, the most general case. These two functions are so similar that they could easily be combined into one function. The type of window (rectangle or ellipse) would be stored with the color data in the memory block associated with each child window. When the child window received a WM_PAINT message, it would determine what shape to paint along with the color data.

MDI Function Summary

Table 29-2 summarizes the MDI support functions.

Function	Purpose
DefFrameProc	Provides default message processing for the window function of the frame window in an MDI application.
DefMDIChildProc	Provides default message processing for the window function of a child window in an MDI application.
TranslateMDISysAccel	Provides default translation of Windows keyboard messages for MDI applications.

Table 29-2. MDI Function Summary.

MDI Function Descriptions

This section contains the detailed descriptions of the MDI support functions.

DEFFRAMEPROC ☐ Win 2.0 ■ Win 3.0 ■ Win 3.1

Purpose   Provides default message processing for the window function of the frame window in an MDI (multiple document interface) application.

Syntax   LONG **DefFrameProc**(HWND *hWnd*, HWND *hWndMDIClient*, WORD *wMsg*, WORD *wParam*, LONG *lParam*);

Description In an MDI application, the frame window is primarily responsible for maintaining the menu. All child windows share the same menu line. The default MDI behavior will add child window names, preceded by a number, to the menu line as the child windows are activated. DefFrameProc() is the equivalent of DefWindowProc(), except that DefFrameProc() provides specialized functions for an MDI frame window as the default. All messages that are not processed by the frame window's message processing logic should be passed to DefFrameProc().

Uses	Used at the bottom of the frame window message processing (window) function to handle messages not explicitly processed by the program's logic.
Returns	LONG. This value is returned to Windows as the returned value from the frame window's message processing (window) function.
See Also	DefMDIChildProc(), CreateWindow()
Parameters	
hWnd	HWND: The MDI frame window handle.
hWndMDIClient	HWND: The MDI client window handle. The client window is normally created during processing of the WM_CREATE message for the frame window. Client windows are created from the class MDICLIENT.
wMsg	WORD: The message ID value (such as WM_MOVE). This value is initially sent from Windows to the frame window function.
wParam	WORD: The 16-bit value passed with the message. This value is initially sent from Windows to the frame window function.
lParam	DWORD: The 32-bit value passed with the message. This value is initially sent from Windows to the frame window function.
Related Messages	All messages that the MDI frame window message processing (window) function receives, but does not act on, are sent to DefFrameProc(). In addition, the following messages should be passed to DefFrameProc() regardless of whether action is taken in the MDI frame window's message processing function: WM_COMMAND, WM_MENUCHAR, WM_NEXTMENU, WM_SET FOCUS, and WM_SIZE.
Example	The MDI example earlier in this chapter uses DefFrameProc() at the bottom of the MDI frame message processing function, FrameWndProc().

DefMDIChildProc □ Win 2.0 ■ Win 3.0 ■ Win 3.1

Purpose	Provides default message processing for the window function of a child window in an MDI (multiple document interface) application.
Syntax	LONG **DefMDIChildProc**(HWND *hWnd*, WORD *wMsg*, WORD *wParam*, LONG *lParam*);
Description	This function takes the place of DefWindowProc() for a child window message function in an MDI window. The default processing notifies the MDI client window when a child is created or closed, and also does the normal chores for sizing the child window, iconizing, etc.
Uses	Used within the child window function of an MDI application.
Returns	LONG. This value is returned to Windows as the returned value from the child message processing (window) function.
See Also	DefFrameProc()
Parameters	
hWnd	HWND: The MDI child window handle.
wMsg	WORD: The message ID value (such as WM_MOVE). This value is initially sent from Windows to the child window function.
wParam	WORD: The 16-bit value passed with the message. This value is initially sent from Windows to the child window function.
lParam	DWORD: The 32-bit value passed with the message. This value is initially sent from Windows to the child window function.

Related Messages The following messages are actively processed by this function: WM_CHILDACTIVATE, WM_GET-MINMAXINFO, WM_MENUCHAR, WM_MOVE,WM_NEXTMENU, WM_SETFOCUS, WM_SIZE, and WM_SYSCOMMAND.

Example Both the RectProc() and ElipProc() window functions in the MDI example earlier in this chapter use this function.

TRANSLATEMDISYSACCEL
☐ Win 2.0 ■ Win 3.0 ■ Win 3.1

Purpose Provides default translation of Windows keyboard messages for MDI applications.

Syntax BOOL **TranslateMDISysAccel**(HWND *hWndClient*, LPMSG *lpMsg*);

Description This function is used within the MDI application's message loop to process system menu input for the MDI frame window. If the message is translated, the function returns 1. In this case, the message should not be passed on to TranslateMessage() and DispatchMessage(), as the translated equivalent to the original message will be placed on the application's message queue.

Uses Used within an MDI application's message loop.

Returns BOOL. TRUE if the message was processed, FALSE if not.

Parameters

hWndClient HWND: The MDI client window handle. Note that this is the client window, not the frame window handle.

lpMsg LPMSG: A pointer to an MSG data structure containing the Windows message. The message is assumed to have been retrieved from Windows with either GetMessage() or PeekMessage().

Related Messages All messages are passed through this function.

Example The general structure for an MDI message loop is as follows:

```
while (GetMessage (&msg, NULL, 0, 0))              /* the message loop */
{
        if (!TranslateMDISysAccel (hWndClient, &msg) &&
                !TranslateAccelerator (hWndFrame, hAccel, &msg))
        {
                TranslateMessage (&msg) ;
                DispatchMessage (&msg) ;
        }
}
```

This example shows both the MDI message translation and accelerator table translations being checked in the message loop. If the MDI application does not use keyboard accelerators, the TranslateAccelerator() function can be omitted.

30

Dynamic Data Exchange (DDE)

Dynamic Data Exchange is a message protocol that allows Windows applications to exchange data. Using DDE is similar to using the clipboard. With the clipboard, the user is normally in charge of controlling the cut and paste operations. With DDE, the application can control the flow of data in the background. DDE is ideal for problems such as displaying stock quotes as they change, or providing links between different types of applications. Microsoft Word for Windows and Excel support DDE links for updating spreadsheet values shown within a word processing document.

DDE is implemented with nine Windows messages. Learning to use DDE in your applications is simply a matter of learning how these nine messages work. You can register your own unique messages for data transmittal to exchange data between two or more programs you are working on. By using the DDE messages defined in the DDE.H header file, your application will be able to exchange data with many other programs that use the DDE standard.

Windows 3.1 includes an alternative method of implementing DDE via a series of about 25 functions that reside in a DLL library called DDEML.LIB. These functions provide a different programmer's interface to DDE, but work on the same principles described in this chapter. DDE data exchange implemented with the DDEML functions is compatible with the conventional DDE implemented with Windows messages. The DDEML functions are not covered in this book.

How DDE Data Is Exchanged

Because DDE is a message-based system, the data must be transmitted with messages. Windows messages allow only two parameter values, a WORD (*wParam*) and a DWORD (*lParam*). That is not enough room to transmit much information. To get around this limit, the *lParam* value is used to hold an indirect address to a block of memory. For short strings used to pass the names of data elements, *lParam* holds one or two global atom values. For larger amounts of data, *lParam* holds the handle of a global memory block allocated using GlobalAlloc() with the GMEM_DDESHARE option.

Global atoms and DDESHARE global memory blocks are used because they are the only two types of data that can be safely used by two separate applications. Trying to read a normal memory block allocated by another application risks the dreaded "Sharing Violation" error message, and/or termination of the program. Future releases of Windows are expected to have even more stringent safeguards against the use of another application's data.

Keep in mind that there are two other ways to exchange data between applications. One is to use the clipboard. The other is to read data maintained by a dynamic link library (DLL).

The DDE protocol requires nine messages because there are several different situations that an application may need to address. One is that the receiving application may not be running. Applications that are not running will not get DDE data. Another problem is that the receiving application may be running, but not ready to receive the data. Also, the receiving application may be able to read several different formats or types of DDE data, and it will need to decide which format to read, and which to reject.

In a DDE conversation, the client is the application that starts the conversation. The server is the application that responds to the client. In most cases, the server will provide data to the client, but this does not have to be the case, as we will see in the first example in this chapter. To keep things simple, we will look at cases where only one DDE conversation is going on at one time. An application can engage in several DDE conversations at once. This means that an application can be both a client and a server at the same time.

Applications, Topics, and Item Identifiers

Because a server may be able to send more than one type of data, DDE messages label data with character strings stored as global atoms. Atoms are used to transmit the name of the application and the name of the data item(s) requested.

Data items are labeled with three levels of identifiers. When the DDE conversation is started, both the client and server must support the same "application" and "topic." "Application" is normally the name of the server program, while "topic" refers to one of a number of DDE subjects that the program may exchange (such as plots, text, bitmaps, etc.). Limiting the conversation to a specific application and topic is important. Otherwise, all running applications that support DDE would respond to all messages. As soon as the DDE conversation is established, the specific data element requested is specified with the "item" name.

Cold DDE Link

The simplest DDE conversation, the cold link, is ideal for sending a packet of information on an infrequent basis. DDE conversations start when the client sends a WM_DDE_INITIATE message. This is the only DDE message that is sent with SendMessage(). The rest are posted with PostMessage(), placing the messages on the message queue of the receiving application. SendMessage() has the handy ability to transmit the same message to every running application on the system.

The WM_DDE_INITIATE message uses the *lParam* parameter to encode the desired application name and topic name as global atoms. An application having the ability to respond to this type of data sends back a WM_DDE_ACK acknowledgement message, as shown in Table 30-1. Other applications running on the system ignore the WM_DDE_INITIATE message.

	Message	From	To	Data Transmitted	⊠
1	WM_DDE_INITIATE	Client	Server	Application name, topic name (as atoms).	
2	WM_DDE_ACK	Server	Client	Echoes application and topic names if server can supply data. Also provides window handle of server.	

Table 30-1. Initiation of a DDE Conversation.

If the client gets a WM_DDE_ACK back, the DDE conversation has started. Now the client can ask for some data. If WM_DDE_ACK is not returned, the server application is probably not running. The client can attempt to start the server by calling WinExec(), or simply give up and display a warning message.

Assuming a link was established, the client requests the data be transmitted by sending a WM_DDE_REQUEST message to the server. A handle to the memory block containing the data is sent back with a WM_DDE_DATA message. The client confirms the receipt of the data with a WM_DDE_ACK message, as shown in Table 30-2.

	Message	From	To	Data Transmitted	⊠
3	WM_DDE_REQUEST	Client	Server	The name of the data item requested (as an atom), and the clipboard format to use for the data.	
4	WM_DDE_DATA	Server	Client	Echoes the data item name (as an atom), and passes a handle to a global memory block containing the data.	
5	WM_DDE_ACK	Client	Server	Echoes the data item name (as an atom), and lets server know if the data was accepted.	

Table 30-2. A DDE Cold Link Data Transmission.

The actual data is passed within a global memory block allocated with GlobalAlloc(). The GMEM_DDESHARE option is used when allocating the memory block to allow the data to be passed without causing a memory error ("sharing violation").

If the server cannot respond to the WM_DDE_REQUEST, the server transmits a WM_DDE_DATA message encoding a zero in one of the bit fields of the data (the *fAck* bit field). This is called a "negative" acknowledgment. If the server can send the requested data item, the bit field is set to one. This is called a "positive" acknowledgment.

The data item name is passed as a global atom with every message. This allows an application involved in several DDE conversations to keep track of which request is being processed. Additional WM_DDE_REQUEST messages can be sent for each data item that the client would like to receive. When all of the data has been collected, the DDE conversation is terminated, as shown in Table 30-3.

	Message	From	To	Data Transmitted	
6	WM_DDE_TERMINATE	Client	Server	The handle of the client window.	
7	WM_DDE_TERMINATE	Server	Client	The handle of the server window.	

Table 30-3. Termination of a DDE Conversation.

Hot DDE Link

The cold link is fine for sending a packet of data at one time, but it is inefficient if the client would like to receive data whenever the data changes. Examples of data that change periodically are links between communications programs and spreadsheets. The classic example is updating an Excel spreadsheet based on the latest stock quotes received over a modem. The hot link is initiated the same way as a cold link. When the conversation is established, the client sends the server a WM_DDE_ADVISE message. This lets the server know that the client would like the data sent every time the data changes. The transmittal of the WM_DDE_DATA messages then goes on as needed, until either the server or the client terminates the conversation.

Table 30-4 shows the message sequence.

	Message	From	To	Data Transmitted	
1	WM_DDE_INITIATE	Client	Server	Application name, topic name (as atoms).	
2	WM_DDE_ACK	Server	Client	Echoes application and topic names if server can supply data. Also provides window handle of server.	
3	WM_DDE_ADVISE	Client	Server	The name of the data item requested (as an atom), the clipboard format to use for the data, and the link type (hot).	
4	WM_DDE_DATA	Server	Client	Echoes the data item name (as an atom), and passes a handle to a global memory block containing the data.	
5	WM_DDE_ACK (optional, depends on the *fAckReq* flag sent with WM_DDE_ADVISE).	Client	Server	Echoes the data item name (as an atom), and lets server know if the data was accepted.	
	(Steps 4-5 continue as the server's data changes.)				
6	WM_DDE_TERMINATE	Client	Server	The handle of the client window.	
7	WM_DDE_TERMINATE	Server	Client	The handle of the server window.	

Table 30-4. Sequence of a Hot DDE Conversation.

The client can temporarily stop updates from the server by posting a WM_DDE_UNADVISE message. This message does not terminate the conversation, but lets the server know that updates are not needed until a WM_DDE_ADVISE message is posted.

Warm DDE Link

The hot DDE link is ideal for intermittent transmittal of small amounts of data. For larger amounts of data, or frequent transmissions, the client may not be able to deal with the data all of the time. The warm DDE link provides a compromise. The server notifies the client with a WM_DDE_DATA message when the data changes, but sends a NULL in place of the handle to the memory block containing the data. If the client is busy, it can ignore the message. If the client has time to read the data, it sends a WM_DDE_REQUEST message back to the server. The server then transmits another WM_DDE_DATA message, this time including the handle to the data.

Table 30-5 shows the warm link message sequence.

	Message	From	To	Data Transmitted	☒
1	WM_DDE_INITIATE	Client	Server	Application name, topic name (as atoms).	
2	WM_DDE_ACK	Server	Client	Echoes application and topic names if server can supply data. Also provides window handle of server.	
3	WM_DDE_ADVISE	Client	Server	The name of the data item requested (as an atom), the clipboard format to use for the data and the link type (warm).	
4	WM_DDE_DATA	Server	Client	Echoes the data item name (as an atom), and passes a NULL in place of the handle to a global memory block containing the data.	
5	WM_DDE_ACK (optional, depends on the *fAckReq* flag sent with WM_DDE_ADVISE). (Steps 4-5 continue as the server's data changes. No data is transmitted until a WM_DDE_REQUEST is posted.)	Client	Server	Echoes the data item name (as an atom), and lets server know if the data was accepted.	
6	WM_DDE_REQUEST	Client	Server	The name of the data item requested (as an atom), and the clipboard format to use for the data.	
7	WM_DDE_DATA	Server	Client	Echoes the data item name (as an atom), and passes a handle to a global memory block containing the data.	
8	WM_DDE_ACK (optional, depends on the *fAckReq* flag sent with WM_DDE_DATA). (The conversation continues with steps 4-5).	Client	Server	Echoes the data item name (as an atom), and lets server know if the data was accepted.	
9	WM_DDE_TERMINATE	Client	Server	The handle of the client window.	
10	WM_DDE_TERMINATE	Server	Client	The handle of the server window.	

Table 30-5. Sequence of a Warm DDE Conversation.

In general, an application supporting DDE should support old, warm, and hot links. The data passed in global memory blocks uses a clipboard data format to structure the data. It is preferable to support the CF_TEXT clipboard data format, as this is the most likely method of transmitting data. Other, more specialized data formats, can be supported in addition to CF_TEXT. CF_TEXT provides the common denominator for exchange of data between programs written by different people.

Generalized DDE Conversations

If you are writing both the client and server application, you can control the names of the application, topics and items. The more general situation occurs when your application needs to be able to exchange data with a range of applications, using topics and items which are not known. There are two types of support for generalized DDE conversations. The first is the use of "wild card names" during the DDE connection step. (Using a wild card name is similar to using the "*.*" notation in DOS when doing a directory search.) If the client specifies NULL in place of the application name atom or topic name atom, all running DDE servers will respond. The client can then look over the application and/or topic names that come back (via WM_DDE_ACK messages) and choose which ones are appropriate to establish DDE links.

The other convention used for generalized DDE conversations is support of the "System" topic. Supporting the system topic is not required, but strongly recommended for any DDE server application. The idea is that all DDE applications support this topic name and provide standard information items to potential clients. The clients can then use the information to narrow the choice of which data to exchange. Table 30-6 shows the recommended "System" topic data items that a server should support. In all cases, the data is transmitted as character strings (CF_TEXT clipboard format). Multiple items in the string are separated by tab characters.

Item Name	Data Transmitted
SysItems	A list of the items that the application supports as part of the system topic.
Topics	A list of the items that the application can support at this time. This may change, depending on what activity the application is doing.
ReturnMessage	Data in support of the last WM_DDE_ACK message. This is a way for the server to transmit additional data.
Status	The application receiving a WM_DDE_REQUEST message for this item should respond with a WM_DDE_DATA message containing either "Busy" or "Ready."
Formats	A list of the clipboard formats that the server supports. The server should list them in the order of preference. The first format should be the format that retains the maximum amount of information.

Table 30-6. "System" Topic Items.

The second example, Listing 30-2, uses Microsoft Excel's support of the System topic to obtain information from Excel. One thing to keep in mind with generalized DDE conversations is that a single initiation of a DDE link using wild cards will result in a large number of messages being transmitted. Processing these messages takes time, and can significantly slow down system performance.

Other DDE Data Transmission Messages

In the descriptions of the three types of links (cold, hot, warm), the data was always transmitted with a WM_DDE_DATA message. This is the general method of sending any type of data. There is an alternative if the data transmitted is a series of one or more character string commands. This is appropriate when one application will control another application's behavior. A good example of this is control of the Windows Program Manager application. The Program Manager responds to five different DDE commands. They are described in Section 22-20 of the Windows SDK manual and are summarized in Table 30-7.

Example Command	Meaning
[CreateGroup(New Group)]	Creates a new program group called "New Group" in the Program Manager window.
[AddItem(FILENAME.EXT, MyFile)]	Adds the application FILENAME.EXT to the group, and names the application icon "MyFile."
[DeleteGroup(Old Group)]	Deletes a program group called "Old Group" in the Program Manager window.

[ShowGroup(New Group,1)]	Displays a group called "New Group. The second value is a code: 1=Show normal, 2=Show iconic, 3=Show maximized, 4=Show last size, 5=Activate, show current size, 6=Show minimized, 7=Minimize, no change in active group, 8=Show current size, no change in active group.
[ExitProgMan(1)]	Exits the Program Manager. 0=Exit without saving, 1=Save state.

Table 30-7. Windows Program Manager DDE Commands.

To use these commands, an application establishes a DDE conversation with the Windows Program Manager application. In this case, the application name and topic are both "PROGMAN." The commands are enclosed in square brackets and sent with a WM_DDE_EXECUTE message. The first example program (Listing 30-1) demonstrates creating a program group using DDE messages.

The other message for sending data is WM_DDE_POKE. It is used when a DDE conversation is in either a warm or hot link, but when data needs to be transmitted without a prompting WM_DDE_DATA message from the client to the server. It can be thought of as an "I know you did not ask for this, but here it is anyway" message.

Adding a New Group to the Program Manager

This example, see Listing 30-1, creates a new program group in the Windows Program Manager window, and adds the WINFILE.EXE program to the group. It is typical of a cold link DDE session that would take place in an install program. Figure 30-1 shows how the Program Manager window will appear after this example program is executed.

The DDE conversation is managed by a hidden window. The hidden window is convenient, as it allows DDE messages to be sent to the "window" without complicating the WndProc() function for the application's main window. The "sender" window class is created in WndProc() when the WM_CREATE message is processed. The "sender"

window class has its own window message processing function SenderProc(), shown at the end of the listing. SenderProc() must be included in the EXPORTS section of the program's .DEF definition file. A function prototype should also be added to the program's header file.

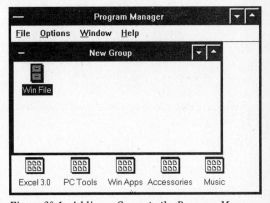

Figure 30-1. Adding a Group to the Program Manager.

The application starts the conversation with Program Manager when SenderProc() processes the WM_CREATE message. The WM_DDE_EXECUTE messages are not sent until SenderProc() receives a WM_USER + 1 message from the application's main window. This message is sent when the user clicks the "Do It!" menu item.

Two WM_DDE_EXECUTE messages are sent to the Program Manager. The first one contains a command string with both the CreateGroup() and ShowGroup() commands. The second message transmits AddItem(). The two messages could have been combined into a single longer message.

WM_DDE_ACK messages received after the initial WM_DDE_INITIATE message, and after the two WM_DDE_EXECUTE messages, are posted. SenderProc() uses Boolean values to take a shortcut when keeping track of which ACK is expected. This is fine for a simple DDE application, but becomes complex if several DDE conversations are happening at the same time. In those cases, use the item name (stored as an atom) to determine which DDE message is being processed.

⇨ Listing 30-1. Creating a Program Group Inside the Program Manager

```
/* generic.c   dde example - creates group in program manager */

#include <windows.h>
#include <dde.h>                          /* note inclusion of DDE.H */
```

```
#include "generic.h"


int PASCAL WinMain (HANDLE hInstance, HANDLE hPrevInstance, LPSTR lpszCmdLine, int nCmdShow)
{
        HWND            hWnd ;
        MSG             msg ;
        WNDCLASS        wndclass ;

        ghInstance = hInstance ;                /* store instance handle as global var. */
        if (!hPrevInstance)
        {
                wndclass.style          = CS_HREDRAW | CS_VREDRAW ;
                wndclass.lpfnWndProc    = WndProc ;
                wndclass.cbClsExtra     = 0 ;
                wndclass.cbWndExtra     = 0 ;
                wndclass.hInstance      = hInstance ;
                wndclass.hIcon          = LoadIcon (hInstance, gszAppName) ;
                wndclass.hCursor        = LoadCursor (NULL, IDC_ARROW) ;
                wndclass.hbrBackground  = GetStockObject (WHITE_BRUSH) ;
                wndclass.lpszMenuName   = gszAppName ;
                wndclass.lpszClassName  = gszAppName ;
                if (!RegisterClass (&wndclass))
                        return FALSE ;
        }

        hWnd = CreateWindow (                   /* create the program's window here */
                gszAppName,                     /* class name */
                gszAppName,                     /* window name */
                WS_OVERLAPPEDWINDOW,            /* window style */
                CW_USEDEFAULT,                  /* x position on screen */
                CW_USEDEFAULT,                  /* y position on screen */
                CW_USEDEFAULT,                  /* width of window */
                CW_USEDEFAULT,                  /* height of window */
                NULL,                           /* parent window handle (null = none) */
                NULL,                           /* menu handle (null = use class menu) */
                hInstance,                      /* instance handle */
                NULL) ;                         /* lpstr (null = not used) */
        ShowWindow (hWnd, nCmdShow) ;
        UpdateWindow (hWnd) ;                   /* send first WM_PAINT message */

        while (GetMessage (&msg, NULL, 0, 0))   /* the message loop */
        {
                TranslateMessage (&msg) ;
                DispatchMessage (&msg) ;
        }
        return msg.wParam ;
}


long FAR PASCAL WndProc (HWND hWnd, unsigned iMessage, WORD wParam, LONG lParam)
{
        WNDCLASS                wndclass ;
        static          HWND    hSender ;

        switch (iMessage)
        {                                       /* create a sever window class */
                case WM_CREATE:
                        wndclass.style          = 0 ;
                        wndclass.lpfnWndProc    = SenderProc ;
                        wndclass.cbClsExtra     = 0 ;
                        wndclass.cbWndExtra     = 0 ;
                        wndclass.hInstance      = ghInstance ;
                        wndclass.hIcon          = NULL ;
                        wndclass.hCursor        = NULL ;
                        wndclass.hbrBackground  = NULL ;
                        wndclass.lpszMenuName   = NULL ;
                        wndclass.lpszClassName  = "sender" ;
```

```
                              /* create a hidden sender window */
                RegisterClass (&wndclass) ;
                hSender = CreateWindow ("sender", NULL, WS_CHILD, 0, 0, 0, 0,
                        hWnd, NULL, ghInstance, NULL) ;
                if (!hSender)
                        MessageBox (hWnd, "Could not create DDE sender window.",
                                "Error Message", MB_OK) ;
                break ;
        case WM_COMMAND:                           /* process menu items */
                switch (wParam)
                {
                case IDM_DOIT:             /* tell sender to make a group */
                        PostMessage (hSender, WM_USER + 1, 0, 0L) ;
                        break ;
                case IDM_QUIT:
                        DestroyWindow (hWnd) ;
                        break ;
                }
                break ;
        case WM_DESTROY:
                PostQuitMessage (0) ;
                break ;
        default:
                return DefWindowProc (hWnd, iMessage, wParam, lParam) ;
        }
        return (0L) ;
}

                /* window procedure for the hidden DDE sender window */

long FAR PASCAL SenderProc (HWND hWnd, unsigned iMessage, WORD wParam, LONG lParam)
{
        ATOM                aApplication, aTopic ;
        static       HWND   hProgMgr = NULL ;
        HANDLE              hMem1, hMem2 ;
        LPSTR               lpMem ;
        char                cBuf1 [] =
                    "[CreateGroup(New Group)][ShowGroup(New Group,1)]" ;
        char                cBuf2 [] = "[AddItem(WINFILE.EXE,Win File)]" ;
        static       BOOL   bInit = FALSE, bExec = FALSE ;

        switch (iMessage)
        {
                case WM_CREATE:          /* initiate dde conversation with prog man */
                        aApplication = GlobalAddAtom ("PROGMAN") ;
                        aTopic = GlobalAddAtom ("PROGMAN") ;
                        bInit = TRUE ;
                        SendMessage (-1, WM_DDE_INITIATE, hWnd,
                                MAKELONG (aApplication, aTopic)) ;
                        GlobalDeleteAtom (aApplication) ;
                        GlobalDeleteAtom (aTopic) ;
                        break ;
                case WM_DDE_ACK:
                        if (bInit)                    /* ACK from a WM_DDE_INITIATE */
                        {
                                bInit = FALSE ;
                                GlobalDeleteAtom (LOWORD (lParam)) ;
                                GlobalDeleteAtom (HIWORD (lParam)) ;
                                if (!(lParam & 0x8000))  /* if ACK is negative */
                                        PostMessage (wParam, WM_DDE_TERMINATE, hWnd, 0L) ;
                                else
                                hProgMgr = wParam ;        /* save program mgr handle */
                        }
                        else if (bExec)            /* ACK from a WM_DDE_EXECUTE */
                        {
                                bExec = FALSE ;
                                if (HIWORD (lParam))
                                        GlobalFree (HIWORD (lParam)) ;
                                PostMessage (wParam, WM_DDE_TERMINATE, hWnd, 0L) ;
                        }
```

```
                        break ;
            case (WM_USER + 1):        /* message from WndProc() - make group */
                    if (hProgMgr)
                    {
                            bExec = TRUE ;
                            hMem1 = GlobalAlloc (GMEM_DDESHARE | GMEM_MOVEABLE,
                                    sizeof (cBuf1) + 1) ;
                            lpMem = GlobalLock (hMem1) ;
                            lstrcpy (lpMem, (LPSTR) cBuf1) ;
                            GlobalUnlock (hMem1) ;   /* send first command string */
                            PostMessage (hProgMgr, WM_DDE_EXECUTE, hWnd,
                                    MAKELONG (0, hMem1)) ;

                            hMem2 = GlobalAlloc (GMEM_DDESHARE | GMEM_MOVEABLE,
                                    sizeof (cBuf2) + 1) ;
                            lpMem = GlobalLock (hMem2) ;
                            lstrcpy (lpMem, (LPSTR) cBuf2) ;
                            GlobalUnlock (hMem2) ;   /* send second command string */
                            PostMessage (hProgMgr, WM_DDE_EXECUTE, hWnd,
                                    MAKELONG (0, hMem2)) ;
                    }
                    break ;
            default:
                    return DefWindowProc (hWnd, iMessage, wParam, lParam) ;
    }
    return (0L) ;
}
```

Obtaining File Names from Microsoft Excel

In this example, the application establishes a DDE link with Microsoft Excel and obtains the current open file names. This is typical of the client side of a cold link DDE session. When executed, this application will display the names of the currently active files, as shown in Figure 30-2.

The DDE abilities of Excel are documented in the Excel user's manual. Excel supports a broad range of DDE links, including cold, warm, and hot data links. This example obtains the file names by posting a WM_DDE_REQUEST for the "System" topic and the item "Topics." Excel responds with a WM_DDE_DATA message containing the file names in the clipboard format CF_TEXT. This text data is saved in a global variable *gcGlobTextBuf[]*, so that the application's window can display the string. In addition, the topic atom is retrieved and stored in the global variable *gcGlobTopicBuf[]*. This string is also displayed at the top of the application's window, primarily to demonstrate manipulating global atoms.

Figure 30-2. Example DDE Session Obtaining Data from Microsoft Excel.

The top part of the listing including the WinMain() function is not repeated here, as it is identical to the previous listing. SenderProc() must be included in the EXPORTS section of the program's .DEF definition file. A function prototype should also be added to the program's header file.

Note the interplay of USER messages being sent between the application's main window and the sender window. Normally, the USER messages would be given names in the application's header file, such as

```
#define SENDDDEREQ            WM_USER + 1
```

In the example in Listing 30-2, the more direct WM_USER + n notation is used for clarity.

▷ **Listing 30-2. DDE Data from Microsoft Excel**

```
HWND      ghWndVisible ;  /* globals */
char      gcGlobTextBuf [128] ;
char      gcGlobTopicBuf [128] ;

long FAR PASCAL WndProc (HWND hWnd, unsigned iMessage, WORD wParam, LONG lParam)
{
```

```
        WNDCLASS                wndclass ;
        static          HWND    hSender ;
        PAINTSTRUCT             ps ;

        switch (iMessage)
        {                                       /* create a sever window class */
                case WM_CREATE:
                        ghWndVisible = hWnd ;
                        wndclass.style          = 0 ;
                        wndclass.lpfnWndProc    = SenderProc ;
                        wndclass.cbClsExtra     = 0 ;
                        wndclass.cbWndExtra     = 0 ;
                        wndclass.hInstance      = ghInstance ;
                        wndclass.hIcon          = NULL ;
                        wndclass.hCursor        = NULL ;
                        wndclass.hbrBackground  = NULL ;
                        wndclass.lpszMenuName   = NULL ;
                        wndclass.lpszClassName  = "sender" ;
                                                /* create a hidden DDE sender window */
                        RegisterClass (&wndclass) ;
                        hSender = CreateWindow ("sender", NULL, WS_CHILD, 0, 0, 0, 0,
                                hWnd, NULL, ghInstance, NULL) ;
                        if (!hSender)
                                MessageBox (hWnd, "Could not create DDE sender window.",
                                        "Error Message", MB_OK) ;
                        break ;

                case WM_COMMAND:                /* process menu items */
                        switch (wParam)
                        {
                        case IDM_DOIT:          /* tell dde wind to get data from excel */
                                PostMessage (hSender, WM_USER + 1, 0, 0L) ;
                                break ;
                        case IDM_QUIT:          /* tell dde wind to terminate dde */
                                PostMessage (hSender, WM_USER + 2, 0, 0L) ;
                                DestroyWindow (hWnd) ;
                                break ;
                        }
                        break ;
                case WM_USER + 3:               /* message from dde wind - data ready */
                        InvalidateRect (hWnd, NULL, TRUE) ;
                        break ;
                case WM_PAINT:
                        BeginPaint (hWnd, &ps) ;
                        TextOut (ps.hdc, 0, 0, gcGlobTopicBuf,
                                lstrlen (gcGlobTopicBuf)) ;
                        TextOut (ps.hdc, 0, 20, gcGlobTextBuf,
                                lstrlen (gcGlobTextBuf)) ;
                        EndPaint (hWnd, &ps) ;
                        break ;
                case WM_DESTROY:
                        PostQuitMessage (0) ;
                        break ;
                default:
                        return DefWindowProc (hWnd, iMessage, wParam, lParam) ;
        }
        return (0L) ;
}


long FAR PASCAL SenderProc (HWND hWnd, unsigned iMessage, WORD wParam, LONG lParam)
{
        ATOM                    aApplication, aTopic, aItem ;
        static          HWND    hExcelWnd = NULL ;
        static          BOOL    bInit = FALSE ;
        DDEDATA FAR             *lpDDEData ;

        switch (iMessage)
```

```
     {
               case WM_CREATE:                      /* start dde conversation */
                    aApplication = GlobalAddAtom ("Excel") ;
                    aTopic = GlobalAddAtom ("System") ;
                    bInit = TRUE ;
                    SendMessage (-1, WM_DDE_INITIATE, hWnd,
                         MAKELONG (aApplication, aTopic)) ;
                    GlobalDeleteAtom (aApplication) ;
                    GlobalDeleteAtom (aTopic) ;
                    break ;
               case WM_DDE_ACK:
                    if (bInit)                      /* ACK from a WM_DDE_INITIATE */
                    {
                         bInit = FALSE ;
                         GlobalDeleteAtom (LOWORD (lParam)) ;
                         GlobalDeleteAtom (HIWORD (lParam)) ;
                         if (!(lParam & 0x8000))  /* if ACK is negative */
                              PostMessage (wParam, WM_DDE_TERMINATE, hWnd, OL) ;
                         else
                              hExcelWnd = wParam ;      /* save excel handle */
                    }
                    else                            /* another ACK */
                         GlobalDeleteAtom (HIWORD (lParam)) ;
                    break ;
               case WM_DDE_DATA:                    /* got data back from excel */
                                                    /* save atom contents in buf */
                    GlobalGetAtomName (HIWORD (lParam), gcGlobTopicBuf, 128) ;
                                                    /* lock the memory buffer */
                    lpDDEData = (DDEDATA FAR *) GlobalLock (LOWORD (lParam)) ;
                                                    /* excel wants ACK ? */
                    if (lpDDEData->fAckReq)
                         PostMessage (hExcelWnd, WM_DDE_ACK, hWnd,
                              MAKELONG (0x8000, HIWORD (lParam))) ;
                    else
                         GlobalDeleteAtom (HIWORD (lParam)) ;
                                                    /* save the data if in CF_TEXT format */
                    if (lpDDEData->cfFormat == CF_TEXT)
                    {
                         lstrcpy (gcGlobTextBuf, lpDDEData->Value) ;
                                                    /* tell visible wind. data is ready */
                         PostMessage (ghWndVisible, WM_USER + 3, 0, OL) ;
                    }
                    if (lpDDEData->fRelease)/* excel wants cleanup ? */
                         GlobalFree (LOWORD (lParam)) ;
                    else
                         GlobalUnlock (LOWORD (lParam)) ;
                    break ;
               case (WM_USER + 1):                  /* message from host - talk to Excel */
                    if (hExcelWnd)
                    {
                         aItem = GlobalAddAtom ("Topics") ;
                         PostMessage (hExcelWnd, WM_DDE_REQUEST, hWnd,
                              MAKELONG (CF_TEXT, aItem)) ;
                    }
                    break ;
               case (WM_USER + 2):                  /* message from host - quit dde */
                    PostMessage (hExcelWnd, WM_DDE_TERMINATE, hWnd, OL) ;

                    break ;
               default:
                    return DefWindowProc (hWnd, iMessage, wParam, lParam) ;
     }
     return (OL) ;
}
```

DDE Message Summary

Table 30-8 summarizes the DDE messages. The detailed message descriptions are in the next section.

Message	Description	
WM_DDE_ACK	Notifies an application that another DDE message was received.	
WM_DDE_ADVISE	The client application sends this message to the server to inform the server that the client would like to receive updated data any time the data changes.	
WM_DDE_DATA	Sends data to the client application, or notifies the client that the data has changed in a warm link.	
WM_DDE_EXECUTE	Sends one or more command strings to the client application.	
WM_DDE_INITIATE	Starts a DDE conversation.	
WM_DDE_POKE	This message is posted by the client application, sending unsolicited data to the server.	
WM_DDE_REQUEST	Posted by the client application to prompt transmittal of a data item from the server.	
WM_DDE_TERMINATE	Stops a DDE conversation.	
WM_DDE_UNADVISE	Sent by the client application to stop updates of a particular item in a warm or hot link.	

Table 30-8. DDE Message Summary.

DDE Message Descriptions

This section contains the detailed descriptions of the DDE messages.

These messages are defined in the DDE.H header file that comes with the software development kit.

WM_DDE_ACK   ■ Win 2.0   ■ Win 3.0   ■ Win 3.1

Purpose   Notifies an application that another DDE message was received.

Syntax   PostMessage (HWND *hWnd*, **WM_DDE_ACK**, WORD *wParam*, DWORD *lParam*);

Discussion   This message is posted in response to receipt of a WM_DDE_INITIATE, WM_DDE_EXECUTE, WM_DDE_DATA, WM_DDE_ADVISE, WM_DDE_UNADVISE, or WM_DDE_POKE message. In some cases, WM_DDE_ACK is also posted in response to a WM_DDE_REQUEST message. (See that message description for details.) The response code with the WM_DDE_ACK message can be either positive or negative. If the *fAck* element (most significant bit) of the DDEACK data structure is zero, the response is negative. If *fAck* is one, the response is positive.

Parameters

hWnd   HWND: The window handle of the window to receive the message.

wParam   WORD: The window handle of the window that sent the message.

lParam   DWORD: The meaning of *lParam* depends on which message the application is responding to.

Responding to WM_DDE_INITIATE: The low-order word of *lParam* should be a global atom that contains the name of the replying application. The high-order word of *lParam* should contain a global atom containing the data topic. If the topic sent with WM_DDE_INITIATE is NULL, a WM_DDE_ACK should be sent back for every topic supported.

Responding to WM_DDE_EXECUTE: The low-order word of *lParam* should contain a bit flag as specified in Table 30-9. The high-order word should contain a global memory handle containing the command string. See WM_DDE_EXECUTE for details on the command string.

Responding to all other DDE messages: The low-order word of *lParam* should contain a bit flag as specified in Table 30-9. The high-order word should contain a global atom contain the data item for which the response is sent.

Bit	Name	Meaning	
15	fAck	1=Request accepted, 0 =Request not accepted.	
14	fBusy	1=Busy. This only has meaning if fAck is zero. The busy flag should be set if the application cannot respond immediately.	
13-8	reserved	Reserved for Microsoft use.	
7-0	bAppReturnCode	Reserved for application-specific return codes.	

Table 30-9. lParam Low-Order Word Flags for WM_DDE_ACK.

These values correspond to the elements of the DDEACK data structure. This structure contains the bit fields, and is defined in DDE.H as follows:

```
typedef struct {
        unsigned        bAppReturnCode:8,
                        reserved:6,
                        fBusy:1,
                        fAck:1;
} DDEACK
```

Posting
PostMessage() should be used to send WM_DDE_ACK. The only exception is when responding to a WM_DDE_INITIATE message. Then use SendMessage(). When responding to a message that contains a global atom, the application can reuse the atom received in responding, or it can delete the atom received, and then create and return a new atom.

When responding to a WM_DDE_EXECUTE message, the application should reuse the *hCommands* global memory object. This basically echoes the commands sent to the sender. The sender is responsible for deleting the *hCommands* object. Once a WM_DDE_TERMINATE message is sent, the application should not acknowledge other messages from the application that sent the WM_DDE_TERMINATE.

Receiving
An application expects to receive a WM_DDE_ACK after sending data to another application. When the ACK is received, the application knows that the other application has received the data, so it is safe to delete global atoms and memory areas containing the data that was sent. The data should be deleted from memory even if the ACK was negative, meaning that the other application could not use the data.

WM_DDE_ADVISE
■ Win 2.0　　■ Win 3.0　　■ Win 3.1

Purpose
The client application sends this message to the server to inform the server that the client would like to receive updated data any time the data changes.

Syntax
PostMessage (HWND *hWnd*, **WM_DDE_ADVISE**, WORD *wParam*, DWORD *lParam*);

Discussion
This message is used to set up both hot and warm DDE links. Hot links involve transmission of the data every time the data changes. Warm links simply notify the client when the data has changed. The client then uses WM_DDE_REQUEST to request the data.

Parameters
hWnd
HWND: The window handle of the window to receive the message.

wParam
WORD: The window handle of the window sending the message.

lParam
DWORD: The high-order word (called *aItem*) contains a global atom containing the name of the data item being requested. The low-order word (called *hOptions*) contains a handle to a global memory block containing a DDEADVISE data structure. This structure contains bit fields described in Table 30-10. The DDEADVISE structure is defined in DDE.H as follows:

```
typedef struct {
      unsigned          reserved:14,        /* bits 0-13 reserved */
                        fDeferUpd:1,        /* warm link request */
                        fAckReq:1;          /* ACK requested ? */
      int               cfFormat;           /* clipboard format */
} DDEADVISE;
```

Bit	Name	Meaning	⊠
15	*fAckReq*	1=Server requested to send WM_DDE_DATA with the *fAckReq* bit set to 1. 0 0=Server requested to send WM_DDE_DATA with the *fAckReq* bit set to 0. This inhibits sending the ACK messages, speeding data transfer	
14	*fDeferUpd*	1=Server is requested to send WM_DDE_DATA with *hData* set to NULL. This starts a warm link, where data is not transferred until the client sends a WM_DDE_REQUEST message. 0=Server is requested to send data with each WM_DDE_DATA message.	
13-0	*reserved*	Reserved for Microsoft use.	

Table 30-10. lParam Low-Order Word Flags for WM_DDE_ADVISE.

> *cfFormat* is the clipboard format used to transmit the data. This can be either a standard clipboard format, or a special format created with RegisterClipboardFormat(). If an application uses more than one clipboard format, it can post multiple WM_DDE_ADVISE messages for separate topics and items.

Posting Use PostMessage(), not SendMessage(), to transmit this message to another application. Be sure that the global memory object pointed to by the low-order word of *lParam* is allocated with GlobalAlloc() using the GMEM_DDE_SHARE option. This memory block should be deleted if the server responds with a WM_DDE_ACK message.

Receiving Always respond to this message by posting a WM_DDE_ACK message. If responding positively, delete the *hOptions* global memory block containing the DDEADVISE structure. If responding negatively, do not delete the *hOptions* memory block, as the sender will delete it when it receives the negative WM_DDE_ACK. The *aItem* global atom can either be reused, or deleted and a new item created in its place.

WM_DDE_DATA   ■ Win 2.0   ■ Win 3.0   ■ Win 3.1

Purpose Sends data to the client application, or notifies the client that the data has changed in a warm link.

Syntax PostMessage (HWND *hWnd*, **WM_DDE_DATA**, WORD *wParam*, DWORD *lParam*);

Discussion This message transfers data from the server to the client in a DDE link. If a warm link has been established, this message simply informs the client that new data is available. It is up to the client to request the data with a WM_DDE_REQUEST message.

Parameters

hWnd HWND: The window handle of the window to receive the message.

wParam WORD: The window handle of the window sending the message.

lParam DWORD: The high-order word (called *aItem*) contains a global atom containing the name of the data item being sent.

> The low-order word (called *hOptions*) contains a handle to a global memory block containing a DDEDATA data structure. This structure contains bit fields, which are described in Table 30-11. The DDEDATA dtructure is defined in DDE.H as follows:

```
typedef struct {
      unsigned          unused:12,
                        fResponse:1,      /* 1 = got REQUEST, 0 = got ADVISE */
                        fRelease:1,       /* 1 = client frees data */
                        reserved:1,
                        fAckReq:1;        /* 1 = expect ACK back */
      int               cfFormat;         /* clipboard format */
      BYTE              Value[1];         /* can be more than one element */
} DDEDATA;
```

Bit	Name	Meaning	☒
15	fAckReq	1=Client is expected to send a WM_DDE_ACK message after receiving the WM_DDE_DATA. 0=Client is not expected to send ACK.	
13	fDeferUpd	1=Client is expected to free the data pointed to by *hData*. 0=Client should not free the data. See the Posting and Receiving notes below for exceptions.	
12	fRequested	1=Data is being sent in response to a WM_DDE_REQUEST message. 0=Data is being sent in response to a WM_DDE_ADVISE message.	
14, 11-0	reserved	Reserved for Microsoft use.	

Table 30-11. lParam Low-Order Word Flags for WM_DDE_DATA.

cfFormat contains the clipboard format being used to store the data. This can be either a standard clipboard format, or a special format created with RegisterClipboardFormat(). *Value[]* is an array of one or more bytes of data being transmitted. This data is in the format specified by *cfFormat*. In a warm link, the high-order word in *lParam* will be NULL. This simply notifies the client that new data is available, but does not transmit the data. It is up to the client to post the WM_DDE_REQUEST message to get the actual data.

Posting   Use PostMessage() to send this message. The *hData* data block containing the DDEDATA data structure must be allocated using GlobalAlloc() with the GMEM_DDESHARE option. If the client receiving the data responds with a negative WM_DDE_ACK message, the server should delete the *hData* memory block. *hData* should also be deleted if the *fRelease* flag is set to zero. Do not set *fAckReq* and *fRelease* to zero. With both set to zero, the server will not know when to delete the *hData* memory block.

Receiving   A client receiving this message must decide whether or not to respond with a WM_DDE_ACK message. If *fAckReq* is 1, post the WM_DDE_ACK, otherwise do not post the message. If *fAckReq* is 0, delete the *aItem* global atom. If *hData* is NULL, a warm link is in progress. The client can ask for the data by sending a WM_DDE_REQUEST message, or simply ignore the WM_DDE_MESS-AGE. If *hData* is not NULL, the *hData* global memory block should be deleted unless *fRelease* is zero, or *fRelease* is 1, and the client decides to respond with a negative WM_DDE_ACK message.

WM_DDE_EXECUTE   ■ Win 2.0   ■ Win 3.0   ■ Win 3.1

Purpose   Sends one or more command strings to the client application.

Syntax   PostMessage (HWND *hWnd*, **WM_DDE_EXECUTE**, WORD *wParam*, DWORD *lParam*);

Discussion   This is a convenient way to send character string commands from the server to the client application. The commands are stored in a global memory block containing a null-terminated character string. The command strings are in the format

```
[command(parameters)]
```

The square brackets are part of the transmitted string. There can be more than one command in the character string. Here are several examples of valid commands

```
[startup][filefunction(data.txt,7)][shutdown]
[passname("This is the string data passed.")]
```

The square brackets are required around each command.

Parameters

hWnd   HWND: The window handle of the window to receive the message.

wParam   WORD: The window handle of the window sending the message.

lParam   DWORD: The low-order word is reserved. The high-order word contains a handle to a global memory block containing the command string. The block must be allocated with the GMEM_DDESHARE option.

Posting   Use PostMessage() to post this message. The server sending this message should wait for the WM_DDE_ACK message to come back from the client before deleting the memory block containing the command string.

Receiving   Respond to receiving this message by posting a WM_DDE_ACK message. Reuse the *hCommands* handle in sending the WM_DDE_ACK message back.

WM_DDE_INITIATE   ■ Win 2.0   ■ Win 3.0   ■ Win 3.1

Purpose   Starts a DDE conversation.

Syntax   SendMessage (HWND *hWnd*, **WM_DDE_INITIATE** , WORD *wParam*, DWORD *lParam*)

Discussion   When an application receives this message, it should check to see if the application name and data name held by the atoms in *lParam* match the application's name and data supported. If so, the application should respond with a WM_DDE_ACK message. Otherwise, the message is ignored.

Parameters

hWnd   HWND: The window handle of the window to receive the message.

wParam   WORD: The window handle of the window sending the message.

lParam   DWORD: The low-order word contains a global atom holding the name of the application. This parameter is called *aApplication*. The application name cannot contain slashes or backslashes, as these characters are reserved for future network support. If *aApplication* is NULL, any application can respond.

                The high-order word contains a global atom holding the name of the data element. This parameter is called *aTopic*. If *aTopic* is NULL, any topic is valid. Upon receiving a WM_DDE_INITIATE message with a NULL value for *aTopic*, the application should send a WM_DDE_ACK message for every topic it supports.

Sending   Use SendMessage() to transmit this message, not PostMessage(). The message can be sent to every application running on the system by setting the first parameter of SendMessage() to –1. The window handle(s) for applications that respond can be obtained from the returning WM_DDE_ACK message(s).

                Delete the two global atoms containing the application and topic names immediately after calling SendMessage(). You do not have to wait for the WM_DDE_ACK message(s) to come back to delete these atoms.

Receiving   Post a WM_DDE_ACK message for each topic supported if the application name matches. If a topic is specified, post a WM_DDE_ACK only if the topic is supported. The receiving application should create new *aApplication* and *aTopic* atoms. Do not use the atoms sent with WM_DDE_INITIATE, as the sending application is expected to delete them.

WM_DDE_POKE

Purpose   This message is posted by the client application sending unsolicited data to the server.

Syntax   PostMessage (HWND *hWnd*, **WM_DDE_POKE**, WORD *wParam*, DWORD *lParam*);

Discussion   WM_DDE_POKE allows the client to send the server data independent of when the server initiates data exchange.

Parameters

hWnd   HWND: The window handle of the window to receive the message.

wParam   WORD: The window handle of the window sending the message.

lParam   DWORD: The high-order word contains a global atom containing the name of the data item being transmitted. This parameter is called *aItem*. The low-order word contains a handle (called *hData*) to a global memory block containing a DDEPOKE data structure. This structure contains bit fields, and is defined in DDE.H as follows:

```
typedef struct {
        unsigned        unused:13,
                        fRelease:1,             /* 1 = receiver frees memory */
                        fReserved:2;
        int             cfFormat;               /* clipboard data format used */
        BYTE            Value[1];               /* this may be > 1 byte */
} DDEPOKE;
```

If the *fReserved* field is set to 1, the application receiving the WM_DDE_POKE message is expected to free the global memory block containing the DDEPOKE data structure. If *fReserved* is 0, the block should not be freed.

cfFormat contains the clipboard format being used to store the data. This can be either a standard clipboard format, or a special format created with RegisterClipboardFormat().

Value[] is an array of one or more bytes of data being transmitted. This data is in the format specified by *cfFormat*.

Posting   Use PostMessage() to transmit this message, not SendMessage(). Use the GMEM_DDESHARE option when calling GlobalAlloc() to allocate memory to hold the DDEPOKE data structure.

The sending application is responsible for deleting the memory block if the *fRelease* flag is set to zero. In this case, the sending application should wait for the WM_DDE_ACK message to come back before deleting the data.

Receiving   An application receiving this message should respond with a WM_DDE_ACK message. The WM_DDE_ACK can reuse the *aItem* atom, or it can delete the received atom and create a new one. After receiving WM_DDE_POKE, the application should delete the global memory block *hData* unless *fRelease* is zero.

WM_DDE_REQUEST

Purpose   Posted by the client application to prompt transmittal of a data item from the server.

Syntax   PostMessage (HWND *hWnd*, **WM_DDE_REQUEST**, WORD *wParam*, DWORD *lParam*);

Discussion   This message is sent as part of a warm link. If the client receives a WM_DDE_DATA message with a NULL data item, the server is indicating that a data item has changed and a new value is available. A WM_DDE_REQUEST can then be sent by the client to prompt for the latest data value.

Parameters

hWnd   HWND: The window handle of the window to receive the message.

wParam   WORD: The window handle of the window sending the message.

lParam	DWORD: The low-order word (called *cfFormat*) contains the clipboard format being used to store the data. This can be either a standard clipboard format, or a special format created with RegisterClipboardFormat(). The high-order word (called *aItem*) contains a global atom containing the data item name being requested.
Posting	Use PostMessage() to transmit this message, not SendMessage().
Receiving	The receiving application normally will respond by posting a WM_DDE_DATA message containing the requested data. Otherwise, it should post a WM_DDE_ACK message containing a negative response. In either case, the global atom *aItem* can either be reused, or deleted and a new atom created.

WM_DDE_TERMINATE　　　　　　　　■ Win 2.0　　■ Win 3.0　　■ Win 3.1

Purpose	Stops a DDE conversation.
Syntax	PostMessage (HWND *hWnd*, **WM_DDE_TERMINATE**, WORD *wParam*, DWORD *lParam*);
Discussion	This message notifies either a client or server application that the DDE conversation is terminated.
Parameters	
hWnd	HWND: The window handle of the window to receive the message.
wParam	WORD: The window handle of the window sending the message.
lParam	DWORD: Not used. Set equal to 0L.
Posting	Use PostMessage() to transmit this message, not SendMessage(). After posting this message, the application should not respond to any other messages from the application receiving the message, other than WM_DDE_TERMINATE.
Receiving	Respond by posting a WM_DDE_TERMINATE message. Do not respond to this message if the receiving application initiated WM_DDE_TERMINATE (to avoid an infinite loop of messages).

WM_DDE_UNADVISE　　　　　　　　■ Win 2.0　　■ Win 3.0　　■ Win 3.1

Purpose	Sent by the client application to stop updates of a particular item in a warm or hot link.
Syntax	PostMessage (HWND *hWnd*, **WM_DDE_UNADVISE**, WORD *wParam*, DWORD *lParam*);
Discussion	After a WM_DDE_ADVISE message is received by the server, the server is expected to send a WM_DDE_DATA message when the data item changes. WM_DDE_UNADVISE stops this process, temporarily stopping hot or warm link WM_DDE_DATA messages.
Parameters	
hWnd	HWND: The window handle of the window to receive the message.
wParam	WORD: The window handle of the window sending the message.
lParam	DWORD: The low-order word (called *cfFormat*) contains the clipboard format being used to store the data. This can be either a standard clipboard format, or a special format created with RegisterClipboardFormat(). The high-order word (called *aItem*) contains a global atom containing the data item name being retracted. If *aItem* is NULL, all WM_DDE_ADVISE conversations associated with the client application are terminated.
Posting	Use PostMessage() to transmit this message, not SendMessage().
Receiving	Post the WM_DDE_ACK message to respond to this message.

Appendix A
Bibliography and Sources
of Additional Information

Books on Windows

Charles Petzold's book is an excellent tutorial on programming under Windows. It covers all the basic elements of Windows and several more advanced topics, including DDE and MDI.

Programming Windows
Charles Petzold
Microsoft Press, 1990

The Norton and Yao book is slower paced and easier to digest than Petzold's book, but it covers less material.

Windows 3.0 Power Programming Techniques
Peter Norton and Paul Yao
Bantam Books, 1990

Jeffrey Richter's book covers a number of advanced topics, including dynamic dialog boxes, custom controls, printer setup, and program installation. It is intended for readers who have already mastered the material in the Petzold, or Norton and Yao books.

Windows 3: A Developer's Guide
Jeffrey M. Richter
M&T Books, 1991

Other Programming Reference Books

This IBM document spells out the rules for programming the user interface for Windows and OS/2 applications. Following these guidelines is strongly encouraged.

Systems Application Architecture,
Common User Access Advanced Interface Design Guide
International Business Machines, 1989

The classic Kerninghan and Ritchie book is the standard reference for the C language.

The C Programming Language, Second Edition
Brian W. Kerninghan and Dennis M. Ritchie
Prentice Hall, 1988

If you need a more readable introduction to the C language, try the Waite and Prata book.

The Waite Group's New C Primer Plus
Mitchell Waite and Stephan Prata
The Waite Group, 1990

For a thorough understanding of the MS-DOS operating system that underlies Windows, refer to the Microsoft Press Encyclopedia.

The MS-DOS Encyclopedia
Ray Duncan, General Editor
Microsoft Press, 1988

For additional background on digital communications, refer to Paul Bate's book.

Practical Digital and Data Communications
Paul Bates
Prentice-Hall, 1987

Sound Driver Support and Information

Users of the popular Sound Blaster and Adlib music cards can obtain an excellent Windows driver that was developed at the University of Wisconson.

Monty Schmidt
1020 E. Johnson #1
Madison, WI 53703
(608) 256-3133
COMPUSERVE 73020, 2770

For more complete control of all of the Sound Blaster features, Creative Labs, Inc. offers a DLL (dynamic link library). The DLL includes support of both the synthesized sound, and voice record/playback functions.

Creative Labs, Inc.
2050 Duane Ave.
Santa Clara, CA 95954
(408) 986-1461

MIDI drivers are available from Microsoft as part of their Multimedia Development Kit, or separately from Playroom Software.

Microsoft Corporation
16011 NE 36th Way
Box 97017
Redmond, WA 98073-9717
(206) 426-9900

Playroom Software
7308-C East Independence Blvd., Suite 310
Charlotte, NC 28227
(704) 536-3093

The MIDI (Musical Instrument Digital Interface) specification is available from the International MIDI Association.

International MIDI Association
5316 W. 57th St.
Los Angeles, CA 90056
(213) 649-6434

Appendix B
Useful Macros from WINDOWS.H

WINDOWS.H contains a number of useful #define statements that define macros. They can be used to improve the clarity of an application's code and maintain strong type checking.

The following three macros extract one of the color values from the composite 32-bit color value used with either the RGB color model, or a color palette.

```
GetBValue(rgb)          ((BYTE)((rgb)>>16))
GetGValue(rgb)          ((BYTE)(((WORD)(rgb)) >> 8))
GetRValue(rgb)          ((BYTE)(rgb))
```

It is frequently necessary to extract one-half of either a 16-bit WORD or a 32-bit DWORD value when processing Windows messages.

```
HIBYTE(w)               ((BYTE)(((WORD)(w) >> 8) & 0xFF))
HIWORD(l)               ((WORD)(((DWORD)(l) >> 16) & 0xFFFF))
LOBYTE(w)               ((BYTE)(w))
LOWORD(l)               ((WORD)(l))
```

WINDOWS.H contains several macros for casting values to different types. The MAKELONG macro combines two WORD values to make a DWORD. Note that the low-order WORD is placed first in the macro.

```
MAKEINTATOM(i)          (LPSTR)((DWORD)((WORD)(i)))
MAKELONG(a, b)          ((LONG)(((WORD)(a)) | ((DWORD)((WORD)(b))) << 16))
MAKEPOINT(l)            (*((POINT FAR *)&(l)))
```

The min and max macros return the smaller or larger of two values.

```
max(a,b)        (((a) > (b)) ? (a) : (b))
min(a,b)        (((a) < (b)) ? (a) : (b))
```

The palette manager uses the high-order byte of the color value to be coded if the color entry is a palette index or a palette RGB value. The RGB macro combines three byte values to make a DWORD color value.

```
PALETTEINDEX(i)         ((DWORD)(0x01000000 | (WORD)(i)))
PALETTERGB(r,g,b)       (0x02000000 | RGB(r,g,b))
RGB(r,g,b)              ((DWORD)(((BYTE)(r)|((WORD)(g)<<8))|(((DWORD)(BYTE)(b))<<16)))
```

Appendix C
Mouse Hit Test Codes

HTERROR	(-2)
HTTRANSPARENT	(-1)
HTNOWHERE	0
HTCLIENT	1
HTCAPTION	2
HTSYSMENU	3
HTGROWBOX	4
HTSIZE	HTGROWBOX
HTMENU	5
HTHSCROLL	6
HTVSCROLL	7
HTREDUCE	8
HTZOOM	9
HTLEFT	10
HTRIGHT	11
HTTOP	12
HTTOPLEFT	13
HTTOPRIGHT	14
HTBOTTOM	15
HTBOTTOMLEFT	16
HTBOTTOMRIGHT	17
HTSIZEFIRST	HTLEFT
HTSIZELAST	HTBOTTOMRIGHT

Appendix D
WINDOWS.H Listing

```
/*-------------------------------------------------------- */
/*                                                         */
/* WINDOWS.H -                                             */
/*                                                         */
/*     Include file for Windows 3.0 applications           */
/*                                                         */
/*-------------------------------------------------------- */

/* If defined, the following flags inhibit definition
 *     of the indicated items.
 *
 * NOGDICAPMASKS          - CC_*, LC_*, PC_*, CP_*, TC_*, RC_
 * NOVIRTUALKEYCODES      - VK_*
 * NOWINMESSAGES          - WM_*, EM_*, LB_*, CB_*
 * NOWINSTYLES            - WS_*, CS_*, ES_*, LBS_*, SBS_*, CBS_*
 * NOSYSMETRICS           - SM_*
 * NOMENUS                - MF_*
 * NOICONS                - IDI_*
 * NOKEYSTATES            - MK_*
 * NOSYSCOMMANDS          - SC_*
 * NORASTEROPS            - Binary and Tertiary raster ops
 * NOSHOWWINDOW           - SW_*
 * OEMRESOURCE            - OEM Resource values
 * NOATOM                 - Atom Manager routines
 * NOCLIPBOARD            - Clipboard routines
 * NOCOLOR                - Screen colors
 * NOCTLMGR               - Control and Dialog routines
 * NODRAWTEXT             - DrawText() and DT_*
 * NOGDI                  - All GDI defines and routines
 * NOKERNEL               - All KERNEL defines and routines
 * NOUSER                 - All USER defines and routines
 * NOMB                   - MB_* and MessageBox()
 * NOMEMMGR               - GMEM_*, LMEM_*, GHND, LHND, associated routines
 * NOMETAFILE             - typedef METAFILEPICT
 * NOMINMAX               - Macros min(a,b) and max(a,b)
 * NOMSG                  - typedef MSG and associated routines
 * NOOPENFILE             - OpenFile(), OemToAnsi, AnsiToOem, and OF_*
 * NOSCROLL               - SB_* and scrolling routines
 * NOSOUND                - Sound driver routines
 * NOTEXTMETRIC           - typedef TEXTMETRIC and associated routines
 * NOWH                   - SetWindowsHook and WH_*
 * NOWINOFFSETS           - GWL_*, GCL_*, associated routines
 * NOHELP                 - Help engine interface.
 * NOPROFILER             - Profiler interface.
 * NODEFERWINDOWPOS       - DeferWindowPos routines
 * NODRIVERS              - Installable driver defines
 * NODBCS                 - DBCS support stuff.
 * NOSYSPARAMSINFO        - SystemParameterInfo (SPI_*)
 * NOSCALABLEFONT         - Scalable font prototypes and data structures
 *
 * USECOMM                - Include COMM driver routines
 *
 * Defining the following allows API's to be included
 * PRINTING               - include printing api's
 */
```

```
#ifdef RC_INVOKED

/* Turn off a bunch of stuff to ensure that RC files compile OK.*/
#define NOATOM
#define NOGDI
#define NOGDICAPMASKS
#define NOMETAFILE
#define NOMINMAX
#define NOMSG
#define NOOPENFILE
#define NORASTEROPS
#define NOSCROLL
#define NOSOUND
#define NOSYSMETRICS
#define NOTEXTMETRIC
#define NOWH
#define NODBCS
#define NOSYSPARAMSINFO

#endif /* RC_INVOKED */


/*--------------------------------------------------------------- */
/*  General Purpose Defines                                       */
/*--------------------------------------------------------------- */

#define NULL            0
#define FALSE           0
#define TRUE            1

#define FAR             far
#define NEAR            near
#define LONG            long
#define VOID            void
#define PASCAL          pascal

#define API             far pascal
#define CALLBACK        far pascal

#ifndef NOMINMAX

#ifndef max
#define max(a,b)        (((a) > (b)) ? (a) : (b))
#endif

#ifndef min
#define min(a,b)        (((a) < (b)) ? (a) : (b))
#endif

#endif  /* NOMINMAX */

#define MAKELONG(a, b)  ((LONG)(((WORD)(a)) | ((DWORD)((WORD)(b))) << 16))
#define LOWORD(l)       ((WORD)(l))
#define HIWORD(l)       ((WORD)(((DWORD)(l) >> 16) & 0xFFFF))
#define LOBYTE(w)       ((BYTE)(w))
#define HIBYTE(w)       ((BYTE)(((WORD)(w) >> 8) & 0xFF))
#define MAKELP(sel, off) ((VOID FAR *)MAKELONG(off, sel))
#define SELECTOROF(lp)  HIWORD(lp)
#define OFFSETOF(lp)    LOWORD(lp)

typedef int             BOOL;
typedef unsigned char   BYTE;
typedef unsigned short  WORD;
typedef unsigned long   DWORD;
typedef char near       *PSTR;
typedef char near       *NPSTR;
typedef char far        *LPSTR;
typedef BYTE near       *PBYTE;
typedef BYTE far        *LPBYTE;
```

```
typedef int near        *PINT;
typedef int far         *LPINT;
typedef WORD near       *PWORD;
typedef WORD far        *LPWORD;
typedef long near       *PLONG;
typedef long far        *LPLONG;
typedef DWORD near      *PDWORD;
typedef DWORD far       *LPDWORD;
typedef void far        *LPVOID;

#ifdef STRICT

#define DECLARE_HANDLE(name)                    \
typedef struct _##name##_ { int dummy; };   \
typedef struct _##name##_ near *name

typedef void near*      HANDLE;

DECLARE_HANDLE(HWND);

#else   /* STRICT */

#define DECLARE_HANDLE(name)        \
typedef WORD name


typedef WORD HANDLE;

DECLARE_HANDLE(HWND);


#endif  /* !STRICT */

/* Special value for CreateWindow, et al. */
#define HWND_DESKTOP        ((HWND)NULL)

typedef HANDLE          *PHANDLE;
typedef HANDLE NEAR     *SPHANDLE;
typedef HANDLE FAR      *LPHANDLE;
typedef HANDLE          GLOBALHANDLE;
typedef HANDLE          LOCALHANDLE;
typedef int (FAR PASCAL *FARPROC)();
typedef int (NEAR PASCAL *NEARPROC)();

DECLARE_HANDLE(HSTR);
DECLARE_HANDLE(HICON);
DECLARE_HANDLE(HDC);
DECLARE_HANDLE(HMENU);
DECLARE_HANDLE(HPEN);
DECLARE_HANDLE(HFONT);
DECLARE_HANDLE(HBRUSH);
DECLARE_HANDLE(HBITMAP);
DECLARE_HANDLE(HCURSOR);
DECLARE_HANDLE(HRGN);
DECLARE_HANDLE(HPALETTE);

typedef DWORD           COLORREF;

typedef struct tagRECT
  {
    int     left;
    int     top;
    int     right;
    int     bottom;
  } RECT;

typedef RECT            *PRECT;
typedef RECT NEAR       *NPRECT;
typedef RECT FAR        *LPRECT;
```

```
typedef struct tagPOINT
  {
    int       x;
    int       y;
  } POINT;
typedef POINT            *PPOINT;
typedef POINT NEAR       *NPPOINT;
typedef POINT FAR        *LPPOINT;


/*-------------------------------------- */
/*  KERNEL Section                       */
/*-------------------------------------- */

#ifndef NOKERNEL

/* Loader Routines */
DWORD    API GetVersion(void);
WORD     API GetNumTasks(void);
HANDLE   API GetCodeHandle(FARPROC);
void     API GetCodeInfo(FARPROC lpProc, LPVOID lpSegInfo);
HANDLE   API GetModuleHandle(LPSTR);
int      API GetModuleUsage(HANDLE);
int      API GetModuleFileName(HANDLE, LPSTR, int);
int      API GetInstanceData(HANDLE, NPSTR, int);
FARPROC  API GetProcAddress(HANDLE, LPSTR);
FARPROC  API MakeProcInstance(FARPROC, HANDLE);
void     API FreeProcInstance(FARPROC);
HANDLE   API LoadLibrary(LPSTR);
HANDLE   API LoadModule(LPSTR, LPVOID);
void     API FreeModule(HANDLE);
void     API FreeLibrary(HANDLE);
DWORD    API GetFreeSpace(WORD);
WORD     API WinExec(LPSTR, WORD);
void     API DebugBreak(void);
void     API OutputDebugString(LPSTR);
void     API SwitchStackBack(void);
void     API SwitchStackTo(WORD, WORD, WORD);
WORD     API GetCurrentPDB(void);
#ifdef WIN31
BOOL     API IsTask(HANDLE);
WORD     API GetFreeSystemResources(WORD);
#endif

#ifndef NOOPENFILE

/* OpenFile() Structure */
typedef struct tagOFSTRUCT
  {
    BYTE          cBytes;
    BYTE          fFixedDisk;
    WORD          nErrCode;
    BYTE          reserved[4];
    BYTE          szPathName[128];
  } OFSTRUCT;
typedef OFSTRUCT         *POFSTRUCT;
typedef OFSTRUCT NEAR    *NPOFSTRUCT;
typedef OFSTRUCT FAR     *LPOFSTRUCT;


/* OpenFile() Flags */
#define OF_READ                 0x0000
#define OF_WRITE                0x0001
#define OF_READWRITE            0x0002
#define OF_SHARE_COMPAT         0x0000
#define OF_SHARE_EXCLUSIVE      0x0010
#define OF_SHARE_DENY_WRITE     0x0020
#define OF_SHARE_DENY_READ      0x0030
#define OF_SHARE_DENY_NONE      0x0040
#define OF_PARSE                0x0100
```

```
#define OF_DELETE              0x0200
#define OF_VERIFY              0x0400      /* Used with OF_REOPEN */
#define OF_SEARCH              0x0400      /* Used without OF_REOPEN */
#define OF_CANCEL              0x0800
#define OF_CREATE              0x1000
#define OF_PROMPT              0x2000
#define OF_EXIST               0x4000
#define OF_REOPEN              0x8000

int     API OpenFile(LPSTR, LPOFSTRUCT, WORD);
int     FAR PASCAL OpenSystemFile(LPSTR, LPOFSTRUCT, WORD);

/* GetTempFileName() Flags */
#define TF_FORCEDRIVE      (BYTE)0x80

BYTE API GetTempDrive(BYTE);
int  API GetTempFileName(BYTE, LPSTR, WORD, LPSTR);
WORD API SetHandleCount(WORD);

WORD API GetDriveType(int);
/* GetDriveType return values */
#define DRIVE_REMOVABLE 2
#define DRIVE_FIXED     3
#define DRIVE_REMOTE    4

#endif /* NOOPENFILE */

#ifndef NOMEMMGR

/* Global Memory Flags */
#define GMEM_FIXED             0x0000
#define GMEM_MOVEABLE          0x0002
#define GMEM_NOCOMPACT         0x0010
#define GMEM_NODISCARD         0x0020
#define GMEM_ZEROINIT          0x0040
#define GMEM_MODIFY            0x0080
#define GMEM_DISCARDABLE       0x0100
#define GMEM_NOT_BANKED        0x1000
#define GMEM_SHARE             0x2000
#define GMEM_DDESHARE          0x2000
#define GMEM_NOTIFY            0x4000
#define GMEM_LOWER             GMEM_NOT_BANKED

#define GHND              (GMEM_MOVEABLE | GMEM_ZEROINIT)
#define GPTR              (GMEM_FIXED | GMEM_ZEROINIT)

#define GlobalDiscard(h) GlobalReAlloc(h, 0L, GMEM_MOVEABLE)

HANDLE  API GlobalAlloc(WORD, DWORD);
DWORD   API GlobalCompact(DWORD);
HANDLE  API GlobalFree(HANDLE);
DWORD   API GlobalHandle(WORD);
LPSTR   API GlobalLock(HANDLE);
HANDLE  API GlobalReAlloc(HANDLE, DWORD, WORD);
DWORD   API GlobalSize(HANDLE);
BOOL    API GlobalUnlock(HANDLE);
WORD    API GlobalFlags(HANDLE);
LPSTR   API GlobalWire(HANDLE);
BOOL    API GlobalUnWire(HANDLE);
HANDLE  API GlobalLRUNewest(HANDLE);
HANDLE  API GlobalLRUOldest(HANDLE);
VOID    API GlobalNotify(FARPROC);
WORD    API GlobalPageLock(HANDLE);
WORD    API GlobalPageUnlock(HANDLE);
VOID    API GlobalFix(HANDLE);
BOOL    API GlobalUnfix(HANDLE);
DWORD   API GlobalDosAlloc(DWORD);
WORD    API GlobalDosFree(WORD);
```

```
/* Flags returned by GlobalFlags (in addition to GMEM_DISCARDABLE) */
#define GMEM_DISCARDED          0x4000
#define GMEM_LOCKCOUNT          0x00FF

#define LockData(dummy)         LockSegment(0xFFFF)
#define UnlockData(dummy)       UnlockSegment(0xFFFF)

HANDLE API LockSegment(WORD);
HANDLE API UnlockSegment(WORD);

#ifdef WIN31

#define GlobalAllocPtr(flags, cb)  \
    ((VOID FAR*)MAKELP(GlobalAlloc((flags), (cb)), 0))
#define GlobalReAllocPtr(lp, cbNew, flags)  \
    ((BOOL)GlobalReAlloc((HANDLE)SELECTOROF(lp), (cbNew), (flags)))
#define GlobalFreePtr(lp)          \
    ((BOOL)GlobalFree((HANDLE)SELECTOROF(lp)))
#define GlobalLockPtr(lp)          \
    ((BOOL)SELECTOROF(GlobalLock((HANDLE)SELECTOROF(lp))))
#define GlobalUnlockPtr(lp)        \
    GlobalUnlock((HANDLE)SELECTOROF(lp))

#endif  /* WIN31 */

/* Local Memory Flags */
#define LMEM_FIXED              0x0000
#define LMEM_MOVEABLE           0x0002
#define LMEM_NOCOMPACT          0x0010
#define LMEM_NODISCARD          0x0020
#define LMEM_ZEROINIT           0x0040
#define LMEM_MODIFY             0x0080
#define LMEM_DISCARDABLE        0x0F00

#define LHND     (LMEM_MOVEABLE | LMEM_ZEROINIT)
#define LPTR     (LMEM_FIXED | LMEM_ZEROINIT)

#define NONZEROLHND      (LMEM_MOVEABLE)
#define NONZEROLPTR      (LMEM_FIXED)

#define LNOTIFY_OUTOFMEM        0
#define LNOTIFY_MOVE            1
#define LNOTIFY_DISCARD         2

#define LocalDiscard(h)     LocalReAlloc(h, 0, LMEM_MOVEABLE)

HANDLE  API LocalAlloc(WORD, WORD);
WORD    API LocalCompact(WORD);
HANDLE  API LocalFree(HANDLE);
HANDLE  API LocalHandle(WORD);
BOOL    API LocalInit( WORD, WORD, WORD);
char NEAR * API LocalLock(HANDLE);
FARPROC API LocalNotify(FARPROC);
HANDLE  API LocalReAlloc(HANDLE, WORD, WORD);
WORD    API LocalSize(HANDLE);
BOOL    API LocalUnlock(HANDLE);
WORD    API LocalFlags(HANDLE);
WORD    API LocalShrink(HANDLE, WORD);

/* Flags returned by LocalFlags (in addition to LMEM_DISCARDABLE) */
#define LMEM_DISCARDED          0x4000
#define LMEM_LOCKCOUNT          0x00FF

#endif /* NOMEMMGR */

LONG    API SetSwapAreaSize(WORD);
VOID    API ValidateFreeSpaces(void);
VOID    API LimitEmsPages(DWORD);
BOOL    API SetErrorMode(WORD);
```

```
VOID     API ValidateCodeSegments(void);

#define UnlockResource(h)  GlobalUnlock(h)

HANDLE  API FindResource(HANDLE, LPSTR, LPSTR);
HANDLE  API LoadResource(HANDLE, HANDLE);
BOOL    API FreeResource(HANDLE);
LPSTR   API LockResource(HANDLE);
FARPROC API SetResourceHandler(HANDLE, LPSTR, FARPROC);
HANDLE  API AllocResource(HANDLE, HANDLE, DWORD);
DWORD   API SizeofResource(HANDLE, HANDLE);
int     API AccessResource(HANDLE, HANDLE);

#define MAKEINTRESOURCE(i)  (LPSTR)((DWORD)((WORD)(i)))

#ifndef NORESOURCE

#define DIFFERENCE  11

/* Predefined Resource Types */
#define RT_CURSOR        MAKEINTRESOURCE(1)
#define RT_BITMAP        MAKEINTRESOURCE(2)
#define RT_ICON          MAKEINTRESOURCE(3)
#define RT_MENU          MAKEINTRESOURCE(4)
#define RT_DIALOG        MAKEINTRESOURCE(5)
#define RT_STRING        MAKEINTRESOURCE(6)
#define RT_FONTDIR       MAKEINTRESOURCE(7)
#define RT_FONT          MAKEINTRESOURCE(8)
#define RT_ACCELERATOR   MAKEINTRESOURCE(9)
#define RT_RCDATA        MAKEINTRESOURCE(10)
/* NOTE: if any new resource types are introduced above this point, then the
** value of DIFFERENCE must be changed.
** (RT_GROUP_CURSOR - RT_CURSOR) must always be equal to DIFFERENCE
** (RT_GROUP_ICON - RT_ICON) must always be equal to DIFFERENCE
*/
#define RT_GROUP_CURSOR (RT_CURSOR + DIFFERENCE)
/* The value 13 is intentionally unused */
#define RT_GROUP_ICON   (RT_ICON + DIFFERENCE)


#endif /* NORESOURCE */

void   API Yield(void);
HANDLE API GetCurrentTask(void);

WORD   API AllocSelector(WORD);
WORD   API FreeSelector(WORD);
WORD   API AllocDStoCSAlias(WORD);
WORD   API ChangeSelector(WORD sourceSel, WORD destSel);

#ifndef NOATOM
typedef WORD     ATOM;

#define MAKEINTATOM(i)     (LPSTR)((DWORD)((WORD)(i)))

BOOL    API InitAtomTable(int);
ATOM    API AddAtom(LPSTR);
ATOM    API DeleteAtom(ATOM);
ATOM    API FindAtom(LPSTR);
WORD    API GetAtomName(ATOM, LPSTR, int);
ATOM    API GlobalAddAtom(LPSTR);
ATOM    API GlobalDeleteAtom(ATOM);
ATOM    API GlobalFindAtom(LPSTR);
WORD    API GlobalGetAtomName(ATOM, LPSTR, int);
HANDLE  API GetAtomHandle(ATOM);

#endif /* NOATOM */

/* User Profile Routines */
```

```
WORD     API GetProfileInt(LPSTR, LPSTR, int);
int      API GetProfileString(LPSTR, LPSTR, LPSTR, LPSTR, int);
BOOL     API WriteProfileString(LPSTR, LPSTR, LPSTR);
WORD     API GetPrivateProfileInt(LPSTR, LPSTR, int, LPSTR);
int      API GetPrivateProfileString(LPSTR, LPSTR, LPSTR, LPSTR, int, LPSTR);
BOOL     API WritePrivateProfileString(LPSTR, LPSTR, LPSTR, LPSTR);

WORD     API GetWindowsDirectory(LPSTR,WORD);
WORD     API GetSystemDirectory(LPSTR,WORD);

/* Catch() and Throw() */
typedef int             CATCHBUF[9];
typedef int FAR         *LPCATCHBUF;

int      API Catch(LPCATCHBUF);
void     API Throw(LPCATCHBUF, int);

void     API SwapRecording(WORD);

#ifdef WIN31

void     API LogError(WORD err, VOID FAR* lpInfo);
void     API LogParamError(WORD err, FARPROC lpfn, VOID FAR* param);

/* LogError and LogParamError constants */

/* Error modifier bits */

#define ERR_WARNING          0x8000
#define ERR_PARAM            0x4000

/* Parameter error values */

#define ERR_BAD_VALUE        0x5001
#define ERR_BAD_FLAGS        0x5002
#define ERR_BAD_INDEX        0x5003
#define ERR_BAD_DVALUE       0x7004
#define ERR_BAD_DFLAGS       0x7005
#define ERR_BAD_DINDEX       0x7006
#define ERR_BAD_PTR          0x7007
#define ERR_BAD_FUNC_PTR     0x7008
#define ERR_BAD_SELECTOR     0x5009
#define ERR_BAD_STRING_PTR   0x700a
#define ERR_BAD_HANDLE       0x700b

/* KERNEL parameter errors */

#define ERR_BAD_HINSTANCE     0x5020
#define ERR_BAD_HMODULE       0x5021
#define ERR_BAD_GLOBAL_HANDLE 0x5022
#define ERR_BAD_LOCAL_HANDLE  0x5023
#define ERR_BAD_ATOM          0x5024

/* USER parameter errors */

#define ERR_BAD_HWND          0x5040
#define ERR_BAD_HMENU         0x5041
#define ERR_BAD_HCURSOR       0x5042
#define ERR_BAD_HICON         0x5043

/* GDI parameter errors */

#define ERR_BAD_COORDS        0x7060
#define ERR_BAD_GDI_OBJECT    0x5061
#define ERR_BAD_HDC           0x5062
#define ERR_BAD_HPEN          0x5063
#define ERR_BAD_HFONT         0x5064
#define ERR_BAD_HBRUSH        0x5065
#define ERR_BAD_HBITMAP       0x5066
```

```
#define ERR_BAD_HRGN          0x5067
#define ERR_BAD_HPALETTE      0x5068

#define ERR_SIZE_MASK         0x3000
#define ERR_SIZE_SHIFT        12
#define ERR_BYTE              0x0000
#define ERR_WORD              0x1000
#define ERR_DWORD             0x3000

/* Debug fill constants */

#define DBGFILL_ALLOC         0xfd
#define DBGFILL_FREE          0xfb
#define DBGFILL_BUFFER        0xf9
#define DBGFILL_STACK         0xf7

#endif  /* WIN31 */

void    API FatalExit(int);
void    API FatalAppExit(WORD, LPSTR);

/* Character Translation Routines */
int     API AnsiToOem(LPSTR, LPSTR);
BOOL    API OemToAnsi(LPSTR, LPSTR);
void    API AnsiToOemBuff(LPSTR, LPSTR, int);
void    API OemToAnsiBuff(LPSTR, LPSTR, int);
LPSTR   API AnsiUpper(LPSTR);
WORD    API AnsiUpperBuff(LPSTR, WORD);
LPSTR   API AnsiLower(LPSTR);
WORD    API AnsiLowerBuff(LPSTR, WORD);
LPSTR   API AnsiNext(LPSTR);
LPSTR   API AnsiPrev(LPSTR, LPSTR);

#ifdef WIN31
#ifndef NODBCS
BOOL API IsDBCSLeadByte( BYTE );
#endif  /* NODBCS */
#endif  /* WIN31 */

/* Keyboard Information Routines */
#ifndef NOKEYBOARDINFO
DWOR    API OemKeyScan(WORD);
WORD    API VkKeyScan(WORD);
int     API GetKeyboardType(int);
int     API GetKBCodePage(void);
int     API GetKeyNameText(LONG, LPSTR, int);
int     API ToAscii(WORD wVirtKey, WORD wScanCode, LPSTR lpKeyState, LPVOID lpChar, WORD wFlags);
#endif

#ifndef NOLANGUAGE
/* Language dependent Routines */
BOOL    FAR  PASCAL IsCharAlpha(char);
BOOL    FAR  PASCAL IsCharAlphaNumeric(char);
BOOL    FAR  PASCAL IsCharUpper(char);
BOOL    FAR  PASCAL IsCharLower(char);
#endif

LONG API GetWinFlags(void);

#define WF_PMODE              0x0001
#define WF_CPU286             0x0002
#define WF_CPU386             0x0004
#define WF_CPU486             0x0008
#define WF_STANDARD           0x0010
#define WF_WIN286             0x0010
#define WF_ENHANCED           0x0020
#define WF_WIN386             0x0020
#define WF_CPU086             0x0040
#define WF_CPU186             0x0080
```

```
#define WF_LARGEFRAME    0x0100
#define WF_SMALLFRAME    0x0200
#define WF_80x87         0x0400
#define WF_PAGING        0x0800
#define WF_WLO           0x8000

/* WEP fSystemExit flag values */
#define WEP_SYSTEM_EXIT 1
#define WEP_FREE_DLL    0

LPSTR API GetDOSEnvironment(void);

#ifdef OEMRESOURCE

/* OEM Resource Ordinal Numbers */
#define OBM_CLOSE        32754
#define OBM_UPARROW      32753
#define OBM_DNARROW      32752
#define OBM_RGARROW      32751
#define OBM_LFARROW      32750
#define OBM_REDUCE       32749
#define OBM_ZOOM         32748
#define OBM_RESTORE      32747
#define OBM_REDUCED      32746
#define OBM_ZOOMD        32745
#define OBM_RESTORED     32744
#define OBM_UPARROWD     32743
#define OBM_DNARROWD     32742
#define OBM_RGARROWD     32741
#define OBM_LFARROWD     32740
#define OBM_MNARROW      32739
#define OBM_COMBO        32738
#ifdef WIN31
#define OBM_UPARROWI     32737
#define OBM_DNARROWI     32736
#define OBM_RGARROWI     32735
#define OBM_LFARROWI     32734
#endif /* WIN31 */

#define OBM_OLD_CLOSE    32767
#define OBM_SIZE         32766
#define OBM_OLD_UPARROW  32765
#define OBM_OLD_DNARROW  32764
#define OBM_OLD_RGARROW  32763
#define OBM_OLD_LFARROW  32762
#define OBM_BTSIZE       32761
#define OBM_CHECK        32760
#define OBM_CHECKBOXES   32759
#define OBM_BTNCORNERS   32758
#define OBM_OLD_REDUCE   32757
#define OBM_OLD_ZOOM     32756
#define OBM_OLD_RESTORE  32755

#define OCR_NORMAL       32512
#define OCR_IBEAM        32513
#define OCR_WAIT         32514
#define OCR_CROSS        32515
#define OCR_UP           32516
#define OCR_SIZE         32640
#define OCR_ICON         32641
#define OCR_SIZENWSE     32642
#define OCR_SIZENESW     32643
#define OCR_SIZEWE       32644
#define OCR_SIZENS       32645
#define OCR_SIZEALL      32646
#define OCR_ICOCUR       32647

#define OIC_SAMPLE       32512
#define OIC_HAND         32513
```

```
#define OIC_QUES          32514
#define OIC_BANG          32515
#define OIC_NOTE          32516

#endif /* OEMRESOURCE */

#endif /* NOKERNEL */

/*-------------------------------------------*/
/* GDI Section                               */
/*-------------------------------------------*/

#ifndef NOGDI

#ifndef NORASTEROPS

/* Binary raster ops */
#define R2_BLACK          1   /*  0        */
#define R2_NOTMERGEPEN    2   /* DPon      */
#define R2_MASKNOTPEN     3   /* DPna      */
#define R2_NOTCOPYPEN     4   /* PN        */
#define R2_MASKPENNOT     5   /* PDna      */
#define R2_NOT            6   /* Dn        */
#define R2_XORPEN         7   /* DPx       */
#define R2_NOTMASKPEN     8   /* DPan      */
#define R2_MASKPEN        9   /* DPa       */
#define R2_NOTXORPEN     10   /* DPxn      */
#define R2_NOP           11   /* D         */
#define R2_MERGENOTPEN   12   /* DPno      */
#define R2_COPYPEN       13   /* P         */
#define R2_MERGEPENNOT   14   /* PDno      */
#define R2_MERGEPEN      15   /* DPo       */
#define R2_WHITE         16   /*  1        */

/*  Ternary raster operations */
#define SRCCOPY          (DWORD)0x00CC0020 /* dest = source                   */
#define SRCPAINT         (DWORD)0x00EE0086 /* dest = source OR dest           */
#define SRCAND           (DWORD)0x008800C6 /* dest = source AND dest          */
#define SRCINVERT        (DWORD)0x00660046 /* dest = source XOR dest          */
#define SRCERASE         (DWORD)0x00440328 /* dest = source AND (NOT dest )   */
#define NOTSRCCOPY       (DWORD)0x00330008 /* dest = (NOT source)             */
#define NOTSRCERASE      (DWORD)0x001100A6 /* dest = (NOT src) AND (NOT dest) */
#define MERGECOPY        (DWORD)0x00C000CA /* dest = (source AND pattern)     */
#define MERGEPAINT       (DWORD)0x00BB0226 /* dest = (NOT source) OR dest     */
#define PATCOPY          (DWORD)0x00F00021 /* dest = pattern                  */
#define PATPAINT         (DWORD)0x00FB0A09 /* dest = DPSnoo                    */
#define PATINVERT        (DWORD)0x005A0049 /* dest = pattern XOR dest         */
#define DSTINVERT        (DWORD)0x00550009 /* dest = (NOT dest)               */
#define BLACKNESS        (DWORD)0x00000042 /* dest = BLACK                    */
#define WHITENESS        (DWORD)0x00FF0062 /* dest = WHITE                    */

#endif /* NORASTEROPS */

/* StretchBlt() Modes */
#define BLACKONWHITE      1
#define WHITEONBLACK      2
#define COLORONCOLOR      3

/* PolyFill() Modes */
#define ALTERNATE         1
#define WINDING           2

/* Text Alignment Options */
#define TA_NOUPDATECP     0x0000
#define TA_UPDATECP       0x0001

#define TA_LEFT           0x0000
#define TA_RIGHT          0x0002
#define TA_CENTER         0x0006
```

```
#define TA_TOP                       0x0000
#define TA_BOTTOM                    0x0008
#define TA_BASELINE                  0x0018

#define ETO_GRAYED        1
#define ETO_OPAQUE        2
#define ETO_CLIPPED       4

#define ASPECT_FILTERING             0x0001

#ifndef NOMETAFILE

/* Metafile Functions */
#define META_SETBKCOLOR              0x0201
#define META_SETBKMODE               0x0102
#define META_SETMAPMODE              0x0103
#define META_SETROP2                 0x0104
#define META_SETRELABS               0x0105
#define META_SETPOLYFILLMODE         0x0106
#define META_SETSTRETCHBLTMODE       0x0107
#define META_SETTEXTCHAREXTRA        0x0108
#define META_SETTEXTCOLOR            0x0209
#define META_SETTEXTJUSTIFICATION    0x020A
#define META_SETWINDOWORG            0x020B
#define META_SETWINDOWEXT            0x020C
#define META_SETVIEWPORTORG          0x020D
#define META_SETVIEWPORTEXT          0x020E
#define META_OFFSETWINDOWORG         0x020F
#define META_SCALEWINDOWEXT          0x0400
#define META_OFFSETVIEWPORTORG       0x0211
#define META_SCALEVIEWPORTEXT        0x0412
#define META_LINETO                  0x0213
#define META_MOVETO                  0x0214
#define META_EXCLUDECLIPRECT         0x0415
#define META_INTERSECTCLIPRECT       0x0416
#define META_ARC                     0x0817
#define META_ELLIPSE                 0x0418
#define META_FLOODFILL               0x0419
#define META_PIE                     0x081A
#define META_RECTANGLE               0x041B
#define META_ROUNDRECT               0x061C
#define META_PATBLT                  0x061D
#define META_SAVEDC                  0x001E
#define META_SETPIXEL                0x041F
#define META_OFFSETCLIPRGN           0x0220
#define META_TEXTOUT                 0x0521
#define META_BITBLT                  0x0922
#define META_STRETCHBLT              0x0B23
#define META_POLYGON                 0x0324
#define META_POLYLINE                0x0325
#define META_ESCAPE                  0x0626
#define META_RESTOREDC               0x0127
#define META_FILLREGION              0x0228
#define META_FRAMEREGION             0x0429
#define META_INVERTREGION            0x012A
#define META_PAINTREGION             0x012B
#define META_SELECTCLIPREGION        0x012C
#define META_SELECTOBJECT            0x012D
#define META_SETTEXTALIGN            0x012E
#define META_DRAWTEXT                0x062F

#define META_CHORD                   0x0830
#define META_SETMAPPERFLAGS          0x0231
#define META_EXTTEXTOUT              0x0a32
#define META_SETDIBTODEV             0x0d33
#define META_SELECTPALETTE           0x0234
#define META_REALIZEPALETTE          0x0035
#define META_ANIMATEPALETTE          0x0436
#define META_SETPALENTRIES           0x0037
```

```
#define META_POLYPOLYGON              0x0538
#define META_RESIZEPALETTE            0x0139

#define META_DIBBITBLT                0x0940
#define META_DIBSTRETCHBLT            0x0b41
#define META_DIBCREATEPATTERNBRUSH    0x0142
#define META_STRETCHDIB               0x0f43

#define META_DELETEOBJECT             0x01f0

#define META_CREATEPALETTE            0x00f7
#define META_CREATEBRUSH              0x00F8
#define META_CREATEPATTERNBRUSH       0x01F9
#define META_CREATEPENINDIRECT        0x02FA
#define META_CREATEFONTINDIRECT       0x02FB
#define META_CREATEBRUSHINDIRECT      0x02FC
#define META_CREATEBITMAPINDIRECT     0x02FD
#define META_CREATEBITMAP             0x06FE
#define META_CREATEREGION             0x06FF

#endif /* NOMETAFILE */

/* GDI Escapes */
#define NEWFRAME                1
#define ABORTDOC                2
#define NEXTBAND                3
#define SETCOLORTABLE           4
#define GETCOLORTABLE           5
#define FLUSHOUTPUT             6
#define DRAFTMODE               7
#define QUERYESCSUPPORT         8
#define SETABORTPROC            9
#define STARTDOC                10
#define ENDDOC                  11
#define GETPHYSPAGESIZE         12
#define GETPRINTINGOFFSET       13
#define GETSCALINGFACTOR14
#define MFCOMMENT               15
#define GETPENWIDTH             16
#define SETCOPYCOUNT            17
#define SELECTPAPERSOURCE       18
#define DEVICEDATA              19
#define PASSTHROUGH             19
#define GETTECHNOLGY            20
#define GETTECHNOLOGY           20
#define SETENDCAP               21
#define SETLINEJOIN             22
#define SETMITERLIMIT           23
#define BANDINFO                24
#define DRAWPATTERNRECT         25
#define GETVECTORPENSIZE        26
#define GETVECTORBRUSHSIZE      27
#define ENABLEDUPLEX            28
#define GETSETPAPERBINS         29
#define GETSETPRINTORIENT       30
#define ENUMPAPERBINS           31
#define SETDIBSCALING           32
#define EPSPRINTING             33
#define ENUMPAPERMETRICS        34
#define GETSETPAPERMETRICS      35
#define POSTSCRIPT_DATA         37
#define POSTSCRIPT_IGNORE       38
#define MOUSETRAILS             39

#define GETEXTENDEDTEXTMETRICS  256
#define GETEXTENTTABLE          257
#define GETPAIRKERNTABLE        258
#define GETTRACKKERNTABLE       259
#define EXTTEXTOUT              512
```

```
#define ENABLERELATIVEWIDTHS      768
#define ENABLEPAIRKERNING         769
#define SETKERNTRACK              770
#define SETALLJUSTVALUES          771
#define SETCHARSET                772

#define GETSETSCREENPARAMS        800

#define STRETCHBLT                2048
#define BEGIN_PATH                4096
#define CLIP_TO_PATH              4097
#define END_PATH                  4098
#define EXT_DEVICE_CAPS           4099
#define RESTORE_CTM               4100
#define SAVE_CTM                  4101
#define SET_ARC_DIRECTION         4102
#define SET_BACKGROUND_COLOR      4103
#define SET_POLY_MODE             4104
#define SET_SCREEN_ANGLE          4105
#define SET_SPREAD                4106
#define TRANSFORM_CTM             4107
#define SET_CLIP_BOX              4108
#define SET_BOUNDS                4109

/* Spooler Error Codes */
#define SP_NOTREPORTED            0x4000
#define SP_ERROR                  (-1)
#define SP_APPABORT               (-2)
#define SP_USERABORT              (-3)
#define SP_OUTOFDISK              (-4)
#define SP_OUTOFMEMORY            (-5)

#define PR_JOBSTATUS              0x0000

/* Object Definitions for EnumObjects() */
#define OBJ_PEN                   1
#define OBJ_BRUSH                 2

/* Bitmap Header Definition */
typedef struct tagBITMAP
  {
    int         bmType;
    int         bmWidth;
    int         bmHeight;
    int         bmWidthBytes;
    BYTE        bmPlanes;
    BYTE        bmBitsPixel;
    LPSTR       bmBits;
  } BITMAP;
typedef BITMAP         *PBITMAP;
typedef BITMAP NEAR    *NPBITMAP;
typedef BITMAP FAR     *LPBITMAP;

typedef struct tagRGBTRIPLE {
      BYTE       rgbtBlue;
      BYTE       rgbtGreen;
      BYTE       rgbtRed;
} RGBTRIPLE;

typedef struct tagRGBQUAD {
      BYTE       rgbBlue;
      BYTE       rgbGreen;
      BYTE       rgbRed;
      BYTE       rgbReserved;
} RGBQUAD;

/* structures for defining DIBs */
typedef struct tagBITMAPCOREHEADER {
```

```
        DWORD      bcSize;                    /* used to get to color table */
        WORD       bcWidth;
        WORD       bcHeight;
        WORD       bcPlanes;
        WORD       bcBitCount;
} BITMAPCOREHEADER;
typedef BITMAPCOREHEADER FAR     *LPBITMAPCOREHEADER;
typedef BITMAPCOREHEADER         *PBITMAPCOREHEADER;


typedef struct tagBITMAPINFOHEADER{
        DWORD      biSize;
        DWORD      biWidth;
        DWORD      biHeight;
        WORD       biPlanes;
        WORD       biBitCount;

        DWORD      biCompression;
        DWORD      biSizeImage;
        DWORD      biXPelsPerMeter;
        DWORD      biYPelsPerMeter;
        DWORD      biClrUsed;
        DWORD      biClrImportant;
} BITMAPINFOHEADER;

typedef BITMAPINFOHEADER FAR     *LPBITMAPINFOHEADER;
typedef BITMAPINFOHEADER         *PBITMAPINFOHEADER;

/* constants for the biCompression field */
#define BI_RGB   0L
#define BI_RLE8  1L
#define BI_RLE4  2L

typedef struct tagBITMAPINFO {
   BITMAPINFOHEADER      bmiHeader;
   RGBQUAD               bmiColors[1];
} BITMAPINFO;
typedef BITMAPINFO FAR           *LPBITMAPINFO;
typedef BITMAPINFO               *PBITMAPINFO;

typedef struct tagBITMAPCOREINFO {
   BITMAPCOREHEADER      bmciHeader;
   RGBTRIPLE             bmciColors[1];
} BITMAPCOREINFO;
typedef BITMAPCOREINFO FAR       *LPBITMAPCOREINFO;
typedef BITMAPCOREINFO           *PBITMAPCOREINFO;

typedef struct tagBITMAPFILEHEADER {
        WORD       bfType;
        DWORD      bfSize;
        WORD       bfReserved1;
        WORD       bfReserved2;
        DWORD      bfOffBits;
} BITMAPFILEHEADER;
typedef BITMAPFILEHEADER FAR     *LPBITMAPFILEHEADER;
typedef BITMAPFILEHEADER         *PBITMAPFILEHEADER;

#define MAKEPOINT(l)        (*((POINT FAR *)&(l)))

#ifndef NOMETAFILE

/* Clipboard Metafile Picture Structure */
typedef struct tagHANDLETABLE
  {
   HANDLE        objectHandle[1];
  } HANDLETABLE;
typedef HANDLETABLE              *PHANDLETABLE;
typedef HANDLETABLE FAR          *LPHANDLETABLE;
```

```
typedef struct tagMETARECORD
  {
    DWORD        rdSize;
    WORD         rdFunction;
    WORD         rdParm[1];
  } METARECORD;
typedef METARECORD                *PMETARECORD;
typedef METARECORD FAR            *LPMETARECORD;

typedef struct tagMETAFILEPICT
  {
    int          mm;
    int          xExt;
    int          yExt;
    HANDLE       hMF;
  } METAFILEPICT;
typedef METAFILEPICT FAR          *LPMETAFILEPICT;

typedef struct tagMETAHEADER
{
    WORD         mtType;
    WORD         mtHeaderSize;
    WORD         mtVersion;
    DWORD        mtSize;
    WORD         mtNoObjects;
    DWORD        mtMaxRecord;
    WORD         mtNoParameters;
} METAHEADER;

#endif /* NOMETAFILE */

#ifndef NOTEXTMETRIC

typedef struct tagTEXTMETRIC
  {
    int   tmHeight;
    int   tmAscent;
    int   tmDescent;
    int   tmInternalLeading;
    int   tmExternalLeading;
    int   tmAveCharWidth;
    int   tmMaxCharWidth;
    int   tmWeight;
    BYTE  tmItalic;
    BYTE  tmUnderlined;
    BYTE  tmStruckOut;
    BYTE  tmFirstChar;
    BYTE  tmLastChar;
    BYTE  tmDefaultChar;
    BYTE  tmBreakChar;
    BYTE  tmPitchAndFamily;
    BYTE  tmCharSet;
    int   tmOverhang;
    int   tmDigitizedAspectX;
    int   tmDigitizedAspectY;
  } TEXTMETRIC;
typedef TEXTMETRIC                *PTEXTMETRIC;
typedef TEXTMETRIC NEAR           *NPTEXTMETRIC;
typedef TEXTMETRIC FAR            *LPTEXTMETRIC;


typedef struct tagNEWTEXTMETRIC
  {
    int   tmHeight;
    int   tmAscent;
    int   tmDescent;
    int   tmInternalLeading;
    int   tmExternalLeading;
    int   tmAveCharWidth;
```

```
      int    tmMaxCharWidth;
      int    tmWeight;
      BYTE   tmItalic;
      BYTE   tmUnderlined;
      BYTE   tmStruckOut;
      BYTE   tmFirstChar;
      BYTE   tmLastChar;
      BYTE   tmDefaultChar;
      BYTE   tmBreakChar;
      BYTE   tmPitchAndFamily;
      BYTE   tmCharSet;
      int    tmOverhang;
      int    tmDigitizedAspectX;
      int    tmDigitizedAspectY;
      DWORD          ntmFlags;          /* various flags (fsSelection) */
      WORD           ntmSizeEM;         /* size of EM */
      WORD           ntmCellHeight;     /* height of font in notional units */
      WORD           ntmAvgWidth;       /* average with in notional units */
    } NEWTEXTMETRIC;
typedef NEWTEXTMETRIC               *PNEWTEXTMETRIC;
typedef NEWTEXTMETRIC NEAR          *NPNEWTEXTMETRIC;
typedef NEWTEXTMETRIC FAR           *LPNEWTEXTMETRIC;

#define NTM_REGULAR      0x00000040    /* possible ntmFlags bits */
#define NTM_BOLD         0x00000020
#define NTM_ITALIC       0x00000001

#endif /* NOTEXTMETRIC */

/* GDI Logical Objects: */

/* Pel Array */
typedef struct tagPELARRAY
  {
    int  paXCount;
    int  paYCount;
    int  paXExt;
    int  paYExt;
    BYTE paRGBs;
  } PELARRAY;
typedef PELARRAY          *PPELARRAY;
typedef PELARRAY NEAR     *NPPELARRAY;
typedef PELARRAY FAR      *LPPELARRAY;

/* Logical Brush (or Pattern) */
typedef struct tagLOGBRUSH
  {
    WORD          lbStyle;
    DWORD         lbColor;
    int           lbHatch;
  } LOGBRUSH;
typedef LOGBRUSH          *PLOGBRUSH;
typedef LOGBRUSH NEAR     *NPLOGBRUSH;
typedef LOGBRUSH FAR      *LPLOGBRUSH;

typedef LOGBRUSH          PATTERN;
typedef PATTERN           *PPATTERN;
typedef PATTERN NEAR      *NPPATTERN;
typedef PATTERN FAR       *LPPATTERN;

/* Logical Pen */
typedef struct tagLOGPEN
  {
    WORD          lopnStyle;
    POINT         lopnWidth;
    DWORD         lopnColor;
  } LOGPEN;
typedef LOGPEN           *PLOGPEN;
typedef LOGPEN NEAR      *NPLOGPEN;
```

```
typedef LOGPEN FAR        *LPLOGPEN;


typedef struct tagPALETTEENTRY {
   BYTE         peRed;
   BYTE         peGreen;
   BYTE         peBlue;
   BYTE         peFlags;
} PALETTEENTRY;
typedef PALETTEENTRY FAR          *LPPALETTEENTRY;

/* Logical Palette */
typedef struct tagLOGPALETTE {
   WORD         palVersion;
   WORD         palNumEntries;
   PALETTEENTRY palPalEntry[1];
} LOGPALETTE;
typedef LOGPALETTE        *PLOGPALETTE;
typedef LOGPALETTE NEAR   *NPLOGPALETTE;
typedef LOGPALETTE FAR    *LPLOGPALETTE;

/* Logical Font */
#define LF_FACESIZE        32

typedef struct tagLOGFONT
  {
   int  lfHeight;
   int  lfWidth;
   int  lfEscapement;
   int  lfOrientation;
   int  lfWeight;
   BYTE lfItalic;
   BYTE lfUnderline;
   BYTE lfStrikeOut;
   BYTE lfCharSet;
   BYTE lfOutPrecision;
   BYTE lfClipPrecision;
   BYTE lfQuality;
   BYTE lfPitchAndFamily;
   BYTE lfFaceName[LF_FACESIZE];
  } LOGFONT;
typedef LOGFONT           *PLOGFONT;
typedef LOGFONT NEAR      *NPLOGFONT;
typedef LOGFONT FAR       *LPLOGFONT;

#define OUT_DEFAULT_PRECIS      0
#define OUT_STRING_PRECIS       1
#define OUT_CHARACTER_PRECIS    2
#define OUT_STROKE_PRECIS       3

#define CLIP_DEFAULT_PRECIS     0
#define CLIP_CHARACTER_PRECIS   1
#define CLIP_STROKE_PRECIS      2

#define DEFAULT_QUALITY         0
#define DRAFT_QUALITY           1
#define PROOF_QUALITY           2

#define DEFAULT_PITCH           0
#define FIXED_PITCH             1
#define VARIABLE_PITCH          2

#define ANSI_CHARSET            0
#define SYMBOL_CHARSET          2
#define SHIFTJIS_CHARSET        128
#define OEM_CHARSET             255

/* Font Families */
#define FF_DONTCARE     (0<<4)  /* Don't care or don't know. */
```

```
#define FF_ROMAN          (1<<4)  /* Variable stroke width, serifed. */
                                  /* Times Roman, Century Schoolbook, etc. */
#define FF_SWISS          (2<<4)  /* Variable stroke width, sans-serifed. */
                                  /* Helvetica, Swiss, etc. */
#define FF_MODERN         (3<<4)  /* Constant stroke width, serifed or sans-serifed. */
                                  /* Pica, Elite, Courier, etc. */
#define FF_SCRIPT         (4<<4)  /* Cursive, etc. */
#define FF_DECORATIVE     (5<<4)  /* Old English, etc. */

/* Font Weights */
#define FW_DONTCARE       0
#define FW_THIN           100
#define FW_EXTRALIGHT     200
#define FW_LIGHT          300
#define FW_NORMAL         400
#define FW_MEDIUM         500
#define FW_SEMIBOLD       600
#define FW_BOLD           700
#define FW_EXTRABOLD      800
#define FW_HEAVY          900

#define FW_ULTRALIGHT     FW_EXTRALIGHT
#define FW_REGULAR        FW_NORMAL
#define FW_DEMIBOLD       FW_SEMIBOLD
#define FW_ULTRABOLD      FW_EXTRABOLD
#define FW_BLACK          FW_HEAVY

/* EnumFonts Masks */
#define RASTER_FONTTYPE       0x0001
#define DEVICE_FONTTYPE       0X0002
#define SCALABLE_FONTTYPE     0x0004

#define RGB(r,g,b)        ((DWORD)(((BYTE)(r)|((WORD)(g)<<8))|(((DWORD)(BYTE)(b))<<16)))
#define PALETTERGB(r,g,b) (0x02000000 | RGB(r,g,b))
#define PALETTEINDEX(i)   ((DWORD)(0x01000000 | (WORD)(i)))

#define GetRValue(rgb)    ((BYTE)(rgb))
#define GetGValue(rgb)    ((BYTE)(((WORD)(rgb)) >> 8))
#define GetBValue(rgb)    ((BYTE)((rgb)>>16))

/* Background Modes */
#define TRANSPARENT       1
#define OPAQUE            2

/* Mapping Modes */
#define MM_TEXT           1
#define MM_LOMETRIC       2
#define MM_HIMETRIC       3
#define MM_LOENGLISH      4
#define MM_HIENGLISH      5
#define MM_TWIPS          6
#define MM_ISOTROPIC      7
#define MM_ANISOTROPIC    8

/* Coordinate Modes */
#define ABSOLUTE          1
#define RELATIVE          2

/* Stock Logical Objects */
#define WHITE_BRUSH       0
#define LTGRAY_BRUSH      1
#define GRAY_BRUSH        2
#define DKGRAY_BRUSH      3
#define BLACK_BRUSH       4
#define NULL_BRUSH        5
#define HOLLOW_BRUSH      NULL_BRUSH
#define WHITE_PEN         6
#define BLACK_PEN         7
#define NULL_PEN          8
```

```
#define OEM_FIXED_FONT          10
#define ANSI_FIXED_FONT         11
#define ANSI_VAR_FONT           12
#define SYSTEM_FONT             13
#define DEVICE_DEFAULT_FONT     14
#define DEFAULT_PALETTE         15
#define SYSTEM_FIXED_FONT       16


/* Brush Styles */
#define BS_SOLID        0
#define BS_NULL         1
#define BS_HOLLOW       BS_NULL
#define BS_HATCHED      2
#define BS_PATTERN      3
#define BS_INDEXED      4
#define BS_DIBPATTERN   5


/* Hatch Styles */
#define HS_HORIZONTAL   0       /* ññ */
#define HS_VERTICAL     1       /* ||||| */
#define HS_FDIAGONAL    2       /* \\\\\ */
#define HS_BDIAGONAL    3       /* ///// */
#define HS_CROSS        4       /* +++++ */
#define HS_DIAGCROSS    5       /* xxxxx */


/* Pen Styles */
#define PS_SOLID        0
#define PS_DASH         1       /* ñññ  */
#define PS_DOT          2       /* ....... */
#define PS_DASHDOT      3       /* _._._._ */
#define PS_DASHDOTDOT   4       /* _.._.._ */
#define PS_NULL         5
#define PS_INSIDEFRAME  6


/* Device Parameters for GetDeviceCaps() */
#define DRIVERVERSION   0       /* Device driver version                  */
#define TECHNOLOGY      2       /* Device classification                  */
#define HORZSIZE        4       /* Horizontal size in millimeters         */
#define VERTSIZE        6       /* Vertical size in millimeters           */
#define HORZRES         8       /* Horizontal width in pixels             */
#define VERTRES         10      /* Vertical width in pixels               */
#define BITSPIXEL       12      /* Number of bits per pixel               */
#define PLANES          14      /* Number of planes                       */
#define NUMBRUSHES      16      /* Number of brushes the device has       */
#define NUMPENS         18      /* Number of pens the device has          */
#define NUMMARKERS      20      /* Number of markers the device has       */
#define NUMFONTS        22      /* Number of fonts the device has         */
#define NUMCOLORS       24      /* Number of colors the device supports   */
#define PDEVICESIZE     26      /* Size required for device descriptor    */
#define CURVECAPS       28      /* Curve capabilities                     */
#define LINECAPS        30      /* Line capabilities                      */
#define POLYGONALCAPS   32      /* Polygonal capabilities                 */
#define TEXTCAPS        34      /* Text capabilities                      */
#define CLIPCAPS        36      /* Clipping capabilities                  */
#define RASTERCAPS      38      /* Bitblt capabilities                    */
#define ASPECTX         40      /* Length of the X leg                    */
#define ASPECTY         42      /* Length of the Y leg                    */
#define ASPECTXY        44      /* Length of the hypotenuse               */

#define LOGPIXELSX      88      /* Logical pixels/inch in X               */
#define LOGPIXELSY      90      /* Logical pixels/inch in Y               */

#define SIZEPALETTE     104     /* Number of entries in physical palette  */
#define NUMRESERVED     106     /* Number of reserved entries in palette  */
#define COLORRES        108     /* Actual color resolution                */

#ifndef NOGDICAPMASKS
```

```
/* Device Capability Masks: */

/* Device Technologies */
#define DT_PLOTTER        0          /* Vector plotter                        */
#define DT_RASDISPLAY     1          /* Raster display                        */
#define DT_RASPRINTER     2          /* Raster printer                        */
#define DT_RASCAMERA      3          /* Raster camera                         */
#define DT_CHARSTREAM     4          /* Character-stream, PLP                  */
#define DT_METAFILE       5          /* Metafile, VDM                         */
#define DT_DISPFILE       6          /* Display-file                          */

/* Curve Capabilities */
#define CC_NONE           0          /* Curves not supported                  */
#define CC_CIRCLES        1          /* Can do circles                        */
#define CC_PIE            2          /* Can do pie wedges                     */
#define CC_CHORD          4          /* Can do chord arcs                     */
#define CC_ELLIPSES       8          /* Can do ellipese                       */
#define CC_WIDE           16         /* Can do wide lines                     */
#define CC_STYLED         32         /* Can do styled lines                   */
#define CC_WIDESTYLED     64         /* Can do wide styled lines              */
#define CC_INTERIORS      128        /* Can do interiors                      */

/* Line Capabilities */
#define LC_NONE           0          /* Lines not supported                   */
#define LC_POLYLINE       2          /* Can do polylines                      */
#define LC_MARKER         4          /* Can do markers                        */
#define LC_POLYMARKER     8          /* Can do polymarkers                    */
#define LC_WIDE           16         /* Can do wide lines                     */
#define LC_STYLED         32         /* Can do styled lines                   */
#define LC_WIDESTYLED     64         /* Can do wide styled lines              */
#define LC_INTERIORS      128        /* Can do interiors                      */

/* Polygonal Capabilities */
#define PC_NONE           0          /* Polygonals not supported              */
#define PC_POLYGON        1          /* Can do polygons                       */
#define PC_RECTANGLE      2          /* Can do rectangles                     */
#define PC_WINDPOLYGON    4          /* Can do winding polygons               */
#define PC_TRAPEZOID      4          /* Can do trapezoids                     */
#define PC_SCANLINE       8          /* Can do scanlines                      */
#define PC_WIDE           16         /* Can do wide borders                   */
#define PC_STYLED         32         /* Can do styled borders                 */
#define PC_WIDESTYLED     64         /* Can do wide styled borders            */
#define PC_INTERIORS      128        /* Can do interiors                      */

/* Polygonal Capabilities */
#define CP_NONE           0          /* No clipping of output                 */
#define CP_RECTANGLE      1          /* Output clipped to rects               */

/* Text Capabilities */
#define TC_OP_CHARACTER   0x0001     /* Can do OutputPrecision    CHARACTER    */
#define TC_OP_STROKE      0x0002     /* Can do OutputPrecision    STROKE       */
#define TC_CP_STROKE      0x0004     /* Can do ClipPrecision      STROKE       */
#define TC_CR_90          0x0008     /* Can do CharRotAbility     90           */
#define TC_CR_ANY         0x0010     /* Can do CharRotAbility     ANY          */
#define TC_SF_X_YINDEP    0x0020     /* Can do ScaleFreedom       X_YINDEPENDENT */
#define TC_SA_DOUBLE      0x0040     /* Can do ScaleAbility       DOUBLE       */
#define TC_SA_INTEGER     0x0080     /* Can do ScaleAbility       INTEGER      */
#define TC_SA_CONTIN      0x0100     /* Can do ScaleAbility       CONTINUOUS   */
#define TC_EA_DOUBLE      0x0200     /* Can do EmboldenAbility    DOUBLE       */
#define TC_IA_ABLE        0x0400     /* Can do ItalisizeAbility   ABLE         */
#define TC_UA_ABLE        0x0800     /* Can do UnderlineAbility   ABLE         */
#define TC_SO_ABLE        0x1000     /* Can do StrikeOutAbility   ABLE         */
#define TC_RA_ABLE        0x2000     /* Can do RasterFontAble     ABLE         */
#define TC_VA_ABLE        0x4000     /* Can do VectorFontAble     ABLE         */
#define TC_RESERVED       0x8000

#endif /* NOGDICAPMASKS */
```

```
/* Raster Capabilities */
#define RC_BITBLT        1           /* Can do standard BLT.          */
#define RC_BANDING       2           /* Device requires banding support */
#define RC_SCALING       4           /* Device requires scaling support */
#define RC_BITMAP64      8           /* Device can support >64K bitmap  */
#define RC_GDI20_OUTPUT  0x0010      /* has 2.0 output calls           */
#define RC_DI_BITMAP     0x0080      /* supports DIB to memory         */
#define RC_PALETTE       0x0100      /* supports a palette             */
#define RC_DIBTODEV      0x0200      /* supports DIBitsToDevice        */
#define RC_BIGFONT       0x0400      /* supports >64K fonts            */
#define RC_STRETCHBLT    0x0800      /* supports StretchBlt            */
#define RC_FLOODFILL     0x1000      /* supports FloodFill             */
#define RC_STRETCHDIB    0x2000      /* supports StretchDIBits         */


/* palette entry flags */

#define PC_RESERVED      0x01        /* palette index used for animation    */
#define PC_EXPLICIT      0x02        /* palette index is explicit to device */
#define PC_NOCOLLAPSE    0x04        /* do not match color to system palette */

/* DIB color table identifiers */

#define DIB_RGB_COLORS   0           /* color table in RGBTriples      */
#define DIB_PAL_COLORS   1           /* color table in palette indices */

/* constants for Get/SetSystemPaletteUse() */

#define SYSPAL_STATIC    1
#define SYSPAL_NOSTATIC 2

/* constants for CreateDIBitmap */
#define CBM_INIT         0x04L       /* initialize bitmap */

#ifndef NODRAWTEXT

/* DrawText() Format Flags */
#define DT_TOP                   0x0000
#define DT_LEFT                  0x0000
#define DT_CENTER                0x0001
#define DT_RIGHT                 0x0002
#define DT_VCENTER               0x0004
#define DT_BOTTOM                0x0008
#define DT_WORDBREAK             0x0010
#define DT_SINGLELINE            0x0020
#define DT_EXPANDTABS            0x0040
#define DT_TABSTOP               0x0080
#define DT_NOCLIP                0x0100
#define DT_EXTERNALLEADING       0x0200
#define DT_CALCRECT              0x0400
#define DT_NOPREFIX              0x0800
#define DT_INTERNAL              0x1000


int     API DrawText(HDC, LPSTR, int, LPRECT, WORD);
BOOL    API DrawIcon(HDC, int, int, HICON);

#endif /* NODRAWTEXT */

/* ExtFloodFill style flags */
#define FLOODFILLBORDER          0
#define FLOODFILLSURFACE         1

HDC     API GetWindowDC(HWND);
HDC     API GetDC(HWND);
int     API ReleaseDC(HWND, HDC);

#ifdef WIN31
```

```
HDC      API GetDCEx(register HWND hwnd, HRGN hrgnClip, DWORD flags);

/* GetDCEx() flags */
#define DCX_WINDOW              0x00000001L
#define DCX_CACHE               0x00000002L
#define DCX_NORESETATTRS        0x00000004L
#define DCX_CLIPCHILDREN        0x00000008L
#define DCX_CLIPSIBLINGS        0x00000010L
#define DCX_PARENTCLIP          0x00000020L

#define DCX_EXCLUDERGN          0x00000040L
#define DCX_INTERSECTRGN        0x00000080L

#define DCX_EXCLUDEUPDATE       0x00000100L
#define DCX_INTERSECTUPDATE     0x00000200L

#define DCX_LOCKWINDOWUPDATE    0x00000400L


#define DCX_USESTYLE            0x00010000L
#define DCX_NORECOMPUTE         0x00100000L
#define DCX_VALIDATE            0x00200000L



#endif  /* WIN31 */


HDC      API CreateDC(LPSTR, LPSTR, LPSTR, LPVOID);
HDC      API CreateIC(LPSTR, LPSTR, LPSTR, LPVOID);
HDC      API CreateCompatibleDC(HDC);
BOOL     API DeleteDC(HDC);
int      API SaveDC(HDC);
BOOL     API RestoreDC(HDC, int);
DWORD    API MoveTo(HDC, int, int);
DWORD    API GetCurrentPosition(HDC);
BOOL     API LineTo(HDC, int, int);
DWORD    API GetDCOrg(HDC);

int      API MulDiv(int, int, int);

BOOL     API ExtTextOut(HDC, int, int, WORD, LPRECT, LPSTR, WORD, LPINT);

BOOL     API Polyline(HDC, LPPOINT, int);
BOOL     API Polygon(HDC, LPPOINT, int);
BOOL     API PolyPolygon(HDC, LPPOINT, LPINT, int);

BOOL     API Rectangle(HDC, int, int, int, int);
BOOL     API RoundRect(HDC, int, int, int, int, int, int);
BOOL     API Ellipse(HDC, int, int, int, int);
BOOL     API Arc(HDC, int, int, int, int, int, int, int, int);
BOOL     API Chord(HDC, int, int, int, int, int, int, int, int);
BOOL     API Pie(HDC, int, int, int, int, int, int, int, int);
BOOL     API PatBlt(HDC, int, int, int, int, DWORD);
BOOL     API BitBlt(HDC, int, int, int, int, HDC, int, int, DWORD);
BOOL     API StretchBlt(HDC, int, int, int, int, HDC, int, int, int, int, DWORD);
BOOL     API TextOut(HDC, int, int, LPSTR, int);
LONG     API TabbedTextOut(HDC, int, int, LPSTR, int, int, LPINT, int);
BOOL     API GetCharWidth(HDC, WORD, WORD, LPINT);
DWORD    API SetPixel( HDC, int, int, DWORD);
DWORD    API GetPixel( HDC, int, int);
BOOL     API FloodFill( HDC, int, int, DWORD);
BOOL     API ExtFloodFill(HDC, int, int, DWORD, WORD);
void     API LineDDA(int, int, int, int, FARPROC, LPSTR);

HANDLE   API GetStockObject(int);

HPEN     API CreatePen(int, int, DWORD);
```

```
HPEN      API CreatePenIndirect(LOGPEN FAR *);

HBRUSH    API CreateSolidBrush(DWORD);
HBRUSH    API CreateHatchBrush(int,DWORD);
DWORD     API SetBrushOrg(HDC, int, int);
DWORD     API GetBrushOrg(HDC);
HBRUSH    API CreatePatternBrush(HBITMAP);
HBRUSH    API CreateBrushIndirect(LOGBRUSH FAR *);

HBITMAP API CreateBitmap(int, int, BYTE, BYTE, LPSTR);
HBITMAP API CreateBitmapIndirect(BITMAP FAR *);
HBITMAP API CreateCompatibleBitmap(HDC, int, int);
HBITMAP API CreateDiscardableBitmap(HDC, int, int);

LONG      API SetBitmapBits(HBITMAP, DWORD, LPSTR);
LONG      API GetBitmapBits(HBITMAP, LONG, LPSTR);
DWORD     API SetBitmapDimension(HBITMAP, int, int);
DWORD     API GetBitmapDimension(HBITMAP);

HFONT     API CreateFont(int, int, int, int, int, BYTE, BYTE, BYTE, BYTE, BYTE, BYTE, BYTE,
BYTE, LPSTR);
HFONT     API CreateFontIndirect(LOGFONT FAR *);

int       API SelectClipRgn(HDC, HRGN);
HRGN      API CreateRectRgn(int, int, int, int);
void      API SetRectRgn(HRGN, int, int, int, int);
HRGN      API CreateRectRgnIndirect(LPRECT);
HRGN      API CreateEllipticRgnIndirect(LPRECT);
HRGN      API CreateEllipticRgn(int, int, int, int);
HRGN      API CreatePolygonRgn(LPPOINT, int, int);
HRGN      API CreatePolyPolygonRgn(LPPOINT, LPINT, int, int);
HRGN      API CreateRoundRectRgn(int, int, int, int, int, int);

BOOL      API IsGDIObject(HANDLE);

int       API GetObject(HANDLE, int, LPVOID);
BOOL      API DeleteObject(HANDLE);
HANDLE    API SelectObject(HDC, HANDLE);
BOOL      API UnrealizeObject(HBRUSH);

DWORD     API SetBkColor(HDC, DWORD);
DWORD     API GetBkColor(HDC);
int       API SetBkMode(HDC, int);
int       API GetBkMode(HDC);
DWORD     API SetTextColor(HDC, DWORD);
DWORD     API GetTextColor(HDC);
WORD      API SetTextAlign(HDC, WORD);
WORD      API GetTextAlign(HDC);
DWORD     API SetMapperFlags(HDC, DWORD);
DWORD     API GetAspectRatioFilter(HDC);
DWORD     API GetNearestColor(HDC, DWORD);
int       API SetROP2(HDC, int);
int       API GetROP2(HDC);
int       API SetStretchBltMode(HDC, int);
int       API GetStretchBltMode(HDC);
int       API SetPolyFillMode(HDC, int);
int       API GetPolyFillMode(HDC);
int       API SetMapMode(HDC, int);
int       API GetMapMode(HDC);
DWORD     API SetWindowOrg(HDC, int, int);
DWORD     API GetWindowOrg(HDC);
DWORD     API SetWindowExt(HDC, int, int);
DWORD     API GetWindowExt(HDC);
DWORD     API SetViewportOrg(HDC, int, int);
DWORD     API GetViewportOrg(HDC);
DWORD     API SetViewportExt(HDC, int, int);
DWORD     API GetViewportExt(HDC);
DWORD     API OffsetViewportOrg(HDC, int, int);
DWORD     API ScaleViewportExt(HDC, int, int, int, int);
```

```
DWORD    API OffsetWindowOrg(HDC, int, int);
DWORD    API ScaleWindowExt(HDC, int, int, int, int);

int      API GetClipBox(HDC, LPRECT);
int      API IntersectClipRect(HDC, int, int, int, int);
int      API OffsetClipRgn(HDC, int, int);
int      API ExcludeClipRect(HDC, int, int, int, int);
BOOL     API PtVisible(HDC, int, int);
int      API CombineRgn(HRGN, HRGN, HRGN, int);
BOOL     API EqualRgn(HRGN, HRGN);
int      API OffsetRgn(HRGN, int, int);
int      API GetRgnBox(HRGN, LPRECT);

#ifdef WIN31

/* Drawing bounds accumulation APIs */
WORD     API SetBoundsRect(HDC hDC, LPRECT lprcBounds, WORD flags);
WORD     API GetBoundsRect(HDC hDC, LPRECT lprcBounds, WORD flags);

#define DCB_RESET        0x0001
#define DCB_ACCUMULATE   0x0002
#define DCB_DIRTY        DCB_ACCUMULATE
#define DCB_SET          (DCB_RESET | DCB_ACCUMULATE)
#define DCB_ENABLE       0x0004
#define DCB_DISABLE      0x0008

#endif /* WIN31 */

int      API SetTextJustification(HDC, int, int);
DWORD    API GetTextExtent(HDC, LPSTR, int);
DWORD    API GetTabbedTextExtent(HDC, LPSTR, int, int, LPINT);
int      API SetTextCharacterExtra(HDC, int);
int      API GetTextCharacterExtra(HDC);

#ifdef WIN31
DWORD    API GetTextExtentEx(HDC, LPSTR, int, int, LPINT, LPINT);
#endif /* WIN31 */

HANDLE   API GetMetaFile(LPSTR);
BOOL     API DeleteMetaFile(HANDLE);
HANDLE   API CopyMetaFile(HANDLE, LPSTR);

#ifndef NOMETAFILE
void     API PlayMetaFileRecord(HDC, LPHANDLETABLE, LPMETARECORD, WORD);
BOOL     API EnumMetaFile(HDC, LOCALHANDLE, FARPROC, BYTE FAR *);
#endif

BOOL     API PlayMetaFile(HDC, HANDLE);
int      API Escape(HDC, int, int, LPSTR, LPSTR);
int      API EnumFonts(HDC, LPSTR, FARPROC, LPSTR);
int      API EnumFontFamilies(HDC, LPSTR, FARPROC, LPSTR);
int      API EnumObjects(HDC, int, FARPROC, LPSTR);
int      API GetTextFace(HDC, int, LPSTR);


#ifndef NOTEXTMETRIC
BOOL     API GetTextMetrics(HDC, LPTEXTMETRIC );
#endif

int      API GetDeviceCaps(HDC, int);

int      API SetEnvironment(LPSTR, LPSTR, WORD);
int      API GetEnvironment(LPSTR, LPSTR, WORD);

BOOL     API DPtoLP(HDC, LPPOINT, int);
BOOL     API LPtoDP(HDC, LPPOINT, int);

HANDLE   API CreateMetaFile(LPSTR);
HANDLE   API CloseMetaFile(HANDLE);
```

```
HANDLE   API GetMetaFileBits(HANDLE);
HANDLE   API SetMetaFileBits(HANDLE);

int      API SetDIBits(HDC,HANDLE,WORD,WORD,LPSTR,LPBITMAPINFO,WORD);
int      API GetDIBits(HDC,HANDLE,WORD,WORD,LPSTR,LPBITMAPINFO,WORD);
int      API SetDIBitsToDevice(HDC,WORD,WORD,WORD,WORD,
                               WORD,WORD,WORD,WORD,
                               LPSTR,LPBITMAPINFO,WORD);
HBITMAP API CreateDIBitmap(HDC,LPBITMAPINFOHEADER,DWORD,LPSTR,
                           LPBITMAPINFO,WORD);
HBRUSH   API CreateDIBPatternBrush(HANDLE,WORD);
int      API StretchDIBits(HDC, WORD, WORD, WORD, WORD, WORD,
             WORD, WORD, WORD, LPSTR, LPBITMAPINFO, WORD, DWORD);

HPALETTE API CreatePalette (LPLOGPALETTE);
HPALETTE API SelectPalette (HDC,HPALETTE, BOOL) ;
WORD     API RealizePalette (HDC) ;
int      API UpdateColors (HDC) ;
void     API AnimatePalette(HPALETTE, WORD, WORD, LPPALETTEENTRY);
WORD     API SetPaletteEntries(HPALETTE,WORD,WORD,LPPALETTEENTRY);
WORD     API GetPaletteEntries(HPALETTE,WORD,WORD,LPPALETTEENTRY);
WORD     API GetNearestPaletteIndex(HPALETTE, DWORD);
BOOL     API ResizePalette(HPALETTE, WORD);

WORD     API GetSystemPaletteEntries(HDC,WORD,WORD,LPPALETTEENTRY);
WORD     API GetSystemPaletteUse(HDC);
WORD     API SetSystemPaletteUse(HDC, WORD);

#ifndef NOSCALABLEFONT

/* GDI scalable font API prototypes and data structures: */

typedef struct _PANOSE { /* panose */
   BYTE bFamilyType;
   BYTE bSerifStyle;
   BYTE bWeight;
   BYTE bProportion;
   BYTE bContrast;
   BYTE bStrokeVariation;
   BYTE bArmStyle;
   BYTE bLetterform;
   BYTE bMidline;
   BYTE bXHeight;
} PANOSE;

#ifndef NOTEXTMETRIC

typedef struct _OUTLINETEXTMETRIC {
   WORD otmSize;                  /* I size of this structure         */
   TEXTMETRIC otmTextMetrics;     /* regular text metrics             */
   BYTE otmFiller;                /* want to be word aligned          */
   PANOSE otmPanoseNumber;        /* Panose number of font            */
   WORD otmfsSelection;           /* B Font selection flags (see #defines) */
   WORD otmfsType;                /* B Type indicators  (see #defines)     */
   WORD otmsCharSlopeRise;        /* Slope angle Rise / Run   1 vertical   */
   WORD otmsCharSlopeRun;         /* O vertical                       */
   WORD otmEMSquare;              /* N size of EM                     */
   WORD otmAscent;                /* D ascent above baseline          */
   WORD otmDescent;               /* D descent below baseline         */
   WORD otmLineGap;               /* D                                */
   WORD otmCapEmHeight;           /* D height of upper case M         */
   WORD otmXHeight;               /* D height of lower case chars in font */
   RECT otmrcFontBox;             /* D Font bounding box              */
   WORD otmMacAscent;             /* D ascent above baseline for Mac  */
   WORD otmMacDescent;            /* D descent below baseline for Mac */
   WORD otmMacLineGap;            /* D                                */
   WORD otmusMinimumPPEM;         /* D Minimum point ppem             */
   POINTotmptSubscriptSize;       /* D Size of subscript              */
   POINTotmptSubscriptOffset;     /* D Offset of subscript            */
```

```
    POINTotmptSuperscriptSize;      /* D Size of superscript      */
    POINTotmptSuperscriptOffset;    /* D Offset of superscript    */
    WORD  otmsStrikeoutSize;        /* D Strikeout size           */
    WORD  otmsStrikeoutPosition;    /* D Strikeout position       */
    WORD  otmsUnderscoreSize;       /* D Underscore size          */
    WORD  otmsUnderscorePosition;   /* D Underscore position      */
    PSTR  otmpFamilyName;           /* offset to family name      */
    PSTR  otmpFaceName;             /* offset to face name        */
    PSTR  otmpStyleName;            /* offset to Style string     */
    PSTR  otmpFullName;             /* offset to full name        */
} OUTLINETEXTMETRIC;

typedef OUTLINETEXTMETRIC        FAR      *LPOUTLINETEXTMETRIC;

#endif /* NOTEXTMETRIC */

typedef struct _FIXED {
    WORD         fract;
    short        value;
} FIXED;

typedef struct _MAT2 {
    FIXED        eM11;
    FIXED        eM12;
    FIXED        eM21;
    FIXED eM22;
} MAT2;

typedef MAT2                     FAR      *LPMAT2;

typedef struct _GLYPHMETRICS {
    WORD         gmBlackBoxX;
    WORD         gmBlackBoxY;
    POINT        gmptGlyphOrigin;
    short        gmCellIncX;
    short        gmCellIncY;
} GLYPHMETRICS;

typedef GLYPHMETRICS             FAR      *LPGLYPHMETRICS;

typedef struct _ABC {
    short        abcA;
    WORD         abcB;
    short        abcC;
} ABC;

typedef ABC                      FAR      *LPABC;
typedef WORD                     FAR      *LPFONTDIR;

typedef struct _RASTERIZER_STATUS {
    short        nSize;
    short        wFlags;
    short        nLanguageID;
} RASTERIZER_STATUS;

typedef RASTERIZER_STATUS        FAR      *LPRASTERIZER_STATUS;

/* bits defined in wFlags of RASTERIZER_STATUS */

#define TT_AVAILABLE      0x0001
#define TT_ENABLED        0x0002

DWORD   API ConvertOutlineFontFile(LPSTR, LPSTR, LPSTR);
DWORD   API GetFontData(HDC, DWORD, DWORD, LPSTR, DWORD);
DWORD   API GetGlyphOutline(HDC, WORD, WORD, LPGLYPHMETRICS, DWORD, LPSTR, LPMAT2);
DWORD   API EngineMakeFontDir(HDC, LPFONTDIR, LPSTR);
BOOL    API CreateScalableFontResource(HDC, LPSTR, LPSTR, LPSTR);
BOOL    API GetCharABCWidths(HDC, WORD, WORD, LPABC);
BOOL    API GetRasterizerCaps(LPRASTERIZER_STATUS, int);
```

```
#ifndef NOTEXTMETRIC

DWORD    API GetOutlineTextMetrics(HDC, WORD, LPOUTLINETEXTMETRIC);

#endif  /* NOTEXTMETRIC */
#endif  /* NOSCALABLEFONT */
#endif  /* NOGDI */


/*------------------------------------- */
/*      USER Section                   */
/*------------------------------------- */

#ifndef NOUSER

int      API wvsprintf(LPSTR,LPSTR,LPSTR);


#ifdef __cplusplus
extern "C"
{
#endif  /* __cplusplus */

int      FAR cdecl wsprintf(LPSTR,LPSTR,...);

#ifdef __cplusplus
}
#endif  /* __cplusplus */

#ifndef NOSCROLL

/* Scroll Bar Constants */
#define SB_HORZ              0
#define SB_VERT              1
#define SB_CTL               2
#define SB_BOTH              3

#define SB_MAX               3

#define ESB_ENABLE_BOTH      0
#define ESB_DISABLE_LTUP     1
#define ESB_DISABLE_RTDN     2
#define ESB_DISABLE_BOTH     3

#define ESB_MAX              3


/* Scroll Bar Commands */
#define SB_LINEUP            0
#define SB_LINEDOWN          1
#define SB_PAGEUP            2
#define SB_PAGEDOWN          3
#define SB_THUMBPOSITION     4
#define SB_THUMBTRACK        5
#define SB_TOP               6
#define SB_BOTTOM            7
#define SB_ENDSCROLL         8


#endif /* NOSCROLL */

#ifndef NOSHOWWINDOW

/* ShowWindow() Commands */
#define SW_HIDE              0
#define SW_SHOWNORMAL        1
#define SW_NORMAL            1
#define SW_SHOWMINIMIZED     2
#define SW_SHOWMAXIMIZED     3
```

```
#define SW_MAXIMIZE            3
#define SW_SHOWNOACTIVATE      4
#define SW_SHOW                5
#define SW_MINIMIZE            6
#define SW_SHOWMINNOACTIVE     7
#define SW_SHOWNA              8
#define SW_RESTORE             9


/* Old ShowWindow() Commands */
#define HIDE_WINDOW            0
#define SHOW_OPENWINDOW        1
#define SHOW_ICONWINDOW        2
#define SHOW_FULLSCREEN        3
#define SHOW_OPENNOACTIVATE    4

/* Identifiers for the WM_SHOWWINDOW message */
#define SW_PARENTCLOSING       1
#define SW_OTHERZOOM           2
#define SW_PARENTOPENING       3
#define SW_OTHERUNZOOM         4

#endif /* NOSHOWWINDOW */

/* Region Flags */
#define ERROR            0
#define NULLREGION       1
#define SIMPLEREGION     2
#define COMPLEXREGION    3

/* CombineRgn() Styles */
#define RGN_AND          1
#define RGN_OR           2
#define RGN_XOR          3
#define RGN_DIFF         4
#define RGN_COPY         5

#ifndef NOVIRTUALKEYCODES

/* Virtual Keys, Standard Set */
#define VK_LBUTTON       0x01
#define VK_RBUTTON       0x02
#define VK_CANCEL        0x03
#define VK_MBUTTON       0x04    /* NOT contiguous with L & RBUTTON */
#define VK_BACK          0x08
#define VK_TAB           0x09
#define VK_CLEAR         0x0C
#define VK_RETURN        0x0D
#define VK_SHIFT         0x10
#define VK_CONTROL       0x11
#define VK_MENU          0x12
#define VK_PAUSE         0x13
#define VK_CAPITAL       0x14
#define VK_ESCAPE        0x1B
#define VK_SPACE         0x20
#define VK_PRIOR         0x21
#define VK_NEXT          0x22
#define VK_END           0x23
#define VK_HOME          0x24
#define VK_LEFT          0x25
#define VK_UP            0x26
#define VK_RIGHT         0x27
#define VK_DOWN          0x28
#define VK_SELECT        0x29
#define VK_PRINT         0x2A
#define VK_EXECUTE       0x2B
#define VK_SNAPSHOT      0x2C
/* #define VK_COPY       0x2C not used by keyboards. */
#define VK_INSERT        0x2D
```

```
#define VK_DELETE          0x2E
#define VK_HELP            0x2F

/* VK_A thru VK_Z are the same as their ASCII equivalents: 'A' thru 'Z' */
/* VK_0 thru VK_9 are the same as their ASCII equivalents: '0' thru '0' */

#define VK_NUMPAD0         0x60
#define VK_NUMPAD1         0x61
#define VK_NUMPAD2         0x62
#define VK_NUMPAD3         0x63
#define VK_NUMPAD4         0x64
#define VK_NUMPAD5         0x65
#define VK_NUMPAD6         0x66
#define VK_NUMPAD7         0x67
#define VK_NUMPAD8         0x68
#define VK_NUMPAD9         0x69
#define VK_MULTIPLY        0x6A
#define VK_ADD             0x6B
#define VK_SEPARATOR       0x6C
#define VK_SUBTRACT        0x6D
#define VK_DECIMAL         0x6E
#define VK_DIVIDE          0x6F
#define VK_F1              0x70
#define VK_F2              0x71
#define VK_F3              0x72
#define VK_F4              0x73
#define VK_F5              0x74
#define VK_F6              0x75
#define VK_F7              0x76
#define VK_F8              0x77
#define VK_F9              0x78
#define VK_F10             0x79
#define VK_F11             0x7A
#define VK_F12             0x7B
#define VK_F13             0x7C
#define VK_F14             0x7D
#define VK_F15             0x7E
#define VK_F16             0x7F

#define VK_NUMLOCK         0x90
#define VK_SCROLL          0x91

#endif /* NOVIRTUALKEYCODES */

typedef struct tagWNDCLASS
  {
    WORD         style;
    LONG         (API *lpfnWndProc)(HWND, unsigned, WORD, LONG);
    int          cbClsExtra;
    int          cbWndExtra;
    HANDLE       hInstance;
    HICON        hIcon;
    HCURSOR      hCursor;
    HBRUSH       hbrBackground;
    LPSTR        lpszMenuName;
    LPSTR        lpszClassName;
  } WNDCLASS;
typedef WNDCLASS          *PWNDCLASS;
typedef WNDCLASS NEAR     *NPWNDCLASS;
typedef WNDCLASS FAR      *LPWNDCLASS;

#ifndef NOMSG

/* Message structure */
typedef struct tagMSG
  {
    HWND         hwnd;
    WORD         message;
    WORD         wParam;
```

```
    LONG          lParam;
    DWORD         time;
    POINT         pt;
 } MSG;
typedef MSG       *PMSG;
typedef MSG NEAR *NPMSG;
typedef MSG FAR  *LPMSG;

#endif /* NOMSG */

#ifndef NOWINOFFSETS

/* Window field offsets for GetWindowLong() and GetWindowWord() */
#define GWL_WNDPROC              (-4)
#define GWW_HINSTANCE            (-6)
#define GWW_HWNDPARENT           (-8)
#define GWW_ID                   (-12)
#define GWL_STYLE                (-16)
#define GWL_EXSTYLE              (-20)

/* Class field offsets for GetClassLong() and GetClassWord() */
#define GCL_MENUNAME             (-8)
#define GCW_HBRBACKGROUND        (-10)
#define GCW_HCURSOR              (-12)
#define GCW_HICON                (-14)
#define GCW_HMODULE              (-16)
#define GCW_CBWNDEXTRA           (-18)
#define GCW_CBCLSEXTRA           (-20)
#define GCL_WNDPROC              (-24)
#define GCW_STYLE                (-26)


#endif /* NOWINOFFSETS */

#ifndef NOWINMESSAGES

/* Window Messages */
#define WM_NULL              0x0000
#define WM_CREATE            0x0001
#define WM_DESTROY           0x0002
#define WM_MOVE              0x0003
#define WM_SIZE              0x0005
#define WM_ACTIVATE          0x0006
#define WM_SETFOCUS          0x0007
#define WM_KILLFOCUS         0x0008
#define WM_ENABLE            0x000A
#define WM_SETREDRAW         0x000B
#define WM_SETTEXT           0x000C
#define WM_GETTEXT           0x000D
#define WM_GETTEXTLENGTH     0x000E
#define WM_PAINT             0x000F
#define WM_CLOSE             0x0010
#define WM_QUERYENDSESSION   0x0011
#define WM_QUIT              0x0012
#define WM_QUERYOPEN         0x0013
#define WM_ERASEBKGND        0x0014
#define WM_SYSCOLORCHANGE    0x0015
#define WM_ENDSESSION        0x0016
#define WM_SHOWWINDOW        0x0018
#define WM_CTLCOLOR          0x0019
#define WM_WININICHANGE      0x001A
#define WM_DEVMODECHANGE     0x001B
#define WM_ACTIVATEAPP       0x001C
#define WM_FONTCHANGE        0x001D
#define WM_TIMECHANGE        0x001E
#define WM_CANCELMODE        0x001F
#define WM_SETCURSOR         0x0020
#define WM_MOUSEACTIVATE     0x0021
#define WM_CHILDACTIVATE     0x0022
```

```
#define WM_QUEUESYNC              0x0023
#define WM_GETMINMAXINFO          0x0024
#define WM_PAINTICON              0x0026
#define WM_ICONERASEBKGND         0x0027
#define WM_NEXTDLGCTL             0x0028
#define WM_SPOOLERSTATUS          0x002A
#define WM_DRAWITEM               0x002B
#define WM_MEASUREITEM            0x002C
#define WM_DELETEITEM             0x002D
#define WM_VKEYTOITEM             0x002E
#define WM_CHARTOITEM             0x002F
#define WM_SETFONT                0x0030
#define WM_GETFONT                0x0031
#define WM_SETHOTKEY              0x0032
#define WM_GETHOTKEY              0x0033
#define WM_QUERYDRAGICON          0x0037

#define WM_COMPAREITEM            0x0039
#define WM_COMPACTING             0x0041

#ifdef WIN31
#define WM_OTHERWINDOWCREATED     0x0042
#define WM_OTHERWINDOWDESTROYED   0x0043
#define WM_COMMNOTIFY             0x0044

#define WM_WINDOWPOSCHANGING      0x0046
#define WM_WINDOWPOSCHANGED       0x0047
#define WM_POWER                  0x0048
#endif  /* WIN31 */

#define WM_NCCREATE               0x0081
#define WM_NCDESTROY              0x0082
#define WM_NCCALCSIZE             0x0083
#define WM_NCHITTEST              0x0084
#define WM_NCPAINT                0x0085
#define WM_NCACTIVATE             0x0086
#define WM_GETDLGCODE             0x0087
#define WM_NCMOUSEMOVE            0x00A0
#define WM_NCLBUTTONDOWN          0x00A1
#define WM_NCLBUTTONUP            0x00A2
#define WM_NCLBUTTONDBLCLK        0x00A3
#define WM_NCRBUTTONDOWN          0x00A4
#define WM_NCRBUTTONUP            0x00A5
#define WM_NCRBUTTONDBLCLK        0x00A6
#define WM_NCMBUTTONDOWN          0x00A7
#define WM_NCMBUTTONUP            0x00A8
#define WM_NCMBUTTONDBLCLK        0x00A9

#define WM_KEYFIRST               0x0100
#define WM_KEYDOWN                0x0100
#define WM_KEYUP                  0x0101
#define WM_CHAR                   0x0102
#define WM_DEADCHAR               0x0103
#define WM_SYSKEYDOWN             0x0104
#define WM_SYSKEYUP               0x0105
#define WM_SYSCHAR                0x0106
#define WM_SYSDEADCHAR            0x0107
#define WM_KEYLAST                0x0108

#define WM_INITDIALOG             0x0110
#define WM_COMMAND                0x0111
#define WM_SYSCOMMAND             0x0112
#define WM_TIMER                  0x0113
#define WM_HSCROLL                0x0114
#define WM_VSCROLL                0x0115
#define WM_INITMENU               0x0116
#define WM_INITMENUPOPUP          0x0117
#define WM_MENUSELECT             0x011F
#define WM_MENUCHAR               0x0120
```

```
#define WM_ENTERIDLE              0x0121


#define WM_MOUSEFIRST             0x0200
#define WM_MOUSEMOVE              0x0200
#define WM_LBUTTONDOWN            0x0201
#define WM_LBUTTONUP              0x0202
#define WM_LBUTTONDBLCLK          0x0203
#define WM_RBUTTONDOWN            0x0204
#define WM_RBUTTONUP              0x0205
#define WM_RBUTTONDBLCLK          0x0206
#define WM_MBUTTONDOWN            0x0207
#define WM_MBUTTONUP              0x0208
#define WM_MBUTTONDBLCLK          0x0209
#define WM_MOUSELAST              0x0209


#define WM_PARENTNOTIFY           0x0210
#define WM_MDICREATE              0x0220
#define WM_MDIDESTROY             0x0221
#define WM_MDIACTIVATE            0x0222
#define WM_MDIRESTORE             0x0223
#define WM_MDINEXT                0x0224
#define WM_MDIMAXIMIZE            0x0225
#define WM_MDITILE                0x0226
#define WM_MDICASCADE             0x0227
#define WM_MDIICONARRANGE         0x0228
#define WM_MDIGETACTIVE           0x0229
#define WM_MDISETMENU             0x0230
#define WM_DROPFILES              0x0233


#define WM_CUT                    0x0300
#define WM_COPY                   0x0301
#define WM_PASTE                  0x0302
#define WM_CLEAR                  0x0303
#define WM_UNDO                   0x0304
#define WM_RENDERFORMAT           0x0305
#define WM_RENDERALLFORMATS       0x0306
#define WM_DESTROYCLIPBOARD       0x0307
#define WM_DRAWCLIPBOARD          0x0308
#define WM_PAINTCLIPBOARD         0x0309
#define WM_VSCROLLCLIPBOARD       0x030A
#define WM_SIZECLIPBOARD          0x030B
#define WM_ASKCBFORMATNAME        0x030C
#define WM_CHANGECBCHAIN          0x030D
#define WM_HSCROLLCLIPBOARD       0x030E
#define WM_QUERYNEWPALETTE        0x030F
#define WM_PALETTEISCHANGING      0x0310
#define WM_PALETTECHANGED         0x0311

#ifdef WIN31
#define WM_PENWINFIRST            0x0380
#define WM_PENWINLAST             0x038F


#define WM_COALESCE_FIRST         0x0390
#define WM_COALESCE_LAST          0x039F


#endif  /* WIN31 */



/* NOTE: All Message Numbers below 0x0400 are RESERVED. */

/* Private Window Messages Start Here: */
#define WM_USER                   0x0400

/* WM_SIZE message wParam values */
```

```
#define SIZENORMAL      0
#define SIZEICONIC      1
#define SIZEFULLSCREEN  2
#define SIZEZOOMSHOW    3
#define SIZEZOOMHIDE    4

#ifdef WIN31

/* WM_WINDOWPOSCHANGING/CHANGED struct pointed to by lParam */
typedef struct tagWINDOWPOS
{
    HWND hwnd;
    HWND hwndInsertAfter;
    int  x;
    int  y;
    int  cx;
    int  cy;
    WORD flags;
} WINDOWPOS;
typedef WINDOWPOS FAR *LPWINDOWPOS;

#endif /* WIN31 */

#ifndef NONCMESSAGES

/* WM_SYNCTASK Commands */
#define ST_BEGINSWP     0
#define ST_ENDSWP       1

/* WinWhere() Area Codes */
#define HTERROR         (-2)
#define HTTRANSPARENT   (-1)
#define HTNOWHERE       0
#define HTCLIENT        1
#define HTCAPTION       2
#define HTSYSMENU       3
#define HTGROWBOX       4
#define HTSIZE          HTGROWBOX
#define HTMENU          5
#define HTHSCROLL       6
#define HTVSCROLL       7
#define HTREDUCE        8
#define HTZOOM          9
#define HTLEFT          10
#define HTRIGHT         11
#define HTTOP           12
#define HTTOPLEFT       13
#define HTTOPRIGHT      14
#define HTBOTTOM        15
#define HTBOTTOMLEFT    16
#define HTBOTTOMRIGHT   17

#ifdef WIN31

/* WM_NCCALCSIZE parameter structure */
typedef struct tagNCCALCSIZE_PARAMS
{
        RECT            rgrc[3];
        WINDOWPOS       FAR*    lppos;
}       NCCALCSIZE_PARAMS;
typedef NCCALCSIZE_PARAMS       FAR*    LPNCCALCSIZE_PARAMS;

/* WM_NCCALCSIZE "window valid rect" return values */
#define WVR_ALIGNTOP    0x0010
#define WVR_ALIGNLEFT   0x0020
#define WVR_ALIGNBOTTOM 0x0040
#define WVR_ALIGNRIGHT  0x0080
#define WVR_HREDRAW     0x0100
#define WVR_VREDRAW     0x0200
```

```
#define WVR_REDRAW        (WVR_HREDRAW | WVR_VREDRAW)
#define WVR_VALIDRECTS    0x0400

#endif  /* WIN31 */

#endif  /* NONCMESSAGES */

/* WM_MOUSEACTIVATE Return Codes */
#define MA_ACTIVATE           1
#define MA_ACTIVATEANDEAT     2
#define MA_NOACTIVATE         3

#ifdef  WIN31
#define MA_NOACTIVATEANDEAT   4
#endif  /* WIN31 */

WORD    API RegisterWindowMessage(LPSTR);

#ifndef NOKEYSTATES

/* Key State Masks for Mouse Messages */
#define MK_LBUTTON        0x0001
#define MK_RBUTTON        0x0002
#define MK_SHIFT          0x0004
#define MK_CONTROL        0x0008
#define MK_MBUTTON        0x0010

#endif /* NOKEYSTATES */

#endif /* NOWINMESSAGES */

#ifndef NOWINSTYLES

/* Window Styles */
#define WS_OVERLAPPED     0x00000000L
#define WS_POPUP          0x80000000L
#define WS_CHILD          0x40000000L
#define WS_MINIMIZE       0x20000000L
#define WS_VISIBLE        0x10000000L
#define WS_DISABLED       0x08000000L
#define WS_CLIPSIBLINGS   0x04000000L
#define WS_CLIPCHILDREN   0x02000000L
#define WS_MAXIMIZE       0x01000000L
#define WS_CAPTION        0x00C00000L        /* WS_BORDER | WS_DLGFRAME  */
#define WS_BORDER         0x00800000L
#define WS_DLGFRAME       0x00400000L
#define WS_VSCROLL        0x00200000L
#define WS_HSCROLL        0x00100000L
#define WS_SYSMENU        0x00080000L
#define WS_THICKFRAME     0x00040000L
#define WS_GROUP          0x00020000L
#define WS_TABSTOP        0x00010000L

#define WS_MINIMIZEBOX    0x00020000L
#define WS_MAXIMIZEBOX    0x00010000L

#define WS_TILED          WS_OVERLAPPED
#define WS_ICONIC         WS_MINIMIZE
#define WS_SIZEBOX        WS_THICKFRAME

/* Common Window Styles */
#define WS_OVERLAPPEDWINDOW (WS_OVERLAPPED | WS_CAPTION | WS_SYSMENU | WS_THICKFRAME |
        WS_MINIMIZEBOX |WS_MAXIMIZEBOX)
#define WS_POPUPWINDOW  (WS_POPUP | WS_BORDER | WS_SYSMENU)
#define WS_CHILDWINDOW  (WS_CHILD)

#define WS_TILEDWINDOW  (WS_OVERLAPPEDWINDOW)

/* Extended Window Styles */
```

```
#define WS_EX_DLGMODALFRAME      0x00000001L
#define WS_EX_NOPARENTNOTIFY     0x00000004L

#ifdef  WIN31
#define WS_EX_TOPMOST            0x00000008L
#define WS_EX_ACCEPTFILES        0x00000010L
#define WS_EX_TRANSPARENT        0x00000020L


#endif /* WIN31 */

/* Class styles */
#define CS_VREDRAW               0x0001
#define CS_HREDRAW               0x0002
#define CS_KEYCVTWINDOW          0x0004
#define CS_DBLCLKS               0x0008

#define CS_OWNDC                 0x0020
#define CS_CLASSDC               0x0040
#define CS_PARENTDC              0x0080
#define CS_NOKEYCVT              0x0100
#define CS_NOCLOSE               0x0200
#define CS_SAVEBITS              0x0800
#define CS_BYTEALIGNCLIENT       0x1000
#define CS_BYTEALIGNWINDOW       0x2000
#define CS_GLOBALCLASS           0x4000   /* Global window class */


#endif /* NOWINSTYLES */

#ifndef NOCLIPBOARD

/* Predefined Clipboard Formats */
#define CF_TEXT          1
#define CF_BITMAP        2
#define CF_METAFILEPICT  3
#define CF_SYLK          4
#define CF_DIF           5
#define CF_TIFF          6
#define CF_OEMTEXT       7
#define CF_DIB           8
#define CF_PALETTE       9
#define CF_PENDATA       10

#define CF_OWNERDISPLAY          0x0080
#define CF_DSPTEXT               0x0081
#define CF_DSPBITMAP             0x0082
#define CF_DSPMETAFILEPICT       0x0083

/* "Private" formats don't get GlobalFree()'d */
#define CF_PRIVATEFIRST          0x0200
#define CF_PRIVATELAST           0x02FF

/* "GDIOBJ" formats do get DeleteObject()'d */
#define CF_GDIOBJFIRST           0x0300
#define CF_GDIOBJLAST            0x03FF

#endif /* NOCLIPBOARD */

typedef struct tagPAINTSTRUCT
  {
    HDC  hdc;
    BOOL fErase;
    RECT rcPaint;
    BOOL fRestore;
    BOOL fIncUpdate;
    BYTE rgbReserved[16];
  } PAINTSTRUCT;
```

```
typedef PAINTSTRUCT        *PPAINTSTRUCT;
typedef PAINTSTRUCT NEAR *NPPAINTSTRUCT;
typedef PAINTSTRUCT FAR  *LPPAINTSTRUCT;

typedef struct tagCREATESTRUCT
  {
        LPSTR           lpCreateParams;
        HANDLE          hInstance;
        HANDLE          hMenu;
        HWND            hwndParent;
        int             cy;
        int             cx;
        int             x;
        int             x;
        LONG            style;
        LPSTR           lpszName;
        LPSTR           lpszClass;
        DWORD           dwExStyle;
  } CREATESTRUCT;
typedef CREATESTRUCT FAR *LPCREATESTRUCT;


/* Owner draw control types */
#define ODT_MENU        1
#define ODT_LISTBOX     2
#define ODT_COMBOBOX    3
#define ODT_BUTTON      4

/* Owner draw actions */
#define ODA_DRAWENTIRE  0x0001
#define ODA_SELECT      0x0002
#define ODA_FOCUS       0x0004

/* Owner draw state */
#define ODS_SELECTED    0x0001
#define ODS_GRAYED      0x0002
#define ODS_DISABLED    0x0004
#define ODS_CHECKED     0x0008
#define ODS_FOCUS       0x0010

/* MEASUREITEMSTRUCT for ownerdraw */
typedef struct tagMEASUREITEMSTRUCT
  {
   WORD         CtlType;
   WORD         CtlID;
   WORD         itemID;
   WORD         itemWidth;
   WORD         itemHeight;
   DWORD        itemData;
  } MEASUREITEMSTRUCT;
typedef MEASUREITEMSTRUCT NEAR   *PMEASUREITEMSTRUCT;
typedef MEASUREITEMSTRUCT FAR    *LPMEASUREITEMSTRUCT;

/* DRAWITEMSTRUCT for ownerdraw */
typedef struct tagDRAWITEMSTRUCT
  {
   WORD         CtlType;
   WORD         CtlID;
   WORD         itemID;
   WORD         itemAction;
   WORD         itemState;
   HWND         hwndItem;
   HDC          hDC;
   RECT         rcItem;
   DWORD        itemData;
  }    DRAWITEMSTRUCT;
typedef DRAWITEMSTRUCT NEAR      *PDRAWITEMSTRUCT;
typedef DRAWITEMSTRUCT FAR       *LPDRAWITEMSTRUCT;
```

```
/* DELETEITEMSTRUCT for ownerdraw */
typedef struct tagDELETEITEMSTRUCT
  {
    WORD         CtlType;
    WORD         CtlID;
    WORD         itemID;
    HWND         hwndItem;
    DWORD        itemData;
  } DELETEITEMSTRUCT;
typedef DELETEITEMSTRUCT NEAR    *PDELETEITEMSTRUCT;
typedef DELETEITEMSTRUCT FAR     *LPDELETEITEMSTRUCT;


/* COMPAREITEMSTUCT for ownerdraw sorting */
typedef struct tagCOMPAREITEMSTRUCT
  {
    WORD         CtlType;
    WORD         CtlID;
    HWND         hwndItem;
    WORD         itemID1;
    DWORD        itemData1;
    WORD         itemID2;
    DWORD        itemData2;
  } COMPAREITEMSTRUCT;
typedef COMPAREITEMSTRUCT NEAR   *PCOMPAREITEMSTRUCT;
typedef COMPAREITEMSTRUCT FAR    *LPCOMPAREITEMSTRUCT;

#ifndef NOMSG

/* Message Function Templates */
BOOL    API GetMessage(LPMSG, HWND, WORD, WORD);
BOOL    API TranslateMessage(LPMSG);
LONG    API DispatchMessage(LPMSG);
BOOL    API PeekMessage(LPMSG, HWND, WORD, WORD, WORD);

/* PeekMessage() Options */
#define PM_NOREMOVE      0x0000
#define PM_REMOVE        0x0001
#define PM_NOYIELD       0x0002

#endif /* NOMSG */


#ifndef NOLSTRING
int     API lstrcmp( LPSTR, LPSTR );
int     API lstrcmpi( LPSTR, LPSTR );
LPSTR   API lstrcpy( LPSTR, LPSTR );
LPSTR   API lstrcat( LPSTR, LPSTR );
int     API lstrlen( LPSTR );
#endif  /* NOLSTRING */

#ifndef NOLFILEIO
int     API _lopen( LPSTR, int );
int     API _lclose( int );
int     API _lcreat( LPSTR, int );
LONG    API _llseek( int, long, int );
WORD    API _lread( int, LPSTR, int );
WORD    API _lwrite( int, LPSTR, int );

#define READ            0   /* Flags for _lopen */
#define WRITE           1
#define READ_WRITE      2
#endif  /* NOLFILEIO */

BOOL    API ExitWindows(DWORD dwReturnCode, WORD wReserved);
#define EW_RESTARTWINDOWS       0x42
#ifdef  WIN31
#define EW_REBOOTSYSTEM         0x43
#endif  /* WIN31 */
```

```
BOOL    API SwapMouseButton(BOOL);
DWORD   API GetMessagePos(void);
LONG    API GetMessageTime(void);

#ifdef WIN31
LONG    API GetMessageExtraInfo(void);
#endif /* WIN31 */

HWND    API GetSysModalWindow(void);
HWND    API SetSysModalWindow(HWND);

LONG    API SendMessage(HWND, WORD, WORD, LONG);
BOOL    API PostMessage(HWND, WORD, WORD, LONG);
BOOL    API PostAppMessage(HANDLE, WORD, WORD, LONG);
void    API ReplyMessage(LONG);
void    API WaitMessage(void);
LONG    API DefWindowProc(HWND, WORD, WORD, LONG);
void    API PostQuitMessage(int);
LONG    API CallWindowProc(FARPROC, HWND, WORD, WORD, LONG);
BOOL    API InSendMessage(void);

WORD    API GetDoubleClickTime(void);
void    API SetDoubleClickTime(WORD);

BOOL    API RegisterClass(LPWNDCLASS);
BOOL    API UnregisterClass(LPSTR, HANDLE);
BOOL    API GetClassInfo(HANDLE, LPSTR, LPWNDCLASS);

BOOL    API SetMessageQueue(int);

#define CW_USEDEFAULT      ((int)0x8000)
HWND    API CreateWindow(LPSTR, LPSTR, DWORD, int, int, int, int, HWND, HMENU, HANDLE, LPSTR);
HWND    API CreateWindowEx(DWORD, LPSTR, LPSTR, DWORD, int, int, int, int, HWND, HMENU, HANDLE,
LPSTR);

BOOL    API IsWindow(HWND);
BOOL    API IsChild(HWND, HWND);
BOOL    API DestroyWindow(HWND);

BOOL    API ShowWindow(HWND, int);
BOOL    API FlashWindow(HWND, BOOL);
void    API ShowOwnedPopups(HWND, BOOL);

BOOL    API OpenIcon(HWND);
void        CloseWindow(HWND);
void    API MoveWindow(HWND, int, int, int, int, BOOL);
void    API SetWindowPos(HWND, HWND, int, int, int, int, WORD);

#ifndef NODEFERWINDOWPOS

HANDLE  API BeginDeferWindowPos(int nNumWindows);
HANDLE  API DeferWindowPos(HANDLE hWinPosInfo, HWND hWnd, HWND hWndInsertAfter, int x, int y,
int cx, int cy, WORD wFlags);
void    API EndDeferWindowPos(HANDLE hWinPosInfo);

#endif /* NODEFERWINDOWPOS */

BOOL    API IsWindowVisible(HWND);
BOOL    API IsIconic(HWND);
BOOL    API AnyPopup(void);
void    API BringWindowToTop(HWND);
BOOL    API IsZoomed(HWND);

/* Special HWND values for SetWindowPos() hwndInsertAfter */
#define HWND_TOP          ((HWND)NULL)
#define HWND_BOTTOM       ((HWND)1)
#define HWND_GROUPTOTOP   ((HWND)-1)

/* SetWindowPos() and WINDOWPOS flags */
```

```
#define SWP_NOSIZE              0x0001
#define SWP_NOMOVE              0x0002
#define SWP_NOZORDER            0x0004
#define SWP_NOREDRAW            0x0008
#define SWP_NOACTIVATE          0x0010
#define SWP_FRAMECHANGED        0x0020  /* The frame changed: send WM_NCCALCSIZE */
#define SWP_SHOWWINDOW          0x0040
#define SWP_HIDEWINDOW          0x0080
#define SWP_NOCOPYBITS          0x0100
#define SWP_NOOWNERZORDER       0x0200  /* Don't do owner Z ordering */

#define SWP_DRAWFRAME           SWP_FRAMECHANGED
#define SWP_NOREPOSITION        SWP_NOOWNERZORDER


#ifndef NOCTLMGR

HWND    API CreateDialog(HANDLE, LPSTR, HWND, FARPROC);
HWND    API CreateDialogIndirect(HANDLE, LPSTR, HWND, FARPROC);
HWND    API CreateDialogParam(HANDLE, LPSTR, HWND, FARPROC, LONG);
HWND    API CreateDialogIndirectParam(HANDLE, LPSTR, HWND, FARPROC, LONG);
int     API DialogBox(HANDLE, LPSTR, HWND, FARPROC);
int     API DialogBoxIndirect(HANDLE, HANDLE, HWND, FARPROC);
int     API DialogBoxParam(HANDLE, LPSTR, HWND, FARPROC, LONG);
int     API DialogBoxIndirectParam(HANDLE, HANDLE, HWND, FARPROC, LONG);
void    API EndDialog(HWND, int);
HWND    API GetDlgItem(HWND, int);
void    API SetDlgItemInt(HWND, int, WORD, BOOL);
WORD    API GetDlgItemInt(HWND, int, BOOL FAR *, BOOL);
void    API SetDlgItemText(HWND, int, LPSTR);
int     API GetDlgItemText(HWND, int, LPSTR, int);
void    API CheckDlgButton(HWND, int, WORD);
void    API CheckRadioButton(HWND, int, int, int);
WORD    API IsDlgButtonChecked(HWND, int);
LONG    API SendDlgItemMessage(HWND, int, WORD, WORD, LONG);
HWND    API GetNextDlgGroupItem(HWND, HWND, BOOL);
HWND    API GetNextDlgTabItem(HWND, HWND, BOOL);
int     API GetDlgCtrlID(HWND);
long    API GetDialogBaseUnits(void);
LONG    API DefDlgProc(HWND, WORD, WORD, LONG);
#define DLGWINDOWEXTRA  30      /* Window extra byted needed for private dialog classes */

#endif  /* NOCTLMGR */

#ifndef NOMSG
BOOL    API CallMsgFilter(LPMSG, int);
#endif

#ifndef NOCLIPBOARD

/* Clipboard Manager Functions */
BOOL    API OpenClipboard(HWND);
BOOL    API CloseClipboard(void);

#ifdef WIN31
HWND    API GetOpenClipboardWindow(void);
#endif  /* WIN31 */

HWND    API GetClipboardOwner(void);
HWND    API SetClipboardViewer(HWND);
HWND    API GetClipboardViewer(void);
BOOL    API ChangeClipboardChain(HWND, HWND);
HANDLE  API SetClipboardData(WORD, HANDLE);
HANDLE  API GetClipboardData(WORD);
WORD    API RegisterClipboardFormat(LPSTR);
int     API CountClipboardFormats(void);
WORD    API EnumClipboardFormats(WORD);
int     API GetClipboardFormatName(WORD, LPSTR, int);
```

```
BOOL    API EmptyClipboard(void);
BOOL    API IsClipboardFormatAvailable(WORD);
int     API GetPriorityClipboardFormat(WORD  FAR *, int);

#endif /* NOCLIPBOARD */

HWND    API SetFocus(HWND);
HWND    API GetFocus(void);
HWND    API GetActiveWindow(void);
int     API GetKeyState(int);
int     API GetAsyncKeyState(int);
void    API GetKeyboardState(BYTE FAR *);
void    API SetKeyboardState(BYTE FAR *);
BOOL    API EnableHardwareInput(BOOL);
BOOL    API GetInputState(void);
HWND    API GetCapture(void);
HWND    API SetCapture(HWND);
void    API ReleaseCapture(void);

#ifdef WIN31

DWORD   API GetQueueStatus(WORD flags);

/* GetQueueStatus flags */
#define QS_KEY          0x0001
#define QS_MOUSEMOVE    0x0002
#define QS_MOUSEBUTTON  0x0004
#define QS_MOUSE        (QS_MOUSEMOVE | QS_MOUSEBUTTON)
#define QS_POSTMESSAGE  0x0008
#define QS_TIMER        0x0010
#define QS_PAINT        0x0020
#define QS_SENDMESSAGE  0x0040


#endif  /* WIN31 */

/* Windows Functions */
WORD    API SetTimer(HWND, int, WORD, FARPROC);
BOOL    API KillTimer(HWND, int);

BOOL    API EnableWindow(HWND,BOOL);
BOOL    API IsWindowEnabled(HWND);

HANDLE  API LoadAccelerators(HANDLE, LPSTR);

#ifndef NOMSG
int     API TranslateAccelerator(HWND, HANDLE, LPMSG);
#endif

#ifndef NOSYSMETRICS

/* GetSystemMetrics() codes */
#define SM_CXSCREEN     0
#define SM_CYSCREEN     1
#define SM_CXVSCROLL    2
#define SM_CYHSCROLL    3
#define SM_CYCAPTION    4
#define SM_CXBORDER     5
#define SM_CYBORDER     6
#define SM_CXDLGFRAME   7
#define SM_CYDLGFRAME   8
#define SM_CYVTHUMB     9
#define SM_CXHTHUMB     10
#define SM_CXICON       11
#define SM_CYICON       12
#define SM_CXCURSOR     13
#define SM_xCYCURSOR    14
#define SM_CYMENU       15
#define SM_CXFULLSCREEN 16
```

```
#define SM_CYFULLSCREEN        17
#define SM_CYKANJIWINDOW       18
#define SM_MOUSEPRESENT        19
#define SM_CYVSCROLL           20
#define SM_CXHSCROLL           21
#define SM_DEBUG               22
#define SM_SWAPBUTTON          23
#define SM_RESERVED1           24
#define SM_RESERVED2           25
#define SM_RESERVED3           26
#define SM_RESERVED4           27
#define SM_CXMIN               28
#define SM_CYMIN               29
#define SM_CXSIZE              30
#define SM_CYSIZE              31
#define SM_CXFRAME             32
#define SM_CYFRAME             33
#define SM_CXMINTRACK          34
#define SM_CYMINTRACK          35

#ifdef WIN31
#define SM_CXDOUBLECLK         36
#define SM_CYDOUBLECLK         37
#define SM_CXICONSPACING       38
#define SM_CYICONSPACING       39
#define SM_MENUDROPALIGNMENT   40
#define SM_PENWINDOWS          41
#endif /* WIN31 */


int     API GetSystemMetrics(int);

#endif /* NOSYSMETRICS */

#ifndef NOMENUS

BOOL    API IsMenu(HMENU);

HMENU   API LoadMenu(HANDLE, LPSTR);
HMENU   API LoadMenuIndirect(LPSTR);
HMENU   API GetMenu(HWND);
BOOL    API SetMenu(HWND, HMENU);
BOOL    API ChangeMenu(HMENU, WORD, LPSTR, WORD, WORD);
BOOL    API HiliteMenuItem(HWND, HMENU, WORD, WORD);
int     API GetMenuString(HMENU, WORD, LPSTR, int, WORD);
WORD    API GetMenuState(HMENU, WORD, WORD);
void    API DrawMenuBar(HWND);
HMENU   API GetSystemMenu(HWND, BOOL);
HMENU   API CreateMenu(void);
HMENU   API CreatePopupMenu(void);
BOOL    API DestroyMenu(HMENU);
BOOL    API CheckMenuItem(HMENU, WORD, WORD);
BOOL    API EnableMenuItem(HMENU, WORD, WORD);
HMENU   API GetSubMenu(HMENU, int);
WORD    API GetMenuItemID(HMENU, int);
WORD    API GetMenuItemCount(HMENU);

BOOL    API InsertMenu(HMENU, WORD, WORD, WORD, LPSTR);
BOOL    API AppendMenu(HMENU, WORD, WORD, LPSTR);
BOOL    API ModifyMenu(HMENU, WORD, WORD, WORD, LPSTR);
BOOL    API RemoveMenu(HMENU, WORD, WORD);
BOOL    API DeleteMenu(HMENU, WORD, WORD);
BOOL    API SetMenuItemBitmaps(HMENU, WORD, WORD, HBITMAP, HBITMAP);
LONG    API GetMenuCheckMarkDimensions(void);

BOOL    API TrackPopupMenu(HMENU, WORD, int, int, int, HWND, LPRECT);
/* Flags for TrackPopupMenu */
#define TPM_LEFTBUTTON  0x0000

#ifdef WIN31
```

```
#define TPM_RIGHTBUTTON 0x0002
#define TPM_LEFTALIGN   0x0000
#define TPM_CENTERALIGN 0x0004
#define TPM_RIGHTALIGN  0x0008


#endif /* WIN31 */

#endif /* NOMENUS */

BOOL    API GrayString(HDC, HBRUSH, FARPROC, DWORD, int, int, int, int, int);
void    API UpdateWindow(HWND);
HWND    API SetActiveWindow(HWND);

HDC     API BeginPaint(HWND, LPPAINTSTRUCT);
void    API EndPaint(HWND, LPPAINTSTRUCT);
BOOL    API GetUpdateRect(HWND, LPRECT, BOOL);
int     API GetUpdateRgn(HWND, HRGN, BOOL);

int     API ExcludeUpdateRgn(HDC, HWND);

void    API InvalidateRect(HWND, LPRECT, BOOL);
void    API ValidateRect(HWND, LPRECT);

void    API InvalidateRgn(HWND, HRGN, BOOL);
void    API ValidateRgn(HWND, HRGN);

#ifdef WIN31

BOOL    API RedrawWindow(HWND hwnd,
        LPRECT lprcUpdate, HRGN hrgnUpdate, WORD flags);

/* RedrawWindow() flags */
#define RDW_INVALIDATE          0x0001
#define RDW_INTERNALPAINT       0x0002
#define RDW_ERASE               0x0004

#define RDW_VALIDATE            0x0008
#define RDW_NOINTERNALPAINT     0x0010
#define RDW_NOERASE             0x0020

#define RDW_NOCHILDREN          0x0040
#define RDW_ALLCHILDREN         0x0080

#define RDW_UPDATENOW           0x0100
#define RDW_ERASENOW            0x0200


/* LockWindowUpdate API */
BOOL API LockWindowUpdate(HWND hwndLock);

#endif /* WIN31 */

void    API ScrollWindow(HWND, int, int, LPRECT, LPRECT);
BOOL    API ScrollDC(HDC, int, int, LPRECT, LPRECT, HRGN, LPRECT);

#ifdef WIN31

int     API ScrollWindowEx(
        HWND hwnd,
        int dx,
        int dy,
        LPRECT prcScroll,
        LPRECT prcClip,
        HRGN hrgnUpdate,
        LPRECT prcUpdate,
        WORD flags);

#define SW_SCROLLCHILDREN       0x0001  /* Scroll children within *lprcScroll. */
```

```
#define SW_INVALIDATE          0x0002  /* Invalidate after scrolling */
#define SW_ERASE               0x0004  /* If SW_INVALIDATE, don't send WM_ERASEBACKGROUND */


#endif /* WIN31 */

#ifndef NOSCROLL
int      API SetScrollPos(HWND, int, int, BOOL);
int      API GetScrollPos(HWND, int);
void     API SetScrollRange(HWND, int, int, int, BOOL);
void     API GetScrollRange(HWND, int, LPINT, LPINT);
void     API ShowScrollBar(HWND, WORD, BOOL);
BOOL     API EnableScrollBar(HWND, WORD, WORD);
#endif

BOOL     API SetProp(HWND, LPSTR, HANDLE);
HANDLE   API GetProp(HWND, LPSTR);
HANDLE   API RemoveProp(HWND, LPSTR);
int      API EnumProps(HWND, FARPROC);
void     API SetWindowText(HWND, LPSTR);
int      API GetWindowText(HWND, LPSTR, int);
int      API GetWindowTextLength(HWND);

void     API GetClientRect(HWND, LPRECT);
void     API GetWindowRect(HWND, LPRECT);
void     API AdjustWindowRect(LPRECT, LONG, BOOL);
void     API AdjustWindowRectEx(LPRECT, LONG, BOOL, DWORD);

#ifndef NOMB

/* MessageBox() Flags */
#define MB_OK                  0x0000
#define MB_OKCANCEL            0x0001
#define MB_ABORTRETRYIGNORE    0x0002
#define MB_YESNOCANCEL         0x0003
#define MB_YESNO               0x0004
#define MB_RETRYCANCEL         0x0005

#define MB_ICONHAND            0x0010
#define MB_ICONQUESTION        0x0020
#define MB_ICONEXCLAMATION     0x0030
#define MB_ICONASTERISK        0x0040

#define MB_ICONINFORMATION  MB_ICONASTERISK
#define MB_ICONSTOP            MB_ICONHAND

#define MB_DEFBUTTON1          0x0000
#define MB_DEFBUTTON2          0x0100
#define MB_DEFBUTTON3          0x0200

#define MB_APPLMODAL           0x0000
#define MB_SYSTEMMODAL         0x1000
#define MB_TASKMODAL           0x2000

#define MB_NOFOCUS             0x8000


int      API MessageBox(HWND, LPSTR, LPSTR, WORD);
void     API MessageBeep(WORD);

#endif /* NOMB */

int      API ShowCursor(BOOL);
void     API SetCursorPos(int, int);

#ifdef WIN31
HCURSOR API GetCursor(void);
```

```
#endif   /* WIN31 */

HCURSOR API SetCursor(HCURSOR);
void    API GetCursorPos(LPPOINT);
void    API ClipCursor(LPRECT);
#ifdef  WIN31
void    API GetClipCursor(LPRECT);
#endif


void    API CreateCaret(HWND, HBITMAP, int, int);
WORD    API GetCaretBlinkTime(void);
void    API SetCaretBlinkTime(WORD);
void    API DestroyCaret(void);
void    API HideCaret(HWND);
void    API ShowCaret(HWND);
void    API SetCaretPos(int, int);
void    API GetCaretPos(LPPOINT);

void    API ClientToScreen(HWND, LPPOINT);
void    API ScreenToClient(HWND, LPPOINT);

#ifdef  WIN31

void    API MapWindowPoints(HWND hwndFrom, HWND hwndTo, LPPOINT lppt, WORD cpt);

#define MapWindowRect(hwndFrom, hwndTo, lprc) \
        MapWindowPoints(hwndFrom, hwndTo, (LPPOINT)&lprc, 2)

#endif   /* WIN31 */

HWND    API WindowFromPoint(POINT);
HWND    API ChildWindowFromPoint(HWND, POINT);

#ifndef NOCOLOR

/* Color Types */
#define CTLCOLOR_MSGBOX         0
#define CTLCOLOR_EDIT           1
#define CTLCOLOR_LISTBOX        2
#define CTLCOLOR_BTN            3
#define CTLCOLOR_DLG            4
#define CTLCOLOR_SCROLLBAR      5
#define CTLCOLOR_STATIC         6
#define CTLCOLOR_MAX            8       /* three bits max */

#define COLOR_SCROLLBAR         0
#define COLOR_BACKGROUND        1
#define COLOR_ACTIVECAPTION     2
#define COLOR_INACTIVECAPTION   3
#define COLOR_MENU              4
#define COLOR_WINDOW            5
#define COLOR_WINDOWFRAME       6
#define COLOR_MENUTEXT          7
#define COLOR_WINDOWTEXT        8
#define COLOR_CAPTIONTEXT       9
#define COLOR_ACTIVEBORDER      10
#define COLOR_INACTIVEBORDER    11
#define COLOR_APPWORKSPACE      12
#define COLOR_HIGHLIGHT         13
#define COLOR_HIGHLIGHTTEXT     14
#define COLOR_BTNFACE           15
#define COLOR_BTNSHADOW         16
#define COLOR_GRAYTEXT          17
#define COLOR_BTNTEXT           18
#ifdef  WIN31
#define COLOR_INACTIVECAPTIONTEXT19
#define COLOR_BTNHIGHLIGHT      20
#endif   /* WIN31 */
```

```
DWORD    API GetSysColor(int);
void     API SetSysColors(int, LPINT, LONG FAR *);

#endif   /* NOCOLOR */

BOOL     API FillRgn(HDC, HRGN, HBRUSH);
BOOL     API FrameRgn(HDC, HRGN, HBRUSH, int, int);
BOOL     API InvertRgn(HDC, HRGN);
BOOL     API PaintRgn(HDC, HRGN);
BOOL     API PtInRegion(HRGN, int, int);

void     API DrawFocusRect(HDC, LPRECT);
int      API FillRect(HDC, LPRECT, HBRUSH);
int      API FrameRect(HDC, LPRECT, HBRUSH);
void     API InvertRect(HDC, LPRECT);
void     API SetRect(LPRECT, int, int, int, int);
void     API SetRectEmpty(LPRECT);
int      API CopyRect(LPRECT, LPRECT);
void     API InflateRect(LPRECT, int, int);
int      API IntersectRect(LPRECT, LPRECT, LPRECT);
int      API UnionRect(LPRECT, LPRECT, LPRECT);
BOOL     API SubtractRect(LPRECT, LPRECT, LPRECT);
void     API OffsetRect(LPRECT, int, int);
BOOL     API IsRectEmpty(LPRECT);
BOOL     API EqualRect(LPRECT, LPRECT);
BOOL     API PtInRect(LPRECT, POINT);
BOOL     API RectVisible(HDC, LPRECT);
BOOL     API RectInRegion(HRGN, LPRECT);

DWORD    API GetCurrentTime(void);
DWORD    API GetTickCount(void);

#ifndef NOWINOFFSETS

WORD     API GetWindowWord(HWND, int);
WORD     API SetWindowWord(HWND, int, WORD);
LONG     API GetWindowLong(HWND, int);
LONG     API SetWindowLong(HWND, int, LONG);
WORD     API GetClassWord(HWND, int);
WORD     API SetClassWord(HWND, int, WORD);
LONG     API GetClassLong(HWND, int);
LONG     API SetClassLong(HWND, int, LONG);
HWND     API GetDesktopHwnd(void);
HWND     API GetDesktopWindow(void);

#endif   /* NOWINOFFSETS */

HWND     API GetParent(HWND);
HWND     API SetParent(HWND, HWND);
BOOL     API EnumChildWindows(HWND, FARPROC, LONG);
HWND     API FindWindow(LPSTR, LPSTR);
BOOL     API EnumWindows(FARPROC, LONG);
BOOL     API EnumTaskWindows(HANDLE, FARPROC, LONG);
int      API GetClassName(HWND, LPSTR, int);
HWND     API GetTopWindow(HWND);
HWND     API GetNextWindow(HWND, WORD);
HANDLE   API GetWindowTask(HWND);
HWND     API GetLastActivePopup(HWND);

/* GetWindow() Constants */
#define GW_HWNDFIRST    0
#define GW_HWNDLAST     1
#define GW_HWNDNEXT     2
#define GW_HWNDPREV     3
#define GW_OWNER        4
#define GW_CHILD        5


HWND     API GetWindow(HWND, WORD);
```

```
#ifndef NOWH

FARPROC API SetWindowsHook(int, FARPROC);
BOOL    API UnhookWindowsHook(int, FARPROC);
DWORD   API DefHookProc(int, WORD, DWORD, FARPROC FAR *);

#ifdef  WIN31

typedef DWORD HHOOK;
typedef DWORD (API *HOOKPROC)(int code, WORD wParam, LONG lParam);

HHOOK   API SetWindowsHookEx(int idHook, HOOKPROC lpfn, HANDLE hModule, HANDLE hTask);
BOOL    API UnhookWindowsHookEx(HHOOK hHook);
DWORD   API CallNextHookEx(HHOOK hHook, int code, WORD wParam, LONG lParam);

#endif  /* WIN31 */

/* SetWindowsHook() codes */
#define WH_MSGFILTER          (-1)
#define WH_JOURNALRECORD       0
#define WH_JOURNALPLAYBACK     1
#define WH_KEYBOARD            2
#define WH_GETMESSAGE          3
#define WH_CALLWNDPROC         4

#ifdef  WIN31

#define WH_CBT                 5
#define WH_SYSMSGFILTER        6
#define WH_MOUSE               7
#define WH_HARDWARE            8
#define WH_DEBUG               9


#endif  /* WIN31 */

/* Hook Codes */

#define HC_GETLPLPFN          (-3)
#define HC_LPLPFNNEXT         (-2)
#define HC_LPFNNEXT           (-1)
#define HC_ACTION              0
#define HC_GETNEXT             1
#define HC_SKIP                2
#define HC_NOREM               3
#define HC_NOREMOVE            3
#define HC_SYSMODALON          4
#define HC_SYSMODALOFF         5

#ifdef  WIN31

/* CBT Hook Codes */
#define HCBT_MOVESIZE          0
#define HCBT_MINMAX            1
#define HCBT_QS                2
#define HCBT_CREATEWND         3
#define HCBT_DESTROYWND        4
#define HCBT_ACTIVATE          5
#define HCBT_CLICKSKIPPED      6
#define HCBT_KEYSKIPPED        7
#define HCBT_SYSCOMMAND        8
#define HCBT_SETFOCUS          9

/* HCBT_CREATEWND parameters pointed to by lParam */
typedef struct tagCBT_CREATEWND
{
   LPCREATESTRUCT        lpcs;
   HWND                  hwndInsertAfter;
} CBT_CREATEWND;
```

```
typedef CBT_CREATEWND   FAR *LPCBT_CREATEWND;

#endif /* WIN31 */

/* WH_MSGFILTER Filter Proc Codes */
#define MSGF_DIALOGBOX  0
#define MSGF_MENU       2
#define MSGF_MOVE       3
#define MSGF_SIZE       4
#define MSGF_SCROLLBAR  5
#define MSGF_NEXTWINDOW 6


/* Window Manager Hook Codes */
#define WC_INIT          1
#define WC_SWP           2
#define WC_DEFWINDOWPROC 3
#define WC_MINMAX        4
#define WC_MOVE          5
#define WC_SIZE          6
#define WC_DRAWCAPTION   7

#ifdef WIN31
typedef struct tagMOUSEHOOKSTRUCT
  {
   POINT       pt;
   HWND        hwnd;
   WORD        wHitTestCode;
   DWORD       dwExtraInfo;
  } MOUSEHOOKSTRUCT;
typedef MOUSEHOOKSTRUCT  FAR *LPMOUSEHOOKSTRUCT;

typedef struct tagCBTACTIVATESTRUCT
  {
   BOOL fMouse;
   HWND hWndActive;
  } CBTACTIVATESTRUCT;

typedef struct tagHARDWAREHOOKSTRUCT
  {
   HWND        hWnd;
   WORD        wMessage;
   WORD        wParam;
   DWORD       lParam;
  } HARDWAREHOOKSTRUCT;

#endif /* WIN31 */

/* Message Structure used in Journaling */
typedef struct tagEVENTMSG
  {
   WORD        message;
   WORD        paramL;
   WORD        paramH;
   DWORD       time;
  } EVENTMSG;
typedef EVENTMSG        *PEVENTMSGMSG;
typedef EVENTMSG NEAR   *NPEVENTMSGMSG;
typedef EVENTMSG FAR    *LPEVENTMSGMSG;

#endif  /* NOWH */

#ifndef NOMENUS

#define MF_INSERT           0x0000
#define MF_CHANGE           0x0080
#define MF_APPEND           0x0100
#define MF_DELETE           0x0200
```

```
#define MF_REMOVE              0x1000

/* Menu flags for Add/Check/EnableMenuItem() */
#define MF_BYCOMMAND           0x0000
#define MF_BYPOSITION          0x0400


#define MF_SEPARATOR           0x0800

#define MF_ENABLED             0x0000
#define MF_GRAYED              0x0001
#define MF_DISABLED            0x0002

#define MF_UNCHECKED           0x0000
#define MF_CHECKED             0x0008
#define MF_USECHECKBITMAPS     0x0200

#define MF_STRING              0x0000
#define MF_BITMAP              0x0004
#define MF_OWNERDRAW           0x0100

#define MF_POPUP0x0010
#define MF_MENUBARBREAK        0x0020
#define MF_MENUBREAK           0x0040

#define MF_UNHILITE            0x0000
#define MF_HILITE              0x0080

#define MF_SYSMENU             0x2000
#define MF_HELP                0x4000
#define MF_MOUSESELECT         0x8000


/* Menu item resource format */
typedef struct
  {
    WORD versionNumber;
    WORD offset;
  } MENUITEMTEMPLATEHEADER;

typedef struct
  {
    WORD         mtOption;
    WORD         mtID;
    LPSTR        mtString;
  } MENUITEMTEMPLATE;

#define MF_END                 0x0080

#endif   /* NOMENUS */

#ifndef NOSYSCOMMANDS

/* System Menu Command Values */
#define SC_SIZE                0xF000
#define SC_MOVE                0xF010
#define SC_MINIMIZE            0xF020
#define SC_MAXIMIZE            0xF030
#define SC_NEXTWINDOW          0xF040
#define SC_PREVWINDOW          0xF050
#define SC_CLOSE               0xF060
#define SC_VSCROLL             0xF070
#define SC_HSCROLL             0xF080
#define SC_MOUSEMENU           0xF090
#define SC_KEYMENU             0xF100
#define SC_ARRANGE             0xF110
#define SC_RESTORE             0xF120
#define SC_TASKLIST            0xF130
```

```
#define SC_SCREENSAVE    0xF140
#define SC_HOTKEY        0xF150

#define SC_ICON          SC_MINIMIZE
#define SC_ZOOM          SC_MAXIMIZE

#endif /* NOSYSCOMMANDS */

/* Resource Loading Routines */
HBITMAP API LoadBitmap(HANDLE, LPSTR);
HCURSOR API LoadCursor(HANDLE, LPSTR);
HCURSOR API CreateCursor(HANDLE, int, int, int, int, LPSTR, LPSTR);
BOOL    API DestroyCursor(HCURSOR);

/* Standard Cursor IDs */
#define IDC_ARROW        MAKEINTRESOURCE(32512)
#define IDC_IBEAM        MAKEINTRESOURCE(32513)
#define IDC_WAIT         MAKEINTRESOURCE(32514)
#define IDC_CROSS        MAKEINTRESOURCE(32515)
#define IDC_UPARROW      MAKEINTRESOURCE(32516)
#define IDC_SIZE         MAKEINTRESOURCE(32640)
#define IDC_ICON         MAKEINTRESOURCE(32641)
#define IDC_SIZENWSE     MAKEINTRESOURCE(32642)
#define IDC_SIZENESW     MAKEINTRESOURCE(32643)
#define IDC_SIZEWE       MAKEINTRESOURCE(32644)
#define IDC_SIZENS       MAKEINTRESOURCE(32645)

HICON   API LoadIcon(HANDLE, LPSTR);
HICON   API CreateIcon(HANDLE, int, int, BYTE, BYTE, LPSTR, LPSTR);
BOOL    API DestroyIcon(HICON);


#define ORD_LANGDRIVER   1  /* The ordinal number for the entry point of
                            ** language drivers.
                            */

#ifndef NOICONS

/* Standard Icon IDs */
#define IDI_APPLICATION MAKEINTRESOURCE(32512)
#define IDI_HAND        MAKEINTRESOURCE(32513)
#define IDI_QUESTION    MAKEINTRESOURCE(32514)
#define IDI_EXCLAMATION MAKEINTRESOURCE(32515)
#define IDI_ASTERISK    MAKEINTRESOURCE(32516)

#endif /* NOICONS */

int     API LoadString(HANDLE, WORD, LPSTR, int);

int     API AddFontResource(LPSTR);
BOOL    API RemoveFontResource(LPSTR);


/* Dialog Box Command IDs */
#define IDOK            1
#define IDCANCEL        2
#define IDABORT         3
#define IDRETRY         4
#define IDIGNORE        5
#define IDYES           6
#define IDNO            7

#ifndef NOCTLMGR

/* Control Manager Structures and Definitions */

#ifndef NOWINSTYLES

/* Edit Control Styles */
```

```
#define ES_LEFT          0x0000L
#define ES_CENTER        0x0001L
#define ES_RIGHT         0x0002L
#define ES_MULTILINE     0x0004L
#define ES_UPPERCASE     0x0008L
#define ES_LOWERCASE     0x0010L
#define ES_PASSWORD      0x0020L
#define ES_AUTOVSCROLL   0x0040L
#define ES_AUTOHSCROLL   0x0080L
#define ES_NOHIDESEL     0x0100L
#define ES_OEMCONVERT    0x0400L

#ifdef  WIN31
#define ES_READONLY      0x0800L
#endif  /* WIN31 */


#endif  /* NOWINSTYLES */

/* Edit Control Notification Codes */
#define EN_SETFOCUS      0x0100
#define EN_KILLFOCUS     0x0200
#define EN_CHANGE        0x0300
#define EN_UPDATE        0x0400
#define EN_ERRSPACE      0x0500
#define EN_MAXTEXT       0x0501
#define EN_HSCROLL       0x0601
#define EN_VSCROLL       0x0602

#ifndef NOWINMESSAGES

/* Edit Control Messages */
#define EM_GETSEL           (WM_USER+0)
#define EM_SETSEL           (WM_USER+1)
#define EM_GETRECT          (WM_USER+2)
#define EM_SETRECT          (WM_USER+3)
#define EM_SETRECTNP        (WM_USER+4)
#define EM_SCROLL           (WM_USER+5)
#define EM_LINESCROLL       (WM_USER+6)
#define EM_GETMODIFY        (WM_USER+8)
#define EM_SETMODIFY        (WM_USER+9)
#define EM_GETLINECOUNT     (WM_USER+10)
#define EM_LINEINDEX        (WM_USER+11)
#define EM_SETHANDLE        (WM_USER+12)
#define EM_GETHANDLE        (WM_USER+13)
#define EM_GETTHUMB         (WM_USER+14)
#define EM_LINELENGTH       (WM_USER+17)
#define EM_REPLACESEL       (WM_USER+18)
#define EM_SETFONT          (WM_USER+19)
#define EM_GETLINE          (WM_USER+20)
#define EM_LIMITTEXT        (WM_USER+21)
#define EM_CANUNDO          (WM_USER+22)
#define EM_UNDO             (WM_USER+23)
#define EM_FMTLINES         (WM_USER+24)
#define EM_LINEFROMCHAR     (WM_USER+25)
#define EM_SETWORDBREAK     (WM_USER+26)
#define EM_SETTABSTOPS      (WM_USER+27)
#define EM_SETPASSWORDCHAR  (WM_USER+28)
#define EM_EMPTYUNDOBUFFER  (WM_USER+29)

#ifdef  WIN31
#define EM_GETFIRSTVISIBLE  (WM_USER+30)
#define EM_SETREADONLY      (WM_USER+31)
#endif  /* WIN31 */
#define EM_MSGMAX           (WM_USER+32)

#endif  /* NOWINMESSAGES */

/* Button Control Styles */
```

```
#define BS_PUSHBUTTON          0x00L
#define BS_DEFPUSHBUTTON       0x01L
#define BS_CHECKBOX            0x02L
#define BS_AUTOCHECKBOX        0x03L
#define BS_RADIOBUTTON         0x04L
#define BS_3STATE              0x05L
#define BS_AUTO3STATE          0x06L
#define BS_GROUPBOX            0x07L
#define BS_USERBUTTON          0x08L
#define BS_AUTORADIOBUTTON     0x09L
#define BS_OWNERDRAW           0x0BL
#define BS_LEFTTEXT            0x20L


/* User Button Notification Codes */
#define BN_CLICKED             0
#define BN_PAINT               1
#define BN_HILITE              2
#define BN_UNHILIITE           3
#define BN_DISABLE             4
#define BN_DOUBLECLICKED       5


/* Button Control Messages */
#define BM_GETCHECK            (WM_USER+0)
#define BM_SETCHECK            (WM_USER+1)
#define BM_GETSTATE            (WM_USER+2)
#define BM_SETSTATE            (WM_USER+3)
#define BM_SETSTYLE            (WM_USER+4)


/* Static Control Constants */
#define SS_LEFT                0x00L
#define SS_CENTER              0x01L
#define SS_RIGHT               0x02L
#define SS_ICON                0x03L
#define SS_BLACKRECT           0x04L
#define SS_GRAYRECT            0x05L
#define SS_WHITERECT           0x06L
#define SS_BLACKFRAME          0x07L
#define SS_GRAYFRAME           0x08L
#define SS_WHITEFRAME          0x09L
#define SS_USERITEM            0x0AL
#define SS_SIMPLE              0x0BL
#define SS_LEFTNOWORDWRAP      0x0CL
#define SS_NOPREFIX            0x80L    /* Don't do "&" character translation */


#ifdef  WIN31
#ifndef NOWINMESSAGES
/* Static Control Mesages */
#define STM_SETICON            (WM_USER+0)
#define STM_GETICON            (WM_USER+1)
#define STM_MSGMAX             (WM_USER+2)
#endif  /* NOWINMESSAGES */
#endif  /* WIN31 */


/* Dialog Manager Routines */

#ifndef NOMSG
BOOL    API IsDialogMessage(HWND, LPMSG);
#endif

void    API MapDialogRect(HWND, LPRECT);

int     API DlgDirList(HWND, LPSTR, int, int, WORD);
BOOL    API DlgDirSelect(HWND, LPSTR, int);
int     API DlgDirListComboBox(HWND, LPSTR, int, int, WORD);
BOOL    API DlgDirSelectComboBox(HWND, LPSTR, int);

/* DlgDirList, DlgDirListComboBox flags values */
```

```
#define DDL_READWRITE          0x0001
#define DDL_READONLY           0x0002
#define DDL_HIDDEN             0x0004
#define DDL_SYSTEM             0x0008
#define DDL_DIRECTORY          0x0010
#define DDL_ARCHIVE            0x0020

#define DDL_POSTMSGS           0x2000
#define DDL_DRIVES             0x4000
#define DDL_EXCLUSIVE          0x8000


/* Dialog Styles */
#define DS_ABSALIGN            0x01L
#define DS_SYSMODAL            0x02L
#define DS_LOCALEDIT           0x20L    /* Edit items get Local storage */
#define DS_SETFONT             0x40L    /* User specified font for Dlg controls */
#define DS_MODALFRAME          0x80L    /* Can be combined with WS_CAPTION  */
#define DS_NOIDLEMSG           0x100L   /* WM_ENTERIDLE message will not be sent */

#define DM_GETDEFID            (WM_USER+0)
#define DM_SETDEFID            (WM_USER+1)
#define DC_HASDEFID            0x534B

/* Dialog Codes */
#define DLGC_WANTARROWS        0x0001      /* Control wants arrow keys */
#define DLGC_WANTTAB           0x0002      /* Control wants tab keys */
#define DLGC_WANTALLKEYS       0x0004      /* Control wants all keys */
#define DLGC_WANTMESSAGE       0x0004      /* Pass message to control */
#define DLGC_HASSETSEL         0x0008      /* Understands EM_SETSEL message */
#define DLGC_DEFPUSHBUTTON     0x0010      /* Default pushbutton */
#define DLGC_UNDEFPUSHBUTTON   0x0020    /* Non-default pushbutton */
#define DLGC_RADIOBUTTON       0x0040      /* Radio button */
#define DLGC_WANTCHARS         0x0080      /* Want WM_CHAR messages */
#define DLGC_STATIC            0x0100      /* Static item: don't include  */
#define DLGC_BUTTON            0x2000      /* Button item: can be checked */

#define LB_CTLCODE       0L

/* Listbox Return Values */
#define LB_OKAY          0
#define LB_ERR           (-1)
#define LB_ERRSPACE      (-2)

/*
** The idStaticPath parameter to DlgDirList can have the following values
** ORed if the list box should show other details of the files along with
** the name of the files;
*/
/* all other details also will be returned */


/* Listbox Notification Codes */
#define LBN_ERRSPACE     (-2)
#define LBN_SELCHANGE    1
#define LBN_DBLCLK       2
#define LBN_SELCANCEL    3
#define LBN_SETFOCUS     4
#define LBN_KILLFOCUS    5

#ifndef NOWINMESSAGES

/* Listbox messages */
#define LB_ADDSTRING           (WM_USER+1)
#define LB_INSERTSTRING        (WM_USER+2)
#define LB_DELETESTRING        (WM_USER+3)
#define LB_RESETCONTENT        (WM_USER+5)
#define LB_SETSEL              (WM_USER+6)
```

```
#define LB_SETCURSEL          (WM_USER+7)
#define LB_GETSEL             (WM_USER+8)
#define LB_GETCURSEL          (WM_USER+9)
#define LB_GETTEXT            (WM_USER+10)
#define LB_GETTEXTLEN         (WM_USER+11)
#define LB_GETCOUNT           (WM_USER+12)
#define LB_SELECTSTRING       (WM_USER+13)
#define LB_DIR                (WM_USER+14)
#define LB_GETTOPINDEX        (WM_USER+15)
#define LB_FINDSTRING         (WM_USER+16)
#define LB_GETSELCOUNT        (WM_USER+17)
#define LB_GETSELITEMS        (WM_USER+18)
#define LB_SETTABSTOPS        (WM_USER+19)
#define LB_GETHORIZONTALEXTENT (WM_USER+20)
#define LB_SETHORIZONTALEXTENT (WM_USER+21)
#define LB_SETCOLUMNWIDTH     (WM_USER+22)
#define LB_SETTOPINDEX        (WM_USER+24)
#define LB_GETITEMRECT        (WM_USER+25)
#define LB_GETITEMDATA        (WM_USER+26)
#define LB_SETITEMDATA        (WM_USER+27)
#define LB_SELITEMRANGE       (WM_USER+28)
#define LB_SETCARETINDEX      (WM_USER+31)
#define LB_GETCARETINDEX      (WM_USER+32)

#ifdef  WIN31
#define LB_SETITEMHEIGHT(WM_USER+33)
#define LB_GETITEMHEIGHT(WM_USER+34)
#endif  /* WIN31 */
#define LB_MSGMAX             (WM_USER+35)

#endif  /* NOWINMESSAGES */

#ifndef NOWINSTYLES

/* Listbox Styles */
#define LBS_NOTIFY            0x0001L
#define LBS_SORT              0x0002L
#define LBS_NOREDRAW          0x0004L
#define LBS_MULTIPLESEL       0x0008L
#define LBS_OWNERDRAWFIXED    0x0010L
#define LBS_OWNERDRAWVARIABLE 0x0020L
#define LBS_HASSTRINGS        0x0040L
#define LBS_USETABSTOPS       0x0080L
#define LBS_NOINTEGRALHEIGHT  0x0100L
#define LBS_MULTICOLUMN       0x0200L
#define LBS_WANTKEYBOARDINPUT 0x0400L
#define LBS_EXTENDEDSEL       0x0800L
#ifdef  WIN31
#define LBS_DISABLENOSCROLL   0x1000L
#endif  /* WIN31 */
#define LBS_STANDARD          (LBS_NOTIFY | LBS_SORT | WS_VSCROLL | WS_BORDER)

#endif  /* NOWINSTYLES */


/* Combo Box return Values */
#define CB_OKAY               0
#define CB_ERR                (-1)
#define CB_ERRSPACE           (-2)


/* Combo Box Notification Codes */
#define CBN_ERRSPACE          (-1)
#define CBN_SELCHANGE         1
#define CBN_DBLCLK            2
#define CBN_SETFOCUS          3
#define CBN_KILLFOCUS         4
#define CBN_EDITCHANGE        5
#define CBN_EDITUPDATE        6
```

```
#define CBN_DROPDOWN            7
#ifdef  WIN31
#define CBN_CLOSEUP             8
#endif  /* WIN31 */

/* Combo Box styles */
#ifndef NOWINSTYLES
#define CBS_SIMPLE                      0x0001L
#define CBS_DROPDOWN                    0x0002L
#define CBS_DROPDOWNLIST                0x0003L
#define CBS_OWNERDRAWFIXED              0x0010L
#define CBS_OWNERDRAWVARIABLE           0x0020L
#define CBS_AUTOHSCROLL                 0x0040L
#define CBS_OEMCONVERT                  0x0080L
#define CBS_SORT                        0x0100L
#define CBS_HASSTRINGS                  0x0200L
#define CBS_NOINTEGRALHEIGHT            0x0400L
#ifdef  WIN31
#define CBS_DISABLENOSCROLL             0x0800L
#endif  /* WIN31 */
#endif  /* NOWINSTYLES */


/* Combo Box messages */
#ifndef NOWINMESSAGES
#define CB_GETEDITSEL                   (WM_USER+0)
#define CB_LIMITTEXT                    (WM_USER+1)
#define CB_SETEDITSEL                   (WM_USER+2)
#define CB_ADDSTRING                    (WM_USER+3)
#define CB_DELETESTRING                 (WM_USER+4)
#define CB_DIR                          (WM_USER+5)
#define CB_GETCOUNT                     (WM_USER+6)
#define CB_GETCURSEL                    (WM_USER+7)
#define CB_GETLBTEXT                    (WM_USER+8)
#define CB_GETLBTEXTLEN                 (WM_USER+9)
#define CB_INSERTSTRING                 (WM_USER+10)
#define CB_RESETCONTENT                 (WM_USER+11)
#define CB_FINDSTRING                   (WM_USER+12)
#define CB_SELECTSTRING                 (WM_USER+13)
#define CB_SETCURSEL                    (WM_USER+14)
#define CB_SHOWDROPDOWN                 (WM_USER+15)
#define CB_GETITEMDATA                  (WM_USER+16)
#define CB_SETITEMDATA                  (WM_USER+17)
#ifdef  WIN31
#define CB_GETDROPPEDCONTROLRECT        (WM_USER+18)
#define CB_SETITEMHEIGHT                (WM_USER+19)
#define CB_GETITEMHEIGHT                (WM_USER+20)
#define CB_SETEXTENDEDUI                (WM_USER+21)
#define CB_GETEXTENDEDUI                (WM_USER+22)
#define CB_GETDROPPEDSTATE              (WM_USER+23)
#endif  /* WIN31 */
#define CB_MSGMAX                       (WM_USER+24)
#endif  /* NOWINMESSAGES */


#ifndef NOWINSTYLES

/* Scroll Bar Styles */
#define SBS_HORZ                        0x0000L
#define SBS_VERT                        0x0001L
#define SBS_TOPALIGN                    0x0002L
#define SBS_LEFTALIGN                   0x0002L
#define SBS_BOTTOMALIGN                 0x0004L
#define SBS_RIGHTALIGN                  0x0004L
#define SBS_SIZEBOXTOPLEFTALIGN         0x0002L
#define SBS_SIZEBOXBOTTOMRIGHTALIGN     0x0004L
#define SBS_SIZEBOX                     0x0008L

#endif /* NOWINSTYLES */
```

```
#endif /* NOCTLMGR */

#ifndef NOSOUND

int     API OpenSound(void);
void    API CloseSound(void);
int     API SetVoiceQueueSize(int, int);
int     API SetVoiceNote(int, int, int, int);
int     API SetVoiceAccent(int, int, int, int, int);
int     API SetVoiceEnvelope(int, int, int);
int     API SetSoundNoise(int, int);
int     API SetVoiceSound(int, LONG, int);
int     API StartSound(void);
int     API StopSound(void);
int     API WaitSoundState(int);
int     API SyncAllVoices(void);
int     API CountVoiceNotes(int);
LPINT   API GetThresholdEvent(void);
int     API GetThresholdStatus(void);
int     API SetVoiceThreshold(int, int);

/* WaitSoundState() Constants */
#define S_QUEUEEMPTY     0
#define S_THRESHOLD      1
#define S_ALLTHRESHOLD   2

/* Accent Modes */
#define S_NORMAL         0
#define S_LEGATO         1
#define S_STACCATO       2

/* SetSoundNoise() Sources */
#define S_PERIOD512      0        /* Freq = N/512 high pitch, less coarse hiss    */
#define S_PERIOD1024     1        /* Freq = N/1024                                */
#define S_PERIOD2048     2        /* Freq = N/2048 low pitch, more coarse hiss    */
#define S_PERIODVOICE    3        /* Source is frequency from voice channel (3)   */
#define S_WHITE512       4        /* Freq = N/512 high pitch, less coarse hiss    */
#define S_WHITE1024      5        /* Freq = N/1024                                */
#define S_WHITE2048      6        /* Freq = N/2048 low pitch, more coarse hiss    */
#define S_WHITEVOICE     7        /* Source is frequency from voice channel (3)   */

#define S_SERDVNA       (-1)     /* Device not available */
#define S_SEROFM        (-2)     /* Out of memory        */
#define S_SERMACT       (-3)     /* Music active         */
#define S_SERQFUL       (-4)     /* Queue full           */
#define S_SERBDNT       (-5)     /* Invalid note         */
#define S_SERDLN        (-6)     /* Invalid note length  */
#define S_SERDCC        (-7)     /* Invalid note count   */
#define S_SERDTP        (-8)     /* Invalid tempo        */
#define S_SERDVL        (-9)     /* Invalid volume       */
#define S_SERDMD        (-10)    /* Invalid mode         */
#define S_SERDSH        (-11)    /* Invalid shape        */
#define S_SERDPT        (-12)    /* Invalid pitch        */
#define S_SERDFQ        (-13)    /* Invalid frequency    */
#define S_SERDDR        (-14)    /* Invalid duration     */
#define S_SERDSR        (-15)    /* Invalid source       */
#define S_SERDST    (-16) /* Invalid state        */

#endif /* NOSOUND */

#ifdef USECOMM

#define NOPARITY         0
#define ODDPARITY        1
#define EVENPARITY       2
#define MARKPARITY       3
#define SPACEPARITY      4

#define ONESTOPBIT       0
```

```
#define ONE5STOPBITS      1
#define TWOSTOPBITS       2

#define IGNORE            0        /* Ignore signal               */
#define INFINITE          0xFFFF   /* Infinite timeout            */

/* Error Flags */
#define CE_RXOVER         0x0001   /* Receive Queue overflow      */
#define CE_OVERRUN        0x0002   /* Receive Overrun Error       */
#define CE_RXPARITY       0x0004   /* Receive Parity Error        */
#define CE_FRAME          0x0008   /* Receive Framing error       */
#define CE_BREAK          0x0010   /* Break Detected              */
#define CE_CTSTO          0x0020   /* CTS Timeout                 */
#define CE_DSRTO          0x0040   /* DSR Timeout                 */
#define CE_RLSDTO         0x0080   /* RLSD Timeout                */
#define CE_TXFULL         0x0100   /* TX Queue is full            */
#define CE_PTO            0x0200   /* LPTx Timeout                */
#define CE_IOE            0x0400   /* LPTx I/O Error              */
#define CE_DNS            0x0800   /* LPTx Device not selected    */
#define CE_OOP            0x1000   /* LPTx Out-Of-Paper           */
#define CE_MODE           0x8000   /* Requested mode unsupported  */

#define IE_BADID          (-1)     /* Invalid or unsupported id   */
#define IE_OPEN           (-2)     /* Device Already Open         */
#define IE_NOPEN          (-3)     /* Device Not Open             */
#define IE_MEMORY         (-4)     /* Unable to allocate queues   */
#define IE_DEFAULT        (-5)     /* Error in default parameters */
#define IE_HARDWARE       (-10)    /* Hardware Not Present        */
#define IE_BYTESIZE       (-11)    /* Illegal Byte Size           */
#define IE_BAUDRATE       (-12)    /* Unsupported BaudRate        */

/* Events */
#define EV_RXCHAR         0x0001   /* Any Character received       */
#define EV_RXFLAG         0x0002   /* Received certain character   */
#define EV_TXEMPTY        0x0004   /* Transmitt Queue Empty        */
#define EV_CTS            0x0008   /* CTS changed state            */
#define EV_DSR            0x0010   /* DSR changed state            */
#define EV_RLSD           0x0020   /* RLSD changed state           */
#define EV_BREAK          0x0040   /* BREAK received               */
#define EV_ERR            0x0080   /* Line status error occurred   */
#define EV_RING           0x0100   /* Ring signal detected         */
#define EV_PERR           0x0200   /* Printer error occured        */
#define EV_CTSS           0x0400   /* CTS state                    */
#define EV_DSRS           0x0800   /* DSR state                    */
#define EV_RLSDS          0x1000   /* RLSD state                   */
#define EV_RingTe         0x2000   /* Ring trailing edge indicator */
#define EV_RINGTE         EV_RingTe

/* Escape Functions */
#define SETXOFF           1        /* Simulate XOFF received      */
#define SETXON            2        /* Simulate XON received       */
#define SETRTS            3        /* Set RTS high                */
#define CLRRTS            4        /* Set RTS low                 */
#define SETDTR            5        /* Set DTR high                */
#define CLRDTR            6        /* Set DTR low                 */
#define RESETDEV          7        /* Reset device if possible    */

#define LPTx              0x80     /* Set if ID is for LPT device */

#ifdef WIN31

/* new escape functions
#define GETMAXLPT         8        /* Max supported LPT id        */
#define GETMAXCOM         9        /* Max supported COM id        */
#define GETBASEIRQ        10       /* Get port base & irq for a port */

/* Comm Baud Rate indices */
#define CBR_110           0xFF10
```

```
#define CBR_300          0xFF11
#define CBR_600          0xFF12
#define CBR_1200         0xFF13
#define CBR_2400         0xFF14
#define CBR_4800         0xFF15
#define CBR_9600         0xFF16
#define CBR_14400        0xFF17
#define CBR_19200        0xFF18
/* #define CBR_RESERVED  0xFF19
#define CBR_RESERVED     0xFF1A */
#define CBR_38400        0xFF1B
/* #define CBR_RESERVED  0xFF1C
#define CBR_RESERVED     0xFF1D
#define CBR_RESERVED     0xFF1E */
#define CBR_56000        0xFF1F
/* #define CBR_RESERVED  0xFF20
#define CBR_RESERVED     0xFF21
#define CBR_RESERVED     0xFF22 */
#define CBR_128000       0xFF23
/* #define CBR_RESERVED  0xFF24
#define CBR_RESERVED     0xFF25
#define CBR_RESERVED     0xFF26 */
#define CBR_256000       0xFF27


/* notifications passed in low word of lParam on WM_COMMNOTIFY messages   */
#define CN_RECEIVE       0x01     /* bytes are available in the input queue*/
#define CN_TRANSMIT      0x02     /* fewer than wOutTrigger bytes still    */
                                  /* remain in the output queue waiting    */
                                  /* to be transmitted.                    */
#endif /* WIN31 */


typedef struct tagDCB
 {
   BYTE Id;                /* Internal Device ID             */
   WORD BaudRate;          /* Baudrate at which runing       */
   BYTE ByteSize;          /* Number of bits/byte, 4-8       */
   BYTE Parity;            /* 0-4=None,Odd,Even,Mark,Space   */
   BYTE StopBits;          /* 0,1,2 = 1, 1.5, 2              */
   WORD RlsTimeout;        /* Timeout for RLSD to be set     */
   WORD CtsTimeout;        /* Timeout for CTS to be set      */
   WORD DsrTimeout;        /* Timeout for DSR to be set      */

   BYTE fBinary: 1;        /* Binary Mode (skip EOF check    */
   BYTE fRtsDisable:1;     /* Don't assert RTS at init time  */
   BYTE fParity: 1;        /* Enable parity checking         */
   BYTE fOutxCtsFlow:1;    /* CTS handshaking on output      */
   BYTE fOutxDsrFlow:1;    /* DSR handshaking on output      */
   BYTE fDummy: 2;         /* Reserved                       */
   BYTE fDtrDisable:1;     /* Don't assert DTR at init time  */

   BYTE fOutX: 1;          /* Enable output X-ON/X-OFF       */
   BYTE fInX: 1;           /* Enable input X-ON/X-OFF        */
   BYTE fPeChar: 1;        /* Enable Parity Err Replacement  */
   BYTE fNull: 1;          /* Enable Null stripping          */
   BYTE fChEvt: 1;         /* Enable Rx character event.     */
   BYTE fDtrflow: 1;       /* DTR handshake on input         */
   BYTE fRtsflow: 1;       /* RTS handshake on input         */
   BYTE fDummy2: 1;

   char XonChar;           /* Tx and Rx X-ON character       */
   char XoffChar;          /* Tx and Rx X-OFF character      */
   WORD XonLim;            /* Transmit X-ON threshold        */
   WORD XoffLim;           /* Transmit X-OFF threshold       */
   char PeChar;            /* Parity error replacement char  */
   char EofChar;           /* End of Input character         */
   char EvtChar;           /* Recieved Event character       */
   WORD TxDelay;           /* Amount of time between chars    */
 } DCB;
```

```
typedef DCB FAR * LPDCB;

typedef struct tagCOMSTAT
  {
    BYTE fCtsHold: 1;       /* Transmit is on CTS hold        */
    BYTE fDsrHold: 1;       /* Transmit is on DSR hold        */
    BYTE fRlsdHold: 1;      /* Transmit is on RLSD hold       */
    BYTE fXoffHold: 1;      /* Received handshake             */
    BYTE fXoffSent: 1;      /* Issued handshake               */
    BYTE fEof: 1;           /* End of file character found    */
    BYTE fTxim: 1;          /* Character being transmitted    */
    WORD cbInQue;           /* count of characters in Rx Queue */
    WORD cbOutQue;          /* count of characters in Tx Queue */
  } COMSTAT;

int     API OpenComm(LPSTR, WORD, WORD);
#ifdef  WIN31
BOOL    API EnableCommNotification(int, HWND, int, int);
#endif  /* WIN31 */
int     API SetCommState(LPDCB);
int     API GetCommState(int, LPDCB);
int     API ReadComm(int, LPSTR, int);
int     API UngetCommChar(int, char);
int     API WriteComm(int, LPSTR, int);
int     API CloseComm(int);
int     API GetCommError(int, COMSTAT FAR *);
int     API BuildCommDCB(LPSTR, LPDCB);
int     API TransmitCommChar(int, char);
WORD    FAR * API SetCommEventMask(int, WORD);
WORD    API GetCommEventMask(int, int);
int     API SetCommBreak(int);
int     API ClearCommBreak(int);
int     API FlushComm(int, int);
LONG    API EscapeCommFunction(int, int);

#endif  /* USECOMM */

#ifdef  WIN31
#ifndef NODRIVERS
#define DRV_LOAD                0x0001
#define DRV_ENABLE              0x0002
#define DRV_OPEN                0x0003
#define DRV_CLOSE               0x0004
#define DRV_DISABLE             0x0005
#define DRV_FREE                0x0006
#define DRV_CONFIGURE           0x0007
#define DRV_QUERYCONFIGURE      0x0008
#define DRV_INSTALL             0x0009
#define DRV_REMOVE              0x000A
#define DRV_POWER               0x000F
#define DRV_RESERVED            0x0800
#define DRV_USER                0x4000

/* Supported return values for DRV_CONFIGURE message */
#define DRVCNF_CANCEL           0x0000
#define DRVCNF_OK               0x0001
#define DRVCNF_RESTART          0x0002

HANDLE  API OpenDriver(LPSTR szDriverName, LPSTR szSectionName, LONG lParam2);
LONG    API CloseDriver(HANDLE hDriver, LONG lParam1, LONG lParam2);
HANDLE  API GetDriverModuleHandle(HANDLE hDriver);
LONG    API SendDriverMessage(HANDLE hDriver, WORD message, LONG lParam1, LONG lParam2);
LONG    API DefDriverProc(DWORD dwDriverIdentifier, HANDLE driverID, WORD message, LONG
        lParam1, LONG lParam2);
HANDLE  API GetNextDriver(HANDLE, DWORD);

/* GetNextDriver flags */
#define GND_FIRSTINSTANCEONLY   0x00000001
#define GND_REVERSE             0x00000002
```

```
typedef struct tagDRIVERINFOSTRUCT
{
  WORD          length;
  HANDLE        hDriver;
  HANDLE        hModule;
  char          szAliasName[128];
} DRIVERINFOSTRUCT;
typedef DRIVERINFOSTRUCT FAR *LPDRIVERINFOSTRUCT;
BOOL    API GetDriverInfo(HANDLE, LPDRIVERINFOSTRUCT);

#endif   /* !NODRIVERS */
#endif   /* WIN31 */

#ifndef NOMDI
#ifdef  WIN31
/* MDI client style bits */
#define MDIS_ALLCHILDSTYLES      0x0001

/* wParam Flags for WM_MDITILE and WM_MDICASCADE messages. */
#define MDITILE_VERTICAL         0x0000
#define MDITILE_HORIZONTAL       0x0001
#define MDITILE_SKIPDISABLED     0x0002
#endif   /* WIN31 */

typedef struct tagMDICREATESTRUCT
  {
  LPSTR         szClass;
  LPSTR         szTitle;
  HANDLE        hOwner;
  int           x,y;
  int           cx,cy;
  LONG          style;
  LONG          lParam;        /* app-defined stuff */
  } MDICREATESTRUCT;

typedef MDICREATESTRUCT FAR * LPMDICREATESTRUCT;

typedef struct tagCLIENTCREATESTRUCT
  {
  HANDLE        hWindowMenu;
  WORD          idFirstChild;
  } CLIENTCREATESTRUCT;

typedef CLIENTCREATESTRUCT FAR * LPCLIENTCREATESTRUCT;

LONG    API DefFrameProc(HWND,HWND,WORD,WORD,LONG);
LONG    API DefMDIChildProc(HWND,WORD,WORD,LONG);

#ifndef NOMSG
BOOL    API TranslateMDISysAccel(HWND,LPMSG);
#endif

WORD    API ArrangeIconicWindows(HWND);

#endif   /* NOMDI */

#ifdef  WIN31
#ifndef NOSYSPARAMSINFO
/* Parameter for SystemParametersInfo() */

#define SPI_GETBEEP              1
#define SPI_SETBEEP              2
#define SPI_GETMOUSE             3
#define SPI_SETMOUSE             4
#define SPI_GETBORDER            5
#define SPI_SETBORDER            6
#define SPI_TIMEOUTS             7
#define SPI_GETKEYBOARDSPEED     10
```

```
#define SPI_SETKEYBOARDSPEED          11
#define SPI_LANGDRIVER                12
#define SPI_ICONHORIZONTALSPACING     13
#define SPI_GETSCREENSAVETIMEOUT      14
#define SPI_SETSCREENSAVETIMEOUT      15
#define SPI_GETSCREENSAVEACTIVE       16
#define SPI_SETSCREENSAVEACTIVE       17
#define SPI_GETGRIDGRANULARITY        18
#define SPI_SETGRIDGRANULARITY        19
#define SPI_SETDESKWALLPAPER          20
#define SPI_SETDESKPATTERN            21
#define SPI_GETKEYBOARDDELAY          22
#define SPI_SETKEYBOARDDELAY          23
#define SPI_ICONVERTICALSPACING       24
#define SPI_GETICONTITLEWRAP          25
#define SPI_SETICONTITLEWRAP          26
#define SPI_GETMENUDROPALIGNMENT      27
#define SPI_SETMENUDROPALIGNMENT      28
#define SPI_SETDOUBLECLKWIDTH         29
#define SPI_SETDOUBLECLKHEIGHT        30
#define SPI_GETICONTITLELOGFONT       31
#define SPI_SETDOUBLECLICKTIME        32
#define SPI_SETMOUSEBUTTONSWAP        33
#define SPI_SETICONTITLELOGFONT       34


BOOL    API SystemParametersInfo(WORD, WORD, LPVOID, WORD);
/* Flags */
#define SPIF_UPDATEINIFILE      0x0001
#define SPIF_SENDWININICHANGE   0x0002

#define SPIF_VALID              0x0003

#endif  /* NOSYSPARAMSINFO */
#endif  /* WIN31 */

#endif  /* NOUSER */

#ifndef NOHELP

/*  Help engine section.  */

/* Commands to pass WinHelp() */
#define HELP_CONTEXT            0x0001  /* Display topic in ulTopic */
#define HELP_QUIT               0x0002  /* Terminate help */
#define HELP_INDEX              0x0003  /* Display index */
#define HELP_CONTENTS           0x0003
#define HELP_HELPONHELP         0x0004  /* Display help on using help */
#define HELP_SETINDEX           0x0005  /* Set the current Index for multi index help */
#define HELP_SETCONTENTS        0x0005
#define HELP_CONTEXTPOPUP       0x0008
#define HELP_FORCEFILE          0x0009
#define HELP_KEY                0x0101  /* Display topic for keyword in offabData */
#define HELP_COMMAND            0x0102
#define HELP_PARTIALKEY         0x0105  /* call the search engine in winhelp */
#define HELP_MULTIKEY           0x0201
#define HELP_SETWINPOS          0x0203

BOOL    API WinHelp(HWND hwndMain, LPSTR lpszHelp, WORD usCommand, DWORD ulData);

typedef struct tagMULTIKEYHELP
  {
    WORD        mkSize;
    BYTE        mkKeylist;
    BYTE        szKeyphrase[1];
  } MULTIKEYHELP;

#endif  /* NOHELP */
```

```
#ifndef NOPROFILER

/* function declarations for profiler routines contained in Windows libraries */
int      API ProfInsChk(void);
void     API ProfSetup(int,int);
void     API ProfSampRate(int,int);
void     API ProfStart(void);
void     API ProfStop(void);
void     API ProfClear(void);
void     API ProfFlush(void);
void     API ProfFinish(void);

#endif   /* NOPROFILER */


#ifdef  PRINTING
typedef struct {
    short        cbSize;
    LPSTR        lpszDocName;
    LPSTR        lpszOutput;
    } DOCINFO, FAR * LPDOCINFO;

int      API StartDoc(HDC, LPDOCINFO);
int      API StartPage(HDC);
int      API EndPage(HDC);
int      API EndDoc(HDC);
int      API SetAbortProc(HDC, FARPROC);
int      API AbortDoc(HDC);
#endif
```

Jim Conger began programming in 1972 while studying Engineering at the University of Southern California. He has been writing programs ever since for a variety of computers. Most of his early work was done on mainframe computer systems using FORTRAN and BASIC for process simulation work. Jim started programming microcomputers in the early 1980s while living in London. These projects were primarily financial models, using BASIC, Pascal and assembly language. His first C programs were written in 1983 while under the CP/M operating system, and has continued using C and C++ under MS-DOS and Windows.

Jim's hobby of playing woodwind instruments lead to his interest in computer music. He is the author of two books on the subject, *C Programming for MIDI* (M&T Books, 1989), and *MIDI Sequencing in C* (M&T Books, 1989). Jim lives in California with his wife and two children.

Colophon

Production for this book used desktop publishing techniques—every phase of the book involved the use of computer technology. Never did production use traditional typesetting, stats, or photos, and virtually everything for this book, from the illustrations to the formatted text, was saved on disk. Only the cover painting was created in the traditional manner.

This book was written on an IBM PC-compatible computer but Apple Macintosh computers were used for desktop publishing. The text was written using Microsoft Word for Windows 1.1 and style sheets. The finished documents were transferred directly to a Macintosh using MacLink Desktop version 5.0.

All book design and page formatting was done in Aldus PageMaker 4.01 for the Macintosh, using the imported Microsoft Word files. Adobe Postscript fonts were used. Design elements and line art work was created in Adobe Illustrator 3.01.

PC screen dumps were captured as .BMP files and then translated to TIFFs using Publisher's Paintbrush, by ZSoft Corporation. The PC TIFF files were transferred directly to Macintosh on a 3.5-inch DOS disk opened under Access PC. The TIFF files were imported into PageMaker.

The cover was created as a traditional airbrush painting and scanned. QuarkXpress 3.0 was used for four-color cover type and layout.

Final files were sent on Syquest 44 Mb removable disk cartridges to the printer, R.R. Donnelley & Sons Co., where they were directly imposed to film through a Macintosh IIfx and Linotronic 530 phototypesetting machine, utilizing Adobe and Monotype fonts. Plates were then made from the film.

AS A PUBLISHER AND WRITER WITH OVER 360,000 BOOKS SOLD EACH YEAR, IT CAME AS A GREAT SHOCK TO DISCOVER THAT OUR RAIN FORESTS, HOME FOR HALF OF ALL LIVING THINGS ON EARTH, ARE BEING DESTROYED AT THE RATE OF 50 ACRES PER MINUTE ☞ AT THIS RATE THE RAIN FORESTS WILL COMPLETELY DISAPPEAR IN JUST 50 YEARS ☞ BOOKS HAVE A LARGE INFLUENCE ON THIS RAMPANT DESTRUCTION ☞ FOR EXAMPLE, SINCE IT TAKES 17 TREES TO PRODUCE ONE TON OF PAPER, A FIRST PRINTING OF 30,000 COPIES OF A TYPICAL 480 PAGE BOOK CONSUMES 108,000 POUNDS OF PAPER WHICH WILL REQUIRE 918 TREES ☞ TO HELP OFFSET THIS LOSS, WAITE GROUP PRESS WILL PLANT TWO TREES FOR EVERY TREE FELLED FOR PRODUCTION OF THIS BOOK ☞ THE DONATION WILL BE MADE TO RAINFOREST ACTION NETWORK (THE BASIC FOUNDATION, P.O. BOX 47012, ST. PETERSBURG, FL 33743), WHICH CAN PLANT 1,000 TREES FOR $250.

BREAK into Windows Programming

Subscribe to **Windows Tech Journal**,
the new magazine of tools and techniques for
Windows programmers.

(see other side for more information)

Plan for a programming breakthrough.

To get your free issue and start your no-risk subscription, simply fill out this form and
send it to **Windows Tech Journal**, PO Box 70087, Eugene OR 97401-0143 or
you can FAX it to 503-746-0071.
You'll get a full year—12 issues in all—of Windows tools and techniques for only **$29.95.**
If you're not completely satisfied write "no thanks" on the subscription bill.
The free issue is yours to keep and you owe nothing.

NAME _____

COMPANY _____

ADDRESS _____

CITY _____ STATE _____ ZIP _____

PHONE _____

For fastest service call **800-234-0386** or FAX this card to **503-746-0071.**

Errata:

The following function was inadvertantly omitted from Chapter 6: Mouse and Cursor functions.

GetCursor

□ Win 2.0   □ Win 3.0   ■ Win 3.1

Purpose	Get the handle of the curent cursor.
Syntax	HCURSOR GetCursor (void);
Description	Retrieves the handle of the curent cursor.
Returns	The handle of the curent cursor, if one exists. Return NULL on error.
Parameters	None (void).
See Also	SetCursor().

MESSAGES

Button Messages

Button Notification Codes

Combo Box Messages

Combo Box Notification Codes

Waite Group Satisfaction Report Card

Please fill out this card if you wish to know of future updates to *The Waite Group's Windows API Bible*, or to receive our catalog.

Company Name: _____

Division: _____ **Mail Stop:** _____

Last Name: _____ **First Name:** _____ **Middle Initial:** _____

Street Address: _____

City: _____ **State:** _____ **Zip:** _____

Daytime telephone: (   )

Date product was acquired: Month _____ **Day** _____ **Year** _____ **Your Occupation:** _____

Overall, how would you rate *The Waite Group's Windows API Bible*?

☐ Excellent   ☐ Very Good   ☐ Good
☐ Fair   ☐ Below Average ☐ Poor

What did you like MOST about this product? _____

_____

What did you like LEAST about this product? _____

_____

How did you use this book (problem-solver, tutorial, reference...)?

_____

_____

What programming language do you use to write Windows applications?

☐ C   ☐ C++   ☐ Pascal
☐ Visual Basic   ☐ Other _____

What is your level of computer expertise?

☐ New   ☐ Know one language   ☐ Know many languages
☐ Hacker   ☐ Guru   ☐ Wizard/Professional

What computer languages are you familiar with? _____

_____

Please describe your computer hardware:

Computer _____   Hard disk _____
5.25" disk drives _____   3.5" disk drives _____
Video card _____   Monitor _____
Printer _____   Peripherals _____

Where did you buy this book?

☐ Bookstore (name: _____)
☐ Discount store (name: _____)
☐ Computer store (name: _____)
☐ Catalog (name: _____)
☐ Direct from WGP   ☐ Other _____

What price did you pay for this book? _____

What influenced your purchase of this book?

☐ Recommendation   ☐ Advertisement
☐ Magazine review   ☐ Store display
☐ Mailing   ☐ Book's format
☐ Reputation of The Waite Group   ☐ **Other** _____

How many computer books do you buy each year? _____

How many other Waite Group books do you own? _____

What is your favorite Waite Group book? _____

_____

Is there any program or subject you would like to see The Waite Group cover in a similar approach? _____

_____

Additional comments? _____

_____

_____

☐ **Check here for a free Waite Group catalog**

Waite Group Press, Inc.
Attention: *Windows API Bible*
200 Tamal Plaza, Suite 101
Corte Madera, CA 94925

- - - - - - - - - - - - - - - - - - FOLD HERE - - - - - - - - - - - - - - - -

GetClipboardData (WORD wFormat) :
HANDLE

GetClipboardFormatName (WORD
wFormat, LPSTR lpFormatName, int
nMaxCount) : int

GetClipboardOwner (void) : HWND

GetClipboardViewer (void) : HWND

GetOpenClipboardWindow (void) : HWND

GetPriorityClipboardFormat (WORD FAR
*lpPriorityList, int nCount) : int

IsClipboardFormatAvailable (WORD
wFormat) : BOOL

OpenClipboard (HWND hWnd) : BOOL

RegisterClipboardFormat (LPSTR
lpFormatName) : WORD

SetClipboardData (WORD wFormat,
HANDLE hMem) : HANDLE

SetClipboardViewer (HWND hWnd) : HWND

Sound Functions

CloseSound (void) : void

CountVoiceNotes (int nVoice) : int

GetThresholdEvent (void) : LPINT

GetThresholdStatus (void) : int

MessageBeep (WORD wType) : void

OpenSound (void) : int

SetSoundNoise (int nSource, int
nDuration) : int

SetVoiceAccent (int nVoice, int nTempo, int
nVolume, int nMode, int nPitch) : int

SetVoiceEnvelope (int nVoice, int nShape,
int nRepeat) : int

SetVoiceNote (int nVoice, int nValue, int
nLength, int nCDots) : int

SetVoiceQueueSize (int nVoice, int nBytes)
: int

SetVoiceSound (int nVoice, LONG
lFrequency, int nDuration) : int

SetVoiceThreshold (int nVoice, int nNotes)
: int

StartSound (void) : int

StopSound (void) : int

SyncAllVoices (void) : int

WaitSoundState (int nState) : int

Character Sets and Strings

AnsiLower (LPSTR lpString) : LPSTR

AnsiLowerBuff (LPSTR lpString, WORD
nLength) : WORD

AnsiNext (LPSTR lpCurrentChar) : LPSTR

AnsiPrev (LPSTR lpStart, LPSTR
lpCurrentChar) : LPSTR

AnsiToOem (LPSTR lpAnsiStr, LPSTR
lpOemStr) : int

AnsiToOemBuff (LPSTR lpAnsiStr, LPSTR
lpOemStr, int nLength) : void

AnsiUpper (LPSTR lpString) : LPSTR

AnsiUpperBuff (LPSTR lpString, WORD
nLength) : WORD

IsCharAlpha (char cChar) : BOOL

IsCharAlphaNumeric (char cChar) : BOOL

IsCharLower (char cChar) : BOOL

IsCharUpper (char cChar) : BOOL

lstrcat (LPSTR lpString1, LPSTR
lpString2) : LPSTR

lstrcmp (LPSTR lpString1, LPSTR
lpString2) : int

lstrcmpi (LPSTR lpString1, LPSTR
lpString2) : int

lstrcpy (LPSTR lpString1, LPSTR lpString2)
: LPSTR

lstrlen (LPSTR lpString) : int

OemToAnsi (LPSTR lpOemStr, LPSTR
lpAnsiStr) : int

OemToAnsiBuff (LPSTR lpOemStr, LPSTR
lpAnsiStr, int nLength) : void

ToAscii (WORD wVirtKey, WORD
wScanCode, LPSTR lpKeyState, LPVOID
lpChar, WORD wFlags) : int

MS-DOS and Disk File Access

DlgDirList (HWND hDlg, LPSTR
lpPathSpec, int nIDListBox, int
nIDStaticPath, WORD wFileType) : int

DlgDirListComboBox (HWND hDlg, LPSTR
lpPathSpec, int nIDListBox, int
nIDStaticPath, WORD wFileType) : int

DlgDirSelect (HWND hDlg, LPSTR lpString,
int nIDListBox) : BOOL

DlgDirSelectComboBox (HWND hDlg,
LPSTR lpString, int nIDComboBox) :
BOOL

GetDOSEnvironment (void) : LPSTR

GetDriveType (int nDrive) : WORD

GetEnvironment (LPSTR lpPortName,
LPSTR lpEnviron, WORD nMaxCount) :
int

GetPrivateProfileInt (LPSTR
lpApplicationName, LPSTR lpKeyName,
int nDefault, LPSTR lpFileName) :
WORD

GetPrivateProfileString (LPSTR
lpApplicationName, LPSTR lpKeyName,
LPSTR lpDefault, LPSTR
lpReturnedString, int nSize, LPSTR
lpFileName) : int

GetProfileInt (LPSTR lpApplicationName,
LPSTR lpKeyName, int nDefault) : WORD

GetProfileString (LPSTR lpApplicationName,
LPSTR lpKeyName, LPSTR lpDefault,
LPSTR lpReturnedString, int nSize) : int

GetSystemDirectory (LPSTR
lpBuffer,WORD nSize) : WORD

GetTempDrive (BYTE cDriveLetter) : BYTE

GetTempFileName (BYTE cDriveLetter,
LPSTR lpPrefixString, WORD wUnique,
LPSTR lpTempFileName) : int

GetWindowsDirectory (LPSTR
lpBuffer,WORD nSize) : WORD

_lclose (int hFile) : int

_lcreat (LPSTR lpPathName, int iAttribute)
: int

_llseek (int hFile, long lOffset, int iOrigin) :
LONG

_lopen (LPSTR lpPathName, int
iReadWrite) : int

_lread (int hFile, LPSTR lpBuffer, int
wBytes) : int

_lwrite (int hFile, LPSTR lpBuffer, int
wBytes) : int

OpenFile (LPSTR lpFileName,
LPOFSTRUCT lpReOpenBuf, WORD
wStyle) : int

SetEnvironment (LPSTR lpPortName,
LPSTR lpEnviron, WORD nCount) : int

SetErrorMode (WORD wMode) : WORD

SetHandleCount (WORD wNumber) :
WORD

WritePrivateProfileString (LPSTR lpApplicationName, LPSTR lpKeyName, LPSTR
lpString, LPSTR lpFileName) : BOOL

WriteProfileString (LPSTR
lpApplicationName, LPSTR lpKeyName,
LPSTR lpString) : BOOL

Communications Functions

BuildCommDCB (LPSTR lpDef, DCB FAR *
lpDCB) : int

ClearCommBreak (int nCid) : int

CloseComm (int nCid) : int

EscapeCommFunction (int nCid, int
nFunc) : int

FlushComm (int nCid, int nQueue) : int

GetCommError (int nCid, COMSTAT FAR
*lpStat) : int

GetCommEventMask (int nCid, int
nEvtMask) : WORD

GetCommState (int nCid, DCB FAR
*lpDCB) : int

OpenComm (LPSTR lpComName, WORD
wInQueue, WORD wOutQueue) : int

ReadComm (int nCid, LPSTR lpBuf, int
nSize) : int

SetCommBreak (int nCid) : int

FAR *SetCommEventMask (int nCid, WORD
nEvtMask) : WORD

SetCommState (DCB FAR *lpDCB) : int

TransmitCommChar (int nCid, char cChar)
: int

UngetCommChar (int nCid, char cChar) :
int

WriteComm (int nCid, LPSTR lpBuf, int
nSize) : int

Atom Functions

AddAtom (LPSTR lpString) : ATOM

DeleteAtom (ATOM nAtom) : ATOM

FindAtom (LPSTR lpString) : ATOM

GetAtomHandle (ATOM wAtom) : HANDLE

GetAtomName (ATOM nAtom, LPSTR
lpBuffer, int nSize) : WORD

DeleteDC (HDC hDC) : BOOL

DeviceCapabilities (LPSTR lpDeviceName, LPSTR lpPort, WORD nIndex, LPSTR lpOutput, LPDEVMODE lpDevMode) : DWORD

DPtoLP (HDC hDC, LPPOINT lpPoints, int nCount) : BOOL

DrawText (HDC hDC, LPSTR lpString, int nCount, LPRECT lpRect, WORD wFormat) : int

EnumFonts (HDC hDC, LPSTR lpFacename, FARPROC lpFontFunc, LPSTR lpData) : int

ExtDeviceMode (HWND hWnd, HANDLE hDriver, LPDEVMODE lpDevModeOutput, LPSTR lpDeviceName, LPSTR lpPort, LPDEVMODE lpDevModeInput, LPSTR lpProfile, WORD wMode) : int

Escape (HDC hDC, int nEscape, int nCount, LPSTR lpInData, LPSTR lpOutData) : int

ExtTextOut (HDC hDC, int X, int Y, WORD wOptions, LPRECT lpRect, LPSTR lpString, WORD nCount, LPINT lpDx) : BOOL

GetBkColor (HDC hDC) : DWORD

GetBkMode (HDC hDC) : int

GetCharWidth (HDC hDC, WORD wFirstChar, WORD wLastChar, LPINT lpBuffer) : BOOL

GetDC (HWND hWnd) : HDC

GetDCOrg (HDC hDC) : DWORD

GetDeviceCaps (HDC hDC, int nIndex) : int

GetMapMode (HDC hDC) : int

GetSystemMetrics (int nIndex) : int

GetTabbedTextExtent (HDC hDC, LPSTR lpString, int nCount, int nTabPositions, LPINT lpnTabStopPositions) : DWORD

GetTextAlign (HDC hDC) : WORD

GetTextCharacterExtra (HDC hDC) : int

GetTextColor (HDC hDC) : DWORD

GetTextExtent (HDC hDC, LPSTR lpString, int nCount) : DWORD

GetTextFace (HDC hDC, int nCount, LPSTR lpFacename) : int

GetTextMetrics (HDC hDC, LPTEXTMETRIC lpMetrics) : BOOL

GetViewportExt (HDC hDC) : DWORD

GetViewportOrg (HDC hDC) : DWORD

GetWindowDC (HWND hWnd) : HDC

GetWindowExt (HDC hDC) : DWORD

GetWindowOrg (HDC hDC) : DWORD

GrayString (HDC hDC, HBRUSH hBrush, FARPROC lpOutputFunc, DWORD lpData, int nCount, int X, int Y, int nWidth, int nHeight) : BOOL

LPtoDP (HDC hDC, LPPOINT lpPoints, int nCount) : BOOL

OffsetViewportOrg (HDC hDC, int X, int Y) : DWORD

OffsetWindowOrg (HDC hDC, int X, int Y) : DWORD

ReleaseDC (HWND hWnd, HDC hDC) : int

RemoveFontResource (LPSTR lpFilename) : BOOL

ResetDC (HDC hDC, LPDEVMODE lpInitData) : HDC

RestoreDC (HDC hDC, int nSavedDC) : BOOL

SaveDC (HDC hDC) : int

ScaleViewportExt (HDC hDC, int Xnum, int Xdenom, int Ynum, int Ydenom) : DWORD

ScaleWindowExt (HDC hDC, int Xnum, int Xdenom, int Ynum, int Ydenom) : DWORD

SetBkColor (HDC hDC, DWORD crColor) : DWORD

SetBkMode (HDC hDC, int nBkMode) : int

SetMapMode (HDC hDC, int nMapMode) : int

SetMapperFlags (HDC hDC, DWORD dwFlag) : DWORD

SetTextAlign (HDC hDC, WORD wFlags) : WORD

SetTextCharacterExtra (HDC hDC, int nCharExtra) : int

SetTextColor (HDC hDC, DWORD crColor) : DWORD

SetTextJustification (HDC hDC, int nBreakExtra, int nBreakCount) : int

SetViewportExt (HDC hDC, int X, int Y) : DWORD

SetViewportOrg (HDC hDC, int X, int Y) : DWORD

SetWindowExt (HDC hDC, int X, int Y) : DWORD

SetWindowOrg (HDC hDC, int X, int Y) : DWORD

TabbedTextOut (HDC hDC, int X, int Y, LPSTR lpString, int nCount, int nTabPositions, LPINT lpnTabStop-Positions, int nTabOrigin) : long

TextOut (HDC hDC, int X, int Y, LPSTR lpString, int nCount) : BOOL

wsprintf (LPSTR lpOutput, LPSTR lpFormat[, argument]...) : int

wvsprintf (LPSTR lpOutput, LPSTR lpFormat, LPSTR lpArglist) : int

Painting the Screen

Arc (HDC hDC, int X1, int Y1, int X2, int Y2, int X3, int Y3, int X4 , int Y4) : BOOL

BeginPaint (HWND hWnd, LPPAINTSTRUCT lpPaint) : HDC

Chord (HDC hDC, int X1, int Y1, int X2, int Y2, int X3, int Y3, int X4 , int Y4) : BOOL

CombineRgn (HRGN hDestRgn, HRGN hSrcRgn1, HRGN hSrcRgn2, int nCombineMode) : int

CopyRect (LPRECT lpDestRect, LPRECT lpSourceRect) : int

CreateBrushIndirect (LOGBRUSH FAR *lpLogBrush) : HBRUSH

CreateEllipticRgn (int X1, int Y1, int X2, int Y2) : HRGN

CreateEllipticRgnIndirect (LPRECT lpRect) : HRGN

CreateHatchBrush (int nIndex,DWORD crColor) : HBRUSH

CreatePatternBrush (HBITMAP hBitmap) : HBRUSH

CreatePen (int nPenStyle, int nWidth, DWORD crColor) : HPEN

CreatePenIndirect (LOGPEN FAR * lpLogPen) : HPEN

CreatePolygonRgn (LPPOINT lpPoints, int nCount, int nPolyFillMode) : HRGN

CreatePolyPolygonRgn (LPPOINT lpPoints, LPINT lpPolyCounts, int nCount, int nPolyFillMode) : HRGN

CreateRectRgn (int X1, int Y1, int X2, int Y2) : HRGN

CreateRectRgnIndirect (LPRECT lpRect) : HRGN

CreateRoundRectRgn (int X1, int Y1, int X2, int Y2, int X3, int Y3) : HRGN

CreateSolidBrush (DWORD crColor) : HBRUSH

DeleteObject (HANDLE hObject) : BOOL

DrawFocusRect (HDC hDC, LPRECT lpRect) : void

Ellipse (HDC hDC, int X1, int Y1, int X2, int Y2) : BOOL

EndPaint (HWND hWnd, LPPAINTSTRUCT lpPaint) : void

EnumObjects (HDC hDC, int nObjectType, FARPROC lpObjectFunct, LPSTR lpData) : int

EqualRect (LPRECT lpRect1, LPRECT lpRect2) : BOOL

EqualRgn (HRGN hSrcRgn1, HRGN hSrcRgn2) : BOOL

ExcludeClipRect (HDC hDC, int X1, int Y1, int X2, int Y2) : int

ExcludeUpdateRgn (HDC hDC, HWND hWnd) : int

ExtFloodFill (HDC hDC, int X, int Y, DWORD crColor, WORD wFillType) : BOOL

FillRect (HDC hDC, LPRECT lpRect, HBRUSH hBrush) : int

FillRgn (HDC hDC, HRGN hRgn, HBRUSH hBrush) : BOOL

FloodFill (HDC hDC, int X, int Y, DWORD crColor) : BOOL

FrameRect (HDC hDC, LPRECT lpRect, HBRUSH hBrush) : int

FrameRgn (HDC hDC, HRGN hRgn, HBRUSH hBrush, int nWidth, int nHeight) : BOOL

GetBrushOrg (HDC hDC) : DWORD

GetBValue (DWORD rgbColor) : BYTE

GetClipBox (HDC hDC, LPRECT lpRect) : int

GetCurrentPosition (HDC hDC) : DWORD

GetNearestColor (HDC hDC, DWORD crColor) : DWORD

GetObject (HANDLE hObject, int nCount, LPSTR lpObject) : int

GetPixel (HDC hDC, int X, int Y) : DWORD

GetPolyFillMode (HDC hDC) : int

GetRgnBox (HRGN hRgn, LPRECT lpRect) : int

GetROP2 (HDC hDC) : int

GetStockObject (int nIndex) : HANDLE

GetSysColor (int nIndex) : DWORD

GetUpdateRect (HWND hWnd, LPRECT lpRect, BOOL bErase) : BOOL

GetUpdateRgn (HWND hWnd, HRGN hRgn, BOOL bErase) : int

InflateRect (LPRECT lpRect, int X, int Y) : void

IntersectClipRect (HDC hDC, int X1, int Y1, int X2, int Y2) : int

IntersectRect (LPRECT lpDestRect, LPRECT lpSrc1Rect, LPRECT lpSrc2Rect) : int

InvalidateRect (HWND hWnd, LPRECT lpRect, BOOL bErase) : void

InvalidateRgn (HWND hWnd, HRGN hRgn, BOOL bErase) : void

InvertRect (HDC hDC, LPRECT lpRect) : void

InvertRgn (HDC hDC, HRGN hRgn) : BOOL

IsRectEmpty (LPRECT lpRect) : BOOL

LineDDA (int X1, int Y1, int X2, int Y2, FARPROC lpLineFunc, LPSTR lpData) : void

LineTo (HDC hDC, int X, int Y) : BOOL

MAKEPOINT (DWORD dwInteger) : POINT

MoveTo (HDC hDC, int X, int Y) : DWORD

OffsetClipRgn (HDC hDC, int X, int Y) : int

OffsetRect (LPRECT lpRect, int X, int Y) : void

OffsetRgn (HRGN hRgn, int X, int Y) : int

PaintRgn (HDC hDC, HRGN hRgn) : BOOL

Pie (HDC hDC, int X1, int Y1, int X2, int Y2, int X3, int Y3, int X4, int Y4) : BOOL

Polygon (HDC hDC, LPPOINT lpPoints, int nCount) : BOOL

Polyline (HDC hDC, LPPOINT lpPoints, int nCount) : BOOL

PolyPolygon (HDC hDC, LPPOINT lpPoints, LPINT lpPolyCounts, int nCount) : BOOL

PtInRect (LPRECT lpRect, POINT Point) : BOOL

PtInRegion (HRGN hRgn, int X, int Y) : BOOL

PtVisible (HDC hDC, int X, int Y) : BOOL

Rectangle (HDC hDC, int X1, int Y1, int X2, int Y2) : BOOL

RectInRegion (HRGN hRgn, LPRECT lpRect) : BOOL

RectVisible (HDC hDC, LPRECT lpRect) : BOOL

RGB (BYTE cRed, BYTE cGreen, BYTE cBlue) : COLORREF

RoundRect (HDC hDC, int X1, int Y1, int X2, int Y3, int X3, int Y3) : BOOL

SelectClipRgn (HDC hDC, HRGN hRgn) : int

SelectObject (HDC hDC, HANDLE hObject) : HANDLE

SetBrushOrg (HDC hDC, int X, int Y) : DWORD

SetPixel (HDC hDC, int X, int Y, DWORD crColor) : DWORD

SetPolyFillMode (HDC hDC, int nPolyFillMode) : int

SetRect (LPRECT lpRect, int X1, int Y1, int X2, int Y2) : void

SetRectEmpty (LPRECT lpRect) : void

SetRectRgn (HRGN hRgn, int X1, int Y1, int X2, int Y2) : void

SetROP2 (HDC hDC, int nDrawMode) : int

SetSysColors (int nChanges, LPINT lpSysColor, DWORD FAR *lpColorValues) : void

UnionRect (LPRECT lpDestRect, LPRECT lpSrc1Rect, LPRECT lpSrc2Rect) : int

UnrealizeObject (HBRUSH hObject) : BOOL

UpdateWindow (HWND hWnd) : void

ValidateRect (HWND hWnd, LPRECT lpRect) : void

ValidateRgn (HWND hWnd, HRGN hRgn) : void

Color Palette Control

AnimatePalette (HPALETTE hPalette, WORD wStartIndex, WORD wNumEntries, LPPALETTEENTRY lpPaletteColors) : void

CreatePalette (LPLOGPALETTE lpLogPalette) : HPALETTE

GetPaletteEntries (HPALETTE hPalette, WORD wStartIndex, WORD wNumEntries, LPPALETTEENTRY lpPaletteEntries) : WORD

GetNearestPaletteIndex (HPALETTE hPalette, DWORD crColor) : WORD

GetSystemPaletteEntries (HDC hDC, WORD wStartIndex, WORD wNumEntries, LPPALETTEENTRY lpPaletteEntries) : WORD

GetSystemPaletteUse (HDC hDC, WORD wUndoc) : WORD

PALETTEINDEX (int nPaletteIndex) : COLORREF

PALETTERGB (BYTE cRed, BYTE cGreen, BYTE cBlue) : COLORREF

RealizePalette (HDC hDC) : int

ResizePalette (HPALETTE hPalette, WORD nNumEntries) : BOOL

SelectPalette (HDC hDC, HPALETTE hPalette, BOOL bForceBackground) : HPALETTE

SetPaletteEntries (HPALETTE hPalette, WORD wStartIndex, WORD wNumEntries, LPPALETTEENTRY lpPaletteEntries) : WORD

SetSysColors (int nChanges, LPINT lpSysColor, DWORD FAR *lpColorValues) : void

SetSystemPaletteUse (HDC hDC, WORD wUsage) : WORD

UpdateColors (HDC hDC) : int

Dialog Boxes

CheckDlgButton (HWND hDlg, int nIdButton, WORD wCheck) : void

CheckRadioButton (HWND hDlg, int nIDFirstButton, int nIDLastButton, int nIDCheckButton) : void

CreateDialog (HANDLE hInstance, LPSTR lpTemplateName, HWND hWndParent, FARPROC lpDialogFunc) : HWND

CreateDialogIndirect (HANDLE hInstance, LPSTR lpDialogTemplate, HWND hWndParent, FARPROC lpDialogFunc) : HWND

CreateDialogIndirectParam (HANDLE hInstance, LPSTR lpDialogTemplate, HWND hWndParent, FARPROC lpDialogFunc, LONG dwInitParam) : HWND

CreateDialogParam (HANDLE hInstance, LPSTR lpTemplateName, HWND hWndParent, FARPROC lpDialogFunc, LONG dwInitParam) : HWND

DefDlgProc (HWND hDlg, WORD wMsg, WORD wParam, LONG lParam) : LONG

DialogBox (HANDLE hInstance, LPSTR lpTemplateName, HWND hWndParent, FARPROC lpDialogFunc) : int

DialogBoxIndirect (HANDLE hInstance, HANDLE hDialogTemplate, HWND hWndParent, FARPROC lpDialogFunc) : int

DialogBoxIndirectParam (HANDLE hInstance, HANDLE hDialogTemplate, HWND hWndParent, FARPROC lpDialogFunc, DWORD dwInitParam) : int

DialogBoxParam (HANDLE hInstance, LPSTR lpTemplateName, HWND hWndParent, FARPROC lpDialogFunc, DWORD dwInitParam) : int

EndDialog (HWND hDlg, int nResult) : void

GetDialogBaseUnits (void) : LONG

GetDlgCtrlID (HWND hWnd) : int

GetDlgItem (HWND hWnd, int nIDDlgItem) : HWND

GetDlgItemInt (HWND hDlg, int nIDDlgItem, BOOL FAR *lpTranslated, BOOL bSigned) : WORD

GetDlgItemText (HWND hDlg, int nIDDlgItem, LPSTR lpString, int nMaxCount) : int

GetNextDlgGroupItem (HWND hDlg, HWND hCtl, BOOL bPrevious) : HWND

GetNextDlgTabItem (HWND hDlg, HWND hCtl, BOOL bPrevious) : HWND

IsDialogMessage (HWND hDlg, LPMSG lpMsg) : BOOL

IsDlgButtonChecked (HWND hDlg, int nIDButton) : WORD

MapDialogRect (HWND hDlg, LPRECT lpRect) : void

MessageBox (HWND hWndParent, LPSTR lpText, LPSTR lpCaption, WORD wType) : int

SendDlgItemMessage (HWND hDlg, int nIDDlgItem, WORD wMsg, WORD wParam, LONG lParam) : DWORD

SetDlgItemInt (HWND hDlg, int nIDDlgItem, WORD wValue, BOOL bSigned) : void

SetDlgItemText (HWND hDlg, int nIDDlgItem, LPSTR lpString) : void

Memory Management

FreeModule (HANDLE hModule) : void

GetCodeHandle (FARPROC lpProc) : HANDLE

GetCodeInfo (FARPROC lpProc, LPVOID lpSegInfo) : void

GetCurrentPDB (void) : WORD

GlobalDosAlloc (DWORD dwBytes) : DWORD

GlobalDosFree (WORD wSelector) : WORD

GlobalFix (HANDLE hMem) : void

GetFreeSpace (WORD wFlags) : DWORD

GetModuleFileName (HANDLE hModule, LPSTR lpFilename, int nSize) : int

GetModuleHandle (LPSTR lpModuleName) : HANDLE

GetModuleUsage (HANDLE hModule) : int

GlobalAlloc (WORD wFlags, DWORD dwBytes) : HANDLE

GlobalCompact (DWORD dwMinFree) : DWORD

GlobalDiscard (DWORD hMem) : HANDLE

GlobalFlags (HANDLE hMem) : WORD

GlobalFree (HANDLE hMem) : HANDLE

GlobalHandle (WORD wMem) : DWORD

GlobalLock (HANDLE hMem) : LPSTR

GlobalLRUNewest (HANDLE hMem) : HANDLE

GlobalLRUOldest (HANDLE hMem) : HANDLE

GlobalNotify (HANDLE lpNotifyProc) : void

GlobalPageLock (WORD wSelector) : WORD

GlobalPageUnlock (WORD wSelector) : WORD

GlobalReAlloc (HANDLE hMem, WORD wBytes, WORD wFlags) : HANDLE

GlobalSize (HANDLE hMem) : DWORD

GlobalUnfix (HANDLE hMem) : BOOL

GlobalUnlock (HANDLE hMem) : BOOL

GlobalUnWire (HANDLE hMem) : BOOL

GlobalWire (HANDLE hMem) : LPSTR

LimitEmsPages (DWORD dwKbytes) : void

LoadModule (LPSTR lpModuleName, LPVOID lpParameterBlock) : HANDLE

LocalAlloc (WORD wFlags, WORD wBytes) : HANDLE

LocalCompact (WORD wMinFree) : WORD

LocalDiscard (HANDLE hMem) : HANDLE

LocalFlags (HANDLE hMem) : WORD

LocalFree (HANDLE hMem) : HANDLE

LocalHandle (WORD wMem) : HANDLE

LocalLock (HANDLE hMem) : PSTR

LocalReAlloc (HANDLE hMem, WORD wBytes, WORD wFlags) : HANDLE

LocalShrink (HANDLE hSeg, WORD wSize) : WORD

LocalSize (HANDLE hMem) : WORD

LocalUnlock (HANDLE hMem) : BOOL

LockSegment (WORD wSegment) : HANDLE

MulDiv (int nNumber, int nNumerator, int nDenominator) : int

UnlockSegment (WORD wSegment) : BOOL

WinExec (LPSTR lpCmdLine, WORD nCmdShow) : WORD

Bitmaps

BitBlt (HDC hDC, int X, int Y, int nWidth, int nHeight, HDC hSrcDC, int XSrc, int YSrc, DWORD dwRop) : BOOL

CreateBitmap (int nWidth, int nHeight, BYTE nPlanes, BYTE nBitCount, LPSTR lpBits) : HBITMAP

CreateBitmapIndirect (BITMAP FAR * lpBitmap) : HBITMAP

CreateCompatibleBitmap (HDC hDC, int nWidth, int nHeight) : HBITMAP

CreateDIBitmap (HDC hDC, LPBITMAPINFOHEADER lpInfoHeader, DWORD dwUsage, LPSTR lpInitBits, LPBITMAPINFO lpInitInfo, WORD wUsage) : HBITMAP

CreateDIBPatternBrush (HANDLE hPackedDIB, WORD wUsage) : HBRUSH

CreateDiscardableBitmap (HDC hDC, int nWidth, int nHeight) : HBITMAP

GetBitmapBits (HBITMAP hBitmap, LONG dwCount, LPSTR lpBits) : DWORD

GetBitmapDimension (HBITMAP hBitmap) : DWORD

GetDIBits (HDC hDC, HANDLE hBitmap, WORD nStartScan, WORD nNumScans, LPSTR lpBits, LPBITMAPINFO lpBitsInfo, WORD wUsage) : int

GetStretchBltMode (HDC hDC) : int

LoadBitmap (HANDLE hInstance, LPSTR lpBitmapName) : HBITMAP

PatBlt (HDC hDC, int X, int Y, int nWidth, int nHeight, DWORD dwRop) : BOOL

SetBitmapBits (HBITMAP hBitmap, DWORD dwCount, LPSTR lpBits) : LONG

SetBitmapDimension (HBITMAP hBitmap, int X, int Y) : LONG

SetDIBits (HDC hDC, HANDLE hBitmap, WORD nStartScan, WORD nNumScans, LPSTR lpBits, LPBITMAPINFO lpBitsInfo, WORD wUsage) : int

SetDIBitsToDevice (HDC hDC, WORD DestX, WORD DestY, WORD nWidth, WORD nHeight, WORD SrcX, WORD SrcY, WORD nStartScan, WORD nNumScans, LPSTR lpBits, LPBITMAPINFO lpBitsInfo, WORD wUsage) : WORD

SetStretchBltMode (HDC hDC, int nStretchMode) : int

StretchBlt (HDC hDestDC, int X, int Y, int nWidth, int nHeight, HDC hSrcDC, int XSrc, int YSrc, int nSrcWidth, int nSrcHeight, DWORD dwRop) : BOOL

StretchDIBits (HDC hDC, WORD DestX, WORD DestY, WORD wDestWidth, WORD wDestHeight, WORD SrcX, WORD SrcY, WORD wSrcWidth, WORD wSrcHeight, LPSTR lpBits, LPBITMAPINFO lpBitsInfo, WORD wUsage, DWORD dwRop) : WORD

Icons

ArrangeIconicWindows (HWND hWnd) : WORD

CreateIcon (HANDLE hInstance, int nWidth, int nHeight, BYTE nPlanes, BYTE nBitsPixel, LPSTR lpANDbits, LPSTR lpXORbits) : HICON

DestroyIcon (HICON hIcon) : BOOL

DrawIcon (HDC hDC, int X, int Y, HICON hIcon) : BOOL

LoadIcon (HANDLE hInstance, LPSTR lpIconName) : HICON

OpenIcon (HWND hWnd) : BOOL

The Clipboard

ChangeClipboardChain (HWND hWnd, HWND hWndNext) : BOOL

CloseClipboard (void) : BOOL

CountClipboardFormats (void) : int

EmptyClipboard (void) : BOOL

EnumClipboardFormats (WORD wFormat) : WORD

GlobalAddAtom (LPSTR lpString) : ATOM
GlobalDeleteAtom (ATOM nAtom) : ATOM
GlobalFindAtom (LPSTR lpString) : ATOM
GlobalGetAtomName (ATOM nAtom,
  LPSTR lpBuffer, int nSize) : WORD
InitAtomTable (int nSize) : BOOL

Metafiles

CloseMetaFile (HANDLE hDC) : HANDLE
CopyMetaFile (HANDLE hSrcMetaFile,
  LPSTR lpFileName) : HANDLE
CreateMetaFile (LPSTR lpFilename) : HDC
DeleteMetaFile (HANDLE hMF) : BOOL
EnumMetaFile (HDC hDC, LOCALHANDLE
  hMF, FARPROC lpCallbackFunc, BYTE
  FAR *lpClientData) : BOOL
GetMetaFile (LPSTR lpFilename) :
  HANDLE
GetMetaFileBits (HANDLE hMF) : HANDLE
PlayMetaFile (HDC hDC, HANDLE hMF) :
  BOOL
PlayMetaFileRecord (HDC hDC,
  LPHANDLETABLE lpHandletable,
  LPMETARECORD lpMetaRecord, WORD
  nHandles) : void
SetMetaFileBits (HANDLE hMem) :
  HANDLE

The Timer

GetCurrentTime (void) : DWORD
GetTickCount (void) : DWORD
KillTimer (HWND hWnd, int nIDEvent) :
  BOOL
SetTimer (HWND hWnd, int nIDEvent,
  WORD wElapse, FARPROC lpTimerFunc)
  : WORD

Resources

AccessResource (HANDLE hInstance,
  HANDLE hResInfo) : int
AllocResource (HANDLE hInstance,
  HANDLE hResInfo, DWORD dwSize) :
  HANDLE
FindResource (HANDLE hInstance, LPSTR
  lpName, LPSTR lpType) : HANDLE
FreeResource (HANDLE hResData) : BOOL
GetInstanceData (HANDLE hInstance,
  NPSTR pData, int nCount) : int
LoadResource (HANDLE hInstance,
  HANDLE hResInfo) : HANDLE
LoadString (HANDLE hInstance, WORD wID,
  LPSTR lpBuffer, int nBufferMax) : int
LockResource (HANDLE hResData) :
  LPSTR
SetResourceHandler (HANDLE hInstance,
  LPSTR lpType, FARPROC lpLoadFunc) :
  FARPROC
SizeofResource (HANDLE hInstance,
  HANDLE hResInfo) : WORD

Execution Profiling and Debugging

DebugBreak (void) : void
FatalExit (int Code) : void
OutputDebugString (LPSTR
  lpOutputString) : void
ProfClear (void) : void
ProfFinish (void) : void
ProfFlush (void) : void
ProfInsChk (void) : int
ProfSampRate (int nRate286,int nRate386)
  : void
ProfSetup (int nBufferSize,int nSamples) :
  void
ProfStart (void) : void
ProfStop (void) : void
ValidateCodeSegments (void) : void
ValidateFreeSpaces (void) : LPSTR

Help File Support

WinHelp (HWND hWnd, LPSTR lpHelpFile,
  WORD wCommand, DWORD dwData) :
  BOOL

Dynamic Link Libraries

FreeLibrary (HANDLE hLibModule) : void
GetProcAddress (HANDLE hModule,
  LPSTR lpProcName) : FARPROC
LoadLibrary (LPSTR lpLibFileName) :
  HANDLE
LocalInit (WORD wSegment, WORD pStart,
  WORD pEnd) : BOOL

Multiple Document Interface

DefFrameProc (HWND hWnd, HWND
  hWndMDIClient, WORD wMsg, WORD
  wParam, LONG lParam) : LONG
DefMDIChildProc (HWND hWnd, WORD
  wMsg, WORD wParam, LONG lParam) :
  LONG
TranslateMDISysAccel (HWND
  hWndClient, LPMSG lpMsg) : BOOL

Messages

Button Messages
BM_GETCHECK
BM_GETSTATE
BM_SETCHECK
BM_SETSTATE
BM_SETSTYLE

Button Notification Codes
BN_CLICKED
BN_DISABLE
BN_DOUBLECLICKED
BN_HILITE
BN_PAINT
BN_UNHILITE

Combo Box Messages
CB_ADDSTRING
CB_DELETESTRING

CB_DIR
CB_FINDSTRING
CB_GETCOUNT
CB_GETCURSEL
CB_GETDROPPEDCONTROLRECT
CB_GETDROPPEDSTATE
CB_GETEDITSEL
CB_GETEXTENDEDUI
CB_GETITEMDATA
CB_GETITEMHEIGHT
CB_GETLBTEXT
CB_GETLBTEXTLEN
CB_INSERTSTRING
CB_LIMITTEXT
CB_MSGMAX
CB_RESETCONTENT
CB_SELECTSTRING
CB_SETCURSEL
CB_SETEDITSEL
CB_SETEXTENDEDUI
CB_SETITEMDATA
CB_SETITEMHEIGHT
CB_SHOWDROPDOWN

Combo Box Notification Codes
CBN_CLOSEUP
CBN_DBLCLK
CBN_DROPDOWN
CBN_EDITCHANGE
CBN_EDITUPDATE
CBN_ERRSPACE
CBN_KILLFOCUS
CBN_SELCHANGE
CBN_SETFOCUS

Dialog Box Messages
DM_GETDEFID
DM_SETDEFID
STM_GETICON
STM_SETICON

Edit Control Messages
EM_CANUNDO
EM_EMPTYUNDOBUFFER
EM_FMTLINES
EM_GETFIRSTVISIBLE
EM_GETHANDLE
EM_GETLINE
EM_GETLINECOUNT
EM_GETMODIFY
EM_GETRECT
EM_GETSEL
EM_GETTHUMB
EM_LIMITTEXT
EM_LINEFROMCHAR
EM_LINEINDEX
EM_LINELENGTH
EM_LINESCROLL
EM_MSGMAX
EM_REPLACESEL
EM_SCROLL

GetMenuString (HMENU hMenu, WORD wIDItem, LPSTR lpString, int nMaxCount, WORD wFlag) : int

GetSubMenu (HMENU hMenu, int nPos) : HMENU

GetSystemMenu (HWND hWnd, BOOL bRevert) : HMENU

HiliteMenuItem (HWND hWnd, HMENU hMenu, WORD wIDHiliteItem, WORD wHilite) : BOOL

InsertMenu (HMENU hMenu, WORD nPosition, WORD wFlags, WORD wIDNewItem, LPSTR lpNewItem) : BOOL

LoadMenu (HANDLE hInstance, LPSTR lpMenuName) : HMENU

LoadMenuIndirect (LPSTR lpMenuTemplate) : HMENU

ModifyMenu (HMENU hMenu, WORD nPosition, WORD wFlags, WORD wIDNewItem, LPSTR lpNewItem) : BOOL

RemoveMenu (HMENU hMenu, WORD nPosition, WORD wFlags) : BOOL

SetMenu (HWND hWnd, HMENU hMenu) : BOOL

SetMenuItemBitmaps (HMENU hMenu, WORD nPosition, WORD wFlags, HBITMAP hBitmapUnchecked, HBITMAP hBitmapChecked) : BOOL

TrackPopupMenu (HMENU hMenu, WORD wFlags, int x, int y, int nReserved, HWND hWnd, LPRECT lpReserved) : BOOL

Scroll Bars

EnableScrollBar (HWND hWnd, WORD wSBFlags, WORD wArrowFlags) : BOOL

GetScrollPos (HWND hWnd, int nBar) : int

GetScrollRange (HWND hWnd, int nBar, LPINT lpMinPos, LPINT lpMaxPos) : void

ScrollDC (HDC hDC, int dx, int dy, LPRECT lprcScroll, LPRECT lprcClip, HRGN hrgnUpdate, LPRECT lprcUpdate) : BOOL

ScrollWindow (HWND hWnd, int XAmount, int YAmount, LPRECT lpRect, LPRECT lpClipRect) : void

SetScrollPos (HWND hWnd, int nBar, int nPos, BOOL bRedraw) : int

SetScrollRange (HWND hWnd, int nBar, int nMinPos, int nMaxPos, BOOL bRedraw) : void

ShowScrollBar (HWND hWnd, WORD wBar, BOOL bShow) : void

Mouse and Cursor Functions

ClientToScreen (HWND hWnd, LPPOINT lpPoint) : void

ClipCursor (LPRECT lpRect) : void

CreateCaret (HWND hWnd, HBITMAP hBitmap, int nWidth, int nHeight) : void

CreateCursor (HANDLE hInstance, int nXhotspot, int nYhotspot, int nWidth, int nHeight, LPSTR lpANDbitPlane, LPSTR lpXORbitPlane) : HCURSOR

DestroyCaret (void) : void

DestroyCursor (HCURSOR hCursor) : BOOL

GetCapture (void) : HWND

GetCaretBlinkTime (void) : WORD

GetCaretPos (LPPOINT lpPoint) : void

GetClipCursor (LPRECT lpRect) : void

GetCursorPos (LPPOINT lpPoint) : void

GetDoubleClickTime (void) : WORD

HideCaret (HWND hWnd) : void

LoadCursor (HANDLE hInstance, LPSTR lpCursorName) : HCURSOR

ReleaseCapture (void) : void

ScreenToClient (HWND hWnd, LPPOINT lpPoint) : void

SetCapture (HWND hWnd) : HWND

SetCaretBlinkTime (WORD wMSeconds) : void

SetCaretPos (int X, int Y) : void

SetCursor (HCURSOR hCursor) : HCURSOR

SetCursorPos (int X, int Y) : void

SetDoubleClickTime (WORD wCount) : void

ShowCaret (HWND hWnd) : void

ShowCursor (BOOL bShow) : int

SwapMouseButton (BOOL bSwap) : BOOL

Keyboard Support

EnableHardwareInput (BOOL bEnableInput) : BOOL

GetAsyncKeyState (int vKey) : int

GetInputState (void) : BOOL

GetKBCodePage (void) : int

GetKeyboardState (BYTE FAR *lpKeyState) : void

GetKeyboardType (int nTypeFlag) : int

GetKeyNameText (LONG lParam, LPSTR lpBuffer, int nSize) : int

GetKeyState (int nVertKey) : int

LoadAccelerators (HANDLE hInstance, LPSTR lpTableName) : HANDLE

MapVirtualKey (WORD wCode, WORD wMapType) : WORD

OemKeyScan (WORD wOemChar) : DWORD

SetKeyboardState (BYTE FAR *lpKeyState) : void

TranslateAccelerator (HWND hWnd, HANDLE hAccTable, LPMSG lpMsg) : int

VkKeyScan (WORD cChar) : int

Message Processing Functions

CallMsgFilter (LPMSG lpMsg, int nCode) : BOOL

CallWindowProc (FARPROC lpPrevWndFunc, HWND hWnd, WORD wMsg, WORD wParam, LONG lParam) : LONG

DefHookProc (int nCode, WORD wParam, DWORD lParam, FARPROC FAR * lplpfnNextHook) : DWORD

DefWindowProc (HWND hWnd, WORD wMsg, WORD wParam, LONG lParam) : LONG

DispatchMessage (LPMSG lpMsg) : LONG

ExitWindows (DWORD dwReserved, WORD wReturnCode) : BOOL

FreeProcInstance (FARPROC lpProc) : void

GetMessage (LPMSG lpMsg, HWND hWnd, WORD wMsgFilterMin, WORD wMsgFilterMax) : BOOL

GetMessagePos (void) : DWORD

GetMessageTime (void) : DWORD

InSendMessage (void) : BOOL

MakeProcInstance (FARPROC lpProc, HANDLE hInstance) : FARPROC

PeekMessage (LPMSG lpMsg, HWND hWnd, WORD wMsgFilterMin, WORD wMsgFilterMax, WORD wRemoveMsg) : BOOL

PostAppMessage (HANDLE hTask, WORD wMsg, WORD wParam, LONG lParam) : BOOL

PostMessage (HWND hWnd, WORD wMsg, WORD wParam, LONG lParam) : BOOL

PostQuitMessage (int nExitCode) : void

RegisterWindowMessage (LPSTR lpString) : WORD

ReplyMessage (LONG lReply) : void

SendMessage (HWND hWnd, WORD wMsg, WORD wParam, LONG lParam) : DWORD

SetMessageQueue (int nMsg) : BOOL

SetWindowsHook (int nFilterType, FARPROC lpFilterFunc) : FARPROC

TranslateMessage (LPMSG lpMsg) : BOOL

UnhookWindowsHook (int nHook, FARPROC lpfnHook) : BOOL

WaitMessage (void) : void

Device Contexts, Text Output, and Printing

AddFontResource (LPSTR lpFilename) : int

CreateDC (LPSTR lpDriverName, LPSTR lpDeviceName, LPSTR lpOutput, LPSTR lpInitData) : HDC

CreateFont (int nHeight, int nWidth, int nEscapement, int nOrientation, int nWeight, BYTE cItalic, BYTE cUnderline, BYTE cStrikeOut, BYTE cCharSet, BYTE cOutputPrecision, BYTE cClipPrecision, BYTE cQuality, BYTE cPitchAndFamily, LPSTR lpFacename) : HFONT

CreateFontIndirect (LOGFONT FAR *lpLogFont) : HFONT

CreateIC (LPSTR lpDriverName, LPSTR lpDeviceName, LPSTR lpOutput, LPSTR lpInitData) : HDC

THE WAITE GROUP'S
WINDOWS API BIBLE
Reference Card

Creating Windows

CreateWindow (LPSTR lpClassName, LPSTR lpWindowName, DWORD dwStyle, int X, int Y, int nWidth, int nHeight, HWND hWndParent, HMENU hMenu, HANDLE hInstance, LPSTR lpParam) : HWND

CreateWindowEx (DWORD dwExStyle,LPSTR lpClassName, LPSTR lpWindowName, DWORD dwStyle, int X, int Y, int nWidth, int nHeight, HWND hWndParent, HMENU hMenu, HANDLE hInstance, LPSTR lpParam) : HWND

RegisterClass (LPWNDCLASS lpWndClass) : BOOL

Window Support Functions

AdjustWindowRect (LPRECT lpRect, LONG dwStyle, BOOL bMenu) : void

AdjustWindowRectEx (LPRECT lpRect, LONG dwStyle, BOOL bMenu, DWORD dwExStyle) : void

AnyPopup (void) : BOOL

BeginDeferWindowPos (int nNumWindows) : HANDLE

BringWindowToTop (HWND hWnd) : void

ChildWindowFromPoint (HWND hWndParent, POINT Point) : HWND

CloseWindow (HWND hWnd) : void

DeferWindowPos (HANDLE hWndPosInfo, HWND hWnd, HWND hWndInsertAfter, int x, int y, int cx, int cy, WORD wFlags) : HANDLE

DestroyWindow (HWND hWnd) : BOOL

EnableWindow (HWND hWnd, BOOL bEnable) : BOOL

EndDeferWindowPos (HANDLE hWinPosInfo) : void

EnumChildWindows (HWND hWndParent, FARPROC lpEnumFunc, LONG lParam) : BOOL

EnumProps (HWND hWnd, FARPROC lpEnumFunc) : int

EnumTaskWindows (HANDLE hTask, FARPROC lpEnumFunc, LONG lParam) : BOOL

EnumWindows (FARPROC lpEnumFunc, LONG lParam) : BOOL

FindWindow (LPSTR lpClassName, LPSTR lpWindowName) : HWND

FlashWindow (HWND hWnd, BOOL bInvert) : BOOL

GetActiveWindow (void) : HWND

GetClassInfo (HANDLE hInstance, LPSTR lpClassName, LPWNDCLASS lpWindClass) : BOOL

GetClassLong (HWND hWnd, int nIndex) : LONG

GetClassName (HWND hWnd, LPSTR lpClassName, int nMaxCount) : int

GetClassWord (HWND hWnd, int nIndex) : WORD

GetClientRect (HWND hWnd, LPRECT lpRect) : void

GetCurrentTask (void) : HANDLE

GetDesktopWindow (void) : HWND

GetFocus (void) : HWND

GetLastActivePopup (HWND hwndOwner) : HWND

GetNextWindow (HWND hWnd, WORD wFlag) : HWND

GetNumTasks (void) : int

GetParent (HWND hWnd) : HWND

GetProp (HWND hWnd, LPSTR lpString) : HANDLE

GetSysModalWindow (void) : HWND

GetTopWindow (HWND hWnd) : HWND

GetVersion (void) : DWORD

GetWindow (HWND hWnd, WORD wCmd) : HWND

GetWindowLong (HWND hWnd, int nIndex) : LONG

GetWindowRect (HWND hWnd, LPRECT lpRect) : void

GetWindowTask (HWND hWnd) : HANDLE

GetWindowText (HWND hWnd, LPSTR lpString, int nMaxCount) : int

GetWindowTextLength (HWND hWnd) : int

GetWindowWord (HWND hWnd, int nIndex) : WORD

GetWinFlags (void) : DWORD

IsChild (HWND hWndParent, HWND hWnd) : BOOL

IsIconic (HWND hWnd) : BOOL

IsWindow (HWND hWnd) : BOOL

IsWindowEnabled (HWND hWnd) : BOOL

IsWindowVisible (HWND hWnd) : BOOL

IsZoomed (HWND hWnd) : BOOL

MoveWindow (HWND hWnd, int X, int Y, int nWidth, int nHeight, BOOL bRepaint) : void

RemoveProp (HWND hWnd, LPSTR lpString) : HANDLE

SetActiveWindow (HWND hWnd) : HWND

SetClassLong (HWND hWnd, int nIndex, LONG dwNewLong) : LONG

SetClassWord (HWND hWnd, int nIndex, WORD wNewWord) : WORD

SetFocus (HWND hWnd) : HWND

SetParent (HWND hWndChild, HWND hWndNewParent) : HWND

SetProp (HWND hWnd, LPSTR lpString, HANDLE hData) : BOOL

SetSysModalWindow (HWND hWnd) : HWND

SetWindowLong (HWND hWnd, int nIndex, LONG dwNewLong) : LONG

SetWindowPos (HWND hWnd, HWND hWndInsertAfter, int X, int Y, int cx, int cy, WORD wFlags) : void

SetWindowText (HWND hWnd, LPSTR lpString) : void

SetWindowWord (HWND hWnd, int nIndex, WORD wNewWord) : WORD

ShowOwnedPopups (HWND hWnd, BOOL bShow) : void

ShowWindow (HWND hWnd, int nCmdShow) : BOOL

SystemParametersInfo (WORD wAction, WORD wParam, LPVOID lpvParam, WORD fWinIni) : BOOL

UnregisterClass (LPSTR lpClassName, HANDLE hInstance) : BOOL

WindowFromPoint (POINT Point) : HWND

Menus

AppendMenu (HMENU hMenu, WORD wFlags, WORD wIDNewItem, LPSTR lpNewItem) : BOOL

CheckMenuItem (HMENU hMenu, WORD wIDCheckItem, WORD wCheck) : BOOL

CreatePopupMenu (void) : HMENU

CreateMenu (void) : HMENU

DeleteMenu (HMENU hMenu, WORD nPosition, WORD wFlags) : BOOL

DestroyMenu (HMENU hMenu) : BOOL

DrawMenuBar (HWND hWnd) : void

EnableMenuItem (HMENU hMenu, WORD wIDEnableItem, WORD wEnable) : WORD

GetMenu (HWND hWnd) : HMENU

GetMenuCheckMarkDimensions (void) : DWORD

GetMenuItemCount (HMENU hMenu) : WORD

GetMenuItemID (HMENU hMenu, int nPos) : WORD

GetMenuState (HMENU hMenu, WORD wID, WORD wFlags) : WORD

Edit Control Notification Codes
EN_CHANGE
EN_ERRSPACE
EN_HSCROLL
EN_KILLFOCUS
EN_MAXTEXT
EN_SETFOCUS
EN_UPDATE
EN_VSCROLL

List Box Messages
LB_ADDSTRING
LB_DELETESTRING
LB_DIR
LB_FINDSTRING
LB_GETCARETINDEX
LB_GETCOUNT
LB_GETCURSEL
LB_GETHORIZONTALEXTENT
LB_GETITEMDATA
LB_GETITEMHEIGHT
LB_GETITEMRECT
LB_GETSEL
LB_GETSELCOUNT
LB_GETSELITEMS
LB_GETTEXT
LB_GETTEXTLEN
LB_GETTOPINDEX
LB_INSERTSTRING
LB_MSGMAX
LB_RESETCONTENT
LB_SELECTSTRING
LB_SELITEMRANGE
LB_SETCARETINDEX
LB_SETCOLUMNWIDTH
LB_SETCURSEL
LB_SETHORIZONTALEXTENT
LB_SETITEMDATA
LB_SETITEMHEIGHT
LB_SETSEL
LB_SETTABSTOPS
LB_SETTOPINDEX

List Box Notification Codes
LBN_DBLCLK
LBN_ERRSPACE
LBN_KILLFOCUS
LBN_SELCANCEL
LBN_SELCHANGE
LBN_SETFOCUS

Windows Messages
WM_ACTIVATE
WM_ACTIVATEAPP
WM_ASKCBFORMATNAME
WM_CANCELMODE
WM_CHANGECBCHAIN
WM_CHAR
WM_CHARTOITEM
WM_CHILDACTIVATE
WM_CLEAR
WM_CLOSE
WM_COMMAND
WM_COMMNOTIFY
WM_COMPACTING
WM_COMPAREITEM

WM_COPY
WM_CREATE
WM_CTLCOLOR
WM_CUT
WM_DEADCHAR
WM_DELETEITEM
WM_DESTROY
WM_DESTROYCLIPBOARD
WM_DEVMODECHANGE
WM_DRAWCLIPBOARD
WM_DRAWITEM
WM_DROPFILES
WM_ENABLE
WM_ENDSESSION
WM_ENTERIDLE
WM_ERASEBKGND
WM_FONTCHANGE
WM_GETDLGCODE
WM_GETFONT
WM_GETHOTKEY
WM_GETMINMAXINFO
WM_GETTEXT
WM_GETTEXTLENGTH
WM_HOTKEYEVENT
WM_HSCROLL
WM_HSCROLLCLIPBOARD
WM_ICONERASEBKGND
WM_INITDIALOG
WM_INITMENU
WM_INITMENUPOPUP
WM_KEYDOWN
WM_KEYUP
WM_KILLFOCUS
WM_LBUTTONDBLCLK
WM_LBUTTONDOWN
WM_LBUTTONUP
WM_MBUTTONDBLCLK
WM_MBUTTONDOWN
WM_MBUTTONUP
WM_MDIACTIVATE
WM_MDICASCADE
WM_MDICREATE
WM_MDIDESTROY
WM_MDIGETACTIVE
WM_MDIICONARRANGE
WM_MDIMAXIMIZE
WM_MDINEXT
WM_MDIRESTORE
WM_MDISETMENU
WM_MDITILE
WM_MEASUREITEM
WM_MENUCHAR
WM_MENUSELECT
WM_MOUSEACTIVATE
WM_MOUSEMOVE
WM_MOVE
WM_NCACTIVATE
WM_NCCALCSIZE
WM_NCCREATE
WM_NCDESTROY
WM_NCHITTEST
WM_NCLBUTTONDBLCLK
WM_NCLBUTTONDOWN
WM_NCLBUTTONUP
WM_NCMBUTTONDBLCLK
WM_NCMBUTTONDOWN

WM_NCMBUTTONUP
WM_NCMOUSEMOVE
WM_NCPAINT
WM_NCRBUTTONDBLCLK
WM_NCRBUTTONDOWN
WM_NCRBUTTONUP
WM_NEXTDLGCTL
WM_NULL
WM_OTHERWINDOWCREATED
WM_OTHERWINDOWDESTROYED
WM_PAINT
WM_PAINTCLIPBOARD
WM_PAINTICON
WM_PALETTECHANGED
WM_PALETTEISCHANGING
WM_PARENTNOTIFY
WM_PASTE
WM_QUERYDRAGICON
WM_QUERYENDSESSION
WM_QUERYNEWPALETTE
WM_QUERYOPEN
WM_QUEUESYNC
WM_QUIT
WM_RBUTTONDBLCLK
WM_RBUTTONDOWN
WM_RBUTTONUP
WM_RENDERALLFORMATS
WM_RENDERFORMAT
WM_SETCURSOR
WM_SETFOCUS
WM_SETFONT
WM_SETHOTKEY
WM_SETREDRAW
WM_SETTEXT
WM_SHOWWINDOW
WM_SIZE
WM_SIZECLIPBOARD
WM_SPOOLERSTATUS
WM_SYSCHAR
WM_SYSCOLORCHANGE
WM_SYSCOMMAND
WM_SYSDEADCHAR
WM_SYSKEYDOWN
WM_SYSKEYUP
WM_TIMECHANGE
WM_TIMER
WM_UNDO
WM_USER
WM_VKEYTOITEM
WM_VSCROLL
WM_VSCROLLCLIPBOARD
WM_WINDOWPOSCHANGED
WM_WINDOWPOSCHANGING
WM_WININICHANGE

DDE Messages
WM_DDE_ACK
WM_DDE_ADVISE
WM_DDE_DATA
WM_DDE_EXECUTE
WM_DDE_INITIATE
WM_DDE_POKE
WM_DDE_REQUEST
WM_DDE_TERMINATE
WM_DDE_UNADVISE